1

American Political Music

ALSO BY DANNY O. CREW
AND FROM McFARLAND

*Ku Klux Klan Sheet Music: An Illustrated Catalogue
of Published Music, 1867–2002* (2003)

*Suffragist Sheet Music: An Illustrated Catalogue
of Published Music Associated with the
Women's Rights and Suffrage Movement in America,
1795–1921, with Complete Lyrics* (2002)

*Presidential Sheet Music: An Illustrated Catalogue
of Published Music Associated with the
American Presidency and Those Who Sought the Office* (2001)

American Political Music

A State-by-State Catalog of Printed and Recorded Music Related to Local, State and National Politics, 1756–2004

Danny O. Crew

Volume 1: Alabama–New York [Frankenthaler]
(Preface; Symbols and Abbreviations;
Introduction; entries AmPM-1 to AmPM-1076)

McFarland & Company, Inc., Publishers
Jefferson, North Carolina, and London

Volume 1

LIBRARY OF CONGRESS CATALOGUING-IN-PUBLICATION DATA

Crew, Danny O., 1947–
American political music : a state-by-state catalog of printed and recorded music related to local, state and national politics, 1756–2004 / Danny O. Crew.
p. cm.
Includes bibliographical references and index.

ISBN 0-7864-2286-6 (2 volume set : softcover : 50# alkaline paper) ∞
ISBN 0-7864-2305-6 (v. 1 : softcover : 50# alkaline paper)
ISBN 0-7864-2306-4 (v. 2 : softcover : 50# alkaline paper)

1. Political ballads and songs — United States — Bibliography.
2. Political ballads and songs — United States — Discography.   I. Title.
ML128.A54C74   2006   016.7815'990973 — dc22   2005029563

British Library cataloguing data are available

©2006 Danny O. Crew. All rights reserved

No part of this book may be reproduced or transmitted in any form or by any means, electronic or mechanical, including photocopying or recording, or by any information storage and retrieval system, without permission in writing from the publisher.

Cover photograph ©2005 Stockbyte

Manufactured in the United States of America

McFarland & Company, Inc., Publishers
Box 611, Jefferson, North Carolina 28640
www.mcfarlandpub.com

VOLUME 1 : 0-7864-2305-6
TWO VOLUME SET : 0-7864-2286-6

To the never-say-die fighting spirit
of American local politics
as typified by former Kentucky State Representative
Cassius Marcellus Clay*

*While attending a political debate in 1843, Clay was shot in the chest by a hired killer. Pulling out his Bowie knife, Clay stabbed the would be assassin in the head and face, gouging out one of the attacker's eyes and slicing up the other. Six years later in 1849, after giving an anti-slavery speech, a pro-slavery supporter attacked Clay, clubbing him and then stabbing him in the lung, severing his breastbone. Severely wounded, Clay wrestled the knife away from the attacker, and in turn stabbed him. As he passed out from loss of blood, Clay was heard to say, "I died in the defense of the liberties of the people." Clay lived until 1903; his second attacker died the next day.

Table of Contents

• **VOLUME 1** •

Acknowledgments viii

Preface ix

Symbols and Abbreviations xi

Introduction xiii

The Catalog: Alabama–New York [Frankenthaler] 1

• **VOLUME 2** •

Symbols and Abbreviations vii

The Catalog: New York [Gadsden]–Wyoming; General 423

Appendices

Appendix A: Publishers by City 735

Appendix B: Parodied Songs 753

Bibliography 771

Indexes

Index of Titles 773

Index of Authors, Composers, Arrangers 827

Index of Politicians 845

Index of Subjects and Offices 863

Acknowledgments

Individuals. Miriam Arcia; Rita Arruda; Michael Berry; Andrea Calhoun; Gale Camarda; Raymond Collins; Maryanne Cornelius; Ryan Coup; Brett Coy; Jay M. Craig; Johnny Crass; Teresa Crew; Craig Cronbaugh; Mike Darrin; Oscar Davis, Jr.; Linda Grant De Pauw; Art Draper; Kathy Elmont; Mary Beth Fine; Ken Florey; Doug French; David and Janice Frent; Carmarda J. Gayle; John Gingerich; Andrea L. Glass; Marillyn Halstead; Beverly Hamer; Sue Hammond; John Hannigan; Joseph E. Hartmann; Patricia Herman; Noel C. Holobeck; Alan January; Michele Karas; Kenneth S. Kozlowski; Brian Krapf; Craig Lacy; Karen Mau; Veronique Le Melle; Frank Loconto; Andrea A. Loyola; Ken Marder; Sandy and Dennis Marrone; Mayor George Matta; Carole McGuire; Dawn Mullin; Eva Murphy; Jim Murray; Susan O'Neill; Dena Naslund; Barbara J. Ottenschot; Dr. Tom Pearson; Raisa Ravinova; Paul Riviere; Joe Rabito; Amy Sarver; David Rushford; Jonathan D. Salant; Sheronda Sanders; Diane Sarver; Henry and Bobbie Shaffner; Sam Shaw; Crystal E. Shell; Jane Shoop; Jim Snow; Kurt Stein; Stacy Stumpf; Elwyn Taylor; David Ware; Marc Wellman; Lawrence Zimmerman.

Institutions. Arkansas Secretary of State's Office; Atlantic County New Jersey, Library; Atlantic County New Jersey Sheriff's Department; Brown University Library; Buffalo & Erie County Public Library; City of Albany, Georgia, Office of the City Clerk; City of Albany, New York; City of Ashland, Kentucky; City of Birmingham, Alabama, Public Library; City of Bowling Green, Kentucky; City of Chicago, Illinois; City of Dowagiac, Michigan; City of Duquesne, Pennsylvania; City of Evansville, Indiana, Mayor's Office; City of Fort Madison, Iowa; City of Fort Wayne, Indiana; City of Los Angeles, California, Public Library; City of Miami, Florida; City of Mount Vernon, New York; City of New Bedford, Massachusetts; City of New Orleans Office of the City Council; City of New York, Public Library; City of Novi, Michigan, Office of City Clerk; City of Ouray, Colorado; City of Pittsburgh, Pennsylvania, Mayor's Office; City of St. Louis Public Library; City of Waterbury, Connecticut, Silas Bronson Library; City of Worcester; Connecticut State Library; Connecticut State Library; Gasconade County Historical Society, Hermann, Missouri; Illinois State Library; Indiana State Archives; Iowa Secretary of State's Office; Iowa State Legislative Information Office; Kentucky Department for Libraries and Archives; Legislative Reference Bureau Library, State of Hawaii; Library of Congress, American Memory; Maryland Historical Society; Massachusetts Archives; Monroe County, New York, Board of Commissioners; Nebraska State Library; New York City Public Library; New York State Library; Office of Commonwealth Libraries, Harrisburg, Pennsylvania; Office of the Queens Borough President, New York; Pennsylvania State Senate Library; Public Library of Cincinnati & Hamilton County; Sagadahoc County, Maine, Sheriff's Department; Selma-Dallas County, Alabama, Public Library; South Carolina State Library; St. Louis, Missouri, Public Library; State Library of Florida; State Library of Louisiana; State Library of Massachusetts; Supreme Court of Ohio Law Library; Town of Winthrop, Massachusetts; State Legislative Library, Pennsylvania; Town of Webster, New York; VA-NC Piedmont Genealogical Society; Wake Forest University, Z. Smith Reynolds Library; Warren Newport Public Library, Gurnee, Illinois; Warren Township, Illinois.

Preface

American Political Music is the fourth in a series of reference books documenting the political music of our nation. This latest work in particular complements and extends the music included in my first book *Presidential Sheet Music* (McFarland, 2000), and should be used in conjunction with the bibliographic data contained therein, as entries are not duplicated.

This bibliography differs from that earlier work in that it includes all forms of music associated with incumbents and candidates for American local, state and federal political offices, as well as high profile political individuals, judges and American diplomats. Music documented includes sheet music, song book contents, broadside songs, songs in newspapers, vinyl records, CDs, piano rolls, wax cylinders and other music recording media.

The book documents each song as fully as possible to include title, authors or composers, publishers, and copyright dates. Where available, it also includes references to a location where such music or lyrics may be found in print, on the Internet as written lyrics or midi or mp3 files.

The lyrical content of over 35,000 individual songs was personally reviewed in order to establish the name references in each piece. A separate entry was made for each person mentioned in a song text so as to try and make each individual's legacy as complete as possible within his or her overall entry. It does not include recordings of a non-musical nature such as speeches, radio spots, etc., unless accompanied by music.

Each entry is as complete as possible; however, since many pieces were identified by reference or from catalogues or other publications, it was occasionally not possible to determine all the usual criteria. When such identification was used, all available data are presented. In many pieces, the printed music contained actual musical notation while others contained only a reference to a popular song of the day to which the lyrics could be sung.

Music Included in This Catalogue

• Music that illustrates on its cover, names in its title, is dedicated to or mentions in the lyrics a politician (except elected presidents, including Jefferson Davis). This includes music published before, during and after the individual held office, and memorial and other posthumous music.

• Music that illustrates on its cover, names in its title, is dedicated to or mentions in the lyrics a member of the immediate family of one of the above.

• Music about a local or state political party or organization.

• Music about city halls, state houses or the U.S. Capitol.

• Individual songs per the above that are contained in otherwise non-songsters and songbooks.

• Songs meeting the above criteria that are printed in newspapers or magazines.

Music Not Included in the Catalogue

- Music about elected presidents. These are to be found in *Presidential Sheet Music* (McFarland, 2000).

Notes on the Music Included

In order to provide continuity and preclude repetition of statistical data, certain editorial assumptions have been incorporated into the catalog. These are listed below and generally apply unless otherwise noted.

1. Music before 1919 is approximately 10¾" × 13¾".
2. Music from 1919 to the present is approximately 9" × 12".
3. Copyright is held by the publisher.
4. The date given is that of the copyright, not the publishing date.
5. Sheet music with multiple songs listed *on* the cover, or where only the title changes from one cover to another, are generally identified as sub-numbers of one reference number.
6. Editions which are identical except for color, publisher, size or non-music related content such as advertising, are generally identified by variation numbers: [V-1: Published by Lee & Walker] [V-2: Published by Oliver Ditson].
7. Non-illustrated covers are black and white unless otherwise noted.
8. Music not related to a particular candidate but which can be attributed to a particular state is located at the end of the respective state's entries under the heading "Miscellaneous Music."

The "General" Category

Music not related to a particular candidate and which cannot be attributed to a particular state, is located under the major heading General, following the entries for Wyoming. This heading is divided into five sub-sections: Judges and Courts; Governors and State Officials; Mayors, Councils, Other Local Offices; and State and Local.

Symbols and Abbreviations

General Key

a.	Arranged by
ab.	About
Adm.	Admiral
Adv.	Advertisement
Ave.	Avenue
Bet.	Between
Bro.	Brother
Bros.	Brothers
c.	Compiled by
ca.	Circa
Capt.	Captain
Co.	Company
Col.	Colonel
Cor.	Corner
Corp.	Corporation
Demo.	Democratic
e.	Edited by
Eng.	Engraving
Etc.	Etcetera
Gen.	General
Genl.	General
Gov.	Governor
Govr.	Governor
Hon.	Honorable
Inc.	Incorporated
Incl.	Including
Lieut.	Lieutenant
Lt.	Lieutenant
Ltd.	Limited
m.	Music by
Maj.	Major
Obv:	Obverse (Front)
Op. ###	Opus number
Opp.	Opposite
pp.	Pages
Pub.	Publishing
Repub.	Republican
Rev.	Revised
Rev:	Reverse (Back)
Sq.	Square
St.	Street
Sts.	Streets
U.S.	United States
w.	Words by
&	And
&c	Etcetera
[ ]	Information not found on the music itself
( )	Information found on the music
" "	Quoted exactly as on the music
' '	Quote within a quote or emphasis as on music

Color Key

Be	Beige
Bk	Black
Bl	Blue
B/W	Black & White
Br	Brown
Gd	Gold
Gn	Green
Gy	Grey
Ma	Maroon
N/c	Natural Color
O	Orange
Pk	Pink
Pl	Purple
R	Red
R/w/b	Red, White & Blue
S	Silver
W	White
Y	Yellow

Reference Key

[AMC] American Memory History Collection. Library of Congress on-line collection @ http://memory.loc.gov/ammem/amhome.html

[Crew/xxx-xxx] Crew, Danny O. *Presidential Sheet Music*. Jefferson, NC: McFarland, 2000.

[Crew/S-xxx] Crew, Danny O. *Suffragist Sheet Music*. Jefferson, NC: McFarland, 2001.

[Crew/K-xxx] Crew, Danny O. *Ku Klux Klan Sheet Music*. Jefferson, NC: McFarland, 2002.

[DOC/PSM-xxx] Crew, Danny O. *Presidential Sheet Music*. Jefferson, NC: McFarland, 2000.

[FOM, p. xx] Levy, Lester S. *Flashes of Merriment, A Century of Humorous Songs in America, 1805–1905*. Norman: University of Oklahoma Press, 1974.

[H-xxx] Hoogerwerf, Frank W. *Confederate Sheet-Music Imprints*. Brooklyn: Brooklyn College, 1984.

[LL/JH] Lester S. Levy Sheet Music Collection. Milton S. Eisenhower Library, Johns Hopkins University. On-line collection @ http://levysheetmusic.mse.jhu.edu/index.html

[M-xxx] Mills, William. *Songs, Odes, Glees and Ballads: A Bibliography of American President Campaign Songsters*. Westport, CT: Greenwood, 1990.

[SBAR, p. xx] Moore, Frank. *Songs and Ballads of the American Revolution*. New York: D. Appleton, 1855.

[S/U, p. x] Sonneck, Oscar George Theodore and William Treat Upton. *A Bibliography of Early Secular Music [18th Century]*. Washington, DC: The Library of Congress, 1945.

[TPL, p. x] Lynch, Timothy P. *Strike Songs of the Depression*. Jackson: University Press of Mississippi, 2001.

[VBL, p. x] Lawrence, Vera Brodsky. *Music of Patriots, Politicians and Presidents*. New York: Macmillan, 1975.

[W-xxxx] Wolfe, Richard J. *Secular Music in America 1801–1825, a Bibliography*. New York: New York Public Library, 1964.

[WFU] Rare Books and Manuscripts Department, Z. Smith Reynolds Library, Wake Forest University, Winston-Salem, North Carolina. On-line collection @ http://www.wfu.edu/Library/rarebook/broads.html

Introduction

Music and politics have always been powerful bedfellows since the beginning of American political activity. In fact, it was a song that captured the public's imagination in 1768 and united a fledgling patriot movement. This song — *The Liberty Song* — was set to the traditional tune of *Hearts of Oak*, and became so popular that even Tories composed parodies of the parody. And who wrote it? — John Dickinson, a Pennsylvania assemblyman and later a member of the Continental Congress.

State and local politicians from mayors to senators have often been the focus, and occasionally even the composers, of many a musical offering. Unfortunately, this unique slice of American political life is relatively unknown among scholars and historians. The wealth of the subject matter is truly staggering, as a primary source of political thought, and is certainly deserving of additional study. It is the goal of this book that by making the academic community aware of this enormous wealth of material, additional scholarship will be conducted.

Early Federal-era politician-composers like John Dickinson were not uncommon. Continental Congressman and signer of the Declaration of Independence Francis Hopkinson composed many stirring tunes for American independence, including the very popular *Battle of the Kegs*. His son, Joseph Hopkinson (later to become a New Jersey assemblyman), wrote one of the most famous songs in American History — *Hail Columbia*. His 1798 words to Philip Phile's earlier *President's March* became America's unofficial national anthem for over 100 years.

In addition to Dickinson and the Hopkinsons, many other politicians have, over the almost 250 years of American political history, taken their turn at penning music — some political tunes, and some not. Other famous songwriter-politicians include William O. Butler, general and Democratic candidate for vice president in 1848, Albert G. Pike, Confederate commissioner and Arkansas Supreme Court justice; Horace Greeley, congressman and Democratic candidate for president in 1872; Queen Liliuokalani of Hawaii; Charles Dawes, general, Nobel Peace Prize winner and vice president; Jimmie Walker, state senator and mayor of New York City; Huey Long, Louisiana governor and U.S. senator; Jimmy Davis, Louisiana lieutenant governor and governor; Mike Curb, California lieutenant governor; Clint Eastwood, mayor of Carmel, California; William Fries (C.W. McCall), mayor of Oray, Colorado; Sonny Bono, mayor and U.S. congressman; Vic Knight, lieutenant governor and secretary of state for Washington State; and W. Lee O'Daniel, Texas governor and U.S. senator, to name only a few.

Another group of songs related to politics that comprise our sub-presidential political music legacy are those songs inspired by the words of America's politicians. Numerous tunes have been written to the words, speeches, ideas and quotes of the famous and the not so famous political figure. These include the famous such as Thomas Jefferson, William H.

Harrison; Zachary Taylor; and Abe Lincoln, and the not-so-famous such as William Ambrose, congressman; James A. Dix, New York senator and governor; George McClellan, general and governor; Upton Sinclair, candidate for governor of California; Dr. Francis Townsend, author of the Townsend Plan, among numerous others.

By far the most popular type of songs related to all politicians are those that seek to either boost or detract from the individual officeseeker. Laudatory musical selections are one of the earliest forms of political expression. Ben Franklin (assemblyman), John Hancock (congressman and governor) and Charles Pinckney (secretary of state) were but a few of our founding fathers heralded and reviled in song. Musical assassination, however, was far more the popular sport during the Federal period (and the subsequent 200+ years). Even though we often think that modern politics is mean, it is hard for us today to comprehend the vileness and viciousness of the parodies of the late 1700s and early 1800s. Hot issues of the times provided fertile ammunition for musical mischief. Of particular interest were those individuals involved in the England-France debates, the XYZ affair, the Alien and Sedition Act and even Thomas Jefferson's alleged affair with his Sally. Nothing was off limits.

The presidential campaigns of the 1830s and 1840s also spawned some of the most contemptible lyrics ever written in American history, and not only towards the presidential candidates themselves. As in the Federal period, issues and individuals involved in the debates were frequently the targets of musical attack: The national bank debate, nullification, Texas independence and slavery all provided ample fodder for the balladeer.

Slavery in particular, and its related issues, would mark the bitter political debate leading up to the Civil War and would dominate political music as well. Bloody Kansas, the Sumner-Brooks affair, the Harpers Ferry raid, and the fight for Maryland's loyalty spawned scores of tunes disparaging everyone from the president down to the city marshal of Baltimore. Personal attacks were the norm, not the exception. On the other hand, politicians at all levels were also praised: Heroes such as loyal governors and congressmen who joined the Union ranks were lauded in the North, while those Baltimore politicians who supported the South and were subsequently imprisoned by Union forces, were praised as heroes of the Southern cause.

Far from quieting the tunesmiths, the onset of the Civil War brought with it new levels of music combat. Every conceivable variety of negative songs was penned about Lincoln, his cabinet and his supporters. Even poor Congressman Ely who was captured at the first Battle of Manassas was ridiculed in song. Conversely, pro–Union songwriters turned out anti-copperhead, anti–Confederate and anti–anyone-connected-with-the-South songs.

Even long after the war, the musical campaign literature continued to focus on those who were loyal to either the North or the South. As late as 1896, politicians at all levels were still producing "look-what-I-did-in-the-war songs." It was also during this period that the political scandal song took a front row in the musical conversation of the day. Ulysses S. Grant and his administration gave the crafty songwriter plenty of ammunition for poison-pen musical treatment. Of course, the Democrats had their own problems with Boss Tweed and his Tammany ilk. In reading the lyrics of the political music of the times, one could easily believe that there was not an honest person left in this nation from city hall to the White House.

In addition to scandal-related music, war is another subject that has traditionally spawned musical outpourings, and politicians at all levels have been both the friendly and unfriendly targets of such music. From the early days of the American Revolution to Vietnam, politicians and the military have been linked. Often these songs praise the military prowess of the individual, many of whom were, or were to be, politicians: Generals Henry Knox (secretary of war), Horatio Gates (state legislator) and Anthony Wayne (state assembly and congressman), have been the subject of songs long after their deaths. Politicians like Col. Edward D. Baker (congressman) were praised when they made the ultimate sacrifice in war. Many governors served with distinction during the Civil War such as Governor Richard Yates (Illinois) and Governor Oliver P. Morton (Indiana). Songs in their praise were plentiful.

Of course, the Spanish American War launched its hero, Teddy Roosevelt, all the way from a lowly police commissioner of New York City to the White House. Seldom in American history has anyone been ensconced in musical legend more than Theodore Roosevelt. Even his daughter's wedding to a young congressman (Nick Longworth) was exploited musically.

While the idea of the "coattail" effect was not new to the 1930s, with the immense popularity of Franklin Roosevelt, many state and local politicians rushed to be seen as being associated with him. Many did this through music, and the "coattail" song became common during this period. Whether a candidate was running for alderman (William Dawson, Chicago) or governor (Culbert L. Olson, California), it did not hurt to have a piece of music published featuring a photograph of the candidate and FDR.

With the rise of radio and especially television, the "golden age" of published sheet music saw a precipitous decline. Political music, especially at the local level, plays in 2005 more of a backdrop role in campaigns. However, one modern invention, the Internet, has actually rekindled an old musical tradition — parody political music.

Numerous web sites and web rings have been developed that feature pro, anti and parody music. Many of these sites specialize in political parody songs. This wealth of political insight and passion is, unfortunately, truly ephemeral. Web sites routinely come and go, and once lost, the music generated through these sites is gone forever. Many of the songs cited in this book are of such music. Preserving these songs in a hard-copy format has been a priority of the author over the past several years. A quick review of such citations contained in this book will give the reader a glimpse into this valuable, fleeting resource of political passion and partisanship and call attention to why it needs to be preserved.

Music is passion. Political music is an important expression of that particular passion that is uniquely American politics. It is hoped that by bringing these resources to the attention of scholars and historians, it will have helped in some small way to open this vast resource for study and analysis so that others may gain important insights into the American political process.

The Catalog

ALABAMA

• **AmPM-1 BAGBY**, Arthur Pendleton (State House, 1821, 1822, 1824 & 1834–1836; State Senate, 1825; Governor, 1837–1841; U.S. Senate, 1841–1848; U.S. Ambassador to Russia, 1848–1849)
1.1 The Alabama State March. m. Arnaud P. Pfister, "of Tuscaloosa, Ala." Published by Geib & Walker, 23 Maiden Lane, New York, NY. [1837–1841]. B/w litho of the Alabama State Capitol building. "Composed and Respectfully Dedicated to His Excellency Arthur P. Bagby, Governor of the State of Alabama." 4pp. Page 4: Blank. [LL/JH].

• **AmPM-2 BAKER**, Wilson (Director of Public Safety, Selma, 1965)
2.1 Oh, Wallace. w.m. Len Chandler. In: *Freedom Is A Constant Struggle, Songs Of The Freedom Movement*, page 168. c. Guy and Candie Carawan. Published by Oak Publications, New York, NY. 1868. 224pp.

• **AmPM-3 BIRNEY**, James Gillespie (General Assembly, Kentucky, 1816; State House, Alabama, 1819; American Colonization Society, 1832–1833; Vice President, American Anti-Slavery Society, 1835; Liberty Party Candidate for President, 1840 & 1844) [ALSO SEE: DOC/PSM-JBR]
3.1 Birney And Liberty. w.m. No composer or tune indicated. In: *The Liberty Minstrel*, page 129. e. George W. Clark. Published by George W. Clark, New York, NY. 1844. [4⅝" × 6¾"]. Non-pictorial songbook with gold leaf title. "And Sold by Wm. Harned, 22 Spruce St., New York and Baltimore and Marsh, Boston, Mass." 230pp. [Crew/JBR-1].
3.2 Hail The Day! w. No composer indicated. m. "Wreath The Bowl or Yankee Doodle." In: *The Liberty Minstrel*, page 180. e. George W. Clark. Published by George W. Clark, New York, NY. 1844. [4⅝" × 6¾"]. Non-pictorial songbook with gold leaf title. "And Sold by Wm. Harned, 22 Spruce St., New York and Baltimore and Marsh, Boston, Mass." 230pp. [Crew/JBR-1].
3.3 Ode To James Birney. w. Elizur Wright. m. G.W.C. In: *The Liberty Minstrel*, page 150. e. George W. Clark. Published by George W. Clark, New York, NY. 1844. [4⅝" × 6¾"]. Non-pictorial songbook with gold leaf title. "And Sold by Wm. Harned, 22 Spruce St., New York and Baltimore and Marsh, Boston, Mass." 230pp. [Crew/JBR-1].
3.4 Slaveholder's Lament. w. L.P. Judson. m. "Music arranged from *Lucy Neal* by G.W.C." In: *The Liberty Minstrel*, page 212. e. George W. Clark. Published by George W. Clark, New York, NY. 1844. [4⅝" × 6¾"]. Non-pictorial songbook with gold leaf title. "And Sold by Wm. Harned, 22 Spruce St., New York and Baltimore and Marsh, Boston, Mass." 230pp. [Crew/JBR-1].
3.5 Stolen We Were. w. "By a Colored Man." m. No composer indicated. In: *The Liberty Minstrel*, page 140. e. George W. Clark. Published by George W. Clark, New York, NY. 1844. [4⅝" × 6¾"]. Non-pictorial songbook with gold leaf title. "And Sold by Wm. Harned, 22 Spruce St., New York and Baltimore and Marsh, Boston, Mass." 230pp. [Crew/JBR-1].
3.6 Vermont Whig Song. w. "That Same Old Whig." m. No tune indicated. No publisher indicated. [1844]. B/w litho of a raccoon, geometric design border. 2pp. Page 2: Blank. [Crew/HC-128]. [AMC].
3.7 We Ask Not Material Glory. w.m. No composer or tune indicated. In: *The Liberty Minstrel*, page 94. e. George W. Clark. Published by George W. Clark, New York, NY. 1844. [4⅝" × 6¾"]. Non-pictorial songbook with gold leaf title. "And Sold by Wm. Harned, 22 Spruce St., New York and Baltimore and Marsh, Boston, Mass." 230pp. [Crew/JBR-1].
3.8 We're For Freedom Through The Land. w. J.E. Robinson. m. "Music arranged from the *Old Granite State*." "Suggested by a song sung by George W. Clark, at a recent convention in Rochester, N.Y." In: *The Liberty Minstrel*, page 173. e. George W. Clark. Published by George W. Clark, New York, NY. 1844. [4⅝" × 6¾"]. Non-pictorial songbook with gold leaf title. "And Sold by Wm. Harned, 22 Spruce St., New York and Baltimore and Marsh, Boston, Mass." 230pp. [Crew/JBR-1].

- **AmPM-4 BOUTWELL**, Albert Burton (State Senate, 1946–1958; Lt. Governor, 1958; Mayor, Birmingham, 1963–1967)

4.1 Go Tell It On The Mountain. w.m. "Adaptions [sic] of old spiritual by Mrs. Halmer and Carlton Reese." In: *Freedom Is A Constant Struggle, Songs Of The Freedom Movement*, page 100. c. Guy and Candie Carawan. Published by Oak Publications, New York, NY. 1968. "Original verses by Florence Reese." 224pp.

4.2 We've Got A Job. w.m. Carlton Reese and Birmingham Choir. In: *Freedom Is A Constant Struggle, Songs Of The Freedom Movement*, page 22. c. Guy and Candie Carawan. Published by Oak Publications, New York, NY. 1968. "Original verses by Florence Reese." 224pp.

- **AmPM-5 BREWER**, Albert (State House, 1955–1967; Lt. Governor, 1967–1968; Governor, 1968–1971)

5.1 Albert Brewer Campaign Song. w. No composer indicated. m. No composer indicated. [ca. 1968]. [3" × 5"]. Published as a post card by Citizens for Albert Brewer, Bob Teel, Chairman. Obv: N/c photo of Albert Brewer, facsimile signature. Rev: Music.

CLARK, George W. (Justice of the Peace, Alabama, 1865–1867) [See: Texas]

- **AmPM-6 CLARK**, James G., Jr. (Sheriff, Dallas County, 1957–1966?)

6.1 National Brotherhood Week. w.m. Tom Lehrer. On 33⅓ rpm LP: *That Was The Year That Was*. Reprise Records #6179. Performed by Tom Lehrer. 1965.

6.2 Oh, Wallace. w.m. Len Chandler. In: *Freedom Is A Constant Struggle, Songs Of The Freedom Movement*, page 168. c. Guy and Candie Carawan. Published by Oak Publications, New York, NY. 1968. 224pp.

- **AmPM-7 COBB**, James Edward (Circuit Judge, 1874–1886; U.S. House, 1887–1895)

7.1 Tom Watson Of Georgia. w. E.J. Seymour. m. "Air—*Marching Through Georgia*." In: *Harrison And Reid Campaign Song Book*, page 11. w. E.J. Seymour. m. Popular Airs. [1892]. [3⅞" × 5⅛"]. Bl/gn non-pictorial, stars, geometric designs. 36pp. [M-316]. [Crew/BFH-35].

- **AmPM-8 CONNER**, Theophilus Eugene 'Bull' (State House, 1935–1937; Commissioner of Public Safety, Birmingham, 1937–1953 & 1957–1963; State Public Service Commission, 1964–1972)

8.1 Bull Conner's Jail. w. Ernie Marrs. m. "Tune—*Down In The Valley, Birmingham Jail.*" In: *We Shall Overcome, Songs Of The Southern Freedom Movement*, page 103. Compiled by Guy and Candie Carawan for The Student Non-Violent Coordinating Committee. Published by Oak Publications, 165 W. 46th Street, New York, NY. [ca. 1968]. [5½" × 8½"]. Bl/bk photo of marchers. 112pp.

8.2 Talking Birmingham Jam. w. Phil Ochs. m. No tune indicated. "Recorded on *I Ain't Marching Anymore*, Electra EKS-7287 (1965)." "Copyright Phil Ochs." Lyrics and sound file published online at <http://www.mudcat.org/kids/@displaysong.cfm?SongID=5668>. [199–].

8.3 We've Got A Job. w.m. Carlton Reese and Birmingham Choir. In: *Freedom Is A Constant Struggle, Songs Of The Freedom Movement*, page 22. c. Guy and Candie Carawan. Published by Oak Publications, New York, NY. 1968. "Original verses by Florence Reese." 224pp.

- **AmPM-9 HEFLIN**, James Thomas, (Mayor, Lafayette, 1893–1894; Register in Chancery, Lafayette, 1894–1896; State House, 1896–1900; Alabama Secretary of State, 1902–1904; U.S. House, 1904–1920; U.S. Senate, 1920–1931)

9.1 The Answer To Heflin. w.m. No composer or tune indicated. No publisher indicated. [1928]. [3½" × 5⅛"]. O/bk non-pictorial. "The New Song Hit." 2pp. Page 2: Blank. [Crew/AES-59].

- **AmPM-10 HOBSON**, Richmond Pearson (U.S. House, 1907–1915)

10.1 For Victory Of Our Country's Flag (Song and Chorus). w.m. Andrew J. Bocx. Published by Ilsen & Company, Nos. 25–27 West 6th Street, Cincinnati, OH. 1899. R/w/b U.S. flag. B/w photos of Theodore "Roosevelt, Admiral Dewey, Commodore Schley, General Shafter, Eghert, General Miles, Lt. Merritt, Lt. Hobson, General Wheeler, General Lee, and General Funston." "Dedicated to the Army and Navy of the United States." 6pp. Page 2: Blank. Page 6: Advertising. [Crew/TR-75].

10.2 The King Of The Sea. w. Charles C. Clark. m. Tony Clark. Published by Charles C. Clark, Proctor, VT. 1900. B/w photos of Theodore Roosevelt, Admiral George "Dewey," Admiral Robley "Evans," Lieutenant "Hobson," Admiral William T. "Sampson," Commodore "Schley," and General William R. "Shafter." R/w/b drawing of a classical archway, flags. "Great National War Song." 6pp. [?]. [Crew/TR-125].

10.3 Hobson Of The Merrimac. m. F.A. Jewell. Published by F. Trifet, Publisher, 36 Broomfield Street, Boston, MA. 1898. Bl/w photo of Richmond Pearson Hobson. Bl/w geometric design frame. "Waltzes for Piano." "No. 173, August 17, 1898, *Boston Journal Of Sheet Music*." 8pp. Pages 2 and 8: Advertising.

10.4 Hobson's Choice (A Song For The Times). w.m. Winthrop. Published by The John Church Company, Cincinnati, OH. R/w/b non-pictorial geometric designs. "To Lieut. Hobson and his Comrades Seven." "The old saying with a new Hobson and a new Choice. 6pp. Pages 2 and 6: Blank.

10.5 I Love The U.S.A. w.m. Will Hardy. Published by Bostonia Publishing Co., Worcester, MA. 1915. B/w photos of "Hon. Richmond Pearson Hobson, Rev. P.A. Baker, D.D., and Rev. Howard H. Russell, D.O." R/w/b drawing of Miss Liberty holding an American Flag, shield. "The Temperance Version of *I Love The U.S.A.*" "A Tremendous feature of the Great Anti-Saloon League Campaign." 6pp.

10.5A Naval Heroes Waltz. m. William J. Carkeek, "Author of *Pompadour Polka, Twilight Schottische, The Derby Two-Step*." Published by Sterling Piano Co., 334 Fulton St., Brooklyn, NY. 1898. Litho of Naval heroes including Schley, Hobson, Watson, Sampson and Dewey. "Dedicated to Our Naval Heores.

10.6 Our Gallant Hobson March And Two Step. m. Cel'ia Walters Harrigan. Published by Windsor Music Company, 266 Wabash Ave., Chicago, IL. 1898. Bl/w/br photo of Lt. Richmond Hobson, stars, anchor, geometric designs. "Dedicated to the American Hero Lieut. Richmond Pearson Hobson and his Brave Associates of the Merrimac." 6pp. Pages 2 and 6: Blank.

10.7 Our Heroes Of To-Day. w.m. W.H. Pease. Published by Eastern Music Publishing Company, New York, NY. Copyright 1909 by W.H. Pease. Gn/w photos of "Theodore Roosevelt (by I.A. Julee), Admiral Dewey (by Clinedinst), Winfield S. Schley by (Pach Bros.), Wilber Wright [and] W.H. Pease." Gn/w drawing of Miss "Liberty," flag, eagle, shield. 6pp. Pages 2 and 6: Blank. [Crew/TR-238].

10.8 Sinking Of The Merrimac. w.m. John T. Hallett. Published by Press of the Skelton Company, Provo, UT. [ca. 1899]. Bl/w photos of William McKinley, Admirals Dewey and Sampson, J.T. Hallett and the U.S.S. Merrimac. Bl/w geometric designs. 4pp. Page 4: "Notice to public: Having lost my eye sight and hands through an explosion, as recreation in some of the dark hours with an earnest desire to do something in the way of helping myself, I have tried composing and now offer my song *Sinking Of The Merrimac*, for sale, feeling confident it will be appreciated by a generous liberty-loving public, Respectfully, J.T. Hallett." [Crew/WM-208].

• **AmPM-11** HUNT, Harold Guy (State Senate, 1962; Probate Judge, 1964–1976; Governor, 1987–1993)

11.1 Congratulations Mr. Guy Hunt. w.m. Happy Hal Burns. Performed by Happy Hal Burns. Cassette tape. Published by Happy Hal Music. 1986. Recorded at Sound of Birmingham. Cassette cover features a b/w photo of Guy Hunt. "A Whimdoozie of a Song."

• **AmPM-12** KING, William Rufus de Vane (State House, North Carolina, 1797–1809; City Solicitor, Wilmington, 1810; U.S. House, 1811–1816; U.S. Senate, Alabama, 1819–1844 & 1848–1852; U.S. Ambassador to France, 1844–1846; Vice-President, 1853) [ALSO SEE: DOC/PSM-FP]

12.1 Four Year's Ago. w. No composer indicated. m. "Air—*Dan Tucker*." In: *The Coon Exterminator Or Polk And Dallas Songster*, page 27. Published by *The Democratic Choir*, No. 15 North 6th Street, Philadelphia, PA. 1844. [3¼" × 4½"]. Non-pictorial black border. "Adapted by *The Democratic Choir* of Philadelphia and by all the Democratic associations throughout the United States." Page 3: Litho of upside down raccoon—"That same old koon." [M-027]. [Crew/JKP-2].

12.2 Hasty Soup. w. "Jersey Blue." m. "Tune—*Auld Lang Syne*." "Trenton, June 25, 1852." In: *Scott And Graham Melodies (Being a Collection of Campaign Songs for 1852)*, page 19. Published by Huestis & Cozans, Nos. 104 and 106 Nassau Street, New York, NY. 1852. [3¹³⁄₁₆" × 6¹⁄₁₆"]. B/w litho of Winfield Scott, geometric design border. "As sung by the Whig Clubs throughout the United States." 76pp. Page 2, 4 and 75: Blank. Page 76: Advertising. [M-086]. [Crew/WS-15].

12.3 Hurrah For Scott And Graham. w. No composer indicated. m. "Tune—*Oh! Susanna*." "Yazoo City, Miss., July 3, 1852." In: *Scott And Graham Melodies (Being a Collection of Campaign Songs for 1852)*, page 31. Published by Huestis & Cozans, Nos. 104 and 106 Nassau Street, New York, NY. 1852. [3¹³⁄₁₆" × 6¹⁄₁₆"]. B/w litho of Winfield Scott, geometric design border. "As sung by the Whig Clubs throughout the United States." 76pp. Page 2, 4 and 75: Blank. Page 76: Advertising. [M-086]. [Crew/WS-15].

12.4 Scott, Who Oft To Victory Led. w. No composer indicated. m. "Tune—*Scots Wha Hae We' Wallace Bled*." "Washington, June 8, 1852." In: *Scott And Graham Melodies (Being a Collection of Campaign Songs for 1852)*, page 62. Published by Huestis & Cozans, Nos. 104 and 106 Nassau Street, New York, NY. 1852. [3¹³⁄₁₆" × 6¹⁄₁₆"]. B/w litho of Winfield Scott, geometric design border. "As sung by the Whig Clubs throughout the United States." 76pp. [M-086]. [Crew/WS-15].

12.5 The Soup Pot. w.m. No composer or tune indicated. In: *Scott And Graham Melodies (Being a Collection of Campaign Songs for 1852)*, page 58. Published by Huestis & Cozans, Nos. 104 and 106 Nassau Street, New York, NY. 1852. [3¹³⁄₁₆" × 6¹⁄₁₆"]. B/w litho of Winfield Scott, geometric design border. "As sung by the Whig Clubs throughout the United States." 76pp. [M-086]. [Crew/WS-15].

12.6 Wait Till November. w. No composer indicated. m. "Tune—*Wait For The Wagon*." In: *Scott And Graham Melodies (Being a Collection of Campaign Songs for 1852)*, page 56. Published by Huestis & Cozans, Nos. 104 and 106 Nassau Street, New York, NY. 1852. [3¹³⁄₁₆" × 6¹⁄₁₆"]. B/w litho of Winfield Scott, geometric design border. "As sung by the Whig Clubs throughout the United States." 76pp. [M-086]. [Crew/WS-15].

12.7 The Workingman's Song. w. J.C. m. "Tune—*The Washing Days*." In: *Scott And Graham Melodies (Being a Collection of Campaign Songs for 1852)*, page 50. Published by Huestis & Cozans, Nos. 104 and 106 Nassau Street, New York, NY. 1852. [3¹³⁄₁₆" × 6¹⁄₁₆"]. B/w litho of Winfield Scott, geometric design border. "As sung by the Whig Clubs throughout the United States." 76pp. [M-086]. [Crew/WS-15].

12.8 Young Whigs' Song. w. No composer indicated. m. "Tune—*Nelly Bly*." In: *Scott And Graham Melodies (Being a Collection of Campaign Songs for 1852)*, page 16. Published by Huestis & Cozans, Nos. 104 and 106 Nassau Street, New York, NY. 1852. [3¹³⁄₁₆" × 6¹⁄₁₆"]. B/w litho of Winfield Scott, geometric design border. "As sung by the Whig Clubs throughout the United States." 76pp. [M-086]. [Crew/WS-15].

• **AmPM-13** LONGO, Albert J. (State Director of Public Safety, 1965)

13.1 Oh, Wallace. w.m. Len Chandler. In: *Freedom Is A Constant Struggle, Songs Of The Freedom Movement*, page 168. c. Guy and Candie Carawan. Published by Oak Publications, New York, NY. 1968. 224pp.

• **AmPM-14** MOORE, Roy (Deputy District Attorney, Etowah County, 1977–1982; Circuit Judge, Gadsden, 1992–2000; State Supreme Court, 2000–2003)

14.1 A-Labama. w. Jim Deken. m. "*Oh, Susanna*, based on a performance by American folk song." Published online at <http://www.amiright.com/parody/misc/americanfolksong0.shtml>. 2003.

14.2 Exodus Of Roy Moore. w. William Tong. m. "*Exodus*, based on a performance by Pat Boone." "Satire of demagogue Alabama Chief Justice Roy Moore, who was recently suspended by a judicial ethics panel for his refusal to obey a federal court order to remove his Ten Commandments granite monument from the Alabama Judicial Building rotunda..." Published by Amiright.com at <http://www.amiright.com/parody/60s/patboone0.shtml>. [ca. 2003].

14.3 The G.O.P. Is On The Eve Of Destruction. w. William Tong. m. "*Eve Of Destruction*, based on a performance by Barry McGuire." Published by Amiright.com at <http://www.amiright.com/parody/60s/barrymcguire3.shtml>. [ca. 2003].

14.4 Moore's Slabs Of Rock. w. William Tong. m. "*I Am A Rock*, based on a performance by Simon & Garfunkel." "Satire of demagogue Alabama Chief Justice Roy Moore, who was recently suspended by a judicial ethics panel for his refusal to obey a federal court order to remove his Ten Commandments granite monument from the Alabama Judicial Building rotunda..." Published by Amiright.com at <http://www.amiright.com/parody/60s/simongarfunkel14.shtml>. [2003].

14.5 Shifty Ways To Lose The Culture. w. Guy DiRito. m. "*Fifty Way To Leave Your Lover*, based on a performance by Paul Simon." "In support of Justice Roy Moore." Published by Amiright.com at <http://www.amiright.com/parody/70s/paulsimon27.shtml>. [ca. 2003].

14.6 Werewolves Of Alabama. w. Steve Kalafut. m. "*Werewolves Of London*, based on a performance by Warren Zevon." "The two songs *Werewolves Of London* and *Sweet Home Alabama* have the same chord patterns and are in the same key. Therefore, they should be combined into one..." Published by Amiright.com at <http://www.amiright.com/parody/70s/warrenzevon5.shtml>. [ca. 2003].

- **AmPM-15 RICE**, Condoleeza (Director of Soviet and East European Affairs, National Security Council, 1989-1991; Special Assistant to the President for National Security Affairs, 2001–Present)

15.1 American Lie. w. Dangers0ne. m. "*American Pie*, based on a performance by Don McLean." "With apologies to Don McLean." Published online at <http://www.amiright.com/parody/70s/donmcclean24.shtml>. [ca. 2003].

15.2 The Christ-What-A-Mess Song. w. Tom Smith. m. *The Christmas Song*. From "*A Very Dubya Xmas*." "Published online at <http://www.tomsmithonline.com/lyrics/very_dubya_xmas.htm>. 2002.

15.3 Condi. w. William Tong. m. "*Windy*, based on a performance by The Association." "National Security Advisor Condi Rice refuses to testify under oath to the 9/11 commission, and keeps tripping over her own words trying to defend the Bush administration's pre-decision to blame 9/11 attacks on Iraq instead of Al Qaida terrorists, as revealed by former counterterrorism official Richard Clarke." Published online at <http://www.amiright.com/parody/60s/theassociation15.shtml>. [2004].

15.4 Condi Rice. w. Leo Jay. m. "*Billie Jean*, based on a performance by Michael Jackson." "Sung by the feerlis U.S. Cummander in Cheef [sic]." Published online at <http://www.amiright.com/parody/80s/michaeljackson69.shtml>. [2004].

15.5 Condoleeza. w. Leo Jay. m. "*Mona Lisa*, based on a performance by Nat 'King' Cole." Published online at <http://www.amiright.com/parody/misc/natkingcole19.shtml>. [2004].

15.6 Condoleeza. w. giblet o'sarcasm. m. "*Wonder Woman TV Theme*, based on a performance by Norman Gimbel and Charles Fox." "A personal commentary, regarding our National Security Advisor's upcoming testimony before the Congressional September 11 Commission." Published online at <http://www.amiright.com/parody/70s/normangimbelndcharlesfox0.shtml>. [2004].

15.7 Condoleeza. w. William K. Tong. m. "Sung to the tune of *Chititquita* by ABBA." Published online at <http://www.bootnewt.envy.nu.scalia.html>.

15.7A Condoleeza. w. John A. Barry. m. "*Camelita*, based on a performance by Warren Zevon." "Just submitted a parody called "Condi" and remembered this one from the 2000 'election.'" Published online at <http://www.amiright.com/parody/70s/warrenzevon12.shtml>. [ca. 2000].

15.8 Condoleeza Rice. w. Bruno the Elder. m. "*Wouldn't It Be Nice*, originally by The Beach Boys." "This one is about African American Republicans or OREOS are they are sometimes known as." Published online at <http://www.amiright.com/parody/misc/thebeachboys5.shtml>. [ca. 2001].

15.8A Dubya. w. Seraph the Comic Artist. m. "*Lucky*, based on a performance by Britney Spears." "Parody No. 2 on the site — there were two reasons in particular why I chose the song this time — a, because I hate it, so I had to make fun out of it, and b, because I wanted to do an anti–Bush song and the lyrics I was thinking of fitted perfectly here, Enjoy." Published online at <http://www.amiright.com/parody/2000s/britneyspears230.shtml>. 2004.

15.9 Dubya's People. w. Alvin Dover and Bill Tong. m. "*Everyday People*, based on a performance by Sly & The Family Stone." Published online at <http://www.amiright.com/parody/2000s/ludacris16.shtml>. 2003.

15.10 Fabulosa Condoleezza. w. Madeleine Begun Kane. Published online at <http://www.madkane.com/yellow.html>. "Feel free to sing *Fabulosa Condoleezza* to *Mona Lisa by* Jay Livingston & Ray Evans, using this midi link which opens a second window. Thanks to reader Warren Woodruff for inspiring this song parody." 2003.

15.11 He's Just A Blight. w. Skisics Surus. m. "*Kryptonite*, originally by Three Doors Down." Published online at <http://www.amiright.com/parody/2000s/threedoorsdown1.shtml>. [ca. 2001].

15.12A How Do You Sleep? w. Ralph Paterno. m. "No tune indicated. "Political Song about Rice, Cheney and Rumsfield at Politicalsong.net." Published online by Politicalsong.net at <http://www.politicalsong.net/how_do_you_sleep>. 2004.

15.12 If Bush Only Had A Brain/The Nerve/A Heart. w. Lco Jay. m. "*If I Only Had The Nerve/A Brain/A Heart*, based on a performance by *Wizard Of Oz* Soundtrack." "I'm really not as partisan as this might sound — all in good fun — sort of...;-) Anyway ... As sung by the Prez-ee-dent of these here U-nited States!" Published online at <http://www.amiright.com/parody/misc/wizardofozsoundtrack0.shtml>. [2004].

15.13 In 2004. From CD: *American Way*. m. "*When I'm 64* by The Beatles." Performed by Dimpled Chad & The Disenfranchised Lyrics. Published at <http:/dimpledchad.net>. [ca. 2001].

15.14 It's Beginning To Look A Lot Like Vietnam. w. William Tong. m. "*It's Beginning To Look A Lot Like Christmas,* based on a performance by X-mas." Published online at <http://www.amiright.com/parody/misc/xmas2.shtml>. [ca. 2003].

15.15 John Ashcroft Is Coming To Town. w. Tom Smith. m. *Santa Claus Is Coming To Town.* From "*A Very Dubya Xmas.*" "Published online at <http://www.tomsmithonline.com/lyrics/very_dubya_xmas.htm>. 2002.

15.15A Killing The Soldiers. w. Bush League. m. "*Killing Me Softly,* based on a performance by Roberta Flack." Published online at <http://www.amiright.com/parody/70s/robertaflack7.shtml>. [2004].

15.16 La Dumbya. w. Alvin Dover. m. "*La Bamba,* originally by Ritchie Valens." Published online at <http://amiright.com/parody/misc/ritchievalens1.shml>. [ca. 2002].

15.17 Putin Busts A Stich. w. Skisics Surus. m. "*Puttin' On The Ritz,* originally by Irving Berlin." Published online at <http://amiright.com/parody/misc/irvingberlin0.shml>. [ca. 2001].

15.18 Republican Girl. w. Mark Hoolihan. m. "*Material Girl,* based on a performance by Madonna." "In honor of Condoleeza Rice's refusal to testify before the commission President Bush appointed." Published online at <http://www.amiright.com/parody/80s/madonna47.shtml>. [2004].

15.19 Rice To W. w. William Tong. m. "*Nice To Be With You,* based on a performance by Gallery." Published online at <http://www.amiright.com/parody/70s/gallery1.shtml>. [2004].

15.20 Shred The Constitution. w. Alvin Dover. m. "*Ball Of Confusion,* originally by The Temptations." Published online at <http://www.amiright.com/parody/70s/thetemptations3.shtml>. [ca. 2002].

15.21 Subterranean Homesick Blues. w. Skisics Surus. m. "*Subterranean Homesick Blues,* originally by Bob Dylan." Published online at <http://amiright.com/parody/60s/bobdylan5.shtml>. [ca. 2001].

15.22 Talking Cabinet Blues. w. Dave Lippman. m. No tune indicated. Published online at <http://www.davelippman.com/Cabinet.html>. N/c photo of Dave Lippman. [ca. 2001].

15.23 Welcome To Your Hell-Hole, Condoleeza. w. Bob Gomez. m. "*Hotel California,* based on a performance by The Eagles." "Responding to public pressure, the President has allowed his national security advisor to testify under oath, as opposed to on *60 Minutes.*'" Published online at <http://www.amiright.com/parody/70s/theeagles97.shtml>. [2004].

• **AmPM-16 RICE**, Samuel F. (State House, 1840–1841, 1859 & 1876; State Supreme Court, 1855–1859; State Senate, 1861–1865?)

16.1 Carve That Possum. In: *Democratic Campaign Songs* [Song Book], page 4. m. "Popular Airs." Published in Madison County, Alabama. [1876]. [3⅝" × 6⁹⁄₁₆"]. Non-pictorial geometric design border. 4pp. [M-2-1]. [Crew/ SJT-11].

• **AmPM-16A SPARKMAN**, John Jackson (U.S. House, 1937–1946; U.S. Senate, 1946–1979; Democratic Candidate for Vice President, 1952) [ALSO SEE: DOC/PSM-AS]

16A.1 March On With Adlai & John (A Campaign Song 1952). w.m. I. Dan Danziger. a. Charles J. Cliff. Published by American Free Enterprises, No. 1025 Vermont Avenue NW., Washington, DC. 1952. [6" × 10"]. B/w photos of Adlai E. Stevenson II and John Sparkman. 4pp. [Crew/AS-2].

• **AmPM-17 SPENCER**, George Eliphaz (U.S. Senate, 1868–1879; Republican National Committee, 1872)

17.1 Captain Grant. w. No composer indicated. m. "*Air — Captain Jenks.*" In: *Tilden And Hendricks' Reform Songs (For The Centennial Campaign Of 1876),* page 33. Published by The National Democratic Committee, Box 3637, New York, NY. 1876. [3⅞" × 5¹⁵⁄₁₆"]. Gn/bk litho of Samuel J. Tilden and Thomas A. Hendricks, geometric design border. 40pp. [M-203]. [Crew/SJT-21].

• **AmPM-18 THOMPSON**, Myron H. (Judge, U.S. District Court, Middle District, Alabama, 1980–Present)

18.1 A-Labama. w. Jim Deken. m. "*Oh, Susanna,* based on a performance by American folk song." Published online at <http://www.amiright.com/parody/misc/americanfolksong0.shtml>. 2003.

• **AmPM-19 UNDERWOOD**, Oscar Wilder (U.S. House, 1895–1896 & 1897–1915; U.S. Senate, 1914–1927)

19.1 Charles E. Hughes (Campaign Song). w. J.L. Feeney. m. "*Air — Baby Shoes.*" In: *Hughes And Fairbanks Campaign Song Book,* page 2. c. James L. Feeney. Published by William H. Delaney, Song Publisher, No. 117 Park Row, New York, NY. Copyright 1916 by William W. DeLaney. [8" × 11"]. R/w/b flags, shield. Bl/w photos of "Charles Evans Hughes" and "Charles Warren Fairbanks." "Preparedness, Protection, Prosperity." R/w/b drawing of flags, shield, geometric designs. 20pp. [M-407]. [Crew/CEH-1].

19.2 Underwood March. m. Caroline Westmoreland Dowman "(Birmingham, Ala)." Published by Roberts and Sons, Birmingham, AL. Copyright 1912 by The Age Herald Publishing Company. Br/w photo of Oscar Underwood. Br/w drawing of leaves. "Dedicated to the Oscar W. Underwood Marching Club of Alabama." 6pp. Page 6: Blank. [Crew/MISC-25].

• **AmPM-20 WALLACE**, George (State House, 1947–1953; Circuit Court Judge, 1953–1958; Governor, 1963–1967 1971–1979, 1983–1987; American Independent Party Candidate for President, 1968) [ALSO SEE: DOC/PSM-GCW]

20.1 Another Day's Journey. w. "New words SCLC." m. "Tune — *Kidnapper.*" In: *Freedom Is A Constant Struggle, Songs Of The Freedom Movement,* page 168. c. Guy and Candie Carawan. Published by Oak Publications, New York, NY. 1968. 224pp.

20.2 The Ballad Of George Wallace {20.2-1}. w.m. Bill Rogers. 45 rpm record. Golden Records, 5919 Belmont, Dallas, TX. Record #GS-339. Performed by Bill Rogers and Julian Thorp on his famous steel guitar. Side 2: **United We Stand** {20.2-2}. w.m. Bill Rogers. [1968].

20.3 Berlin Wall. w. "James Orange and other Young People." m. "Tune — *Joshua Fit The Battle.*" In: *Freedom Is A Constant Struggle, Songs Of The Freedom Movement,* page 154. c. Guy and Candie Carawan. Published by Oak Publications, New York, NY. 1968. 224pp.

20.3A By George, There's A Way {20.3A-1}. w.m. J. Joiner and O. Perden. 45 rpm 7" vinyl record. PJ Records, Florence, AL. #1001/PRP 4771. Performed by Henry Cramer. [1968]. Side 2: **Stand Up For America** {20.3A-2}.

20.4 The Fighting Little Man From Alabam. w.m. Merritt Jordan. Universal Records, 2401 Belcher Ave., Montgomery, AL. Record #45-111. Performed by Merritt Jordan. "Promotional Copy." [1968–1972]. Side 2: *My World Is Like The Night*.

20.5 Go Tell It On The Mountain. w.m. "Adaptions [sic] of old spiritual by Mrs. Halmer and Carlton Reese." In: *Freedom Is A Constant Struggle, Songs Of The Freedom Movement*, page 100. c. Guy and Candie Carawan. Published by Oak Publications, New York, NY. 1968. "Original verses by Florence Reese." 224pp.

20.5A Lay Him Down (George Wallace). w.m. Bob McKee. Audio Cassette. First Man Publishers, P.O. Box 424, Montgomery. Alabama 36101. Performed by Bib McKee. Side 2: **Lay Him Down** (Star Spangled Banner).

20.6 Murder On The Road In Alabama. w.m. Len Chandler. In: *Freedom Is A Constant Struggle, Songs Of The Freedom Movement*, page 172. c. Guy and Candie Carawan. Published by Oak Publications, New York, NY. 1968. 224pp.

20.7 Nobody Likes A Smart Ass. w. Sam Adams. m. Wurlitzer and Plagiarize. 33⅓ rpm LP (2-Vols). Spade Records, POB 2306, Baton Rouge, LA. Spade Records LP/101&LP/102. Original Cast, *The Fudgeripple Follies Or Nobody Likes A Smart Ass*. [196–].

20.8 Oh, Wallace. w.m. Len Chandler. In: *Freedom Is A Constant Struggle, Songs Of The Freedom Movement*, page 159. c. Guy and Candie Carawan. Published by Oak Publications, New York, NY. 1968. 224pp.

20.9 Our Man From Alabam {20.9-1}. w.m. Harry Glenn and Paul Parker. 45 rpm vinyl record. Harry Glenn Presents Souvenir Record, Box 841, Hammond, Indiana 46325. #Mv-GL 3202-G/M. Performed by Paul Parker & The Unpredictables. Side 2: **An Open Letter To All** (The George Wallace Pledge to All Americans) {20.9-2}. w.m. Harry Glenn & Bruce Wyatt. Narrated by Doug Benton. [1968?].

20.10 Right! Right! w.m. Len Chandler. In: *Freedom Is A Constant Struggle, Songs Of The Freedom Movement*, page 159. c. Guy and Candie Carawan. Published by Oak Publications, New York, NY. 1968. 224pp.

20.10A Send Wallace To The White House Election Day (Wallace Song). 45 rpm vinyl record. Produced by Stallings & Atherton, Box 111, Nacogdoches, TX. [ca. 1968].

20.11 Talking Birmingham Jam. w. Phil Ochs. m. No tune indicated. "Recorded on *I Ain't Marching Anymore*." Electra EKS-7287. 1965. "Copyright Phil Ochs." Lyrics and sound file published online at <http://www.mudcat.org/kids/@displaysong.cfm?SongID=5668>. [199–].

20.12 This Is George Wallace (Send Them A Message). 33⅓ rpm LP. Published by Music City Records, Nashville, TN. and Jimmy Velvet Productions. 1972. #MCR 1001. Album Cover: N/c photo of The White House, George Wallace. Songs include: **Stand Up For America** (Little Man) {20.12-1}. w.m. Dave Rich and Jimmy Velvet, and **Little Men Needing A Good Friend** {20.12-2}. w.m. Dave Rich and Jimmy Velvet.

20.13 Vote Wallace In 72. w.m. L. Leblanc. 45 rpm record. Reb Rebel Records, POB 769, Crowley, LA. Leber Music #No. 519-Side 2. Performed by Happy Fats. 1972. Record label: Drawing of two r/w/b Confederate flags.

20.14 Wallace '68 Campaign Favorites — George C. Wallace. w.m. Lamar Morris. 33⅓ rpm LP. Record #XTBV-132593-1A. Published by Wallace Campaign Headquarters, POB 1968, Montgomery, AL. 1968. Album Cover: Br/w photo of George Wallace. "Stand Up For America." Song include: **Stand Up For America** {20.14-1}; **Let The People Speak** {20.14-2}; **Wallace Cannon Ball** {20.14-3}; **Wallace In The White House** {20.14-4}; **America, The Beautiful**; **My Country Tis Of Thee** {20.14-5}; **Open Letters To All** {20.14-6}; **Wallace Victory Wagon** {20.14-7}; **By George, There's A Way** {20.14-8}.

20.15 Wallace For '72' {20.15-1}. w.m. Bob Brock. 45 rpm record. Vote Records #s-1/S-2. Printed by Universal Dynamic Industries, Inc., Atlanta, GA. 1972. Performed by Chuck Atha. Side B: **I'm A Sick American** {20.15-2}. w.m. "Writer Unknown." Performed by Frank W. Morris. Sleeve: R/w/b drawing of George Wallace, historical characters, American flag. "Wallace to Washington '72."

20.16 Way Over Yonder In Montgomery. w.m. "Adapted from religious song, Church Bells Tolling, by James Orange." In: *Freedom Is A Constant Struggle, Songs Of The Freedom Movement*, page 164. c. Guy and Candie Carawan. Published by Oak Publications, New York, NY. 1968. "Original verses by Florence Reese." 224pp.

20.17 We Shall Not Be Moved. w. Noel E. Parmentel, Jr. and Marshall J. Dodge. In: *Folk Songs For Conservatives*, page 27. Published by Unicorn Press, Inc., No. 790 Madison Avenue, New York, NY. 10021. 1964. [5" × 8⅜"]. Bl/w drawings of Barry Goldwater, Bill Buckley, Ray Cohn, eagle. List of contents. "Sung by Noel E. Parmentel, Jr. and His Unbleached Muslims, Greatest Political Satirists Since Cohn and Schine." "Right Wing Hootenanny." 36pp. [Crew/BMG-13].

20.18 Werewolves Of Alabama. w. Steve Kalafut. m. "*Werewolves Of London*, based on a performance by Warren Zevon." "The two songs *Werewolves Of London* and *Sweet Home Alabama* have the same chord patterns and are in the same key. Therefore, they should be combined into one..." Published by Amiright.com at <http://www.amiright.com/parody/70s/warrenzevon5.shtml>. [ca. 2003].

20.19 We've Got A Job. w.m. Carlton Reese and Birmingham Choir. In: *Freedom Is A Constant Struggle, Songs Of The Freedom Movement*, page 22. c. Guy and Candie Carawan. Published by Oak Publications, New York, NY. 1968. "Original verses by Florence Reese." 224pp.

20.20 Which Side Are You On? w.m. Len Chandler. In: *Freedom Is A Constant Struggle, Songs Of The Freedom Movement*, page 160. c. Guy and Candie Carawan. Published by Oak Publications, New York, NY. 1968. "Original verses by Florence Reese." 224pp.

20.21 You Should Have Been There. w.m. "Adaption [sic] of spiritual by Virginia Davis and Amanda Bowens. In: *Freedom Is A Constant Struggle, Songs Of The Freedom Movement*, page 44. c. Guy and Candie Carawan. Published by Oak Publications, New York, NY. 1968. "Original verses by Florence Reese." 224pp.

- **AmPM-21 WALLACE**, Lurleen (Governor, 1967–1968) [ALSO SEE: DOC/PSM-GCW and JGS]

21.1 Stand Up For Schmitz. w.m. Joseph Erdelyi, Jr. (March 28, 1968, U.S.A.). Copyright 1968 by Erdelyi Music Publishing Company, Room 600, No. 1697 Broadway, New York, NY. 10019. [1972 Edition]. Y/bk Non-pictorial. Old dedication and text related to George and Lurleen Wallace crossed out — "~~Name of John G. Schmitz substituted for that of George C. Wallace. Schmitz is the American Party candidate for the Presidency of the U.S., Nominated at the American Party Convention in Louisville, Kentucky, August 4, 1972, Campaign Song. For technical reasons, the American Party is known as the Courage Party in New York State~~." "Dedicated to the Memory of Governor Lurleen Wallace." Advertising. 2pp. Page 2: Blank. [Crew/JGS-1].

21.2 Stand Up For Schmitz And Anderson. w.m. Joseph Erdelyi, Jr. (March 28, 1968, U.S.A.). Copyright 1968 by Erdelyi Music Publishing Company, Room 600, No. 1697 Broadway, New York, NY. 10019. [1972 edition]. Gn/bk non-pictorial. "Dedicated to the memory of Governor Lurleen Wallace." Old dedication and text related to George Wallace crossed out — "~~Campaign Song for John G. Schmitz, Presidential Candidate and Tom Anderson, Vice-Presidential Candidate of the American Party U.S.A. — Nationwide (In NY State it is called The Courage Party)~~." Advertising. 2pp. Page 2: Blank. [Crew/JGS-2].

21.3 Stand Up For Wallace (Campaign Song for George C. Wallace). w.m. Joseph Erdelyi, Jr. Published by Erdelyi Music Publishing Company, Room 600, No. 1697 Broadway, New York, NY. 10019. 1968. Bl/w photo of George Wallace. R/w/b cover. "Win With Wallace." "Courage-Character." 4pp. Page 2: "Dedicated to Her Excellency, Governor Lurleen Wallace, of the State of Alabama. "Campaign Song for Ex-Governor George C. Wallace of Alabama." Page 4: "The Story of George C. Wallace" reprinted from the Liberty Lobby Research Staff Report. [Crew/GCW-5].

21.4 Stand Up For Wallace. w.m. Joseph Erdelyi, Jr. "(March 28, 1968, U.S.A.)." Copyright 1968 by Erdelyi Music Publishing Company, Room 600, No. 1697 Broadway, New York, NY. 10019. [8½" × 11"]. Y/bk non-pictorial. "Dedicated to Her Excellency, Governor Lurleen Wallace, of the State of Alabama." "Campaign Song for Ex-Governor George C. Wallace of Alabama." "Note: It is suggested that each verse be repeated." 2pp. Page 2: Blank. [Crew/GCW-4].

- **AmPM-22 WHEELER**, Joseph (U.S. House, 1881–1883 & 1885–1900)

22.1 General Jo Wheeler's March. m. Ella Nichols. Published by John F. Ellis & Co., No. 937 Penn. Ave., NW, Washington, DC. 1899. B/w litho of bugler on horseback at grave, pile of wood labeled with state names, U.S. flag on pole, compass without arrows. "Respectfully dedicated to the President of the United States Wm. McKinley." 6pp. Page 6: Long narrative on the meaning of the piece. Quote from President McKinley. [Crew/WM-349].

- **AmPM-22A WILLIAMS**, Aubrey (Deputy Administrator, WPA; Director, National Youth Administration, 1935–1945?)

22A.1 He's Got Them On The List. w. No composer indicated. m. "Tune — *I've Got A Little List*." In: *Again And Again And Again Or All At Sea*, page 13. Published by Albany Legislative Correspondents' Association of New York State, Albany, NY. 1945. [8¾" × 11"]. N/c drawing of Franklin Roosevelt as pirate, Thomas Dewey as "Black Tom," Henry Wallace, Sidney Hillman, others on ship — "Union Ship C.I.O.-P.A.C." "Black Tom" Dewey walking plank. "Featuring Political Craft and Cunning and Contortions; Also Summoned by Subpoena, and Hit-Toddy and the Shady Lady, the Indestructible Dame Known as Lu-Lu; Together with Mystical Midsummer Mummery of '46, in a Roaring and Raucous and Revealing Racing Scene Entitled 'Hoots and Straddles.'" "All Done with Music, Magic, and Mirrors — In Three Acts at Hotel Ten Eyck, Albany, March 15, 1945." [Crew/FDR-371].

- **AmPM-23 YANCEY**, William Lowndes (State House, 1841; State Senate, 1843; U.S. House, 1844–1846; Confederate Senate, 1862)

23.1 Advice To The Rebels. w. No composer indicated. m. "Air — *Dan Tucker*." In: *Beadle's Dime Knapsack Songster: Containing The Choicest Patriotic Songs, Together With Many New And Original Ones, Set To Old Melodies*, page 70. Published by Beadle and Company, No. 141 William Street, New York, NY. 1862. [3¾" × 5¾"]. Litho of coin — "One Dime, United States of America." 74pp. [Crew/GBM-78].

23.2 Anxious Stephen! w. No composer indicated. m. "Air — *Cynthia Sue*." In: *The Wide Awake Vocalist (Or Rail Splitters' Song Book)*, page 31. Published by E.A. Daggett, No. 333 Broadway, New York, NY. 1860. Non-pictorial geometric design border. "Words and Music for the Republican Campaign of 1860, Embracing a Great Variety of Songs, Solos, Duets and Choruses Arranged for Piano or melodeon; The best collection of Words and Music ever published for a campaign, Every Club and Family should have copies, so as to join in the choruses; The Ladies are invited to join in the choruses at the meetings." 68pp. [M-116]. [Crew/AL-59].

23.3 The Carte-De-Visite Album. w. No composer indicated. m. "Air — *Chanting Benny*." Published by H. De Marsan, 60 Chatham Street, New York, NY. [1861–1865]. [Approx. 6" × 9"]. B/w litho border of theatrical-type people, lion's heard, geometric designs. "A Comic Song written for Tony Pastor." 2pp. Page 2: Blank. [AMC].

23.4 I Want To Be A Soldier. w.m. No composer indicated. m. Air — [V-1, V-2 & V-3: *I Want To Be An Angel*]. [V-4: *Wait For The Wagon.*]. [V-1: No publisher indicated] [V-2 & V-4: A.W. Auner, Song Publisher, 110 N. 10th St., ab. Arch, Philadelphia, PA] [V-3: Johnson, Song Publisher, 7 Tenth St., Philadelphia, PA]. [ca. 1861]. B/w litho of [V-1 & V-3: Battle scene] [V-2: Soldier, eagle] [V-4: Soldier, tent, rifle], geometric design border. [V-3: "See Johnson's New Catalogue of Songs] [V-4: Additional verses]. 2pp. Page 2: Blank. [AMC].

23.5 Jeff Davis (Or The King Of The Southern Dominions). w. No composer indicated. m. "Air — *The King Of The Cannibal Island.*" Published by H. De Marsan, Publisher, No. 54 Chatham Street, New York, NY. [1863?]. [6¾" × 9¾"]. B/w penny song sheet with litho border of caricatures of musicians, Black man and children, jesters. 2pp. Page 2: Blank. [Crew/JD-52].

23.6 Jeff Davis (Or The King Of The Southern Dominion). w. No composer indicated. m. "Air — *The King Of The Cannibal Island.*" Published by J. Wrigley, Publisher, No. 27 Chatham Street, New York, NY. [186–]. [6" × 9"]. R/w/b hand colored star and stripe border. "No. 799." "J. Wrigley, Publisher of Songs, Ballads, and Toy Books, Conversation, Age, and Small Playing Cards, Alphabet Wood Blocks, Valentines, Motto Verses, and Cut Motto Paper, &c." 2pp. Page 2: Blank.

23.7 Jeff Davis' Last Proclamation To His Council. w. No composer indicated. m. "Air — *The Girl I Left Behind Me.*" [186–]. Non-pictorial geometric design border. 2pp. Page 2: Blank.

23.8 Old Abe And The Fire-Eaters. w. R. Colby. m. "Air — *Dearest May.*" In: *The Republican Campaign Songster For 1860*, page 39. c. W.H. Burleigh. Published by [V-1 and V-2: H. Dayton, No. 36 Howard Street, New York, NY] [V-3: McNally & Company, No. 81 Dearborn Street, Chicago, IL]. 1860. [V-1: Gn/bk] [V-2: Y/bk] [V-3: Be/bk] [V-4: Bl/bk]. "Price 10 cents." [3¹³⁄₁₆" × 6"]. 72pp. [M-104]. [Crew/AL-57].

23.9 The People Are A-Coming. w. No composer indicated. m. No composer indicated. In: *The Republican Campaign Songster For 1860*, page 29. c. W.H. Burleigh. Published by [V-1 and V-2: H. Dayton, No. 36 Howard Street, New York, NY] [V-3: McNally & Company, No. 81 Dearborn Street, Chicago, IL]. 1860. [V-1: Gn/bk] [V-2: Y/bk] [V-3: Be/bk] [V-4: Bl/bk]. "Price 10 cents." [3¹³⁄₁₆" × 6"]. 72pp. [M-104]. [Crew/AL-57].

23.10 Secessia Land. w. No composer indicated. m. "Air — *Promised Land.*" Published by A.W. Auner, Song Publisher, Auner's Printing Office, 110 North Tenth Street, above Arch, Philadelphia, PA. [1862–1864]. B/w litho border. 2pp. Page 2: Blank. [AMC].

23.11 Shool. w.m. No composer or tune indicated. In: *Republican Song Book*, page 6. c. Thomas Drew "(Late Editor of *The Massachusetts Spy*)." Published by Thayer and Eldridge, Boston, MA. 1860. [3⅞" × 5⅞"].

Br/bk litho of beardless Abraham Lincoln, vignettes of young Lincoln chopping rails, polling raft. 68pp. "The Campaign of 1860, Republican Songs for the People, Original and Selected." [M-108]. [Crew/AL-8].

23.12 The Song Of The Democracy. w.m. No composer or tune indicated. In: *The Democratic Campaign Songster, No. #1*, page 5. Published by American Publishing House, No. 60 West Fourth Street, Cincinnati, OH. 1860. [3⅞" × 5¹¹⁄₁₆"]. Pk/bk litho of "Stephen A. Douglas," black line border. At top of cover — "No. 1, Price 10 Cents." 52pp. [M-118]. [Crew/SAD-12].

23.13 Stand By The Flag. w.m. No composer or tune indicated. In: *The Democratic Campaign Songster: Douglas & Johnson Melodies,* page 10. Published by P.J. Cozans, Publisher, New York, NY. [1860]. [3⅞" × 6"]. Y/bk litho of an eagle with ribbon — "Douglas & Johnson," train, ships, monument — "Liberty" sitting on rock base — "The Constitution." 40pp. [M-117]. [Crew/SAD-5].

• **AmPM-24   MISCELLANEOUS MUSIC**
24.1 Alabama. w. Julia Tutwiler. m. Edna Gockel-Gussen. Published by Janeal Music Publishing Company. Sole selling agent Educators Music Supply, Inc., Sylacauga, AL. 1958. [Edition ca. 1969]. [6⅞" × 10¼"]. Bl/w photo of the State Capitol building. R/w/b drawing of St. Andrews flags, seal of the Sesquicentennial. "Sesquicentennial Celebration Edition — Alabama 150 1819–1969." "Adopted as the State Song of Alabama by Act of Legislature, March 3, 1931." "Mixed Voices SATB." 12pp. Pages 2 and 3: Narratives. Page 16: Blank.

24.2 The Mayor Of Alabam. w.m. Frank Trumbauer and George Redmond. Published by Robbins Music Corp., 700 Seventh Avenue, New York, NY. 1936. [6⅞" × 10⅞"]. Bl/pk/w drawing of instruments. "A Ken Star arrangement, Robbins Series of Modern Orchestra Novelties by Leading American Modern Composers." Parts set for band.

24.3 Montgomery. m. S.L. Tyler. Published by W.H. Boner & Co., 1102 Chestnut Street, Philadelphia, PA. 1886. B/w litho of various state capitol buildings: "Madison, Wis., Harrisburg, Pa., Hartford, Conn., Columbus, O., Lansing, Mich., Washington, D.C., St. Paul, Minn., Richmond Va., Sacramento, Cal., Albany, NY., Boston, Mass., Montgomery, Ala." "The Capitol Collection." 8pp. Page 2: Blank. Page 3: At top of music — "To my Brother, C.A. Tyler." Page 8: Advertising.

ALASKA

• **AmPM-25   KNAPP**, Lyman E. (Territorial Governor, 1889–1893)
25.1 Columbia My Country (American Anthem). w.m. George M. Vickers "(Composer of *Guard The Flag, God Bless Our Land*, &c)." [ca. 1893]. Bl/w litho of Miss Columbia, two women, steamboat. "The New Patriotic Song Approved by People from New England to Alaska." "The sentiment of this song will, I am sure, be indorsed by every true American — William McKinley; Full of Patriotic sentiment, well expressed — Governor Wm. E. Russell, Massachusetts; It is patriotic in sentiment and the music is charming, Governor

J.M. Stone, Mississippi; It is a patriotic gem and will probably remain one of the patriotic songs of our country — Governor Elisha P. Ferry, Washington; I trust it may be welcomed by an appreciative public with the favour it deserves — Gen. Lyman E. Knapp, Alaska; I regard such music as a important part of the education of the young people of the land — Hon. John Wanamaker, and representative Americans in all parts of the United States." 4pp. Page 2: Facsimile letter releasing copyright. Page 4: Blank. [Crew/WM-145].

LUTTRELL, John King (Treasury Agent for Alaska, 1893) [See: California]

• AmPM-26 MARROU, Andre (State House, 1980–1982; Libertarian Candidate for Vice President, 1988; Libertarian Candidate for President, 1992)

26.1 Swing On A Politician. w. Dave Aronson. m. "Chorus from *Swing On A Star*." "I wrote this, about the less well-known candidates of the 1992 Presidential election..." Published online at <http://www.speaeasy.org/~dacearonson/personal/old/swingpol.html>. 1992.

ARIZONA

FRÉMONT, John Charles (Governor, Arizona Territory, 1878–1881) [See: California]

• AmPM-27 GOLDWATER, Barry M. (City Council, Phoenix 1949-1952; U.S. Senator, 1953–1965 & 1969–1987) [ALSO SEE: DOC/PSM-BMG]

27.1 All Things Considered. w.m. Mighty Mighty Bosstones. Lyrics published online at <http://www.plyrics.com/lyrics/mightymightybosstones/allthingsconsidered.html>. [ca. 198–].

27.1A Barry's Boys. w.m. June Reizner. On 33⅓ rpm LP: *Reflecting* by The Chad Mitchell Trio. Performed by The Chad Mitchell Trio. Mercury Records #SR 60891/MG 20891. [ca. 1964]. Lyrics published online by Mudcat Café at <http://mudcat.org/@displaysong.cfm?SongID=519>. 1997.

27.2 Cool Goldwater. w. Noel E. Parmentel, Jr. and Marshall J. Dodge. In: *Folk Songs For Conservatives*, page 11. Published by Unicorn Press, Inc., No. 790 Madison Avenue, New York, NY. 10021. 1964. [5" × 8⅜"]. Bl/w drawings of Barry Goldwater, Bill Buckley, Ray Cohn, eagle. List of contents. "Sung by Noel E. Parmentel, Jr. and His Unbleached Muslims, Greatest Political Satirists Since Cohn and Schine." "Right Wing Hootenanny." 36pp. [Crew/BMG-13].

27.3 Dance Of The Liberal Republicans. w.m. Gerald Gardner. In: *These Are The Songs That Were* [Song Book], page 10. e. Gerald Gardner "(Writer of *Who's In Charge Here?*, *News-Reals*, and *That Was The Week That Was*)." Published by Edwin H. Morris and Company, No. 31 West 54th Street, New York, NY. 10019. 1965. B/w photo of Lyndon B. Johnson, Hubert Humphrey, Everett Dirksen, others. R/w/bk cover. List of contents. 36pp. Pages 8, 23 and 25: Photos of politicians. [Crew/LBJ-6].

27.4 Go Goldwater! w. No composer indicated. 33⅓ rpm 6⅞" record. Copyright Vera Nova Music. Republican National Committee #ET-2. Produced by RKO Studios, New York, NY. #133256. 1964. Both sides identical. Various cuts and timings of the song for radio play.

27.5 Goldwater. w.m. Hazel E. Davis. 45 rpm gold vinyl record. Faith & Freedom Records, 5901 Rose Avenue, Long Beach, CA. [1964]. Performed by The Citizens.

27.6 The Goldwater Anthem {27.6-1}. w.m. Lafayett Sammons. 45 rpm record. Gold-Teen Records, Box 75, Jonesboro, AR. Record #641. Performed by The Mason-Dixon Quartet. Side 2: *The Goldwater Swing* {27.6-2}. w.m. Lafayett Sammons. 1964.

27.7 Goldwater Victory Song. 45 rpm vinyl record. Published by Ra-Q Record Company, Scottsdale, AZ. 1964.

27.8 The Goldwaters Sing Folk Songs To Bug The Liberals. w.m. The Goldwaters. 33⅓ rpm LP. Published by Greenleaf Records #M101-63A. (SoN #4931-2). 1964. Songs include: *It's Over Now*; *Win In–64* {27.8-1}; *Barry's Moving In* {27.8-2}; *What Have You Done* {27.8-3}; *Farewell Serenade* {27.8-4}; *Bobby Bobby* {27.8-5}; *White House Goodbye* {27.8-6}; *The Campaign Trail* {27.8-7}; *Down In Havana* {27.8-8}; *The End Of The Monk* {27.8-9}; *The Rejected Song* {27.8-10}; and *Row Our Own Boat* {27.8-11}.

27.9 The Good Times Train. w. Johnny Lehmann. m. Jimmie Driftwood. Copyright 1960 by Worden Music Co., Inc. In: *Welcome GOP To The Jumbo Jamboree Uline Arena, April 4, 1960, Washington, DC*. [Program], page 4. R/w/b elephant. 4pp. Page 3 and 4: "Elected dignitaries in attendance — Senators Thurston Morton, Barry Goldwater, and Everett M. Dirksen; Congressmen William Miller and Charles Halleck." [Crew/MISC-154].

27.10 Hubert Humphrey — The President For You And Me. w. *Joe Glazer*. m. *"Tune—Davy Crockett."* In: *Sing And Win With Hubert Humphrey*, page 1. [1960]. [8½" × 13"]. B/w photo of Hubert H. Humphrey in front of a poster of Franklin D. Roosevelt. "These songs (except for one) were made up by Joe Glazer for the next President of the United States, Hubert Humphrey. *The President For You And Me* was written by Wisconsin's wonderful Lt. Governor and strong Humphrey supporter, Phileo Nash." 2pp. Page 2: Blank. [Crew/HHH-4].

27.11 I'm For Barry {27.11-1}. w.m. John Wilson, Antoni Gollan, Robert Nickels and John Miller. 45 rpm vinyl record. Published by the National Youth For Goldwater. Record #801Y=3396/R4KB-3396&7. Followed on side 1 by: *Back Again* {27.11-2} and *Hold*

On {27.11-3}. Side 2: Songs are: *Talking Blues* {27.11-4}; *Good News* {27.11-5}; and *Budapest* {27.11-6}. 1964.

27.12 Let's Test Again. w. Noel E. Parmentel, Jr. and Marshall J. Dodge. m. *Let's Twist Again.* In: *Folk Songs For Conservatives*, page 31. Published by Unicorn Press, Inc., No. 790 Madison Avenue, New York, NY. 10021. 1964. [5" × 8⅜"]. Bl/w drawings of Barry Goldwater, Bill Buckley, Ray Cohn, eagle. List of contents. "Sung by Noel E. Parmentel, Jr. and His Unbleached Muslims, Greatest Political Satirists Since Cohn and Schine." "Right Wing Hootenanny." 36pp. [Crew/BMG-13].

27.13 Long, Long Ago (Barry's Lament). w. Milton M. Schwartz. a. Danny Hurd. m. Tune—*Long, Long Ago.* In: *Sing Along With Jack* [Song Book], page 24. Published by Pocket Books, Inc., New York, NY. B/w drawing of Barry Goldwater as a minuteman guarding the U.S. Treasury. Copyright 1963 by Bonny Publishing Corporation. [9" × 11⅞"]. R/w/bk drawing of sheet music *Vive La Dynasty*, silhouette of John F. Kennedy in chair with conductor's baton, caricature of Kennedy family. "Hit Songs from the New Frontier." 36pp. Page 3: "Illustrations by David Gantz." Page 36: Drawing of John F. Kennedy in chair with baton. Song titles. [Crew/JFK-17].

27.14 On Top Of Goldwater (JFK's Lament). m. "To the tune of *On Top Of Old Smokey.*" In: *Sing Along With Jack* [Song Book], page 22. w. Milton M. Schwartz. a. Danny Hurd. Published by Pocket Books, Inc., New York, NY. Copyright 1963 by Bonny Publishing Corporation. [9" × 11⅞"]. R/w/bk drawing of sheet music "*Vive La Dynasty,*" silhouette of John F. Kennedy in chair with conductor's baton, caricature of Kennedy family. "Hit Songs from the New Frontier." 36pp. Page 3: "Illustrations by David Gantz." Page 36: Drawing of John F. Kennedy in chair with baton. Song titles. [Crew/ JFK-17].

27.15 Red River Valley (T.V.A.). w. Noel E. Parmentel, Jr. and Marshall J. Dodge. In: *Folk Songs For Conservatives*, page 17. Published by Unicorn Press, Inc., No. 790 Madison Avenue, New York, NY. 10021. 1964. [5" × 8⅜"]. Bl/w drawings of Barry Goldwater, Bill Buckley, Ray Cohn, eagle. List of contents. "Sung by Noel E. Parmentel, Jr. and His Unbleached Muslims, Greatest Political Satirists Since Cohn and Schine." "Right Wing Hootenanny." 36pp. [Crew/BMG-13].

27.16 Return To Proven Ways (The Rev. B.M. Goldwater). w.m. Hank Levine. On LP: *Washington Is For The Birds.* 33⅓ rpm LP. Reprise Records # RS-6212. Album cover: N/c drawings of Lyndon and Lady Bird Johnson. "The Authentic voices of Lady Bird Johnson, L.B.J. and People like That."

27.17 Sweet Selma Levine. w. Noel E. Parmentel, Jr. and Marshall J. Dodge. In: *Folk Songs For Conservatives*, page 23. Published by Unicorn Press, Inc., No. 790 Madison Avenue, New York, NY. 10021. 1964. [5" × 8⅜"]. Bl/w drawings of Barry Goldwater, Bill Buckley, Ray Cohn, eagle. List of contents. "Sung by Noel E. Parmentel, Jr. and His Unbleached Muslims, Greatest Political Satirists Since Cohn and Schine." "Right Wing Hootenanny." 36pp. [Crew/BMG-13].

27.18 Talking Vietnam. w. Julius Lester, 1965. m. *Talking Blues.* "Written shortly after the U.S. started bombing North Vietnam in 1965..." In: *The Vietnam Songbook*, page 120. c. Barbara Dane and Irwin Silber. Published by The Guardian, No. 32 West 22nd Street, New York, NY. Copyright 1969 by Barbara Dane and Irwin Silber. [7" × 10"]. B/w photo of a protest march. O/y/r/bk cover. 228pp.

27.19 We Shall Not Be Moved. w. Noel E. Parmentel, Jr. and Marshall J. Dodge. In: *Folk Songs For Conservatives*, page 27. Published by Unicorn Press, Inc., No. 790 Madison Avenue, New York, NY. 10021. 1964. [5" × 8⅜"]. Bl/w drawings of Barry Goldwater, Bill Buckley, Ray Cohn, eagle. List of contents. "Sung by Noel E. Parmentel, Jr. and His Unbleached Muslims, Greatest Political Satirists Since Cohn and Schine." "Right Wing Hootenanny." 36pp. [Crew/BMG-13].

27.20 Where I Stand—Ha Ha!. w. No composer indicated. In: Unknown newspaper. [1964]. Non-pictorial. "Campaign Hootenanny: Two of a group of parodies from the Reporter, reprinted with permission of that magazine and of the author."

• **AmPM-28** MCCAIN, John Sidney, III (U.S. House, 1983–1987; U.S. Senate, 1987–Present)

28.1 Another Trick In The Fall, Part 1. w. Skisics Surus, "skisics@yahoo.com." m. "Parody of song from *Another Brick In The Wall, Part 1* by Pink Floyd." Published online at <http://www.geocities.com/wmktong/bootnewt/trick1.htm>. [ca. 2000].

28.2 Back To 1999. w. Skisics Surus, "skisics@yahoo.com." m. "Sung to the tune of *1999* by Prince." Published online at <http://www.geocities.com/wmktong/bootnewt/back1999.htm>. [ca. 2000].

28.3 Bush, Whore Son. w. Skisics Surus, "skisics@yahoo.com." m. "Sung to the tune of *Black Hole Sun* by Soundgarden." Published online at <http://www.geocities.com/wmktong/bootnewt/bush-son.htm>. [ca. 2000].

28.4 Daddy. w. Skisics Surus, "skisics@yahoo.com." m. "Parody of *Mother* from *The Wall* by Pink Floyd." Published online at <http://www.geocities.com/wmktong/bootnewt/trick1.htm>. [ca. 2000].

28.5 Electoral Rhapsody 2000. w. Kevin Dunlap. m. "Sung to the tune of *Bohemian Rhapsody* by Queen." Published online at <http://www.analyticalq.com/music/parodies/rhapsody.htm>. 2000.

28.6 Friends In Loaded Place. w. Tim Wilson. m. "Original: *Friends In Low Places* written and performed by Garth Brooks." Published by the Georgy Bush Project online at <http://www.georgybush.com/lyrics3.html>. [2000].

28.7 Goodbye, Fool. w. Skisics Surus, "skisics@yahoo.com." m. "Parody of song from *Goodbye Cruel World* by Pink Floyd." Published online at <http://www.geocities.com/wmktong/bootnewt/goodbyefool.htm>. [ca. 2000].

28.8 Hello, Bob Jones. w. Skisics Surus, "skisics@yahoo.com." m. "Parody of *Goodbye, Blue Sky* from *The Wall* by Pink Floyd." Published online at <http://www.geocities.com/wmktong/bootnewt/hellobobjones.htm>. [ca. 2000].

28.9 I Can See Clearly Now, McCain Is Gone. w. "George W." m. Tune—*I Can See Clearly Now.* Published online by PoliticsOL.com at <www.presidential

election2000.com/I_can_see_clearly_now.html>. [Crew/GWB-3].

28.10 I Hear McCain A Comin.' w. No composer indicated. m. "Parody of *Folsom Prison Blues* by Johnny Cash." Lyrics published by *The Bob Rivers Show* with Bob, Spike & Joe and Twisted Tunes online at <http://www.twistedradio.com/player/lyrics.asp?songID=663>. [2000].

28.11 I'm In Love With John McCain. w. Paul Shaklin. On CD: *Vice Vice Baby*. Published by Narodniki Records. CD Cover: Caricature of composer. See: <www.paulShaklin.com>. 2001.

28.12 McCain. w. William K. Tong. m. "Sung to the tune of *Cocaine* by Eric Clapton." Published online at <http://www.geocities.com/wmktong/bootnewt/mccain.htm>. [ca. 2000].

28.13 McCain As Patton. w. Paul Shaklin. On CD: *The Usual Suspects*. Published by Goes Around Records. CD Cover: N/c drawing of Bill Clinton, Jesse Jackson, and others. See: <www.paulShaklin.com>. 2001.

28.14 The McCain Mutiny. w. Paul Shaklin. On CD: *Vice Vice Baby*. Published by Narodniki Records. CD Cover: Caricature of composer. See: <www.paulShaklin.com>. 2001.

28.15 One Of My Burns. w. Skisics Surus, "skisics@yahoo.com." m. "Parody of *One Of My Turns* from *The Wall* by Pink Floyd." Published online at <http://www.geocities.com/wmktong/bootnewt/oneburns.htm>. [ca. 2000].

28.16 Shrub Is In Despair. w. William K. Tong. m. "Sung to the tune of *Love Is In The Air* by John Paul Young." Published online at <http://www.geocities.com/wmktong/bootnewt/shrubdes.htm>. [ca. 2000].

28.17 Sixteen Scandals. w. Michael Pacholek. m. "*Sixteen Candles*, based on a performance by Johnny Maestro & The Crests." Published online at <http://www.amiright.com/parody/misc/johnnymaestrothecrests.shtml>. [ca. 2003].

28.18 Texas Swing. w. Ice Bielefeldt. m. "*Midwest Swing* originally by St. Lunatics." "If four well-known Texas Republicans became a rap group, what would it sound like?" Published online at <http://www.amiright.com/parody/2000s/stlunatics0.shtml>. 2003.

28.19 The Thin Vice. w. Skisics Surus, "skisics@yahoo.com." m. "Parody of song from *The Wall* by Pink Floyd." Published online at <http://www.geocities.com/wmktong/bootnewt/thinvice.htm>. [ca. 2000].

28.20 Vote McCaine [sic]. w. No composer indicated. m. "To the tune of *Cocaine*." Published online at <http://www.wwirr.com/wcr/parody/mccain.html>. [199-]

28.21 Voting Places. w. Skisics Surus, "skisics@yahoo.com." m. "Parody of *Empty Spaces* from *The Wall* by Pink Floyd." Published online at <http://www.geocities.com/wmktong/bootnewt/votingplaces.htm>. [ca. 2000].

• **AmPM-29** O'CONNOR, Sandra Day (Assistant State Attorney General, 1965-1969; State Senate, 1969-1974; Superior Court Judge, Maricopa County, 1974-1979; State Court of Appeals, 1979-1981; U.S. Supreme Court, 1981-Present)

29.1 Dubya, The Bogus POTUS. w. William Tong. m. "*Rudolph The Red-Nosed Reindeer*, originally by Gene Autry." Published online at <http://amiright.com/parody/misc/geneautry0.shml>. [ca. 2000].

29.2 Failure Boy. w. Michael Pacholek. m. Tune — "*Sk8er Boi* originally by Avril Lavigne." "This is what my life has come to: Ripping off a girl who wasn't even old enough to vote when she wrote the original (and can't vote in the U.S. anyway). Naming the song *Failyr Boi* was considered, but quickly dropped." Published online at <http://www.amiright.com/parody/2000s/avrillavigne67/shtml>. 2003

• **AmPM-30** REHNQUIST, William Hubbs (Assistant U.S. Attorney General, 1969-1972, U.S. Supreme Court, 1972-Present)

30.1 Dubya, The Bogus POTUS. w. William Tong. m. "*Rudolph The Red-Nosed Reindeer*, originally by Gene Autry." Published online at <http://amiright.com/parody/misc/geneautry0.shml>. [ca. 2000].

30.2 Indecision 2000. w. Gary S. O'Connor. m. Tune —"*Mack The Knife*, based on a performance by Bobby Darin." "I finally got to write my editorial on the Presidential Election of 2000. This is political fodder for your ears. The story of Al, Walker, Kathy, Hillary, Jessie and all the rest is set to the melody of *Mack The Knife* in this parody. By the way, this is not the Rush Limbaugh theme song, but it could be!" Published online at <http://www.amiright.com/parody/60s/bobbydarin2.shtml>. [ca. 2003].

30.3 Mr. Rehnquist's Neighborhood. w. Bill Strauss and Elaina Newport. On Cassette: *Thank God I'm A Contra Boy*. Published by Capitol Steps Productions, 1505 King Street, Alexandria, VA. 1986. Cassette Cover: Capitol building.

30.4 Rehnquist's Song. w. Mark McGuffin. m. *I Am The Very Model Of A Modern Major General* by Sir. Author Sullivan. "Inspired by Judge Rehnquist's gold-striped judge's robe, which was in turn inspired by Judge Rehnquist's love of Gilbert & Sullivan. Send kudos, comments or complaints to mcguffin@foolmoon.com care of Mark McGuffin." Published online at <http://www.lightjunkie.org/parody/rehnquist.html>. [ca. 2001].

30.5 To Hell With Vote Machines. w. William Tong. m. Tune —"*Yellow Submarine*, originally by The Beatles." Published online at <http://amiright.com/parody/misc/thebeatles7.shml>. [ca. 2000].

• **AmPM-30A** RIMSZA, Skip (City Council, Phoenix, 1990-1994; Mayor, Phoenix, 1994-Present)

30A.1 Light Rail Man. w. Fordo-HartleyX. m. "Sung to the tune of *Nowhere Man* by the Beatles." Lyrics and sound file published onlibe at <http://www.phxnews.com/fullstory.php?article=3344>. 2003.

ARKANSAS

• **AmPM-31 BERRY**, James Henderson (State House, 1866 & 1872–1874; State Court Judge, 1878; Governor, 1883–1885; U.S. Senate, 1885–1907)

31.1 Gov. Berry's Grand March. m. Alex. G. Black. Published by Peel & Clark, Publishers, Bentonville, AR. 1884. B/w non-pictorial geometric designs. "Dedicated to James H. Berry, Gov. of Arkansas." 6pp. Page 6: Blank.

• **AmPM-32 BROUGH**, Charles Hillman (Governor, 1917–1921)

32.1 America My Country (The New National Anthem). w. Jens K. Grondahl. m. E.F. Maetzold. Published by The Red Wing Printing Co., Red Wing, MN. 1917. R/w/b litho of a shield, geometric designs. "Long paragraph on the song—*America, My Country* is said to be the greatest patriotic song-poem of the war..." 4pp. Page 4: Testimonial signed by officers of the National Editorial Association. List of Governors who had "written letters commending the nation-wide use of this song" including "Gov. Brough of Arkansas."

• **AmPM-32A BRYANT**, Kelly (Arkansas Secretary of State, 1963)

32A.1 Arkansas. w.m. Eva Ware Barnett. Published by Kelly Bryant, Secretary of State, Little Rock, AR. 1963. N/c picture of a pastoral mountain scene. "The official State Song." 6pp. Page 2: Narrative on song history. Page 6: N/c photo of Arkansas scenes, State symbols.

• **AmPM-33 CLARK**, Wesley (Candidate for the Democratic Nomination for President, 2004)

33.1 The Ballad Of Wesley Clark. w. Mac195. m. Tune—"*The Ballad Of Davy Crockett,* based on a performance by The Kentucky Headhunters." Published online at <http://amiright.com/parody/misc/thekentuckyheadhunters0.shtml>. [2004].

33.2 Bushlicker. w. "Political Prankster." m. "*Complicated,* based on the performance by Avril Lavigne." Published online at <http://amiright.com/parody/2000s/avrillavigne175.shml>. [2003].

33.3 Dashing Through The States. w. John Jenkins. m. Tune—"*Jingle Bells,* based on the performance by Traditional." "The Democratic field of presidential candidates has been reduced from 10 to 7 with more candidates expected to withdraw this week. Will the selection process eventually narrow down to two candidates in a replay of the Super Bowl with the upstart from Carolina going against the veteran from Massachusetts?" Published online at <http://www.amiright.com/parody/misc/traditional437.shtml>. 2004.

33.4 The Democratic Presidential Candidate Show. w. Laurence Dunne. m. "*The Muppet Show* by The Muppets." "I'm not a Republican by and certainly I'm not a Dubya fan, as my Bush parodies will attest <http://www.amiright.com/parody/60s/thebradybunchtvshow0.shtml>." Published online at <http://amiright.com/parody/70s/muppets0.shtml>. [ca. 2003].

33.5 Fifty Guys Runnin' 'Gainst Dubya. w. Charlie Decker. m. "*Fifty Ways To Leave Your Lover,* based on the performance by Paul Simon." Published online at <http://amiright.com/parody/70s/paulsimon28.shml>. [2003].

33.6 Gov'nor Arnold/General Wesley. w. Johnny D. m. "*Uncle Albert/Admiral Halsey,* based on a performance by Paul McCartney." Published online at <http://www.amiright.com/parody/70s/paulmccartney23.shtml>. 2003.

33.7 Green Party Man. w. Charlie Decker. m. "*Street Fighting Man,* based on a performance by Rolling Stones." "Although I am a Democrat politically, I sympathize with the Green Party, even if only to keep Dems honest." Published online at <http://www.amiright.com/parody/60s/rollingstones34.shtml>. [ca. 2003].

33.8 New Hampshire Primary Marching Cadence. w. Guy DiRito. m. "*Military Cadence (Sound Off),* based on a performance by Traditional." "This song is done to the traditional military cadence beat. Practice marching as you sound off to this." Published online at <http://www.amiright.com/parody/misc/traditional430.shtml>. 2004.

33.9 Pal Wesley Clark. w. Michael Pacholek. m. "*Palisades Park,* based on the performance by Freddy Cannon." "I should have written this weeks ago. The flavor of the month has melted. Not that this was an endorsement anyway." "And now Clark's fade is well underway. Maybe Kerry will appoint him Secretary of Defense, after all, Clark shouldn't have trouble getting his fellow Republicans to confirm him in the Senate." Published online at <http://www.amiright.com/parody/60s/freddycannon0.shtml>. 2003.

33.10 People Who Tried (Political). w. Malcolm Higgins. m. "*People Who Died,* based on a performance by Jim Carroll." Published online at <http://www.amiright.com/parody/misc/jimcarroll0.shtml>. [ca. 2003].

33.11 Vote. w. Moscowman. m. "*Vogue,* based on a performance by Madonna." "The Election is coming in November, voters reading the magazines and think what's their decision on the upcoming election." Published online at <http://amiright.com/parody/90s/thekinks3.shtml>. [2004].

33.12 We Want Howard Dean. w.m. Denny Zartman. m. No tune indicated. "Spread The Word Through Song and Music! Songs For Dean, Songs to get elected by." N/c photo of Howard Dean. Lyrics and sound file published online at <http://songsfordean.com/so/lyrics/somethingtosee.php>. 2004.

33.13 Yell Like Howard Dean. w. John Jenkins. m. "*Yellow Submarine,* based on the performance by The Beatles." "As the race for the Democratic presidential nomination approaches the first two voter tests, the Iowa caucus and the New Hampshire primary (both in January), Dr. Howard Dean is combining his fire breathing campaign rhetoric and his unique internet appeal to lead the polls in both states. Will he stay there?" Published online at <http://amiright.com/parody/60s/thebeatles415.shml>. [ca. 2004].

• **AmPM-34 CLAYTON**, Powell (Governor, 1868; U.S. Senate, 1871–1877)

34.1 Governor Clayton's Quick Step. m. Mrs. Lizzie Bowers "(Author of *Ever Onward March, General Sherman's Savannah March, etc., etc., etc.*)." Published by Balmer & Weber, 209 Fourth Street, St. Louis, MO. 1868. B/w geometric design frame. "To General Powell Clayton, Governor of Arkansas." 6pp. Pages 2 and 6: Blank.

- **AmPM-34x** CLINTON, William Jefferson (State Attorney General, 1977–1979; Governor, 1979–1981 & 1983–1992; President, 1993–2001) [SEE: DOC/PSM-WJC]
- **AmPM-35** DAVIS, Jeff (Prosecuting Attorney, 1892–1896; State Attorney General, 1898–1900; Governor, 1901–1906; U.S. Senate, 1907–1913)

35.1 The Great Bear State Dance. w. Mattie Webb. m. Maggie Hambaugh Dandoe "(Author of *The Copper King, The Twentieth Century Waltz*)." Published by A.W. Perry & Sons Music Co., Sedalia, MO. [1901–1906]. Bl/w geometric designs. "Dedicated to Governor Jefferson Davis, of Arkansas." 6pp. Pages 2 and 6: Blank.

- **AmPM-36** DORSEY, Stephen Wallace (U.S. Senator, 1873–1879)

36.1 Mary Blaine. w. Ben Warren. m. Air—*Mary Blane*. Published by Hitchcock's Music Store, No. 166 Nassau Street, New York, NY. 1884. Litho of James G. Blaine in woman's dress, slogans—"Side Contracts," "Sentenced to Go Up Salt River, Nov. 6, 1884." "Little Rock RR Bonds." "20 Years in Congress." "Mulligan Letters." "To J.G.B. form the King of the Lobby." "Belmont." "Crooked Paths." "Self." Oriental man with sign inscribed "Blain-E Must-E Go-E." "Utilizing the old air of *Mary Blane* for Patriot Purposes." 4pp. Page 4: Blank. [Crew/GC-70].

- **AmPM-37** FAUBUS, Orval E. (Governor, 1955–1967; National States Rights Candidate for President, 1960)

37.1 The Johnson Victory Hymn. w. W.L. White. [1964]. [8½" × 11"]. Non-pictorial. "W.L. White in *The Emporia Gazette*." 2pp. Page 2: Reprint of an anti-Johnson editorial by W.L. White in the *Emporia Gazette*. [Crew/LBJ-38].

37.2 We Like Faubus. w.m. Nick Morris. Published by Morrissey Music Co., Little Rock, AR. 1958. Bl/w photo of "The Hon. Orval E. Faubus, Governor of Arkansas." "Recorded by The Warners on President Record #No. 581." 4pp. Page 4: Orchestration for small ensemble.

- **AmPM-38** GARLAND, Augustus Hill (Confederate Provisional Congress, 1861; Confederate Congress, 1861–1865; Governor, 1874–1876; U.S. Senate, 1877–1885; U.S. Attorney General, 1885–1889)

38.1 Good Bye, Old Grover, Good Bye. w. A.A. Rowley (Beloit, Kansas). m. "Air—*Good-Bye, My Lover, Good-Bye*." In: *Republican Campaign Songs*, page 2. Published by The Western News Company, Chicago, IL. 1888. [5¼" × 7½"]. B/w litho of "The Author, in '63, 17th Illinois Cav." "Original, Pointed and Spicy ... Set to Old Familiar Tunes, Suitable for Glee Clubs and Marching Clubs." "Look at it and you will buy it." 36pp. [M-283]. [Crew/BFH-64].

- **AmPL-38A** JONES, James Kimbrough (State Senate, 1873–1879; U.S. House, 1881–1885; U.S. Senate, 1885–1903)

38A.1 Ben And Levi. w. No composer indicated. m. "Air—*Solomon And Levi*." In: *Democratic Song Book For The Campaign Of 1888*, page 8. c. John R. East. Published by John R. East, Bloomington, IN. 1888. [4¼" × 5¹³⁄₁₆"]. Bl/bl litho of Grover Cleveland and Allen Thurman. "Price 10 cents, postage prepaid, Liberal Discounts to Dealers." 20pp. [Crew/GC-140].

38A.2 The Cuckoos. w. No composer indicated. m. "Tune—*Billy Magee McGaw*." In: *The Rough Rider (Republican Campaign Song Book)*, page 8. c. J. Burgess Brown. Published by J. Burgess Brown, Indianapolis, IN. 1900. [6" × 9"]. Br/bk non-pictorial. "ROUGH ON DemocRATS." 28pp. Page 3: B/w litho of William McKinley. Page 28: "Republican National Ticket—1900. [Crew/WM-330].

38A.3 He Will Never Come Here Anymore. w. E.J. Seymour. m. Tune—*On The Bowery*." In: *Campaign Songs, 1896* [Song Sheet], page 2. Published by Wholesale Dry Goods Republican Club, New York, NY. 1896. [12" × 18¼"]. Non-pictorial. 2pp. [Six songs per page]. [Crew/WM-128].

38A.4 John Brown's Body. w. Gen. Stillman F. Kneeland. m. *Glory, Glory, Hallelujah*. In: *Campaign College Songs 1900* [Song Book], page 5. w. Gen. Stillman F. Kneeland. Published for the Wholesale Dry Goods Republican Club, No. 350 Broadway, New York, NY. 1900. [5⅞" × 9⅛"]. Y/bk photos of William "McKinley" and Theodore "Roosevelt." Y/bk drawings of eagle, shield, flags. "A bird that can sing and won't sing must be made to sing." 16pp. Page 16: "If any one pulls down the Flag, shoot him on the spot—John A. Dix." "Will you vote for a man who will pull down the American Flag in the Philippines?" [Crew/WM-214].

38A.5 Marching To The Bugle Call. w. No composer indicated. m. "Tune—*Swinging In The Grape Vine Swing*." In: *The Rough Rider (Republican Campaign Song Book)*, page 19. c. J. Burgess Brown. Published by J. Burgess Brown, Indianapolis, IN. 1900. [6" × 9"]. Br/bk non-pictorial. "ROUGH ON DemocRATS." 28pp. [Crew/WM-330].

38A.6 The Menagerie. w. Gen. Stillman F. Kneeland. m. "Page 243, *Carmina Collegensia*." In: *Campaign College Songs 1900* [Song Book], page 2. Published for the Wholesale Dry Goods Republican Club, No. 350 Broadway, New York, NY. 1900. [5⅞" × 9⅛"]. Y/bk photos of William "McKinley" and Theodore "Roosevelt." Y/bk drawings of eagle, shield, flags. "A bird that can sing and won't sing must be made to sing." 16pp. Page 16: "If any one pulls down the Flag, shoot him on the spot—John A. Dix." "Will you vote for a man who will pull down the American Flag in the Philippines?" [Crew/WM-214].

38A.7 The New Dollar. w. E.J. Seymour. m. "Tune—*The New Bully*." In: *Campaign Songs, 1896* [Song Sheet]. Published by Wholesale Dry Goods Republican Club, New York, NY. 1896. [12" × 18¼"]. Non-pictorial. 2pp. [Six songs per page]. [Crew/WM-128].

38A.8 The Son Of A Gambolier. w. Gen. Stillman F. Kneeland. m. "*The Son Of A Gambolier*." In: *Campaign College Songs 1900* [Song Book], page 6. Published for the Wholesale Dry Goods Republican Club, No. 350 Broadway, New York, NY. 1900. [5⅞" ×

9⅛"]. Y/bk photos of William "McKinley" and Theodore "Roosevelt." Y/bk drawings of eagle, shield, flags. "A bird that can sing and won't sing must be made to sing." 16pp. Page 16: "If any one pulls down the Flag, shoot him on the spot — John A. Dix." "Will you vote for a man who will pull down the American Flag in the Philippines?" [Crew/WM-214].

38A.9 We've Waited, Billy, Waited Long For You. w. Stephen Laskey. m. "Tune — *I've Waited, Honey, Waited Long For You.*" In: *McKinley & Roosevelt Campaign 1900* [Song Book], page 16. Published for the Wholesale Dry Goods Republican Club, No. 350 Broadway by C.G. Burgoyne, New York, NY. 1900. [4¾" × 7"]. Y/bk litho of William McKinley and Theodore Roosevelt, eagle, shield. "Meetings daily from 12 Noon until 2 p.m." "A bird that can sing and won't must be made to sing." 20pp. [M-376]. [Crew/WM-84].

• **AmPM-39 MACARTHUR,** Douglas (America First Party Candidate for President, 1952) [ALSO SEE: DOC/PSM-DAM]

39.1 All-Out For MacArthur. w.m. Ralph Barfell. Published by Ralph Barfell, Appleton, WI. 1942. R/w/b drawing of Douglas MacArthur, ships, Nazi submarine sinking, tank, planes, large "V." "Victory United Nations." 6pp. Page 6: Blank. 2pp insert on Mr. Barfell and learning to plan Hawaiian or Spanish Guitar.

39.2 But He Wouldn't Say Yes! w. No composer indicated. m. "Air — *I Can't Say No.*" In: *Dealers Choice Or Back-To-Back Biting,* page 15. Published by the Albany Legislative Correspondent's Association of New York State, Albany, NY. 1944. [8" × 11¾"]. N/c drawing of Franklin Roosevelt, Thomas Dewey, "Chiang," "Winnie" and "Joe" playing cards — "Featuring the World's Most Exciting Egomaniacs in a Marvelous Musical of Messianic and Mystery: Showing Sinners, Sycophants, Suckers, and Sleuths Saving Civilization with Sound; or Find the Joker!" "Dealt Off the Bottom of a Hot Deck — In Three Acts at Ten Eyck, Albany, March 9, 1944." [Crew/FDR-364].

39.3 Duty, Honor, Country. w. Douglas MacArthur. m. Harold L. Walters. Published by Rubank, Inc. [ca. 1962]. Bl/w photo of Douglas MacArthur, bunting. "Conductor-Narrator." "Rubank Symphonic Band Library No. 142." "Adapted by B.G. Cook from an Address by General of the Army Douglas MacArthur at the U.S. Military Academy, May 12, 1962." Conductor's score. 10pp. [Crew/DAM-70].

39.4 Gen. Douglas MacArthur. m. Robert Russel Bennett. Published by Chapell & Co., Inc., No. 609 Fifth Avenue, New York, NY. 1965. [7" × 10½"]. Bk/bl/w drawing by Ron Chereswin of members of a marching band. "Theme from NBC-TV *That War In Korea.*" Parts set for band. [Crew/DAM-64].

39.5 General Mac Will Never Fade Away. w.m. Seymour Schwartz. 78 rpm record. Rondo Records #628A. Performed by Booker T. Washington and the Pacific Sextette. [195–].

39.6 General MacArthur's Promise. w. Roy Parton. m. Lew Tobin. Published by Nordyke Publishing Company, Hollywood, CA. 1943. R/w/b drawing of an eagle. "Victory Edition." 4pp. Page 4: Advertising. [Crew/DAM-68].

39.6A Harry Done 'Em Wrong. w.m. Lee Thornsby. On: *Grand Old Party Songs.* 33⅓ rpm 10" record. Published by Middlesex Trading Company, #G8-OL-7518. Performed by Eli Frantz and his Magic Guitar. [ca. 195–].

39.7 I'm The Guy. w.m. No composer or tune indicated. [ca. 1944]. [8½" × 11"]. Bl/w non-pictorial line border. 2pp. Page 2: Blank. [Crew/DAM-62].

39.8 Letter To General MacArthur. w.m. Harold J. Rome. Published by Musette Publishers, Inc., Steinway Hall, New York, NY. 1942. R/w/bl/y drawing by Drusin of three children drawing. 6pp. Pages 2 and 6: Advertising. [Crew/DAM-60].

39.9 Let's Dig In And Dig Out. w.m. Billy Hays (A.S.C.A.P.). m. Frank Capano. (A.S.C.A.P.). Published by Tin Pan Alley, No. 1011 Chestnut Street, Philadelphia, PA. [V-1: 9" × 12"] [V-2: 8½" × 11"]. 1942. B/w geometric designs. "Title suggested by Elwood Hagy." [V-2: At top — "This is a Tin Pan Alley Publication"]. 4pp. [Crew/DAM-63].

39.10 MacArthur At Manila (Descriptive Battle Scene). m. Eugene V. Clark. Published by Chart Music Publishing House, Chicago, IL. 1942. Pl/w non-pictorial. "Series of Drum Publication." "Snare Drum Solos." List of other tunes in the series. 4pp. Page 4: Advertising. [Crew/DAM-67].

39.11 MacArthur's Men. w.m. Carl Sobie and Gertrude Antczak. Published by Carl Sobie, Music Publisher, No. 1509 Broadway, Detroit, MI. 1942. Bk/bl/w drawing of General MacArthur, soldiers, palm tree. 6pp. Pages 2 and 6: Advertising. [Crew/DAM-69].

39.12 MacArthur's Return To The Philippines. w.m. Charlie Hodgkins. Published by Charlie Hodgkins, Salem, MA. 1945. Bl/w non-pictorial geometric border, stars. "Dedicated to the Allied Armed Forces of the World." 6pp. Pages 2 and 6: Blank. [Crew/DAM-65].

39.13 The Rising Sun Has Gone Down For All Time. w.m. Jimmy Lawson. Published by Lawson Publications. [1945]. Br/w photo of General Douglas A. MacArthur. "Featured by Carl Saunders and Sunway Vitamins." 4pp. Page 4: Blank. [Crew/DAM-66].

39.14 You Can't Win A War Without The Irish. w.m. Harold Curran and Wallace Garland. Published by Murray Singer Music Publishing Company, No. 1647 Broadway, New York, NY. 1942. R/gn/br/w drawings of soldiers, General Douglas Mac Arthur, "Father Duffy." "Dedicated to the Rainbow Division and the fighting men in every branch of the service." 4pp. Page 4: Advertising. [Crew/DAM-61].

• **AmPM-40 MORSE,** Wayne Lyman (U.S. Senate, 1945–1969)

40.1 The Johnson Victory Hymn. w. W.L. White. [1964]. [8½" × 11"]. Non-pictorial. "W.L. White in *The Emporia Gazette.*" 2pp. Page 2: Reprint of an anti-Johnson editorial by W.L. White in the *Emporia Gazette.* [Crew/LBJ-38].

• **AmPM-42 PIKE,** Albert G. (Reporter, Arkansas Supreme Court, 1836–1844; Confederate Commissioner to the Tribes of Indian Territory, 1861–1862; State Supreme Court, 1864)

42.1 The Bonnie Blue Flag. w.m. Harry Macarthy. Published by A.E. Blackmar & Bro., 74 Camp Street,

New Orleans, LA. 1861. R/w/b litho of the Confederate Bonny Blue and Stars and Bars flags. "Composed, arranged and sung at his Personation Concerts by Harry Macarthy, The Arkansas Comedian." "To Albert G. Pike, The Poet Lawyer of Arkansas." 6pp. [H-3331-3333, 3335-3339 & 3340].

42.2 Buena Vista. w.m. No composer or tune indicated. In: *The Patriot's Songster*, page 13. Published by Mumford & Company, Cincinnati, OH. 1862. [3½" × 6"]. Non-pictorial. 48pp.

42.3 Song, After The Midnight Cometh Morn. w. Albert Pike. m. No tune indicated. No publisher indicated. January 22, 1870. Non-pictorial. "For Señorita Carolina Cassard." 2pp. [AMC].

42.4 Southrons. Hear Your Country Call You! w. Albert Pike. m. No tune indicated. In: *War Songs Of The Blue And The Gray*, page 26. Published by Hurst & Co., Publishers, New York, NY. [ca. 1880]. [4⅜" × 6½"]. Bl/k lithos of "Grant," "Robert E. Lee," "Johnston," and "Sherman," 72pp. [Crew/USG-299].

42.5 The War Song Of Dixie (Southrons, Hear Your Country Call You). w. Albert Pike. m. J.C. Vierick. Published by P.P. Werlein & Halsey, 3 & 5 Camp Street, New Orleans, LA. 1861. B/w non-pictorial geometric designs. "Inscribed to our Gallant Volunteers." "Op. 562." 8pp. Page 8: Blank. [AMC].

- **AmPM-43** **RIVIERE**, Paul (Arkansas Secretary of State, 1979)

43.1 Arkansas. w.m. Eva Ware Barnett. Published and Distributed by Paul Riviere, Secretary of State, [Little Rock, AR.]. [ca. 1979]. B/w drawing by Jan Barger of a family, home. "The Official Arkansas State Song." 4pp.

- **AmPM-44** **ROBINSON**, Joseph Taylor (General Assembly, 1895; U.S. House, 1903–1913, Governor; 1913; U.S. Senate, 1913–1937)

44.1 Welcome Song To Huey Long (Our U.S. Senator). w.m. Tom McNelly. a. Joseph Garrow. Published by Tom McNelly, Music Publishers, New Orleans, LA. 1931. Photo of Huey Long. Drawings of the "Louisiana State Capitol" building and the "U.S. Capitol" building, geometric designs. 8pp. Page 8: Blank.

- **AmPM-44A** **ROCKEFELLER**, Winthrop (Republican National Committee, 1961; Delegate, Republican National Convention, 1964; Governor, 1967–1971)

44A.1 Democrats For Rockefeller. w. Helen and Dan Mathes. m. No tune indicated. In: *WR Campaign Songs 1968* [Songbook], page 6. w. "Parodies composed by Helen and Dan Mathes." m. Popular songs. No publisher indicated. 1968. [8½" × 7"]. R/w/b cover. 16pp. Page 2: "Introduced by the Mathes Family, Dan (father), Helen (mother), Mike (14), Kathy (12), Francis (10)." Pages 2, 4, 15 and 16: Blank.

44A.2 [Listen To The Issues Goin' 'Round The Land]. w. Helen and Dan Mathes. m. "Tune—*Crawdad Song*." In: *WR Campaign Songs 1968* [Songbook], page 8. w. "Parodies composed by Helen and Dan Mathes." m. Popular songs. No publisher indicated. 1968. [8½" × 7"]. R/w/b cover. 16pp. Page 2: "Introduced by the Mathes Family, Dan (father), Helen (mother), Mike (14), Kathy (12), Francis (10)." Pages 2, 4, 15 and 16: Blank.

44A.3 The Man By The Name Of Win. w. Helen and Dan Mathes. m. No tune indicated. In: *WR Campaign Songs 1968* [Songbook], page 12. w. "Parodies composed by Helen and Dan Mathes." m. Popular songs. No publisher indicated. 1968. [8½" × 7"]. R/w/b cover. 16pp. Page 2: "Introduced by the Mathes Family, Dan (father), Helen (mother), Mike (14), Kathy (12), Francis (10)." Pages 2, 4, 15 and 16: Blank.

44A.4 Rockefeller. w. Helen and Dan Mathes. m. No tune indicated. In: *WR Campaign Songs 1968* [Songbook], page 5. w. "Parodies composed by Helen and Dan Mathes." m. Popular songs. No publisher indicated. 1968. [8½" × 7"]. R/w/b cover. 16pp. Page 2: "Introduced by the Mathes Family, Dan (father), Helen (mother), Mike (14), Kathy (12), Francis (10)." Pages 2, 4, 15 and 16: Blank.

44A.5 [Win Has Come From The Mountain]. w. Helen and Dan Mathes. m. No Tune indicated. In: *WR Campaign Songs 1968* [Songbook], page 10. w. "Parodies composed by Helen and Dan Mathes." m. Popular songs. No publisher indicated. 1968. [8½" × 7"]. R/w/b cover. 16pp. Page 2: "Introduced by the Mathes Family, Dan (father), Helen (mother), Mike (14), Kathy (12), Francis (10)." Pages 2, 4, 15 and 16: Blank.

44A.6 WR Campaign Songs 1968 [Songbook]. w. "Parodies composed by Helen and Dan Mathes." m. Popular songs. No publisher indicated. 1968. [8½" × 7"]. R/w/b cover. 16pp. Page 2: "Introduced by the Mathes Family, Dan (father), Helen (mother), Mike (14), Kathy (12), Francis (10)." Pages 2, 4, 15 and 16: Blank.

CALIFORNIA

- **AmPM-45** **BALL**, Danney (Candidate for Governor, 2002; Candidate for Senate, 2004)

45.1 All It Takes. w.m. Danney Ball. CD. CitySong Records, 140 E. Stetson Ave., #133, Hemet, CA. 92543. [199-].

45.2 Catch The Danney Ball Concert Tonight. w.m. Danney Ball. VHS tape. Jimmy Mac Productions c/o CitySong Records, 140 E. Stetson Ave., #133, Hemet, CA. 92543. [ca. 199-].

45.3 The Danney Ball Country Songbook. w.m. Danney Ball. CD. Songwrangler Music Publishing Company c/o CitySong Records, 140 E. Stetson Ave., #133, Hemet, CA. 92543. [ca. 199-].

45.4 The Danney Ball Gospel Songbook. w.m.

Danney Ball. CD. Songwrangler Music Publishing Company c/o CitySong Records, 140 E. Stetson Ave., #133, Hemet, CA. 92543. [ca. 199-].

45.5 *I'm Coming Back To Church*. w.m. Danney Ball. CD. CitySong Records, 140 E. Stetson Ave., #133, Hemet, CA. 92543. [199-].

45.6 *Palm Springs I Love You*. w.m. Danney Ball. CD. CitySong Records, 140 E. Stetson Ave., #133, Hemet, CA. 92543. [ca. 1999].

45.7 *Temecula*. w.m. Danney Ball. CD. CitySong Records, 140 E. Stetson Ave., #133, Hemet, CA. 92543. 1999.

45.8 *This Is My Country*. w.m. Danney Ball. CD. CitySong Records, 140 E. Stetson Ave., #133, Hemet, CA. 92543. 2005.

45.9 *[3 People Are Afraid Of Danney Ball]*. w.m. Danney Ball. "I though my campaign needed a little campaign song. I woke up last night with these words on my mind." Published online at <http://www.beatboxer.com/campsong.html>.

45.10 *Welcome To Hemet*. w.m. Danney Ball. CD. CitySong Records, 140 E. Stetson Ave., #133, Hemet, CA. 92543. 2004.

- **AmPM-45A BIDWELL**, John (State Senate, 1849; U.S. House, 1865–1867; Anti-Monopoly Candidate for Governor, 1875; Prohibition Candidate for Governor, 1888; Prohibition Candidate for President, 1892)

45A.1 *We'll Make California Dry!* w. Rev. R.A.M. Browne. m. S. Maxwell. a. Horner Yourjee. Published by The Tribune Song Company, Publishers, 322 California Building, Los Angeles, CA. 1914. W/br/y/gn drawings of four California bears, flowers, geometric designs. "California Dry Federation Official Campaign Song." "Vote California Dry, November 2, 1914." 8pp. Pages 2, 7 and 8: Blank. Page 3: "This song is dedicated to Gen. And Mrs. John Bidwell, Chico, California, whose unswerving loyalty to the Temperance Cause in California has been the means of bringing about much of the interest and sympathy that is being shown in this fight for California State-wide Prohibition." Page 6: Narrative on the goals of the Federation. [Crew/S-1914-19].

- **AmPM-46 BONO**, Sonny (Mayor, Palm Springs, 1988–1992; U.S. House, 1995–1998)

46.1 *All I Ever Need Is You*. w.m. Jimmy Holliday & Eddie Reeves. Published by United Artists Music Group, New York, NY. 1970. R/b photo of Sonny Bono & Cher. "Recorded by Sonny & Cher on Kapp Records."

46.2 *And The Beat Goes On* (2002). w. Tim Hall. m. Tune—"*And The Beat Goes On* originally by Sonny & Cher." "This autobiographical version of *And The Beat Goes On* highlights the lives of Sonny and Cher from the 1950's to today." Published online at <http://www.amiright.com/parody/60s/sonnyandcher0.shtml>.

46.3 *Bang Bang* (My Baby Shot Me). w.m. Sonny Bono. 1966. Sheet Music. Bl/w photo of Cher. "Recorded by Cher on Imperial Records."

46.4 *The Beat Goes On*. w.m. Sonny Bono. Published at Belinda Limited, 17 Savile Row, London, England. 1967. B/w photo of "Sonny & Cher." Gn/bk/w cover. 4pp.

46.5 *But You're Mine*. w.m. Sonny Bono. Published by Belinda Limited, 17 Savile Row, London, England. 1965. B/w photo of Sonny & Cher." Recorded by Sonny & Cher."

46.6 *A Cowboy's Work Is Never Done*. w.m. Sonny Bono. Sheet music. N/c photo of Sonny and Cher. Chris-Mark Music. 1971. "As recorded by Sonny & Cher."

46.6A *Fuck Hollywood*. w.m. Anti-Heros. Lyrics published online at <http://www.plyrics.com/lyrics/antoheros/fuckhollywood.html>. [ca. 198-].

46.7 *Good Combination*. w.m. Mark Barkan. Sheet music. Published by Tri-Parte Music, Inc. 1968. B/w photo of Sonny and Cher. Pl/gy geometric designs. "Recorded by Sonny & Cher."

46.8 *I Can't Ski, Babe*. w. No composer indicated. m. "Parody of *I Got You Babe* by Sonny & Cher." Lyrics published by *The Bob Rivers Show* with Bob, Spike & Joe and Twisted Tunes online at <http://www.twistedradio.com/player/lyrics.asp?songID=656>. [ca. 2000].

46.8A *I Love Lake Tahoe*. w.m. A. On CD: '*A*' Vs Monkey Kong. Lyrics published online at <http://www.plyrics.com/lyrics/a/ilovelaketahoe.html>. 1990.

46.9 *It's Gonna Rain*. w.m. Sonny Bono. Published by Edward Kassner Music Co., Ltd. Sole selling agents: Kassner Associated Publishers, Ltd., Kassner House, 25, Denmark Street, W.C.2, London, England. Copyright 1965 by Five West Music/Laughter Music. Ma/bk photo of Sonny Bono and Cher. "Recorded by Sonny and Cher on Atlantic 4035." 4pp.

46.9A *It's Over*. w.m. Mest. Lyrics published online at <http://www.plyrics.com/lyrics/mest/itsover.html>. [ca. 198-].

46.10 *I've Got You Babe*. w.m. Sonny Bono. Published by Belinda Music PTY, Ltd., 3rd Floor, MacDonell House, 321 Pitt Street, Sydney, Australia. 1965. B/w photo of Sonny and Cher Bono. "Recorded on Atlantic Records by Sonny and Cher." 4pp.

46.11 *Laugh At Me*. w.m. Sony Bono. Published by West One Music, 17 Savile Row, London, England. 1965. [8½" × 11"]. B/w photo of Sonny Bono. Gn/w geometric designs. "Recorded by Sonny on Atlantic." 4pp. Page 4: Advertising.

46.12 *Little Man*. w.m. Sonny Bono. w. [French] Michel Taittinger. Published by Les Editions & Productions Musicales Gerard Tornuier, Paris, France. 1966. O/bk/w photo of Sonny & Cher. "Recorded by Sonny and Cher on Atlantic." 4pp. + insert of French lyrics.

46.13 *Mama Was A Rock And Roll Singer*. w.m. Sonny Bono. Published by Charles Hansen Educational Music & Books, 1860 Broadway, New York, NY. Copyright 1973 by Chris-Marc Music. B/w photos of "Sonny & Cher." 6pp. Page 2: Blank. Page 6: B/w geometric design.

46.14 *Needles And Pins*. w.m. Sonny Bono and Jack Nitzsche. Published by Metric Music Co., Sole Selling Agent: Criterion Music Corp., 150 West 55th Street, New York, NY. 1963. Bl/w photo of The Searchers. "Recorded by The Searchers on Kapp Records and Jackie DeShannon on Liberty Records." 6pp. Page 6: Blank.

46.15 *Sing 'C'est La Vie.'* w.m. Sonny Bono,

Charles Green and Brian Stone. Published by Belinda Music PTY, Ltd., 3rd Floor, MacDonell House, 321 Pitt Street, Sydney, Australia. Copyright 1965 by Cotillion Music. Br/w photo of Sonny and Cher Bono. "Recorded on Atlantic Records by Sonny and Cher." 6pp. Page 6: Blank.
46.16 When You Say Love. w.m. Jerry Foster and Bill Rice. B/bl photo of Sonny Bono and Cher. Published by Charles Hansen Music and Books, 1860 Broadway, New York, NY. 10023. 1972. "Jack & Bill Music Company." "As recorded by Sonny & Cher on KAPP Records." 4pp.

• **AmPM-47** BOOTH, Newton (State Senate, 1863; Governor, 1871–1875; U.S. Senator, 1875–1881)
47.1 Hurrah Song. w. N.G. Sawyer. m. No tune indicated. In: *Grant And Wilson Campaign Songster*, page 33. Published by Frank Eastman, Book and Job Printer, No. 509 Clay Street, San Francisco, CA. [4¼" × 5⅜"]. 1872. Bk/bl geometric design border. 40pp. [Crew/USG-69].

• **AmPM-48** BOXER, Barbara (Congressional Aide, 1974–1976; Board of Supervisors, Marin County, 1976–1982; U.S. House, 1983–1993; U.S. Senate, 1993–Present)
48.1 Babs Boxer. w. "Laz." m. *The Boxer* by Simon & Garfunkel. Published by FreeRepublic.com at <http://www.freerepublic.com/forum/a373bfb5b2bf1.htm>. [199-].
48.1A The Boxer (Barbara, lie, lie, lie). w. "Doug from Upland." m. *The Boxer* by Simon & Garfunkel. Published by FreeRepublic.com at <http://www.freerepublic.com/forum/a36365032755e.htm>. 1998.
48.2 [3 People Are Afraid Of Danney Ball]. w.m. Danney Ball. "I though my campaign needed a little campaign song. I woke up last night with these words on my mind." Published online at <http://www.beatboxer.com/campsong.html>.

• **AmPM-49** BROWN, Edmund G. 'Pat' (State Attorney General, 1951–1959; Governor, 1959–1967)
49.1 The Party With A Heart (Democratic Victory Waltz). w.m. Paul Brock Killeen. Published by Golden Harp Publishing Co., 638 Montgomery Street, San Francisco, CA. 1958. B/w photo of "Pat Brown, Governor." 4pp. Page 4: Blank.

• **AmPM-50** BROWN, Edmund Gerald, Jr. "Jerry" (California Secretary of State, 1971–1975; Governor, 1975–1983; Candidate for Democratic Nomination for President, 1976, 1980, 1992; Candidate for U.S. Senate, 1982; Mayor, Oakland, 1998–Present)
50.1 California Sucks. w.m. Screeching Weasel. On LP: *Screeching Weasel.* Lyrics published online at <http://www.plyrics/lyrics/screechingweasel/californiasucks.html>. 1987.
50.1A California Über Alles. w.m. Dead Kennedys. Lyrics published onlkine at <http://www.geocities.com/SunsetStrip/Pit/9613/lyricsfresh.html>. On: LP: *Fresh Fruit For Rotting Vegetables* by the Dead Kennedys. Cherry Red Records #155. 1980.
50.1B Jerry Brown. w. No composer indicated. m. "Parody of *Charlie Brown* by The Coasters." Lyrics published by *The Bob Rivers Show* with Bob, Spike & Joe and Twisted Tunes online at <http://www.twistedradio.com/player/lyrics.asp?songID=538>. [199-].
50.2 Olie And The Brown Campaign Song. w. Mike Huben. m. "To the tune of *Pinkey And The Brain Theme Song.*" Published online by Mike Huben at <http://www.world.std.com/~mhuben/song.html>. 2000. "The 'Meet John Brain' episode of *Pinkey And The Brain* is strikingly close to the mouse-scale antics of the Libertarian Party. The public cheerfully misinterprets Brain's honest declarations of his evil intent to be the things they desire. When they finally see him in real life, they realize 'why, he's just a mouse!' and abandon him for rival Chicken Boo (perhaps Perot)." "Part of the 'Critiques of Libertarianism' site." [Crew/MISC-197].

• **AmPM-51** BUSTAMONTE, Cruz M. (State Assembly, 1993–1998; Lt. Governor, 1998–Present)
51.1 Back (Bragging By Arnold Schwarzenegger). w. Ethan Mawyer. m. "*Bad*, based on a performance by Michael Jackson." "I don't do political parodies too often but this idea seemed too good to pass up when it came to me Wednesday night." Published online at <http://www.amiright.com/parody/80s/michaeljackson50.shtml>. 2003.
51.2 The Ballot Of Arnold Schwarzenegger. w. Bob Gomez. m. "*The Ballad Of Davy Crockett*, based on the performance by George Burns/Tom Blackburn." "Great. Now we can look forward to three years of gridlock and Really Bad pronunciation." Published online at <http://www.amiright.com/parody/misc/georgeburnstomblackburn0.shtml>. 2003.
51.3 California Screaming. w. Loose Bruce Kerr. m. Tune — "*California Dreaming* by The Mamas and the Popas [sic]." "About California's recall campaign for governor, contains the names of the top runners and a little angst. Played on Jim Bohannon Show on Westwood One; upcoming on Dr. Demento." Published online at <http://www.amiright.com/parody/60s/mamaspopas0.shtml>. 2003.
51.4 Cruz Bustamante. w. Bob Gomez. m. "*Guantanamera*, originally by The Sandpipers." "Quoted parts are spoken by the probable next Governor of California. I can translate this into Spanish if you really want me to." Published online at <http://amiright.com/parody/60s/thesandpipers0.shml>. [ca. 2000].
51.5 Recall California. w. Bob Gomez. m. "*Sweet Home Alabama*, originally by Lynyrd Skinner." "Darrell Issa spent nearly two million dollars to gather enough signatures for the recall. No he is out of the race and so is Bill Simon. In the latest polls, the number of Republicans who are afraid that Arnold will win roughly equals the number who are afraid he will lose." Published online at <http://www.amiright.com/parody/70s/lynyrdskynyrd12.shtml>. 2003.
51.6 Recalling Gray. w. Alex Murray. m. "*Auf Wiedersehen*, based on a performance by Cheap Trick." "Haven't done a parody in a while, so this is a bit rusty. To clarify, all bye-byes, goodbyes, so longs, etc are directed towards Red Davis." Published online at <http://www.amiright.com/parody/70s/cheaptrick3.shtml>. 2003.
51.7 Sweet Home California. w. "Static." m. "*Sweet Home Alabama* by Lynyrd Skynyrd." "Inspired by X games' sweet home calif. Tony hawk 900! Booya! Back from vaca and better than ever. Must have been that smelly bear poo by the dumpster. Here goes nothing

... [sic]." Published online at <http://www.amiright.com/parody/70s/lynyrdskynyrd11.shtml>. 2003.

51.8 *Vote For The Terminator*. w. Rice Cube & Walt Daddy. m. "Tune — *We Didn't Start The Fire* originally by Billy Joel." "We're not completely endorsing Schwarzenegger because we don't know his complete platform, but considering that voting for Bustamonte will be worse than keeping Davis in power, and Ahnuld is the leading Republican candidate who has a ghost's chance in hell of becoming governor ..." Published online at Published online at <http://www.amiright.com/parody/80s/billyjoel62.shtml>. 2003.

- **AmPM-51A   BYRON**, Michael (Candidate for U.S. House, 2004)

51A.1 *The Tail Of Darrell Issa* (The Car Thief Who Went Bad). w. Stephen Baird. m. No tune indicated. N/c photo of Mike Byron — "Human need above political greed." Lyrics published online at <http://byron.blogcap.com/archive/campaign_song_the_tale_of_darrell_issa.php>. 2004.

- **AmPM-52   CARPENTER**, G.J. (State Assembly, 1875–1877; Candidate for U.S. House, 1876)

52.1 *The Republican Ticket*. w. Sam Booth. m. "Tune — *Rosin The Bow*." In: *Campaign Songs*, page 4. [1876]. [6" × 9⅜"]. Non-pictorial. "Supplement to *Hayes And Wheeler Songster*." 4pp. [Verses for local Congressional candidates]. [Crew/RBH-56].

- **AmPM-53   CONDIT**, Gary Adrian (City Council, Ceres, 1972–1976; Mayor, Ceres, 1974–1976; Board of Supervisors, Stanislaus County, 1976–1982; State Assembly, 1982–1989; U.S. House, 1989–2003)

53.1 *The Ballad Of Chandra Levy*. w. Jeff Wilder. m. "*MTA*, originally by Kingston Trio." Published online at <http://www.amiright.com/parody/60s/kingstontrio0.shml>. [ca. 2002].

53.2 *Ballad Of Gary Condit*. w. No composer indicated. m. "Parody of *Ballad Of Davy Crockett* by Buddy Ebsen." Lyrics published by *The Bob Rivers Show* with Bob, Spike & Joe and Twisted Tunes online at <http://www.twistedradio.com/player/lyrics.asp?songID=583>. [ca. 2001].

53.3 *Chandra Levy's Gone*. w. Sharon Krebs. m. "*Gone*, originally N'Sync." Published online at <http://www.amiright.com/parody/90s/nsync25.shml>. [ca. 2002].

53.4 *The Condit Lie Detector Test*. w. Paul Shaklin. On CD: *The Usual Suspects*. Published by Goes Around Records. CD Cover: N/c drawing of Bill Clinton, Jesse Jackson, and others. See: <www.paulShaklin.com>. 2001.

53.5 *Condit Love*. w. Darrell Decker. m. "*Puppy Love*, originally by Donnie Osmond." Published online at <http://amiright.com/parody/70s/donnieosmond0.shml>. [ca. 2001].

53.6 *Congressman* (Condit). w. Bruce Decker. m. "*Pianoman* originally by Billy Joel." Published online at <http://www.amiright.com/parody/60s/tonybennett2.shml>. [ca. 2002].

53.7 *Just Like Gary Condit Blues*. w. Maria Weir Werth. m. "*Just Like Tom Thumb Blues*, originally by Bob Dylan." Published online at <http://www.amiright.com/parody/misc/bobdylan6.shml>. [ca. 2002].

53.8 *99 Gruff Balloons*. w. Malcolm Higgins. m. "*99 Red Balloons,* originally by Nena." Published online at <http://www.amiright.com/parody/80s/nena1.shtml>. [ca. 2001].

53.9 *She's Gone* (Gary Condit's Song). w. Tallteen16. m. "*She's Gone,* originally by Hall & Oats." Published online at <http://www.amiright.com/parody/70s/hallandoats0.shtml>. [ca. 2001].

- **AmPM-54   CURB**, Michael (Lt. Governor, 1979–1983)

54.1 *Burning Bridges*. w. Mike Curb. m. Lalo Schifrin. Published by Hastings Music Corp., 1350 Avenue of the Americas, New York, NY. 10019. 1970. R/bk/w drawing of a tank, stars of the film including Clint Eastwood, Telly Savalas, Don Rickles, Donald Sutherland. "Recorded by The Mike Curb Congregation on M-G-M Records and [by] Clint Eastwood on Certron Records." "*Kelly's Heroes*, Metro-Goldwyn-Mayer Presents a Katzka-Loeb Production." "Distributed by Big 3." 4pp. Page 4: Advertising.

54.2 *Dirty Dingus Magee*. w.m. Mack Davis and Mike Curb. Published by Leo Feist, New York, NY. 1070. Pl/w drawings of movie scenes. From the movie Dirt Dinguss Magee starring Frank Sinatra, George Kennedy and Lois Nettleton." 4pp. Page 4: Advertising.

54.3 *It Was A Good Time* (Rosy's Theme). w. Mike Curb and Mack Davis. m. Maurice Jarre. Published by Leo Feist, Inc., New York, NY. 1970. Gd/gn/w drawing of scene from the film. "From the M-G-M Film *Ryan's Daughter*" "From MGM A Story of Love Filmed by David Lean *Ryan's Daughter* starring Robert Mitchum, Trevor Howard, Christopher Jones, John Mills, Leo McKern and Sarah Miles; Original Screenplay by Robert Bolt; Produced by Anthony Havelock-Allan; Music by Maurice Jarre; Metrocolor and Superpanvision 70mm." 4pp, Page 4: Advertising.

54.4 *Nixon Now Rally Song* {54.4–1}. w.m. Jerry Jerome. a. Bob Summers. 45 rpm record. MGM Records, 7165 Sunset Boulevard, Hollywood, CA. #PK1007/72 L 3912&13. [1972]. Performed by The Mike Curb Congregation. Side B: *More Than Ever* (Theme Song) {54.4–2}. w.m. Ken Southerland.

54.5 *Sweet Gingerbread Man*. w. Alan & Marilyn Bergman. m. Michel Legrand. Published by Robbins Music Corp., Ltd., 35 Soho Square, London, England. 1970. B/w photo of "The Mike Curb Congregation." "Recorded on MGM by The Mike Curb Congregation." O/bk/w cover. 4pp.

54.6 *Where Was I When The Parade Went By*. w.m. Mack David, Mike Curb and Maurice Jarre. Published by Hastings Music Corp., New York, NY. 1971. Pl/w drawing of a woman walking by a seashore. "From the M-G-M Film *Ryan's Daughter*" "From MGM A Story of Love Filmed by David Lean *Ryan's Daughter* starring Robert Mitchum, Trevor Howard, Christopher Jones, John Mills, Leo McKern and Sarah Miles; Original Screenplay by Robert Bolt; Produced by Anthony Havelock-Allan; Music by Maurice Jarre; Metrocolor and Superpanvision 70mm."

- **AmPM-55   DAVIS**, Angela (Communist Party Candidate for Vice President, 1980 & 1984)

55.1 *From Joan To Angela*. w. Bill Conway. m. Waldemar Hille. In: *From Joan To Angela, A Bitter Ballad Of Oppression And Martyrs*, page 33 [attached].

Book by Bill Conway. Published by Fad Publishers, P.O. B 62950, Los Angeles, CA. 90062. 1971. [5½" × 8⅜"]. Y/bk photo of Angela Davis. Y/bk drawing of Joan Of Arc. 34pp.

• **AmPM-56 DAVIS**, Horace (U.S. House, 1877–1881; President Chamber of Commerce, San Francisco, 1883–1884; Board of Trustees, Sanford University, 1885–1916; President, UC-Berkeley, 1887–1890)

56.1 The Republican Ticket. w. Sam Booth. m. "Tune — *Rosin The Bow*." In: *Campaign Songs*, page 4. [1876]. [6" × 9⅜"]. Non-pictorial. "Supplement to *Hayes And Wheeler Songster*." 4pp. [Verses for local Congressional candidates]. [Crew/RBH-56].

56.2 Vote For Horace Davis. w. Sam Booth. m. No tune indicated. In: *Campaign Songs*. [1876]. [6" × 9⅜"]. Non-pictorial. "Supplement to *Hayes And Wheeler Songster*." 4pp. [Crew/RBH-56].

• **AmPM-57 DAVIS**, Joseph Graham, Jr. 'Gray' (State Assembly, 1982–1986; State Controller, 1986–1994; Lt. Governor, 1994–1998; Governor, 1999–2003)

57.1 A Boy Named Gray. w. Michael Pacholek. m. "*A Boy Named Sue* originally by Johnny Cash." "For the record, his real name is Joseph Graham Davis, Jr. Originally written by Shel Silverstein." Published online at <http://www.amiright.com/parody/60s/johnnycash10.shtml>. 2003.

57.2 After The Votin.' w. Malcolm Higgins. m. "*After The Lovin,'* based on a performance by Engelbert Humperdinck. "Sorry folks, I have to backlash at the loonie left who flood this site with anti right crap ... what's good for the gander ..." Published online at <http://www.amiright.com/parody/70s/engelberthumperdinck3.shtml>. [ca. 2003].

57.2A Anrold [sic] *Goes To Californeeya.* w. Lionel Mertens. m. "*All The Gold In California*, based on a performance by *Gatlin Brothers*." Published online at <http://www.amiright.com/parody/70s/gatlinbrothersl.shtml>. [2004].

57.3 Arnie. w. Malcolm Higgins. m. "*Sunny*, based on a performance by Bobby Hebb. Published online at <http://www.amiright.com/parody/60s/bobbyhebb2.shtml>. [ca. 2003].

57.4 Arnie, Blow Away That Whore. w. Malcolm Higgins. m. "*Michael Row The Boat Ashore* originally by 'Traditional.'" Published online at <http://www.amiright.com/parody/misc/miscl.html>. 2003.

57.5 Arnie's Song (Turf Him Out). w. Malcolm Higgins. m. "*Anthony's Song (Movin' On)*, based on a performance by Billy Joel." Published online at <http://www.amiright.com/parody/70s/billyjoel84.shtml>. [ca. 2003].

57.6 Baby, I'm Back. w. William Tong. m. "*Baby Come Back*, based on the performance by Player." "As sung by Arnold Schwarzenegger, Republican candidate for governor of California." Published online at <http://www.amiright.com/parody/70s/player2.shtml>. 2003.

57.7 Back (Bragging By Arnold Schwarzenegger). w. Ethan Mawyer. m. "*Bad*, based on a performance by Michael Jackson." "I don't do political parodies too often but this idea seemed too good to pass up when it came to me Wednesday night." Published online at <http://www.amiright.com/parody/80s/michaeljackson50.shtml>. 2003.

57.8 The Ballot Of Arnold Schwarzenegger. w. Bob Gomez. m. "*The Ballad Of Davy Crockett*, based on the performance by George Burns/Tom Blackburn." "Great. Now we can look forward to three years of gridlock and Really Bad pronunciation." Published online at <http://www.amiright.com/parody/misc/georgeburnstomblackburn0.shtml>. 2003.

57.9 The Battle Hymn Of The Republicans. w. Phil Alexander. m. "*The Battle Hymn Of The Republic*, based on a performance by Traditional." " ... given that *The Battle Hymn Of The Republic* is in essence a parody of the tune *John Brown's Body*, this is a parody to a mixture of the two ..." Published online at <http://www.amiright.com/parody/misc/traditional272.shtml>. 2003.

57.10 A Boy Named Gray. w. Michael Pacholek. m. "*A Boy Named Sue*, based on a performance by Johnny Cash." "For the record, his full name is Joseph Graham Davis Jr." Published online at <http://www.amiright.com/parody/60s/johnnycash10.shtml>. 2003.

57.11 California Governor Song. w. "Static." m. "*The Chanukah Song* by Adam Sandler. "Typical sandler song. too many syllables in places, too little, and alternate endings. Static out." Published online at <http://www.amiright.com/parody/misc/adamsandler0.shtml>. 2003.

57.12 California Screaming. w. Loose Bruce Kerr. m. "*California Dreaming* by The Mamas and the Popas [sic]." "About California's recall campaign for governor, contains the names of the top runners and a little angst. Played on Jim Bohannon Show on Westwood One; upcoming on Dr. Demento." Published online at <http://www.amiright.com/parody/60s/mamaspopas0.shtml>. 2003.

57.13 California Screaming. w. Michael Pacholek. m. "*California Dreaming* by The Mamas and the Papas." "Dedicated to all those morons who don't know who's really to blame for California's budget woes. And every other State's budget woes." Published online at <http://www.amiright.com/parody/60s/themamasthepapas1.shtml>. 2003.

57.14 California's Dumb. w. Michael Pacholek. m. "*California Sun*, based on a performance by Joe Jones." " ... If you're dumb enough to vote for a guy with no political experience and who thinks budget deficits can be reduced by cutting taxes, then you deserve the disaster to come ..." Published online at <http://www.amiright.com/parody/60s/joejones2.shtml>. 2003.

57.15 Cruz Bustamante. w. Bob Gomez. m. "*Guantanamera*, originally by The Sandpipers." "Quoted parts are spoken by the probable next Governor of California. I can translate this into Spanish if you really want me to." Published online at <http://amiright.com/parody/60s/thesandpipers0.shml>. [ca. 2000].

57.16 Davis Needs To Go Right Now (Political). w. Malcolm Higgins. m. "*No One Needs To Know Right Now*, based on a performance by Shania Twain. Published online at <http://www.amiright.com/parody/misc/shaniatwain1.shtml>. [ca. 2003].

57.17 Destined To Win. w. Malcolm Higgins. m.

"*Dust In The Wind,* based on a performance by Kansas. Published online at <http://www.amiright.com/parody/70s/kansas12.shtml>. [ca. 2003].

57.18 Dupes In California Wishing To Replace Gray Davis. w. William Tong. m. *Supercalifragilisticexpalidocious,* originally by Julie Andrews." "The California blackouts were rigged by Bush cronies at Enron by manipulating the demand on the electric grid from out of the state, and then selling extra power to the state at loan shark prices. On 9/16/03, the Federal 9th Circuit Court of Appeals barred the California recall election ... stay tuned for the U.S. Supreme Court." Published online at <http://www.amiright.com/parody/60s/julieandrews9/ html>. 2003.

57.19 A Few Short Years Ago. From CD: *American Way.* Performed by Dimpled Chad & The Disenfranchised. Lyrics published at <http://dimpledchad.net>. [ca. 2000].

57.20 50 Candidates For Gov'ner. w. Michael Florio. m. "*50 Ways To Leave Your Lover* originally by Paul Simon." Published online at <http://www.amiright.com/parody/70s/paulsimon26.shtml>. 2003.

57.21 Gave Gray Defeat. w. Malcolm Higgins. m. "*Eight Days A Week,* based on a performance by The Beatles." Published online at <http://www.amiright.com/parody/60s/thebeatles273.shtml>. 2003.

57.22 Get Grey [sic] **Davis Fired.** w. Stanuman. m. "*Great Balls Of Fire,* based on a performance by Jerry Lee Lewis." Published online at <http://www.amiright.com/parody/misc/jerryleelewis6.shtml>. 2003.

57.23 Goodbye T' Gray. w. Malcolm Higgins. m. "*Goodbye T' Jane,* based on a performance by Traditional." Published online at <http://www.amiright.com/parody/70s/0.shtml>. [ca. 2003].

57.24 Govern California. w. Aaron Saraco. m. "*Hotel California,* based on a performance by The Eagles." "Okay, so I took a little too long on this one ... but it's pretty different from the other California recall parodies. This one is all Schwarzenegger!" Published online at <http://www.amiright.com/parody/70s/theeagles65.shtml>. [ca. 2003].

57.25 Governor Gray. w. Charlie Decker. m. "*Ruby Tuesday* originally by the Rolling Stones." "California is mocking the United States, removing an elected official to replace him with an actor or a porn tycoon or a guy who smashes watermelons." Published online at <http://www.amiright.com/parody/60s/rollingstones31.shtml>. 2003.

57.26 Gray Tuesday. w. Paul Robinson. m. "*Ruby Tuesday,* based on a performance by The Rolling Stones." "California recently had the recall election in which Governor Gray Davis was removed and replaced by some guy named Arnold with a funny last name." Published online at <http://www.amiright.com/parody/60s/therollingstones17.shtml>. [ca. 2003].

57.27 How Come There's A Recall, California. w. William Tong. m. "*Hotel California,* based on the performance by The Eagles." "Satire about the Enron-rigged electrical blackouts in California, the right wing funded recall campaign for governor, and the behind-the-scenes scheming by the Bush White House to steal political power [in] California, a state the GOP has repeatedly lost in elections." Published online at <http://www.amiright.com/parody/70s/theeagles54.shtml>. 2003.

57.28 I Run For Gov'nor, Maria. w. Michael Pacholek. m. "*Take A Letter Maria,* originally by R.B. Greaves." Published online at <http://www.amiright.com/parody/60s/rbgreaves0.shtml>. 2003

57.29 I Second That Emotion. w. Malcolm Higgins. m. "*I Second That Emotion,* based on a performance by Smokey Robinson." Published online at <http://www.amiright.com/parody/60s/smokeyrobinson2.shtml>. [ca. 2003].

57.30 I'll Be Gov, Bush Wishes. w. William Tong. m. "*I'll Be Home For Christmas,* based on the performance by Bing Crosby." "As sung by the Republican gubernatorial candidate Arnold Schwarzenegger." Published online at <http://www.amiright.com/parody/misc/bingcrosby15/html>. 2003.

57.31 I'm Just Not Running. w. "Crazydon". m. "*It Keep You Running,* originally by The Doobie Brothers.*" "As we all know, California governor Gray Davis has been subjected to a recall, and lots of candidates have come out to run for governor, including Arnold Schwarzenegger, Gary Coleman and Angelyne. I don't live in California, I live in West Virginia, where our governor should be recalled due to some hanky-panky. But at least he's not running for re-election. What a relief ..." Published online at <http://www.amiright.com/parody/70s/thedoobiebrothers8.shtml>.2003.

57.32 Leader (Aisle Be Bach). w. Guy DiRito. m. Tune — "*Leader Of The Pack,* based on a performance by The Shangri-Las." Published online at <http://www.amiright.com/parody/60s/theshrangilas0.shml>. 2003.

57.33 Misdeeds In Office High. w. Ken Jorgensen. m. "*Ghost Riders In The Sky,* based on a performance by Frankie Lane." "Tax and spend Democrats, what else is new?" Published online at <http://www.amiright.com/parody/60s/frankielane0.shtml>. 2003.

57.34 Objection (To The Election). w. Malcolm Higgins. m. "*Objection,* based on a performance by Sakira. Published online at <http://www.amiright.com/parody/2000s/shakira35.shtml>. [ca. 2003].

57.35 Oh Arnold. w. William Tong. m. "*Oh Carol,* Based on a performance by Neil Sedaka." "As sung by California Republican fat cats to their gubernatorial candidate, Arnold Schwarzenegger." Published online at <http://www.amiright.com/parody/60s/neilsedaka4.shtml>. 2003

57.36 Oh Little Town Of Anaheim. w. Malcolm Higgins. m. "*Oh Little Town Of Bethlehem,* based on a performance by Traditional Christmas." "Written in 1992, with a beer on a friend's dock ... yeah right." Published online at <http://www.amiright.com/parody/misc/traditionalchristmas2.shtml>. [ca. 2003].

57.37 Please Don't Vote For Arnie. w. No composer indicated. m. Parody of *Don't Look Back In Anger* by Oasis." "Surprisingly, you might think, this song doesn't relate to the election of the most moronic, brain-dead, cringeingly [sic] right-wing actor ever to waist screen time in our cinemas. No, this isn't anything to do with Ronald Reagan — it's a song about Arnold Schwarzenegger for president in 2008? Stranger things have happened ..." Published online at <http://www.chu.cam.ac.uk/~TSK23/Songs/original.html>. [ca. 2003].

57.38 Pursuing Democrats. w. Fitu Petaia. m. "*I Wish,* based on a performance by Stevie Wonder. Published online at <http://www.amiright.com/parody/70s/steviewonder17.shtml>. [ca. 2003].

57.39 Recall California. w. Bob Gomez. m. "*Sweet Home Alabama,* originally by Lynyrd Skinner." "Darrell Issa spent nearly two million dollars to gather enough signatures for the recall. No he is out of the race and so is Bill Simon. In the latest polls, the number of Republicans who are afraid that Arnold will win roughly equals the number who are afraid he will lose." Published online at <http://www.amiright.com/parody/70s/lynyrdskynyrd12.shtml>. 2003.

57.40 Recall Vote Is Back Today (Political). w. Malcolm Higgins. m. "*Rock And Roll Is Here To Stay,* originally by Danny and the Juniors." Published online at <http://www.amiright.com/parody/misc/dannyandthejuniors8.shtml>. 2003.

57.41 Re-callin' (The Gray Davis Song). w. Malcolm Higgins. m. "*Free Fallin,'* originally by Tom Petty." Published online at <http://www.amiright.com/parody/90s/tompetty11.shtml>. 2003.

57A.41 Recalling. w. William Tong. m. "*Free Falling,* based on the performance by Tom Petty & The Heartbreakers." Published online at <http://www.amiright.com/parody/80s/tompettyheartbreakers2.shtml>. 2003.

57.42 Recalling Gray. w. Alex Murray. m. "*Auf Wiedersehen,* based on a performance by Cheap Trick." "Haven't done a parody in a while, so this is a bit rusty. To clarify, all bye-byes, goodbyes, so longs, etc are directed towards Red Davis." Published online at <http://www.amiright.com/parody/70s/cheaptrick3.shtml>. 2003.

57.43 The Right Before. w. Malcolm Higgins. m. "*The Night Before,* based on a performance by The Beatles." Published online at <http://www.amiright.com/parody/60s/beatles206.shtml>. [ca. 2003].

57.44 Right Wing Wants To Reign In All Of California. w. William Tong. m. "*It Never Rains In Southern California* originally by Albert Hammond." Published online at <http://www.amiright.com/parody/70s/alberthammond4.shtml>. 2003.

57.45 Sacramento In My Mind. w. Bubba. m. "*Carolina In My Mind,* based on a performance by James Taylor." "As sung by Arnold Schwarzenegger (the next Governor of California)." Published online at <http://www.amiright.com/parody/70s/jamestaylor12.shtml>. 2003.

57.46 Schwarzenegger. w. William Tong. m. "*Operator,* Based on a performance by Jim Croce." "As sung by California Republican fat cats to Arnold Schwarzenegger." Published online at <http://www.amiright.com/parody/70s/jimcroce13.shtml>. 2003

57.47 Schwarzenegger. w. Malcolm Higgins. m. "*Come Together* originally by The Beatles." Published online at <http://www.amiright.com/parody/60s/thebeatles193.shtml>. 2003

57.48 Schwarzenegger. w. Michael Pacholek. m. "*Get Together,* based on a performance by The Youngbloods." "I don't think the Youngbloods had the original, but until I can find out for sure, I'll list them as such. As I said, Ahnold is begging for one of these, and he's getting lots of them, and here's my swing at the pitch." Published online at <http://www.amiright.com/parody/60s/theyoungbloods0.shtml>. 2003

57.49 Schwarzenegger Got Stoned. w. Adam Bernstein. m. "*Like A Rolling Stone* originally by Bob Dylan." Published online at <http://www.amiright.com/parody/60s/bobdylan25.shtml>. 2003.

57.50 Sweet Home California. w. "Static." m. "*Sweet Home Alabama* by Lynyrd Skynyrd." "Inspired by X games' sweet home calif. Tony hawk 900! Booya! Back from vaca and better than ever. Must have been that smelly bear poo by the dumpster. Here goes nothing ... [sic]." Published online at <http://www.amiright.com/parody/70s/lynyrdskynyrd11.shtml>. 2003.

57.51 The Terminator. w. William Tong. m. "*My Generation,* Based on a performance by The Who." "Satire about Republican candidate for Governor of California, Arnold Schwarzenegger." Published online at <http://www.amiright.com/parody/60s/thewho22.shtml>. 2003

57.52 This Year's Misses (The Gray Davis Song). w. Malcolm Higgins. m. "*This Year's Kisses,* based on a performance by Dick Powell." Published online at <http://www.amiright.com/parody/misc/dickpowell19370.shtml>. [ca. 2003].

57.53 Total Recall Of The Gray. w. Michael Pacholek. m. "*Total Eclipse Of The Heart,* originally by Bonnie Tyler." Published online at <http://www.amiright.com/parody/80s/bonnietyler8.shtml>. 2003.

57.54 Turfin' Gray Today. w. Malcolm Higgins. m. "*Surfin' USA,* based on a performance by The Beach Boys. Published online at <http://www.amiright.com/parody/60s/thebeachboys19.shtml>. [ca. 2003].

57.55 Vote For Schwarzenegger. w. Mike Armstrong. m. "*Walk A Little Straighter,* based on a performance by Billy Currington." "Though a registered republican, I, Jordan do not mean this as a slam on his chances nor an endorsement to his candidacy. It's more a mock of the whole debacle going on out there." Published online at <http://www.amiright.com/parody/2000s/0.shtml>. [ca. 2003].

57.56 Vote For The Terminator. w. Rice Cube & Walt Daddy. m. "*We Didn't Start The Fire,* originally by Billy Joel." "We're not completely endorsing Schwarzenegger because we don't know his complete platform, but considering that voting for Bustamontte will be worse than keeping Davis in power, and Ahnuld is the leading Republican candidate who has a ghost's chance in hell of becoming governor ..." Published online at Published online at <http://www.amiright.com/parody/80s/billyjoel62.shtml>. 2003.

57.57 Vote Well, California. w. Jim Deken. m. "*Hotel California,* based on a performance by Eagles." Published online at <http://www.amiright.com/parody/70s/eagles15.shtml>. 2003.

57.58 We Can Kick Him Out (Gray Davis Recall). w. Jamie L. m. "*We Can Work It Out,* originally by Beatles." "Inspired by California's recall of Governor Davis." Published online at Published online at <http://www.amiright.com/parody/60s/beatles70.shtml>. 2003.

57.59 Wish They All Could Lead California. w. m. Spaff Sumsion. m. "Parody of *California Girls.*" "Recorded by Robert Lund' on MP3. Published online at <http://www.spaff.com/posey/california.html>. 2003.

57.60 *With A Little Help From The Reds*. w. Malcolm Higgins. m. "*With A Little Help From my Friends*, based on a performance by The Beatles. Published online at <http://www.amiright.com/parody/60s/thebeatles209.shtml>. [ca. 2003].

- **AmPM-58 DEAN**, John (Chief Minority Counsel to the House Judiciary Committee; Associate Deputy U.S. Attorney General; Legal Counsel to Richard Nixon)

58.1 *Haldeman, Ehrlichman, Mitchell And Dean*. w. Bob Warren. m. "Sung by The Creep. Mr. G. Records. #G-826. ca. 1973. Transcribed by <ahs@nevada.edu>." Published online at <http://php.indiana-edu/~jbmorris/LYRICS/hemd.html>. [ca. 1973].

58.1A *Feel Like I'm Nixon, I Lie*. w. Michael Pacholek. m. "*Feel Like I'm Fixin' To Die*, based on the performance by Country Joe & the Fish." "'Let me just say this' (as Nixon would say): He would not appreciate this, he earned it. When the transcripts of the Oval Office tapes were released, the constant profanities were edited so that they read "(expletive deleted)," hence the alteration of Country Joe's 'Fish Cheer.' 'Just one more thing' (as Nixon would say), if you think Bush is the worst president we've had, take a look at Nixon's record..., then read *Worse Than Watergate* by John Dean who would know." Published online at <http://amiright.com/parody/60s/countryjoethefish1.shml>. 2004.

58.2 *Watergate Bug*. w. David Arkin. m. "Tune — Tam Pearce." In: *Sing Out! The Folk Song Magazine*, Volume 22, Number 3, 1973, page 23. Published by *Sing Out!*, No. 595 Broadway, New York, NY. 1979. [7" × 10"]. [Crew/RMN-43].

- **AmPM-59 DOOLITTLE**, John Taylor (State Senate, 1981–1990; U.S. House, 1991–Present)

59.1 *Gingrich The White-Hared Speaker*. w. William K. Tong. m. "*Rudolph The Red-Nosed Reindeer*, based on a performance by Gene Autry." Published online at <http://www.amiright.com/parody/misc/geneautry14.shtml>. [ca. 1996].

- **AmPM-60 DORNAN**, Robert Kenneth (U.S. House, 1977–1983 & 1985–1997)

60.1 *Gingrich The White-Hared Speaker*. w. William K. Tong. m. "*Rudolph The Red-Nosed Reindeer*, based on a performance by Gene Autry." Published online at <http://www.amiright.com/parody/misc/geneautry14.shtml>. [ca. 1996].

60.2 *Nine Little Leaders*. w. William K. Tong. m. "Sung to the tune of *Nine Little Reindeers* by Gene Autry." In: *The Sting The Right Wing Song Book* at <http://www.geocities.com/wmktong/bootnewt/9litlead.htm>. [ca. 1996].

- **AmPM-61 EASTWOOD**, Clint (Mayor, Carmel, 1986–1988)

61.1 *Another Autumn*. w. Alan Jay Lerner. m. Frederick Loewe. Published by Chappell & Co., 609 Fifth Avenue, New York, NY. 1952. N/c drawings of stars — Clint Eastwood, Lee Marvin, Jean Seberg. "Based on the Lerner and Loewe Broadway musical play [*Paint Your Wagon*]."

61.2 *Best Things*. w. Alan Jay Lerner. m. Frederick Loewe. Published by Chappell & Co., [V-1: 609 Fifth Avenue, New York, NY] [V-2: 50 New Bond St., London W.1. England]. Copyright 1951 & 1969. [V-1: N/c] [V-2: Y/br] drawings of Clint Eastwood, Lee Marvin, Jean Seberg. "Paramount Pictures presents Clint Eastwood, Lee Marvin, Jean Seberg in *Paint Your Wagon* based on the Lerner and Loewe Broadway musical play; Co-starring Ray Walston, Harve Presnell; Featuring the Nitty Gritty Dirt Band; Screenplay and lyrics by Alan Jay Lerner; Directed by Joshua Logan; Music for additional songs by Andre Previn." 6pp. Page 6: Advertising.

61.3 *Burning Bridges*. w. Mike Curb. m. Lalo Schifrin. Published by Hastings Music Corp., 1350 Avenue of the Americas, New York, NY. 10019. 1970. R/bk/w drawing of a tank, stars of the film including Clint Eastwood, Telly Savalas, Don Rickles, Donald Sutherland. "Recorded by The Mike Curb Congregation on M-G-M Records and [by] Clint Eastwood on Certron Records." "*Kelly's Heroes*, Metro-Goldwyn-Mayer Presents a Katzka-Loeb Production." "Distributed by Big 3." 4pp. Page 4: Advertising.

61.4 *Espacio*. m. Clint Eastwood. Published by Warner Bros. Publications, 15800 N.W. 48th Avenue, Miami, FL. 33014. Copyright 2000 by Cibie Music/WB Music Corp. N/c photos of the stars from the movie *Space Cowboys* including Clint Eastwood and James Garner. "Original Sheet Music Edition." 4pp. Page 2: At top of music — "From Warner Bros. Pictures *Space Cowboys*." Page 4: Advertising.

61.4A *Every Which Way But Loose*. w.m. Stephen Dorff, Milton Brown and T.L. Garrett. Published by Campbell, Connelly & Co., Ltd., London, England. 1978; Nc drawing of characters and scenes from the movie "*Every Which Way But Loose*, a Malpaso Compant Film, Starring Clint Eastwood, Co-Starring Sonda Locke, Geoffrey Lewis, Beverly D'Angelo and Ruth Gordon as Ma; Written by Jeremy Joe Kronsberg; Produced by Robert Daley; Directed by James Fargo; Color by Deluxe." "Recorded on Elektra Records by Eddie Rabbitt." 4pp.

61.5 *The First Thing You Know*. w. Alan Jay Lerner. m. Frederick Loewe. Published by Chappell & Co., [V-1: 609 Fifth Avenue, New York, NY] [V-2: 50 New Bond St., London W.1. England]. Copyright 1951 & 1969. [V-1: N/c] [V-2: Y/br] drawings of Clint Eastwood, Lee Marvin, Jean Seberg. "Paramount Pictures presents Clint Eastwood, Lee Marvin, Jean Seberg in *Paint Your Wagon* Based on the Lerner and Loewe Broadway musical play; Co-starring Ray Walston, Harve Presnell; Featuring the Nitty Gritty Dirt Band; Screenplay and lyrics by Alan Jay Lerner; Directed by Joshua Logan; Music for additional songs by Andre Previn." 6pp. Page 6: Advertising.

61.6 *A Fistful Of Dollars*. w. Robert Mellin. m. Ennio Morricone. Published by Franco-London Music, Ltd., 64 Bond Street, London, England. 1965. O/bk drawing of Clint Eastwood, scenes from the movie. "Starring Clint Eastwood and Marianne Koch; directed by Sergio Leone; released through United Artists." "*A Fistful Of Dollars* Original Soundtrack Recording by the Ennio Morricone Orchestra on R.C.A. Records." 6pp.

61.6A *Frontier Justice*. w.m. D.O.A. On CD: *Fes*-

tival Of Atheists. Lyrics published online at http://www.plyrics.com/lyrics/doa/frontoerjustice.html. 1998.

61.7 Gold Fever. w. Alan Jay Lerner. m. Frederick Loewe. Published by Chappell & Co., [V-1: 609 Fifth Avenue, New York, NY] [V-2: 50 New Bond St., London W.1. England]. Copyright 1951 & 1969. [V-1: N/c] [V-2: Y/br] drawings of Clint Eastwood, Lee Marvin, Jean Seberg. "Paramount Pictures presents Clint Eastwood, Lee Marvin, Jean Seberg in *Paint Your Wagon* Based on the Lerner and Loewe Broadway musical play; Co-starring Ray Walston, Harve Presnell; Featuring the Nitty Gritty Dirt Band; Screenplay and lyrics by Alan Jay Lerner; Directed by Joshua Logan; Music for additional songs by Andre Previn." 6pp. Page 6: Advertising.

61.8 The Good, Bad And The Ugly (Il Buono, Il Brutto, Il Cattivo). w.m. Ennio Morricone. Published by Unart Music Corp., New York, NY. 1968. O/w/bk drawings of scenes from the movie. "Clint Eastwood in *The Good, The Bad, And The Ugly*, co-starring Lee Van Cleef, Also Giuffre and with Mario Brega; also starring Eli Wallach in the role of Tuco; Screenplay by Age-Scarpelli, Luciano Vincenzoni and Dergio Leone; Directed by Sergio Leone; Techniscope Technicolor; Released thru United Artists." "Recorded by Leroy Holmes Orchestra and Chorus on United Artists Records; Recorded by Hugo Montenegro His Orchestra and Chorus on RCA Victor Records." 6pp. Page 6: Advertising.

61.9 The Gospel Of No Name City. w. Alan Jay Lerner. m. Frederick Loewe. Published by Chappell & Co., [V-1: 609 Fifth Avenue, New York, NY] [V-2: 50 New Bond St., London W.1., England]. Copyright 1951 & 1969. [V-1: N/c] [V-2: Y/br] drawings of Clint Eastwood, Lee Marvin, Jean Seberg. "Paramount Pictures presents Clint Eastwood, Lee Marvin, Jean Seberg in *Paint Your Wagon* Based on the Lerner and Loewe Broadway musical play; Co-starring Ray Walston, Harve Presnell; Featuring the Nitty Gritty Dirt Band; Screenplay and lyrics by Alan Jay Lerner; Directed by Joshua Logan; Music for additional songs by Andre Previn." 6pp. Page 6: Advertising.

61.10 Hang 'Em High. m. Dominic Frontiere. Published by Unart Music Corp., New York, NY. 1968. Bk/w/y drawing of scenes from the movie. "Piano Solo." "Clint Eastwood in *Hang 'Em High*, a Leonard Freeman Production co-staring Inger Stevens, Ed Begley, Pat Hingle as Judge Fenton; Screenplay by Leonard Freeman and Mel Goldberg; Directed by Ted Post; Produced by Leonard Freeman; Color by Deluxe; United Artists Music." 4pp. Page 4: Advertising.

61.11 I Still See Elisa. w. Alan Jay Lerner. m. Frederick Loewe. Published by Chappell & Co., [V-1: 609 Fifth Avenue, New York, NY] [V-2: 50 New Bond St., London W.1. England]. Copyright 1951 & 1969. [V-1: N/c] [V-2: Y/br] drawings of Clint Eastwood, Lee Marvin, Jean Seberg. "Paramount Pictures presents Clint Eastwood, Lee Marvin, Jean Seberg in *Paint Your Wagon* Based on the Lerner and Loewe Broadway musical play; Co-starring Ray Walston, Harve Presnell; Featuring the Nitty Gritty Dirt Band; Screenplay and lyrics by Alan Jay Lerner; Directed by Joshua Logan; Music for additional songs by Andre Previn." 6pp. Page 6: Advertising.

61.12 I Talk To The Trees. w. Alan Jay Lerner. m. Frederick Loewe. Published by Chappell & Co., [V-1: 609 Fifth Avenue, New York, NY] [V-2: 50 New Bond St., London W.1. England]. Copyright 1951 & 1969. [V-1: N/c] [V-2: Y/br] drawings of Clint Eastwood, Lee Marvin, Jean Seberg. "Paramount Pictures presents Clint Eastwood, Lee Marvin, Jean Seberg in *Paint Your Wagon* Based on the Lerner and Loewe Broadway musical play; Co-starring Ray Walston, Harve Presnell; Featuring the Nitty Gritty Dirt Band; Screenplay and lyrics by Alan Jay Lerner; Directed by Joshua Logan; Music for additional songs by Andre Previn." 6pp. Page 6: Advertising.

61.13 I Talk To The Trees. w. Alan Jay Lerner. m. Frederick Loewe. Published by Chappell & Co., 609 Fifth Avenue, New York, NY. 1952. N/c drawings of stars — Clint Eastwood, Lee Marvin, Jean Seberg. "Based on the Lerner and Loewe Broadway musical play [*Paint Your Wagon*]."

61.14 I'll Wake You Up When I Get Home. w.m. Stephen Dorff and Milton Brown. Published by Warner Bros. Publications, Inc., 75 Rockefeller Plaza, New York, NY. 10019. 1979. Br/w drawing of Clint Eastwood, monkey, other scenes from the movie. Br/w photo of Charlie Rich." From the Malpaso Company-Warner Bros. Film Release *Every Which Way But Loose*." "Recorded by Charlie Rich on Electra Records." 6pp. Page 6: "This sheet should sell for no more than one dollar and fifty cents."

61.15 I'm On My Way. w. Alan Jay Lerner. m. Frederick Loewe. Published by Chappell & Co., 609 Fifth Avenue, New York, NY. 1952. N/c drawings of stars — Clint Eastwood, Lee Marvin, Jean Seberg. "Based on the Lerner and Loewe Broadway musical play [*Paint Your Wagon*]."

61.16 A Million Miles Away Behind The Door. w. Alan Jay Lerner. m. Frederick Loewe. Published by Chappell & Co., [V-1: 609 Fifth Avenue, New York, NY] [V-2: 50 New Bond St., London W.1. England]. Copyright 1951 & 1969. [V-1: N/c] [V-2: Y/br] drawings of Clint Eastwood, Lee Marvin, Jean Seberg. "Paramount Pictures presents Clint Eastwood, Lee Marvin, Jean Seberg in *Paint Your Wagon* Based on the Lerner and Loewe Broadway musical play; Co-starring Ray Walston, Harve Presnell; Featuring the Nitty Gritty Dirt Band; Screenplay and lyrics by Alan Jay Lerner; Directed by Joshua Logan; Music for additional songs by Andre Previn." 6pp. Page 6: Advertising.

61.17 Misty. w. Johnny Burke. m. Erroll Garner. Published by Charles Hansen Music and Books, 1860 Broadway, New York, NY. Copyright 1955 by Vernon Music Corp. Bl/w photo of Clint Eastwood. "From the Universal Film *Play Misty For Me*." "Clint Eastwood in *Play Misty For Me* ... the most frightening words you'll ever hear! Co-starring Jessica Walter, Donna Mills, John Larch; Screenplay by Jo Heims and Deal Riesner; Story by Jo Heims; Directed by Clint Eastwood; Produced by Robert Daley; A Jennings Lang Presentation; A Malpaso Company Production; A Universal-Malpaso Company Picture; Technicolor." 4pp. Page 4: Litho of a treble clef.

61.18 Paint Your Wagon (Piano Selection). w. Alan Jay Lerner. m. Frederick Loewe. Published by Chappell & Co., 609 Fifth Avenue, New York, NY. 1952. N/c drawings of stars — Clint Eastwood, Lee Marvin, Jean Seberg. "Based on the Lerner and Loewe Broadway musical play." 14pp.

61.19 Pursuing Democrats. w. Fitu Petaia. m. "*I Wish,* based on a performance by Stevie Wonder." Published online at <http://www.amiright.com/parody/70s/steviewonder17.shtml>. [ca. 2003].

61.20 They Call The Wind Maria. w. Alan Jay Lerner. m. Frederick Loewe. Published by Chappell & Co., [V-1: 609 Fifth Avenue, New York, NY] [V-2: 50 New Bond St., London W.1. England]. Copyright 1951 & 1969. [V-1: N/c] [V-2: Y/br] drawings of Clint Eastwood, Lee Marvin, Jean Seberg. "Paramount Pictures presents Clint Eastwood, Lee Marvin, Jean Seberg in *Paint Your Wagon* Based on the Lerner and Loewe Broadway musical play; Co-starring Ray Walston, Harve Presnell; Featuring the Nitty Gritty Dirt Band; Screenplay and lyrics by Alan Jay Lerner; Directed by Joshua Logan; Music for additional songs by Andre Previn." 6pp. Page 6: Advertising.

61.21 Wande'rin' Star. w. Alan Jay Lerner. m. Frederick Loewe. Published by Chappell & Co., [V-1: 609 Fifth Avenue, New York, NY] [V-2: 50 New Bond St., London W.1. England]. Copyright 1951 & 1969. [V-1: N/c] [V-2: Y/br] drawings of Clint Eastwood, Lee Marvin, Jean Seberg. "Paramount Pictures presents Clint Eastwood, Lee Marvin, Jean Seberg in *Paint Your Wagon* Based on the Lerner and Loewe Broadway musical play; Co-starring Ray Walston, Harve Presnell; Featuring the Nitty Gritty Dirt Band; Screenplay and lyrics by Alan Jay Lerner; Directed by Joshua Logan; Music for additional songs by Andre Previn." 6pp. Page 6: Advertising.

• **AmPM-62 FAZIO**, Victor Herbert, Jr. (Charter Commission, Sacramento County, 1972–1974; Planning Commission, Sacramento County, 1975; State Assembly, 1975–1978; U.S. House, 1979–1999)

62.1 The Little First Lady With Megalomania. w. Paul Silhan. m. "Sung to *The Little Old Lady From Pasadena* by Jan & Dean." On: Cassette: *Lie-A-lot.* Lyrics published at <http://www.paulsilhan.com/lal-1.htm>. 1995.

• **AmPM-62A FOOTE**, W.W. (Anti-Monopoly Party Candidate for Railroad Commission, 1882)

62A.1 Anti-Monopoly War Song. w.m. No composers indicated. Copyright 1882 by J.R. Harrison. Non-pictorial geometric designs. "Composed for The Anti-Monopoly Party of California." "Dedicated to R.J. Harrison." 4pp. Page 4: "Vote for W.W. Foote, Regular Nominee, Railroad Commissioner, Third District, Anti-Monopoly Ticket." "A Vote for Foote is a Vote for Liberty Against Railroad Tyranny."

• **AmPM-63 FRÉMONT**, John Charles (Governor of California, 1846; U.S. Senate, 1850–1851; Candidate for President, 1856; Governor, Arizona Territory, 1878–1881) [ALSO SEE: DOC/PSM-JCF]

63.1 Abram's Band. w. No composer indicated. m. "Air — *Gideon's Band.*" In: *The Lincoln And Johnson Union Campaign Songster,* page 28. Published by A. Winch, No. 505 Chestnut Street, Philadelphia, PA. 1864. [3⅞" × 6"]. Be/bk lithos of Abraham Lincoln and Andrew Johnson, geometric design border. 58pp. [M-124] [Crew/AL-379].

63.2 Advance, Boys, Advance. w. No composer indicated. m. "Air — *Boatmen Dance.*" In: *The Lincoln And Johnson Union Campaign Songster,* page 35. Published by A. Winch, No. 505 Chestnut Street, Philadelphia, PA. 1864. [3⅞" × 6"]. Be/bk lithos of Abraham Lincoln and Andrew Johnson, geometric design border. 58pp. [M-124] [Crew/AL-379].

63.3 Anti-Buchanan Song. w. No composer indicated. m. "Air — *Old Dan Tucker.*" In: *The Fremont Songster,* page 42. Published by [V-1: H.S. Riggs & Company, Publishers, No. 4 Cortland Street] [V-2: P.J. Cozans, No. 107 Nassau Street], New York, NY. 1856. [V-1: 3⅝" × 5¾"] [V-2: 3½" × 5⅝"]. Be/bk litho of wreath, John C. Fremont. "With a current likeness of John C. Fremont, The People's Candidate for the Presidency." 40pp. [M-094, 095]. [Crew/JCF-45].

63.4 [As Buchanan Was Walking By The White house One Day] (Campaign Song). w. No composer indicated. m. "Air — *Vilikins And His Dinah.*" In: *The Republican Campaign Songster, A Collection Of Lyrics, Original And Selected, Specifically Prepared For The Friends Of Freedom In The Campaign Of Fifty-Six,* page 93. Published by Miller, Orton & Mulligan, No. 25 Park Row, New York, NY. 1856. [3¹³⁄₁₆" × 6"]. Be/bk litho of "Colonel John C. Fremont" facing to viewer's left, black line border. 112pp. [M-097]. [Crew/JCF-24].

63.5 Away, Boys, Away. w. No composer indicated. m. "Air — *Away Over Mountain.*" In: *The Fremont Songster,* page 34. Published by [V-1: H.S. Riggs & Company, Publishers, No. 4 Cortland Street] [V-2: P.J. Cozans, No. 107 Nassau Street], New York, NY. 1856. [V-1: 3⅝" × 5¾"] [V-2: 3½" × 5⅝"]. Be/bk litho of wreath, John C. Fremont. "With a current likeness of John C. Fremont, The People's Candidate for the Presidency." 40pp. [M-094, 095]. [Crew/JCF-45].

63.6 The Bachelor Candidate. w. No composer indicated. m. "Air — *Rory O'More.*" Published by Andrews, Printer, No. 38 Chatham Street, New York, NY. [1856]. B/w penny song sheet with litho border of geometric designs. "Andrews, Printer, No. 38 Chatham Street, N.Y. Dealer in Songs, Games, Toy Books, Mottos, Verses, Valentines, &c." 2pp. Page 2: Blank. [Crew/JCF-59].

63.7 The Bachelor Candidate. w. No composer indicated. m. "Air — *The Campbells Are Coming.*" In: *Fremont Songs For The People (Original And Selected),* page 43. c. Thomas Drew "(Editor of *The Massachusetts Spy*)." Published by John P. Jewett & Company, Boston, MA. Copyright 1856 by Thomas Drew. [3⅝" × 5½"]. B/w litho of "J.C. Fremont." "The Campaign of 1856." 68pp. [Crew/JCF-18].

63.8 The Ballot Battle. w. No composer indicated. m. "Air — *Wait For The Wagon.*" In: *Fremont Songs For The People (Original And Selected),* page 60. c. Thomas Drew "(Editor of *The Massachusetts Spy*)." Published by John P. Jewett & Company, Boston, MA. Copyright 1856 by Thomas Drew. [3⅝" × 5½"]. B/w litho of "J.C. Fremont." "The Campaign of 1856." 68pp. [Crew/JCF-18].

63.9 Banner Song. w. No composer indicated. m. "Air — *From Greenland's Icy Mountains.*" In: *The Fre-*

mont Songster*, page — inside cover. Published by [V-1: H.S. Riggs & Company, Publishers, No. 4 Cortland Street] [V-2: P.J. Cozans, No. 107 Nassau Street], New York, NY. 1856. [V-1: 3⅝" × 5¾"] [V-2: 3½" × 5⅝"]. Be/bk litho of wreath, John C. Fremont. "With a current likeness of John C. Fremont, The People's Candidate for the Presidency." 40pp. [M-094, 095]. [Crew/JCF-45].

63.10 The Battle Cry. w. W.I. Stillman. m. No tune indicated. "From the *N.Y. Evening Post.*" In: *The Republican Campaign Songster, A Collection Of Lyrics, Original And Selected, Specifically Prepared For The Friends Of Freedom In The Campaign Of Fifty-Six*, page 36. Published by Miller, Orton & Mulligan, No. 25 Park Row, New York, NY. 1856. [3¹³⁄₁₆" × 6"]. Be/bk litho of "Colonel John C. Fremont" facing to viewer's left, black line border. 112pp. [M-097]. [Crew/JCF-24].

63.11 The Bay State Hurrah. w.m. No composer or tune indicated. In: *Fremont Songs For The People (Original And Selected)*, page 37. c. Thomas Drew "(Editor of *The Massachusetts Spy*)." Published by John P. Jewett & Company, Boston, MA. Copyright 1856 by Thomas Drew. [3⅝" × 5½"]. B/w litho of "J.C. Fremont." "The Campaign of 1856." 68pp. [Crew/JCF-18].

63.12 [Behold! The Furious Storm Is Rolling] (Rallying Song). w. No composer indicated. m. "Air — *The Marsellaise Hymn.*" In: *The Republican Campaign Songster, A Collection Of Lyrics, Original And Selected, Specifically Prepared For The Friends Of Freedom In The Campaign Of Fifty-Six*, page 5. Published by Miller, Orton & Mulligan, No. 25 Park Row, New York, NY. 1856. [3¹³⁄₁₆" × 6"]. Be/bk litho of "Colonel John C. Fremont" facing to viewer's left, black line border. 112pp. [M-097]. [Crew/JCF-24].

63.13 Behold The Man! w. No composer indicated. m. "Air — *A Little More Cider Too.*" In: *The Republican Campaign Songster, A Collection Of Lyrics, Original And Selected, Specifically Prepared For The Friends Of Freedom In The Campaign Of Fifty-Six*, page 105. Published by Miller, Orton & Mulligan, No. 25 Park Row, New York, NY. 1856. [3¹³⁄₁₆" × 6"]. Be/bk litho of "Colonel John C. Fremont" facing to viewer's left, black line border. 112pp. [M-097]. [Crew/JCF-24].

63.14 The Bill-Poster's Dream (Or Cross Readings). w. No composer indicated. m. "Air — *The Captain With His Whiskers.*" Published by H. De Marsan, Publisher, 54 Chatham Street, New York, NY. [ca. 1859]. [Approx. 6" × 9½"]. B/w litho border of four characters intertwined with star-studded ribbon, floral and geometric designs. 2pp. Page 2: Blank. [AMC].

63.15 Bold Fremont Of The West. w. No composer indicated. m. "Air — *The Fine Old English Gentleman.*" In: *The Fremont Songster*, page 24. Published by [V-1: H.S. Riggs & Company, Publishers, No. 4 Cortland Street] [V-2: P.J. Cozans, No. 107 Nassau Street], New York, NY. 1856. [V-1: 3⅝" × 5¾"] [V-2: 3½" × 5⅝"]. Be/bk litho of wreath, John C. Fremont. "With a current likeness of John C. Fremont, The People's Candidate for the Presidency." 40pp. [M-094, 095]. [Crew/JCF-45].

63.16 The Brave Old Men. w. No composer indicated. m. "Air — *The Brave Old Oak.*" In: *The Fremont Songster*, page 26. Published by [V-1: H.S. Riggs & Company, Publishers, No. 4 Cortland Street] [V-2: P.J. Cozans, No. 107 Nassau Street], New York, NY. 1856. [V-1: 3⅝" × 5¾"] [V-2: 3½" × 5⅝"]. Be/bk litho of wreath, John C. Fremont. "With a current likeness of John C. Fremont, The People's Candidate for the Presidency." 40pp. [M-094, 095]. [Crew/JCF-45].

63.17 Buchanan And Fremont. w. No composer indicated. m. "Air — *Vilikins And His Dinah.*" In: *Fremont Songs For The People (Original And Selected)*, page 13. c. Thomas Drew "(Editor of *The Massachusetts Spy*)." Published by John P. Jewett & Company, Boston, MA. Copyright 1856 by Thomas Drew. [3⅝" × 5½"]. B/w litho of "J.C. Fremont." "The Campaign of 1856." 68pp. [Crew/JCF-18].

63.18 Buck, Buck Never Had Luck. w. A. Oakley Hall. m. "Air — *Tippecanoe And Tyler, Too.*" In: *The Republican Campaign Songster, A Collection Of Lyrics, Original And Selected, Specifically Prepared For The Friends Of Freedom In The Campaign Of Fifty-Six*, page 95. Published by Miller, Orton & Mulligan, No. 25 Park Row, New York, NY. 1856. [3¹³⁄₁₆" × 6"]. Be/bk litho of "Colonel John C. Fremont" facing to viewer's left, black line border. 112pp. [M-097]. [Crew/JCF-24].

63.19 Campaign Song. w. No composer indicated. m. "Air — *A Little More Cider.*" In: *The Freeman's Glee Book, A Collection Of Songs, Odes, Glees And Ballads With Music, Original And Selected, Harmonized And Arranged For Each. Published Under The Auspices Of The Central Fremont And Dayton Glee Club Of The City Of New York, And Dedicated To All, Who, Cherishing Republican Liberty Consider Freedom Worth A Song*, page 24. Published by Miller, Orton & Mulligan, No. 25 Park Row, New York, NY. [and Auburn, NY]. 1856. [4⅕⁄₁₆" × 6"]. Pk/bk litho of man on mountain peak, music sheets, geometric designs. 112pp. [Crew/JCF-16].

63.20 Campaign Song. Published from *American Purpose Newsletter*. [1964]. [2" × 3½"]. Non-pictorial. Obv: Song. Rev: Blank. [Crew/BMG-14].

63.21 Charley Our Hero. w. No composer indicated. m. "Air — *My Boy Tommy.*" In: *The Republican Campaign Songster, A Collection Of Lyrics, Original And Selected, Specifically Prepared For The Friends Of Freedom In The Campaign Of Fifty-Six*, page 66. Published by Miller, Orton & Mulligan, No. 25 Park Row, New York, NY. 1856. [3¹³⁄₁₆" × 6"]. Be/bk litho of "Colonel John C. Fremont" facing to viewer's left, black line border. 112pp. [M-097]. [Crew/JCF-24].

63.22 A Cheer For Freedom. w. No composer indicated. m. "Air — *Good Night.*" In: *The Freeman's Glee Book, A Collection Of Songs, Odes, Glees And Ballads With Music, Original And Selected, Harmonized And Arranged For Each. Published Under The Auspices Of The Central Fremont And Dayton Glee Club Of The City Of New York, And Dedicated To All, Who, Cherishing Republican Liberty Consider Freedom Worth A Song*, page 76. Published by Miller, Orton & Mulligan, No. 25 Park Row, New York, NY. [and Auburn, NY]. 1856. [4⅕⁄₁₆" × 6"]. Pk/bk litho of man on mountain peak, music sheets, geometric designs. 112pp. [Crew/JCF-16].

63.23 Clear The Track! w. No composer indicated.

m. "Music—*Begone, Dull Care!*" Published in the *New York Weekly Times, And National Democrat*, July 26, 1856. [VBL, p. 334].

63.24 Colored Volunteer. w. Tom Craig. m. No tune indicated. Published by [V-1: Johnson, No. 7 Tenth Street] [V-2: A.W. Auner, N.E. Cor. Of Eleventh and Market], Philadelphia, PA. [186-]. [Approx. 6" × 9"]. B/e geometric design border. [V-1: "See Prof. Brooks' Ball Room Monitor, it will give you more Instruction in Dancing than say book ever Published. Sold by Johnson, No. 7 North Tenth Street, Phila. Price 15 cts."]. 2pp. Page 2: Blank. [V-1 & 2: AMC]. [V-2: VBL, p. 385].

63.25 The Colored Volunteers. w. No composer indicated. m. No tune indicated. Published by Charles Magnus, 12 Frankfort Street, New York, NY. [186-]. H/c litho of a Black man on stage playing a banjo. "500 Illustrated Ballads, lithographed and printed by Charles Magnus, No. 12 Frankfort Street, New York. Branch Office: No. 520 7th St., Washington, D.C." 2pp. Page 2: Blank. [AMC].

63.26 Come Away. w.m. No composer or tune indicated. In: *The Fremont Campaign Songster*, page 30. Published by Frost & Dory, Publishers, No. 140–142 Vine Street, Cincinnati, OH. 1856. [3½" × 5½"]. B/w litho of John C. Fremont. 32pp. [M-093]. [Crew/JCF-42].

63.27 Contraband Now (Song and Chorus). w.m. Frank Wardlaw. Published by Miller & Beacham, Baltimore MD. 1861. Non-pictorial.

63.28 The Contrast. w. No composer indicated. m. "Air—*Lesbia Hath A Beaming Eye*." In: *The Republican Campaign Songster, A Collection Of Lyrics, Original And Selected, Specifically Prepared For The Friends Of Freedom In The Campaign Of Fifty-Six*, page 87. Published by Miller, Orton & Mulligan, No. 25 Park Row, New York, NY. 1856. [3$^{13}/_{16}$" × 6"]. Be/bk litho of "Colonel John C. Fremont" facing to viewer's left, black line border. 112pp. [M-097]. [Crew/JCF-24].

63.29 Darkly Frowns The Rocky Heights. w. A Lady. m. "Air—*Nelly Bly Shuts Her Eye When She Goes To Sleep*." "Two songs by a Lady, Song No. 1." In: *The Republican Campaign Songster, A Collection Of Lyrics, Original And Selected, Specifically Prepared For The Friends Of Freedom In The Campaign Of Fifty-Six*, page 67. Published by Miller, Orton & Mulligan, No. 25 Park Row, New York, NY. 1856. [3$^{13}/_{16}$" × 6"]. Be/bk litho of "Colonel John C. Fremont" facing to viewer's left, black line border. 112pp. [M-097]. [Crew/JCF-24].

63.30 The Dawn Of Liberty. w. No composer indicated. m. "Air—*Star Spangled Banner*." "Suggested by the picture of Fremont planting the American flag on the summit of the Rocky Mountains." In: *The Freeman's Glee Book, A Collection Of Songs, Odes, Glees And Ballads With Music, Original And Selected, Harmonized And Arranged For Each. Published Under The Auspices Of The Central Fremont And Dayton Glee Club Of The City Of New York, And Dedicated To All, Who, Cherishing Republican Liberty Consider Freedom Worth A Song*, page 66. Published by Miller, Orton & Mulligan, No. 25 Park Row, New York, NY. [and Auburn, NY]. 1856. [4$^{15}/_{16}$" × 6"]. Pk/bk litho of man on mountain peak, music sheets, geometric designs. 112pp. [Crew/JCF-16].

63.31 De Nigger On De Fence. w. No composer indicated. m. "Air—*All Round My Hat*." No publisher indicated. [ca. 1864]. H/c litho of two Black men. 2pp. Page 2: Blank. [AMC].

63.32 De Union's De Best Road To Trabbel. w. No composer indicated. m. "Air—*Other Side Ob Jordan*." In: *The Lincoln And Johnson Union Campaign Songster*, page 36. Published by A. Winch, No. 505 Chestnut Street, Philadelphia, PA. 1864. [3⅞" × 6"]. Be/bk lithos of Abraham Lincoln and Andrew Johnson, geometric design border. 58pp. [M-124] [Crew/AL-379].

63.33 The Dirge Of The Doughface. w. No composer indicated. m. "Air—*Ben Bolt*." "A song to be learned before November next, as it will then be extensively needed." In: *The Republican Campaign Songster, A Collection Of Lyrics, Original And Selected, Specifically Prepared For The Friends Of Freedom In The Campaign Of Fifty-Six*, page 16. Published by Miller, Orton & Mulligan, No. 25 Park Row, New York, NY. 1856. [3$^{13}/_{16}$" × 6"]. Be/bk litho of "Colonel John C. Fremont" facing to viewer's left, black line border. 112pp. [M-097]. [Crew/JCF-24].

63.34 The Exodus. w. No composer indicated. m. "Air—*The Soldier's Tear*." "To take place on the evening of next 3d of March." In: *The Republican Campaign Songster, A Collection Of Lyrics, Original And Selected, Specifically Prepared For The Friends Of Freedom In The Campaign Of Fifty-Six*, page 17. Published by Miller, Orton & Mulligan, No. 25 Park Row, New York, NY. 1856. [3$^{13}/_{16}$" × 6"]. Be/bk litho of "Colonel John C. Fremont" facing to viewer's left, black line border. 112pp. [M-097]. [Crew/JCF-24].

63.35 Extract From 'Pope.' w.m. No composer or tune indicated. In: *The Freeman's Glee Book, A Collection Of Songs, Odes, Glees And Ballads With Music, Original And Selected, Harmonized And Arranged For Each. Published Under The Auspices Of The Central Fremont And Dayton Glee Club Of The City Of New York, And Dedicated To All, Who, Cherishing Republican Liberty Consider Freedom Worth A Song*, page 73. Published by Miller, Orton & Mulligan, No. 25 Park Row, New York, NY. [and Auburn, NY]. 1856. [4$^{15}/_{16}$" × 6"]. Pk/bk litho of man on mountain peak, music sheets, geometric designs. 112pp. [Crew/JCF-16].

63.36 For Freedom And Fremont (The Hurrah Song). w. No composer indicated. m. Air—*The Hurrah Song*. In: *Fremont Songs For The People (Original And Selected)*, page 24. c. Thomas Drew "(Editor of *The Massachusetts Spy*)." Published by John P. Jewett & Company, Boston, MA. Copyright 1856 by Thomas Drew. [3⅝" × 5½"]. B/w litho of "J.C. Fremont." "The Campaign of 1856." 68pp. [Crew/JCF-18].

63.37 For Fremont And Freedom. w. No composer indicated. m. "Air—*Rory O'More*." In: *The Republican Campaign Songster, A Collection Of Lyrics, Original And Selected, Specifically Prepared For The Friends Of Freedom In The Campaign Of Fifty-Six*, page 20. Published by Miller, Orton & Mulligan, No. 25 Park Row, New York, NY. 1856. [3$^{13}/_{16}$" × 6"]. Be/bk litho of "Colonel John C. Fremont" facing to viewer's left, black line border. 112pp. [M-097]. [Crew/JCF-24].

63.38 For Fremont, The Choice Of The Nation. w.

J.F. Crosby. m. "Air—*The Red, White And Blue.*" In: *The Freeman's Glee Book, A Collection Of Songs, Odes, Glees And Ballads With Music, Original And Selected, Harmonized And Arranged For Each. Published Under The Auspices Of The Central Fremont And Dayton Glee Club Of The City Of New York, And Dedicated To All, Who, Cherishing Republican Liberty Consider Freedom Worth A Song*, page 18. Published by Miller, Orton & Mulligan, No. 25 Park Row, New York, NY. [and Auburn, NY]. 1856. [4¹⁵⁄₁₆" × 6"]. Pk/bk litho of man on mountain peak, music sheets, geometric designs. 112pp. [Crew/JCF-16].

63.39 The Four Years' Race. w. No composer indicated. m. "Air—*Few Days.*" In: *The Freeman's Glee Book, A Collection Of Songs, Odes, Glees And Ballads With Music, Original And Selected, Harmonized And Arranged For Each. Published Under The Auspices Of The Central Fremont And Dayton Glee Club Of The City Of New York, And Dedicated To All, Who, Cherishing Republican Liberty Consider Freedom Worth A Song*, page 40. Published by Miller, Orton & Mulligan, No. 25 Park Row, New York, NY. [and Auburn, NY]. 1856. [4¹⁵⁄₁₆" × 6"]. Pk/bk litho of man on mountain peak, music sheets, geometric designs. 112pp. [Crew/JCF-16].

63.40 A Fourth Of July Ode For The Freemen Of Fifty-Six. w. No composer indicated. m. "Air—*Scots Wha Hae.*" In: *The Republican Campaign Songster, A Collection Of Lyrics, Original And Selected, Specifically Prepared For The Friends Of Freedom In The Campaign Of Fifty-Six*, page 13. Published by Miller, Orton & Mulligan, No. 25 Park Row, New York, NY. 1856. [3¹³⁄₁₆" × 6"]. Be/bk litho of "Colonel John C. Fremont" facing to viewer's left, black line border. 112pp. [M-097]. [Crew/JCF-24].

63.41 Franklin Pierce's Farewell. w. No composer indicated. m. "Air—*Araby's Daughter.*" In: *Fremont Songs For The People (Original And Selected)*, page 36. c. Thomas Drew "(Editor of *The Massachusetts Spy*)." Published by John P. Jewett & Company, Boston, MA. Copyright 1856 by Thomas Drew. [3⅜" × 5½"]. B/w litho of "J.C. Fremont." "The Campaign of 1856." 68pp. [Crew/JCF-18].

63.42 [Free Soil We Claim For Freedom's Sons] (A New Song to an Old Tune). w. No composer indicated. m. "Air—*Yankee Doodle.*" In: *The Republican Campaign Songster, A Collection Of Lyrics, Original And Selected, Specifically Prepared For The Friends Of Freedom In The Campaign Of Fifty-Six*, page 60. Published by Miller, Orton & Mulligan, No. 25 Park Row, New York, NY. 1856. [3¹³⁄₁₆" × 6"]. Be/bk litho of "Colonel John C. Fremont" facing to viewer's left, black line border. 112pp. [M-097]. [Crew/JCF-24].

63.43 Freedom. w.m. No composer or tune indicated. From the "*N.Y. Evening Post.*" In: *The Republican Campaign Songster, A Collection Of Lyrics, Original And Selected, Specifically Prepared For The Friends Of Freedom In The Campaign Of Fifty-Six*, page 46. Published by Miller, Orton & Mulligan, No. 25 Park Row, New York, NY. 1856. [3¹³⁄₁₆" × 6"]. Be/bk litho of "Colonel John C. Fremont" facing to viewer's left, black line border. 112pp. [M-097]. [Crew/JCF-24].

63.44 Freedom And Fremont. w. No composer indicated. m. "Air—*Yankee Doodle.*" In: *The Freeman's Glee Book, A Collection Of Songs, Odes, Glees And Ballads With Music, Original And Selected, Harmonized And Arranged For Each. Published Under The Auspices Of The Central Fremont And Dayton Glee Club Of The City Of New York, And Dedicated To All, Who, Cherishing Republican Liberty Consider Freedom Worth A Song*, page 82. Published by Miller, Orton & Mulligan, No. 25 Park Row, New York, NY. [and Auburn, NY]. 1856. [4¹⁵⁄₁₆" × 6"]. Pk/bk litho of man on mountain peak, music sheets, geometric designs. 112pp. [Crew/JCF-16].

63.45 Freedom And Fremont. w.m. No composer or tune indicated. In: *The Fremont Songster*, page 43. Published by [V-1: H.S. Riggs & Company, Publishers, No. 4 Cortland Street] [V-2: P.J. Cozans, No. 107 Nassau Street], New York, NY. 1856. [V-1: 3⅝" × 5¾"] [V-2: 3½" × 5⅝"]. Be/bk litho of wreath, John C. Fremont. "With a current likeness of John C. Fremont, The People's Candidate for the Presidency." 40pp. [M-094, 095]. [Crew/JCF-45].

63.46 Freedom's Anthem. w. No composer indicated. m. "Air—*God Save The King.*" In: *The Republican Campaign Songster, A Collection Of Lyrics, Original And Selected, Specifically Prepared For The Friends Of Freedom In The Campaign Of Fifty-Six*, page 91. Published by Miller, Orton & Mulligan, No. 25 Park Row, New York, NY. 1856. [3¹³⁄₁₆" × 6"]. Be/bk litho of "Colonel John C. Fremont" facing to viewer's left, black line border. 112pp. [M-097]. [Crew/JCF-24].

63.47 Freedom's Soldiers On Kansas. w. No composer indicated. m. "Air—*The Brave Old Oak.*" "By permission of the Author." In: *The Freeman's Glee Book, A Collection Of Songs, Odes, Glees And Ballads With Music, Original And Selected, Harmonized And Arranged For Each. Published Under The Auspices Of The Central Fremont And Dayton Glee Club Of The City Of New York, And Dedicated To All, Who, Cherishing Republican Liberty Consider Freedom Worth A Song*, page 105. Published by Miller, Orton & Mulligan, No. 25 Park Row, New York, NY. [and Auburn, NY]. 1856. [4¹⁵⁄₁₆" × 6"]. Pk/bk litho of man on mountain peak, music sheets, geometric designs. 112pp. [Crew/JCF-16].

63.48 Freedom's Songs! (For The Campaign Of 1856!). w.m. No composers indicated. Published by Higgins & Bradley, No. 20 Washington Street, Boston, MA. 1856. B/w litho of John C. Fremont. "John C. Fremont, An Acrostic." Song sheet with four Fremont-related campaign songs. "Let Friends of freedom send in their orders early." 2pp. Page 2: Blank. [Crew/JCF-57].

63.49 The Freemen Of The North. w. No composer indicated. m. "Air—*Auld Lang Syne.*" In: *Fremont Songs For The People (Original And Selected)*, page 9. c. Thomas Drew "(Editor of *The Massachusetts Spy*)." Published by John P. Jewett & Company, Boston, MA. Copyright 1856 by Thomas Drew. [3⅜" × 5½"]. B/w litho of "J.C. Fremont." "The Campaign of 1856." 68pp. [Crew/JCF-18].

63.50 Freemen Win Where Fremont Leads. w. No composer indicated. m. "Air—*Lutzow's Wild Hunt.*" In: *The Freeman's Glee Book, A Collection Of Songs, Odes, Glees And Ballads With Music, Original And Selected, Harmonized And Arranged For Each. Published*

Under The Auspices Of The Central Fremont And Dayton Glee Club Of The City Of New York, And Dedicated To All, Who, Cherishing Republican Liberty Consider Freedom Worth A Song, page 89. Published by Miller, Orton & Mulligan, No. 25 Park Row, New York, NY. [and Auburn, NY]. 1856. [4 15/16" × 6"]. Pk/bk litho of man on mountain peak, music sheets, geometric designs. 112pp. [Crew/JCF-16].

63.51 Freemen's Rally. w. No composer indicated. m. "Air—*Here's A Health To All Good Lassies.*" In: *Fremont Songs For The People (Original And Selected),* page 47. c. Thomas Drew "(Editor of *The Massachusetts Spy*)." Published by John P. Jewett & Company, Boston, MA. Copyright 1856 by Thomas Drew. [3⅝" × 5½"]. B/w litho of "J.C. Fremont." "The Campaign of 1856." 68pp. [Crew/JCF-18].

63.52 The Freeman's Vow. w. No composer indicated. m. "Air—*Oh! Hard Times Come Again No More.*" "By permission of the Author." In: *The Freeman's Glee Book, A Collection Of Songs, Odes, Glees And Ballads With Music, Original And Selected, Harmonized And Arranged For Each. Published Under The Auspices Of The Central Fremont And Dayton Glee Club Of The City Of New York, And Dedicated To All, Who, Cherishing Republican Liberty Consider Freedom Worth A Song,* page 100. Published by Miller, Orton & Mulligan, No. 25 Park Row, New York, NY. [and Auburn, NY]. 1856. [4 15/16" × 6"]. Pk/bk litho of man on mountain peak, music sheets, geometric designs. 112pp. [Crew/JCF-16].

63.53 Fremont. w.m. No composer or tune indicated. "The following originally appeared in the *National Era,* published in Washington, D.C." In: *The Republican Campaign Songster, A Collection Of Lyrics, Original And Selected, Specifically Prepared For The Friends Of Freedom In The Campaign Of Fifty-Six,* page 47. Published by Miller, Orton & Mulligan, No. 25 Park Row, New York, NY. 1856. [3 13/16" × 6"]. Be/bk litho of "Colonel John C. Fremont" facing to viewer's left, black line border. 112pp. [M-097]. [Crew/JCF-24].

63.54 Fremont. w. No composer indicated. m. "Music arranged by J.M. Hagar, Music Conductor of the Church of the Pilgrim, Brooklyn, for the *Freeman's Glee Book.*" "By permission of Oliver Ditson." In: *The Freeman's Glee Book, A Collection Of Songs, Odes, Glees And Ballads With Music, Original And Selected, Harmonized And Arranged For Each. Published Under The Auspices Of The Central Fremont And Dayton Glee Club Of The City Of New York, And Dedicated To All, Who, Cherishing Republican Liberty Consider Freedom Worth A Song,* page 46. Published by Miller, Orton & Mulligan, No. 25 Park Row, New York, NY. [and Auburn, NY]. 1856. [4 15/16" × 6"]. Pk/bk litho of man on mountain peak, music sheets, geometric designs. 112pp. [Crew/JCF-16].

63.55 Fremont And Dayton. w. No composer indicated. m. "Air—*O, What Has Caused This Great Commotion.*" In: *Fremont Songs For The People (Original And Selected),* page 22. c. Thomas Drew "(Editor of *The Massachusetts Spy*)." Published by John P. Jewett & Company, Boston, MA. Copyright 1856 by Thomas Drew. [3⅝" × 5½"]. B/w litho of "J.C. Fremont." "The Campaign of 1856." 68pp. [Crew/JCF-18].

63.56 Fremont And Dayton. w. No composer indicated. m. "Air—*Yankee Doodle.*" In: *The Freeman's Glee Book, A Collection Of Songs, Odes, Glees And Ballads With Music, Original And Selected, Harmonized And Arranged For Each. Published Under The Auspices Of The Central Fremont And Dayton Glee Club Of The City Of New York, And Dedicated To All, Who, Cherishing Republican Liberty Consider Freedom Worth A Song,* page 70. Published by Miller, Orton & Mulligan, No. 25 Park Row, New York, NY. [and Auburn, NY]. 1856. [4 15/16" × 6"]. Pk/bk litho of man on mountain peak, music sheets, geometric designs. 112pp. [Crew/JCF-16].

63.57 Fremont And Dayton (Or Yankee Doodle Revised). w. No composer indicated. m. Air—*Yankee Doodle.* In: *Fremont Songs For The People (Original And Selected),* page 54. c. Thomas Drew "(Editor of *The Massachusetts Spy*)." Published by John P. Jewett & Company, Boston, MA. Copyright 1856 by Thomas Drew. [3⅝" × 5½"]. B/w litho of "J.C. Fremont." "The Campaign of 1856." 68pp. [Crew/JCF-18].

63.58 Fremont And Freedom. w. No composer indicated. m. "Air—*Right Over Wrong.*" In: *Fremont Songs For The People (Original And Selected),* page 18. c. Thomas Drew "(Editor of *The Massachusetts Spy*)." Published by John P. Jewett & Company, Boston, MA. Copyright 1856 by Thomas Drew. [3⅝" × 5½"]. B/w litho of "J.C. Fremont." "The Campaign of 1856." 68pp. [Crew/JCF-18].

63.59 Fremont And Liberty. w. Joseph Gutman, Jr. m. No tune indicated. In: *The Republican Campaign Songster, A Collection Of Lyrics, Original And Selected, Specifically Prepared For The Friends Of Freedom In The Campaign Of Fifty-Six,* page 48. Published by Miller, Orton & Mulligan, No. 25 Park Row, New York, NY. 1856. [3 13/16" × 6"]. Be/bk litho of "Colonel John C. Fremont" facing to viewer's left, black line border. 112pp. [M-097]. [Crew/JCF-24].

63.60 Fremont And Victory (A Rallying Song). w. No composer indicated. m. "Tune of *Marseilles* Hymn." Published by Andrews, Printer, No. 38 Chatham Street, New York, NY. [1856]. B/w penny song sheet with litho border of geometric designs. "Andrews, Printer, No. 38 Chatham Street, N.Y. Dealer in Songs, Games, Toy Books, Mottos, Verses, Valentines, &c." 2pp. Page 2: Blank. [Crew/JCF-58].

63.61 Fremont And Victory. w. No composer indicated. m. "Air—*Banks Of Banna.*" In: *The Fremont Campaign Songster,* page 10. Published by Frost & Dory, Publishers, No. 140–142 Vine Street, Cincinnati, OH. 1856. [3½" × 5½"]. B/w litho of John C. Fremont. 32pp. Page 2: "To the Fremont Clubs and the Republican Party throughout the Union, this little volume is Respectfully Dedicated by the Publishers." [M-093]. [Crew/JCF-42].

63.62 Fremont Boys, Come Out Tonight. w. A. Oakley Hall. m. "Air—*Buffalo Gals.*" In: *The Republican Campaign Songster, A Collection Of Lyrics, Original And Selected, Specifically Prepared For The Friends Of Freedom In The Campaign Of Fifty-Six,* page 100. Published by Miller, Orton & Mulligan, No. 25 Park Row, New York, NY. 1856. [3 13/16" × 6"]. Be/bk litho of "Colonel John C. Fremont" facing to viewer's left, black line border. 112pp. [M-097]. [Crew/JCF-24].

63.63 The Fremont Crusader's Song. w. Francis C. Woodworth. m. "Air—*Sparkling And Bright.*" In: *The Freeman's Glee Book, A Collection Of Songs, Odes, Glees And Ballads With Music, Original And Selected, Harmonized And Arranged For Each. Published Under The Auspices Of The Central Fremont And Dayton Glee Club Of The City Of New York, And Dedicated To All, Who, Cherishing Republican Liberty Consider Freedom Worth A Song*, page 56. Published by Miller, Orton & Mulligan, No. 25 Park Row, New York, NY. [and Auburn, NY]. 1856. [4$\frac{15}{16}$" × 6"]. Pk/bk litho of man on mountain peak, music sheets, geometric designs. 112pp. [Crew/JCF-16].

63.64 The Fremont Freedman's Battle Cry. w. No composer indicated. m. "Air—*The Ivy Green.*" In: *The Republican Campaign Songster, A Collection Of Lyrics, Original And Selected, Specifically Prepared For The Friends Of Freedom In The Campaign Of Fifty-Six*, page 62. Published by Miller, Orton & Mulligan, No. 25 Park Row, New York, NY. 1856. [3$\frac{13}{16}$" × 6"]. Be/bk litho of "Colonel John C. Fremont" facing to viewer's left, black line border. 112pp. [M-097]. [Crew/JCF-24].

63.65 Fremont Gathering Song. w. No composer indicated. m. "Air—*Highland Fling.*" In: *Fremont Songs For The People (Original And Selected)*, page 50. c. Thomas Drew "(Editor of *The Massachusetts Spy*)." Published by John P. Jewett & Company, Boston, MA. Copyright 1856 by Thomas Drew. [3⅝" × 5½"]. B/w litho of "J.C. Fremont." "The Campaign of 1856." 68pp. [Crew/JCF-18].

63.66 Fremont Glees. w. No composer indicated. m. "Air—*Jordan Is A Hard Road To Travel.*" In: *The Fremont Campaign Songster*, page 23. Published by Frost & Dory, Publishers, No. 140–142 Vine Street, Cincinnati, OH. 1856. [3½" × 5½"]. B/w litho of John C. Fremont. 32pp. Page 2: "To the Fremont Clubs and the Republican Party throughout the Union, this little volume is Respectfully Dedicated by the Publishers." [M-093]. [Crew/JCF-42].

63.67 A Fremont Lyric For Free Men. w. No composer indicated. m. "Air—*Lucy Long.*" In: *The Fremont Campaign Songster*, page 13. Published by Frost & Dory, Publishers, No. 140–142 Vine Street, Cincinnati, OH. 1856. [3½" × 5½"]. B/w litho of John C. Fremont. 32pp. Page 2: "To the Fremont Clubs and the Republican Party throughout the Union, this little volume is Respectfully Dedicated by the Publishers." [M-093]. [Crew/JCF-42].

63.68 Fremont Rally Song. w. No composer indicated. m. "Air—*Kinloch Of Kinloch.*" In: *The Freeman's Glee Book, A Collection Of Songs, Odes, Glees And Ballads With Music, Original And Selected, Harmonized And Arranged For Each. Published Under The Auspices Of The Central Fremont And Dayton Glee Club Of The City Of New York, And Dedicated To All, Who, Cherishing Republican Liberty Consider Freedom Worth A Song*, page 58. Published by Miller, Orton & Mulligan, No. 25 Park Row, New York, NY. [and Auburn, NY]. 1856. [4$\frac{15}{16}$" × 6"]. Pk/bk litho of man on mountain peak, music sheets, geometric designs. 112pp. [Crew/JCF-16].

63.69 Fremont Rallying Song. w. No composer indicated. m. "Air—*Old Folks At Home.*" In: *Fremont Songs For The People (Original And Selected)*, page 29. c. Thomas Drew "(Editor of *The Massachusetts Spy*)." Published by John P. Jewett & Company, Boston, MA. Copyright 1856 by Thomas Drew. [3⅝" × 5½"]. B/w litho of "J.C. Fremont." "The Campaign of 1856." 68pp. [Crew/JCF-18].

63.70 Fremont Rallying Song. w. No composer indicated. m. "Air—*Vive La Companie.*" In: *Fremont Songs For The People (Original And Selected)*, page 6. c. Thomas Drew "(Editor of *The Massachusetts Spy*)." Published by John P. Jewett & Company, Boston, MA. Copyright 1856 by Thomas Drew. [3⅝" × 5½"]. B/w litho of "J.C. Fremont." "The Campaign of 1856." 68pp. [Crew/JCF-18].

63.71 Fremont, The Choice Of The Nation. w. No composer indicated. m. "Air—*The Red, White And Blue.*" B/w litho of an American flag inscribed—"Freedom's Standard." In: *Fremont Songs For The People (Original And Selected)*, page 26 c. Thomas Drew "(Editor of *The Massachusetts Spy*)." Published by John P. Jewett & Company, Boston, MA. Copyright 1856 by Thomas Drew. [3⅝" × 5½"]. B/w litho of "J.C. Fremont." "The Campaign of 1856." 68pp. [Crew/JCF-18].

63.72 Fremont The True And The Bold. w. No composer indicated. m. "Air—*Lutzow's Wild Hunt.*" In: *The Freeman's Glee Book, A Collection Of Songs, Odes, Glees And Ballads With Music, Original And Selected, Harmonized And Arranged For Each. Published Under The Auspices Of The Central Fremont And Dayton Glee Club Of The City Of New York, And Dedicated To All, Who, Cherishing Republican Liberty Consider Freedom Worth A Song*, page 92. Published by Miller, Orton & Mulligan, No. 25 Park Row, New York, NY. [and Auburn, NY]. 1856. [4$\frac{15}{16}$" × 6"]. Pk/bk litho of man on mountain peak, music sheets, geometric designs. 112pp. [Crew/JCF-16].

63.73 The Fremont Train. w. No composer indicated. m. "Air—*Old Dan Tucker.*" In: *The Freeman's Glee Book, A Collection Of Songs, Odes, Glees And Ballads With Music, Original And Selected, Harmonized And Arranged For Each. Published Under The Auspices Of The Central Fremont And Dayton Glee Club Of The City Of New York, And Dedicated To All, Who, Cherishing Republican Liberty Consider Freedom Worth A Song*, page 48. Published by Miller, Orton & Mulligan, No. 25 Park Row, New York, NY. [and Auburn, NY]. 1856. [4$\frac{15}{16}$" × 6"]. Pk/bk litho of man on mountain peak, music sheets, geometric designs. 112pp. [Crew/JCF-16].

63.74 Fremont's The Choice Of The Nation. w.m. No composer or tune indicated. "Sung first at the Brooklyn Ratification Meeting." In: *The Fremont Songster*, page 30. Published by [V-1: H.S. Riggs & Company, Publishers, No. 4 Cortland Street] [V-2: P.J. Cozans, No. 107 Nassau Street], New York, NY. 1856. [V-1: 3⅝" × 5¾"] [V-2: 3½" × 5⅝"]. Be/bk litho of wreath, John C. Fremont. "With a current likeness of John C. Fremont, The People's Candidate for the Presidency." 40pp. [M-094, 095]. [Crew/JCF-45].

63.75 Get Out Of The Way, Old Buchanan. w. No composer indicated. m. "Air—*Old Dan Tucker.*" In: *Fremont Songs For The People (Original And Selected)*, page 56. c. Thomas Drew "(Editor of *The Massachu-*

setts Spy)." Published by John P. Jewett & Company, Boston, MA. Copyright 1856 by Thomas Drew. [3⅝" × 5½"]. B/w litho of "J.C. Fremont." "The Campaign of 1856." 68pp. [Crew/JCF-18].

63.76 Get Out Of The Way, 'Ten-Cent Jimmy.' w.m. No composer or tune indicated [*Old Dan Tucker*]. In: *Fremont Songs For The People (Original And Selected)*, page 52. c. Thomas Drew "(Editor of *The Massachusetts Spy*)." Published by John P. Jewett & Company, Boston, MA. Copyright 1856 by Thomas Drew. [3⅝" × 5½"]. B/w litho of "J.C. Fremont." "The Campaign of 1856." 68pp. [Crew/JCF-18].

63.77 Give 'Em Jesse. w. No composer indicated. m. "Air — *Yankee Doodle*." In: *Fremont Songs For The People (Original And Selected)*, page 61. c. Thomas Drew "(Editor of *The Massachusetts Spy*)." Published by John P. Jewett & Company, Boston, MA. Copyright 1856 by Thomas Drew. [3⅝" × 5½"]. B/w litho of "J.C. Fremont." "The Campaign of 1856." 68pp. [Crew/JCF-18].

63.78 Give 'Em Jesse And Fremont. w. No composer indicated. m. "Air — *Jessie, The Flower Of Dumblane*." "From the *N.Y. Evening Mirror*." In: *The Republican Campaign Songster, A Collection Of Lyrics, Original And Selected, Specifically Prepared For The Friends Of Freedom In The Campaign Of Fifty-Six*, page 38. Published by Miller, Orton & Mulligan, No. 25 Park Row, New York, NY. 1856. [3¹³⁄₁₆" × 6"]. Be/bk litho of "Colonel John C. Fremont" facing to viewer's left, black line border. 112pp. [M-097]. [Crew/JCF-24].

63.79 God And The Right. w. No composer indicated. m. "Air — *America*." In: *The Freeman's Glee Book, A Collection Of Songs, Odes, Glees And Ballads With Music, Original And Selected, Harmonized And Arranged For Each.* Published Under The Auspices Of The Central Fremont And Dayton Glee Club Of The City Of New York, And Dedicated To All, Who, Cherishing Republican Liberty Consider Freedom Worth A Song, page 61. Published by Miller, Orton & Mulligan, No. 25 Park Row, New York, NY. [and Auburn, NY]. 1856. [4⁵⁄₁₆" × 6"]. Pk/bk litho of man on mountain peak, music sheets, geometric designs. 112pp. [Crew/JCF-16].

63.80 God Made Us Free! w. No composer indicated. m. "Air — *America*." a. S.J. In: *The Freeman's Glee Book, A Collection Of Songs, Odes, Glees And Ballads With Music, Original And Selected, Harmonized And Arranged For Each.* Published Under The Auspices Of The Central Fremont And Dayton Glee Club Of The City Of New York, And Dedicated To All, Who, Cherishing Republican Liberty Consider Freedom Worth A Song, page 12. Published by Miller, Orton & Mulligan, No. 25 Park Row, New York, NY. [and Auburn, NY]. 1856. [4⁵⁄₁₆" × 6"]. Pk/bk litho of man on mountain peak, music sheets, geometric designs. 112pp. [Crew/JCF-16].

63.81 Grasshopper Pie. w. "By one who has eaten it." m. "Air — *Old Dan Tucker*." "Fort Hall, 1856." In: *The Republican Campaign Songster, A Collection Of Lyrics, Original And Selected, Specifically Prepared For The Friends Of Freedom In The Campaign Of Fifty-Six*, page 102. Published by Miller, Orton & Mulligan, No. 25 Park Row, New York, NY. 1856. [3¹³⁄₁₆" × 6"]. Be/bk litho of "Colonel John C. Fremont" facing to viewer's left, black line border. 112pp. [M-097]. [Crew/JCF-24].

63.82 Grim Truth In Masquerade. w. No composer indicated. m. "Air — *Alley Croaker*." "Dedicated (without permission) to the Signer of the Fugitive Slave Bill." In: *The Republican Campaign Songster, A Collection Of Lyrics, Original And Selected, Specifically Prepared For The Friends Of Freedom In The Campaign Of Fifty-Six*, page 10. Published by Miller, Orton & Mulligan, No. 25 Park Row, New York, NY. 1856. [3¹³⁄₁₆" × 6"]. Be/bk litho of "Colonel John C. Fremont" facing to viewer's left, black line border. 112pp. [M-097]. [Crew/JCF-24].

63.83 The Gudgeon Of Democracy And The Southern Ark. w. No composer indicated. m. "Air — *The Cruel Troopers Riding By*." In: *The Republican Campaign Songster, A Collection Of Lyrics, Original And Selected, Specifically Prepared For The Friends Of Freedom In The Campaign Of Fifty-Six*, page 7. Published by Miller, Orton & Mulligan, No. 25 Park Row, New York, NY. 1856. [3¹³⁄₁₆" × 6"]. Be/bk litho of "Colonel John C. Fremont" facing to viewer's left, black line border. 112pp. [M-097]. [Crew/JCF-24].

63.84 Hail To Fremont. w. No composer indicated. m. "Air — *Hail Columbia*." In: *The Republican Campaign Songster, A Collection Of Lyrics, Original And Selected, Specifically Prepared For The Friends Of Freedom In The Campaign Of Fifty-Six*, page 57. Published by Miller, Orton & Mulligan, No. 25 Park Row, New York, NY. 1856. [3¹³⁄₁₆" × 6"]. Be/bk litho of "Colonel John C. Fremont" facing to viewer's left, black line border. 112pp. [M-097]. [Crew/JCF-24].

63.85 Have You Heard Of One Fremont? w. No composer indicated. m. "Air — *Tippecanoe And Tyler, Too*." In: *The Freeman's Glee Book, A Collection Of Songs, Odes, Glees And Ballads With Music, Original And Selected, Harmonized And Arranged For Each.* Published Under The Auspices Of The Central Fremont And Dayton Glee Club Of The City Of New York, And Dedicated To All, Who, Cherishing Republican Liberty Consider Freedom Worth A Song, page 68. Published by Miller, Orton & Mulligan, No. 25 Park Row, New York, NY. [and Auburn, NY]. 1856. [4⁵⁄₁₆" × 6"]. Pk/bk litho of man on mountain peak, music sheets, geometric designs. 112pp. [Crew/JCF-16].

63.86 Heads We Win — Tails You Lose. w. No composer indicated. m. "Air — *Dearest May*." "The delightful game suggested by Millard Fillmore to the South, in his celebrated Albany Speech." "By permission of O. Ditson." In: *The Freeman's Glee Book, A Collection Of Songs, Odes, Glees And Ballads With Music, Original And Selected, Harmonized And Arranged For Each.* Published Under The Auspices Of The Central Fremont And Dayton Glee Club Of The City Of New York, And Dedicated To All, Who, Cherishing Republican Liberty Consider Freedom Worth A Song, page 52. Published by Miller, Orton & Mulligan, No. 25 Park Row, New York, NY. [and Auburn, NY]. 1856. [4⁵⁄₁₆" × 6"]. Pk/bk litho of man on mountain peak, music sheets, geometric designs. 112pp. [Crew/JCF-16].

63.87 The Homesick Candidate. w. No composer indicated. m. "Air — *Carry Me Back*, &c." In: *The Republican Campaign Songster, A Collection Of Lyrics,*

Original And Selected, Specifically Prepared For The Friends Of Freedom In The Campaign Of Fifty-Six, page 72. Published by Miller, Orton & Mulligan, No. 25 Park Row, New York, NY. 1856. [3¹³⁄₁₆" × 6"]. Be/bk litho of "Colonel John C. Fremont" facing to viewer's left, black line border. 112pp. [M-097]. [Crew/JCF-24].

63.88 Hurrah For Fremont! w.m. No composer or tune indicated. In: *The Freeman's Glee Book, A Collection Of Songs, Odes, Glees And Ballads With Music, Original And Selected, Harmonized And Arranged For Each. Published Under The Auspices Of The Central Fremont And Dayton Glee Club Of The City Of New York, And Dedicated To All, Who, Cherishing Republican Liberty Consider Freedom Worth A Song*, page 22. Published by Miller, Orton & Mulligan, No. 25 Park Row, New York, NY. [and Auburn, NY]. 1856. [4¹⁵⁄₁₆" × 6"]. Pk/bk litho of man on mountain peak, music sheets, geometric designs. 112pp. [Crew/JCF-16].

63.89 Hurrah! For Fremont The Brave (To The Republicans Of The Union). w.m. Annie Page. Published by L. Carleton, No. 58 North 8th Street, Philadelphia, PA. 1856. Non-pictorial geometric designs. "To the Hon. N.P. Banks." "Here's A Health To Freemont [sic]." "Campaign Song No. 1." 6pp. Pages 2 and 6: Blank. [Crew/JCF-56].

63.90 Hurrah For The Man We Love. w. No composer indicated. m. "Air—*Vive L'Amour.*" In: *McClellan And Liberty* [Song Sheet]. Published by Frank McElroy, No. 113 Nassau Street, New York, NY. 1864. [7" × 17"]. Non-pictorial. "Stand by the Union and I'll Stand by you." "The Work before us; To suppress the Rebellion, To preserve the Union, To maintain the sovereignty of the People!" "Let us apply ourselves to the duty of uniting all the conservative elements of the country, in the effort to place in the Presidential Chair a man who will revere the Constitution as his highest political authority—Such a man is George B. McClellan." "The following is ... from a recent letter of the Hon. Amos Kendall: I am losing my patience in reading Gen. McClellan's report. The injustice to him, and the atrocious wrong to his noble army and the country, are enough to make the blood of honest and patriotic men boil within them." 2pp. [Crew/GBM-61].

63.91 Hurrah Song For Fremont. w. No composer indicated. m. "Air—*Lucy Neal.*" In: *The Fremont Campaign Songster*, page 8. Published by Frost & Dory, Publishers, No. 140–142 Vine Street, Cincinnati, OH. 1856. [3½" × 5½"]. B/w litho of John C. Fremont. 32pp. Page 2: "To the Fremont Clubs and the Republican Party throughout the Union, this little volume is Respectfully Dedicated by the Publishers." [M-093]. [Crew/JCF-42].

63.92 I Dreamed In The White House That I Was Installed w. No composer indicated. m. "Air—*I Dreamed That I Dwelt In Marble Halls.*" "Sung with immense applause by the Doughface Doeless Buck, on board the steamboat 'Misery,' during her voyage Up Salt River." In: *The Republican Campaign Songster, A Collection Of Lyrics, Original And Selected, Specifically Prepared For The Friends Of Freedom In The Campaign Of Fifty-Six*, page 28. Published by Miller, Orton & Mulligan, No. 25 Park Row, New York, NY. 1856. [3¹³⁄₁₆" × 6"]. Be/bk litho of "Colonel John C. Fremont" facing to viewer's left, black line border. 112pp. [M-097]. [Crew/JCF-24].

63.93 Intercepted Dispatch. w. No composer indicated. m. "Air—*The Darkie's Break Down.*" In: *The Republican Campaign Songster, A Collection Of Lyrics, Original And Selected, Specifically Prepared For The Friends Of Freedom In The Campaign Of Fifty-Six*, page 58. Published by Miller, Orton & Mulligan, No. 25 Park Row, New York, NY. 1856. [3¹³⁄₁₆" × 6"]. Be/bk litho of "Colonel John C. Fremont" facing to viewer's left, black line border. 112pp. [M-097]. [Crew/JCF-24].

63.94 Jacky Boy. w. No composer indicated. m. "Air—*Nelly Bly.*" In: *Fillmore And Donelson Songs For The Campaign* (Songster), page 6. Published by Robert M. De Witt, Nos. 160 and 162 Nassau Street, New York, NY. November 4, 1856. [4¾" × 7⅛"]. Bl/bk litho of George Washington—"July 4, 1776," wreath, geometric design border. "This is the only authorized edition containing Duganne's Songs. Price 6 cts. each, $4 per 100. Discount to trade." Long quote from George Washington's "Farewell Address." 40pp. Page 3: "Union and Peace." [M-101, 102]. [Crew/MF-10].

63.95 Jesse. w. No composer indicated. m. "Air—*Peg Of Inverlochy.*" In: *The Republican Campaign Songster, A Collection Of Lyrics, Original And Selected, Specifically Prepared For The Friends Of Freedom In The Campaign Of Fifty-Six*, page 82. Published by Miller, Orton & Mulligan, No. 25 Park Row, New York, NY. 1856. [3¹³⁄₁₆" × 6"]. Be/bk litho of "Colonel John C. Fremont" facing to viewer's left, black line border. 112pp. [M-097]. [Crew/JCF-24].

63.96 Jesse Fremont. w. No composer indicated. m. "Air—*Jesse, The Flower Of Dumblane.*" In: *Fremont Songs For The People (Original And Selected)*, page 28 c. Thomas Drew "(Editor of *The Massachusetts Spy*)." Published by John P. Jewett & Company, Boston, MA. Copyright 1856 by Thomas Drew. [3⅝" × 5½"]. B/w litho of "J.C. Fremont." "The Campaign of 1856." 68pp. [Crew/JCF-18].

63.97 Joe Terrapin's Fremont Song. w. No composer indicated. m. "Air—*In A Few Days.*" In: *Fremont Songs For The People (Original And Selected)*, page 10. c. Thomas Drew "(Editor of *The Massachusetts Spy*)." Published by John P. Jewett & Company, Boston, MA. Copyright 1856 by Thomas Drew. [3⅝" × 5½"]. B/w litho of "J.C. Fremont." "The Campaign of 1856." 68pp. [Crew/JCF-18].

63.98 John Fremont's Coming. w. No composer indicated. m. "Air—*Old Dan Tucker.*" In: *Fremont Songs For The People (Original And Selected)*, page 16. c. Thomas Drew "(Editor of *The Massachusetts Spy*)." Published by John P. Jewett & Company, Boston, MA. Copyright 1856 by Thomas Drew. [3⅝" × 5½"]. B/w litho of "J.C. Fremont." "The Campaign of 1856." 68pp. [Crew/JCF-18].

63.99 Jordan. w.m. No composer or tune indicated. In: *The Fremont Songster*, page 44. Published by [V-1: H.S. Riggs & Company, Publishers, No. 4 Cortland Street] [V-2: P.J. Cozans, No. 107 Nassau Street], New York, NY. 1856. [V-1: 3⅝" × 5¾"] [V-2: 3½" × 5⅝"]. Be/bk litho of wreath, John C. Fremont. "With a current likeness of John C. Fremont, The People's Candidate for the Presidency." 40pp. [M-094, 095]. [Crew/JCF-45].

63.100 The Kansas Pioneers. w. James A. Boone. m. "Air — *The Days When We Went Gypsying.*" In: *The Republican Campaign Songster, A Collection Of Lyrics, Original And Selected, Specifically Prepared For The Friends Of Freedom In The Campaign Of Fifty-Six*, page 104. Published by Miller, Orton & Mulligan, No. 25 Park Row, New York, NY. 1856. [3 13/16" × 6"]. Be/bk litho of "Colonel John C. Fremont" facing to viewer's left, black line border. 112pp. [M-097]. [Crew/JCF-24].

63.101 The March Of Freedom. w. No composer indicated. m. "Air — *Old Dan Tucker.*" In: *The Republican Campaign Songster, A Collection Of Lyrics, Original And Selected, Specifically Prepared For The Friends Of Freedom In The Campaign Of Fifty-Six*, page 50. Published by Miller, Orton & Mulligan, No. 25 Park Row, New York, NY. 1856. [3 13/16" × 6"]. Be/bk litho of "Colonel John C. Fremont" facing to viewer's left, black line border. 112pp. [M-097]. [Crew/JCF-24].

63.102 Most Miserable Consolation (Stool-Pigeon Forney To Jim Trencents Buck). w. No composer indicated. m. "Air — *Wind Thy Horn, My Hunter Boy.*" In: *The Republican Campaign Songster, A Collection Of Lyrics, Original And Selected, Specifically Prepared For The Friends Of Freedom In The Campaign Of Fifty-Six*, page 27. Published by Miller, Orton & Mulligan, No. 25 Park Row, New York, NY. 1856. [3 13/16" × 6"]. Be/bk litho of "Colonel John C. Fremont" facing to viewer's left, black line border. 112pp. [M-097]. [Crew/JCF-24].

63.103 The Name Of Fremont. w. No composer indicated. m. "Air — *Battle Of The Baltie.*" In: *The Freeman's Glee Book, A Collection Of Songs, Odes, Glees And Ballads With Music, Original And Selected, Harmonized And Arranged For Each. Published Under The Auspices Of The Central Fremont And Dayton Glee Club Of The City Of New York, And Dedicated To All, Who, Cherishing Republican Liberty Consider Freedom Worth A Song*, page 99. Published by Miller, Orton & Mulligan, No. 25 Park Row, New York, NY. [and Auburn, NY]. 1856. [4 5/16" × 6"]. Pk/bk litho of man on mountain peak, music sheets, geometric designs. 112pp. [Crew/JCF-16].

63.104 The Nebraskaites Think. w. No composer indicated. m. "Air — *Jordan Is A Hard Road To Travel.*" "By permission of Oliver Ditson." In: *The Freeman's Glee Book, A Collection Of Songs, Odes, Glees And Ballads With Music, Original And Selected, Harmonized And Arranged For Each. Published Under The Auspices Of The Central Fremont And Dayton Glee Club Of The City Of New York, And Dedicated To All, Who, Cherishing Republican Liberty Consider Freedom Worth A Song*, page 44. Published by Miller, Orton & Mulligan, No. 25 Park Row, New York, NY. [and Auburn, NY]. 1856. [4 5/16" × 6"]. Pk/bk litho of man on mountain peak, music sheets, geometric designs. 112pp. [Crew/JCF-16].

63.105 The North Is Discovered! w. No composer indicated. m. "Air — *The Star Spangled Banner.*" In: *The Republican Campaign Songster, A Collection Of Lyrics, Original And Selected, Specifically Prepared For The Friends Of Freedom In The Campaign Of Fifty-Six*, page 3. Published by Miller, Orton & Mulligan, No. 25 Park Row, New York, NY. 1856. [3 13/16" × 6"]. Be/bk litho of "Colonel John C. Fremont" facing to viewer's left, black line border. 112pp. [M-097]. [Crew/JCF-24].

63.106 Nursery Rhymes For Young America. w. No composer indicated. m. "Air — *A Frog He Would A Wooing Go, Heigho, Says Rowley.*" In: *The Republican Campaign Songster, A Collection Of Lyrics, Original And Selected, Specifically Prepared For The Friends Of Freedom In The Campaign Of Fifty-Six*, page 31. Published by Miller, Orton & Mulligan, No. 25 Park Row, New York, NY. 1856. [3 13/16" × 6"]. Be/bk litho of "Colonel John C. Fremont" facing to viewer's left, black line border. 112pp. [M-097]. [Crew/JCF-24].

63.107 O Come, Come Away. w.m. No composer or tune indicated. In: *The Fremont Songster*, page 10. Published by [V-1: H.S. Riggs & Company, Publishers, No. 4 Cortland Street] [V-2: P.J. Cozans, No. 107 Nassau Street], New York, NY. 1856. [V-1: 3 5/8" × 5 3/4"] [V-2: 3 1/2" × 5 5/8"]. Be/bk litho of wreath, John C. Fremont. "With a current likeness of John C. Fremont, The People's Candidate for the Presidency." 40pp. [M-094, 095]. [Crew/JCF-45].

63.107A [O, The Sunlight Of Freedom Shines Out Once Again]. In: *The True Issue* [A Cloth Bandanna/Songster]. Published by the Shawmut Chemical Printing Company, Boston, MA. [1856]. [10 1/4" × 10 3/4"]. Cloth bandanna printed with illustration of John C. Fremont. Narrative to either side. Three campaign songs. Rev: Blank. [Crew-JCF-12].

63.108 O, What Is That Sound. w. No composer indicated. m. "Air — *Star Spangled Banner.*" In: *The Fremont Songster*, page 30. Published by [V-1: H.S. Riggs & Company, Publishers, No. 4 Cortland Street] [V-2: P.J. Cozans, No. 107 Nassau Street], New York, NY. 1856. [V-1: 3 5/8" × 5 3/4"] [V-2: 3 1/2" × 5 5/8"]. Be/bk litho of wreath, John C. Fremont. "With a current likeness of John C. Fremont, The People's Candidate for the Presidency." 40pp. [M-094, 095]. [Crew/JCF-45].

63.109 Ode To Freedom w. S.R. Hemenway. m. "Air — *Scots Wha Hae.*" "From the *Boston Atlas.*" In: *The Republican Campaign Songster, A Collection Of Lyrics, Original And Selected, Specifically Prepared For The Friends Of Freedom In The Campaign Of Fifty-Six*, page 40. Published by Miller, Orton & Mulligan, No. 25 Park Row, New York, NY. 1856. [3 13/16" × 6"]. Be/bk litho of "Colonel John C. Fremont" facing to viewer's left, black line border. 112pp. [M-097]. [Crew/JCF-24].

63.110 Oh! Hope For The Triumph. w. No composer indicated. m. "Air — *Believe Me, If All Those Endearing Young Charms.*" In: *The Republican Campaign Songster, A Collection Of Lyrics, Original And Selected, Specifically Prepared For The Friends Of Freedom In The Campaign Of Fifty-Six*, page 84. Published by Miller, Orton & Mulligan, No. 25 Park Row, New York, NY. 1856. [3 13/16" × 6"]. Be/bk litho of "Colonel John C. Fremont" facing to viewer's left, black line border. 112pp. [M-097]. [Crew/JCF-24].

63.111 Oh Jemmy Buchan! w.m. No composer or tune indicated. In: *The Freeman's Glee Book, A Collection Of Songs, Odes, Glees And Ballads With Music,*

Original And Selected, Harmonized And Arranged For Each. Published Under The Auspices Of The Central Fremont And Dayton Glee Club Of The City Of New York, And Dedicated To All, Who, Cherishing Republican Liberty Consider Freedom Worth A Song*, page 62. Published by Miller, Orton & Mulligan, No. 25 Park Row, New York, NY. [and Auburn, NY]. 1856. [4$\frac{15}{16}$" × 6"]. Pk/bk litho of man on mountain peak, music sheets, geometric designs. 112pp. [Crew/JCF-16].

63.112 Oh, Jessie Is A Sweet, Bright Lady. w. No composer indicated. m. "Air — *Comin' Through The Rye*." In: *The Freeman's Glee Book, A Collection Of Songs, Odes, Glees And Ballads With Music, Original And Selected, Harmonized And Arranged For Each. Published Under The Auspices Of The Central Fremont And Dayton Glee Club Of The City Of New York, And Dedicated To All, Who, Cherishing Republican Liberty Consider Freedom Worth A Song*, page 35. Published by Miller, Orton & Mulligan, No. 25 Park Row, New York, NY. [and Auburn, NY]. 1856. [4$\frac{15}{16}$" × 6"]. Pk/bk litho of man on mountain peak, music sheets, geometric designs. 112pp. [Crew/JCF-16].

63.113 Oh, You Can't Go The Caper, Stephen. w.m. No composer or tune indicated. In: *The Wide Awake Vocalist (Or Rail Splitters' Song Book)*, page 23. Published by E.A. Daggett, No. 333 Broadway, New York, NY. 1860. Non-pictorial geometric design border. "Words and Music for the Republican Campaign of 1860, Embracing a Great Variety of Songs, Solos, Duets and Choruses Arranged for Piano or melodeon; The best collection of Words and Music ever published for a campaign, Every Club and Family should have copies, so as to join in the choruses; The Ladies are invited to join in the choruses at the meetings." 68pp. [M-116]. [Crew/AL-59].

63.114 Old Abe They Said Was An Honest Man (Song). w. J.W. Jarboe, Esq. m. F. Lafayette. Published by Firth, Son & Company, No. 563 Broadway, New York, NY. 1864. Non-pictorial geometric designs. "Words Composed and Sung with Great Applause by J.W. Jarboe, Esq. at the Great McClellan Union Meeting, Union Square." "To the McClellan Union Clubs." 6pp. Pages 2 and 6: Blank. [Crew/GBM-48].

63.115 The Old Time And The New. w. No composer indicated. m. "Air — *Old English Gentleman*." In: *The Freeman's Glee Book, A Collection Of Songs, Odes, Glees And Ballads With Music, Original And Selected, Harmonized And Arranged For Each. Published Under The Auspices Of The Central Fremont And Dayton Glee Club Of The City Of New York, And Dedicated To All, Who, Cherishing Republican Liberty Consider Freedom Worth A Song*, page 38. Published by Miller, Orton & Mulligan, No. 25 Park Row, New York, NY. [and Auburn, NY]. 1856. [4$\frac{15}{16}$" × 6"]. Pk/bk litho of man on mountain peak, music sheets, geometric designs. 112pp. [Crew/JCF-16].

63.116 Our Champions — Fremont And Dayton. w. No composer indicated. m. No tune indicated. In: *The Fremont Campaign Songster*, page 4. Published by Frost & Dory, Publishers, No. 140–142 Vine Street, Cincinnati, OH. 1856. [3½" × 5½"]. B/w litho of John C. Fremont. 32pp. Page 2: "To the Fremont Clubs and the Republican Party throughout the Union, this little volume is Respectfully Dedicated by the Publishers." [M-093]. [Crew/JCF-42].

63.117 Our Jessie. w. George W. Bungay. m. No tune indicated. In: *The Republican Campaign Songster, A Collection Of Lyrics, Original And Selected, Specifically Prepared For The Friends Of Freedom In The Campaign Of Fifty-Six*, page 59. Published by Miller, Orton & Mulligan, No. 25 Park Row, New York, NY. 1856. [3$\frac{13}{16}$" × 6"]. Be/bk litho of "Colonel John C. Fremont" facing to viewer's left, black line border. 112pp. [M-097]. [Crew/JCF-24].

63.118 Our Jessie. w. A Lady. m. "Air — *Jessie, The Flower Of Dumblane*." "Song No. 2." In: *The Republican Campaign Songster, A Collection Of Lyrics, Original And Selected, Specifically Prepared For The Friends Of Freedom In The Campaign Of Fifty-Six*, page 71. Published by Miller, Orton & Mulligan, No. 25 Park Row, New York, NY. 1856. [3$\frac{13}{16}$" × 6"]. Be/bk litho of "Colonel John C. Fremont" facing to viewer's left, black line border. 112pp. [M-097]. [Crew/JCF-24].

63.119 A Party Like Buchanan's. w. No composer indicated. m. "Air — *The Rose That All Are Praising*." In: *The Fremont Songster*, page 12. Published by [V-1: H.S. Riggs & Company, Publishers, No. 4 Cortland Street] [V-2: P.J. Cozans, No. 107 Nassau Street], New York, NY. 1856. [V-1: 3⅝" × 5¾"] [V-2: 3½" × 5⅝"]. Be/bk litho of wreath, John C. Fremont. "With a current likeness of John C. Fremont, The People's Candidate for the Presidency." 40pp. [M-094, 095]. [Crew/JCF-45].

63.120 The Pass Of The Sierra. w.m. No composer or tune indicated. In: *Fremont Songs For The People (Original And Selected)*, page 58. c. Thomas Drew "(Editor of *The Massachusetts Spy*)." Published by John P. Jewett & Company, Boston, MA. Copyright 1856 by Thomas Drew. [3⅝" × 5½"]. B/w litho of "J.C. Fremont." "The Campaign of 1856." 68pp. [Crew/JCF-18].

63.121 The Pathfinder's Prayer On The Mountain. w. No composer indicated. m. "Air — *Remember The Glories Of Brian The Brave*." In: *The Republican Campaign Songster, A Collection Of Lyrics, Original And Selected, Specifically Prepared For The Friends Of Freedom In The Campaign Of Fifty-Six*, page 89. Published by Miller, Orton & Mulligan, No. 25 Park Row, New York, NY. 1856. [3$\frac{13}{16}$" × 6"]. Be/bk litho of "Colonel John C. Fremont" facing to viewer's left, black line border. 112pp. [M-097]. [Crew/JCF-24].

63.122 Political Pastry (A Crusty Joke Done Brown). w. No composer indicated. m. "Air — *The Minstrel Boy*." In: *The Republican Campaign Songster, A Collection Of Lyrics, Original And Selected, Specifically Prepared For The Friends Of Freedom In The Campaign Of Fifty-Six*, page 37. Published by Miller, Orton & Mulligan, No. 25 Park Row, New York, NY. 1856. [3$\frac{13}{16}$" × 6"]. Be/bk litho of "Colonel John C. Fremont" facing to viewer's left, black line border. 112pp. [M-097]. [Crew/JCF-24].

63.123 The Presidential Track. w. No composer indicated. m. "Air — *Old Dan Tucker*." In: *Fillmore And Donelson Songs For The Campaign* (Songster), page 35. Published by Robert M. De Witt, Nos. 160 and 162 Nassau Street, New York, NY. November 4, 1856. [4¾" × 7⅛"]. Bl/bk litho of George Washington —

"July 4, 1776," wreath, geometric design border. "This is the only authorized edition containing Duganne's Songs. Price 6 cts. each, $4 per 100. Discount to trade." Long quote from George Washington's "Farewell Address." 40pp. Page 3: "Union and Peace." [M-101, 102]. [Crew/MF-10].

63.124 Quamdiu Yendem Abutere Patientiae Nostra? Ad Quen Finem Sese Jactabit Audacia? (Come gentle muse, Give me Your Aid). w. "B." m. No tune indicated. No publisher indicated. Published in Baltimore, June 30, 1861. B/w geometric design border. 2pp. Page 2: Blank. [AMC].

63.125 Rallying Song. w. No composer indicated. m. "Air—*Susannah.*" In: *Fremont Songs For The People (Original And Selected)*, page 42. c. Thomas Drew "(Editor of *The Massachusetts Spy*)." Published by John P. Jewett & Company, Boston, MA. Copyright 1856 by Thomas Drew. [3⅝" × 5½"]. B/w litho of "J.C. Fremont." "The Campaign of 1856." 68pp. [Crew/JCF-18].

63.126 Rallying Song. w. No composer indicated. m. "Air—*A Life On The Ocean Wave.*" In: *Fremont Songs For The People (Original And Selected)*, page 51. c. Thomas Drew "(Editor of *The Massachusetts Spy*)." Published by John P. Jewett & Company, Boston, MA. Copyright 1856 by Thomas Drew. [3⅝" × 5½"]. B/w litho of "J.C. Fremont." "The Campaign of 1856." 68pp. [Crew/JCF-18].

63.127 A Rallying Song For Charlie. w. J.E. Snodgrass. m. "Air—*Who'll Be King But Charlie.*" In: *The Freeman's Glee Book, A Collection Of Songs, Odes, Glees And Ballads With Music, Original And Selected, Harmonized And Arranged For Each. Published Under The Auspices Of The Central Fremont And Dayton Glee Club Of The City Of New York, And Dedicated To All, Who, Cherishing Republican Liberty Consider Freedom Worth A Song*, page 21. Published by Miller, Orton & Mulligan, No. 25 Park Row, New York, NY. [and Auburn, NY]. 1856. [4¹⁵⁄₁₆" × 6"]. Pk/bk litho of man on mountain peak, music sheets, geometric designs. 112pp. [Crew/JCF-16].

63.128 The Republican Ball. w. James A. Boone. m. "Air—*Rosin The Bow.*" In: *The Republican Campaign Songster, A Collection Of Lyrics, Original And Selected, Specifically Prepared For The Friends Of Freedom In The Campaign Of Fifty-Six*, page 90. Published by Miller, Orton & Mulligan, No. 25 Park Row, New York, NY. 1856. [3¹³⁄₁₆" × 6"]. Be/bk litho of "Colonel John C. Fremont" facing to viewer's left, black line border. 112pp. [M-097]. [Crew/JCF-24].

63.129 Republican Song Of Freedom. w. No composer indicated. m. "Air—*E. Pluribus Unum.*" In: *The Fremont Campaign Songster*, page 15. Published by Frost & Dory, Publishers, No. 140-142 Vine Street, Cincinnati, OH. 1856. [3½" × 5½"]. B/w litho of John C. Fremont. 32pp. Page 2: "To the Fremont Clubs and the Republican Party throughout the Union, this little volume is Respectfully Dedicated by the Publishers." [M-093]. [Crew/JCF-42].

63.130 The Retrospect. w. No composer indicated. m. "Air—*The Old Oaken Bucket.*" In: *The Republican Campaign Songster, A Collection Of Lyrics, Original And Selected, Specifically Prepared For The Friends Of Freedom In The Campaign Of Fifty-Six*, page 9. Published by Miller, Orton & Mulligan, No. 25 Park Row, New York, NY. 1856. [3¹³⁄₁₆" × 6"]. Be/bk litho of "Colonel John C. Fremont" facing to viewer's left, black line border. 112pp. [M-097]. [Crew/JCF-24].

63.131 Rise Ye Freemen. w. No composer indicated. m. "Air—*Marseilles Hymn.*" In: *The Fremont Songster*, page 20. Published by [V-1: H.S. Riggs & Company, Publishers, No. 4 Cortland Street] [V-2: P.J. Cozans, No. 107 Nassau Street], New York, NY. 1856. [V-1: 3⅝" × 5¾"] [V-2: 3½" × 5⅝"]. Be/bk litho of wreath, John C. Fremont. "With a current likeness of John C. Fremont, The People's Candidate for the Presidency." 40pp. [M-094, 095]. [Crew/JCF-45].

63.132 [Rouse Ye, Freemen, From Your Slumbers] (Campaign Song). w. E.W. Locke. m. "Air—*Old Dan Tucker.*" In: *The Fremont Songster*, page 46. Published by [V-1: H.S. Riggs & Company, Publishers, No. 4 Cortland Street] [V-2: P.J. Cozans, No. 107 Nassau Street], New York, NY. 1856. [V-1: 3⅝" × 5¾"] [V-2: 3½" × 5⅝"]. Be/bk litho of wreath, John C. Fremont. "With a current likeness of John C. Fremont, The People's Candidate for the Presidency." 40pp. [M-094, 095]. [Crew/JCF-45].

63.133 The Sale Of Kansas. w. No composer indicated. m. "Air—*Villikens And His Dinah.*" In: *Fillmore And Donelson Songs For The Campaign* (Songster), page 23. Published by Robert M. De Witt, Nos. 160 and 162 Nassau Street, New York, NY. November 4, 1856. [4¾" × 7⅛"]. Bl/bk litho of George Washington—"July 4, 1776," wreath, geometric design border. "This is the only authorized edition containing Duganne's Songs. Price 6 cts. each, $4 per 100. Discount to trade." Long quote from George Washington's "Farewell Address." 40pp. [M-101, 102]. [Crew/MF-10].

63.134 Should Antecedents Be Forgot? w. No composer indicated. m. "Air—*Should Auld Acquaintance Be Forgot.*" In: *The Republican Campaign Songster, A Collection Of Lyrics, Original And Selected, Specifically Prepared For The Friends Of Freedom In The Campaign Of Fifty-Six*, page 64. Published by Miller, Orton & Mulligan, No. 25 Park Row, New York, NY. 1856. [3¹³⁄₁₆" × 6"]. Be/bk litho of "Colonel John C. Fremont" facing to viewer's left, black line border. 112pp. [M-097]. [Crew/JCF-24].

63.135 The Slave-Driver Monody. w. No composer indicated. m. "Air—*Old Dog Tray.*" In: *The Republican Campaign Songster, A Collection Of Lyrics, Original And Selected, Specifically Prepared For The Friends Of Freedom In The Campaign Of Fifty-Six*, page 54. Published by Miller, Orton & Mulligan, No. 25 Park Row, New York, NY. 1856. [3¹³⁄₁₆" × 6"]. Be/bk litho of "Colonel John C. Fremont" facing to viewer's left, black line border. 112pp. [M-097]. [Crew/JCF-24].

63.136 Slavery Embarkation. w. No composer indicated. m. "Air—*Fisherman's Bark.*" In: *Fremont Songs For The People (Original And Selected)*, page 48. c. Thomas Drew "(Editor of *The Massachusetts Spy*)." Published by John P. Jewett & Company, Boston, MA. Copyright 1856 by Thomas Drew. [3⅝" × 5½"]. B/w litho of "J.C. Fremont." "The Campaign of 1856." 68pp. [Crew/JCF-18].

63.137 Song. w. No composer indicated. m. "Air—*Sparkling And Bright.*" In: *Fremont Songs For The People (Original And Selected)*, page 44. c. Thomas Drew

"(Editor of *The Massachusetts Spy*)." Published by John P. Jewett & Company, Boston, MA. Copyright 1856 by Thomas Drew. [3⅝" × 5½"]. B/w litho of "J.C. Fremont." "The Campaign of 1856." 68pp. [Crew/JCF-18].

63.138 A Song Dedicated To The Colored Volunteer. w. Tom Craig. m. No tune indicated. Published by J. Mc. C. Crummill, Printer, No, 449 N. 3d St. [186-]. B/e geometric design border. 2pp. Page 2: Blank. [AMC].

63.139 Song For Freedom. w.m. No composer or tune indicated. In: *The Republican Campaign Songster, A Collection Of Lyrics, Original And Selected, Specifically Prepared For The Friends Of Freedom In The Campaign Of Fifty-Six*, page 65. Published by Miller, Orton & Mulligan, No. 25 Park Row, New York, NY. 1856. [3¹³⁄₁₆" × 6"]. Be/bk litho of "Colonel John C. Fremont" facing to viewer's left, black line border. 112pp. [M-097]. [Crew/JCF-24].

63.139A [A Song For The Brave Fremont]. In: *The True Issue* [A Cloth Bandanna/Songster]. Published by the Shawmut Chemical Printing Company, Boston, MA. [1856]. [10¼" × 10¾"]. Cloth bandanna printed with illustration of John C. Fremont. Narrative to either side. Three campaign songs. Rev: Blank. [Crew/JCF-12].

63.140 Song For The People. w.m. No composer or tune indicated. Published by Andrews, Printer, 38 Chatham Street, New York, NY. [1856]. [Approx. 6" × 10"]. B/w non-pictorial geometric design litho border. "Andrews, Printer, 38 Chatham Street, N.Y., Songs, Games, Toy Books, Motto Verses, &c., Wholesale and Retail." 2pp. Page 2: Blank. [AMC].

63.141 Song For The People. w. No composer indicated. m. "Air — *Tippecanoe And Tyler Too*." In: *Fremont Songs For The People (Original And Selected)*, page 11. c. Thomas Drew "(Editor of *The Massachusetts Spy*)." Published by John P. Jewett & Company, Boston, MA. Copyright 1856 by Thomas Drew. [3⅝" × 5½"]. B/w litho of "J.C. Fremont." "The Campaign of 1856." 68pp. [Crew/JCF-18].

63.142 The Song Of Fifty-Six. w. No composer indicated. m. "Air — *Oh! Hard Times Come Again no More*." In: *The Republican Campaign Songster, A Collection Of Lyrics, Original And Selected, Specifically Prepared For The Friends Of Freedom In The Campaign Of Fifty-Six*, page 21. Published by Miller, Orton & Mulligan, No. 25 Park Row, New York, NY. 1856. [3¹³⁄₁₆" × 6"]. Be/bk litho of "Colonel John C. Fremont" facing to viewer's left, black line border. 112pp. [M-097]. [Crew/JCF-24].

63.143 A Song Of Freedom. w. John G. Whittier. m. "Air — *Suoni La Tromba*." In: *The Fremont Songster*, page 41. Published by [V-1: H.S. Riggs & Company, Publishers, No. 4 Cortland Street] [V-2: P.J. Cozans, No. 107 Nassau Street], New York, NY. [V-1: 3⅜" × 5¾"] [V-2: 3½" × 5⅝"]. Be/bk litho of wreath, John C. Fremont. "With a current likeness of John C. Fremont, The People's Candidate for the Presidency." 40pp. [M-094, 095]. [Crew/JCF-45].

63.144 Sons Of Freedom. w. No composer indicated. m. "Air — *Yankee Doodle*." In: *The Fremont Songster*, page 3. Published by [V-1: H.S. Riggs & Company, Publishers, No. 4 Cortland Street] [V-2: P.J. Cozans, No. 107 Nassau Street], New York, NY. 1856. [V-1: 3⅜" × 5¾"] [V-2: 3½" × 5⅝"]. Be/bk litho of wreath, John C. Fremont. "With a current likeness of John C. Fremont, The People's Candidate for the Presidency." 40pp. [M-094, 095]. [Crew/JCF-45].

63.145 Sons Of Liberty. w. No composer indicated. m. "Air — *Hail Columbia*." In: *The Fremont Songster*, page 14. Published by [V-1: H.S. Riggs & Company, Publishers, No. 4 Cortland Street] [V-2: P.J. Cozans, No. 107 Nassau Street], New York, NY. 1856. [V-1: 3⅜" × 5¾"] [V-2: 3½" × 5⅝"]. Be/bk litho of wreath, John C. Fremont. "With a current likeness of John C. Fremont, The People's Candidate for the Presidency." 40pp. [M-094, 095]. [Crew/JCF-45].

63.146 The Southern Serpent. w. No composer indicated. m. "Air — *The Valley Lay Smiling Before Me*." In: *The Republican Campaign Songster, A Collection Of Lyrics, Original And Selected, Specifically Prepared For The Friends Of Freedom In The Campaign Of Fifty-Six*, page 85. Published by Miller, Orton & Mulligan, No. 25 Park Row, New York, NY. 1856. [3¹³⁄₁₆" × 6"]. Be/bk litho of "Colonel John C. Fremont" facing to viewer's left, black line border. 112pp. [M-097]. [Crew/JCF-24].

63.147 The Statesman Most True. w. No composer indicated. m. "Air — *Away Over Mountain*." In: *The Fremont Songster*, page 36. Published by [V-1: H.S. Riggs & Company, Publishers, No. 4 Cortland Street] [V-2: P.J. Cozans, No. 107 Nassau Street], New York, NY. 1856. [V-1: 3⅜" × 5¾"] [V-2: 3½" × 5⅝"]. Be/bk litho of wreath, John C. Fremont. "With a current likeness of John C. Fremont, The People's Candidate for the Presidency." 40pp. [M-094, 095]. [Crew/JCF-45].

63.148 A Story About Jordan. w. No composer indicated. m. "Air — *Jordan Is A Hard Road To Travel*." In: *The Fremont Campaign Songster*, page 28. Published by Frost & Dory, Publishers, No. 140–142 Vine Street, Cincinnati, OH. 1856. [3½" × 5½"]. B/w litho of John C. Fremont. 32pp. [M-093]. [Crew/JCF-42].

63.149 Strike Now Or Never — Now And Forever. w. No composer indicated. m. "Air — *The Marsellaise Hymn*." In: *The Republican Campaign Songster, A Collection Of Lyrics, Original And Selected, Specifically Prepared For The Friends Of Freedom In The Campaign Of Fifty-Six*, page 78. Published by Miller, Orton & Mulligan, No. 25 Park Row, New York, NY. 1856. [3¹³⁄₁₆" × 6"]. Be/bk litho of "Colonel John C. Fremont" facing to viewer's left, black line border. 112pp. [M-097]. [Crew/JCF-24].

63.150 Strike Together. w. No composer indicated. m. "Air — *Men Of Labor*." "Forget, forgive, unite — Whittier." In: *The Freeman's Glee Book, A Collection Of Songs, Odes, Glees And Ballads With Music, Original And Selected, Harmonized And Arranged For Each. Published Under The Auspices Of The Central Fremont And Dayton Glee Club Of The City Of New York, And Dedicated To All, Who, Cherishing Republican Liberty Consider Freedom Worth A Song*, page 79. Published by Miller, Orton & Mulligan, No. 25 Park Row, New York, NY. [and Auburn, NY]. 1856. [4¹⁵⁄₁₆" × 6"]. Pk/bk litho of man on mountain peak, music sheets, geometric designs. 112pp. [Crew/JCF-16].

63.151 [Take Down The Harp Of The Last Cam-

paign] (A Campaign Song). w. No composer indicated. m. "Air—*The Harp That Once In Tara's Halls.*" In: *Republican Song Book*, page 46. c. Thomas Drew "(Late Editor of *The Massachusetts Spy*)." Published by Thayer and Eldridge, Boston, MA. 1860. [3⅞" × 5⅞"]. Br/bk litho of beardless Abraham Lincoln, vignettes of young Lincoln chopping rails, polling raft. 68pp. [M-108]. [Crew/AL-8].

63.152 [They're Rousing, They're Rousing In The Valley And Glen] (Rallying Song). w. H. Greeley. m. No tune indicated. In: *The Fremont Songster* page 62. Published by [V-1: H.S. Riggs & Company, Publishers, No. 4 Cortland Street] [V-2: P.J. Cozans, No. 107 Nassau Street], New York, NY. 1856. [V-1: 3⅝" × 5¾"] [V-2: 3½" × 5⅝"]. Be/bk litho of wreath, John C. Fremont. "With a current likeness of John C. Fremont, The People's Candidate for the Presidency." 40pp. [M-094, 095]. [Crew/JCF-45].

63.153 Those Noble Old Statesmen. w. No composer indicated. m. "Air—*Araby's Daughter.*" In: *The Fremont Songster*, page 18. Published by [V-1: H.S. Riggs & Company, Publishers, No. 4 Cortland Street] [V-2: P.J. Cozans, No. 107 Nassau Street], New York, NY. 1856. [V-1: 3⅝" × 5¾"] [V-2: 3½" × 5⅝"]. Be/bk litho of wreath, John C. Fremont. "With a current likeness of John C. Fremont, The People's Candidate for the Presidency." 40pp. [M-094, 095]. [Crew/JCF-45].

63.154 'Tis Time That Freemen Raise A Hand. w. No composer indicated. m. "Air—*Yankee Doodle.*" In: *The Fremont Campaign Songster*, page 20. Published by Frost & Dory, Publishers, No. 140–142 Vine Street, Cincinnati, OH. 1856. [3½" × 5½"]. B/w litho of John C. Fremont. 32pp. [M-093]. [Crew/JCF-42].

63.155 To The Work. w.m. No composer or tune indicated. In: *The Fremont Songster*, page 43. Published by [V-1: H.S. Riggs & Company, Publishers, No. 4 Cortland Street] [V-2: P.J. Cozans, No. 107 Nassau Street], New York, NY. 1856. [V-1: 3⅝" × 5¾"] [V-2: 3½" × 5⅝"]. Be/bk litho of wreath, John C. Fremont. "With a current likeness of John C. Fremont, The People's Candidate for the Presidency." 40pp. [M-094, 095]. [Crew/JCF-45].

63.156 The Toast. w. No composer indicated. m. "Air—*Vive La Companie.*" In: *The Freeman's Glee Book, A Collection Of Songs, Odes, Glees And Ballads With Music, Original And Selected, Harmonized And Arranged For Each. Published Under The Auspices Of The Central Fremont And Dayton Glee Club Of The City Of New York, And Dedicated To All, Who, Cherishing Republican Liberty Consider Freedom Worth A Song*, page 94. Published by Miller, Orton & Mulligan, No. 25 Park Row, New York, NY. [and Auburn, NY]. 1856. [4 15/16" × 6"]. Pk/bk litho of man on mountain peak, music sheets, geometric designs. 112pp. [Crew/JCF-16].

63.157 The Union And Freedom. w. No composer indicated. m. Wm. Berge. In: *The Freeman's Glee Book, A Collection Of Songs, Odes, Glees And Ballads With Music, Original And Selected, Harmonized And Arranged For Each. Published Under The Auspices Of The Central Fremont And Dayton Glee Club Of The City Of New York, And Dedicated To All, Who, Cherishing Republican Liberty Consider Freedom Worth A Song*, page 50. Published by Miller, Orton & Mulligan, No. 25 Park Row, New York, NY. [and Auburn, NY]. 1856. [4 15/16" × 6"]. Pk/bk litho of man on mountain peak, music sheets, geometric designs. 112pp. [Crew/JCF-16].

63.158 The Voice Of Freedom. w. No composer indicated. m. "Air—*Partant Pour La Syrie.*" In: *Fremont Songs For The People (Original And Selected)*, page 19. c. Thomas Drew "(Editor of *The Massachusetts Spy*)." Published by John P. Jewett & Company, Boston, MA. Copyright 1856 by Thomas Drew. [3⅝" × 5½"]. B/w litho of "J.C. Fremont." "The Campaign of 1856." 68pp. [Crew/JCF-18].

63.159 The Voice Of Freedom. w. No composer indicated. m. "Air—*Mourir La Patriæ.*" In: *The Freeman's Glee Book, A Collection Of Songs, Odes, Glees And Ballads With Music, Original And Selected, Harmonized And Arranged For Each. Published Under The Auspices Of The Central Fremont And Dayton Glee Club Of The City Of New York, And Dedicated To All, Who, Cherishing Republican Liberty Consider Freedom Worth A Song*, page 16. Published by Miller, Orton & Mulligan, No. 25 Park Row, New York, NY. [and Auburn, NY]. 1856. [4 15/16" × 6"]. Pk/bk litho of man on mountain peak, music sheets, geometric designs. 112pp. [Crew/JCF-16].

63.160 Volunteer Song. w. By A Lady. m. "Air—*Ole Dan Tucker.*" In: *The Republican Campaign Songster, A Collection Of Lyrics, Original And Selected, Specifically Prepared For The Friends Of Freedom In The Campaign Of Fifty-Six*, page 75. Published by Miller, Orton & Mulligan, No. 25 Park Row, New York, NY. 1856. [3 13/16" × 6"]. Be/bk litho of "Colonel John C. Fremont" facing to viewer's left, black line border. 112pp. [M-097]. [Crew/JCF-24].

63.161 A Warning To The South. w. No composer indicated. m. "Air—*Oh Woodman, Spare That Tree.*" "Loud were the Boohoos when Senator Seward hinted that the day of compromise would soon be over if the South persisted in the present bad faith." In: *The Republican Campaign Songster, A Collection Of Lyrics, Original And Selected, Specifically Prepared For The Friends Of Freedom In The Campaign Of Fifty-Six*, page 101. Published by Miller, Orton & Mulligan, No. 25 Park Row, New York, NY. 1856. [3 13/16" × 6"]. Be/bk litho of "Colonel John C. Fremont" facing to viewer's left, black line border. 112pp. [M-097]. [Crew/JCF-24].

63.162 We'll Give 'Em Jessie. w. No composer indicated. m. "Air—*Wait For The Wagon.*" In: *The Freeman's Glee Book, A Collection Of Songs, Odes, Glees And Ballads With Music, Original And Selected, Harmonized And Arranged For Each. Published Under The Auspices Of The Central Fremont And Dayton Glee Club Of The City Of New York, And Dedicated To All, Who, Cherishing Republican Liberty Consider Freedom Worth A Song*, page 26. Published by Miller, Orton & Mulligan, No. 25 Park Row, New York, NY. [and Auburn, NY]. 1856. [4 15/16" × 6"]. Pk/bk litho of man on mountain peak, music sheets, geometric designs. 112pp. [Crew/JCF-16].

63.163 We're For Freedom Through This Land. w. No composer indicated. m. "Air—*The Old Granite State.*" In: *The Freeman's Glee Book, A Collection Of*

Songs, Odes, Glees And Ballads With Music, Original And Selected, Harmonized And Arranged For Each. Published Under The Auspices Of The Central Fremont And Dayton Glee Club Of The City Of New York, And Dedicated To All, Who, Cherishing Republican Liberty Consider Freedom Worth A Song, page 84. Published by Miller, Orton & Mulligan, No. 25 Park Row, New York, NY. [and Auburn, NY]. 1856. [4¹⁵⁄₁₆" × 6"]. Pk/bk litho of man on mountain peak, music sheets, geometric designs. 112pp. [Crew/JCF-16].

63.164 Wha'll Be Our But Charlie. w.m. No composer or tune indicated. In: *The Fremont Campaign Songster*, page 6. Published by Frost & Dory, Publishers, No. 140–142 Vine Street, Cincinnati, OH. 1856. [3½" × 5½"]. B/w litho of John C. Fremont. 32pp. [M-093]. [Crew/JCF-42].

63.165 What Bursts On Our Sight. w. No composer indicated. m. "Air—*Lutzow's Wild Hunt*." In: *The Fremont Songster*, page 33. Published by [V-1: H.S. Riggs & Company, Publishers, No. 4 Cortland Street] [V-2: P.J. Cozans, No. 107 Nassau Street], New York, NY. 1856. [V-1: 3⅝" × 5¾"] [V-2: 3½" × 5⅝"]. Be/bk litho of wreath, John C. Fremont. "With a current likeness of John C. Fremont, The People's Candidate for the Presidency." 40pp. [M-094, 095]. [Crew/JCF-45].

63.166 [What Has Caused This Great Commotion] (A Campaign Song). w. No composer indicated. m. "Air—*Oh! What Has Caused This Great Commotion?*" "From the *Boston Atlas*." In: *The Republican Campaign Songster, A Collection Of Lyrics, Original And Selected, Specifically Prepared For The Friends Of Freedom In The Campaign Of Fifty-Six*, page 40. Published by Miller, Orton & Mulligan, No. 25 Park Row, New York, NY. 1856. [3¹³⁄₁₆" × 6"]. Be/bk litho of "Colonel John C. Fremont" facing to viewer's left, black line border. 112pp. [M-097]. [Crew/JCF-24].

63.167 What Miss Columbia Did When She Came Of Age. w. No composer indicated. m. "Air—*Duncan Gray Came Here To Woo*." In: *The Republican Campaign Songster, A Collection Of Lyrics, Original And Selected, Specifically Prepared For The Friends Of Freedom In The Campaign Of Fifty-Six*, page 29. Published by Miller, Orton & Mulligan, No. 25 Park Row, New York, NY. 1856. [3¹³⁄₁₆" × 6"]. Be/bk litho of "Colonel John C. Fremont" facing to viewer's left, black line border. 112pp. [M-097]. [Crew/JCF-24].

63.168 What Sam Tells The People. w. No composer indicated. m. "Air—*Dandy Jim*." In: *Fillmore And Donelson Songs For The Campaign* (Songster), page 8. Published by Robert M. De Witt, Nos. 160 and 162 Nassau Street, New York, NY. November 4, 1856. [4¾" × 7⅛"]. Bl/bk litho of George Washington—"July 4, 1776," wreath, geometric design border. "This is the only authorized edition containing Duganne's Songs. Price 6 cts. each, $4 per 100. Discount to trade." Long quote from George Washington's "Farewell Address." 40pp. Page 3: "Union and Peace." [M-101, 102]. [Crew/MF-10].

63.168A [When Forth To The Battle The Bold Warrior Rode]. In: *The True Issue* [A Cloth Bandanna/Songster]. Published by the Shawmut Chemical Printing Company, Boston, MA. [1856]. [10¼" × 10¾"]. Cloth bandanna printed with illustration of John C. Fremont. Narrative to either side. Three campaign songs. Rev: Blank. [Crew-JCF-12].

63.169 When Fremont Is Elected. w. No composer indicated. m. "Air—*Hold Your Horses*." In: *The Freeman's Glee Book, A Collection Of Songs, Odes, Glees And Ballads With Music, Original And Selected, Harmonized And Arranged For Each. Published Under The Auspices Of The Central Fremont And Dayton Glee Club Of The City Of New York, And Dedicated To All, Who, Cherishing Republican Liberty Consider Freedom Worth A Song*, page 80. Published by Miller, Orton & Mulligan, No. 25 Park Row, New York, NY. [and Auburn, NY]. 1856. [4¹⁵⁄₁₆" × 6"]. Pk/bk litho of man on mountain peak, music sheets, geometric designs. 112pp. [Crew/JCF-16].

63.170 When We Met In Convention. w. No composer indicated. m. "Air—*'Tis My Delight Of A Shiny Night*." In: *Fillmore And Donelson Songs For The Campaign* (Songster), page 21. Published by Robert M. De Witt, Nos. 160 and 162 Nassau Street, New York, NY. November 4, 1856. [4¾" × 7⅛"]. Bl/bk litho of George Washington—"July 4, 1776," wreath, geometric design border. "This is the only authorized edition containing Duganne's Songs. Price 6 cts. each, $4 per 100. Discount to trade." Long quote from George Washington's "Farewell Address." 40pp. Page 3: "Union and Peace." [M-101, 102]. [Crew/MF-10].

63.171 The White House. w. G.R. Edeson. m. "Air—*Root, Hog, Or Die!*" Published by H. De Marsan, 54 Chatham Street, New York, NY. [1861–1862]. B/w litho border of minstrels, geometric designs. 2pp. Page 2: Blank. [AMC].

63.172 The White House Race. w. No composer indicated. m. "Air—*Camptown Races*." In: *The Freeman's Glee Book, A Collection Of Songs, Odes, Glees And Ballads With Music, Original And Selected, Harmonized And Arranged For Each. Published Under The Auspices Of The Central Fremont And Dayton Glee Club Of The City Of New York, And Dedicated to All, Who, Cherishing Republican Liberty Consider Freedom Worth A Song*, page 54. Published by Miller, Orton & Mulligan, No. 25 Park Row, New York, NY. [and Auburn, NY]. 1856. [4¹⁵⁄₁₆" × 6"]. Pk/bk litho of man on mountain peak, music sheets, geometric designs. 112pp. [Crew/JCF-16].

63.173 The Withering November Leaves. w. No composer indicated. m. "Air—*Katy Darling*." In: *Fillmore And Donelson Songs For The Campaign* (Songster), page 5. Published by Robert M. De Witt, Nos. 160 and 162 Nassau Street, New York, NY. November 4, 1856. [4¾" × 7⅛"]. Bl/bk litho of George Washington—"July 4, 1776," wreath, geometric design border. "This is the only authorized edition containing Duganne's Songs. Price 6 cts. each, $4 per 100. Discount to trade." Long quote from George Washington's "Farewell Address." 40pp. Page 3: "Union and Peace." [M-101, 102]. [Crew/MF-10].

63.174 The Woolly Horse. w. A Lady. m. "Air—*Yankee Doodle*." "Song No. 2." In: *The Republican Campaign Songster, A Collection Of Lyrics, Original And Selected, Specifically Prepared For The Friends Of Freedom In The Campaign Of Fifty-Six*, page 70. Published by Miller, Orton & Mulligan, No. 25 Park Row, New York, NY. 1856. [3¹³⁄₁₆" × 6"]. Be/bk litho of "Colonel

John C. Fremont" facing to viewer's left, black line border. 112pp. [M-097]. [Crew/JCF-24].

GEARY, John White (Mayor, San Francisco, 1850–1851) [See: Pennsylvania]

• **AmPM-64 GODDARD**, A.E. (Mayor, Sacramento, 1927; Delegate to Republican National Convention, 1936)

64.1 Camellia City March. w. Mrs. A.A. Goddard. m. Arthur C. Blank. Published by Camellia City Publishing Co., 819 Sixteenth Street, Sacramento, CA. 1927. B/w photo of the State Capitol. R/w/gn drawing of camellias. "To The Veterans of All Wars." 6pp. Page 6: Facsimile of a handwritten letter to Blake from "A.E. Goddard, Mayor, Sacramento."

• **AmPM-65 GOODCELL**, Rex B. (Judge; Candidate for Governor, 1926; State Insurance Commissioner, 1938–1939)

65.1 What Does Old Glory Say To The Rest Of The World. w. James B. Gaughen. m. Fred L. Hakel. Published by James B. Gaughen, Music Publisher, No. 4046 3rd Street, San Diego, CA. 1926. [10⅜" × 13$\frac{13}{16}$"]. Bl/w photos of Abraham Lincoln, world military leaders—"Pershing," "Foch," "Diaz," "Haig." "If you want world peace, keep me on your piano." R/w/b flag border. 12pp. Page 2: Advertising for "Judge Rex B. Goodcell—Our Next Governor." [Crew/AL-312].

• **AmPM-66 GWIN**, William McKendree (U.S. Marshal, Mississippi, 1833; U.S. House, Mississippi, 1841–1843; U.S. Senate, California, 1850–1855 & 1857–1861)

66.1 Chappaqua. w.m. No composer or tune indicated. In: *Grant And Wilson Campaign Songster*, page 2. Published by Frank Eastman, Book and Job Printer, No. 509 Clay Street, San Francisco, CA. [4¼" × 5⅝"]. 1872. Bk/bl geometric design border. 40pp. [Crew/USG-69].

66.2 Wilson And Grant. w. Sam Booth. m. "Tune—*Bonnie Dundee*." In: *Grant And Wilson Campaign Songster*, page 2. Published by Frank Eastman, Book and Job Printer, No. 509 Clay Street, San Francisco, CA. [4¼" × 5⅝"]. 1872. Bk/bl geometric design border. 40pp. [Crew/USG-69].

• **AmPM-67 HALDEMAN**, Harry Robbins (Nixon Campaign Manager, 1968; White House Chief of Staff, 1969–1973)

67.1 Down At The Old Watergate. w. Congressman William L. Hungate, Democrat, Missouri. Copyright 1973 by Popdraw, Inc., No. 165 West 46th Street, New York, NY. "Recorded by Perception Records, 165 West 46th Street, New York, NY." In: *Poor Richard's Watergate*, page 8. e. Roy Kammerman. Published by Price/Stern/Sloan, Publishers, Los Angeles, CA. 1973. [5¼" × 6¾"]. Bl/w photo of Richard Nixon. 68pp.

67.2 Haldeman, Ehrlichman, Mitchell And Dean. w. Bob Warren. m. "Sung by The Creep. Mr. G. Records. #G-826. [ca. 1973]. Transcribed by <ahs@nevada.edu>." Published online at <http://php.indiana-edu/~jbmorris/LYRICS/hemd.html>. [ca. 1973].

67.3 I'm So Lonesome Tonight. w. No composer indicated. m. "Tune—*Are You Lonesome Tonight*." In: *Thoroughly Mad-ern Malcolm or He Didn't Need A Course In Forensics To Become A Famous Public Speaker*, page 13. Published by the New York State Legislative Correspondents' Association, Albany, NY. 1974. N/w photo of Malcolm Wilson as Alfred E. Newman—"What—Me Governor?" "Featuring the New York Correspondents' Association, March 16. 1974." 32pp.

67.4 Watergate Bug. w. David Arkin. m. "Tune—*Tam Pearce*." In: *Sing Out! The Folk Song Magazine*, Volume 22, Number 3, 1973, page 23. Published by *Sing Out!*, No. 595 Broadway, New York, NY. 1979. [7" × 10"]. [Crew/RMN-43].

• **AmPM-68 HAYES**, Everis Anson (U.S. House, 1905–1919)

68.1 Our Starry Flag (A New National Flag Song). w.m. Alfred Beirly, Mus. Doc. Published by Alfred Beirly Music Co., Chicago, IL. 1911. R/w/b litho of a proposed new configuration of the American as proposed by Representative E.A. Hayes. "Respectfully Inscribed to the Sixty-Second Congress of the Great American Republic." 8pp. Page 2: "Our New National Flag—The following Flag Resolution was introduced in Congress by the Hon. E.A. Hayes, Member from California." Facsimile printing of the "Concurrent Resolution, in the House of Representatives, August 8, 1911." Pages 7 and 8: Blank.

• **AmPM-69 HOGE**, Joseph Pendleton (U.S. House, Illinois, 1843–1847; Candidate for U.S. Senate, California, 1869; President of the State Constitutional Convention, 1878; Board of Freeholders, San Francisco, 1880; Judge of the Superior Court, San Francisco, 1889–1891)

69.1 Hoist Up The Flag. w.m. No composer or tune indicated. In: *Grant And Wilson Campaign Songster*, page 31. Published by Frank Eastman, Book and Job Printer, No. 509 Clay Street, San Francisco, CA. [4¼" × 5⅝"]. 1872. Bk/bl geometric design border. 40pp. [Crew/USG-69].

• **AmPM-70 HUFFINGTON,** Arianna (Candidate for Governor, 2003)

70.1 California Governor Song. w. "Static." m. Tune—"*The Chanukah Song* by Adam Sandler. "Typical Sandler song. too many syllables in places, too little, and alternate endings. Static out." Published online at <http://www.amiright.com/parody/misc/adamsandler0.shtml>. 2003.

70.2 California Screaming. w. Loose Bruce Kerr. m. Tune—"*California Dreaming* by The Mamas and the Popas [sic]." "About California's recall campaign for governor, contains the names of the top runners and a little angst. Played on Jim Bohannon Show on Westwood One; upcoming on Dr. Demento." Published online at <http://www.amiright.com/parody/60s/mamaspopas0.shtml>. 2003.

70.3 I Love DC. w. William Ross. m. "To the tune of *I Love L.A.* by Randy Newman." Lyrics and sound file published online at <http://www.seanet.com/~billr/ilovedc.htm>. 1996.

70.4 Recall California. w. Bob Gomez. m. "*Sweet Home Alabama*, originally by Lynyrd Skinner." "Darrell Issa spent nearly two million dollars to gather enough signatures for the recall. No he is out of the race and so is Bill Simon. In the latest polls, the number of Republicans who are afraid that Arnold will win roughly equals the number who are afraid he will lose." Published online at <http://www.amiright.com/parody/70s/lynyrdskynyrd12.shtml>. 2003.

70.5 Recalling Gray. w. Alex Murray. m. "*Auf*

Wiedersehen, based on a performance by Cheap Trick." "Haven't done a parody in a while, so this is a bit rusty. To clarify, all bye-byes, goodbyes, so longs, etc are directed towards Red Davis." Published online at <http://www.amiright.com/parody/70s/cheaptrick3.shtml>. 2003.

70.6 Speaker Of The House. w. William Ross. m. "To the tune of *Leader Of The Pack.*" "Sung in a female voice impersonating Arianna Huffington." Lyrics and sound file published online at <http://www.seanet.com/-billr/speaker.htm>. 1996.

70.7 Schwarzenegger Got Stoned. w. Adam Bernstein. m. "*Like A Rolling Stone* originally by Bob Dylan." Published online at <http://www.amiright.com/parody/60s/bobdylan25.shtml>. 2003.

70.8 Vote For The Terminator. w. Rice Cube & Walt Daddy. m. "*We Didn't Start The Fire,* originally by Billy Joel." "We're not completely endorsing Schwarzenegger because we don't know his complete platform, but considering that voting for Bustamonte will be worse than keeping Davis in power, and Ahnuld is the leading Republican candidate who has a ghost's chance in hell of becoming governor..." Published online at Published online at <http://www.amiright.com/parody/80s/billyjoel62.shtml>. 2003.

• **AmPM-71** HUFFINGTON, Michael (Deputy Assistant Secretary, Department of Defense, 1986–1987; U.S. House, 1993–1995)

71.1 Republican Clowns. w. H.R. Yeager. m. "Sung to the tune of *Send In The Clowns.*" Published online at <http://www.geocities.com/CapitolHill/Congress/3950>. 1998.

• **AmPM-72** HYDE, James M. (Councilman, Hollywood, 1930)

72.1 My Spanish Bird Of Paradise (Spanish Fox-Trot). w.m. Charles Alphin and F. Alva Stone. Published by Chas. F. Loveland, 520 South Broadway, Los Angeles, CA. 1930. Br/w photo of Nellie Fernandez. "Dedicated to Nellie Fernandez Spanish Star of the Stage and Screen." 1930. 6pp. Page 2: Blank. Page 6: Br/w photo of James Hyde. "Presented with the Compliments of Citizens of Hollywood in appreciation of 'The best Councilman Hollywood ever had.' Trusting you will help to Re-Elect James M. Hyde, Councilman District No. 2."

• **AmPM-72A** ISSA, Darrell (U.S. House, 2001–Present; Candidate for Governor, 2003)

72A.1 California Screaming. w. Loose Bruce Kerr. m. Tune — "*California Dreaming* by The Mamas and the Poppas." "About California's recall campaign for governor, contains the names of the top runners and a little angst. Played on Jim Bohannon Show on Westwood One; upcoming on Dr. Demento." Published online at <http://www.amiright.com/parody/60s/mamaspopas0.shtml>. 2003.

72A.2 Recall California. w. Bob Gomez. m. "*Sweet Home Alabama,* originally by Lynyrd Skinner." "Darrell Issa spent nearly two million dollars to gather enough signatures for the recall. No he is out of the race and so is Bill Simon. In the latest polls, the number of Republicans who are afraid that Arnold will win roughly equals the number who are afraid he will lose." Published online at <http://www.amiright.com/parody/70s/lynyrdskynyrd12.shtml>. 2003.

72A.3 Recalling. w. William Tong. m. "*Free Falling,* based on the performance by Tom Petty & The Heartbreakers." Published online at <http://www.amiright.com/parody/80s/tompettyheartbreakers2.shtml>. 2003.

72A.4 Right Wing Wants To Reign In All Of California. w. William Tong. m. Tune — "*It Never Rains In Southern California,* originally by Albert Hammond." Published online at <http://www.amiright.com/parody/70s/alberthammond4.shtml>. 2003.

72A.5 The Tail Of Darrell Issa (The Car Thief Who Went Bad). w. Stephen Baird. m. No tune indicated. N/c photo of Mike Byron — "Human need above political greed." Lyrics published online at <http://byron.blogcap.com/archive/campaign_song_the_tale_of_darrell_issa.php>. 2004.

72A.6 Total Recall Of The Gray. w. Michael Pacholek. m. "*Total Eclipse Of The Heart,* originally by Bonnie Tyler." Published online at <http://www.amiright.com/parody/80s/bonnietyler8.shtml>. 2003.

• **AmPM-73** JOHNSON, Hiram Warren (Governor, 1911–1917; Candidate for Vice-President, 1912; U.S. Senate, 1917–1945) [ALSO SEE: DOC/PSM-TR]

73.1 Hiram, Oh Hiram (I'll Hit The Trail With You). w.m. John J. Jones. Published by John J. Jones, 2460 Washington Avenue, New York, NY. 1920. Br/w photo of Hiram W. Johnson. "Respectfully dedicated to Senator Hiram W. Johnson of California." 4pp. Page 2: At top of music — "Respectfully dedicated to Senator Hiram W. Jones of California." Page 4: Advertising.

73.2 Wait For The Wagon. w. "Words adapted by C.H. Congdon." m. Notation. "The first three stanzas were used in *The Rail-Splitters Song Book,* Campaign of 1860." In: *Progressive Battle Hymns,* page 28. Published by C.H. Congdon. 1912. Bk/w photos of Theodore Roosevelt and Hiram Johnson. R/w/bk bandanna, Kipling quote. 68pp. [M-403]. [Crew/TR-117].

• **AmPM-74** KENNEDY, Anthony McLeod (U.S. Court of Appeals, 1975–1988; U.S. Supreme Court, 1988–Present)

74.1 Dubya, The Bogus POTUS. w. William Tong. m. "*Rudolph The Red-Nosed Reindeer,* originally by Gene Autry." Published online at <http://amiright.com/parody/misc/geneautry0.shml>. [ca. 2000].

74.2 Failure Boy. w. Michael Pacholek. m. Tune — "*Sk8er Boi* originally by Avril Lavigne." "This is what my life has come to: Ripping off a girl who wasn't even old enough to vote when she wrote the original (and can't vote in the U.S. anyway). Naming the song *Failyr Boi* was considered, but quickly dropped." Published online at <http://www.amiright.com/parody/2000s/avrillavigne67/shtml>. 2003

• **AmPM-74A** KENNEDY, Scott (Mayor, Santa Cruz, 2000–Present)

74A.1 God Rest Ye Merry Gentlemen. w. Becky A. Johnson. m. "*God Rest Ye Merry Gentlemen.*" "Here is one we update every year to accommodate the new mayor." Published online at <http://projects.is.asu.edu/pipermail/hpn/2003-December/007852.html>. 2003.

• **AmPM-75** KENTFIELD, David (Candidate for State Controller, 1876)

75.1 The Republican Ticket. m. "Tune—*Rosin The Bow*." In: *Campaign Songs*, page 4. w. Sam Booth. [1876]. [6" × 9⅜"]. Non-pictorial. "Supplement to *Hayes And Wheeler Songster*." 4pp. [Verses for local Congressional candidates]. [Crew/RBH-56].

• **AmPM-76 KNIGHT**, Goodwin J. (Superior Court Judge, 1935–1946; Lt. Governor, 1947–1953; Governor, 1953–1959)

76.1 The Goodwin Knight Victory March. w. Edgar Hervey. m. James Lee MacDonald (ASCAP). No publisher indicated. Copyright 1958 by James Lee MacDonald, 16110 Argyle Avenue, Hollywood, CA. B/w litho of a lyre, scroll, quill. "Special Campaign Edition by ATM." 4pp. Page 4: "Campaign records may be ordered through ATM, 1610 Argyle, Hollywood, 28, California."

• **AmPM-77 LEWINSKY**, Monica (White House Intern, 1996–1998)

77.1 All I'm Turning To (Is Rush Limbaugh). w. S.T.G. m. "*All I Wanna Do* (Is Have Some Fun), originally by Sheryl Crow Published online at <http://www.amiright.com/parody/90s/shetylcrow0.shtml>. [199-].

77.2 Amazing Bush. w. Static. m. "*Amazing Grace*, based on the performance by Traditional." "Gotta flip it around this time for personal reasons." Published online at <http://www.amiright.com/parody/misc/traditional304.shtml>. 2003.

77.3 Bill And Hillary. w. Scott Loeb. m. "This is a parody of *Jack & Diane* by John Cougar about our President & Co." Published online at <http://www.geocities.com/sldice/bill_hillary.htm>. [199-].

77.4 Bill Clinton Got Run Over By A Taxi. w. Billy Florio. m. "*Grandma Got Run Over By A Reindeer*, originally by Elmo & Patsy." Published online at <http://amiright.com/parody/80s/elmoandpatsy0.shml>. [ca. 2001].

77.5 A Bill Clinton Parody. w. Billy Florio. m. "*Crocodile Rock*, originally by Elton John." Published online at <http://amiright.com/parody/70s/eltonjohn6.shml>. [ca. 2001].

77.6 Bill Clinton Rhapsody. w. Tom Stevens. m. "*Another Bohemian Rhapsody*, originally by Queen." Published online at <http://www.amiright.com/parody/70s/queen14.shtml>. [ca. 2000].

77.7 Bill So Horney. w.m. Mark Ross, Chris Wong Won, David Hobbs and Luther Campbell. On 33⅓ rpm EP: *Bill So Horney* by 2 Live Crew. Lil' Joe Records, 6157 NW 167th St., Miami, FL. Record #LJR 900–1. 1998. Performed by 2 Live Crew and Amos Braxton. Cover art: Drawing of Bill Clinton and Monica Lewinsky; 2 Live Crew. [2 versions — Clean and Explicit]. 1998.

77.8 Bleaque Alley. w. "Melhi." m. "*Creeque Alley*, originally by The Mamas and Papas." Written as the Monica Lewinsky scandal was fading." Published online at <http://amiright.com/parody/60s/themamasandpapas0.shml>. [ca. 2000].

77.9 The Clinton's Theme. w. Josh Kane. m. Tune—"*The Flintstones Theme*, originally by Theme Song." Published online at <http://amiright.com/parody/misc/themesong4.shml>. [ca. 2000].

77.10 Democracy Bites. w. S.G.T. m. "*Misc Songs*, originally by Pearl Jam." Published online at <http://amiright.com/parody/90s/pearljam6.shml>. [ca. 2001].

77.11 Falling Away From Me. w. S.G.T. m. "*Retiring Away Form Me*, originally by Korn." Published online at <http://www.amiright.com/parody/2000s/korn2.shtml>. [ca. 2001].

77.12 Hail To The Chief, O. w. Raymond Frost. m. No tune indicated. [Sir Arthur Sullivan]. Published online at <http://lightjunkie.org/parody/starr2.html>. 1998.

77.13 Happy Monica. w. Bill Strauss and Elaina Newport. On CD: *Unzippin' My Doo-Dah*. Published by Capitol Steps Productions, 1505 King Street, Alexandria, VA. 1998. CD Cover: Gn/bl/y drawing of George Bush and George W. Bush as Seuss characters.

77.13A Here Comes Clinton's Paws. w. Papi Sorrelis. m. "*Here Comes Santa Claus*, based on a performance by Traditional." "This is one of my songs from my History of the Presidents series. Enjoy!" Published online at <http://www.amiright.com/parody/misc/traditional492.shtml>. 2004.

77.14 Hey Now (Your [sic] an Ex Pres). w. Vermonter. m. "*Hey Now (Your* [sic] *An All Star)*, originally by Smash Mouth." Published online at <http://www.amiright.com/parody/90s/smashmouth2.shtml>. [ca. 2001].

77.15 Hillary. w. "S.G.T." m. "Parody of Pearl Jam's *Jeremy*." Published online at <http://www.angelfire.com.music/parodies/sentinpearljamparody.html>. [199-].

77.16 Hillary (You're A Fine Girl). w. Mediamike. m. "*Brandy (You're A Fine Girl)*, based on a performance by Looking Glass." "This was the first song I did for the Album." Published online at <http://www.amiright.com/parody/70s/lookingglass7.shtml>. 2003.

77.17 Hillary's Song (Open Fire). w. S.T.G. m. *Ana's Song* (Open) originally by Silverchair." Published over the Internet online by Amiright.com at <http://www.amiright.com/parody/90s/silverchair0.shtml>. 2000. "Please make sure you take time to vote on the parodies you read, the parody authors appreciate the feedback!" [Crew/WJC-16].

77.18 Hotel Lincoln Bedroom. w. Billy Florio. m. "*Hotel California*, originally by The Eagles." Published online at <http://www.amiright.com/parody/70s/theeagles7.shtml>. [199-].

77.19 I Am A Prime Example Of Transactional Immunity. w. Lady Gale [Gale Stevenson]. m. Sir Arthur Sullivan. Published online at <http://lightjunkie.org/parody/major-intern.html>. 1998.

77.20 I Got You Bill. w. Malcolm Higgins. m. Tune—"*I Got You Babe*, originally by Sonny and Cher." Published online at <http://amiright.com/parody/misc/sonnyandcher1.shtml>. [ca. 1999].

77.21 I Think Lewinsky's Sexy. w. Becca. m. "*She Thinks My Tractor's Sexy*, originally by Kenny Chesney." This parody is in Bill Clinton persona (Bill Clinton's point-of-view)... Both parodies contain how he feels about Mademoiselle Lewinsky." Published online at <http://www.amiright.com/parody/2000s/kennychesney0.shtml>. [ca. 2001].

77.22 I'm Monica Lewinsky. w. Duncan McNab. m. No tune indicated. Duncan McNab of the River

Police on the Forth. McNab is on the committee of Glenfarg Folk Club and, I'm reliably informed, writes very funny songs..." Lyrics published online at <http://www.mudcat.org/kids/@displaysong.cfm?SongID=2989>. 1999.

77.23 Instant Clinton. w. Tom Smith. m. "*Where The Hell Is Bill?* by Camper Van Beethoven." "This mid–80s demented classic ... is a perfect forum for riffing on the Clinton Administration." "Published online at <http://www.tomsmithonline.com/lyrics/instantclinton.htm>. 1999.

77.24 Itsy Bitsy Teenie Weenie Yellow Spot Of Something Seamy. w. Paul Silhan. m. "Sung to *Itsy Bitsy Teenie Weenie Yellow Polk Dot Bikini* by Bryan Hyland." On CD: *Scandal In The Wind*. Lyrics published online at <http://www.paulsilhan.com/itsy.htm>. 1998.

77.25 Ken's Obsession, Night And Day. w. H.R. Yeager. m. "Sung to the tune of *Santa Claus Is Coming To Town*." Published online at <http://www.geocities.com/CapitolHill/Congress/3950>. 1998.

77.26 Lirty Dies: Imbos In The Office. w.m. The Capitol Steps. Published by The Capitol Steps online at <http://capsteps.com/lirty/imbos.html>. 1998.

77.27 Love In The Oval Office. w. No composer indicated. m. "Parody of *Love In The Elevator* by Aerosmith." Lyrics published by *The Bob Rivers Show* with Bob, Spike & Joe and Twisted Tunes online at <http://www.twistedradio.com/player/lyrics.asp?songID=694>. [199-].

77.28 Miss Lewinsky (The Opera). w. No composer indicated. m. "Tune of *Miss Gradenko* by The Police." "The Half-Baked Institute for Political Parody." "The following duet was inspired by *Miss Gradenko* by The Police. It is the writer's opinion that Bill, Hillary, Monica, Paula and Gennifer should all go into group therapy together to uncover their past-life karma." Published online at <http://www.houstonprogressive.org/parody2.html>. [ca. 1997–1998].

77.29 Mrs. Lewis, You've Got A Naughty Daughter. w. Paul Silhan. m. "Sung *Mrs. Brown, You've Got A Lovely Daughter* by Herman's Hermits." Lyrics published online at <http://www.paulsilhan.com/mrslewis.htm>. 1998.

77.29A Monica (The Stinkweed Of The West). w. 2Eagle. m. "*Flora (The Lily Of The West)*, based on the performance by Peter, Paul and Mary." Published online at <http://amiright.com/parody/60s/peterpaulandmary17.shml>. 2004.

77.30 Name Is Bill Clinton. w. S.T.G. m. "*Dreams In Digital (Fiction)*, originally by Orgy." Published online at <http://amiright.com/parody/2000s/orgy0.shml>. [ca. 2001].

77.31 Oops He Did Her Again. w. Alex. m. "*Oops I Did It Again*, originally by Britney Spears." Published online at <http://www.amiright.com/parody/90s/britneyspears25.shtml>. [ca. 1999].

77.32 Oval Office Thumpin.' w. Mel. m. "This is to the tune of that old *Tubthumping* song." Published online at <http://foreardgarden.com/forward/6625.html>. [199-].

77.32 Poor Bill Can't Tell The Truth. w. Peter Hicks and Geoff Francis. m. No tune indicated. "Isn't it heart warming to know that the man responsible for the continuing genocide against the Iraqi people has finally come clean about his little dalliances — or has he?" Published online at <http://www.trump.net.au/glazfolk/songs/clinton.htm>. [ca. 1999].

77.33 The Scandal (Reprise). w. Jason Frazier. m. "Adapted from *Prince Ali (Reprise)* from *Aladdin*." Published online at <http://geocities.com/Hollywood/5082/scandal.html>. [ca. 2002].

77.34 Schizophrenicville. w. Billy Florio. m. Tune — "*Margaritaville*, originally by Jimmy Buffet." Published online at <http://www.amiright.com/parody/70s/jimmybuffet0.shtml>. [ca. 2001].

77.35 Some Wail Away. w. Malcolm Higgins. m. "*Come Sail Away*, based on a performance by Styx." "Written of yourse [sic] by the ultimate lefty ... me." Published online at <http://www.amiright.com/parody/misc/styx0.shtml>. [ca. 2003].

77.36 The President's Aren't Alright. w. "YASMR." m. "*The Kids Aren't Alright* originally by The Offspring." Published online at <http://www.amiright.com/parody/2000s/theoffspring13.shtml>. 2003.

77.37 Tap My Phone Line. w. James E.F. Landau. m. "*Steal My Sunshine*, originally by Len." Published online at <http://www.amiright.com/parody/90s/len0.shtml>. [ca. 1999].

77.38 There's The Game That Ol Bill Played. w. Terry Parish. m. "*Amarillo In The Morning*, originally by George Strait." Published online at <http://www.amiright.com/parody/misc/georgestrait1.shml>. August 16, 2000.

77.39 Tie A Yellow Ribbon 'Round The Ol' Pee-Pee. w. Paul Silhan. m. "Sung to *Tie A Yellow Ribbon 'Round The Ol' Oak Tree* by Tony Orlando & Dawn." On CD: *Scandal In The Wind*. Lyrics published online at <http://www.paulsilhan.com/yellow.htm>. 1998.

77.40 Was Bill Clinton Blown. w. S.G.T. m. "*Is Anybody Home*, originally by Our Lady Peace." Published online at <http://amiright.com/parody/2000s/ourladypeace0.shml>. [ca. 2001].

77.41 What's New Democrat? w. Adam Moses. m. "*What's New Pussycat?* based on a performance by Tom Jones. "A look back at a certain happy hands former President." Published online at <http://www.amiright.com/parody/60s/tomjones10.shtml>. [ca. 2004].

77.42 Where' Slick Willie Lay. w. Joseph Hayes. m. "*Barbara Allen*, based on a performance by Dolly Parton. "The oldest known song that the Pilgrims brought over. Go to <http://theromanceclub.com/aurthirs/lauramillsalcott/lyrics.htm> and see the original lyrics and scroll down to a choice of three who sing it." Published online at <http://www.amiright.com/parody/misc/dollyparton0.shtml>. [ca. 2004].

77.43 The (Willie) White House. w. Leo Jay. m. "*Copacabana*, based on a performance by Barry Manilow." "I know this is ancient history, but a little nostalgia never hurt...;-) it came to me while I was working on something else, and figured I might as well publish it — I'm trying to rack up 10 parodies. Plus, this looks forward to what may be yet to come...;-) Besides, I've done some bush-wacking, so I owe a bit to the left. I mean. 'left of Center' ... Or is that 'Left-inching-toward-center-while-pandering-to-the-base? Whatever ..." Published online at <http://www.

amiright.com/parody/70s/barrymanilow27.shtml>. [2004].

77.44 Your Cheatin' Parts. w. Paul Silhan. m. "Sung to Hank William's *Your Cheatin' Heart*." On: Cassette: *Spinball Wizard*. "As heard on Rush's Radio Show." Lyrics published at <http://www.paulsilhan.com/cheatin.htm>. 1998.

• **AmPM-78 LUTTRELL**, John King (Justice of the Peace, Brooklyn [Oakland], 1856–1857; State House, 1871–1872; U.S. House, 1873–1879; Treasury Agent for Alaska, 1893)

78.1 The Republican Ticket. m. "Tune—*Rosin The Bow*." In: *Campaign Songs*, page 4. w. Sam Booth. [1876]. [6" × 9⅜"]. Non-pictorial. "Supplement to *Hayes And Wheeler Songster*." 4pp. [Verses for local Congressional candidates]. [Crew/RBH-56].

• **AmPM-79 MCNAMARA**, Robert S. (President Ford Motor Company, 1960; U.S. Secretary of Defense, 1960–1968; President World Bank, 1968–1981)

79.1 All The King's Horses. w.m. Skip Storey and Joe Mazo, 1968. "L.B.J. made a classic speech... 'All the King's horses and all the King's men are not going to move us...'" In: *The Vietnam Songbook*, page 35. c. Barbara Dane and Irwin Silber. Published by The Guardian, No. 32 West 22nd Street, New York, NY. Copyright 1969 by Barbara Dane and Irwin Silber. [7" × 10"]. B/w photo of a protest march. O/y/r/bk cover. 228pp.

79.2 Beware: Here Come Friends. w.m. Richard Kohler and Barbara Dane, 1968. In: *The Vietnam Songbook*, page 100. c. Barbara Dane and Irwin Silber. Published by The Guardian, No. 32 West 22nd Street, New York, NY. Copyright 1969 by Barbara Dane and Irwin Silber. [7" × 10"]. B/w photo of a protest march. O/y/r/bk cover. 228pp.

79.3 Cool Goldwater. w. Noel E. Parmentel, Jr. and Marshall J. Dodge. In: *Folk Songs For Conservatives*, page 11. Published by Unicorn Press, Inc., No. 790 Madison Avenue, New York, NY. 10021. 1964. [5" × 8⅜"]. Bl/w drawings of Barry Goldwater, Bill Buckley, Ray Cohn, eagle. List of contents. "Sung by Noel E. Parmentel, Jr. and His Unbleached Muslims, Greatest Political Satirists Since Cohn and Schine." "Right Wing Hootenanny." 36pp. [Crew/BMG-13].

79.4 Demonstrating G.I. w.m. Matthew Jones. In: *Freedom Is A Constant Struggle, Songs Of The Freedom Movement*, page 23. c. Guy and Candie Carawan. Published by Oak Publications, New York, NY. 1968. "Original verses by Florence Reese." 224pp.

79.5 Ghost Advisors. w. Charlie Eberhardt. m. "Tune—*Ghost Riders*." From The Longest Year by Bowen and Fish." Lyrics and sound file published on-line at <http://www.mudcat.org/kids/@displaysong.cfm?SongID=2230>. [199-].

79.6 Include Me Out. w.m. Tuli Kupferberg, 1968. "Take-off from J.J. Rousseau..." In: *The Vietnam Songbook*, page 44. c. Barbara Dane and Irwin Silber. Published by The Guardian, No. 32 West 22nd Street, New York, NY. Copyright 1969 by Barbara Dane and Irwin Silber. [7" × 10"]. B/w photo of a protest march. O/y/r/bk cover. 228pp.

79.7 Mac The Knife. w. No composer indicated. m. *Mack The Knife*. In: *The Vietnam Songbook*, page 125. c. Barbara Dane and Irwin Silber. Published by The Guardian, No. 32 West 22nd Street, New York, NY. Copyright 1969 by Barbara Dane and Irwin Silber. [7" × 10"]. B/w photo of a protest march. O/y/r/bk cover. 228pp.

79.8 McNamara's Brand. w.m. Mortimer Frankel, "1965." "Secretary of Defense Robert McNamara, who later gained a phony reputation as a dove, was in fact one of the chief architects of the war..." In: *The Vietnam Songbook*, page 100. c. Barbara Dane and Irwin Silber. Published by The Guardian, No. 32 West 22nd Street, New York, NY. Copyright 1969 by Barbara Dane and Irwin Silber. [7" × 10"]. B/w photo of a protest march. O/y/r/bk cover. 228pp.

79.9 No More Johnson (Oh Freedom). w. No composer indicated. m. No tune indicated. "Learned in Italy from two American girls." In: *The Vietnam Songbook*, page 129. c. Barbara Dane and Irwin Silber. Published by The Guardian, No. 32 West 22nd Street, New York, NY. Copyright 1969 by Barbara Dane and Irwin Silber. [7" × 10"]. B/w photo of a protest march. O/y/r/bk cover. 228pp.

79.10 Stamattina E Morto. w. No composer indicated. m. *Michael Row The Boat Ashore*. "One of the two most popular songs of the Italian Left today." In: *The Vietnam Songbook*, page 181. c. Barbara Dane and Irwin Silber. Published by The Guardian, No. 32 West 22nd Street, New York, NY. Copyright 1969 by Barbara Dane and Irwin Silber. [7" × 10"]. B/w photo of a protest march. O/y/r/bk cover. 228pp.

79.11 There Ain't No Bugs On Me. w. Jack Warshaw, 1968. m. "Traditional." In: *The Vietnam Songbook*, page 142. c. Barbara Dane and Irwin Silber. Published by The Guardian, No. 32 West 22nd Street, New York, NY. Copyright 1969 by Barbara Dane and Irwin Silber. [7" × 10"]. B/w photo of a protest march. O/y/r/bk cover. 228pp.

• **AmPM-80 MCADOO**, William Gibbs (U.S. Secretary of the Treasury, 1913–1918; U.S. House, 1933–1938)

80.1 [Bring Back The G.O.P.'s Of Childhood]. w. I.E. Henry. m. "Tune—*Bring Back Those Wonderful Days*." In: *Republican Campaign Songs*, page 6. Published by Republican State Committee Headquarters, Topeka, Kansas. 1920. [5⁵⁄₁₆" × 7¹³⁄₁₆"]. Be/bk photos of "Warren G. Harding" and "Calvin Coolidge"—"Our Country Needs Them." "Sing and Smile on to Victory." 24pp. [Crew/WGH-63].

80.2 How Do You Do Mr. Mcadoo? w. Wilie Weston and Herman Ruby. m. Mike Bernard. Published by Waterson, Berlin & Snyder Co., Music Publishers, Strand Theatre Building, Broadway at 47th Street, New York, NY. 1918. R/bk/w drawing by Barbelle of William McAdoo on pedestal, cheering crowd. 4pp. Page 4: Advertising.

80.3 If You Can't Enlist Buy A Liberty Bond (And Help The U.S.A.). w. Joseph M. Davis. m. J. Fred Coots. Published by Triangle Music Pub. Co., 145 West 45th Street, New York, NY. R/w/l/b drawing of Miss Liberty with gun, facsimile letter from the Treasury Department. "The Song of the Nation." 4pp. Page 2: At top of music—"Respectfully dedicated to the Hon. W.G. McAdoo." Page 4: Advertising. [LL/JH].

80.4 Party Pals. w. No composer indicated. m. "Air—*I Just Couldn't Say Good-Bye*." In: *Foam Sweet Foam*, page 7. Published by Albany Legislative Correspondents' Association, Albany, NY. 1933. [8" × 11¾"]. N/c drawing by Jerry Costello of Franklin D. Roosevelt, Al Smith and other politicians riding a bottle of beer—"The Lager Limited." "A Rollicking Review Rotating on Resurrection of Bouncing Beverages, Tipsily Tapped at Ten Eyck Hotel Rathskeller, Albany, New York, the evening of Thursday, February 23, 1933, at Seven-Thirty o'clock." 20pp. [Crew/FDR-277].

- **AmPM-81   MCCLINTOCK**, Thomas (State House, 1982–1992 & 1996–Present, Candidate for Governor, 2003)

81.1 California Screaming. w. Loose Bruce Kerr. m. "*California Dreaming* by The Mamas and the Popas [sic]." "About California's recall campaign for governor, contains the names of the top runners and a little angst. Played on Jim Bohannon Show on Westwood One; upcoming on Dr. Demento." Published online at <http://www.amiright.com/parody/60s/mamaspopas0.shtml>. 2003.

81.2 Recalling Gray. w. Alex Murray. m. "*Auf Wiedersehen,* based on a performance by Cheap Trick." "Haven't done a parody in a while, so this is a bit rusty. To clarify, all bye-byes, goodbyes, so longs, etc are directed towards Red Davis." Published online at <http://www.amiright.com/parody/70s/cheaptrick3.shtml>. 2003.

81.3 Vote For The Terminator. w. Rice Cube & Walt Daddy. m. Tune—"*We Didn't Start The Fire* originally by Billy Joel." "We're not completely endorsing Schwarzenegger because we don't know his complete platform, but considering that voting for Bustamontte will be worse than keeping Davis in power, and Ahnuld is the leading Republican candidate who has a ghost's chance in hell of becoming governor ..." Published online at Published online at <http://www.amiright.com/parody/80s/billyjoel62.shtml>. 2003.

- **AmPM-82   MCCOPPIN**, Frank (Mayor, San Francisco, 1867–1869)

82.1 Wilson And Grant. w. Sam Booth. m. "Tune—*Bonnie Dundee*." In: *Grant And Wilson Campaign Songster*, page 2. Published by Frank Eastman, Book and Job Printer, No. 509 Clay Street, San Francisco, CA. [4¼" × 5⅝"]. 1872. Bk/bl geometric design border. 40pp. [Crew/USG-69].

- **AmPM-83   MCKENNA**, Joseph (State Assembly, 1875–1877; U.S. House, 1885–1892; U.S. Court of Appeals, 1892–1897; U.S. Attorney General, 1897–1898; U.S. Supreme Court, 1898–1925)

83.1 The Cabinet Grand March. m. Hans S. Line, Op. 64. Published by National Music Company, Nos. 215–221 Wabash Avenue, Chicago, IL. 1897. R/w cover. B/w photo of William McKinley and eight Cabinet members. "Dedicated to Hon. Lyman J. Gage." 6pp. Page 6: Advertising. [Crew/WM-15].

83.2 The Republican Ticket. w. No composer indicated. m. "Tune—*Rosin The Bow*." In: *Campaign Songs*, page 4. w. Sam Booth. [1876]. [6" × 9⅜"]. Nonpictorial. "Supplement to *Hayes And Wheeler Songster*." 4pp. [Verses for local Congressional candidates]. [Crew/RBH-56].

83.3 Vote For Horace Davis. In: *Campaign Songs*. w. Sam Booth. [1876]. [6" × 9⅜"]. Non-pictorial. "Supplement to *Hayes And Wheeler Songster*." 4pp. [Verses for local Congressional candidates]. [Crew/RBH-56].

- **AmPM-84   MURPHY**, George Lloyd (U.S. Senate, 1965–1971)

84.1 American Eagles. w.m. Irving Berlin. Published by [V-1: This Is The Army, Inc., Music Publishing Division, No. 799 Seventh Avenue, New York, NY. 1943] [V-2: Chappell, No. 50 New Bond St., London, England. 1942]. Gn/w/y drawing of soldiers as title. "Irving Berlin's *This Is The Army*, Presented by Warner Bros., In Technicolor, Starring men of the Armed Forces with George Murphy, Joan Leslie, Lt. Ronald Reagan and George Tobias, Alan Hale, Charles Butterworth and Kate Smith, Directed by Michel Curtiz, Produced by Jack L. Warner and Hal B. Wallis, Screen Play by Casey Robinson and Cpt. Claude Binyon, Based on the Stage Show Irving Berlin's *This Is The Army*." "All profits will be turned over to The Army Emergency Relief Fund." 4pp. Page 4: Advertising.

84.2 Amor. w. [English] Sunny Skylar. w. [Spanish] Ricardo Lopez Mendez. m. Gabriel Ruiz. Published by Melody Lane Publications, Inc., 1619 Broadway, New York, NY. Copyright 1943 by Promotora Hispano Americana de Musica. O/bl/w photos of George Murphy, Ginny Sims and Tommy Dorsey, two scenes from the movie. "*Broadway Rhythm* Starring George Murphy, Ginny Simms, Charles Winninger, Nancy Walker, Lena Horne, Gloria DeHaven, Ben Blue, Eddie (Rochester) Anderson and Tommy Dorsey and His Orchestra; Directed by Rou Del Ruth; Produced by Jack Cummings; Photographed in Technicolor; A Metro-Golden-Mayer Picture." 6pp. Page 6: Bl/w photo of "Jimmie Costello—Sincerely."

84.3 Amor Amor. w. [English] Sunny Skylar. w. [Spanish] Ricardo Lopez Mendez. m. Gabriel Ruiz. Published by Southern Music Publishing Co., Ltd., Denmark Street, London. W.C.2. England. 1943. [6¼" × 9½"]. O/bk/w photo of George Murphy and Ginny Sims]. "From the Metro-Goldwyn-Mayer Picture in Technicolor *Broadway Rhythm* Starring George Murphy, Ginny Simms and Tommy Dorsey and His Orchestra; Directed by Rou Del Ruth; Produced by Jack Cummings." "Buy War Savings Certificates." 4pp.

84.4 And Then You Kissed Me. w. Sammy Cahn. m. Jule Styne. Published by Miller Music Corp., 1619 Broadway, New York, NY. 1944. N/c photo of Frank Sinatra. O/y/br drawing of music notes, stars, hearts. "Sinatra." "Frank Sinatra, George Murphy, Adolphe Menjou, Gloria De Haven, Walter Slezak, Eugene Pallette in *Step Lively* with Wally Brown, Alan Carney, Grant Mitchell, Anne Jefferys; Produced by Robert Fellows; Directed by Tim Whelan; RKO Radio Pictures." 4pp. Page 4: Advertising.

84.5 The Army's Made A Man Out Of Me. w.m. Irving Berlin. Published by [V-1: This Is The Army, Inc., Music Publishing Division, No. 799 Seventh Avenue, New York, NY. 1943] [V-2: Chappell, No. 50 New Bond St., London, England. 1942]. Gn/w/y drawing of soldiers as title. "Irving Berlin's *This Is The Army*, Presented by Warner Bros., In Technicolor, Starring men of the Armed Forces with George Murphy, Joan Leslie, Lt. Ronald Reagan and George Tobias, Alan Hale, Charles Butterworth and Kate Smith, Directed by Michel Curtiz, Produced by Jack L. Warner and Hal B. Wallis, Screen Play by Casey Robinson and Cpt. Claude Binyon, Based on the Stage Show Irving Berlin's *This Is The Army*." "All profits will be turned over to The Army Emergency Relief Fund." 4pp. Page 4: Advertising.

84.6 *As Long As There's Music*. w. Sammy Cahn. m. Jule Styne. Published by Miller Music Corp., 1619 Broadway, New York, NY. 1944. N/c photo of Frank Sinatra. O/y/br drawing of music notes, stars, hearts. "Sinatra." "Frank Sinatra, George Murphy, Adolphe Menjou, Gloria De Haven, Walter Slezak, Eugene Pallette in *Step Lively* with Wally Brown, Alan Carney, Grant Mitchell, Anne Jefferys; Produced by Robert Fellows; Directed by Tim Whelan; RKO Radio Pictures." 6pp. Page 6: Advertising.

84.7 *Begin The Beguine*. w.m. Cole Porter. Published by Harms, Inc., New York, NY. 1935. [Edition 1940]. Bl/w photo of Fred Astaire and Eleanor Powell, other scene from movie. "Fred Astaire, Eleanor Powell in *Broadway Melody Of 1940* with George Murphy, Frank Morgan, Ian Hunter, Florence Rice, Lynne Carver; Screen Play Leon Gordon and George Oppenheimer; Directed by Norman Taurog; Produced by Jack Cummings." "As Featured in the MGM Picture." 8pp. Page 8: Advertising.

84.8 *Bird In A Gilded Cage*. w. Arthur J. Lamb. m. Harry Von Tilzer. Published by Harry Von Tilzer Music Publishing Co., [V-1: 1619] [V-2: 1697] Broadway, New York 19, NY. 1900. [Edition ca. 1950]. [V-1: Bl/w] [V-2: B/w] photos from the movie. "From the MGM Picture *Ringside Maisie* staring Ann Southern and George Murphy, Robert Sterling, Virginia O'Brien, Natalie Thompson, Original Screenplay by Mary C. McCall, Jr., Directed by Edwin L. Marin; Produced by J. Walter Ruben." 4pp.

84.9 *Blame It On The Rhumba*. w. Harold Adamson. m. Jimmy McHugh. Published by Leo Feist, Inc., 1629 Broadway, New York, NY. 1936. Pk/bl/w drawings of dancers, buildings. "A Universal Picture *Top Of The Town*, [with] Doris Nolan, George Murphy, Hugh Herbert, Gregory Ratoff, Gertrude Niesen, Ella Logan, Henry Armetta, Ray Mayer, Mischa Auer, The Three Sailors; Charles R. Rogers, Executive Producer." List of other titles in the film. 6pp. Pages 2 and 6: Advertising.

84.10 *Broadway Jamboree*. w. Harold Adamson. m. Jimmie McHugh. Published by Robbins Music Corp., 799 Seventh Avenue, New York, NY. 1937. Pl/w photos of stars "Alice Faye, George Murphy, Ken Murray, Oswald, Frances Hunt, Charles Winninger, Andy Devine." "The New Universal Picture presents Alice Faye in *You're A Sweetheart*, a Buddy De Sylvia Musical with George Murphy, Ken Murray and his stooge Oswald, Frances Hunt, Charles Winninger, Andy Devine, William Gargan, Frank Jenks; Charles R. Rogers, Executive Vice-President in Charge of Production."

84.11 *Come Out, Come Out Wherever You Are*. w. Sammy Cahn. m. Jule Styne. Published by Miller Music Corp., 1619 Broadway, New York, NY. 1944. N/c photo of Frank Sinatra. O/y/br drawing of music notes, stars, hearts. "Sinatra." "Frank Sinatra, George Murphy, Adolphe Menjou, Gloria De Haven, Walter Slezak, Eugene Pallette in *Step Lively* with Wally Brown, Alan Carney, Grant Mitchell, Anne Jefferys; Produced by Robert Fellows; Directed by Tim Whelan; RKO Radio Pictures." 8pp. Pages and 8: Advertising.

84.12 *Dinah*. w. Sam M. Lewis and Joe Young. m. Harry Akst. Published y Mills Music, Inc., Music Publishers, 1619 Broadway, New York, NY. 1925. [Edition ca. 1940]. B/w photos of Eddie Cantor, scene from the movie, bar of music. R/w/bk stars and music notes. "*Show Business*, Starring Eddie Cantor, George Murphy, Joan Davis, Nancy Kelly, Constance Moore, with Don Douglas; Directed by Edwin L. Marin; Produced by Eddie Cantor; RKO Pictures. 4pp. Page 4: Advertising.

84.13 *Don't Blame Me*. w. Dorothy Fields. m. Jimmie McHugh. Published by Robbins Music Corporation, 799 Seventh Avenue, New York, NY. 1933. R/w photo of star from the film. "M-G-M Presents *Big City* Starring Margaret O'Brien, Robert Preston Danny Thomas, George Murphy, Karin Booth, Edward Arnold, Butch Jenkins, and introducing to the screen Betty Garrett and Lotte Lehmann; Screen play by Whitfield Cook and Anne Morrison Chapin; Additional dialogue by Aben Kandel; Based on a story by Miklos Laszlo; Directed by Norman Taurog, Joe Pasternak." 6pp. Pages 2 and 6: Advertising.

84.14 *Everybody Sing*. w. Arthur Freed. m. Nacio Herb Brown. Published by Robbins Music Corp., 799 Seventh Avenue, New York, NY. Bl/w photos of stars "Sophie Tucker, George Murphy, Buddy Ebsen, Judy Garland, Charles Igor Gorin, Robert Taylor, Eleanor Powell." "Robert Taylor, Eleanor Powell in *Broadway Melody Of 1938*, A Metro-Goldwyn-Mayer Picture; Dances Directed by Dave Gould." "Songs by Brown and Freed." 6pp. Pages 2 and 6: Advertising.

84.15 *For Me And My Gal*. w. Edgar Leslie and E. Ray Goetz. m. George W. Meyer. Published by Mills Music, Inc., 1619 Broadway, New York, NY. 1932. [Edition ca. 194-]. [V-1: B/w tinted photo of Judy Garland. R/w cover] [V-2: Pl/gy photos of the various stars from the film]. "Judy Garland in *For Me And My Gal* with George Murphy, Gene Kelly, Marta Eggberth, Ben Blue; Directed by Busby Berkeley; A Metro-Goldwyn-Mayer Picture." [V-2: "Buy United States War Savings Bonds and Stamps"]. 4pp. Page 4: Advertising.

84.16 *George Murphy*. w.m. Tom Lehrer. On 33⅓ rpm LP: *That Was The Year That Was*. Reprise Records #6179. Performed by Tom Lehrer. 1965. Lyrics available online at <http://php.indiana.edu/~jbmorris.LYRICS/lehrer.tw3>.

84.17 *Got A Pair Of New Shoes*. w. Arthur Freed. m. Nacio Herb Brown. Published by Robbins Music Corp., 799 Seventh Avenue, New York, NY. Bl/w photos of stars "Sophie Tucker, George Murphy, Buddy Ebsen, Judy Garland, Charles Igor Gorin, Robert Taylor, Eleanor Powell." "Robert Taylor, Eleanor Powell in *Broadway Melody Of 1938*, A Metro-Goldwyn-Mayer Picture; Dances Directed by Dave Gould." "Songs by Brown and Freed." 6pp. Pages 2 and 6: Advertising.

84.18 Heavenly, Isn't It? w. Mort Greene. m. Harry Revel. Published by Greene-Revel, Inc., Music Publishers, 580 5th Avenue, New York, NY. 1942. B/w drawings of scenes from the film. "The RKO Picture *The Mayor Of 44th Street*, Starring George Murphy, Anne Shirley; Featuring Freddy Martin and His Record Breaking Orchestra, and Joan Merrill. 4pp. Page 4: Advertising.

84.19 How About A Cheer For The Navy. w.m. Irving Berlin. Published by [V-1: This Is The Army, Inc., Music Publishing Division, No. 799 Seventh Avenue, New York, NY. 1943] [V-2: Chappell, No. 50 New Bond St., London, England. 1942]. Gn/w/y drawing of soldiers as title. "Irving Berlin's *This Is The Army*, Presented by Warner Bros., In Technicolor, Starring men of the Armed Forces with George Murphy, Joan Leslie, Lt. Ronald Reagan and George Tobias, Alan Hale, Charles Butterworth and Kate Smith, Directed by Michel Curtiz, Produced by Jack L. Warner and Hal B. Wallis, Screen Play by Casey Robinson and Cpt. Claude Binyon, Based on the Stage Show Irving Berlin's *This Is The Army*. "All profits will be turned over to The Army Emergency Relief Fund." 4pp. Page 4: Advertising.

84.20 I Left My Heart At The Stage Door Canteen. w.m. Irving Berlin. Published by [V-1: This Is The Army, Inc., Music Publishing Division, No. 799 Seventh Avenue, New York, NY. 1943] [V-2: Chappell, No. 50 New Bond St., London, England. 1942]. Gn/w/y drawing of soldiers as title. "Irving Berlin's *This Is The Army*, Presented by Warner Bros., In Technicolor, Starring men of the Armed Forces with George Murphy, Joan Leslie, Lt. Ronald Reagan and George Tobias, Alan Hale, Charles Butterworth and Kate Smith, Directed by Michel Curtiz, Produced by Jack L. Warner and Hal B. Wallis, Screen Play by Casey Robinson and Cpt. Claude Binyon, Based on the Stage Show Irving Berlin's *This Is The Army*." "All profits will be turned over to The Army Emergency Relief Fund." 4pp. Page 4: Advertising.

84.21 I Want A Girl (Just Like The Girl That Married Dear Old Dad). w. William Dillon. m. Harry Von Tilzer. Published by Harry Von Tilzer Music Pub. Co., 1697 Broadway, New York, NY. 1911. [Edition ca. 1940]. B/w photo of Eddie Cantor. "Featured in RKO Radio Pictures *Show Business*, Starring Eddie Cantor with George Murphy, Joan Davis, Nancy Kelly, Constance Moore." "Harry Von Tilzer's Famous Hit." 6pp. Pages 2 and 6: Advertising.

84.22 I'm Feelin' Like A Million. w. Arthur Freed. m. Nacio Herb Brown. Published by Robbins Music Corp., 799 Seventh Avenue, New York, NY. 1937. [V-1: Bl/w photos of stars "Sophie Tucker, George Murphy, Buddy Ebsen, Judy Garland, Charles Igor Gorin, Robert Taylor, Eleanor Powell." "Robert Taylor, Eleanor Powell in *Broadway Melody Of 1938*, A Metro-Goldwyn-Mayer Picture; Dances Directed by Dave Gould." "Songs by Brown and Freed"] [V-2: Bl/w non-pictorial geometric design border. "Advanced Artist Copy." "Please announce title of production when broadcasting this number." "Sung by Eleanor and George Murphy in the MGM production of *Broadway Melody Of 1938*"]. [V-1: 6pp. Pages 2 and 6: Advertising] [V-2: 4pp.].

84.23 I'm Getting Tired So I Can Sleep. w.m. Irving Berlin. Published by [V-1: This Is The Army, Inc., Music Publishing Division, No. 799 Seventh Avenue, New York, NY. 1943] [V-2: Chappell, No. 50 New Bond St., London, England. 1942]. Gn/w/y drawing of soldiers as title. "Irving Berlin's *This Is The Army*, Presented by Warner Bros., In Technicolor, Starring men of the Armed Forces with George Murphy, Joan Leslie, Lt. Ronald Reagan and George Tobias, Alan Hale, Charles Butterworth and Kate Smith, Directed by Michel Curtiz, Produced by Jack L. Warner and Hal B. Wallis, Screen Play by Casey Robinson and Cpt. Claude Binyon, Based on the Stage Show Irving Berlin's *This Is The Army*." "All profits will be turned over to The Army Emergency Relief Fund." 4pp. Page 4: Advertising.

84.24 Irresistible You. w. Don Raye and Gene De Paul. Published by Leo Feist, Inc., 1619 Broadway, New York, NY. 1944. R/w photos of Ginny Sims and Tommy Dorsey. "*Broadway Rhythm* Starring George Murphy, Ginny Simms, Charles Winninger, Nancy Walker, Lena Horne, Gloria DeHaven, Ben Blue, Eddie (Rochester) Anderson, Hazel Scott, Kenny Bowers, The Ross Sisters, Dean Murphy and Tommy Dorsey and His Orchestra; Directed by Rou Del Ruth; Produced by Jack Cummings; Photographed in Technicolor; A Metro-Golden-Mayer Picture." 6pp. Page 6: Advertising.

84.25 It Had To Be You. w. Gus Kahn. m. Isham Jones. Published by Remick Music Corp., Inc., New York 19, NY. 1939. B/w photos of Eddie Cantor, George Murphy, Joan Davis, Nancy Kelly. R/w/bk printing. "*Show Business*, Starring Eddie Cantor, George Murphy, Joan Davis, Nancy Kelly, Constance Moore, with Don Douglas; Directed by Edwin L Marin; Produced by Eddie Cantor; Screen Play by Joseph Quillan and Dorothy Bennett. RKO Pictures." 6pp. Page 6: Advertising.

84.26 Jamboree. w. Harold Adamson. m. Jimmy McHugh. Published by Leo Feist, Inc., 1629 Broadway, New York, NY. 1936. Pk/bl/w drawings of dancers, buildings. "A Universal Picture *Top Of The Town*, [with] Doris Nolan, George Murphy, Hugh Herbert, Gregory Ratoff, Gertrude Niesen, Ella Logan, Henry Armetta, Ray Mayer, Mischa Auer, The Three Sailors; Charles R. Rogers, Executive Producer." List of other titles in the film. 6pp. Pages 2 and 6: Advertising.

84.27 Milkman, Keep Those Bottles Quiet. w.m. Don Raye and Gene De Paul. Published by Leo Feist, Inc., 1619 Broadway, New York, NY. 1944. R/w photos of Ginny Sims and Tommy Dorsey. "*Broadway Rhythm* Starring George Murphy, Ginny Simms, Charles Winninger, Nancy Walker, Lena Horne, Gloria DeHaven, Ben Blue, Eddie (Rochester) Anderson, Hazel Scott, Kenny Bowers, The Ross Sisters, Dean Murphy and Tommy Dorsey and His Orchestra; Directed by Rou Del Ruth; Produced by Jack Cummings; Photographed in Technicolor; A Metro-Golden-Mayer Picture." 6pp. Pages 2 and 6: Advertising.

84.28 A Million Miles From Manhattan. w. Mort Greene. m. Harry Revel. Published by Greene-Revel, Inc., Music Publishers, 580 5th Avenue, New York, NY. 1942. B/w drawings of scenes from the film. "The

RKO Picture *The Mayor Of 44th Street*, Starring George Murphy, Anne Shirley; Featuring Freddy Martin and His Record Breaking Orchestra, and Joan Merrill.

84.29 The Lady Who Didn't Believe In Love. w. Kim Gannon (ASCAP). m. Julie Styne (ASCAP). Published by Remick Music Corp., New York, NY. 1942. B/w photos of stars from the movie including George Murphy, Anne Shirley, Carole Landis, Dennis Day and Benny Goodman. "Charles R. Rogers presents *The Powers Girl*, with George Murphy, Anne Shirley, Carole Landis, Dennis Day and Benny Goodman and his Orchestra; Produced by Charles R. Rogers; Directed by Norman Z. McLeod; Released thru United Artists." "Buy United States War Savings Bonds and Stamps."

84.30 My Fine Feathered Friend. w. Harold Adamson. m. Jimmie McHugh. Published by Robbins Music Corp., 799 Seventh Avenue, New York, NY. 1937. Pl/w photos of stars "Alice Faye, George Murphy, Ken Murray, Oswald, Frances Hunt, Charles Winninger, Andy Devine." "The New Universal Picture presents Alice Faye in *You're A Sweetheart*, a Buddy De Sylvia Musical with George Murphy, Ken Murray and his stooge Oswald, Frances Hunt, Charles Winninger, Andy Devine, William Gargan, Frank Jenks; Charles R. Rogers, Executive Vice-President in Charge of Production."

84.31 My Wonderful One Let's Dance. w.m. Nacio Herb Brown, Arthur Freed and Roger Edens. Published by Leo Feist, Inc., 1629 Broadway, New York, NY. 1940. B/w photos of "Lana Turner, George Murphy and Joan Blondell in *Two Girls On Broadway*, A Metro-Goldwin-Mayer Picture." R/w/bk drawings of New York scenes. 6pp. Page 2: At top of music — "Sung by George Murphy." Page 6: Advertising.

84.32 Out Of This World. w. Kim Gannon (ASCAP). m. Julie Styne (ASCAP). Published by Remick Music Corp., New York, NY. 1942. B/w photos of stars from the movie including George Murphy, Anne Shirley, Carole Landis, Dennis Day and Benny Goodman. "Charles R. Rogers presents *The Powers Girl*, with George Murphy, Anne Shirley, Carole Landis, Dennis Day and Benny Goodman and his Orchestra; Produced by Charles R. Rogers; Directed by Norman Z. McLeod; Released thru United Artists." "Buy United States War Savings Bonds and Stamps." 4pp. Page 4: Advertising.

84.33 Partners. w. Kim Gannon (ASCAP). m. Julie Styne (ASCAP). Published by Remick Music Corp., New York, NY. 1942. B/w photos of stars from the movie including George Murphy, Anne Shirley, Carole Landis, Dennis Day and Benny Goodman. "Charles R. Rogers presents *The Powers Girl*, with George Murphy, Anne Shirley, Carole Landis, Dennis Day and Benny Goodman and his Orchestra; Produced by Charles R. Rogers; Directed by Norman Z. McLeod; Released thru United Artists." "Buy United States War Savings Bonds and Stamps."

84.34 Pretty Baby. w. Gus Kahn. m. Tony Jackson and Egbert Van Alstyne. Published by Francis, Day & Hunter, Ltd., 138–140, Charing Cross Road, London. W.C.2., England. 1916 [ca. 1943 edition]. [8⅛" × 10¼"]. Gn/bk/w photo from the movie of George Murphy and Ginny Simms. "*Broadway Rhythm* starring George Murphy, Ginny Simms with Charles Winninger, Gloria De Haven, Nancy Walker, Ben Blue, Lena Horne, Eddie 'Rochester' Anderson, Hazel Scott, Kenny Bowers, The Ross Sisters, Dean Murphy and Tommy Dorsey and His Orchestra." "A Metro Goldwyn Mayer Picture; Directed by Roy Del Ruth; Produced by Jack Cummings." 4pp.

84.35 Put Your Arms Around Me, Honey. w. Junie McCree. m. Albert Von Tilzer. Published by Broadway Music Corp., Will Von Tilzer, President, 1619 Broadway, New York, NY. 1937. B/w photo of Betty Grable, George Murphy and Cesar Romero. "Betty Grable, George Murphy and Cesar Romero in the 20th Century-Fox picture *Coney Island*, in Technicolor, with Charles Winninger, Phil Silvers' Directed by Walter Land' Produced by William Perlberg; Original Screen Play by George Seaton." "Decca Record #4337 by Dick Kuhn with his Orchestra." R/w/bk drawings of music notes, Coney Island scenes. 4pp. Page 4: Advertising.

84.36 That Foolish Feeling. w. Harold Adamson. m. Jimmy McHugh. Published by Leo Feist, Inc., 1629 Broadway, New York, NY. 1936. Pk/bl/w drawings of dancers, buildings. "A Universal Picture *Top Of The Town*, [with] Doris Nolan, George Murphy, Hugh Herbert, Gregory Ratoff, Gertrude Niesen, Ella Logan, Henry Armetta, Ray Mayer, Mischa Auer, The Three Sailors; Charles R. Rogers, Executive Producer." List of other titles in the film. 6pp. Pages 2 and 6: Advertising.

84.37 That's What The Well Dressed Man In Harlem Will Wear. w.m. Irving Berlin. Published by [V-1: This Is The Army, Inc., Music Publishing Division, No. 799 Seventh Avenue, New York, NY. 1943] [V-2: Chappell, No. 50 New Bond St., London, England. 1942]. Gn/w/y drawing of soldiers as title. "Irving Berlin's *This Is The Army*, Presented by Warner Bros., In Technicolor, Starring men of the Armed Forces with George Murphy, Joan Leslie, Lt. Ronald Reagan and George Tobias, Alan Hale, Charles Butterworth and Kate Smith, Directed by Michel Curtiz, Produced by Jack L. Warner and Hal B. Wallis, Screen Play by Casey Robinson and Cpt. Claude Binyon, Based on the Stage Show Irving Berlin's *This Is The Army*." "All profits will be turned over to The Army Emergency Relief Fund." 4pp. Page 4: Advertising.

84.38 There's No Two Ways About It. w. Harold Adamson. m. Jimmy McHugh. Published by Leo Feist, Inc., 1629 Broadway, New York, NY. 1936. Pk/bl/w drawings of dancers, buildings. "A Universal Picture *Top Of The Town*, [with] Doris Nolan, George Murphy, Hugh Herbert, Gregory Ratoff, Gertrude Niesen, Ella Logan, Henry Armetta, Ray Mayer, Mischa Auer, The Three Sailors; Charles R. Rogers, Executive Producer." List of other titles in the film. 6pp. Pages 2 and 6: Advertising.

84.39 This Is The Army Mr. Jones. w.m. Irving Berlin. Published by [V-1: This Is The Army, Inc., Music Publishing Division, No. 799 Seventh Avenue, New York, NY. 1943] [V-2: Chappell, No. 50 New Bond St., London, England. 1942]. Gn/w/y drawing of soldiers as title. "Irving Berlin's *This Is The Army*, Presented by Warner Bros., In Technicolor, Starring men of the Armed Forces with George Murphy, Joan

Leslie, Lt. Ronald Reagan and George Tobias, Alan Hale, Charles Butterworth and Kate Smith, Directed by Michel Curtiz, Produced by Jack L. Warner and Hal B. Wallis, Screen Play by Casey Robinson and Cpt. Claude Binyon, Based on the Stage Show Irving Berlin's *This Is The Army*." "All profits will be turned over to The Army Emergency Relief Fund." 4pp. Page 4: Advertising.

84.40 Three Dreams. w. Kim Gannon (ASCAP). m. Julie Styne (ASCAP). Published by Remick Music Corp., New York, NY. 1942. B/w photos of stars from the movie including George Murphy, Anne Shirley, Carole Landis, Dennis Day and Benny Goodman. "Charles R. Rogers presents *The Powers Girl*, with George Murphy, Anne Shirley, Carole Landis, Dennis Day and Benny Goodman and his Orchestra; Produced by Charles R. Rogers; Directed by Norman Z. McLeod; Released thru United Artists." "Buy United States War Savings Bonds and Stamps." 4pp. Page 4: Advertising.

84.41 Top Of The Town. w. Harold Adamson. m. Jimmy McHugh. Published by Leo Feist, Inc., 1629 Broadway, New York, NY. 1936. Pk/bl/w drawings of dancers, buildings. "A Universal Picture *Top Of The Town*, [with] Doris Nolan, George Murphy, Hugh Herbert, Gregory Ratoff, Gertrude Niesen, Ella Logan, Henry Armetta, Ray Mayer, Mischa Auer, The Three Sailors; Charles R. Rogers, Executive Producer." List of other titles in the film. 6pp. Pages 2 and 6: Advertising.

84.42 What Does He Look Like? (That Boy of Mine). w.m. Irving Berlin. Published by [V-1: This Is The Army, Inc., Music Publishing Division, No. 799 Seventh Avenue, New York, NY. 1943] [V-2: Chappell, No. 50 New Bond St., London, England. 1942]. Gn/w/y drawing of soldiers as title. "Irving Berlin's *This Is The Army*, Presented by Warner Bros., In Technicolor, Starring men of the Armed Forces with George Murphy, Joan Leslie, Lt. Ronald Reagan and George Tobias, Alan Hale, Charles Butterworth and Kate Smith, Directed by Michel Curtiz, Produced by Jack L. Warner and Hal B. Wallis, Screen Play by Casey Robinson and Cpt. Claude Binyon, Based on the Stage Show Irving Berlin's *This Is The Army*." "All profits will be turned over to The Army Emergency Relief Fund." 4pp. Page 4: Advertising.

84.43 When There's A Breeze On Lake Louise. w. Mort Greene. m. Harry Revel. Published by Greene-Revel, Inc., Music Publishers, 580 5th Avenue, New York, NY. 1942. B/w drawings of scenes from the film. "The RKO Picture *The Mayor Of 44th Street*, Starring George Murphy, Anne Shirley; Featuring Freddy Martin and His Record Breaking Orchestra, and Joan Merrill. 4pp. Page 4: Advertising.

84.44 Where Are You? w. Harold Adamson. m. Jimmy McHugh. Published by Leo Feist, Inc., 1629 Broadway, New York, NY. 1936. Pk/bl/w drawings of dancers, buildings. "A Universal Picture *Top Of The Town*, [with] Doris Nolan, George Murphy, Hugh Herbert, Gregory Ratoff, Gertrude Niesen, Ella Logan, Henry Armetta, Ray Mayer, Mischa Auer, The Three Sailors; Charles R. Rogers, Executive Producer." List of other titles in the film. 6pp. Pages 2 and 6: Advertising. Page 3: Sung by Gertrude Niesen."

84.45 With My Head In The Clouds. w.m. Irving Berlin. Published by [V-1: This Is The Army, Inc., Music Publishing Division, No. 799 Seventh Avenue, New York, NY. 1943] [V-2: Chappell, No. 50 New Bond St., London, England. 1942]. Gn/w/y drawing of soldiers as title. "Irving Berlin's *This Is The Army*, Presented by Warner Bros., In Technicolor, Starring men of the Armed Forces with George Murphy, Joan Leslie, Lt. Ronald Reagan and George Tobias, Alan Hale, Charles Butterworth and Kate Smith, Directed by Michel Curtiz, Produced by Jack L. Warner and Hal B. Wallis, Screen Play by Casey Robinson and Cpt. Claude Binyon, Based on the Stage Show Irving Berlin's *This Is The Army*." "All profits will be turned over to The Army Emergency Relief Fund." 4pp. Page 4: Advertising.

84.46 You're Bad For Me. w. Mort Greene. m. Harry Revel. Published by Greene-Revel, Inc., Music Publishers, 580 5th Avenue, New York, NY. 1942. B/w drawings of scenes from the film. "The RKO Picture *The Mayor Of 44th Street*, Starring George Murphy, Anne Shirley; Featuring Freddy Martin and His Record Breaking Orchestra, and Joan Merrill.

84.47 You May Not Remember. w. George Jessel. m. Ben Oakland. Published by Southern Music Publishing Co., Inc., 1619 Broadway, New York 19, NY. 1925. [Edition ca. 1940]. B/w photos of Eddie Cantor. R/w/bk dancer, stars and music notes. "*Show Business*, Starring Eddie Cantor, George Murphy, Joan Davis, Nancy Kelly, Constance Moore, with Don Douglas; Directed by Edwin L Marin; Produced by Eddie Cantor; RKO Pictures. 4pp. Page 4: B/w photo of "Dan Ryan."

84.48 You're A Sweetheart. w. Harold Adamson. m. Jimmie McHugh. Published by Robbins Music Corp., 799 Seventh Avenue, New York, NY. 1937. Pl/w photos of stars "Alice Faye, George Murphy, Ken Murray, Oswald, Frances Hunt, Charles Winninger, Andy Devine." "The New Universal Picture presents Alice Faye in *You're A Sweetheart*, a Buddy De Sylvia Musical with George Murphy, Ken Murray and his stooge Oswald, Frances Hunt, Charles Winninger, Andy Devine, William Gargan, Frank Jenks; Charles R. Rogers, Executive Vice-President in Charge of Production." 6pp. Pages 2 and 6: Advertising.

84.49 Yours And Mine. w. Arthur Freed. m. Nacio Herb Brown. Published by Robbins Music Corp., 799 Seventh Avenue, New York, NY. Bl/w photos of stars "Sophie Tucker, George Murphy, Buddy Ebsen, Judy Garland, Charles Igor Gorin, Robert Taylor, Eleanor Powell." "Robert Taylor, Eleanor Powell in *Broadway Melody Of 1938*, A Metro-Goldwyn-Mayer Picture; Dances Directed by Dave Gould." "Songs by Brown and Freed."

• **AmPM-84A** NEWSOM, Gavin (Parking and Traffic Commission, San Francisco, 1996; Board of Supervisors, San Francisco, 1996–2004; Mayor, San Francisco, 2004–Present)

84A.1 Marryin' Libertarians. w. John A. Barry. "*Marian The Librarian* (From *The Music Man*), base4d on the performance by Robert Preston." "From The Bu'shit Man my unfinished parody of *The Music Man*. This is an extended take on the original, combined with the part of *Gary, Indiana*." Published online at

<http://amiright.com/parody/misc/robertpreston0/ shtml>. 2004.
- **AmPM-84x NIXON**, Richard Milhous (U.S. House, 1947–1950; U.S. Senate, 1950–1957; Vice President, 1957–1961; President, 1969–1974) [SEE: DOC-/PSM-DDE & RMN]
- **AmPM-85 OLIVIER**, Arthur (Mayor and City Council, Bellflower, 1994–1999; Libertarian Candidate for Vice President, 2000)

85.1 Olie And The Browne Campaign Song. w. No composer indicated. m. "To the tune of the *Pinky And The Brain Theme Song*." "'The Meet John Brain' episode of *Pinky And The Brain* is strikingly close to the mouse-scale antics of the Libertarian Party. The public cheerfully misinterprets Brain's honest declarations of his evil intent to be the things they desire. When they finally see him in real life, the realize 'why, he's just a mouse!' and abandon him for rival Chicken Boo (perhaps Perot...)." Published online by Critiques of Libertarianism at <http://www.world.std.com/ ~mhuben/song.html>. 2000.

- **AmPM-86 OLSON**, Culbert Levy (State Senate, Utah, 1916–1920; State Senate, California, 1935–1939; Governor, 1939–1943)

86.1 He's O-L-S-O-N (Elect Him Governor Of Our State) (A Senator Olson Campaign Song). w. Georgie Jackson. m. Nathan Davis. Published by Nathan Davis, P.O. Box 524, Hollywood, CA. 1938. Bl/w photo of Culbert Olson. "The Next Governor of California. Hear this song on Olson Program, KFVD 1000 Kilocycles, Daily at 6 P.M." "Senator Culbert L. Olson Democratic Candidate for Governor of California." 4pp. Page 4: Advertising.

86.2 I Am Proud To Be A Democrat. w. Adeleide Davenport Armstrong. m. Louis Oscar Karzag. Published by Karzag Publishing House, 621 West Fourth Street, Los Angeles, CA. 1938. Br/w photo of "Our Next Governor, Senator Culbert L. Olson." 4pp. + 2pp. insert. Page 4 and page 2 (insert): Blank.

86.3 Oh, Bring Back Dick Nixon To Me. w. Milton M. Schwartz. m. "To the tune of *My Bonnie*." In: *Sing Along With Jack* [Song Book], page 30. a. Danny Hurd. Published by Pocket Books, Inc., New York, NY. Copyright 1963 by Bonny Publishing Corporation. [9" × 11⅞"]. R/w/bk drawing of sheet music "Vive La Dynasty," silhouette of John F. Kennedy in chair with conductor's baton, caricature of Kennedy family. "Hit Songs from the New Frontier." 36pp. Page 3: "Illustrations by David Gantz." Page 36: Drawing of John F. Kennedy in chair with baton. Song titles. [Crew/JFK-17].

86.4 The Roosevelt Song. w. Sasha Stone. m. Lou Halmy. Published by Sasha Stone, Hollywood, CA. 1940. R/w/b flag, eagle. Bl/w photo of Franklin D. Roosevelt. Slogans based on the letters in "F.D. Roosevelt" — "'Fighting for right against all that is wrong; Daring to some, but unfair to none; Rays of sunshine bringing where needed; On is your by-word — never defeated; On please don't stop — so on with your work; Serve your Country — bring peace to the world; End all miseries as you wish to do; Voices of millions are praying for you; Efforts are made to discredit what you do; Let them do what they may for they are very few; To ignore the cause of the Red, White and Blue." 4pp. Page 2: "A Tribute to a great humanitarian." Page 4: B/w photo of "Honorable Culbert L. Olson, Governor of California for Vice President of the United States." [Crew/FDR-52].

86.5 We'll Meet In Sacramento (Bye And Bye). w. Capt. A.W. Lewis. m. "Music Adapted." Published by National Music Publishers & Distributors, 532 16th Street, Oakland, CA. 1938. Bk/pk photo of "Senator Culbert L. Olson, Democratic Candidate for Governor of California, 1938." "Official Campaign Song of [Senator Olson]." Bk/pk photo of an African-American singing group — "Introduced and Sung by Southern Lighthouse Singers." 4pp. Page 4: Blank.

- **AmPM-87 PACHECO**, Romualdo (State Senate, 1851 & 1861; State Assembly, 1853–1855 & 1868–1870; County Judge, Santa Barbara, 1855–1859; State Treasurer, 1863–1866; Lt. Governor, 1871–1875; Governor, 1875; U.S. House, 1877–1883; U.S. Ambassador to Central America, 1890–1893)

87.1 The Republican Ticket. w. Sam Booth. m. "Tune — *Rosin The Bow*." In: *Campaign Songs*, page 4. [1876]. [6" × 9⅜"]. Non-pictorial. "Supplement to *Hayes And Wheeler Songster*." 4pp. [Verses for local Congressional candidates]. [Crew/RBH-56].

- **AmPM-88 PAGE**, Horace Francis (U.S. House, 1873–1883)

88.1 The Republican Ticket. w. Sam Booth. m. "Tune — *Rosin The Bow*." In: *Campaign Songs*, page 4. [1876]. [6" × 9⅜"]. Non-pictorial. "Supplement to *Hayes And Wheeler Songster*." 4pp. [Verses for local Congressional candidates]. [Crew/RBH-56].

- **AmPM-89 PARKER**, William (Police Chief, Los Angeles, 1950–1966)

89.1 The Ballad Of The DPO (Or I Got 92 Kids!). w. Vern Partlow. m. "With apologies to Tennesse [sic] Ernie and *His Sixteen Tons*." Published by Public Relations Dept., Local 685, Los Angeles County Probation Officers, AFL-CIO, Los Angeles, CA. [ca. 197-]. [8½" × 11"]. B/w drawing of a treble and bass clef. "Cultural Memo, Please Post." "Awake and Sing: But Don't Sing Solo! Join the mixed chorus at your union membership meeting, Monday, Jan. 11, 7:30 p.m., 7th Floor Hearing Room, New Hall of Records, Every Voice Helps! E Pluribus Unum — As it says on every Penny!" 2pp. Page 2: Blank.

- **AmPM-90 PELOSI**, Nancy (Chairwoman California State Democratic Party, 1981–1983; U.S. House, 1987–Present)

90.1 California Girls. w. John Jenkins. m. "*California Girls*, based on the performance by Beach Boys." The last four leaders of the Democratic Party in the House of Representatives have been Tip O'Neill (Massachusetts, 1977–87), Jim Wright (Texas, 87–89), Tom Foley (Washington, 89–94), and Dick Gephardt (Missouri, 94–2002)..." Published online at <http:// amiright.com/parody/60s/beachboys17.shml>. [2003].

90.2 That Leftist Tart From San Francisco. w. John Jenkins. m. Tune — "*I Left My Heart In San Francisco* originally by Tony Bennett." "A duet with the last two lines of each verse (after the introduction) sung by Nancy Pelosi and the balance sung by an anonymous Democrat Congressman." Published online at <http:// www.amiright.com/parody/60s/tonybennett2.shml>. [ca. 2003].

- **AmPM-91 PERKINS**, George Clement (State Senate, 1869–1876; Governor, 1879–1883; U.S. Senate, 1893–1915)
91.1 When The Boodler's Fade. w. Gerald Grey. m. J.A. Parks. In: *Parks' Democratic Campaign Songs (For Male Voices)*, page 25. Published by The J.A. Parks Company, York, NE. 1912. [7" × 9½"]. Gn/bl non-pictorial geometric designs. 36pp. [M-399]. [Crew/WW-178].
- **AmPM-92 PIPER**, William Adam (U.S. House, 1875–1877)
92.1 Democratic Reform. m. "Tune — *Taffy Was A Welshman*." In: *Campaign Songs*, page 2. w. Sam Booth. [1876]. [6" × 9⅜"]. Non-pictorial. "Supplement to *Hayes And Wheeler Songster*." 4pp. [Verses for local Congressional candidates]. [Crew/RBH-56].
92.2 The Republican Ticket. w. Sam Booth. m. "Tune — *Rosin The Bow*." In: *Campaign Songs*, page 4. [1876]. [6" × 9⅜"]. Non-pictorial. "Supplement to *Hayes And Wheeler Songster*." 4pp. [Crew/RBH-56].
- **AmPM-93 PIXLEY**, Frank M. (State Assembly, 1859–1860; State Attorney General, 1862–1863; U.S. District Attorney for the Northern District of California, 1869; Delegate, Republican National Convention, 1880 & 1884)
93.1 Hoist Up The Flag. w.m. No composer or tune indicated. In: *Grant And Wilson Campaign Songster*, page 31. Published by Frank Eastman, Book and Job Printer, No. 509 Clay Street, San Francisco, CA. [4¼" × 5⅝"]. 1872. Bk/bl geometric design border. 40pp. [Crew/USG-69].
93.2 Wilson And Grant. w. Sam Booth. m. "Tune — *Bonnie Dundee*." In: *Grant And Wilson Campaign Songster*, page 2. Published by Frank Eastman, Book and Job Printer, No. 509 Clay Street, San Francisco, CA. [4¼" × 5⅝"]. 1872. Bk/bl geometric design border. 40pp. [Crew/USG-69].
- **AmPM-94 RAFFERTY**, Max (Superintendent of Public Instruction, 1963–1971)
94.1 We Shall Not Be Moved. w. Noel E. Parmentel, Jr. and Marshall J. Dodge. In: *Folk Songs For Conservatives*, page 27. Published by Unicorn Press, Inc., No. 790 Madison Avenue, New York, NY. 10021. 1964. [5" × 8⅜"]. Bl/w drawings of Barry Goldwater, Bill Buckley, Ray Cohn, eagle. List of contents. "Sung by Noel E. Parmentel, Jr. and His Unbleached Muslims, Greatest Political Satirists Since Cohn and Schine." "Right Wing Hootenanny." 36pp. [Crew/BMG-13].
- **AmPM-94x REAGAN**, Ronald Wilson (President, Screen Actors Guild, 1947–1952 & 1959–1960; Governor, 1967–1975; President, 1981–1989) [SEE: DOC/PSM-RR]
  ROBINSON, Charles Lawrence (State Assembly, California, 1851–1852) [See: Kansas]
- **AmPM-94A REID**, Jim (Candidate for Mayor, San Francisco, 1999 & 2003)
94A.1 B-Sides. w. Stephen Capozzola. m. No tune indicated. "A playful song about relaxation without interruption, even by the mayor." Produced by Alex James Muscat, Last Stop Records. Sound file published online <http://www.sfmayor.com/dark_horse_campaign_songs.htm>. 2003.
94A.2 Homelessness Opus 2004. w. Stephen Capozzola. m. No tune indicated. "A San Francisco homeless history in words and classical music." Produced by Alex James Muscat, Last Stop Records. Sound file published online <http://www.sfmayor.com/dark_horse_campaign_songs.htm>. 2003.
94A.3 Parking Ticket Musical Chairs. w. Stephen Capozzola. m. No tune indicated. "No solutions to parking problems from City Hall, just more fines & fees." Produced by Alex James Muscat, Last Stop Records. Sound file published online <http://www.sfmayor.com/dark_horse_campaign_songs.htm>. 2003.
94A.4 Unaffordable Housing. w. Stephen Capozzola. m. No tune indicated. "The truth about affordable housing is that it isn't. It's unaffordable!" Produced by Alex James Muscat, Last Stop Records. Sound file published online <http://www.sfmayor.com/dark_horse_campaign_songs.htm>. 2003.
94A.5 We Need Reid. w. Bill Olsen. m. No composer indicated. m. "Old church song." "A old church song with new political words sung by a retired teacher." Produced by Alex James Muscat, Last Stop Records. Sound file published online <http://www.sfmayor.com/dark_horse_campaign_songs.htm>. 2003.
94A.6 Who's Looking Out For Us. w.m. No composer or tune indicated. "A MUNI fare-increase protest song about waiting on the N-Judah." Produced by Alex James Muscat, Last Stop Records. Sound file published online <http://www.sfmayor.com/dark_horse_campaign_songs.htm>. 2003.
- **AmPM-95 ROLPH**, Jr., James (Mayor, San Francisco, 1911–1931; Governor, 1931–1934)
95.1 California. w. Roy H. McCray. m. Keaumoku Louis. Published by Keaumoku Louis, 373 West California Avenue, Glendale, CA. 1931. B/w photo of "Hon Jas. Rolph, Jr., Governor of California." Bl/w/o drawing of Spanish-style home. "Dedicated to Hon Jas. Rolph, Jr., Governor of California." 6pp. Page 6: Reproduction of a newspaper article titled "Governor's Song Born at Banquet."
95.2 My California (March Fox Trot). m. Ethel Morgan Tebbetts. a. [Ukulele] "Doc" Morris. Published by George W. Tebbetts, Los Angeles, CA. 1930. B/w photo of James Rolph, Jr.—[facsimile handwriting]: "To Mr. George W. Tebbetts, James Rolph, Jr., May." O/bk/w cover. "Dedicated to Mayor James Rolph, Jr., our future Governor." "Distributed by Harry G. Neville, Los Angeles, Calif." 6pp. Page 5: Blank. Page 6: Advertising.
95.3 Our Governor. w. Iva Holtz Woolley, "Ogden, Utah." m. Henry Starr, "San Francisco, Calif." Published by Chas. W. Rollinson, 1080 Lincoln Building, Los Angeles, CA. Bl/w photo of James Rolph, Jr. R/w/b drawings of California State flag, shield. "Dedicated to the Great Humane Governor of California, James Rolph, Jr." 4pp. Page 4: Blank.
95.4 San Francisco, I Love You. w.m. Elizabeth S. Cooper and Elmer J. Esperance. Published by Cooper and Esperance, San Francisco, CA. 1930. B/w photos of "Mayor James Rolph," "Elizabeth S. Cooper" and "Elmer J. Esperance." O/bl/w drawing of San Francisco skyline; official seal of the City. "Dedicated to His Honor the Mayor, James Rolph." 6pp. Pages 5 and 6: Blank.
95.5 A Smile Will Go A Long Long Way. w.m. Benny Davis and Harry Akst. Published by Waterson,

Berlin & Snyder Co., Strand Theatre Building, New York, NY. 1928. R/w/bk floral and geometric designs. "Dedicated to His Honor Smiling Jimmie Rolph, Mayor of San Francisco. The Song with the Spirit of the West." 6pp. Pages 2 and 6: Advertising.

• **AmPM-96 ROSECRANS**, William Starke (U.S. House, 1881–1885; Register of the Treasury 1885–1893)

96.1 Garfield's At The Front! (Campaign Song and Chorus). w. No composer indicated. m. J. Maurice Hubbard. Published by S. Brainard's Sons, Cleveland, OH. 1880. Non-pictorial geometric design frame. "Gen. Garfield Proceeded to the Front (Gen. Rosecran's official report of the battle of Chickamauga)." "Written for, and dedicated to The Illinois Campaign Glee Club." 6pp. Page 6: Advertising. [Crew/JAG-149].

96.2 The Good Old Union Wagon. w.m. S. Matthews. Published by A.C. Peters & Bro., Cincinnati, OH. 1863. R/w/b litho of an American flag. "Music of the Union." List of titles in the series. [AMC].

96.3 Hurrah! w.m. No composer or tune indicated. In: *Beadle's Dime Knapsack Songster: Containing The Choicest Patriotic Songs, Together With Many New And Original Ones, Set To Old Melodies*, page 27. Published by Beadle and Company, No. 141 William Street, New York, NY. 1862. [3¾" × 5¾"]. Litho of coin—"One Dime, United States of America." 74pp. [Crew/GBM-78].

96.4 Jim Garfield's At The Front. w. No composer indicated. m. "Tune—*The Old English Gentleman*." "Gen. Garfield proceeded to the front—Gen. Rosecrans' official Report of Battle of Chickamauga." In: *Garfield And Arthur Campaign Song Book*, page 6. Published by The Republican Congressional Committee, Washington, DC. 1880. [5¹³⁄₁₆" × 9¹⁄₁₆"]. [V-1: Bl/bk] [V-2: Pk/bk] [V-3: Be/bk] [V-4: Gy/bk] litho of James A. Garfield and Chester A. Arthur, palm tree, plants and small animals, geometric designs. 28pp. [M-210]. [Crew/JAG-62].

96.5 Our General's Grand March {96.5–1}. m. C.S. Grafulla. Published by E.A. Daggett, New York, NY. 1861. N/c litho [horizontal format] of Union generals, including "Scott, Butler, McClellan, Sprague, Prentiss, Tyler, Burnside, Hunter, Blenker, M'Dowell, Anderson, M'Call, Woll, Rosecrans, Lander, Dix, Curtis, Stone, Heintzelman, Banks, and Fremont." 8pp. Pages 2 and 8: Blank. Page 3: Title—*Our General's Quickstep* {96.5–2}. "As Performed by the 7th Reg. National Guard Band." [Crew/WS-14].

96.6 Rebellion's Weak Back. w.m. F. Wilmarth. Published by Russell & Patee, Boston, MA. [ca. 1862]. Non-pictorial geometric designs. "As sung by Billy Morris at Morris Bros., Pell and Trowbridge." [AMC].

96.7 Rosecrans' Victory March. m. Charles R.C. Published by John Church, Cincinnati, OH 1863. N/c litho of General Rosecrans on horseback directing troops in battle. 6pp.

96.8 The Soldier's Song. w. A. Stuart, Co. I, 9th Ind. Regiment. m. No tune indicated. Published by Enterprise Print, Mishawaka, IN. [186–]. [6¾" × 15"]. Pk/bk litho of toy soldier, American flag, geometric design border. 2pp. Page 2: Blank. [WFU].

96.9 Three Cheers For Abe And Andy (A Song For The Times). w.m. Chas. B. Brigham. Published by H.M. Higgins, No. 117 Randolph Street, Chicago, IL. 1964. Non-pictorial geometric designs. "Inscribed to Capt. H.G. Brigham, 107 N.Y. Vol." 6pp. Pages 2 and 6: Blank. [Crew/AL-540].

96.10 The Union Army March. a. George A. Mietzke, Op. 11. Published by Schuberth & Company, No. 98 Spring Street, New York, NY. 1861. N/c lithos by Shearman and Hart of George McClellan, U.S. and German flags, cannons, Union Generals—"Woll," "Rosecrans," "Siegl," and "Blenker." "Introducing the German National Air—*What Is The German's Fatherland?* and the American Patriotic Song—*Columbia The Gem Of The Ocean*." "Dedicated to the Commanders, Officers, and Privates of the Army & Navy." Page 2: Blank. [Crew/GBM-58].

96.11 White Star Division. w. "Composed by a member of Knapp's Penn's Battery." m. "Air—*Sword Of Bunker Hill*." No publisher indicated. [1864–1865]. Non-pictorial black line border. 2pp. Page 2: Blank. [AMC].

• **AmPM-97 ROSSI**, Angelo (Mayor, San Francisco, 1931–1944)

97.1 On The Streets Of San Francisco. w.m. Selma Behringer. Published by West Coast Music Publishing Co., 942 Market Street, San Francisco, CA. 1937. Bl/w photo of Angelo Rossi. Y/bl/w geometric designs, printing. "Respectfully dedicated to Mayor Angelo Rossi." 6pp. Pages 2 and 6: Advertising.

• **AmPM-98 SALINGER**, Pierre (White House Press Secretary, 1961–1964; U.S. Senate, 1964)

98.1 Cool Goldwater. w. Noel E. Parmentel, Jr. and Marshall J. Dodge. In: *Folk Songs For Conservatives*, page 11. Published by Unicorn Press, Inc., No. 790 Madison Avenue, New York, NY. 10021. 1964. [5" × 8⅜"]. Bl/w drawings of Barry Goldwater, Bill Buckley, Ray Cohn, eagle. List of contents. "Sung by Noel E. Parmentel, Jr. and His Unbleached Muslims, Greatest Political Satirists Since Cohn and Schine." "Right Wing Hootenanny." 36pp. [Crew/BMG-13].

98.2 I'm Called Little Caroline. w. Milton M. Schwartz. m. "Tune—*I'm Called Little Buttercup*." In: *Sing Along With Jack* [Song Book], page 10. Published by Pocket Books, Inc., New York, NY. Copyright 1963 by Bonny Publishing Corporation. [9" × 11⅞"]. R/w/bk drawing of sheet music *Vive La Dynasty*, silhouette of John F. Kennedy in chair with conductor's baton, caricature of Kennedy family. "Hit Songs from the New Frontier." 36pp. Page 3: "Illustrations by David Gantz." Page 36: Drawing of John F. Kennedy in chair with baton. Song titles. [Crew/JFK-17].

98.3 Plucky Pierre. w.m. Gerald Gardner. In: *These Are The Songs That Were*, page 22. Published by Edwin H. Morris & Co., Inc., 31 West 54th Street, New York, NY. 1965. B/w photo of Lyndon Johnson, Mike Mansfield, Everett Dirksen and Hubert Humphrey. R/w/bk printing. "*Writer Of Who's In Charge Here?, News-Reals*, and *That Was The Week That Was*." List of titles in the songbook. 36pp.

• **AmPM-99 SCHMITZ**, Eugene E. (Mayor, San Francisco, 1902–1907; Board of Supervisors, San Francisco, 1921?–1925)

99.1 The Yankee Hustler (Tribute to American

Progress) (March). m. Eugene E. Schmitz, Mayor of San Francisco. Published by Sam Davis, 421 Post Street, San Francisco, CA. 1902. B/w photo of "Eugene E. Schmitz, Mayor of San Francisco." B/w litho of a man in the clouds giving electricity to a train. 6pp. Page 2: Narrative on the derivation of the title *Yankee Hustler.* Page 6: Advertising.

- **AmPM-99A SCHMITZ**, John George (State Senate, 1964–1970 & 1978–1982; U.S. House, 1970–1973; Candidate for President, 1972) [SEE: DOC/PSM-JGS]
- **AmPM-100 SCHWARZENEGGER**, Arnold (Governor, 2003–Present)

100.1 After The Votin.' w. Malcolm Higgins. m. *"After The Lovin,'* based on a performance by Engelbert Humperdinck. "Sorry folks, I have to backlash at the loonie left who flood this site with anti right crap ... what's good for the gander..." Published online at <http://www.amiright.com/parody/70s/engelberthumperdinck3.shtml>. [ca. 2003].

100.2 Ahnie. w. Malcolm Higgins. m. *"Money* originally by The Beatles." Published online at <http://www.amiright.com/parody/60s/thebeatles196.shml>.

100.3 Ahnold's On De Airwayffs. w. Malcolm Higgins. m. *"Pilot Of The Airwaves,* based on a performance by Charlie Dore." Published online at <http://www.amiright.com/parody/70s/thevillagepeople16/html>. 2003.

100.4 Ah-nuld The Austrian. w. Jack Wilson. m. *"Ahab The Arab,* based on a performance by Ray Stevens." "My first Ah-nuld parody!" Published online at <http://www.amiright.com/parody/60s/raystevens2.shtml>. 2003.

100.5 All My Gropin (Or, The Arnie 'Hands On' Style of Governing). w. Malcolm Higgins. m. *"All My Lovin,'* based on a performance by The Beatles. Published online at <http://www.amiright.com/parody/60s/thebeatles269.shtml>. [ca. 2003].

100.6 American Pie 2. w. Codeman. m. *"American Pie,* Based on a performance by Don McLean." Published online at <http://www.amiright.com/parody/70s/donmclean4.shtml>. 2003

100.6A Anrold [sic] *Goes To Californeeya*. w. Lionel Mertens. m. *"All The Gold In California,* based on a performance by *Gatlin Brothers."* Published online at <http://www.amiright.com/parody/70s/gatlinbrothers1.shtml>. [2004].

100.7 Are You Still Arnold? w. Michael. m. *"Are You Happy Now?,* based on the performance by Michelle Branch." Published online at <http://www.amiright.com/parody/2000s/michellebranch22.shtml>. 2003.

100.8 Arnie. w. Malcolm Higgins. m. *"Sunny,* based on a performance by Bobby Hebb. Published online at <http://www.amiright.com/parody/60s/bobbyhebb2.shtml>. [ca. 2003].

100.9 Arnie, Blow Away That Whore. w. Malcolm Higgins. m. *"Michael Row The Boat Ashore* originally by 'Traditional.'" Published online at <http://www.amiright.com/parody/misc/misc/1.html>. 2003.

100.10 Arnie's Song (Turf Him Out). w. Malcolm Higgins. m. *"Anthony's Song (Movin' On),* based on a performance by Billy Joel." Published online at <http://www.amiright.com/parody/70s/billyjoel84.shtml>. [ca. 2003].

100.11 Arnold Schwarzenegger's Total Body Workout (With and Without Weights). m. Popular Tunes. 33⅓ rpm LP. Columbia Records #FC 3998, AL 39298 & BL 39298. m. Popular songs. Includes 4 page booklet. Album cover: N/c photo of Arnold Schwarzenegger in workout clothes.1984.

100.12 Arnoldwood. w. Aaron Dodson. m. *"Hollywood,* based on a performance by Madonna." Published online at <http://www.amiright.com/parody/2000s/madonna21.shtml>. [ca. 2002].

100.13 Baby, I'm Back. w. William Tong. m. *"Baby Come Back,* based on the performance by Player." "As sung by Arnold Schwarzanegger, Republican candidate for governor of California." Published online at <http://www.amiright.com/parody/70s/player2.shtml>. 2003.

100.14 Back (Bragging By Arnold Schwarzenegger). w. Ethan Mawyer. m. *"Bad,* based on a performance by Michael Jackson." "I don't do political parodies too often but this idea seemed too good to pass up when it came to me Wednesday night." Published online at <http://www.amiright.com/parody/80s/michaeljackson50.shtml>. 2003.

100.15 The Ballot Of Arnold Schwarzenegger. w. Bob Gomez. m. *"The Ballad Of Davy Crockett,* based on the performance by George Burns/Tom Blackburn." "Great. Now we can look forward to three years of gridlock and Really Bad pronunciation." Published online at <http://www.amiright.com/parody/misc/georgeburnstomblackburn0.shtml>. 2003.

100.16 The Battle Hymn Of The Republicans. w. Phil Alexander. m. *"The Battle Hymn Of The Republic,* based on a performance by Traditional." "...given that *The Battle Hymn Of The Republic* is in essence a parody of the tune *John Brown's Body,* this is a parody to a mixture of the two..." Published online at <http://www.amiright.com/parody/misc/traditional272.shtml>. 2003.

100.17 A Boy Named Gray. w. Michael Pacholek. m. *"A Boy Named Sue,* based on a performance by Johnny Cash." "For the record, his full name is Joseph Graham Davis Jr. Original written by Shel Silverstein." Published online at <http://www.amiright.com/parody/60s/johnnycash10.shtml>. 2003.

100.18 Boxing Lady. w. Bob Gomez. m. *"Foxy Lady,* based on a performance by Jimi Hendricks." "Crank it all the way up." Published online at <http://www.amiright.com/parody/60s/jimihendricks8.shtml>. 2003

100.19 California Gov. w. Jack Wilson. m. *"California Girls,* based on a performance by The Beach Boys." "A new Arnold parody." Published online at <http://www.amiright.com/parody/60s/thebeachboys36.shtml>. 2003.

100.20 California Governor Song. w. "Static." m. *"The Chanukah Song* by Adam Sandler. "Typical Sandler song. too many syllables in places, too little, and alternate endings. Static out." Published online at <http://www.amiright.com/parody/misc/adamsandler0.shtml>. 2003.

100.21 California Screaming. w. Loose Bruce Kerr. m. Tune — *"California Dreaming* by The Mamas and the Popas [sic]." "About California's recall campaign for governor, contains the names of the top runners and a little angst. Played on *Jim Bohannon Show* on Westwood One; upcoming on *Dr. Demento*." Published online at <http://www.amiright.com/parody/60s/mamaspopas0.shtml>. 2003.

100.22 California Screaming. w. Michael Pacholek. m. Tune—"*California Dreaming* by The Mamas and the Papas." "Dedicated to all those morons who don't know who's really to blame for California's budget woes. And every other State's budget woes." Published online at <http://www.amiright.com/parody/60s/themamasthepapas1.shtml>. 2003.

100.23 California Uber Alles. w. Adam Bernstein. m. "*Deutschland Uber Alles* originally by Franz Joseph Haydn and Hoffman von Fallersleben." Published online at <http://www.amiright.com/parody/misc/FranzJosephHaydnandHoffmanvonFallersleben0.shtml>. 2003

100.24 California's Governor Is Arnold Schwarzenegger. w. Johnny D. m. "*Supercalifragilisticexpialidocious*, based on a performance by Julie Andrews (Mary Poppins)." Published online at <http://www.amiright.com/parody/60s/julieandrewsmarypopkins1.shtml>. 2003

100.25 California's Dumb. w. Michael Pacholek. m. "*California Sun*, based on a performance by Joe Jones." "...If you're dumb enough to vote for a guy with no political experience and who thinks budget deficits can be reduced by cutting taxes, then you deserve the disaster to come..." Published online at <http://www.amiright.com/parody/60s/joejones2.shtml>. 2003.

100.26 Campaign California. w. Michael Pacholek. m. "*Hotel California*, based on a performance by The Eagles." "'Conan,' of course is ... the Barbarian, not O'Brien. Proposition 13, the biggest bullet in California's foot, was passed in 1978, hence the reference to no property taxes since 1979." Published online at <http://www.amiright.com/parody/70s/theeagles51.shtml>. [ca. 2001].

100.27 Cruz Bustamante. w. Bob Gomez. m. "*Guantanamera*, originally by The Sandpipers." "Quoted parts are spoken by the probable next Governor of California. I can translate this into Spanish if you really want me to." Published online at <http://amiright.com/parody/60s/thesandpipers0.shml>. [ca. 2000].

100.28 Davis Needs To Go Right Now (Political). w. Malcolm Higgins. m. "*No One Needs To Know Right Now*, based on a performance by Shania Twain. Published online at <http://www.amiright.com/parody/misc/shaniatwain1.shtml>. [ca. 2003].

100.29 Democratic Boo Boo. w. Malcolm Higgins. m. "*Chattanooga Choo Choo*, based on a performance by Glenn Miller. Published online at <http://www.amiright.com/parody/misc/glennmiller0.shtml>. [ca. 2003].

100.30 Destined To Win. w. Malcolm Higgins. m. "*Dust In The Wind*, based on a performance by Kansas. Published online at <http://www.amiright.com/parody/70s/kansas12.shtml>. [ca. 2003].

100.31 A Detective Named Dirty Harry. w. Fitu Petaia. m. "*A Horse With No Name*, based on a performance by America." Published online at <http://www.amiright.com/parody/70s/america12.shtml>. 2003.

100.32 Do You Vant To Know A Secret? w. Malcolm Higgins. m. "*Do You Want To Know A Secret*, based on the performance by The Beatles." Published online at <http://www.amiright.com/parody/60s/thebeatles263.html>. 2003.

100.33 Don't Stand For Election. w. Michael Pacholek. m. "*Don't Stand So Close To Me*, based on a performance by The police. "A British woman, whose name I've forgotten, once said that the difference between Brits and Americans is that Americans feel the need, the need for speed. For example, she points out, Brits 'stand for election,' while Americans run for office.'" Published online at <http://www.amiright.com/parody/80s/thepolice30.shtml>. [ca. 2003].

100.34 Dufusrider. w. Fitu Petaia. m. "*Lowrider*, based on a performance by WAR." Published online at <http://www.amiright.com/parody/70s/war15.shtml>. 2003.

100.35 Dupes In California Wishing To Replace Gray Davis. w. William Tong. m. "*Supercalifragilisticexpalidocious* originally by Julie Andrews." "The California blackouts were rigged by Bush cronies at Enron by manipulating the demand on the electric grid from out of the state, and then selling extra power to the state at loan shark prices. On 9/16/03, the Federal 9th Circuit Court of Appeals barred the California recall election ... stay tuned for the U.S. Supreme Court." Published online at <http://www.amiright.com/parody/60s/julieandrews9.shtml>. 2003.

100.36 Earthquake. w. Michael. m. "*Landslide*, based on a performance by Stevie Nicks. Published online at <http://www.amiright.com/parody/70s/stevienicks0.shtml>. [ca. 2003].

100.37 End Of Days — A Tribute To Arnold Schwarzenegger. w. "Bloody & SLNinho." m. "*Come What May*, based on the performance by Ewan McGregor & Nichole Kidman." "Do you thing [sic] that Moulin Rouge's hit single *Come What May* would have been such a success if it were performed by, say ... Arnold Schwarzenegger? Yeah, we think so!" Published online at <http://www.amiright.com/parody/2000s/ewanmcgregornicholekidman0.shtml>. [ca. 2002].

100.38 A Few Short Years Ago. From CD: *American Way*. Performed by Dimpled Chad & The Disenfranchised. Lyrics published at <http:/dimpledchad.net>. [ca. 2000].

100.39 50 Candidates For Gov'ner. w. Michael Florio. m. "*50 Ways To Leave Your Lover* originally by Paul Simon." Published online at <http://www.amiright.com/parody/70s/paulsimon26.html>. 2003.

100.40 The 59th Schwarznegger [sic] **Bridge Song**. w. "Doug." m. "*The 59th Street Bridge Song*, based on the performance by Simon and Garfunkel." "They're used to me [be] singing at the gym, and even to me making up songs as I go. On the eve of the recall election, this one caught them by surprise." Published online at <http://www.amiright.com/parody/60s/simonandgarfunkel17.shtml>. [ca. 2002].

100.40A Fuck Hollywood. w.m. Anti-Heros. Lyrics published online at <http://www.plyrics.com/lyrics/antiheros/fuckhollywood.html>. [ca. 198-].

100.41 Gave Gray Defeat. w. Malcolm Higgins. m. "*Eight Days A Week*, based on a performance by The

Beatles." Published online at <http://www.amiright.com/parody/60s/thebeatles273.shtml>. 2003.

100.42 Goodbye T' Gray. w. Malcolm Higgins. m. *"Goodbye T' Jane,* based on a performance by Traditional." Published online at <http://www.amiright.com/parody/70s/0.shtml>. [ca. 2003].

100.43 G.O.P. w. Malcolm Higgins. m. *"TNT,* based on a performance by AC/DC." Published online at <http://www.amiright.com/parody/70s/acdc30.shtml>. [ca. 2003].

100.44 Govern California. w. Aaron Saraco. m. *"Hotel California,* based on a performance by The Eagles." "Okay, so I took a little too long on this one ... but it's pretty different from the other California recall parodies. This one is all Schwarzenegger!" Published online at <http://www.amiright.com/parody/70s/theeagles65.shtml>. [ca. 2003].

100.45 Governor Gray. w. Charlie Decker. m. *"Ruby Tuesday* originally by the Rolling Stones." "California is mocking the United States, removing an elected official to replace him with an actor or a porn tycoon or a guy who smashes watermelons." Published online at <http://www.amiright.com/parody/60s/rollingstones31.shtml>. 2003.

100.46 The Governor Is Mister Freeze. w. Jared. m. *"Another Postcard,* based on the performance by Barenaked Ladies." "Arnold Schwarzanegger played Mister Freeze in the fourth Batman movie..." Published online at <http://www.amiright.com/parody/2000s/barenakedladies13.shtml>. 2003.

100.47 Gov'nor Arnold/General Wesley. w. Johnny D. m. *"Uncle Albert/Admiral Halsey,* based on a performance by Paul McCartney." Published online at <http://www.amiright.com/parody/70s/paulmccartney23.shtml>. 2003.

100.48 Gray Tuesday. w. Paul Robinson. m. *"Ruby Tuesday,* based on a performance by The Rolling Stones." "California recently had the recall election in which Governor Gray Davis was removed and replaced by some guy named Arnold with a funny last name." Published online at <http://www.amiright.com/parody/60s/therollingstones17.shtml>. [ca. 2003].

100.49 Grizzly Bear Song. w.m. Don Ohman. On Cassette Tape: *Memories Of Montana.* Performed by "Amtrak" Don Ohman. "Gov. Schwarzenegger Gift. All profits go to Don's Nursing Home Entertainment Fund." 2004.

100.50 The Groper. w. William Tong. m. *"The Joker,* based the performance by Steve Miller Band." "Satire about Arnold Schwarzenegger GOP candidate for governor, who is known to have groped female actresses and talk show hosts. As sung by Arnold Schwarzenegger." Published online at <http://www.amiright.com/parody/70s/stevemillerband4.html>. 2003.

100.51 He's Got The Poll Girls In His Hands. w. Malcolm Higgins. m. *"He's Got The Whole World In His Hands,* based on a performance by Traditional." "The Arnie 'touchy feely' way to do things." Published online at <http://www.amiright.com/parody/misc/traditional267.shtml>. [ca. 2003].

100.52 How Come There's A Recall, California. w. William Tong. m. *"Hotel California,* based on the performance by The Eagles." "Satire about the Enron-rigged electrical blackouts in California, the right wing funded recall campaign for governor, and the behind-the-scenes scheming by the Bush White House to steal political power [in] California, a state the GOP has repeatedly lost in elections." Published online at <http://www.amiright.com/parody/70s/theeagles54/ html>. 2003.

100.53 I Am Ahhnold. w. Johnny D. m. *"I Am Woman,* based on a performance by Helen Reddy." Published online at <http://www.amiright.com/parody/70s/helenreddy7.shtml>. [ca. 2002].

100.54 I Am Governor Schwarzenegger. w. Paul Robinson. m. Tune — *"Mr. Zebra,* based on a performance by Tori Amos." "I know Rhonda Miller of Burbank, CA, who is the one suing the Governor... I can tell you that unless she has changed drastically that she is not a liar... The malicious and misleading smear the Governor's campaign henchmen laid on her is basically inexcusable as far as I'm concerned. I hop the Gov. can pull this State out of it's troubles but I can't say I have much respect or trust for him." Published online at <http://amiright.com/parody/60s/thenewchristieminstrels1.shtml. [ca. 2003].

100.55 I Run For Gov'nor, Maria. w. Michael Pacholek. m. Tune — *"Take A Letter Maria* originally by R.B. Greaves." Published online at <http://www.amiright.com/parody/60s/rbgreaves0.shtml>. 2003.

100.56 I Second That Emotion. w. Malcolm Higgins. m. *"I Second That Emotion,* based on a performance by Smokey Robinson." Published online at <http://www.amiright.com/parody/60s/smokeyrobinson2.shtml>. [ca. 2003].

100.57 If I Was The Governor. w. Malcolm Higgins. m. *"If I Had A Hammer,* based on the performance by Trini Lopez." Published online at <http://www.amiright.com/parody/60s/trinilopez1.shtml>. 2003.

100.58 I'll Be Back (The Arnold Schwarzenegger Song). w. Malcolm Higgins. m. *"I'll Be Back,* Based on a performance by The Beatles." "As you might have guessed, sung by Ahnold." Published online at <http://www.amiright.com/parody/60s/thebeatles172.shtml>. 2003

100.59 I'll Be Gov, Bush Wishes. w. William Tong. m. *"I'll Be Home For Christmas,* based on the performance by Bing Crosby." "As sung by the Republican gubernatorial candidate Arnold Schwarzenegger." Published online at <http://www.amiright.com/parody/misc/bingcrosby15.html>. 2003.

100.60 I'm Just Not Running. w. "crazydon." m. Tune — *"It Keep You Running* originally by The Doobie Brothers." "As we all know, California governor Gray Davis has been subjected to a recall, and lots of candidates have come out to run for governor, including Arnold Schwarzenegger, Gary Coleman and Angelyne. I don't live in California, I live in West Virginia, where our governor should be recalled due to some hanky-panky. But at least he's not running for re-election. What a relief ..." Published online at <http://www.amiright.com/parody/70s/thedoobiebrothers8.shtml>. 2003.

100.61 Leader (Aisle Be Bach). w. Guy DiRito. m. Tune — *"Leader Of The Pack,* based on a performance by The Shangri-Las." Published online at <http://

www.amiright.com/parody/60s/theshrangilas0.shml>. 2003.

100.62 Losin.' w. Malcolm Higgins. m. "*Groovin,'* based on a performance by The Rascals." Published online at <http://www.amiright.com/parody/60s/therascals4.shtml>. [ca. 2003].

100.63 Mambo #5-Plex. w. Sparki. m. "*Mambo #5,* based on a performance by Lou Bega." Published online at <http://www.amiright.com/parody/90s/loubega6.shtml>. [ca. 2003].

100.64 Mr. Universe. w. Malcolm Higgins. m. "*Across The Universe,* based on the performance by The Beatles." " Kongradulations Mr. Ahnold ... may I swear you in for your deposition ... tell us in your own words what happened." Published online at <http://www.amiright.com/parody/60s/thebeatles262.shtml>. [ca. 2002].

100.65 No Thanks To You. w. JamToafitu Petaia. m. "*Then Came You,* based on a performance by Spinners featuring Dionne Warrick." Published online at <http://www.amiright.com/parody/60s/spinnersfeaturingdionnewarrick0.shtml>. [ca. 2003].

100.66 Objection (To The Election). w. Malcolm Higgins. m. "*Objection,* based on a performance by Sakira." Published online at <http://www.amiright.com/parody/2000s/shakira35.shtml>. [ca. 2003].

100.67 Ode To The Terminator. w. Bob O'Mara. m. "*American Pie,* based on a performance by Don McLean." "This parody is dedicated to Arnie and all the other characters that brought the *Terminator* films to life ... If you have not seen the 3rd film, and want to, do not read." Published online at <http://www.amiright.com/parody/60s/donmclean2.shtml>. 2003.

100.68 Oh Arnold. w. William Tong. m. "*Oh Carol,* based on a performance by Neil Sedaka." "As sung by California Republican fat cats to their gubernatorial candidate, Arnold Schwarzenegger." Published online at <http://www.amiright.com/parody/60s/neilsedaka4.shtml>. 2003

100.69 Oh Little Town Of Anaheim. w. Malcolm Higgins. m. "*Oh Little Town Of Bethlehem,* based on a performance by Traditional Christmas." "Written in 1992, with a beer on a friend's dock ... yeah right." Published online at <http://www.amiright.com/parody/misc/traditionalchristmas2.shtml>. [ca. 2003].

100.70 Pine Cones And Halle Berry. w. Spaff.com. m. "*It's Beginning To Look A Lot Like Christmas/Pine Cones And Holly Berries,* originally by Meredith Willson." "Is it December yet? Robert Lund could release a Christmas CD this year, so I'm throwing lyrics at him." Published online at <http://www.amiright.com/parody/misc/meredithwillson0.shtml>. 2003

100.71 Please Don't Vote For Arnie. w. No composer indicated. m. Parody of *Don't Look Back In Anger* by Oasis." "Surprisingly, you might think, this song doesn't relate to the election of the most moronic, brain-dead, cringeingly [sic] right-wing actor ever to waist screen time in our cinemas. No, this isn't anything to do with Ronald Reagan — it's a song about Arnold Schwarzenegger for president in 2008? Stranger things have happened..." Published online at <http://www.chu.cam.ac.uk/~TSK23/Songs/original.html>. [ca. 2003].

100.72 Please Vote For Me California. w. Mark Hoolihan. m. "*Don't Cry For Me Argentina,* based on the performance by Madonna." "Just some campaign music for Arnold Schwarzenegger. Why? Because I Can." Published online at <http://www.amiright.com/parody/90s/madonna4.shtml>. 2003.

100.73 Pursuing Democrats. w. Fitu Petaia. m. "*I Wish,* based on a performance by Stevie Wonder." Published online at <http://www.amiright.com/parody/70s/steviewonder17.shtml>. [ca. 2003].

100.74 Recall California. w. Bob Gomez. m. "*Sweet Home Alabama,* originally by Lynyrd Skinner." "Darrell Issa spent nearly two million dollars to gather enough signatures for the recall. No he is out of the race and so is Bill Simon. In the latest polls, the number of Republicans who are afraid that Arnold will win roughly equals the number who are afraid he will lose." Published online at <http://www.amiright.com/parody/70s/lynyrdskynyrd12.shtml>. 2003.

100.75 Recall Vote Is Back Today (Political). w. Malcolm Higgins. m. "*Rock And Roll Is Here To Stay,* originally by Danny and the Juniors." Published online at <http://www.amiright.com/parody/misc/dannyandthejuniors8.shtml>. 2003.

100.76 Re-callin' (The Gray Davis Song). w. Malcolm Higgins. m. "*Free Fallin'* originally by Tom Petty." Published online at <http://www.amiright.com/parody/90s/tompetty11.shtml>. 2003.

100.77 Recalling Gray. w. Alex Murray. m. "*Auf Wiedersehen,* based on a performance by Cheap Trick." "Haven't done a parody in a while, so this is a bit rusty. To clarify, all bye-byes, goodbyes, so longs, etc are directed towards Red Davis." Published online at <http://www.amiright.com/parody/70s/cheaptrick3.shtml>. 2003.

100.78 The Right Before. w. Malcolm Higgins. m. "*The Night Before,* based on a performance by The Beatles." Published online at <http://www.amiright.com/parody/60s/beatles206.shtml>. [ca. 2003].

100.79 Right Wing Wants To Reign In All Of California. w. William Tong. m. "*It Never Rains In Southern California,* originally by Albert Hammond." Published online at <http://www.amiright.com/parody/70s/alberthammond4.shtml>. 2003.

100.80 Sacramento In My Mind. w. Bubba. m. "*Carolina In My Mind,* based on a performance by James Taylor." "As sung by Arnold Schwarzenegger (the next Governor of California)." Published online at <http://www.amiright.com/parody/70s/jamestaylor12.shtml>. 2003.

100.81 Schwarzenegger. w. Phil Nelson. m. "*Baba O'riley,* based on a performance by The Who." Published online at <http://www.amiright.com/parody/70s/thewho30.shtml>. 2003

100.82 Schwarzenegger. w. William Tong. m. "*Operator,* based on a performance by Jim Croce." "As sung by California Republican fat cats to Arnold Schwarzenegger." Published online at <http://www.amiright.com/parody/70s/jimcroce13.shtml>. 2003

100.83 Schwarzenegger. w. Michael Pacholek. m. "*Get Together,* based on a performance by The Youngbloods." "I don't think the Youngbloods had the original, but until I can find out for sure, I'll list them as such. As I said, Ahnold is begging for one of these, and he's getting lots of them, and here's my swing at the pitch." Published online at <http://www.amiright.com/parody/60s/theyoungbloods0.shtml>. 2003

100.84 Schwarzenegger. w. Malcolm Higgins. m. "*Come Together,* originally by The Beatles." Published online at <http://www.amiright.com/parody/60s/thebeatles193.shtml>. 2003

100.85 Schwarzenegger. w. Malcolm Higgins. m. "*Oh Susanna,* originally by Traditional." Published online at <http://www.amiright.com/parody/misc/publicdomain2.shtml>. 2003

100.86 Schwarzenegger Got Stoned. w. Adam Bernstein. m. "*Like A Rolling Stone,* originally by Bob Dylan." Published online at <http://www.amiright.com/parody/60s/bobdylan25.shtml>. 2003.

100.87 Squishin And Gropin. w. Malcolm Higgins. m. "*Wishin And Hopin,* based on the performance by Dusty Springfield." Published online at <http://www.amiright.com/parody/60s/dustyspringfield8/html>. [ca. 2002].

100.88 Sweet Home California. w. "Static." m. Tune — "*Sweet Home Alabama* by Lynyrd Skynyrd." "Inspired by X games' sweet home calif. Tony hawk 900! Booya! Back from vaca and better than ever. Must have been that smelly bear poo by the dumpster. Here goes nothing ... [sic]." Published online at <http://www.amiright.com/parody/70s/lynyrdskynyrd11.shtml>. 2003.

100.88A The Tail Of Darrell Issa (The Car Thief Who Went Bad). w. Stephen Baird. m. No tune indicated. N/c photo of Mike Byron — "Human need above political greed." Lyrics published online at <http://byron.blogcap.com/archive/campaign_song_the_tale_of_darrell_issa.php>. 2004.

100.89 Terminator. w. Susanna Viljanen. m. "*Conquistador,* based on a performance by Procol Harem." Published online at <http://www.amiright.com/parody/60s/procolharem0.shtml>. 2003

100.90 The Terminator. w. William Tong. m. "*My Generation,* based on a performance by The Who." "Satire about Republican candidate for Governor of California, Arnold Schwarzenegger." Published online at <http://www.amiright.com/parody/60s/thewho22.shtml>. 2003

100.91 This Year's Misses (The Gray Davis Song). w. Malcolm Higgins. m. "*This Year's Kisses,* based on a performance by Dick Powell." Published online at <http://www.amiright.com/parody/misc/dickpowell19370.shtml>. [ca. 2003].

100.92 Total Recall Of The Gray. w. Michael Pacholek. m. "*Total Eclipse Of The Heart,* originally by Bonnie Tyler." Published online at <http://www.amiright.com/parody/80s/bonnietyler8.shtml>. 2003.

100.93 Trendy Mane (A Valley Girl Saga). w. Mary & Pippen. m. "*Ariel,* based on a performance by Dean Friedman." "If you aren't familiar with the song, please download it — it's a treat! We left the 'vertical hold' line alone with one slight change — it was too good to mess with...." Published online at <http://www.amiright.com/parody/70s/deanfriedman0.shtml>. 2003

100.94 Try The Spinach. w. DJ-Johnny & Lars. m. "*Go The Distance,* based on a performance by Michael Bolton." "One of my top favorites that I've ever written, It's in my long line of songs about food. Enjoy." Published online at <http://www.amiright.com/parody/90s/michaelbolton0.shtml>. [ca. 2003].

100.95 Turfin' Gray Today. w. Malcolm Higgins. m. "*Surfin' USA,* based on a performance by The Beach Boys." Published online at <http://www.amiright.com/parody/60s/thebeachboys19.shtml>. [ca. 2003].

100.96 Vote. w. Moscowman. m. "*Vogue,* based on a performance by Madonna." "The Election is coming in November, voters reading the magazines and think what's their decision on the upcoming election." Published online at <http://amiright.com/parody/90s/thekinks3.shtml. [2004].

100.97 Vote For Schwarzenegger. w. Mike Armstrong. m. "*Walk A Little Straighter,* based on a performance by Billy Currington." "Though a registered republican, I, Jordan do not mean this as a slam on his chances nor an endorsement to his candidacy. It's more a mock of the whole debacle going on out there." Published online at <http://www.amiright.com/parody/2000s/0.shtml>. [ca. 2003].

100.98 Vote For The Terminator. w. Rice Cube & Walt Daddy. m. "*We Didn't Start The Fire,* originally by Billy Joel." "We're not completely endorsing Schwarzenegger because we don't know his complete platform, but considering that voting for Bustamontte will be worse than keeping Davis in power, and Ahnuld is the leading Republican candidate who has a ghost's chance in hell of becoming governor..." Published online at Published online at <http://www.amiright.com/parody/80s/billyjoel62.shtml>. 2003.

100.99 We Can Kick Him Out (Gray Davis Recall). w. Jamie L. m. "*We Can Work It Out,* based on a performance by Beatles." "Inspired by California's recall of Governor Davis." Published online at <http://www.amiright.com/parody/60s/beatles70.shtml>. [ca. 2003].

100.100 Wish They All Could Lead California. w. M. Spaff Sumsion. m. "Parody of *California Girls.*" "'Recorded by Robert Lund' on MP3." Published online at <http://www.spaff.com/posey/california.html>. 2003.

100.101 With A Little Help From The Reds. w. Malcolm Higgins. m. "*With A Little Help From My Friends,* based on a performance by The Beatles. Published online at <http://www.amiright.com/parody/60s/thebeatles209.shtml>. [ca. 2003].

• AmPM-101 SINCLAIR, Upton (Candidate for U.S. House, 1920; Candidate for U.S. Senate, 1922; Candidate for Governor, 1928 & 1934)

101.1 Anthem Of Freedom. w.m. Margaret J. Honn. Published by Hollywood Publishers, Hollywood, CA. 1934. Bl/w photos/drawings of Franklin D. Roosevelt and Upton Sinclair. R/w/b drawing of the Statue of Liberty, stars and stripes. "Dedicated to Franklin D. Roosevelt and Upton Sinclair." 6pp. Page 6: Blank. [Crew/FDR-246].

101.2 End Poverty In California (And Upton Sinclair Will Show The Way). w.m. No composer indicated. Published by End Poverty League, Inc., 1245 South Flower Street, Los Angeles, CA. 1934. B/w photo of — "Upton Sinclair" [facsimile signature]. Bl/w drawing of a bee — "E-P-I-C, I Produce, I Defend."

"End Poverty In California Official Campaign Song, Upton Sinclair." 4pp. Page 4: Blank.

101.3 *Epic Plan Song*. w.m. Ray D. Woodruff. Published by Ray Music Co., P.O. Box 41, Long Beach, CA. 1934. Bl/w photo of "Upton Sinclair" Bl/w geometric designs. 4pp. Page 2: At top of music—"Dedicated to the Epic Plan."

101.4 *The Reveille* (Song) w. Bret Harte. m. John Bartow Montell. Published by Edward Schuberth & Co., 11 East 22nd Street, New York, NY. 1918. [Donated for sale probably ca. 1934]. B/w non-pictorial geometric designs. Music was counter stamped with the following message: "Epic Auction Sale, Campaign Fund, Upton Sinclair for Governor, 2826 S. Vermont—Every Wednesday, 1 p.m., If you will donate merchandise, phone *MO*rningside 16121 or *RE*public 9618 [?]." 8pp. Pages 2 and 7: Blank. Page 8: Advertising.

- **AmPM-102 SNEDDON, Thomas W., Jr.** (District Attorney, Santa Barbara County, 1983–Present)

102.1 *D.S.* w.m. Michael Jackson. On CD: *HIStory: Past, Present And Future, Book 1*. Sony #0000029LG. 2 CDs. 1995. Lyrics printed at <http://lyricscafe.com/jackson_michael/ds.html>.

- **AmPM-103 STANFORD, Sally** (Vice-President, Chamber of Commerce, Sausalito; City Council, Sausalito, 1972–1976; Mayor, Sausalito, 1976–?)

103.1 *Lady Of The House*. w.m. Dyke Davis, Myron Crandall, Minco De Burvin and William Aaron. No publisher indicated. Copyright 1978 by Dyke Davis, Myron Crandall, Minco De Burvin and William Aaron. [8½" × 11"]. Gd/ma photo of Sally Stanford against a backdrop of sheet music. "Dedicated to Sally Stanford." "Introduced by Pamela Brooks." 6pp.

103.2 *Lady Of The House*. w.m. Dyke Davis, Myron Crandall, Minco De Burvin and William Aaron. No publisher indicated. Copyright 1978 by Dyke Davis, Myron Crandall, Minco De Burvin and William Aaron. [8½" × 11"]. Non-pictorial. "Dedicated to Sally Stanford." "Introduced by Pamela Brooks." 2pp.

103.3 *Re-Elect Sally Stanford Sausalito Councilwoman*. w.m. No composers indicated. No publisher indicated. Copyright 1979 by Dyke Davis, Myron Crandall, Minco De Burvin and William Aaron. [8½" × 11"]. Bl/bk star and stripes. "Dedicated to Sally Stanford." "Introduced by Pamela Brooks." 2pp.

- **AmPM-104 TOWNSEND, Francis Everett** (Pension Reformer; Author of the Townsend Plan for Old Age Assistance, 1930s)

104.1 *America My America* (March Song). w.m. Zena Stevens, Stevens, South Dakota "(Also Author of *Heads Up America*)." Published by the Townsend National Recovery Plan, 450 East Ohio Street, Chicago, IL. 1940. Pl/w photo of "Doctor Francis E. Townsend, A Man With A Plan." "Featured by Verna (Tootie) Stevens, Chicago; Madame Mamie Stark, Los Angeles." "Official Song." 4pp.

104.2 *America Stand Up Today* (March Song). w.m. William Tansey. Published by Leftwich Publishing Company, 846 Broadway, Los Angeles, CA. Copyright 1938 by Townsend National Recovery Plan, Inc. Bl/w photo of Dr. Francis Townsend. Bl/w stars, stripes. "Featured by Mamie Stark, Third Townsend National Convention, June, 1938, Los Angeles, California." "Official Song Townsend National Plan." 4pp. Page 4: Logo of the Townsend Plan.

104.3 *Heads Up America* (March Song). w.m. Zena Stevens, Stevens, South Dakota. Published by Zena Stevens, Stevens, SD. 1939. Bl/w photo of Verna Stephens. "Featured by Verna (Tootie) Stevens, Chicago." "Official Song Townsend National Recovery Plan, Convention Edition." 4pp. Page 3: At bottom of music—"Copies of this song may be purchased from the Publisher, Zena Stevens, Stevens, So. Dakota, or National Representatives at all Townsend Clubs, or direct from National Headquarters, 450 East Ohio Street, Chicago," Page 4: Printer's address.

104.4 *Hello! Good Times* (To The Townsend-Plan Let's Go) (March Song). w.m. Norman Moray. Published by Paul Music Co., Indianapolis, IN. 1935. B/w non-pictorial geometric designs. 4pp. Page 2: Inside subtitle—"To the O-A-R-P" Let's Go." Page 4: Blank.

104.5 *Just Over The Hill* (The Townsend Plan Song). w.m. R.E. Higley. Published by Higley Music Company, 210 Olive Street, St. Louis, MO. 1935. Bl/w photo of Mr. and Mrs. Higley. "Featured by The Higleys." Bl/w drawing of a meadow, trees, flowers. 4pp. Page 2: At top of music—"Dedicated to Geo. C. Higley, President Club 93, Los Angeles, Cal." Page 4: Blank.

104.6 *March Of The Townsendites*. w.m. U.S.A. Heggbolm, Max Bates and Harmon Charles. Published by The National Recovery Music Publishing Co., Detroit. MI. 1940. Y/bk photo of Dr. Townsend, geometric design frame. 6pp. Page 2: Blank. Page 6: *America* with words and music. "Records of this song and talks by Dr. Townsend are Available."

104.7 *Put Over The Townsend Plan*. w.m. Charlotte Rogers Palmer. Published by Dasch, Reed and Love, Music Library of Chicago, 64 East Jackson Boulevard, Chicago, IL. May, 1936. Bl/w non-pictorial. "The Townsend Rally Song." "Dedicated to Dr. Francis E. Townsend." 4pp. Page 4: Blank.

104.8 *Song Poems*. w. Coribel Shantz, Boulder, Colorado. Copyright by Coribel Shantz [1935]. [5⅜" × 8¾"]. Bk/be litho of floral and geometric design, deer. 20pp. Songs include: *[In Nineteen Thirty Five]*. {104.8-1}. w. Townsend lyrics. m. "Tune, *America*." Page 2; *[Hail, Hail, The Townsend Plan]* {104.8-2}. w. Townsend lyrics. m. "Tune—*Hail, Hail, The Gangs All Here*." Page 2; *[Goodnight, Members]* {104.8-3}. w. Townsend lyrics. m. "Tune—*Goodnight, Ladies*." Page 2; *[Gone Are The Days]* {104.8-4}. w. Townsend lyrics. m. "Tune—*Old Black Joe*." Page 3; *[There Are Smiles]* {104.8-5}. w. Townsend lyrics. m. "Tune—*Smiles*." Page 4; *[In The Evening By The Moonlight]* {104.8-6}. w. Townsend lyrics. m. "Tune—*In The Evening By The Moonlight*." Page 4; *[We're Singing Tonight]* {104.8-7}. w. Townsend lyrics. m. "Tune—*We're Tenting Tonight*." Page 5; *[Here Townsend Comes]* {104.8-8}. w. Townsend lyrics. m. "Tune—Bridal Chorus from *Lohengrin*." Page 6; *[Townsend Will Shine Tonight]* {104.8-9}. w. Townsend lyrics. m. "Tune—*Our Boys Will Shine Tonight*." Page 6; *[We Should Not Turn A Deaf Ear To Townsend]*

{104.8-10}. w. Townsend lyrics. m. "Tune — *The Little Brown Church.*" Page 7; *[Right, Left — Right, Left!]* {104.8-11}. w. Townsend lyrics. m. "Tune — *The Sidewalks Of New York.*" Page 8; *[Far O'er The Mountain]* {104.8-12}. w. Townsend lyrics. m. Tune — *Juanita.*" Page 9; *[If A Body Wants A Thriller]* {104.8-13}. w. Townsend lyrics. m. "Tune — *Comin' Thro' The Rye.*" Page 10; *[Sacred Days Of Happy Meeting]* {104.8-14}. w. Townsend lyrics. m. "Tune — *Love Devine* and *Hail Thou Once Despised.*" Page 10; *[Forging Right Ahead]* {104.8-15}. w. Townsend lyrics. m. "Tune — *Jingle Bells.*" Page 11; *[Onward Townsend Soldiers]* {104.8-16}. w. Townsend lyrics. m. "Tune — *Onward Christian Soldiers.*" Page 12; *[Our Townsend's Not Overly Troubled]* {104.8-17}. w. Townsend lyrics. m. "Tune — *Bring Back My Bonnie.*" Page 13; *[Hello, Townsends, Glad To Meet You]* {104.8-18}. w. Townsend lyrics. m. "*Goodbye, Dolly Gray.*" Page 14; *[The Townsends Gain Momentum]* {104.8-19}. w. Townsend lyrics. m. "Tune — *The Soldier's Farewell.*" Page 14; *[Believe Me When I Tell You This Is Your Day]* {104.8-20}. w. Townsend lyrics. m. "Tune — *Believe Me, If All Those Endearing Young Charms.*" Page 15; *[It's A Long Hard Road For Townsend]* {104.8-21}. w. Townsend lyrics. m. "Tune — *There's A Long, Long Trail A-Winding.*" Page 16; *[Here Dem Bells]* {104.8-22}. w. Townsend lyrics. m. "Tune — *Hear Dem Bells.*" Page 16; *[The Bells Ring Of Townsend]* {104.8-23}. w. Townsend lyrics. m. "Tune — *The Bells Of St. Mary's.*" Page 17; *[Put On Your Bright New Armor]* {104.8-24}. w. Townsend lyrics. m. "Tune — *Put On Your Old Gray Bonnet.*" Page 18; *[The Sun Shines Bright In Each And Every State]* {104.8-25}. w. Townsend lyrics. m. "Tune — *My Old Kentucky Home.*" Page 19; *[T-Is For The Thousand Things 'T will Give Us]* {104.8-26}. w. Townsend lyrics. m. "Tune — *Mother.*" Page 20; *[There Is No Easy Path To Glory Or To Fame]* {104.8-27}. w. Townsend lyrics. m. "Tune — *Drink to Me Only With Thine Eyes.*" Page 20.

104.9 35 Townsend Songs To Be Used At Townsend Meetings. c. J.F. Winneur, "Lecturer, Musician & Song Leader, Giving full time for our cause." Published by the Kingston Townsend Glee, Detroit, MI. [1937-1941]. [9" × 12¾"]. B/w photo of "J.F. Winneur & Trombone, Organizer." "To be used at Townsend Meetings." 4pp. Page 4: At bottom of music — "5 cents each, $4.00 per hundred, J.F. Winneur, 96 Avalon, Detroit (Highland Park, Mich)." Songs include: **God Bless America** {104.9-1}. w. Traditional. m. *God Bless America.* Page 1; **America** {104.9-2}. w. Traditional. m. *America.* Page 1; **Star-Spangled Banner** {104.9-3}. w. Traditional. m. *Star-Spangled Banner.* Page 1; **God Be With You** {104.9-4}. w. Traditional. m. *God Be With You.* Page 1; **When The Roll Is Called** {104.9-5}. w. Townsend lyrics. m. *When The Roll Is Called.* Page 1; **Be A Townsend Man** {104.9-6}. w. Townsend lyrics. m. "Tune — *Coming Through The Rye.*" Page 1; **My Country Lies Over** {104.9-7}. w. Townsend lyrics. m. *My Bonnie.* Page 1; **Smiles** {104.9-8}. w. Townsend lyrics. m. *Smiles.* Page 1; **Long Long Trail** {104.9-9}. w. Townsend lyrics. m. *Long Long Trail.* Page 2; **Old Gray Bonnet** {104.9-10}. w. Townsend lyrics. m. *Old Gray Bonnet.* Page 2; **My Old Kentucky Home** {104.9-11}. w. Traditional. m. *My Old Kentucky Home.* Page 2; **The Townsend Battle Cry** {104.9-12}. w. Townsend lyrics. m. No tune indicated. Page 2; **Stand By America** {104.9-13}. w. Traditional. m. *Stand By America.* Page 2; **Loves Old Sweet Song** {104.9-14}. w. Townsend lyrics. m. *Loves Old Sweet Song.* Page 2; **Tramp, Tramp, Tramp** {104.9-15}. w. Townsend lyrics. m. *Tramp, Tramp, Tramp.* Page 2; **Stand Up, Stand Up For Townsend** {104.9-16}. w. Townsend lyrics. m. No tune indicated. Page 2; **Townsend Soldiers** {104.9-17}. w. Traditional. m. *Onward Christian Soldiers.* Page 2; **Yankee Doodle** {104.9-18}. w. Townsend lyrics. m. *Yankee Doodle.* Page 3; **March Of The Townsendites** {104.9-19}. w. Townsend lyrics. m. No tune indicated. Page 3; **Vision Of Hope** {104.9-20}. w. Townsend lyrics. m. "Tune — *Columbia Gem Of The Ocean.*" Page 3; **Work For The Townsend Plan.** {104.9-21}. w. Townsend lyrics. m. "Tune — *Night Is Coming.*" Page 3; **The Townsend Plan** {104.9-22}. w. Townsend lyrics. m. "Tune — *America The Beautiful.*" Page 3; **Pack Up Your Troubles** {104.9-23}. w. Townsend lyrics. m. *Pack Up Your Troubles.* Page 3; **All-Hail!** {104.9-24}. w. Townsend lyrics. m. *All-Hail!* Page 3; **Keep The Old Folks Happy** {104.9-25}. w. Townsend lyrics. m. No tune indicated. Page 3; **Townsend Plan Is Here To Stay** {104.9-26}. w. Townsend lyrics. m. "Tune — *Maryland, My Maryland.*" Page 3; **Almost Persuaded** {104.9-27}. w. Townsend lyrics. m. *Almost Persuaded.* Page 4; **Dixie** {104.9-28}. w. Townsend lyrics. m. *Dixie.* Page 4; **Old Black Joe** {104.9-29}. w. Townsend lyrics. m. *Old Black Joe.* Page 4; **Blest Be The Tie** {104.9-30}. w. Townsend lyrics. m. *Blest Be The Tie.* Page 4; **Old Rugged Cross** {104.9-31}. w. Townsend lyrics. m. *Old Rugged Cross.* Page 4; **Battle Cry Of Freedom** {104.9-32}. w. Townsend lyrics. m. *Battle Cry Of Freedom.* Page 4; **Marching Through Georgia** {104.9-33}. w. Townsend lyrics. m. *Marching Through Georgia.* Page 4; **Townsend Battle Cry Of Republic** {104.9-34}. w. Townsend lyrics. m. *Battle Hymn Of The Republic.* Page 4; **Auld Lang Syne** {104.9-35}. w. Townsend lyrics. m. *Auld Lang Syne.* Page 4.

104.10 Three Cheers For Dr. Townsend. w.m. M.A. Coffey and M.M. Currie. Published by M.A. Coffey, 3629 East 8th Street, Long Beach, CA. 1936. Bl/w drawing of a horn of plenty with coins spilling. 4pp. Page 4: Blank.

104.11 Three Cheers For Dr. Townsend. w.m. Kenneth M. Day. Published by Radio Music Guild, 1650 Broadway, New York, NY. Copyright 1936 by Kenneth M. Day. [8½" × 11"]. B/w litho of two men at a piano. "Professional Copy Tax Free." "Vocal arrangement with piano accompaniment." "Issued for the convenience of Singing Artists of the Screen Radio Stage." 4pp. Page 4: Blank.

104.12 Townsend Campaign Hymn. w. No composer indicated. m. No composer indicated. Published in *Time Magazine*, December 23, 1935, page 50. B/w photo of "Dr. Francis Townsend" and two supporters. Narrative on *Time's* upcoming examination of The Townsend Plan. Musical notation for two lines of the music.

104.13 Townsend Convention Song Book. Published by the Townsend National Recovery Plan for the

Cleveland, Ohio, Convention, 1936. Copyright 1936 by Frank Dryer. [4⅜" × 8¼"]. Be/r geometric design border, Townsend Plan logos. 34pp. Page 2: Letter "To The Townsend Family." Page 3: At bottom of music—"Please note, the entire proceeds from the sale of this book go toward expenses of our convention." Page 32: Blank. Townsend related songs include: *That Townsend Man* {104.13-1}. w. Mamie Stark, Los Angeles, CA. m. "Tune—*Ol Man River.*" Page 1; *Townsend Legion* {104.13-2}. w. Frank Dryer, D.D. m. "Tune—*Onward Christian Soldiers.*" Page 2; *Our Plan Is Marching On* {104.13-3}. w. Mrs. Riches and Mrs. Burnham, Los Angeles, CA. m. "Tune—*The Battle Hymn Of The Republic.*" Page 2; *Work, Work, Work* {104.13-4}. w. Judge John Carabine, Springfield, MA. m. "Tune—*Tramp, Tramp, Tramp.*" Page 3; *Townsend Home Song* {104.13-5}. w. C.H. Johnson, Colorado. m. "Tune—*Home On The Range.*" Page 3; *On To Victory* {104.13-6}. w. E.T. Zimmerman, Los Angeles, CA. m. "Tune—*The Battle Hymn Of The Republic.*" Page 4; *The Townsend Plan Of Freedom* {104.13-7}. w. Ada Williams, Seattle, WA. m. "Tune—*The Battle Cry Of Freedom.*" Page 4; *Dedicated To The Townsend Plan* {104.13-8}. w. "Townsend Club No. 1, San Pedro, CA." m. "Tune—*The Battle Hymn Of The Republic.*" Page 5; *The Townsend Plan* {104.13-9}. w. Frank Dryer. m. "Tune—*America.*" Page 5; *The Battle Cry Of Townsend* {104.13-10}. w. Wm. Anwyl Jones, Oaks, CA. m. "Tune—*The Battle Cry Of Freedom.*" Page 6; *Townsend Rally Song* {104.13-11}. w. G.C. Burton, Los Angeles, CA. m. "Tune—*The Battle Hymn Of The Republic.*" Page 6; *Around The Corner* {104.13-12}. w. H.W. Sample, Hastings, NB. m. "Tune—*Marching Through Georgia.*" Page 7; *Be A Townsend Man* {104.13-13}. w. Belle Lammers. m. "Tune—*Coming Through The Rye.*" Page 7; *The Townsend Song* {104.13-14}. w. Mrs. Burr S. Rogers, Lindsey, OH. m. "Tune—*Marching Through Georgia.*" Page 8; *Love's Old Sweet Song* {104.13-15}. w. J.L. Molloy. m. "Tune—*Love's Old Sweet Song.*" Page 8; *Prosperity* {104.13-16}. w. Mrs. P.W. Miller and Mrs. Clara Taylor, New Smyrna, FL. m. "Tune—*Auld Lang Syne.*" Page 9; *Freedom* {104.13-17}. w. William Kennedy Mason. m. "Tune—*America The Beautiful.*" Page 9; *The Townsend Plan* {104.13-18}. w. Chauncey H. King, Glendale, CA. m. "Tune—*The Battle Hymn Of The Republic.*" Page 10; *A Challenge To Congress* {104.13-19}. w. No composer indicated. m. "Adapted from the old *Trelawney Cry.*" Page 10; *Rally For The Plan* {104.13-20}. w. S.J. Eddy, Lansing, MI. m. "Tune—*The Battle Cry Of Freedom.*" Page 11; *Cheer Up* {104.13-21}. w. Mamie Stark, Los Angeles, CA. m. No tune indicated. Page 11; *We Are Coming, Dr. Townsend* {104.13-22}. w. Dr. W.J. Rhynsburger, Los Angeles, CA. m. "Tune—*It's A Long Way To Tipperary.*" Page 12; *The Townsend Pension* {104.13-23}. w. Dr. E. Billman, St. Petersburg, FL. m. "Tune—*Old-Time Religion.*" Page 12; *Marching To Victory* {104.13-24}. w. S.J. Eddy, Lansing, MI. m "Tune—*Marching Through Georgia.*" Page 13; *The Old Oaken Bucket* {104.13-25}. w. Samuel Woodworth. m. Tune—*The Old Oaken Bucket.* Page 13; *The Cleveland Convention* {104.13-26}. w. Dr. W.J. Rhynsburger, Los Angeles, CA. m. "Tune—*Over There.*" Page 14; *Vision Of Hope* {104.13-27}. w. William Kennedy Mason. m. "Tune—*Columbia The Gem Of The Ocean.*" Page 14; *The Star Spangled Banner* {104.13-28}. w. Francis Scott Key. "Tune—*The Star Spangled Banner.*" Page 15; *The Dr. Townsend Spirit* {104.13-29}. w. Dr. W.J. Rhynsburger, Los Angeles, CA. m. No tune indicated. Page 15; *Oh, Give Us A Plan* {104.13-30}. w. Mrs. O.L. Barnes, Denver, CO. m. "Tune—*Home On The Range.*" Page 16; *The Morning Light Is Breaking* {104.13-31}. w. J.J. Phare, Berea, OH. m. "Tune—*Old Church Tune.*" Page 16; *Get Behind The Townsend Plan* {104.13-32}. w. Joseph E. Harvey. m. "Tune—*Quilting Party—I Was Seeing Nellie Home.*" Page 17; *Home, Sweet Home* {104.13-33}. w. John Howard Payne. Tune—*Home, Sweet Home.* Page 17; *Convention Rally Song* {104.13-34}. w. Frank Dyer. m. "Tune—*Coming 'Round The Mountain.*" Page 120; *Have Faith* {104.13-35}. w. Frank Dyer, D.D. m. "Gospel hymn tune *Have Faith In God.*" Page 20; *Townsend Cheer Song* {104.13-36}. w. Miss Bessie Whitfield. m. "*Marching Through Georgia.*" Page 21; *Our Plan Is Marching On* {104.13-37}. w. William Kennedy Mason. m. "Tune—*The Battle Hymn Of The Republic.*" Page 22; *Townsend Plan Is Here To Stay* {104.13-38}. w. Mrs. Nellie Plath. m. "Tune—*Maryland, My Maryland.*" Page 22; *How Do Ye Do!* {104.13-39}. w. Rev. O.L. Barnes, Denver, CO. m. No tune indicated. Page 23; *The Townsend Trail* {104.13-40}. w. Mrs. Al. T. Fox, San Diego, CA. m. "Tune—*Long, Long Trail.*" Page 23; *Pack Up Your Troubles* {104.13-41}. w. Mary E. Klinsmann, Fargo, ND. m. "Tune—*Pack Up Your Troubles.*" Page 24; *Marching To Congress* {104.13-42}. w. Cordelia Jewett Harvey, Canon City, CO. m. "Tune—*Marching Through Georgia.*" Page 24; *Blest Be The Tie* {104.13-43}. w. No composer indicated. m. *Blest Be The Tie.* Page 25; *New Battle Hymn Of The Republic* {104.13-44}. w. H.C. Hughes. m. "Tune—*The Battle Hymn Of The Republic.*" Page 25; *Back To Congress* {104.13-45}. w. Adis Logan, Kansas City. m. "Tune—*Hold The Fort.*" Page 26; *The Townsend Plan* {104.13-46}. w. Carey E. Swinington, Cleveland, OH. m. "Tune—*America The Beautiful.*" Page 26; *Is That So!* {104.13-47}. w. Mrs. Adelia Fuller, Michigan Center, MI. m. No tune indicated. Page 26. *God Be With You* {104.13-48}. w. No composer indicated. m. No tune indicated. Page 27; *Ruben And Rachel* {104.13-49}. w. Mrs. A.C. Bailey, Burley, ID. m. "Tune—*Ruben And Rachel.*" Page 27; *Prosperity* {104.13-50}. w. Mrs. P.W. Miller and Mrs. Clara Taylor. m. "Tune—*Auld Lang Syne.*" Page 28; *Praise To Our Leader* {104.13-51}. w. Orpha Estelle PeGan, Cleveland, OH. m. "Tune—*My Country 'Tis Of Thee.*" Page 28; *Working For The Townsend* {104.13-52}. w. Dr. H. Raider Morgan, Los Angeles, CA. m. "Tune—*Marching Through Georgia.*" Page 29; *We Are Here, Dr. Townsend* {104.13-53}. w. Mamie Stark, Los Angeles, CA. m. "Tune—*Howdy Everybody.*" Page 29; *One Land Are We* {104.13-54}. w. Frank Dyer, D.D. m. "Tune National Hymn 10, 10, 10, 10." Page 30; *Two Short Years* {104.13-55}. w. Charles Mason, Roush, Chicago, IL. m. "Tune—*Three Blind Mice.*" Page 30; *On To Washington* {104.13-56}. w. No composer indicated. m. "Tune—*Hold The Fort.*" Page 30;

Townsend Soldiers {104.13-57}. w. Ethna F. Benedict, Yucapia, CA. m. "Tune—*Onward Christian Soldiers.*" Page 31; **Hail Dr. Townsend** {104.13-58}. w. Evangeline Burnham, Los Angeles, CA. m. "Tune—*Over There.*" Page 31; **On With Townsend** {104.13-59}. w. Josephine G. Whittemore, Chatsworth, CA. m. "Tune—*On Wisconsin.*" Page 32; **Walk Out** {104.13-60}. w. Mrs. Frank Dryer. m. "Tune—*My Bonnie Lies Over The Ocean.*" Page 32 **Ye Townsend People** {104.13-61}. w. Alice Spencer French. m. "Tune—*Onward Christian Soldiers.*" Page 32.

104.14 Townsend O.A.R.P. Campaign Song. w. A. John Engler. Published by A. John Engler, M.E. Church, Franklin, IN. [1936]. [5" × 7⅜"]. Bl/bk nonpictorial geometric design border. "The Spirit of Modern Evolution." 4pp. Page 3: At bottom of music—"Dedicated to Dr. F.E. Townsend, founder of the O.A.R.P. and National Townsend Clubs in the U.S.A." Page 4: "Order this O.A.R.P. Campaign song for your Townsend Clubs. It will serve to put life and enthusiasm into your O.A.R.P. endeavor."

104.15 Townsend Official Song Book. Published for the Third Townsend National Convention, June 1938, Los Angeles, CA. 1938. [5" × 6⅞"]. R/bl lines, stars, official Townsend seal. 44pp; **America** {104.15-1}. w.m. Standard patriotic song. Page 1; **The Battle-Cry Of Townsend!** {104.15.2} w. Townsend lyrics. m. "Tune—*Battle-Cry Of Freedom.*" Page 3; **God Be With you** {104.15-3}. w. Townsend lyrics. m. No tune indicated. Page 3; **Townsend Soldiers** {104.15-4}. w. Townsend lyrics. m. "Tune—*Onward Christian Soldiers.*" Page 4; **Work For The Townsend Plan** {104.15-5}. w. Townsend lyrics. m. "Tune—*Work For The Night Is Coming.*" Page 5; **When The Roll Is Called Up Yonder** {104.15-6}. w. Townsend lyrics. m. Tune—*When The Roll Is Called Up Yonder.* Page 5; **That Man Townsend** {104.15-7}. w. Townsend lyrics. m. No tune indicated. Page 6; **Oh! Say But I'm Glad** {104.15-8}. w. Townsend lyrics. m. No tune indicated. Page 7; **The Townsend Plan** {104.15-9}. w. Townsend lyrics. m. "Tune—*Auld Lang Syne.*" Page 7; **Townsend Song** {104.15-10}. w. Townsend lyrics. m. "Tune—*My Maryland.*" Page 8; **Victory Song** {104.15-11}. w. Townsend lyrics. m. "Tune—*Marching Through Georgia.*" Page 8; **Home Sweet Home** {104.15-12}. w.m. Standard popular song. Page 9; *[Now Remember To Boost The Plan]* {104.15-13}. w. Townsend lyrics. m. "Tune—*In The Shade Of The Old Apple Tree.*" Page 9; *[The Townsend Plan Is Here To Stay]* {104.15-14}. w. Townsend lyrics. m. "Tune—*Maryland, My Maryland.*" Page 10; *[There's A Gold Mine In The Sky]* {104.15-15}. w. Townsend lyrics. m. "Tune—*There's A Gold Mine In The Sky.*" Page 10; **Star Spangled Banner** {104.15-16}. w.m. Standard patriotic song. Page 11; **Three Cheers For The Great Townsend Plan** {104.15-17}. w. Townsend lyrics. m. "Tune—*Old Rugged Cross.*" Page 12; *[The Fight Is On]* {104.15-18}. w. Townsend lyrics. m. "Tune—*The Fight Is On.*" Page 12; **America Invincible** {104.15-19}. w.m. Standard patriotic song. Page 13; **Blest Be The Tie** {104.15-20}. w.m. Standard religious song. Page 14; **Four Short Years** {104.15-21}. w. Townsend lyrics. m. "Tune—*Three Blind Mice.*" Page 14; **Working For The Townsend** {104.15-22}. w. Townsend lyrics. m. "Tune—*Marching Through Georgia.*" Page 15; **Love's Old Sweet Song** {104.15-23}. w.m. Standard popular song. Page 16; *[With The Loyal Townsend Workers]* {104.15-24}. w. Townsend lyrics. m. "Tune—*When The Roll-Call Is Called Up Yonder.*" Page 16; **On With Townsend** {104.15-25}. w. Townsend lyrics. m. "Tune—*On Wisconsin.*" Page 17; *[Dr. Townsend Has A Plan]* {104.15-26}. w. Townsend lyrics. m. "Tune—*Tramp, Tramp, Tramp.*" Page 17; **The Fight Is On** {104.15-27}. w. Townsend lyrics. m. "Tune—*Under Own Music By Same Name.*" Page 18; *[We Are Nearing The End Of A Townsend Day]* {104.15-28}. w. Townsend lyrics. m. "Tune—*Perfect Day.*" Page 18; **The Townsend Plan** {104.16-29}. w. Townsend lyrics. m. "Tune—*Battle Hymn Of The Republic.*" Page 19; **A Song Of Hope** {104.15-30}. w. Townsend lyrics. m. "Tune—*Old Black Joe.*" Page 22; *[Pack Up Your Troubles In A Townsend Bag]* {104.15-31}. w. Townsend lyrics. m. "Tune—*Pack Up Your Troubles.*" Page 22; **Marching Together In Union** {104.15-32}. w. Townsend lyrics. m. "Tune—*Marching Through Georgia.*" Page 23; *[In Every Time Of Trouble, God Has Chosen A Great Man]* {104.15-33}. w. Townsend lyrics. m. "Tune—*Marching Through Georgia.*" Page 23; *[When Townsend Helps Me Get Dat Pension]* {104.15-34}. w. Townsend lyrics. m. "Tune—*Dixie.*" Page 24; **Loyalty And Harmony** {104.15-35}. w. Townsend lyrics. m. "Tune—*Moonlight And Roses.*" "The Biltmore Club Theme Song." Page 24; **The Doctor Has Found A Good Way** {104.15-36}. w. Townsend lyrics. m. "Tune—*Home On The Range.*" Page 25; *[Bring The Good Old Townsend Plan]* {104.16-37}. w. Townsend lyrics. m. "Tune—*Marching Through Georgia.*" Page 25; *[The Gen'ral Welfare Act Is Here]* {104.15-38}. w. Townsend lyrics. m. "Tune—*Marching Through Georgia.*" Page 26; *[Bring The Good Old Bugle Folks]* {104.15-39}. w. Townsend lyrics. m. "Tune—*Marching Through Georgia.*" Page 26; *[God Bless And Aid This Happy Band]* {104.15-40}. w. Townsend lyrics. m. "Tune—*Drink To Me Only With Thine Eyes.*" Page 27; *[East, West, North, South—Everywhere You Go]* {104.15-41}. w. Townsend lyrics. m. "Tune—*East Side, West Side.*" Page 27; *[Our Plan Is Like A Mountain Railroad]* {104.15-42}. w. Townsend lyrics. m. "Tune—*Life's Railway To Heaven.*" Page 28; *[America, America, Thy People Must Be Free]* {104.15-43}. w. Townsend lyrics. m. "Tune—*America The Beautiful.*" Page 29; **Townsend Marching Song** {104.15-44}. w. Townsend lyrics. m. "Tune—*Jolly Coppersmith.*" Page 30; **The Townsend Campaign Song** {104.15-45}. w. Townsend lyrics. m. "Tune—*Marching Through Georgia.*" Page 30; **God's Plan** {104.15-46}. w. Townsend lyrics. m. "Tune—*Battle Hymn Of The Republic.*" Page 31; **Townsend Home Song** {104.15-47}. w. Townsend lyrics. m. "Tune—*Home On The Range.*" Page 32; **Townsend Party Song** {104.15-48}. w. Townsend lyrics. m. "Tune—*Battle Hymn Of The Republic.*" Page 33; **America The Beautiful** {104.15-49}. w.m. Standard patriotic song. Page 34; **Get Behind The Townsend Plan** {104.15-50}. w. Townsend lyrics. m. "Tune—*Quilting Party—I Was Seeing Nellie Home.*" Page 35; **Plans** {104.15-51}. w. Townsend lyrics. m. "Tune—*Smiles.*" Page 35; **The Townsend Battle Cry**

{104.15-52}. w. Townsend lyrics. m. "Tune—*John Brown's Body.*" Page 36; ***Politics*** {104.15-53}. w. Townsend lyrics. m. "Tune—*Yankee Doodle.*" Page 36; ***Cheer Up! Townsend Army*** {104.15-54}. w. Townsend lyrics. m. "Tune—*Tramp, Tramp, Tramp.*" Page 37; ***[Townsendites! Townsendites!]*** {104.15-55}. w. Townsend lyrics. m. "Tune—*Redwing.*" Page 37; ***There's A Great Day Coming*** {104.15-56}. w. Townsend lyrics. m. "Tune—*Long, Long Trail.*" Page 38; ***[Just Keep On A Working For The Townsend Plan]*** {104.15-57}. w. Townsend lyrics. m. "Tune—*Let Me Call You Sweetheart.*" Page 38; ***[Put On Your Townsend Bonnet]*** {104.15-58}. w. Townsend lyrics. m. "Tune—*Old Grey Bonnet.*" Page 38.

104.16 Townsend Old Age Revolving Plan. w. Jesse Minor. m. Vashti Rogers Griffin. Published by Saunders Publishing Company, 2832 Beech Street, San Diego, CA. Copyright 1936 by Jesse Minor. Bl/w geometric design border. "Dedicated to Dr. Townsend." 6pp. Page 6: Advertising.

104.17 The Townsend Plan Is Here To Stay (Our Challenge). w. Charles Dalziel. m. Don Parker. Published by The Don Parker Music Publishing Co., 4016 Santa Monica Boulevard, Hollywood, CA. 1936. B/w drawing of thousands of people marching on the U.S. Capitol building. 4pp. Page 4: B/w photo of Don Parker. Biography of Parker.

104.18 Townsend Plan March Song. w.m. William J. Tansey. Published by Golden Music Pub. Co., 752 Haight Street, San Francisco, CA. 1934. B/w geometric and floral design border. [V-1: Small geometric design in center of page with 'March Song' above] [V-2: Small geometric design in the center of the page with 'March Song' as part of the design. 4pp. Page 4: [V-1: Blank with a paste-on page long narrative on the "Townsend Old Age Pension Revolving Fund Plan"] [V-2: Same narrative as V-1 except it is printed on the page].

104.19 The Townsend Plan National March (Official Townsend National Theme Song). w.m. Clayton A. Sanders. Published by CAS, Publisher, Indianapolis, IN. 1952. Ma/w photo within a drawing of a television set, of "Mother Townsend." Ma/w drawing of man at a microphone saying "Ladies and Gentlemen we now Present." "Dedicated to the Memory of 'Mother' Townsend, Mother and Sweetheart of the Townsend Movement." 6pp. Page 2: Blank. Page 6: Advertising.

104.20 Townsend Song Sheet. Published by The Ryan Sanitarium and The Gould Funeral Service, Binghamton, NY. [ca. 1940]. [5½" × 8½"]. B/w non-pictorial. "Furnished Free to Local Clubs." Advertising. 4pp. Songs include: ***America*** {104.20-1}. w. Francis Scott Key. m. *America.* Page 2; ***[Raise Now High The Townsend Standard]*** {104.20-2}. w. Townsend lyrics. m. "Tune—*Tramp, Tramp, Tramp.*" Page 2; ***Onward Townsend Soldiers*** {104.20-3}. w. Townsend lyrics. m. "Tune—*Onward Christian Soldiers.*" Page 2; ***Down In Lovers Lane*** {104.20-4}. w. No composer indicated. w. *Down In Lovers Lane.* Page 2; ***[In Visions Now I Plainly See]*** {104.20-5}. w. Townsend lyrics. m. "Tune—*In The Shade Of The Old Apple Tree.*" Page 2; ***[When Townsend Plan Is Adopted]*** {104.20-6}. w. Townsend lyrics. m. "Tune—*Marching Through Georgia.*" Page 3; ***All Hail*** {104.20-7}. w. No composer indicated. m. No tune indicated. Page 3; ***Old Gray Bonnet*** {104.20-8}. w. No composer indicated. m. *Old Gray Bonnet.* Page 3; ***Townsend Right*** {104.20-9}. w. Townsend lyrics. m. "Tune—*Jingle Bells.*" Page 3; ***We Should Not Turn A Deaf Ear To Townsend*** {104.20-10}. w. Townsend lyrics. m. "Tune—*The Little Brown Church.*" Page 3; ***God Be With You*** {104.20-11}. w. No composer indicated. m. *God Be With You.* Page 4; ***[What Townsend's Doing There]*** {104.20-12}. w. No composer indicated. m. "Tune—*Coming Thro' The Rye.*" Page 4; ***[Hail, Hail, The Townsend Plan]*** {104.20-13}. w. Townsend lyrics. m. "Tune—*Hail, Hail, The Gang's All Here.*" Page 4; ***Here Dem Bells*** {104.20-14}. w. No composer indicated. m. *Here Dem Bells.* Page 4.

104.21 Townsend Songs. Published by Edna L. Eaton. [ca. 1936]. [5½" × 8½"]. Pl/w non-pictorial mimeograph cover. "Compliments of Edna L. Eaton, National Representative." 8pp; ***America*** {104.21-1}. Page 2; ***[We Have Fought]*** {104.21-2}. w. Townsend lyrics. m. "Melody—*U.S. Marine Song.*" Page 2; ***Our Townsend Plan*** {104.21-3}. w. Townsend lyrics. m. "Melody—*My Maryland.*" Page 3; ***The American Plan*** {104.21-4}. w. Townsend lyrics. m. "Melody—*America, The Beautiful.*" Page 3; ***Loyalty Song*** {104.21-5}. w. Townsend lyrics. m. "Melody—*Juanita.*" Page 4; ***God To Be With You*** {104.21-6}. w. Townsend lyrics. m. "Melody—*Good To Be With You.*" Page 4; ***Love's Old Sweet Song*** {104.21-7}. Page 5; ***Townsend Theme Song*** {104.21.8}. w. Townsend lyrics. m. "Melody—*The Woody Woodpecker Song.*" Page 5; ***Onward Townsend Soldiers*** {104.21-9}. w. Townsend lyrics. m. "Melody—*Onward Christian Soldiers.*" Page 6; ***Townsend Battle Song*** {104.21-10}. w. Townsend lyrics. m. "Melody—*Battle Hymn Of The Republic.*" Page 7; ***On To Washington*** {104.21-11}. w. Townsend lyrics. m. "Melody—*Loyalty to Christ.* Page 8.

104.22 Townsend Victory March. m. Maude L. Landes. Published by Maude L. Landes, Route 9, Box 500, Portland, OR. 1935. B/w litho of an eagle, black line border. 8pp. Page 8: Blank.

104.23 [Untitled Townsend Song Sheet]. w. No composer indicated. Printed by J.F. Winneur, 96 Avalon, Detroit, MI. [1937-1941]. [9" × 12¾"]. Non-pictorial. At top of page 1: "Pledge of Allegiance." Bottom of page 1—"Townsend Pledge." Songs include: ***Long Long Trail*** {104.23-1}. w. Townsend lyrics. m. *Long Long Trail.* Page 1; ***Old Gray Bonnet*** {104.21-2}. w. Townsend lyrics. m. *Old Gray Bonnet.* Page 1; ***Battle ... Republic*** {104.23-3}. w. Townsend lyrics. m. *Battle Hymn Of The Republic.* Page 1; ***Marching Through Georgia*** {104.23-4}. w. Townsend lyrics. m. *Marching Through Georgia.* Page 1; ***Old Black Joe*** {104.23-5}. w. Townsend lyrics. m. *Old Black Joe.* Page 1; ***Loves Old Sweet Song*** {104.23-6}. w. Townsend lyrics. m. *Loves Old Sweet Song.* Page 1; ***Tramp, Tramp, Tramp*** {104.23-7}. w. Townsend lyrics. m. *Tramp, Tramp, Tramp.* Page 1; ***Stand Up, Stand Up For Townsend*** {104.23-8}. w. Townsend lyrics. m. No tune indicated. Page 1; ***Townsend Soldiers*** {104.23-9}. w. Townsend lyrics. m. *Onward Christian Soldiers.* Page 1; ***Yankee Doodle*** {104.23-10}. w. Townsend lyrics. m. *Yankee Doodle*. Page 2; **Smiles** {104.23–11}. w. Townsend lyrics. m. *Smiles*. Page 2; **Be A Townsend Man** {104.23–12}. w. Townsend lyrics. m. "Tune — Coming Through The Rye." Page 2; **The Townsend Plan** {104.23–13}. w. Townsend lyrics. m. "Tune — America The Beautiful." Page 2; **Pack Up Your Troubles** {104.23–14}. w. Townsend lyrics. m. *Pack Up Your Troubles*. Page 2; **Prosperity** {104.23–15}. w. Townsend lyrics. m. *Auld Lang Syne*. Page 2; **Praise To Our Leader** {104.21–16}. w. Townsend lyrics. m. *America*. Page 2; **Townsend Plan Is Here To Stay** {104.23–17}. w. Townsend lyrics. m. "Tune — *Maryland, My Maryland*." Page 2.

104.24 When Our Old-Age Pension Check Comes To Our Door. w.m. Manny Stone. Published by Stone & Stone, Music Publishers, 3900 Ocean View Boulevard, Montrose, CA. 1934. Bl/w/o drawing of retired couple meeting the mailman, geometric designs. "Originally Introduced Over the Air by Diamond 'D' Cowboys of Radio Station K.G.E.R., Long Beach, Calif." 6pp. Page 6: Advertising.

- **AmPM-105   WARREN**, Earl (District Attorney, Alameda County; State Attorney General, 1939–1943; Candidate for Vice President, 1948; Governor, 1943–1953; U.S. Supreme Court, 1953–1969) [ALSO SEE: DOC/PSM-TED]

105.1 Always True To Fashion. w. No composer indicated. m. "Tune — *Always True To You In My Fashion*." "Quartette — Stassen, Taft, Warren and Martin." In: *Alice In Blunderland Or Through The Rooking Class* [Program and Songbook], page 6. Published by The Legislative Correspondents' Association of New York State, Albany, NY. 1949. [8⅝" × 11"]. N/c drawings of Harry Truman, Thomas Dewey, Franklin Roosevelt, Henry Wallace, Harold Stassen, Alben Barkley, Robert Taft, Earl Warren, other politicians. "A Scintillating Satire of Sadistic Surprises and Surprising Successes Featuring a Dramatic Disclosure of How Tom Did Not Go Down to D.C. in Slips; Together with a Give-Away-Nothing Radio Broadcast and Epic Melodrama of the Indian Wars Entitled 'When the Cat's Away the Mice Will Play.'" "Done With Music and Mirrors — Particularly Mirrors in Three Acts at Hotel Ten Eyck, Albany, March 12, 1949." [Crew/HST-20].

105.2 Hang Earl Warren. w. Noel E. Parmentel, Jr. and Marshall J. Dodge. In: *Folk Songs For Conservatives*, page 29. Published by Unicorn Press, Inc., No. 790 Madison Avenue, New York, NY. 10021. 1964. [5" × 8⅜"]. Bl/w drawings of Barry Goldwater, Bill Buckley, Ray Cohn, eagle. List of contents. "Sung by Noel E. Parmentel, Jr. and His Unbleached Muslims, Greatest Political Satirists Since Cohn and Schine." "Right Wing Hootenanny." 36pp. [Crew/BMG-13].

105.3 I Can Pass On My Troubles. w. No composer indicated. m. "Tune — *I've Got The Sun In The Morning*." In: *Visions And Revisions*, page 8. Published by The Albany Legislative Correspondents' Association, Albany, NY. March 6, 1947. [8½" × 11"]. R/w/gn/y/bk drawing of Thomas "Dewey" as Santa Claus, sign — "Santa's Workshop," other New York politicians. "Revealing in Rhapsodic Revelry of Song and Stunt How a Political Scrooge Became a Political Saint; or, What Happened When Many Paws Raided the Wonderful Workshop of Santa Claus Dewey; Together with Other Strange and Silly Scenes." "Hotel Ten Eyck, Albany, March 6, 1947." 24pp. [Crew/TED-34].

105.4 The John Birch Society. w.m. Michael Brown. In: *The Mitchell Trio Song Book*, page 42. Published by Quadrangle Books, Inc., No. 180 North Wacker, Chicago, IL. 50505. 1964. R/w/b drawings of the members of The Chad Mitchell Trio. 146pp. [Crew/JFK-70].

105.5 The Johnson Victory Hymn. w. W.L. White. [1964]. [8½" × 11"]. Non-pictorial. "W.L. White in *The Emporia Gazette*." 2pp. Page 2: Reprint of an anti-Johnson editorial by White in the *Emporia Gazette*. [Crew/LBJ-38].

105.6 [Sound Off]. w. No composer indicated. m. "Tune — *Sound Off*." In: *Eisenhower Song Book*, page 8. [1952]. [5" × 9"]. R/w/b non-pictorial lines. 13pp. 24pp. Ten songs written to popular tunes. [M-430]. [Crew/DDE-23].

- **AmPM-106   WESTENBERG**, J.C. (Prohibition Party Candidate For Congress, 1915)

106.1 We'll Make California Dry! w. Rev. R.A.M. Browne. m. S. Maxwell. a. Horner Yourjee. Published by The Tribune Song Company, Publishers, 322 California Building, Los Angeles, CA. 1914. W/br/y/gn drawings of four California bears, flowers, geometric designs. "California Dry Federation Official Campaign Song." "Vote California Dry, November 2, 1914." 8pp. Pages 2. 7 and 8: Blank. Page 3: "This song is dedicated to Gen. And Mrs. John Bidwell, Chico, California, whose unswerving loyalty to the Temperance Cause in California has been the means of bringing about much of the interest and sympathy that is being shown in this fight for California State-wide Prohibition." Page 6: Narrative on the goals of the Federation. Page 8: Photo of and campaign advertisement for "J.C. Westenberg, Candidate for Congress, Fourth District, Prohibition Ticket." Platform includes "Extension of Suffrage to Women." [Crew/S-1914–19].

- **AmPM-107   WILSON**, J. Stitt (Mayor, Berkeley, 1911–1913)

107.1 Have You Heard About Milwaukee? w.m. Harvey P. Moyer. In: *Socialist Campaign Songs*, page 9. Published by The Co-Operative Printing Company, No. 5443 Drexel Avenue, Chicago, IL. [ca. 1910]. [7¾" × 5¼"]. R/br non-pictorial. "Music fills all Hearts with Fire." "Have your branch get a lot of these matchless, stirring, yet low priced booklets and start the whole community to singing these thrilling Socialist songs. That's the way to make your campaign a glorious success. Do It Now." 18pp. Page 18: Advertising for *Moyer's Songs Of Socialism* songbook. [M-398, 404]. [Crew/SP-1].

- **AmPM-108   WILSON**, Peter Barton (State Assembly, 1967–1971; Mayor, San Diego, 1971–1982; U.S. Senate, 1983–1991; Governor, 1991–1999)

108.1 The Ballot Of Arnold Schwarzenegger. w. Bob Gomez. m. "*The Ballad Of Davy Crockett,* based on the performance by George Burns/Tom Blackburn." "Great. Now we can look forward to three years of gridlock and Really Bad pronunciation." Published online at <http://www.amiright.com/parody/misc/georgeburnstomblackburn0.html>. 2003.

108.2 Battle Hymn Of The Republicans. w. No composer indicated. m. Tune — *Battle Hymn Of The*

Republic. N/c photos of George Bush. Ronald Reagan, Willie Horton, peacemaker missile, clear-cut forest, Dick Armey, Bill Archer, Pete Wilson, H. Ross Perot and George W. Bush. "The Washington press corps serenaded president-elect George Bush on his campaign plane with the first verse and refrain of this hymn in 1988. We added a few more stanzas." Published online by PoliticsOL.com at <http://www.presidentialelection2000.com/battle_hymn_of_the_republicans.html>. 2000.

108.3 Campaign California. w. Michael Pacholek. m. "*Hotel California*, based on a performance by The Eagles." "'Conan,' of course is ... the Barbarian, not O'Brien. Proposition 13, the biggest bullet in California's foot, was passed in 1978, hence the reference to no property taxes since 1979." Published online at <http://www.amiright.com/parody/70s/theeagles51.shtml>. [ca. 2001].

108.4 Get Grey [sic] *Davis Fired*. w. Stanuman. m. "*Great Balls Of Fire*, based on a performance by Jerry Lee Lewis." Published online at <http://www.amiright.com/parody/misc/jerryleelewis6.shtml>. 2003.

108.5 Gov'nor Arnold/General Wesley. w. Johnny D. m. "*Uncle Albert/Admiral Halsey*, based on a performance by Paul McCartney." Published online at <http://www.amiright.com/parody/70s/paulmccartney23.shtml>. 2003.

• **AmPM-109** YORTY, Samuel William (State Assembly, 1936–1940 & 1949–1950; U.S. House, 1951–1955; Mayor, Los Angeles, 1961–1973)

109.1 Sam Yorty's Here To Stay. w. Sammy Cahn. m. "To the tune of *Our Love Is Here To Stay*." [196-]. [8½" × 11"]. Non-pictorial. 2pp. Page 2: Blank.

109.2 Take'A Me Backa Tony! (Fox-Trot). w. Sam W. Yorty. m. Frank P. Marini. Published by Marini & Yorty Co., 3229 N. Main Street, Los Angeles, CA. 1930. B/w photo of Dan Cervo—"Featured by Dan Cervo The Accordion Wizard." R/w/gn drawings of organ grinder man and his monkey. "With Ukulele Arrangement." 1930. 6pp. Page 2: Blank. Page 6: Advertising.

• **AmPM-110** MISCELLANEOUS MUSIC

110.1 Anti-Monopoly War Song. w.m. R.J. Harrison. Copyright 1882 by R.J. Harrison. B/w non-pictorial geometric designs. "Composed for the Anti-Monopoly Party of California." 4pp. Page 4: Blank. [AMC].

110.2 Election Song. w. No composer indicated. m. "No tune indicated. MP3 file provided online." Published online by the California Voter Foundation at <http://calvoter.org/2002/primary/song>. [ca. 2001].

110.3 Sacramento. m. S.L. Tyler. Published by W.H. Boner & Co., 1102 Chestnut Street, Philadelphia, PA. 1886. B/w litho of various state capitol buildings: "Madison, Wis., Harrisburg, Pa., Hartford, Conn., Columbus, O., Lansing, Mich., Washington, D.C., St. Paul, Minn., Richmond Va., Sacramento, Cal., Albany, NY., Boston, Mass., Montgomery, Ala." "The Capitol Collection." 8pp. Page 2: Blank. Page 3: At top of music—"To my Brother, C.A. Tyler." Page 8: Advertising.

110.4 Sacramento At The Big State Fair. w.m. Olla Hewitt. Published by Olla Hewitt, Dunsmur, CA. 1926. B/w photo for the state capitol building. B/w floral and geometric designs. 4pp. Page 4: Advertising.

110.5 Vote Our California Dry. w.m. Asbury Shumard. Published by Asbury Shumard, Box 350, R.F.D. 2, Long Beach, CA. 1916. B/w non-pictorial geometric designs. 6pp. Pages 2 and 6: Blank. Page 3: At top of music—"Dedicated to the W.C.T.U., Long Beach, California."

COLORADO

• **AmPM-111** COSTIGAN, Edward Prentiss (Candidate for Governor, 1912 & 1914; U.S. Senate, 1931–1937)

111.1 Pass The Prosperity Around [Song Sheet]. [Published in Colorado]. [1912]. [5⅜" × 7⅞"]. Non-pictorial. "Vote for Roosevelt, Johnson and Costigan—They will pass prosperity around." 4pp.

• **AmPM-112** FRIES, William D. "Bill" [Aka: C.W. McCall] (Mayor, Ouray, 1982)

112.1 Best Of C.W. McCall. w.m. C.W. McCall. CD published by Mercury Records, Nashville, TN. "825793. 1993. Songs include: *Convoy* {112.1–1}; *Silverton* {112.1–2}; *Four Wheel Drive* {112.1–3}; *Wolf Creek Pass* {112.1–4}; *Classified* {112.1–5}; *There Won't Be No Country Music* {112.1–6}; *Old Home Filler-Up An' Keep On A-Truckin Café* {112.1–7}; *Crispy Critters* {112.1–8}; *Round The World With The Rubber Duck* {112.1–9}; *Black Bear Road* {112.1–10}; *Roses For Mama* {112.1–11}; and *Aurora Borealis* {112.1–12}.

112.2 Convoy. w.m. C.W. McCall, Bill Fries and Chip Davis. Published by Chappell Music Co., 810 Seventh Avenue, New York., NY. 10019. 1975. B/w photo of C.W. McCall. Y/r cover. "Recorded by C.W. McCall on MGM Records." 10pp. Page 2: Blank. Page 10: Definitions for C.B. radio terms.

112.3 C.W. McCall—Greatest Hits. w.m. C.W. McCall. CD published by Phd Special Markets #520394. 1998. Songs include: *Convoy* {112.3–1}; *Jackson Hole* {112.3–2}; *Four Wheel Cowboy* {112.3–3}; *Wolf Creek Pass* {112.3–4}; *Old Home Filler-Up An' Keep On A-Truckin Café* {112.3–5}; *Gallopin' Goose* {112.3–6}; *Audubon* {112.3–7}; *There Won't Be No Country Music* {112.3–8}; *Long Lonesome Road* {112.3–9}; *Green River* {112.3–10}; *Black Bear Road* {112.3–11}.

112.4 There Won't Be No Country Music (There Won't Be No Rock And Roll). w.m. Bill Fries and Louis F. Davis. Published by Chappell Music Co., 810 Seventh Avenue, New York, NY. 10019. 1976. B/w photo of C.W. McCall, a.k.a. Bill Fries. "Recorded by C.W. McCall on Polydor Records." 6pp.
• **AmPM-114** HART, Gary Warren (U.S. Senate, 1975–1987) [See: DOC/PSM-MISC]
114.1 Bob Graham The Only Candidate. On CD: *The Bob Graham Charisma Tour Album.* CD. 2004. Lyrics published online at <http://nbc6.net/politics/2264430/detail.htm>.
114.2 Broken Gary Heart. w. No composer indicated. m. "Parody of *How Can You Mend A Broken Heart?* by The BeeGees." Lyrics published by *The Bob Rivers Show* with Bob, Spike & Joe and Twisted Tunes online at <http://www.twistedradio.com/player/lyrics.asp?songID=525>. [199-].
114.3 Hart Attack. w. Bill Strauss and Elaina Newport. On Cassette: *Workin' 9 To 10.* Published by Capitol Steps Productions, 1505 King Street, Alexandria, VA. 1987. Cassette Cover: N/c drawing of Ronald Reagan at desk.
114.4 If You Want To Be President. w. No composer indicated. m. "Parody of *If You Want To Be Happy* by Jimmy Soul." Lyrics published by *The Bob Rivers Show* with Bob, Spike & Joe and Twisted Tunes online at <http://www.twistedradio.com/player/lyrics.asp?songID=680>. [ca. 1992].
114.5 Keep Your Pants On. w. No composer indicated. m. "Parody of *Give Peace A Chance* by John Lennon." Lyrics published by *The Bob Rivers Show* with Bob, Spike & Joe and Twisted Tunes online at <http://www.twistedradio.com/player/lyrics.asp?songID=541>. [199-].
MCCALL, C.W. (Mayor, Ouray, 1982) [See: William D. Fries]
• **AmPM-115** TABOR, Horace Austin Warner (State House, Kansas, 1856–1857; Mayor, Leadville; 1878–1879; Treasurer, Lake County; 1879; Lt. Governor 1879–1883; U.S. Senate, 1883)
115.1 Our President Roosevelt's Colorado Hunt (March Song). w. Silver Echo Tabor "(Author of *Spirits, Love And Likes*, and *In A Dream I Loved You*)." m. Professor A.S. Lohmann. Published by Silver Echo Tabor, Denver, CO. 1908. O/bk/w drawing of Theodore Roosevelt. "To the Memory of the Late U.S. Senator H.A.W. Tabor." "Dedicated to my Beloved Father H.A.W. Tabor." 8pp. Pages 2, 7 and 8: Blank. [Crew/TR-212].
• **AmPM-116** TELLER, Henry Moore (U.S. Senate; 1876–1882 & 1885–1909; U.S. Secretary of the Interior, 1882–1885; Member, U.S. Monetary Commission, 1908–1912)
116.1 Exit Old Party. w. No composer indicated. m. "Tune—*Good-By, My Lover, Good-By.*" In: *Republican Campaign Parodies And Songs* [Songster], page 20. Published by Betts and Burnett, South Butler, Wayne County, NY. 1896. [7¾" × 5½"]. Be/bk non-pictorial. "McKinley and Hobart." "1896." 28pp. [M-340]. [Crew/WM-67].
116.2 Split Up The Back. w. H.W. Taylor. m. J.B. Herbert. "Male Voices." In: *Red-Hot Democratic Campaign Songs For 1896*, page 16. c. J.B. Herbert. Published by The S. Brainard's Sons Company, Nos. 151 and 153 Wabash Avenue, Chicago, IL. 1896. [5¼" × 7"]. R/be litho of ribbon, geometric designs. 28pp. [M-355]. [Crew/WJB-18].
• **AmPM-117** WAITE, Davis Hanson (State Assembly, Wisconsin, 1857; State Legislature, Kansas, 1879; Governor, Colorado, 1893–1895)
117.1 When The Votes Are Counted. w.m. J.A. Parks. In: *Park's Republican Campaign Songs (For Male Voices)*, page 26. e. James Asher Parks. Published by The J.A. Parks Company, York, NE. 1900. Gn/bk non-pictorial. "Respectfully inscribed to Gen. Chas. F. Manderson." 40pp. [M-371]. [Crew/WM-106].

CONNECTICUT

• **AmPM-118** BEECHER, Henry Ward (American Congregational preacher, Abolitionist, Editor of the *Independent*, 1861, and the *Christian Union*, 1870)
118.1 Audax Omnia Perpeti Gens Lincolna Ruit Per Vetitum Nefas. w.m. No composers or tune indicated. No publisher indicated. [1861–1862]. B/w non-pictorial geometric design border. 2pp. Page 2: Blank. [AMC].
118.2 Cabinet Pictures. w.m. No composer or tune indicated. In: *Copperhead Minstrel (A Choice Collection Of Democratic Poems & Songs)*, page 24. Published by Feeks and Bancker, Wholesale Agents, No. 24 Ann Street, New York. 1863. [4¾" × 7¼"]. O/bk non-pictorial. "For the use of Political Clubs and the Social Circle." "Price 25 cents." 64pp. [M-133] [Crew/GBM-64].
118.3 Cleveland's Lullaby. w. M.H. m. Tune—*Baby Mine.* Published in an unknown newspaper [probably Detroit] as being "From the *Chicago Tribune.*" [1884].
118.4 De Nigger On De Fence. w. No composer indicated. m. "Tune—*All Round My Hat.*" In: *Copperhead Minstrel (A Choice Collection Of Democratic Poems & Songs)*, page 38. Published by Feeks and Bancker, Wholesale Agents, No. 24 Ann Street, New York. 1863. [4¾" × 7¼"]. O/bk non-pictorial. "For the use of Political Clubs and the Social Circle." "Price 25 cents." 64pp. [M-133] [Crew/GBM-64].
118.5 De Nigger On De Fence. w. No composer indicated. m. "Air—*All Round My Hat.*" No publisher indicated. [ca. 1864]. H/c litho of two Black men. 2pp. Page 2: Blank. [AMC].
118.6 De Serenade. w.m. No composer or tune in-

dicated. In: *Copperhead Minstrel (A Choice Collection Of Democratic Poems & Songs)*, page 10. Published by Feeks and Bancker, Wholesale Agents, No. 24 Ann Street, New York. 1863. [4¾" × 7¼"]. O/bk non-pictorial. "For the use of Political Clubs and the Social Circle." "Price 25 cents." 64pp. [M-133] [Crew/GBM-64].

118.7 ***Don't Mix Your Liquor Boys***. w. No composer indicated. m. "*Low-Backed Car* or *Wait For The Wagon*." Published by Andrews, Printer, 38 Chatham Street, New York, NY. [185-]. B/w non-pictorial geometric design border. "Andrews, Printer, 38 Chatham St., N.Y., Dealer in Songs, Games Books, Toy Motto Verses, &c., Wholesale and Retain." 2pp. Page 2: Blank. [AMC].

118.8 ***The Gallant Colonel***. w.m. No composers or tune indicated. No publisher indicated. [1862-1863]. B/w litho of the Confederate stars and bars flag, geometric design border. 2pp. Page 2: Blank. [AMC].

118.9 ***Gen. Johnston***. w. No composer indicated. m. "Air—*American Star*." No publisher indicated. [1861-1862]. B/w litho of an exploding cannon ball, geometric design border. 2pp. Page 2: Blank. [AMC].

118.10 ***General Beauregard*** (Song). w. No composer indicated. m. "Air—*Scots Wha Hae*." [ca. 1861]. [Approx. 4¾" × 10"]. Litho of bugler on horseback, geometric design border. 2pp. Page 2: Blank. [WFU].

118.11 ***Greeley And Gratz Campaign Song***. w.m. No composer indicated. m. "Air—*When This Cruel War Is Over*." In: *The Sun's Greeley Campaign Songster*, page 32. c. Amos J. Cumming. Published from *The Sun* Office, New York, NY. 1872. [4⅛" × 6½"]. Be/bk litho of Horace Greeley, wreath. "He shines for all." 64pp. [Crew/HG-5].

118.12 ***Hey! Uncle Abe, Are You Joking Yet?*** w. No composer indicated. m. "Tune—*Johnny Cope*." Published by J.F. Feeks, 26 Ann Street, and 636 Broadway, New York, NY. 1864. B/w non-pictorial geometric design border. 2pp. Page 2: Blank. [AMC].

118.13 ***Hey! Uncle Abe, Are You Joking Yet?*** w. No composer indicated. m. "Air—*Johnny Cope*." In: *Democratic Presidential Campaign Songster (No. 1)*, page 30. Published by J.F. Feeks, No. 26 Ann Street, New York, NY. 1864. [3¾" × 5½"]. Y/bk litho of George B. McClellan, chain link frame. "McClellan & Pendleton." "Original Campaign Songs, Choruses, &c." 74pp. [M-135, 136]. [Crew/GBM-23].

118.14 ***John Brown Song***. w. No composer indicated. m. *Glory Hallelujah*. In: *Copperhead Minstrel (A Choice Collection Of Democratic Poems & Songs)*, page 36. Published by Feeks and Bancker, Wholesale Agents, No. 24 Ann Street, New York. 1863. [4¾" × 7¼"]. O/bk non-pictorial. "For the use of Political Clubs and the Social Circle." "Price 25 cents." 64pp. [M-133] [Crew/GBM-64].

118.15 ***My God! What Is All This For?*** w. No composer indicated. m. "Air—*Rosseau's Dream*." No publisher indicated. [1861-1862]. [V-1: B/w geometric design border] [V-2: Pk/bk line border]. "The above is the dying words of a Federal soldier on the Battle field of Manassas, 1861." 2pp. Page 2: Blank. [V-1: AMC] [V-2: WFU].

118.16 ***Nursery Ballad For The Wide-Awakes*** (The Rail That Abe Split). w.m. No composer or tune indicated. In: *The Democratic Campaign Songster, No. #1*, page 6. Published by American Publishing House, No. 60 West Fourth Street, Cincinnati, OH. 1860. [3⅞" × 5¹⁵⁄₁₆"]. Pk/bk litho of "Stephen A. Douglas," black line border. At top of cover—"No. 1, Price 10 Cents." 52pp. [M-118]. [Crew/SAD-12].

118.17 ***The President's Ball***. w. No composer indicated. m. "Air—*Lannegan's Ball*." Published by H. De Marsan, 54 Chatham Street, New York, NY. [1860-1862]. [Approx. 6" × 9"]. B/w litho border of theatrical-type figures, leaves, lion's head, stars. "Sung by Joe English." 2pp. Page 2: Blank. [AMC].

118.18 ***Sherman's March***. w. Michael Fee. m. "*Ginger Blue*." Published by H. De Marsan, Dealer in Songs Toy-Books &c., 54 Chatham Street, New York, NY. [1863-1865]. B/w non-pictorial geometric design border. 2pp. Page 2: Blank. [AMC].

118.19 ***Southern Sentiments***. w.m. No composers or tune indicated. Published in Baltimore. 1861. B/w litho of man on horse with a trumpet, geometric design border. "October 9th, 1861." Preceded on page 1 by *Hark! The Summons*. 2pp. Page 2: Blank. [AML].

118.20 ***Southern Sentiments***. w. "B." m. "Air—*Let Haughty Gaul Invasion Threat*." Published in Baltimore. 1861. [Approx. 3½" × 6⅝"]. Non-pictorial. "October 6th, 1861." 2pp. Page 2: Blank. [AML] [WFU].

118.21 ***Swinging Around The Circle***. w.m. E.W. Locke. Published by G.D. Russel & Company, No. 126 Tremont, Opp. Park Street, Boston, MA. 1866. B/w non-pictorial geometric designs. "Sung at the Soldiers & Sailors Convention at Pittsburgh, Sept. 1866 by the Author, and received with unbounded applause." 6pp. Pages 2 and 6: Blank. [Crew/AJN-26].

118.22 ***Upside Down***. w.m. Howard Paul. Published by Wm. A. Pond & Co., 547 Broadway, New York, NY. [187-]. B/w litho of Sol Smith Russell. "Comic song sung with great success by Sol Smith Russell, and the Author." [FOM, p. 221].

• **AmPM-119** **BINGHAM**, Hiram (Lt. Governor, 1922-1924; Governor, 1924; U.S. Senate, 1924-1933)

119.1 ***Oh Connecticut, My Connecticut*** (Song). w.m. William Gerhardt. Published by William B. Gerhardt, Colchester, CT. 1931. B/w photo of Hiram Bingham. Bl/br/w drawing of the Capitol dome, airplanes, grapes, geometric designs, seal of the State of Connecticut. "Dedicated to Senator Hiram Bingham." 6pp. Pages 2 and 6: Blank.

119.2 ***Republican Campaign Songs***. Published by the Seventh Senatorial District Republican Association, Connecticut. [1932]. [8½" × 14"]. Non-pictorial mimeograph. 4pp. Pages 1 and 3: Music. Pages 2 and 4: Blank.

• **AmPM-120** **BOWLES**, Chester Bliss (State Rationing Office, 1942-1943; Administrator, U.S. Office of Price Administration, 1943-1946; U.S. War Production Board and Petroleum Board, 1943-1946; U.S. Economic Stabilization Board, 1946; U.S. Delegate to the United Nations Economic, Scientific and Cultural Organization Conference at Paris, 1946; Governor, 1949-1951; U.S. Ambassador to India and Nepal, 1951-1953 & 1963 to 1969; U.S. House, 1959-1961; U.S. Under Secretary of State, 1961; Presidential Advisor, 1961-1963).

120.1 Cool Goldwater. w. Noel E. Parmentel, Jr. and Marshall J. Dodge. In: *Folk Songs For Conservatives*, page 11. Published by Unicorn Press, Inc., No. 790 Madison Avenue, New York, NY. 10021. 1964. [5" × 8⅜"]. Bl/w drawings of Barry Goldwater, Bill Buckley, Ray Cohn, eagle. List of contents. "Sung by Noel E. Parmentel, Jr. and His Unbleached Muslims, Greatest Political Satirists Since Cohn and Schine." "Right Wing Hootenanny." 36pp. [Crew/BMG-13].

120.2 We Are Democrats, Too. w. No composer indicated. m. "Tune—*I'm An Indian, Too.*" In: *Alice In Blunderland Or Through The Rooking Class* [Program and Songbook], page 22. Published by The Legislative Correspondents' Association of New York State, Albany, NY. 1949. [8⅝" × 11"]. N/c drawings of Harry Truman, Thomas Dewey, Franklin Roosevelt, Henry Wallace, Harold Stassen, Alben Barkley, Robert Taft, Earl Warren, other politicians. "A Scintillating Satire of Sadistic Surprises and Surprising Successes Featuring a Dramatic Disclosure of How Tom Did Not Go Down to D.C. in Slips; Together with a Give-Away-Nothing Radio Broadcast and Epic Melodrama of the Indian Wars Entitled 'When the Cat's Away the Mice Will Play.'" "Done With Music and Mirrors—Particularly Mirrors in Three Acts at Hotel Ten Eyck, Albany, March 12, 1949." [Crew/HST-20].

• **AmPM-121 BROWN**, John (Abolitionist; "Captain" of a Colony on the Osawatomie River, Kansas, 1855; Leader, Harper's Ferry Raid, 1859)

121.1 The Black Brigade (Plantation Song & Dance). w.m. Dan D. Emmett. Published by Wm. A. Pond & Co., 547 Broadway, New York, NY. 1863. Non-pictorial geometric designs. "Sung with Great Success at Bryant's Minstrels." 6pp. Pages 2 and 6: Blank.

121.2 Call All! Call All! w. "Georgia." m. No tune indicated. In: *War Songs Of The Blue And The Gray*, page 23. Published by Hurst & Co., Publishers, New York, NY. [ca. 1880]. [4⅜" × 6½"]. Bl/k lithos of "Grant," "Robert E. Lee," "Johnston," and "Sherman," 72pp. [Crew/USG-299].

121.2A Everybody Knows The Reason Why. w. D. Clyde Lloyd, 1952. m. "Tune—*John Brown's Body.*" In: *We Like Ike*, page 4. Copyright 1952 by D. Clyde Lloyd, Salt Lake, UT. R/w/bl/pl drawing of an American flag, hands touching the flag. "Republican Party Campaign Song—1952." 4pp. [Crew/DDE-117].

121.3 The Fate Of John Brown {121.3–1}. w. No composer indicated. m. "Air—*John Anderson, My Jo.*" Published by H. De Marsan, 54 Chatham Street, New York, NY. [Approx. 6" × 9½"]. B/w litho border of minstrels, geometric designs. Followed on page 1 by ***John Brown*** {121.3–2}. w. P.H. Matthews. 2pp. Page 2: Blank. [AMC].

121.4 The Fright Of Old Virginia (Being A Condensed Account of the Harper's Ferry Insurrection, October 16th, 1859). w. Walter W. Warren. m. "Air—*Teddy The Tiller.*" No publisher indicated. [1859–1860]. [Approx. 6½" × 12"?]. Non-pictorial. 2pp. Page 2: Blank. [AMC].

121.5 Glory Hallelujah! w. No composer indicated. m. Tune—*Glory Hallelujah.* In: *Hayes & Wheeler Song Book*, page 5. Published by The Union Republican Congressional Committee, Washington, DC. 1876. [5¾" × 9¼"]. Br/bk litho of Rutherford B. Hayes and William A. Wheeler, shield, geometric design border. "I'll be on hand again shortly." [V-1: "Series I" under title on cover] [V-2: Series not indicated on cover]. 52pp. Page 2: Contents. Page 52: State-by-state electoral vote totals for 1876. [M-196, 197]. [Crew/RBH-20].

121.6 Glory Hallelujah! (No. 1). w. No composer indicated. m. "Air—*Glory Hallelujah!*" In: *The Grant Campaign Songster, Containing All The Most Popular Original Songs, Ballads And Recitations That Will Be Most Sung During This Presidential Campaign, Adapted To Very Popular And Well-Known Airs And Choruses*, page 55. Published by Robert M. Dewitt, Publisher, No. 13 Frankfort Street, New York, NY. 1868. [4¼" × 5¾"]. [V-1: Be/bk] [V-2: Gn/bk] litho of Ulysses S. Grant. 76pp. [M-155]. [Crew/USG-75].

121.7 Glory Hallelujah! (No. 2). w. No composer indicated. m. "Air—*Glory Hallelujah!*" In: *The Grant Campaign Songster, Containing All The Most Popular Original Songs, Ballads And Recitations That Will Be Most Sung During This Presidential Campaign, Adapted To Very Popular And Well-Known Airs And Choruses*, page 56. Published by Robert M. Dewitt, Publisher, No. 13 Frankfort Street, New York, NY. 1868. [4¼" × 5¾"]. [V-1: Be/bk] [V-2: Gn/bk] litho of Ulysses S. Grant. 76pp. [M-155]. [Crew/USG-75].

121.8 Glory Hallelujah No. 3 (Or New John Brown Song). w. No composer indicated. m. *Battle Hymn Of The Republic.* Published by H. De Marsan, Publisher, 54 Chatham Street, New York, NY. [ca. 1860]. [Approx. 6" × 9½"]. B/w litho border of minstrels, geometric designs. 2pp. Page 2: Blank. [AMC].

121.9 Glory Hally, Hallelujah! (Or John Brown Song). w. No composer indicated. m. *Battle Hymn Of The Republic.* Published by Horace Partridge, No. 27 Hanover Street, Boston, MA. [ca. 1860]. [Approx. 6" × 9½"]. B/w geometric designs litho border. "Hip, Hip, Hip Hurrah!" 2pp. Page 2: Blank. [AMC].

121.10 Grand Vocal Medley. a. P.P. Bliss. Published by Root & Cady, 67 Washington Street, Chicago, IL. 1863. B/w non-pictorial geometric designs. "Arranged from Root & Cady's most popular publications." 10pp. [AMC].

121.11 Hoist Up The Flag. w. No composer indicated. m. No tune indicated. Published by H. De Marsan, No. 60 Chatham Street, New York, NY. [ca. 1863]. [Approx. 6" × 9"]. B/w non-pictorial border of naval scenes. "The music can be obtained of the publishers, Winner & Co., No. 933 Spring Garden Street, Philadelphia, Pa." 2pp. Page 2: Blank. [AMC].

121.12 Hoist Up The Flag, Long May It Wave. w. No composer indicated. m. No tune indicated. Published by Johnson Song Publisher, No. 7 No. 10th Street, Philadelphia, PA. [ca. 1863]. [Approx. 6" × 9"]. B/w non-pictorial geometric design border. 2pp. Page 2: Blank. [AMC].

121.13 The Irish Wide-Awake. w. Harry M. Parker. m. "Air—*Billy O. Rourke.*" Published by H. De Marsan, 54 & 60 Chatham Street, New York, NY. [ca. 1860]. [Approx. 6¼" × 9½"]. H/c litho border of minstrels, animals. 2pp. Page 2: Blank. [AMC].

121.14 John Brown. w. No composer indicated m. *Battle Hymn Of The Republic.* Published by Charles

Magnus, 12 Franklin Street, New York, NY. [1863–1864]. N/c lithos of an Indian with a American flag inscribed "For The Union," and a litho of a bull and man chopping a tree, vignette labeled—"Indiana." 2pp. Page 2: Blank. [AMC].

121.15 John Brown. w. No composer indicated. m. "Arranged by C.B. Marsh." Published by C.S. Hall, 256 Main Street, Charlestown, MA. 1861. B/w litho of an eagle at top of music. "Origin, Fort Warren." 2pp. Page 2: Blank. [AMC]. [VBL, p. 357].

121.16 John Brown {121.16–1}. w. P.H. Matthews. m. No tune indicated. Published by H. De Marsan, 54 Chatham Street, New York, NY. [Approx. 6" × 9½"]. B/w litho border of minstrels, geometric designs. Followed on page 1 by ***The Fate Of John Brown*** {121.16–2}. 2pp. Page 2: Blank. [AMC].

121.17 John Brown. w. John L. Zieber. m. "Can be sung to the tune of *Caroline Of Edinburgtown, New Jersa*, or *Root, Hog Or Die*." Published by John L. Zieber, Publisher, Philadelphia, PA. [ca. 1860]. [Approx. 5½" × 9"]. B/w non-pictorial geometric design border. "Zieber's Popular Editions." "Look out for the original song, called *Handy Andy*." 2pp. Page 2: Blank. [AMC].

121.18 John Brown Song. w. No composer indicated. m. *Glory Hallelujah*. In: *Copperhead Minstrel (A Choice Collection Of Democratic Poems & Songs)*, page 36. Published by Feeks and Bancker, Wholesale Agents, No. 24 Ann Street, New York. 1863. [4¾" × 7¼"]. O/bk non-pictorial. "For the use of Political Clubs and the Social Circle." "Price 25 cents." 64pp. [M-133] [Crew/GBM-64].

121.19 The John Brown Song. w. Henry H. Brownell. m. *Glory Hallelujah*. In: *Songs For The Union*, page 4. "Printed for the Union Congressional Committee by John A. Gray & Geen, New York," NY. [ca. 1864]. Non-pictorial. 8pp. [AMC].

121.20 The John Brown Song. w. No composer indicated. m. *Battle Hymn*. Published by S. Brainard's Sons, Publishers, Cleveland, OH. 1885. N/c litho by Goes & Quensel of mounted soldiers. "Our National War Songs." List of other songs.

121.21 John Brown's Body Lies A Mouldering. w. No composer indicated. m. *Glory Hallelujah*. In: *American War Songs For School Rooms*, page 12. Published by The Toledo Chewing Gum Company, Toledo, OH. [ca. 1898]. [4¼" × 6¾"]. R/w/b litho of a cherub driving a chariot being drawn by a red lion, Civil War medals, flag, clouds. "Woman's Relief Corps; Soldiers and Marines; Army and Navy; Sons of Veterans; Spanish War Veterans; G.A.R. and All Patriotic and Fraternal Societies." 28pp. Page 28: N/c lithos of Civil War "Army Corps Badges."

121.22 John Brown's Entrance Into Hell. w.m. No composers or tune indicated. No publisher indicated. [ca. 1861–1865]. 2pp. Non-pictorial. Page 2: Blank. [AMC].

121.23 John Brown's Original Marching Song. w. No composer indicated. m. "*Brothers, Will You Meet Me*." Published by Johnson, Song Publisher, Stationer & Printer, No. 7 N. Tenth Street, 3 doors above Market, Philadelphia, PA. [ca. 1860]. [Approx. 6" × 9½"]. B/w non-pictorial geometric design border. 2pp. Page 2: Blank. [AMC].

121.24 John Brown's Song. w.m. No composers or tune indicated. Published by J. Wrigley, Publisher of Songs, Ballads, and Toy Books, Conversation, Age and Small Playing Cards, Alphabet Wood Blocks, Valentines, Motto Verses, and Cut Paper, &c., No. 27 Chatham Street. (Opposite City Hall Park) New York." [ca. 1860–1861]. B/w litho border of cherubs, minstrels, geometric designs. 2pp. Page 2: Blank. [AMC].

121.25 The Movement's Moving On. w. Len Chandler, Jr. m. "Tune Traditional—*John Brown's Body*." In: *Freedom Is A Constant Struggle, Songs Of The Freedom Movement*, page 223. c. Guy and Candie Carawan. Published by Oak Publications, New York, NY. 1968. 224pp.

121.26 My God! What Is All This For? w. No composer indicated. m. "Air—*Rosseau's Dream*." No publisher indicated. [1861–1862]. [V-1: B/w geometric design border] [V-2: Pk/bk line border]. "The above is the dying words of a Federal soldier on the Battle field of Manassas, 1861." 2pp. Page 2: Blank. [V-1: AMC] [V-2: WFU].

121.27 Nobody Knows Where John Brown Went. w.m. Arthur Longbake. Published by Jos. Morris Co., Philadelphia, PA. 1909. N/c litho of a Black man looking at the grave of John Brown—Here Lies John Brown, Prepare ye all to Follow Me." 6pp. Pages 2 and 6: Advertising. [AMC].

121.28 Old John Brown (A Song For Every Southern Man). w.m. No composers or tune indicated. No publisher indicated. [ca. 1860]. [5" × 7¾"]. B/w non-pictorial geometric design border. 2pp. Page 2: Blank. [AMC].

121.29 The Original John Brown's Song. w. No composer indicated. m. Air—*Glory Hallelujah*. In: *Beadle's Dime Knapsack Songster: Containing The Choicest Patriotic Songs, Together With Many New And Original Ones, Set To Old Melodies*, page 7. Published by Beadle and Company, No. 141 William Street, New York, NY. 1862. [3¾" × 5¾"]. Litho of coin—"One Dime, United States of America." 74pp. [Crew/GBM-78].

121.30 Poem. w. Eugene J. Hall. m. "Air—*The Grave Of Bonaparte*." "Written by Eugene J. Hall, and read at a meeting held in Ogden Park, Chicago, 1882, at which the widow of John Brown was present." In: *Patriotic Song Book For The G.A.R., For The Use Of The G.A.R. In Their Post-Meeting, Reunions, Camp-Fires, Installation Exercises, Fourth Of July Celebrations, And Memorial Service*, page 95. Published by Orwell Blake, Des Moines, IA. 1883. [5¹⁵⁄₁₆" × 9⅜"]. R/gd litho of a G.A.R. badge. 116pp.

121.31 Sam. Houston And The People. w. No composer indicated. m. No tune indicated. Published by H. De Marsan, Publisher, 60 Chatham Street, New York, NY. [ca. 1860]. [Approx. 6½" × 9¾"]. H/c border design of naval scenes. "H. De Marsan, Publisher of Songs & Ballads—Toy-books, paper dolls." 2pp. Page 2: Blank. [AMC].

121.32 A Song For The Times (Or John Brown No. 4). w.m. No composers or tune indicated. Published by H. De Marsan, Dealer in Songs, Toy Books, &c., 54 Chatham Street, New York, NY. [5½" × 9"]. B/w litho border of cherubs, minstrels, geometric designs. 2pp. Page 2: Blank.

121.33 Witches' Scene From MacGreeley (Which is Seen to be a Fact). w.m. No composer or tune indicated. From the "*New York Standard.*" In: *National Republican Grant And Wilson Campaign Song-Book*, page 34. From the *New York Standard*. Published by The Union Republican Congressional Committee, Washington, DC. 1872. [3¹³⁄₁₆" × 8⅝"]. Be/bk litho of Ulysses S. Grant. "We'll Sing a Song for U.S. Grant." 100pp. [M-182]. [Crew/USG-110].

• **AmPM-122 BUCKINGHAM**, William Alfred (Mayor, Norwich, 1849–1850 & 1856–1857; Governor, 1858–1866; U.S. Senate, 1869–1875)

122.1 Forward, The Ninth! w. No composer indicated. m. "Tune—*Excelsior*." "This was the watchword of the Flunkies (i.e. Seymour Democrats) during the last election in Connecticut, in which contest the Republicans were victorious. Three cheers for 'Buckingham' and the 'Old Nutmeg State.'" In: *Hutchinson's Republican Songster For 1860*, page 55. e. John W. Hutchinson" (of the Hutchinson Family Singers)." Published by O. Hutchinson, Publisher, No. 272 Greenwich Street, New York, NY. 1860. B/w floral design border. "Lincoln and Liberty." 76pp. [M-110]. [Crew/AL-317].

• **AmPM-122A BULKELEY**, Morgan Gardner (City Council, Hartford, 1874; Alderman, Hartford, 1875–1876; Mayor, Hartford, 1880–1888; Governor, 1889–1893; U.S. Senate, 1905–1911)

122A.1 Wide Awakes 1869 Re-Union At The Armory, Hartford, Nov. 1, 1888 (Republican Songs for the Campaign of 1888). Published by The Case Lockwood and Brainard Co., Hartford, CT. 1888. B/w vignette of an arm with a hammer at the bottom of page. "For President Benjamin Harrison of Indiana. For Governor Hon. Morgan G. Bulkeley of Hartford." 4pp.

• **AmPM-123 DODD**, Thomas Joseph (Special Agent for Federal Bureau of Investigation, 1933–1934; Connecticut Director of National Youth Administration, 1935–1938; U.S. House, 1953–1957; U.S. Senate, 1958–1971)

123.1 Draft Dodger Rag. w.m. Phil Ochs. In: *Broadside, Volume 2*, page 36. Published by Oak Publications, 33 West 60th Street, New York, NY. 1968. 96pp. and online at <http://www.sfheart.com/protese/Draft_Dodger_Rag.html>. Lyrics also published online by Mudcat Café at <http://mudcat.org/@displaysong.cfm?SongID=1703>. [199-].

• **AmPM-124 EATON**, William Wallace (Clerk of Courts, Tolland County, 1846–1847; State House, 1847–1848, 1853, 1863, 1870–1871, & 1873–1874; State Senate, 1850; Clerk of Courts, Hartford, 1851 & 1854; City Attorney, Hartford, 1857–1858; City Court Judge, Hartford, 1863–1864 & 1867–1872; U.S. Senate, 1875–1881; U.S. House, 1883–1885)

124.1 Concerning The War We Are In. w. W.A. Croffut. m. "Air—*Meg Maguire.*" "As sung by Senator Thurman, basso; Senator Hill, tenor; Senator Beck, soprano; Accompanied by Eaton with Trombone, and Proctor Knott with piccolo." In: *Bourbon Ballads*, page 2. Published in the *New York Tribune*, Extra No. 52, September, 1879. Non-pictorial newspaper supplement. "Songs for the Stump." 4pp. [Crew/MISC-226]. [AMC].

• **AmPM-125 ENGLISH**, James Edward (Board of Selectmen, New Haven, 1847–1861; Common Council, 1848–1849, State House, 1855 & 1872; State Senate, 1856–1858; U.S. House, 1861–1865; Governor, 1867–1868 & 1870; U.S. Senate, 1875–1876)

125.1 Forward, The Ninth! w. No composer indicated. m. "Air—*Excelsior*." "This was the watchword of the Flunkies (i.e. Seymour Democrats) during the last election in Connecticut, in which contest the Republicans were victorious. Three cheers for Buckingham, and the Old Nutmeg State." In: *Hutchinson's Republican Songster For 1860*, page 55. e. John W. Hutchinson "(of the Hutchinson Family Singers)." Published by O. Hutchinson, Publisher, No. 272 Greenwich Street, New York, NY. 1860. B/w floral design border. "Lincoln and Liberty." 76pp. [M-110]. [Crew/AL-317].

• **AmPM-126 GRISWOLD**, Roger (U.S. House, 1795–1805; State Supreme Court, 1807; Lt. Governor, 1809–1811; Governor, 1811–1812)

126.1 The Legislative Pugilists. w. Francis Guy, "A Patriot Exile." m. "Tune—*The Night Before Larry Was Fetch'd.*" In: *The Republican Harmonist (Being A Select Collection Of Republican, Patriotic, And Sentimental Songs, Odes, Sonnets, &c, American And European: Some Of Which Are Original, And Most Of The Others Now Come For The First Time From An American Press)*, page 81. c. D.E. [Daniel Ebsworth] "(A Citizen of the World)." Printed "for the People," Boston, MA. 1801. Non-pictorial. 152pp. [Crew/TJ-10].

• **AmPM-127 HARDY**, Guy Urban (Publisher; Postmaster, Canon City, 1900–1904; U.S. House, 1919–1933)

127.1 America My Country (The New National Anthem). w. Jens K. Grondahl. m. E.F. Maetzold. Published by The Red Wing Printing Co., Red Wing, MN. 1917. R/w/b litho of a shield, geometric designs. Long paragraph on the song—"*America, My Country* is said to be the greatest patriotic song-poem of the war..." 4pp. Page 4: Testimonial signed by officers of the National Editorial Association including Guy W. [sic] Hardy, Colorado, Vice President. List of Governors who had "written letters commending the nationwide use of this song."

• **AmPM-128 HENNEY**, William F. (Mayor, Hartford, 1904–1908)

128.1 Our Mayor (March Two-Step). m. Samuel H. Brigham. a. Harry Walters. Published by Cook's Music House, 251 Asylum Street, Hartford, CT. 1907. B/w photo of Wm. Henney. Bl/w torches, geometric designs. "Respectfully dedicated to Hon. Wm. F. Henney, Mayor of Hartford, Conn." "Sam'l. H. Brigham, Sergeant Fifer of the Putnam Phalanx, Hartford, Conn." 6pp. Page 6: Blank.

HODGE, Orlando J. (State Senate, Connecticut, 1864–1865) [See: Ohio]

• **AmPM-129 HOLCOMB**, Marcus H. (Probate Court Judge, Southington, 1893–1910; City Treasurer, Hartford, 1893–1908; State Senate, 1893–1894; State House, 1905–1906; State Attorney General, 1906–1907; Judge, Southington Borough, 1905–1909; State Superior Court, 1906–1915; Governor, 1915–1921)

129.1 My America. w.m. Frank Peer Beal. Published by The Boston Music Company, 26 & 28 West Street

Boston, MA. Copyright 1917 by Frank Beal. [8¾" × 10½"]. Bl/w litho of American flag, stars, geometric designs. "Endorsed by the Governors of New Hampshire, Connecticut & Massachusetts. Sung on the floor of the House of Congress, April 4, 1917." "All benefits from the sale of this publication are to be donated to the American Red Cross." List of Arrangements available." 4pp. Page 2: Endorsements by "H.M. Keyes, Governor of New Hampshire," "Samuel W. McCall, Governor of Massachusetts," and "Marcus H. Holcomb, Governor of Connecticut," and "F.H. Gallinger, United States Senator." Page 4: Bl/e geometric design.

- **AmPM-130 HUNTINGTON**, Samuel (Executive Councilor, Norwich, 1763; Colonial Assembly, 1764; Crown Attorney, 1765; Superior Court, 1774–1784; Continental Congress, 1776, 1778–1781 & 1783; Signer of the Declaration of Independence, 1776; Lt. Governor, 1785, Governor, 1786–1796)

130.1 The Declaration Of Independence Of The United States Of North America, July 4, 1776. w. From the Declaration of Independence. m. John E. Wilson. Published by John E. Wilson, Baltimore, MD. 1863. B/w litho of the interior of Independence Hall. "Arranged and adapted for Vocal and Instrumental Music as the Great National Chant." 4pp. [?]. Page 4: Facsimile signatures of all signers.

130.2 Old Independence Hall. w. A. Fletcher Stayman. m. Francis Weiland. Published by Stayman & Brothers, No. 210 Chesnut Street, Philadelphia, PA. 1855. Non-pictorial. "Respectfully dedicated to the Memory of the Signers of the Declaration of Independence." "Fac Simile of their signatures" including John Adams, Sam Adams, Elbridge Gerry, Thomas Jefferson. 8pp. Pages 2 and 8: Blank. [Crew/MISC-34].

- **AmPM-131 JEWELL**, Marshall (Governor, 1869–1870 & 1871–1873; U.S. Minister to Russia, 1873–1874; U.S. Postmaster General, 1874–1876)

131.1 Hurrah For Garfield (Republican Campaign Song). m. J.N. Pattison. Published by J.N. Pattison, No. 24 Union Square, New York, NY. 1880. Non-pictorial geometric frame. "Approved and Recommended by the Republican National Committee." List of "Executive Committee" member. 6pp. Page 2: "To Ex-Gov. Marshall Jewell." "Approved and Recommended by the Republican National Committee." Page 6: Advertising.

- **AmPM-132 LAKE**, Everett J. (State House, 1903–1905; State Senate, 1905–1907; Lt. Governor, 1907–1909; Governor, 1921–1923)

132.1 Governor's March. m. W.M. Redfield. Published by C.C. Church & Co., Hartford, CT. 1921. Br/w photo of "Governor Everett J. Lake, of Connecticut." Br/w geometric design border. "Popular Edition." 4pp. Page 2: At top of music — "Dedicated by permission to Governor Everett J. Lake, of Connecticut." Page 4: Advertising.

- **AmPM-133 LIEBERMAN**, Joseph I. (State Senate, 1970–1980; State Attorney General, 1983 & 1986–1988; U.S. Senate, 1988–Present; Candidate for Vice President, 2000; Candidate for Democratic Nomination for President, 2004)

133.1 All You Democrats. w. Adam Bernstein. m. Tune — "*Mr. Tambourine Man* originally by Bob Dylan." Published online at <http://www.amiright.com/parody/60s/bobdylan17/ shtml>. [ca. 2003].

133.2 The Ballad Of The War Protesters. w. Michael Pacholek. m. Tune — "*The Ballad Of John And Yoko* originally by The Beatles." "'Finks' is the plural of 'fink,' not somebody's name. 'The wife,' like the President, and his reasons for going to war, is fictional — in each case, unfortunately. And if I keep writing this stuff, well, all three Dixie Chicks are married, so I guess I'm stuck. For Now." Published online at <http://www.amiright.com/parody/60s/thebeatles102.shtml>. [ca. 2003].

133.3 Bush And Gore. w. Western River. m. "*Black Hole Sun* by Soundgarden." Published online at <http://www.amiright.com/parody/90s/soundgarder1.shml>. [ca. 2000].

133.4 Dashing Through The States. w. John Jenkins. m. Tune — "*Jingle Bells*, based on the performance by Traditional." "The Democratic field of presidential candidates has been reduced from 10 to 7 with more candidates expected to withdraw this week. Will the selection process eventually narrow down to two candidates in a replay of the Super Bowl with the upstart from Carolina going against the veteran from Massachusetts?" Published online at <http://www.amiright.com/parody/misc/traditional437.shtml>. 2004.

133.5 The Day Gore Tried To Win. w. "S.G.T." m. "Parody of Soundgarden's *The Day I Tried To Live.*" Published online at <http://www.angelfire.com.music/parodies/sentinsounfgardenparody.html>. [ca. 2001].

133.6 Dean, Dean. w. Bob Gomez. m. "*Green, Green*, based on a performance by The New Christie Minstrels." "Please check out Stray Pooch's parody version of this song which he did last June. Oh, and happy Thank Your Mentor Day. I would like to take this opportunity to thank the editors and writers of *Mad Magazine*, without whose crazy parodies, I never would have had the guts to write something this silly." Published online at <http://amiright.com/parody/60s/thenewchristieminstrels1.shtml. [ca. 2003].

133.7 The Democratic Presidential Candidate Show. w. Laurence Dunne. m. "*The Muppet Show* by The Muppets." "I'm not a Republican by and certainly I'm not a Dubya fan, as my Bush parodies will attest <http://www.amiright.com/parody/60s/thebradybunchtvshow0.shtml>." Published online at <http://amiright.com/parody/70s/muppets0.shtml. [ca. 2003].

133.8 Democracy Bites. w. S.G.T. m. "*Misc Songs*, originally by Pearl Jam." Published online at <http://amiright.com/parody/90s/pearljam6.shml>. [ca. 2001].

133.9 Election City. w. Michael Pacholek. m. "*Atlantic City,* based on a performance by Bruce Springsteen." "For the record, it was Pierre Ambroise Francois Choderios de LaClos (1741–1803), author of *Dangerous Liaisons*, who said, Revenge is a dish best served cold.' Not an old Klingon proverb, as Gene Roddenberry (or Quinton Tarantino) would have us believe. And while governing should not be, politics is often all about revenge. Burr..." Published online at <http://www.amiright.com/parody/80s/brucespringsteen22.shtml>. [ca. 2003].

133.10 Electoral Rhapsody 2000. w. Kevin Dunlap.

m. "Sung to the tune of *Bohemian Rhapsody* by Queen." Published online at <http://www.analyticalq.com/music/parodies/rhapsody.htm>. 2000.

133.11 A Few Short Years Ago. From CD: *American Way.* Performed by Dimpled Chad & The Disenfranchised. Lyrics published at <http:/dimpledchad.net>. [ca. 2000].

133.12 Glorified D (Lieberman). w. MrMacphisto. m. Tune — "*Glorified G*, based on the performance by Pearl Jam." "Come this November, I'll be supporting the 'anyone but Bush' ticket, but Lieberman is one of the few people that I wouldn't want as a substitute to Bush ... Note, also that I don't have a problem with the Jewish community, but he seems like one of the few fanatical Jews out there..." Published online at <http://www.amiright.com/parody/90s/pearljam32.shtml>. [ca. 2003].

133.13 Head Just Like A Rock. w. Michael Pacholek. m. Tune — "*Loves Me Like A Rock* originally by Paul Simon." "Yeah, I know, Kerry's still gotta get through the primaries against those heavyweights Howard Dean, John Edwards, and Joe Lie-berman. If Lieberman is a Democrat, then I'm the center fielder for the Yankees. But Kerry vs. Bush? That debate will make Bartlet vs. Richie (On *The West Wing*) look like Ali v. Frazier!" Published online at <http://www.amiright.com/parody/70s/paulsimon15.shtml>. 2003

133.14 Howard Dean's Leading In Taxachusetts. w. Michael McVey. m. "*Massachusetts*, based on a performance by The Bee Gees." "As for the other 49 states, well, does the name McGovern ring a bell?" Published online at <http://www.amiright.com/parody/70s/thebeegees23.shtml>. 2003.

133.15 If I Were The V.P. w. No composer indicated. m. "Parody of *If I Were A Rich Man* from *Fiddler On The Roof*." Lyrics published by *The Bob Rivers Show* with Bob, Spike & Joe and Twisted Tunes online at <http://www.twistedradio.com/player/lyrics.asp?songID=678>. [2000].

133.16 I'm Just A Guy, A Guy Named Joe. w. Henry and Bobbie Shaffner. m. "*Melody — I Can't Say No.*" Published as a Press Release by Luckman Associates, 134 West Houston Street, Suite 1, New York, NY. 10012. [8½" × 11"]. Non-pictorial. "Public Relations News Flash! — Senator Lieberman 'Can't say no' to Funny New Song Names '*A Guy Named Joe.*'" 2pp. Page 2: Blank.

133.17 It Ain't Me (In 2004) Babe. w. "Bubba." m. Tune — "*It Ain't Me Babe* originally by Bob Dylan." Published online at <http://www.amiright.com/parody/60s/bobdylan5.shtml>. [ca. 2003].

133.18 Lieberman Bites The Dust. w. Steve Kalafut. m. Tune — "*Another One Bites The Dust*, based on the performance by Queen." "Joe Lieberman withdraws from the campaign to win his party's presidential nomination." Published online at <http://www.amiright.com/parody/80s/queen47.shtml>. 2004.

133.19 Lieberman In 2004. w. Alan Friedman, Southern Discomfort. m. Tune — "*Everything's Coming Up Roses* originally by Rosalind Russell." "Joe Lieberman's advisors position him for a run at the White House in 2004." Published online at <http://www.amiright.com/parody/misc/rosalindrussell0.shtml>. 2003

133.20 Lieberman Killed The Video Games. w. Larcen Tyler. m. Tune — "*Video Killed The Radio Star*, originally by The Buggles." Published online at <http://amiright.com/parody/80s/thebuggles1.shml>. [ca. 2000].

133.21 New Hampshire Primary Marching Cadence. w. Guy DiRito. m. "*Military Cadence (Sound Off)*, based on a performance by Traditional." "This song is done to the traditional military cadence beat. Practice marching as you sound off to this." Published online at <http://www.amiright.com/parody/misc/traditional430.shtml>. 2004.

133.22 '04 Elections Are Coming. w. KAH & Ana. m. "*Santa Clause Is Coming To Town*, based on a performance by Traditional." "For the Holidays, our AP Gov teacher gave us an assignment to write some holiday song political song parodies ... and here's what we came up with. Enjoy!" Published online at <http://amiright.com/parody/misc/traditional387.shtml>. 2003.

133.23 People Who Tried (Political). w. Malcolm Higgins. m. "*People Who Died*, based on a performance by Jim Carroll." Published online at <http://www.amiright.com/parody/misc/jimcarroll0.shtml>. [ca. 2003].

133.24 Season On The Trail. w. Michael Pacholek. m. "*Season's In The Sun*, based on a performance by Terry Jacks." "The Campaign trail, that is. Oy, oy, Joe, another one bites the dust." Published online at <http://www.amiright.com/parody/70s/terryjacks5.shtml>. [ca. 2004].

133.25 Some Wail Away. w. Malcolm Higgins. m. "*Come Sail Away*, based on a performance by Styx." "Written of yourse [sic] by the ultimate lefty ... me." Published online at <http://www.amiright.com/parody/misc/styx0.shtml>. [ca. 2003].

133.26 Stupid (Go Cast Your Vote). w. Bruce Decker. m. "*Cupid* originally by The Spinners." Published online at <http://www.amiright.com/parody/misc/thespinners0.shtml>. [ca. 2000]

133.27 33.3% Sure (I Won't Lose It In '04). w. Mike Armstrong. m. "*99.9% Sure (I've Never Been Here Before)* originally by Brian McComas." "Yea, so, this is a really cool country song — idea just kind of hit me while I was listening to it, hopefully you like it. With questions surrounding the '04 election, the fact that the presidency is up in the air is what I'm trying to convey." Published online at <http://www.amiright.com/parody/2000s/brianmccomas0.shtml>. [ca. 2003].

133.28 Uncle Albert/Whiney Joe. w. Greek Geek. m. "*Uncle Albert/Admiral Halsey*, originally by Wings. Published online at <http://www.amiright.com/parody/70s/wings1.shtml>. [ca. 2000].

133.29 Vote. w. Jennifer Pozner. m. "To the tune of Madonna's *Vogue*. " Lyrics published online by <billionairesforbushorgore@topica.com>. 2000.

133.30 Vote. w. Moscowman. m. Tune — "*Vogue*, based on a performance by Madonna." "The Election is coming in November, voters reading the magazines and think what's their decision on the upcoming election." Published online at <http://amiright.com/parody/90s/thekinks3.shtml>. [2004].

133.31 We Want Howard Dean. w.m. Denny Zartman. m. No tune indicated. "Spread The Word Through Song and Music! Songs For Dean, Songs to get elected by." N/c photo of Howard Dean. Lyrics and sound file published online at <http://songsfordean.com/so/lyrics/somethingtosee.php>. 2004.

133.32 *West Palm Beach.* w. Weird O'l Yankee Vic. m. "*Green Acres,* originally by Theme." Published online at <http://www.amiright.com/parody/misc/theme0.shml>. [ca. 2000].

- AmPM-134   MARIGOLD, W.H. (State Senate, 1895 & 1897)

134.1 *The Marigold Two Step*. m. Harry E. Jeroy. Published by Alfred Fox, Bridgeport, CT. and Thomas B. Fox, 273 Brixton Road, London, England. 1895. B/w flowers, geometric designs. "Dedicated to Senator W.H. Marigold." 6pp. Page 6: Blank.

- AmPM-135   MCCURDY, Charles J. (State Senate, 1832; Lt. Governor, 1847–1849; U.S. Ambassador to Austria, 1850–1852)

135.1 *The Dying Soldier Of Buena Vista*. w. Col. Henry Petrikin. m. Orramel Whittlesey, of Salem, Conn. [facsimile signature]. No publisher indicated. 1849. B/w litho by Wm. Endicott of a battle scene, dying man lying on an American flag, soldier in attendance. "The music Composed and most respectfully dedicated to His Honor Charles J. McCurdy, Lt. Governor of the State of Connecticut." 10pp. Pages 2 and 10: Blank.

- AmPM-136   MIDDENDORF, John William, II (U.S. Ambassador to the Netherlands, 1969–1973; U.S. Secretary of the Navy, 1974–1977)

136.1 *Thumbs Up, America!* w. Sammy Cahn "(Director of ASCAP, President Song Writer's Hall of Fame)." m. Hon. J. William Middendorff II, "(Former Secretary of the Navy)." Published by The Presidential Inaugural Committee, Washington, DC. 1981. N/c photo of Ronald Reagan. "Inaugural Theme Song for President Ronald Reagan and his First Lady, Nancy, January 20, 1981." B/w Presidential Seal inscribed "Inauguration of The President and The Vice-President." 4pp. Page 2: "Dedicated to the President and First Lady." Page 3: "Music Production Coordinator: Richard A. McCraken." Page 4: Inaugural and song credits. R/w/b drawing of Presidential seal, fingerprints. [Crew/RR-1].

136.2 *The U.S. Capitol March* (For Concert Band). m. J. William Middendorff II. a. Richard Hayman. Published by Bourne Co., New York, NY. 1980. R/w/b eagle. Parts set for concert band.

MORGAN, Edwin Dennison (City Council, Hartford, 1832) [See: New York]

- AmPM-137   NADER, Ralph (Consumers Advocate; Author; Green Party Candidate for President, 1992, 1996, 2000 & 2004)

137.1 *Blame Florida*. w. Caitlin, "Falaen@aol.com." m. "Sung to the tune of *Blame Canada* from the *South Park: The Movie*." Published online at <http://www.geocities.com/wmktong/bootnewt/blame-fl.htm>. [ca. 2000].

137.2 *Bushlicker*. w. "Political Prankster." m. "*Complicated,* based on the performance by Avril Lavigne." Published online at <http://amiright.com/parody/2000s/avrillavigne175.shml>. [2003].

137.3 *Election Impossible*. w. S.T.G. m. "*Mission Impossible 2 Theme,* originally by Limp Bizkit." "It does not follow exactly to River of Dreams because I cut out a verse or two in the middle." Published online at <http://www.amiright.com/parody/2000s/limpbizkit2.shml>. [ca. 2000].

137.4 *Green Party Man*. w. Charlie Decker. m. "*Street Fighting Man,* based on a performance by Rolling Stones." "Although I am a Democrat politically, I sympathize with the Green Party, even if only to keep Dems honest." Published online at <http://www.amiright.com/parody/60s/rollingstones34.shtml>. [ca. 2003].

137.5 *Hand Count*. w. Keith K. Higa. m. "*Convoy,* originally by C.W. McCall." Published online at <http://www.amiright.com/parody/70s/cwmccall0.shtml>. [2000].

137.6 *J.F. Kerryville*. w. Kelly S. Solid. m. "*Margaritaville,* based on a performance by Jimmy Buffet." Published online at <http://amiright.com/parody/70s/jimmybuffet14.shtml>. [2004].

137.7 *Kerry*. w. Johnny D. m. "*Sherry,* based on a performance by Frankie Valli and the Four Seasons." "I'm not saying I'll vote for Kerry or Bush or Nader or Lyndon LaRouche ... It's just that politicians are always fair game on Amiright ... heh heh heh..." Published online at <http://www.amiright.com/parody/60s/frankievalliandthefourseasons2.shtml>. [2004].

137.8 *Kerry, Kerry* (A Progressive's Lament). w. Ravyn Rant. m. "*Momma Mia,* based on a performance by Abba." "I started this right after Super Tuesday, when the Democratic candidate was announced months before the convention." Published online at <http://www.amiright.com/parody/70s/abba61.shtml>. [2004].

137.9 *Mrs. Naders*. w. Mrs. Janiskewicz. m. No tune indicated. "Permission granted to use in Nader's Campaign, with proper credit, but not for personal profit." "Mrs. Janiskewicz is a older hardworking Polish American who is fed-up with what is happening in 'Her American Democracy.' She does not like living in a Corpocracy. She is outraged that Mr. Nader was not permitted to debate. She originally wrote *Mrs. Naders,* symbolic of all women backing Nader with her 60's friends in mind. Older now, they wanted to do a video-song rapping..." Lyrics published online by <billionairesforbushorgore@topica.com>. 2000.

137.10 *My Name Is Ralph Nader*. w. Joe. m. "*My Name Is Joe,* based on a performance by Weezer." "I'm not making fun of the song *My Name Is Jones* because it kicks butt." "Nader as president ... when pigs fly." Published by Amiright.com at <http://www.amiright.com/parody/90s/weezer3.shtml>. [ca. 2003].

137.11 *Ralph Nader*. w. Billy Florio. m. "*Around The World,* originally by Red Hot Chili Peppers." Published online at <http://amiright.com/parody/90s/redhotchilipeppers2.shtml>. [ca. 2001].

137.12 *Ralph Nader Rap*. w. Ron Presley. m. "*Party Up,* originally by DMX." Published online at <http://amiright.com/parody/2000s/dmx0.shml>. [ca. 2001].

137.13 *Return Of Nader*. w. Phil Nelson. m. "*Eye Of The Tiger,* based on a performance by Survivor." "Ralph Nader's Running Again." Published online at <http://www.amiright.com/parody/80s/survivor.shtml>. 2004.

137.14 Sing We Sing [Song Book]. Published online by Radio IUMA at <http://www.artists2.iuma.com/IUMA/Bands/Sng_We_Sing/lyrics-0.html>. 2000. Eleven songs. "Click this link to purchase *Sing We Sing* for $10 + $5 shipping and handling. All profits generated from the sale of *Sing We Sing* will be donated to Green Party causes and the Vote Nader 2004 Campaign." Gn/w photo of a "Vote Nader & LaDuke" campaign button. [Crew/MISC-198].

137.15 Vote. w. Jennifer Pozner. m. "To the tune of Madonna's *Vogue*. " Lyrics published online by <billionairesforbushorgore@topica.com>. 2000.

• **AmPM-138 NILES**, John Milton (Associate Judge, Hartford County, 1821–1826; State House, 1826; Postmaster, Hartford, 1829–1836; U.S. Senate, 1835–1839 & 1843–1849; U.S. Postmaster General, 1840–1841)

138.1 All Round My 'At I Vers A Veeping Villow. w.m. No composer or tune indicated. "A Song to be Sung at Van Buren's Indignation meetings." In: *Songs For The People (Or Tippecanoe Melodies)* [Songster], page 27. "Dedicated to the Democratic Whig Young Men of the City and County of New York." Published for the Authors by James P. Giffing, No. 56 Gold Street, New York, NY. 1840. [3¾" × 6"]. Litho of William Henry Harrison, log cabin, flag. "Original and Selected." 76pp. [M-019]. [Crew/WHH-63].

138.2 Beggar's Petition. w. No composer indicated. m. "Tune — *All On Hobbies*." "A very pathetic and musical appeal to the Dear People, by an Ex-Postmaster General." In: *Tippecanoe Song-Book (A Collection Of Log Cabin And Patriotic Melodies)*, page 14. Published by Marshall, Williams & Butler, Philadelphia, PA. 1840. White on black litho of log cabin, plow, flags, eagle. 180pp. [M-024]. [Crew/WHH-61].

138.3 Martin Van Buren To John M. Niles. w. No composer indicated. m. "Air — *Come Rest In This Bosom*." In: *Harrison Melodies (Original And Selected)*, page 17. Published by Weeks, Jordan & Co., Boston, MA. 1840. [3⅜" × 6"]. B/w litho of William Henry Harrison. "Published under the direction of the Boston Harrison Club." 76pp. [M-001, 002, 003]. [Crew/WHH-86].

138.4 Mr. Van Buren's Farewell To The Palace. w.m. No composers or tune indicated. No publisher indicated. [1840]. [Approx. 5" × 12"]. Non-pictorial. 2pp. Page 2: Blank. [AMC]. [Crew/MVB-19].

138.5 Song Of The Pauper. w. No composer indicated. m. "Tune — *Up Salt River*." "As sung by the late P.M.G." In: *Songs For The People (Or Tippecanoe Melodies)* [Songster], page 46. "Dedicated to the Democratic Whig Young Men of the City and County of New York." Published for the Authors by James P. Giffing, No. 56 Gold Street, New York, NY. 1840. [3¾" × 6"]. Litho of William Henry Harrison, log cabin, flag. "Original and Selected." 76pp. [M-019]. [Crew/WHH-63].

• **AmPM-139 SCULLY**, Martin (Mayor, Waterbury, 1914–1918)

139.1 You're A Million Dollar Doll. w.m. James A. Lonergan. Published by James A. Lonergan Publishing Co., Waterbury, CT. 1915. Bl/w photo of "Mayor Martin Scully" and "Chas. A. Collier," woman bowing; "Municipal Building, Waterbury, Conn." Bl/w geometric designs. 6pp. Page 2: At top of music — "Respectfully dedicated to Miss Irene Keefe (Miss Waterbury)." Page 6: Blank.

• **AmPM-140 SHERMAN**, Roger (Surveyor of New Haven County, 1745; Connecticut Assembly, 1755–1756, 1758–1761, 1764–1766; Justice of the Peace, Litchfield County, 1755–1761; Justice of the Peace, New Haven, 1765–1766; State Senate, 1766–1785; Superior Court, 1766–1767 & 1773–1788; State Council of Safety, 1777–1779; Continental Congress, 1774–1781, & 1784; Signer, Declaration of Independence, 1776; Mayor, New Haven, 1784–1793; U.S. House, 1789–1791; U.S. Senate, 1791–1793)

140.1 The Declaration Of Independence Of The United States Of North America, July 4, 1776. w. From the Declaration of Independence. m. John E. Wilson. Published by John E. Wilson, Baltimore, MD. 1863. B/w litho of the interior of Independence Hall. "Arranged and adapted for Vocal and Instrumental Music as the Great National Chant." 4pp. [?]. Page 4: Facsimile signatures of all signers.

140.2 Old Independence Hall. w. A. Fletcher Stayman. m. Francis Weiland. Published by Stayman & Brothers, No. 210 Chesnut Street, Philadelphia, PA. 1855. Non-pictorial. "Respectfully dedicated to the Memory of the Signers of the Declaration of Independence." "Fac Simile of their signatures" including John Adams, Sam Adams, Elbridge Gerry, Thomas Jefferson. 8pp. Pages 2 and 8: Blank. [Crew/MISC-34].

• **AmPM-141 SMITH**, John Cotton (State House, 1793, 1796 & 1800; U.S. House, 1800–1806; State Supreme Court, 1809; Lt. Governor, 1810; Governor, 1813–1818)

141.1 My Mother's Bible (A Ballad). w. George P. Morris, Esq. m. Henry Russell. Published by Firth & Hall, 1 Franklin Square, New York, NY. 1841. B/w litho of a family gathered around a table in Bible study. "This song is respectfully dedicated to Hon. John Cotton Smith of Sharon, Ct." [V-1: Dedication Above the lithograph] [V-2: Dedication below the lithograph]. 8pp. Pages 2 and 8: Blank. [LL/JH].

• **AmPM-142 STOWE**, Harriet Beecher (Abolitionist; Author, *Uncle Toms Cabin*, 1850)

142.1 The Georgian Slave (Ballad). w. [Charles Jefferys]. m.a. S. Glover. Published by S. Brainard & Co., Cincinnati, OH. 1852. B/w non-pictorial geometric designs. "To Mrs. Harriet Beecher Stowe." Printed verse. [AMC].

142.2 Little Eva; Uncle Tom's Guardian Angel. w. John G. Whittier. m. Manuel Emilio. Published by John P. Jewett & Co., Boston, MA. 1852. B/w litho of Uncle Tom and Eva, geometric design border. "Little Eva, Song Composed and most Respectfully dedicated to Mrs. Harriet Beecher Stowe, author of *Uncle Tom's Cabin*."

142.3 Poor Uncle Tom. w.m. No composers or tune indicated. Published by Andrews, Printer, No. 38 Chatham Street, New York, NY. [185-]. [Approx. 6" × 9½"]. Non-pictorial geometric design border. "This song suggested by the incidents to be found in Mrs. Harriet Beecher Stowe's celebrated work entitled *Uncle Tom's Cabin*, and sung nightly, with tremendous applause, by Wood's celebrated Minstrels, at 444 Broadway, N.Y." 2pp. Page 2: Blank.

142.4 Southern Sentiments. w.m. No composers or tune indicated. Published in Baltimore. 1861. B/w litho of man on horse with a trumpet, geometric design border. "October 9th, 1861." Preceded on page 1 by *Hark! The Summons.* 2pp. Page 2: Blank. [AML].

142.5 Southern Sentiments. w.m. "B." m. "Air—*Let Haughty Gaul Invasion Threat.*" Published in Baltimore. 1861. [Approx. 3½" × 6⅝"]. Non-pictorial. "October 6th, 1861." 2pp. Page 2: Blank. [AML] [WFU].

142.6 Uncle Tom's Glimpse Of Glory. w. Eliza. m. Frank Howard. Published by E.H. Wade, 197 Washington Street, Boston, MA. 1852. B/w non-pictorial geometric designs. "Respectfully dedicated to Mrs. Harriet Beecher Stowe (Author of *Uncle Tom's Cabin*)." "For sale by Horace Waters, 333 Broadway, New York."

• **AmPM-144** TOUCEY, Isaac (Prosecuting Attorney, Hartford County, 1822–1835 & 1842–1844; U.S. House, 1835–1839; Governor, 1846–1847; U.S. Attorney General, 1848–1849; State Senate, 1850; State House, 1852; U.S. Senate, 1852–1857; U.S. Secretary of the Navy, 1857–1861)

144.1 Song Of The Office Holder. w. No composer indicated. m. "Air—*A Few Days.*" In: *Republican Song Book*, page 8. c. Thomas Drew "(Late Editor of *The Massachusetts Spy*)." Published by Thayer and Eldridge, Boston, MA. 1860. [3⅞" × 5⅞"]. Br/bk litho of beardless Abraham Lincoln, vignettes of young Lincoln chopping rails, polling raft. 68pp. [M-108]. [Crew/AL-8].

• **AmPM-145** TRACY, Uriah (State House, 1788; U.S. House, 1793–1796; U.S. Senate, 1796–1807)

145.1 The Governmental Chair. w. No composer indicated. m. "Tune—*Mrs. Casey.*" In: *The Republican Harmonist (Being A Select Collection Of Republican, Patriotic, And Sentimental Songs, Odes, Sonnets, &c, American And European: Some Of Which Are Original, And Most Of The Others Now Come For The First Time From An American Press)*, page 24. c. D.E. [Daniel Ebsworth] "(A Citizen of the World)." Printed "for the People," Boston, MA. 1801. Non-pictorial. 152pp. [Crew/TJ-10].

145.2 The Retrospect: Or A Touch On The Tories. w. No composer indicated. m. "Tune—*Pretty Work For Twelve Dollars A Day.*" In: *The Republican Harmonist (Being A Select Collection Of Republican, Patriotic, And Sentimental Songs, Odes, Sonnets, &c, American And European: Some Of Which Are Original, And Most Of The Others Now Come For The First Time From An American Press)*, page 20. c. D.E. [Daniel Ebsworth] "(A Citizen of the World)." Printed "for the People," Boston, MA. 1801. Non-pictorial. 152pp. [Crew/TJ-10].

TREAT, Robert (Surveyor of Milford Lands, 1639–1640 & 1652; Tax Collector, Wethersfield, 1647; Deputy, New Haven Colony General Court, 1653, 1655–1659; Chief Military Officer of Milford, 1654; Magistrate, New Haven Colony, 1660–1664; Founder and Town Clerk, Newark, New Jersey, 1666–1667; State Legislature, New Jersey, 1667–1672; Assistant, General Court of the Colony of Connecticut, 1673–1676; Deputy Governor, Colony of Connecticut, 1676–1683, 1699–1709; Governor, Colony of Connecticut, 1683–1698) [See: New Jersey]

• **AmPM-146** TRUMBULL, John H. (Governor, 1926–1930; Candidate for Governor, 1932)

146.1 Republican Campaign Songs. Published by the Seventh Senatorial District Republican Association, Connecticut. [1932]. [8½" × 14"]. Non-pictorial mimeograph. 4pp. Pages 1 and 3: Music. Pages 2 and 4: Blank.

• **AmPM-147** WALLER, Thomas M. (State House, 1867–1868, 1872, 1876; Secretary of State, Connecticut, 1870–1871; Mayor, New London, 1873; Governor, 1883–1885)

147.1 Governor Waller's March. m. Fred C. Wight. Published by Jean M. Missud Pub., Salem, MA. 1891. [7" × 10¾"]. Non-pictorial band part set.

• **AmPM-148** WELLES, Gideon (State House, 1826; Postmaster, Hartford, 1836–1841; U.S. Secretary of the Navy, 1871–1869)

148.1 Cabinet Pictures. w.m. No composer or tune indicated. In: *Copperhead Minstrel (A Choice Collection Of Democratic Poems & Songs)*, page 24. Published by Feeks and Bancker, Wholesale Agents, No. 24 Ann Street, New York. 1863. [4¾" × 7¼"]. O/bk non-pictorial. "For the use of Political Clubs and the Social Circle." "Price 25 cents." 64pp. [M-133] [Crew/GBM-64].

148.2 The Carte-De-Visite Album. w. No composer indicated. m. "Air—*Chanting Benny.*" Published by H. De Marsan, 60 Chatham Street, New York, NY. [1861–1865]. [Approx. 6" × 9"]. B/w litho border of theatrical-type people, lion's heard, geometric designs. "A Comic Song written for Tony Pastor." 2pp. Page 2: Blank. [AMC].

148.3 Fourth Of July (Song). w.m. No composer or tune indicated. No publisher indicated. [ca. 1862]. [Approx. 4¾" 8¾"]. Non-pictorial geometric design border. "Gotten up expressly for those who have an appreciative mind." 2pp. Page 2: Blank. [WFU].

148.4 How Are You Greenbacks? w. No composer indicated. m. *How Are You Greenbacks?* In: *Copperhead Minstrel (A Choice Collection Of Democratic Poems & Songs)*, page 34. Published by Feeks and Bancker, Wholesale Agents, No. 24 Ann Street, New York. 1863. [4¾" × 7¼"]. O/bk non-pictorial. "For the use of Political Clubs and the Social Circle." "Price 25 cents." 64pp. [M-133] [Crew/GBM-64].

148.5 A Hundred Years Hence. w. Tony Pastor. m. No tune indicated. Published by Charles Magnus, 12 Franklin Street, New York, NY. [1863–1864]. N/c lithos of an Indian with a American flag inscribed "For The Union," and a litho of a bull, man chopping a tree, vignette titled "Indiana." 2pp. Page 2: Blank. [AMC].

148.6 Old Abe They Said Was An Honest Man (Song). w. J.W. Jarboe, Esq. m. F. Lafayette. Published by Firth, Son & Company, No. 563 Broadway, New York, NY. 1864. Non-pictorial geometric designs. "Words Composed and Sung with Great Applause by J.W. Jarboe, Esq. at the Great McClellan Union Meeting, Union Square." "To the McClellan Union Clubs." 6pp. Pages 2 and 6: Blank. [Crew/GBM-48].

148.7 Old Abe And Old Nick. w. No composer indicated. m. "Tune—*Lord Lovel.*" In: *Copperhead Min-*

strel *(A Choice Collection Of Democratic Poems & Songs)*, page 34. Published by Feeks and Bancker, Wholesale Agents, No. 24 Ann Street, New York. 1863. [4¾" × 7¼"]. O/bk non-pictorial. "For the use of Political Clubs and the Social Circle." "Price 25 cents." 64pp. [M-133] [Crew/GBM-64].

148.8 Old Lincoln And His Fellows, Is The Abolitionist's Government! w.m. No composers or tune indicated. No publisher indicated. [1861–1862]. B/w litho of a man's head which can be seen also if the music is turned upside down. "What a precious set!" 2pp. Page 2: Blank. [AMC].

148.9 Sic Semper. w. "By A Virginian." m. No tune indicated. No publisher indicated. [1861–1862]. [Approx. 6" × 9½"]. Non-pictorial geometric design border. 2pp. Page 2: Blank. [AMC].

148.10 The White House. w. G.R. Edeson. m. "Air—*Root, Hog, Or Die!*" Published by H. De Marsan, 54 Chatham Street, New York, NY. [1861–1862]. B/w litho border of minstrels, geometric designs. 2pp. Page 2: Blank. [AMC].

- **AmPM-149 WILLIAMS**, William (Town Clerk, Lebanon, 1753–1796; State House, 1757–1762, 1763–1776, & 1780–1784; Continental Congress, 1776–1777; Signer of the Declaration of Independence, 1776; Council of Safety, 1776–1783 [?]; County Court, Windham, 1776–1804; Judge of Probate, Windham, 1776–1808; Assistant Councilor/Councilor, Windham, 1780–1800)

149.1 The Declaration Of Independence Of The United States Of North America, July 4, 1776. w. From the Declaration of Independence. m. John E. Wilson. Published by John E. Wilson, Baltimore, MD. 1863. B/w litho of the interior of Independence Hall. "Arranged and adapted for Vocal and Instrumental Music as the Great National Chant." 4pp. [?]. Page 4: Facsimile signatures of all signers.

149.2 Old Independence Hall. w. A. Fletcher Stayman. m. Francis Weiland. Published by Stayman & Brothers, No. 210 Chesnut Street, Philadelphia, PA. 1855. Non-pictorial. "Respectfully dedicated to the Memory of the Signers of the Declaration of Independence." "Fac Simile of their signatures" including John Adams, Sam Adams, Elbridge Gerry, Thomas Jefferson. 8pp. Pages 2 and 8: Blank. [Crew/MISC-34].

- **AmPM-150 WOLCOTT**, Oliver (Sheriff, Litchfield County, 1751; State Council 1774–1786; Judge Common Pleas & Probate, Litchfield County 1774–1786 [?]; Continental Congress Commissioner of Indian Affairs for the Northern Department, 1776; Continental Congress, 1776–1778 & 1780–1783; Signer, Declaration of Independence, 1776; Lt. Governor, 1786–1796; Governor, 1796–1797)

150.1 The Declaration Of Independence Of The United States Of North America, July 4, 1776. w. From the Declaration of Independence. m. John E. Wilson. Published by John E. Wilson, Baltimore, MD. 1863. B/w litho of the interior of Independence Hall. "Arranged and adapted for Vocal and Instrumental Music as the Great National Chant." 4pp. [?]. Page 4: Facsimile signatures of all signers.

150.2 Old Independence Hall. w. A. Fletcher Stayman. m. Francis Weiland. Published by Stayman & Brothers, No. 210 Chesnut Street, Philadelphia, PA. 1855. Non-pictorial. "Respectfully dedicated to the Memory of the Signers of the Declaration of Independence." "Fac Simile of their signatures" including John Adams, Sam Adams, Elbridge Gerry, Thomas Jefferson. 8pp. Pages 2 and 8: Blank. [Crew/MISC-34].

150.3 The Retrospect: Or A Touch On The Tories. w. No composer indicated. m. "Tune—*Pretty Work For Twelve Dollars A Day.*" In: *The Republican Harmonist (Being A Select Collection Of Republican, Patriotic, And Sentimental Songs, Odes, Sonnets, &c, American And European: Some Of Which Are Original, And Most Of The Others Now Come For The First Time From An American Press)*, page 20. c. D.E. [Daniel Ebsworth] "(A Citizen of the World)." Printed "for the People," Boston, MA. 1801. Non-pictorial. 152pp. [Crew/TJ-10].

- **AmPM-150A WOOSTER**, David (Collector of the Customs, New Haven. 1760s; General Assembly, 1775)

150A.1 General Wooster March. m. B.C. Baker. Published by Wooster Board of Trade Band, Wooster, OH. 1925. B/w drawing of General Wooster on Horseback. "Compliments of Freedlanders." 4pp. Page 4: B/w photo of "Wooster Board of Trade Band."

- **AmPM-151 MISCELLANEOUS MUSIC**

151.1 The Capitol Three- Step (With Description). m. G. Prutting, Jr. Published by G. Prutting, Jr., Hartford, CT. [ca. 1898]. B/w photo of the State Capitol building at Hartford. "The latest Society Dance, As Danced at the 20th Annual Convention of the American Society of Professors of Dancing, held at Boston, Sept. 8, 1897." 4pp. Page 4: Blank.

151.2 City Of Waterbury, Our Home Town. w. Frank Stuart and Neil Maloney. m. Frank Cola Santo (Frank Colasanto-Ficeto). Published by Frank Cola Santo, 347 West 46th Street, New York, NY. 1958. Pl/w photos of various sights in Waterbury including the Waterbury City Hall building. 6pp. Page 2: At top of music—"March-Song Dedicated to the City of Waterbury."

151.3 Dear Old Hartford, Conn. w.m. Alonzo J. Ross. Published by Alonzo J. Ross, 11 Roosevelt Street, Hartford, CT. 1928. Br/w photo of "State Capitol, Hartford, Conn." R/w/b eagle, flags, shield, stripe border. 6pp. Page 6: Narrative on Hartford's history.

151.4 Foot Guard Quick Step. m. C.S. Grafulla. Published by Danforth & Brewer, No. 6 State Street, Hartford, CT. 1845. H/c litho of military unit assembled in front of the state capitol building. "Arranged for the Piano Forte, and Dedicated to Major Commandant L.H. Bacon, and the Officers and Members of the First Company Gov's Foot Guard of Connecticut." 4pp. Page 4: Blank. [LL/JH].

151.5 Genl. King's Quick Step. m. James M. Hubbard. Published by Wm. Hall & Son, No. 239 Broadway, New York, NY. 1848. B/w tinted litho by Sarony & Major of General King, eagle, fancy geometric frame. "As performed at the Governor's Inauguration (3rd May, 1848) in New Haven, Conn., by Bloomfield's United States Band." 6pp. Pages 2 and 6: Blank.

151.6 Hartford. m. S.L. Tyler. Published by W.H. Boner & Co., 1102 Chestnut Street, Philadelphia, PA. 1886. B/w litho of various state capitol buildings: "Madison, Wis., Harrisburg, Pa., Hartford, Conn.,

Columbus, O., Lansing, Mich., Washington, D.C., St. Paul, Minn., Richmond Va., Sacramento, Cal., Albany, NY., Boston, Mass., Montgomery, Ala." "The Capitol Collection." 8pp. Page 2: Blank. Page 3: At top of music—"To my Brother, C.A. Tyler." Page 8: Advertising.

151.7 Republican Campaign Songs. Published by the Seventh Senatorial District Republican Association, Connecticut. [1932]. [8½" × 14"]. Non-pictorial mimeograph. 4pp. Pages 1 and 3: Music. Pages 2 and 4: Blank.

DELAWARE

• **AmPM-152** BAYARD, Thomas Francis, Sr. (U.S. Senate, 1869–1885; U.S. Secretary of State, 1885–1889; U.S. Ambassador to Great Britain, 1893–1897)
152.1 The Betters In Our Block. w. Frank N. Scott. m. No tune indicated. In: *P.T. Schultz & Co's Blaine And Logan Bugle Call,* page 8. Published by P.T. Schultz & Company, No. 172 Race Street, Cincinnati, OH. 1881. [1884 Edition]. [5⅞" × 7⅜"]. Bk/gn litho of James G. Blaine and John A. Logan, flags and eagle, geometric design border. 36pp. Page 36: Advertising. [M-245]. [Crew/JGB-67].
152.2 Bryan's Dream. w. Stephe Bonbright. m. No tune indicated. In: *Republican Victory Campaign Songs,* page 24. c. F.F. Gilbert. Published by Home Music Company, No. 41 East Randolph Street, Chicago, IL. [5⅜" × 7¾"]. 1896. B/w photo of William McKinley. R/w/b drawing of U.S. Flags. 36pp. [Crew/WM-251].
152.3 Good Bye, Old Grover, Good Bye. w. A.A. Rowley. m. "Air—*Good-Bye, My Lover, Good-Bye.*" In: *Republican Campaign Songs,* page 2. w. A.A. Rowley (Beloit, Kas). Published by The Western News Company, Chicago, IL. 1888. [5¼" × 7½"]. B/w litho of "The Author, in '63, 17th Illinois Cav." "Original, Pointed and Spicy ... Set to Old Familiar Tunes, Suitable for Glee Clubs and Marching Clubs." "Look at it and you will buy it." 36pp. [M-283]. [Crew/BFH-64].
152.4 Political Barber Shop. w.m. No composer or tune indicated. "Male Voices." In: *True Blue Republican Campaign Songs For 1896,* page 12. c. J.B. Herbert. Published by The S. Brainard's Sons Company, Chicago, IL. 1896. [5⅜" × 6⅞"]. R/w/b drawing of crossed flags, wreath, ribbons. Bl/w photo of "Hon. Wm. McKinley." "Protection." 36pp. [M-328]. [Crew/WM-169].
• **AmPM-153** BIDEN, Joseph Robinette, Jr. (County Council, New Castle County, 1970–1972; U.S. Senate, 1973–Present)
153.1 Biden Time. w. Bill Strauss and Elaina Newport. On Cassette: *Workin' 9 To 10.* Published by Capitol Steps Productions, 1505 King Street, Alexandria, VA. 1987. Cassette Cover: N/c Reagan at desk.
• **AmPM-154** CLARKE, John (Justice of the Peace, 1805; Governor, 1817–1820)
154.1 Governor John Clarke's Grand March. m. J.F. Goneke. Published and sold by Geo. Willig, 171 Chesnut Street, Philadelphia, PA. [1819–1820]. Non-pictorial. "Composed for the Piano Forte." 2pp. Page 2: Blank.
• **AmPM-155** CLAYTON, John Middleton (State House, 1824; Delaware Secretary of State, 1826–1828; U.S. Senate, 1829–1836, 1845–1849 & 1853–1856; U.S. Secretary of State, 1849–1850)
155.1 Clayton Bulwer Polka. m. L.C. Haugawout. Published by Edward L. Walker, 142 Chesnut Street, Philadelphia, PA. 1856. B/w non-pictorial geometric designs. "The Prize Polka—A Premium of $50 was awarded for this Polka." 6pp. Pages 2 and 6: Blank.
155.2 Harmonious Coons. w. No composer indicated. m. *Dame Durden.* Published in the *Richmond Enquirer,* Richmond, VA., September 22, 1848. [VBL, p. 322].
• **AmPM-156** DICKINSON, John (State Assembly, Lower Counties, 1760; Pennsylvania Assembly, 1762 & 1764; Colonial Congress, 1765; Continental Congress, Pennsylvania, 1774–1776; Continental Congress, Delaware, 1776–1777, 1779–1780; President, State of Delaware, 1781; President, State of Pennsylvania, 1782–1785)
156.1 American Liberty (Or the Sovereign Right of Thinking) (A New Song). w. No composer indicated. m. "Tune—*Nancy Dawson.*" Published in the Newark *Centinel Of Freedom,* August 14, 1798. [VBL, p. 150].
156.2 The Liberty Song. w. John Dickinson. m. Air—*Hearts Of Oak.* Published in the *Boston Gazette,* July 18, 1768. [SBAR, p. 36].
156.3 The Liberty Song. w. John Dickinson. m. Air—*Hearts Of Oak.*" In: *Bickerstaff's Boston Almanac For The Year Of Our Lord 1779, Being The Second Year After Leap Year.* Printed by Mein and Flemming, and sold by John Mein, at the London Book-Store, North side of King Street, Philadelphia, PA. 1769. B/w woodblock of "The Hon. James Otis, Jun, Esq." on the cover. [SABR, p. 36].
156.4 The Liberty Song. w. John Dickinson. m. "A Colonial (1768) parody on *Hearts Of Oak.*" Lyrics and sound file published by Mudcat Café online at <http://www.mudcat.org/kids/@displaysong.cfm?SongID=6596>. [199-].
• **AmPM-157** MCKEAN, Thomas (Deputy Prothonotary & Register for the Probate of Wills, New Castle County; Deputy Attorney General, Sussex County, 1756–1758; House of Assembly, 1762–1775; Stamp-Act Congress, 1765; Notary for the Lower Counties, 1765; Justice of the Peace for the Common

Pleas, Quarter Sessions, and the Orphans' Court, New Castle County, 1765; Collector of the Port of New Castle, 1771; Continental Congress, 1774–1776, 1778–1782; Signer of the Declaration of Independence, 1776; State House 1776–1777; President, State of Delaware, 1777) [Also See: Pennsylvania]

157.1 The Declaration Of Independence Of The United States Of North America, July 4, 1776. w. From the Declaration of Independence. m. John E. Wilson. Published by John E. Wilson, Baltimore, MD. 1863. B/w litho of the interior of Independence Hall. "Arranged and adapted for Vocal and Instrumental Music as the Great National Chant." 4pp. [?]. Page 4: Facsimile signatures of all signers.

157.2 Old Independence Hall. w. A. Fletcher Stayman. m. Francis Weiland. Published by Stayman & Brothers, No. 210 Chesnut Street, Philadelphia, PA. 1855. Non-pictorial. "Respectfully dedicated to the Memory of the Signers of the Declaration of Independence." "Fac Simile of their signatures" including John Adams, Sam Adams, Elbridge Gerry, Thomas Jefferson. 8pp. Pages 2 and 8: Blank. [Crew/MISC-34].

• **AmPM-158** MCLANE, Louis (U.S. House, 1817–1827; U.S. Senate; 1827–1829; U.S. Envoy Extraordinary and Minister Plenipotentiary to England, 1829–1831 & 1845–1846; U.S. Secretary of the Treasury, 1831–1833; U.S. Secretary of State, 1833–1834)

158.1 King Andrew (Glee). w. No composer indicated. m. "Tune—*Dame Durden*." Published by S.H. Parker, No. 141 Washington Street, Boston, MA. August, 1834. Non-pictorial. "As Sung at the Salem Whig Festival." 4pp. Pages 1 and 4: Blank. [Crew/AJK-7].

• **AmPM-159** READ, George (Attorney General for Lower Delaware, 1763–1774; Provincial Assembly, 1765–1777; Continental Congress 1774–1777; Signer of the Declaration of Independence, 1776; Vice President of Delaware; State House, 1779–1780; U.S. Court of Appeals, 1782; U. S. Senate, 1789–1793, Chief Justice of Delaware, 1793–1798)

159.1 The Declaration Of Independence Of The United States Of North America, July 4, 1776. w. From the Declaration of Independence. m. John E. Wilson. Published by John E. Wilson, Baltimore, MD. 1863. B/w litho of the interior of Independence Hall. "Arranged and adapted for Vocal and Instrumental Music as the Great National Chant." 4pp. [?]. Page 4: Facsimile signatures of all signers.

159.2 Old Independence Hall. w. A. Fletcher Stayman. m. Francis Weiland. Published by Stayman & Brothers, No. 210 Chesnut Street, Philadelphia, PA. 1855. Non-pictorial. "Respectfully dedicated to the Memory of the Signers of the Declaration of Independence." "Fac Simile of their signatures" including John Adams, Sam Adams, Elbridge Gerry, Thomas Jefferson. 8pp. Pages 2 and 8: Blank. [Crew/MISC-34].

• **AmPM-160** RODNEY, Caesar (High Sheriff, Kent County, 1755–1758; Justice of the Peace, Judge of all Lower Courts, 1756; Superintendent of the Printing of Delaware Currency, 1759; State Assembly, 1762–1769; Superintendent of the State Loan Office, 1769; Delaware Supreme Court, 1769–1777; Continental Congress, 1774–1776; Signer, Declaration of Independence, 1776; President, State of Delaware, 1778–1782)

160.1 The Declaration Of Independence Of The United States Of North America, July 4, 1776. w. From the Declaration of Independence. m. John E. Wilson. Published by John E. Wilson, Baltimore, MD. 1863. B/w litho of the interior of Independence Hall. "Arranged and adapted for Vocal and Instrumental Music as the Great National Chant." 4pp. [?]. Page 4: Facsimile signatures of all signers.

160.2 Old Independence Hall. w. A. Fletcher Stayman. m. Francis Weiland. Published by Stayman & Brothers, No. 210 Chesnut Street, Philadelphia, PA. 1855. Non-pictorial. "Respectfully dedicated to the Memory of the Signers of the Declaration of Independence." "Fac Simile of their signatures" including John Adams, Sam Adams, Elbridge Gerry, Thomas Jefferson. 8pp. Pages 2 and 8: Blank. [Crew/MISC-34].

DISTRICT OF COLUMBIA

Individuals

• **AmPM-161** BOHLEN, Charles Eustis (U.S. Ambassador to Soviet Union, 1953–1957; U.S. Ambassador to Philippines, 1957–1959; U.S. Ambassador to France, 1962–1968)

161.1 Cool Goldwater. w. Noel E. Parmentel, Jr. and Marshall J. Dodge. In: *Folk Songs For Conservatives*, page 11. Published by Unicorn Press, Inc., No. 790 Madison Avenue, New York, NY. 10021. 1964. [5" × 8⅜"]. Bl/w drawings of Barry Goldwater, Bill Buckley, Ray Cohn, eagle. List of contents. "Sung by Noel E. Parmentel, Jr. and His Unbleached Muslims, Greatest Political Satirists Since Cohn and Schine." "Right Wing Hootenanny." 36pp. [Crew/BMG-13].

• **AmPM-162** BUCHANAN, Patrick J. (White House Political Advisor, 1971–1974; Assistant to the President, 1985–1987; Director of White House Communications, 1985–1989; Candidate for Republican Nomination for President, 1992 & 1996; Candidate for President, 2000)

162.1 Ballot Box Blues. w. No composer indicated. m. "Parody of *Summertime Blues* by Eddie Cochran." Lyrics published by *The Bob Rivers Show* with Bob, Spike & Joe and Twisted Tunes online at <http://

www.twistedradio.com/player/lyrics.asp?songID=584>. [ca. 2000].

162.2 Ballot Mix Up. w. A.n.d.y.H. m. "*Cheers Theme*, originally by Theme Song." Published online at <http://www.amiright.com/parody/80s/themesong0.html>. [ca. 2000].

162.3 Battle Hymn Of The Republicans. w. No composer indicated. m. Tune—*Battle Hymn Of The Republic.* N/c photos of George Bush. Ronald Reagan, Willie Horton, peacemaker missile, clear-cut forest, Dick Armey, Bill Archer, Pete Wilson, H. Ross Perot and George W. Bush. "The Washington press corps serenaded president-elect George Bush on his campaign plane with the first verse and refrain of this hymn in 1988. We added a few more stanzas." Published online by PoliticsOL.com at <http://www.presidentialelection2000.com/battle_hymn_of_the_republicans.html>. 2000.

162.4 Buchanan. w. No composer indicated. m. "Parody of *Rhianon* by Fleetwood Mac." Lyrics published by *The Bob Rivers Show* with Bob, Spike & Joe and Twisted Tunes online at <http://www.twistedradio.com/player/lyrics.asp?songID=593>. [199-].

162.5 Buchanan's Gonna Fall. w. William K. Tong. m. "Sung to the tune of *Rockin' Pneumonia & The Boogie Woogie Flu* by Johnny Rivers." In: *The Sting The Right Wing Song Book* at <http://www.geocities.com/wmktong/bootnewt/buchfall.htm>.

162.6 Bush The Panderer. w. William Tong. m. "*The Wanderer*, originally by Dion." Published online at <http://amiright.com/parody/misc/dion0.shml>. [ca. 2000].

162.7 Election. w. "MedicManager." m. "*Eighteen*, originally by Alice Cooper." Published online at <http://www.amiright.com/parody/70s/alicecooper0.shtml>. [2000].

162.8 Electoral Rhapsody 2000. w. Kevin Dunlap. m. "Sung to the tune of *Bohemian Rhapsody* by Queen." Published online at <http://www.analyticalq.com/music/parodies/rhapsody.htm>. 2000.

162.9 A Few Short Years Ago. From CD: *American Way.* Performed by Dimpled Chad & The Disenfranchised. Lyrics published at <http:/dimpledchad.net>. [ca. 2000].

162.10 Georgie Got A Bush. w.m. Mondo Fax. On CD: *Music To Pee Your Pants By.* RavenHill Records. Performed by Mondo Max. Lyrics and MP3 file published by MP3.com at <http://www.artists.mp3.com/artist_song/609/609276.html>. [ca. 2000].

162.11 Grand Old Party. w. William K. Tong. m. "Sung to the tune of *Garden Party* by Rick Nelson." In: *The Sting The Right Wing Song Book* at <http://www.geocities.com/wmktong/bootnewt/goparty.htm>.

162.12 Hand Count. w. Keith K. Higa. m. "*Convoy*, originally by C.W. McCall." Published online at <http://www.amiright.com/parody/70s/cwmccall0.shtml>. [2000].

162.13 I Can't Stand Him. w. William K. Tong. m. "Sung to the tune of *I'm Still Standing* by Elton John." In: *The Sting The Right Wing Song Book* at <http://www.geocities.com/wmktong/bootnewt/cantstnd.htm>.

162.14 Imagine. w. William K. Tong. m. "*Imagine*, based on a performance by John Lennon." "Written in 1996 ... and since that time: Gingrich quit Congress in disgrace, Helms retired, Thurmond died, and Buchanan is hated by the G.O.P. for his criticism of Bush." <http://www.geocities.com/wmktong/bootnewt/imagine.htm>.

162.15 Just Vote For Me. w. Angela Kuo "(axk23@psu.edu)." m. "To the tune of *Under The Sea* from *The Little Mermaid.*" "Well, it's less than a month to go and with the recent presidential and vice-presidential debates, I thought it might be appropriate to post this [song]. Right now I am still undecided which candidate I will vote for. Somehow I doubt much will happen in the next month to change that. But I will vote anyway. At least it gives me the right to complain." Published online at <http://geocities.com/Hollywood/5082/vote.html>. 1996.

162.16 The Palm Beach Pokey. w. No composer indicated. m. *Hokie Pokie.* Published on the Internet at <www.dovewinds.com/duba/alshokeypokey.html>. 2000. Verses to the tune of The Hokey Pokey. N/c photos of Al Gore as dancing doll, crowd of people with sign reading :I only got to vote once." With sound. "Click here to help us buy Newspaper Advertisement's [sic] to expose the Democrats Voter Fraud!" 3pp. [Crew/AG-1].

162.16A Pat Buchanan. w. Paul Shanklin. On CD: *Bill Clinton Comeback Kid Tour.* Published by Narodniki Records. CD Cover: Caricature of Bill Clinton. See: www.paulshanklin.com. 2002.

162.17 The Search For A Likely Candidate. w.m. Henry and Bobbie Shaffner. Published as a photocopy by Henry and Bobbie Shaffner and Saul Broudy, Bala Cynwyd, PA. 1991. [8½" × 11"]. Non-pictorial. 2pp. Page 2: Blank.

162.18 Stuck Inside A Chimney (With the Christmas Blues Again). w. Outfidel. m. Tune—"*Stuck Inside Of Mobile (With The Memphis Blues Again)*, originally by Bob Dylan." Published online at <http://amiright.com/parody/misc/bobdylan3.shml>. [ca. 2000].

162.19 Stupid (Go Cast Your Vote). w. Bruce Decker. m. Tune—"*Cupid* originally by The Spinners." Published online at <http://www.amiright.com/parody/misc/thespinners0.shtml>. [ca. 2000]

162.20 Vote Palm Beach. w. Billy Florio. m. "*Sloop John B*, originally by The Beach Boys." Published online at <http://amiright.com/parody/misc/thebeachboys1.shml>. [ca. 2000].

162.21 Voting For Albert Gore. w. Ian Highet. m. "*Knocking On Heaven's Door*, originally by Bob Dylan." Published online at <http://www.amiright.com/parody/70s/bobdylan0.shtml>. [2000].

162.22 What Becomes Of The Double Punched Ballots. w. Billy Florio. m. "*What Becomes Of The Broken Hearted*, originally by Jimmy Ruffin." Published online at <http://www.amiright.com/parody/misc/jimmyriffin0.shml>. [ca. 2000].

162.23 Zany Politics. w. Edward Goldstein. m. "Parody of Animaniac's opening theme song." Published online at <http://www.bagelfather.com/funstuff/parody/parody12.htm>. [199-].

• **AmPM-163 CHOATE**, Pat (State Economic Planner, Oklahoma, 1965; Regional Administrator,

U.S. Department of Commerce; State Commissioner of Economic Development, Tennessee; Reform Party Candidate for Vice President, 1996)

163.1 Going To Bat For Ross And Pat. w. Linda Grant De Pauw. m. "Melody—*Take Me Out To The Ball Game*." In: *Rhythm Of Reform: Song Lyrics For Reform Party Volunteers*, page 17. Published by Peacock Press, 20 Granada Road, Pasadena, MD. 21122. 1996. [5½" × 8½"]. Pl/bk drawing of two bunnies playing drums, musical notes. [Crew/RP-1].

163.2 The Reform Party Platform. w. Linda Grant De Pauw. m. "Melody—*Maryland, My Maryland* a.k.a. *Oh, Tannenbaum*." In: *Rhythm Of Reform: Song Lyrics For Reform Party Volunteers*, page 27. Published by Peacock Press, 20 Granada Road, Pasadena, MD. 21122. 1996. [5½" × 8½"]. Pl/bk drawing of two bunnies playing drums, musical notes. [Crew/RP-1].

163.3 The Solitary Bard' Ballad. w. Linda Grant De Pauw. m. "Melody—*The Minstrel Boy*." In: *Rhythm Of Reform: Song Lyrics For Reform Party Volunteers*, page 14. Published by Peacock Press, 20 Granada Road, Pasadena, MD. 21122. 1996. [5½" × 8½"]. Pl/bk drawing of two bunnies playing drums, musical notes. [Crew/RP-1].

163.4 Sousa Lovers For Perot (Medley). w. Linda Grant De Pauw. m. "Melodies—*The Stars And Stripes Forever* and *The Washington Post*." In: *Rhythm Of Reform: Song Lyrics For Reform Party Volunteers*, page 18. Published by Peacock Press, 20 Granada Road, Pasadena, MD. 21122. 1996. [5½" × 8½"]. Pl/bk drawing of two bunnies playing drums, musical notes. [Crew/RP-1].

163.5 When Reform Goes Marching In. w. Linda Grant De Pauw. m. "Melody—*When The Saints Go Marching In*." In: *Rhythm Of Reform: Song Lyrics For Reform Party Volunteers*, page 19. Published by Peacock Press, 20 Granada Road, Pasadena, MD. 21122. 1996. [5½" × 8½"]. Pl/bk drawing of two bunnies playing drums, musical notes. [Crew/RP-1].

• **AmPM-164   DOUGLAS, William Orville** (Securities and Exchange Commission, 1936–1939; U.S. Supreme Court, 1939–1975.

164.1 Hang Earl Warren. w. Noel E. Parmentel, Jr. and Marshall J. Dodge. In: *Folk Songs For Conservatives*, page 29. Published by Unicorn Press, Inc., No. 790 Madison Avenue, New York, NY. 10021. 1964. [5" × 8⅜"]. Bl/w drawings of Barry Goldwater, Bill Buckley, Ray Cohn, eagle. List of contents. "Sung by Noel E. Parmentel, Jr. and His Unbleached Muslims, Greatest Political Satirists Since Cohn and Shine." "Right Wing Hootenanny." 36pp. [Crew/BMG-13].

164.2 Having A Time. w. No composer indicated. m. "Tune—*Bidin' My Time*." In: *Thoroughly Mad-Ern Malcolm Or He Didn't Need A Course In Forensics To Become A Famous Public Speaker*, page 12. Published by the New York State Legislative Correspondents' Association, Albany, NY. 1974. N/w photo of Malcolm Wilson as Alfred E. Newman—"What—Me Governor?" "Featuring the New York Correspondents' Association, March 16. 1974." 32pp.

• **AmPM-165   DOUGLASS, Frederick** (Publisher of *The North Star*, 1847; Delegate, First Women's Rights Convention, 1848; President of the Freedman's Savings and Trust Company, 1874; U.S. Marshal, 1877; Recorder of Deeds, Washington, D.C., 1880; U.S. Consul-General to Haiti, 1889)

165.1 [Down With Douglass, Pierce And Shannon]. w.m. No composer or tune indicated. In: *Fremont Glees* [Song Sheet]. [1856]. [9¾" × 15½"]. Nonpictorial cloth. "As Sung by the Centerville Republican Club." 2pp. Page 2: Blank. [Crew/JCF-38].

165.2 Frederick Douglass Funeral March. m. N. Clark Smithe. Published by The S. Brainard's Sons Co., Chicago, IL. [ca. 1895]. B/w photo of Frederick Douglass. Four b/w vignettes of "Slave Trade, Bondage, Auction Block, Freedom" with litho of Abraham Lincoln and Black children. 6pp. Pages 2 and 6: Blank.

165.3 The Grundys. w. No composer indicated. m. "Air—*Comin' Thro' The Rye*." Published in *Woodhull And Claflin's Weekly*, June 1, 1872. [VBL, p. 453].

165.4 Hail To The Spirit Of Freedom (March). m. W.C. Handy. Published by [V-1: Pace and Handy Music, Memphis, TN. 1915] [V-2: Handy Brothers Music Company, Inc., Publishers, No. 1650 Broadway, New York, NY. 1943]. [V-1: O/w/bl] [V-2: B/w] photos of "Abraham Lincoln," "Frederick Douglass," flags, eagle, man—"50 years of freedom, ladder with rungs inscribed "Labor, Religion, Education, wealth, art, music, science." "1865–1915," woman with scales and shield—"Ethiopia shall stretch forth her hand." "Souvenir of the Lincoln Jubilee." Bl/w photo of "W.C. Handy." 6pp. Page 2: "Dedicated to the ten million Afro-Americans and to the immortal Lincoln." Lincoln quote—"Let us keep step to the music of the Republic." Page 6: Advertising. [Crew/AL-245].

165.5 Political Millenium (In Posse). w. S.N. Holmes. m. "Tune—*Common Meter*." In: *The Republican Campaign Song Book, With Music, 1892*, page 52. e. Samuel Newall Holmes. Published by Samuel Newall Holmes, Syracuse, NY. 1892. Be/bk nonpictorial. "Composed and especially prepared by Judge S.N. Holmes of Syracuse, N.Y." "Headquarters: Syracuse, N.Y." "Price twenty-five cents." 60pp. [M-308]. [Crew/BFH-107].

165.6 Underground Rail Car! (Or Song of the Fugitive!). w.m. George N. Allen. Published by S. Brainard & Co., 77 Superior Street, Cleveland, OH. 1854. B/w litho of a Black man meeting a train. "To Fred Douglass, Esq." 6pp. Pages 2 and 6: Blank.

165.7 The Veto Galop! m. "Make Peace." Published by McCarrell & Mininger, No. 91 West Jefferson Street, Louisville, KY. 1866. B/w litho by Bennett, Donaldson & Elmes of "Andy" Johnson holding a document inscribed "Veto" and riding a horse named "Constitution," men labeled "Dead Ducks" including "W. Phillips," "Wade," "Stevens, "Fr. Douglass," "Freedmans Bureau;" Crowd cheering—"Hurrah for Andy," "See the Lame Ducks." Litho of building in the background—"Forney & Co., Dealers in Game." 6pp. Pages 2 and 6: Blank. [Crew/AJN-17].

165.8 Victoria's Banner. w. No composer indicated. m. "Tune—*Comin' Thro' The Rye*." [1872]. Original not located. Lyric sheet published in *Election Songs Of The United States*. Sung by Oscar Brand; Accompanied on Guitar and Banjo by Billy Faier; Notes by Irwin Silber. 33⅓ rpm LP. Produced by Folkways Records FH 5280. Scholastic Records, Englewood Cliffs, NJ. 1963.

165.9 Victory For Victoria (The 1872 Campaign

Song). w. No composer indicated. m. Tune—*Comin' Thro' The Rye*. [1872]. Original not located. Lyrics published online at <http://www.victoria-woodhull.com/song.html>. [Probably the same song as 1317.3].

• **AmPM-166 FAUNTROY**, Walter Edward (City Council, District of Columbia, 1967–1969; Delegate, U.S. House, 1971–1991)

166.1 The Congressional Record (The Living Legacy of Dr. Martin Luther King, Jr.). 33⅓ rpm LP, 2 Vols.). Respect Stax Records #STS-5525. 1975. Produced by Hon. Walter E. Fauntroy. Popular and religious songs in tribute to Dr. King. Album cover: N/c photos of Dr. King and Congressman Fauntroy. Includes the song: *Abraham, Martin, John* (Malcolm, Martin, John, Bobby).

• **AmPM-167 FRANKFURTER**, Felix (Assistant U.S. Attorney; U.S. Supreme Court, 1939–1962)

167.1 Hang Earl Warren. w. Noel E. Parmentel, Jr. and Marshall J. Dodge. In: *Folk Songs For Conservatives*, page 29. Published by Unicorn Press, Inc., No. 790 Madison Avenue, New York, NY. 10021. 1964. [5" × 8⅜"]. Bl/w drawings of Barry Goldwater, Bill Buckley, Ray Cohn, eagle. List of contents. "Sung by Noel E. Parmentel, Jr. and His Unbleached Muslims, Greatest Political Satirists Since Cohn and Schine." "Right Wing Hootenanny." 36pp. [Crew/BMG-13].

167.2 [The Nation Of Our Fathers Is Assailed By Foes Within]. w. No composer indicated. m. "Air—*Battle Hymn Of The Republic*." In: *Campaign Songs For The Liberty Quartette*, page 8. Published for The Liberty Quartette, Utica, NY. [1936]. [4¼" × 8¹⁄₁₆"]. Bk/br litho of four men singing, eagle. 18pp. [Crew/AML-36].

167.3 [O Give Me A Home Where No Brain Trusters Roam]. w. No composer indicated. m. "Air—*Home On The Range*." In: *Campaign Songs For The Liberty Quartette*, page 5. Published for The Liberty Quartette, Utica, NY. [1936]. [4¼" × 8¹⁄₁₆"]. Bk/br litho of four men singing, eagle. 18pp. [Crew/AML-36].

• **AmPM-168 HOOVER**, John Edgar (Director, Federal Bureau of Investigation, 1924–1972)

168.1 Daily News, Daily Blues. w.m. Tom Paxton. In: *Broadside, Volume 2*, page 31. Published by Oak Publications, 33 West 60th Street, New York, NY. 1968. 96pp.

168.2 The Government Indirect. w. No composer indicated. m. "Tune—*The Emperor Of Japan*." "Duet—Ike and JE Hoover." In: *Socialist Song Book*, page 53. e. Owen Fleischman. Published by The Young People's Socialist League, No. 303 Fourth Avenue, New York, NY. 1959. [8½" 11"]. B/w drawing of person playing the guitar. 74pp. [Crew/SP-8].

168.3 Luci Had A Baby. w. Barbara Dane. m. No tune indicated. In: *The Vietnam Songbook*, page 128. c. Barbara Dane and Irwin Silber. Published by The Guardian, No. 32 West 22nd Street, New York, NY. Copyright 1969 by Barbara Dane and Irwin Silber. [7" × 10"]. B/w photo of a protest march. O/y/r/bk cover. 228pp.

168.4 The New Century. w. Blaine Selkirk. m. Sara Jordan. On Cassette: *The Presidents' Rap*. Jordan Music Productions, Toronto, Canada. 1992 & 1994.

168.5 Song Of JE Hoover. w.m. No composer or tune indicated. In: *Socialist Song Book*, page 52. e. Owen Fleischman. Published by The Young People's Socialist League, No. 303 Fourth Avenue, New York, NY. 1959. [8½" × 11"]. B/w drawing of person playing the guitar. 74pp. [Crew/SP-8].

168.5A Übermensch. w.m. Turbonegro. Lyrics published online at <http://www.plyrics.com/lyrics/turbonegro/bermensch.html>. [ca. 198-].

168.6 What A Friend We Have In Hoover. w. Tom Paxton. m. Tune—*What A Friend We Have In Jesus*. Lyrics and sound file published online at <http://www.mudcat.org/kids/@displaysong.cfm?SongID=7719>. [199-].

168.7 White House Blues (#2). w. No composer indicated. m. Tune in sound file. "*From The American History Songbook by Silverman*." Lyrics and sound file published online at <http://www.mudcat.org/kids/@displaysong.cfm?SongID=7843>. [199-].

• **AmPM-169 WILSON**, Frank J. (Chief, U.S. Secret Service, 1937–1946)

169.1 United States Secret Service March. m. William A. Boos. No publisher indicated. Copyright 1943 by William A. Boos. R/w/b American flags, outline may of the United States, "Secret Service" cadge. "Dedicated to Chief Frank J. Wilson." "50th Annual I.A.C.P. Conference, Hotel Statler, Detroit, 1943." 6pp. Page 2: Narrative on the Secret Service. Page 6: Bl/w litho of the "United States Treasury Seal."

• **AmPM-170 KISSINGER**, Henry Alfred (Assistant to the President for National Security Affairs, 1969–1975; U.S. Secretary of State, 1973–1977; Winner, Nobel Peace Prize, 1973)

170.1 Brain-Dead Whine. w. Michael Pacholek. w. Tune—"*Red, Red Wine* originally by Neil Diamond." Published online at <http://amiright.com/parody/60s/neildiamond2.shml>.

170.2 Convention '72. w.m. N. Canel and N. Kousaloos. 45 rpm record. Mainstream Records, MRL 5525/ZT8P 224228. Performed by The Delegates. 1972.

170.2A Feel Like I'm Nixon, I Lie. w. Michael Pacholek. m. "*Feel Like I'm Fixin' To Die*, based on the performance by Country Joe & the Fish." "'Let me just say this' (as Nixon would say): He would not appreciate this, he earned it. When the transcripts of the Oval Office tapes were released, the constant profanities were edited so that they read "(expletive deleted),' hence the alteration of Country Joe's 'Fish Cheer.' 'Just one more thing' (as Nixon would say), if you think Bush is the worst president we've had, take a look at Nixon's record ... then read *Worse Than Watergate* by John Dean who would know." Published online at <http://amiright.com/parody/60s/countryjoethefish1.shml>. 2004.

170.3 I Wonder Who's Kissinger Now. w. Dave Lippman. w. [Original] Will Hough and Frank Adams. m. [Original] Joseph E. Howard and Harold Orlob. "Deep Apologies! [To the original composers]." Published online at <http://www.davelippman.com/iwonder.html>. B/w photo of Dave Lippman? [ca. 2001].

170.4 I'm Henry The Ace, I Am. w. William K. Tong. m. Tune—"*I'm Henry VIII, I Am* originally by Herman's Hermits." "As sung by Henry Kissinger, recently appointed to lead the 9/11 whitewash, er, investigation." Published online at <http://amiright.com/parody/60s/hermanshermits4.shtml>. 2002.

170.5 The Ribald Rebel's Song (Fight For Liberation). w. No composer indicated. m. *Tramp Tramp*. Lyrics and sound file published online at <http://www.mudcat.org/kids/@displaysong.cfm?SongID=6892>. [199-].

170.6 Stepped Down. w. William K. Tong. m. Tune — "*Get Down* originally by Gilbert O'Sullivan." "Due to lack of public credibility, Henry Kissinger steps down as Bush's hand-picked head of the federal commission to investigate 9/11." Published online at <http://amiright.com/parody/60s/gilbertosullivan5.shtml>.

170.6A Vietnam Serenade. w.m. Conflict. On LP: *It's Time To See Who's Who*. Lyrics published online at <http://www.plyrics.com/lyrics/conflict/vietnamserenade.html>. 1981.

170.7 Whitewash The Investigation. w. William K. Tong. m. Tune — "*My Generation*, originally by The Who." "Satire about former Secretary of State Henry Kissinger, a known liar and wanted as a war criminal by many nations, recently appointed by Dubya Bush to head (head off?) the 9/11 investigation." Published online at <http://amiright.com/parody/60s/thewho3.shml>. 2002.

- **AmPM-171** VAN NESS, John Peter (Alderman, Washington D.C., 1829; Mayor, Washington, D.C., 1830–1834; President of the Washington Branch of the Bank of the U.S. and Metropolitan Bank, 1814–1846)

171.1 When This Old Hat Was New. w.m. No composer or tune indicated. In: *The Log Cabin & Hard Cider Melodies, A Collection Of Popular And Patriotic Songs*, page 47. Published by Charles Adams, No. 23 Tremont Street, Boston, MA. 1840. [3¾" × 6"]. [V-1: Pk/bk] [V-2: Gn/bk] litho of William Henry Harrison. "The Freeman's glittering Sword be Blest, For ever blest the Freeman's Lyre." 78pp. Pages 2 and 77: Blank. Page 3: Inside title page. B/w litho of log cabin. "Respectfully Dedicated to the Friends of Harrison and Tyler." Page 78: Advertising. [M-012]. [Crew/WHH-68].

171.2 When This Old Hat Was New. w.m. No composer or tune indicated. In: *Whig Songs For 1844* [Songster], page 9. Published by Greeley & McElrath, New York, NY. 1844. [5⅞" × 9³⁄₁₆"]. Non-pictorial. 16pp. Page 16: "Odes and Poems." [M-061]. [Crew/HC-35].

- **AmPM-171A** WILSON, Frank R. (Director of Publicity, U.S. Treasury Department, 1919?)

171A.1 We'll Bring Our Heroes Home. w. m. Elizabeth Clayton Bacon. a. R.M. Stults. Published by Theo. Presser Co., Philadelphia, PA. 1919. B/w drawing of a mother holding a service star flag. "Official Victory Loan Campaign Song of the 3rd Federal Reserve District, Approved by Frank R. Wilson, National Director of Publicity, U.S. Treasury Dept." 4pp. Page 4: Advertising.

- **AmPM-172** WOLFOWITZ, Paul D. (Deputy Assistant Secretary of Defense, 1977–1980; U.S. Ambassador to Indonesia; 1986–1989; 1989–1993; Under Secretary of Defense; Deputy Secretary of Defense, 2001–Present)

172.1 American Lie. w. Dangers0ne. m. "*American Pie*, based on a performance by Don McLean." "With apologies to Don McLean." Published online at <http://www.amiright.com/parody/70s/donmcclean24.shtml>. [ca. 2003].

172.2 Attacking And Fighting Again. w. William Tong. m. "*Back In The High Life Again*, based on the performance by Steve Winwood." "Emperor Dubya, with a cabinet packed full of Daddy Bush's old war hawk relics (Rumsfeld, Powell, Wolfowitz, etc.), is hell-bent on war, undeterred by worldwide opposition from governments and 10 million marchers in 600 cities." Published online at <http://www.amiright.com/parody/80s/stevewinwood5.shtml>. [ca. 2003].

172.3 Bush's Brain. w. William Tong. m. "*Penny Lane*, based on a performance by Beatles." Published online at <http://www.amiright.com/parody/60s/beatles137.shtml>. [ca. 2003].

172.4 What's War All About, Wolfie? w. William Tong. m. "*What's It All About, Alfie?*, based on a performance by Dionne Warwick." "A shaken Deputy Secretary of Defense Paul Wolfowitz recently survived an Iraqi rocket attack while staying at a hotel near American Military headquarters in Baghdad." Published online at <http://www.amiright.com/parody/60s/dionnewarwick7.shtml>. [ca. 2003].

172.5 Wolfowitz Is Gunnin.' w. Mac195. m. Tune — "*Werewolves Of London*, based on a performance by Warren Zevon." "In honor of America's beloved Deputy Sec. Of Defense, Paul Wolfowitz." Published online at <http://amiright.com/parody/70s/warrenzevon9.shtml>. 2004.

- **AmPM-173** WASHINGTON CITY

173.1 America's Anthem Of Peace (The National Prayer). w.m. Louis Coleman St. Claire and Irma Wocher Woollen. No publisher indicated. Copyright 1933 by St. Claire Publishing Co., Indianapolis, IN. [10" × 13"]. Bl/s photo of the U.S. Capitol building. "A Tribute to American Patriotism." 8pp. Page 2: Poem. Page 3: "Dedication." Page 6: Quartette arrangement. Pages 7 and 8: Blank.

173.2 The Capitol (March). m. No composer indicated. In: *Little Patriots, A Book Of American Sons For Children*, page 29. Published by ABC Music Corporation, No. 799 7th Avenue, New York, NY. 1941. [6" × 9"]. R/w/b drawing of child. 44pp. [Crew/MISC-185].

173.3 Capitol City (March Two-Step). m. Harry Lincoln. Published by Vandersloot Music Co., Williamsport, PA. 1911. O/w/bk drawing by W.I. Dittmar of the U.S. Capitol building. List of other songs composed by Harry Lincoln. 6pp. Page 6: Advertising.

173.4 Capitol March. m. Arno Rapee and William Axt. Published by Richmond-Robbins, 1658 Broadway, New York, NY. 1923. B/w photo of Roxy Rothafel. Gy/w drawing of the U.S. Capitol dome, geometric designs. 6pp. Page 6: Advertising. "Respectfully dedicated to S.L. Rothafel."

173.5 Capture Of Washington. w. No composer indicated. m. No tune indicated. "On Wednesday, August 24, there was a severe action at Bladenburgh, six miles from the Capitol. Baltimore has acquired immortal honor by the brave resistance of Commodore

Barney, his sailors and the bold volunteers. The same day in solid column the enemy succeeded in taking the City of Washington. Their number supposed to be from 8 to 15,000 — ours 3 or 4,000. The British destroyed considerable private property and most of the public property, at the City — Navy-Yard, Georgetown, &c. though some was destroyed by our own citizens. The British Army under the command of Gen. Ross — The United States' troops commanded by Gen. Winder." Printed by Nathaniel Coverly, Jr., Milk Street, Boston, MA. 1814. B/w wood block of fighting, ships burning. 2pp. Page 2: Blank.

173.6 Detroit-Washington March. m. Carry Baxter Jennings. Published by Carrie B. Jennings, Howard City, MI. 1923. Bl/w drawings of U.S. Capitol building, Detroit skyline with municipal building. 6pp. Page 2: At top of music — "In pleasant recollection of the trip from Detroit, Michigan, to Washington, D.C. in company with the Michigan delegation, organized by W.C. Hollands, Past Grand Patron O.E.S., to attend the seventeenth Triennial Assembly of the General Chapter in November, 1923." Page 6: Advertising.

173.7 The District Of Columbia Is My Home Town. w.m. James L. Dixon. Published by James L. Dixon, 1022 Seventeenth Street, N.W., Washington, DC. 1950. Bl/bk/w drawings of U.S. Capitol, Lincoln Memorial, Washington Memorial. "Souvenir Copy." 4pp. [Crew/MISC-186].

173.8 Give The Stars And Stripes A Permanent Wave. w.m. Moe Jaffe and Harold Green. Published by Mills Music, Inc., Music Publishers, 1619 Broadway, New York, NY. 1940. Bl/w photo of the U.S. Capitol building. R/w/b star and stripe background.

173.9 The Goddess Of Liberty (The Queen Of Our Land). w.m. H. George Schuette. Published by Crown Music Co., New York, NY. 1907. R/w/b litho of Miss Liberty standing on a eagle holding an American flag; "Dome part of U.S. Capitol, Washington, D.C.," "Statue of Liberty, New York Harbor. Refrain printed on cover. 6pp. Page 2: Blank. Page 6: Advertising.

173.10 Hilbus's Musical Boquet, Vol 1. Published by George Hilbus, Washington, DC. 1857. B/w litho of the U.S. Capitol building, geometric designs.

173.11 Homeland Waltzes. m. Harry J. Lincoln. Published by Vandersloot Music Pub. Co., Williamsport, PA. 1910. Pl/gn/w drawing of the Capitol at Washington, axes, eagles, floral designs. "Composer of *A Southern Dream, A Dream Of The South, Garden Of Dreams*, etc., etc., etc." 8pp. Page 8: Advertising.

173.12 The Man Of The Hour Two Step. m. Frank Sherman. Published by The John Franklin Music Co., New York, NY. 1907. O/bk/w drawing of a man in front of the U.S. Capitol dome, "The March of the Minute." "Dedicated by him [Frank Sherman] to his friend George Broadhurst. 6pp. Page 6: Advertising.

173.13 Music From Washington: Behind Closed Doors. m. Dominic Frontiere. a. Warren Barker. Published by Hal Leonard Publishing Corp., Winona, MN. 55987. 1979. Y/w/gn litho background of the word "Encore" repeated over the page. "From the Paramount Television Production *Washington: Behind Closed Doors*." "Encore for Concert Band." "Parts set for concert band."

173.14 The Old Spirit Of Seventy Six. w.m. J. Frank Butts. Published by Joseph D. Kaufman, Washington, DC. 1919. Bl/w drawing of U.S. Capitol dome, fife and drum players. "Dedicated to Voteless Washington." 6pp. Page 2: Acknowledgements. Page 6: Bl/w photo of Walt Mason. Narrative on voteless Washington. "Poor Washington."

173.15 Our Capitol (A March of Excitement) (Two Step). m. Jas. N. Harrington. Published by The John Franklin Music Co., Boston, MA. 1905. Bl/gd/w litho of the U.S. Capitol Dome. 6pp. Pages 2 and 6: Advertising.

173.16 Our Nation Grand. w.m. H. George Schuette. Published by H. George Schuette, Manitowoc, WI. 1907. R/w/b litho of Uncle Sam, map of "United States of America," geometric designs. B/w photo of the Capitol building at Washington. Chorus printed on the cover. 6pp. Page 2: Blank. Page 6: Advertising.

173.17 Stars Over Capitol Hill. w. Fred Hillebrand. m. Adam Carroll. No publisher indicated. Copyright 1943 by Alliance Music Co., 1658 Broadway, New York, NY. 4pp. Pages 1 and 4: Blank.

173.18 The Song Of Liberty (Or The March Of 'Concord'!). w.m. C.A. Hill, "Author of *The American Marseillaise*, &c., &c.," Washington, D.C., March 4th, 1854. B/w litho by D. McLellan, Litho., 26 Spruce Street, N.Y. of "United States Capitol, eagle, geometric designs. 1854. "A Favorite National Air Dedicated to The Nations Weal." 4pp. Page 4: Blank.

173.19 That's The Meaning Of Uncle Sam. w. Frank Davis. m. Win Brookhouse. Published by Shapiro, Bernstein & Co., Music Publishers, 224 West 47th Street, New York, NY. 1916. R/w/b litho of Uncle Sam standing in front of the U.S. Capitol building, father and son, eagle, shields, axe. 6pp. Pages 2 and 6: Advertising.

173.20 This Is America (Song). w. John McLaughlin. m. Maurice Gardner. Published by Sam Fox Pub. Co., Cleveland, OH 1956. Bl/bk/w drawing of the U.S. Capitol building. 6pp. Page 6: Advertising.

173.21 The Tourist Souvenir (March and Two Step). m. Edw. Bergenholtz. Published by E.F. Droop & Sons, 925 Penn. Ave., Washington, DC. 1901. Gn/w/bk drawing of the U.S. Capitol dome. B/w photo of the "Congressional Library." 6pp. Pages 2 and 6: Advertising.

173.22 Washington (Comic Song). w. Vincent Bryan. m. Gertrude Hoffman. Published by Jerome H. Remick & Co., New York, NY. 1906. O/bk/w drawing of the U.S. Capitol building. "Sung by Charles Bigelow and Anna Held in *The Parisian Model*, Management of F. Ziegfield, Jr." 6pp. Pages 2 and 6: Advertising.

173.23 The U.S. Capitol March (For Concert Band). m. J. William Middendorff II. a. Richard Hayman. Published by Bourne Co., New York, NY. 1980. R/w/b eagle. Parts set for concert band.

173.24 Washington. m. S.L. Tyler. Published by W.H. Boner & Co., 1102 Chestnut Street, Philadelphia, PA. 1886. B/w litho of various state capitol buildings: "Madison, Wis., Harrisburg, Pa., Hartford, Conn., Columbus, O., Lansing, Mich., Washington, D.C., St. Paul, Minn., Richmond Va., Sacramento, Cal., Albany, NY., Boston, Mass., Montgomery, Ala."

"The Capitol Collection." 8pp. Page 2: Blank. Page 3: At top of music — "To my Brother, C.A. Tyler." Page 8: Advertising.

173.25 Washington. w.m. Jimmie Dodd. Published by Remick Music Corp, New York, NY. 1951. R/w/b drawing of the U.S. Capitol building, silhouette of people. "The Official Song of Washington, D.C." 4pp. Page 4: Advertising.

173.26 Washington. w. Jessie I. Pierson. m. William T. Pierson. Published by W.T. Pierson & Company, Washington, DC. 1919. Br/w photo of the skyline of Washington. Br/w geometric design frame. 8pp. Pages 2 and 8: Advertising. Page 4: At top of music — "Dedicated with reverent love and profound respect to the Capitol City of the United States of America."

173.27 The Washington Evening Star March. m. W.J. Stannard, Leader of the Army Band. Published as a supplement of the *Washington Sunday Star*. Copyright 1924. B/w litho of the U.S. Capitol, bear holding a one-star flag. 4pp. Page 4: B/w litho of a building [*Star* Offices?].

173.28 Washington Fair Capitol. w.m. Dr. Edwin N.C. Barnes. Published by Music Education Publications, Washington, DC. 1927. Bl/w shield. "Dedicated to the School Children of Washington." 6pp. Page 6: Advertising.

173.29 The Washington Waltzes (Nos. 1 & 2). m. William Cooper Glynn. Published by Henry Prentiss, 32 Court Street, Boston, MA. 1844. B/w green-tinted litho by Thayer & Co. of the U.S. Capitol building. "Arranged for the Piano Forte and respectfully inscribed to Miss Mary Lancaster of Lexington, Kentucky." 6pp. Page 6: Blank.

- **AmPM-174 DIPLOMATIC/JUDICIAL/ADMINISTRATIVE OFFICES — GENERAL**

174.1 Al Gore. w. Jack Rudd. m. *James Dean* originally by The Eagles." Published online by Amiright.com at <http://www.amiright.com/parody/70s/theeagles3.shtml>. 2000. [Crew/WJC-16].

174.2 Appointed Forever. w. Bar and Grill Singers. m. "Sung to the tune of the Turtles' classic *Happy Together*." "A group of performers known as the Bar And Grill Singers has put together a truly hilarious set of lyrics poking fun at federal judges ... David Post." Published by The Volokh Conspiracy online at <http://volokh.blogspot.com/2003_04_13_volokh_archive.html>. 2003.

174.3 Baby Bush. w. William Tong. m. "*Baby Face*, originally by Unknown." Published online at <http://www.amiright.com/parody/misc/unknown0.shtml>. [ca. 2001].

174.4 Back The Red White And Blue With Gold. w.m. Al Hoffman, Mann Curtis and Jerry Livingston. Published by World Music, Inc., 607 Fifth Avenue, New York, NY. 1942. R/w/bl/y/gd drawing of a Continental soldier against a stripe background. "Adopted for the Official Campaign by the Treasury Dep't Defense Savings Staff." 6pp. Pages 2 and 6: Blank.

174.5 The Bankers And The Diplomats. w. Malvina Reynolds, from Faith Petric, 1977. m. Tune file available. Copyright Schroder Music Co., 1959. Lyrics and sound file published by Mudcat Café online at <http://www.mudcat.org/kids/@displaysong.cfm?SongID=5819>. [199-].

174.6 A Boy Named Bush. w. Sharon Krebs. m. "*The Beverly Hillbillies*, originally by Theme Song." Published online at <http://amiright.com/parody/misc/themesong7.shml>. [ca. 2000].

174.7 The Broom. w.m. No composer or tune indicated. In: *Republican Song Book*, page 44. c. Thomas Drew "(Late Editor of *The Massachusetts Spy*)." Published by Thayer and Eldridge, Boston, MA. 1860. [3 7/8" × 5 7/8"]. Br/bk litho of beardless Abraham Lincoln, vignettes of young Lincoln chopping rails, polling raft. 68pp. [M-108]. [Crew/AL-8].

174.8 The Cheater Is Named George W. w. William Tong. m. "Sung to the tune of *How Sweet It Is (To Be Loved By You)* by James Taylor." Published online at <http://geocities.com/wmtong/bootnewt/cheater-gw.htm>. 2001.

174.9 Cheating Skills. w. William K. Tong. m. "Originally by Jimmy Buffet." Published online (lyrics only) by Amiright.com at <http://www.amiright.com/parody/70s/jimmybuffett1.shtml>. 2000. "Please make sure you take time to vote on the parodies you read, the parody authors appreciate the feedback! [Crew/GWB-21].

174.10 Crime Of The Season. w. William Tong. m. "*Time Of The Season*, originally by The Zombies." Published online at <http://amiright.com/parody/misc/thezombies1.shml>. [ca. 2000].

174.11 The Diplomat March. m. John Philip Sousa. Published by The John Church Company, Cincinnati, OH. 1904. B/w litho of John Philip Sousa, leaves, geometric designs. List other Sousa titles available.

174.12 Diplomat March And Two Step. m. Gustavio Brighami. Published by The Thompson Music Co., 269 Wabash Avenue, Chicago, IL. 1900. B/w photo of the U.S. Capitol building. B/w litho of a sword, palm leaves. 8pp. Pages 2 and 7: Blank. Page 8: Advertising.

174.13 Do What I Like. w. William Tong. m. Tune — "*My Life*, originally by Billy Joel." Published online at <http://www.amiright.com/parody/70s/billyjoel5.shtml>. [ca. 2001].

174.14 Dubya, The Bogus POTUS. w. William Tong. m. "*Rudolph The Red-Nosed Reindeer*, originally by Gene Autry." Published online at <http://amiright.com/parody/misc/geneautry0.shml>. [ca. 2000].

174.15 Even Though He Hasn't A Clue. w. Mariah. m. "*Hopelessly Devoted To You*, originally by Olivia Newton John." Published online at <http://amiright.com/parody/80s/olivianewtonjohn0.shtml>. [ca. 2000].

174.16 George Bush Was Crowned President. w. William Tong. m. Tune — "*God Rest Ye, Merry Gentlemen*, originally by Traditional." Published online at <http://amiright.com/parody/misc/traditional14.shml>. [ca. 2000].

174.17 Georgie Bush Coup. w. William Tong. m. "*The Mickey Mouse Club March*, originally by Theme Song." Published online at <http://amiright.com/parody/misc/themesong10.shml>. [ca. 2000].

174.18 Gore Got Screwed By 5 To 4. w. Skisics Surus, "skisics@yahoo.com." m. "Sung to the tune of *25 Or 6 To 4* by Chicago." Published online at <http://www.geocities.com/wmktong/bootnewt/gore5to4.htm>. [ca. 2000].

174.19 Got Him In. w. William Tong. m. "*Let 'Em In*, originally by Wings." Published by Amiright.com at <http://www.amiright.com/parody/70s/wing3.shtml>. [ca. 2001].

174.20 Hear The Call. w. Herbert N. Casson. m. No tune indicated. In: *Labor Songs*, page 16. c. Herbert N. Casson. Published by Lynn Labor Press, 153 Oxford Street, Lynn, MA. [189-]. [3¾" × 5¾"]. Gn/bk geometric designs. 36pp. [Crew/ SLP-3]

174.21 He's Going To The Supreme Court. w. Richard Toomer. m. Tune—"*Graceland* originally by Paul Simon." Published online at <http://www.amiright.com/parody/80s/paulsimon1.shtml>. [ca. 2000].

174.22 Indecision 2000. w. Gary S. O'Connor. m. Tune—"*Mack The Knife,* based on a performance by Bobby Darin." "I finally got to write my editorial on the Presidential Election of 2000. This is political fodder for your ears. The story of Al, Walker, Kathy, Hillary, Jessie and all the rest is set to the melody of Mack the Knife in this parody. By the way, this is not the Rush Limbaugh theme song, but it could be!" Published online at <http://www.amiright.com/parody/60s/bobbydarin2.shtml>. [ca. 2003].

174.23 Odor In The Supreme Court. w. William K. Tong. m. "Sung to the tune of *Owner Of A Lonely Heart* by Yes." "Dedicated to the Felonious Five who appointed Bush President." Published online at <http://bootnewt.envy.nu/odorscotus.htm>. [ca. 2000].

174.24 The Raising (A New Song For Federal Mechanics). w. Francis Hopkinson. m. No tune indicated. Published in the *Pennsylvania Gazette,* February 6, 1788. [VBL, p. 106].

174.25 SCROTUM (Supreme Courts Resident of the United Millionaires). w. Skisics Surus. m. "*All Star,* originally by Smashmouth." Published online at <http://www.amiright.com/parody/2000s/smashmouth1.shtml>. [ca. 2000].

174.26 Shrub Pretender. w. William Tong. m. "*Love Me Tender,* originally by Elvis Presley." Published online at <http://www.amiright.com/parody/misc/elvispresley3.shtml>. [ca. 2001].

174.27 Shrub's Team Made Enemies. w. William Tong. m. "*Sweet Dreams Are Made Of This*, originally by Eurythmics." Published online at <http://amiright.com/parody/80s/eurythmics0.shml>. [ca. 2001].

174.28 Six Thousand Millions Strong! w. No composer indicated. m. "Tune—*Le Petit Tambour.*" "Letter from the Secretary of the Treasury, transmitting—in response to the Senate Resolution of March 8, 1880—'A statement showing the Expenditures of the Government on account of the War of the Rebellion, from July 1, 1861, to June 30, 1879, inclusive—$6,189,929,908.58." In: *Garfield And Arthur Campaign Song Book*, page 20. Published by The Republican Congressional Committee, Washington, DC. 1880. [$5\frac{13}{16}$" × $9\frac{1}{16}$"]. [V-1: Bl/bk] [V-2: Pk/bk] [V-3: Be/bk] [V-4: Gy/bk] litho of James A. Garfield and Chester A. Arthur, palm tree, plants and small animals, geometric designs. 28pp. Page 2: Index. Page 28: "The Electoral Vote for 1880." [M-210]. [Crew/ JAG-62].

174.29 Smut. w.m. Tom Lehrer. In: *Tom Lehrer's Second Song Book*, page 20. Published by Crown Publishers, Inc., New York, NY. 1968. [7⅜" × 10¼"]. Gn/w/bk litho of musical instruments, floral designs. 64pp.

174.30 Supreme Court's Installation. w. William Tong. m. "*You're My Soul And Inspiration,* originally by The Righteous Brothers." "Sung by Scalia to Dubya." Published online at <http://www.amiright.com/parody/misc/therighteousbrothers0.shtml>. [ca. 2000]

174.31 Uncle Sam A Drummer. w.m. W.A. Williams. "The State Department requested our South American consuls to solicit information that would help the brewers enlarge their trade there." In: *Silver Tones, A New Temperance And Prohibition Song Book Containing The Most Popular Songs Sung by The Silver Lake Quartette, For Use In W.C.T.U., Temperance, And Prohibition Party Work, Religious Meetings, Entertainments, Evenings Of Song, Etc.*, page 7. Edited by Rev. C.H. Mead, G.E. Chambers, and Rev. W.A. Williams. Published by W.A. Williams, Publisher, Warnock, Ohio. 1892. [$5\frac{11}{16}$" × 8"]. Be/bk geometric design border. 132pp. [Crew/S-1892-1] [Crew/BFH-133].

174.32 Unlearned Pretender. w. William Tong. m. "*Return To Sender,* originally by Elvis Presley." Published online at <http://amiright.com/parody/misc/elvispresley2.shml>. [ca. 2000].

174.33 U.S. Supreme Court March Two-Step. m. S.H. Keeney. a. J.H. Bell. Published by S.H. Kenney, Wellsboro, PA. 1896. Gn/w flags, geometric designs. 6pp. Pages 2 and 6: Blank.

174.34 Usurper Smirk. w. William Tong. m. "*Surfer Girl,* originally by The Beach Boys." Published online at <http://www.amiright.com/parody/misc/thebeachboys7.shtml>. [ca. 2000].

174.35 The Yankee Consul [Opera Title]. w. Henry M. Blossom, Jr. m. Alfred G. Robyn. Published by M. Witmark & Sons, New York, NY. 1903. R/w/bl/bk drawing of palm trees, star and stripe shield, two cherubs on the shield. "A Comic Opera In 2 Acts." "Management—Henry W. Savage." List of titles from the opera: ***Ain't It Funny What A Difference Just A Few Hours Make?*** {174.35-1}; ***Con, Con, Con*** {174.35-2}; ***Cupid Has Found My Heart*** {174.35-3}; ***The Hammers Will Go Rap, Rap, Rap*** {174.35-4}; ***Hark, While I Sing To Thee!*** {174.25-5}; ***Hola!*** {174.35-6}; ***I'd Like To Be A Soldier*** {174.35-7}; ***In Old Madrid*** {174.25-8}; ***In Old New York*** {174.35-9}; ***In The Days Of Old*** {174.35-10}. 6pp. Page 6: Advertising; ***Lanciers*** {174.35-12}; ***The Mermaid And The Lobster*** {174.35-13}; ***Mosquito And The Midge*** {174.35-14}; ***My San Domingo Maid*** {174.36-15}. 6pp. Page 6: Advertising; ***Nina*** {174.35-16}; ***Tell Me*** {174.35-17}; ***We Come Of Castilian Blood*** {174.35-18}; ***We Were Taught To Walk Demurely*** {174.35-19}; ***When The Goblins Are At Play*** {174.35-20}; ***Ye Ho! Oh Glad Is The Life Of A Sailor At Sea*** {174.35-21}.

• AmPM-175 CONGRESS—GENERAL

175.1 American Freedom. w. E. Rushton. m. No tune indicated. In: *The New National Song Book, Containing Songs, Odes, And Other Poems on National Subjects Compiled from Various Sources*, page 23. Published by Leavitt and Allen, No. 379 Broadway, New York, NY. [1841]. [3½" × 5¼"]. Gd/br non-pictorial designs on hardback cover. Spine printed with title. 172pp. [Crew/GW-675].

175.2 Back To Congress. w. Adis Logan, "Kansas City." m. "Tune—*Hold The Fort.*" In: *Townsend Con-*

vention *Song Book*, page 26. Published by the Townsend National Recovery Plan for the Cleveland, Ohio, Convention, 1936. Copyright 1936 by Frank Dryer. [4⅜" × 8¼"]. B/e/r geometric design border, Townsend Plan logos. 34pp. Page 2: Letter "To The Townsend Family." Page 3: At bottom of music — "Please note, the entire proceeds from the sale of this book go toward expenses of our convention." Page 32: Blank.

175.3 Battle Of Leesburgh! w. No composer indicated. m. "Tune — *Wait For The Wagon*." [1861–1862]. [[Approx. 4" × 8¾"]. Non-pictorial geometric design border. 2pp. Page 2: Blank. [WFU].

175.4 Boyz On The Hill. w. "Antic the Fearless." m. Tune — "*Boyz In The Hood* originally by Dynamite Hack." Published online at <http://www.amiright.com/parody/2000s/dynamitehack0.shtml>. 2003

175.5 Bull Run. w. No composer indicated. m. "Tune — *Wait For The Wagon*." No publisher indicated. [ca. 1861]. [Approx. 4½" × 7¾"]. B/w non-pictorial double line border. 2pp. Page 2: Blank. [WFU].

175.6 Bull's Run. w. No composer indicated. m. "Tune — *Wait For The Wagon*." No publisher indicated. [1861–1862]. [4" × 8½"]. Non-pictorial geometric design border. 2pp. Page 2: Blank. [WFU].

175.7 A Challenge To Congress. w. No composer indicated. m. "Adapted from the old *Trelawney Cry*." In: *Townsend Convention Song Book*, page 10. Published by the Townsend National Recovery Plan for the Cleveland, Ohio, Convention, 1936. Copyright 1936 by Frank Dryer. [4⅜" × 8¼"]. B/e/r geometric design border, Townsend Plan logos. 34pp. Page 2: Letter "To The Townsend Family." Page 3: At bottom of music — "Please note, the entire proceeds from the sale of this book go toward expenses of our convention." Page 32: Blank.

175.7A Civil Rap. w. Emily Nghiem. m. "Set to the tune of *Tom's Diner*, originally by Suzanne Vega and later re-mixed by D.N.A." Lyrics and wave file published online at <http://www.houstonprogressive.org/isocracy.html>. 1999.

175.8 The Congress. m. No composer indicated. In: *The Compleat Tutor For The Fife, Containing Ye Best & Easiest Instructions For Learners To Obtain A Proficiency. To Which Is Added A Choice Collection Of Ye Most Celebrated Marches, Airs, &c. Properly Adapted To That Instrument, With Several Choice Pieces For Two Flutes)*, page 30. Printed for & sold by George Willig, No. 12 South Fourth Street, Philadelphia [PA], where also may had a great variety of other music, musical instruments, strings, &c., &c. [ca. 1805]. 30pp. [S/U, p. 84] [W-9425].

175.9 The Congress. w. No composer indicated. m. *Nancy Dawson*. "From *Songs Of The American Revolution* by Rabson." Lyrics and sound file published online at <http://www.mudcat.org/kids/@displaysong.cfm?SongID=6077>. [199-].

175.10 Congress Grand March. m. J.Z. Hesser. Published by Atwill, 201 Broadway, New York, NY. [ca. 1830]. Non-pictorial. 4pp. Pages 1 and 4: Blank.

175.11 Congress Grand March. m. J.Z. Hesser. Published by David P. Faulds, Louisville, KY. [ca. 1840]. Non-pictorial. "Composed and Arranged for the Piano Forte."

175.12 Congress Grand March. m. J.Z. Hesser. Published by E. Riley & Co, 297 Broadway, New York, NY. [ca. 1850]. Non-pictorial. 4pp. Pages 1 and 4: Blank.

175.13 Congress Grand March. Published by Firth & Pond, New York. [ca. 1840].

175.14 Congress Grand March. m. J.Z. Hesser. Published Firth, Pond & Co., 1 Franklin Square, New York, NY. [1831–1843]. Non-pictorial geometric designs. 4pp. Pages 1 and 4: Blank.

175.15 Congress Grand March. m. Jupiter Zeus Hesser. Published by G.P. Reed, 17 Tremont Row, Boston, MA. [ca. 1840]. Non-pictorial. "Composed for the Piano Forte." 4pp. Pages 1 and 4: Blank.

175.16 Congress Grand March. m. J.Z. Hesser. Published by Keith's Music Publishing House, 67 & 69 Court Street, Boston, MA. [ca. 1840]. Non-pictorial. 4pp. Pages 1 and 4: Blank.

175.17 Congress Grand March. m. Jupiter Zeus Hesser. Published by Oliver Ditson, 115 Broadway, New York, NY. [ca. 1840]. Non-pictorial. 4pp. Pages 1 and 4: Blank.

175.18 Congress Grand March. m. Jupiter Zeus Hesser. In: *Drawing Room Gems, A Collection Of Popular Marches, Waltzes, Polkas, Galops, &c*. Published by Oliver Ditson & Co., 277 Washington Street, Boston, MA. [ca. 1850]. B/w geometric design frame. List of other titles in the series. 6pp. Page 2: Blank. Page 6: Advertising.

175.19 Congress Grand March. m. No composer indicated. In: *Centennial Chimes!* (Song Book), page 31. w.m. Patriotic songs with music. Published by John Church & Co., Cincinnati, OH. 1876. [9" × 11½"]. R/w/b litho of eagle, Liberty bell, star boarder. Hard cover. 54pp. [Crew/GW-690].

175.20 Congress March. m. J.Z. Hesser. Published by J.L. Peters, New York, NY. [ca. 1850]. Non-pictorial geometric designs. "Floating Gems, A Collection of Easy Pieces by Various Authors." List of other titles in the series. 4pp. Page 4: Blank.

175.21 Congress March. m. J.Z. Hesser. Published by Balmer & Weber, 311 N. Fifth Street, St. Louis, MO. 1865. Non-pictorial black border. "Universal Favorites by Various Authors." List of other titles in the series. 4pp. Page 4: Advertising.

175.22 Congress March. m. J.Z. Hesser. In: *Very Best Set , Of Easy Airs For Small Hands*. Published by Lee & Walker, 922 Chestnut Street, Philadelphia, PA. [ca. 1870]. "Arranged expressly for learners."

175.23 Congress March. m. J.Z. Hesser. Published by Published by S. Brainard & Co., 77 Superior Street, Cleveland, OH. [ca. 1850]. Non-pictorial. 4pp. Pages 1 and 4: Blank.

175.24 Congress March. m. J.Z. Hesser. Published by W.C. Peters & Sons, Cincinnati, OH. [ca. 1850]. Non-pictorial. 4pp. Pages 1 and 4: Blank.

175.25 Congress Waltz. m. Ch. Zeuner. Published by Parker & Ditson, 107 Washington Street, Boston, MA. 1836. Non-pictorial geometric designs. "Composed for the Piano Forte and dedicated to Miss Elizabeth Bradlee." 4pp. Pages 1 and 4: Blank.

175.26 Congressional Polka. m. Joseph Ascher. Published by Geo. Hilbus, Music Department, Washington, DC. [ca. 1840]. B/w litho of the U.S. Capitol building, geometric designs. 6pp. Pages 2 and 6: Blank.

175.27 Congressional Scumbag. w. Andy Moon. m. "*Teenage Dirtbag*, based on a performance by Wheatus." Published online at <http://www.amiright.com/parody/2000s/wheatus29.shtml>. [ca. 2003].

175.28 The Democrat Congress. w. No composer indicated. m. "Tune—*Old Oaken Bucket*." In: *New People's Party Songster*, page 14. e. Theodore Parish Stelle. Published in Mt. Vernon, IL. [ca. 1894]. 32pp. [M-361]. [Crew/WJB-62].

175.29 Destroying The US Constitution. w. No composer indicated. m. "To the tune of *Stairway to Heaven*." Published online at <http://www.wwirr.com/wcr/parody/constitution.html>. [199-]

175.30 Eight Dollars A Day. w. Jesse Hutchinson, Jr. m. J.J. Hutchinson. Published by Oliver Ditson, 115 Washington Street, Boston, MA. 1848. Non-pictorial geometric designs. "Written & Dedicated to the Congress of the U.S." "As sung in all the concerts of the Hutchinson Family. 6pp. Page 6: Blank.

175.31 Filibuster. w.m. Gerald Gardner. In: *These Are The Songs That Were* [Song Book], page 4. e. Gerald Gardner "(Writer *Of Who's In Charge Here?, News-Reals*, and *That Was The Week That Was*)." Published by Edwin H. Morris and Company, No. 31 West 54th Street, New York, NY. 10019. 1965. B/w photo of Lyndon B. Johnson, Hubert Humphrey, Everett Dirksen, others. R/w/bk cover. List of contents. 36pp. Pages 8, 23 and 25: Photos of politicians. [Crew/LBJ-6].

175.32 The Game Of Wills. w. William K. Tong. m. Sung to the tune of *The Game Of Love* by Wayne Fontana & The Mindbenders." In: *The Sting The Right Wing Song Book* at <http://www.geocities.com/wmktong/bootnewt/gamewill>.

175.33 Grand National Medley Overture [On The Airs *Hail Columbia, Major Andre's Complaint* and *Yankee Doodle*]. Published by Geib & Walker, 23 Maiden Lane, New York, NY. Non-pictorial. Composed and Arranged for the Piano Forte and is most respectfully inscribed to the President and Members of Congress of the United States of America by the Publisher." 12pp. [?].

175.33A I'm An Amendment. From TV Show: *The Simpsons*. Lyrics published online at <http://snpp.com/guides/lyrics_list.html>. [199-].

175.34 In The Name Of Jehovah Our Banner We Raise. w. Rev. T.H. Stockton, Chaplin to Congress. m. Leopold Meihnen, Doct. Of Music. Published by J.E. Gould, 7th and Chesnut Streets, Philadelphia, PA. 1854. "In the name of our God we will set up our banners." "Music composed and dedicated to his [Stockton] friend William Wallace Keys, Esqr." 6pp. Pages 2 and 6: Blank.

175.35 It's Up To You, Mr. Voter! w. J.L. Feeney. m. "Air—*Onward, Christian Soldiers*." In: *Hughes And Fairbanks Campaign Song Book*, page 6. c. James L. Feeney. Published by William H. Delaney, Song Publisher, No. 117 Park Row, New York, NY. Copyright 1916 by William W. DeLaney. [8" × 11"]. R/w/b flags, shield. Bl/w photos of "Charles Evans Hughes" and "Charles Warren Fairbanks." "Preparedness, Protection, Prosperity." R/w/b drawing of flags, shield, geometric designs. 20pp. [M-407]. [Crew/CEH-1].

175.36 The Legislator. w. Michael Pacholek. m. "*The Entertainer* originally by Billy Joel." Published online at <http://www.amiright.com/parody/70s/billyjoel43.shml>. [ca. 2002].

175.37 Marching To Congress. w. Cordelia Jewett Harvey, Canon City, CO. m. "Tune—*Marching Through Georgia*." In: *Townsend Convention Song Book*, page 24. Published by the Townsend National Recovery Plan for the Cleveland, Ohio, Convention, 1936. Copyright 1936 by Frank Dryer. [4⅜" × 8¼"]. Be/r geometric design border, Townsend Plan logos. 34pp.

175.38 Mr. Congressman. w. No composer indicated. m. No tune indicated. In: *National Youth Lobby*, page 25. Published by The Young Progressive Citizens of America. 1947. [8½" × 11"]. B/w drawing of man, the Capitol. "Jobs! Peace! Freedom!" "Hear Henry Wallace Keynote the National Youth Lobby." "Sponsored by Y.P.C.A. in Washington, D.C., on June 15 and 16, 1947." 30pp. Pages 25 to 27: Songs. [Crew/HAW-9].

175.38A My Congressman. w.m. Fifteen. Lyrics published online at <http://www.plyrics.com/lyrics/fifteen/mycongressman.html>. [ca. 198-].

175.39 A New Song. w. "Colon and Spondee." [Joseph Dennie and Royall Tyler]. m. "To the tune of *O Dear What Can The Matter Be?*" "As sung with applause at Congress Garden." Published in the *Farmer's Weekly Museum: Newhampshire [sic] And Vermont Journal*, June 26, 1797. [VBL, p. 138].

175.40 Not By My Vote. w.m. Charles M. Fillmore. In: *Fillmore's Prohibition Songs*, page 75. "These four words will answer all arguments on this question—Not By My Vote. If they say to us: Men will have it. We can answer: Not By My Vote. If another say men will sell it. Again we reply, Not By My Vote. I am not bound to abolish the saloon, but only my interest in it. My vote may not hurt the saloon, but I am bound to vote it right all the same. Saloons may go on, like the brook forever. Men may die in them like flies and hell grow fat on drunkards. Girls may be betrayed and boys baited hellward. Faith may be weakened and character dismantled. Homes may be destroyed and women and children beggared. Soldier's Homes may still sell drinks to the old veterans, and Army canteens debauch the young ones. Our national Capitol may have a saloon at either end. Senators and Representatives may be drunk on the floors of Congress, But Not By My Vote."—Hale [Johnson]." Published by Fillmore Brothers Company, No. 421 Elm Street, Cincinnati, OH. 1903. 230pp.

175.41 Oh Congress, It Is Up To You. w.m. Morris Siegel. No publisher indicated. Copyright 1932 by Morris Siegel, 1870 East 12th Street, Brooklyn, NY. Bl/w drawing of veterans marching, soldiers in battle—"Our country may it always be right." "Special Edition for Bonus Expeditionary Forces, Washington, D.C." "15¢ Pay No More." 4pp.

175.42 Oh Dear! What Can The Matter Be? (Congress Won't Give Me The Votes). w. Milton m. Schwartz. m. "To the Tune of *Where Is My Little Dog Gone*." In: *Sing Along With Jack*, page 24. Published by Bonny Publishing Corp. 1963. R/b/e silhouette of John F. Kennedy, drawing his family. "Hit Songs From The New Frontier." 32pp.

175.43 Oh Where, Oh Where Has The Congress Gone? m. "To the tune of *Where Has My Little Dog*

Gone?" In: *Sing Along With Jack* [Song Book], page 26. w. Milton M. Schwartz. a. Danny Hurd. Published by Pocket Books, Inc., New York, NY. Copyright 1963 by Bonny Publishing Corporation. [9" × 11⅞"]. R/w/bk drawing of sheet music "Vive La Dynasty," silhouette of John F. Kennedy in chair with conductor's baton, caricature of Kennedy family. "Hit Songs from the New Frontier." 36pp. Page 3: "Illustrations by David Gantz." Page 36: Drawing of John F. Kennedy in chair with baton. Song titles. [Crew/JFK-17].

175.44 Old Party Congressmen. w. No composer indicated. m. "Tune—*We're Going Home.*" In: *New People's Party Songster*, page 25. w. Theo. P. Stelle. m. Popular tunes. Published by Theo. P. Stelle, Mt. Vernon, IL. [ca. 1892]. 36pp. Pages 2, 35 and 36: Advertising. [Crew/JBW-13].

175.45 On Meeting Of Congress At Washington City. (Song). w. No composer indicated. m. No tune indicated. Published in the *Boston Gazette*, December 4, 1800. [VBL, p. 164].

175.46 Our Starry Flag (A New National Flag Song). w.m. Alfred Beirly, Mus. Doc. Published by Alfred Beirly Music Co., Chicago, IL. 1911. R/w/b litho of a proposed new configuration of the American as proposed by Representative E.A. Hayes. "Respectfully Inscribed to the Sixty-Second Congress of the Great American Republic." 8pp. Page 2: "Our New National Flag—The following Flag Resolution was introduced in Congress by the Hon. E.A. Hayes, Member from California." Facsimile printing of the "Concurrent Resolution, in the House of Representatives, August 8, 1911." Pages 7 and 8: Blank.

175.46A Peter Bazooka. w.m. Dead Milkmen. Lyrics published online at <http://www.plyrics.com/lyrics/dealmilkmen/peterbazooka.html>. [ca. 198-].

175.47 Protect The Freedman. (Song And Chorus). w. Luke Collin. m. J.P. Webster. Published by Oliver Ditson & Co., 277 Washington Street, Boston, MA. 1866. B/w geometric and floral design frame. "To the Honorable the Thirty-Ninth Congress." "Sung by Skiff & Gaylord's Minstrels." 6pp. Pages 2 and 6: Blank.

175.48 Republican Congress. w. William K. Tong. m. "Sung to the tune of *American Woman* by The Guess Who." In: *The Sting The Right Wing Song Book* at <http://www.geocities.com/wmktong/bootnewt/congress.html>. [199-].

175.49 A Salute To Congress. 33⅓ rpm LP. Published by the White House Historical Association. 1965. Program for The White House, October 7, 1965. [Popular tunes].

175.50 So You Want To Be A Congressman. w.m. Arthur Korb. In: *Songs For Political Action*, page 2. Published by National Citizens Political Action Committee, No. 205 East 42nd Street, New York, NY. 1944. Drawing of man, guitar, singers. Narrative. 4pp. [Crew/FDR-197].

175.51 Song (On The Meeting of Congress at Washington City). w. No. composer indicated. m. No tune indicated. Published in the *Boston Gazette*, December 4, 1800, [VBL, p. 164].

175.52 A Song. w. No composer indicated. m. "Tune—*Hearts Of Oak.*" Published in Rivington's *Royal Gazette.* 1779. "A Song, written by a refugee on reading the King's speech, and sung at the Refugee Club, in the City of New York." [SBAR, p. 253].

175.53 Tea Pot Blues (Fox Trot Song). w.m. Leona Lovell "(Writer of *My Dixie Rose*)." Published by Leona Lovell Music Publishing Company, No. 303–4 Melbourne Hotel, St. Louis, MO. 1924. R/w/b drawing of Uncle Sam, arm inscribed "Congress" pouring oil from teapot inscribed "Teapot Dome" onto group of men. 6pp. Pages 2 and 6: Advertising. [Crew/WGH-40].

175.54 Things That I'd Like To See. w. "Composed and Sung by Dan Rice." m. "Tune—*Irish Washerwoman.*" In: *Dan Rice's Great American Humorist Song Book*, page 11. 1866. [4⅛" × 5¾"]. Br/bk drawing of an actor. "Containing Original and Selected Songs, Carefully Revised & Corrected." 34pp.

175.55 The War-Worn Soldier. w.m. No composer or tune indicated. "Written under the reign of Anglo-Federalism." In: *The Republican Harmonist (Being A Select Collection Of Republican, Patriotic, And Sentimental Songs, Odes, Sonnets, &c, American And European: Some Of Which Are Original, And Most Of The Others Now Come For The First Time From An American Press)*, page 77. c. D.E. [Daniel Ebsworth] "(A Citizen of the World)." Printed "for the People," Boston, MA. 1801. Non-pictorial. 152pp. [Crew/TJ-10].

175.56 We've Got Our Eyes On You. w. No composer indicated. m. No tune indicated. In: *National Youth Lobby*, page 25. Published by The Young Progressive Citizens of America. 1947. [8½" × 11"]. B/w drawing of man, the Capitol. "Jobs! Peace! Freedom!" "Hear Henry Wallace Keynote the National Youth Lobby." "Sponsored by Y.P.C.A. in Washington, D.C., on June 15 and 16, 1947." 30pp. [Crew/HAW-9].

175.57 What Is Congress Doing Now? w. Charles A. Mulliner. m. J.W. Reitmeyer. Published by The Zabel-Worley Co., Philadelphia, PA. 1893. Gn/w geometric designs. B/w photo of either Mulliner or Reitmeyer. "Composer of the Latest Success of the Day." 6pp. Pages 2 and 6: Blank.

175.58 What Is Congress Doing Now? (Song). w.m. Charles A. Mulliner. m. J.W. Reitmeyer. No publisher indicated. For sale at Kirk Johnson & Co., Music House, 24 West King Street, Lancaster, PA. Copyright 1893 by Charles Mulliner. B/w geometric designs. 6pp. Pages 2 and 6: Blank.

175.59 When Congress Closed. w. Major W.T. Anderson. m. "Tune—*When Johnny Comes Marching Home.*" In: *Hayes & Wheeler Song Book*, page 30. Published by The Union Republican Congressional Committee, Washington, DC. 1876. [5¾" × 9¼"]. Br/bk litho of Rutherford B. Hayes and William A. Wheeler, shield, geometric design border. "I'll be on hand again shortly." [V-1: "Series I" under title on cover] [V-2: Series not indicated on cover]. 52pp. [M-196, 197]. [Crew/RBH-20].

• **AmPM-176   CONGRESSMEN**

176.1 Mr. Congressman. w. Agnes Cummingham. m. "Tune—*Little Brown Jug.*" In: *The People's Song Book*, 117. e. Waldemar Hille. Published by Boni & Gaer, Inc., New York, NY. 1948. [7" × 10½"]. R/w/b music notes and keyboard. "Forward by Alan Lomax; Preface by B.A. Botkin." 128pp.

176.2 Mr. Congressman. w. No composer indicated. m. "Parody of *Mr. Tambourine Man* by The Byrds." Lyrics published by *The Bob Rivers Show* with Bob, Spike & Joe and Twisted Tunes online at <http://www.twistedradio.com/player/lyrics.asp?songID=932>. [199-].

176.3 What Have They Got On You Mr. Congressman? w. Mark Swan. m. Raymond Hubbell, Published by T.B. Harms and Francis, Day & Hunter, New York, NY. 1920. R/w/bk geometric designs, large "?." 6pp. Page 6: Blank. Page 6: Advertising.

176.4 When I'm A Congressman. w. Harriet D. Castle. m. Ira B. Wilson. In: *The Suffragettes* (A Musical Comedy), page 29. Published by Lorenz Publishing Company, Dayton, Ohio; 150 Fifth Avenue, New York, New York; and 218 S. Wabash Avenue, Chicago, Illinois. 1914. [6¾" × 9⅞"]. Br/bk drawing of three women carrying signs reading "Votes For Women" and "We Demand The Ballot." "Price $1.00 per copy, postpaid, without right to perform publicly. Six copies with right of two public performances, $5.00." 62pp. [Crew/S-1914-16(L)].

- **AmPM-177 SENATE/SENATORS**

177.1 Carousel Of Love. w. Mitchel Herman. m. Al Goodman. 1949. B/w photos of television stars including Fred Allen, Portland Hoffa, Al Goodman, Mrs. Nussbaum and Senator Claghorn. "As introduced on the *Fred Allen Show*."

177.1A The Fondler. w. No composer indicated. m. "Parody of *The Wanderer* by Dion & The Belmonts." Lyrics published by *The Bob Rivers Show* with Bob, Spike & Joe and Twisted Tunes online at <http://www.twistedradio.com/player/lyrics.asp?songID=1003>. [199-].

177.2 The Glorious Nineteen. Published by N. Car**?, Washington, DC. [1868]. B/w litho of U.S. flag, eagle with ribbon inscribed "U.S. Supreme Court." Star inscribed "U.S. Constitution." Wreath with the number "19" within. 6pp. Page 2: "Legend — In 1868 before the nation had time to recover from the effects of the great Rebellion when the hearts of men were still torn, and their minds still confused with the horrors of '64, the reins of government were seized by a fanatical crew, who threatened once more to plunge the country into civil war. All was gloom and despondency, thinking man dreaded the future still more than the past, the Head of the Nation, was arranged before a partisan tribunal, the Palladium of our liberty was stormed, when seven noble patriots threw themselves into the breach, and striking for God and their Country, scoring alike the threats and imprecations, bribes and promises of their party, pushed forward to the rescue and, by their timely efforts in behalf of law and order and the Rights of the People, gave the nation once more the blessings of Tranquility and Peace." 6pp. Page 6: Blank. [Crew/AJN-22].

177.3 Mistress Of The Senator. Audra McDonald. In: *Way Back To Paradise.* Published by Hal Leonard. 199-.

177.4 Mr. So And So. w. J.W.B. Siders. m. "Air — From W.S. Gilbert's *Iolanthe.*" In: *Blaine And Logan Campaign Songster,* page 11. Published by American News Company, New York, NY. 1884. 36pp. [M-249]. [Crew/JGB-84].

177.5 Peace On Honorable Terms To America. w. No composer indicated. m. No tune indicated. Published as a broadsheet by Nathaniel Coverly, Jun., Milk Street, Boston, MA. 1815. B/w engraving of Miss Liberty and Miss Justice, eagle and shield, rising sun. "Signed by our Commissioners at Ghent, Dec. 24, 1814, Prince Regent, Dec. 28, Ratified by the President and Senate, of the United States, Feb. 17, 1815. [VLB, p. 216].

177.6 President Harrison's Grand Military Waltz. Published by G.P. Reed, No. 17 Tremont Row, Boston, MA. [1841]. Non-pictorial. "Respectfully Dedicated by the Publisher to the Senators of the U.S." "Pr. 25. Nett [sic]." 4pp. [Crew/WHH-95].

177.7 The Senator Waltzes. m. I. Benedict. Published by F.B. Haviland Pub. Co., Music Publishers, 114 West 44th Street, New York, NY. 1921. Gn/w litho of the U.S. Capitol building, geometric design frame. 6pp. Page 6: Advertising.

177.8 The Senator Waltzes. m. I Benedict. Published by Willis Woodward & Co., 842 & 844 Broadway, New York, NY. 1890. Bl/w litho of Wm. H. Crane as "The Senator," U.S. Capitol dome in background. "Respectfully dedicated by permission to 'The Senator, W.H. Crane." Facsimile handwriting on calling card — "With best wishes of the 'Senator,' Wm. H. Crane." 8pp. Pages 2 and 8: Advertising. [Crane was an actor famous for his portrayal of fictional Western senator, Senator Hannibal Rivers].

177.9 The Senator Waltzes. m. I Benedict. Published by Willis Woodward & Co., 842 & 844 Broadway, New York, NY. 1890. B/w flowers, geometric designs. "Respectfully dedicated by permission to 'The Senator,' W.H. Crane." Facsimile handwriting on calling card — "With best wishes of the 'Senator,' Wm. H. Crane." 10pp. Pages 2 and 10: Blank.

177.10 The Senator March. m. H. Braham. Published by Willis Woodward & Co., 842 & 844 Broadway, New York, NY. 1890. Bl/w litho of Wm. H. Crane as "The Senator," U.S. Capitol dome in background. "Respectfully dedicated by permission to 'The Senator, W.H. Crane." Facsimile handwriting on calling card — "With best wishes of the 'Senator,' Wm. H. Crane." [Crane was an actor famous for his portrayal of fictional Western senator, Senator Hannibal Rivers].

177.11 38 Senators. w. A.J. Kiser. m. Edouard Hesselberg. Published by A.J. Kiser, Colorado Springs, CO. 1920.

177.12 We 38 Senators Must Win The Day. w. A.J. Kiser. m. Edouard Hesselberg. Published by A.J. Kiser, Colorado Springs, CO. 1920.

FLORIDA

• **AmPM-178 ANDREWS**, Charles Oscar (Criminal Court Judge, Walton County, 1910–1911; Assistant State Attorney General, 1912–1919; Circuit Judge, 1919–1925; State House, 1927; State Supreme Court Commissioner, 1929–1932; U.S. Senate, 1936–1946)

178.1 The American Creed Song Sheet. w. No composer indicated. m. "*Bear Came Over The Mountain*." [1936]. [8½" × 14"]. Non-pictorial typed. Various patriotic, popular and pro-Roosevelt songs. At top of page 1—"The American Creed." 2pp.

• **AmPM-178A BRAVO**, Vanessa (City Council, Hialeah, 2004–Present)

178A.1 Seis Milliones. w.m. Elio Rodriguez. Published in *The Miami Herald* and online at *Herald.com*. April 2, 2004. "Radio Jingle On Controversy — Here are excerpts from a radio jingle on the controversy over the pledge by council members Vanessa Bravo and Cindy Miel to refund $6 million. It was written by Elio Rodreguez and produced by Gerardo Peña." "Translated by Herald staff writer Elaine de Vaille." Lyrics and midi file published online at <http://miami. com/mld/miamiherald/news/local/8334546.htm>.

• **AmPM-178B BRUDERLY**, David E. (Candidate for U.S. House, 2004)

178B.1 Bruderly Campaign Song. w.m. Cathy DeWitt. "Recorded by Cathy DeWitt." Lyrics and mp3 file published at <http://www.bruderly.com/song. html>. 2003.

• **AmPM-179 BUSH**, Jeb (Governor, 1999–Present)

179.1 The Ballad Of Jeb Bush. w. Alan C. Bessey. m. "Sung to the tune of *Ballad Of Jed Clampett* from the Beverly Hillbillies." Published online at <http:// www.geocities.com/wmktong/bootnewt/balladjeb. htm>. [ca. 2000].

179.2 The Ballad Of Jeb Bush. w. R. Winters. m. Tune —"*The Ballad Of Jed Clampett*, based on the performance by Paul Henning." "Jeb Bush is still getting heat for Florida vote irregularities. Expected to be issue in his gubernatorial race in 2002." Published online at <http://www.amiright.com/parody/misc/paulhenning 0.shtml>. [ca. 2001].

179.3 The Ballad Of Jeb Bush. w. Darrell Decker. m. "Sung to the tune of *Ballad Of Jed Clampett* from the Beverly Hillbillies." Published online at <http:// www.geocities.com/wmktong/bootnewt/jeb2.htm>. [ca. 2000].

179.4 The Ballad Of Jeb's Brother. w. William Tong. m. "*The Ballad Of Jed Clampett*, based on a performance by Lester Flatt and Earl Skruggs." Published online at <http://www.amiright.com/parody/60s/ lesterflattandearlskruggs0.shtml>. [ca. 2003].

179.5 Ballots Of Jeb Bush. w. Bill Tong. m. "*The Beverly Hillbillies*, originally by Theme Song." Published online at <http://amiright.com/parody/misc/ themesong0.shml>. [ca. 2000].

179.6 Banana Republic. w. William Tong. m. "Sung to the tune of *The Chiquita Banana Jingle*, from a suggestion by Laurie from Florida." N/c photo of Jeb Bush and Katherine Harris in Banana suits in front of a map of Florida. Published online at <http://geo cities.com/wmtong/bootnewt/banana.htm>. [ca. 2000].

179.7 The Boy Dubya. w. Skisics Surus, "skisics@ yahoo.com." m. "Sung to the tune of *The Jean Genie* by David Bowie." Published online at <http://www. geocities.com/wmktong/bootnewt/boydubya.htm>. [ca. 2000].

179.8 Brain-Dead Whine. w. Michael Pacholek. w. Tune —"*Red, Red Wine* originally by Neil Diamond." Published online at <http://www.amiright.com/ parody/60s/neildiamond2.shml>.

179.9 Bush Boys Hijacked The Crown. w. Skisics Surus, "skisics@yahoo.com." m. "Sung to the tune of *The Boys Are Back In Town* by Thin Lizzy." Published online at <http://www.geocities.com/wmktong/boot newt/bushboys.htm>. [ca. 2000].

179.10 Bush Brothers' Unraveling Nation Show. w. William Tong. m. "*Brother Love's Traveling Salvation Show*, originally by Neil Diamond." Published online at <http://www.amiright.com/parody/70s/neil diamond4.shtml>. [2000].

179.11 Bush Inaugural Theme Song. w. Gloria Messer. m. "To the tune of *What A Wonderful World* by Sam Cooke. " Lyrics published online at <http:// www.topica.com/lists/billionairesforbushorgore>. 2000.

179.12 Bush On Trial. w. Skisics Surus, "skisics@ yahoo.com." m. "Parody of *The Trial* from *The Wall* by Pink Floyd." Published online at <http://www. geocities.com/wmktong/bootnewt/bushtrial.htm>. [ca. 2000].

179.13 Bush The Deceiver. w. Skisics Surus, "skisics@yahoo.com." m. "Sung to the tune of *I'm A Believer* by Monkees." Published online at <http:// www.geocities.com/wmktong/bootnewt/bushdeceiver. htm>. [ca. 2000].

179.14 Country Under Dubya w. Skisics Surus, "skisics@yahoo.com." m. "Sung to the tune of *Hotel California* by The Eagles." Published online at <http:// www.geocities.com/wmktong/bootnewt/country-w. htm>. [ca. 2000].

179.15 The Day The Vote Was Swiped w. Skisics Surus, "skisics@yahoo.com." m. "Sung to the tune of *American Pie, Part 1 & 2* by Don McLean." Published online at <http://www.geocities.com/wmktong/boot newt/voteswiped.htm>. [ca. 2000].

179.16 Do You Want To Know A Secret? (Jeb's Confession To Brother Smirk). w. Skisics Surus and Bill Tong." m. "Sung to the tune of *Do You Want To Know A Secret?* by The Beatles." Published online at <http://www.geocities.com/ wmktong/bootnewt/jeb secret.htm>. [ca. 2000].

179.17 Don't Cry For Me, Tallahassee. w. William Tong. m. "*Don't Cry For Me, Argentina*, originally by

Madonna." "As sung by Katherine Harris." Published online at <http://amiright.com/parody/90s/madonna0.shml>. [ca. 2000].

179.18 Dub-ba-yoo. w. Lyndia Theys. m. "*Peggy Sue*, originally by Buddy Holly." Published online at <http://amiright.com/parody/misc/buddyholly1.shml>. [ca. 2001].

179.19 Dubya, The Bogus POTUS. w. William Tong. m. "*Rudolph The Red-Nosed Reindeer*, originally by Gene Autry." Published online at <http://amiright.com/parody/misc/geneautry0.shml>. [ca. 2000].

179.20 Dubya's Dumber Than Dirt. w. Sara Rose. m. "*Another One Bites The Dust*, originally by Queen." Published online at <http://amiright.com/parody/70s/queen11.shml>. [ca. 2001].

179.21 Dumb King Medley. (Ode to Smirk). w. Skisics Surus, "skisics@yahoo.com." m. "Sung to the tune of *Sun King Medley* by the Beatles." Published online at <http://www.geocities.com/wmktong/bootnewt/dumbking.htm>. [ca. 2000].

179.22 Dubya Can't Wait (Ode to the Florida Recount). w. Skisics Surus, "skisics@yahoo.com." m. "Sung to the tune of *Carry That Weight* by the Beatles." Published at <geocities.com/wmktong/bootnewt/dumbking.htm>. [2000].

179.23 An Election That's Fair. w. Sara Rose. m. "*Mercedes Benz*, originally by Janis Joplin." Published online at <http://amiright.com/parody/misc/janisjoplin0.shml>. [ca. 2000].

179.24 The End (Ode to the American Voter). w. Skisics Surus, "skisics@yahoo.com." m. "Sung to the tune of *The End* by the Beatles." Published at <geocities.com/wmktong/bootnewt/dumbking.htm>. [2000].

179.25 Every Breath You Take. w. Skisics Surus, "skisics@yahoo.com." m. "Sung to the tune of *Every Breath You Take* by The Police." Published online at <http://www.geocities.com/wmktong/bootnewt/breathtake.htm>. [ca. 2000].

179.26 Faking On His Part Won't Do. w. William Tong. m. "*Breaking Up Is Hard To Do*, originally by Neil Sedaka." Published online at <http://www.amiright.com/parody/misc/neilsedaka1.shtml>. [ca. 2001].

179.27 Florida. w. Skisics Surus, "skisics@yahoo.com." m. "Sung to the tune of *Panama* by Van Halen." Published online at <http://www.geocities.com/wmktong/bootnewt/florida.htm>. [ca. 2000].

179.28 George Bush Is Done. w. Charlie Decker. m. "*It's All Been Done*, based on the performance by Barenaked Ladies." "Pretty Self-explanatory." Published online at <http://www.amiright.com/parody/90s/barenakedladies24.shtml>. 2004.

179.29 George Bush Was Crowned President. w. William Tong. m. Tune — "*God Rest Ye, Merry Gentlemen*, originally by Traditional." Published online at <http://amiright.com/parody/misc/traditional14.shml>. [ca. 2000].

179.30 George W. Bush Inaugural Theme Song. w. Joel Landy. m. "Tune — *What A Wonderful Life* by San Cooke." Published online by the Centre for Political Song at <http://polsong.gcal.ac.uk/songs/landy.html>. [ca. 2001].

179.31 Getting' Wronger Every Day. w. Skisics Surus, "skisics@yahoo.com." m. "Sung to the tune of *Feelin' Stronger Every Day* by Chicago." Published online at <http://www.geocities.com/wmktong/bootnewt/getwronger.htm>. [ca. 2000].

179.32 Going Up The Pharmacy. w. Alvin Dover. m. "Sung to the tune of *Going Up The Country* by Canned Heat." "As sung by Jeb's daughter, Noelle Bush." N/c mug shot of Noelle Bush at the Tallahassee Police Department holding a sign that reads, "Vote for my dad for Governor of Florida." Published online by alvindover@hotmail.com at <http://bootnewt.tripod.com/pharmacy.htm>. [ca. 2002].

179.33 Golden Numbers (Ode to Poppy Bush). w. Skisics Surus, "skisics@yahoo.com." m. "Sung to the tune of *Golden Slumbers* by the Beatles." Published at <geocities.com/wmktong/bootnewt/dumbking.htm>. [2000].

179.34 Got Him In. w. William Tong. m. "*Let 'Em In*, originally by Wings." Published by Amiright.com at <http://www.amiright.com/parody/70s/wing3.shtml>. [ca. 2001].

179.35 Harris Get Slammed (Ode to Katherine Harris). w. Skisics Surus, "skisics@yahoo.com." m. "Sung to the tune of *Polythene Pam* by the Beatles." Published at <geocities.com/wmktong/bootnewt/dumbking.htm>. [2000].

179.36 Harris Is Just All Right With Me. w. William Tong. m. "*Jesus Is Just Alright*, originally by The Doobie Brothers." Published online at <http://amiright.com/parody/70s/thedoobiebrothers.shml>. [ca. 2000].

179.37 Have A Cigar. w. Skisics Surus, "skisics@yahoo.com." m. "Sung to the tune of *Have A Cigar* by Pink Floyd." "As sung by the G.O.P. Leadership." Published online at <http://www.geocities.com/wmktong/bootnewt/havacigar.htm>. [ca. 2000].

179.38 Have You Ever Seen A Race. w. Skisics Surus, "skisics@yahoo.com." m. "Sung to the tune of *Have You Ever Seen The Rain* by Creedence Clearwater Revival." Published online at <http://www.geocities.com/wmktong/bootnewt/havaseenracecigar.htm>. [ca. 2000].

179.39 He Ain't Ready, He's Jeb's Brother. w. William Tong. m. "*He Ain't Heavy, He's My Brother*, originally by The Hollies." Published online at <http://www.amiright.com/parody/misc/thehollies0.shtml>. [ca. 2001].

179.40 He Came In Through The Backdoor Window (Ode to Jeb Bush). w. Skisics Surus, "skisics@yahoo.com." m. "Sung to the tune of *She Came In Through The Backdoor Window* by the Beatles." Published at <www.geocities.com/wmktong/bootnewt/dumbking.htm>. [2000].

179.41 House Of The Lying Dunce. w. William Tong. m. "*House Of The Rising Sun* by The Animals." Published online at <http://www.amiright.com/parody/60s/theanimals1.shtml>. [ca. 2001].

179.42 I Stole It. w. "Weird Alan." m. "Parody of Dave Matthews Band's *I Did It*." "I know this is kind of outdated to be doing an election controversy parody, but the premise is 100 days or so later, George W. Bush finally admits how he became president..." Published online at <http://www.angelfire.com.music/parodies/davematthewsparody.html>. [2001].

179.43 I'll Leave It Up To You. w. Skisics Surus, "skisics@yahoo.com." m. "Sung to the tune of *I'd Love To Change The World* by Ten Years After." Published online at <http://www.geocities.com/wmktong/bootnewt/leaveitup.htm>. [ca. 2000].

179.44 I'm An American Fraud. w. Skisics Surus, "skisics@yahoo.com." m. "Sung to the tune of *We're An American Band* by Grand Funk Railroad." Published online at <http://www.geocities.com/wmktong/bootnewt/amerfraud.htm>. [ca. 2000].

179.45 I'm In The White House Now. w. Sara Rose. m. "*I've Got My Mind Set On You,* originally by George Harrison." "Sung by the Shrub." Published online at <http://amiright.com/parody/80s/georgeharrison0.shml>. [ca. 2000].

179.46 Indecision 2000. w. Gary S. O'Connor. m. "*Mack The Knife,* based on a performance by Bobby Darin." "I finally got to write my editorial on the Presidential Election of 2000. This is political fodder for your ears. The story of Al, Walker, Kathy, Hillary, Jessie and all the rest is set to the melody of Mack the Knife in this parody. By the way, this is not the Rush Limbaugh theme song, but it could be!" Published online at <http://www.amiright.com/parody/60s/bobbydarin2.shtml>. [ca. 2003].

179.47 Jeb Stole The Votes For Me. w. William Tong. m. "*Brand New Key,* based on the performance by Melanie." "As sung by Dubya." Published online at <http://www.amiright.com/parody/70s/melonie0.shtml>. [ca. 2000].

179.48 Jeb Took Care Of Business. w. Skisics Surus, "skisics@yahoo.com." m. "Sung to the tune of *Takin' Care Of Business* by Bachman-Turner Overdrive." Published online at <http://www.geocities.com/wmktong/bootnewt/jebtookcare.htm>. [ca. 2000].

179.49 Litigator. w. William Tong. m. "*Operator,* originally by Jim Croce." "As sung by Dubya." Published online at <http://www.amiright.com/parody/70s/jimcroce0.shml>. [ca. 2000].

179.50 Mean Mr. Bastard (Ode to Tom Delay). w. Skisics Surus, "skisics@yahoo.com." m. "Sung to the tune of *Mean Mr. Mustard* by the Beatles." Published at <geocities.com/wmtong/bootnewt/dumbking.htm>. [2000].

179.51 Move Bush. w. John Spoof. m. "*Move Bitch,* based on a performance by Ludacris." Published online at <http://www.amiright.com/parody/2000s/ludacris16.shtml>. 2003.

179.52 The Name Of Shrub. w. William Tong. m. "*The Game Of Love,* originally by Wayne Fontana & The Mindbenders." Published online by Amiright.com at <http://amiright.com/parody/misc/waynefontanathemindbenders0.shml>. [ca. 2000].

179.53 The New So Long It's Been [Good] To Know You. w. Joel Landy and Stephen L. Suffet. m. "Original words and music by Woodie Guthrie." Published by the Centre For Political Song online at <http://polsong.ac.uk/songs/guthrie.htm>. 2001, 2002 & 2003.

179.54 No JFK. w. Michael Pacholek. m. "*YMCA,* based on a performance by The Village People." "After three years of watching George W. Bush's stupidities and sanctuary, I'm beginning to think America owes Dan Quayle an apology. Because, after 40 years, every- one [is] 'no Jack Kennedy.' The closest we've come to JFK is Bill Clinton. Except the press was nicer to JFK. Then, the reporters really were liberal, even if the editorial pages weren't." Published online at <http://www.amiright.com/parody/70s/thevillagepeople16.shtml>. 2003.

179.55 Partisan Woman. w. William Tong. m. "Sung to the tune of *Hard Headed Woman* by Elvis Presley." Published online at <http://geocities.com/wmtong/bootnewt/partisan.htm>. [ca. 2000].

179.56 Polluted Rivers And Clear Cut Woods. w. William Tong. m. "*Over The River And Through The Woods,* based on a performance by Traditional." Published online at <http://www.amiright.com/parody/misc/traditional435.shtml>. [ca. 2003].

179.57 Poppy Bush's Boys. w. William Tong. m. "*The Dukes Of Hazard Theme Song,* originally by Waylon Jennings." "Dubya and Jeb ... just two good ol' frauds." Published online at <http://amiright.com/parody/70s/waylonjennings0.shtml>. 2000.

179.58 Pretty Woman. w. Skisics Surus, "skisics@yahoo.com." m. "Sung to the tune of *Oh Pretty Woman* by Roy Orbison." N/c photo of Katherine Harris with a "W" branded on her forehead, "Florida Sec. Of State & Bush Campaign Co-Chair." Published online at <http://www.geocities.com/wmktong/bootnewt/prettywoman.htm>. [ca. 2000].

179.59 Shrub Has A Head Of Stone. w. Darrell Decker. m. "*Like A Rolling Stone,* originally by Bob Dylan." Published online at <http://www.amiright.com/parody/misc/bobdylan7.shtml>. [ca. 2000].

179.60 Shrub's Wrong. w. William Tong. m. "*Love Song,* originally by Anne Murray." Published online at <http://www.amiright.com/parody/70s/annemurray0.shtml>. [ca. 2001].

179.61 The Things He Did For Lust. w. Skisics Surus, "skisics@yahoo.com." m. "Sung to the tune of *The Things We Do For Love* by 10 CC." Published online at <http://www.geocities.com/wmktong/bootnewt/thinglust.htm>. [ca. 2000].

179.62 We Stole This City. w. Skisics Surus. m. "*We Built This City,* originally by Starship." Published online at <http://amiright.com/parody/80s/starship0.shml>. [ca. 2001].

179.63 What A Lucky Man. w. William Tong. m. "*Lucky Man* originally by Emerson, Lake and Palmer." Published online at <http://www.amiright.com/parody/70s/emersonlakepalmer0.shtml>. [ca. 2000].

179.64 What's Brains Got To Do With It. w. Jorge Enrique D'range. m. "*What's Love Got To Do With It,* originally by Tina Turner." Published online at <http://amiright.com/parody/80s/tinaturner0.shml>. [ca. 2001].

• **AmPM-180** CATTS, Sidney Johnston, Jr. (Delegate to Democratic National Convention, 1936[?] & 1940)

180.1 [The Old G.O.P.]. w. Sidney J. Catts, Jr. "(of the Florida Delegation)." m. "Sing to the Tune of *The Old Grey Mare.*" [1936]. [8½" × 11"]. Non-pictorial. 2pp. Page 2: Blank. [Crew/FDR-283].

• **AmPM-181** CONE, Frederick P. (Mayor, Lake City; State Senate, 1907–1913; Governor, 1937–1941)

181.1 The American Creed Song Sheet. w. No composer indicated. m. "*Bear Came Over The Mountain.*"

[1936]. [8½" × 14"]. Non-pictorial typed. Various patriotic, popular and pro-Roosevelt songs. At top of page 1—"The American Creed." 2pp.
• **AmPM-182** DUNN, John Franklin (State Senate, 1889)
182.1 My Florida Home. w. J. Mortimer Murphy. m. Mrs. J. Mortimer Murphy. Published by J. Mortimer Murphy, Anclote, FL. 1891. [V-1: N/c] [V-2: B/w] litho of a Florida home scene with palms, cabin, sailboat. "Dedicated to Hon. John F. Dunn." 6pp.
• **AmPM-183** GRAHAM, Daniel Robert (State House, 1966–1970, State Senate, 1970–1978; Governor, 1979–1986; U.S. Senate, 1986–Present)
183.1 All You Democrats. w. Adam Bernstein. m. *"Mr. Tambourine Man,* based on a performance by Bob Dylan." Published online at <http://www.amiright.com/parody/60s/bobdylan17.shtml>. [ca. 2003].
183.2 The Ballad Of The War Protestors. w. Michael Pacholek. m. *"The Ballad Of John And Yoko* originally by The Beatles." "'Finks' is the plural of 'fink,' not somebody's name. 'The wife,' like the President, and his reasons for going to war, is fictional — in each case, unfortunately. And if I keep writing this stuff, well, all three Dixie Chicks are married, so I guess I'm stuck. For Now." Published online at <http://www.amiright.com/parody/60s/thebeatles102.shtml>. [ca. 2003].
183.3 The Bob Graham Charisma Tour Album. CD. FLX Records #04–2622. Recorded at Sunrise Studio, Sunrise, FL. 2004. Songs include: *We've Got A Friend In Bob Graham* {183.3–1}. w.m. Frank Loconto and Bob Graham; *Arriba Bob* (Bob Graham For President) {183.3–2}. w.m. Frank Loconto, Matt Calderin and Rosco Martinez; *Get Up, Get Out & Vote For Bob Graham* {183.3–3}. w.m. Frank Loconto; *I've Done Every Job, Man* (Bob Graham Work Days) {183.3–4}. w.m. Frank Loconto, Mark Goeff and Bob Graham; *Graham Country USA* (NASCAR Song) {183.3–5}. w.m. Frank Loconto and Bob Graham; *My Beautiful Adele* (Bob's Love Song To Adele) {183.3–6}. w.m. Frank Loconto; *(You've Gotta) Believe In America* {183.3–7}. w.m. Frank Loconto; *G.W. Bushonomics, Supply Side, Economic Blues* {183.3–8}. w.m. Frank Loconto; *Friend In Bob Graham* {183.3–9}; *Bob Graham March* {183.3–10}. a. A. Gelt.
183.4 Bob Graham The Only Candidate. Lyrics published online at <http://nbc6.net/politics/2264430/detail.htm>.
183.5 Bushlicker. w. "Political Prankster." m. *"Complicated,* based on the performance by Avril Lavigne." Published online at <http://amiright.com/parody/2000s/avrillavigne175.shtml>. [2003].
183.6 My Black And White Friend. Lyrics published online at <http://nbc6.net/politics/2264430/detail.htm>.
183.7 People Who Tried (Political). w. Malcolm Higgins. m. Tune—*"People Who Died,* based on a performance by Jim Carroll." Published online at <http://www.amiright.com/parody/misc/jimcarroll0.shtml>. [ca. 2003].
183.8 Single Honest Dem. w. Mark Snyder? m. "To the tune of *Smoky Mountain Rain."* Published by FreeRepublic.com online at <http://www.freerepublic.com/forum/a36dlbbc65015.htm>. 1999.
183.9 We Want Howard Dean. w.m. Denny Zartman. m. No tune indicated. "Spread The Word Through Song and Music! Songs For Dean, Songs to get elected by." N/c photo of Howard Dean. Lyrics and sound file published online at <http://songsfordean.com/so/lyrics/somethingtosee.php>. 2004.
• **AmPM-184** GREEN, Robert Alexis (State House, 1918–1920, U.S. House, 1925–1944)
184.1 The American Creed Song Sheet. w. No composer indicated. m. *"Bear Came Over The Mountain."* [1936]. [8½" × 14"]. Non-pictorial typed. Various patriotic, popular and pro-Roosevelt songs. At top of page 1—"The American Creed." 2pp.
• **AmPM-185** HARRIS, Katherine (State Senate, 1994–1998; Florida Secretary of State, 1999–2002; U.S. House, 2003–Present)
185.1 Ballots Of Jeb Bush. w. Bill Tong. m. *"The Beverly Hillbillies,* originally by Theme Song." Published online at <http://amiright.com/parody/misc/themesong0.shml>. [ca. 2000].
185.2 Banana Republic. w. William Tong. m. "Sung to the tune of *The Chiquita Banana Jingle,* from a suggestion by Laurie from Florida." N/c photo of Jeb Bush and Katherine Harris in Banana suits in front of a map of Florida. Published online at <http://geocities.com/wmtong/bootnewt/banana.htm>. [ca. 2000].
185.3 Blame Florida. w. Caitlin, "Falaen@aol.com." m. "Sung to the tune of *Blame Canada* from the *South Park: The Movie."* Published online at <http://www.geocities.com/wmktong/bootnewt/blame-fl.htm>. [ca. 2000].
185.4 Bush Boys Hijacked The Crown. w. Skisics Surus, "skisics@yahoo.com." m. "Sung to the tune of *The Boys Are Back In Town* by Thin Lizzy." Published online at <http://www.geocities.com/wmktong/bootnewt/bushboys.htm>. [ca. 2000].
185.5 Bush Brothers' Unraveling Nation Show. w. William Tong. m. *"Brother Love's Traveling Salvation Show,* originally by Neil Diamond." Published online at <http://www.amiright.com/parody/70s/neildiamond4.shtml>. [2000].
185.6 Bush Had A Fun Time All His Life. w. William Tong. m. *"You Are The Sunshine Of My Life,* originally by Stevie Wonder." Published online at <http://amiright.com/parody/70s/steviewonder0.shml>. [ca. 2000].
185.7 Butterfly Ballots. w. Bruce Decker. m. *"Butterfly Kisses,* originally by Bob Carlisle." Published online at <http://www.amiright.com/parody/misc/bobcarlisle0.shtml>. [2000].
185.8 Cheating Skills. w. William K. Tong. m. "Originally by Jimmy Buffett [sic]." Published online (lyrics only) by Amiright.com at <http://www.amiright.com/parody/70s/jimmybuffett1.shtml>. 2000. [Crew/GWB-21].
185.9 Country Under Dubya. w. Skisics Surus, "skisics@yahoo.com." m. "Sung to the tune of *Hotel California* by The Eagles." Published online at <http://www.geocities.com/wmktong/bootnewt/country-w.htm>. [ca. 2000].
185.10 The Day The Vote Was Swiped w. Skisics

Surus, "skisics@yahoo.com." m. "Sung to the tune of *American Pie, Part 1 & 2* by Don McLean." Published online at <http://www.geocities.com/wmktong/bootnewt/voteswiped.htm>. [ca. 2000].

185.11 *Do You Want To Know A Secret?* (Jeb's Confession To Brother Smirk). w. Skisics Surus and Bill Tong." m. "Sung to the tune of *Do You Want To Know A Secret?* by The Beatles." Published online at <http://www.geocities.com/wmktong/bootnewt/jebsecret.htm>. [ca. 2000].

185.12 *Don't Cry For Me, Tallahassee*. w. William Tong. m. "*Don't Cry For Me, Argentina*, originally by Madonna." "As sung by Katherine Harris." Published online at <http://amiright.com/parody/90s/madonna0.shml>. [ca. 2000].

185.13 *Dubya The Big Eared Liar*. w. Mariah. m. "*Rudolph The Red-Nosed Reindeer*, originally by Traditional." Published online at <http://amiright.com/parody/misc/traditional27.shml>. [ca. 2000].

185.14 *Dubya, The Bogus POTUS*. w. William Tong. m. "*Rudolph The Red-Nosed Reindeer*, originally by Gene Autry." Published online at <http://amiright.com/parody/misc/geneautry0.shml>. [ca. 2000].

185.15 *Dubya's Dumber Than Dirt*. w. Sara Rose. m. "*Another One Bites The Dust*, originally by Queen." Published online at <http://amiright.com/parody/70s/queen11.shml>. [ca. 2001].

185.16 *Dumb King Medley* (Ode to Smirk). w. Skisics Surus, "skisics@yahoo.com." m. "Sung to the tune of *Sun King Medley* by the Beatles." Published online at <http://www.geocities.com/wmktong/bootnewt/dumbking.htm>. [ca. 2000].

185.17 *Dubya Can't Wait* (Ode to the Florida Recount). w. Skisics Surus, "skisics@yahoo.com." m. "Sung to the tune of *Carry That Weight* by the Beatles." Published online at <geocities.com/wmtong/bootnewt/dumbking.htm>. [2000].

185.18 *The Election Song*. w. Tom Bracewell. m. "*The Galaxy Song*, originally by Monty Python." Published online at <http://amiright.com/parody/80s/montypython0.shml>. [ca. 2000].

185.19 *An Election That's Fair*. w. Sara Rose. m. "*Mercedes Benz*, originally by Janis Joplin." Published online at <http://amiright.com/parody/misc/janisjoplin0.shml>. [ca. 2000].

185.20 *The End* (Ode to the American Voter). w. Skisics Surus, "skisics@yahoo.com." m. "Sung to the tune of *The End* by the Beatles." Published online at <geocities.com/wmtong/bootnewt/dumbking.htm>. [2000].

185.21 *Fraud In Town*. w. William Tong. m. "*Allentown*, originally by Billy Joel." Published online at <http://www.amiright.com/parody/80s/billyjoel1.html>. [ca. 2001].

185.22 *Getting' Wronger Every Day*. w. Skisics Surus, "skisics@yahoo.com." m. "Sung to the tune of *Feelin' Stronger Every Day* by Chicago." Published online at <http://www.geocities.com/wmktong/bootnewt/getwronger.htm>. [ca. 2000].

185.23 *Give Back The Votes*. w. William Tong. m. "Sung to the tune of *Hit The Road, Jack* by Ray Charles." Published online at <http://geocities.com/wmtong/bootnewt/votesback.htm>. [ca. 2000].

185.24 *Golden Numbers* (Ode to Poppy Bush). w. Skisics Surus, "skisics@yahoo.com." m. "Sung to the tune of *Golden Slumbers* by the Beatles." Published online at <geocities.com/wmtong/bootnewt/dumbking.htm>. [ca. 2000].

185.25 *Hail To The Thief*. w. Lydia Theys. m. "*Hail to The Chief*, originally by Traditional." Published online at <http://amiright.com/parody/misc/traditional29.shml>. [ca. 2000].

185.26 *Hand Count*. w. Keith K. Higa. m. "*Convoy*, originally by C.W. McCall." Published online at <http://www.amiright.com/parody/70s/cwmccall0.shtml>. [2000].

185.27 *Harris Get Slammed* (Ode to Katherine Harris). w. Skisics Surus, "skisics@yahoo.com." m. "Sung to the tune of *Polythene Pam* by the Beatles." Published online at <geocities.com/wmtong/bootnewt/dumbking.htm>. [ca. 2000].

185.28 *Harris Is Just All Right With Me*. w. William Tong. m. "*Jesus Is Just Alright*, originally by The Doobie Brothers." Published online at <http://amiright.com/parody/70s/thedoobiebrothers.shml>. [ca. 2000].

185.29 *He Came In Through The Backdoor Window* (Ode to Jeb Bush). w. Skisics Surus, "skisics@yahoo.com." m. "Sung to the tune of *She Came In Through The Backdoor Window* by the Beatles." Published online at <geocities.com/wmtong/bootnewt/dumbking.htm>. [2000].

185.30 *He's Dumb, But He's Grateful*. w. William Tong. m. Tune—"*O Come All Ye Faithful*, originally by Traditional." "As sung by Dubya." Published online at <http://amiright.com/parody/misc/traditional16.shml>. [ca. 2000].

185.31 *He's Mr. Sleaze*. w. William K. Tong. m. "Sung to the tune of *Please, Mister, Please* by Olivia Newton-John." Published online at <http://www.geocities.com/wmktong/bootnewt/mr-sleaze.htm>. 2000. [Crew/GWB-21].

185.32 *I'll Leave It Up To You*. w. Skisics Surus, "skisics@yahoo.com." m. "Sung to the tune of *I'd Love To Change The World* by Ten Years After." Published online at <http://www.geocities.com/wmktong/bootnewt/leaveitup.htm>. [ca. 2000].

185.33 *I'm An American Fraud*. w. Skisics Surus, "skisics@yahoo.com." m. "Sung to the tune of *We're An American Band* by Grand Funk Railroad." Published online at <http://www.geocities.com/wmktong/bootnewt/amerfraud.htm>. [ca. 2000].

185.34 *I'm In The White House Now*. w. Sara Rose. m. "*I've Got My Mind Set On You*, originally by George Harrison." "Sung by the Shrub." Published online at <http://amiright.com/parody/80s/georgeharrison0.shml>. [ca. 2000].

185.35 *Indecision 2000*. w. Gary S. O'Connor. m. Tune—"*Mack The Knife*, based on a performance by Bobby Darin." "I finally got to write my editorial on the Presidential Election of 2000. This is political fodder for your ears. The story of Al, Walker, Kathy, Hillary, Jessie and all the rest is set to the melody of *Mack the Knife* in this parody. By the way, this is not the Rush Limbaugh theme song, but it could be!" Published online at <http://www.amiright.com/parody/60s/bobbydarin2.shtml>. [ca. 2003].

185.36 *Litigator*. w. William Tong. m. "*Operator*,

originally by Jim Croce." "As sung by Dubya." Published online at <http://amiright.com/parody/70s/jimcroce0.shml>. [ca. 2000].
185.37 Mean Mr. Bastard (Ode to Tom Delay). w. Skisics Surus, "skisics@yahoo.com." m. "Sung to the tune of *Mean Mr. Mustard* by the Beatles." Published online at <geocities.com/wmtong/bootnewt/dumbking.htm>. [2000].
185.38 Partisan Woman. w. William Tong. m. "Sung to the tune of *Hard Headed Woman* by Elvis Presley." Published online at <http://geocities.com/wmtong/bootnewt/partisan.htm>. [ca. 2000].
185.39 Pretty Woman. w. Skisics Surus, "skisics@yahoo.com." m. "Sung to the tune of *Oh Pretty Woman* by Roy Orbison." N/c photo of Katherine Harris with a "W" branded on her forehead, "Florida Sec. Of State & Bush Campaign Co-Chair." Published online at <http://www.geocities.com/wmktong/bootnewt/prettywoman.htm>. [ca. 2000].
185.40 The Right Wing Tricksters Came To Town. w. William Tong. m. "*The Night They Drove Old Dixie Down,* originally by Joan Baez." Published online at <http://www.amiright.com/parody/70s/joanbaez0.shtml>. [ca. 2001].
185.41 Schizophrenicville. w. Billy Florio. m. Tune—"*Margaritaville,* originally by Jimmy Buffet." Published online at <http://www.amiright.com/parody/70s/jimmybuffet0.shtml>. [ca. 2001].
185.42 Tainted Lady. w. William K. Tong. m. "Originally by Ian Thomas." Published online by Amiright.com at <http://www.amiright.com/parody/70s/ianthomas0.shtml>. 2000. "Please make sure you take time to vote on the parodies you read, the parody authors appreciate the feedback!" [ca. 2000]. [Crew/GWB-20].
185.43 Vote Busters. w. William Tong. m. "*Ghostbusters,* originally by Ray Parker, Jr." Published online at <http://www.amiright.com/parody/80s/rayparkerjr0.shtml>. [ca. 2001].
185.44 What The Shrub Has Planned. w. Skisics Surus, "skisics@yahoo.com." m. "Sung to the tune of *Kokomo* by The Beach Boys." Published online at <http://www.geocities.com/wmktong/bootnewt/shrubplan.htm>. [ca. 2000].
185.45 Who Stole The White House. w. Skisics Surus. m. "*Who Let The Dogs Out?,* originally by The Baha Men." Published online at <http://www.amiright.com/parody/2000s/thebagamen0.shtml>. [ca. 2000].
• **AmPM-186** HOLLAND, Spessard Lindsey (Prosecuting Attorney, Polk County, 1919–1920; County Judge, Polk County, 1921–1929; State Senate, 1932–1940; Governor, 1941–1945; U.S. Senate 1946–1971)
186.1 Ahead With Holland. w. No composer indicated. m. No tune indicated. [ca. 1940]. [8½" × 14"]. Non-pictorial mimeograph. 2pp. Page 2: Blank.
JACKSON, Andrew (Territorial Governor, Florida, 1821) [See: Tennessee] [ALSO SEE: DOC/PSM-AJL]
• **AmPM-186A** JURI, Nilo (Candidate for Mayor, Hialeah, 1993)
186A.1 Seis Milliones. w.m. Elio Rodriguez. Published in *The Miami Herald* and online at Herald.com. April 2, 2004. "Radio Jingle On Controversy — Here are excerpts from a radio jingle on the controversy over the pledge by council members Vanessa Bravo and Cindy Miel to refund $6 million. It was written by Elio Rodriguez and produced by Gerardo Peña." "Translated by Herald staff writer Elaine de Vaille." Lyrics and midi file published online at <http://miami.com/mld/miamiherald/news/local/8334546.htm>.
• **AmPM-186B** MARTINEZ, Raul (City Council, Hialeah, 1977–1981; Mayor, Hialeah, 1981–Present)
186B.1 Seis Milliones. w.m. Elio Rodriguez. Published in *The Miami Herald* and online at *Herald.com.* April 2, 2004. "Radio Jingle On Controversy — Here are excerpts from a radio jingle on the controversy over the pledge by council members Vanessa Bravo and Cindy Miel to refund $6 million. It was written by Elio Rodriguez and produced by Gerardo Peña." "Translated by Herald staff writer Elaine de Vaille." Lyrics and midi file published online at <http://miami.com/mld/miamiherald/news/local/8334546.htm>.
• **AmPM-186C** MIEL, Cindy (City Council, Hialeah, 2004–Present)
186C.1 Seis Milliones. w.m. Elio Rodriguez. Published in *The Miami Herald* and online at *Herald.com.* April 2, 2004. "Radio Jingle On Controversy — Here are excerpts from a radio jingle on the controversy over the pledge by council members Vanessa Bravo and Cindy Miel to refund $6 million. It was written by Elio Rodriguez and produced by Gerardo Peña." "Translated by Herald staff writer Elaine de Vaille." Lyrics and midi file published online at <http://miami.com/mld/miamiherald/news/local/8334546.htm>.
• **AmPM-187** PEPPER, Claude Denson (State House, 1929–1930; State Board of Public Welfare, 1931–1932; State Board of Law Examiners, 1933; U.S. Senate, 1936–1951 & 1963–1989)
187.1 DDT. w. No composer indicated. m. "*Bury Me Not On The Lone Parie* [sic]." In: *National Youth Lobby* [Program with Songs], page 27. Published by The Young Progressive Citizens of America. 1947. [8½" × 11"]. B/w drawing of man, the Capitol. "Jobs! Peace! Freedom!" "Hear Henry Wallace Keynote the National Youth Lobby." "Sponsored by Y.P.C.A. in Washington, D.C., on June 15 and 16, 1947." 30pp. Pages 25 to 27: Songs. [Crew/HAW-9].
187.2 The American Creed Song Sheet. w. No composer indicated. m. "*Bear Came Over The Mountain.*" [1936]. [8½" × 14"]. Non-pictorial typed. Various patriotic, popular and pro-Roosevelt songs. At top of page 1—"The American Creed." 2pp.
• **AmPM-188** REEDER, C.H. (City Commissioner, Miami, 1933–1935 & 1943–1945; Mayor, Miami; 1920–1931 & 1941–1943)
188.1 Miami, Playground Of The U.S.A. (Fox Trot). w. Teresa Conner. m. Caesar La Monaca. No publisher indicated. 1929. [V-1: Standard size] [V-2: Pre–1919 size]. B/w photos of "Mayor C.H. Reeder," and "Caesar La Monaca." B/w drawing of bathing beauties, beach, Miami skyline. "Respectfully Dedicated to Mayor C.H. Reeder." 6pp. Page 6: Blank.
• **AmPM-189** RENO, Janet (Staff Director, Florida House Judiciary Committee, 1971–1973; State Attorney General, Dade County, 1978–1993; U.S. Attorney General, 1993–2001; Candidate for Governor, 2002)

189.1 All Those Chads. w. William Strader. m. "*All That Jazz,* originally from the musical *Chicago.*" Published online at <http://www.amiright.com/parody/misc/fromthemusicalchicago0.shtml>. [ca. 2001].

189.2 Bald Head. w. "Weird Alan." m. "Parody of Sum41's *Fat Lip.*" Published online at <http://www.angelfire.com/music/parodies/sum41parody.html>. [199-].

189.2A B.A.T.F. w.m. Aus Rotten. Lyrics published online at <http://www.plyrics.com/lyrics/ausrotten/batf.html>. [ca. 199-].

189.3 Big, Bad Jan Reno. w. William K. Tong. m. "Sung to the tune of *Bad, Bad Leroy Brown* by Jim Croce." In: *The Sting The Right Wing Song Book* at <http://www.geocities.com/wmktong/bootnewt/badreno.htm>.

189.4 Bill So Horney. w.m. Mark Ross, Chris Wong Won, David Hobbs and Luther Campbell. On 33⅓ rpm EP: *Bill So Horney* by 2 Live Crew. Lil' Joe Records, 6157 NW 167th St., Miami, FL. Record #LJR 900-1. 1998. Performed by 2 Live Crew and Amos Braxton. Cover art: Drawing of Bill Clinton and Monica Lewinsky; 2 Live Crew. [2 versions — Clean and Explicit]. 1998.

189.5 Democratic Party Blues. w. Guy DiRito. m. Tune — "*Folsom Prison Blues* originally by Johnny Cash." "It's the lame leading the blind." Published online at <http://amiright.com/parody/60s/rollingstones.shtml>. [199-].

189.6 El Reno. w. Paul Silhan. m. "Sung to Walt Disney's *Zorro* theme." Lyrics published online at <http://www.paulsilhan.com/el-reno.htm>. 1997.

189.7 Hey Now (Your [sic] an Ex Pres). w. Vermonter. m. "*Hey Now (Your* [sic] *An All Star),* originally by Smash Mouth." Published online at <http://www.amiright.com/parody/90s/smashmouth2.shtml>. [ca. 2001].

189.8 Instant Clinton. w. Tom Smith. m. "*Where The Hell Is Bill?* by Camper Van Beethoven." "This mid-80s demented classis ... is a perfect forum for riffing on the Clinton Administration." "Published online at <http://www.tomsmithonline.com/lyrics/instantclinton.htm>. 1999.

189.9 Janet Angel. w. Paul Shaklin. On CD: *Executive Privileges.* Published by Narodniki Records. CD Cover: N/c drawing of a naked Bill Clinton covered by presidential seal. See: <www.paulShaklin.com>. 2001.

189.10 Middle-Aged Lady Named Janet Reno. w. Bill Strauss and Elaina Newport. On CD: *Lord Of The Fries.* Published by Capitol Steps Productions, 1505 King Street, Alexandria, VA. 1994. Record # CSCD-1014. CD Cover: N/c drawing of Bill Clinton, White House.

189.11 1. .2. .3 Volunteer Some More. w. Paul Silhan. m. "Sung to (As is commonly known) *1. .2. .3. . What Are We Fighting For?* (although — as Country Joe fans know- the song's real title is the *I-Feel-Like-I'm-Fixin'-To-Die-Rag*) by Country Joe & The Fish." On: Cassette: *Spinball Wizard.* "As heard on Rush's Radio Show." Lyrics published at <http://www.paulsilhan.com/1-2-3.htm>. 1997.

189.11A Original Prankster. w.m. Offspring. Lyrics published online at <http://www.plyrics.com/lyrics/offspring/priginalprankster.html>. [ca. 199-].

189.12 Pretty Fly (For Janet Reno). w. Jimmy Crackcorn. m. "*Pretty Fly For A White Guy,* originally by The Offspring." Published online at <http://www.amiright.com/parody/2000s/theoffspring38.shtml>. [ca. 2001].

189.13 They're Mad At Reno Now. w. William K. Tong. m. "Sung to the tune of *Bad, Bad Leroy Brown* by Jim Croce." In: *The Sting The Right Wing Song Book* at <http://www.geocities.com/wmktong/bootnewt/mad-reno.htm>. [199-].

189.14 Whitewater Debacle. w. Paul Silhan. m. "Sung to *Winchester Cathedral* by The New Vaudeville Band." On: Cassette: *Lie-A-lot.* Lyrics published at <http://www.paulsilhan.com/lal-4.htm>. 1994.

• **AmPM-190 WEXLER,** Robert (State Senate, 1990–1996; U.S. House, 1997–Present)

190.1 Vote Palm Beach. w. Billy Florio. m. "*Sloop John B,* originally by The Beach Boys." Published online at <http://amiright.com/parody/misc/thebeachboys1.shml>. [ca. 2000].

• **AmPM-191 WOLFARTH,** William (Mayor, Miami, 1951)

191.1 Bayfront Park Gold And Silver Shell (March). m. Joseph La Monaca. Copyright 1951 by Ceaser La Monaca. Ma/w photos of Joseph and Ceaser La Monaca, "Bayfront Park Gold and Silver Shell." Gd/w/ma drawing of band shell. "Respectfully dedicated to his honor The Mayor of Miami." 4p. Page 2: "Respectfully Dedicated to His Honor Mayor William M. Wolfarth of Miami, Fla." Page 4: Blank.

• **AmPM-192 MISCELLANEOUS MUSIC**

192.1 For The Florida Supreme Court. w. Bruce Decker. m. Tune — "*Let's Call The Whole Thing Off* originally by Fred Astaire." Published online at <http://www.amiright.com/parody/misc/fredastaire0.shtml>. [ca. 2000]

GEORGIA

• **AmPM-193 BARR,** Robert (U.S. Attorney, 1986–1990; U.S. House, 1995–2003)

193.1 Georgia Voters Drove Out Barr. w. William K. Tong. m. "Sung to the tune of *Drive My Car* by The Beatles." "Good riddance to Congressman Bob Barr (R-GA), defeated in a recent primary election." Published online at <http://www.bootnewt.envy.nu.droveoutbarr.htm>. [199-].

193.2 Welfare For Big Business. w. William K. Tong. m. "Sung to the tune of *Takin' Care Of Business*

Bachman Turner Overdrive." In: *The Sting The Right Wing Song Book* at <http://www.geocities.com/wmktong/bootnewt/business.htm>. [199-].

• **AmPM-194** BROWN, Joseph E. (State Senate, 1849; State Superior Court, 1855; Governor, 1857–1865; State Supreme Court, 1868–1870; U.S. Senate, 1881–1891)

194.1 Empire State Grand March. m. Hermann L. Schreiner. Published by J.C. Schreiner & Son, Macon, GA. 1864. B/w litho of Joseph Brown, arch, Confederate flags, floral and geometric designs. "To his Excellency Gov. Joseph E. Brown." "Dates of office: October 1857 to 1859; October 1859 to 1861; October 1861 to 1863; October 1863–1865." 6pp. Pages 5 and 6: Blank.

BROWN, Lee P. (Commissioner of Public Safety, Atlanta) [See: Texas]

• **AmPM-194x** CARTER, James Earl, Jr. (State Senate, 1963–1966; Governor, 1971–1975; President, 1977–1981; Winner, Nobel Peace Prize, 2002) [SEE: DOC/PSM-JEC]

• **AmPM-196** CLELAND, Joseph Maxwell "Max" (State Senate, 1971–1975; Administrator of U.S. Veterans Administration, 1977; Georgia Secretary of State, 1982–1996; U.S. Senate, 1997–2003)

196.1 Sixteen Scandals. w. Michael Pacholek. m. "*Sixteen Candles,* based on a performance by Johnny Maestro & The Crests." Published online at <http://www.amiright.com/parody/misc/johnnymaestrothecrests.shtml>. [ca. 2003].

• **AmPM-197** COBB, Howell (U.S. Solicitor General, 1837–1841; U.S. House, 1843–1851 & 1855–1857; Governor, 1851–1853; U.S. Secretary of the Treasury, 1857–1860; Confederate Provisional Congress, 1861)

197.1 Bully For You. w. John L. Zieber. m. No tune indicated. Published by J.H. Johnson, Philadelphia, PA. [1861]. [Approx. 6" × 9"]. Non-pictorial geometric design border. "Written expressly for J.H. Johnson." 2pp. Page 2: Blank. [AMC].

197.2 Dis-Union Dixie Land. w. No composer indicated. m. Air—*Dixie.* Published by J.W. DuBree, Printer, No. 1169 South Eleventh Street, Philadelphia, PA. [1860–1861]. Non-pictorial. "J.W. DuBree, Song Publisher, Card and Job Printer, No. 1169 South Eleventh Street, Philadelphia." "Union." "Badges, Letter and Note Paper, Envelopes, Shields, Stars, Flags, all sizes, Cockades, and Rosettes. Songs of all kinds for the Union, Wholesale & Retail." 2pp. Page 2: Blank. [AMC].

197.3 I Want To Be A Soldier. w.m. No composer indicated. m. "Air—[V-1, V-2 & V-3: *I Want To Be An Angel*]. [V-4: *Wait For The Wagon.*]. [V-1: No publisher indicated] [V-2 & V-4: A.W. Auner, Song Publisher, 110 N. 10th St., ab. Arch, Philadelphia, PA] [V-3: Johnson, Song Publisher, 7 Tenth St., Philadelphia, PA]. [ca. 1861]. B/w litho of [V-1 & V-3: Battle scene] [V-2: Soldier, eagle] [V-4: Soldier, tent, rifle], geometric design border. [V-3: "See Johnson's New Catalogue of Songs] [V-4: Additional verses]. 2pp. Page 2: Blank. [AMC].

197.4 National Cement. w. George W. Bungay. m. No tune indicated. In: *The Republican Campaign Songster For 1860,* page 48. c. W.H. Burleigh. Published by [V-1 and V-2: H. Dayton, No. 36 Howard Street, New York, NY] [V-3: McNally & Company, No. 81 Dearborn Street, Chicago, IL]. 1860. [V-1: Gn/bk] [V-2: Y/bk] [V-3: Be/bk] [V-4: Bl/bk]. "Price 10 cents." [3¹³⁄₁₆" × 6"]. 72pp. [M-104]. [Crew/AL-57].

197.5 [Our Good Old Uncle Sam Is Sick] (A Campaign Song). w.m. No composer or tune indicated. In: *The Republican Campaign Songster No. #1,* page 30. Published by American Publishing House, No. 60 West Fourth Street, Cincinnati, OH. [1860]. [3¾" × 5¾"]. B/w litho of Abraham Lincoln. 48pp. [?]. [M-113]. [Crew/AL-298].

197.6 A Peep At Washington. w. "Composed and Sung by Mr. Rice, in Washington, D.C., during the session of Congress, 1850." m. "Tune—*Susannah.*" In: *Dan Rice's Great American Humorist Song Book,* page 23. 1866. [4⅛" × 5¾"]. Br/bk drawing of an actor. "Containing Original and Selected Songs, Carefully Revised & Corrected." 34pp.

• **AmPM-198** COLQUITT, Alfred Holt (U.S. House, 1853–1855; State House, 1859; State Secession Convention, 1861; Governor, 1876–1882; U.S. Senate, 1883–1894)

198.1 The Bradbury Schottische. m. Dayton Vreeland. Published by F.G. Smith, 109 & 111 Broadway, Paterson, NJ. 1897. B/w geometric designs. "Dedicated to H.N. Lakeham." 4pp. Page 4: Advertising for Bradbury pianos with photo of "Famous Patrons of Bradbury Pianos" including: "U.S. Grant, J.A. Garfield, C.A. Arthur, Benj. Harrison, R.B. Hayes, Grover Cleveland, Stanley Mathews, J.M Rusk, Benj. Tracy, Levi Morton, Thos. B. Reed, J.W. Noble, William Windom, John G. Carlisle, C.C. McCabe, A.H. Colquitt [and] Walter Q. Gresham." [Crew/MISC-142]

• **AmPM-199** CRAWFORD, William Harris (State House, 1803–1807; U.S. Senate, 1807–1813; U.S. Minister to France, 1813–1815; U.S. Secretary of War, 1815–1816; U.S. Secretary of the Treasury, 1816–1825; Judge of the Northern Circuit Court, 1827–1834)

199.1 Presidential Cotillion. w.m. No composer or tune indicated. Published in the *New York Statesman,* September 24, 1824. [VBL, p. 226].

CRISP, Charles Frederick (Solicitor General of the Southwestern Judicial Circuit, 1872–1877; Superior Court Judge, 1877–1882; U.S. House, 1883–1896)

199.2 Grandfather's Hat. w. No composer indicated. m. Notation. In: *True Blue Republican Campaign Songs For 1892,* page 6. Published by [V-1: Oliver Ditson Company, Boston, MA] [V-2: The S. Brainard's Son's Company, Chicago, IL]. 1892. [5⅜" × 7¼"]. Bl/bk litho of Benjamin F. Harrison, eagle, flag, geometric designs. 36pp. [M-307]. [Crew/BFH-47].

199.3 Harrison Will Hold The Job. w. E.J. Seymour. m. "Air—*When McGinnis Gets A Job.*" In: *Harrison And Reid Campaign Song Book,* page 13. w. E.J. Seymour. m. Popular Airs. [1892]. [3⅞" × 5⅛"]. Bl/gn non-pictorial, stars, geometric designs. 36pp. Pages 2 and 35: Blank. Page 36: Advertising for this songbook. [M-316]. [Crew/BFH-35].

• **AmPM-200** EVANS, Clement Anselm (State Senate, 1859; Inferior Court Judge, Stewart County, 1854)

200.1 Leesburg March. m. F. Sulzner. Published by J.A. McClure, Nashville, TN. and Memphis, TN. 1861. "McClure's Collection of National Melodies." 6pp. Page 6: Blank. [H-3597].

• **AmPM-201   FORSYTH**, John (State Attorney General, 1808; U.S. House, 1813–1818 & 1823–1827; U.S. Senate, 1818–1819 & 1829–1834; U.S. Ambassador to Spain, 1819–1823; Governor, 1827–1829; U.S. Secretary of State, 1834–1841)

201.1 All Round My 'At I Vers A Veeping Villow. w.m. No composer or tune indicated. "A Song to be Sung at Van Buren's Indignation meetings." In: *Songs For The People (Or Tippecanoe Melodies)* [Songster], page 27. "Dedicated to the Democratic Whig Young Men of the City and County of New York." Published for the Authors by James P. Giffing, No. 56 Gold Street, New York, NY. 1840. [3¾" × 6"]. Litho of William Henry Harrison, log cabin, flag. "Original and Selected." 76pp. [M-019]. [Crew/WHH-63].

201.2 The Farmer Of North Bend. w.m. No composer or tune indicated. Published by Charles T. Geslain, No. 357 Broadway, New York, NY. 1840. B/w litho of a log cabin, horse and buggy, steamboat. "The Patriot's Home." "A Very Popular Whig Song Respectfully Dedicated to the Log Cabin Association of the United States by the Publisher." "Pr. 50 cts." 6pp. Pages 2 and 6: Blank. [Crew/WHH-9].

201.3 The Last Cabinet Council. w. No composer indicated. m. "Tune—*There's Nae Luck About The House.*" "A Very Pathetic and musical appeal to the Dear People, by an Ex-Post Master General." In: *Tippecanoe Song-Book (A Collection Of Log Cabin And Patriotic Melodies)*, page 45. Published by Marshall, Williams & Butler, Philadelphia, PA. 1840. White on black litho of log cabin, plow, flags, eagle. 180pp. [M-024]. [Crew/WHH-61].

201.4 The Last Cabinet Council. w. No composer indicated. m. "Air—*There's Nae Luck About The House.*" In: *The Log Cabin & Hard Cider Melodies, A Collection Of Popular And Patriotic Songs,* page 30. Published by Charles Adams, No. 23 Tremont Street, Boston, MA. 1840. [3¾" × 6"]. [V-1: Pk/bk] [V-2: Gn/bk] litho of William Henry Harrison. "The Freeman's glittering Sword be Blest, For ever blest the Freeman's Lyre." 78pp. Pages 2 and 77: Blank. Page 3: Inside title page. B/w litho of log cabin. "Respectfully Dedicated to the Friends of Harrison and Tyler." Page 78: Advertising. [M-012]. [Crew/WHH-68].

201.5 Mr. Van Buren's Farewell To The Palace. w.m. No composers or tune indicated. No publisher indicated. [1840]. [Approx. 5" × 12"]. Non-pictorial. 2pp. Page 2: Blank. [AMC]. [Crew/MVB-19].

201.6 Van And The Farmer. w. No composer indicated. m. "Tune—*King And The Countryman.*" In: *The Log Cabin & Hard Cider Melodies, A Collection Of Popular And Patriotic Songs,* page 22. Published by Charles Adams, No. 23 Tremont Street, Boston, MA. 1840. [3¾" × 6"]. [V-1: Pk/bk] [V-2: Gn/bk] litho of William Henry Harrison. "The Freeman's glittering Sword be Blest, For ever blest the Freeman's Lyre." 78pp. Pages 2 and 77: Blank. Page 3: Inside title page. B/w litho of log cabin. "Respectfully Dedicated to the Friends of Harrison and Tyler." Page 78: Advertising. [M-012]. [Crew/WHH-68].

• **AmPM-202   GILMER**, Geo. R. (State House, 1818, 1819 & 1824; U.S. House, 1821–1823, 1827–1829 & 1833–1835; Governor, 1829–1831 & 1837–1839)

202.1 Governor Gilmer's Grand March. m. W.W. Waddell. Published and sold by Geo. Willig, 171 Chesnut Street, Philadelphia, PA. 1830. B/w litho of a gazebo with soldier standing guard. "As performed at the concert in Athens, Geo., Aug. 4th, 1830." "Composed & Arranged for the Piano Forte with accompaniment for the Flute." 4pp.

• **AmPM-203   GINGRICH**, Newt (U.S. House, 1979–1999)

203.1 Ain't He Fruity. w. William K. Tong. m. "Sung to the tune of *Tutti Fruity* by Little Richard." Published online at <http://www.geocities.com/wmktong/bootnewt/fruity.htm>. [ca. 2000].

203.2 Antagonist Congress. w. ParodyKeet. m. "*American Woman,* based on a performance by Guess Who." "I may have set this tune to words before but I'm on a political roll in the name of dumping our present Kaiser." Published online at <http://amiright.com/parody/70s/guesswho5.shtml>. 2003.

203.3 Bad Newt Rising. w. William K. Tong. m. "Sung to the tune of *Bad Moon Rising* by Creedence Clearwater Revival." <http://www.geocities.com/wmktong/bootnewt/badnewt.htm>. [ca. 2000].

203.4 Bad Water. w. William K. Tong. m. "Sung to the tune of *Black Water* by the Doobie Brothers." Published online at <http://www.geocities.com/wmktong/bootnewt/badwater.htm>. [ca. 2000].

203.5 Ban The Cities. w. William K. Tong. m. "Sung to the tune of *Kansas City* by Wilbert Harrison." Published online at <http://www.geocities.com/wmktong/bootnewt/bancity.htm>. [ca. 2000].

203.6 Band Of Goons. w. William K. Tong. m. "Sung to the tune of *Band Of Gold* by Freda Payne." Published online at <http://www.geocities.com/wmktong/bootnewt/bandgoon.htm>. [ca. 2000].

203.7 Barge On Polluted Water. w. William K. Tong. m. "Sung to the tune of *Bridge Over Troubled Waters* by Simon & Garfunkel." Published online at <http://www.geocities.com/wmktong/bootnewt/bargeon.htm>. [ca. 2000].

203.8 Bill So Horney. w.m. Mark Ross, Chris Wong Won, David Hobbs and Luther Campbell. On 33⅓ rpm EP: *Bill So Horney* by 2 Live Crew. Lil' Joe Records, 6157 NW 167th St., Miami, FL. Record #LJR 900-1. 1998. Performed by 2 Live Crew and Amos Braxton. Cover art: Drawing of Bill Clinton and Monica Lewinsky; 2 Live Crew. [2 versions—Clean and Explicit]. 1998.

203.9 Blew By You. w. William K. Tong. m. "Sung to the tune of *Blue Bayou* by Linda Ronstadt/Roy Orbison." Published online at <http://www.geocities.com/wmktong/bootnewt/blewbyou.htm>. [ca. 2000].

203.10 The Boot Newt Songbook. w. William K. Tong. m. Popular tunes. Published online at <http://www.geocities.com/wmktong/bootnewt/newtsong/htm>. [ca. 2000]. Electronic songbook consisting of 72 songs. December, 2000. All selections by Wm. K. Tong unless otherwise noted. Full text available online.

203.11 Boot That Newt. w. William K. Tong. m. "Sung to the tune of *Blue Suede Shoes* by Carl Perkins."

Published online at <http://www.geocities.com/wmktong/bootnewt/bootnewt.htm>. [199-].

203.12 Budgetary Hell. w. William K. Tong. m. "Sung to the tune of *Heartbreak Hotel* by Elvis Presley." Published online at <http://www.geocities.com/wmktong/bootnewt/budghell.htm>. [199-].

203.13 Can't Buy My Vote. w. William K. Tong. m. "Sung to the tune of *Can't Buy Me Love* by the Beatles." Published online at <http://www.geocities.com/wmktong/bootnewt/cant-buy.htm>. [199-].

203.14 Come Together. w. Skisics Surus, "skisics@yahoo.com." m. "Sung to the tune of *Come Together* by The Beatles." Published online at <http://www.geocities.com/wmktong/bootnewt/cometogether.htm>. [ca. 2000].

203.15 Connie, Do You Want To Know A Secret? w. No composer indicated. m. "Parody of *Do You Want To Know A Secret?* by The Beatles." Lyrics published by *The Bob Rivers Show* with Bob, Spike & Joe and Twisted Tunes online at <http://www.twistedradio.com/player/lyrics.asp?songID=838>. [199-].

203.16 Could They All Be Following Newt? w. William K. Tong. m. "Sung to the tune of *Could It Be I'm Falling In Love?* by the Spinners." Published online at <http://www.geocities.com/wmktong/bootnewt/follnewt.htm>. [199-].

203.17 Cry Baby. w. William K. Tong. m. "Sung to the tune of *Heartbreak Hotel* by Elvis Presley." Published online at <http://www.geocities.com/wmktong/bootnewt/crybaby.htm>. Illustrated with a facsimile headline from *The Daily News*. [199-].

203.18 Do You Fear What I Fear? w. William K. Tong. m. "Sung to the tune of *Do You Hear What I Hear.*" Published online at <http://www.geocities.com/wmktong/bootnewt/doyufear.htm>. [199-].

203.19 Doesn't Mr. Gingrich Understand. w. William K. Tong. m. "Sung to the tune of *Winter Wonderland.*" Published online at <http://www.geocities.com/wmktong/bootnewt/undrstnd.htm>. [199-].

203.20 Dumpster Trash. w. William K. Tong. m. "Sung to the tune of *Monster Mash* by Bobby 'Boris' Picket." Published online at <http://www.geocities.com/wmktong/bootnewt/dmptrash.htm>. [199-].

203.21 Everybody's Scanning Newt's Phone. w. Paul Silhan. m. "Sung to Bob (Zimmerman) Dylan's *Rainy Day Women #12 & #35 (Everybody Must Get Stoned!).*" "As heard on Rush's radio Show." Lyrics published online at <http://www.paulsilhan.com/dylan3.htm>. 1997.

203.22 Fool On The Hill. w. William K. Tong. m. "Sung to the tune of *Fool On The Hill* by the Beatles." Published online at <http://www.geocities.com/wmktong/bootnewt/foolhill.htm>. [199-].

203.23 Furlough Shuffle. w. William K. Tong. m. "Sung to the tune of *The Curly Shuffle* by Jump 'N' the Saddle." Published online at <http://www.geocities.com/wmktong/bootnewt/furshufl.htm>. [199-].

203.23A Get Away. w.m. D.O.A. On CD: *The Black Spot.* Lyrics published online at <http://www.plyrics.com/lyrics/doa/getaway.html>. 1995.

203.24 Get Back. w. William K. Tong. m. "Sung to the tune of *Get Back By The Beatles.*" Published online at <http://www.geocities.com/wmktong/bootnewt/getback.htm>. [199-].

203.25 Get Lost. w. William K. Tong. m. "Sung to the tune of *Get Down* by Gilbert O'Sullivan." Published online at <http://www.geocities.com/wmktong/bootnewt/getlost.htm>. [199-].

203.26 Get Ready. w. William K. Tong. m. "Sung to the tune of *Get Ready* by the Temptations." Published online at <http://www.geocities.com/wmktong/bootnewt/getready.htm>. [199-].

203.27 The Gingrich Song. w. William K. Tong. m. "Sung to the tune of *The Christmas Song.*" Published online at <http://www.geocities.com/wmktong/bootnewt/gingsong.htm>. [199-].

203.28 Gingrich The Showman. w. William K. Tong. m. "Sung to the tune of *Frosty The Snowman.*" Published online at <http://www.geocities.com/wmktong/bootnewt/showman.htm>. [199-].

203.29 Gingrich The White-Hared Speaker. w. William K. Tong. m. "Sung to the tune of *Rudolph The Red-Nosed Reindeer.*" Published online at <http://www.geocities.com/wmktong/bootnewt/whspeaker.htm>. N/c photo of Newt Gingrich with a distorted face. [199-].

203.30 Gingrich Was A Flop. w. William K. Tong. m. "Sung to the tune of *At The Hop* by Danny and the Juniors." Published online at <http://www.geocities.com/wmktong/bootnewt/gingflop.htm>. [199-].

203.31 G.O.P. Is Running This Town. w. William K. Tong. m. "Sung to the tune of *Santa Claus Is Coming to Town.*" Published online at <http://www.geocities.com/wmktong/bootnewt/thistown.htm>. [199-].

203.32 GOPAC. w. William K. Tong. m. "Sung to the tune of *Get Back* by the Beatles." Published online at <http://www.geocities.com/wmktong/bootnewt/gopac.htm>. [199-].

203.33 Great Balls Of Sewage. w. William K. Tong. m. "Sung to the tune of *Great Balls Of Fire* by Jerry Lee Lewis." Published online at <http://www.geocities.com/wmktong/bootnewt/greatbal.htm>. [199-].

203.34 He's Evil. w. William K. Tong. m. "Sung to the tune of *Boll Weevil* by Fats Domino." Published online at <http://www.geocities.com/wmktong/bootnewt/hes-evil.htm>. [199-].

203.35 Hey Gingrich! Leave Our Lunch Alone. w. No composer indicated. m. "Parody of *Another Brick In The Wall Part Two* by Pink Floyd." Lyrics published by *The Bob Rivers Show* with Bob, Spike & Joe and Twisted Tunes online at <http://www.twistedradio.com/player/lyrics.asp?songID=649>. [199-].

203.36 Hey Newt. w. William K. Tong. m. "Sung to the tune of *Hey Jude* by the Beatles." Published online at <http://www.geocities.com/wmktong/bootnewt/hey-newt.htm>. [199-].

203.37 Hit The Road, Newt. w. William K. Tong. m. "Sung to the tune of *Hit The Road Jack* by Ray Curtis." Published online at <http://www.geocities.com/wmktong/bootnewt/hit-road.htm>. [199-].

203.38 House Of The White-Haired One. w. William K. Tong. m. "Sung to the tune of *House Of The Rising Sun* by the Animals." Published online at <http://www.geocities.com/wmktong/bootnewt/housewht.htm>. [199-].

203.39 House Republican. w. William K. Tong. m. "Sung to the tune of *Hoochie-Koochie Man* by Muddy

Waters." Published online at <http://www.geocities.com/wmktong/bootnewt/houserep.htm>. [199-].

203.40 How Gingrich Stole Congress. w. Bill Strauss and Elaina Newport. On CD: *A Whole Newt World.* Published by Capitol Steps Productions, 1505 King Street, Alexandria, VA. 1995. CD Cover: Gn/bl/y drawing of George Bush and George W. Bush as Seuss characters. [199-].

203.41 How Wild Are They? w. William K. Tong. m. "Sung to the tune of *What Child Is This?*" In: *The Sting The Right Wing Song Book* published online at <http:www.geocities.com/wmktong/bootnewt/howwild.htm>. [199-].

203.42 I Can't Vote For That (No Can Do). w. William K. Tong. m. "Sung to the tune of *I Can't Go For That* (No Can Do) by Daryl Hall & John Oats." In: *The Sting The Right Wing Song Book* published online at <http://www.geocities.com/wmktong/bootnewt/nocan-do.htm>.

203.43 I Hate You Abe. w. William K. Tong. m. "*I Got You Babe* by Sonny and Cher." Published online at <http://www.amiright.com/parody/misc/sonnyandcher0.shml>. [ca. 2000].

203.44 I Just Can't Wait To Beat Ging. w. Tom Smith. m. "*I Just Can't Wait To Be King* by Elton John." "From the Hypothetical Musical *The Lyin' Ging.*" "I firmly believe that Bill Clinton has gotten the worst shafting of any president in recent memory." "Published online at <http://www.tomsmithonline.com/lyrics/beatging.htm>. 1995.

203.45 I Just Groan At Gingrich. w. William K. Tong. m. "Sung to the tune of *I'll Be Home For Christmas.*" Published online at <http://www.geocities.com/wmktong/bootnewt/jstgroan.htm>. [199-].

203.46 I Love DC. w. William Ross. m. "To the tune of *I Love L.A. by Randy Newman.*" Lyrics and sound file published online at <http://www.seanet.com/-billr/ilovedc.htm>. 1996.

203.47 I Saw Three Newts. w. William K. Tong. m. "Sung to the tune of *I Saw Three Ships.*" N/c photo of Newt Gingrich with children captioned "Newt explains to the children that elephants are not reptiles, but Newts are." Published online at <http://www.geocities.com/wmktong/bootnewt/3-newts.htm>. [199-].

203.48 I Want The Newt Drugged. w. William K. Tong. m. "Sung to the tune of I *Want A New Drug* by Huey Lewis & the News." Published online at <http://www.geocities.com/wmktong/bootnewt/newtdrug.html>. [199-].

203.49 I'm Steaming Mad At Newt Gingrich. w. William K. Tong. m. "Sung to the tune of *White Christmas.*" Published online at <http://www.geocities.com/wmktong/bootnewt/steaming.htm>. [199-].

203.50 Imagine. w. William K. Tong. m. "Sung to the tune of *Imagine* by John Lennon." Published online at <http://www.geocities.com/wmktong/bootnewt/imagine.htm>. [199-].

203.51 Imagine (Revised). w. William K. Tong. m. "*Imagine,* based on a performance by John Lennon." "Written in 1996 ... and since that time: Gingrich quit Congress in disgrace, Helms retired, Thurmond died, and Buchanan is hated by the G.O.P. for his criticism of Bush." Published online at <http://www.geocities.com/wmktong/bootnewt/imagine.htm>. 2003.

203.52 Industry Machine. w. William K. Tong. m. "Sung to the tune of *Yellow Submarine* by The Beatles." In: *The Sting The Right Wing Song Book* published online at <http://www.geocities.com/wmktong/bootnewt/inmachin.htm>.

203.53 Jesse's World. w. William K. Tong. m. "Sung to the tune of *Jessie's Girl* by Rick Springfield." In: *The Sting The Right Wing Song Book* published online at <http://www.geocities.com/wmktong/bootnewt/jessewld.htm>, and at <http://www.amiright.com/parody/80s/rickspringfield2.shtml>. 1999.

203.54 Just Vote For Me. w. Angela Kuo (axk23@psu.edu). m. "To the tune of *Under The Sea* from *The Little Mermaid.*" "Well, it's less than a month to go and with the recent presidential and vice-presidential debates, I thought it might be appropriate to post this [song]. Right now I am still undecided which candidate I will vote for. Somehow I doubt much will happen in the next month to change that. But I will vote anyway. At least it gives me the right to complain." Published online at <http://geocities.com/Hollywood/5082/vote.html>. 1996.

203.55 Knockin' Around The Budget Bill. w. William K. Tong. m. "Sung to the tune of *Rockin' Around The Christmas Tree* by Brenda Lee." Published online at <http://www.geocities.com/wmktong/bootnewt/knocking.htm>. [199-].

203.56 The Legislator. w. Michael Pacholek. m. "*The Entertainer,* based on a performance by Billy Joel." "This is an update of a piece I did way back in 1995, when we were all afraid of Newt Gingrich and what he could do if he got one of his own guys in the White House. Now we know." Published online at <http://www.amiright.com/parody/70s/billyjoel43.shml>. [ca. 2002].

203.57 Let It Bleed. w. William K. Tong. m. "Sung to the tune of *Let It Be* by the Beatles." Published online at <http://www.geocities.com/wmktong/bootnewt/letbleed.htm>. [199-].

203.58 Leaving All The Kook Right Wing For Georgia. w. William K. Tong. m. "Sung to the tune of *Midnight Train To Georgia* by Gladys Knight and the Pips." Published online at <http://www.geocities.com/wmktong/bootnewt/leave-ga.htm>. [199-].

203.58A The Little First Lady With Megalomania. w. Paul Silhan. m. "Sung to *The Little Old Lady From Pasadena* by Jan & Dean." On: Cassette: *Lie-A-lot.* Lyrics published at <http://www.paulsilhan.com/lal-1.htm>. 1995.

203.59 Mangle Bills. w. William K. Tong. m. "Sung to the tune of *Jingle Bells.*" Published online at <http://www.geocities.com/wmktong/bootnewt/mangbill.htm>. [199-].

203.60 Maniac From Georgia. w. William K. Tong. m. "Sung to the tune of *Rainy Night In Georgia* by Brook Benton." Published online at <http://www.geocities.com/wmktong/bootnewt/mangeorg.htm>. [199-].

203.61 Money For Nothing. w. William K. Tong. m. "Sung to the tune of m. "Sung to the tune of *Money For Nothing* by Dire Straits." Published online at <http://www.geocities.com/wmktong/bootnewt/moneyfrm.htm>. [199-].

203.62 The Most Crude Politician. w. William K. Tong. m. "Sung to the tune of *The Most Beautiful Girl* by Charlie Rich." Published online at <http://www.geocities.com/wmktong/bootnewt/crudepol.htm>. [199-].

203.63 My Reward. w. William K. Tong. m. "Sung to the tune of *My Sweet Lord* by George Harrison." Published online at <http://www.geocities.com/wmktong/bootnewt/myreward.htm>. [199-].

203.64 Never In Newt's Dreams. w. William K. Tong. m. "Sung to the tune of *Forever In Blue Jeans* by Neil Diamond." Published online at <http://www.geocities.com/wmktong/bootnewt/nwtdream.htm>. [199-].

203.65 Newt Don't Have No Powers. w. William K. Tong. m. "Sung to the tune of *You Don't Bring Me Flowers* by Neil Diamond & Barbara Streisand." Published online at <http://www.geocities.com/wmktong/bootnewt/nopower.htm>. [199-].

203.66 Newt Gingrich & The Right Wing. w. William K. Tong. m. "Sung to the tune of *The Holly & The Ivy*." Published online at <http://www.geocities.com/wmktong/bootnewt/gingrigh.htm>. [199-].

203.67 Newt Gingrich Does The Hanky Panky. w. No composer indicated. m. "Parody of *Hanky Panky* by Tommy James & The Shondells." Lyrics published by *The Bob Rivers Show* with Bob, Spike & Joe and Twisted Tunes online at <http://www.twistedradio.com/player/lyrics.asp?songID=940>. [199-].

203.68 Newt Got No Wins For The Right Wing. w. William K. Tong. m. "Sung to the tune of *Wind Beneath My Wings* by Bette Midler." Published online at <http://www.geocities.com/wmktong/bootnewt/newtwing.htm>. [199-].

203.69 Newt Had No Shame. w. William K. Tong. m. "Sung to the tune of *Ain't That A Shame* by Fats Domino." Published online at <http://www.geocities.com/wmktong/bootnewt/noshame.htm>. [199-].

203.70 Newt Is On A Roll. w. William K. Tong. m. "Sung to the tune of *Heart Of Rock A & Roll* by Huey Lewis and the News." Published online at <http://www.geocities.com/wmktong/bootnewt/newtroll.htm>. [199-].

203.71 Newt, Newt, Newt Goin' Out My Back Door. w. Bill Strauss and Elaina Newport. On CD: *Return To Center.* Published by Capitol Steps Productions, 1505 King Street, Alexandria, VA. 1996. CD Cover: Gn/bl/y drawing of George Bush and George W. Bush as Seuss characters.

203.72 Newt's A Real Nowhere Man. w. William K. Tong. m. "Sung to the tune of *Nowhere Man* by the Beatles." Published online at <http://www.geocities.com/wmktong/bootnewt/nowhere.htm>. [199-].

203.73 No No No Newt (Kiss Him Goodbye). w. William K. Tong. m. "Sung to the tune of *Na Na Hey Hey* (Kiss Him Goodbye) by Steam." Published online at <http://www.geocities.com/wmktong/bootnewt/no-newt.htm>. [199-].

203.74 Not A Believer. w. William K. Tong. m. "Sung to the tune of *I'm A Believer* by Neil Diamond/The Monkees." Published online at <http://www.geocities.com/wmktong/bootnewt/nbelieve.htm>. [199-].

203.75 Polluter's Song. w. William K. Tong. m. "Sung to the tune of *Annie's Song* by John Denver." Published online at <http://www.geocities.com/wmktong/bootnewt/pollsong.htm>. [199-].

203.76 The Power Of Newt. w. William K. Tong. m. "Sung to the tune of *The Power Of Love* by Huey Lewis and the News." Published online at <http://www.geocities.com/wmktong/bootnewt/powernwt.htm>. [199-].

203.77 Remember The Alamo. w. Tony Ryals "(ryals@angelfire.com)." m. No tune indicated. Published online at <www.anglefore.com>. [1990s].

203.78 Rescue Me. w. William K. Tong. m. "Sung to the tune of *Rescue Me* by Fontella Bass." In: *The Sting The Right Wing Song Book* published online at <http://www.geocities.com/wmktong/bootnewt/rescueme.htm>. [199-].

203.79 Scum On The Water. w. William Tong. m. Tune — "*Smoke On The Water,* based on a performance by Deep Purple." "Written in 1999, satire about one of the least popular parts of the Republicans' agenda, their assault on environmental protection, part of which led to the government shutdown of 1995." Published online at <http://www.amiright.com/parody/70s/deeppurple6.shtml>. 1999.

203.80 Send Their Green, Green Asses Home. w. Darrell Decker. m. "*Green Grass Of Home,* based on the performance by Tom Jones." Published online at <http://amiright.com/parody/70s/tomjones0.shml>. [2001].

203.81 The Speaker & The President Should Be Friends. w. Paul Silhan. m. "Sung to *The Farmer & The Cowman Should Be Friends* from the Broadway classic *Oklahoma!*" On: Cassette: *Brother Lib.* Lyrics published at <http://www.paulsilhan.com/bl-8.htm>. 1995.

203.82 Show Down. w. William K. Tong. m. "Sung to the tune of *Small Town* by John Mellencamp." Published online at <http://www.geocities.com/wmktong/bootnewt/showdown.htm>. [199-].

203.83 Some Will Chant Impeachment. w. William K. Tong. m. "Sung to the tune of *Some Enchanted Evening* from *South Pacific.*" Published online at <http://www.geocities.com/wmktong/bootnewt/somechant.htm>. [199-].

203.84 Speaker Of The House. w. William Ross. "To the tune of *Leader Of The Pack.*" "Sung in a female voice impersonating Arianna Huffington." Lyrics and sound file published online at <http://www.seanet.com/-billr/speaker.htm>. 1996.

203.85 Steaming Mad At Newt Gingrich. w. William Tong. m. "*White Christmas,* based on a performance by Bing Crosby." "Written in 1996." Published online at <http://www.amiright.com/parody/misc/bingcrosby18.shtml>. [1996].

203.86 Take For A Ride. w. William K. Tong. m. "Sung to the tune of *Ticket To Ride* by the Beatles." Published online at <http://www.geocities.com/wmktong/bootnewt/takeride.htm>. [199-].

203.87 Tap My Phone Line. w. James E.F. Landau. m. "*Steal My Sunshine,* originally by Len." Published online at <http://www.amiright.com/parody/90s/len0.shtml>. [ca. 1999].

203.88 That Newt Was Sent A-Walking. w. William K. Tong. m. "Sung to the tune of *These Books Were Made For Walking* by Nancy Sinatra." Published online at <http://www.geocities.com/wmktong/bootnewt/sentwalk.htm>. [199-].

203.89 They Shouldn't Run The U.S.A. w. William K. Tong. m. "Sung to the tune of *Back In The U.S.A.* by Chuck Berry." Published online at <http://www.geocities.com/wmktong/bootnewt run-usa.htm>. [ca. 2000].

203.90 They Tried To Railroad Bill. w. William K. Tong. m. "Sung to the tune of *Railroad Bill.*" Published online at <http://www.geocities.com/wmktong/bootnewt/railbill.htm>. [ca. 2000].

203.91 They Want Newt So Bad. w. Paul Silhan. m. "Sung to Bob (Zimmerman) Dylan's *I Want You So Bad.*" "As heard on Rush's radio Show." Lyrics published online at <http://www.paulsilhan.com/dylan 3.htm>. 1996.

203.92 They Will Go Down In History. w. William K. Tong. m. "Sung to the tune of *Rockin' Around The Christmas Tree* by Brenda Lee." Published online at <http://www.geocities.com/wmktong/bootnewt/history.htm>. [199-].

203.93 They're The G.O.P. w. William Tong. m. "*You're A Grand Old Flag,* originally by Traditional." Published online at <http://www.amiright.com/parody/misc/traditional25/ html>. [ca. 199-].

203.94 Tie Adhesive Tape Around The Mouth Of Newt. w. William K. Tong. m. "Sung to the tune of *Tie A Yellow Ribbon Round The Old Oak Tree* by Tony Orlando & Dawn." Illustrated with a picture of Newt Gingrich with yellow tape across the mouth. Published online at <http://www.geocities.com/wmktong/bootnewt/tie-tape.htm>. [199-].

203.95 Unexciting Right-Wing Zany Former Congressman Dick Cheney. w. Don Clinchy. m. "Original: *Itsy-Bitsy Tweeny-Weeny Yellow Polka-Dot Bikini* written and performed by Bryan Hyland." Published by the Georgy Bush Project online at <http://www.georgybush.com/lyrics2.html>. [2000].

203.96 We Are In Grave Danger. w. William K. Tong. m. "Sung to the tune of *Away In The Manger.*" Published online at <http://www.geocities.com/wmktong/bootnewt/grdanger.htm>. [199-].

203.97 We Are In Shock. w. William K. Tong. m. "Sung to the tune of *Jingle Bells Rock.*" Photo of Newt Gingrich on a facsimile magazine cover with the headline "The Loser." Published online at <http://www.geocities.com/wmktong/bootnewt/werinshk.htm>. [199-].

203.98 We Can See Clearly Now. w. William K. Tong. m. "Sung to the tune of *I Can See Clearly Now* by Johnny Nash." Published online at <http://www.geocities.com/wmktong/bootnewt/clearly.htm>. [199-].

203.99 When I'm Sixty-Five. w. William K. Tong. m. "Sung to the tune of *When I'm Sixty-Four* by the Beatles." Published online at <http://www.geocities.com/wmktong/bootnewt/whenim65.htm>. [199-].

203.100 Whole Lotta Fakin' Goin' On. w. William K. Tong. m. "Sung to the tune of *Whole Lotta Shakin' Goin' On* by Jerry Lee Lewis." Published online at <http://www.geocities.com/wmktong/bootnewt/wholelot.htm>. [199-].

203.101 You're Insane. w. William K. Tong. m. "Sung to the tune of *You're So Vain* by Carly Simon." Published online at <http://www.geocities.com/wmktong/bootnewt/yoinsane.htm>. [199-].

203.102 You've Lost At Budget Dealing. w. William K. Tong. m. "Sung to the tune of *You've Lost That Loving Feeling* by the Righteous Brothers." Published online at <http://www.geocities.com/wmktong/bootnewt/youvlost.htm>. [199-].

203.103 Zany Politics. w. Edward Goldstein. m. "Parody of *Animaniac*'s opening theme song." Published online at <http://www.bagelfather.com/funstuff/parody/parody12.htm>. [199-].

• **AmPM-204 GWINNETT**, Button (Commons House of Assembly, 1769; Provincial Congress at Savannah, 1776; Continental Congress, 1776; Signer, Declaration of Independence, 1776; Acting President and Commander-in-Chief, Georgia, 1777)

204.1 The Declaration Of Independence Of The United States Of North America, July 4, 1776. w. From the Declaration of Independence. m. John E. Wilson. Published by John E. Wilson, Baltimore, MD. 1863. B/w litho of the interior of Independence Hall. "Arranged and adapted for Vocal and Instrumental Music as the Great National Chant." 4pp. [?]. Page 4: Facsimile signatures of all signers.

204.2 Old Independence Hall. w. A. Fletcher Stayman. m. Francis Weiland. Published by Stayman & Brothers, No. 210 Chesnut Street, Philadelphia, PA. 1855. Non-pictorial. "Respectfully dedicated to the Memory of the Signers of the Declaration of Independence." "Fac Simile of their signatures" including John Adams, Sam Adams, Elbridge Gerry, Thomas Jefferson. 8pp. Pages 2 and 8: Blank. [Crew/MISC-34].

• **AmPM-205   HALL**, Lyman (Continental Congress, 1775–1777; Signer of the Declaration of Independence, 1776; Governor, 1783; Judge of the Inferior Court, Chatham County)

205.1 The Declaration Of Independence Of The United States Of North America, July 4, 1776. w. From the Declaration of Independence. m. John E. Wilson. Published by John E. Wilson, Baltimore, MD. 1863. B/w litho of the interior of Independence Hall. "Arranged and adapted for Vocal and Instrumental Music as the Great National Chant." 4pp. [?]. Page 4: Facsimile signatures of all signers.

205.2 Old Independence Hall. w. A. Fletcher Stayman. m. Francis Weiland. Published by Stayman & Brothers, No. 210 Chesnut Street, Philadelphia, PA. 1855. Non-pictorial. "Respectfully dedicated to the Memory of the Signers of the Declaration of Independence." "Fac Simile of their signatures" including John Adams, Sam Adams, Elbridge Gerry, Thomas Jefferson. 8pp. Pages 2 and 8: Blank. [Crew/MISC-34].

• **AmPM-206   HILL**, Benjamin (State House, 1851; State Senate, 1859–1860; Confederate Provisional Congress, 1861; Confederate Senate, 1861–1865; U.S. House, 1875–1877; U.S. Senate, 1877–1882)

206.1 Concerning The War We Are In. w. W.A. Croffut. m. "Air—*Meg Maguire.*" "As sung by Senator Thurman, basso; Senator Hill, tenor; Senator Beck, soprano; Accompanied by Eaton with Trombone, and Proctor Knott with piccolo." In: *Bourbon Ballads*, page 2. Published in the *New York Tribune*, Extra No. 52, September, 1879. Non-pictorial newspaper supplement. "Songs for the Stump." 4pp. [Crew/MISC-226]. [AMC].

206.2 Good-Bye, Old Grover. w. "Revised by Prof. J.A. Adams." m. "Tune—*Good-Bye, My Lover, Good-*

Bye. Key C." In: Cam*paign Songs Wholesale Dry Goods Republican Club* [Song Book], page 6. Published by Wholesale Dry Goods Republican Club, New York, NY. [1892]. [5¾" × 9"]. Non-pictorial. Music starts on page 1. 8pp.

206.3 Tilden's Dream. w. No composer indicated. a. A. Watt. In: *Helmick's Republican Campaign Song Book*, page 7. Published by F.W. Helmick, Music dealer and Publisher, No. 50 West 4th Street, Cincinnati, OH. 1876. [5¼" × 7½"]. [V-1: Y/bk] [V-2: Pl/bk] lithos of Rutherford B. Hayes and William A. Wheeler, geometric design border. "Arranged for Four Voices." "As Sung by the Springfield, (O.) Glee Club." 24pp. [M-198]. [Crew/RBH-14].

• **AmPM-207 JOHNSON**, Herschel Vespasian (U.S. Senate, 1848–1849; Superior Court, Ocmulgee Circuit, 1849–1853; Presidential Elector, 1852; Governor, 1853–1857; Democratic Candidate for Vice President, 1860; Delegate to the State Secession Convention, Milledgeville, 1861; Confederate Senate, 1862–1865; State Middle Circuit Court, 1873–1880)

207.1 Cheer Up, My Lively Lads. w.m. No composer or tune indicated. In: *The Democratic Campaign Songster: Douglas & Johnson Melodies,* page 4. Published by P.J. Cozans, Publisher, New York, NY. [1860]. [3⅞" × 6"]. Y/bk litho of an eagle with ribbon—"Douglas & Johnson," train, ships, monument—"Liberty" sitting on rock base—"The Constitution." 40pp. [M-117]. [Crew/SAD-5].

207.2 [Come All True Democrats And Join] (Campaign Song For 1860). w.m. No composer or tune indicated. In: *The Democratic Campaign Songster, No. #1,* page 46. Published by American Publishing House, No. 60 West Fourth Street, Cincinnati, OH. 1860. [3⅞" × 5$^{11}/_{16}$"]. Pk/bk litho of "Stephen A. Douglas," black line border. At top of cover—"No. 1, Price 10 Cents." 52pp. [M-118]. [Crew/SAD-12].

207.3 [Come All Ye Noble Democrats] (Campaign Song). w.m. No composer or tune indicated. In: *The Democratic Campaign Songster, No. #1,* page 47. Published by American Publishing House, No. 60 West Fourth Street, Cincinnati, OH. 1860. [3⅞" × 5$^{11}/_{16}$"]. Pk/bk litho of "Stephen A. Douglas," black line border. At top of cover—"No. 1, Price 10 Cents." 52pp. [M-118]. [Crew/SAD-12].

207.4 [Come Join Our Throng, Ye Patriots True] (A Rallying Song). w. No composer indicated. m. "Air—*Dan Tucker.*" In: *The Democratic Campaign Songster, No. #1,* page 35. Published by American Publishing House, No. 60 West Fourth Street, Cincinnati, OH. 1860. [3⅞" × 5$^{11}/_{16}$"]. Pk/bk litho of "Stephen A. Douglas," black line border. At top of cover—"No. 1, Price 10 Cents." 52pp. [M-118]. [Crew/SAD-12].

207.5 Democratic Huzza. w. No composer indicated. m. "Air—*Foot Travellor—Alpine Glee Singer,* page 70." In: *The Democratic Campaign Songster, No. #1,* page 21. Published by American Publishing House, No. 60 West Fourth Street, Cincinnati, OH. 1860. [3⅞" × 5$^{11}/_{16}$"]. Pk/bk litho of "Stephen A. Douglas," black line border. At top of cover—"No. 1, Price 10 Cents." 52pp. [M-118]. [Crew/SAD-12].

207.6 A Democrat's Dream. w. No composer indicated. m. "Air—*Yankee Doodle.*" In: *The Democratic Campaign Songster: Douglas & Johnson Melodies,* page 11. Published by P.J. Cozans, Publisher, New York, NY. [1860]. [3⅞" × 6"]. Y/bk litho of an eagle with ribbon—"Douglas & Johnson," train, ships, monument—"Liberty" sitting on rock base—"The Constitution." 40pp. [M-117]. [Crew/SAD-5].

207.7 Douglas And Johnson. w. J.F.R. m. No tune indicated. In: *The Democratic Campaign Songster: Douglas & Johnson Melodies,* page 13. Published by P.J. Cozans, Publisher, New York, NY. [1860]. [3⅞" × 6"]. Y/bk litho of an eagle with ribbon—"Douglas & Johnson," train, ships, monument—"Liberty" sitting on rock base—"The Constitution." 40pp. [M-117]. [Crew/SAD-5].

207.8 Douglas And Johnson Song. w. No composer indicated. m. "Air—*Star Spangled Banner.*" In: *The Democratic Campaign Songster, No. #1,* page 30. Published by American Publishing House, No. 60 West Fourth Street, Cincinnati, OH. 1860. [3⅞" × 5$^{11}/_{16}$"]. Pk/bk litho of "Stephen A. Douglas," black line border. At top of cover—"No. 1, Price 10 Cents." 52pp. [M-118]. [Crew/SAD-12].

207.9 Douglas And Union. w. Michael Doheny. m. "Air—*Star Spangled Banner.*" In: *The Democratic Campaign Songster, No. #1,* page 23. Published by American Publishing House, No. 60 West Fourth Street, Cincinnati, OH. 1860. [3⅞" × 5$^{11}/_{16}$"]. Pk/bk litho of "Stephen A. Douglas," black line border. At top of cover—"No. 1, Price 10 Cents." 52pp. [M-118]. [Crew/SAD-12].

207.10 Douglas Going Home (National Song). w. No composer indicated. m. "Air—*Few Days.*" In: *The Democratic Campaign Songster: Douglas & Johnson Melodies,* page 24. Published by P.J. Cozans, Publisher, New York, NY. [1860]. [3⅞" × 6"]. Y/bk litho of an eagle with ribbon—"Douglas & Johnson," train, ships, monument—"Liberty" sitting on rock base—"The Constitution." 40pp. [M-117]. [Crew/SAD-5].

207.11 Douglas Is The Man. w. No composer indicated. m. "Tune—*Dearest Mae.*" In: *The Democratic Campaign Songster, No. #1,* page 45. Published by American Publishing House, No. 60 West Fourth Street, Cincinnati, OH. 1860. [3⅞" × 5$^{11}/_{16}$"]. Pk/bk litho of "Stephen A. Douglas," black line border. At top of cover—"No. 1, Price 10 Cents." 52pp. [M-118]. [Crew/SAD-12].

207.12 Douglas Our Choice. w. No composer indicated. m. "Tune—*Old Dan Tucker.*" In: *The Democratic Campaign Songster, No. #1,* page 25. Published by American Publishing House, No. 60 West Fourth Street, Cincinnati, OH. 1860. [3⅞" × 5$^{11}/_{16}$"]. Pk/bk litho of "Stephen A. Douglas," black line border. At top of cover—"No. 1, Price 10 Cents." 52pp. [M-118]. [Crew/SAD-12].

207.13 Douglas Shall Be President. w. No composer indicated. m. "Air—*Yankee Doodle.*" In: *The Democratic Campaign Songster, No. #1,* page 39. Published by American Publishing House, No. 60 West Fourth Street, Cincinnati, OH. 1860. [3⅞" × 5$^{11}/_{16}$"]. Pk/bk litho of "Stephen A. Douglas," black line border. At top of cover—"No. 1, Price 10 Cents." 52pp. [M-118]. [Crew/SAD-12].

207.14 Douglas The Patriot Honest And True. w.m. No composer or tune indicated. In: *The Democratic Campaign Songster, No. #1,* page 26. Published by American Publishing House, No. 60 West Fourth Street, Cincinnati, OH. 1860. [3⅞" × 5$^{11}/_{16}$"]. Pk/bk litho of "Stephen A. Douglas," black line border. At top of cover—"No. 1, Price 10 Cents." 52pp. [M-118]. [Crew/SAD-12].

207.15 Douglas's Going Home. w. No composer indicated. m. "Air—*Yankee Doodle.*" In: *The Democratic Campaign Songster, No. #1,* page 39. Published by American Publishing House, No. 60 West Fourth Street, Cincinnati, OH. 1860. [3⅞" × 5$^{11}/_{16}$"]. Pk/bk litho of "Stephen A. Douglas," black line border. At top of cover—"No. 1, Price 10 Cents." 52pp. [M-118]. [Crew/SAD-12].

207.16 Hurra For Douglas! w. No composer indicated. m. "Tune—*A Little More Cider.*" In: *The Democratic Campaign Songster, No. #1,* page 8. Published by American Publishing House, No. 60 West Fourth Street, Cincinnati, OH. 1860. [3⅞" × 5$^{11}/_{16}$"]. Pk/bk litho of "Stephen A. Douglas," black line border. At top of cover—"No. 1, Price 10 Cents." 52pp. [M-118]. [Crew/SAD-12].

207.17 O! Poor Old Abe! w. No composer indicated. m. "Tune—*Nelly Gray.*" In: *The Democratic Campaign Songster, No. #1,* page 14. Published by American Publishing House, No. 60 West Fourth Street, Cincinnati, OH. 1860. [3⅞" × 5$^{11}/_{16}$"]. Pk/bk litho of "Stephen A. Douglas," black line border. At top of cover—"No. 1, Price 10 Cents." 52pp. [M-118]. [Crew/SAD-12].

207.18 [Oh Greeley, I Leave The Course] (Campaign Song). w. Col. George S. Hickox. m. "Air—*Oh, Carry Me Till I Die.*" "Dedicated to the Douglas and Johnson Club, of Olean." In: *The Democratic Campaign Songster: Douglas & Johnson Melodies,* page 21. Published by P.J. Cozans, Publisher, New York, NY. [1860]. [3⅞" × 6"]. Y/bk litho of an eagle with ribbon—"Douglas & Johnson," train, ships, monument—"Liberty" sitting on rock base—"The Constitution." 40pp. [M-117]. [Crew/SAD-5].

207.19 Our Champions. w.m. No composer or tune indicated. In: *The Democratic Campaign Songster, No. #1,* page 43. Published by American Publishing House, No. 60 West Fourth Street, Cincinnati, OH. 1860. [3⅞" × 5$^{11}/_{16}$"]. Pk/bk litho of "Stephen A. Douglas," black line border. At top of cover—"No. 1, Price 10 Cents." 52pp. [M-118]. [Crew/SAD-12].

207.20 Red, White And Blue. w.m. No composer or tune indicated. In: *The Democratic Campaign Songster, No. #1,* page 19. Published by American Publishing House, No. 60 West Fourth Street, Cincinnati, OH. 1860. [3⅞" × 5$^{11}/_{16}$"]. Pk/bk litho of "Stephen A. Douglas," black line border. At top of cover—"No. 1, Price 10 Cents." 52pp. [M-118]. [Crew/SAD-12].

207.21 Then Rally! w. No composer indicated. m. "Tune—*Bonnie Eloise.*" In: *The Democratic Campaign Songster, No. #1,* page 17. Published by American Publishing House, No. 60 West Fourth Street, Cincinnati, OH. 1860. [3⅞" × 5$^{11}/_{16}$"]. Pk/bk litho of "Stephen A. Douglas," black line border. At top of cover—"No. 1, Price 10 Cents." 52pp. [M-118]. [Crew/SAD-12].

207.22 We Mean To Win The Day. w. No composer indicated. m. "Air—*Yankee Doodle.*" In: *The Democratic Campaign Songster, No. #1,* page 31. Published by American Publishing House, No. 60 West Fourth Street, Cincinnati, OH. 1860. [3⅞" × 5$^{11}/_{16}$"]. Pk/bk litho of "Stephen A. Douglas," black line border. At top of cover—"No. 1, Price 10 Cents." 52pp. [M-118]. [Crew/SAD-12].

• **AmPM-208 KELLY,** Asa D. (Mayor, Albany, 1962)

208.1 Ain't Gonna Let Nobody Turn Me Round. w. "Members of the Albany [Ga.] Movement." m. Traditional. In: *We Shall Overcome, Song Of The Southern Freedom Movement,* page 61. Compiled by Guy and Candie Carawan for The Student Non-Violent Coordinating Committee. Published by Oak Publications, 165 W. 46th Street, New York, NY. [ca. 1968]. [5½" × 8½"]. Bl/bk photo of marchers. 112pp.

208.2 Ain't Gonna Let Nobody Turn Me Round. w. "Members of the Albany [Ga.] Movement." m. Traditional. w.m. Bill Blake. Copyright 1963 by Stormking Music, Inc. Published in: *Sing Out! The Folksong Magazine,* Vol. 14, No. 1, February-March 1964, page 7. Published by Sing Out Inc., No. 165 West 46th Street, New York, NY. 1964. [5½" × 8¼"]. Song copyright 1963 by Stormking Music, Inc.

208.3 Oh Pritchett, Oh Kelly. w. Bertha Gober and Janie Culbreath. m. *Oh Mary, Oh Martha.* "They sing to Chief of Police Laurie Pritchett and Mayor Asa D. Kelly." In: *We Shall Overcome, Song Of The Southern Freedom Movement,* page 62. Compiled by Guy and Candie Carawan for The Student Non-Violent Coordinating Committee. Published by Oak Publications, 165 W. 46th Street, New York, NY. [ca. 1968]. [5½" × 8½"]. Bl/bk photo of marchers. 112pp.

• **AmPM-209 KING,** Martin Luther (Civil Rights Leader; President of the Southern Christian Leadership Conference, 1970–1968; Winner, Nobel Peace Prize, 1964)

209.1 Abraham, Martin And John. w.m. Dick Holler. Published by [V-1: Roznique Music Inc., 8th Floor, No. 17 West 60th Street, New York, NY] [V-2: The Goodman Group]. [V-1: B/w/r/bl] [V-2: Bl/bk] photo/drawing of Mt. Rushmore with busts of John F. Kennedy, Martin Luther King, Robert Kennedy and Abraham Lincoln. [V-2: "Exclusively distributed by Hal Leonard Publishing Corporation, 777 West Bluemound Rd., Milwaukee, WI."]. 6pp. [V-1: B/w photo of "Moms Mabley" and advertisement for her recording of above title] [V-1 & V-2: Page 6: Cover photo]. [Crew/JFK-30].

209.2 Abraham, Martin And John. w.m. Dick Holler. Published by Roznique Music Inc., West 46th Street, Suite 1200, New York, NY. 10036. 1968. [V-1: 9" × 12"] [V-2: 7" × 10½"]. B/w silhouette of man. [V-1: Quotes by John Kennedy—"Ask not what your country can do for you, Ask what you can do for your country," Martin Luther King—"I have a dream," and Abraham Lincoln—"Of the people, by the people, for the people."] [V-2: "AMLO Choral, The Authentic Record Sound!" "S.A.T.B. with optional Guitar, Bass and Drums"]. [V-1: 6pp] [V-2: 8pp]. [Crew/JFK-31].

209.3 Abraham, Martin And John. w.m. Richard Holler. a. Anita Kerr. Copyright 1968, 1970 and 1984 by Regent Music Corporation. Non-pictorial. "Pop Choral Showcase." Publisher logos—"The Goodman Group," "Cherry Lane Music Company, Inc.," Jenson Publications, Inc." List of arrangements. Page 2: "S.S.A. Accompanied." 12pp. [Crew/JFK-60].

209.4 Abraham, Martin And John. w.m. Dick Holler. a. Ed Lojeski. Published by [V-1: Roznique Music Inc., No. 1516 Broadway, New York, NY. Distributed by: West Coast Publications, Inc., No. 4423 West Jefferson Boulevard, Los Angeles, CA. 90016. 1968 and 1971. Bk/br/pk/w drawing of Mt. Rushmore with busts of John Kennedy, Martin Luther King, Robert Kennedy and Abraham Lincoln. "SATB For Mixed Chorus with Piano and Optional Percussion, Guitar and String Bass." 16pp. [Crew/JFK-62].

209.5 Abraham, Martin And John. w.m. Dick Holler. a. Matt Dennis. Published by Roznique Music Inc., No. 165 West 46th Street, New York, NY. 10036. Copyright 1968 and 1971. [8½" × 11"]. Be/bk drawing of Mt. Rushmore with busts of John F. Kennedy, Martin Luther King, Robert Kennedy and Abraham Lincoln. "Big Note Easy Piano." 4pp. [Crew/JFK-66].

209.6 Abraham, Martin And John. w.m. Dick Holler. Published by Screen Gems-Columbia Publications, A Division of Columbia Pictures Industries, Inc., No. 6744 N.E. 4th Avenue, Miami, FL. Copyright 1968 and 1972 by Roznique Music Inc., New York, NY. [8½" × 11"]. Pk/br drawings of John Kennedy, Abraham Lincoln and Martin Luther King, piano keyboard. "Bradley Easy Piano Series." 4pp. Page 4: Blank. [Crew/JFK-69].

209.7 Abraham, Martin And John. w.m. Dick Holler. a. John Brimhall. Published by Charles Hansen, Distributor, Educational Sheet Music & Books, No. 1860 Broadway, New York, NY. 10023. Copyright 1968 by Roznique Music Inc., New York, NY. [8½" × 11"]. R/w/b/gn/pl/y drawing of two children, one dressed as Abraham Lincoln. "Brimhall Piano Series." 4pp. [Crew/JFK-78].

209.8 Abraham, Martin And John. w.m. Dick Holler. In: *Fife 'N' Drums*, page 2. Published by Hal Leonard Publishing Corp., Winona, MN 55987. 1976. [8½" × 11"]. R/w/b litho of Colonial fife and drummers pattern. List of titles. 48pp. Page 3: "Sounder Music Notation copyright 1973 by Hammond Organ Company, Division of Hammond Corporation." [Crew/JFK-82].

209.9 Abraham, Martin And John. w.m. Dick Holler. In: *The All-American Patriotic Song Book*, page 6. Published by Creative Concepts Publishing Corp., No. 154 El Roblar Drive, Box 848, Ojai, CA. 93023. R/w/b flag design. "Complete Sheet Music Edition." 100pp. [Crew/JFK-84].

209.10 Abraham, Martin And John. w.m. Dick Holler. 45 rpm record. Laurie Records, New York, NY. Record #3464/W4KM. Performed by Dion. 1968.

209.11 Abraham, Martin And John. w.m. Dick Holler. a. Leroy Glover. 45 rpm record. Mercury Records #72935/1-44167. Performed by Moms Mabley. 1968.

209.12 Abraham, Martin And John. w.m. Dick Holler. On LP: *JP & The Silver Stars.* 33⅓ rpm LP. Lesco Records, 725 No. Western Ave., Los Angeles, CA. Lesco #LP-1001. "Steel Band From Trinidad."

209.13 Allelujah Dr. Martin Luther King, Jr. w.m. Jean-Claude Petion. 33⅓ rpm LP. Pecord Production #11873-1. Rara 'N' Roll Beat From Haiti. 1984. Album cover: B/w photo of Jean-Claude Petion.

209.14 Ballad Of The Student Sit-Ins. w.m. Guy Carawan, Eve Merriam and Norman Curtis. In: *We Shall Overcome, Song Of The Southern Freedom Movement*, page 38. Compiled by Guy and Candie Carawan for The Student Non-Violent Coordinating Committee. Published by Oak Publications, 165 W. 46th Street, New York, NY. [ca. 1968]. [5½" × 8½"]. Bl/bk photo of marchers. 112pp.

209.15 The Congressional Record (The Living Legacy of Dr. Martin Luther King, Jr.). 33⅓ rpm LP 2 Vols.). Respect Stax Records #STS-5525. 1975. Produced by Hon. Walter E. Fauntroy. Popular and religious songs in tribute to Dr. King. Album cover: N/c photos of Dr. King and Congressman Fauntroy. Includes the song: *Abraham, Martin, John* (Malcolm, Martin, John, Bobby) {209.15–1}.

209.16 Don't The Angels Sing For Martin Luther King. w. Noble Sissle. m. Eubie Blake. Published by Leo Feist, Inc., New York, NY. 1968. [8½" × 11"]. B/w photo of Martin Luther King, Jr. 4pp. Page 4: Publisher logo.

209.17 Dr. Martin Luther King. w.m. Thomas L. a. T. Loveless and G. McCoy. 45 rpm record. Valbrest Records, Chicago, IL. T. Little Production #TM-4739. Performed by Swan Mellarks. [196-].

209.18 Dr. Martin Luther King Jr. Funeral Services. 33⅓ rpm LP. Brotherhood Records LP-2001. From the "Funeral Service's Ebenezer Baptist Church, April 9, 1968." Side B: Speeches of Dr. King — Washington, August 28, 1963 and I have a Dream.

209.19 Elegy For Martin Luther King, Jr. m. David Ward-Steinman. Published by Highgate Press, Galaxy Music Corporation, New York, NY. 1969. Non-pictorial black line border. 4pp.

209.20 Every One Hundred Years. w. Mildred Bailey and Joseph Bailey. m. Joseph Bailey. Published by Yoshema Music, Inc., 66 St. Nicholas Place, Suite B-36, New York, NY. 1968. Bl/w photo of Martin Luther King, geometric designs. "Eulogy to Dr. Martin Luther King." 4pp.

209.21 Free At Last. a. Jay Arnold. Published by Chas. H. Hansen Music Corp., 1842 West Avenue, Miami, FL. 33139. 4pp. Page 2: At top of music — "Dedicated to the memory of Dr. Martin Luther King, Jr." Page 4: B/w geometric design.

209.21A Freedmen's Town. a. No composer indicated. m. "Inspired by *Allentown* by Billy Joel." Lyrics and sound file published at <http://houstonprogressive.org/4d-song.html>. [ca. 1999].

209.22 Freedom. w.m. Frederick Tillis. Published by Southern Music Publishing Co., Inc., New York, NY. 1974. [7¼" × 10½"]. B/w publisher logo. "For Mixed Chorus (a capella)." 32pp. Page 3: "Commissioned by the Kentucky State College Concert Choir In Memory of Dr. Martin Luther King."

209.23 Gonna Be A Meetin' Over Yonder. w. [New] Chicago Movement. m. The Impressions. In: *Freedom Is A Constant Struggle, Songs Of The Freedom Movement*, page 196. c. Guy and Candie Carawan. Published by Oak Publications, New York, NY. 1968. 224pp.

209.23A I Have A Dream. w. Martin Luther King, Jr. m. Phyllis Luidens Reed. Published by Galaxy Music Corp., New York, NY., and Galaxy Limited, London. 1970. Non-pictorial stripe cover. "For

Medium Voice and Piano." **209.24 I Remember Martin Luther King, Jr.** (An American Celebration of Freedom) [Song Books and Performance Guidelines]. a.e. Ruth Roberts. Published by Michel Brent Publications, Inc., Box 1186, Port Chester, NY. 10573. 1986. R/w/gy/bk drawing of Martin Luther King, children. 30pp.

209.25 The Johnson Victory Hymn. w. W.L. White. [1964]. [8½" × 11"]. Non-pictorial. "W.L. White in *The Emporia Gazette*." 2pp. Page 2: Reprint of an anti-Johnson editorial by W.L. White in the *Emporia Gazette*. [Crew/LBJ-38].

209.26 A Man Named King. w.m. Greg Scelsa. A. Andrea Klouse. Published by Hal Leonard Corp., 7777 W. Bluemound Rd., P.O. Box 13819, Milwaukee, WI. 1989. Bk/w/pl non-pictorial. "Hal Leonard Concert Festival Choral Series." Available for SATB, SAB and 2-Part." 12pp.

209.27 Martin Luther King (A Man With So Much Love). w.m. James Weldon Lane. Published by J. Weldon Lane Music Co., 6056 Market Street, Philadelphia, PA. 1978. B/w drawing of Martin Luther King, Jr. 8pp. Page 8: Blank.

209.28 Martin Luther King. On CD: *When The Rain Comes Down*. Performed by Cathy Fink. [ca. 200-].

209.29 Martin Luther King Day. w.m. Kelvin Pope. 33⅓ rpm Album. On LP: *Calypso Forever*. Performed by Kelvin Pope (Mighty Duke). Straker's Records #GS 2253. [1980s]. Album cover: N/c photo of Mighty Duke.

209.30 Martin Luther King For President. w.m. Slinger Francisco "(The Mighty Sparrow)." a. Bert Inniss. 33⅓ rpm LP. On LP: *The Outcast*. National Recording Company, Kingston, Jamaica. #NLP 4199. [196-].

209.31 Martin Luther King For President. w.m. Slinger Francisco "The Mighty Sparrow)." "From LP: *The Mighty Sparrow Sings True Life Stories Of Passion, People And Politics*, 1964, Mace Records #M10002." Lyrics published by Mudcat Café online at <http://www.mudcat.org/kids/@displaysong.cfm?SongID=6596>. [1998].

209.32 Martin Luther King Jr. w.m. Cecil Payne. On CD: *Payne's Window*. Performed by Cecil Payne. 1999.

209.33 Martin Luther King Southside. w.m. Joe Turner. On CD: *Everyday I Have The Blues*. Performed by Joe Turner with Pee Wee Crayton and Sonny Stitt. 1991.

209.34 Martin Luther King's Dream. On CD: *Just A Collection Of Antiques*. Performed by the Strawbs. [ca. 1990s?]. Published in Germany.

209.35 Marty & His Travelin' Beatnik Band. w.m. Norris. 45 rpm record. Reb Rebel Records, Crowley, LA. Leber Music #No. 506. Performed by The Multiple Voices of The Son of Mississippi. [196-]. Label: Two r/w/b Confederate flags. Side 2: *Joining The Big Society*.

209.35A MLK. w. Bono. m. U2. On LP: *The Unforgettable Fire*. Performed by U2. 33 13/rpm LP. Island Records. 1984.

209.36 My Country. w. Jud Strunk. m. Dennis McCarthy. Published by Every Little Tune, Inc., No. 9200 Sunset Boulevard, Los Angeles, CA. Copyright 1974 by Every Little Tune, Inc., Kayteekay Music and Pierre Cossette Music Company — "A Product of the Wes Ferrell Organization." Multicolor drawings of Abraham Lincoln, John F. Kennedy, Martin Luther King, homes, flag, flute, heart, football game, hamburger, canyon, skyline — "Rock — Jazz — Soul — Country & Western — Folk — Blues." "Recorded by Jud Strunk on Capitol Records." "Distributed by Big 3." 6pp. Page 6: Advertising. [Crew/MISC-93].

209.37 Never Too Much Love. w. [New] Chicago Movement. m. The Impressions. In: *Freedom Is A Constant Struggle, Songs Of The Freedom Movement*, page 194. c. Guy and Candie Carawan. Published by Oak Publications, New York, NY. 1968. 224pp.

209.37A 911 For Peace. w.m. Anti-Flag. On CD: *Mobilize*. Lyrics published online at <http://www.plyrics.com/lyrics/antiflag/011firpeace.html>. 2002.

209.38 Nobody Likes A Smart Ass. w. Sam Adams. m. Wurlitzer and Plagiarize. 33⅓ rpm LP (2-Vols). Spade Records, POB 2306, Baton Rouge, LA. Spade Records #LP/101&LP/102. Original Cast, *The Fudgeripple Follies Or Nobody Likes A Smart Ass*. [1964–1968].

209.39 Oh, Wallace. w.m. Len Chandler. In: *Freedom Is A Constant Struggle, Songs Of The Freedom Movement*, page 168. c. Guy and Candie Carawan. Published by Oak Publications, New York, NY. 1968. 224pp.

209.39A One People, One Struggle. w.m. Anti-Flag. Lyrics published online at <http://www.plyrics.com/lyrics/antiflag/onepeopleonestruggle.html>. [ca. 198-].

209.39B Resolution. w.m. Fifteen. Lyrics published online at <http://www.plyrics.com/lyrics/fifteen/resolution.html>. [ca. 198-].

209.40 The Rev. King Suite. m. Jack DeJohnette and John Coltrane. 33⅓ rpm LP. On LP: *Sorcery*. Prestige Records, #P-10081. Performed by Jack DeJohnette. 1974.

209.41 A Season Of Hope (Ten Spots to Celebrate the January Birthday of Dr. Martin Luther King, Jr.). 33⅓ rpm LP. SandCastles Records. "Hosted by Steve Allen." "Each of the ten 30-second spots opens with a sound image followed by a voice-over by Steve Allen, a 5-second excerptation from Dr. Martin Luther King, Jr., and closing tag." 1968.

209.42 Selma. w.m. Tommy Butler. On: 8-Track Cassette: *The Selma Album*. Cotillion Records #TC 2-110. A Warner Communications Company. 1976. Album cover: O/bk drawing of marchers. "Original Cast Album from the inspiring musical Selma by Tommy Butler, A Musical Tribute to Dr. Martin Luther King."

209.43 This Was A Man. w.m. Marta Keen. A. Carl Stroman. Published by Shawnee Press, Inc., Delaware Water Gap, PA. 18327. [7" × 10⅜"]. Bk/w/gn drawing of Martin Luther King. "50th Anniversary Publication." "Cassettes Available." 8pp. Page 2: At top of music — "For 2-part voices and piano with optional cassette."

209.44 Wade In The Water. w. No composer indicated. m. "Traditional Spiritual." In: *Freedom Is A Constant Struggle, Songs Of The Freedom Movement*, page 28. c. Guy and Candie Carawan. Published by

Oak Publications, New York, NY. 1968. "Original verses by Florence Reese." 224pp.

209.45 We Got The Whole World Shakin.' w. [New] Chicago Movement. Original — "Sam Cooke." m. *We Got The Whole World Shakin'*. In: *Freedom Is A Constant Struggle, Songs Of The Freedom Movement*, page 204. c. Guy and Candie Carawan. Published by Oak Publications, New York, NY. 1968. 224pp.

209.46 We Shall Overcome. w.m.a. Zilphia Horton, Frank Hamilton, Guy Carawan and Pete Seeger. Published by TRO, The Richmond Organization. Copyright 1960 & 1963 by Ludlow Music Inc., New York, NY. [ca. 1968]. [8½" × 11"]. B/w photo of "Martin Luther King, Jr. 1929–1968." 4pp. Page 4: Same as page 1.

209.47 What A Friend We Have In Hoover. w. Tom Paxton. m. Tune — *What A Friend We Have In Jesus*. Lyrics and sound file published online at <http://www.mudcat.org/kids/@displaysong.cfm?SongID=7719>. [199-].

209.48 Who Killed J.F.K., R.F.K., M.L.K., M.J.K? Published by Cutter Designs, Box 1465, Manchester, MA. as a post card. [3" × 5"]. Obv: N/c photo of Rush Harp in front of billboard featuring song title. Five bars of music below — "Not LHO; not JER; not SBS; not EMK not any way." Rev: Description of obverse of post card — "Researcher Rush Harp conducting his Bearsville (NY) 'Symphonie Conspiracie' in the Vale of Truth and Light along Rte. 28 near Woodstock (NY)." [Crew/JFK-50].

209.49 Why? (The King Of Love Is Dead). w.m. Calvin E. (Gene) Taylor. a. Hale Smith. Published by Ninandy Music Co. Sole selling agent Sam Fox Publishing Company, Inc., 140 Broadway, New York, NY. 1970. B/w non-pictorial geometric design border. "Mixed (S.A.B.T.) Voices." 12pp.

LAMAR, Mirabeau Bonaparte (State Senate, Georgia, 1829) [See: Texas]

• **AmPM-210   LUMPKIN**, Wilson (State House, 1804–1812; U.S. House, 1815–1817 & 1827–1831; Governor, 1831–1835; U.S. Senate, 1837–1841)

210.1 Governour Lumpkin's March. m. Victor Lataste. No publisher indicated. [1831–1835]. Non-pictorial geometric designs. "Composed & Arranged for the Piano Forte." 2pp. Page 2: Blank.

MACADOO, William Gibbs [See: California]

• **AmPM-211   MADDOX**, Lester Garfield (Governor, 1967–1971; Lt. Governor, 1971–1975; Candidate for President, 1968) [SEE: DOC/PSM-LGM]

211.1 God, Family & Country. 33⅓ rpm LP. Published by Lefevre Sound #MLSP 3485. [ca. 197-]. Various religious songs performed by Lester Maddox. "Lester Maddox Sings, Whistles, Speaks, and Plays Harmonica." Songs include: ***Epitaph*** {211.1-1}; ***Medley*** {211.1-2}. Traditional religious songs. Lester Maddox on harmonica; ***I Love My Country*** {211.1-3}. w.m. Lester Maddox. Lester Maddox on harmonica with the Goss Bros; ***Be A Real Man*** {211.1-4}. w.m. Lester Maddox. Lester Maddox on harmonica with the Goss Bros.

211.2 Lester Maddox. 45 rpm vinyl record. Published by Lefevre Records, SO 13364/MLFP 300. [ca. 1960s].

211.3 Rednecks {211.1.5}. w.m. Randy Newman. On LP: *Good Old Boys*. Warner Bros. Records #MS 2193. Performed by Randy Newman. Lyrics on Album cover reverse. 1974.

• **AmPM-212   MCDONALD**, Charles J. (Solicitor General, Flint Circuit, 1822–1825; Judge, Flint Circuit, 1825–1828; State House, 1830; State Senate, 1834–1837; Governor, 1839–1843; Georgia Supreme Court, 1855–1859)

212.1 Governor McDonald's Quick Step. m. Francis E. Brown. Published by Hewitt & Jaques, 239 Broadway, New York, NY. [1839–1843]. Non-pictorial geometric designs. "Composed & Arranged for the Piano Forte and Respectfully Dedicated to His Excellency Charles J. McDonald, Governor of Georgia." 4pp. Page 4: Blank.

212.2 Southern Rights March. m. B.R. Lignoski. Published by George Willig, Baltimore, MD. 1853. B/w geometric designs. "Composed and Arranged for the Piano and Respectfully Dedicated to his Excellency Ex-Gov. C.J. McDonald of Ga." 6pp. Pages 2 and 6: Blank. [LL, JH].

• **AmPM-212A   MILLER**, Zell Bryan (Mayor, Young Harris, 1959–1961; State Senate, 1961–1965; State Board of Pardons and Paroles, 1973–1975; Lt. Governor, Georgia, 1975–1991; Governor, 1991–1999; U.S. Senate, 2000–Present)

212A.1 Psycho Miller. w. William Tong. m. "*Psycho Killer*, based on the performance by Talking Heads." "Inspired by the title of a column written by Tamara Baler in American Politics Journal — dedicated to Sen. Zell Miller (S-GA), who have a hate-filled keynote speech attacking John Kerry and his own party at the Republican National Convention." Published online at <http://www.amiright.com/parody/70s/talkngheads1.shtml>. 2004.

• **AmPM-213   NISBET**, Eugenius Aristides (State House, 1827–1830; State Senate, 1830–1837; U.S. House, 1839–1841; State Supreme Court, 1845–1853; State Secession Convention, 1861; Candidate for Governor, 1861)

213.1 Song Of The Southern Boys (Cheer, Boys, Cheer). a. Herman L. Schreiner. Published by John C. Schreiner & Sons, Macon, GA. [ca. 1861]. Gn/w non-pictorial geometric design border. "To Judge E.A. Nisbet, Macon, Ga." 6pp. Pages 2 and 6: Blank. [H-3823].

• **AmPM-214   PRITCHETT**, Laurie (Chief of Police, Albany, 1962)

214.1 Ain't Gonna Let Nobody Turn Me Round. w. "Members of the Albany [Ga.] Movement." m. Traditional. In: *We Shall Overcome, Song Of The Southern Freedom Movement*, page 61. Compiled by Guy and Candie Carawan for The Student Non-Violent Coordinating Committee. Published by Oak Publications, 165 W. 46th Street, New York, NY. [ca. 1968]. [5½" × 8½"]. Bl/bk photo of marchers. 112pp.

214.2 Ain't Gonna Let Nobody Turn Me Round. w. "Members of the Albany [Ga.] Movement." m. "Traditional." w.m. Bill Blake. Copyright 1963 by Stormking Music, Inc. Published in: *Sing Out! The Folksong Magazine*, Vol. 14, No. 1, February-March 1964, page 7. Published by Sing Out Inc., No. 165 West 46th Street, New York, NY. 1964. [5½" × 8¼"]. Song copyright 1963 by Stormking Music, Inc.

214.3 Oh Pritchett, Oh Kelly. w. Bertha Gober and Janie Culbreath. m. *Oh Mary, Oh Martha.* "They sing to Chief of Police Laurie Pritchett and Mayor Asa D. Kelly." In: *We Shall Overcome, Song Of The Southern Freedom Movement*, page 62. Compiled by Guy and Candie Carawan for The Student Non-Violent Coordinating Committee. Published by Oak Publications, 165 W. 46th Street, New York, NY. [ca. 1968]. [5½" × 8½"]. Bl/bk photo of marchers. 112pp.

214.4 This Little Light Of Mine. w. Bob Gibson and members of SCLC. m. Traditional. In: *We Shall Overcome, Song Of The Southern Freedom Movement*, page 23. Compiled by Guy and Candie Carawan for The Student Non-Violent Coordinating Committee. Published by Oak Publications, 165 W. 46th Street, New York, NY. [ca. 1968]. [5½" × 8½"]. Bl/bk photo of marchers. 112pp.

• **AmPM-215** RUSK, Dean (Assistant U.S. Secretary of State, 1950–1952; U.S. Secretary of State, 1961–1969)

215.1 All The King's Horses. w.m. Skip Storey and Joe Mazo, 1968. "L.B.J. made a classic speech... 'All the King's horses and all the King's men are not going to move us...'" In: *The Vietnam Songbook*, page 35. c. Barbara Dane and Irwin Silber. Published by The Guardian, No. 32 West 22nd Street, New York, NY. Copyright 1969 by Barbara Dane and Irwin Silber. [7" × 10"]. B/w photo of a protest march. O/y/r/bk cover. 228pp.

215.2 Beware: Here Come Friends. w.m. Richard Kohler and Barbara Dane, 1968. In: *The Vietnam Songbook*, page 100. c. Barbara Dane and Irwin Silber. Published by The Guardian, No. 32 West 22nd Street, New York, NY. Copyright 1969 by Barbara Dane and Irwin Silber. [7" × 10"]. B/w photo of a protest march. O/y/r/bk cover. 228pp.

215.3 Cool Goldwater. w. Noel E. Parmentel, Jr. and Marshall J. Dodge. In: *Folk Songs For Conservatives*, page 11. Published by Unicorn Press, Inc., No. 790 Madison Avenue, New York, NY. 10021. 1964. [5" × 8⅜"]. Bl/w drawings of Barry Goldwater, Bill Buckley, Ray Cohn, eagle. List of contents. "Sung by Noel E. Parmentel, Jr. and His Unbleached Muslims, Greatest Political Satirists Since Cohn and Schine." "Right Wing Hootenanny." 36pp. [Crew/BMG-13].

215.4 Dean Rusk Song. w.m. Bill Frederick, Copyright 1967 by Futura Music Publishers. "This song is based on [a] news item from the *New York Times*, January 1, 1966: Weary Rusk Tells Of World's Mischief ..." In: *The Vietnam Songbook*, page 32. c. Barbara Dane and Irwin Silber. Published by The Guardian, No. 32 West 22nd Street, New York, NY. Copyright 1969 by Barbara Dane and Irwin Silber. [7" × 10"]. B/w photo of a protest march. O/y/r/bk cover. 228pp.

215.5 Hell No! We Won't Go! w.m. Barbara Dane, 1967. "This is remark of Stokley Carmichael's which was taken up by a lot of people..." In: *The Vietnam Songbook*, page 12. c. Barbara Dane and Irwin Silber. Published by The Guardian, No. 32 West 22nd Street, New York, NY. Copyright 1969 by Barbara Dane and Irwin Silber. [7" × 10"]. B/w photo of a protest march. O/y/r/bk cover. 228pp.

215.6 Honor Our Commitment. w.m. Jacqueline Sharpe, Copyright 1966 by Marks Music. "This has been one of the stock phrases used by Johnson and Rusk (Humphrey too, I believe) to justify our war against Vietnam." In: *The Vietnam Songbook*, page 52. c. Barbara Dane and Irwin Silber. Published by The Guardian, No. 32 West 22nd Street, New York, NY. Copyright 1969 by Barbara Dane and Irwin Silber. [7" × 10"]. B/w photo of a protest march. O/y/r/bk cover. 228pp.

215.7 I'm Called Little Caroline. w. Milton M. Schwartz. m. "Tune—*I'm Called Little Buttercup.*" In: *Sing Along With Jack* [Song Book], page 10. Published by Pocket Books, Inc., New York, NY. Copyright 1963 by Bonny Publishing Corporation. [9" × 11⅞"]. R/w/bk drawing of sheet music *Vive La Dynasty*, silhouette of John F. Kennedy in chair with conductor's baton, caricature of Kennedy family. "Hit Songs from the New Frontier." 36pp. Page 3: "Illustrations by David Gantz." Page 36: Drawing of John F. Kennedy in chair with baton. Song titles. [Crew/JFK-17].

• **AmPM-215A** STEPHENS, Alexander H. (State House, 1836; State Senate, 1842; U.S. House, 1843–59, 1873–82; Confederate House, 1861–1862; Confederate Vice President, 1861–1865; Governor, 1882–1883) [ALSO SEE: DOC/PSM-JD]

215A.1 The Bonnie Blue Flag. w.m. No composer indicated. m. *Bonny Blue Flag.* Published by H.J. Wehman, P.O. Box 1823, New York, NY. [ca. 1861]. [Approx. 6¼" × 10¼"]. Non-pictorial geometric design border. "The words and Music of this song will be sent to any address, post-paid, on receipt of 40 cents, by H.J. Wehman, P.O. Box 1823, New York City. A Complete Catalogue of Songs sent free to any address." 2pp. Page 2: Blank. [VBL, p. 359].

215A.2 Freeman, Rally! w. No composer indicated. m. "Air—*Rosin The Bow.*" Published by H. De Marsan, Publisher, 54 Chatham Street, New York, NY. [186-]. [Approx. 6" × 9¼"]. H/c litho border of American flags, eagle, soldier, slave. 2pp. Page 2: Blank. [AMC].

215A.3 Georgia Sequi-Centennial March. m. Miss Florence Colding. Published by E.D. Irvine & Co., Music Publishers, Macon, GA. 1883. R/w/b Confederate Stars and Bars background with an arch and a soldier superimposed over the blue field. "Respectfully inscribed to the Memory of Hon. A.H. Stephens, late Governor of Georgia." "Engraved on wood at E.D. Irvine & Bro's Job Office, Macon, Ga." 6pp. Page 6: Advertising.

215A.4 Hoist Up The Flag! w.m. No composer or tune indicated. In: *Grant And Wilson Campaign Songster*, page 31. Published by Frank Eastman, Book and Job Printer, No. 509 Clay Street, San Francisco, CA. [4¼" × 5⅝"]. 1872. Bk/bl geometric design border. 40pp. [Crew/USG-69].

215A.5 Jeff Davis' Last Proclamation To His Council. w. No composer indicated. m. "Air—*The Girl I Left Behind Me.*" No publisher indicated. Penny song sheet. [186-]. Non-pictorial geometric design border. 2pp. Page 2: Blank.

215A.6 Old Shady. w. No composer indicated. m. Notation. In: *Patriotic Song Book For The G.A.R., For The Use Of The G.A.R. In Their Post-Meeting, Reunions, Camp-Fires, Installation Exercises, Fourth Of July Celebrations, And Memorial Service*, page 28. Published by Orwell Blake, Des Moines, IA. 1883. [5 13/16" × 9 1/16"]. R/gd litho of a G.A.R. badge. 116pp.

215A.7 [Our Good Old Uncle Sam Is Sick] (A Campaign Song). w.m. No composer or tune indicated. In: *The Republican Campaign Songster No. #1*, page 30. Published by American Publishing House, No. 60 West Fourth Street, Cincinnati, OH. [1860]. [3¾" × 5¾"]. B/w litho of Abraham Lincoln. 48[?]pp. [M-113]. [Crew/AL-298].

215A.8 Over The Left. w. No composer indicated. m. "Air—*Sweet Kitty Clover.*" No publisher indicated. [186-]. [Approx. 6" × 9"]. B/w litho of a hand holding two crossed American flags and a ribbon inscribed "God and our Native Land," geometric design border. 2pp. Page 2: Blank. [AMC].

215A.9 Southern Song. w. No composer indicated. m. "Air—*Wait For The Wagon.*" In: *War Songs Of The Blue And The Gray*, page 59. Published by Hurst & Co., Publishers, New York, NY. [ca. 1880]. [4⅜" × 6½"]. Bl/k lithos of "Grant," "Robert E. Lee," "Johnston," and "Sherman," 72pp. [Crew/USG-299].

215A.10 The Southern Wagon. w.m. No composer or tune indicated. No publisher indicated. [ca. 1861]. [Approx. 5" × 7¾"]. Litho geometric design border. 2pp. Page 2: Blank. [WFU].

215A.11 Traitors March To The White House. w. Albert F. Dawson. m. "Air—*Irishman's Shanty.*" Published by J. Wrigley, No. 27 Chatham Street, New York, NY. [1861–1865]. R/w/b litho border of stars and stripes. "J. Wrigley, Publisher of Songs, Ballad's [sic], and Toy Books, Conversation, Age, and Small Playing Cards, Alphabet Wood Blocks, Valentines, Motto Verses, and Cut Paper &c., No. 27 Chatham Street. (Opposite City Hall Park) New York." 2pp. Page 2: Blank. [AMC].

215A.12 12th Regiment New-York State Militia. w. Archibald Scott. m. "Air—*Viva La.*" Published by H. De Marsan, Publisher, Songs, Ballads, Toy Books, 60 Chatham Street, New York, NY. [ca. 1861]. [5½" × 9"]. B/w litho border of columns, two soldiers, eagles with harp and shield, lyre. 2pp. Page 2: Blank. [AMC].

• **AmPM-216 TOOMBS**, Robert Augustus (State House 1837–1843; U.S. House, 1841–1843; 1845–1853; U.S. Senate, 1853–1861; Confederate Provisional Congress, 1861–1862; Confederate Secretary of State, 1861)

216.1 All Come To Smash! O Boo-Hoo! w. W.A. Croffut. m. L. Lafayette Sykes. Notation. "Dedicated to Robert Toombs, who desires his name ever to stand as a traitor." In: *My Country 'Tis Of Thee Sweet Land Of Liberty Of Thee I Sing (Republican Campaign Song Book 1880)*, page 22. c. L. Fayette Sykes. Published by The Republican Central Campaign Club of New York, Headquarters, Coleman House, No. 1169 Broadway, New York, NY. 1880. [5 13/16" × 9⅛"]. Gn/bk non-pictorial geometric designs. "For President Gen'l. James A. Garfield of Ohio, For Vice-President Gen'l. Chester A. Arthur of New York." 52pp. [M-211, 212]. [Crew/JAG-41].

216.2 Democratic Reform. w. No composer indicated. m. "Tune—*Taffy Was A Welshman.*" In: *Campaign Songs*, page 2. w. Sam Booth. [1876]. [6" × 9⅜"]. Non-pictorial. "Supplement to *Hayes And Wheeler Songster.*" 4pp. [Verses for local Congressional candidates also, including Horace Davis, Frank Page, Joseph McKenna, Romualdo Pacheco and Dave Kentfield]. [Crew/RBH-56].

216.3 [Free Soil We Claim For Freedom's Sons] (A New Song to an Old Tune). w. No composer indicated. m. "Air—*Yankee Doodle.*" In: *The Republican Campaign Songster, A Collection Of Lyrics, Original And Selected, Specifically Prepared For The Friends Of Freedom In The Campaign Of Fifty-Six*, page 60. Published by Miller, Orton & Mulligan, No. 25 Park Row, New York, NY. 1856. [3 13/16" × 6"]. Be/bk litho of "Colonel John C. Fremont" facing to viewer's left, black line border. 112pp. [M-097]. [Crew/JCF-24].

216.4 The Friends Of Old Buchan. w. No composer indicated. m. No composer indicated. In: *The Fremont Songster*, page 6. Published by [V-1: H.S. Riggs & Company, Publishers, No. 4 Cortland Street] [V-2: P.J. Cozans, No. 107 Nassau Street], New York, NY. 1856. [V-1: 3⅝" × 5¾"] [V-2: 3½" × 5⅝"]. Be/bk litho of wreath, John C. Fremont. "With a current likeness of John C. Fremont, The People's Candidate for the Presidency." 40pp. [M-094, 095]. [Crew/JCF-45].

216.5 Jeff Davis' Last Proclamation To His Council. w. No composer indicated. m. "Air—*The Girl I Left Behind Me.*" [186-]. Non-pictorial geometric design border. 2pp. Page 2: Blank. [AMC].

216.6 Lines To A Copperhead. w. Enarc. m. No tune indicated. No publisher indicated. [ca. 1863]. Non-pictorial. "An editor in Southern Illinois, in reply to a Union editor who had called him a Copperhead, replied—'Yes, sir, we are a Copperhead, and so are Vallandigham and Dan Voorhees Copperheads, and we and the glory in it! What are you going to do about it?' To them, and like all men, these lines were addressed by a western soldier, while lying wounded in a hospital in Collierville, Tenn." 2pp. Page 2: Blank. [AMC].

216.7 Overtures From Richmond. w. Francis J. Child. m. "*Liliburloro* by Henry Purcell, c. 1686." In: *No More Booze! And After Ribtickling, Knee Stomping, Gut Busting, High Stepping, Side Splitting, Tow Tapping, Fantastically Funny! Folk Songs For Guitar*, page 54. c.a. Jerry Silverman. Published by G. Shirmer, New York, NY. 1978. Pl/o/bk/w geometric designs. 68pp. [Crew/WM-257].

216.8 Patent Chivalry. w. No composer indicated. m. "Air—*A Highland Lad My Love was Born.*" In: *Fremont Songs For The People (Original And Selected)*, page 39. c. Thomas Drew "(Editor of *The Massachusetts Spy*)." Published by John P. Jewett & Company, Boston, MA. Copyright 1856 by Thomas Drew. [3⅝" × 5½"]. B/w litho of "J.C. Fremont." "The Campaign of 1856." 68pp. [Crew/JCF-18].

216.9 The Toast. w. No composer indicated. m. "Air—*Vive La Companie.*" In: *The Freeman's Glee Book, A Collection Of Songs, Odes, Glees And Ballads With Music, Original And Selected, Harmonized And Arranged For Each. Published Under The Auspices Of The Central Fremont And Dayton Glee Club Of The City Of New York, And Dedicated To All, Who, Cherishing Republican Liberty Consider Freedom Worth A Song*, page 94. Published by Miller, Orton & Mulligan, No. 25 Park Row, New York, NY. [and Auburn,

NY]. 1856. [4¹⁵⁄₁₆" × 6"]. Pk/bk litho of man on mountain peak, music sheets, geometric designs. 112pp. [Crew/JCF-16].

216.10 What Has Caused This Great Commotion. w. No composer indicated. m. No composer indicated. In: *The Fremont Songster*, page 8. Published by [V-1: H.S. Riggs & Company, Publishers, No. 4 Cortland Street] [V-2: P.J. Cozans, No. 107 Nassau Street], New York, NY. 1856. [V-1: 3⅝" × 5¾"] [V-2: 3½" × 5⅝"]. Be/bk litho of wreath, John C. Fremont. "With a current likeness of John C. Fremont, The People's Candidate for the Presidency." 40pp. [M-094, 095]. [Crew/JCF-45].

216.11 When Fremont Is Elected. w. No composer indicated. m. "Air — *Hold Your Horses.*" In: *The Freeman's Glee Book, A Collection Of Songs, Odes, Glees And Ballads With Music, Original And Selected, Harmonized And Arranged For Each. Published Under The Auspices Of The Central Fremont And Dayton Glee Club Of The City Of New York, And Dedicated To All, Who, Cherishing Republican Liberty Consider Freedom Worth A Song*, page 80. Published by Miller, Orton & Mulligan, No. 25 Park Row, New York, NY. [and Auburn, NY]. 1856. [4¹⁵⁄₁₆" × 6"]. Pk/bk litho of man on mountain peak, music sheets, geometric designs. 112pp. [Crew/JCF-16].

216.12 Witches' Scene From MacGreeley (Which is Seen to be a Fact). w.m. No composer or tune indicated. From the "*New York Standard.*" In: *National Republican Grant And Wilson Campaign Song-Book*, page 34. From the *New York Standard*. Published by The Union Republican Congressional Committee, Washington, DC. 1872. [3¹³⁄₁₆" × 8⅝"]. Be/bk litho of Ulysses S. Grant. "We'll Sing a Song for U.S. Grant." 100pp. [M-182]. [Crew/USG-110].

• **AmPM-216A UPSHAW**, William David (U.S. House, 1919–1927; Prohibition Party Candidate for President, 1932)

216A.1 The Outlaw. w.m. J.G. Dailey, "Our most versatile song writer ... Rev. McDonald." Published by J.G. Dailey Music, 4734 Kingsessing Ave., Philadelphia, PA. 1926. 6¼ × 9⅜]. R/w non-pictorial geometric design border. "Dedicated to Hon. Wm. D. Upshaw, Congressman from Georgia." "J.G. Dailey's Songs." 4pp. Page 2: At top of music — "Inscribed to my esteemed friend, Hon. Wm. D. Upshaw, Congressman from Georgia 'The Cyclonic Champion of the Eighteenth Amendment to the Constitution.'" Page 4: Advertising.

• **AmPM-217 WALTON**, George (Secretary, Provincial Congress, 1775; Council of Safety, 1775; State House, 1775; Continental Congress, 1776–1777, 1780, & 1781; Signer, Declaration of Independence, 1776; Governor, 1779 & 1789; Commissioner to Treat with the Indians, 1783; Chief Justice of Georgia, 1783–1789; Board of Commissioners, Augusta, 1784–1785; Judge of the Superior, 1790 & 1799–1804; U.S. Senate, 1795–1796)

217.1 The Declaration Of Independence Of The United States Of North America, July 4, 1776. w. From the Declaration of Independence. m. John E. Wilson. Published by John E. Wilson, Baltimore, MD. 1863. B/w litho of the interior of Independence Hall. "Arranged and adapted for Vocal and Instrumental Music as the Great National Chant." 4pp. [?]. Page 4: Facsimile signatures of all signers.

217.2 Old Independence Hall. w. A. Fletcher Stayman. m. Francis Weiland. Published by Stayman & Brothers, No. 210 Chesnut Street, Philadelphia, PA. 1855. Non-pictorial. "Respectfully dedicated to the Memory of the Signers of the Declaration of Independence." "Fac Simile of their signatures" including John Adams, Sam Adams, Elbridge Gerry, Thomas Jefferson. 8pp. Pages 2 and 8: Blank. [Crew/MISC-34].

• **AmPM-218 WATSON**, Thomas Edward (State House, 1882–1883; U.S. House, 1891–1893; Candidate for Vice-President, 1896; Candidate for President, 1904; U.S. Senate, 1921–1922)

218.1 Gold And McKinley For Me. w. E.G. Hanford. m. "Air — *Bring Back My Bonnie To Me.*" In: *McKinley & Roosevelt Campaign 1900* [Song Book], page 3. Published for the Wholesale Dry Goods Republican Club, No. 350 Broadway by C.G. Burgoyne, New York, NY. 1900. [4¾" × 7"]. Y/bk litho of William McKinley and Theodore Roosevelt, eagle, shield. "Meetings daily from 12 Noon until 2 p.m." "A bird that can sing and won't must be made to sing." 20pp. [M-376]. [Crew/WM-84].

218.2 Other Side Of Jordan. w.m. No composer indicated. m. "Tune — *Other Side Of Jordan.*" In: *Republican Campaign Songs*, page 1. c. J. Burgess Brown. Published for The State Central Committee, Indianapolis, IN. 1896. [5¼" × 7⅜"]. Pk/bk litho of William McKinley and Garret Hobart, eagle, geometric design border. "We love the old Red, White and Blue, That freedom long ago unfurled, We love the glorious Country too, The fairest one in all the World, We love our mines, We love our mills, With fervor that our heart-strings thrills, therefore, 'Tis taken by consent McKinley for Our President." "Up to date." "Second Edition." 24pp. [M-322]. [Crew/WM-134].

218.3 The Second Battle. w.m. J.A. Parks. In: *Park's Republican Campaign Songs (For Male Voices)*, page 28. e. James Asher Parks. Published by The J.A. Parks Company, York, NE. 1900. Gn/bk non-pictorial. "Respectfully inscribed to Gen. Chas. F. Manderson." 40pp. [M-371]. [Crew/WM-106].

218.4 Tom Watson Of Georgia. w. E.J. Seymour. m. "Air — *Marching Through Georgia.*" In: *Harrison And Reid Campaign Song Book*, page 11. w. E.J. Seymour. m. Popular Airs. [1892]. [3⅞" × 5⅛"]. Bl/gn non-pictorial, stars, geometric designs. 36pp. [M-316]. [Crew/BFH-35].

218.5 We'll All Be Happy Them. w.m. J.A. Parks. m. Notation. In: *Park's Republican Campaign Songs (For Male Voices)*, page 16. e. James Asher Parks. Published by The J.A. Parks Company, York, NE. 1900. Gn/bk non-pictorial. "Respectfully inscribed to Gen. Chas. F. Manderson." 40pp. [M-371]. [Crew/WM-106].

218.6 The White House Gate (Solo and Chorus). w.m. Logan S. Porter. In: *Roosevelt Campaign Songster 1904 (For Male Voices)*, page 26. c. Logan S. Porter. Published by The Home Music Company, Logansport, IN. 1904. [6" × 9"]. Be/bk photos of Theodore Roosevelt and Charles Fairbanks. Be/bk drawing of a star, geometric designs. "Single Copy 15 cts — $1.60 per Dozen." 36pp. [M-391]. [Crew/TR-356].

WAYNE, Anthony (U.S. House, Georgia, 1791–1792) [See: Pennsylvania]

- **AmPM-219 WILDE**, Richard Henry (Solicitor General/State Attorney General, Richmond County, 1811–1813; U.S. House, 1815–1817, 1925 & 1827–1835)
219.1 My Life Is Like The Summer Rose. w. "The Honble. Rd. Wilde of Georgia." m. John Bianchi Taylor, Esqr., "protégé of Mr. Incledon." Published by G.E. Blake, No. 13 South 5th Street, Philadelphia, PA. [1818?]. Non-pictorial. "Blake's Musical Miscellany." "The music Composed and Inscribed to Miss Catherine Potter." 4pp. Page 4: Blank. [W-9223].

- **AmPM-219A WRIGHT**, James (South Carolina Attorney General, 1747–1757; South Carolina Chief Justice & Lt. Governor, 1760–1764; Royal Governor of Georgia, 1764–1782)
219A.1 Ethiopian Quadrilles. a. A. Nagerj Onyqjva. Published by Firth & Hall, Broadway, New York, NY. 1843. B/w litho vignettes of African-American scenes: Playing banjo, dancing, fighting and riding an alligator, plantation life with a building labeled "J. Wright." "Virginia Minstrels."

- **AmPM-220 MISCELLANEOUS MUSIC**
220.1 The Georgia Waltz. w.m. Remus Harris and Irving Melsher. Published by Mills Music, Inc., Music Publishers, 1619 Broadway, New York, NY. 1939. Bl/w/br litho of sun, rays, clouds behind a facsimile of a Resolution, adopting "*The Georgia Waltz* as the official Waltz of the State of Georgia." Resolution signed by the president of the Georgia Senate. 6pp. Pages 2 and 6: Advertising. Page 3: At top of music — "The Official Song for the Dance Sensation The Georgia Waltz, Dance Created by Georgia Dancing Master' Association."

HAWAII

- **AmPM-220A BLAIR**, Russell (State House, 1980s; State Senate, 1990?–2000?; Executive Director, State Office of Consumer Protection, 1995?; District Court Judge, 2000?)
220A.1 Man Of Campaign Sorrow. w. John S. Pritchett. m. "Sung to the tune of *Man Of Constant Sorrow* from the album of the year *O Brother Where Art Thou.*" Lyrics published online at <htttp://www.pritchettcartoons.com/sorrow.htm>. [ca. 200-].

- **AmPM-221 BURNS**, John A. (Traffic Safety Commission, Honolulu, 1950–1954; U.S. House Territorial Delegate, 1957–1959; Governor, 1962–1974)
221.1 Hawaii Is Calling. w.m. E.Z. Martin. Published by Dr. E.Z. Martin, New Holland, PA. 17557. 1968. N/c photo of Hawaiian woman in hula skirt. "Dedicated to John A. Burns, Governor of Hawaii." "Photo courtesy of Visitors Bureau Hawaiian State Department." "Hawaii's Motto: The Life of the land is perpetuated in righteousness." 4pp. Page 4: Facsimile of a letter from Governor Burns to E.Z. Martin.

- **AmPM-222 DOLE**, Sanford B. (President, Republic of Hawaii, 1894–1900; Territorial Governor, 1900–1903; U.S. District Court Judge, 1903–1915)
222.1 March: Republic Of Hawaii. m. H. Berger. Published by Hawaiian News Co. 1896. B/w litho by Schmidt Lith. Co., San Francisco, of Sanford B. Dole, Hawaiian flags, palms. "Respectfully dedicated to Sanford B. Dole, First President of the Republic of Hawaii." 4pp. Page 4: Blank.

- **AmPM-223 FARRINGTON**, Wallace Rider (Governor, 1921–1929)
223.1 That's What The Lei Said To Me. w.m. Alfred Perez. Published by Alfred Perez, 836–11th Avenue, Honolulu, HI. 1927. R/w photo of a Hawaiian woman with lei. 6pp. Page 2: "Re-Dedicated to the Late Governor Wallace Rider Farrington and to all other lei lovers of the world." Page 6: Advertising.

- **AmPM-223A FASI**, Frank F. (Candidate for State House, 1950; State Senate, 1958–1959; Candidate for U.S. Senate, 1959; Mayor, Honolulu, 1969–1981 & 1985–1994)
223A.1 The Ballad Of Jeremy Harris. w. John S. Pritchett. m. "Sung to the tune of *Davy Crockett.*" Lyrics published online at <htttp://www.pritchettcartoons.com/ballad.htm>. [ca. 200-].

- **AmPM-223B GRUALTY**, Reynaldo (State Senate, 1993–1997; State Insurance Commissioner, 1997–2000; Circuit Court Judge, 2000–?)
223B.1 The Ballad Of Jeremy Harris. w. John S. Pritchett. m. "Sung to the tune of *Davy Crockett.*" Lyrics published online at <htttp://www.pritchettcartoons.com/ballad.htm>. [ca. 200-].

- **AmPM-223C HARRIS**, Jeremy (Delegate, Hawaii Constitutional Convention, 1978; Kauai County Council, 1979–1983?; Mayor, Honolulu, 1994–Present)
223C.1 The Ballad Of Jeremy Harris. w. John S. Pritchett. m. "Sung to the tune of *Davy Crockett.*" Lyrics published online at <htttp://www.pritchettcartoons.com/ballad.htm>. [ca. 200-].
223C.2 Man Of Campaign Sorrow. w. John S. Pritchett. m. "Sung to the tune of *Man Of Constant Sorrow* from the album of the year *O Brother Where Art Thou.*" Lyrics published online at <htttp://www.pritchettcartoons.com/sorrow.htm>. [ca. 200-].

- **AmPM-223D INOUYE**, Daniel Ken (Territorial House, 1954–1958; Territorial Senate, 1958–1959; U.S. House, 1959–1963; U.S. Senate, 1993–Present)
223D.1 Man Of Campaign Sorrow. w. John S. Pritchett. m. "Sung to the tune of *Man Of Constant Sorrow* from the album of the year *O Brother Where Art Thou.*" Lyrics published online at <htttp://www.pritchettcartoons.com/sorrow.htm>. [ca. 200-].

- **AmPM-224 KALAKAUA** (King, Hawaii, 1874–1891)

224.1 Hawaii Ponoi. w. King Kalakaua. m. H. Berger. Published by J.H. Soper, Honolulu, HI. Copyright 1884 and 1888 by H. Berger. B/w litho by Schmidt Label & Litho Co., San Francisco, Cal., of Diamond Head, palm trees. "Mele Hawaii." List of other titles in the series. 4pp. Page 4: Blank.

224.2 Kalakaua March. m. Louis Bodecker. Published by M. Gray, San Francisco, CA. 1874. B/W sepia toned photo of King Kalakaua. R/w geometric designs. "The Photograph is respectfully dedicated to His Majesty by Bradley & Rulofson." 6pp. Page 2: Blank.

- **AmPM-225 LILIUOKALANI** (Queen, Hawaii, 1891–1893)

225.1 Aloha Oe (Farewell To Thee). w.m. H.M. Queen Liliuokalani. a. Arthur Lange. Published by the Popular Music Pub. Co., Philadelphia, PA. 1913. Gn/w litho of palm trees, ocean. 6pp. Pages 2 and 6: Advertising.

225.2 Aloha Oe (Farewell To Thee). w. [English] J. Will Callahan. w.m. Queen Liliuokalani. e. Henry S. Sawyer. Published by McKinley Music Co., Chicago, IL. 1916. R/w/bk litho of palm trees, ocean, sun. 6pp. Pages 2 and 6: Advertising.

225.3 Cuckoo! Cuckoo! All Sing Cuckoo! (Republican Campaign Song) (Song and Chorus). w. C. Sharp, Junior. m. B. Flat, Senior. Published by Emil Wulschner & Son, Indianapolis, IN. 1894. Gn/ma/w cartoon drawings of rooster speaking sayings including "1893–4, Cuckoo Over There!," "1893–4, Yes Sir, Cuckoo, Cuckoo, Cuckoo," "Nov. 1894, I Didn't Cuckoo," and "1897, I C-C-Cant Ck-Ck-Cuckoo, I'm D-D-Dead," Uncle Sam saying "Now You Just Get Out Of Here." "To the Indianapolis Bald-Headed Glee Club." 6pp. Includes solo arrangement and arrangement for Male choruses. Page 6: Narrative on the origin of "Cuckoo." [Crew/WM-322].

225.4 The Democrat Congress. w. No composer indicated. m. "Tune—*Old Oaken Bucket.*" In: *New People's Party Songster*, page 14. e. Theodore Parish Stelle. Published in Mt. Vernon, IL. [ca. 1894]. 32pp. [M-361]. [Crew/WJB-62].

225.5 Lilikaloo. w. John Wilson. "The ex-Queen Liliuokalani was so unwise as to embarrass President Cleveland in his efforts in her behalf by amiably wishing that power were hers to cut off the heads of certain refractory subjects who are directing the present Hawaiian Government recognized by the United States. She is a foolish woman who simply threw her crown away." In: *National Campaigner (Marching Songs Republican Clubs)* [Song Book], page 10. Published by Dudley T. Limerick & Company, No. 4031 Locust Street, Philadelphia, PA. 1896. [6⅜" × 9¾"]. Non-pictorial. "The slogan: McKinley is Coming! O! ho! O! ho!" List of contents Long narrative on marching songs. 24pp. [M-336]. [Crew/WM-271].

225.6 Liliuokalani's Prayer And Serenade. w.m. Liliuokalani. Published by John H. Wilson, Honolulu, HI. 1895. B/w photos of "Liliuokalani" and "Victoria Kaulani." R/w/b litho of the seal of Hawaii, crown, bibles, geometric designs. "Composed by Her Majesty during her imprisonment by the Republican Govt. of Hawaii." "Sung with great success by the Royal Hawaiian Glee Club on its tour of the World." 6pp. Page 2: Song—*Aloha Oe* (Song and Chorus) {225.6-1}. Page 5: Song—*Liliuoklani's Prayer* (He Aloha o ka Haku). (The Lord's Mercy) {225.6-2}. "Lovingly Dedicated to her niece Victoria Kalulani." Page 6: Blank.

225.6A Queen Liliuokalani March And Songs. w. E.K. Defries. m. J.S. Libornio. Published by Chas. Scharf & Co., Music Publishers, Arlington Hotel Block, Honolulu, HI. and Broder & Schlam, 26, 28 & 30 O'Farrell St., San Francisco, CA. 1894. Bl/w photo of Queen Liliuokalani, facsimile autograph. B/w geometric designs. 6pp.

225.7 That's What's Worrying. w. J.W. Matthews. m. "Tune—*We Won't Go Home Till Morning.*" "For Male Voices." In: *True Blue Republican Campaign Songs For 1896*, page 18. c. J.B. Herbert. Published by The S. Brainard's Sons Company, Chicago, IL. 1896. [5⅜" × 6⅞"]. R/w/b drawing of crossed flags, wreath, ribbons. Bl/w photo of "Hon. Wm. McKinley." "Protection." 36pp. [M-328]. [Crew/WM-169].

IDAHO

- **AmPM-226 ALEXANDER**, Moses (Mayor, Chillicothe, 1888; Mayor, Boise, 1897–1899 & 1901–1903; Governor, 1915–1919)

226.1 America My Country (The New National Anthem). w. Jens K. Grondahl. m. E.F. Maetzold. Published by The Red Wing Printing Co., Red Wing, MN. 1917. R/w/b litho of a shield, geometric designs. "Long paragraph on the song—*America, My Country* is said to be the greatest patriotic song-poem of the war ..." 4pp. Page 4: Testimonial signed by officers of the National Editorial Association. List of Governors who had "written letters commending the nation-wide use of this song" including "Gov. Alexander of Idaho."

- **AmPM-227 BORAH**, William Edgar (U.S. Senate 1907–1940)

227.1 Keep 'Em Pure. w. No composer indicated. m. "Air—*If I Had Rhythm In My Nursery Rhymes.*" In: *Tory, Tory Hallelujah*, page 9. Published by Albany Legislative Correspondents' Association, Albany, NY. 1936. [8" × 11¾"]. N/c drawing of Franklin D. Roosevelt, other politicians dressed as Revolutionary soldiers in battle scene—"A Dashing Delirious Drama, Lampooning Loyalists and Liberty Leaguers, Daggering Despots, Dictators and Dummy Donkey-Drivers to music by Red-Coats and Lyrics by Turn-Coats, the Combat Being Played Against a Spangled Back-Drop."

"Furiously Fought at Ten Eyck Hotel, Albany, New York, The Evening of Thursday, March 12, 1936, at Seven-Thirty o'clock." [Crew/FDR-325].

227.2 *[They May Put Jim Over And In]*. w. No composer indicated. m. "Tune—*Good Night, Little Girl, Good Night.*" In: *Gridiron Nights*, page 319. Published by Frederick A. Stokes Company, Publishers, New York, New York. Copyright 1915 by Arthur Wallace Dunn. [7½" × 10½"]. B/gd imprinting of comedy mask, lamps, floral designs. 406pp.

227.3 *Welcome Song To Huey Long*. (Our U.S. Senator). w.m. Tom McNelly. a. Joseph Garrow. Published by Tom McNelly, Music Publishers, New Orleans, LA. 1931. Photo of Huey Long. Drawings of the "Louisiana State Capitol" building and the "U.S. Capitol" building, geometric designs. 8pp. Page 8: Blank.

• **AmPM-228   CAMPBELL**, Arthur (Candidate for State Mine Inspector, 1936)

228.1 *We Are New Deal Democratic* (A Campaign March Song). w. E.T. Cooke. m. Bert Sams. Published and Distributed by The Young Men's and Women's Democratic Club of Shoshone County, [ID]. [1936]. [8¼" × 13½"]. Non-pictorial. "Published and Distributed by The Young Men's and Women's Democratic Club of Shoshone County who endorse the following Nominees for Public Service." Slate of candidates for Idaho "State Officers" and "County Officers." 8pp. Pages 2, 7 and 8: Local advertising. Page 3: B/w drawing of "Franklin D. Roosevelt." Page 6: Blank. [Crew/FDR-337].

• **AmPM-229   CONDIE**, John W. (Candidate for State Superintendent of Public Instruction, 1936)

229.1 *We Are New Deal Democratic* (A Campaign March Song). w. E.T. Cooke. m. Bert Sams. Published and Distributed by The Young Men's and Women's Democratic Club of Shoshone County, [ID]. [1936]. [8¼" × 13½"]. Non-pictorial. "Published and Distributed by The Young Men's and Women's Democratic Club of Shoshone County who endorse the following Nominees for Public Service." Slate of candidates for Idaho "State Officers" and "County Officers." 8pp. Pages 2, 7 and 8: Local advertising. Page 3: B/w drawing of "Franklin D. Roosevelt." Page 6: Blank. [Crew/FDR-337].

• **AmPM-230   EGBERT**, A.C. (Candidate for County Assessor, Shoshone County, 1936)

230.1 *We Are New Deal Democratic* (A Campaign March Song). w. E.T. Cooke. m. Bert Sams. Published and Distributed by The Young Men's and Women's Democratic Club of Shoshone County, [ID]. [1936]. [8¼" × 13½"]. Non-pictorial. "Published and Distributed by The Young Men's and Women's Democratic Club of Shoshone County who endorse the following Nominees for Public Service." Slate of candidates for Idaho "State Officers" and "County Officers." 8pp. Pages 2, 7 and 8: Local advertising. Page 3: B/w drawing of "Franklin D. Roosevelt." Page 6: Blank. [Crew/FDR-337].

• **AmPM-231   ENKING**, Myrtle P. (Candidate for County Prosecuting Attorney, Shoshone County, 1936)

231.1 *We Are New Deal Democratic* (A Campaign March Song). w. E.T. Cooke. m. Bert Sams. Published and Distributed by The Young Men's and Women's Democratic Club of Shoshone County, [ID]. [1936]. [8¼" × 13½"]. Non-pictorial. "Published and Distributed by The Young Men's and Women's Democratic Club of Shoshone County who endorse the following Nominees for Public Service." Slate of candidates for Idaho "State Officers" and "County Officers." 8pp. Pages 2, 7 and 8: Local advertising. Page 3: B/w drawing of "Franklin D. Roosevelt." Page 6: Blank. [Crew/FDR-337].

• **AmPM-232   FITZGERALD**, John L. (Candidate for County Commission, Shoshone County, 1936)

232.1 *We Are New Deal Democratic* (A Campaign March Song). w. E.T. Cooke. m. Bert Sams. Published and Distributed by The Young Men's and Women's Democratic Club of Shoshone County, [ID]. [1936]. [8¼" × 13½"]. Non-pictorial. "Published and Distributed by The Young Men's and Women's Democratic Club of Shoshone County who endorse the following Nominees for Public Service." Slate of candidates for Idaho "State Officers" and "County Officers." 8pp. Pages 2, 7 and 8: Local advertising. Page 3: B/w drawing of "Franklin D. Roosevelt." Page 6: Blank. [Crew/FDR-337].

• **AmPM-233   FURGUSON**, Natalie (Candidate for County Superintendent of Public Instruction, Shoshone County, 1936)

233.1 *We Are New Deal Democratic* (A Campaign March Song). w. E.T. Cooke. m. Bert Sams. Published and Distributed by The Young Men's and Women's Democratic Club of Shoshone County, [ID]. [1936]. [8¼" × 13½"]. Non-pictorial. "Published and Distributed by The Young Men's and Women's Democratic Club of Shoshone County who endorse the following Nominees for Public Service." Slate of candidates for Idaho "State Officers" and "County Officers." 8pp. Pages 2, 7 and 8: Local advertising. Page 3: B/w drawing of "Franklin D. Roosevelt." Page 6: Blank. [Crew/FDR-337].

• **AmPM-234   GIRARD**, Franklin (Secretary of State, 1933–1938; State Forester, 1938–1943)

234.1 *We Are New Deal Democratic* (A Campaign March Song). w. E.T. Cooke. m. Bert Sams. Published and Distributed by The Young Men's and Women's Democratic Club of Shoshone County, [ID]. [1936]. [8¼" × 13½"]. Non-pictorial. "Published and Distributed by The Young Men's and Women's Democratic Club of Shoshone County who endorse the following Nominees for Public Service." Slate of candidates for Idaho "State Officers" and "County Officers." 8pp. Pages 2, 7 and 8: Local advertising. Page 3: B/w drawing of "Franklin D. Roosevelt." Page 6: Blank. [Crew/FDR-337].

• **AmPM-235   HALLY**, Matt (Candidate for County Surveyor, Shoshone County, 1936)

235.1 *We Are New Deal Democratic* (A Campaign March Song). w. E.T. Cooke. m. Bert Sams. Published and Distributed by The Young Men's and Women's Democratic Club of Shoshone County, [ID]. [1936]. [8¼" × 13½"]. Non-pictorial. "Published and Distributed by The Young Men's and Women's Democratic Club of Shoshone County who endorse the following Nominees for Public Service." Slate of candidates for

Idaho "State Officers" and "County Officers." 8pp. Pages 2, 7 and 8: Local advertising. Page 3: B/w drawing of "Franklin D. Roosevelt." Page 6: Blank. [Crew/FDR-337].

• **AmPM-236** HANSON, William (Candidate for County Commission, Shoshone County, 1936)

236.1 We Are New Deal Democratic (A Campaign March Song). w. E.T. Cooke. m. Bert Sams. Published and Distributed by The Young Men's and Women's Democratic Club of Shoshone County, [ID]. [1936]. [8¼" × 13½"]. Non-pictorial. "Published and Distributed by The Young Men's and Women's Democratic Club of Shoshone County who endorse the following Nominees for Public Service." Slate of candidates for Idaho "State Officers" and "County Officers." 8pp. Pages 2, 7 and 8: Local advertising. Page 3: B/w drawing of "Franklin D. Roosevelt." Page 6: Blank. [Crew/FDR-337].

• **AmPM-237** KELLY, Thomas B. (Candidate for County Probate Judge, Shoshone County, 1936)

237.1 We Are New Deal Democratic (A Campaign March Song). w. E.T. Cooke. m. Bert Sams. Published and Distributed by The Young Men's and Women's Democratic Club of Shoshone County, [ID]. [1936]. [8¼" × 13½"]. Non-pictorial. "Published and Distributed by The Young Men's and Women's Democratic Club of Shoshone County who endorse the following Nominees for Public Service." Slate of candidates for Idaho "State Officers" and "County Officers." 8pp. Pages 2, 7 and 8: Local advertising. Page 3: B/w drawing of "Franklin D. Roosevelt." Page 6: Blank. [Crew/FDR-337].

• **AmPM-238** MILLER, Bert Henry (Candidate for U.S. House, 1914, 1938; State Attorney General, 1932–1936 & 1940–1944)

238.1 We Are New Deal Democratic (A Campaign March Song). w. E.T. Cooke. m. Bert Sams. Published and Distributed by The Young Men's and Women's Democratic Club of Shoshone County, [ID]. [1936]. [8¼" × 13½"]. Non-pictorial. "Published and Distributed by The Young Men's and Women's Democratic Club of Shoshone County who endorse the following Nominees for Public Service." Slate of candidates for Idaho "State Officers" and "County Officers." 8pp. Pages 2, 7 and 8: Local advertising. Page 3: B/w drawing of "Franklin D. Roosevelt." Page 6: Blank. [Crew/FDR-337].

• **AmPM-239** MITSON, Harry (Candidate for District Court Clerk, Shoshone County, 1936)

239.1 We Are New Deal Democratic (A Campaign March Song). w. E.T. Cooke. m. Bert Sams. Published and Distributed by The Young Men's and Women's Democratic Club of Shoshone County, [ID]. [1936]. [8¼" × 13½"]. Non-pictorial. "Published and Distributed by The Young Men's and Women's Democratic Club of Shoshone County who endorse the following Nominees for Public Service." Slate of candidates for Idaho "State Officers" and "County Officers." 8pp. Pages 2, 7 and 8: Local advertising. Page 3: B/w drawing of "Franklin D. Roosevelt." Page 6: Blank. [Crew/FDR-337].

• **AmPM-240** MIX, Gainford P. (Lt. Governor, 1931–1933 & 1935–1937)

240.1 We Are New Deal Democratic (A Campaign March Song). w. E.T. Cooke. m. Bert Sams. Published and Distributed by The Young Men's and Women's Democratic Club of Shoshone County, [ID]. [1936]. [8¼" × 13½"]. Non-pictorial. "Published and Distributed by The Young Men's and Women's Democratic Club of Shoshone County who endorse the following Nominees for Public Service." Slate of candidates for Idaho "State Officers" and "County Officers." 8pp. Pages 2, 7 and 8: Local advertising. Page 3: B/w drawing of "Franklin D. Roosevelt." Page 6: Blank. [Crew/FDR-337].

• **AmPM-241** MURPHY, Dan (Candidate for County Commission, Shoshone County, 1936)

241.1 We Are New Deal Democratic (A Campaign March Song). w. E.T. Cooke. m. Bert Sams. Published and Distributed by The Young Men's and Women's Democratic Club of Shoshone County, [ID]. [1936]. [8¼" × 13½"]. Non-pictorial. "Published and Distributed by The Young Men's and Women's Democratic Club of Shoshone County who endorse the following Nominees for Public Service." Slate of candidates for Idaho "State Officers" and "County Officers." 8pp. Pages 2, 7 and 8: Local advertising. Page 3: B/w drawing of "Franklin D. Roosevelt." Page 6: Blank. [Crew/FDR-337].

• **AmPM-242** PARSONS, Henry C. (Candidate for State Auditor, 1936)

242.1 We Are New Deal Democratic (A Campaign March Song). w. E.T. Cooke. m. Bert Sams. Published and Distributed by The Young Men's and Women's Democratic Club of Shoshone County, [ID]. [1936]. [8¼" × 13½"]. Non-pictorial. "Published and Distributed by The Young Men's and Women's Democratic Club of Shoshone County who endorse the following Nominees for Public Service." Slate of candidates for Idaho "State Officers" and "County Officers." 8pp. Pages 2, 7 and 8: Local advertising. Page 3: B/w drawing of "Franklin D. Roosevelt." Page 6: Blank. [Crew/FDR-337].

• **AmPM-243** POPE, James Pinckney (Board of Education, Boise, 1924–1929; Mayor, Boise, 1929–1933; U.S. Senate, 1933–1939)

243.1 Over Here. w. "A Descendent of New England Pioneers, 1634." m. "A World War Veteran." Published by Patriotic Songs Publications, No. 351 West 52nd Street, New York, NY. 1935. Bl/w drawing of Statue of Liberty, man on hill. "Dedicated To Youth In This World Crisis." 4pp. Page 4: List of crises — "Italy and Ethiopia, League of Nations," "Roosevelt and Red Peril," "Kemal, Dictator of Turkey," "Senator Pope and Anti-Neutrality." "Attention, Immediately write or wire the President, Washington, D.C., Urge America's entrance into the League of Nations." [Crew/FDR-203].

• **AmPM-244** ROSS, C. Ben (County Commission, Canyon County, 1915–1921; Mayor, Pocatello, 1921–1930; Governor, 1931–1937; Candidate for U.S. Senate, 1936)

244.1 We Are New Deal Democratic (A Campaign March Song). w. E.T. Cooke. m. Bert Sams. Published and Distributed by The Young Men's and Women's Democratic Club of Shoshone County, [ID]. [1936]. [8¼" × 13½"]. Non-pictorial. "Published and Distributed by The Young Men's and Women's Democratic

Club of Shoshone County who endorse the following Nominees for Public Service." Slate of candidates for Idaho "State Officers" and "County Officers." 8pp. Pages 2, 7 and 8: Local advertising. Page 3: B/w drawing of "Franklin D. Roosevelt." Page 6: Blank. [Crew/FDR-337].

• **AmPM-245** RYAN, Philip (Candidate for State Senator, 1936)
245.1 We Are New Deal Democratic (A Campaign March Song). w. E.T. Cooke. m. Bert Sams. Published and Distributed by The Young Men's and Women's Democratic Club of Shoshone County, [ID]. [1936]. [8¼" × 13½"]. Non-pictorial. "Published and Distributed by The Young Men's and Women's Democratic Club of Shoshone County who endorse the following Nominees for Public Service." Slate of candidates for Idaho "State Officers" and "County Officers." 8pp. Pages 2, 7 and 8: Local advertising. Page 3: B/w drawing of "Franklin D. Roosevelt." Page 6: Blank. [Crew/FDR-337].

• **AmPM-246** RYAN, Thomas (Candidate for County Treasurer, Shoshone County, 1936)
246.1 We Are New Deal Democratic (A Campaign March Song). w. E.T. Cooke. m. Bert Sams. Published and Distributed by The Young Men's and Women's Democratic Club of Shoshone County, [ID]. [1936]. [8¼" × 13½"]. Non-pictorial. "Published and Distributed by The Young Men's and Women's Democratic Club of Shoshone County who endorse the following Nominees for Public Service." Slate of candidates for Idaho "State Officers" and "County Officers." 8pp. Pages 2, 7 and 8: Local advertising. Page 3: B/w drawing of "Franklin D. Roosevelt." Page 6: Blank. [Crew/FDR-337].

• **AmPM-246A** SMYLIE, Robert E. (Governor, 1955–1967)
246A.1 We Sing Of Idaho (Centennial March). w.m. Merrill D. Tonning. Published by Treasure Valley Songs, 1129 Denver Street, Bosie, ID. 1961. Br/w photo of Idaho mountain scene. "Distributed by State Department of Education." "An Idaho Souvenir." "Designated as the Official Idaho Centennial March by Governor Robert E. Smylie." 4pp. + band parts.

• **AmPM-247** STARK, Kirby (Candidate for County Commission, Shoshone County, 1936)
247.1 We Are New Deal Democratic (A Campaign March Song). w. E.T. Cooke. m. Bert Sams. Published and Distributed by The Young Men's and Women's Democratic Club of Shoshone County, [ID]. [1936]. [8¼" × 13½"]. Non-pictorial. "Published and Distributed by The Young Men's and Women's Democratic Club of Shoshone County who endorse the following Nominees for Public Service." Slate of candidates for Idaho "State Officers" and "County Officers." 8pp. Pages 2, 7 and 8: Local advertising. Page 3: B/w drawing of "Franklin D. Roosevelt." Page 6: Blank. Page 7: B/w photo and advertising for Kirby Stark for Sheriff. [Crew/FDR-337].

• **AmPM-248** TAYLOR, Glen Hearst (U.S. Senate, 1945–1951; Candidate for Vice President, 1948) [ASLO SEE: DOC/PSM-HAW]
248.1 I've Got A Ballot. w. E.Y. Harburg. m. "Tune—*I've Got A Six-Pence*." [1948]. Original not located. Lyric sheet published in *Election Songs Of The United States*. Sung by Oscar Brand; Accompanied on Guitar and Banjo by Billy Faier; Notes by Irwin Silber. 33⅓ rpm LP. Produced by Folkways Records FH 5280. Scholastic Records, Englewood Cliffs, NJ. 1963.
248.2 Vote For Henry Wallace. w.m. Carl Leon Eddy. Published by House of Carleon, No. 2439 Park Avenue, Indianapolis 5, IN. 1948. Bl/w photos of "Henry Wallace" and "Senator Glen Taylor." O/bl/w geometric designs. "The House of Carleon, Publishers of Songs You'll Always Love." 4pp.

• **AmPM-249** THORNBURG, L.H. (Candidate for State House, 1936)
249.1 We Are New Deal Democratic (A Campaign March Song). w. E.T. Cooke. m. Bert Sams. Published and Distributed by The Young Men's and Women's Democratic Club of Shoshone County, [ID]. [1936]. [8¼" × 13½"]. Non-pictorial. "Published and Distributed by The Young Men's and Women's Democratic Club of Shoshone County who endorse the following Nominees for Public Service." Slate of candidates for Idaho "State Officers" and "County Officers." 8pp. Pages 2, 7 and 8: Local advertising. Page 3: B/w drawing of "Franklin D. Roosevelt." Page 6: Blank. [Crew/FDR-337].

• **AmPM-250** TURK, Joe (Candidate for State House, 1936)
250.1 We Are New Deal Democratic (A Campaign March Song). w. E.T. Cooke. m. Bert Sams. Published and Distributed by The Young Men's and Women's Democratic Club of Shoshone County, [ID]. [1936]. [8¼" × 13½"]. Non-pictorial. "Published and Distributed by The Young Men's and Women's Democratic Club of Shoshone County who endorse the following Nominees for Public Service." Slate of candidates for Idaho "State Officers" and "County Officers." 8pp. Pages 2, 7 and 8: Local advertising. Page 3: B/w drawing of "Franklin D. Roosevelt." Page 6: Blank. [Crew/FDR-337].

• **AmPM-251** WELKER, Herman (Prosecuting Attorney, Moscow, 1929–1935; State Senate, 1948–1950; U.S. Senate, 1951–1957)
251.1 Nobody's For McCarthy (But The People). In: *Rally For McCarthy*, page 4. Published by The Joint Committee Against Communism. 1954. [5½" × 8¾"]. Non-pictorial geometric frame. "Rally For McCarthy and Against Present Congressional Committees, Constitution Hall, Washington, D.C., Thursday, November 11, 1954, at 8:00 P.M." 4pp. Page 3: Program. Speakers include "Hon. Herman Welker, U.S. Senator, Idaho."

• **AmPM-252** WHITE, Compton Ignatius, Jr. (School Board and Clark Fork Board of Trustees, 1947–1950; Mayor, Clark Fork, 1958–1962; U.S. House, 1963–1967)
252.1 We Are New Deal Democratic (A Campaign March Song). w. E.T. Cooke. m. Bert Sams. Published and Distributed by The Young Men's and Women's Democratic Club of Shoshone County, [ID]. [1936]. [8¼" × 13½"]. Non-pictorial. "Published and Distributed by The Young Men's and Women's Democratic Club of Shoshone County who endorse the following Nominees for Public Service." Slate of candidates for Idaho "State Officers" and "County Officers." 8pp. Pages 2, 7 and 8: Local advertising. Page 3: B/w draw-

ing of "Franklin D. Roosevelt." Page 6: Blank. [Crew/FDR-337].
- **AmPM-253 WILKERSON, A.E.** (Candidate for County Coroner, Shoshone County, 1936)
253.1 We Are New Deal Democratic (A Campaign March Song). w. E.T. Cooke. m. Bert Sams. Published and Distributed by The Young Men's and Women's Democratic Club of Shoshone County, [ID]. [1936]. [8¼" × 13½"]. Non-pictorial. "Published and Distributed by The Young Men's and Women's Democratic Club of Shoshone County who endorse the following Nominees for Public Service." Slate of candidates for Idaho "State Officers" and "County Officers." 8pp. Pages 2, 7 and 8: Local advertising. Page 3: B/w drawing of "Franklin D. Roosevelt." Page 6: Blank. [Crew/FDR-337].

ILLINOIS

- **AmPM-254 ALTGELD, John Peter** (District Attorney, Andrew County, Missouri, 1874–1875; Superior Court Judge, Cook County, 1886–1891; Governor, 1893–1897)

254.1 An Auspicious Occasion. w. No composer indicated. m. "Tune—*Odd Fellows' Hall.*" In: *Republican Campaign Parodies And Songs* [Songster], page 13. Published by Betts and Burnett, South Butler, Wayne County, NY. 1896. [7¾" × 5½"]. Be/bk non-pictorial. "McKinley and Hobart." "1896." 28pp. [M-340]. [Crew/WM-67].

254.2 The Banner Ratification Song. w.m. No composer or tune indicated. [1892]. [4⁹⁄₁₆" × 8½"]. Non-pictorial. 2pp. Page 2: Blank. [Crew/GC-119].

254.3 Boy Bryan's Epitaph. w. No composer indicated. m. "Tune—*Upidee.*" In: *Republican Campaign Parodies And Songs* [Songster], page 12. Published by Betts and Burnett, South Butler, Wayne County, NY. 1896. [7¾" × 5½"]. Be/bk non-pictorial. "McKinley and Hobart." "1896." 28pp. [M-340]. [Crew/WM-67].

254.4 Exit Old Party. w. No composer indicated. m. "Tune—*Good-By, My Lover, Good-By.*" In: *Republican Campaign Parodies And Songs* [Songster], page 20. Published by Betts and Burnett, South Butler, Wayne County, NY. 1896. [7¾" × 5½"]. Be/bk non-pictorial. "McKinley and Hobart." "1896." 28pp. [M-340]. [Crew/WM-67].

254.5 Gold And McKinley For Me. w. E.G. Hanford. m. "Air—*Bring Back My Bonnie To Me.*" In: *McKinley & Roosevelt Campaign 1900* [Song Book], page 3. Published for the Wholesale Dry Goods Republican Club, No. 350 Broadway by C.G. Burgoyne, New York, NY. 1900. [4¾" × 7"]. Y/bk litho of William McKinley and Theodore Roosevelt, eagle, shield. "Meetings daily from 12 Noon until 2 p.m." "A bird that can sing and won't must be made to sing." 20pp. [M-376]. [Crew/WM-84].

254.6 Other Side Of Jordan. w. No composer indicated. m. "Tune—*Other Side Of Jordan.*" In: *Republican Campaign Songs*, page 1. c. J. Burgess Brown. Published for The State Central Committee, Indianapolis, IN. 1896. [5¼" × 7⅜"]. Pk/bk litho of William McKinley and Garret Hobart, eagle, geometric design border. "We love the old Red, White and Blue, That freedom long ago unfurled, We love the glorious Country too, The fairest one in all the World, We love our mines, We love our mills, With fervor that our heart-strings thrills, therefore, 'Tis taken by consent McKinley for Our President." "Up to date." "Second Edition." 24pp. [M-322]. [Crew/WM-134].

254.7 Our Governors March (Or Two Step) m. Joseph Gearen. Published by Lyon & Healy, Chicago, IL. 1897. Bk/w/gn/br drawings of all Illinois Governors, Illinois capitol building, farm scene, law books. 6pp. Page 2: Blank. Page 6: Advertising. [Crew/JMP-1].

254.8 Our Governor's March. m. George Stahl. Published by National Music Co., 215–221 Wabash Avenue, Chicago, IL. And Benj. W. Hitchcock, 385 Sixth Avenue, New York, NY. 1893. 6pp. Page 6: Blank. B/w litho of John P. Altgeld. "Respectfully Dedicated to His Excellency John P. Altgeld, Governor of the State of Illinois." "For Piano Forte."

254.9 We've Waited, Billy, Waited Long For You. w. Stephen Laskey. m. "Tune—*I've Waited, Honey, Waited Long For You.*" In: *McKinley & Roosevelt Campaign 1900*, page 16. Published for the Wholesale Dry Goods Republican Club, No. 350 Broadway by C.G. Burgoyne, New York, NY. 1900. [4¾" × 7"]. Y/bk litho of William McKinley and Theodore Roosevelt, eagle, shield. "Meetings daily from 12 Noon until 2 p.m." "A bird that can sing and won't must be made to sing." 20pp. [M-376]. [Crew/WM-84].

254.10 When The Poppies Fade. w.m. J.A. Parks. In: *Park's Republican Campaign Songs (For Male Voices)*, page 10. e. James Asher Parks. Published by The J.A. Parks Company, York, NE. 1900. Gn/bk non-pictorial. "Respectfully inscribed to Gen. Chas. F. Manderson." 40pp. [M-371]. [Crew/WM-106].

254.11 When The Votes Are Counted. w.m. J.A. Parks. In: *Park's Republican Campaign Songs (For Male Voices)*, page 26. e. James Asher Parks. Published by The J.A. Parks Company, York, NE. 1900. Gn/bk non-pictorial. "Respectfully inscribed to Gen. Chas. F. Manderson." 40pp. [M-371]. [Crew/WM-106].

254.12 The White House. w. No composer indicated. m. "Tune—*I'se Gwine Back To Dixie.*" In: *The Rough Rider (Republican Campaign Song Book)*, page 10. c. J. Burgess Brown. Published by J. Burgess Brown, Indianapolis, IN. 1900. [6" × 9"]. Br/bk non-pictorial. "ROUGH ON DemocRATS." 28pp. Page 3:

B/w litho of William McKinley. Page 28: "Republican National Ticket—1900. [Crew/WM-330].

BAKER, Edward Dickinson (State House, Illinois, 1837; State Senate, Illinois, 1840–1844; U.S. House, Illinois, 1845–1847 & 1849–1851; U.S. Senate, Oregon, 1860–1861) [See: Oregon]

• **AmPM-255 BERGER**, Henry A. (Board of County Commissioners, Cook County, 1926?; Candidate Trustee Sanitary District, Chicago, 1928)

255.1 Get Yourself A Nice Brown Derby (And Fall In Line for Al). w.m. Walter Goodwin "(Writer of *Back In The Old Neighborhood*)." 1928. Br/w photos of "Alfred E. Smith," "T.J. Crowe," "James M. Whalen," "Henry A. Berger" and "Ald. Ross A. Woodhull "(To fill vacancy)." 4pp. Page 4: Biographies of "Democratic Nominees for Trustees Sanitary District of Chicago." "For Your Health's Sake." [Crew/AES-26].

• **AmPM-255A BEVERIDGE**, John Lourie (Sheriff, Cook County, 1866; State Senate, 1871; U.S. House, 1871–1873, Lt. Governor, 1872–1873; Governor, 1873–1877; U.S. Sub-Treasurer, Chicago, 1877–1881)

255A.1 Our Governors March (Or Two Step) m. Joseph Gearen. Published by Lyon & Healy, Chicago, IL. 1897. Bk/w/gn/br drawings of all Illinois Governors, Illinois capitol building, farm scene, law books. 6pp. Page 2: Blank. Page 6: Advertising. [Crew/JMP-1].

• **AmPM-256 BISSELL**, William Harrison (State House, 1840–1842; Prosecuting Attorney, St. Clair County, 1844; U.S. House, 1849–1855; Governor, 1857–1860)

256.1 Buena Vista. w.m. No composer or tune indicated. In: *The Patriot's Songster*, page 13. Published by Mumford & Company, Cincinnati, OH. 1862. [3½" × 6"]. Non-pictorial. 48pp.

256.2 Our Governors March (Or Two Step). m. Joseph Gearen. Published by Lyon & Healy, Chicago, IL. 1897. Bk/w/gn/br drawings of all Illinois Governors, Illinois capitol building, farm scene, law books. 6pp. Page 2: Blank. Page 6: Advertising. [Crew/JMP-1].

• **AmPM-257 BOND**, Shadrack (Legislative Council of Indiana Territory, 1805–1808; Delegate to Congress, Illinois, 1812–1813; Receiver of Public Moneys, Kaskaskia, 1814–1818; Governor, 1818 to 1822; Register of the Land Office, Kaskaskia, 1823–1832)

257.1 Our Governors March (Or Two Step) m. Joseph Gearen. Published by Lyon & Healy, Chicago, IL. 1897. Bk/w/gn/br drawings of all Illinois Governors, Illinois capitol building, farm scene, law books. 6pp. Page 2: Blank. Page 6: Advertising. [Crew/JMP-1].

• **AmPM-258 BUSSE**, Fred A. (State Treasurer, 1903–1905; Mayor, Chicago, 1907–1911)

258.1 Triumphal March. m. Julia L. Lange. Published by Teller Publishing Co., 6060 State Street, Chicago, IL. 1907. B/w photo of Mayor F.A. Busse. Bl/w geometric and floral designs. "Respectfully dedicated to Chicago's Mayor F.A. Busse." 6pp. Pages 2 and 6: Blank. Page 3: At top of music: "Dedicated to Fred A. Busse."

• **AmPM-259 CANNON**, Joseph Gurney (State's Attorney, 1861–1868; U.S. House, 1873–1891, 1893–1913 & 1915–1923)

259.1 The North American March. m. Marie Louka "(Composer of *The Rajah March And Two Step* and *A Silent Prayer Reverie*)." Published by H.A. Weymann and Son, 923 Market Street, Philadelphia, PA. 1904. R/e/bk drawings of Joe Cannon and John Williams on the front page of the newspaper The North American. Drawing titled "After-Dinner faces of 'Uncle Joe' Cannon, Speaker of the House and John Williams, Leader of the House Democrats." Four drawings of Indian Chiefs. "Its all here and it's all true." 6pp. Page 6: Advertising.

259.2 Roosevelt's Shadow. w. No composer indicated. m. "Music—*When The Flowers Bloom In The Spring Time*." In: *Bryan Electors (Pithy Pointers For The Campaign Of 1908)* [Song Book], page 7. Published by Holt County Democrat, O'Neill, NB. 1908. [6$\frac{5}{16}$" × 8⅛"]. Gn/bk/r drawing of "William Jennings Bryan—Our Next President." 16pp. [Crew/WJB-100].

259.3 Tammany. w. No composer indicated. m. No tune indicated. In: *The Red Book, Containing Portraits And Biographies Of Some Persons More Or Less Prominent Public Life Written Entirely Without Respect To The Libel Laws, In A Studious Effort To Conceal Everything But The Truth; Some Songs Built Upon The Same Principle, And Other Important (?) Material Entirely Unfit To Print*, page 17. Published by Legislative Correspondents' Association of the State of New York, Albany, NY. 1913. [5" × 7¼"]. R/w/bk hardback book with drawing of State House, seal of New York, geometric designs. 90pp.

259.4 Teddy's Boy Billy. w. No composer indicated. m. "Tune—*Waltz Me Around Again Willie*." In: *Bryan Electors (Pithy Pointers For The Campaign Of 1908)*, page 4. Published by Holt County Democrat, O'Neill, NB. 1908. [6$\frac{5}{16}$" × 8⅛"]. Gn/bk/r drawing of "William Jennings Bryan—Our Next President." 16pp. [Crew/WJB-100].

259.5 [Though I Am Up In The Speaker's Chair, I'm Lonely]. w.m. No composer or tune indicated. In: *Gridiron Nights*, page 141. Published by Frederick A. Stokes Company, Publishers, New York, NY. Copyright 1915 by Arthur Wallace Dunn. [7½" × 10½"]. B/gd imprinting of comedy mask, lamps, floral designs. 406pp.

259.6 When Bryan Is At The Wheel. w. No composer indicated. m. "Music—*Why Don't You Try*." In: *Bryan Electors (Pithy Pointers For The Campaign Of 1908)* [Song Book], page 5. Published by Holt County Democrat, O'Neill, NB. 1908. [6$\frac{5}{16}$" × 8⅛"]. Gn/bk/r drawing of "William Jennings Bryan—Our Next President." 16pp. [Crew/WJB-100].

259.7 The White House Gate. w.m. Logan S. Porter. In: *Parker Campaign Songster, 1904*, page 26. e. Logan S. Porter. Published by The Home Music Company, Logansport, IN. 1904. [6" × 9"]. O/bk litho of Alton Parker and Henry Gassaway Davis. 36pp. [M-394]. [Crew/ABP-7]

• **AmPM-260 CARLIN**, Thomas (Sheriff, Greene County, 1821; State Senate, 1824–1828; Receiver of Public Monies, Quincy, 1834–1838; Governor, 1838–1842; State House, 1849)

260.1 Our Governors March (Or Two Step) m. Joseph Gearen. Published by Lyon & Healy, Chicago, IL. 1897. Bk/w/gn/br drawings of all Illinois Governors, Illinois capitol building, farm scene, law books. 6pp. Page 2: Blank. Page 6: Advertising. [Crew/JMP-1].

• **AmPM-261 CARPENTIER**, Charles Francis (Mayor, East Moline, 1929–1938; State Senate, 1939–1953; Illinois Secretary of State, 1953–1964)
261.1 Illinois. w. C.H. Chamberlin. m. "Air—*Baby Mine*." Published by Paul Powell, Secretary of State, Springfield, IL. [1890–1894] [Edition ca. 1970]. [8½" × 11¼"]. R/w/b drawing—"Seal of the State of Illinois, Aug. 26th, 1818," with a red bar diagonally across the seal reading "Illinois." "Issued by, Charles F. Carpentier, Secretary of State." 4pp. [Crew/AL-340].
• **AmPM-262 CAULFIELD**, Bernard Gregory (U.S. House, 1875–1877)
262.1 The Presidential Racecourse. w. No composer indicated. m. "Tune—*Camptown Races*." "From the *Graphic*." In: *Hayes & Wheeler Song Book*, page 40. Published by The Union Republican Congressional Committee, Washington, DC. 1876. [5¾" × 9¼"]. Br/bk litho of Rutherford B. Hayes and William A. Wheeler, shield, geometric design border. "I'll be on hand again shortly." [V-1: "Series I" under title on cover] [V-2: Series not indicated on cover]. 52pp. [M-196, 197]. [Crew/RBH-20].
• **AmPM-263 CERMAK**, Anton J. (State House, 1902; Chief Bailiff, Chicago, 1915; County Board, Cook County; Alderman, Chicago; Candidate for U.S. Senator, 1928; Mayor, Chicago, 1931–1933)
263.1 Century Of Progress March. m. Frank W. Geiger. Published by Frank W. Geiger, Whitehouse Station, NJ. 1933. B/w photo of scene at the 1933 Chicago Exposition. "Composed for the Chicago Exposition of 1933 and dedicated to Mayor Anton Cermak." 6pp. Page 6: Blank.
263.2 Cermak For Mayor. w.m. Casper Nathan. Published by Silvie Ferretti's Booster Club, Chicago, IL. 1931. B/w photo of Anton Cermak. O/bl/w geometric designs.
263.3 Greetings (Chicago Welcomes You). w.m. Col. George D. Gaw. a. Frank Barden. Published by George Frank Publishers, 500 North Sacramento, Chicago, IL. 1932. Pl/y/w/bk drawing of scenes from the 1933 Chicago World's Fair, statue, skyline. B/w photo of "Hon. A.J. Cermak, Mayor," "Col. George D. Gaw," and "Rufus C. Dawes, Pres. Of Century of Progress." "Chicago's Official Song." "1833–CHICAGO–1933." 8pp. Pages 2, 7 and 8: Narratives on Chicago.
263.4 Let's Back Cermak To Win (Song-Fox Trot). w. Anna Donoghue and William McNamara. m. Ted Hay. No publisher indicated. 1928. B/w photo of Anthony Cermak. Gn/w/bk geometric designs. "Dedicated to 'The Man of the Hour.'" "To Anthony J. Cermak—Personal Liberty Champion with the Compliments of his many friends." 4pp. Page 4: Biography of Anthony Cermak.
• **AmPM-264 CLEMENTS**, Isaac (Register in Bankruptcy, 1867; U.S. House, 1873–1875; U.S. Penitentiary Commissioner, 1877; U.S. Pension Agent, Chicago, 1890–1893; Superintendent of the Soldiers' Orphans' Home, Normal, 1899)
264.1 Colonel Clements Two-Step March. m. G.E. Holmes. Published by Benjamin's Temple of Music in Danville, IL. Copyright 1899 by G.E. Holmes. Bl/w cover. "Dedicated to Col. Isaac Clements, Governor of National Soldiers Home in Danville, Illinois." 8pp. Pages 2, 7 and 8: Blank.
• **AmPM-265 COLES**, Edward (Private Secretary to President James Madison, 1809–1815; Registrar of the Land Office, Edwardsville, 1819–1822; Governor, 1822–1826)
265.1 Freedom Country. w. Win Stracke and Norman Luboff. m. Norman Luboff. Published by Walton Music Corporation, 17 West 60th Street, New York, NY. 1967. [8" × 11⅛"]. B/w drawing of "Edward Coles, Second Governor of Illinois, b. 1786–d. 1868." "A cantata about the great freedom struggle in early Illinois, 1822–1824." 60pp.
265.2 Our Governors March (Or Two Step) m. Joseph Gearen. Published by Lyon & Healy, Chicago, IL. 1897. Bk/w/gn/br drawings of all Illinois Governors, Illinois capitol building, farm scene, law books. 6pp. Page 2: Blank. Page 6: Advertising. [Crew/JMP-1].
• **AmPM-266 CRANFIELD**, Mrs. A.R. (Mayor, Warren, 1918)
266.1 U.S. National Guard March. m. Gene Swinbank. Published by Gene Swinbank, Warren, IL. 1915. B/w photo of Mrs. A.R. Canfield." Bl/w drawings of American flags, ribbons. "Respectfully Dedicated to the Hon. Mrs. A.R. Canfield, first Lady Mayor of Illinois." 6pp. Pages 2 and 6: Blank.
• **AmPM-266A CROWE**, T.J. (Delegate, Democratic National Convention, 1924; Candidate Trustee Sanitary District, Chicago, 1928)
266A.1 Get Yourself A Nice Brown Derby (And Fall In Line for Al). w.m. Walter Goodwin "(Writer of *Back In The Old Neighborhood*)." 1928. Br/w photos of "Alfred E. Smith," "T.J. Crowe," "James M. Whalen," "Henry A. Berger" and "Ald. Ross A. Woodhull "(To fill vacancy)." 4pp. Page 4: Biographies of "Democratic Nominees for Trustees Sanitary District of Chicago." "For Your Health's Sake." [Crew/AES-26].
• **AmPM-267 CULLOM**, Shelby Moore (City Attorney, Springfield, 1855; State House, 1856, 1860–1861 & 1873–1874, U.S. House, 1865–1871); Governor, 1877–1883; U.S. Senate, 1883–1913)
267.1 Git On Board. w. J.W. Matthews. m. Notation. "Old Melody." "For Male Voices." In: *True Blue Republican Campaign Songs For 1896*, page 19. c. J.B. Herbert. Published by The S. Brainard's Sons Company, Chicago, IL. 1896. [5⅜" × 6⅞"]. R/w/b drawing of crossed flags, wreath, ribbons. Bl/w photo of "Hon. Wm. McKinley." "Protection." 36pp. [M-328]. [Crew/WM-169].
267.2 Our Governors March (Or Two Step) m. Joseph Gearen. Published by Lyon & Healy, Chicago, IL. 1897. Bk/w/gn/br drawings of all Illinois Governors, Illinois capitol building, farm scene, law books. 6pp. Page 2: Blank. Page 6: Advertising. [Crew/JMP-1].
• **AmPM-268 DALEY**, Richard Michael (State Senate, 1972–1980; State's Attorney, Cook County, 1980–1989; Mayor, 1989–Present)
268.1 Werewolves Of Chicago. w. J. Phillip. m. "*Werewolves Of London*, based on a performance by Warren Zevon." "A humorous parody of the song and an attack on Chicago Politics." Published online at <http://www.amiright.com/parody/70s/warren-zevon2.shtml>. [ca. 2003].

• **AmPM-269 DAWSON**, William Levi (Alderman, Chicago 1933–1939; U.S. House, 1943–1970)

269.1 On With Roosevelt. w. J.B. Crawford. m. "Tune—*On Wisconsin.*" In: *Our Heroes* [Song Sheet], page 1. [1940]. Non-pictorial. "Campaign Songs for the Election of Franklin D. Roosevelt, Songs will be introduced by Julma B. Crawford." 2pp. Page 2: Blank. [Crew/FDR-181].

• **AmPM-270 DIRKSEN**, Everett McKinley (Commissioner of Finance, Pekin, 1927–1931; U.S. House, 1933–1949; U.S. Senate, 1951–1969)

270.1 Dance Of The Liberal Republicans. w.m. Gerald Gardner. In: *These Are The Songs That Were* [Song Book], page 10. e. Gerald Gardner (Writer *Of Who's In Charge Here?, News-Reals,* and *That Was The Week That Was*). Published by Edwin H. Morris and Company, No. 31 West 54th Street, New York, NY. 10019. 1965. B/w photo of Lyndon B. Johnson, Hubert Humphrey, Everett Dirksen, others. R/w/bk cover. List of contents. 36pp. Pages 8, 23 and 25: Photos of politicians. [Crew/LBJ-6].

270.2 E.M.D. w.m. Bob Rhines, 509 West Muller Road, East Peoria, IL. No publisher indicated. [ca. 1969]. [8½" × 11"]. B/w photos of Everett Dirksen and Bob Rhynes. B/w litho border of American flags. 6pp.

270.3 Man Is Not Alone. w. Everett McKinley Dirksen and Charles Wood. m. John Cacavas. Published by Chappel & Co., Inc., 609 Fifth Avenue, New York, NY. 1967. N/c reproduction of an "Original painting from life by Louis Lupas" of Everett McKinley Dirksen. "From the Capitol Recording by Senator Everett McKinley Dirksen." 6pp. Page 2: Blank. Page 6: Advertising.

270.4 Gallant Men. w. Charles Wood. m. John Cacavas. Published by Chappel & Co., 609 Fifth Avenue, New York, NY. 1966. N/c photos of Everett Dirksen, U.S. Capitol building. "From the Capitol Recording: *Gallant Men—Stories Of The American Adventure Told By Senator Everett McKinley Dirksen.*" 6pp. Page 6: Blank.

270.5 Gallant Men (Songs Of The American Adventure) (Souvenir Folio). w. Charles Wood. m. John Cacavas. Published by Chappel & Co., 609 Fifth Avenue, New York, NY. 1966. N/c photos of Everett Dirksen, U.S. Capitol building. "Adapted From the Capitol Recording Album: *Gallant Men—Stories Of The American Adventure Told By Senator Everett McKinley Dirksen.*"

270.6 Gallant Men {270.6–1}. w. Charles Wood. m. John Cacavas. 45 rpm record. Capitol Records #5805/45–26495. Performed by Senator Everett McKinley Dirksen. Arranged and conducted by John Cacavas. Side 2: ***The New Colossus*** (Statue of Liberty) {270.6–2}. w.m. John Cacavas. [196-].

270.8 The Good Times Train. w. Johnny Lehmann. m. Jimmie Driftwood. Copyright 1960 by Worden Music Co., Inc. In: *Welcome GOP To The Jumbo Jamboree Uline Arena, April 4, 1960, Washington, DC.* [Program], page 4. R/w/b elephant. 4pp. Pages 3 and 4: Elected dignitaries in attendance—Senators Thurston Morton, Barry Goldwater, and Everett M. Dirksen; Congressmen William Miller and Charles Halleck.

270.9 On Top Of Goldwater (JFK's Lament). w. Milton M. Schwartz. m. "To the tune of *On Top Of Old Smokey.*" In: *Sing Along With Jack*, page 22. a. Danny Hurd. Published by Pocket Books, Inc., New York, NY. Copyright 1963 by Bonny Publishing Corporation. [9" × 11⅞"]. R/w/bk drawing of sheet music "Vive La Dynasty," silhouette of John F. Kennedy in chair with conductor's baton, caricature of Kennedy family. "Hit Songs from the New Frontier." 36pp. Page 3: "Illustrations by David Gantz." Page 36: Drawing of John F. Kennedy in chair with baton. Song titles. [Crew/ JFK-17].

• **AmPM-271 DOUGLAS**, Stephen A. (State's Attorney, Morgan County, 1835; State House, 1836–1837; Secretary of State, Illinois, 1840–1841; U.S. House, 1843–1847; U.S. Senate, 1847–1861; Democratic Candidate for President, 1860) [ALSO SEE: DOC/PSM-SAD]

271.1 Abe Lincoln's Excelsior. w. Lm'n Peel. m. No tune indicated. In: *The Great Republican Campaigns Of 1860 And 1896*, page 179. e. Osborn H. Oldroyd. Published by Laird & Lee, Chicago, IL. 1896. [5$\frac{3}{16}$" × 7$\frac{7}{16}$"]. Gn/r/bk photos of Abraham Lincoln, William McKinley and Garrett Hobart. "Sound Money, Protection, Prosperity." 208pp. [Crew/AL-574].

271.2 Anxious Stephen! w. No composer indicated. m. "Air—*Cynthia Sue.*" In: *The Wide Awake Vocalist (Or Rail Splitters' Song Book)*, page 31. Published by E.A. Daggett, No. 333 Broadway, New York, NY. 1860. Non-pictorial geometric design border. "Words and Music for the Republican Campaign of 1860, Embracing a Great Variety of Songs, Solos, Duets and Choruses Arranged for Piano or melodeon; The best collection of Words and Music ever published for a campaign, Every Club and Family should have copies, so as to join in the choruses; The Ladies are invited to join in the choruses at the meetings." 68pp. [M-116]. [Crew/AL-59].

271.3 The Baltimore Convention. w. "B." m. "Tune—*Tip And Ty.*" In: *The Wide Awake Vocalist (Or Rail Splitters' Song Book)*, page 26. Published by E.A. Daggett, No. 333 Broadway, New York, NY. 1860. Non-pictorial geometric design border. "Words and Music for the Republican Campaign of 1860, Embracing a Great Variety of Songs, Solos, Duets and Choruses Arranged for Piano or melodeon; The best collection of Words and Music ever published for a campaign, Every Club and Family should have copies, so as to join in the choruses; The Ladies are invited to join in the choruses at the meetings." 68pp. [M-116]. [Crew/AL-59].

271.4 The Bay State Hurrah. w.m. No composer or tune indicated. In: *Fremont Songs For The People (Original And Selected)*, page 37. c. Thomas Drew "(Editor of *The Massachusetts Spy*)." Published by John P. Jewett & Company, Boston, MA. Copyright 1856 by Thomas Drew. [3⅝" × 5½"]. B/w litho of "J.C. Fremont." "The Campaign of 1856." 68pp. [Crew/JCF-18].

271.5 Banner Of Freedom. w.m. No composer or tune indicated. In: *Republican Song Book*, page 51. c. Thomas Drew "(Late Editor of *The Massachusetts Spy*)." Published by Thayer and Eldridge, Boston, MA. 1860. [3⅞" × 5⅞"]. Br/bk litho of beardless Abraham Lincoln, vignettes of young Lincoln chopping rails, polling raft. 68pp. [M-108]. [Crew/AL-8].

271.6 Behold The Man! w. No composer indicated. m. "Air—*A Little More Cider Too.*" In: *The Republican Campaign Songster, A Collection Of Lyrics, Original And Selected, Specifically Prepared For The Friends Of Freedom In The Campaign Of Fifty-Six,* page 105. Published by Miller, Orton & Mulligan, No. 25 Park Row, New York, NY. 1856. [3 13/16" × 6"]. Be/bk litho of "Colonel John C. Fremont" facing to viewer's left, black line border. 112pp. [M-097]. [Crew/JCF-24].

271.7 Buck, Buck Never Had Luck. w. A. Oakley Hall. m. "Air—*Tippecanoe And Tyler, Too.*" In: *The Republican Campaign Songster, A Collection Of Lyrics, Original And Selected, Specifically Prepared For The Friends Of Freedom In The Campaign Of Fifty-Six,* page 95. Published by Miller, Orton & Mulligan, No. 25 Park Row, New York, NY. 1856. [3 13/16" × 6"]. Be/bk litho of "Colonel John C. Fremont" facing to viewer's left, black line border. 112pp. [M-097]. [Crew/JCF-24].

271.8 Buck Shooting. w. No composer indicated. m. "Air—*Will They Miss Me.*" In: *The Republican Campaign Songster, A Collection Of Lyrics, Original And Selected, Specifically Prepared For The Friends Of Freedom In The Campaign Of Fifty-Six,* page 67. Published by Miller, Orton & Mulligan, No. 25 Park Row, New York, NY. 1856. [3 13/16" × 6"]. Be/bk litho of "Colonel John C. Fremont" facing to viewer's left, black line border. 112pp. [M-097]. [Crew/JCF-24].

271A.1 [The Campaign Opens Brightly] (Campaign Song). w. No composer indicated. m. "Air—*Benny Haven.*" Published in the *Louisville Daily Courier,* August 16, 1860. Lyrics published online at <http://lincoln.lib.niu.edu/498R/danielle/Breckinridge-CampSong.html>.

271.9 Campaign Song. w. No composer indicated. m. "Air—*Hurrah, Hurrah, Hurrah.*" In: *The Great Republican Campaigns Of 1860 And 1896,* page 176. e. Osborn H. Oldroyd. Published by Laird & Lee, Chicago, IL. 1896. [5 5/16" × 7 7/16"]. Gn/r/bk photos of Abraham Lincoln, William McKinley and Garrett Hobart. "Sound Money, Protection, Prosperity." 208pp. [Crew/AL-574].

271.10 Cheer Up, My Lively Lads. w.m. No composer or tune indicated. In: *The Democratic Campaign Songster: Douglas & Johnson Melodies,* page 4. Published by P.J. Cozans, Publisher, New York, NY. [1860]. [3 7/8" × 6"]. Y/bk litho of an eagle with ribbon—"Douglas & Johnson," train, ships, monument—"Liberty" sitting on rock base—"The Constitution." 40pp. [M-117]. [Crew/SAD-5].

271.11 [Come All True Democrats] (Campaign Song for 1860). w.m. No composer or tune indicated. In: *The Democratic Campaign Songster: Douglas & Johnson Melodies,* page 3. Published by P.J. Cozans, Publisher, New York, NY. [1860]. [3 7/8" × 6"]. Y/bk litho of an eagle with ribbon—"Douglas & Johnson," train, ships, monument—"Liberty" sitting on rock base—"The Constitution." 40pp. [M-117]. [Crew/SAD-5].

271.12 [Come All True Democrats And Join] (Campaign Song For 1860). w.m. No composer or tune indicated. In: *The Democratic Campaign Songster, No. #1,* page 46. Published by American Publishing House, No. 60 West Fourth Street, Cincinnati, OH. 1860. [3 7/8" × 5 11/16"]. Pk/bk litho of "Stephen A. Douglas," black line border. At top of cover—"No. 1, Price 10 Cents." 52pp. [M-118]. [Crew/SAD-12].

271.13 [Come All Ye Noble Democrats] (Campaign Song). w.m. No composer or tune indicated. In: *The Democratic Campaign Songster, No. #1,* page 47. Published by American Publishing House, No. 60 West Fourth Street, Cincinnati, OH. 1860. [3 7/8" × 5 11/16"]. Pk/bk litho of "Stephen A. Douglas," black line border. At top of cover—"No. 1, Price 10 Cents." 52pp. [M-118]. [Crew/SAD-12].

271.14 Come And Vote For Me. w.m. No composer or tune indicated. In: *The Great Republican Campaigns Of 1860 And 1896,* page 158. e. Osborn H. Oldroyd. Published by Laird & Lee, Chicago, IL. 1896. [5 5/16" × 7 7/16"]. Gn/r/bk photos of Abraham Lincoln, William McKinley and Garrett Hobart. "Sound Money, Protection, Prosperity." 208pp. [Crew/AL-574].

271.15 [Come Join Our Throng, Ye Patriots True] (A Rallying Song). w. No composer indicated. m. "Air—*Dan Tucker.*" In: *The Democratic Campaign Songster, No. #1,* page 35. Published by American Publishing House, No. 60 West Fourth Street, Cincinnati, OH. 1860. [3 7/8" × 5 11/16"]. Pk/bk litho of "Stephen A. Douglas," black line border. At top of cover—"No. 1, Price 10 Cents." 52pp. [M-118]. [Crew/SAD-12].

271.16 The Democratic Battle Hymn. w. No composer indicated. m. "Air—*Marseillaise Hymn.*" In: *The Democratic Campaign Songster, No. #1,* page 28. Published by American Publishing House, No. 60 West Fourth Street, Cincinnati, OH. 1860. [3 7/8" × 5 11/16"]. Pk/bk litho of "Stephen A. Douglas," black line border. At top of cover—"No. 1, Price 10 Cents." 52pp. [M-118]. [Crew/SAD-12].

271.17 Democratic Huzza. w. No composer indicated. m. "Air—*Foot Travellor—Alpine Glee Singer,* page 70." In: *The Democratic Campaign Songster, No. #1,* page 21. Published by American Publishing House, No. 60 West Fourth Street, Cincinnati, OH. 1860. [3 7/8" × 5 11/16"]. Pk/bk litho of "Stephen A. Douglas," black line border. At top of cover—"No. 1, Price 10 Cents." 52pp. [M-118]. [Crew/SAD-12].

271.18 A Democrat's Dream. w. No composer indicated. m. "Air—*Yankee Doodle.*" In: *The Democratic Campaign Songster: Douglas & Johnson Melodies,* page 11. Published by P.J. Cozans, Publisher, New York, NY. [1860]. [3 7/8" × 6"]. Y/bk litho of an eagle with ribbon—"Douglas & Johnson," train, ships, monument—"Liberty" sitting on rock base—"The Constitution." 40pp. [M-117]. [Crew/SAD-5].

271.19 Douglas. w.m. No composer or tune indicated. In: *The Democratic Campaign Songster: Douglas & Johnson Melodies,* page 23. Published by P.J. Cozans, Publisher, New York, NY. [1860]. [3 7/8" × 6"]. Y/bk litho of an eagle with ribbon—"Douglas & Johnson," train, ships, monument—"Liberty" sitting on rock base—"The Constitution." 40pp. [M-117]. [Crew/SAD-5].

271.20 A Douglas! A Douglas! w.m. No composer or tune indicated. In: *The Democratic Campaign Songster: Douglas & Johnson Melodies,* page 5. Published by P.J. Cozans, Publisher, New York, NY. [1860]. [3 7/8" × 6"]. Y/bk litho of an eagle with ribbon—"Douglas & Johnson," train, ships, monument—"Liberty" sitting

(Illinois) DOUGLAS / AmPM-271.21

on rock base — "The Constitution." 40pp. [M-117]. [Crew/SAD-5].

271.21 Douglas And His Dinah (Song or Duet, and Chorus for Male Voices). w. No composer indicated. m.a. A. Cull. In: *The Wide Awake Vocalist (Or Rail Splitters' Song Book)*, page 52. Published by E.A. Daggett, No. 333 Broadway, New York, NY. 1860. Non-pictorial geometric design border. "Words and Music for the Republican Campaign of 1860, Embracing a Great Variety of Songs, Solos, Duets and Choruses Arranged for Piano or melodeon; The best collection of Words and Music ever published for a campaign, Every Club and Family should have copies, so as to join in the choruses; The Ladies are invited to join in the choruses at the meetings." 68pp. [M-116]. [Crew/AL-59].

271.22 Douglas And Johnson. w. J.F.R. m. No tune indicated. In: *The Democratic Campaign Songster: Douglas & Johnson Melodies*, page 13. Published by P.J. Cozans, Publisher, New York, NY. [1860]. [3⅞" × 6"]. Y/bk litho of an eagle with ribbon — "Douglas & Johnson," train, ships, monument — "Liberty" sitting on rock base — "The Constitution." 40pp. [M-117]. [Crew/SAD-5].

271.23 Douglas And Johnson Song. w. No composer indicated. m. "Air — *Star Spangled Banner.*" In: *The Democratic Campaign Songster, No. #1*, page 30. Published by American Publishing House, No. 60 West Fourth Street, Cincinnati, OH. 1860. [3⅞" × 5¹⁵⁄₁₆"]. Pk/bk litho of "Stephen A. Douglas," black line border. At top of cover — "No. 1, Price 10 Cents." 52pp. [M-118]. [Crew/SAD-12].

271.24 Douglas And Reform. w. No composer indicated. m. "Air — *We're A Band Of Freemen.*" In: *The Democratic Campaign Songster: Douglas & Johnson Melodies*, page 27. Published by P.J. Cozans, Publisher, New York, NY. [1860]. [3⅞" × 6"]. Y/bk litho of an eagle with ribbon — "Douglas & Johnson," train, ships, monument — "Liberty" sitting on rock base — "The Constitution." 40pp. [M-117]. [Crew/SAD-5].

271.25 Douglas And Union. w. Michael Doheny. m. "Air — *Star Spangled Banner.*" In: *The Democratic Campaign Songster, No. #1*, page 23. Published by American Publishing House, No. 60 West Fourth Street, Cincinnati, OH. 1860. [3⅞" × 5¹⁵⁄₁₆"]. Pk/bk litho of "Stephen A. Douglas," black line border. At top of cover — "No. 1, Price 10 Cents." 52pp. [M-118]. [Crew/SAD-12].

271.26 The Douglas Campaign Rolling. w. Michael Doheny. m. "Air — *Irish Molly O!*" In: *The Democratic Campaign Songster: Douglas & Johnson Melodies*, page 7. Published by P.J. Cozans, Publisher, New York, NY. [1860]. [3⅞" × 6"]. Y/bk litho of an eagle with ribbon — "Douglas & Johnson," train, ships, monument — "Liberty" sitting on rock base — "The Constitution." 40pp. [M-117]. [Crew/SAD-5].

271.27 The Douglas Cause Is Growing. w. No composer indicated. m. "Air — *Free And Easy.*" In: *The Democratic Campaign Songster: Douglas & Johnson Melodies*, page 35. Published by P.J. Cozans, Publisher, New York, NY. [1860]. [3⅞" × 6"]. Y/bk litho of an eagle with ribbon — "Douglas & Johnson," train, ships, monument — "Liberty" sitting on rock base — "The Constitution." 40pp. [M-117]. [Crew/SAD-5].

271.28 The Douglas Flag. w. No composer indicated. m. "Air — *The Minstrel Boy.*" In: *The Democratic Campaign Songster: Douglas & Johnson Melodies*, page 26. Published by P.J. Cozans, Publisher, New York, NY. [1860]. [3⅞" × 6"]. Y/bk litho of an eagle with ribbon — "Douglas & Johnson," train, ships, monument — "Liberty" sitting on rock base — "The Constitution." 40pp. [M-117]. [Crew/SAD-5].

271.29 Douglas Going Home (National Song). w. No composer indicated. m. "Air — *Few Days.*" In: *The Democratic Campaign Songster: Douglas & Johnson Melodies*, page 24. Published by P.J. Cozans, Publisher, New York, NY. [1860]. [3⅞" × 6"]. Y/bk litho of an eagle with ribbon — "Douglas & Johnson," train, ships, monument — "Liberty" sitting on rock base — "The Constitution." 40pp. [M-117]. [Crew/SAD-5].

271.30 The Douglas Is Coming. w. No composer indicated. m. "Tune — *The Campbells Are Coming.*" In: *The Democratic Campaign Songster: Douglas & Johnson Melodies*, page 1. Published by P.J. Cozans, Publisher, New York, NY. [1860]. [3⅞" × 6"]. Y/bk litho of an eagle with ribbon — "Douglas & Johnson," train, ships, monument — "Liberty" sitting on rock base — "The Constitution." 40pp. [M-117]. [Crew/SAD-5].

271.31 Douglas Is The Man. w. No composer indicated. m. "Tune — *Dearest Mae.*" In: *The Democratic Campaign Songster, No. #1*, page 45. Published by American Publishing House, No. 60 West Fourth Street, Cincinnati, OH. 1860. [3⅞" × 5¹⁵⁄₁₆"]. Pk/bk litho of "Stephen A. Douglas," black line border. At top of cover — "No. 1, Price 10 Cents." 52pp. [M-118]. [Crew/SAD-12].

271.32 A Douglas Lay. w.m. No composer or tune indicated. In: *The Democratic Campaign Songster: Douglas & Johnson Melodies*, page 33. Published by P.J. Cozans, Publisher, New York, NY. [1860]. [3⅞" × 6"]. Y/bk litho of an eagle with ribbon — "Douglas & Johnson," train, ships, monument — "Liberty" sitting on rock base — "The Constitution." 40pp. [M-117]. [Crew/SAD-5].

271.33 Douglas Our Choice. w. No composer indicated. m. "Tune — *Old Dan Tucker.*" In: *The Democratic Campaign Songster, No. #1*, page 25. Published by American Publishing House, No. 60 West Fourth Street, Cincinnati, OH. 1860. [3⅞" × 5¹⁵⁄₁₆"]. Pk/bk litho of "Stephen A. Douglas," black line border. At top of cover — "No. 1, Price 10 Cents." 52pp. [M-118]. [Crew/SAD-12].

271.34 Douglas — Our Union Right Or Wrong. w.m. No composer or tune indicated. In: *The Democratic Campaign Songster: Douglas & Johnson Melodies*, page 2. Published by P.J. Cozans, Publisher, New York, NY. [1860]. [3⅞" × 6"]. Y/bk litho of an eagle with ribbon — "Douglas & Johnson," train, ships, monument — "Liberty" sitting on rock base — "The Constitution." 40pp. [M-117]. [Crew/SAD-5].

271.35 Douglas Shall Be President. w. No composer indicated. m. "Air — *Yankee Doodle.*" In: *The Democratic Campaign Songster, No. #1*, page 39. Published by American Publishing House, No. 60 West Fourth Street, Cincinnati, OH. 1860. [3⅞" × 5¹⁵⁄₁₆"]. Pk/bk litho of "Stephen A. Douglas," black line border. At top of cover — "No. 1, Price 10 Cents." 52pp. [M-118]. [Crew/SAD-12].

271.36 Douglas The Patriot Honest And True. w.m. No composer or tune indicated. In: *The Democratic Campaign Songster, No. #1,* page 26. Published by American Publishing House, No. 60 West Fourth Street, Cincinnati, OH. 1860. [3⅞" × 5¹¹⁄₁₆"]. Pk/bk litho of "Stephen A. Douglas," black line border. At top of cover—"No. 1, Price 10 Cents." 52pp. [M-118]. [Crew/SAD-12].

271.37 Douglas To The Rescue. w.m. No composer or tune indicated. In: *The Democratic Campaign Songster, No. #1,* page 24. Published by American Publishing House, No. 60 West Fourth Street, Cincinnati, OH. 1860. [3⅞" × 5¹¹⁄₁₆"]. Pk/bk litho of "Stephen A. Douglas," black line border. At top of cover—"No. 1, Price 10 Cents." 52pp. [M-118]. [Crew/SAD-12].

271.38 Douglas's Going Home. w. No composer indicated. m. "Air—*Yankee Doodle.*" In: *The Democratic Campaign Songster, No. #1,* page 39. Published by American Publishing House, No. 60 West Fourth Street, Cincinnati, OH. 1860. [3⅞" × 5¹¹⁄₁₆"]. Pk/bk litho of "Stephen A. Douglas," black line border. At top of cover—"No. 1, Price 10 Cents." 52pp. [M-118]. [Crew/SAD-12].

271.39 Douglas's Home. w. No composer indicated. m. "Air—*Few Days.*" In: *The Democratic Campaign Songster, No. #1,* page 37. Published by American Publishing House, No. 60 West Fourth Street, Cincinnati, OH. 1860. [3⅞" × 5¹¹⁄₁₆"]. Pk/bk litho of "Stephen A. Douglas," black line border. At top of cover—"No. 1, Price 10 Cents." 52pp. [M-118]. [Crew/SAD-12].

271.40 [Down With Douglass, Pierce And Shannon]. w.m. No composer or tune indicated. In: *Fremont Glees* [Song Sheet]. [1856]. [9¾" × 15½"]. Non-pictorial cloth. "As Sung by the Centerville Republican Club." 2pp. Page 2: Blank. [Crew/JCF-38].

271.41 Du Da. w. No composer indicated. m. "Air—*Camptown Races.*" "Sung at the Republican Ratification Meeting, at Springfield, Illinois." In: *Republican Song Book,* page 41. c. Thomas Drew "(Late Editor of *The Massachusetts Spy*)." Published by Thayer and Eldridge, Boston, MA. 1860. [3⅞" × 5⅞"]. Br/bk litho of beardless Abraham Lincoln, vignettes of young Lincoln chopping rails, polling raft. 68pp. [M-108]. [Crew/AL-8].

271.42 The Fate Of Fowler. w. No composer indicated. m. "Tune—*Lord Lovel.*" "Showing how it is best to be off with the Old Love before you are on with the new." In: *Connecticut Wide-Awake Songster,* page 49. e. John W. Hutchinson "(of Hutchinson Family Singers)" and Benjamin Jepson. Published by O. Hutchinson, Publisher, No. 272 Greenwich Street, New York, NY. 1860. [4" × 6"]. Bl/bk non-pictorial line border. "Lincoln and liberty." 76pp. [M-109]. [Crew/AL-175].

271.43 A Fine Old Gentleman. w. No composer indicated. m. "Air—*The Fine Old English Gentleman.*" In: *The Great Republican Campaigns Of 1860 And 1896,* page 168. e. Osborn H. Oldroyd. Published by Laird & Lee, Chicago, IL. 1896. [5⁵⁄₁₆" × 7⁵⁄₁₆"]. Gn/r/bk photos of Abraham Lincoln, William McKinley and Garrett Hobart. "Sound Money, Protection, Prosperity." 208pp. [Crew/AL-574].

271.44 For Abe Shall Have The Belt. w. "S." m.a. Henry Tucker. In: *The Wide Awake Vocalist (Or Rail Splitters' Song Book),* page 30. Published by E.A. Daggett, No. 333 Broadway, New York, NY. 1860. Non-pictorial geometric design border. "Words and Music for the Republican Campaign of 1860, Embracing a Great Variety of Songs, Solos, Duets and Choruses Arranged for Piano or melodeon; The best collection of Words and Music ever published for a campaign, Every Club and Family should have copies, so as to join in the choruses; The Ladies are invited to join in the choruses at the meetings." 68pp. [M-116]. [Crew/AL-59].

271.45 For Freedom And Fremont (The Hurrah Song). w. No composer indicated. m. Air—*The Hurrah Song.* In: *Fremont Songs For The People (Original And Selected),* page 24. c. Thomas Drew "(Editor of *The Massachusetts Spy*)." Published by John P. Jewett & Company, Boston, MA. Copyright 1856 by Thomas Drew. [3⅝" × 5½"]. B/w litho of "J.C. Fremont." "The Campaign of 1856." 68pp. [Crew/JCF-18].

271.46 Freedom. w.m. No composer or tune indicated. From the "*N.Y. Evening Post.*" In: *The Republican Campaign Songster, A Collection Of Lyrics, Original And Selected, Specifically Prepared For The Friends Of Freedom In The Campaign Of Fifty-Six,* page 46. Published by Miller, Orton & Mulligan, No. 25 Park Row, New York, NY. 1856. [3¹³⁄₁₆" × 6"]. Be/bk litho of "Colonel John C. Fremont" facing to viewer's left, black line border. 112pp. [M-097]. [Crew/JCF-24].

271.47 Freedom And Fremont. w.m. No composer or tune indicated. In: *The Fremont Songster,* page 43. Published by [V-1: H.S. Riggs & Company, Publishers, No. 4 Cortland Street] [V-2: P.J. Cozans, No. 107 Nassau Street], New York, NY. 1856. [V-1: 3⅝" × 5¾"] [V-2: 3½" × 5⅝"]. Be/bk litho of wreath, John C. Fremont. "With a current likeness of John C. Fremont, The People's Candidate for the Presidency." 40pp. [M-094, 095]. [Crew/JCF-45].

271.48 Fremont And Dayton. w. No composer indicated. m. "Air—*O, What Has Caused This Great Commotion.*" In: *Fremont Songs For The People (Original And Selected),* page 22. c. Thomas Drew "(Editor of *The Massachusetts Spy*)." Published by John P. Jewett & Company, Boston, MA. Copyright 1856 by Thomas Drew. [3⅝" × 5½"]. B/w litho of "J.C. Fremont." "The Campaign of 1856." 68pp. [Crew/JCF-18].

271.49 Fremont And Dayton. w. No composer indicated. m. "Air—*Yankee Doodle.*" In: *The Freeman's Glee Book, A Collection Of Songs, Odes, Glees And Ballads With Music, Original And Selected, Harmonized And Arranged For Each. Published Under The Auspices Of The Central Fremont And Dayton Glee Club Of The City Of New York, And Dedicated To All, Who, Cherishing Republican Liberty Consider Freedom Worth A Song,* page 70. Published by Miller, Orton & Mulligan, No. 25 Park Row, New York, NY. [and Auburn, NY]. 1856. [4¹⁵⁄₁₆" × 6"]. Pk/bk litho of man on mountain peak, music sheets, geometric designs. 112pp. [Crew/JCF-16].

271.50 Fremont And Dayton (Or Yankee Doodle Revised). w. No composer indicated. m. "Air—*Yankee Doodle.*" In: *Fremont Songs For The People (Original And Selected),* page 54. c. Thomas Drew "(Editor of *The Massachusetts Spy*)." Published by John P. Jewett & Company, Boston, MA. Copyright 1856 by Thomas Drew. [3⅝" × 5½"]. B/w litho of "J.C. Fremont." "The Campaign of 1856." 68pp. [Crew/JCF-18].

271.51 The Friends Of Old Buchan. w. No composer indicated. m. No composer indicated. In: *The Fremont Songster*, page 6. Published by [V-1: H.S. Riggs & Company, Publishers, No. 4 Cortland Street] [V-2: P.J. Cozans, No. 107 Nassau Street], New York, NY. 1856. [V-1: 3⅝" × 5¾"] [V-2: 3½" × 5⅝"]. Be/bk litho of wreath, John C. Fremont. "With a current likeness of John C. Fremont, The People's Candidate for the Presidency." 40pp. [M-094, 095]. [Crew/JCF-45].

271.52 [Friends Of The Union] (Song). w. No composer indicated. m. "Air—*Dixey's Land*." In: *The Democratic Campaign Songster: Douglas & Johnson Melodies,* page 18. Published by P.J. Cozans, Publisher, New York, NY. [1860]. [3⅞" × 6"]. Y/bk litho of an eagle with ribbon—"Douglas & Johnson," train, ships, monument—"Liberty" sitting on rock base—"The Constitution." 40pp. [M-117]. [Crew/SAD-5].

271.53 [From Every Mountain-Top And Valley] (Douglas Rallying Song). w. No composer indicated. m. "Air—*Old Folks At Home*." In: *The Democratic Campaign Songster, No. #1*, page 40. Published by American Publishing House, No. 60 West Fourth Street, Cincinnati, OH. 1860. [3⅞" × 5¹¹⁄₁₆"]. Pk/bk litho of "Stephen A. Douglas," black line border. At top of cover—"No. 1, Price 10 Cents." 52pp. [M-118]. [Crew/SAD-12].

271.54 Gaily Did Little Dug. w. No composer indicated. m. "Air—*Gaily The Troubadour*." In: *The Democratic Campaign Songster, No. #1*, page 41. Published by American Publishing House, No. 60 West Fourth Street, Cincinnati, OH. 1860. [3⅞" × 5¹¹⁄₁₆"]. Pk/bk litho of "Stephen A. Douglas," black line border. At top of cover—"No. 1, Price 10 Cents." 52pp. [M-118]. [Crew/SAD-12].

271.55 Get Out Of The Way, Old Buchanan. w. No composer indicated. m. "Air—*Old Dan Tucker*." In: *Fremont Songs For The People (Original And Selected)*, page 56. c. Thomas Drew "(Editor of *The Massachusetts Spy*)." Published by John P. Jewett & Company, Boston, MA. Copyright 1856 by Thomas Drew. [3⅝" × 5½"]. B/w litho of "J.C. Fremont." "The Campaign of 1856." 68pp. [Crew/JCF-18].

271.56 Get Out Of The Way, 'Ten-Cent Jimmy.' w.m. No composer or tune indicated. In: *Fremont Songs For The People (Original And Selected)*, page 52. c. Thomas Drew "(Editor of *The Massachusetts Spy*)." Published by John P. Jewett & Company, Boston, MA. Copyright 1856 by Thomas Drew. [3⅝" × 5½"]. B/w litho of "J.C. Fremont." "The Campaign of 1856." 68pp. [Crew/JCF-18].

271.57 Get Out Of The Way, You Little Giant (Solo or Duet with Male Chorus). w. B.G.W. a. A. Cull. In: *The Wide Awake Vocalist (Or Rail Splitters' Song Book)*, page 24. Published by E.A. Daggett, No. 333 Broadway, New York, NY. 1860. Non-pictorial geometric design border. "Words and Music for the Republican Campaign of 1860, Embracing a Great Variety of Songs, Solos, Duets and Choruses Arranged for Piano or melodeon; The best collection of Words and Music ever published for a campaign, Every Club and Family should have copies, so as to join in the choruses; The Ladies are invited to join in the choruses at the meetings." 68pp. [M-116]. [Crew/AL-59].

271.58 Give Us Abe And Hamlin Too. w. Mrs. L.L. Deming. m. "Air—*A Wet Sheet And A Flowing Sea*." In: *The Great Republican Campaigns Of 1860 And 1896*, page 170. e. Osborn H. Oldroyd. Published by Laird & Lee, Chicago, IL. 1896. [5⁵⁄₁₆" × 7⁷⁄₁₆"]. Gn/r/bk photos of Abraham Lincoln, William McKinley and Garrett Hobart. "Sound Money, Protection, Prosperity." 208pp. [Crew/AL-574].

271.59 Great Ratification Song For The Buchaniers. w. No composer indicated. m. "Air—*Yankee Doodle*." In: *The Freeman's Glee Book, A Collection Of Songs, Odes, Glees And Ballads With Music, Original And Selected, Harmonized And Arranged For Each. Published Under The Auspices Of The Central Fremont And Dayton Glee Club Of The City Of New York, And Dedicated To All, Who, Cherishing Republican Liberty Consider Freedom Worth A Song*, page 78. Published by Miller, Orton & Mulligan, No. 25 Park Row, New York, NY. [and Auburn, NY]. 1856. [4¹⁵⁄₁₆" × 6"]. Pk/bk litho of man on mountain peak, music sheets, geometric designs. 112pp. [Crew/JCF-16].

271.60 The Gudgeon Of Democracy And The Southern Ark. w. No composer indicated. m. "Air—*The Cruel Troopers Riding By*." In: *The Republican Campaign Songster, A Collection Of Lyrics, Original And Selected, Specifically Prepared For The Friends Of Freedom In The Campaign Of Fifty-Six*, page 7. Published by Miller, Orton & Mulligan, No. 25 Park Row, New York, NY. 1856. [3¹³⁄₁₆" × 6"]. Be/bk litho of "Colonel John C. Fremont" facing to viewer's left, black line border. 112pp. [M-097]. [Crew/JCF-24].

271.61 Hail! The Little Giant, Hail! w. No composer indicated. m. "Tune—*Hail Columbia*." In: *The Democratic Campaign Songster, No. #1*, page 16. Published by American Publishing House, No. 60 West Fourth Street, Cincinnati, OH. 1860. [3⅞" × 5¹¹⁄₁₆"]. Pk/bk litho of "Stephen A. Douglas," black line border. At top of cover—"No. 1, Price 10 Cents." 52pp. [M-118]. [Crew/SAD-12].

271.62 [Hear The Shout Of Freedom Rising] (Republican Campaign Son No. 2). w.m. No composer indicated. m. "Tune—*That Old Tall Man 'Bout Fifty-Two*." In: *The Republican Campaign Songster No. #1*, page 16. Published by American Publishing House, No. 60 West Fourth Street, Cincinnati, OH. [1860]. [3¾" × 5¾"]. B/w litho of Abraham Lincoln. 48pp. [?]. [M-113]. [Crew/AL-298].

271.63 Here's To You General Scott. w.m. No composer or tune indicated. In: *Scott And Graham Melodies (Being A Collection Of Campaign Songs For 1852)*, page 8. Published by Huestis & Cozans, Nos. 104 and 106 Nassau Street, New York, NY. 1852. [3¹³⁄₁₆" × 6⅙"]. B/w litho of Winfield Scott, geometric design border. "As sung by the Whig Clubs throughout the United States." 76pp. [M-086]. [Crew/WS-15].

271.64 The Hero Of Chippewa. w. No composer indicated. m. "Tune—*Lucy Neal*." In: *Scott And Graham Melodies* (Being a Collection of Campaign Songs for 1852), page 28. Published by Huestis & Cozans, Nos. 104 and 106 Nassau Street, New York, NY. 1852. [3¹³⁄₁₆" × 6⅙"]. B/w litho of Winfield Scott, geometric design border. "As sung by the Whig Clubs throughout the United States." 76pp. [M-086]. [Crew/WS-15].

271.65 The Hero With Never A Scar. w. No composer indicated. m. "Tune — *The Low-Back'd Car.*" In: *Scott And Graham Melodies (Being A Collection Of Campaign Songs For 1852)*, page 34. Published by Huestis & Cozans, Nos. 104 and 106 Nassau Street, New York, NY. 1852. [3 13/16" × 6 3/16"]. B/w litho of Winfield Scott, geometric design border. "As sung by the Whig Clubs throughout the United States." 76pp. [M-086]. [Crew/WS-15].

271.66 High Old Abe Shall Win (Quartette). w. G.W. Bungay. m.a. Henry Tucker. In: *The Wide Awake Vocalist (Or Rail Splitters' Song Book)*, page 14. Published by E.A. Daggett, No. 333 Broadway, New York, NY. 1860. Non-pictorial geometric design border. "Words and Music for the Republican Campaign of 1860, Embracing a Great Variety of Songs, Solos, Duets and Choruses Arranged for Piano or melodeon; The best collection of Words and Music ever published for a campaign, Every Club and Family should have copies, so as to join in the choruses; The Ladies are invited to join in the choruses at the meetings." 68pp. [M-116]. [Crew/AL-59].

271.67 Hurra For Douglas! w. No composer indicated. m. "Tune — *A Little More Cider.*" In: *The Democratic Campaign Songster, No. #1*, page 8. Published by American Publishing House, No. 60 West Fourth Street, Cincinnati, OH. 1860. [3 7/8" × 5 1/16"]. Pk/bk litho of "Stephen A. Douglas," black line border. At top of cover — "No. 1, Price 10 Cents." 52pp. [M-118]. [Crew/SAD-12].

271.68 Hurrah Chorus. w.m. No composer or tune indicated. In: *Connecticut Wide-Awake Songster*, page 11. e. John W. Hutchinson "(of Hutchinson Family Singers)" and Benjamin Jepson. Published by O. Hutchinson, Publisher, No. 272 Greenwich Street, New York, NY. 1860. [4" × 6"]. Bl/bk non-pictorial line border. "Lincoln and liberty." 76pp. [M-109]. [Crew/AL-175].

271.69 Hurrah For Abe Lincoln! w. No composer indicated. m. "Tune — *Boatman Dance.*" In: *Connecticut Wide-Awake Songster*, page 12. e. John W. Hutchinson "(of Hutchinson Family Singers)" and Benjamin Jepson. Published by O. Hutchinson, Publisher, No. 272 Greenwich Street, New York, NY. 1860. [4" × 6"]. Bl/bk non-pictorial line border. "Lincoln and liberty." 76pp. [M-109]. [Crew/AL-175].

271.70 I'll Bet My Money On The Douglas Nag. w. No composer indicated. m. "Tune — *Camptown Races.*" In: *The Democratic Campaign Songster, No. #1*, page 34. Published by American Publishing House, No. 60 West Fourth Street, Cincinnati, OH. 1860. [3 7/8" × 5 1/16"]. Pk/bk litho of "Stephen A. Douglas," black line border. At top of cover — "No. 1, Price 10 Cents." 52pp. [M-118]. [Crew/SAD-12].

271.71 [In Illinois, There Can Be Found] (Campaign Song). w. No composer indicated. m. "Air — *Camptown Races.*" In: *The Democratic Campaign Songster, No. #1*, page 3. Published by American Publishing House. No. 60 West Fourth Street, Cincinnati, OH. 1860. [3 7/8" × 5 1/16"]. Pk/bk litho of "Stephen A. Douglas," black line border. At top of cover — "No. 1, Price 10 Cents." 52pp. [M-118]. [Crew/SAD-12].

271.72 [In Poor Democratic Times] (Song). w. No composer indicated. m. "Air — *Good Old Colony Times.*" In: *Republican Song Book*, page 39. c. Thomas Drew "(Late Editor of *The Massachusetts Spy*)." Published by Thayer and Eldridge, Boston, MA. 1860. [3 7/8" × 5 7/8"]. Br/bk litho of beardless Abraham Lincoln, vignettes of young Lincoln chopping rails, polling raft. 68pp. [M-108]. [Crew/AL-8].

271.73 John Fremont's Coming. w. No composer indicated. m. "Air — *Old Dan Tucker.*" In: *Fremont Songs For The People (Original And Selected)*, page 16. c. Thomas Drew "(Editor of *The Massachusetts Spy*)." Published by John P. Jewett & Company, Boston, MA. Copyright 1856 by Thomas Drew. [3 3/8" × 5 1/2"]. B/w litho of "J.C. Fremont." "The Campaign of 1856." 68pp. [Crew/JCF-18].

271.74 A Jolly Good Crew We'll Have. w. W.S. Sanford. m. "Air — *Little More Cider.*" In: *Connecticut Wide-Awake Songster*, page 71. e. John W. Hutchinson "(of Hutchinson Family Singers)" and Benjamin Jepson. Published by O. Hutchinson, Publisher, No. 272 Greenwich Street, New York, NY. 1860. [4" × 6"]. Bl/bk non-pictorial line border. "Lincoln and liberty." 76pp. [M-109]. [Crew/AL-175].

271.75 Jordan. w. J.J. Hutchinson. m. *Jordan Is A Hard Road to Travel*. In: *Hutchinson's Republican Songster For 1860*, page 25. e. John W. Hutchinson "(of the Hutchinson Family Singers)." Published by O. Hutchinson, Publisher, No. 272 Greenwich Street, New York, NY. 1860. B/w floral design border. "Lincoln and Liberty." 76pp. [M-110]. [Crew/AL-317].

271.76 Last Hope Of Buchanan. w. No composer indicated. m. "Air — *Last Rose Of Summer.*" In: *Fremont Songs For The People (Original And Selected)*, page 41. c. Thomas Drew "(Editor of *The Massachusetts Spy*)." Published by John P. Jewett & Company, Boston, MA. Copyright 1856 by Thomas Drew. [3 3/8" × 5 1/2"]. B/w litho of "J.C. Fremont." "The Campaign of 1856." 68pp. [Crew/JCF-18].

271.77 Lincoln Is The Man. w. Greenhorn. m. No tune indicated. In: *The Great Republican Campaigns Of 1860 And 1896*, page 165. e. Osborn H. Oldroyd. Published by Laird & Lee, Chicago, IL. 1896. [5 3/16" × 7 1/16"]. Gn/r/bk photos of Abraham Lincoln, William McKinley and Garrett Hobart. "Sound Money, Protection, Prosperity." 208pp. [Crew/AL-574].

271.78 The Lincoln Wedge. w. No composer indicated. m. "Air — *Maggie Lauder.*" "Respectfully dedicated to Gen. Clark of the Burlington, Vermont, Times." In: *The Great Republican Campaigns Of 1860 And 1896*, page 180. e. Osborn H. Oldroyd. Published by Laird & Lee, Chicago, IL. 1896. [5 3/16" × 7 1/16"]. Gn/r/bk photos of Abraham Lincoln, William McKinley and Garrett Hobart. "Sound Money, Protection, Prosperity." 208pp. [Crew/AL-574].

271.79 Little Dug. w. No composer indicated. m. "Tune — *Uncle Ned.*" In: *Republican Song Book*, page 35. c. Thomas Drew "(Late Editor of *The Massachusetts Spy*)." Published by Thayer and Eldridge, Boston, MA. 1860. [3 7/8" × 5 7/8"]. Br/bk litho of beardless Abraham Lincoln, vignettes of young Lincoln chopping rails, polling raft. 68pp. [M-108]. [Crew/AL-8].

271.80 The Loco Foco National Convention. w. J. Covert. m. "Tune — *Camptown Races.*" In: *Scott And*

Graham Melodies (Being A Collection Of Campaign Songs For 1852), page 22. Published by Huestis & Cozans, Nos. 104 and 106 Nassau Street, New York, NY. 1852. [3 13/16" × 6 1/16"]. B/w litho of Winfield Scott, geometric design border. "As sung by the Whig Clubs throughout the United States." 76pp. [M-086]. [Crew/WS-15].

271.81 The Long And Short Of It (Or The Complaint of Douglas). w. "B." m. Henry Tucker. In: *The Wide Awake Vocalist (Or Rail Splitters' Song Book)*, page 45. Published by E.A. Daggett, No. 333 Broadway, New York, NY. 1860. Non-pictorial geometric design border. "Words and Music for the Republican Campaign of 1860, Embracing a Great Variety of Songs, Solos, Duets and Choruses Arranged for Piano or melodeon; The best collection of Words and Music ever published for a campaign, Every Club and Family should have copies, so as to join in the choruses; The Ladies are invited to join in the choruses at the meetings." 68pp. [M-116]. [Crew/AL-59].

271.82 The Neb-Rascality. w. No composer indicated. m. Various popular tunes. "As Sung by the Hutchinson Family." In: *Hutchinson's Republican Songster For 1860*, page 38. e. John W. Hutchinson (of the Hutchinson Family Singers). Published by O. Hutchinson, Publisher, No. 272 Greenwich Street, New York, NY. 1860. B/w floral design border. "Lincoln and Liberty." 76pp. [M-110]. [Crew/AL-317].

271.83 The Neb-Rascality. w. No composer indicated. m. Various popular tunes. "As Sung by the Hutchinson Family." In: *Connecticut Wide-Awake Songster*, page 38. e. John W. Hutchinson "(of the Hutchinson Family Singers)" and Ben Jepson. Published by O. Hutchinson, Publisher, No. 272 Greenwich Street, New York, NY. 1860. [4" × 6"]. Bl/bk non-pictorial line border. "Lincoln and Liberty." 76pp. Pages 2, 75 and 76: Advertising. Pages 5 and 6: Contents. Pages 7 to 10: Republican platform. [M-109]. [Crew/AL-175].

271.84 New Nursery Ballads (For Good Little Democrats). w.m. No composer or tune indicated. In: *Hutchinson's Republican Songster For 1860*, page 72. e. John W. Hutchinson "(of the Hutchinson Family Singers)." Published by O. Hutchinson, Publisher, No. 272 Greenwich Street, New York, NY. 1860. B/w floral design border. "Lincoln and Liberty." 76pp. [M-110]. [Crew/AL-317].

271.85 The Night Of The Secession. w. No composer indicated. m. "Tune—*The Night Before Her Bridal.*" In: *Republican Song Book*, page 21. c. Thomas Drew "(Late Editor of *The Massachusetts Spy*)." Published by Thayer and Eldridge, Boston, MA. 1860. [3 7/8" × 5 7/8"]. Br/bk litho of beardless Abraham Lincoln, vignettes of young Lincoln chopping rails, polling raft. 68pp. [M-108]. [Crew/AL-8].

271.86 O Come, Come Away. w.m. No composer or tune indicated. In: *The Fremont Songster*, page 10. Published by [V-1: H.S. Riggs & Company, Publishers, No. 4 Cortland Street] [V-2: P.J. Cozans, No. 107 Nassau Street], New York, NY. 1856. [V-1: 3 5/8" × 5 3/4"] [V-2: 3 1/2" × 5 5/8"]. Be/bk litho of wreath, John C. Fremont. "With a current likeness of John C. Fremont, The People's Candidate for the Presidency." 40pp. [M-094, 095]. [Crew/JCF-45].

271.87 O! Poor Abraham! w. No composer indicated. m. "Tune—*O, Dearest Mae!*" In: *The Democratic Campaign Songster, No. #1*, page 12. Published by American Publishing House, No. 60 West Fourth Street, Cincinnati, OH. 1860. [3 7/8" × 5 11/16"]. Pk/bk litho of "Stephen A. Douglas," black line border. At top of cover—"No. 1, Price 10 Cents." 52pp. [M-118]. [Crew/SAD-12].

271.88 O Poor Douglas, You Cannot Follow Me. w. No composer indicated. m. "Air—*O, Susanna.*" In: *The Wide Awake Vocalist (Or Rail Splitters' Song Book)*, page 63. Published by E.A. Daggett, No. 333 Broadway, New York, NY. 1860. Non-pictorial geometric design border. "Words and Music for the Republican Campaign of 1860, Embracing a Great Variety of Songs, Solos, Duets and Choruses Arranged for Piano or melodeon; The best collection of Words and Music ever published for a campaign, Every Club and Family should have copies, so as to join in the choruses; The Ladies are invited to join in the choruses at the meetings." 68pp. [M-116]. [Crew/AL-59].

271.89 O! Poor Old Abe! w. No composer indicated. m. "Tune—*Nelly Gray.*" In: *The Democratic Campaign Songster, No. #1*, page 14. Published by American Publishing House, No. 60 West Fourth Street, Cincinnati, OH. 1860. [3 7/8" × 5 11/16"]. Pk/bk litho of "Stephen A. Douglas," black line border. At top of cover—"No. 1, Price 10 Cents." 52pp. [M-118]. [Crew/SAD-12].

271.90 O This Is Not My Own Native Land. w. No composer indicated. m. "Tune—*Nelly Gray.*" In: *The Democratic Campaign Songster, No. #1*, page 15. Published by American Publishing House, No. 60 West Fourth Street, Cincinnati, OH. 1860. [3 7/8" × 5 11/16"]. Pk/bk litho of "Stephen A. Douglas," black line border. At top of cover—"No. 1, Price 10 Cents." 52pp. [M-118]. [Crew/SAD-12].

271.91 O! Then Hurra! w. No composer indicated. m. "Tune—*Mary Blane.*" In: *The Democratic Campaign Songster, No. #1*, page 13. Published by American Publishing House, No. 60 West Fourth Street, Cincinnati, OH. 1860. [3 7/8" × 5 11/16"]. Pk/bk litho of "Stephen A. Douglas," black line border. At top of cover—"No. 1, Price 10 Cents." 52pp. [M-118]. [Crew/SAD-12].

271.92 [Oh, Douglas! The Choice Of The People] (Campaign Song). w. Miss R.H. m. No tune indicated. In: *The Democratic Campaign Songster: Douglas & Johnson Melodies*, page 14. Published by P.J. Cozans, Publisher, New York, NY. [1860]. [3 7/8" × 6"]. Y/bk litho of an eagle with ribbon—"Douglas & Johnson," train, ships, monument—"Liberty" sitting on rock base—"The Constitution." 40pp. [M-117]. [Crew/SAD-5].

271.93 [Oh Greeley, I Leave The Course] (Campaign Song). w. Col. George S. Hickox. m. "Air—*Oh, Carry Me Till I Die.*" "Dedicated to the Douglas and Johnson Club, of Olean." In: *The Democratic Campaign Songster: Douglas & Johnson Melodies*, page 21. Published by P.J. Cozans, Publisher, New York, NY. [1860]. [3 7/8" × 6"]. Y/bk litho of an eagle with ribbon—"Douglas & Johnson," train, ships, monument—"Liberty" sitting on rock base—"The Constitution." 40pp. [M-117]. [Crew/SAD-5].

271.94 Oh, You Can't Go The Caper, Stephen.

w.m. No composer or tune indicated. In: *The Wide Awake Vocalist (Or Rail Splitters' Song Book)*, page 23. Published by E.A. Daggett, No. 333 Broadway, New York, NY. 1860. Non-pictorial geometric design border. "Words and Music for the Republican Campaign of 1860, Embracing a Great Variety of Songs, Solos, Duets and Choruses Arranged for Piano or melodeon; The best collection of Words and Music ever published for a campaign, Every Club and Family should have copies, so as to join in the choruses; The Ladies are invited to join in the choruses at the meetings." 68pp. [M-116]. [Crew/AL-59].

271.95 Old Abe And His Fights. w. No composer indicated. m. "Air—*Roger De Coverly.*" Published in the *New York Herald*, August 30, 1860. [VBL, p. 343].

271.96 Old Abe And Little Dug w.m. No composer or tune indicated. In: *The Wide Awake Vocalist (Or Rail Splitters' Song Book)*, page 51. Published by E.A. Daggett, No. 333 Broadway, New York, NY. 1860. Non-pictorial geometric design border. "Words and Music for the Republican Campaign of 1860, Embracing a Great Variety of Songs, Solos, Duets and Choruses Arranged for Piano or melodeon; The best collection of Words and Music ever published for a campaign, Every Club and Family should have copies, so as to join in the choruses; The Ladies are invited to join in the choruses at the meetings." 68pp. [M-116]. [Crew/AL-59].

271.97 Old Abe Lincoln Is The Man w. No composer indicated. m. "Air—*Dandy Jim Of Caroline.*" In: *The Wide Awake Vocalist (Or Rail Splitters' Song Book)*, page 51. Published by E.A. Daggett, No. 333 Broadway, New York, NY. 1860. Non-pictorial geometric design border. "Words and Music for the Republican Campaign of 1860, Embracing a Great Variety of Songs, Solos, Duets and Choruses Arranged for Piano or melodeon; The best collection of Words and Music ever published for a campaign, Every Club and Family should have copies, so as to join in the choruses; The Ladies are invited to join in the choruses at the meetings." 68pp. [M-116]. [Crew/AL-59].

271.98 Old Abe's Preliminary Visit To The White House. w. No composer indicated. m. "Tune—*The King And Countryman.*" In: *Republican Song Book*, page 810 c. Thomas Drew "(Late Editor of *The Massachusetts Spy*)." Published by Thayer and Eldridge, Boston, MA. 1860. [3⅞" × 5⅞"]. Br/bk litho of beardless Abraham Lincoln, vignettes of young Lincoln chopping rails, polling raft. 68pp. [M-108]. [Crew/AL-8].

271.99 Old Abe's Preliminary Visit To The White House. w. No composer indicated. m. "Air—*Villikins And His Dinah.*" In: *The Great Republican Campaigns Of 1860 And 1896*, page 151. e. Osborn H. Oldroyd. Published by Laird & Lee, Chicago, IL. 1896. [5$\frac{5}{16}$" × 7$\frac{7}{16}$"]. Gn/r/bk photos of Abraham Lincoln, William McKinley and Garrett Hobart. "Sound Money, Protection, Prosperity." 208pp. [Crew/AL-574].

271.100 Old Uncle Abe. w. No composer indicated. m. "Air—*My Old Kentucky Home.*" In: *The Democratic Campaign Songster: Douglas & Johnson Melodies*, page 30. Published by P.J. Cozans, Publisher, New York, NY. [1860]. [3⅞" × 6"]. Y/bk litho of an eagle with ribbon—"Douglas & Johnson," train, ships, monument—"Liberty" sitting on rock base—"The Constitution." 40pp. [M-117]. [Crew/SAD-5].

271.101 Our Champions. w.m. No composer or tune indicated. In: *The Democratic Campaign Songster, No. #1*, page 43. Published by American Publishing House, No. 60 West Fourth Street, Cincinnati, OH. 1860. [3⅞" × 5$\frac{11}{16}$"]. Pk/bk litho of "Stephen A. Douglas," black line border. At top of cover—"No. 1, Price 10 Cents." 52pp. [M-118]. [Crew/SAD-12].

271.102 [Our Good Old Uncle Sam Is Sick] (A Campaign Song). w.m. No composer or tune indicated. In: *The Republican Campaign Songster No. #1*, page 30. Published by American Publishing House, No. 60 West Fourth Street, Cincinnati, OH. [1860]. [3¾" × 5¾"]. B/w litho of Abraham Lincoln. 48pp. [?]. [M-113]. [Crew/AL-298].

271.103 Our Standard Bearer. w. Robert A. Cumming. m. No tune indicated. In: *The Republican Campaign Songster For 1860*, page 41. c. W.H. Burleigh. Published by [V-1 and V-2: H. Dayton, No. 36 Howard Street, New York, NY] [V-3: McNally & Company, No. 81 Dearborn Street, Chicago, IL]. 1860. [V-1: Gn/bk] [V-2: Y/bk] [V-3: Be/bk] [V-4: Bl/bk]. "Price 10 cents." [3$\frac{13}{16}$" × 6"]. 72pp. [M-104]. [Crew/AL-57].

271.104 [Our Sucker Pole Is Planted] (Organization Song). w.m. No composer or tune indicated. In: *The Republican Campaign Songster No. #1*, page 21. Published by American Publishing House, No. 60 West Fourth Street, Cincinnati, OH. [1860]. [3¾" × 5¾"]. B/w litho of Abraham Lincoln. 48pp. [?]. [M-113]. [Crew/AL-298].

271.105 Patent Chivalry. w. No composer indicated. m. "Air—*A Highland Lad My Love Was Born.*" In: *Fremont Songs For The People (Original And Selected)*, page 39. c. Thomas Drew "(Editor of *The Massachusetts Spy*)." Published by John P. Jewett & Company, Boston, MA. Copyright 1856 by Thomas Drew. [3⅝" × 5½"]. B/w litho of "J.C. Fremont." "The Campaign of 1856." 68pp. [Crew/JCF-18].

271.106 The People Had Five Candidates (Or The Medley Crew). w. No composer indicated. m.a. Henry Tucker. In: *The Wide Awake Vocalist (Or Rail Splitters' Song Book)*, page 42. Published by E.A. Daggett, No. 333 Broadway, New York, NY. 1860. Non-pictorial geometric design border. "Words and Music for the Republican Campaign of 1860, Embracing a Great Variety of Songs, Solos, Duets and Choruses Arranged for Piano or melodeon; The best collection of Words and Music ever published for a campaign, Every Club and Family should have copies, so as to join in the choruses; The Ladies are invited to join in the choruses at the meetings." 68pp. [M-116]. [Crew/AL-59].

271.107 The People's Nominee. w. Karl Kriton. m. "Tune—*Boatman Dance.*" In: *Connecticut Wide-Awake Songster*, page 15. e. John W. Hutchinson "(of Hutchinson Family Singers)" and Benjamin Jepson. Published by O. Hutchinson, Publisher, No. 272 Greenwich Street, New York, NY. 1860. [4" × 6"]. Bl/bk non-pictorial line border. "Lincoln and liberty." 76pp. [M-109]. [Crew/AL-175].

271.108 The People's Nominee. w. Karl Kriton. m. "Tune—*Nelly Bly.*" In: *Hutchinson's Republican Songster For 1860*, page 15. e. John W. Hutchinson "(of the

Hutchinson Family Singers)." Published by O. Hutchinson, Publisher, No. 272 Greenwich Street, New York, NY. 1860. B/w floral design border. "Lincoln and Liberty." 76pp. [M-110]. [Crew/AL-317].

271.109 The Philistines And Goliath. w.m. No composer or tune indicated. In: *The Democratic Campaign Songster, No. #1,* page 22. Published by American Publishing House, No. 60 West Fourth Street, Cincinnati, OH. 1860. [3⅞" × 5^11^/16"]. Pk/bk litho of "Stephen A. Douglas," black line border. At top of cover—"No. 1, Price 10 Cents." 52pp. [M-118]. [Crew/SAD-12].

271.110 Pierce's Lament. w. No composer indicated. m. "Tune—*Oh, Boys, Carry Me 'Long.*" In: *Scott And Graham* Melodies *(Being A Collection Of Campaign Songs For 1852),* page 35. Published by Huestis & Cozans, Nos. 104 and 106 Nassau Street, New York, NY. 1852. [3 13/16" × 6 1/16"]. B/w litho of Winfield Scott, geometric design border. "As sung by the Whig Clubs throughout the United States." 76pp. [M-086]. [Crew/WS-15].

271.111 Poor Little Doug. w. No composer indicated. m. "Air—*Uncle Ned.*" In: *The Wide Awake Vocalist (Or Rail Splitters' Song Book),* page 60. Published by E.A. Daggett, No. 333 Broadway, New York, NY. 1860. Non-pictorial geometric design border. "Words and Music for the Republican Campaign of 1860, Embracing a Great Variety of Songs, Solos, Duets and Choruses Arranged for Piano or melodeon; The best collection of Words and Music ever published for a campaign, Every Club and Family should have copies, so as to join in the choruses; The Ladies are invited to join in the choruses at the meetings." 68pp. [M-116]. [Crew/AL-59].

271.112 Poor Little Doug (A New Nigger Song to an Old Nigger Tune). w.m. No composer or tune indicated. In: *The Great Republican Campaigns Of 1860 And 1896,* page 161. e. Osborn H. Oldroyd. Published by Laird & Lee, Chicago, IL. 1896. [5 5/16" × 7 7/16"]. Gn/r/bk photos of Abraham Lincoln, William McKinley and Garrett Hobart. "Sound Money, Protection, Prosperity." 208pp. [Crew/AL-574].

271.113 Poor Little Dug (A New Nigger Song to an Old Nigger Tune). w. No composer indicated. m. "Air—*Uncle Ned.*" In: *The Republican Campaign Songster No. #1,* page 23. Published by American Publishing House, No. 60 West Fourth Street, Cincinnati, OH. [1860]. [3¾" × 5¾"]. B/w litho of Abraham Lincoln. 48pp. [?]. [M-113]. [Crew/AL-298].

271.114 Presidential Aspirants. w. No composer indicated. m. "Air—*Ho! For The White House.*" Published in the *New York Herald,* August 30, 1860. [VBL, p. 342].

271.115 The Presidential Track. w. No composer indicated. m. "Air—*Old Dan Tucker.*" In: *Fillmore And Donelson Songs For The Campaign,* page 35. Published by Robert M. De Witt, Nos. 160 and 162 Nassau Street, New York, NY. November 4, 1856. [4¾" × 7⅛"]. Bl/bk litho of George Washington—"July 4, 1776," wreath, geometric design border. "This is the only authorized edition containing Duganne's Songs. Price 6 cts. each, $4 per 100. Discount to trade." Long quote from George Washington's "Farewell Address." 40pp. [M-101, 102]. [Crew/MF-10].

271.116 The Presidential Track. w. No composer indicated. m. "Air—*Camptown Races.*" In: *The Democratic Campaign Songster: Douglas & Johnson Melodies,* page 15. Published by P.J. Cozans, Publisher, New York, NY. [1860]. [3⅞" × 6"]. Y/bk litho of an eagle with ribbon—"Douglas & Johnson," train, ships, monument—"Liberty" sitting on rock base—"The Constitution." 40pp. [M-117]. [Crew/SAD-5].

271.117 The Rail Splitters. w. No composer indicated. m. "Air—*Uncle Ned.*" In: *The Great Republican Campaigns Of 1860 And 1896,* page 164. e. Osborn H. Oldroyd. Published by Laird & Lee, Chicago, IL. 1896. [5 5/16" × 7 7/16"]. Gn/r/bk photos of Abraham Lincoln, William McKinley and Garrett Hobart. "Sound Money, Protection, Prosperity." 208pp. [Crew/AL-574].

271.118 The Rally. w.m. No composer or tune indicated. In: *The Democratic Campaign Songster: Douglas & Johnson Melodies,* page 32. Published by P.J. Cozans, Publisher, New York, NY. [1860]. [3⅞" × 6"]. Y/bk litho of an eagle with ribbon—"Douglas & Johnson," train, ships, monument—"Liberty" sitting on rock base—"The Constitution." 40pp. [M-117]. [Crew/SAD-5].

271.119 Rally For Breckenridge And Lane. w. No composer indicated. m. "Air—*The Low Back'd Car.*" Published by H. De Marsan, Publisher, No. 60 Chatham Street, New York, NY. [1860]. R/w/b hand-colored penny song sheet with litho order of cherubs, sailor, Miss Liberty, geometric designs. 2pp. Page 2: Blank. [Crew/JCB-7]. [AMC].

271.120 Rally For Douglas. w. No composer indicated. m. "Air—*Washing Day.*" In: *The Democratic Campaign Songster: Douglas & Johnson Melodies,* page 34. Published by P.J. Cozans, Publisher, New York, NY. [1860]. [3⅞" × 6"]. Y/bk litho of an eagle with ribbon—"Douglas & Johnson," train, ships, monument—"Liberty" sitting on rock base—"The Constitution." 40pp. [M-117]. [Crew/SAD-5].

271.121 Red, White And Blue. w.m. No composer or tune indicated. In: *The Democratic Campaign Songster, No. #1,* page 19. Published by American Publishing House, No. 60 West Fourth Street, Cincinnati, OH. 1860. [3⅞" × 5 11/16"]. Pk/bk litho of "Stephen A. Douglas," black line border. At top of cover—"No. 1, Price 10 Cents." 52pp. [M-118]. [Crew/SAD-12].

271.122 Red, White And Blue. w.m. No composer or tune indicated. In: *The Democratic Campaign Songster, No. #1,* page 32. Published by American Publishing House, No. 60 West Fourth Street, Cincinnati, OH. 1860. [3⅞" × 5 11/16"]. Pk/bk litho of "Stephen A. Douglas," black line border. At top of cover—"No. 1, Price 10 Cents." 52pp. [M-118]. [Crew/SAD-12].

271.123 The Republican Ball. w. James A. Boone. m. "Air—*Rosin The Bow.*" In: *The Republican Campaign Songster, A Collection Of Lyrics, Original And Selected, Specifically Prepared For The Friends Of Freedom In The Campaign Of Fifty-Six,* page 90. Published by Miller, Orton & Mulligan, No. 25 Park Row, New York, NY. 1856. [3 13/16" × 6"]. Be/bk litho of "Colonel John C. Fremont" facing to viewer's left, black line border. 112pp. [M-097]. [Crew/JCF-24].

271.124 [Rouse Ye, Freemen, From Your Slumbers] (Campaign Song). w. E.W. Locke. m. "Air—*Old*

Dan Tucker." In: *The Fremont Songster*, page 46. Published by [V-1: H.S. Riggs & Company, Publishers, No. 4 Cortland Street] [V-2: P.J. Cozans, No. 107 Nassau Street], New York, NY. 1856. [V-1: 3⅝" × 5¾"] [V-2: 3½" × 5⅝"]. Be/bk litho of wreath, John C. Fremont. "With a current likeness of John C. Fremont, The People's Candidate for the Presidency." 40pp. [M-094, 095]. [Crew/JCF-45].

271.125 The Senator's Lament. w. No composer indicated. m. "Tune—*Robinson Crusoe.*" In: *Republican Song Book*, page 58. c. Thomas Drew "(Late Editor of *The Massachusetts Spy*)." Published by Thayer and Eldridge, Boston, MA. 1860. [3⅞" × 5⅞"]. Br/bk litho of beardless Abraham Lincoln, vignettes of young Lincoln chopping rails, polling raft. 68pp. "The Campaign of 1860, Republican Songs for the People, Original and Selected." Page 2: B/w litho of Abraham Lincoln. Pages 62–64: Republican platform. [M-108]. [Crew/AL-8].

271.126 Shool. w.m. No composer or tune indicated. In: *Republican Song Book*, page 6. c. Thomas Drew "(Late Editor of *The Massachusetts Spy*)." Published by Thayer and Eldridge, Boston, MA. 1860. [3⅞" × 5⅞"]. Br/bk litho of beardless Abraham Lincoln, vignettes of young Lincoln chopping rails, polling raft. 68pp. "The Campaign of 1860, Republican Songs for the People, Original and Selected." Page 2: B/w litho of Abraham Lincoln. [M-108]. [Crew/AL-8].

271.127 Sing A Song Of Charleston. w. M.D. m. "Air—*Sing A Song Of Sixpence.*" In: *The Wide Awake Vocalist (Or Rail Splitters' Song Book)*, page 61. Published by E.A. Daggett, No. 333 Broadway, New York, NY. 1860. Non-pictorial geometric design border. "Words and Music for the Republican Campaign of 1860, Embracing a Great Variety of Songs, Solos, Duets and Choruses Arranged for Piano or melodeon; The best collection of Words and Music ever published for a campaign, Every Club and Family should have copies, so as to join in the choruses; The Ladies are invited to join in the choruses at the meetings." 68pp. [M-116]. [Crew/AL-59].

271.128 Slavery Embarkation. w. No composer indicated. m. "Air—*Fisherman's Bark.*" In: *Fremont Songs For The People (Original And Selected)*, page 48. c. Thomas Drew "(Editor of *The Massachusetts Spy*)." Published by John P. Jewett & Company, Boston, MA. Copyright 1856 by Thomas Drew. [3⅝" × 5½"]. B/w litho of "J.C. Fremont." "The Campaign of 1856." 68pp. [Crew/JCF-18].

271.129 Song. w. No composer indicated. m. "Air—*Sparkling And Bright.*" In: *Fremont Songs For The People (Original And Selected)*, page 44. c. Thomas Drew "(Editor of *The Massachusetts Spy*)." Published by John P. Jewett & Company, Boston, MA. Copyright 1856 by Thomas Drew. [3⅝" × 5½"]. B/w litho of "J.C. Fremont." "The Campaign of 1856." 68pp. [Crew/JCF-18].

271.130 Song For The Times (On The State of the Union). w. Judson. m. "Tune—*Axes To Grind.*" In: *Hutchinson's Republican Songster For 1860*, page 30. e. John W. Hutchinson "(of the Hutchinson Family Singers)." Published by O. Hutchinson, Publisher, No. 272 Greenwich Street, New York, NY. 1860. B/w floral design border. "Lincoln and Liberty." 76pp. [M-110]. [Crew/AL-317].

271.131 A Song Of The Campaign. w. No composer indicated. m. "Air—*Wait For The Wagon.*" In: *Republican Song Book*, page 55. c. Thomas Drew "(Late Editor of *The Massachusetts Spy*)." Published by Thayer and Eldridge, Boston, MA. 1860. [3⅞" × 5⅞"]. Br/bk litho of beardless Abraham Lincoln, vignettes of young Lincoln chopping rails, polling raft. 68pp. [M-108]. [Crew/AL-8].

271.132 The Song Of The Democracy. w.m. No composer or tune indicated. In: *The Democratic Campaign Songster, No. #1*, page 5. Published by American Publishing House, No. 60 West Fourth Street, Cincinnati, OH. 1860. [3⅞" × 5¹¹⁄₁₆"]. Pk/bk litho of "Stephen A. Douglas," black line border. At top of cover—"No. 1, Price 10 Cents." 52pp. [M-118]. [Crew/SAD-12].

271.133 Song Of The Office Holder. w. No composer indicated. m. "Air—*A Few Days.*" In: *Republican Song Book*, page 8. c. Thomas Drew "(Late Editor of *The Massachusetts Spy*)." Published by Thayer and Eldridge, Boston, MA. 1860. [3⅞" × 5⅞"]. Br/bk litho of beardless Abraham Lincoln, vignettes of young Lincoln chopping rails, polling raft. 68pp. [M-108]. [Crew/AL-8].

271.134 Sons Of Freedom. w. No composer indicated. m. "Air—*Yankee Doodle.*" In: *The Fremont Songster*, page 3. Published by [V-1: H.S. Riggs & Company, Publishers, No. 4 Cortland Street] [V-2: P.J. Cozans, No. 107 Nassau Street], New York, NY. 1856. [V-1: 3⅝" × 5¾"] [V-2: 3½" × 5⅝"]. Be/bk litho of wreath, John C. Fremont. "With a current likeness of John C. Fremont, The People's Candidate for the Presidency." 40pp. [M-094, 095]. [Crew/JCF-45].

271.135 Stand By The Flag. w.m. No composer or tune indicated. In: *The Democratic Campaign Songster: Douglas & Johnson Melodies*, page 10. Published by P.J. Cozans, Publisher, New York, NY. [1860]. [3⅞" × 6"]. Y/bk litho of an eagle with ribbon—"Douglas & Johnson," train, ships, monument—"Liberty" sitting on rock base—"The Constitution." 40pp. [M-117]. [Crew/SAD-5].

271.136 The Taller Man Well Skilled (For Male Voices). w. "G." m.a. Henry Tucker. In: *The Wide Awake Vocalist (Or Rail Splitters' Song Book)*, page 28. Published by E.A. Daggett, No. 333 Broadway, New York, NY. 1860. Non-pictorial geometric design border. "Words and Music for the Republican Campaign of 1860, Embracing a Great Variety of Songs, Solos, Duets and Choruses Arranged for Piano or melodeon; The best collection of Words and Music ever published for a campaign, Every Club and Family should have copies, so as to join in the choruses; The Ladies are invited to join in the choruses at the meetings." 68pp. [M-116]. [Crew/AL-59].

271.137 That Old Man 'Bout Fifty-Two. w.m. No composer or tune indicated. In: *Republican Song Book*, page 57. c. Thomas Drew "(Late Editor of *The Massachusetts Spy*)." Published by Thayer and Eldridge, Boston, MA. 1860. [3⅞" × 5⅞"]. Br/bk litho of beardless Abraham Lincoln, vignettes of young Lincoln chopping rails, polling raft. 68pp. [M-108]. [Crew/AL-8].

271.138 Then Rally! w. No composer indicated. m.

"Tune—*Bonnie Eloise.*" In: *The Democratic Campaign Songster, No. #1,* page 17. Published by American Publishing House, No. 60 West Fourth Street, Cincinnati, OH. 1860. [3⅞" × 5¹⁵⁄₁₆"]. Pk/bk litho of "Stephen A. Douglas," black line border. At top of cover—"No. 1, Price 10 Cents." 52pp. [M-118]. [Crew/SAD-12].

271.139 [There's An Old Plow Hoss Whose Name Is Dug] (Campaign Song). w.m. No composer indicated. m. "Tune—*Du Da.*" In: *The Republican Campaign Songster No. #1,* page 15. Published by American Publishing House, No. 60 West Fourth Street, Cincinnati, OH. [1860]. [3¾" × 5¾"]. B/w litho of Abraham Lincoln. 48pp. [?]. [M-113]. [Crew/AL-298].

271.140 They Will Miss You At Home. w.m. No composer or tune indicated. In: *The Democratic Campaign Songster: Douglas & Johnson Melodies,* page 30. Published by P.J. Cozans, Publisher, New York, NY. [1860]. [3⅞" × 6"]. Y/bk litho of an eagle with ribbon—"Douglas & Johnson," train, ships, monument—"Liberty" sitting on rock base—"The Constitution." 40pp. [M-117]. [Crew/SAD-5].

271.141 Those Noble Old Statesmen. w. No composer indicated. m. "Air—*Araby's Daughter.*" In: *The Fremont Songster,* page 18. Published by [V-1: H.S. Riggs & Company, Publishers, No. 4 Cortland Street] [V-2: P.J. Cozans, No. 107 Nassau Street], New York, NY. 1856. [V-1: 3⅝" × 5¾"] [V-2: 3½" × 5⅝"]. Be/bk litho of wreath, John C. Fremont. "With a current likeness of John C. Fremont, The People's Candidate for the Presidency." 40pp. [M-094, 095]. [Crew/JCF-45].

271.142 Three Cheers For Douglas. w.m. No composer or tune indicated. In: *The Democratic Campaign Songster: Douglas & Johnson Melodies,* page 16. Published by P.J. Cozans, Publisher, New York, NY. [1860]. [3⅞" × 6"]. Y/bk litho of an eagle with ribbon—"Douglas & Johnson," train, ships, monument—"Liberty" sitting on rock base—"The Constitution." 40pp. [M-117]. [Crew/SAD-5].

271.143 To Stephen A. Douglas. w.m. No composer or tune indicated. In: *The Democratic Campaign Songster: Douglas & Johnson Melodies,* page 28. Published by P.J. Cozans, Publisher, New York, NY. [1860]. [3⅞" × 6"]. Y/bk litho of an eagle with ribbon—"Douglas & Johnson," train, ships, monument—"Liberty" sitting on rock base—"The Constitution." 40pp. [M-117]. [Crew/SAD-5].

271.144 To The Work. w.m. No composer or tune indicated. In: *The Fremont Songster,* page 43. Published by [V-1: H.S. Riggs & Company, Publishers, No. 4 Cortland Street] [V-2: P.J. Cozans, No. 107 Nassau Street], New York, NY. 1856. [V-1: 3⅝" × 5¾"] [V-2: 3½" × 5⅝"]. Be/bk litho of wreath, John C. Fremont. "With a current likeness of John C. Fremont, The People's Candidate for the Presidency." 40pp. [M-094, 095]. [Crew/JCF-45].

271.145 The Toast. w. No composer indicated. m. "Air—*Vive La Companie.*" In: *The Freeman's Glee Book, A Collection Of Songs, Odes, Glees And Ballads With Music, Original And Selected, Harmonized And Arranged For Each. Published Under The Auspices Of The Central Fremont And Dayton Glee Club Of The City Of New York, And Dedicated To All, Who, Cherishing Republican Liberty Consider Freedom Worth A Song,* page 94. Published by Miller, Orton & Mulligan, No. 25 Park Row, New York, NY. [and Auburn, NY]. 1856. [4¹⁵⁄₁₆" × 6"]. Pk/bk litho of man on mountain peak, music sheets, geometric designs. 112pp. [Crew/JCF-16].

271.146 Uncle Abe And Johnny Breck. w. No composer indicated. m. "Air—*Robin Ruff.*" In: *The Democratic Campaign Songster: Douglas & Johnson Melodies,* page 29. Published by P.J. Cozans, Publisher, New York, NY. [1860]. [3⅞" × 6"]. Y/bk litho of an eagle with ribbon—"Douglas & Johnson," train, ships, monument—"Liberty" sitting on rock base—"The Constitution." 40pp. [M-117]. [Crew/SAD-5].

271.147 Unroll The Republican Stars (Solo or Duet, with mixed Chorus). w. George W. Bungay. m.a. A. Cull. In: *The Wide Awake Vocalist (Or Rail Splitters' Song Book),* page 32. Published by E.A. Daggett, No. 333 Broadway, New York, NY. 1860. Non-pictorial geometric design border. "Words and Music for the Republican Campaign of 1860, Embracing a Great Variety of Songs, Solos, Duets and Choruses Arranged for Piano or melodeon; The best collection of Words and Music ever published for a campaign, Every Club and Family should have copies, so as to join in the choruses; The Ladies are invited to join in the choruses at the meetings." 68pp. [M-116]. [Crew/AL-59].

271.148 Vive La Honest Abe (A Wide-Awake Song). w. C.L. Russell. m. "Air—*Vive La Companie.*" In: *Connecticut Wide-Awake Songster,* page 29. e. John W. Hutchinson "(of Hutchinson Family Singers)" and Benjamin Jepson. Published by O. Hutchinson, Publisher, No. 272 Greenwich Street, New York, NY. 1860. [4" × 6"]. Bl/bk non-pictorial line border. "Lincoln and liberty." 76pp. [M-109]. [Crew/AL-175].

271.149 Vote For Bell Of Tennessee. w. No composer indicated. m. "Air—*Harlem National Union Glee Club No. 1.*" Published in the *New York Herald,* 1860. [VBL, p. 343].

271.150 The War-Cry. w. No composer indicated. m. "Air—*There's Nae Luck About The House.*" In: *The Democratic Campaign Songster: Douglas & Johnson Melodies,* page 19. Published by P.J. Cozans, Publisher, New York, NY. [1860]. [3⅞" × 6"]. Y/bk litho of an eagle with ribbon—"Douglas & Johnson," train, ships, monument—"Liberty" sitting on rock base—"The Constitution." 40pp. [M-117]. [Crew/SAD-5].

271.151 We Mean To Win The Day. w. No composer indicated. m. "Air—*Yankee Doodle.*" In: *The Democratic Campaign Songster, No. #1,* page 31. Published by American Publishing House, No. 60 West Fourth Street, Cincinnati, OH. 1860. [3⅞" × 5¹⁵⁄₁₆"]. Pk/bk litho of "Stephen A. Douglas," black line border. At top of cover—"No. 1, Price 10 Cents." 52pp. [M-118]. [Crew/SAD-12].

271.152 We're Bound To Work. w. No composer indicated. m. "Air—*Camptown Races.*" "The Springfield Glee Club sang the above song at a ratification meeting, Springfield, Ill., June 7, 1860." In: *The Great Republican Campaigns Of 1860 And 1896,* page 171. e. Osborn H. Oldroyd. Published by Laird & Lee, Chicago, IL. 1896. [5⁵⁄₁₆" × 7⁷⁄₁₆"]. Gn/r/bk photos of Abraham Lincoln, William McKinley and Garrett Hobart. "Sound Money, Protection, Prosperity." 208pp. [Crew/AL-574].

271.153 We're Bound To Work All Night. w. No composer indicated. m. "Air—*Du Da.*" In: *The Wide Awake Vocalist (Or Rail Splitters' Song Book)*, page 22. Published by E.A. Daggett, No. 333 Broadway, New York, NY. 1860. Non-pictorial geometric design border. "Words and Music for the Republican Campaign of 1860, Embracing a Great Variety of Songs, Solos, Duets and Choruses Arranged for Piano or melodeon; The best collection of Words and Music ever published for a campaign, Every Club and Family should have copies, so as to join in the choruses; The Ladies are invited to join in the choruses at the meetings." 68pp. [M-116]. [Crew/AL-59].

271.154 [What Has Caused This Great Commotion] (A Campaign Song). w. No composer indicated. m. "Air—*Oh! What Has Caused This Great Commotion?*" "From the *Boston Atlas.*" In: *The Republican Campaign Songster, A Collection Of Lyrics, Original And Selected, Specifically Prepared For The Friends Of Freedom In The Campaign Of Fifty-Six*, page 40. Published by Miller, Orton & Mulligan, No. 25 Park Row, New York, NY. 1856. [3 13/16" × 6"]. Be/bk litho of "Colonel John C. Fremont" facing to viewer's left, black line border. 112pp. [M-097]. [Crew/JCF-24].

271.155 When The Late Autumn Comes. w. No composer indicated. m. "Tune—*Gentle Annie.*" In: *The Democratic Campaign Songster, No. #1*, page 11. Published by American Publishing House, No. 60 West Fourth Street, Cincinnati, OH. 1860. [3 7/8" × 5 11/16"]. Pk/bk litho of "Stephen A. Douglas," black line border. At top of cover—"No. 1, Price 10 Cents." 52pp. [M-118]. [Crew/SAD-12].

271.156 When We Met In Convention. w. No composer indicated. m. "Air—*'Tis My Delight Of A Shiny Night.*" In: *Fillmore And Donelson Songs For The Campaign* (Songster), page 21. Published by Robert M. De Witt, Nos. 160 and 162 Nassau Street, New York, NY. November 4, 1856. [4 3/4" × 7 1/8"]. Bl/bk litho of George Washington—"July 4, 1776," wreath, geometric design border. "This is the only authorized edition containing Duganne's Songs. Price 6 cts. each, $4 per 100. Discount to trade." Long quote from George Washington's "Farewell Address." 40pp. Page 3: "Union and Peace." [M-101, 102]. [Crew/MF-10].

271.157 Where Are They? w. No composer indicated. m. "Tune—*Where, Oh Where Are The Hebrew Children?*" In: *Republican Song Book*, page 28. c. Thomas Drew "(Late Editor of *The Massachusetts Spy*)." Published by Thayer and Eldridge, Boston, MA. 1860. [3 7/8" × 5 7/8"]. Br/bk litho of beardless Abraham Lincoln, vignettes of young Lincoln chopping rails, polling raft. 68pp. [M-108]. [Crew/AL-8].

271.158 Where, Oh, Where! w.m. No composer or tune indicated. In: *The Great Republican Campaigns Of 1860 And 1896*, page 166. e. Osborn H. Oldroyd. Published by Laird & Lee, Chicago, IL. 1896. [5 5/16" × 7 7/16"]. Gn/r/bk photos of Abraham Lincoln, William McKinley and Garrett Hobart. "Sound Money, Protection, Prosperity." 208pp. [Crew/AL-574].

271.159 Where, Oh! Where Is Jimmy Buchanan? w. No composer indicated. m. "Air—*Where, Oh Where Are The Hebrew Children?* In: *The Wide Awake Vocalist (Or Rail Splitters' Song Book)*, page 40. Published by E.A. Daggett, No. 333 Broadway, New York, NY. 1860. Non-pictorial geometric design border. "Words and Music for the Republican Campaign of 1860, Embracing a Great Variety of Songs, Solos, Duets and Choruses Arranged for Piano or melodeon; The best collection of Words and Music ever published for a campaign, Every Club and Family should have copies, so as to join in the choruses; The Ladies are invited to join in the choruses at the meetings." 68pp. [M-116]. [Crew/AL-59].

271.160 Wide Awake (Campaign Song). w. No composer indicated. m. "Tune—*A Wet Sheet And A Flowing Sea.*" In: *Republican Song Book*, page 27. c. Thomas Drew "(Late Editor of *The Massachusetts Spy*)." Published by Thayer and Eldridge, Boston, MA. 1860. [3 7/8" × 5 7/8"]. Br/bk litho of beardless Abraham Lincoln, vignettes of young Lincoln chopping rails, polling raft. 68pp. [M-108]. [Crew/AL-8].

271.161 Wide-Awake Club Song. w. No composer indicated. m. "Air—*A Wet Sheet And A Flowing Sea.*" In: *Connecticut Wide-Awake Songster*, page 70. e. John W. Hutchinson "(of Hutchinson Family Singers)" and Benjamin Jepson. Published by O. Hutchinson, Publisher, No. 272 Greenwich Street, New York, NY. 1860. [4" × 6"]. Bl/bk non-pictorial line border. "Lincoln and liberty." 76pp. [M-109]. [Crew/AL-175].

• **AmPM-272 DUNCAN**, Joseph (Justice of the Peace, Jackson County, 1821–1823; State Senate, 1824–1826; U.S. House, 1827–1834, Governor, 1834–1838)

272.1 Here's To Van Buren, The Chief Of Our Land. w. No composer indicated. m. "Tune—*Here's To The Maiden Of Blushing Fifteen.*" In: *Songs For The People (Or Tippecanoe Melodies)* [Songster], page 24. "Dedicated to the Democratic Whig Young Men of the City and County of New York." Published for the Authors by James P. Giffing, No. 56 Gold Street, New York, NY. 1840. [3 3/4" × 6"]. Litho of William Henry Harrison, log cabin, flag. "Original and Selected." 76pp. [M-019]. [Crew/WHH-63].

272.2 The Locofoco Exit, On The Fourth Of March, 1841. w. No composer indicated. m. "Tune—*I See Them On Their Winding Way.*" In: *Songs For The People (Or Tippecanoe Melodies)* [Songster], page 33. "Dedicated to the Democratic Whig Young Men of the City and County of New York." Published for the Authors by James P. Giffing, No. 56 Gold Street, New York, NY. 1840. [3 3/4" × 6"]. Litho of William Henry Harrison, log cabin, flag. "Original and Selected." 76pp. [M-019]. [Crew/WHH-63].

272.3 Our Governors March (Or Two Step) m. Joseph Gearen. Published by Lyon & Healy, Chicago, IL. 1897. Bk/w/gn/br drawings of all Illinois Governors, Illinois capitol building, farm scene, law books. 6pp. Page 2: Blank. Page 6: Advertising. [Crew/JMP-1].

272.4 The Spoilsmen. w.m. No composer or tune indicated. In: *Songs For The People (Or Tippecanoe Melodies)* [Songster], page 31. "Dedicated to the Democratic Whig Young Men of the City and County of New York." Published for the Authors by James P. Giffing, No. 56 Gold Street, New York, NY. 1840. [3 3/4" × 6"]. Litho of William Henry Harrison, log cabin, flag. "Original and Selected." 76pp. [M-019]. [Crew/WHH-63].

- **AmPM-273 EDWARDS**, Ninian (State House, Kentucky, 1796–1797; General Court Judge, Kentucky, 1803; Circuit Court Judge, Kentucky, 1804; Judge, Court of Appeals, Kentucky, 1806; State Supreme Court, Kentucky, 1808; Governor, Territory of Illinois, 1809–1818; U.S. Senate, Illinois, 1818–1824; U.S. Minister to Mexico, 1824; Governor, Illinois, 1826–1831)

273.1 Governors March (Or Two Step) m. Joseph Gearen. Published by Lyon & Healy, Chicago, IL. 1897. Bk/w/gn/br drawings of all Illinois Governors, Illinois capitol building, farm scene, law books. 6pp. Page 2: Blank. Page 6: Advertising.

- **AmPM-274 FIFER**, Joseph Wilson (State Senate, 1881–1883; Governor, 1889–1893)

274.1 Our Governors March (Or Two Step) m. Joseph Gearen. Published by Lyon & Healy, Chicago, IL. 1897. Bk/w/gn/br drawings of all Illinois Governors, Illinois capitol building, farm scene, law books. 6pp. Page 2: Blank. Page 6: Advertising. [Crew/JMP-1].

- **AmPM-275 FLEISCHMAN**, Harry (Candidate for U.S. House, 1940)

275.1 Socialist Songs [Song Sheet]. Published as a handout for a dinner for Harry Fleischman, Denver, Colorado, Oct. 1946. [8½" × 11"]. Non-pictorial r/w printing. 2pp. Page 2: Blank.

- **AmPM-276 FORD**, Thomas (State Court Judge, 1837; State Supreme Court, 1841–1842; Governor, 1842–1846)

276.1 On The Road To California. w. No composer indicated. m. "Sung to *Old Dan Tucker*." "Purportedly sung by the Mormons after their expulsion from Nauvoo, Illinois in the winter and spring of 1846. Thomas Ford was the governor of Illinois who acquiesced to the murder of Mormon Prophet Joseph Smith in 1844, and expressed satisfaction upon the Mormon expulsion from the state two years later. Recorded on *They Think We Live On Carrots In Utah* ... recorded in 1995 by Cody Webster at the University of Utah." Lyrics and sound file published online at <http://www.mudcat.org/kids/@displaysong.cfm?SongID=5953>. [199-].

276.2 Our Governors March (Or Two Step) m. Joseph Gearen. Published by Lyon & Healy, Chicago, IL. 1897. Bk/w/gn/br drawings of all Illinois Governors, Illinois capitol building, farm scene, law books. 6pp. Page 2: Blank. Page 6: Advertising. [Crew/JMP-1].

- **AmPM-277 FRENCH**, Augustus C. (State Legislature, 1830s; Receiver of the United States Land Office, Palestine, 1839; Governor, 1846–1853)

277.1 Our Governors March (Or Two Step) m. Joseph Gearen. Published by Lyon & Healy, Chicago, IL. 1897. Bk/w/gn/br drawings of all Illinois Governors, Illinois capitol building, farm scene, law books. 6pp. Page 2: Blank. Page 6: Advertising. [Crew/JMP-1].

- **AmPM-278 GAGE**, Lyman Judson (U.S. Secretary of the Treasury, 1897–1902)

278.1 The Cabinet Grand March. m. Hans S. Line, Op. 64. Published by National Music Company, Nos. 215–221 Wabash Avenue, Chicago, IL. 1897. R/w cover. B/w photo of William McKinley and eight Cabinet members. "Dedicated to Hon. Lyman J. Gage." 6pp. Page 6: Advertising. [Crew/WM-15].

- **AmPM-279 GOLDBERG**, Arthur (U.S. Secretary of Labor, 1961–1962; U.S. Supreme Court, 1962–1965; U.S. Ambassador to the United Nations, 1965–1968)

279.1 Is It A Race War? w.m. Fred Garner, 1968. In: *The Vietnam Songbook*, page 88. c. Barbara Dane and Irwin Silber. Published by The Guardian, No. 32 West 22nd Street, New York, NY. Copyright 1969 by Barbara Dane and Irwin Silber. [7" × 10"]. B/w photo of a protest march. O/y/r/bk cover. 228pp.

- **AmPM-279x GRANT**, Ulysses Simpson (President, 1869–1877) [SEE: DOC/PSM-USG]
- **AmPM-280 GREEN**, Dwight H. (Candidate for Mayor, Chicago; 1939; Governor, 1941–1949)

280.1 Illinois. w.m. Jay Livingston and Ray Evans. Published by Paramount Music Corp., 1619 Broadway, New York, NY. 1948. Bl/w photos of Illinois scenes. Bl/w map of the state of Illinois. 4pp. Page 2: At top of music — "Inspired by Governor Dwight H. Green." Page 4: B/w photo of "Governor Dwight H. Green of Illinois," facsimile signature.

280.2 Illinois {280.2-1}. w.m. Jay Livingston and Ray Evans. 78 rpm record. Mercury Records, Chicago, IL. [ca. 1948]. *Fox Trot* arrangement Played by George Olsen and his Orchestra. Vocals by Ray Adams, Betty Norman and Wally Jylha. "A musical salute to the State Inspired by Governor Dwight H. Green." Side 2: *March* {280.2-2} arrangement.

- **AmPM-281 HAMILTON**, John Marshall (State Senate, 1877–1881; Lt. Governor, 1881–1883; Governor, 1883–1885)

281.1 Our Governors March (Or Two Step) m. Joseph Gearen. Published by Lyon & Healy, Chicago, IL. 1897. Bk/w/gn/br drawings of all Illinois Governors including John M. Palmer, Illinois capitol building, farm scene, law books. 6pp. Page 2: Blank. Page 6: Advertising. [Crew/JMP-1].

- **AmPM-282 HARRISON**, Carter Henry (County Commission, Cook County, 1874–1876; U.S. House, 1875–1879; Mayor, Chicago, 1879–1887 & 1893)

282.1 Carter H. Harrison's Funeral March. m. Geo. Schleiffarth "(Author of *Gen. Grant's* and *Gen. Sherman's Funeral Marches*, etc.)." Published by S. Brainard's Sons Co., Chicago, IL. 1898. B/w litho of "Carter H. Harrison, Born in Fayette Co., Ky., Feb. 15, 1825; Assassinated in Chicago, Oct 28, 1893," black line border. "Dedicated to the Memory of The World's Fair Mayor." 8pp. Pages 2, 6, 7 and 8: Blank.

282.2 Funeral March (In Memoriam Carter H. Harrison). m. Herbert Lanyon. Published by Wm. V. McKinley & Co., 3305 Cottage Grove Avenue, Chicago, IL. 1893. B/w photo of Carter Harrison. "Carter H. Harrison, Mayor of Chicago, World's Fair Year, 1893." "In the hearts of the people." 6pp. Pages 2 and 6: Blank.

282.3 The Garden City Waltz. m. Albert Woellhaf. a. Alice R. Smythe. Published by Noble Publishing Co., 185 Van Buren Street, Chicago, IL. 1899. B/w litho of Carter Harrison [facsimile signature], geometric design border. "Respectfully dedicated to Hon. Carter H. Harrison." 1899. 6pp. Page 6: Blank.

282.4 The Hat He Never Ate. w. Dr. Howard S. Taylor. m. Ben Harney. Published by Home Music Co., 126 Washington Street, Chicago, IL. 1899. B/w photo of "Carter H. Harrison." B/w photo of Ben Harney. "Dedicated to Chicago's greatest mayor, honest fearless and upright." R/w printing. 6pp. Page 2: Blank. Page 3: Words by Horace S. Taylor [sic]. Page 6: "Remember Election Day Tuesday, April 2, 1901."

282.5 Ode To Carter H. Harrison. w. Gertrude Godard. m. Dwight W. Godard. Published by D.W. Godard, Aurora, IL. 1893. B/w litho of Carter Harrison, black border. "Chicago's Columbian Mayor." "His life was gentle, and the elements so mix'd in him That Nature might stand up and say to all the world, *This was A man.*" "Dedicated to Miss Annie Howard." 6pp. Page 6: Blank.

282.6 We'll Try To Get Along. w.m. J.A. Parks. In: *Park's Republican Songs Campaign Of 1904 (For Male Voices)* [Song Book], page 26. Published by J.A. Parks Company, York, NE. 1904. [6^{15}/$_{16}$" × 9¾"]. Br/br nonpictorial geometric design border. 40pp. [M-390]. [Crew/TR-157].

• **AmPM-283   HASTERT**, John Dennis (State House, 1980–1986; U.S. House, 1987–Present)

283.1 Budget Surplus w. John Jenkins. m. "*American Pie,* based on the performance by Don McLean." "After suffering through 38 consecutive years of budget deficits, the United States government achieved surpluses in 1999 — $1.8 billion — and 2000 — $87 billion..." Published online at <http://www.amiright.com/parody/70s/donmclean28.shtml>. [ca. 2003].

283.2 The Dennis Hastert Blues. w. Kneton Ngo. m. "*Where Everybody Knows Your Name* originally by Gary Portnoy and Judy Hart Angelo." Published online at <http://www.amiright.com/parody/80s/garyportnoyandjudyhartangelo0.shml>. [ca. 2002].

283.3 Georgy Bush's Smarmy Jerks Club Band. w. Bo 'Ice' Bielefeldt. m. "*Sergeant Pepper's Lonely Hearts Club Band* by Beatles." Published online by Amiright. com at <http://www.amiright.com/parody/misc/beatles1.shml>. [ca. 2002].

283.4 Fallin' Fumblin' Trippin.' w. Skisics Surus, "skisics@yahoo.com." m. "Sung to the tune of *Lovin' Touchin' Squeezin'* by Journey." "As sung by Trent Lott and Dennis Hastert." Published online at <http://www.geocities.com/wmktong/bootnewt/fallfumb.htm>. [ca. 2000].

283.5 Send Their Green, Green Asses Home. w. Darrell Decker. m. "*Green Grass Of Home,* based on the performance by Tom Jones." Published online at <http://amiright.com/parody/70s/tomjones0.shml>. [2001].

283.6 Super Duper Tuesday. w. ParodyKeet. m. "*If I Were A Rich Man,* based on a performance by Tevye, star of *Fiddler On The Roof.*" Published online at <http://amiright.com/parody/misc/tevyestaroffidlerontheroof0.shtml>. 2003.

• **AmPM-284   HAY**, John (Private Secretary to Abraham Lincoln, 1861–1865; Asst. U.S. Secretary of State, 1879–1881; U.S. Secretary of State, 1898–1905)

284.1 Hurrah For Billy Bryan! w. R.J.P. m. Logan S. Porter. In: *Bryan Campaign Songster For 1900 (For Male Voices)*, page 22. e. Logan S. Porter. Published by Home Music Company, Logansport, IN. 1900. Pk/bk litho of William Jennings Bryan and Adlai E. Stevenson. 36pp. [M-386]. [Crew/WJB-71].

284.2 I Wonder What He'd Do. w. J.J. Javanaugh.

m. W.A. Sullenbarger. In: *The National Democratic Song Book For 1900*, page 2. w. J.J. Kavanaugh. m. W.A. Sullenbarger. Published by The S. Brainard's Sons Company, Chicago, IL. Copyright 1900 by Kavanaugh and Sullenbarger. Be/bk photos of William J. Bryan and Adlai E. Stevenson. Be/bk geometric designs. "No. 1." 20pp. [M-382]. [Crew/WJB-8].

284.3 John Hay March. m. M.A. Althouse. Published by Penn Music Publishing Co., Reading, PA. 1916. B/w litho of John Hay, Lincoln at his desk, Queen, box of "John Hay" cigars. "Dedicated to W.W. Stewart & Sons, Reading, PA., Manufactures of the John Hay Cigar." R/w/b stripe border. 6pp. Pages 2 and 6: Blank. [Also in a Piano Roll by Q.R.S. #32510].

284.4 Old Abe They Said Was An Honest Man (Song). w. J.W. Jarboe, Esq. m. F. Lafayette. Published by Firth, Son & Company, No. 563 Broadway, New York, NY. 1864. Non-pictorial geometric designs. "Words Composed and Sung with Great Applause by J.W. Jarboe, Esq. at the Great McClellan Union Meeting, Union Square." "To the McClellan Union Clubs." 6pp. Pages 2 and 6: Blank. [Crew/GBM-48].

284.5 When The Boys Come Home. 1917.

• **AmPM-285   HERTZ**, Henry L. (State Treasurer, 1897–1899)

285.1 Hurrah For All The Ticket. w. W.A.P. In: *Republican Campaign Songs (As Sung By The Marquette Club Quartette)*, page 6. Published by the Marquette Club of Chicago, Dearborn Avenue and Maple Street, Chicago, IL. 1888. [3½" × 6¼"]. Be/bl geometric design border. "W.A. Paulson, 1st Bass; R.J. Wherry, 1st Tenor; M.O. Naramore, 2nd Bass; O.B. Knight, 2nd Tenor." "Music and Instructions Cheerfully Furnished on Application." 28pp. [Crew/BFH-129].

• **AmPM-286   HILLMAN**, Sidney (President, Amalgamated Clothing Workers, 1914; NRA Labor Advisory Board, 1933; National Industrial Recovery Board, 1934; Founder, Congress of Industrial Organizations, 1935–1940; Associate Director General, Office of Production Management, 1940–1942; Founder, American Labor Party, 1944–1945)

286.1 Clear It With Sidney. w. No composer indicated. m. "Tune — *Bellbottom Trousers.*" In: *Again And Again And Again Or All At Sea*, page 10. Published by Albany Legislative Correspondents' Association of New York State, Albany, NY. 1945. [8¾" × 11"]. N/c drawing of Franklin Roosevelt as a pirate, Thomas Dewey as "Black Tom," Henry Wallace, Sidney Hillman, others on ship — "Union Ship C.I.O.-P.A.C." "Black Tom" Dewey walking plank. "Featuring Political Craft and Cunning and Contortions; Also Summoned by Subpoena, or Hit-Toddy and the Shady Lady, the Indestructible Dame Known as Lu-Lu; Together with Mystical Midsummer Mummery of '46, in a Roaring and Raucous and Revealing Racing Scene Entitled 'Hoots and Straddles.'" "All Done with Music, Magic, and Mirrors — In Three Acts at Hotel Ten Eyck, Albany, March 15, 1945." [Crew/FDR-371].

286.2 Swing, Baby, Swing. w. No composer indicated. m. "Air — *Danny Deever.*" In: *Lehman Unlimited*, page 8. Published by The Legislative Correspondents' Association of New York, Albany, NY. 1942. [7¾" × 10½"]. N/c drawing of Herb Lehman as a train engineer, others dressed as bandits trying to block the way including Dewey, Mead, Poletti, Willkie, Marvin Bennett and Farley—"The Great Train Hold-Up!" "Featuring that Famous Political Personality and Star of 'There'll Always be a Herbie' on an Uncensored Double Bill with 'Fifty Million Candidates Won't be Wronged.'" "Exploded At Hotel Ten Eyck, Albany, New York, on the evening of Thursday, March 12th, 1942, at seven-thirty o'clock."

286.3 *Poor Jim*. w. No composer indicated. m. "Tune—*Poor Jud Is Dead*." In: *Dealers Choice Or Back-To-Back Biting*, page 9. Published by the Albany Legislative Correspondent's Association of New York State, Albany, NY. 1944. [8" × 11¾"]. N/c drawing of Franklin Roosevelt, Thomas Dewey, "Chiang," "Winnie" and "Joe" playing cards—"Featuring the World's Most Exciting Egomaniacs in a Marvelous Musical of Messianic and Mystery: Showing Sinners, Sycophants, Suckers, and Sleuths Saving Civilization with Sound; or Find the Joker!" "Dealt Off the Bottom of a Hot Deck—In Three Acts at Ten Eyck, Albany, March 9, 1944." [Crew/FDR-364].

286.4 *Spring Fantasy!* w. No composer indicated. m. "Air—*Flowers That Bloom In The Spring*." In: *Sock-A-Bye Baby, A No Punches-Pulled Potpourri, Pillorying Political Palookas On Parade And Set To 'Swing' Time, Plus that Mad Maternal Masterpiece—Labor's Love Lost*, page 11. Published by The Legislative Correspondents' Association of New York, Albany, NY. 1938. [7¾" × 10½"]. N/c drawing of politicians as boxers: "Tom Dewey, Gotham Gamecock, Morry Tremaine Queen City's Idol, Bob-Jackson, Jamestown's Mighty Atom, Ripper Rolly Marvin, Syracuse Fistic Sensation, Jabber Bennett, Brooklyn Bomber and Promoter's Dream, Billy Bleakley, Westchester Wildcat, Killer Lehman, Knockerouter De Luxe." "Ace Cards for 1838 Golden Gloves Combat." "At Ten Eyck Hotel, Albany, New York, the evening of Thursday, March Tenth, 1938, at seven o'clock." 16pp. [Crew/TED-28].

286.5 *Swing, Baby, Swing*. w. No composer indicated. m. "Air—*Danny Deever*." In: *Lehman Unlimited*, page 8. Published by The Legislative Correspondents' Association of New York, Albany, NY. 1942. [7¾" × 10½"]. N/c drawing of Herb Lehman as a train engineer, others dressed as bandits trying to block the way including Dewey, Mead, Poletti, Willkie, Marvin Bennett and Farley—"The Great Train Hold-Up!" "Featuring that Famous Political Personality and Star of 'There'll Always be a Herbie' on an Uncensored Double Bill with 'Fifty Million Candidates Won't be Wronged.'" "Exploded At Hotel Ten Eyck, Albany, New York, on the evening of Thursday, March 12th, 1942, at seven-thirty o'clock."

286.6 *We're All For F.D.R.* w. No composer indicated. m. "Tune—*By The Beautiful Sea*." In: *Again And Again And Again Or All At Sea*, page 9. Published by Albany Legislative Correspondents' Association of New York State, Albany, NY. 1945. [8¾" × 11"]. N/c drawing of Franklin Roosevelt as pirate, Thomas Dewey as "Black Tom," Henry Wallace, Sidney Hillman, others on ship—"Union Ship C.I.O.-P.A.C." "Black Tom" Dewey walking plank. "Featuring Political Craft and Cunning and Contortions; Also Summoned by Subpoena, or Hit-Toddy and the Shady Lady, the Indestructible Dame Known as Lu-Lu; Together with Mystical Midsummer Mummery of '46, in a Roaring and Raucous and Revealing Racing Scene Entitled 'Hoots and Straddles.'" "All Done with Music, Magic, and Mirrors—In Three Acts at Hotel Ten Eyck, Albany, March 15, 1945." [Crew/FDR-371].

HOGE, Joseph Pendleton (U.S. House, Illinois) [See: California]

• **AmPM-287 HORNER**, Henry (Probate Judge, 1915–1931; Governor, 1933–1940)

287.1 *The Elephant And The Mule*. w.m. James L. Walls. Published by James L. Walls, No. 1616 South Seventh Street, Springfield, IL. 1936. B/w drawing of crossed American and eagle flags, donkey. "1936 Roosevelt and Horner." 4pp. Page 4: Eight b/w photos of Franklin D. Roosevelt and seven Illinois candidates. [Crew/FDR-427].

287.2 *Marching On With Horner* (March Song). w.m. Paul G. Nesgen. a. Ralph McFadden. Published by The Veterans' Fund. Copyright 1936 by Horner Veteran's Organizations, Springfield, IL. [6¾" × 9"]. B/w photo of "Governor Horner." "B/w drawing of soldier, veteran in a parade. "Dedicated and Distributed Free to all Illinois Veterans and their Friends." 4pp.

287.3 *We Are Marching Over Here* (Song Of The Democrats). w. Kitty Keepers Voss and Billie Poczulp. m. Kitty Keepers Voss. Published by Henry H. Voss, 6924 South Fairfield Avenue, Chicago, IL. 1932. B/w drawing of "Judge Henry Horner." Bl/w drawings of factory, farm, home, couple with child, airplane, sun inscribed—"Democratic Victory." "Democratic Landslide will bury Depression, Unemployment, Worry." 4pp. + 2pp. insert. Page 4: Narrative on Judge Horner. Page 1 of insert: Extra verses. Page 2 of insert: Blank.

• **AmPM-288 HYDE**, Henry John (State House, 1967–1974; U.S. House 1975–Present)

288.1 *Destroying The US Constitution*. w. No composer indicated. m. "To the tune of *Stairway To Heaven*." Published online at <http://www.wwirr.com/wcr/parody/constitution.html>. [199-]

288.2 *Election Impossible*. w. S.T.G. m. Tune— "*Mission Impossible 2 Theme*, originally by Limp Bizkit." "It does not follow exactly to River of Dreams because I cut out a verse or two in the middle." Published online at <http://www.amiright.com/parody/2000s/limpbizkit2.shml>. [ca. 2000].

288.3 *The Henry Hyde Song Book*. w. William K. Tong. m. Popular tunes. N/c photo of Henry Hyde. "The infamous hypocrite and leader of the House gang of Managers drives towards oblivion." Published online at <http://www.geocities.com/wmktong/bootnewt/hydesong.htm>. [199-]:

288.4 *Henry The Hyde, I Am*. w. William K. Tong. m. "Sung to the tune of *I'm Henry VIII, I Am* by Herman's Hermits." Published online at <http://www.geocities.com/wmktong/bootnewt/ henryhyd.htm>. [199-].

288.5 *Hide Willie Hide*. w. Charles Baum. m. "My son about Bill and Monica el al, parodying *The Two Magicians*." "This was written in February 1998, before most of the events happened as a short shelf-life song that just lasted longer than I thought possible ..." Lyrics and sound file published online at <http://www.mudcat.org/kids/@displaysong.cfm?SongID=8883>. 1998.

288.6 House Gang Henry. w. William K. Tong. m. "Sung to the tune of *Mustang Sally* by Wilson Pickett." <http://www.geocities.com/wmktong/bootnewt/hg-henry.htm>. N/c photo of Henry Hyde. [199-].

288.7 Hyde, Why Don't You Go Get A Life. w. William K. Tong. m. "Sung to the tune of *Got to Get You Into My Life* by the Beatles." Published online at <http://www.geocities.com/wmktong/bootnewt/hydelife.htm>. [199-].

288.8 Hyde's Not Embarrassed. w. William K. Tong. m. "Sung to the tune of *I Shot The Sheriff* by Eric Clapton/Bob Marley." Published online at <http://www.geocities.com/wmktong/bootnewt/notembar.htm>. [199-].

288.9 Hyde's Talkin.' w. William K. Tong. m. "Sung to the tune of *Jive Talking* by the Bee Gees." Published online at <http://www.geocities.com/wmktong/bootnewt/hydetalk.htm>. [199-].

288.10 Who Can They Beat Now? w. William K. Tong. m. "Sung to the tune of *Who Can It Be Now All* by Men At Work." Published online at <http://www.geocities.com/wmktong/bootnewt/beatnow.htm>. [ca. 2000].

• **AmPM-289** ICKES, Harold LeClair (Delegate, Republican National Convention, 1920; U.S. Secretary of the Interior, 1933–1946; Delegate, Democratic National Convention, 1936–1944)

289.1 He's Got Them On The List. w. No composer indicated. m. Arthur Sullivan. "Tune—*I've Got A Little List.*" In: *Again And Again And Again Or All At Sea,* page 13. Published by Albany Legislative Correspondents' Association of New York State, Albany, NY. 1945. [8¾" × 11"]. N/c drawing of Franklin Roosevelt as pirate, Thomas Dewey as "Black Tom," Henry Wallace, Sidney Hillman, others on ship—"Union Ship C.I.O.-P.A.C." "Black Tom" Dewey walking plank. "Featuring Political Craft and Cunning and Contortions; Also Summoned by Subpoena, or Hit-Toddy and the Shady Lady, the Indestructible Dame Known as Lu-Lu; Together with Mystical Midsummer Mummery of '46, in a Roaring and Raucous and Revealing Racing Scene Entitled 'Hoots and Straddles.'" "All Done with Music, Magic, and Mirrors—In Three Acts at Hotel Ten Eyck, Albany, March 15, 1945." [Crew/FDR-371].

289.2 Stalling Stanzas. w. No composer indicated. m. "Air—*The Little Man Who Wasn't There* and *I'm Bidin' My Time.*" "Sung by Hanley and Lehman." In: *So You Won't Talk, A Rollicking Rhapsody Ribbing Strong Silent Statesmen With Twelve Year Itch, Twitting Third Termites And Starring The G.O.P. White House Hopeful In 'Mr. Myth Goes To Washington.' Plus That Pari-Muted Phantasy, 'Three Million Men On A Horse,'* page 12. Published by The Legislative Correspondents' Association of New York, Albany, NY. 1942. [7¾" × 10½"]. N/c drawing of two Veiled brides labeled "Democratic Presidential Nominee" and "Republican Presidential Nominee" and a donkey and elephant dressed as grooms standing on the street at "1940" Convention Corner." Drawing titled "Blind Dates." "Daringly Unreeled at Hotel Ten Eyck, Albany, New York, on the evening of Thursday, February 29th, 1940, at seven-thirty o'clock."16pp.

289.3 We're All For F.D.R. w. No composer indicated. m. "Tune—*By The Beautiful Sea.*" In: *Again And Again And Again Or All At Sea,* page 9. Published by Albany Legislative Correspondents' Association of New York State, Albany, NY. 1945. [8¾" × 11"]. N/c drawing of Franklin Roosevelt as pirate, Thomas Dewey as "Black Tom," Henry Wallace, Sidney Hillman, others on ship—"Union Ship C.I.O.-P.A.C." "Black Tom" Dewey walking plank. "Featuring Political Craft and Cunning and Contortions; Also Summoned by Subpoena, or Hit-Toddy and the Shady Lady, the Indestructible Dame Known as Lu-Lu; Together with Mystical Midsummer Mummery of '46, in a Roaring and Raucous and Revealing Racing Scene Entitled 'Hoots and Straddles.'" "All Done with Music, Magic, and Mirrors—In Three Acts at Hotel Ten Eyck, Albany, March 15, 1945." [Crew/FDR-371].

• **AmPM-290** JACKSON, Jesse Lewis, Sr. (Civil Rights Activist; Founder Operation PUSH, 1971; Candidate for Democratic Presidential Nomination, 1984 &1988)

290.1 Ballot Box Blues. w. No composer indicated. m. "Parody of *Summertime Blues* by Eddie Cochran." Lyrics published by *The Bob Rivers Show* with Bob, Spike & Joe and Twisted Tunes online at <http://www.twistedradio.com/player/lyrics.asp?songID=584>. [ca. 2000].

290.2 Crackhouse (Crack MC). Consolidated. On CD: *Play More Music.* #X2-0777-7-13171-25. Amusement Control Records, Universal City, California. 1992.

290.3 Democracy Bites. w. S.G.T. m. "*Misc Songs,* originally by Pearl Jam." Published online at <http://amiright.com/parody/90s/pearljam6.shml>. [ca. 2001].

290.4 Don't Stop (Counting The Chads). w. Chris Pyhtila. m. "*Don't Stop (Thinking About Tomorrow),* originally by Fleetwood Mac." Published online at <http://amiright.com/parody/70s/fleetwoodmac0.shml>. [ca. 2000].

290.5 An Election Shanty. w. The Civil Serpents. m. "To the tune of *Roll The Woodpile Down.*" "The Civil Serpents asked not to be named." Lyrics and sound file published online at <http://www.mudcat.org/kids/@displaysong.cfm?SongID=8948>. 2000.

290.6 Hey Now (Your [sic] an Ex Pres). w. Vermonter. m. "*Hey Now (Your* [sic] *An All Star),* originally by Smash Mouth." Published online at <http://www.amiright.com/parody/90s/smashmouth2.shtml>. [ca. 2001].

290.7 I Am (The President). w. Mike Florio. m. "*I Am (Superman),* originally by NYC." Published online at <http:// www.amiright.com/parody/90/nyc10.shtml>. [ca. 2000].

290.8 Indecision 2000. w. Gary S. O'Connor. m. "*Mack The Knife,* based on a performance by Bobby Darin." "I finally got to write my editorial on the Presidential Election of 2000. This is political fodder for your ears. The story of Al, Walker, Kathy, Hillary, Jessie [sic] and all the rest is set to the melody of *Mack the Knife* in this parody. By the way, this is not the Rush Limbaugh theme song, but it could be!" Published online at <http://www.amiright.com/parody/60s/bobbydarin2/shtml>. [ca. 2003].

290.9 Jesse Jackson. w. No composer indicated. m.

"Parody of *Foxey Lady* by Jimmy Hendrix." Lyrics published by *The Bob Rivers Show* with Bob, Spike & Joe and Twisted Tunes online at <http://www.twistedradio.com/player/lyrics.asp?songID=539>. [1992].

290.10 *Jesse Jackson's Girl*. w.m. Johnny Crass. Published as a MP3 file online by johnnycrass.com at <http://comcast.net/~johnnycrass2/newjc.htm>. 2001.

290.11 *Jesse Jackson's Thighs*. w. No composer indicated. m. "Parody of *Bette Davis Eyes* by Kim Carnes." Lyrics published by *The Bob Rivers Show* with Bob, Spike & Joe and Twisted Tunes online at <http://www.twistedradio.com/player/lyrics.asp?songID=911>. [199-].

290.12 *Lirty Dies: Gush, Bore, Jeverend Rackson*. w. Bill Strauss and Elaina Newport. Published by The Capitol Steps online at<http://capsteps.com/lirty/gushbore.html>. 2001.

290.13 *Was Bill Clinton Blown*. w. S.G.T. m. "*Is Anybody Home*, originally by Our Lady Peace." Published online at <http://amiright.com/parody/2000s/ourladypeace0.shml>. [ca. 2001].

290.14 *Win Jesse Win*. w.m. Van Alexander, Richard Alexander and Phil Ashley. 33⅓ EP. Blue Parrot Records #BP-204. [198-]. Performed by The Public. Seedsong Music.

• **AmPM-291** JOHNSON, Hale (Candidate for Vice President, 1896) [ALSO SEE: DOC/PSM-JL]

291.1 *Not By My Vote*. w.m. Charles M. Fillmore. In: *Fillmore's Prohibition Songs*, page 75. "These four words will answer all arguments on this question — Not By My Vote. If they say to us: Men will have it. We can answer: Not By My Vote. If another say men will sell it. Again we reply, Not By My Vote. I am not bound to abolish the saloon, but only my interest in it. My vote may not hurt the saloon, but I am bound to vote it right all the same. Saloons may go on, like the brook forever. Men may die in them like flies and hell grow fat on drunkards. Girls may be betrayed and boys baited hellward. Faith may be weakened and character dismantled. Homes may be destroyed and women and children beggared. Soldier's Homes may still sell drinks to the old veterans, and Army canteens debauch the young ones. Our national Capitol may have a saloon at either end. Senators and Representatives may be drunk on the floors of Congress, But Not By My Vote."— Hale [Johnson]." Published by Fillmore Brothers Company, No. 421 Elm Street, Cincinnati, OH. 1903. 230pp. [Crew/JL-1].

• **AmPM-292** KELLY, Edward J. (Mayor, Chicago, 1933–1947)

292.1 *Greetings* (Chicago Welcomes You). w.m. Col. George D. Gaw. a. Frank Barden. Published by George Frank Publishers, 500 North Sacramento, Chicago, IL. 1932. Pl/y/w/bk drawing of scenes from the 1933 Chicago World's Fair, statue, skyline. B/w photo of "Hon. Edward J. Kelly, Mayor [paste-on photo over photo of Anthony Cermak after Cermak was assassinated]," "Col. George D. Gaw," and "Rufus C. Dawes, Pres. Of Century of Progress." "Chicago's Official Song." "1833–CHICAGO–1933." 8pp. Pages 2, 7 and 8: Narratives on Chicago.

292.2 *The Rhythm Of State Street*. w.m. Wendell Hall. Published by Paull-Pioneer Music Corp., 1657 Broadway, New York, NY. 1937. B/w photo of State Street in Chicago. R/w/bk printing. 6pp. Page 2: B/w photos of "Presentation to Chicago's Mayor, Hon. Edward J. Kelly, of the Original Manuscript of Wendell Hall's song, *The Rhythm Of State Street*, Adopted by the State Street Council as the Official Song. B/w photo of Chicago from the air. Facsimile of the letter from Kelly to Hall about the song. Page 6: Advertising.

• **AmPM-293** KERN, Jacob J. (State's Attorney, Cook County, 1892–1896)

293.1 *National Democratic March*. m. L.C. Wiesler. Published by National Music Co., 215–221 Wabash Avenue, Chicago, IL. 1891. Non-pictorial geometric designs. "Dedicated to Hon. Jacob J. Kern." 6pp. Page 2: Blank. Page 6: Advertising.

• **AmPM-294** KERNER, Otto, Jr. (County Judge, 1954–1960; Governor, 1961–1968)

294.1 *Governor Otto Kerner March*. m. D.M. Alberti. No publisher indicated. 1961. [8½" × 11"]. B/w litho of trees, outline of the State of Illinois with the words to the "Illinois — State Song" contained within. "Illinois State Song, Music by Archibald Johnston in 1879; Illinois State Song Lyrics by Charles H. Charmbelin 1880–1892." "This march was composed and written expressly and dedicated to Governor Otto Kerner of Illinois. It was presented on Governor's Day on Thursday, August 17, 1961— Illinois State Fair, at Springfield, Illinois; Hon Ralph S. Bradley, Director of Agriculture; Hon Franklin H. Rust, General Manager State Fair." "Professional Copy." 4pp. Page 4: Blank.

294.2 *Ok ... Otto Kerner*. w.m. Norman Heyne. No publisher indicated. [1964]. Br/w photo of Otto Kerner. 4pp. Page 4: Facsimile of a newspaper article from the *Illinois State Register* on Governor Kerner's record.

294.3 *Ok ... Otto Kerner*. w.m. Norman Heyne. 45 rpm vinyl record. [1964]. Performed by Lurlean Hunter with Jerry Abbott Orchestra. #C-97184. Side 2: Instrumental version.

294.4 *Illinois* (By The Rivers Gently Flowing). w. Charles H. Chamberlin. w. [New] Win Stracke. m. Archibald Johnson. a. Norman Luboff. Published by the State of Illinois. Copyright 1966 by Otto Kerner, Governor of Illinois. Bl/w logo of the "Illinois Sesquicentennial 1818–1968." "Official State Song." Long narrative on the history of the song. 4pp. Page 4: Narrative on the "Illinois Sesquicentennial."

• **AmPM-295** KIRK, Mark Steven (Special Assistant, U.S. Department of State, 1992–1993; Staff Member for U.S. House International Relations Committee, 1995; U.S. House, 2001–Present)

295.1 *Texas Swing*. w. Ice Bielefeldt. m. "*Midwest Swing* originally by St. Lunatics." "If four well-known Texas Republicans became a rap group, what would it sound like?" Published online at <http://www.amiright.com/parody/2000s/stlunatics0.shtml>. 2003.

• **AmPM-295x** LINCOLN, Abraham (State House, 1834–1841; U.S. House, 1847–1849; President, 1861–1865) [SEE: DOC/PSM-AL]

• **AmPM-296** LINCOLN, Robert Todd (U.S. Secretary of War, 1881–1885; U.S. Minister to Great Britain, 1889–1893)

296.1 *Massa Linkum's Boy* (Song & Chorus). w. H. Parker. m. Malcolm S. Gordon. Published by John

Church & Co., No. 66 West Fourth Street, Cincinnati, OH. 1884. Non-pictorial geometric designs. "To Robert T. Lincoln." 6pp. Pages 2 and 6: Blank. [Crew/MISC-201].
- **AmPM-297 LINDSAY, William J.** (Superior Court Judge; Cook County; Candidate for Cook County State Attorney, Chicago, 1928)

297.1 Here's To Judge Lindsay (Fox Trot Song). w. Billy Meyers and William McNamara. m. Al Norman. No publisher indicated. Copyright 1928 by Meyers, McNamara and Norman. Br/w photo of Judge Lindsay. Br/w geometrical designs. "Dedicated to the Finest Man on the Bench." "To Judge Lindsay with the Compliments of his many friends." 4pp. Page 4: Narrative on "Judge William J. Lindsay, Democratic Nominee for State's Attorney of Cook County."

297.2 $weet Memorie$. w. No composer indicated. m. "Tune—*Thanks For The Memories.*" As sung by "Rockefeller, Wilson and Chorus." In: *Thoroughly Mad-ern Malcolm or He Didn't Need A Course In Forensics To Become A Famous Public Speaker*, page 15. Published by the New York State Legislative Correspondents' Association, Albany, NY. 1974. N/w photo of Malcolm Wilson as Alfred E. Newman—"What—Me Governor?" "Featuring the New York Correspondents' Association, March 16. 1974." 32pp.

- **AmPM-298 LOGAN, John Alexander** (State House, 1852–1853 & 1856–1857; Prosecuting Attorney, Illinois, 1853–1857; U.S. House, 1859–1862 & 1867–1871; U.S. Senate, 1871–1877 & 1879–1886; Candidate for Vice President, 1884) [ALSO SEE: DOC-JGB]

298.1 All They Want's An Office To Fill. w. Dan Yell. m. "Tune—*Pop Goes The Weasel.*" In: *Cleveland & Hendricks Songster*, page 34. Copyright 1884 by E.Y. Landis. R/w/bl/gn/br drawing of Grover Cleveland, Thomas Hendricks, George "Washington," Thomas "Jefferson," Andrew "Jackson," ribbons, geometric designs. 64pp. [M-230]. [Crew/GC-46].

298.2 The Archipelago. w. Gen. Stillman F. Kneeland. m. "Tune—*The Alma Matter O.*" Page 243, *Carmina Collegensia.* In: *Campaign College Songs* 1900 [Song Book], page 4. w. Gen. Stillman F. Kneeland. Published for the Wholesale Dry Goods Republican, No. 350 Broadway, New York, NY. 1900. [5⅞" x 9⅛"]. Y/bk photos of William "McKinley" and Theodore "Roosevelt." Y/bk drawings of eagle, shield, flags. "A bird that can sing and won't sing must be made to sing." 16pp. [Crew/WM-214].

298.3 [Arise! Ye Brave, Your Country Calls You] (Rallying Song). w. No composer indicated. m. "Air—*The Marseillaise.*" In: *P.T. Schultz & Co's Blaine And Logan Bugle Call*, page 23. Published by P.T. Schultz & Company, No. 172 Race Street, Cincinnati, OH. 1881. [1884 Edition]. [5⅞" x 7⅝"]. Bk/gn litho of James G. Blaine and John A. Logan, flags and eagle, geometric design border. 36pp. [M-245]. [Crew/JGB-67].

298.4 Arlington Funeral March. m. Comrade Henry Fries. Published by John F. Ellis, 306 Pennsylvania Avenue, Washington, DC. 1870. B/w litho of column, sword, doves. "Written expressly for the exercises at National Cemetery Decoration Day, May 30th, 1870, and respectfully dedicated to Hon. John A. Logan." 6pp. Pages 2 and 6: Blank. [LL/JH].

298.5 The Banner Of Blaine And Logan. w. No composer indicated. m. "Air—*Flag Of The Constellation.*" In: *Blaine And Logan Campaign Songster*, page 40. Published by John Church & Company, Cincinnati, OH. 1884. [4⅞" x 5¹³⁄₁₆"]. Y/bk non-pictorial geometric design border. "Including Biographical Sketches & Constitution for Campaign Clubs." 52pp. [M-233?]. [Crew/JGB-29].

298.6 The Battle Cry. w. J.W.B. Siders. m. "Air—*Battle Cry Of Freedom.*" In: *Blaine And Logan Campaign Songster*, page 10. Published by American News Company, New York, NY. 1884. 36pp. [M-249]. [Crew/JGB-84].

298.7 Battle Cry Of Freedom. w. No composer indicated. m. "Air—*Battle Cry Of Freedom.*" B/w litho of "Maj.-Gen. John A. Logan." In: *The Good Old Songs We Used To Sing, ('61 to '65)* [Song Book], page 23. Published by O.H. Oldroyd. Lincoln Homestead, Springfield, IL. [ca. 1880]. [5¹⁵⁄₁₆" x 8⅝"]. Ma/bl litho from "Photo from Life—1864—General Ulysses S. Grant." 36pp. [Crew/JGB-100].

298.8 Battle Cry Of Freemen. w. No composer indicated. m. "Air—*Battle Cry Of Freedom.*" In: *Blaine And Logan Campaign Songster*, page 36. Published by John Church & Company, Cincinnati, OH. 1884. [4⅞" x 5¹³⁄₁₆"]. Y/bk non-pictorial geometric design border. "Including Biographical Sketches & Constitution for Campaign Clubs." 52pp. [M-233?]. [Crew/JGB-29].

298.9 Blaine And Logan (A Campaign Song). w. Fred Layton. w. "Air—*The Star Spangled Banner.*" In: *Blaine And Logan Campaign Songster*, page 17. Published by American News Company, New York, NY. 1884. 36pp. [M-249]. [Crew/JGB-84].

298.10 Blaine And Logan Rallying Song. w.m. Chas. B. Morrell. Published by Geo. D. Newhall Co., Cincinnati, OH. 1884. B/w geometric design and line border. "Republican Campaign Songs." "The Newest, Sprightliest and the Best." List of other songs in the series. [Crew/JGB-101].

298.11 Blaine And Logan Song. w. N.B. Milliken. m. "Air—*John Brown.*" In: *Blaine And Logan Campaign Song-Book*, page 18. e. Prof. F. Widdows. Published by The Republican National Committee, New York, NY. 1884. [4⅜" x 5¹¹⁄₁₆"]. [V-1: Bk/y] [V-2: Pk/bk] litho of James G. Blaine and John A. Logan. "From the School—House to the Cabinet, From the Cabin to the Senate." 52pp. [M-251]. [Crew/JGB-32].

298.12 Blaine And Logan, Too. w.m. No composers indicated. m. Notation. In: *Blaine And Logan Campaign Songster*, page 21. Published by John Church & Company, Cincinnati, OH. 1884. [4⅞" x 5¹³⁄₁₆"]. Y/bk non-pictorial geometric design border. "Including Biographical Sketches & Constitution for Campaign Clubs." 52pp. [M-233?]. [Crew/JGB-29].

298.13 Blaine And Victory. w. Capt. P. Kelly. m. "Air—*Wearing Of The Green.*" In: *Blaine And Logan Campaign Song-Book*, page 34. e. Prof. F. Widdows. Published by The Republican National Committee, New York, NY. 1884. [4⅜" x 5¹¹⁄₁₆"]. [V-1: Bk/y] [V-2: Pk/bk] litho of James G. Blaine and John A. Logan. "From the School—House to the Cabinet, From the Cabin to the Senate." 52pp. [M-251]. [Crew/JGB-32].

298.14 Blaine, Logan, Victory (Song And Chorus). w.m. J.M. Jolley. Published by John Church & Co., No. 66 West Fourth Street, Cincinnati, OH. 1884. Non-pictorial. 8pp. Pages 7 and 8: Advertising. [Crew/JGB-102].

298.15 Blaine's Rallying Song. w. No composer indicated. m. "Air—*Marching Through Georgia*." In: *Blaine And Logan Campaign Songster*, page 42. Published by John Church & Company, Cincinnati, OH. 1884. [4⅞" × 5¹³⁄₁₆"]. Y/bk non-pictorial geometric design border. "Including Biographical Sketches & Constitution for Campaign Clubs." 52pp. [M-233?]. [Crew/JGB-29].

298.16 Blaine's The People's Choice. w. J.W.B. Siders. m. "Air—*Hail Jerusalem Morn*." In: *Blaine And Logan Campaign Songster*, page 9. Published by American News Company, New York, NY. 1884. 36pp. [M-249]. [Crew/JGB-84].

298.17 Blow The Bugle Call Again. w. Mose M. Bigue. m. No tune indicated. "Written for the Mississippi Republican Association." In: *Blaine And Logan Campaign Song-Book*, page 26. e. Prof. F. Widdows. Published by The Republican National Committee, New York, NY. 1884. [4⅜" × 5¹¹⁄₁₆"]. [V-1: Bk/y] [V-2: Pk/bk] litho of James G. Blaine and John A. Logan. "From the School—House to the Cabinet, From the Cabin to the Senate." 52pp. [M-251]. [Crew/JGB-32].

298.18 The Boys For Us. w. No composer indicated. m. "Air—*John Brown's Body, etc.*" In: *Beulah's Blaine And Logan Original Campaign Song Book 1884*, page 18. Printed and Published by Birnie Paper Company, Springfield, MA. 1884. [4" × 5¾"]. Gy/bk litho of James G. Blaine and John A. Logan, eagle, flags, shield, line border. 36pp. [M-232]. [Crew/JGB-41].

298.19 Boys In Blue. w. J.W.B. Siders. w. "Air—*Hold The Fort*." In: *Blaine And Logan Campaign Songster*, page 15. Published by American News Company, New York, NY. 1884. 36pp. [M-249]. [Crew/JGB-84].

298.20 Boys In Blue. w. Peter Maithre. m. "Air—*Hold The Fort*." In: *Blaine And Logan Campaign Song-Book*, page 16. e. Prof. F. Widdows. Published by The Republican National Committee, New York, NY. 1884. [4⅜" × 5¹¹⁄₁₆"]. [V-1: Bk/y] [V-2: Pk/bk] litho of James G. Blaine and John A. Logan. "From the School—House to the Cabinet, From the Cabin to the Senate." 52pp. [M-251]. [Crew/JGB-32].

298.21 Brave Hosts Are Coming. w. No composer indicated. m. "Air—*Tramp, Tramp, Tramp*." In: *Beulah's Blaine And Logan Original Campaign Song Book 1884*, page 29. Printed and Published by Birnie Paper Company, Springfield, MA. 1884. [4" × 5¾"]. Gy/bk litho of James G. Blaine and John A. Logan, eagle, flags, shield, line border. 36pp. [M-232]. [Crew/JGB-41].

298.22 Bring The Starry Banner Boys. w.m. A.T. Gorham, Oliver Ditson & Co., 451 Washington Street, Boston, MA. 1884. Non-pictorial geometric designs. "Dedicated to The Grand Old Party." "Blaine And Logan Rallying Song." 6pp. Pages 2 and 6: Blank. [Crew/JAG-108].

298.23 [Bring Your Honest Hearts, My Boys] (Rallying Song). w. No composer indicated. m. "Air—*Marching Through Georgia*." In: *P.T. Schultz & Co's Blaine And Logan Bugle Call*, page 20. Published by P.T. Schultz & Company, No. 172 Race Street, Cincinnati, OH. 1881. [1884 Edition]. [5⅞" × 7⅝"]. Bk/gn litho of James G. Blaine and John A. Logan, flags and eagle, geometric design border. 36pp. [M-245]. [Crew/JGB-67].

298.24 Campaign Song No. 1. w. George H. Leithead. m. "Air—*Hoist Up The Flag*." No publisher indicated. [5" × 7½"]. Non-pictorial. "1884." "Copyright secured August 18th, 1884." 2pp. Page 2: Blank.

298.25 Chalk It Down. w. "By Demo." m. "Tune—*Bobbin' Round*." In: *Cleveland & Hendricks Songster*, page 20. Copyright 1884 by E.Y. Landis. R/w/bl/gn/br drawing of Grover Cleveland, Thomas Hendricks, George "Washington," Thomas "Jefferson," Andrew "Jackson," ribbons, geometric designs. 64pp. [M-230]. [Crew/GC-46].

298.26 Champions Of Liberty. w. No composer indicated. m. "Air—*America*." In: *Blaine And Logan Songster*, page 3. Published by Thomas Hunter, Philadelphia, PA. 1884. [5½" × 7¼"]. N/c litho of Abraham Lincoln and James Garfield—"Our Martyred Presidents." Br/w litho of James G. Blaine—"Our Next President," and John A. Logan—"Our Next Vice-President," George Washington, Ulysses S. Grant. 68pp [M-237]. [Crew/JGB-35].

298.27 Cheer, Freemen, Cheer! w. No composers indicated. m. "Air—*Marseilles Hymn*." In: *Blaine And Logan Campaign Songster*, page 23. Published by John Church & Company, Cincinnati, OH. 1884. [4⅞" × 5¹³⁄₁₆"]. Y/bk non-pictorial geometric design border. "Including Biographical Sketches & Constitution for Campaign Clubs." 52pp. [M-233?]. [Crew/JGB-29].

298.28 Choice Of The Fearless Free. w. No composers indicated. m. "Air—*America*." In: *Blaine And Logan Campaign Songster*, page 22. Published by John Church & Company, Cincinnati, OH. 1884. [4⅞" × 5¹³⁄₁₆"]. Y/bk non-pictorial geometric design border. "Including Biographical Sketches & Constitution for Campaign Clubs." 52pp. [M-233?]. [Crew/JGB-29].

298.29 Climbing Jacob's Ladder. w. J.W.B. Siders. w. No tune indicated. In: *Blaine And Logan Campaign Songster*, page 22. Published by American News Company, New York, NY. 1884. 36pp. [M-249]. [Crew/JGB-84].

298.30 Come Gather Round. w. No composer indicated. m. "Air—*Auld Lang Syne*." In: *Blaine And Logan Campaign Songster*, page 28. Published by John Church & Company, Cincinnati, OH. 1884. [4⅞" × 5¹³⁄₁₆"]. Y/bk non-pictorial geometric design border. "Including Biographical Sketches & Constitution for Campaign Clubs." 52pp. [M-233?]. [Crew/JGB-29].

298.31 Come Rally For Blaine And For Logan. w. M.S. Gordon. m. "Air—*Old Rosin The Bow*." In: *Blaine And Logan Campaign Songster*, page 3. Published by John Church & Company, Cincinnati, OH. 1884. [4⅞" × 5¹³⁄₁₆"]. Y/bk non-pictorial geometric design border. "Including Biographical Sketches & Constitution for Campaign Clubs." 52pp. [M-233?]. [Crew/JGB-29].

298.32 Come, Wake Up, Voters. w. No composer indicated. m. "Air—*The Girl I Left Behind Me*." In: *Blaine And Logan Campaign Song-Book*, page 33. e.

Prof. F. Widdows. Published by The Republican National Committee, New York, NY. 1884. [4⅜" × 5¹¹⁄₁₆"]. [V-1: Bk/y] [V-2: Pk/bk] litho of James G. Blaine and John A. Logan. "From the School — House to the Cabinet, From the Cabin to the Senate." 52pp. [M-251]. [Crew/JGB-32].

298.33 Come, Ye Freemen! w. No composer indicated. m. "Air — *Hail, Columbia.*" In: *Blaine And Logan Campaign Songster*, page 19. Published by John Church & Company, Cincinnati, OH. 1884. [4⅞" × 5¹³⁄₁₆"]. Y/bk non-pictorial geometric design border. "Including Biographical Sketches & Constitution for Campaign Clubs." 52pp. [M-233?]. [Crew/JGB-29].

298.34 Dinna Ye Hear The Slogan? w. Prof. F. Widdows. m. "Air — *Johnny Comes Marching Home.*" In: *Blaine And Logan Campaign Song-Book*, page 11. e. Prof. F. Widdows. Published by The Republican National Committee, New York, NY. 1884. [4⅜" × 5¹¹⁄₁₆"]. [V-1: Bk/y] [V-2: Pk/bk] litho of James G. Blaine and John A. Logan. "From the School — House to the Cabinet, From the Cabin to the Senate." 52pp. [M-251]. [Crew/JGB-32].

298.35 Do You See Our Banner Floating. w. No composer indicated. m. "Air — *Comin' Through The Rye.*" In: *Blaine And Logan Campaign Songster*, page 27. Published by John Church & Company, Cincinnati, OH. 1884. [4⅞" × 5¹³⁄₁₆"]. Y/bk non-pictorial geometric design border. "Including Biographical Sketches & Constitution for Campaign Clubs." 52pp. [M-233?]. [Crew/JGB-29].

298.36 Fling Out Your Broad Banner. w. No composer indicated. m. Notation. In: *The People's Songs For Blaine & Logan*, page 20. Published by Acme Publishing Bureau, J.C.O. Redington, General Manager, No. 252 Broadway, New York, NY. Copyright 1884 by J.C.O. Redington. [4⅞" × 6⅝"]. B/w litho of James G. Blaine. "Adopted by the General Republican Committees in New York City and elsewhere." "Adapted for every Voice in the Glorious Land of Freedom. All the Nation may Sing." "Come, join that Columbia's blessings increase, All Singing for Liberty, Glory and Peace." "Acme Songs." 32pp. [M-246]. [Crew/JGB-45].

298.37 For Blaine And Logan Still. w. No composer indicated. m. "Air — *Gay And Happy.*" In: *Blaine And Logan Campaign Song-Book*, page 22. e. Prof. F. Widdows. Published by The Republican National Committee, New York, NY. 1884. [4⅜" × 5¹¹⁄₁₆"]. [V-1: Bk/y] [V-2: Pk/bk] litho of James G. Blaine and John A. Logan. "From the School — House to the Cabinet, From the Cabin to the Senate." 52pp. [M-251]. [Crew/JGB-32].

298.38 For Victory Again. w. No composer indicated. m. "Air – *Marching Through Georgia.*" In: *Blaine And Logan Songster*, page 20. Published by Thomas Hunter, Philadelphia, PA. 1884. [5½" × 7¼"]. N/c litho of Abraham Lincoln and James Garfield — "Our Martyred Presidents." Br/w litho of James G. Blaine — "Our Next President," and John A. Logan — "Our Next Vice-President," George Washington, Ulysses S. Grant. 68pp [M-237]. [Crew/JGB-35].

298.39 Forward! See The White Plumes Waving! w. Frank P. Cleary, M.D. m. "Air — *Tramp, Tramp, The Boys Are Marching.*" In: *Blaine And Logan Campaign Song-Book*, page 15. e. Prof. F. Widdows. Published by The Republican National Committee, New York, NY. 1884. [4⅜" × 5¹¹⁄₁₆"]. [V-1: Bk/y] [V-2: Pk/bk] litho of James G. Blaine and John A. Logan. "From the School — House to the Cabinet, From the Cabin to the Senate." 52pp. [M-251]. [Crew/JGB-32].

298.40 Freeman's Shout For Freedom's Heroes. w. A. Wood. m. "Air — *Old Folks At Home.*" In: *Blaine And Logan Campaign Song-Book*, page 25. e. Prof. F. Widdows. Published by The Republican National Committee, New York, NY. 1884. [4⅜" × 5¹¹⁄₁₆"]. [V-1: Bk/y] [V-2: Pk/bk] litho of James G. Blaine and John A. Logan. "From the School — House to the Cabinet, From the Cabin to the Senate." 52pp. [M-251]. [Crew/JGB-32].

298.41 General Logan And The Fifteenth Army Corps. w. Capt. R.W. Burt, 76th Ohio V.V.I. m. "Tune — *The Kingdom Am A Comin.*" Published by Charles Magnus, No. 12 Frankfort Street, New York, NY. [ca. 1863]. [5" × 8"]. Non-pictorial bl/w geometric design border. Lines note paper. "Ten illustrated Songs on Notepaper, mailed to any Address on receipt of 50 cts." 2pp. Page 2: Blank. [Crew/JGB-112].

298.42 Get In Line For The Fray. w. P.H. Bristow, "(Des Moines)." m.a. J. Woollett, "(Chicago)." In: *Republican League Harrison And Morton Song Book, 1888*, page 6. Printed by Register Press Printing House, Des Moines, IA. Copyright 1888 by P.H. Bristow. [6" × 9¼"]. Bl/bk non-pictorial geometric designs, League logo. "The ball it goes rolling from the Gulf to The Lakes, From Maine in the East out to Oregon's peaks, Get out of its way for 'tis rolling along, You tell of its coming, by music & Song." 44pp. [M-256]. [Crew/BFH-50].

298.43 Glory, Hallelujah! (Our Blaine & Logan Lead). w. No composer indicated. m. Tune — *Glory Hallelujah*. In: *The People's Songs For Blaine & Logan*, page 15. Published by Acme Publishing Bureau, J.C.O. Redington, General Manager, No. 252 Broadway, New York, NY. Copyright 1884 by J.C.O. Redington. [4⅞" × 6⅝"]. B/w litho of James G. Blaine. "Adopted by the General Republican Committees in New York City and elsewhere." "Adapted for every Voice in the Glorious Land of Freedom. All the Nation may Sing." "Come, join that Columbia's blessings increase, All Singing for Liberty, Glory and Peace." "Acme Songs." 32pp. [M-246]. [Crew/JGB-45].

298.44 Hail To The Plumbed Knight! And Logan! w. Col. Thad. K. Preuss. m. "Air — *Columbia, The Gem Of The Ocean.*" In: *Blaine And Logan Campaign Song-Book*, page 8. e. Prof. F. Widdows. Published by The Republican National Committee, New York, NY. 1884. [4⅜" × 5¹¹⁄₁₆"]. [V-1: Bk/y] [V-2: Pk/bk] litho of James G. Blaine and John A. Logan. "From the School — House to the Cabinet, From the Cabin to the Senate." 52pp. [M-251]. [Crew/JGB-32].

298.45 Hayes. w. No composer indicated. m. "Air — *Life On The Ocean Wave.*" In: *Hayes & Wheeler Campaign Song Book (For The Centennial Year)*, page 37. Published by the American News Company, Nos. 117, 119, 121, 123 Nassau Street, New York, NY. 1876. [3⅞" × 6⅛"]. Y/bk litho of Rutherford B. Hayes and William A. Wheeler, liberty cap, geometric designs. 74pp. Pages 2, 4, 73 and 74: Blank. Page 3: "Containing Over Sixty Original Songs Adapted to Popular Melodies." [M-193]. [Crew/RBH-11].

298.46 Hear! Hear The Shout. w. No composer indicated. m. "Air—*Tramp, Tramp, Tramp.*" In: *Blaine And Logan Campaign Songster*, page 17. Published by John Church & Company, Cincinnati, OH. 1884. [4⅞" × 5¹³⁄₁₆"]. Y/bk non-pictorial geometric design border. "Including Biographical Sketches & Constitution for Campaign Clubs." 52pp. [M-233?]. [Crew/JGB-29].

298.47 Hold The Fort For Blaine And Logan. w. No composer indicated. m. "Air—*Hold The Fort.*" In: *Blaine And Logan Campaign Songster*, page 30. Published by John Church & Company, Cincinnati, OH. 1884. [4⅞" × 5¹³⁄₁₆"]. Y/bk non-pictorial geometric design border. "Including Biographical Sketches & Constitution for Campaign Clubs." 52pp. [M-233?]. [Crew/JGB-29].

298.48 How Bright To-night. w. No composer indicated. m. "Air—*Flag Of Constellation.*" In: *Blaine And Logan Campaign Songster*, page 37. Published by John Church & Company, Cincinnati, OH. 1884. [4⅞" × 5¹³⁄₁₆"]. Y/bk non-pictorial geometric design border. "Including Biographical Sketches & Constitution for Campaign Clubs." 52pp. [M-233?]. [Crew/JGB-29].

298.49 Hurrah For Blaine And Logan. w. F.N.S. m. "Music—*Soldier's Farewell.*" In: *P.T. Schultz & Co's Blaine And Logan Bugle Call*, page 6. Published by P.T. Schultz & Company, No. 172 Race Street, Cincinnati, OH. 1881. [1884 Edition]. [5⅞" × 7⅝"]. Bk/gn litho of James G. Blaine and John A. Logan, flags and eagle, geometric design border. 36pp. [M-245]. [Crew/JGB-67].

298.50 Hurrah! For The Army Of Blue. w. No composer indicated. m. "Air—*Life On The Ocean Wave.*" In: *Blaine And Logan Campaign Songster*, page 25. Published by John Church & Company, Cincinnati, OH. 1884. [4⅞" × 5¹³⁄₁₆"]. Y/bk non-pictorial geometric design border. "Including Biographical Sketches & Constitution for Campaign Clubs." 52pp. [M-233?]. [Crew/JGB-29].

298.51 In Praise Of Blaine Of Maine. w. No composer indicated. m. "Air—*When Johnny Comes Marching Home.*" In: *Blaine And Logan Campaign Song-Book*, page 31. e. Prof. F. Widdows. Published by The Republican National Committee, New York, NY. 1884. [4⅜" × 5¹¹⁄₁₆"]. [V-1: Bk/y] [V-2: Pk/bk] litho of James G. Blaine and John A. Logan. "From the School—House to the Cabinet, From the Cabin to the Senate." 52pp. [M-251]. [Crew/JGB-32].

298.52 The Irishman's Greeting To The Ticket. w. A. Wood. m. "Air—*Rory O'More.*" In: *Blaine And Logan Campaign Song-Book*, page 14. e. Prof. F. Widdows. Published by The Republican National Committee, New York, NY. 1884. [4⅜" × 5¹¹⁄₁₆"]. [V-1: Bk/y] [V-2: Pk/bk] litho of James G. Blaine and John A. Logan. "From the School—House to the Cabinet, From the Cabin to the Senate." 52pp. [M-251]. [Crew/JGB-32].

298.53 A Land Called Washington. w. No composer indicated. m. "Air—*There's A Land, etc.*" In: *Beulah's Blaine And Logan Original Campaign Song Book 1884*, page 30. Printed and Published by Birnie Paper Company, Springfield, MA. 1884. [4" × 5¾"]. Gy/bk litho of James G. Blaine and John A. Logan, eagle, flags, shield, line border. 36pp. [M-232]. [Crew/JGB-41].

298.54 Led By Blaine And Logan. w. Dr. Frank P. Cleary. m. "Air—*Marching Through Georgia.*" In: *Blaine And Logan Campaign Song-Book*, page 36. e. Prof. F. Widdows. Published by The Republican National Committee, New York, NY. 1884. [4⅜" × 5¹¹⁄₁₆"]. [V-1: Bk/y] [V-2: Pk/bk] litho of James G. Blaine and John A. Logan. "From the School—House to the Cabinet, From the Cabin to the Senate." 52pp. [M-251]. [Crew/JGB-32].

298.55 A Life In The White House Halls. w. Dan Yell. m. "Tune—*Life On The Ocean Wave.*" In: *Cleveland & Hendricks Songster*, page 36. Copyright 1884 by E.Y. Landis. R/w/bl/gn/br drawing of Grover Cleveland, Thomas Hendricks, George "Washington," Thomas "Jefferson," Andrew "Jackson," ribbons, geometric designs. 64pp. [M-230]. [Crew/GC-46].

298.56 Logan's Grand March. m. John Mack. Published by White, Smith & Co., Chicago, IL. 1884. B/w litho of John A. Logan. "Respectfully Dedicated to Gen. John A. Logan," geometric design border. 6pp. Page 2: Blank. Page 6: Advertising. [Crew/JGB-103].

298.57 Loyal And True. w. No composer indicated. m. "Tune—*Sweet Bye And Bye.*" In: *Blaine And Logan Songster*, page 43. Published by Thomas Hunter, Philadelphia, PA. 1884. [5½" × 7¼"]. N/c litho of Abraham Lincoln and James Garfield—"Our Martyred Presidents." Br/w litho of James G. Blaine—"Our Next President," and John A. Logan—"Our Next Vice-President," George Washington, Ulysses S. Grant. 68pp [M-237]. [Crew/JGB-35].

298.58 Marching Through Georgia. w. J.W.B. Siders ("New Version"). m. Air—*Marching Through Georgia.*" In: *Blaine And Logan Campaign Songster*, page 7. Published by American News Company, New York, NY. 1884. 36pp. [M-249]. [Crew/JGB-84].

298.59 Marching To The White House. w. Frank N. Scott. m. No tune indicated. In: *P.T. Schultz & Co's Blaine And Logan Bugle Call*, page 21. Published by P.T. Schultz & Company, No. 172 Race Street, Cincinnati, OH. 1881. [1884 Edition]. [5⅞" × 7⅝"]. Bk/gn litho of James G. Blaine and John A. Logan, flags and eagle, geometric design border. 36pp. [M-245]. [Crew/JGB-67].

298.60 Marching To Victory. w. J.K. Tyler. m. "Air—*Marching Through Georgia.*" In: *Blaine And Logan Campaign Song-Book*, page 43. e. Prof. F. Widdows. Published by The Republican National Committee, New York, NY. 1884. [4⅜" × 5¹¹⁄₁₆"]. [V-1: Bk/y] [V-2: Pk/bk] litho of James G. Blaine and John A. Logan. "From the School—House to the Cabinet, From the Cabin to the Senate." 52pp. [M-251]. [Crew/JGB-32].

298.61 The Nation Loves Its Soldiers Still. w.m. T.P. Westendorf. In: *Blaine And Logan Campaign Songster*, page 8. Published by John Church & Company, Cincinnati, OH. 1884. [4⅞" × 5¹³⁄₁₆"]. Y/bk non-pictorial geometric design border. "Including Biographical Sketches & Constitution for Campaign Clubs." 52pp. [M-233?]. [Crew/JGB-29].

298.62 Now, Three Times Three. w.m. No composers indicated. m. Notation. In: *Blaine And Logan Campaign Songster*, page 35. Published by John Church & Company, Cincinnati, OH. 1884. [4⅞" × 5¹³⁄₁₆"]. Y/bk non-pictorial geometric design border. "Including Biographical Sketches & Constitution for Campaign Clubs." 52pp. [M-233?]. [Crew/JGB-29].

298.63 O Bring Out Your Banners! w.m. No composer or tune indicated. In: *Blaine And Logan Songster*, page 19. Published by Thomas Hunter, Philadelphia, PA. 1884. [5½" × 7¼"]. N/c litho of Abraham Lincoln and James Garfield—"Our Martyred Presidents." Br/w litho of James G. Blaine—"Our Next President," and John A. Logan—"Our Next Vice-President," George Washington, Ulysses S. Grant. 68pp [M-237]. [Crew/JGB-35].

298.64 One Trial More. w. C.L.S. m. "Air—*Upidee*." In: *P.T. Schultz & Co's Blaine And Logan Bugle Call*, page 31. Published by P.T. Schultz & Company, No. 172 Race Street, Cincinnati, OH. 1881. [1884 Edition]. [5⅞" × 7⅝"]. Bk/gn litho of James G. Blaine and John A. Logan, flags and eagle, geometric design border. 36pp. [M-245]. [Crew/JGB-67].

298.65 Our Candidates. w. No composer indicated. m. "Tune—*Johnny Comes Marching Home*." In: *Facts And Songs For The People*, page 17. Published by C.E. Bolton, Cleveland, OH. 1884. [5" × 7⅛"]. R/w/bl drawing of Miss Liberty, flag, scroll—"Vox populi, Vox Dei, 1884." 54pp. Pages 2 and 53: Advertising. Page 3: B/w photo of "Hon. James G. Blaine." Page 4: Photo of "Gen. John A. Logan." Page 5: Title—*Facts & Songs For The People Prepared Specially For Use In The Blaine And Logan Campaign*. [M-239]. [Crew/JGB-65].

298.66 Our Candidates. w. No composer indicated. m. "Tune—*Hold The Fort*." In: *Blaine And Logan Songster*, page 45. Published by Thomas Hunter, Philadelphia, PA. 1884. [5½" × 7¼"]. N/c litho of Abraham Lincoln and James Garfield—"Our Martyred Presidents." Br/w litho of James G. Blaine—"Our Next President," and John A. Logan—"Our Next Vice-President," George Washington, Ulysses S. Grant. 68pp [M-237]. [Crew/JGB-35].

298.67 Our Choice. w. No composer indicated. m. "Air—*Maxwelton's Braes Are Bonnie*." "August, 1884." In: *Beulah's Blaine And Logan Original Campaign Song Book 1884*, page 6. Printed and Published by Birnie Paper Company, Springfield, MA. 1884. [4" × 5¾"]. Gy/bk litho of James G. Blaine and John A. Logan, eagle, flags, shield, line border. 36pp. [M-232]. [Crew/JGB-41].

298.68 Our Good Old Democrats. w. "By Demo." m. "Tune—*King Of The Cannibal Islands*." In: *Cleveland & Hendricks Songster*, page 12. Copyright 1884 by E.Y. Landis. R/w/bl/gn/br drawing of Grover Cleveland, Thomas Hendricks, George "Washington," Thomas "Jefferson," Andrew "Jackson," ribbons, geometric designs. 64pp. [M-230]. [Crew/GC-46].

298.69 Our Jack. w. No composer indicated. m. "Air—*Tenting To-Night*." In: *Beulah's Blaine And Logan Original Campaign Song Book 1884*, page 19. Printed and Published by Birnie Paper Company, Springfield, MA. 1884. [4" × 5¾"]. Gy/bk litho of James G. Blaine and John A. Logan, eagle, flags, shield, line border. 36pp. [M-232]. [Crew/JGB-41].

298.70 Our Leaders. w. No composer indicated. m. "Tune—*Maryland, My Maryland*." In: *Blaine And Logan Songster*, page 47. Published by Thomas Hunter, Philadelphia, PA. 1884. [5½" × 7¼"]. N/c litho of Abraham Lincoln and James Garfield—"Our Martyred Presidents." Br/w litho of James G. Blaine—"Our Next President," and John A. Logan—"Our Next Vice-President," George Washington, Ulysses S. Grant. 68pp [M-237]. [Crew/JGB-35].

298.71 Our Nominations. w. Frank N. Scott. m. "Air—*The One Horse Chaise*." In: *P.T. Schultz & Co's Blaine And Logan Bugle Call*, page 13. Published by P.T. Schultz & Company, No. 172 Race Street, Cincinnati, OH. 1881. [1884 Edition]. [5⅞" × 7⅝"]. Bk/gn litho of James G. Blaine and John A. Logan, flags and eagle, geometric design border. 36pp. [M-245]. [Crew/JGB-67].

298.72 Over The Left. w. "By Demo." m. "Tune—*Sweet Kitty Clover*." In: *Cleveland & Hendricks Songster*, page 50. Copyright 1884 by E.Y. Landis. R/w/bl/gn/br drawing of Grover Cleveland, Thomas Hendricks, George "Washington," Thomas "Jefferson," Andrew "Jackson," ribbons, geometric designs. 64pp. [M-230]. [Crew/GC-46].

298.73 Peace, Order And Stability. w. No composer indicated. m. "Air—*Yankee Doodle*." In: *Blaine And Logan Songster*, page 10. Published by Thomas Hunter, Philadelphia, PA. 1884. [5½" × 7¼"]. N/c litho of Abraham Lincoln and James Garfield—"Our Martyred Presidents." Br/w litho of James G. Blaine—"Our Next President," and John A. Logan—"Our Next Vice-President," George Washington, Ulysses S. Grant. 68pp [M-237]. [Crew/JGB-35].

298.74 The People Are Shouting. w. No composer indicated. m. "Air—*The Campbells Are Coming*." In: *Blaine And Logan Campaign Songster*, page 9. Published by John Church & Company, Cincinnati, OH. 1884. [4⅞" × 5¹³⁄₁₆"]. Y/bk non-pictorial geometric design border. "Including Biographical Sketches & Constitution for Campaign Clubs." 52pp. [M-233?]. [Crew/JGB-29].

298.75 The Plumed Knight. w. No composer indicated. m. "Tune—*Battle Cry Of Freedom*. In: *Facts And Songs For The People*, page 16. Published by C.E. Bolton, Cleveland, OH. 1884. [5" × 7⅛"]. R/w/bl drawing of Miss Liberty, flag, scroll—"Vox populi, Vox Dei, 1884." 54pp. Pages 2 and 53: Advertising. Page 3: B/w photo of "Hon. James G. Blaine." Page 4: Photo of "Gen. John A. Logan." Page 5: Title—*Facts & Songs For The People Prepared Specially For Use In The Blaine And Logan Campaign*. [M-239]. [Crew/JGB-65].

298.76 The Presidential Racecourse. w. No composer indicated. m. "Air—*Camptown Races*." In: *Blaine And Logan Campaign Songster*, page 5. Published by John Church & Company, Cincinnati, OH. 1884. [4⅞" × 5¹³⁄₁₆"]. Y/bk non-pictorial geometric design border. "Including Biographical Sketches & Constitution for Campaign Clubs." 52pp. [M-233?]. [Crew/JGB-29].

298.77 Rally, Rally, Republicans, Rally. w. No composer indicated. m. Notation. In: *The People's Songs For Blaine & Logan*, page 3. Published by Acme Publishing Bureau, J.C.O. Redington, General Manager, No. 252 Broadway, New York, NY. Copyright 1884 by J.C.O. Redington. [4⅞" × 6⅝"]. B/w litho of James G. Blaine. "Adopted by the General Republican Committees in New York City and elsewhere." "Adapted for every Voice in the Glorious Land of Freedom. All the Nation may Sing." "Come, join that Columbia's blessings increase, All Singing for Liberty, Glory and Peace." "Acme Songs." 32pp. [M-246]. [Crew/JGB-45].

298.78 Rallying Song, 1884. w. J.H. Coggswell. m. "Air—*Marching Through Georgia.*" In: *Blaine And Logan Campaign Song-Book*, page 5. e. Prof. F. Widdows. Published by The Republican National Committee, New York, NY. 1884. [4⅜" × 5¹¹⁄₁₆"]. [V-1: Bk/y] [V-2: Pk/bk] litho of James G. Blaine and John A. Logan. "From the School—House to the Cabinet, From the Cabin to the Senate." 52pp. [M-251]. [Crew/JGB-32].

298.79 The Republican Slogan. w. Dr. H.A. Dobson. "Air—*Yankee Doodle.*" In: *Blaine And Logan Campaign Song-Book*, page 27. e. Prof. F. Widdows. Published by The Republican National Committee, New York, NY. 1884. [4⅜" × 5¹¹⁄₁₆"]. [V-1: Bk/y] [V-2: Pk/bk] litho of James G. Blaine and John A. Logan. "From the School—House to the Cabinet, From the Cabin to the Senate." 52pp. [M-251]. [Crew/JGB-32].

298.80 Republican Watchword. w. Prof. F. Widdows. m. No tune indicated. "Let us have a Peace." In: *Blaine And Logan Campaign Song-Book*, page 21. e. Prof. F. Widdows. Published by The Republican National Committee, New York, NY. 1884. [4⅜" × 5¹¹⁄₁₆"]. [V-1: Bk/y] [V-2: Pk/bk] litho of James G. Blaine and John A. Logan. "From the School—House to the Cabinet, From the Cabin to the Senate." 52pp. [M-251]. [Crew/JGB-32].

298.81 Serenade. w. J.W.B. Siders. w. No composer indicated. In: *Blaine And Logan Campaign Songster*, page 12. Published by American News Company, New York, NY. 1884. 36pp. [M-249]. [Crew/JGB-84].

298.82 The Ship Of State. w. J.W.B. Siders. m. "Air—*Sail On, My Bark.*" In: *Blaine And Logan Campaign Songster*, page 13. Published by American News Company, New York, NY. 1884. 36pp. [M-249]. [Crew/JGB-84].

298.83 Shouting For Blaine And Logan. w. No composer indicated. m. "Air—*Battle Cry Of Freedom.*" In: *Blaine And Logan Campaign Songster*, page 16. Published by John Church & Company, Cincinnati, OH. 1884. [4⅞" × 5¹³⁄₁₆"]. Y/bk non-pictorial geometric design border. "Including Biographical Sketches & Constitution for Campaign Clubs." 52pp. [M-233?]. [Crew/JGB-29].

298.84 Shouting The Cry Of Blaine And Logan. w. Frank N. Scott. m. No tune indicated. In: *P.T. Schultz & Co's Blaine And Logan Bugle Call*, page 17. Published by P.T. Schultz & Company, No. 172 Race Street, Cincinnati, OH. 1881. [1884 Edition]. [5⅞" × 7⅝"]. Bk/gn litho of James G. Blaine and John A. Logan, flags and eagle, geometric design border. 36pp. [M-245]. [Crew/JGB-67].

298.85 Singing For Blaine And Logan. w. No composer indicated. m. "Air—*Battle Cry Of Freedom.*" In: *Blaine And Logan Songster*, page 18. Published by Thomas Hunter, Philadelphia, PA. 1884. [5½" × 7¼"]. N/c litho of Abraham Lincoln and James Garfield—"Our Martyred Presidents." Br/w litho of James G. Blaine—"Our Next President," and John A. Logan—"Our Next Vice-President," George Washington, Ulysses S. Grant. 68pp [M-237]. [Crew/JGB-35].

298.86 The Soldier's Rally. w. Dr. H.A. Dobson. m. "Air—*Marching Through Georgia.*" In: *Blaine And Logan Campaign Song-Book*, page 32. e. Prof. F. Widdows. Published by The Republican National Committee, New York, NY. 1884. [4⅜" × 5¹¹⁄₁₆"]. [V-1: Bk/y] [V-2: Pk/bk] litho of James G. Blaine and John A. Logan. "From the School—House to the Cabinet, From the Cabin to the Senate." 52pp. [M-251]. [Crew/JGB-32].

298.87 Song Of Eighty-Four. m. William E. Chandler. Published by Russell Brothers, No. 126 Tremont Street, Boston, MA. B/w lithos of James G. Blaine and John A. Logan, lyre, wreath. "Russell's Musical Library." "Campaign Songs, 1884." [Crew/JGB-104].

298.88 The Soreheads On Our Block. w. No composer indicated. m. Dave Braham, "Air—*Babies on our Block.*" In: *Hancock And English Campaign Songster*, page 4. Published by New York Popular Publishing Company, A.J. Dick, Manager, No. 32 Beekman Street, New York, NY. 1880. Be/bk litho of Winfield Scott Hancock. "Containing the Largest and Most Complete Collection of Songs, All Written to the Most Popular Airs of the Day." "The Most Popular Edition Of Hancock And English Campaign Songster." 68pp. Page 68: Be/bk litho of William H. English. [M-217]. [Crew/WSH-41].

298.89 Stand, Comrades, Stand. w. C.L.S. m. "Air—*The Marseillaise.*" In: *P.T. Schultz & Co's Blaine And Logan Bugle Call*, page 23. Published by P.T. Schultz & Company, No. 172 Race Street, Cincinnati, OH. 1881. [1884 Edition]. [5⅞" × 7⅝"]. Bk/gn litho of James G. Blaine and John A. Logan, flags and eagle, geometric design border. 36pp. [M-245]. [Crew/JGB-67].

298.90 [A Statesman For Our Leader Is What We Want Today]. w. No composer indicated. m. "Air—*Marching Through Georgia.*" In: *P.T. Schultz & Co's Blaine And Logan Bugle Call*, page 15. Published by P.T. Schultz & Company, No. 172 Race Street, Cincinnati, OH. 1881. [1884 Edition]. [5⅞" × 7⅝"]. Bk/gn litho of James G. Blaine and John A. Logan, flags and eagle, geometric design border. 36pp. [M-245]. [Crew/JGB-67].

298.91 A Struggle For Victory. w. No composer indicated. m. "Tune—*Marching Through Georgia.*" In: *Facts And Songs For The People*, page 16. Published by C.E. Bolton, Cleveland, OH. 1884. [5" × 7⅛"]. R/w/bl drawing of Miss Liberty, flag, scroll—"Vox populi, Vox Dei, 1884." 54pp. Pages 2 and 53: Advertising. Page 3: B/w photo of "Hon. James G. Blaine." Page 4: Photo of "Gen. John A. Logan." Page 5: Title—*Facts & Songs For The People Prepared Specially For Use In The Blaine And Logan Campaign.* [M-239]. [Crew/JGB-65].

298.92 That Man Jimmy Blaine. w. "By Demo." m. "Tune—*Widow Malone.*" In: *Cleveland & Hendricks Songster*, page 3. Copyright 1884 by E.Y. Landis. R/w/bl/gn/br drawing of Grover Cleveland, Thomas

Hendricks, George "Washington," Thomas "Jefferson," Andrew "Jackson," ribbons, geometric designs. 64pp. [M-230]. [Crew/GC-46].

298.93 There They Stand. w. No composer indicated. m. "Air—*Hail, Columbia.*" In: *Blaine And Logan Campaign Songster,* page 24. Published by John Church & Company, Cincinnati, OH. 1884. [4⅞" × 5¹³⁄₁₆"]. Y/bk non-pictorial geometric design border. "Including Biographical Sketches & Constitution for Campaign Clubs." 52pp. [M-233?]. [Crew/JGB-29].

298.94 There's Vict'ry In The Air. w. H.E. Gordon. m. "Air—*Tramp, Tramp, Tramp.*" In: *Blaine And Logan Campaign Song-Book,* page 46. e. Prof. F. Widdows. Published by The Republican National Committee, New York, NY. 1884. [4⅜" × 5¹¹⁄₁₆"]. [V-1: Bk/y] [V-2: Pk/bk] litho of James G. Blaine and John A. Logan. "From the School—House to the Cabinet, From the Cabin to the Senate." 52pp. [M-251]. [Crew/JGB-32].

298.95 'Tis For Blaine And Logan. w.m. Chas. B. Morrell. Published by Geo. D. Newhall Co., Cincinnati, OH. 1884. B/w geometric design and line border. "Republican Campaign Songs." "The Newest, Sprightliest and the Best." List of other songs in the series. [Crew/JGB-101].

298.96 The Toiler's Golden Day. w. No composer indicated. m. "Air—*Wearing Of The Green.*" In: *Blaine And Logan Campaign Song-Book,* page 40. e. Prof. F. Widdows. Published by The Republican National Committee, New York, NY. 1884. [4⅜" × 5¹¹⁄₁₆"]. [V-1: Bk/y] [V-2: Pk/bk] litho of James G. Blaine and John A. Logan. "From the School—House to the Cabinet, From the Cabin to the Senate." 52pp. [M-251]. [Crew/JGB-32].

298.97 Tramp, Tramp. w. Frank N. Scott. m. Air—*Tramp, Tramp, Tramp.* In: *P.T. Schultz & Co's Blaine And Logan Bugle Call,* page 24. Published by P.T. Schultz & Company, No. 172 Race Street, Cincinnati, OH. 1881. [1884 Edition]. [5⅞" × 7⅝"]. Bk/gn litho of James G. Blaine and John A. Logan, flags and eagle, geometric design border. 36pp. [M-245]. [Crew/JGB-67].

298.98 Uncle Sam's Choice Of Blaine And Logan. w. No composer indicated. m. Notation. In: *The People's Songs For Blaine & Logan,* page 7. Published by Acme Publishing Bureau, J.C.O. Redington, General Manager, No. 252 Broadway, New York, NY. Copyright 1884 by J.C.O. Redington. [4⅞" × 6⅝"]. B/w litho of James G. Blaine. "Adopted by the General Republican Committees in New York City and elsewhere." "Adapted for every Voice in the Glorious Land of Freedom. All the Nation may Sing." "Come, join that Columbia's blessings increase, All Singing for Liberty, Glory and Peace." "Acme Songs." 32pp. [M-246]. [Crew/JGB-45].

298.99 Upidee! w. J.W.B. Siders. m. No tune indicated. In: *Blaine And Logan Campaign Songster,* page 5. Published by American News Company, New York, NY. 1884. 36pp. [M-249]. [Crew/JGB-84].

298.100 Victory Rests With You. w. No composer indicated. m. "Air—*Hold The Fort.*" In: *Blaine And Logan Songster,* page 15. Published by Thomas Hunter, Philadelphia, PA. 1884. [5½" × 7¼"]. N/c litho of Abraham Lincoln and James Garfield—"Our Martyred Presidents." Br/w litho of James G. Blaine—"Our Next President," and John A. Logan—"Our Next Vice-President," George Washington, Ulysses S. Grant. 68pp [M-237]. [Crew/JGB-35].

298.101 Wait. w. H.E. Gordon. m. "Air—*Wait Till The Clouds Roll By.*" In: *Blaine And Logan Campaign Song-Book,* page 42. e. Prof. F. Widdows. Published by The Republican National Committee, New York, NY. 1884. [4⅜" × 5¹¹⁄₁₆"]. [V-1: Bk/y] [V-2: Pk/bk] litho of James G. Blaine and John A. Logan. "From the School—House to the Cabinet, From the Cabin to the Senate." 52pp. [M-251]. [Crew/JGB-32].

298.102 We Are Followers Of Blaine And Logan. w. No composer indicated. m. "Air—*Old Dan Tucker.*" In: *Beulah's Blaine And Logan Original Campaign Song Book 1884,* page 16. Printed and Published by Birnie Paper Company, Springfield, MA. 1884. [4" × 5¾"]. Gy/bk litho of James G. Blaine and John A. Logan, eagle, flags, shield, line border. 36pp. [M-232]. [Crew/JGB-41].

298.103 We Remember The Days, Etc. w. No composer indicated. m. "Air—*Tenting To-Night, etc.*" In: *Beulah's Blaine And Logan Original Campaign Song Book 1884,* page 13. Printed and Published by Birnie Paper Company, Springfield, MA. 1884. [4" × 5¾"]. Gy/bk litho of James G. Blaine and John A. Logan, eagle, flags, shield, line border. 36pp. [M-232]. [Crew/JGB-41].

298.104 We'll Carry O-HI-O! w. J.W.B. Siders. m. "Air—*Aunt Jemimah.*" In: *Blaine And Logan Campaign Songster,* page 6. Published by American News Company, New York, NY. 1884. 36pp. [M-249]. [Crew/JGB-84].

298.105 We'll Run 'Em In! w. Prof. F. Widdows. m. "Air—*Genevieve Guards Duet.*" In: *Blaine And Logan Campaign Song-Book,* page 3. e. Prof. F. Widdows. Published by The Republican National Committee, New York, NY. 1884. [4⅜" × 5¹¹⁄₁₆"]. [V-1: Bk/y] [V-2: Pk/bk] litho of James G. Blaine and John A. Logan. "From the School—House to the Cabinet, From the Cabin to the Senate." 52pp. [M-251]. [Crew/JGB-32].

298.106 We'll Vote The Straight Ticket. w. No composer indicated. m. "Air—*We're Going To The Cotton Fields.*" In: *Blaine And Logan Songster,* page 10. Published by Thomas Hunter, Philadelphia, PA. 1884. [5½" × 7¼"]. N/c litho of Abraham Lincoln and James Garfield—"Our Martyred Presidents." Br/w litho of James G. Blaine—"Our Next President," and John A. Logan—"Our Next Vice-President," George Washington, Ulysses S. Grant. 68pp [M-237]. [Crew/JGB-35].

298.107 What Means This Raising Of Banners. w. No composer indicated. m. "Air—*The Red, White And Blue.*" In: *Beulah's Blaine And Logan Original Campaign Song Book 1884,* page 14. Printed and Published by Birnie Paper Company, Springfield, MA. 1884. [4" × 5¾"]. Gy/bk litho of James G. Blaine and John A. Logan, eagle, flags, shield, line border. 36pp. [M-232]. [Crew/JGB-41].

298.108 When Election Day Is Over. w. J.W.B. Siders. m. "Air—*Glory, Glory, Hallelujah!*" In: *Blaine And Logan Campaign Songster,* page 4. Published by American News Company, New York, NY. 1884. 36pp. [M-249]. [Crew/JGB-84].

298.109 When Voting Day Shall Come. w. No composer indicated. m. "Air—*When Johnny Comes Marching Home*." In: *Blaine And Logan Campaign Song-Book*, page 41. e. Prof. F. Widdows. Published by The Republican National Committee, New York, NY. 1884. [4⅜" × 5 11/16"]. [V-1: Bk/y] [V-2: Pk/bk] litho of James G. Blaine and John A. Logan. "From the School—House to the Cabinet, From the Cabin to the Senate." 52pp. [M-251]. [Crew/JGB-32].

298.110 Where Will They Be? w. Walter Neville. m. "Air—*Where Will I Be?*" In: *P.T. Schultz & Co's Blaine And Logan Bugle Call*, page 31. Published by P.T. Schultz & Company, No. 172 Race Street, Cincinnati, OH. 1881. [1884 Edition]. [5⅞" × 7⅝"]. Bk/gn litho of James G. Blaine and John A. Logan, flags and eagle, geometric design border. 36pp. [M-245]. [Crew/JGB-67].

298.111 With Blaine And Jack We'll Clear The Track (Song & Chorus). w.m. W.B. Richardson. John Church & Co., No. 66 W. Fourth Street, Cincinnati, OH. 1884. Non-pictorial geometric designs. 6pp. Pages 2 and 6: Blank. [Crew/JGB-113].

298.112 Work For Blaine And Logan. w. Michigander. m.a. F. Widdows. In: *Blaine And Logan Campaign Song-Book*, page 10. e. Prof. F. Widdows. Published by The Republican National Committee, New York, NY. 1884. [4⅜" × 5 11/16"]. [V-1: Bk/y] [V-2: Pk/bk] litho of James G. Blaine and John A. Logan. "From the School—House to the Cabinet, From the Cabin to the Senate." 52pp. [M-251]. [Crew/JGB-32].

298.113 The Workingman's Campaign Song. w. Frank P. Cleary, M.D. m. "Air—*Away Down South In Dixie*." In: *Blaine And Logan Campaign Song-Book*, page 24. e. Prof. F. Widdows. Published by The Republican National Committee, New York, NY. 1884. [4⅜" × 5 11/16"]. [V-1: Bk/y] [V-2: Pk/bk] litho of James G. Blaine and John A. Logan. "From the School—House to the Cabinet, From the Cabin to the Senate." 52pp. [M-251]. [Crew/JGB-32].

298.114 Yankee Doodle At Chicago. w. No composer indicated. m. "Tune—*Yankee Doodle*." In: *Blaine And Logan Songster*, page 46. Published by Thomas Hunter, Philadelphia, PA. 1884. [5½" × 7¼"]. N/c litho of Abraham Lincoln and James Garfield—"Our Martyred Presidents." Br/w litho of James G. Blaine—"Our Next President," and John A. Logan—"Our Next Vice-President," George Washington, Ulysses S. Grant. 68pp [M-237]. [Crew/JGB-35].

298.115 Yankee Doodle At St. Louis. w. No composer indicated. m. "Tune—*Yankee Doodle*." In: *Republican Campaign Parodies And Songs* [Songster], page 14. Published by Betts and Burnett, South Butler, Wayne County, NY. 1896. [7¾" × 5½"]. Be/bk non-pictorial. "McKinley and Hobart." "1896." 28pp. [M-340]. [Crew/WM-67].

298.116 A Yankee Doodle Tariff. w. Mouse-in-the-Corner. m. No tune indicated. In: *Blaine And Logan Campaign Song-Book*, page 37. e. Prof. F. Widdows. Published by The Republican National Committee, New York, NY. 1884. [4⅜" × 5 11/16"]. [V-1: Bk/y] [V-2: Pk/bk] litho of James G. Blaine and John A. Logan. "From the School—House to the Cabinet, From the Cabin to the Senate." 52pp. [M-251]. [Crew/JGB-32].

• **AmPM-299 LOVEJOY**, Owen (State House, 1854; U.S. House, 1857–1864)

299.1 [Our Good Old Uncle Sam Is Sick] (A Campaign Song). w.m. No composer or tune indicated. In: *The Republican Campaign Songster No. #1*, page 30. Published by American Publishing House, No. 60 West Fourth Street, Cincinnati, OH. [1860]. [3¾" × 5¾"]. B/w litho of Abraham Lincoln. 48pp. [?]. [M-113]. [Crew/AL-298].

299.2 The White House. w. G.R. Edeson. m. "Air—*Root, Hog, Or Die!*" Published by H. De Marsan, 54 Chatham Street, New York, NY. [1861–1862]. B/w litho border of minstrels, geometric designs. 2pp. Page 2: Blank. [AMC].

• **AmPM-300 LUCAS**, Scott Wike (State's Attorney, Mason County, 1920–1925; State Tax Commission, 1933–1935; U.S. House, 1935–1939; U S. Senate, 1939–1951)

300.1 On With Roosevelt. w. J.B. Crawford. m. "Tune—*On Wisconsin*." In: *Our Heroes* [Song Sheet], page 1. [1940]. Non-pictorial. "Campaign Songs for the Election of Franklin D. Roosevelt, Songs will be introduced by Julma B. Crawford." 2pp. Page 2: Blank. [Crew/FDR-181].

300.2 Victory. w. Julma B. Crawford. m. No tune indicated. In: *Our Heroes* [Song Sheet], page 1. [1940]. Non-pictorial. "Campaign Songs for the Election of Franklin D. Roosevelt, Songs will be introduced by Julma B. Crawford." 2pp. Page 2: Blank. [Crew/FDR-181].

• **AmPM-301 MASON**, William Ernest (State House, 1879; State Senate, 1882–1885; U.S. House, 1887–1891; U.S. Senate, 1897–1903 & 1917–1921)

301.1 Our Senator (March And Two Step). m. G.J. Couchois. Published by Sol. Bloom, Chicago, IL. 1897. Pl/w photo of William E. Mason. Pl/w geometric designs. 8pp. Pages 2, 7 and 8: Blank. Page 3: Inside title—***Senator March And Two Step***. Pages 4 and 5: Advertising for Zimmerman carpets. Page 5: "Souvenir of Carpet Dep't Booth, County Fair, 1901."

• **AmPM-302 MATTESON**, Joel A. (State Senate, 1842–1884; Governor, 1853–1857)

302.1 Our Governors March (Or Two Step) m. Joseph Gearen. Published by Lyon & Healy, Chicago, IL. 1897. Bk/w/gn/br drawings of all Illinois Governors, Illinois capitol building, farm scene, law books. 6pp. Page 2: Blank. Page 6: Advertising. [Crew/JMP-1].

• **AmPM-303 MCCORMACK**, Ruth Hanna (U.S. House, 1929–1931; Candidate for U.S. Senate, 1930)

303.1 Ruth Hanna McCormick. w. Tom Lemonier. No publisher indicated. [ca. 1930]. [8½" × 11"]. Non-pictorial carbon copy. 2pp. Page 2: Blank.

• **AmPM-304 MCDONOUGH**, Joseph B. (Candidate for Treasurer, Cook County, 1930)

304.1 What Are You Going To Do For McDonough? w.m. Walter Goodwin. Published by Walter Goodwin, Chicago, IL. 1930. O/w/bk geometric design border. 6pp. Page 2: Blank. Page 6: "Dedicated to Joseph B. McDonough, Candidate for County Treasurer."

• **AmPM-305 MOSELEY-BRAUN**, Carol (State House, 1978–1988; Recorder of Deeds, Cook County,

1988–1992; U.S. Senate, 1993 1999; U.S. Ambassador to New Zealand, 1999–2001)

305.1 All You Democrats. w. Adam Bernstein. m. "*Mr. Tambourine Man,* based on a performance by Bob Dylan." Published online at <http://www.amiright.com/parody/60s/bobdylan17.shtml>. [ca. 2003].

305.2 Kerry. w. Dave Rackmales. m. "Sung to the tune of *Carey* by Joni Mitchell." "Spread The Word Through Song and Music! Songs For Dean, Songs to get elected by." N/c photo of Howard Dean. Lyrics published online at <http://songsfordean.com/so/lyrics/somethingtosee.php>. 2004.

305.3 Moseley My Dear (The Braun Song). w. Malcolm Higgins. m. Tune—"*Martha My Dear,* based on a performance by The Beatles." Published online at <http://www.amiright.com/parody/misc/thebeatles103.shtml>. [ca. 2003].

305.4 Onto Braun. w. Malcolm Higgins. m. "*On And On,* based on a performance by Steven Bishop." Published online at <http://www.amiright.com/parody/70s/stevenbishop0.shtml>. [ca. 2003].

305.5 People Who Tried (Political). w. Malcolm Higgins. m. "*People Who Died,* based on a performance by Jim Carroll." Published online at <http://www.amiright.com/parody/misc/jimcarroll0.shtml>. [ca. 2003].

305.6 Some Wail Away. w. Malcolm Higgins. m. "*Come Sail Away,* based on a performance by Styx." "Written of yourse [sic] by the ultimate lefty ... me." Published online at <http://www.amiright.com/parody/misc/styx0.shtml>. [ca. 2003].

305.7 We Want Howard Dean. w.m. Denny Zartman. m. No tune indicated. "Spread The Word Through Song and Music! Songs For Dean, Songs to get elected by." N/c photo of Howard Dean. Lyrics and sound file published online at <http://songsfordean.com/so/lyrics/somethingtosee.php>. 2004.

• **AmPM-306 OGDEN**, William Butler (State Assembly, 1834–1835; Mayor, Chicago, 1837–1838)

306.1 North Western Railway Polka. m. Mrs. Delia B. Ward. Published by H.M. Higgins, 45 Lake Street, Chicago, IL. 1859. N/c litho of two soldiers, two railroad scenes, ballroom dance. Dedicated to the Officers of the Chicago North Western Railway, Wm. B. Ogden, Geo. L. Dunlap, Geo. P. Lee, E. Dewitt. Robinson, and the Excursionists of the 12th of October 1859." 6pp. Page 2: Blank.

• **AmPM-307 OGLESBY**, Richard J. (State Senate, 1860; Governor, 1865–1869, 1873 & 1885–1889; US Senate, 1873–1879)

307.1 Our Governors March (Or Two Step) m. Joseph Gearen. Published by Lyon & Healy, Chicago, IL. 1897. Bk/w/gn/br drawings of all Illinois Governors, Illinois capitol building, farm scene, law books. 6pp. Page 2: Blank. Page 6: Advertising. [Crew/JMP-1].

• **AmPM-308 PALMER**, John McAuley (Probate Judge, Macoupin County, 1843–1847; County Judge, Macoupin County, 1849–1852; State Senate, 1852–1854 & 1855–1856; Governor, 1869–1873; Candidate for Vice President, 1872; U.S. Senate, 1891–1897; Candidate for President, 1896) [SEE: DOC-/PSM-JMP]

308.1 The Demopublican Party. w. H.S. Taylor. m. J.B. Herbert. In: *The Battle Cry, A New Collection Of Temperance And Prohibition Songs*, page 117. Published by Fillmore Bros., Publishers, 141 West Sixth Street, Cincinnati, and No. 40 Bible House, New York, New York. 1887. [5 1⅝" × 7¼"]. R/w flag, sword and rifle, geometric designs. 168pp.

308.2 From Cincinnati To The White House. w.m. No composer or tune indicated. In: *The Sun's Greeley Campaign Songster*, page 61. c. Amos J. Cumming. Published from *The Sun* Office, New York, NY. 1872. [4⅛" × 6½"]. Be/bk litho of Horace Greeley, wreath. "He shines for all." 64pp. [Crew/HG-5].

308.3 Witches' Scene From MacGreeley (Which is Seen to be a Fact). w.m. No composer or tune indicated. From the "*New York Standard.*" In: *National Republican Grant And Wilson Campaign Song-Book*, page 34. From the *New York Standard.* Published by The Union Republican Congressional Committee, Washington, DC. 1872. [313/16" × 8 3/16"]. Be/bk litho of Ulysses S. Grant. "We'll Sing a Song for U.S. Grant." 100pp. [M-182]. [Crew/USG-110].

• **AmPM-309 PEARSON**, Isaac N. (Illinois Secretary of State, 1889–1893)

309.1 Hurrah For All The Ticket. w. W.A.P. m. No tune indicated. In: *Republican Campaign Songs (As Sung By The Marquette Club Quartette)*, page 6. Published by the Marquette Club of Chicago, Dearborn Avenue and Maple Street, Chicago, IL. 1888. [3½" × 6¼"]. Be/bl geometric design border. "W.A. Paulson, 1st Bass; R.J. Wherry, 1st Tenor; M.O. Naramore, 2nd Bass; O.B. Knight, 2nd Tenor." "Music and Instructions Cheerfully Furnished on Application." 28pp. [Crew/BFH-129].

• **AmPM-310 POWELL**, Paul Taylor (State House, 1959–1963; Illinois Secretary of State, 1965–1970)

310.1 Illinois. w. C.H. Chamberlin. m. "Air—*Baby Mine.*" Published by Paul Powell, Secretary of State, Springfield, IL. [1890–1894] [Edition ca. 1970]. [8½" × 11¼"]. R/w/b drawing—"Seal of the State of Illinois, Aug. 26th, 1818." Issued by Paul Powell, Secretary of State." "Official State Song." 4pp. Page 2: "By permission of Clayton F. Summy Co." Page 3: Narrative—"The State Song." "By Act of the Fifty-fourth General Assembly the song *Illinois* became the official State song." Page 4: Bl/w outline of state, Abraham Lincoln—"Illinois, Land of Lincoln." [Crew/AL-340].

• **AmPM-311 RAUM**, Green Berry (U.S. House, 1867–1869; U.S. Commissioner Internal Revenue, 1876–1883; U.S. Commissioner of Pensions, 1889–1893)

311.1 Du-Da. w. No composer indicated. m. "Tune—*Camptown Races.*" In: *Red Hot Democratic Campaign Songs For 1892*, page 24. c. John Bunyon Herbert. Published by The S. Brainard's Sons Company, Chicago, IL. 1892. [5½" × 7¼"]. R/bk litho of Grover Cleveland on a banner, Capitol building, marchers, geometric design border. 36pp. Pages 2, 31 and 32: Advertising. Page 3: Contents. [M-299]. [Crew/GC-82].

311.2 Ta-Ra-Ra, Boom-De-Ay. w. No composer indicated. m. Notation. "Male Voices." In: *Red Hot Democratic Campaign Songs For 1892*, page 28. c. John

Bunyon Herbert. Published by The S. Brainard's Sons Company, Chicago, IL. 1892. [5½" × 7¼"]. R/bk litho of Grover Cleveland on a banner, Capitol building, marchers, geometric design border. 36pp. [M-299]. [Crew/GC-82].

• **AmPM-312   RAY**, Lyman B. (Lt. Governor, 1889–1893)

312.1 *Hurrah For All The Ticket*. w. W.A.P. m. No tune indicated. In: *Republican Campaign Songs (As Sung By The Marquette Club Quartette)*, page 6. Published by the Marquette Club of Chicago, Dearborn Avenue and Maple Street, Chicago, IL. 1888. [3½" × 6¼"]. Be/bl geometric design border. "W.A. Paulson, 1st Bass; R.J. Wherry, 1st Tenor; M.O. Naramore, 2nd Bass; O.B. Knight, 2nd Tenor." "Music and Instructions Cheerfully Furnished on Application." 28pp. [Crew/BFH-129].

• **AmPM-313   REYNOLDS**, John (State Supreme Court, 1818–1825; Candidate for U.S. Senate, 1823; State House, 1827–1829, 1846, 1852; Governor, 1830–1834; U.S. House, 1834–1837 & 1839–1843)

313.1 *Our Governors March* (Or Two Step) m. Joseph Gearen. Published by Lyon & Healy, Chicago, IL. 1897. Bk/w/gn/br drawings of all Illinois Governors, Illinois capitol building, farm scene, law books. 6pp. Page 2: Blank. Page 6: Advertising. [Crew/JMP-1].

313.2 *The Pioneers Home*. w. T.E. Garrett. m. F. Woolcott. Published by G.F. Ritz, 52 Fourth Street, St. Louis, MO. 1858. B/w non-pictorial geometric designs. "Dedicated to the Hon. John Reynolds, Ex Gov. of Illinois." 6pp. Pages 2 and 6: Blank. [LL/JH].

• **AmPM-314   ROCKWELL**, George Lincoln (Founder, American Nazi Party, 1958)

314.1 *National Socialist Battle Song*. w. Lincoln Rockwell. m. Horst-Wessel-Lied. No publisher indicated. [ca. 1960]. [8½" × 11"]. Non-pictorial mimeograph. 2pp. Page 2: Blank. [Crew/MISC-228].

• **AmPM-315   ROSTENKOWSKI**, Daniel David (State House, 1952; Delegate, Democratic National Convention, 1960, 1964, 1968, 1972 & 1976; State Senate, 1954–1956; U.S. House, 1959–1995)

315.1 *Rosty The Chairman*. w. Bill Strauss and Elaina Newport. On CD: *All I Want For Christmas Is A Tax Increase*. Published by Capitol Steps Productions, 1505 King Street, Alexandria, VA. 1993. CD Cover: N/c drawing of Santa and helpers.

• **AmPM-316   ROWAN**, William A. (Alderman, 1927–1942; U.S. House, 1943–1947; U.S. Comptroller of Customs, Chicago, 1947–1953)

316.1 *On With Roosevelt*. w. J.B. Crawford. m. "Tune—*On Wisconsin*." In: *Our Heroes* [Song Sheet], page 1. [1940]. Non-pictorial. "Campaign Songs for the Election of Franklin D. Roosevelt, Songs will be introduced by Julma B. Crawford." 2pp. Page 2: Blank. [Crew/FDR-181].

316.2 *Victory*. w. Julma B. Crawford. m. No tune indicated. In: *Our Heroes* [Song Sheet], page 1. [1940]. Non-pictorial. "Campaign Songs for the Election of Franklin D. Roosevelt, Songs will be introduced by Julma B. Crawford." 2pp. Page 2: Blank. [Crew/FDR-181].

• **AmPM-317   RUMSFELD**, Donald Henry (U.S. House, 1963–1969; Assistant/Director, Office of Economic Opportunity, 1969–1970; Presidential Counselor, 1970–1973; Director, Cost of Living Council, 1971–1973; U.S. Ambassador to the North Atlantic Treaty Organization, 1973–1974; White House Chief of Staff, 1974–1975; U.S. Secretary of Defense, 1975–1977 & 2001–Present; Special Presidential Ambassador to the Middle East, 1983–1984)

317.1 *American Lie*. w. Dangers0ne. m. "*American Pie*, based on a performance by Don McLean." "With apologies to Don McLean." Published online at <http://www.amiright.com/parody/70s/donmcclean24.shtml>. [ca. 2003].

317.1A *American Lie*. w. LionMArk Hoolihan-Mertens. m. "*American Pie*, based on a performance by Don Mclean." "I wrote this after I saw the Justice Department explaining why it was OK for the, to ignore the constitutional rights of US citizens when they felt like it. Well I felt like writing this. Why... because I can." Published online at <http://www.amiright.com/parody/70s/donmclean48.shtml>. Copyright 2004 by Boniface Bugle Productions.

317.2 *Attacking And Fighting Again*. w. William Tong. m. "*Back In The High Life Again*, based on the performance by Steve Winwood." "Emperor Dubya, with a cabinet packed full of Daddy Bush's old war hawk relics (Rumsfeld, Powell, Wolfowitz, etc.), is hell-bent on war, undeterred by worldwide opposition from governments and 10 million marchers in 600 cities." Published online at <http://www.amiright.com/parody/80s/stevewinwood5.shtml>. [ca. 2003].

317.2A *The Ballad Of Abu Grurayb*. w. Bob Gomez. m. "*The Ballad Of The Green Berets*, based on the performance by Barry Sadler." Published online at <http://www.amiright.com/parody/60s/barrysadler2.shtml>. 2004.

317.3 *Brain-Dead Whine*. w. Michael Pacholek. w. "*Red, Red Wine* originally by Neil Diamond." Published online at <http://www.amiright.com/parody/60s/neildiamond2.shml>.

317.4 *Celebration*. w. Fred Stanton. m. No tune indicated. Published by the Centre for Political Song online at <http://polsong.gcal.ac.uk/songs/stanton.html>. [ca. 2003].

317.5 *The Cheney Bunch*. w. Laurence Dunne. m. "*The Brady Bunch*, based on a performance by *The Brady Bunch* TV show." Published online at <http://amiright.com/parody/60s/thebradybunchtvshow0.shtml>. [ca. 2004].

317.6 *C.R.A.B.* (Cheney, Rumsfeld, Ashcroft & Bush). w. Todd Samusson. m. "No tune indicated. Published online by the Centre for Political Song at <http://polsong.gcal.ac.uk/songs/samusson.html>. 2002.

317.6A *Dubya, No*. w. Michael Pacholek. m. "*Kokomo*, based on a performance by The Beach Boys." "Aruba, Jamaica, Bermuda, Bahama, which one will he invade next? Key Largo? Wait, that's Florida, the Bushes invaded that years ago. Another place that needs regime change. Another one that William Tong will kick himself for not thinking of first." Published online at <http://www.amiright.com/parody/80s/thebeachboys7.shtml>. 2004.

317.7 *Duct And Cover* (A Catacalypso). w. Mark Levy. m. No tune indicated. Published by the Centre for Political Song online at <http://polsong.gcal.ac.uk/songs/levy.html>. [ca. 2003].

317.8 The George W Bush Movie. w. Laurence Dunne. m. "*Theme From Star Wars,* based on a performance by John Williams." "Imagine this text floating away from your wide screen in ten million years against a dark starry background with the theme from *Star Wars* playing, with George Bush instead of the Emperor and Donald Rumsfeld instead of Darth Vader." Published online at <http://amiright.com/parody/70s/johnwilliams0.shtml>. [ca. 2004].

317.9 High Treason. w. Emiloca. m. "*The Reason,* based on the performance by Hoobastank." "I'd like to take this time to apologize once and for all for my country. Tis whole thing in Iraq is embarrassing the red, white and blue out of me. I hope this song isn't too controversial ... it's about as controversial as I get, anyway." "Please post a comment. I'll hunt you down. With a pitchfork." Published online at <http://www.amiright.com/parody/2000s/hoobastank14.shml>. 2004.

317.9A How Do You Sleep? w. Ralph Paterno. m. "No tune indicated. "Political Song about Rice, Cheney and Rumsfeld at Politicalsong.net." Published online by Politicalsong.net at <http://www.politicalsong.net/how_do_you_sleep>. 2004.

317.10 I Got Big Bombs. w. Ashley Smit. m. "*I Like Big Butts,* based on the performance by Sir Raps-A-Lot." "I just love this version to the song." Published online at <http://www.amiright.com/parody/90s/sirrapsalot0.shtml>. 2003.

317.11 Imaginary Budget. w. William Tong. m. "*Imaginary Lover,* originally by Atlanta Rhythm Section." "Satire about how Bush, Rummy, and his Big Business cronies have looted our national treasury." Published online at <http://www.amiright.com/parody/70s/theatlantarhythmsection1.shtml>. [ca. 2002].

317.12 In 2004. From CD: *American Way.* m. "*When I'm 64* by The Beatles." Performed by Dimpled Chad & The Disenfranchised. Lyrics published at <http:/dimpledchad.net>. [ca. 2000].

317.13 John Ashcroft Is Hunting You Down. w. William Tong. m. "*Santa Claus Is Coming To Town,* originally by Traditional." Published online at <http://www.amiright.com/parody/misc/traditional59.html>. [ca. 2002].

317.14 Killing The Soldiers. w. Bush League. m. "*Killing Me Softly,* based on a performance by *Roberta Flack.*" Published online at <http://www.amiright.com/parody/70s/robertaflack7.shtml>. [2004].

317.15 Lirty Dies: Maddam And Yubble-Doo. w.m. The Capitol Steps. Published by The Capitol Steps online at<http://capsteps.com/lirty/maddam.html>. 2003

317.16 Move Bush. w. John Spoof. m. "*Move Bitch,* based on a performance by Ludacris." Published online at <http://www.amiright.com/parody/2000s/ludacris16.shtml>. 2003.

317.16A Rummy, A Message To You. w. Charlie Decker. m. "*Rudi, A Message To You,* based on a performance by Specials." "A message to Donald Rumsfeld, Secretary of Defense." Published online at <http://www.amiright.com/parody/70s/specials0.shtml>. 2004.

317.16B Rummy Please. w. William Tong. m. "*Summer Breeze,* based on a performance by Seals & Crofts." "Satire about Bush's embattled Secretary of Defense Donald Rumsfeld, loathed by U.S> Military professionals for creating the quagmire in Iraq and setting conditions for the Abu Ghraib prison scandal." Published online at <http://www.amiright.com/parody/70s/sealscrifts1.shtml>. 2004.

317.17 Rummy, Rummy, Rummy. w. John A. Barry. m. "*Yummy, Yummy, Yummy,* based on the performance by Ohio Express." Published online at <http://www.amiright.com/parody/60s/ohioexpress2.shtml>. 2004.

317.17A Rummy's Mind. w. John A. Barry. m. "*Summertime,* based on the performance by George Gershwin." "Helen Thomas, 84 year-old reporter columnist, known for her aggressiveness in going after a story." Published online at <http://www.amiright.com/parody/misc/georgegershwin1.shtml>. 2004.

317.18 Rumsey Boy. w. Bob Gomez. m. "*Soldier Boy,* based on the performance by The Shirelles." "Happy Veterans Day" Published online at <http://www.amiright.com/parody/60s/theshirelles2.shtml>. 2003.

317.19 Rumsey's Dummy. w. Michael Pacholek. m. "*Wooly Bully,* based on the performance by Sam the Sham & the Pharaohs." "Since I was the first to use that pairing, on The *Little Drummer Boy* (Rum the Dumb), I don't think William Tong will mind if I pick up where he left off with 'Prison Bullies.'" Published online at <http://www.amiright.com/parody/60s/samtheshamthepharoshs2.shtml>. 2004.

317.20 Rums On The Rocks. w. William Tong. m. "*Love On The Rocks,* based on the performance by Gar- Neil Diamond." "The military torture scandal at Abu Ghraid prison in Iraq has led to world-wide calls for the resignation of Bush's Secretary of Defense, Donald Rumsfeld." Published online at <http://www.amiright.com/parody/70s/neildiamond51.shtml>. 2004.

317.21 Rumsfeld. w. William Tong. m. "*Young Girl,* based on the performance by Gary Puckett & The Union Gap." "Satire about Bush's Secretary of Defense Donald Rumsfeld, now facing calls for his resignation by Congress and by the entire world for allowing and covering up the Abu Ghraib military prison torture scandal in Iraq." Published online at <http://www.amiright.com/parody/60s/garypuckettheuniongap1.shtml>. 2004.

317.22 Shred The Constitution. w. Alvin Dover. m. "*Ball Of Confusion,* originally by The Temptations." Published online at <http://www.amiright.com/parody/70s/thetemptations3.shtml>. [ca. 2002].

317.23 Subterranean Homesick Blues. w. Skisics Surus. m. Tune—"*Subterranean Homesick Blues,* originally by Bob Dylan." Published online at <http://amiright.com/parody/60s/bobdylan5.shml>. [ca. 2001].

317.24 Super-US-Made-Ballistic-Missiles-are-Atrocious. w. No composer indicated. m. "Parody of Supercalifragilisticexpialidocious by Richard M. Sherman and Robert B. Sherman, performed by Julie Andrews, Dick Van Dyke and others." "For those of you who couldn't guess from my appalling impression (i.e.

all of you), the bloke with the American accent is supposed to be Donald Rumsfeld, US Secretary of State for Defence [sic] ..." Published online at <http://www.chu.cam.ac.uk/~TSK23/Songs/original.html>. [ca. 2003].

317.25 *Talking Cabinet Blues*. w. Dave Lippman. m. No tune indicated. Published online at <http://www.davelippman.com/Cabinet.html>. N/c photo of Dave Lippman. [ca. 2001].

317.26 *We're So Sorry 'Bout The Prisoners*. w. Bob Gomez. m. "*Uncle Albert/Admiral Halsey*, based on a performance by Paul McCartney and Wings." "I read the news today, oh, boy." "Now we know how many holes it takes to fill the Oval Office." Published online at <http://www.amiright.com/parody/70s/paulmccartneyandwings18.shtml>. 2004.

317.27 *Workin' Without Karen Hughes*. w. William Tong. m. "*Workin' At The Carwash Blues*, originally by Jim Croce.""Bush advisor Karen Hughes abruptly resigns from the White House staff to return to Texas." Published online at <http://www.amiright.com/parody/70s/jimcroce6.shtml>. [2002].

• **AmPM-318** SMALL, Lennington (State Republican State Central Committee, 1899 & 1919; State Senate, 1901–1903; State Treasurer, 1905–1907 & 1917–1919; Governor, 1921–1929)

318.1 *The Farmer's Prayer*. w. No composer indicated. m. "Sung to the tune *After The Ball*." In: *Democratic Song Book*, page 5. Published by Charles W. Stewart, No. 439 Arlington Place, Chicago, IL. July 21, 1928. [3¾" × 6⅛"]. Non-pictorial geometric design border. "Dedicated to sane government and honest administration with 'Life, Liberty and The Pursuit of Happiness' without blue laws or fool laws. The most damnable tyranny is the tyranny of small things. 'Give me the writing of a nation's songs and I care not who writes its laws.' The best way to cure a fool of his folly—to Laugh him out of it." "Sing Brother Sing!" 6pp. Various Christian and anti-prohibition sayings throughout—"Would Christ have joined the Ku Klux Klan or the Anti-Saloon League?, &c." [M-418]. [Crew/AES-70].

• **AmPM-318A** STEVENSON, Adlai Ewing (U.S. House, 1875–1877 & 1879–1881; Vice President, 1893–1897; Candidate for Vice President, 1900; Candidate for Governor, 1908) [ALSO SEE: DOC/PSM-WJB]

318A.1 *The Ballot's Power*. w. S.N. Holmes. m. "Tune—*The Red, White And Blue*." In: *The Republican Campaign Song Book, With Music, 1892*, page 38. e. Samuel Newall Holmes. Published by Samuel Newall Holmes, Syracuse, NY. 1892. Be/bk non-pictorial. "Composed and especially prepared by Judge S.N. Holmes of Syracuse, N.Y." "Headquarters: Syracuse, N.Y." "Price twenty-five cents." 60pp. [M-308]. [Crew/BFH-107].

318A.2 *Bryan And Stevenson* (Campaign Rallying Song). w.m. Sep. Winner. Published in an unknown newspaper of the time. 1900. [7½" × 11¼"]. B/w photo of "Sep. Winner." Long article on his life. Additional lyrics to the song. Musical notation. [Crew/WJB-98].

318A.3 *The Bryan Ticket We Can't Do*. w.m. Geo. B. Chase. In: *Republican Hot Shot (A Campaign Songster for 1900)*, page 20. e.a. George B. Chase and J.F. Kinsey. Published by Echo Music Company. 1900. [6" × 8¾"]. Bk/r lithos of William McKinley and Theodore Roosevelt. "Second Edition." 28pp. [M-365]. [Crew/WM-238].

318A.4 *Cleveland's White House Home*. w. "Demo." m. "Air—*Maggie Murphy's Home*." In: *Cleveland And Stevenson Songster*, page 4. Copyright 1892 by W.F. Shaw. [6¹³⁄₁₆" × 8"]. R/w/bl/gn litho of flags, wreath, Grover Cleveland and Adlai Stevenson. 68pp. [M-298]. [Crew/GC-2].

318A.5 *The Cuckoos*. w. No composer indicated. m. "Tune—*Billy Magee McGaw*." In: *The Rough Rider (Republican Campaign Song Book)*, page 8. c. J. Burgess Brown. Published by J. Burgess Brown, Indianapolis, IN. 1900. [6" × 9"]. Br/bk non-pictorial. "ROUGH ON DemocRATS." 28pp. Page 3: B/w litho of William McKinley. Page 28: "Republican National Ticket—1900. [Crew/WM-330].

318A.6 *Democratic Boum-Te-Ay*. w. "Demo." m. "Arr. With Chorus by T. O'Neil." In: *Cleveland And Stevenson Songster*, page 3. Copyright 1892 by W.F. Shaw. [6¹³⁄₁₆" × 8"]. R/w/bl/gn litho of flags, wreath, Grover Cleveland and Adlai Stevenson. 68pp. [M-298]. [Crew/GC-2].

318A.7 *Drive The High Tariff Tinkers To The Wall*. w. "Demo." m. "Air—*The Picture That Is Turned To The Wall*." In: *Cleveland And Stevenson Songster*, page 5. Copyright 1892 by W.F. Shaw. [6¹³⁄₁₆" × 8"]. R/w/bl/gn litho of flags, wreath, Grover Cleveland and Adlai Stevenson. 68pp. [M-298]. [Crew/GC-2].

318A.8 *Glory! Glory! Hallelujah*. w. E.J. Seymour. m. Air—*Glory Hallelujah*. In: *Harrison And Reid Campaign Song Book*, page 27. w. E.J. Seymour. m. Popular Airs. No publisher indicated. [1892]. [3⅞" × 5⅛"]. Bl/gn non-pictorial, stars, geometric designs. 36pp. Pages 2 and 35: Blank. Page 36: Advertising for this songbook. [M-316]. [Crew/BFH-35].

318A.9 *Gold And McKinley For Me*. w. E.G. Hanford. m. "Air—*Bring Back My Bonnie To Me*." In: *McKinley & Roosevelt Campaign 1900* [Song Book], page 3. Published for the Wholesale Dry Goods Republican Club, No. 350 Broadway by C.G. Burgoyne, New York, NY. 1900. [4¾" × 7"]. Y/bk litho of William McKinley and Theodore Roosevelt, eagle, shield. "Meetings daily from 12 Noon until 2 p.m." "A bird that can sing and won't must be made to sing." 20pp. [M-376]. [Crew/WM-84].

318A.10 *Harrison And Reid*. w. E.J. Seymour. m. "Air—*Ta-Ra-Ra-Boom Ter Ree*." In: *Harrison And Reid Campaign Song Book*, page 3. w. E.J. Seymour. m. Popular Airs. No publisher indicated. [1892]. [3⅞" × 5⅛"]. Bl/gn non-pictorial, stars, geometric designs. 36pp. Pages 2 and 35: Blank. Page 36: Advertising for this songbook. [M-316]. [Crew/BFH-35].

318A.11 *His Raven Locks Are Hanging Down His Back*. w. Stephen Laskey. m. "Tune—*Her Golden Hair, &c*." In: *McKinley & Roosevelt Campaign 1900*, page 8. Published for the Wholesale Dry Goods Republican Club, No. 350 Broadway by C.G. Burgoyne, New York, NY. 1900. [4¾" × 7"]. Y/bk litho of William McKinley and Theodore Roosevelt, eagle, shield. "Meetings daily from 12 Noon until 2 p.m." "A bird that can sing and won't must be made to sing." 20pp. [M-376]. [Crew/WM-84].

318A.12 Hoosier Voters. w. No composer indicated. m. "Tune—*Old Granite State.*" In: *The Rough Rider (Republican Campaign Song Book)*, page 15. c. J. Burgess Brown. Published by J. Burgess Brown, Indianapolis, IN. 1900. [6" × 9"]. Br/bk non-pictorial. "ROUGH ON DemocRATS." 28pp. Page 3: B/w litho of William McKinley. Page 28: "Republican National Ticket—1900. [Crew/WM-330].

318A.13 Innocuous Desurtude. w. S.N. Holmes. m. "Tune—*Old Dan Tucker.*" In: *The Republican Campaign Song Book, With Music, 1892*, page 48. e. Samuel Newall Holmes. Published by Samuel Newall Holmes, Syracuse, NY. 1892. Be/bk non-pictorial. "Composed and especially prepared by Judge S.N. Holmes of Syracuse, N.Y." "Headquarters: Syracuse, N.Y." "Price twenty-five cents." 60pp. [M-308]. [Crew/BFH-107].

318A.14 Listen To My Tale Of Woe. w. A.B. Sloan, "186 W. 70th St.." m. No tune indicated. In: *McKinley & Roosevelt Campaign 1900,* page 6. Published for the Wholesale Dry Goods Republican Club, No. 350 Broadway by C.G. Burgoyne, New York, NY. 1900. [4¾" × 7"]. Y/bk litho of William McKinley and Theodore Roosevelt, eagle, shield. "Meetings daily from 12 Noon until 2 p.m." "A bird that can sing and won't must be made to sing." 20pp. [M-376]. [Crew/WM-84].

318A.15 Marching To The Bugle Call. w. No composer indicated. m. "Tune—*Swinging In The Grape Vine Swing.*" In: *The Rough Rider (Republican Campaign Song Book)*, page 19. c. J. Burgess Brown. Published by J. Burgess Brown, Indianapolis, IN. 1900. [6" × 9"]. Br/bk non-pictorial. "ROUGH ON DemocRATS." 28pp. Page 3: B/w litho of William McKinley. Page 28: "Republican National Ticket—1900. [Crew/WM-330].

318A.16 Oh! What A Difference In The Morning. w. No composer indicated. m. Notation, Tune—*Oh! What A Difference In The Morning.* In: *Red Hot Democratic Campaign Songs For 1892*, page 25. c. John Bunyon Herbert. Published by The S. Brainard's Sons Company, Chicago, IL. 1892. [5½" × 7¼"]. R/bk litho of Grover Cleveland on a banner, Capitol building, marchers, geometric design border. 36pp. Pages 2, 31 and 32: Advertising. Page 3: Contents. [M-299]. [Crew/GC-82].

318A.17 Our Candidates. w. J.J. Kavanaugh. m. W.A. Sullenbarger. "Sung with Expression." In: *The National Democratic Song Book For 1900*, page 12. w. J.J. Kavanaugh. m. W.A. Sullenbarger. Published by The S. Brainard's Sons Company, Chicago, IL. Copyright 1900 by Kavanaugh and Sullenbarger. Be/bk photos of William J. Bryan and Adlai E. Stevenson. Be/bk geometric designs. "No. 1." 20pp. [M-382]. [Crew/WJB-8].

318A.18 The Republican Train. w. No composer indicated. m. "Tune—*The Gospel Train Am Coming.*" In: *The Rough Rider (Republican Campaign Song Book)*, page 4. c. J. Burgess Brown. Published by J. Burgess Brown, Indianapolis, IN. 1900. [6" × 9"]. Br/bk non-pictorial. "ROUGH ON DemocRATS." 28pp. Page 3: B/w litho of William McKinley. Page 28: "Republican National Ticket—1900. [Crew/WM-330].

318A.19 There'll Be A Hot Time This Fall. w. Stephen R. Royce, "Author of *We Want You, McKinley*, the great campaign song of 1896." m. "Tune—*There'll Be A Hot Time In The Old Town Tonight.*" In: *McKinley & Roosevelt Campaign 1900,* page 15. Published for the Wholesale Dry Goods Republican Club, No. 350 Broadway by C.G. Burgoyne, New York, NY. 1900. [4¾" × 7"]. Y/bk litho of William McKinley and Theodore Roosevelt, eagle, shield. "Meetings daily from 12 Noon until 2 p.m." "A bird that can sing and won't must be made to sing." 20pp. [M-376]. [Crew/WM-84].

318A.20 They Won't Be There. w. No composer indicated. m. Notation. In: *McKinley Campaign Songster For 1900 (For Male Voices)*, page 30. e. W.G. Thomas. Published by The Home Music Company, Logansport, IN. 1900. Gn/bk litho of "William McKinley for President" and "Theo. Roosevelt For Vice President," eagle, flags, shield. "Send cash with order." "All orders will be promptly filled if accompanied by cash." "Single copy 15 cts. $.50 per dozen." "Note: Our McKinley Campaign Songster No. 2, Entirely Different from this will be issued September 10th. Same Price." 36pp. [M-373]. [Crew/WM-275].

318A.21 [We Labored Long And Hard, You Know]. w. No composer indicated. m. "Air—*The Daughter Of The Regiment.*" In: *Gridiron Nights*, page 287. Published by Frederick A. Stokes Company, Publishers, New York, NY. Copyright 1915 by Arthur Wallace Dunn. [7½" × 10½"]. B/gd imprinting of comedy mask, lamps, floral designs. 406pp.

318A.22 [When Bill Bryan Talks About The Presidential Chair]. w. H.D. Tutewiler. m. "To the tune *There'll Be A Hot Time In The Old Town Tonight.*" In: *The March Of The Flag Songbook*, 11. Published by H.D. Tutewiler, No. 133 West Market Street, Indianapolis, IN. 1900. [5" × 7⅜"]. Be/bk litho of flag. "The Only Republican Campaign Songs for 1900 Having the Authorized Endorsement [sic] of Both National Republican Committees." 28pp. [M-374]. [Crew/WM-155].

318A.23 When Bryan Goes Marching Home. w. Hugh A. McCord. m. "Tune—*When Johnny Comes Marching Home.*" In: *McCord's Republican Club Songs (Campaign Of 1900)*, page 14. e. Hugh A. McCord. Published and for Sale by McCord & McCord, Emporia, KS. 1900. [4³⁄₁₆" × 6¹³⁄₁₆"]. Bl/w litho of William "McKinley" and Theodore "Roosevelt," "Prosperity" and "Protection," geometric border. "Price 10 Cents; $1.00 per Dozen." 22pp. [Crew/WM-347].

318A.24 The Whole Thing. w. Hugh A. McCord. m. "Tune—*Charming Billy.*" In: *McCord's Republican Club Songs (Campaign Of 1900)*, page 7. e. Hugh A. McCord. Published and for Sale by McCord & McCord, Emporia, KS. 1900. [4³⁄₁₆" × 6¹³⁄₁₆"]. Bl/w litho of William "McKinley" and Theodore "Roosevelt," "Prosperity" and "Protection," geometric border. "Price 10 Cents; $1.00 per Dozen." 22pp. [Crew/WM-347].

• **AmPM-319** STEVENSON, Adlai E., II. (Governor, 1949–1953; Democratic Candidate for President, 1952 & 1956; U.S. Ambassador to the United Nations, 1961–1965) [ALSO SEE: DOC/PSM-AS]

319.1 All Men On Earth Are Brothers. w.m. Julian Wright. Published by Nordyke Songs & Music Publishers, 6000 Sunset Boulevard, Hollywood 28, CA. [ca. 1966]. "A United Nations Anthem or Pledge." "All Rights Donated to the Adlai Stevenson Memorial U.N. Fund." [Crew/AS-15].

319.2 Cool Goldwater. w. Noel E. Parmentel, Jr. and Marshall J. Dodge. In: *Folk Songs For Conservatives*, page 11. Published by Unicorn Press, Inc., No. 790 Madison Avenue, New York, NY. 10021. 1964. [5" × 8⅜"]. Bl/w drawings of Barry Goldwater, Bill Buckley, Ray Cohn, eagle. List of contents. "Sung by Noel E. Parmentel, Jr. and His Unbleached Muslims, Greatest Political Satirists Since Cohn and Schine." "Right Wing Hootenanny." 36pp. [Crew/BMG-13].

319.3 Don't Let 'Em Take It Away! (A Democratic Campaign Song). w. Robert Sour. m. Bernie Wayne. Published by Meridian Music Corporation, No. 1619 Broadway, New York 19, NY. 1952. [3" × 6"]. Non-pictorial. "Join Phil Regan in Singing a Democratic Campaign Song." 2pp. [Crew/AS-16].

319.3A Illinois. (By The Rivers Gently Flowing). w. Charles H. Chamberlin. m. Archibald Johnson. In: *Souvenir And Historic Illinois*. "Panorama of History. Published by Adlai E. Stevenson, Governor, State of Illinois, Springfield, IL. [ca. 1950]. Gn/w drawing of state. B/w drawing of famous Illinoisans, including Abraham Lincoln.

319.4 I'm Called Little Caroline. w. Milton M. Schwartz. m. "Tune — *I'm Called Little Buttercup.*" In: *Sing Along With Jack* [Song Book], page 10. Published by Pocket Books, Inc., New York, NY. Copyright 1963 by Bonny Publishing Corporation. [9" × 11⅞"]. R/w/bk drawing of sheet music *Vive La Dynasty*, silhouette of John F. Kennedy in chair with conductor's baton, caricature of Kennedy family. "Hit Songs from the New Frontier." 36pp. Page 3: "Illustrations by David Gantz." Page 36: Drawing of John F. Kennedy in chair with baton. Song titles. [Crew/JFK-17].

319.5 Songs Of The New Campaign For America. 45 rpm record #ZTSP-25402. Published by Volunteers for Stevenson. 1956. Side 1 songs: ***Stevenson, Stevenson*** {319.5-1}; ***All The Way With Adlai*** {319.5-2}; ***Adlai Is Gonna Win This Time*** {319.5-3}. Side 2: ***Democratic March*** {319.5-4}.

319.6 We Are Democrats, Too. w. No composer indicated. m. "Tune — *I'm An Indian, Too.*" In: *Alice In Blunderland Or Through The Rooking Class* [Program and Songbook], page 22. Published by The Legislative Correspondents' Association of New York State, Albany, NY. 1949. [8⅝" × 11"]. N/c drawings of Harry Truman, Thomas Dewey, Franklin Roosevelt, Henry Wallace, Harold Stassen, Alben Barkley, Robert Taft, Earl Warren, other politicians. "A Scintillating Satire of Sadistic Surprises and Surprising Successes Featuring a Dramatic Disclosure of How Tom Did Not Go Down to D.C. in Slips; Together with a Give-Away-Nothing Radio Broadcast and Epic Melodrama of the Indian Wars Entitled 'When the Cat's Away the Mice Will Play.'" "Done With Music and Mirrors — Particularly Mirrors in Three Acts at Hotel Ten Eyck, Albany, March 12, 1949." [Crew/HST-20].

319.7 We're Madly For Adlai. w.m. Gilbert S. Watson. Published by Tweed Enterprises, Inc., P.O.B. 392, Lake Forest, IL. 1956. B/w photo of Adlai E. Stevenson II. B/w drawing of flag, The White House, ladder with rungs labeled "Our Next President," "Nominee For President," "Governor of Illinois," "Representative To U.N.," "Ass't. Secretary of State," "Ass't. to Secretary of Navy," 'Private Citizen." Song Lyrics. 2pp. Page 2: Blank.

• **AmPM-320 STRATTON,** William Grant (U.S. House, 1941–1943 & 1947–1949; State Treasurer, 1943–1944 & 1950–1952; Governor, 1953–1961)

320.1 Our Illinois. w. Maude Lanhan. m. Ruth S. Gaudlitz. Copyright 1956 by Ruth S. Gaudlitz, 2027 Illini Road, Springfield, IL. Bl/w/gd drawing of Illinois State flag, stars. "Souvenir Copy." 6pp. Page 2: "Dedicated to Honorable William G. Stratton, Governor, at the 60th Annual State Conference of the Daughters of the American Revolution at Springfield, March 12–14, 1956..." Page 6: Blank.

• **AmPM-321 TANNER,** John Riley (State Senate, 1881; State Treasurer, 1887–1889; Governor, 1897–1901)

321.1 Our Governors March (Or Two Step) m. Joseph Gearen. Published by Lyon & Healy, Chicago, IL. 1897. Bk/w/gn/br drawings of all Illinois Governors, Illinois capitol building, farm scene, law books. 6pp. Page 2: Blank. Page 6: Advertising. [Crew/JMP-1].

• **AmPM-322 THOMPSON,** William Hale (Mayor, Chicago, 1915–1923, 1927–1931)

322.1 America First Last And Always. w.m. Bernie Grossman, Arthur Sizemore and Larry Shay. Published by Milton Weil Music Co., 54 Randolph Street, Chicago, IL. 1926. Bl/w photo of "Big Bill, America First." R/w/b flag and star design. "A Worth Weil Song." 6pp. Page 2: At top of music — "Dedicated to a great American William Hale Thompson." Page 6: Advertising.

322.2 Big Bill The Builder. w.m. Milton Weil, Bernie Grossman and Larry Shay. Published by Milton Weil Music Company, Inc., No. 54 West Randolph Street, Chicago, IL. 1928. B/w photo of Chicago Mayor Bill Thompson — "America First, Big Bill The Builder" [facsimile handwriting]. R/w/b drawings of Big Bill with a portrait of George Washington — "No entangling alliances," Uncle Sam, soldier — "Not for foreign shores," Big Bill Thompson with child and with Charles Lindbergh, boat — "Cape Girardeau." "We are indebted to Corporation Counsel Samuel A. Ettelson for the original suggestion for this song and many of its phrases." "America First." 6pp. Page 3: "Respectfully Dedicated to our dear friend, The Hon. William Hale Thompson." Page 6: Advertising.

322.3 The Farmer's Prayer. w. No composer indicated. m. "Sung to the tune *After The Ball.*" In: *Democratic Song Book*, page 5. Published by Charles W. Stewart, No. 439 Arlington Place, Chicago, IL. July 21, 1928. [3¾" × 6⅛"]. Non-pictorial geometric design border. "Dedicated to sane government and honest administration with 'Life, Liberty and The Pursuit of Happiness' without blue laws or fool laws. The most damnable tyranny is the tyranny of small things. 'Give me the writing of a nation's songs and I care not who writes its laws.' The best way to cure a fool of his folly — to Laugh him out of it." "Sing Brother Sing!" 6pp. Various Christian and anti-prohibition sayings throughout — "Would Christ have joined the Ku Klux

Klan or the Anti-Saloon League?, &c." [M-418]. [Crew/AES-70].

322.4 The Man From The South (With A Big Cigar In His Mouth). w.m. Rube Bloom and Harry Woods. Published by Skidmore Music Co., Music Publishers, 218 West 47th Street, New York, NY. Selling agents: Shapiro, Bernstein & Co., Music Publishers, Cor. Broadway & 47th Streets, New York, NY. 1930. O/bk/w/b drawing of Big Bill Thompson. Br/w tinted photo of Ted Weems—"Introduced by Ted Weems and his Orchestra." 6pp. Page 6: Advertising.

322.5 That's You Bill Thompson, That's You (Song). w. Stephen A. Doyle. m. Buren Van Buren. Published by Stephen A. Doyle, 8 South Dearborn Street, Chicago, IL. 1928. Br/be photo of William H. Thompson. B/be geometric design border. 1928. 8pp. Page 2: Narrative titled "The Second Lincoln Of Illinois," comparing of the two. "Dedicated to His Honor The Mayor of Chicago, William Hale Thompson." Page 7: Blank. Page 8: Advertising.

• **AmPM-323** THOMPSON, Floyd E. (Justice, State Supreme Court, 1919–1928; Candidate for Governor, 1928)

323.1 Floyd Thompson, You're The Man (Song Fox Trot). w.m. Fred Rose and Al. Norman. No Publisher indicated. 1928. B/w photo of Floyd Thompson. Bl/w line drawing of trees, geometric designs. "Dedicated to the Justice of the Supreme Court." "To Floyd Thompson with the Compliments of his many friends." 4pp. Page 4: Blank.

• **AmPM-324** TRUMBULL, Lyman (State house, 1840–1841; Illinois Secretary of State, 1841 & 1843; State Supreme Court, 1848–1853; U.S. Senate, 1855–1873; Candidate for Governor, 1880)

324.1 Old Men's Grant Meeting. w. No composer indicated. m. "Air—*Bennie Havens, O!*" In: *National Republican Grant And Wilson Campaign Song-Book*, page 39. From the *New York Standard.* Published by The Union Republican Congressional Committee, Washington, DC. 1872. [3 13/16" × 8 9/16"]. Be/bk litho of Ulysses S. Grant. "We'll Sing a Song for U.S. Grant." 100pp. [M-182]. [Crew/USG-110].

324.2 Seven Men! Seven Men! w. No composer indicated. m. "Air—*Maryland, My Maryland.*" In: *The Grant Campaign Songster, Containing All The Most Popular Original Songs, Ballads And Recitations That Will Be Most Sung During This Presidential Campaign, Adapted To Very Popular And Well-Known Airs And Choruses*, page 10. Published by Robert M. Dewitt, Publisher, No. 13 Frankfort Street, New York, NY. 1868. [4¼" × 5¾"]. [V-1: Be/bk] [V-2: Gn/bk] litho of Ulysses S. Grant. 76pp. [M-155]. [Crew/USG-75].

324.3 The Stately Statesman. w. No composer indicated. m. "Air—*The Minstrel Boy.*" In: *National Republican Grant And Wilson Campaign Song-Book*, page 2. Published by The Union Republican Congressional Committee, Washington, DC. 1872. [3 13/16" × 8 9/16"]. Be/bk litho of Ulysses S. Grant. "We'll Sing a Song for U.S. Grant." 100pp. [M-182]. [Crew/USG-110].

324.4 Viva La Companie. w.m. No composer or tune indicated. In: *Grant And Wilson Campaign Songster*, page 16. Published by Frank Eastman, Book and Job Printer, No. 509 Clay Street, San Francisco, CA. [4¼" × 5⅝"]. 1872. Bk/bl geometric design border. 40pp. [Crew/USG-69].

324.5 Witches' Scene From MacGreeley (Which is Seen to be a Fact). w.m. No composer or tune indicated. From the "*New York Standard.*" In: *National Republican Grant And Wilson Campaign Song-Book*, page 34. From the *New York Standard.* Published by The Union Republican Congressional Committee, Washington, DC. 1872. [3 13/16" × 8 9/16"]. Be/bk litho of Ulysses S. Grant. "We'll Sing a Song for U.S. Grant." 100pp. [M-182]. [Crew/USG-110].

324.6 Who Shall Rule This American Nation? (Song And Chorus). w.m. Henry C. Work. Published by Root & Cady, 67 Washington Street, Chicago, IL. 1866. B/w non-pictorial geometric designs. "To the Hon. Lyman Trumbull of Chicago." 6pp. Pages 2 and 6: Blank. [LL/JH].

• **AmPM-325** WASHBURNE, Elihu Benjamin (U.S. House, 1853–1869; U.S. Minister to France, 1869–1877)

325.1 Lesh Us Have Peash! w. No composer indicated. m. "Air—*Old Dan Tucker.*" "Verses from a Radical Campaign Song, as sung by Simpson after one of his One-Horse Acts." In: *Seymour Campaign Songster*, page 18. Published by Pattee & Hubbard, Democratic State Committee Rooms, World Building, No. 37 Park Row, New York, NY. 1868. [4" × 5¼"]. Gn/bk litho of Horatio Seymour and Francis Blair. "In the spirit of George Washington and the Patriots of the Revolution, Let us take the steps to re-inaugurate our Government, to start it once again on its course to greatness and prosperity—Horatio Seymour." 38pp. [M-173]. [Crew/HS-8].

• **AmPM-326** WENTWORTH, John (U.S. House, 1843–1851, 1853–1855 & 1865–1867; Mayor, Chicago, 1857–1858 & 1860–1861)

326.1 Long John Polka. m. J.B. Doninker of Geo. Christy's Minstrels. a. Chas. C. Smith. Published by H.M. Higgins, 117 Randolph St., Chicago, IL. 1860. B/w litho of John Wentworth. "To the Hon. John Wentworth, Mayor of Chicago"—[facsimile signature]. 8pp. Pages 2, 7 and 8: Blank.

• **AmPM-326A** WHALEN, James M. (Delegate, Democratic National Convention, 1932–1948; Candidate Trustee Sanitary District, Chicago, 1928)

326A.1 Get Yourself A Nice Brown Derby (And Fall In Line for Al). w.m. Walter Goodwin "(Writer of *Back In The Old Neighborhood*)." 1928. Br/w photos of "Alfred E. Smith," "T.J. Crowe," "James M. Whalen," "Henry A. Berger" and "Ald. Ross A. Woodhull "(To fill vacancy)." 4pp. Page 4: Biographies of "Democratic Nominees for Trustees Sanitary District of Chicago." "For Your Health's Sake." [Crew/AES-26].

• **AmPM-327** WICKE, William (Mayor, Des Plaines, 1915–1923)

327.1 Des Plaines. w. "By a Member of the Des Plaines State Bld'g and Loan Ass'n." m. "Original Hymn by Wm. J. Kirkpatric." m. "Adapted to music by Savena Ahbe." No publisher indicated. 1924. Br/w/gn drawing of river, trees, logo—"You Will Like Des Plaines." Three b/w photos of various scenes in Des Plaines. 4pp. Page 2: Narratives on Des Plaines—"You Will Like Des Plaines Because..." and "Fifty Reasons why You Will Like Des Plaines." Page 3: At bottom of music — "This song adopted by the Lions Club of Des Plaines, Illinois." "You Will Like Des Plaines slogan adopted 1919, suggested by Robert F. Risser." "Hymn of Des Plaines Dedicated to William Wicke, Mayor of Des Plaines, 1915–1923." Page 4: Fifteen b/w photos of various scenes in Des Plaines.

- AmPM-328 WILLETTS or WILLITS, George S. (Candidate for U.S. House, 1892)

328.1 Hurrah For All The Ticket. w. W.A.P. m. No tune indicated. In: *Republican Campaign Songs (As sung By The Marquette Club Quartette)*, page 6. Published by the Marquette Club of Chicago, Dearborn Avenue and Maple Street, Chicago, IL. 1888. [3½" × 6¼"]. Be/bl geometric design border. "W.A. Paulson, 1st Bass; R.J. Wherry, 1st Tenor; M.O. Naramore, 2nd Bass; O.B. Knight, 2nd Tenor." "Music and Instructions Cheerfully Furnished on Application." 28pp. [Crew/BFH-129].

- AmPM-329 WOOD, John (State Senate, 1850; Lt. Governor, 1857–1860; Governor, 1860–1861)

329.1 Our Governors March (Or Two Step) m. Joseph Gearen. Published by Lyon & Healy, Chicago, IL. 1897. Bk/w/gn/br drawings of all Illinois Governors, Illinois capitol building, farm scene, law books. 6pp. Page 2: Blank. Page 6: Advertising. [Crew/JMP-1].

- AmPM-330 WOODHULL, Ross A. (Alderman, Chicago, 1928; Candidate Trustee Sanitary District, Chicago, 1928)

330.1 Get Yourself A Nice Brown Derby (And Fall In Line for Al). w.m. Walter Goodwin "(Writer of *Back In The Old Neighborhood*)." 1928. Br/w photos of "Alfred E. Smith," "T.J. Crowe," "James M. Whalen," "Henry A. Berger" and "Ald. Ross A. Woodhull "(To fill vacancy)." 4pp. Page 4: Biographies of "Democratic Nominees for Trustees Sanitary District of Chicago." "For Your Health's Sake." [Crew/AES-26].

- AmPM-330A WRIGHT, Warren (Candidate for Congress, 1934)

330A.1 Republicans Will Win This Fall (Republican Rally Song). w.m. C.P. Siegfried. Copyright 1934 by C.P. Siegfried, Jacksonville, IL. [8½" × 11"]. Bl/w photo of "Woods Brothers, G.O.P. Quartette." Bl/w drawing of elephant. "Successfully introduced and featured at Republican State Convention, Springfield, Ill., Aug. 9, 1934." 4pp. Page 4: B/w photo of Warren E. Wright. "Warren E. Wright for Congress, 20th Congressional District, Illinois." R/w/b flags. Extra verses for Warren E. Wright. [Crew/MISC-54].

- AmPM-331 YATES, Richard (State House, 1842–1845 & 1848–1849; U.S. House, 1851–1855; Governor, 1861–1865; U.S. Senate, 1865–1871)

331.1 Governor Yates Grand March. m. E. Saylor. Published by Lee & Walker, 722 Chestnut Street, Philadelphia, PA. 1862. B/w tinted litho by T. Sinclair's Litho., Philadelphia, of Richard Yates. "Composed and respectfully dedicated to Gov. Richard Yates of Illinois." 6pp. Page 6: Advertising.

331.2 Our Governors March (Or Two Step) m. Joseph Gearen. Published by Lyon & Healy, Chicago, IL. 1897. Bk/w/gn/br drawings of all Illinois Governors, Illinois capitol building, farm scene, law books. 6pp. Page 2: Blank. Page 6: Advertising. [Crew/JMP-1].

331.3 Our Governor's Schottische! m. Louis H. Rink. Published by S. Brainard & Co., 203 Superior Street, Cleveland, OH. [1861–1865]. B/w geometric design border. "Respectfully Dedicated to Hon. Richard Yates, Governor of Ohio." 6pp. Pages 2 and 6: Blank. [LL/JH].

331.4 Soldier's Friend Polka Quickstep. m. I.W. Gougler. Published by Root & Cady, 95 Clark Street, Chicago, IL. 1863. Non-pictorial fancy geometric design "S" in the title. "Respectfully Dedicated to our 'Gallant Governor' Hon. Richard Yates, the 'Soldier's Friend' by the Author." 6pp. Pages 2 and 6: Blank.

- AmPM-332 YATES, Richard (City Attorney, Jacksonville, 1885–1890; Candidate for U.S. House, 1892 & 1919–1933; Judge, Morgan County, 1894–1897; Governor, 1901–1904; State Public Utilities Commission, 1914–1917; Assistant State Attorney General, 1917–1918)

332.1 Dick Yates Is Bound To Win (Or We'll Take The Demmies In). a. Geo. B. Chase. In: *Republican Hot Shot (A Campaign Songster For 1900)*, page 10. e.a. George B. Chase and J.F. Kinsey. Published by Echo Music Company. 1900. [6" × 8¾"]. Bk/r lithos of William McKinley and Theodore Roosevelt. "Second Edition." 28pp. [M-365]. [Crew/WM-238].

332.2 Hurrah For All The Ticket. w. W.A.P. m. No tune indicated. In: *Republican Campaign Songs (As sung By The Marquette Club Quartette)*, page 6. Published by the Marquette Club of Chicago, Dearborn Avenue and Maple Street, Chicago, IL. 1888. [3½" × 6¼"]. Be/bl geometric design border. "W.A. Paulson, 1st Bass; R.J. Wherry, 1st Tenor; M.O. Naramore, 2nd Bass; O.B. Knight, 2nd Tenor." "Music and Instructions Cheerfully Furnished on Application." 28pp. [Crew/BFH-129].

332.3 Illinois Rally Song — 1900. w. G.A.R. m. a. G.B.C. "Air — *Baby Mine.*" In: *Republican Hot Shot (A Campaign Songster For 1900)*, page 3. e.a. George B. Chase and J.F. Kinsey. Published by Echo Music Company. 1900. [6" × 8¾"]. Bk/r lithos of William McKinley and Theodore Roosevelt. "Second Edition." 28pp. [M-365]. [Crew/WM-238].

332.4 Marchin' Wid De Yates Phalanx! w. C.C. Hassler. m. Geo. B. Chase. In: *Republican Hot Shot (A Campaign Songster For 1900)*, page 16. e.a. George B. Chase and J.F. Kinsey. Published by Echo Music Company. 1900. [6" × 8¾"]. Bk/r lithos of William McKinley and Theodore Roosevelt. "Second Edition." 28pp. [M-365]. [Crew/WM-238].

332.5 Souvenir Of Patriotic Songs. w.m. Popular Tunes. No publisher indicated. [1900]. [6" × 9"]. B/w litho of "Richard Yates." "Judge Richard Yates, Republican Candidate for Governor, will address the meeting on the Political Issues and Mr. Lem Wiley, late bugler in the National Commander of the G.A.R. will play the old army bugle calls and lead the singing of patriotic songs." Long quote by Richard Yates. 4pp.

- AmPM-333 MISCELLANEOUS MUSIC

333.1 Booster March. m. C.H. Stoddard, "Composer of *Capitol City March, Booster Waltzes, Gala Polka, Rena May, Cuban Liberty Two Step, U.S. Victory Two Step.*" Published by The Booster Music Co., Indianapolis, IN. Bl/w photo of "Crawford County Court House." R/w/b advertisements from numerous Robinson, Illinois, businesses. 8pp. Pages 2 and 7: Blank. Page 8: B/w photo of "High School, Oblong."

Numerous advertisements for Robinson and Oblong, Illinois, businesses.

333.2 Governor's Guard (Burlesque Song). m. L.M. French. Published by Kunkle Brothers, St. Louis, MO. 1872. Non-pictorial. "Respectfully Dedicated to the Officers and Members ... Governor's Guards, Springfield, Ill." 6pp. Page 2: Blank. Page 6: Advertising.

333.3 Illinois, Sweet Illinois. w. Morris S. Silver. m. George Fletcher. Published by Fred W. King Music Co., Chicago, IL. 1902. Bl/w photo of the Illinois State House at Springfield and "W.C. DeBaugh, Band Director." R/w b geometric and floral designs. "The first ballad success written on the State of Illinois." 6pp. [?].

333.4 March Capitol City (Springfield, Illinois). m. Wesley Hampton. Published by Wesley Hampton, Centralia, IL. 1911. Ma/w drawing of the Capitol building, shield, geometric designs. 6pp. Page 6: Blank.

INDIANA

- **AmPM-334 BARRETT**, Edward (Candidate for State Geologist, 1918)

334.1 Till Over The Top We Go. w.m. Roy L. Burtch "(Composer of *When The Bugle Calls, Peace On Earth And Liberty, Think Of Me, Tell Me, The Organ And The Choir, Bye Bye Baby Dear*)." Published by The Halcyon Publishing Company, Indianapolis, IN. 1918. Drawing of soldier — "U.S. Marine," machine gun. "The Song Our Allies, Lodges and Glee Clubs are Singing." "State Campaign Song — Democratic State Committee, Denison Hotel, Indianapolis, Ind." "Extra copies of this March Song mailed free on request." 4pp. Page 4: Photos of Woodrow Wilson and 13 State Democratic candidates. "The Party with a Purpose." Text on 11 reasons to vote Democratic. [Crew/WW-121].

- **AmPM-335 BAYH**, Birch Evan (State, 1954–1962; U.S. Senate, 1963–1981)

335.1 Hey Look Him Over (Campaign Jingle). 33⅓ rpm. 6⅞" vinyl record. Senator Birch Bayh Birthday Celebration. #R4LH-1924. Side 2: *U.S. Senator Birch Bayh Birthday Celebration*, Saturday, February 1, 1964. Performed by Cadle Tabernacle, Indianapolis. Sponsored by the 6th District Bayh for Senator Committee. 1964.

- **AmPM-336 BENDER**, Frank J. (Candidate for Commissioner, Porter County, 1934)

336.1 Roosevelt We Hand The Flag To You! w. William Foster. m. Edna May Foster. Published by Calumet Music Publishers, Gary, IN. 1934. R/w/b eagle, trees, geometric designs. Bl/w photo of Franklin D. Roosevelt. 6pp. Page 2: Advertisement for Carroll Holly for Sheriff. Page 6: Advertisements for various office seekers including "Frank J. Bender, Democratic Candidate for Commissioner, North District, Porter County, Election, Tuesday, November 4, 1934. Re-Elect."

- **AmPM-337 BILLHEIMER**. (Candidate, 1908)

337.1 The Hoosier Boom De-Aye. w. No composer indicated. m. "Tune–*Ta-ra-ra-ra Boom-de-aye*." In: *Up-To-Date Republican Campaign Songs*, page 3. Published by J. Burgess Brown "(Leader of the Celebrated Bald-Headed Glee Club), [Indianapolis, IN.]." 1908. [8" × 11"]. B/w photos of William H. Taft and John Sherman. B/w drawing of American Flag — "We'll rally 'round the flag, boys." Verse. "Written and compiled for the State Central Committee." [Crew/WHT-66].

- **AmPM-338 BINGHAM**, James (County Auditor, Wayne County, 1910; Candidate, 1924)

338.1 The Hoosier Boom De-Aye. w. No composer indicated. m. "Tune–*Ta-Ra-Ra-Ra Boom-De-Aye*." In: *Up-To-Date Republican Campaign Songs*, page 3. Published by J. Burgess Brown "(Leader of the Celebrated Bald-Headed Glee Club), [Indianapolis, IN.]." 1908. [8" × 11"]. B/w photos of William H. Taft and John Sherman. B/w drawing of American Flag — "We'll rally 'round the flag, boys." Verse. "Written and compiled for the State Central Committee." [Crew/WHT-66].

- **AmPM-339 BOHMAN**, Lewis S. (Candidate, 1924)

339.1 Rally The Standard Of "Abe" Lincoln. w. Mrs. S.R. Artma "(Composer of *Guess, One Who Cares For Me, The Organ And The Choir*)." m. Roy L. Burtch. Published by Halcyon Publishing Company, No. 307 East North Street, Indianapolis, IN. 1924. Br/w photos of "Calvin Coolidge," "Charles G. Dawes," "Abraham Lincoln" and "Ed Jackson" [Republican nominee for Governor of Indiana], geometric design border. "American Campaign March Song." 4pp. + Insert letter. Page 4: Biographies of candidates and other Republicans from Indiana, including "Ed Jackson, F. Harold Van Orman, Frederick E. Schortmeier, Lewis S. Bohman, Ben H. Urbahns, Arthur L. Gillam, F.M. Thompson, Willard R. Gimmill, Judge Willoughby, E.A. Dausman, Noble Sherwood, Mrs. Edward F. White." Insert — Page 1: Letter from composer to Republican State Committee. Page 2: Advertising.

BOND, Shadrack (Legislative Council of Indiana Territory, 1805–1808) [See: Illinois]

- **AmPM-340 BONHAM**, George (Mayor, Evansville [?])

340.1 G.O.P. March. m. Gust Safstrom "(Writer of *Just Remember You Can Smile, Dearest I Always Dream Of You, Mother's Love* (Lullaby)." Published by De Motte Music Company, De Motte, IN. 1940. R/w/b drawing of an elephant playing a drum, eagle, crossed flags, silhouettes of Abraham "Lincoln," George "Washington." "Willkie Official Souvenir Issue."

'Notification Ceremonies, Elwood, IN. Aug. 17th, 1940." "Endorsed by Wendell L. Willkie Notification Committee, Homer Capehart Grand Chairman, George Bonham, Mayor, City of Evansville, Ind., Honorary Grand Chairman." "The Elwood H.S. Band will participate in the proceeds of the sale of the G.O.P. March." 4pp. Page 4: Bl/w drawings of Wendell L. Willkie residence, Capitol building. "A True American," "Like Lincoln From a Humble Home To the White House," "A Business Man to Run the Biggest Business in the World." [Crew/WLW-2].

• **AmPM-341 BRODY**, Arthur M. (Candidate for County Recorder, Porter County, 1934)
341.1 Roosevelt We Hand The Flag To You! w. William Foster. m. Edna May Foster. Published by Calumet Music Publishers, Gary, IN. 1934. R/w/b eagle, trees, geometric designs. Bl/w photo of Franklin D. Roosevelt. 6pp. Page 2: Advertisement for Carroll Holly for Sheriff. Page 6: Advertisements for various office seekers including "Arthur M. Brody, Democratic Candidate for Recorder of Porter County, Election Tues., Nov. 6, 1934. Vote for Arthur M. Brody." B/w photo of Arthur Brody.

BROWN, Ethan Allen. (State House, Indiana, 1842) [See: Ohio]

• **AmPM-342 BROWNE**, Thomas McClellan (Republican Candidate for Governor, 1872)
342.1 Browne's Grand March. m. Carl Renbort. Published by Benham Bros., Indianapolis, IN. 1872. Non-pictorial geometric design. "To Gen. Thomas M. Browne, Republican Candidate for Governor." "Arranged for Full Band, with Solo parts for Alto and Baritone, with Tenor parts arranged in both clefs, 75 Cts." 6pp. Page 6: Advertising.

• **AmPM-343 BURRUS**, Franklin J. (Candidate for Treasurer, Porter County, 1934)
343.1 Roosevelt We Hand The Flag To You! w. William Foster. m. Edna May Foster. Published by Calumet Music Publishers, Gary, IN. 1934. R/w/b eagle, trees, geometric designs. Bl/w photo of Franklin D. Roosevelt. 6pp. Page 2: Advertisement for Carroll Holly for Sheriff. Page 6: Advertisements for various office seekers including "Franklin J. Burrus, Democratic Candidate for Treasurer, Porter County, Election, Tuesday, November 4, 1934. Be Honest with yourself— Don't be misled, Vote for the party that has helped you. Elect Franklin J. Burrus."

• **AmPM-344 BURTON**, Danny Lee (State House, 1967–1968 & 1977–1980; State Senate, 1969–1972 & 1981–1982; U.S. House, 1983–Present).
344.1 Dan — Watermelon Man. w. William Tong. m. "*Watermelon Man*, based on a performance by Mongo Santamaria." "Dedicated to Rep. Dan Burton (R-IN) who once fired pistols at watermelons to prove 'Clinton murders.' Ironically, Burton is now a vocal critic of the Bush Administration's imperial presidency and repressive policies under the USA Patriot Act." Published online at <http://amiright.com/parody/60s/mongosantamaria0.shtml>. 2003.
344.2 Super Duper Tuesday. w. ParodyKeet. m. "*If I Were A Rich Man*, based on a performance by Tevye, star of *Fiddler On The Roof*." Published online at <http://amiright.com/parody/misc/tevyestaroffidlerontheroof0.shtml>. 2003.

• **AmPM-345 BUSSE**, Benjamin (Mayor, Evansville)
345.1 Sleep, Soldier Sleep! w.m. Thomasanne Payne. Published by Thomasanne Payne, Grayville, IL. [ca. 1925]. B/w photo by Mason of cross inscribed "The Way of the Cross Leads to God," monument inscribed "Payne," Red Cross woman [Thomasanne Payne], dead soldier with flag, wreath inscribed "The President, Mrs. Harding." "Posed by Thomasanne Payne, Authoress, and Carl Stickleman, Sculptor, beside the first monument dedicated to Peace, November 11, 1918 (By The Authoress). The picture includes the President's wreath and the Gresham flag." "Endorsed by the Evansville Chamber of Commerce, the Service Star Legion, Gresham Chapter, Vanderburg County, Indiana, and Mayor Benjamin Busse, of Evansville, Indiana." "The Hero's Song — Just back to dust at the foot of the cross let my body crumble away — For my soul could find no place so sweet to rise on that last great day; Let me lay up my treasures safely where may be found neither moth nor rust — If my treasures be safe, What need I care that my body turns back to dust — by Thomasanne Payne." 4pp. Page 4: B/w photo of "The Tomb of Lafayette, Paris, France." "Narrative and facsimile of song— *We Have Come Lafayette*" by Thomasanne Payne. Four B/w photos of "James Bethel Gresham — America's First Dead;" "Alice Gresham Hood — Mother of James Bethel Gresham;" "Thomasanne Payne — The Authoress and her only son;" "Mrs. E.E. Hoskinson — Sung 'Sleep, Soldier, Sleep' at Gresham's Funeral;" "Rev. Frank Lenig, Ph.D., Gresham's minister, Simpson M.E. Church, Evansville, Ind." Advertisement; Information on and photo of James Bethel Gresham — "America's First Dead."

• **AmPM-346 CALDWELL**, Frederick S. (Candidate for Appellate Court, 1918)
346.1 Till Over The Top We Go. w.m. Roy L. Burtch "(Composer of *When The Bugle Calls, Peace On Earth And Liberty, Think Of Me, Tell Me, The Organ And The Choir, Bye Bye Baby Dear*)." Published by The Halcyon Publishing Company, Indianapolis, IN. 1918. Drawing of soldier — "U.S. Marine," machine gun. "The Song Our Allies, Lodges and Glee Clubs are Singing." "State Campaign Song — Democratic State Committee, Denison Hotel, Indianapolis, Ind." "Extra copies of this March Song mailed free on request." 4pp. Page 4: Photos of Woodrow Wilson and 13 State Democratic candidates. "The Party with a Purpose." Text on 11 reasons to vote Democratic. [Crew/WW-121].

• **AmPM-347 CALLAWAY**, Sam L. (Candidate for Clerk of Supreme and Appellate Courts, 1918)
347.1 Till Over The Top We Go. w.m. Roy L. Burtch "(Composer of *When The Bugle Calls, Peace On Earth And Liberty, Think Of Me, Tell Me, The Organ And The Choir, Bye Bye Baby Dear*)." Published by The Halcyon Publishing Company, Indianapolis, IN. 1918. Drawing of soldier — "U.S. Marine," machine gun. "The Song Our Allies, Lodges and Glee Clubs are Singing." "State Campaign Song — Democratic State Committee, Denison Hotel, Indianapolis, Ind." "Extra copies of this March Song mailed free on request." 4pp. Page 4: Photos of Woodrow Wilson and

13 State Democratic candidates. "The Party with a Purpose." Text on 11 reasons to vote Democratic. [Crew/WW-121].

• **AmPM-348 CAPEHART**, Homer Earl (U.S. Senate, 1945–1963)

348.1 G.O.P. March. m. Gust Safstrom "(Writer of *Just Remember You Can Smile, Dearest I Always Dream Of You, Mother's Love* (Lullaby)." Published by De Motte Music Company, De Motte, IN. 1940. R/w/b drawing of an elephant playing a drum, eagle, crossed flags, silhouettes of Abraham "Lincoln," George "Washington." "Willkie Official Souvenir Issue." 'Notification Ceremonies, Elwood, IN. Aug. 17th, 1940." "Endorsed by Wendell L. Willkie Notification Committee, Homer Capehart Grand Chairman, George Bonham, Mayor, City of Evansville, Ind., Honorary Grand Chairman." "The Elwood H.S. Band will participate in the proceeds of the sale of the G.O.P. March." 4pp. Page 4: Bl/w drawings of Wendell L. Willkie residence, Capitol building. "A True American," "Like Lincoln From a Humble Home To the White House," "A Business Man to Run the Biggest Business in the World." [Crew/WLW-2].

• **AmPM-348A COLFAX**, Schuyler (U.S. House, 1865–1869; Vice President, 1869–1877) [SEE: DOC/PSM-USG]

348A.1 All Hail To Ulysses! w.m. No composer or tune indicated. "By permission of Root & Cady." In: *The Grant And Colfax Republican Songster, Containing Campaign Songs, Ballads And Choruses. Adapted To The Most Popular And Stirring Tunes*, page 31. Published by R.M. Dewitt, Publisher, No. 13 Frankfort Street, New York, NY. 1868. [4" × 6$\frac{5}{16}$"]. R/w/b litho of flag. Advertising. 100pp. [M-150]. [Crew/USG-63].

348A.2 A Big Thing Coming. w. No composer indicated. m. "Air—*A Good Time Coming, Boys*." In: *The Grant & Colfax Spread-Eagle Songster*, page 19. Published by Beadle & Company, No. 98 William Street, and American News Company, No. 121 Nassau Street, New York, NY. 1868. O/bk litho of a man at political rally with arms in a spread-eagle position. "Beadle's Dime Series." "Songs for the hour!" 68pp. Inside title—*The Grant & Colfax Songster (Comprising A Choice Selection Of New And Popular Songs And Ballads For The Campaign)*. [M-151]. [Crew/USG-65].

348A.3 A Campaign Rattler. w.m. No composer or tune indicated. "Music of the Song published in the *Radical Drum Call*." In: *The Grant And Colfax Republican Songster, Containing Campaign Songs, Ballads And Choruses. Adapted To The Most Popular And Stirring Tunes*, page 16. Published by R.M. Dewitt, Publisher, No. 13 Frankfort Street, New York, NY. 1868. [4" × 6$\frac{5}{16}$"]. R/w/b litho of flag. Advertising. 100pp. [M-150]. [Crew/USG-63].

348A.4 Columbia's Appeal. w. No composer indicated. m. "Air—*Vive La Campagnie*." In: *The Grant And Colfax Republican Songster, Containing Campaign Songs, Ballads And Choruses. Adapted To The Most Popular And Stirring Tunes*, page 21. Published by R.M. Dewitt, Publisher, No. 13 Frankfort Street, New York, NY. 1868. [4" × 6$\frac{5}{16}$"]. R/w/b litho of flag. Advertising. 100pp. [M-150]. [Crew/USG-63].

348A.5 The Column Moving. w. No composer indicated. m. "Air—*Over The Mountain*." In: *The Grant & Colfax Spread-Eagle Songster*, page 6. Published by Beadle & Company, No. 98 William Street, and American News Company, No. 121 Nassau Street, New York, NY. 1868. O/bk litho of a man at political rally with arms in a spread-eagle position. "Beadle's Dime Series." "Songs for the hour!" 68pp. Inside title—*The Grant & Colfax Songster (Comprising A Choice Selection Of New And Popular Songs And Ballads For The Campaign)*. [M-151]. [Crew/USG-65].

348A.6 [Come, Boys, Let's Have A Union Song] (Campaign Song). w.m. No composer or tune indicated. In: *Greeley Campaign Songster*, page 33. "Respectfully dedicated to the Greeley Clubs of the Country." Published by Halpin & McClure, Chicago, IL. 1872. [4" × 5$\frac{11}{16}$"]. Pl/bk litho of Horace Greeley, geometric design border. "Chicago: Western News Company, Wholesale Agents." 72pp. [M-187]. [Crew/HG-21].

348A.7 Following Our Leader. w. No composer indicated. m. "Air—*Free And Easy*." In: *The Grant & Colfax Spread-Eagle Songster*, page 30. Published by Beadle & Company, No. 98 William Street, and American News Company, No. 121 Nassau Street, New York, NY. 1868. O/bk litho of a man at political rally with arms in a spread-eagle position. "Beadle's Dime Series." "Songs for the hour!" 68pp. Inside title—*The Grant & Colfax Songster* (Comprising a Choice Selection of New and Popular Songs and Ballads for the Campaign). [M-151]. [Crew/USG-65].

348A.8 Freemen Rally Round The Flag. w. No composer indicated. m. "Air—*Landlord Fill The Flowing Bowl*." In: *The Grant Campaign Songster, Containing All The Most Popular Original Songs, Ballads And Recitations That Will Be Most Sung During This Presidential Campaign, Adapted To Very Popular And Well-Known Airs And Choruses*, page 33. Published by Robert M. Dewitt, Publisher, No. 13 Frankfort Street, New York, NY. 1868. [4¼" × 5¾"]. [V-1: Be/bk] [V-2: Gn/bk] litho of Ulysses S. Grant. 76pp. [M-155]. [Crew/USG-75].

348A.9 Garfield And Colfax. w. No composer indicated. m. "Tune—*Nelly Bly*." In: *Music For The Campaign (A Collection Of Original And Selected Songs, Adapted To Familiar Tunes For Use At Campaign Meetings, For 1880)*, page 5. Published by The *Indianapolis Sentinel* as a newspaper supplement, Indianapolis, IN. 1880. [7¾" × 10⅝"]. B/w lithos of Winfield Scott Hancock and William H. English. "This Collection of fifty one first-class Campaign Songs will be sent to any address, postage paid as follows: 25 for 30 cts.; 50 for 60 cts.; 100 for $1.00. Address Sentinel Company, Indianapolis, Ind." 8pp. Foldover. [Crew/WSH-11].

348A.10 General Grant's The Man. w.m. No composer or tune indicated. "Music of the song published in the *Radical Drum Call*." In: *The Grant And Colfax Republican Songster, Containing Campaign Songs, Ballads And Choruses. Adapted To The Most Popular And Stirring Tunes*, page 27. Published by R.M. Dewitt, Publisher, No. 13 Frankfort Street, New York, NY. 1868. [4" × 6$\frac{5}{16}$"]. R/w/b litho of flag. Advertising. 100pp. [M-150]. [Crew/USG-63].

348A.11 God—Grant—Victory! w. No composer indicated. m. "Air—*Come, Come Away!*" In: *The Grant And Colfax Republican Songster, Containing Campaign*

Songs, Ballads And Choruses. Adapted To The Most Popular And Stirring Tunes, page 8. Published by R.M. Dewitt, Publisher, No. 13 Frankfort Street, New York, NY. 1868. [4" × 6 3/16"]. R/w/b litho of flag. Advertising. 100pp. [M-150]. [Crew/USG-63].

348A.12 Grant And Colfax. w. No composer indicated. m. "Air — *Here's A Health Bonnie Scotland To Thee.*" In: *The Grant Campaign Songster, Containing All The Most Popular Original Songs, Ballads And Recitations That Will Be Most Sung During This Presidential Campaign, Adapted To Very Popular And Well-Known Airs And Choruses*, page 69. Published by Robert M. Dewitt, Publisher, No. 13 Frankfort Street, New York, NY. 1868. [4 1/4" × 5 3/4"]. [V-1: Be/bk] [V-2: Gn/bk] litho of Ulysses S. Grant. 76pp. [M-155]. [Crew/USG-75].

348A.13 Grant And Colfax Are Coming. w. No composer indicated. m. "Air — *Jordan.*" In: *The Grant & Colfax Spread-Eagle Songster*, page 7. Published by Beadle & Company, No. 98 William Street, and American News Company, No. 121 Nassau Street, New York, NY. 1868. O/bk litho of a man at political rally with arms in a spread-eagle position. "Beadle's Dime Series." "Songs for the hour!" 68pp. Inside title — *The Grant & Colfax Songster (Comprising a Choice Selection of New and Popular Songs and Ballads for the Campaign)*. [M-151]. [Crew/USG-65].

348A.14 Grant's The Man. w.m. No composer or tune indicated. "By permission of J. Marsh." In: *The Grant And Colfax Republican Songster, Containing Campaign Songs, Ballads And Choruses. Adapted To The Most Popular And Stirring Tunes*, page 22. Published by R.M. Dewitt, Publisher, No. 13 Frankfort Street, New York, NY. 1868. [4" × 6 3/16"]. R/w/b litho of flag. Advertising. 100pp. [M-150]. [Crew/USG-63].

348A.15 The Great Gunning Match. w. No composer indicated. m. "Air — *Johnny Stole The Ham.*" In: *The Grant & Colfax Spread-Eagle Songster*, page 30. Published by Beadle & Company, No. 98 William Street, and American News Company, No. 121 Nassau Street, New York, NY. 1868. O/bk litho of a man at political rally with arms in a spread-eagle position. "Beadle's Dime Series." "Songs for the hour!" 68pp. Inside title — *The Grant & Colfax Songster (Comprising a Choice Selection of New and Popular Songs and Ballads for the Campaign)*. [M-151]. [Crew/USG-65].

348A.16 Hail To The Chief. w.m. No composer or tune indicated. In: *The Grant And Colfax Republican Songster, Containing Campaign Songs, Ballads And Choruses. Adapted To The Most Popular And Stirring Tunes*, page 50. Published by R.M. Dewitt, Publisher, No. 13 Frankfort Street, New York, NY. 1868. [4" × 6 3/16"]. R/w/b litho of flag. Advertising. 100pp. [M-150]. [Crew/USG-63].

348A.17 Hark! How Sweet Those Organs Play! w. No composer indicated. m. "Air — *Hieland Laddie, Bonnie Laddie!*" In: *Tilden And Hendricks' Reform Songs (For The Centennial Campaign Of 1876)*, page 8. Published by The National Democratic Committee, Box 3637, New York, NY. 1876. [3 7/8" × 5 15/16"]. Gn/bk litho of Samuel J. Tilden and Thomas A. Hendricks, geometric design border. 40pp. [M-203]. [Crew/SJT-21].

348A.18 The Hat Of Chappaqua. w.m. No composer or tune indicated. In: *The Sun's Greeley Campaign Songster*, page 28. c. Amos J. Cumming. Published from *The Sun* Office, New York, NY. 1872. [4 1/8" × 6 1/2"]. Be/bk litho of Horace Greeley, wreath. "He shines for all." 64pp. [Crew/HG-5].

348A.19 How Do You Vote. w. No composer indicated. m. "Air — *Cruel War* and *Not For Joseph.*" "Music of the Song published in the *Radical Drum Call.*" In: *The Grant And Colfax Republican Songster, Containing Campaign Songs, Ballads And Choruses. Adapted To The Most Popular And Stirring Tunes*, page 15. Published by R.M. Dewitt, Publisher, No. 13 Frankfort Street, New York, NY. 1868. [4" × 6 3/16"]. R/w/b litho of flag. Advertising. 100pp. [M-150]. [Crew/USG-63].

348A.20 Hurrah Song. w. No composer indicated. m. "Air — *Low Back Car.*" In: *The Grant And Colfax Republican Songster, Containing Campaign Songs, Ballads And Choruses. Adapted To The Most Popular And Stirring Tunes*, page 6. Published by R.M. Dewitt, Publisher, No. 13 Frankfort Street, New York, NY. 1868. [4" × 6 3/16"]. R/w/b litho of flag. Advertising. 100pp. [M-150]. [Crew/USG-63].

348A.21 Let Every Republican Rally Round. w. No composer indicated. m. "Air — *Vive La Champagne.*" In: *The Grant Campaign Songster, Containing All The Most Popular Original Songs, Ballads And Recitations That Will Be Most Sung During This Presidential Campaign, Adapted To Very Popular And Well-Known Airs And Choruses*, page 24. Published by Robert M. Dewitt, Publisher, No. 13 Frankfort Street, New York, NY. 1868. [4 1/4" × 5 3/4"]. [V-1: Be/bk] [V-2: Gn/bk] litho of Ulysses S. Grant. 76pp. [M-155]. [Crew/USG-75].

348A.22 Marching Along. w.m. No composer or tune indicated. "By permission of Wm. A. Pond & Co." In: *The Grant And Colfax Republican Songster, Containing Campaign Songs, Ballads And Choruses. Adapted To The Most Popular And Stirring Tunes*, page 35. Published by R.M. Dewitt, Publisher, No. 13 Frankfort Street, New York, NY. 1868. [4" × 6 3/16"]. R/w/b litho of flag. Advertising. 100pp. [M-150]. [Crew/USG-63].

348A.23 Marching Glee. w. No composer indicated. m. "Air — *Pirate's Serenade.*" In: *The Grant Campaign Songster, Containing All the Most Popular Original Songs, Ballads and Recitations that will be most sung during this Presidential Campaign, Adapted to Very Popular and Well-Known Airs and Choruses*, page 47. Published by Robert M. Dewitt, Publisher, No. 13 Frankfort Street, New York, NY. 1868. [4 1/4" × 5 3/4"]. [V-1: Be/bk] [V-2: Gn/bk] litho of Ulysses S. Grant. 76pp. [M-155]. [Crew/USG-75].

348A.24 Marching Through Georgia. w.m. No composer or tune indicated. "By permission of Root & Cady." In: *The Grant And Colfax Republican Songster, Containing Campaign Songs, Ballads And Choruses. Adapted To The Most Popular And Stirring Tunes*, page 67. Published by R.M. Dewitt, Publisher, No. 13 Frankfort Street, New York, NY. 1868. [4" × 6 3/16"]. R/w/b litho of flag. Advertising. 100pp. [M-150]. [Crew/USG-63].

348A.25 Old Glory And U.S. Grant. w. L.J. Bates. m. J.P. Webster. In: *The Grant And Colfax Republican Songster, Containing Campaign Songs, Ballads And Choruses. Adapted To The Most Popular And Stirring Tunes,* page 44. Published by R.M. Dewitt, Publisher, No. 13 Frankfort Street, New York, NY. 1868. [4" × 6³⁄₁₆"]. R/w/b litho of flag. Advertising. 100pp. [M-150]. [Crew/USG-63].

348A.26 Our Leader. w. No composer indicated. m. "Air—*Tara's Halls.*" In: *The Grant Campaign Songster, Containing All The Most Popular Original Songs, Ballads And Recitations That Will Be Most Sung During This Presidential Campaign, Adapted To Very Popular And Well-Known Airs And Choruses,* page 47. Published by Robert M. Dewitt, Publisher, No. 13 Frankfort Street, New York, NY. 1868. [4¼" × 5¾"]. [V-1: Be/bk] [V-2: Gn/bk] litho of Ulysses S. Grant. 76pp. [M-155]. [Crew/USG-75].

348A.27 The Presidential Race Course. w. No composer indicated. m. "Air—*Camptown Race Course.*" In: *The Grant Campaign Songster, Containing All The Most Popular Original Songs, Ballads And Recitations That Will Be Most Sung During This Presidential Campaign, Adapted To Very Popular And Well-Known Airs And Choruses,* page 17. Published by Robert M. Dewitt, Publisher, No. 13 Frankfort Street, New York, NY. 1868. [4¼" × 5¾"]. [V-1: Be/bk] [V-2: Gn/bk] litho of Ulysses S. Grant. 76pp. [M-155]. [Crew/USG-75].

348A.28 Riding To Election. w. No composer indicated. m. "Air—*Wait For The Wagon.*" In: *The Grant & Colfax Spread-Eagle Songster,* page 34. Published by Beadle & Company, No. 98 William Street, and American News Company, No. 121 Nassau Street, New York, NY. 1868. O/bk litho of a man at political rally with arms in a spread-eagle position. "Beadle's Dime Series." "Songs for the hour!" 68pp. Inside title—*The Grant & Colfax Songster (Comprising a Choice Selection of New and Popular Songs and Ballads for the Campaign).* [M-151]. [Crew/USG-65].

348A.29 Sherman's March To The Sea. w.m. No composer or tune indicated. In: *The Grant And Colfax Republican Songster, Containing Campaign Songs, Ballads And Choruses. Adapted To The Most Popular And Stirring Tunes,* page 66. Published by R.M. Dewitt, Publisher, No. 13 Frankfort Street, New York, NY. 1868. [4" × 6³⁄₁₆"]. R/w/b litho of flag. Advertising. 100pp. [M-150]. [Crew/USG-63].

248A.30 The Soldier's Vote. w. Dick Elmore. m. No tune indicated. In: *The Grant And Colfax Republican Songster, Containing Campaign Songs, Ballads And Choruses. Adapted To The Most Popular And Stirring Tunes,* page 32. Published by R.M. Dewitt, Publisher, No. 13 Frankfort Street, New York, NY. 1868. [4" × 6³⁄₁₆"]. R/w/b litho of flag. Advertising. 100pp. [M-150]. [Crew/USG-63].

348A.31 Song Of The Hoosier. w. No composer indicated. m. "Air—*Pen-syl-va-nia.*" In: *The Grant And Colfax Republican Songster, Containing Campaign Songs, Ballads And Choruses. Adapted To The Most Popular And Stirring Tunes,* page 20. Published by R.M. Dewitt, Publisher, No. 13 Frankfort Street, New York, NY. 1868. [4" × 6³⁄₁₆"]. R/w/b litho of flag. Advertising. 100pp. [M-150]. [Crew/USG-63].

348A.32 Star-Crested Wagon. w. No composer indicated. m. "Air—*Wait For The Wagon.*" In: *The Grant & Colfax Spread-Eagle Songster,* page 48. Published by Beadle & Company, No. 98 William Street, and American News Company, No. 121 Nassau Street, New York, NY. 1868. O/bk litho of a man at political rally with arms in a spread-eagle position. "Beadle's Dime Series." "Songs for the hour!" 68pp. Inside title—*The Grant & Colfax Songster (Comprising A Choice Selection Of New And Popular Songs And Ballads For The Campaign).* [M-151]. [Crew/USG-65].

348A.33 The Sword Of Ulysses. w. No composer indicated. m. "Air—*Sword Of My Father.*" In: *The Grant And Colfax Republican Songster, Containing Campaign Songs, Ballads And Choruses. Adapted To The Most Popular And Stirring Tunes,* page 30. Published by R.M. Dewitt, Publisher, No. 13 Frankfort Street, New York, NY. 1868. [4" × 6³⁄₁₆"]. R/w/b litho of flag. Advertising. 100pp. [M-150]. [Crew/USG-63].

348A.34 Tanners' Chorus. w. No composer indicated. m. "Air—*Tippecanoe And Tyler, Too!*" In: *The Grant and Colfax Republican Songster, Containing Campaign Songs, Ballads and Choruses. Adapted to the Most Popular and Stirring Tunes,* page 4. Published by R.M. Dewitt, Publisher, No. 13 Frankfort Street, New York, NY. 1868. [4" × 6³⁄₁₆"]. R/w/b litho of flag. Advertising. 100pp. [M-150]. [Crew/USG-63].

348A.35 Three Hundred And Twenty-Nine Dollars. m. "Tune—*They Drafted Him Into The Army.*" In: *Music For The Campaign (A Collection Of Original And Selected Songs, Adapted To Familiar Tunes For Use At Campaign Meetings, For 1880),* page 7. Published by *The Indianapolis Sentinel* as a newspaper supplement, Indianapolis, IN. 1880. [7¾" × 10⅝"]. B/w lithos of Winfield Scott Hancock and William H. English. "This Collection of fifty one first-class Campaign Songs will be sent to any address, postage paid as follows: 25 for 30 cts.; 50 for 60 cts.; 100 for $1.00. Address Sentinel Company, Indianapolis, Ind." 8pp. Foldover. [Crew/WSH-11].

348A.36 Tilden And Reform. w. No composer indicated. m. "Air—*The Wearing Of The Green.*" In: *Tilden And Hendricks' Reform Songs (For The Centennial Campaign of 1876),* page 3. Published by The National Democratic Committee, Box 3637, New York, NY. 1876. [3⅞" × 5¹⁵⁄₁₆"]. Gn/bk litho of Samuel J. Tilden and Thomas A. Hendricks, geometric design border. 40pp. [M-203]. [Crew/SJT-21].

348A.37 Treason's Fate. w. S.N. Holmes. m. "Tune—*A Thousand Years,* &c." In: *The Republican Campaign Song Book, With Music, 1892,* page 15. e. Samuel Newall Holmes. Published by Samuel Newall Holmes, Syracuse, NY. 1892. Be/bk non-pictorial. "Composed and especially prepared by Judge S.N. Holmes of Syracuse, N.Y." "Headquarters: Syracuse, N.Y." "Price twenty-five cents." 60pp. [M-308]. [Crew/BFH-107].

348A.38 Union And Liberty. w. No composer indicated. m. "Air—*Crambambule.*" In: *The Grant Campaign Songster, Containing All The Most Popular Original Songs, Ballads And Recitations That Will Be Most Sung During This Presidential Campaign, Adapted To Very Popular And Well-Known Airs And Choruses,* page 43. Published by Robert M. Dewitt, Publisher, No. 13 Frankfort Street, New York, NY. 1868. [4¼" × 5¾"]. [V-1: Be/bk] [V-2: Gn/bk] litho of Ulysses S. Grant. 76pp. [M-155]. [Crew/USG-75].

348A.39 Victory's Band. w. No composer indicated.

m. "Air—*Dixie's Land.*" In: T*he Grant & Colfax Spread-Eagle Songster*, page 31. Published by Beadle & Company, No. 98 William Street, and American News Company, No. 121 Nassau Street, New York, NY. 1868. O/bk litho of a man at political rally with arms in a spread-eagle position. "Beadle's Dime Series." "Songs for the hour!" 68pp. Inside title—*The Grant & Colfax Songster* (Comprising a Choice Selection of New and Popular Songs and Ballads for the Campaign). [M-151]. [Crew/USG-65].

348A.40 *We Are Coming, Father Greeley*. w. Lewis Herbert. m. "Air—*Wait For The Wagon.*" In: *Greeley Campaign Songster*, page 53. "Respectfully dedicated to the Greeley Clubs of the Country." Published by Halpin & McClure, Chicago, IL. 1872. [4" × 5¹⁵⁄₁₆"]. Pl/bk litho of Horace Greeley, geometric design border. "Chicago: Western News Company, Wholesale Agents." 72pp. [M-187]. [Crew/HG-21].

348A.41 *We'll Go With Grant Again*. w.m. No composer or tune indicated. "Music of the song published in the *Radical Drum Call.*" In: *The Grant And Colfax Republican Songster, Containing Campaign Songs, Ballads And Choruses. Adapted To The Most Popular And Stirring Tunes*, page 19. Published by R.M. Dewitt, Publisher, No. 13 Frankfort Street, New York, NY. 1868. [4" × 6³⁄₁₆"]. R/w/b litho of flag. Advertising. 100pp. [M-150]. [Crew/USG-63].

348A.42 *When We Went 'Lectioneering*. w. No composer indicated. m. "Air—*Evacuation Day.*" In: *Tilden And Hendricks' Reform Songs (For The Centennial Campaign Of 1876)*, page 20. Published by The National Democratic Committee, Box 3637, New York, NY. 1876. [3⅞" × 5⅛"]. Gn/bk litho of Samuel J. Tilden and Thomas A. Hendricks, geometric design border. 40pp. [M-203]. [Crew/SJT-21].

348A.43 *A White House Epilogue*. w.m. No composer or tune indicated. In: *The Sun's Greeley Campaign Songster*, page 45. c. Amos J. Cumming. Published from *The Sun* Office, New York, NY. 1872. [4⅛" × 6½"]. Be/bk litho of Horace Greeley, wreath. "He shines for all." 64pp. [Crew/HG-5].

348A.44 *Who Shall Rule This American Nation?* w.m. No composer or tune indicated. "By permission of Root & Cady." In: *The Grant And Colfax Republican Songster, Containing Campaign Songs, Ballads And Choruses. Adapted To The Most Popular And Stirring Tunes*, page 25. Published by R.M. Dewitt, Publisher, No. 13 Frankfort Street, New York, NY. 1868. [4" × 6³⁄₁₆"]. R/w/b litho of flag. Advertising. 100pp. [M-150]. [Crew/USG-63].

348A.45 *The Yankee Boy*. w. No composer indicated. m. "Air—*Yankee Doodle.*" In: T*he Grant & Colfax Spread-Eagle Songster*, page 45. Published by Beadle & Company, No. 98 William Street, and American News Company, No. 121 Nassau Street, New York, NY. 1868. O/bk litho of a man at political rally with arms in a spread-eagle position. "Beadle's Dime Series." "Songs for the hour!" 68pp. Inside title—*The Grant & Colfax Songster* (Comprising a Choice Selection of New and Popular Songs and Ballads for the Campaign). [M-151]. [Crew/USG-65].

348A.46 *Young Men's Grant Meeting*. w. No composer indicated. m. "Air—*Bennie Havens, O!*" In: *National Republican Grant And Wilson Campaign Song Book*, page 41. From the *New York Standard.* Published by The Union Republican Congressional Committee, Washington, DC. 1872. [3¹³⁄₁₆" × 8³⁄₁₆"]. Be/bk litho of Ulysses S. Grant. "We'll Sing a Song for U.S. Grant." 100pp. [M-182]. [Crew/USG-110].

348A.47 *Your Mission* (Song). w.m. S.M. Grannis "(Author of *Do They Miss Me At Home, What I Live For, People Will Talk, We All Wear Cloaks, Only Waiting, Strike For The Right*, &c.)." Published by S. Brainard &Company, No. 203 Superior Street, Cleveland, OH. 1862. [Edition ca. 1866]. Non-pictorial geometric design border. "To Miss L.A. Gillett, Saline, Mich." 6pp. Page 2: Narrative: "At the closing anniversary of the U.S. Christian Commission held at Washington on the 11th February, 1866, the Hon. Shuyler Colfax said: 'At the last anniversary of the Commission on the Sabbath January, 1865, the striking Ode *Your Mission* was sung. Abraham Lincoln, with his tall form, his care furrowed face, and his nobly-throbbing heart, was here, and listened to it; the tears coursing down his cheeks.' Subsequently he sent up a programme which Mr. Colfax exhibited; on which appears the following request in his familiar handwriting—written by that hand now lying cold in the grave—'Near the close, let us have *Your Mission* repeated by Mr. Phillips. Don't say I called for it—Lincoln.' Mr. Phillips, of Cincinnati, then sung, amidst profound silence, this beautiful Ode." Page 6: Music catalog. [Crew/AL-272].

• **AmPM-349 CONTER,** Herman L. (Candidate for Indiana Secretary of State, 1918)

349.1 *Till Over The Top We Go*. w.m. Roy L. Burtch "(Composer of *When The Bugle Calls, Peace On Earth And Liberty, Think Of Me, Tell Me, The Organ And The Choir, Bye Bye Baby Dear*)." Published by The Halcyon Publishing Company, Indianapolis, IN. 1918. Drawing of soldier—"U.S. Marine," machine gun. "The Song Our Allies, Lodges and Glee Clubs are Singing." "State Campaign Song—Democratic State Committee, Denison Hotel, Indianapolis, Ind." "Extra copies of this March Song mailed free on request." 4pp. Page 4: Photos of Woodrow Wilson and 13 State Democratic candidates. "The Party with a Purpose." Text on 11 reasons to vote Democratic. [Crew/WW-121].

• **AmPM-349A DANIELS,** Mitch E., Jr. (Aide to the Mayor of Indianapolis, 1971–1975; Executive Director, National Republican Senatorial Committee, 1983–1984; Assistant to the President, 1984–1987; Director, Office of Management and Budget, 2001–2003)

349A.1 *Bye Bye Mitch*. w. Madeleine Begun Kane. m. *Bye Bye Birdie.* Published online at <http://www.madkane.com/mitch_daniels.html>. "In honor of Mitch Daniel's resignation as head of OMB, I present my *Bye Bye Mitch*, to be sung to *Bye Bye Birdie* by Boudleaux & Felice Bryant and first performed by the Everly Brothers. Feel free to use this midi link." [ca. 2002].

• **AmPM-350 DAUSMAN,** E.A. (State Senate, 1900–1904; State House, 1904–1906; City Attorney, Goshen, 1910–1916; State Appeals Court Judge, 1916–1924?)

350.1 *Rally The Standard Of "Abe" Lincoln*. w.

Mrs. S.R. Artma "(Composer of *Guess, One Who Cares For Me, The Organ And The Choir*)." m. Roy L. Burtch. Published by Halcyon Publishing Company, No. 307 East North Street, Indianapolis, IN. 1924. Br/w photos of "Calvin Coolidge," "Charles G. Dawes," "Abraham Lincoln" and "Ed Jackson" [Republican nominee for Governor of Indiana], geometric design border. "American Campaign March Song." 4pp. + Insert letter. Page 4: Biographies of candidates and other Republicans from Indiana, including "Ed Jackson, F. Harold Van Orman, Frederick E. Schortmeier, Lewis S. Bohman, Ben H. Urbahns, Arthur L. Gillam, F.M. Thompson, Willard R. Gimmill, Judge Willoughby, E.A. Dausman, Noble Sherwood, Mrs. Edward F. White." Insert — Page 1: Letter from composer to Republican State Committee. Page 2: Advertising.

DAVIS, James John (City Clerk, Elwood, Indiana, 1898–1902; Recorder, Madison County, Indiana, 1903–1907; U.S. Secretary of Labor, 1921–1930) [See Pennsylvania]

• **AmPM-351 DEBS**, Eugene Victor (State House, 1885; Founder, American Railway Union, 1893; Socialist Candidate for President, 1900, 1904, 1908, 1912, & 1920; Founder, Industrial Workers of the World, 1905) [SEE: DOC/PSM-EVD]

351.1 An Auspicious Occasion. w. No composer indicated. m. "Tune—*Odd Fellows' Hall*." In: *Republican Campaign Parodies And Songs* [Songster], page 13. Published by Betts and Burnett, South Butler, Wayne County, NY. 1896. [7¾" × 5½"]. Be/bk non-pictorial. "McKinley and Hobart." "1896." 28pp. [M-340]. [Crew/WM-67].

• **AmPM-352 DIEKMANN**, E.F. (Mayor, Evansville, ca. 1951).

352.1 Evansville (In Old Indiana). w.m. Col. R.H. (Dick) Sturges, "Box 1228, Atlanta, Ga." Published by Harding & Miller Music Co., 518 Main Street, Evansville, IN. 1951. B/w aerial photo of downtown Evansville. Gn/w/bk cover. "Evansville's Own Song." 6pp. Page 2: "Official Song of Evansville, Indiana." "By official proclamation of the Honorable E.F. Diekmann, Mayor, reproduced below, the song *Evansville, In Old Indiana* is declared to be Evansville's official song. It should be sung on all civic and patriotic occasions and taught in the Evansville schools." History of the song. Page 6: Advertising.

• **AmPM-353 DOYLE**, Joseph L. (Candidate for County Clerk, Porter County, 1934)

353.1 Roosevelt We Hand The Flag To You! w. William Foster. m. Edna May Foster. Published by Calumet Music Publishers, Gary, IN. 1934. R/w/b eagle, trees, geometric designs. Bl/w photo of Franklin D. Roosevelt. 6pp. Page 2: Advertisement for Carroll Holly for Sheriff. Page 6: Advertisements for various office seekers including "Joseph L. Doyle, Democratic Candidate for County Clerk, Porter County, Election Tues., Nov. 6, 1934. Experienced — Courteous — Dependable. Re-Elect Joseph L. Doyle." B/w photo of Joseph Doyle.

• **AmPM-354 DURBIN**, Winfield Taylor (Governor, 1901–1905)

354.1 Battle At The Polls. w. T.S. Williamson. m. H.G. Neely. Published by Anderson Music Publishing Company, No. 928 Main Street, Anderson, IN. [1900]. [17⅝" × 17⅝"]. R/w/b litho on cloth of William McKinley, Theodore Roosevelt, Col. Durbin — "Our Leaders — Our Leaders." "Dedicated to Col. Durbin." Rev: Blank. [Crew/WM-253].

354.2 Our Candidates. w. No composer indicated. m. "Tune—*Boom De-Ay*." In: *The Rough Rider (Republican Campaign Song Book)*, page 6. c. J. Burgess Brown. Published by J. Burgess Brown, Indianapolis, IN. 1900. [6" × 9"]. Br/bk non-pictorial. "ROUGH ON DemocRATS." 28pp. Page 3: B/w litho of William McKinley. Page 28: "Republican National Ticket—1900. [Crew/WM-330].

354.3 The Republican Train. w. No composer indicated. m. "Tune—*The Gospel Train Am Coming*." In: *The Rough Rider (Republican Campaign Song Book)*, page 4. c. J. Burgess Brown. Published by J. Burgess Brown, Indianapolis, IN. 1900. [6" × 9"]. Br/bk non-pictorial. "ROUGH ON DemocRATS." 28pp. Page 3: B/w litho of William McKinley. Page 28: "Republican National Ticket—1900. [Crew/WM-330].

• **AmPM-355 ENGLAND**, Douglas (Mayor, New Albany, 1994–1998?)

355.1 My New Albany Home. Janet Rae and Ron Timberlake. Cassette tape. Music Man Productions. 1998. Side B: *A Message From Mayor Doug England*." "Thanks to Mayor Doug England and the City of New Albany." Cassette cover: Photo of Janet Rae and Mayor England.

• **AmPM-356 ENGLISH**, William Hayden (State House, 1851–1852; U.S. House, 1853–1861; Democratic Candidate for Vice President, 1880) [ALSO SEE: DOC/PSM-WSH]

356.1 The Banner Of Hancock And Freedom. w.m. No composer or tune indicated. "Published in sheet music form." In: *Hancock And English Campaign Songster*, page 3. Published by John Church & Company, Cincinnati, OH. 1880. [4" × 5¾"]. Pk/bk geometric design cover. "Including Biographical Sketches & Constitution for Campaign Clubs." 52pp. Page 3: Title—*Democratic Campaign Carols*. [M-214]. [Crew/WSH-38].

356.2 The Battle Cry Of Freemen. w. No composer indicated. m. "Air—*Battle Cry Of Freedom*." In: *Hancock And English Campaign Songster*, page 47. Published by New York Popular Publishing Company, A.J. Dick, Manager, No. 32 Beekman Street, New York, NY. 1880. Be/bk litho of Winfield Scott Hancock. "Containing the Largest and Most Complete Collection of Songs, All Written to the Most Popular Airs of the Day." "The Most Popular Edition Of Hancock And English Campaign Songster." 68pp. Page 68: Be/bk litho of William H. English. [M-217]. [Crew/WSH-41].

356.3 The Battle Cry Of Hancock. w. No composer indicated. m. "Air—*Rally Round The Flag*." In: *The Campaign Songster (Containing A Choice Selection Of Songs Suited To All Political Parties)*, page 8. Published by J.P. Coats, Flint, MI. 1880. [3¾" × 5"]. Gn/bk non-pictorial. "Compliments of B.F. Cotharin, Wholesale and Retail Furniture, Flint, Michigan." Advertising. 46pp. [Crew/JAG-86].

356.4 A Campaign Carol. w. No composer indicated. m. "Air—*The Star Spangled Banner*." In: *The*

Hancock And English Democratic Campaign Song Book, page 26. Published by W.R. Swane & Company, No. 174 Race Street, Cincinnati, OH. 1880. [4⅛" × 6"]. B/w litho of "Winfield S. Hancock" and "W.H. English," eagle, shield, flags. 34pp. [M-216]. [Crew/WSH-39].

356.5 Campaign Rallying Song. w.m. E.C. Carr. Published by Oliver Ditson & Co., No. 451 Washington Street, Boston, MA. 1880. Non-pictorial geometric designs. "Respectfully dedicated to W.S. Hancock and W.H. English, the Next President and Vice-President of the United States." 6pp. Pages 2 and 6: Blank. [Crew/WSH-61].

356.6 Champions Of Liberty. w. No composer indicated. m. "Air—*America.*" In: *The Hancock And English Democratic Campaign Song Book*, page 18. Published by W.R. Swane & Company, No. 174 Race Street, Cincinnati, OH. 1880. [4⅛" × 6"]. B/w litho of "Winfield S. Hancock" and "W.H. English," eagle, shield, flags. 34pp. [M-216]. [Crew/WSH-39].

356.7 Choice Of The Fearless Free. w. No composer indicated. m. "Air—*America.*" In: *Hancock And English Campaign Songster*, page 25. Published by New York Popular Publishing Company, A.J. Dick, Manager, No. 32 Beekman Street, New York, NY. 1880. Be/bk litho of Winfield Scott Hancock. "Containing the Largest and Most Complete Collection of Songs, All Written to the Most Popular Airs of the Day." "The Most Popular Edition Of Hancock And English Campaign Songster." 68pp. Page 68: Be/bk litho of William H. English. [M-217]. [Crew/WSH-41].

356.8 Columbia's Call. w. No composer indicated. m. "Air—*Our Starry Banner.*" In: *Hancock And English Campaign Songster*, page 18. Published by John Church & Company, Cincinnati, OH. 1880. [4" × 5¾"]. Pk/bk geometric design cover. "Including Biographical Sketches & Constitution for Campaign Clubs." 52pp. Page 3: Title—*Democratic Campaign Carols*. [M-214]. [Crew/WSH-38].

356.9 Come Gather Round. w. No composer indicated. m. "Air—*Auld Lang Syne.*" In: *Hancock And English Campaign Songster*, page 15. Published by New York Popular Publishing Company, A.J. Dick, Manager, No. 32 Beekman Street, New York, NY. 1880. Be/bk litho of Winfield Scott Hancock. "Containing the Largest and Most Complete Collection of Songs, All Written to the Most Popular Airs of the Day." "The Most Popular Edition Of Hancock And English Campaign Songster." 68pp. Page 68: Be/bk litho of William H. English. [M-217]. [Crew/WSH-41].

356.10 Come Ye Freemen! w. No composer indicated. m. "Air—*Hail, Columbia.*" In: *Hancock And English Campaign Songster*, page 55. Published by New York Popular Publishing Company, A.J. Dick, Manager, No. 32 Beekman Street, New York, NY. 1880. Be/bk litho of Winfield Scott Hancock. "Containing the Largest and Most Complete Collection of Songs, All Written to the Most Popular Airs of the Day." "The Most Popular Edition Of Hancock And English Campaign Songster." 68pp. Page 68: Be/bk litho of William H. English. [M-217]. [Crew/WSH-41].

356.11 The Coming Man. w. No composer indicated. m. "Air—*Tara's Halls.*" In: *Hancock And English Campaign Songster*, page 29. Published by New York Popular Publishing Company, A.J. Dick, Manager, No. 32 Beekman Street, New York, NY. 1880. Be/bk litho of Winfield Scott Hancock. "Containing the Largest and Most Complete Collection of Songs, All Written to the Most Popular Airs of the Day." "The Most Popular Edition Of Hancock And English Campaign Songster." 68pp. Page 68: Be/bk litho of William H. English. [M-217]. [Crew/WSH-41].

356.12 Democratic Rallying Song. w. No composer indicated. m. "Air—*Battle Cry Of Freedom.*" In: *The Hancock And English Democratic Campaign Song Book*, page 8. Published by W.R. Swane & Company, No. 174 Race Street, Cincinnati, OH. 1880. [4⅛" × 6"]. B/w litho of "Winfield S. Hancock" and "W.H. English," eagle, shield, flags. 34pp. [M-216]. [Crew/WSH-39].

356.13 Democratic Voters. w. No composer indicated. m. "Air—*Battle Cry Of Freedom.*" In: *Hancock And English Campaign Songster*, page 32. Published by John Church & Company, Cincinnati, OH. 1880. [4" × 5¾"]. Pk/bk geometric design cover. "Including Biographical Sketches & Constitution for Campaign Clubs." 52pp. Page 3: Title—*Democratic Campaign Carols*. [M-214]. [Crew/WSH-38].

356.14 For Hancock And English. w. No composer indicated. m. "Air—*Battle Cry Of Freedom.*" In: *The Hancock And English Democratic Campaign Song Book*, page 9. Published by W.R. Swane & Company, No. 174 Race Street, Cincinnati, OH. 1880. [4⅛" × 6"]. B/w litho of "Winfield S. Hancock" and "W.H. English," eagle, shield, flags. 34pp. [M-216]. [Crew/WSH-39].

356.15 The Freeman's Choice. w. No composer indicated. m. "Air—*Nancy Lee.*" In: *Hancock And English Campaign Songster*, page 35. Published by John Church & Company, Cincinnati, OH. 1880. [4" × 5¾"]. Pk/bk geometric design cover. "Including Biographical Sketches & Constitution for Campaign Clubs." 52pp. Page 3: Title—*Democratic Campaign Carols*. [M-214]. [Crew/WSH-38].

356.16 Hail Again Hancock And English. w. No composer indicated. m. "Air—*Hold The Fort.*" In: *Hancock And English Campaign Songster*, page 13. Published by John Church & Company, Cincinnati, OH. 1880. [4" × 5¾"]. Pk/bk geometric design cover. "Including Biographical Sketches & Constitution for Campaign Clubs." 52pp. Page 3: Title—*Democratic Campaign Carols*. [M-214]. [Crew/WSH-38].

356.17 Hail The Republic. w. No composer indicated. m. "Air—*Hail To The Chief.*" In: *Hancock And English Campaign Songster*, page 19. Published by John Church & Company, Cincinnati, OH. 1880. [4" × 5¾"]. Pk/bk geometric design cover. "Including Biographical Sketches & Constitution for Campaign Clubs." 52pp. Page 3: Title—*Democratic Campaign Carols*. [M-214]. [Crew/WSH-38].

356.18 Hancock And English (Quartet and Chorus). w.m. R.A. Glenn. In: *The Hancock And English Democratic Campaign Song Book*, page 16. Published by W.R. Swane & Company, No. 174 Race Street, Cincinnati, OH. 1880. [4⅛" × 6"]. B/w litho of "Winfield S. Hancock" and "W.H. English," eagle, shield, flags. 34pp. [M-216]. [Crew/WSH-39].

356.19 Hancock And English. w. No composer indicated. m. "Air—*Hold The Fort.*" In: *The National Democratic Campaign Songster*, page 7. Printed by The Courier Printing Company, Syracuse, NY. Copyright 1880 by G.N. Harding. [3¾" × 5⅚"]. B/w litho of Winfield S. Hancock and William H. English, eagle, flag. Winfield S. Hancock quote. "1880 Hancock & English." 52pp. [M-218]. [Crew/WSH-2].

356.20 Hancock And English Forever. w. No composer indicated. m. "Air—*Battle Cry Of Freedom.*" In: *The National Democratic Campaign Songster*, page 16. Printed by The Courier Printing Company, Syracuse, NY. Copyright 1880 by G.N. Harding. [3¾" × 5⅚"]. B/w litho of Winfield S. Hancock and William H. English, eagle, flag. Winfield S. Hancock quote. "1880 Hancock & English." 52pp. [M-218]. [Crew/WSH-2].

356.21 Hancock And English, Too. w. No composer indicated. m. Notation. In: *Hancock And English Campaign Songster*, page 41. Published by John Church & Company, Cincinnati, OH. 1880. [4" × 5¾"]. Pk/bk geometric design cover. "Including Biographical Sketches & Constitution for Campaign Clubs." 52pp. Page 3: Title—*Democratic Campaign Carols*. [M-214]. [Crew/WSH-38].

356.22 Hancock Will Carry The Day. w. Wm. McVey. m. Dave Braham, "Air—*Little Widow Dunn.*" In: *Hancock And English Campaign Songster*, page 34. Published by New York Popular Publishing Company, A.J. Dick, Manager, No. 32 Beekman Street, New York, NY. 1880. Be/bk litho of Winfield Scott Hancock. "Containing the Largest and Most Complete Collection of Songs, All Written to the Most Popular Airs of the Day." "The Most Popular Edition Of Hancock And English Campaign Songster." 68pp. Page 68: Be/bk litho of William H. English. [M-217]. [Crew/WSH-41].

356.23 Hancock's The Man. w. No composer indicated. m. "Air—*Pull For The Shore.*" In: *Hancock And English Campaign Songster*, page 36. Published by John Church & Company, Cincinnati, OH. 1880. [4" × 5¾"]. Pk/bk geometric design cover. "Including Biographical Sketches & Constitution for Campaign Clubs." 52pp. Page 3: Title—*Democratic Campaign Carols*. [M-214]. [Crew/WSH-38].

356.24 Hancock's Rallying Song. w. No composer indicated. m. "Air—*Marching Through Georgia.*" In: *Hancock And English Campaign Songster*, page 50. Published by New York Popular Publishing Company, A.J. Dick, Manager, No. 32 Beekman Street, New York, NY. 1880. Be/bk litho of Winfield Scott Hancock. "Containing the Largest and Most Complete Collection of Songs, All Written to the Most Popular Airs of the Day." "The Most Popular Edition Of Hancock And English Campaign Songster." 68pp. Page 68: Be/bk litho of William H. English. [M-217]. [Crew/WSH-41].

356.25 Hark, The Bugle Call. w. No composer indicated. m. "Air—*See The People Turning Out.*" In: *Hancock And English Campaign Songster*, page 49. Published by New York Popular Publishing Company, A.J. Dick, Manager, No. 32 Beekman Street, New York, NY. 1880. Be/bk litho of Winfield Scott Hancock. "Containing the Largest and Most Complete Collection of Songs, All Written to the Most Popular Airs of the Day." "The Most Popular Edition Of Hancock And English Campaign Songster." 68pp. Page 68: Be/bk litho of William H. English. [M-217]. [Crew/WSH-41].

356.26 An Honest Man For President. w. No composer indicated. m. "Air—*Bonnie Blue Flag.*" In: *Hancock And English Campaign Songster*, page 25. Published by John Church & Company, Cincinnati, OH. 1880. [4" × 5¾"]. Pk/bk geometric design cover. "Including Biographical Sketches & Constitution for Campaign Clubs." 52pp. Page 3: Title—*Democratic Campaign Carols*. [M-214]. [Crew/WSH-38].

356.27 Hurrah! For The Army Blue. w. No composer indicated. m. "Air—*Life On The Ocean Wave.*" In: *Hancock And English Campaign Songster*, page 17. Published by New York Popular Publishing Company, A.J. Dick, Manager, No. 32 Beekman Street, New York, NY. 1880. Be/bk litho of Winfield Scott Hancock. "Containing the Largest and Most Complete Collection of Songs, All Written to the Most Popular Airs of the Day." "The Most Popular Edition Of Hancock And English Campaign Songster." 68pp. Page 68: Be/bk litho of William H. English. [M-217]. [Crew/WSH-41].

356.28 Hurrah For The Noble Democrats. w. Wm. McVey. m. J.P. Skelly, "Air—*Irish Regiment.*" In: *Hancock And English Campaign Songster*, page 35. Published by New York Popular Publishing Company, A.J. Dick, Manager, No. 32 Beekman Street, New York, NY. 1880. Be/bk litho of Winfield Scott Hancock. "Containing the Largest and Most Complete Collection of Songs, All Written to the Most Popular Airs of the Day." "The Most Popular Edition Of Hancock And English Campaign Songster." 68pp. Page 68: Be/bk litho of William H. English. [M-217]. [Crew/WSH-41].

356.29 Jamie G. Good-Night. w. No composer indicated. m. "Air—*Hold The Fort.*" In: *The Hancock And English Democratic Campaign Song Book*, page 28. Published by W.R. Swane & Company, No. 174 Race Street, Cincinnati, OH. 1880. [4⅛" × 6"]. B/w litho of "Winfield S. Hancock" and "W.H. English," eagle, shield, flags. 34pp. [M-216]. [Crew/WSH-39].

356.30 Loyal And True. w. No composer indicated. m. "Air—*Sweet Bye And Bye.*" In: *Hancock And English Campaign Songster*, page 44. Published by John Church & Company, Cincinnati, OH. 1880. [4" × 5¾"]. Pk/bk geometric design cover. "Including Biographical Sketches & Constitution for Campaign Clubs." 52pp. Page 3: Title—*Democratic Campaign Carols*. [M-214]. [Crew/WSH-38].

356.31 Marching Home. w. No composer indicated. m. "Air—*In The Morning By The Bright Light.*" In: *Hancock And English Campaign Songster*, page 43. Published by New York Popular Publishing Company, A.J. Dick, Manager, No. 32 Beekman Street, New York, NY. 1880. Be/bk litho of Winfield Scott Hancock. "Containing the Largest and Most Complete Collection of Songs, All Written to the Most Popular Airs of the Day." "The Most Popular Edition Of Hancock And English Campaign Songster." 68pp. Page 68: Be/bk litho of William H. English. [M-217]. [Crew/WSH-41].

356.32 The Old Banner's Waving. w. No composer indicated. m. Florence Harper, "Air—*Old Wooden*

Rocker." In: *Hancock And English Campaign Songster*, page 10. Published by New York Popular Publishing Company, A.J. Dick, Manager, No. 32 Beekman Street, New York, NY. 1880. Be/bk litho of Winfield Scott Hancock. "Containing the Largest and Most Complete Collection of Songs, All Written to the Most Popular Airs of the Day." "The Most Popular Edition Of Hancock And English Campaign Songster." 68pp. Page 68: Be/bk litho of William H. English. [M-217]. [Crew/WSH-41].

356.33 The Old Banner's Waving. w. George Cooper. m. Florence Harper, "Air—*Old Wooden Rocker.*" In: *Garfield & Arthur Campaign Songster*, page 14. Published by New York Publishing Company, No. 32 Beekman Street, New York, NY. [1880]. [4" × 6⅜"]. Hand colored litho of James A. Garfield. 68pp. Page 68: Hand colored litho of Chester Arthur. [Crew/JAG-27].

356.34 On That Morning. w. No composer indicated. m. James Bland, "Air—*In The Morning By The Bright Light.*" In: *Garfield & Arthur Campaign Songster*, page 16. Published by New York Publishing Company, No. 32 Beekman Street, New York, NY. [1880]. [4" × 6⅜"]. Hand colored litho of James A. Garfield. 68pp. Page 68: Hand colored litho of Chester Arthur. [Crew/JAG-27].

356.35 On To Victory. w. No composer indicated. m. "Air—*Hold The Fort.*" In: *The Hancock And English Democratic Campaign Song Book*, page 29. Published by W.R. Swane & Company, No. 174 Race Street, Cincinnati, OH. 1880. [4⅛" × 6"]. B/w litho of "Winfield S. Hancock" and "W.H. English," eagle, shield, flags. 34pp. [M-216]. [Crew/WSH-39].

356.36 Our Country To Thee. w. No composer indicated. m. "Air—*Star Spangled Banner.*" In: *Hancock And English Campaign Songster*, page 56. Published by New York Popular Publishing Company, A.J. Dick, Manager, No. 32 Beekman Street, New York, NY. 1880. Be/bk litho of Winfield Scott Hancock. "Containing the Largest and Most Complete Collection of Songs, All Written to the Most Popular Airs of the Day." "The Most Popular Edition Of Hancock And English Campaign Songster." 68pp. Page 68: Be/bk litho of William H. English. [M-217]. [Crew/WSH-41].

356.37 The Power Of Hancock's Name. w. No composer indicated. m. "Air—*Coronation.*" In: *Hancock And English Campaign Songster*, page 24. Published by John Church & Company, Cincinnati, OH. 1880. [4" × 5¾"]. Pk/bk geometric design cover. "Including Biographical Sketches & Constitution for Campaign Clubs." 52pp. Page 3: Title—*Democratic Campaign Carols*. [M-214]. [Crew/WSH-38].

356.38 The Presidential Racecourse. w. No composer indicated. m. "Air—*Camptown Races.*" In: *Hancock And English Campaign Songster*, page 53. Published by New York Popular Publishing Company, A.J. Dick, Manager, No. 32 Beekman Street, New York, NY. 1880. Be/bk litho of Winfield Scott Hancock. "Containing the Largest and Most Complete Collection of Songs, All Written to the Most Popular Airs of the Day." "The Most Popular Edition Of Hancock And English Campaign Songster." 68pp. Page 68: Be/bk litho of William H. English. [M-217]. [Crew/WSH-41].

356.39 Shouting For Hancock And English. w. No composer indicated. m. "Air—*Battle Cry Of Freedom.*" In: *Hancock And English Campaign Songster*, page 27. Published by New York Popular Publishing Company, A.J. Dick, Manager, No. 32 Beekman Street, New York, NY. 1880. Be/bk litho of Winfield Scott Hancock. "Containing the Largest and Most Complete Collection of Songs, All Written to the Most Popular Airs of the Day." "The Most Popular Edition Of Hancock And English Campaign Songster." 68pp. Page 68: Be/bk litho of William H. English. [M-217]. [Crew/WSH-41].

356.40 The Soreheads On Our Block. w. George Cooper. m. Dave Braham. "Air—*Babies On Our Block.*" In: *Garfield & Arthur Campaign Songster*, page 6. Published by New York Publishing Company, No. 32 Beekman Street, New York, NY. [1880]. [4" × 6⅜"]. Hand colored litho of James A. Garfield. 68pp. Page 68: Hand colored litho of Chester Arthur. [Crew/JAG-27].

356.41 The Soreheads On Our Block. w. No composer indicated. m. Dave Braham, "Air—*Babies On Our Block.*" In: *Hancock And English Campaign Songster*, page 4. Published by New York Popular Publishing Company, A.J. Dick, Manager, No. 32 Beekman Street, New York, NY. 1880. Be/bk litho of Winfield Scott Hancock. "Containing the Largest and Most Complete Collection of Songs, All Written to the Most Popular Airs of the Day." "The Most Popular Edition Of Hancock And English Campaign Songster." 68pp. Page 68: Be/bk litho of William H. English. [M-217]. [Crew/WSH-41].

356.42 A Stainless Name. w. No composer indicated. m. "Air—*Maryland, My Maryland.*" In: *Hancock And English Campaign Songster*, page 39. Published by John Church & Company, Cincinnati, OH. 1880. [4" × 5¾"]. Pk/bk geometric design cover. "Including Biographical Sketches & Constitution for Campaign Clubs." 52pp. Page 3: Title—*Democratic Campaign Carols*. [M-214]. [Crew/WSH-38].

356.43 That's What's The Matter. w. No composer indicated. m. "Air—*What's The Matter?*" In: *Hancock And English Campaign Songster*, page 28. Published by John Church & Company, Cincinnati, OH. 1880. [4" × 5¾"]. Pk/bk geometric design cover. "Including Biographical Sketches & Constitution for Campaign Clubs." 52pp. Page 3: Title—*Democratic Campaign Carols*. [M-214]. [Crew/WSH-38].

356.44 The Three Names. w. No composer indicated. m. "Air—*America.*" In: *Hancock And English Campaign Songster*, page 38. Published by John Church & Company, Cincinnati, OH. 1880. [4" × 5¾"]. Pk/bk geometric design cover. "Including Biographical Sketches & Constitution for Campaign Clubs." 52pp. Page 3: Title—*Democratic Campaign Carols*. [M-214]. [Crew/WSH-38].

356.45 Vote For Hancock. w. No composer indicated. m. "Air—*Hail Columbia.*" In: *The Hancock And English Democratic Campaign Song Book*, page 19. Published by W.R. Swane & Company, No. 174 Race Street, Cincinnati, OH. 1880. [4⅛" × 6"]. B/w litho of "Winfield S. Hancock" and "W.H. English," eagle, shield, flags. 34pp. [M-216]. [Crew/WSH-39].

356.46 Voting For Hancock. w. No composer indicated. m. "Air—*Marching Through Georgia.*" In: *Hancock And English Campaign Songster*, page 27. Published by John Church & Company, Cincinnati, OH. 1880. [4" × 5¾"]. Pk/bk geometric design cover. "Including Biographical Sketches & Constitution for Campaign Clubs." 52pp. Page 3: Title—*Democratic Campaign Carols*. [M-214]. [Crew/WSH-38].

356.47 *Voting For Hancock And English*. w. No composer indicated. m. "Air—*Marching Through Georgia.*" In: *The Hancock And English Democratic Campaign Song Book*, page 12. Published by W.R. Swane & Company, No. 174 Race Street, Cincinnati, OH. 1880. [4⅛" × 6"]. B/w litho of "Winfield S. Hancock" and "W.H. English," eagle, shield, flags. 34pp. [M-216]. [Crew/WSH-39].

356.48 *We Are Marching*. w. No composer indicated. m. "Air—*Marching Along.*" In: *The National Democratic Campaign Songster*, page 19. Printed by The Courier Printing Company, Syracuse, NY. Copyright 1880 by G.N. Harding. [3¾" × 5⁵⁄₁₆"]. B/w litho of Winfield S. Hancock and William H. English, eagle, flag. Winfield S. Hancock quote. "1880 Hancock & English." 52pp. [M-218]. [Crew/WSH-2].

356.49 *The William H. English Marsellaise*. w. No composer indicated. m. "Air—*The Marsellaise.*" In: *The National Democratic Campaign Songster*, page 27. Printed by The Courier Printing Company, Syracuse, NY. Copyright 1880 by G.N. Harding. [3¾" × 5⁵⁄₁₆"]. B/w litho of Winfield S. Hancock and William H. English, eagle, flag. Winfield S. Hancock quote. "1880 Hancock & English." 52pp. [M-218]. [Crew/WSH-2].

356.50 *Yankee Doodle At Cincinnati*. w. No composer indicated. m. "Air—*Yankee Doodle.*" In: *Hancock And English Campaign Songster*, page 42. Published by John Church & Company, Cincinnati, OH. 1880. [4" × 5¾"]. Pk/bk geometric design cover. "Including Biographical Sketches & Constitution for Campaign Clubs." 52pp. Page 3: Title—*Democratic Campaign Carols*. [M-214]. [Crew/WSH-38].

• **AmPM-356A FAIRBANKS**, Charles Warren (U.S. Senate, 1897–1905; Vice-President, 1905–1909; Candidate for Vice President, 1916) [SEE: DOC-/PSM-TR]

356A.1 *Charles Evans Hughes* (A Patriotic Acrostic). w. J.L. Feeney. m. No tune indicated. In: *Hughes And Fairbanks Campaign Song Book*, page 2. c. James L. Feeney. Published by William H. Delaney, Song Publisher, No. 117 Park Row, New York, NY. Copyright 1916 by William W. DeLaney. [8" × 11"]. R/w/b flags, shield. Bl/w photos of "Charles Evans Hughes" and "Charles Warren Fairbanks." "Preparedness, Protection, Prosperity." R/w/b drawing of flags, shield, geometric designs. 20pp. [M-407]. [Crew/CEH-1].

356A.2 *Dixie Land* (Revised). w.m. "Arr. From Dan Emmett." In: *Roosevelt Campaign Songster 1904 (For Male Voices)*, page 24. c. Logan S. Porter. Published by The Home Music Company, Logansport, IN. 1904. [6" × 9"]. Be/bk photos of Theodore Roosevelt and Charles Fairbanks. Be/bk drawing of a star, geometric designs. "Single Copy 15 cts—$1.60 per Dozen." 36pp. [M-391]. [Crew/TR-356].

356A.3 *Fairbanks' Battle Song*. w. No composer indicated. m. "Air—*A Warrior Bold.*" In: *Gridiron Nights, Humorous And Satirical Views Of Politics And Statesmen As Presented By The Famous Dining Club*, page 196. Published by Frederick A. Stokes Co., Publishers, New York, NY. 1915. 372pp.

356A.4 *Indiana*. w.m. W.T. Giffe. In: *Roosevelt Campaign Songster 1904 (For Male Voices)*, page 20. c. Logan S. Porter. Published by The Home Music Company, Logansport, IN. 1904. [6" × 9"]. Be/bk photos of Theodore Roosevelt and Charles Fairbanks. Be/bk drawing of a star, geometric designs. "Single Copy 15 cts—$1.60 per Dozen." 36pp. [M-391]. [Crew/TR-356].

356A.5 *An Irish Democrat's Complaint*. w. Maj. J.H. Durham. m. George A. Barker. Published by Howard Publishing Company, Baltimore, MD. 1904. Bl/w non-pictorial. "The Most Rousing Campaign Song Ever Put Before The People." "A Sure Winner, and Vote Getter for Roosevelt and Fairbanks." "Sung by George Barker." 6pp. Pages 2 and 6: Blank. [Crew/TR-391].

356A.6 *Lay Them In The Tomb*. w. Logan S. Porter. m. "Arr. From *Patience* by W.T. Giffe." In: *Parker Campaign Songster, 1904*, page 14. e. Logan S. Porter. Published by The Home Music Company, Logansport, IN. 1904. [6" × 9"]. O/bk litho of Alton Parker and Henry Gassaway Davis. 36pp. [M-394]. [Crew/ABP-7].

356A.7 *Marching To Victory* (Campaign Song). w. J.L. Feeney. m. "Air—*Marching Through Georgia.*" In: *Hughes And Fairbanks Campaign Song Book*, page 2. c. James L. Feeney. Published by William H. Delaney, Song Publisher, No. 117 Park Row, New York, NY. Copyright 1916 by William W. DeLaney. [8" × 11"]. R/w/b flags, shield. Bl/w photos of "Charles Evans Hughes" and "Charles Warren Fairbanks." "Preparedness, Protection, Prosperity." R/w/b drawing of flags, shield, geometric designs. 20pp. [M-407]. [Crew/CEH-1].

356A.8 *Old Folks At Home* (Revised). w. Logan S. Porter. m. "Arr. From Foster by W.T. Giffe." In: *Parker Campaign Songster, 1904*, page 4. e. Logan S. Porter. Published by The Home Music Company, Logansport, IN. 1904. [6" × 9"]. O/bk litho of Alton Parker and Henry Gassaway Davis. 36pp. [M-394]. [Crew/ABP-7].

356A.9 *Onward, Every Voter* (Campaign Song). w. J.L. Feeney. m. "Air—*Onward, Christian Soldiers.*" In: *Hughes And Fairbanks Campaign Song Book*, page 5. c. James L. Feeney. Published by William H. Delaney, Song Publisher, No. 117 Park Row, New York, NY. Copyright 1916 by William W. DeLaney. [8" × 11"]. R/w/b flags, shield. Bl/w photos of "Charles Evans Hughes" and "Charles Warren Fairbanks." "Preparedness, Protection, Prosperity." R/w/b drawing of flags, shield, geometric designs. 20pp. [M-407]. [Crew/CEH-1].

356A.10 *We Will Win With Hughes And Fairbanks* (Campaign Song). w. J.L. Feeney. m. "Air—*It's A Long Way To Tipperary.*" In: *Hughes And Fairbanks Campaign Song Book*, page 3. c. James L. Feeney. Published by William H. Delaney, Song Publisher, No. 117 Park Row, New York, NY. Copyright 1916 by William W. DeLaney. [8" × 11"]. R/w/b flags, shield. Bl/w photos of "Charles Evans Hughes" and "Charles

Warren Fairbanks." "Preparedness, Protection, Prosperity." R/w/b drawing of flags, shield, geometric designs. 20pp. [M-407]. [Crew/CEH-1].

356A.11 We'll Rally For Our Leaders. w. "Arr. From Mrs. Hattie O. Langley." m. W.T. Giffe. In: *Roosevelt Campaign Songster 1904 (For Male Voices)*, page 6. c. Logan S. Porter. Published by The Home Music Company, Logansport, IN. 1904. [6" x 9"]. Be/bk photos of Theodore Roosevelt and Charles Fairbanks. Be/bk drawing of a star, geometric designs. "Single Copy 15 cts — $1.60 per Dozen." 36pp. [M-391]. [Crew/TR-356].

356A.12 The White House Gate (Solo and Chorus). w.m. Logan S. Porter. In: *Roosevelt Campaign Songster 1904 (For Male Voices)*, page 26. c. Logan S. Porter. Published by The Home Music Company, Logansport, IN. 1904. [6" x 9"]. Be/bk photos of Theodore Roosevelt and Charles Fairbanks. Be/bk drawing of a star, geometric designs. "Single Copy 15 cts — $1.60 per Dozen." 36pp. [M-391]. [Crew/TR-356].

• **AmPM-357 FOX**, Willis A. (Candidate for Superintendent of Public Instruction, 1918)
357.1 Till Over The Top We Go. w.m. Roy L. Burtch "(Composer of *When The Bugle Calls, Peace On Earth And Liberty, Think Of Me, Tell Me, The Organ And The Choir, Bye Bye Baby Dear*)." Published by The Halcyon Publishing Company, Indianapolis, IN. 1918. Drawing of soldier — "U.S. Marine," machine gun. "The Song Our Allies, Lodges and Glee Clubs are Singing." "State Campaign Song — Democratic State Committee, Denison Hotel, Indianapolis, Ind." "Extra copies of this March Song mailed free on request." 4pp. Page 4: Photos of Woodrow Wilson and 13 State Democratic candidates. "The Party with a Purpose." Text on 11 reasons to vote Democratic. [Crew/WW-121].

• **AmPM-357A FRY**, Neil (Sheriff, Porter County)
357A.1 Roosevelt We Hand The Flag To You! w. William Foster. m. Edna May Foster. Published by Calumet Music Publishers, Gary, IN. 1934. R/w/b eagle, trees, geometric designs. Bl/w photo of Franklin D. Roosevelt. 6pp. Page 2: Advertisement for Neil Fry for Sheriff. "Re-Elect Neil Fry Democratic Candidate for Sheriff, Porter County, Honest-Efficient-Worthy, Your Support Will be Appreciated." Page 6: Advertisements for various Porter County office seekers.

• **AmPM-358 GILBERT**, Newton Whiting (State Senate, 1897–1899; Lt. Governor, 1901–1905; U.S. House, 1905–1907)
358.1 Our Candidates. w. No composer indicated. m. "Tune — *Boom De-Ay*." In: *The Rough Rider (Republican Campaign Song Book)*, page 6. c. J. Burgess Brown. Published by J. Burgess Brown, Indianapolis, IN. 1900. [6" x 9"]. Br/bk non-pictorial. "ROUGH ON DemocRATS." 28pp. Page 3: B/w litho of William McKinley. Page 28: "Republican National Ticket — 1900. [Crew/WM-330].

• **AmPM-359 GILLAM**, Arthur L. (Candidate, 1924)
359.1 Rally The Standard Of "Abe" Lincoln. w. Mrs. S.R. Artma "(Composer of *Guess, One Who Cares For Me, The Organ And The Choir*)." m. Roy L. Burtch. Published by Halcyon Publishing Company, No. 307 East North Street, Indianapolis, IN. 1924. Br/w photos of "Calvin Coolidge," "Charles G. Dawes," "Abraham Lincoln" and "Ed Jackson" [Republican nominee for Governor of Indiana], geometric design border. "American Campaign March Song." 4pp. + Insert letter. Page 4: Biographies of candidates and other Republicans from Indiana, including "Ed Jackson, F. Harold Van Orman, Frederick E. Schortmeier, Lewis S. Bohman, Ben H. Urbahns, Arthur L. Gillam, F.M. Thompson, Willard R. Gimmill, Judge Willoughby, E.A. Dausman, Noble Sherwood, Mrs. Edward F. White." Insert — Page 1: Letter from composer to Republican State Committee. Page 2: Advertising.

• **AmPM-360 GIMMILL**, Willard R. (State House, 1908; State Senate, 1914–1915 & 1915; City Attorney, Marion, 1918; Deputy State Attorney General; Candidate, 1924)
360.1 Rally The Standard Of "Abe" Lincoln. w. Mrs. S.R. Artma "(Composer of *Guess, One Who Cares For Me, The Organ And The Choir*)." m. Roy L. Burtch. Published by Halcyon Publishing Company, No. 307 East North Street, Indianapolis, IN. 1924. Br/w photos of "Calvin Coolidge," "Charles G. Dawes," "Abraham Lincoln" and "Ed Jackson" [Republican nominee for Governor of Indiana], geometric design border. "American Campaign March Song." 4pp. + Insert letter. Page 4: Biographies of candidates and other Republicans from Indiana, including "Ed Jackson, F. Harold Van Orman, Frederick E. Schortmeier, Lewis S. Bohman, Ben H. Urbahns, Arthur L. Gillam, F.M. Thompson, Willard R. Gimmill, Judge Willoughby, E.A. Dausman, Noble Sherwood, Mrs. Edward F. White." Insert — Page 1: Letter from composer to Republican State Committee. Page 2: Advertising.

• **AmPM-361 GOODRICH**, James Putnam (Republican Party State Chairman, 1901–1910 & 1912; Governor, 1917–1921)
361.1 Republican Train. w. No composer indicated. m. "Tune — *The Gospel Train Am Coming*." In: *Up-To-Date Republican Campaign Songs*, page 3. Published by J. Burgess Brown "(Leader of the Celebrated Bald-Headed Glee Club), [Indianapolis, IN.]." 1908. [8" x 11"]. B/w photos of William H. Taft and John Sherman. B/w drawing of American Flag — "We'll rally 'round the flag, boys." Verse. "Written and compiled for the State Central Committee." [Crew/WHT-66].

• **AmPM-362 GOODWINE**. (Candidate, 1908)
362.1 The Hoosier Boom De-Aye. w. No composer indicated. m. "Tune — *Ta-Ra-Ra-Ra Boom-De-Aye*." In: *Up-To-Date Republican Campaign Songs*, page 3. Published by J. Burgess Brown "(Leader of the Celebrated Bald-Headed Glee Club), [Indianapolis, IN.]." 1908. [8" x 11"]. B/w photos of William H. Taft and John Sherman. B/w drawing of American Flag — "We'll rally 'round the flag, boys." Verse. "Written and compiled for the State Central Committee." [Crew/WHT-66].

• **AmPM-363 GRAY**, Isaac Pusey (State Senate, 1869–1871; Lt. Governor, 1877–1880; Governor, 1880–1881 & 1885–1889; U.S. Minister to Mexico, 1893–1895)
363.1 The Democratic Showman. w. No composer

indicated. m. "Air — *There's One More River To Cross.*" In: *Republican League Harrison And Morton Song Book, 1888,* page 34. Printed by Register Press Printing House, Des Moines, IA. Copyright 1888 by P.H. Bristow. [6" × 9¼"]. Bl/bk non-pictorial geometric designs, League logo. "The ball it goes rolling from the Gulf to The Lakes, From Maine in the East out to Oregon's peaks, Get out of its way for 'tis rolling along, You tell of its coming, by music & Song." 44pp. [M-256]. [Crew/BFH-50].

363.2 I Am Mighty Grover. w. P.H. Bristow, "(Des Moines)." m. J. Woollett, "(Chicago)." In: *Republican League Harrison And Morton Song Book, 1888,* page 14. Printed by Register Press Printing House, Des Moines, IA. Copyright 1888 by P.H. Bristow. [6" × 9¼"]. Bl/bk non-pictorial geometric designs, League logo. "The ball it goes rolling from the Gulf to The Lakes, From Maine in the East out to Oregon's peaks, Get out of its way for 'tis rolling along, You tell of its coming, by music & Song." 44pp. [M-256]. [Crew/BFH-50].

363.3 I Am The Boss Of My Party. w. P.H. Bristow, "(Des Moines)." m.a. J. Woollett, "(Chicago)." In: *Republican League Harrison And Morton Song Book, 1888,* page 16. Printed by Register Press Printing House, Des Moines, IA. Copyright 1888 by P.H. Bristow. [6" × 9¼"]. Bl/bk non-pictorial geometric designs, League logo. "The ball it goes rolling from the Gulf to The Lakes, From Maine in the East out to Oregon's peaks, Get out of its way for 'tis rolling along, You tell of its coming, by music & Song." 44pp. [M-256]. [Crew/BFH-50].

363.4 Not A Word. w. D.E. Bryer ("Arranged from Fritz Nigel"). m. D.E. Bryer. In: *The Harrison Campaign Songster,* page 10. w. D.E. Bryer (The Old Campaigner). m. Popular tunes. Published by The Home Music Company, No. 200 Fourth Street, Logansport, IN. 1892. [5¾" × 8½"]. Non-pictorial. Table of Contents. 36pp. Page 36: Advertising. [M-301]. [Crew/BFH-87].

363.5 We Want A Hoosier President. w. Thomas F. Byron. m. "Air — *Sing Song, Polly, Won't You Try Me, O.*" In: *Republican Club Campaign Song Book For 1888,* page 18. a. Thomas Byron. Published by Protection Publication Company, South Central Street, Chicago, IL. 1888. [6⅛" × 8⅞"]. Be/bk litho of Benjamin F. Harrison — "For President" and Levi P. Morton — "For Vice-President," eagle, flags, geometric designs. "Thirty Rousing Songs Written to Popular Airs." 36pp. [M-257]. [Crew/BFH-20].

• **AmPM-364   GRESHAM,** Walter Quintin (U.S. District Court Judge, 1869–1883; U.S. Postmaster General, 1883–1884; U.S. Secretary of the Treasury, 1884; U.S. Court of Appeals, 1884–1893; U.S. Secretary of State, 1893–1895)

364.1 The Bradbury Schottische. m. Dayton Vreeland. Published by F.G. Smith, 109 & 111 Broadway, Paterson, NJ. 1897. B/w geometric designs. "Dedicated to H.N. Lakeham." 4pp. Page 4: Advertising for Bradbury pianos with photo of "Famous Patrons of Bradbury Pianos" including "U.S. Grant, J.A. Garfield, C.A. Arthur, Benj. Harrison, R.B. Hayes, Grover Cleveland, Stanley Mathews, J.M Rusk, Benj. Tracy, Levi Morton, Thos. B. Reed, J.W. Noble, William Windom, John G. Carlisle, C.C. McCabe, A.H. Colquitt [and] Walter Q. Gresham." [Crew/MISC-142]

• **AmPM-365   HADLEY.** (Candidate, 1908)

365.1 The Hoosier Boom De-Aye. w. No composer indicated. m. "Tune — *Ta-Ra-Ra-Ra Boom-De-Aye.*" In: *Up-To-Date Republican Campaign Songs,* page 3. Published by J. Burgess Brown "(Leader of the Celebrated Bald-Headed Glee Club), [Indianapolis, IN.]." 1908. [8" × 11"]. B/w photos of William H. Taft and John Sherman. B/w drawing of American Flag — "We'll rally 'round the flag, boys." Verse. "Written and compiled for the State Central Committee." [Crew/WHT-66].

• **AmPM-366   HALLECK,** Charles Abraham (Prosecuting Attorney, 1924–1934; U.S. House, 1935–1969)

366.1 Dance Of The Liberal Republicans. w.m. Gerald Gardner. In: *These Are The Songs That Were* [Song Book], page 10. e. Gerald Gardner "(Writer *Of Who's In Charge Here?, News-Reals,* and *That Was The Week That Was*)." Published by Edwin H. Morris and Company, No. 31 West 54th Street, New York, NY. 10019. 1965. B/w photo of Lyndon B. Johnson, Hubert Humphrey, Everett Dirksen, others. R/w/bk cover. List of contents. 36pp. Pages 8, 23 and 25: Photos of politicians. [Crew/LBJ-6].

366.2 The Good Times Train. w. Johnny Lehmann. m. Jimmie Driftwood. Copyright 1960 by Worden Music Co., Inc. In: *Welcome GOP to The Jumbo Jamboree Uline Arena, April 4, 1960, Washington, DC.* [Program], page 4. R/w/b elephant. 4pp. Page 3 and 4: — Elected dignitaries in attendance — Senators Thurston Morton, Barry Goldwater, and Everett M. Dirksen; Congressmen William Miller and Charles Halleck.

366.3 How Are Things With You? w. No composer indicated. m. "Tune — *How Are Things In Glocca Morra?*" In: *Visions And Revisions,* page 18. Published by The Albany Legislative Correspondents' Association, Albany, NY. March 6, 1947. [8½" × 11"]. R/w/gn/y/bk drawing of Thomas "Dewey" as Santa Claus, sign — "Santa's Workshop," other New York politicians. "Revealing in Rhapsodic Revelry of Song and Stunt How a Political Scrooge Became a Political Saint; or, What Happened When Many Paws Raided the Wonderful Workshop of Santa Claus Dewey; Together with Other Strange and Silly Scenes." "Hotel Ten Eyck, Albany, March 6, 1947." 24pp. [Crew/TED-34].

366.4 On Top Of Goldwater (JFK's Lament). m. "To the tune of *On Top Of Old Smokey.*" In: *Sing Along With Jack* [Song Book], page 22. w. Milton M. Schwartz. a. Danny Hurd. Published by Pocket Books, Inc., New York, NY. Copyright 1963 by Bonny Publishing Corporation. [9" × 11⅞"]. R/w/bk drawing of sheet music "Vive La Dynasty," silhouette of John F. Kennedy in chair with conductor's baton, caricature of Kennedy family. "Hit Songs from the New Frontier." 36pp. Page 3: "Illustrations by David Gantz." Page 36: Drawing of John F. Kennedy in chair with baton. Song titles. [Crew/ JFK-17].

• **AmPM-366x   HARRISON,** Benjamin (Reporter of the Decisions of the State Supreme Court, 185- & 1865–1869; Mississippi River Commission,

1879; U. S. Senate, 1881–1887; President, 1889–1893) [SEE: DOC/PSM-BFH]

• **AmPM-366xx HARRISON**, William Henry (Delegate from the Northwest Ohio Territory, 1799–1800; Territorial Governor, Indiana, 1801–1813; U.S. House, 1816–1819; State Senate, 1819–1821; U.S. Senate, 1825–1828; President, 1841) [SEE: DOC/PSM-WHH]

• **AmPM-367 HART**, William H. (State Auditor, 1899)

367.1 Our Candidates. w. No composer indicated. m. "Tune—*Boom De-Ay*." In: *The Rough Rider (Republican Campaign Song Book)*, page 6. c. J. Burgess Brown. Published by J. Burgess Brown, Indianapolis, IN. 1900. [6" × 9"]. Br/bk non-pictorial. "ROUGH ON DemocRATS." 28pp. Page 3: B/w litho of William McKinley. Page 28: "Republican National Ticket—1900. [Crew/WM-330].

• **AmPM-367A HENDRICKS**, Thomas Andrews (State House, 1848; State Senate, 1849; U.S. House, 1851–1855; Commissioner General Land Office, 1855–1859; U.S. Senate, 1863–1869; Governor, 1873–1877; Democratic Candidate for Vice President, 1876; Vice President, 1885) [SEE: DOC/PSM-SJT & GC]

367A.1 As We Go Marching On. w. E.W.H. Ellis. m. "Air—*John Brown*." In: *Hayes & Wheeler Campaign Song Book (For the Centennial Year)*, page 64. Published by the American News Company, Nos. 117, 119, 121, 123 Nassau Street, New York, NY. 1876. [3⅞" × 6¹⁄₁₆"]. Y/bk litho of Rutherford B. Hayes and William A. Wheeler, liberty cap, geometric designs. 74pp. Pages 2, 4, 73 and 74: Blank. Page 3: "Containing Over Sixty Original Songs Adapted to Popular Melodies." [M-193]. [Crew/RBH-11].

367A.2 The Betters In Our Block. w. Frank N. Scott. m. No composer indicated. In: *P.T. Schultz & Co's Blaine And Logan Bugle Call*, page 8. Published by P.T. Schultz & Company, No. 172 Race Street, Cincinnati, OH. 1881. [1884 Edition]. [5⅞" × 7⅝"]. Bk/gn litho of James G. Blaine and John A. Logan, flags and eagle, geometric design border. 36pp. Page 36: Advertising. [M-245]. [Crew/JGB-67].

367A.3 Blaine And Logan Song. w. N.B. Milliken. m. "Air—*John Brown*." In: *Blaine And Logan Campaign Song-Book*, page 18. e. Prof. F. Widdows. Published by The Republican National Committee, New York, NY. 1884. [4⅜" × 5¹¹⁄₁₆"]. [V-1: Bk/y] [V-2: Pk/bk] litho of James G. Blaine and John A. Logan. "From the School—House to the Cabinet, From the Cabin to the Senate." 52pp. [M-251]. [Crew/JGB-32].

367A.4 Bring Out Your Campaign Banners. w. "By Demo." m. "Tune—*Marching Through Georgia*." In: *Cleveland & Hendricks Songster*, page 45. Copyright 1884 by E.Y. Landis. R/w/bl/gn/br drawing of Grover Cleveland, Thomas Hendricks, George "Washington," Thomas "Jefferson," Andrew "Jackson," ribbons, geometric designs. 64pp. [M-230]. [Crew/GC-46].

367A.5 The Champions Of Reform. w. No composer indicated. m. "Air—*The Old Oaken Bucket*." In: *Tilden And Hendricks' Reform Songs (For The Centennial Campaign of 1876)*, page 12. Published by The National Democratic Committee, Box 3637, New York, NY. 1876. [3⅞" × 5¹⁵⁄₁₆"]. Gn/bk litho of Samuel J. Tilden and Thomas A. Hendricks, geometric design border. 40pp. [M-203]. [Crew/SJT-21].

367A.6 Cleveland And Hendricks Came To Town. w. No composer indicated. m. "Air—*Yankee Doodle*." In: *Beulah's Blaine And Logan Original Campaign Song Book 1884*, page 15. Printed and Published by Birnie Paper Company, Springfield, MA. 1884. [4" × 5¾"]. Gy/bk litho of James G. Blaine and John A. Logan, eagle, flags, shield, line border. 36pp. [M-232]. [Crew/JGB-41].

367A.7 Crow! w. No composer indicated. m. "Air—*Billy Barlow*." In: *Hayes & Wheeler Campaign Song Book (For the Centennial Year)*, page 56. Published by the American News Company, Nos. 117, 119, 121, 123 Nassau Street, New York, NY. 1876. [3⅞" × 6¹⁄₁₆"]. Y/bk litho of Rutherford B. Hayes and William A. Wheeler, liberty cap, geometric designs. 74pp. Pages 2, 4, 73 and 74: Blank. Page 3: "Containing Over Sixty Original Songs Adapted to Popular Melodies." [M-193]. [Crew/RBH-11].

367A.8 The Day Will Come At Last. w. "By Demo." m. "Tune—*A Daddy I'm At Last*." In: *Cleveland & Hendricks Songster*, page 44. Copyright 1884 by E.Y. Landis. R/w/bl/gn/br drawing of Grover Cleveland, Thomas Hendricks, George "Washington," Thomas "Jefferson," Andrew "Jackson," ribbons, geometric designs. 64pp. [M-230]. [Crew/GC-46].

367A.9 A Democratic Toast. w. No composer indicated. m. "Arr. By Tariff Reform." In: *Red Hot Democratic Campaign Songs For 1888*, page 6. e. John Bunyon Herbert. Published by The S. Brainard's Sons Company, Chicago, IL. 1888. [5⅜" × 7⁷⁄₁₆"]. R/bk geometric designs. 36pp. [M-294]. [Crew/GC-141].

367A.10 Democratic Voters. w. No composer indicated. m. "Tune—*Battle Cry Of Freedom*." In: *Cleveland & Hendricks Songster*, page 29. Copyright 1884 by E.Y. Landis. R/w/bl/gn/br drawing of Grover Cleveland, Thomas Hendricks, George "Washington," Thomas "Jefferson," Andrew "Jackson," ribbons, geometric designs. 64pp. [M-230]. [Crew/GC-46].

367A.11 Don't Worry About That Surplus. w. No composer indicated. m. Notation. In: *Young Republican Campaign Song Book*, page 66. c. Henry Camp. Published by the Brooklyn Young Republican Club, Brooklyn, NY. 1888. [4⅜" × 6½"]. R/w/b litho of a U.S. flag. "Campaign 1888." 100pp. Page 100: B/w lithos of Benjamin Harrison and Levi Morton. [M-258, 259]. [Crew/BFH-53].

367A.12 Fall In Line. w. H.E. Gordon. m. No composer indicated. In: *Hayes & Wheeler Song Book*, page 43. Published by The Union Republican Congressional Committee, Washington, DC. 1876. [5¾" × 9¼"]. Br/bk litho of Rutherford B. Hayes and William A. Wheeler, shield, geometric design border. "I'll be on hand again shortly." [V-1: "Series I" under title on cover] [V-2: Series not indicated on cover]. 52pp. Page 2: Contents. Page 52: State-by-state electoral vote totals for 1876. [M-196, 197]. [Crew/RBH-20].

367A.13 For Old Democracy. w. "Dan Yell." m. "Tune—*Marching Through Georgia*." In: *Cleveland & Hendricks Songster*, page 47. Copyright 1884 by E.Y. Landis. R/w/bl/gn/br drawing of Grover Cleveland, Thomas Hendricks, George "Washington," Thomas

"Jefferson," Andrew "Jackson," ribbons, geometric designs. 64pp. [M-230]. [Crew/GC-46].

367A.14 For Tilden And Hendricks, Hurrah! w.m. No composer or tune indicated. In: *Illustrated Campaign Song And Joke*, page 24. Published by The American News Company, New York, NY. [4¾" × 7½"]. 1876. Y/bk litho of Samuel J. Tilden, geometric design border. 50pp. [?]. Page 5: Title—*The Illustrated Campaign Tilden Song And Joke Book*. [Crew/SJT-8].

367A.15 Freemen, Rally! w.m. No composers or tune indicated. In: *Illustrated Campaign Song And Joke*, page 28. Published by The American News Company, New York, NY. [4¾" × 7½"]. 1876. Y/bk litho of Samuel J. Tilden, geometric design border. 50pp. [?]. Page 5: Title—*The Illustrated Campaign Tilden Song And Joke Book*. [Crew/SJT-8].

367A.16 The Gathering. w. No composer indicated. m. "Air—*The Coming Of The Clans*." In: *Tilden And Hendricks' Reform Songs (For The Centennial Campaign of 1876)*, page 13. Published by The National Democratic Committee, Box 3637, New York, NY. 1876. [3⅞" × 5 15/16"]. Gn/bk litho of Samuel J. Tilden and Thomas A. Hendricks, geometric design border. 40pp. [M-203]. [Crew/SJT-21].

367A.17 Gov. Hendrick's Quick Step. m. A. Schuman. Litho of Governor Thomas Hendricks.

367A.18 Hold The Fort For Tilden. w. No composer indicated. m. Air—*Hold The Fort*. "Campaign Song for Democratic Meetings—1876." In: *Illustrated Campaign Song And Joke*, page 7. Published by The American News Company, New York, NY. [4¾" × 7½"]. 1876. Y/bk litho of Samuel J. Tilden, geometric design border. 50pp. [?]. Page 5: Title—*The Illustrated Campaign Tilden Song And Joke Book*. [Crew/SJT-8].

367A.19 It Might Have Been. w. No composer indicated. m. "Tune—*Paddy O'Rafferty*. In: *Hayes & Wheeler Song Book*, page 44. Published by The Union Republican Congressional Committee, Washington, DC. 1876. [5¾" × 9¼"]. Br/bk litho of Rutherford B. Hayes and William A. Wheeler, shield, geometric design border. "I'll be on hand again shortly." [V-1: "Series I" under title on cover] [V-2: Series not indicated on cover]. 52pp. [M-196, 197]. [Crew/RBH-20].

367A.20 Lines To Gubenor Hayes. w.m. No composers or tune indicated. In: *Illustrated Campaign Song And Joke*, page 29. Published by The American News Company, New York, NY. [4¾" × 7½"]. 1876. Y/bk litho of Samuel J. Tilden, geometric design border. 50pp. [?]. Page 5: Title—*The Illustrated Campaign Tilden Song And Joke Book*. [Crew/SJT-8].

367A.21 Marching Along. w. "By Quartermaster General Schley, of the Baltimore Boys in Blue." m. "Tune—*John Brown's Body Lies Mouldering In The Grave*." B/w litho of a drummer. Drum inscribed—Hayes and Wheeler Drum Corp." "Hayes & Wheeler, Our Leaders Gallant and True." In: *Hayes And Wheeler Song Book Of The Baltimore Boys In Blue*, page 7. e. Quartermaster General, Wm. Louis Schley. Published by Maydwell & Thompson, No. 20 Second Street, Baltimore, MD. 1876. [5⅝" × 9"]. Y/bk litho of Hayes and Wheeler, geometric design border. "Hold The Fort." 20pp. [Crew/RBH-77].

367A.22 The New Head And The Old Tail. w.m. No composer or tune indicated. In: *Blaine And Logan Campaign Songster*, page 24. Published by American News Company, New York, NY. 1884. 36pp. [M-249]. [Crew/JGB-84].

367A.23 A New Yankee Doodle. w. No composer indicated. m. Air—*Yankee Doodle*. In: *Tilden And Hendricks' Reform Songs (For The Centennial Campaign of 1876)*, page 36. Published by The National Democratic Committee, Box 3637, New York, NY. 1876. [3⅞" × 5 15/16"]. Gn/bk litho of Samuel J. Tilden and Thomas A. Hendricks, geometric design border. 40pp. [M-203]. [Crew/SJT-21].

367A.24 Noble, Honest Men. w. Dan Yell. m. "Tune—*Bonnie Blue Flag*." In: *Cleveland & Hendricks Songster*, page 43. Copyright 1884 by E.Y. Landis. R/w/bl/gn/br drawing of Grover Cleveland, Thomas Hendricks, George "Washington," Thomas "Jefferson," Andrew "Jackson," ribbons, geometric designs. 64pp. [M-230]. [Crew/GC-46].

367A.25 [Now The Country Sees The Signal] (Campaign Song). w. No composer indicated. m. "Air—*Hold The Fort*." In: *Illustrated Campaign Song And Joke*, page 17. Published by The American News Company, New York, NY. [4¾" × 7½"]. 1876. Y/bk litho of Samuel J. Tilden, geometric design border. 50pp. [?]. Page 5: Title—*The Illustrated Campaign Tilden Song And Joke Book*. [Crew/SJT-8].

367A.26 The Old White Hat. w. No composer indicated. m. "Air—*When This Old Hat Was New*." In: *National Republican Grant And Wilson Campaign Song-Book*, page 42. From the *Chattanooga Herald*. Published by The Union Republican Congressional Committee, Washington, DC. 1872. [3 13/16" × 8 9/16"]. Be/bk litho of Ulysses S. Grant. "We'll Sing a Song for U.S. Grant." 100pp. [M-182]. [Crew/USG-110].

367A.27 Onward Now For Tilden. w. No composer indicated. m. "Air—*Hold The Fort*." In: *Tilden And Hendricks' Reform Songs (For The Centennial Campaign of 1876)*, page 2. Published by The National Democratic Committee, Box 3637, New York, NY. 1876. [3⅞" × 5 15/16"]. Gn/bk litho of Samuel J. Tilden and Thomas A. Hendricks, geometric design border. 40pp. [M-203]. [Crew/SJT-21].

367A.28 The Psalm Of Sammy Tilden. w. No composer indicated. m. "Air—*Auld Lang Syne*." In: *Hayes & Wheeler Campaign Song Book (For the Centennial Year)*, page 9. Published by the American News Company, Nos. 117, 119, 121, 123 Nassau Street, New York, NY. 1876. [3⅞" × 6 1/16"]. Y/bk litho of Rutherford B. Hayes and William A. Wheeler, liberty cap, geometric designs. 74pp. [M-193]. [Crew/RBH-11].

367A.29 Reform. w.m. No composer or tune indicated. In: *Illustrated Campaign Song And Joke*, page 20. Published by The American News Company, New York, NY. [4¾" × 7½"]. 1876. Y/bk litho of Samuel J. Tilden, geometric design border. 50pp. [?]. Page 5: Title—*The Illustrated Campaign Tilden Song And Joke Book*. [Crew/SJT-8].

367A.30 Reform Not Running With Tilden. w. No composer indicated. m. "Air—*Fine Old English Gentleman*." In: *Hayes & Wheeler Campaign Song Book (For the Centennial Year)*, page 63. Published by the American News Company, Nos. 117, 119, 121, 123 Nassau Street, New York, NY. 1876. [3⅞" × 6 1/16"]. Y/bk litho of Rutherford B. Hayes and William A. Wheeler, liberty cap, geometric designs. 74pp. [M-193]. [Crew/RBH-11].

367A.31 Requiescat. w. Mack. m. "This obstreperous Campaign Duett utterly refuses to be harmonized." In: *Hayes & Wheeler Song Book*, page 48. Published by The Union Republican Congressional Committee, Washington, DC. 1876. [5¾" × 9¼"]. Br/bk litho of Rutherford B. Hayes and William A. Wheeler, shield, geometric design border. "I'll be on hand again shortly." [V-1: "Series I" under title on cover] [V-2: Series not indicated on cover]. 52pp. Page 2: Contents. Page 52: State-by-state electoral vote totals for 1876. [M-196, 197]. [Crew/RBH-20].

367A.32 Song Of Victory. w. "By Demo." m. "Tune—*Hold The Fort.*" In: *Cleveland & Hendricks Songster*, page 28. Copyright 1884 by E.Y. Landis. R/w/bl/gn/br drawing of Grover Cleveland, Thomas Hendricks, George "Washington," Thomas "Jefferson," Andrew "Jackson," ribbons, geometric designs. 64pp. [M-230]. [Crew/GC-46].

367A.33 The Soreheads On Our Block. w. George Cooper. m. Dave Braham. "Air—*Babies On Our Block.*" In: *Garfield & Arthur Campaign Songster*, page 6. Published by New York Publishing Company, No. 32 Beekman Street, New York, NY. [1880]. [4" × 6⅜"]. Hand colored litho of James A. Garfield. 68pp. Page 68: Hand colored litho of Chester Arthur. [Crew/JAG-27].

367A.34 Sound The Alarm! w.m. H.E. Gordon, "of Norristown, Pa." In: *Hayes & Wheeler Song Book*, page 45. Published by The Union Republican Congressional Committee, Washington, DC. 1876. [5¾" × 9¼"]. Br/bk litho of Rutherford B. Hayes and William A. Wheeler, shield, geometric design border. "I'll be on hand again shortly." [V-1: "Series I" under title on cover] [V-2: Series not indicated on cover]. 52pp. Page 2: Contents. Page 52: State-by-state electoral vote totals for 1876. [M-196, 197]. [Crew/RBH-20].

367A.35 The Tail Of The Democratic Ticket. w. No composer indicated. m. "Air—*Home, Sweet Home.*" In: *Beulah's Blaine And Logan Original Campaign Song Book 1884*, page 9. Printed and Published by Birnie Paper Company, Springfield, MA. 1884. [4" × 5¾"]. Gy/bk litho of James G. Blaine and John A. Logan, eagle, flags, shield, line border. 36pp. [M-232]. [Crew/JGB-41].

367A.36 Three Cheers To Hayes And Wheeler. w. No composer indicated. m. "Air—*Wait For The Wagon.*" In: *Hayes & Wheeler Campaign Song Book (For the Centennial Year)*, page 53. Published by the American News Company, Nos. 117, 119, 121, 123 Nassau Street, New York, NY. 1876. [3⅞" × 6¹⁄₁₆"]. Y/bk litho of Rutherford B. Hayes and William A. Wheeler, liberty cap, geometric designs. 74pp. Pages 2, 4, 73 and 74: Blank. Page 3: "Containing Over Sixty Original Songs Adapted to Popular Melodies." [M-193]. [Crew/RBH-11].

367A.37 Tilden And Hendricks. w. William A. Clark. m. No tune indicated. "Good tune for crow-eating party—Spittoon." In: *Illustrated Campaign Song And Joke*, page 12. Published by The American News Company, New York, NY. [4¾" × 7½"]. 1876. Y/bk litho of Samuel J. Tilden, geometric design border. 50pp. [?]. Page 5: Title—*The Illustrated Campaign Tilden Song And Joke Book.* [Crew/SJT-8].

367A.38 Tilden And Reform. w.m. Will S. Hayes. "John L. Peters, music publisher, No. 843 Broadway, New York, is publishing 100,000 copies of this new campaign song... This song is destine to become very popular, and will be sung all over this broad land of ours during the present campaign." In: *Tilden And Hendricks' Reform Songs (For The Centennial Campaign of 1876)*, page 9. Published by The National Democratic Committee, Box 3637, New York, NY. 1876. [3⅞" × 5¹⁵⁄₁₆"]. Gn/bk litho of Samuel J. Tilden and Thomas A. Hendricks, geometric design border. 40pp. [M-203]. [Crew/SJT-21].

367A.39 Tilden The Pride Of The Nation. w. No composer indicated. m. "Air—*Columbia, The Gem Of The Ocean.*" In: *Illustrated Campaign Song And Joke*, page 38. Published by The American News Company, New York, NY. [4¾" × 7½"]. 1876. Y/bk litho of Samuel J. Tilden, geometric design border. 50pp. [?]. Page 5: Title—*The Illustrated Campaign Tilden Song And Joke Book.* [Crew/SJT-8].

367A.40 To My Friends I Must Be Faithful (Tilden's Wail). w. No composer indicated. m. "Air—*Old Dog Tray.*" In: *Hayes & Wheeler Campaign Song Book (For the Centennial Year)*, page 52. Published by the American News Company, Nos. 117, 119, 121, 123 Nassau Street, New York, NY. 1876. [3⅞" × 6¹⁄₁₆"]. Y/bk litho of Rutherford B. Hayes and William A. Wheeler, liberty cap, geometric designs. 74pp. [M-193]. [Crew/RBH-11].

367A.41 Voting For Cleveland. w. No composer indicated. m. "Tune—*Marching Through Georgia.*" In: *Cleveland & Hendricks Songster*, page 30. Copyright 1884 by E.Y. Landis. R/w/bl/gn/br drawing of Grover Cleveland, Thomas Hendricks, George "Washington," Thomas "Jefferson," Andrew "Jackson," ribbons, geometric designs. 64pp. [M-230]. [Crew/GC-46].

367A.42 Wait. w. H.E. Gordon. m. "Air—*Wait Till The Clouds Roll By.*" In: *Blaine And Logan Campaign Song-Book*, page 42. e. Prof. F. Widdows. Published by The Republican National Committee, New York, NY. 1884. [4⅜" × 5¹⁵⁄₁₆"]. [V-1: Bk/y] [V-2: Pk/bk] litho of James G. Blaine and John A. Logan. "From the School—House to the Cabinet, From the Cabin to the Senate." 52pp. [M-251]. [Crew/JGB-32].

367A.43 We'll Fight The Traitors To The Death. w. Mrs. A.B.G. m. "Adapted to a Scotch melody." In: *Hayes & Wheeler Song Book*, page 24. Published by The Union Republican Congressional Committee, Washington, DC. 1876. [5¾" × 9¼"]. Br/bk litho of Rutherford B. Hayes and William A. Wheeler, shield, geometric design border. "I'll be on hand again shortly." [V-1: "Series I" under title on cover] [V-2: Series not indicated on cover]. 52pp. [M-196, 197]. [Crew/RBH-20].

367A.44 We'll Put Him In His Little Bed. w. No composer indicated. m. "Air—*Put Me In My Little Bed.*" In: *Hayes & Wheeler Campaign Song Book (For the Centennial Year)*, page 55. Published by the American News Company, Nos. 117, 119, 121, 123 Nassau Street, New York, NY. 1876. [3⅞" × 6¹⁄₁₆"]. Y/bk litho of Rutherford B. Hayes and William A. Wheeler, liberty cap, geometric designs. 74pp. [M-193]. [Crew/RBH-11].

367A.45 We're Going To Haze 'Em. w. No composer indicated. m. "Air—*The Cmpbells Are Coming.*" In: *Hayes & Wheeler Campaign Song Book (For The Centennial Year)*, page 62. Published by the American News Company, Nos. 117, 119, 121, 123 Nassau Street, New York, NY. 1876. [3⅞" × 6⁵⁄₁₆"]. Y/bk litho of Rutherford B. Hayes and William A. Wheeler, liberty cap, geometric designs. 74pp. [M-193]. [Crew/RBH-11].

367A.46 What's The Cause? w. No composer indicated. m. "Air—*Tippecanoe And Tyler, Too.*" In: *Illustrated Campaign Song And Joke*, page 44. Published by The American News Company, New York, NY. [4¾" × 7½"]. 1876. Y/bk litho of Samuel J. Tilden, geometric design border. 50pp. [?]. Page 5: Title—*The Illustrated Campaign Tilden Song And Joke Book*. [Crew/SJT-8].

367A.47 When Election Day Is Over. w. "By Demo." m. "Tune—*When This Cruel War Is Over.*" In: *Cleveland & Hendricks Songster*, page 49. Copyright 1884 by E.Y. Landis. R/w/bl/gn/br drawing of Grover Cleveland, Thomas Hendricks, George "Washington," Thomas "Jefferson," Andrew "Jackson," ribbons, geometric designs. 64pp. [M-230]. [Crew/GC-46].

367A.48 Where We'll Send Him. w. No composer indicated. m. "Air—*Up In A Balloon.*" In: *Hayes & Wheeler Campaign Song Book (For The Centennial Year)*, page 58. Published by the American News Company, Nos. 117, 119, 121, 123 Nassau Street, New York, NY. 1876. [3⅞" × 6⁵⁄₁₆"]. Y/bk litho of Rutherford B. Hayes and William A. Wheeler, liberty cap, geometric designs. 74pp. [M-193]. [Crew/RBH-11].

367A.49 Who'll Not Vote For Cleveland Now? w. "By Demo." m. "Tune—*Who Will Care For Mother Now?*" In: *Cleveland & Hendricks Songster*, page 18. Copyright 1884 by E.Y. Landis. R/w/bl/gn/br drawing of Grover Cleveland, Thomas Hendricks, George "Washington," Thomas "Jefferson," Andrew "Jackson," ribbons, geometric designs. 64pp. [M-230]. [Crew/GC-46].

367A.50 Witches' Scene From MacGreeley (Which is Seen to be a Fact). w.m. No composer or tune indicated. From the "*New York Standard.*" In: *National Republican Grant And Wilson Campaign Song-Book*, page 34. From the *New York Standard*. Published by The Union Republican Congressional Committee, Washington, DC. 1872. [3¹³⁄₁₆" × 8⁵⁄₁₆"]. Be/bk litho of Ulysses S. Grant. "We'll Sing a Song for U.S. Grant." 100pp. [M-182]. [Crew/USG-110].

• **AmPM-368 HOFFMAN**, Balthasar (Candidate for Joint State Representative, Lake and Porter Counties, 1934)

368.1 Roosevelt We Hand The Flag To You! w. William Foster. m. Edna May Foster. Published by Calumet Music Publishers, Gary, IN. 1934. R/w/b eagle, trees, geometric designs. Bl/w photo of Franklin D. Roosevelt. 6pp. Page 2: Advertisement for Carroll Holly for Sheriff. Page 6: Advertisements for various office seekers including "Balthasar Hoffman, Liberal Democratic Candidate for Joint Representative, Lake and Porter Counties, Election, Nov. 6, 1934. Re-Elect." B/w photo of Balthasar Hoffman.

• **AmPM-369 HOLLOWAY**, David Pierson (Editor, *Richmond Palladium*, 1832; State House, 1843 & 1844; State Senate, 1844–1850; Examiner of Land Offices, 1849; U.S. House, 1855–1857)

369.1 The Dirge Of The Doughface. w. No composer indicated. m. "Air—*Ben Bolt.*" "A song to be learned before November next, as it will then be extensively needed." In: *The Republican Campaign Songster, A Collection Of Lyrics, Original And Selected, Specifically Prepared For The Friends Of Freedom In The Campaign Of Fifty-Six*, page 16. Published by Miller, Orton & Mulligan, No. 25 Park Row, New York, NY. 1856. [3¹³⁄₁₆" × 6"]. Be/bk litho of "Colonel John C. Fremont" facing to viewer's left, black line border. 112pp. [M-097]. [Crew/JCF-24].

• **AmPM-370 HOLLY**, Carroll (Sheriff, Porter County, 1934)

370.1 Roosevelt We Hand The Flag To You! w. William Foster. m. Edna May Foster. Published by Calumet Music Publishers, Gary, IN. 1934. R/w/b eagle, trees, geometric designs. Bl/w photo of Franklin D. Roosevelt. 6pp. Page 2: Advertisement and song for M. Clifford Townsend, Democratic Candidate for Governor of Indiana. Page 6: Advertisement for Carroll Holly for Sheriff. [Crew/GC-84].

• **AmPM-371 HOLMAN**, William Steele (Judge, Franklin County, 1843–1846 & 1852–1856; Prosecuting Attorney, Franklin County, 1847–1849; State House, 1851–1852; U.S. House, 1859–1865, 1867–1877, 1881–1895 & 1897)

371.1 Daddy Holman's Cheese-Knife (Solo and Chorus for Male Voices). w.m. No composer or tune indicated. In: *True Blue Republican Campaign Songs For 1892*, page 8. Published by [V-1: Oliver Ditson Company, Boston, MA] [V-2: The S. Brainard's Son's Company, Chicago, IL]. 1892. [5⅜" × 7¼"]. Bl/bk litho of Benjamin F. Harrison, eagle, flag, geometric designs. 36pp. [M-307]. [Crew/BFH-47].

371.2 Harrison Will Hold The Job. w. E.J. Seymour. m. "Air—*When McGinnis Gets A Job.*" In: *Harrison And Reid Campaign Song Book*, page 13. w. E.J. Seymour. m. Popular Airs. [1892]. [3⅞" × 5⅛"]. Bl/gn non-pictorial, stars, geometric designs. 36pp. [M-316]. [Crew/BFH-35].

371.3 Per Die-'Em Bill. w. H.C. Burns, "Pittsburgh, Pa." m. No tune indicated. In: *Acme Songs, Republican Glee Book, And Cartridge Box Of Truth* (Campaign of 1888), page 60. Published by The Acme Publishing Bureau, J.C.O. Redington, General Manager, No. 35 University Avenue, Syracuse, NY. Copyright 1888 by J.C.O. Redington. [5⅛" × 6¹³⁄₁₆"]. Gy/bk lithos of eagle, shield, tent, flag, soldiers, Uncle Sam. "With Music and 20 Illustrations by Nast and others." "Price 10 cents." "Only Book Prepared by Soldiers, The Only Illustrated Campaign Glee Book Ever Printed." "With Music and 20 Illustrations." "Illustrated by Nast and Others." "A Filled Pocket Haversack of Loyalty, Glory, Song, Fun and Facts for Every Individual, Whether Singer or Not." 68pp. [M-255]. [Crew/BFH-25].

• **AmPM-372 HOTTEL**, Milton B. (Candidate for Appellate Court, 1918)

372.1 Till Over The Top We Go. w.m. Roy L. Burtch "(Composer of *When The Bugle Calls*, *Peace On Earth And Liberty*, *Think Of Me*, *Tell Me*, *The Organ And The Choir*, *Bye Bye Baby Dear*)." Published by The Halcyon Publishing Company, Indianapolis, IN. 1918. Drawing of soldier—"U.S. Marine," machine gun. "The Song Our Allies, Lodges and Glee Clubs are Singing." "State Campaign Song—Democratic State Committee, Denison Hotel, Indianapolis, Ind." "Extra copies of this March Song mailed free on request." 4pp. Page 4: Photos of Woodrow Wilson and 13 State Democratic candidates. "The Party with a Purpose." Text on 11 reasons to vote Democratic. [Crew/WW-121].

• **AmPM-373 HOVEY**, Alvin Peterson (Circuit Judge 1851-1854; State Supreme Court, 1854; U.S. District Attorney, 1856; U.S. Minister to Peru, 1865; U.S. House, 1887-1889, Governor, 1889-1891)

373.1 Washington's Birthday Celebration [Program and Song Booklet]. Published by United Soldier's and Sailors' Organizations of Indianapolis, Indianapolis, IN. 1891. [5¼" x 6"]. Non-pictorial geometric design border. List of officers of the association including Gov. Alvin P. Hovey, President. "Tromlinson Hall, Sunday Afternoon, Feb. 22, 1891." "Vose Piano and Programmes kindly furnished by Emil Wulschner, 42 & 44 N. Pennsylvania St., op. Post office." 4pp. Page 2: Programme. Page 3: Songs *America* and *The Star Spangled Banner*. Page 4: Advertising. [Crew/GW-700].

• **AmPM-374 HUCKER**, Carlton C. (Candidate for Surveyor, Porter County, 1934)

374.1 Roosevelt We Hand The Flag To You! w. William Foster. m. Edna May Foster. Published by Calumet Music Publishers, Gary, IN. 1934. R/w/b eagle, trees, geometric designs. Bl/w photo of Franklin D. Roosevelt. 6pp. Page 2: Advertisement for Carroll Holly for Sheriff. Page 6: Advertisements for various office seekers including "Carlton C. Hucker, Democratic Candidate for Surveyor, Porter County, Election, Tuesday, November 4, 1934. Re-Elect. I will appreciate your vote and support."

• **AmPM-375 HUNT**, Union B. (Indiana Secretary of State, 1899-1903)

375.1 Our Candidates. w. No composer indicated. m. "Tune—*Boom De-Ay*." In: *The Rough Rider (Republican Campaign Song Book)*, page 6. c. J. Burgess Brown. Published by J. Burgess Brown, Indianapolis, IN. 1900. [6" x 9"]. Br/bk non-pictorial. "ROUGH ON DemocRATS." 28pp. Page 3: B/w litho of William McKinley. Page 28: "Republican National Ticket—1900. [Crew/WM-330].

• **AmPM-376 JACKSON**, Edward (Prosecuting Attorney, Henry County, 1900-1904; Circuit Judge, 1907-1912; Indiana Secretary of State, 1916-1917 & 1919?-1925; Governor, 1925-1929)

376.1 Rally The Standard Of "Abe" Lincoln. w. Mrs. S.R. Artma "(Composer of *Guess, One Who Cares For Me, The Organ And The Choir*)." m. Roy L. Burtch. Published by Halcyon Publishing Company, No. 307 East North Street, Indianapolis, IN. 1924. Br/w photos of "Calvin Coolidge," "Charles G. Dawes," "Abraham Lincoln" and "Ed Jackson" [Republican nominee for Governor of Indiana], geometric design border. "American Campaign March Song." 4pp. + Insert letter. Page 4: Biographies of candidates and other Republicans from Indiana, including "Ed Jackson, F. Harold Van Orman, Frederick E. Schort- meier, Lewis S. Bohman, Ben H. Urbahns, Arthur L. Gillam, F.M. Thompson, Willard R. Gimmill, Judge Willoughby, E.A. Dausman, Noble Sherwood, Mrs. Edward F. White." Insert—Page 1: Letter from composer to Republican State Committee. Page 2: Advertising.

• **AmPM-377 JENNER**, William Ezra (State Senate, 1934-1942, U.S. Senate, 1944-1945 & 1947-1959)

377.1 [Hurrah For Kennedy Trala]. w. No composer indicated. m. *Solomon Levi*. In: *Untitled John F. Kennedy Song Sheet*, page 1. [1952]. Non-pictorial. 2pp.

• **AmPM-378 JENNINGS**, Jonathan (Governor, 1816-1822)

378.1 Hoosier State (You're Just One Century Old) (Centennial Marching Song). w. Earl E. Crooke. m. Eugene E. Noel. Copyright 1916 by Warner C. Williams, Indianapolis, Ind. R/w/b litho of crossed American flags, state seal, Governor Jonathan Jennings—"Governor 1816." Bl/w photo of Samuel Ralston—"Governor 1916." "Indiana Centennial Souvenir 1816-1916, Containing the Song *Hoosier State*. 6pp. Page 2: List of Committee members. Page 5: Popular songs for singing. Page 6: Events program for Centennial.

378.2 Indianapolis (A Booster Song For The Capitol Of Indiana). w.m. Stella Hall Millikan. Published by S.H. Millikan, 632 Occidental Building, Indianapolis, IN. 1916. Bl/w photos of Jonathan Jennings, "Governor, 1816" and Samuel Ralston, "Governor, 1916." R/w/b crossed American flags, state map of Indiana as background. "Dedicated to Indianapolis, No Mean City." 6pp. Page 2: At top of music—"Dedicated to Indianapolis, No Mean City and written in Honor of the Hundredth Anniversary of the admission of the Hoosier State to the U.S.A." Page 6: Blank.

• **AmPM-379 JONES**, Frank L. (Superintendent of Public Instruction, 1899)

379.1 Our Candidates. w. No composer indicated. m. "Tune—*Boom De-Ay*." In: *The Rough Rider (Republican Campaign Song Book)*, page 6. c. J. Burgess Brown. Published by J. Burgess Brown, Indianapolis, IN. 1900. [6" x 9"]. Br/bk non-pictorial. "ROUGH ON DemocRATS." 28pp. Page 3: B/w litho of William McKinley. Page 28: "Republican National Ticket—1900. [Crew/WM-330].

• **AmPM-380 JONES**, William M. (Candidate for State Auditor, 1919)

380.1 Till Over The Top We Go. w.m. Roy L. Burtch "(Composer of *When The Bugle Calls, Peace On Earth And Liberty, Think Of Me, Tell Me, The Organ And The Choir, Bye Bye Baby Dear*)." Published by The Halcyon Publishing Company, Indianapolis, IN. 1918. Drawing of soldier—"U.S. Marine," machine gun. "The Song Our Allies, Lodges and Glee Clubs are Singing." "State Campaign Song—Democratic State Committee, Denison Hotel, Indianapolis, Ind." "Extra copies of this March Song mailed free on request." 4pp. Page 4: Photos of Woodrow Wilson and 13 State Democratic candidates. "The Party with a Purpose." Text on 11 reasons to vote Democratic. [Crew/WW-121].

• **AmPM-381 KERN**, John Worth (State Senate, 1893-1897; Candidate for Governor, 1900, 1904; Democratic Candidate for Vice President, 1908; U.S. Senate, 1911–1917) [ALSO SEE: DOC/PSM-WJB]

381.1 Banks on The Wabash. w. No composer indicated. m. "Music — *On The Banks Of The Wabash.*" In: *Bryan Electors (Pithy Pointers For The Campaign Of 1908)* [Song Book], page 3. Published by Holt County Democrat, O'Neill, NB. 1908. [6⁵⁄₁₆" × 8⅛"]. Gn/bk/r drawing of "William Jennings Bryan — Our Next President." 16pp. [Crew/WJB-100].

381.2 Bryan's Mule. w. No composer indicated. m. "Tune — *Old Thompson's Mule.*" In: *Up-To-Date Republican Campaign Songs,* page 2. Published by J. Burgess Brown "(Leader of the Celebrated Bald-Headed Glee Club), [Indianapolis, IN]." 1908. [8" × 11"]. B/w photos of William H. Taft and John Sherman. B/w drawing of American Flag — "We'll rally 'round the flag, boys." Verse. "Written and compiled for the State Central Committee." [Crew/WHT-66].

381.3 The Gullible Guy. w. E.P. McCaslin. m. No tune indicated. In: *Republican Campaign Songs,* page 3. e. P. McCaslin, Indianapolis. Published by E.S. McCaslin, Indianapolis, 5901 Dewey Avenue, Indianapolis, IN. 1914. [6¼" × 8½"]. B/w litho of an eagle, shield. "Everyone a political address set to music of fitted to popular tunes." 8pp. + 4pp insert.

381.4 Three Crows. w. No composer indicated. m. "Tune — *Billy McGee McGaw.*" In: *Up-To-Date Republican Campaign Songs,* page 5. Published by J. Burgess Brown "(Leader of the Celebrated Bald-Headed Glee Club), [Indianapolis, IN]." 1908. [8" × 11"]. B/w photos of William H. Taft and John Sherman. B/w drawing of American Flag — "We'll rally 'round the flag, boys." Verse. "Written and compiled for the State Central Committee." [Crew/WHT-66].

381.5 The Winning Ticket. w. No composer indicated. m. "Air — *When Johnny Comes Marching Home.*" In: *Democratic Song Book For The Campaign Of 1888,* page 3. c. John R. East. Published by John R. East, Bloomington, IN. 1888. [4¼" × 5¹³⁄₁₆"]. Bl/bl litho of Grover Cleveland and Allen Thurman. "Price 10 cents, postage prepaid, Liberal Discounts to Dealers." 20pp. [Crew/GC-140].

• **AmPM-382 KORBLY,** Charles Alexander (U.S. House, 1909–1915; Receiver General of Insolvent National Banks, Washington, 1915–1917)

382.1 Republican Train. w. No composer indicated. m. "Tune — *The Gospel Train Am Coming.*" In: *Up-To-Date Republican Campaign Songs,* page 3. Published by J. Burgess Brown "(Leader of the Celebrated Bald-Headed Glee Club), [Indianapolis, IN.]." 1908. [8" × 11"]. B/w photos of William H. Taft and John Sherman. B/w drawing of American Flag — "We'll rally 'round the flag, boys." Verse. "Written and compiled for the State Central Committee." [Crew/WHT-66].

• **AmPM-383 LANDERS,** Franklin (State Senate, 1860; U.S. House, 1875–1877)

383.1 Porter's Invitation To The Boys (As Bennie Beat Blue Jeans). w. No composer indicated. m. "Tune — *Walker In.*" In: *Music For The Campaign (A Collection Of Original And Selected Songs, Adapted to Familiar Tunes For Use at Campaign Meetings, For 1880),* page 7. Published by *The Indianapolis Sentinel* as a newspaper supplement, Indianapolis, IN. 1880. [7¾" × 10⅝"]. B/w lithos of Winfield Scott Hancock and William H. English. "This Collection of fifty one first-class Campaign Songs will be sent to any address, postage paid as follows: 25 for 30 cts.; 50 for 60 cts.; 100 for $1.00. Address Sentinel Company, Indianapolis, Ind." 8pp. Foldover. [Crew/WSH-11].

• **AmPM-384 LANDIS,** Kenesaw Mountain (Judge, District of Northern Illinois, 1905–1922)

384.1 The National Game. m. John Philip Sousa. Published by Sam Fox, Inc., Cleveland, OH. 1925. "Dedicated to Judge Kennesaw Mountain Landis."

384.2 Native Hoosier. w. Grace Patterson Lopez-Dias. m. Mae Doelling Schmidt. Published by Clayton F. Summy Company, Chicago, IL. 1940. R/w/b drawing of the State of Indiana with a list of famous Hoosiers — "James Whitcomb Riley, Thomas Marshall, Gene Stratton Porter, Wendell L. Willkie, John T. McCutcheon, George Ade, General Lew Wallace, Booth Tarkington, Meredith Nicholson, Claude Wickard, William Lowe Bryan, Paul McNutt, Kenesaw Mountain Landis, ad-infinitum." 6pp. Page 2: Blank. Page 6: Advertising. [Crew/WLW-61].

384.3 Standard Oil (Oils Well That Ends Well, A Gusher). w. F.L. Hill. m. A.F. Scheu "(Writer of *Dreaming, Jack Frost, When, Sleepy Sidney, Smiling Sadie,* &c.)." Published by Hill Music Publishing Co., Mercantile Building, Cincinnati, OH. 1907. R/w/bk drawing of Uncle Sam, Oil can driving a broken auto labeled "J.D.R.," large oil slick. "Dedicated to Judge Kenesaw Mountain Landis." 6pp. Page 6: Blank.

LANE, Joseph (State House, Indiana, 1822; State Senate, Indiana, 1844–1846; Territorial Governor of Oregon, 1849–1850; Territorial Delegate to Congress, Oregon, 1851–1859; U.S. Senate 1859–1861; Candidate for Vice President, 1860) [See: Oregon] [ALSO SEE: DOC/PSM-JCB]

• **AmPM-385 LEASE,** Royal L. (Candidate for Prosecuting Attorney, Porter County, 1934)

385.1 Roosevelt We Hand The Flag To You! w. William Foster. m. Edna May Foster. Published by Calumet Music Publishers, Gary, IN. 1934. R/w/b eagle, trees, geometric designs. Bl/w photo of Franklin D. Roosevelt. 6pp. Page 2: Advertisement for Carroll Holly for Sheriff. Page 6: Advertisements for various office seekers including "Royal L. Lease, Democratic Candidate for Prosecuting Attorney, Porter County, A Lawyer interested in honest and efficient management of public office. Your vote and friendly influence will be appreciated."

• **AmPM-386 LESLIE,** Harry Guyer (County Treasurer, Tippecanoe County, 1912–1916; State House, 1923–1927; Governor, 1929–1933)

386.1 On The Banks Of The Wabash, Far Away. w.m. Paul Dresser. In: *Indiana Day* [Booklet], page 4. Printed by the State Board of Public Printing, State House, Indianapolis, IN. [ca. 1930]. 8pp. Non-pictorial. "A birthday anniversary is always an event of importance in the life of any one. It should be a much more important event in the life of a state ... It is entirely proper that we should stop to emphasize the place in our national life that Indiana occupies — Harry G. Leslie, Governor." Pages 2 and 3: Narratives on Indiana. Page 4: Song — *On The Banks Of The Wabash, Far Away.* Page 7: Poems on Indiana. Page 8:

Song: *Hymn To Indiana*. w. Wm. Langdon. m. Charles D. Campbell.

• **AmPM-387 LUGAR**, Richard Green (Board of School Commissioners, Indianapolis, 1964–1967; Mayor, Indianapolis, 1968–1975; U.S. Senate 1977–Present)

387.1 Nine Little Leaders. w. William K. Tong. m. "Sung to the tune of *Nine Little Reindeers* by Gene Autry." In: *The Sting The Right Wing Song Book* at <http://www.geocities.com/wmktong/bootnewt/9litlead.htm>.

• **AmPM-387A MARSHALL**, Thomas Riley (Governor, 1909–1913; Vice President, 1913–1921) [ALSO SEE: DOC/PSM-WW]

387A.1 Native Hoosier. w. Grace Patterson Lopez-Dias. m. Mae Doelling Schmidt. Published by Clayton F. Summy Company, Chicago, IL. 1940. R/w/b drawing of the State of Indiana with a list of famous Hoosiers—"James Whitcomb Riley, Thomas Marshall, Gene Stratton Porter, Wendell L. Willkie, John T. McCutcheon, George Ade, General Lew Wallace, Booth Tarkington, Meredith Nicholson, Claude Wickard, William Lowe Bryan, Paul McNutt, Kenesaw Mountain Landis, ad-infinitum." 6pp. Page 2: Blank. Page 6: Advertising. [Crew/WLW-61].

387A.2 We'll Win With Watson. w. No composer indicated. m. "Tune—*Every Day Will Be Sunday Bye And Bye*." In: *Up-To-Date Republican Campaign Songs*, page 3. Published by J. Burgess Brown (Leader of the Celebrated Bald-Headed Glee Club), [Indianapolis, IN.]. 1908. [8" × 11"]. B/w photos of William H. Taft and John Sherman. B/w drawing of American Flag—"We'll rally 'round the flag, boys." Verse. "Written and compiled for the State Central Committee." [Crew/WHT-66].

• **AmPM-388 MATSON**, Courtland Cushing (Prosecuting Attorney, Putnam County; Chairman of the Democratic State Central Committee, 1878; U.S. House, 1881–1889; Candidate for Governor, 1888; Board of Tax Commissioners, Greencastle, 1909–1913)

388.1 Ben And Levi. w. No composer indicated. m. "Air—*Solomon And Levi*." In: *Democratic Song Book For The Campaign Of 1888*, page 8. c. John R. East. Published by John R. East, Bloomington, IN. 1888. [4¼" × 5¹³⁄₁₆"]. Bl/bl litho of Grover Cleveland and Allen Thurman. "Price 10 cents, postage prepaid, Liberal Discounts to Dealers." 20pp. [Crew/GC-140].

388.2 The Winning Ticket. w. No composer indicated. m. "Air—*When Johnny Comes Marching Home*." In: *Democratic Song Book For The Campaign Of 1888*, page 3. c. John R. East. Published by John R. East, Bloomington, IN. 1888. [4¼" × 5¹³⁄₁₆"]. Bl/bl litho of Grover Cleveland and Allen Thurman. "Price 10 cents, postage prepaid, Liberal Discounts to Dealers." 20pp. [Crew/GC-140].

• **AmPM-389 MATTHEWS**, Claude (State House, 1876; Indiana Secretary of State, 1891–1893; Governor, 1893–1897)

389.1 An Auspicious Occasion. w. No composer indicated. m. "Tune—*Odd Fellows' Hall*." In: *Republican Campaign Parodies And Songs* [Songster], page 13. Published by Betts and Burnett, South Butler, Wayne County, NY. 1896. [7¾" × 5½"]. Be/bk non-pictorial. "McKinley and Hobart." "1896." 28pp. [M-340]. [Crew/WM-67].

389.2 Bryan Walked Off With The Coveted Prize. w. No composer indicated. m. "Tune—*The Band Played On*." In: *Republican Campaign Parodies And Songs* [Songster], page 5. Published by Betts and Burnett, South Butler, Wayne County, NY. 1896. [7¾" × 5½"]. Be/bk non-pictorial. "McKinley and Hobart." "1896." 28pp. [M-340]. [Crew/WM-67].

• **AmPM-390 MCCABE**, Edwin F. (Candidate for Appellate Court, 1918)

390.1 Till Over The Top We Go. w.m. Roy L. Burtch "(Composer of *When The Bugle Calls, Peace On Earth And Liberty, Think Of Me, Tell Me, The Organ And The Choir, Bye Bye Baby Dear*)." Published by The Halcyon Publishing Company, Indianapolis, IN. 1918. Drawing of soldier—"U.S. Marine," machine gun. "The Song Our Allies, Lodges and Glee Clubs are Singing." "State Campaign Song—Democratic State Committee, Denison Hotel, Indianapolis, Ind." "Extra copies of this March Song mailed free on request." 4pp. Page 4: Photos of Woodrow Wilson and 13 State Democratic candidates. "The Party with a Purpose." Text on 11 reasons to vote Democratic. [Crew/WW-121].

• **AmPM-391 MCCARTHY**, John B. (Candidate for Treasurer of State, 1918)

391.1 Till Over The Top We Go. w.m. Roy L. Burtch "(Composer of *When The Bugle Calls, Peace On Earth And Liberty, Think Of Me, Tell Me, The Organ And The Choir, Bye Bye Baby Dear*)." Published by The Halcyon Publishing Company, Indianapolis, IN. 1918. Drawing of soldier—"U.S. Marine," machine gun. "The Song Our Allies, Lodges and Glee Clubs are Singing." "State Campaign Song—Democratic State Committee, Denison Hotel, Indianapolis, Ind." "Extra copies of this March Song mailed free on request." 4pp. Page 4: Photos of Woodrow Wilson and 13 State Democratic candidates. "The Party with a Purpose." Text on 11 reasons to vote Democratic. [Crew/WW-121].

• **AmPM-392 MCCONKEY**, Glenn (Candidate for Commissioner, Porter County, 1934)

392.1 Roosevelt We Hand The Flag To You! w. William Foster. m. Edna May Foster. Published by Calumet Music Publishers, Gary, IN. 1934. R/w/b eagle, trees, geometric designs. Bl/w photo of Franklin D. Roosevelt. 6pp. Page 2: Advertisement for Carroll Holly for Sheriff. Page 6: Advertisements for various office seekers including "Glenn McConkey, Democratic Candidate for Commissioner, South District, Porter County, Election, Tuesday, November 4, 1934."

• **AmPM-393 MCCULLOCH**, Carleton B. (Candidate for Governor 1920 & 1924)

393.1 Home Rule March Song. w.m. Roy L. Burtch. Published by Democratic State Committee, Indianapolis, IN. Copyright 1920 by Halcyon Pub. Co. [5½" × 8½"]. B/w photos of Carleton McCulloch, State Capitol building. "Democratic State Campaign Song." 4pp. Page 4: Narrative—"Who is Dr. Carleton B. McCulloch?"

• **AmPM-394 MCDONALD**, Joseph Ewing (Prosecuting Attorney, Lafayette, 1843–1847; U.S. House, 1849–1851; State Attorney General, 1856–1860; Candidate for Governor, 1864; U.S. Senate, 1875–1881)

394.1 We Want A Hoosier President. w. Thomas F. Byron. m. "Air—*Sing Song, Polly, Won't You Try Me, O.*" In: *Republican Club Campaign Song Book For 1888*, page 18. a. Thomas Byron. Published by Protection Publication Company, South Central Street, Chicago, IL. 1888. [6⅛" × 8⅞"]. Be/bk litho of Benjamin F. Harrison—"For President" and Levi P. Morton—"For Vice-President," eagle, flags, geometric designs. "Thirty Rousing Songs Written to Popular Airs." 36pp. [M-257]. [Crew/BFH-20].

• **AmPM-395** MCNUTT, John C. (Candidate for Supreme Court, 1918)
395.1 Till Over The Top We Go. w.m. Roy L. Burtch "(Composer of *When The Bugle Calls, Peace On Earth And Liberty, Think Of Me, Tell Me, The Organ And The Choir, Bye Bye Baby Dear*)." Published by The Halcyon Publishing Company, Indianapolis, IN. 1918. Drawing of soldier—"U.S. Marine," machine gun. "The Song Our Allies, Lodges and Glee Clubs are Singing." "State Campaign Song—Democratic State Committee, Denison Hotel, Indianapolis, Ind." "Extra copies of this March Song mailed free on request." 4pp. Page 4: Photos of Woodrow Wilson and 13 State Democratic candidates. "The Party with a Purpose." Text on 11 reasons to vote Democratic. [Crew/WW-121].

• **AmPM-396** MCTURNAN. (Candidate for State Superintendent of Schools, 1908)
396.1 The Hoosier Boom De-Aye. w. No composer indicated. m. "Tune—*Ta-Ra-Ra-Ra Boom-De-Aye*." In: *Up-To-Date Republican Campaign Songs*, page 3. Published by J. Burgess Brown "(Leader of the Celebrated Bald-Headed Glee Club), [Indianapolis, IN.]." 1908. [8" × 11"]. B/w photos of William H. Taft and John Sherman. B/w drawing of American Flag—"We'll rally 'round the flag, boys." Verse. "Written and compiled for the State Central Committee." [Crew/WHT-66].

• **AmPM-397** MINTON, Sherman (Public Counselor, 1933–1934; U.S. Senate, 1935–1941; U.S. Circuit Court of Appeals, 1941–1949; U.S. Supreme Court, 1949–1956)
397.1 We Can Win With Roosevelt. w.m. Daniel P. O'Donnell. Published by Indiana Democratic State Central Committee, Fred Bays, State Chairman. 1940. B/w photos of "President Franklin D. Roosevelt" and "Vice-President Henry A. Wallace," Capitol building. B/w drawing of two flags. 6pp. Page 2: Campaign advertising for "Lieut. Gov. Henry Schricker" and "Senator Minton." Page 6: State Democratic ticket.

• **AmPM-398** MORAN, James J. (Candidate for State Supreme Court, 1918)
398.1 Till Over The Top We Go. w.m. Roy L. Burtch "(Composer of *When The Bugle Calls, Peace On Earth And Liberty, Think Of Me, Tell Me, The Organ And The Choir, Bye Bye Baby Dear*)." Published by The Halcyon Publishing Company, Indianapolis, IN. 1918. Drawing of soldier—"U.S. Marine," machine gun. "The Song Our Allies, Lodges and Glee Clubs are Singing." "State Campaign Song—Democratic State Committee, Denison Hotel, Indianapolis, Ind." "Extra copies of this March Song mailed free on request." 4pp. Page 4: Photos of Woodrow Wilson and 13 State Democratic candidates. "The Party with a Purpose." Text on 11 reasons to vote Democratic. [Crew/WW-121].

• **AmPM-399** MORTON, Oliver Hazard Perry Throck (Circuit Judge, 1852; Lt. Governor, 1860–1861; Governor, 1861–1867; U.S. Senate, 1867–1877)
399.1 Carry The New To 'Lysses. w. No composer indicated. m. "Air—*Carry The News To Mary.*" In: *Greeley Campaign Songster*, page 40. "Respectfully dedicated to the Greeley Clubs of the Country." Published by Halpin & McClure, Chicago, IL. 1872. [4" × 5¼₆"]. Pl/bk litho of Horace Greeley, geometric design border. "Chicago: Western News Company, Wholesale Agents." 72pp. [M-187]. [Crew/HG-21].

399.2 Cottage Of The Dear Ones Left At Home. w.m. Major John Hogarth Lozier, of his staff. Published by J.A. Butterfield, Cincinnati, OH. 1865. B/w tinted litho by Ehrgott, Forbriger & Co. of Oliver Morton. "Composed and respectfully dedicated to Governor O.P. Morton." Chorus printed on the cover. 6pp. Pages 2 and 6: Blank.

399.3 The Flag Of Our Union. w. Jno. I. Underwood. m. A. Von Schmit. Published by A.C. Peters & Bro., 94 West 4th Street, Cincinnati, OH. 1862. R/w/b litho of an American flag. "To Governor Morton." 8pp. Pages 2, 7 and 8: Blank. Page 3: At top of music—"Patriotic Song, with Chorus Ad Lib."

399.4 God Save The Country (A National Anthem). w.m. Emanuel Marquis. Published by A.C. Peters & Bro., Cincinnati, OH. 1863. Non-pictorial geometric designs. "To Gov: Morton." 6pp. Page 6: Blank.

399.5 Hayes. w. No composer indicated. m. "Air—*Life On The Ocean Wave.*" In: *Hayes & Wheeler Campaign Song Book (For The Centennial Year)*, page 37. Published by The American News Company, Nos. 117, 119, 121, 123 Nassau Street, New York, NY. 1876. [3⅞" × 6³⁄₁₆"]. Y/bk litho of Rutherford B. Hayes and William A. Wheeler, liberty cap, geometric designs. 74pp. [M-193]. [Crew/RBH-11].

399.6 Hayes, Make Way For Tilden. w. No composer indicated. m. "Air—*Tommy, Make Room For Your Auntie.*" In: *Illustrated Campaign Song And Joke*, page 36. Published by The American News Company, New York, NY. [4¾" × 7½"]. 1876. Y/bk litho of Samuel J. Tilden, geometric design border. 50pp. [?]. Page 5: Title—*The Illustrated Campaign Tilden Song And Joke Book*. [Crew/SJT-8].

399.7 The Heavenly Flag (March And Two Step). m. Sig. Giuseppe Marone. Published by Signor Guiseppe Marone, No. 521 East 12th Street, Indianapolis, IN. 1903. B/w litho of allegorical patriotic scene—"Description: Central group in heaven. The Infant Jesus waving the American Flag, sitting on His Mother's lap, the Holy Father is Crowning Her, and the angels are singing and playing about and holding the table of commandments. On the left is the emancipation of Abraham Lincoln and his cabinet, on the right are angels turning the old world to the new. The U.S. Capitol, the Navy and War Building; on the Avenue are the U.S. Military marching and the Marine Brigade with [Theodore] Roosevelt at the head, his private secretary, the Colonel of the National Park, General F. Lee, and different officers from Illinois, Senator Platt with the silk hat on, Rear Admiral Dewey near Governor Morton's Monument, and the fine monument to Christopher Columbus, showing to the Powers thee greatness of this country. In the river stand a majestic angel with the flower of everlasting peace on the left hand, on the right hand the beautiful American flag sent from heaven to be given to Uncle Sam, Miss Indiana on his right, the favorite state. To help receive the present; the young American boy is ready to defend the matchless flag. The powers of the world with their guns turning towards U.S. are looking with great surprise at the gift. The Author has composed this march to describe in music his painting. The introduction being played by trumpets in heaven, first part is the marching of the soldiers, the trio is the conversation between the angel with Uncle Sam and Miss Indiana." "The painting and music is original, ideal by the noted harpist, Sig. Guiseppe Marone, an American citizen, Indianapolis, Ind." 6pp. Pages 2 and 6: Blank. [Crew/TR-375].

399.8 *Inflation Galop!* m. W. Stuckenholz. Published by Wm. A. Pond & Company, No. 547 Broadway, New York, NY. 1874. B/w litho [horizontal format] from a cartoon by W.H. Sheldon of Ulysses S. Grant, Ben Butler, Oliver P. Morton and Matthew Hale Carpenter blowing up large balloon labeled "Inflation," "$400,000,000" and "$44,000,000 Legalized." 6pp. [Crew/USG-15].

399.9 *My Country Dear, I'd Die For Thee* (Song and Chorus). w. Will P. Wallace. m. Charles E. Ballard. Published by Horace Waters, 481 Broadway, NY. 1864. B/w tinted litho by Major & Knapp of O.P. Morton. "To O.P. Morton, Gov. of Ind." 6pp. Page 6: Blank.

399.10 *O, The Crow, The Beautiful Crow*. w. No composer indicated. m. "Air — *O, The Snow, The Beautiful Snow*." "As sung by the Blaine men, Conklingites, Morton men and other defeated Republican leaders." In: *Illustrated Campaign Song And Joke*, page 26. Published by The American News Company, New York, NY. [4¾" × 7½"]. 1876. Y/bk litho of Samuel J. Tilden, geometric design border. 50pp. [?]. Page 5: Title — *The Illustrated Campaign Tilden Song And Joke Book*. [Crew/SJT-8].

399.11 *Our Wagon*. w. No composer indicated. m. "Air — *Red, White And Blue*." In: *The Grant Songster (For The Campaign Of 1868)*, page 7. Published by Root & Cady, No. 67 Washington Street, Chicago, IL. 1868. [4¾" × 6⅜"]. O/bk litho of Ulysses S. Grant. "A Collection of Campaign Songs for 1868." 48pp. Page 48: Advertising for Grant Campaign music. [M-158, 159]. [Crew/USG-113].

399.12 *Uncle Sam's A Coming*. w. No composer indicated. m. "Air — *Babylon Is Fallen*." In: *Tilden And Hendricks' Reform Songs (For The Centennial Campaign Of 1876)*, page 19. Published by The National Democratic Committee, Box 3637, New York, NY. 1876. [3⅞" × 5¹⁵⁄₁₆"]. Gn/bk litho of Samuel J. Tilden and Thomas A. Hendricks, geometric design border. 40pp. [M-203]. [Crew/SJT-21].

• **AmPM-400 NIBLACK**, Mason Jenks (State House, 1887–1891 & 1915)

400.1 *The Winning Ticket*. w. No composer indicated. m. "Air — *When Johnny Comes Marching Home*." In: *Democratic Song Book For The Campaign Of 1888*, page 3. c. John R. East. Published by John R. East, Bloomington, IN. 1888. [4¼" × 5¹³⁄₁₆"]. Bl/bl litho of Grover Cleveland and Allen Thurman. "Price 10 cents, postage prepaid, Liberal Discounts to Dealers." 20pp. [Crew/GC-140].

• **AmPM-401 ORTH**, Godlove Stein (State Senate, 1843–1848; U.S. House, 1863–1871, 1873–1875 & 1879–1882; U.S. Ambassador, Austria-Hungary, 1875–1876)

401.1 *Tilden And Hendricks' Democratic Centennial Campaign March* (With Radical Accompaniments). m. A. Lutz. Published by St. Louis Music Publishing Company, No. 9 North 15th Street, St. Louis, MO. Copyright 1876 by R. Staples. B/w litho of political caricatures including marching rats poking fun at Republican scandals — Benjamin Butler — "Loyal Mashtub." James G. Blaine — "Maine stock jobber $60,000." John A. Logan — "Our Darling." Ulysses S. Grant — "Let Us Have (a) Peace." Rutherford B. Hayes — "The Cooped Chickens." 8pp. Page 2: Blank. Page 3 Title: ***Democratic Centinial*** [sic] ***March***. Page 8: More drawings. List of Republican scandals: Ben Butler as a frog — "Brother-In-Law Casey and the New Orleans Custom House;" James G. Blaine — "A Bird Who Has Lost its Plumage;" "We Heartily Endorse Bab, Belknap & Blaine and Oppose Further Investigation;" "Godless S. Orth." [Crew/SJT-7].

• **AmPM-402 OVERSTREET**, Jesse (U.S. House, 1895–1909)

402.1 *Loyalty*. w. No composer indicated. m. "Tune — *Little More Cider*." In: *The Rough Rider (Republican Campaign Song Book)*, page 18. c. J. Burgess Brown. Published by J. Burgess Brown, Indianapolis, IN. 1900. [6" × 9"]. Br/bk non-pictorial. "ROUGH ON DemocRATS." 28pp. Page 3: B/w litho of William McKinley. Page 28: "Republican National Ticket — 1900. [Crew/WM-330].

402.2 *Republican Train*. w. No composer indicated. m. "Tune — *The Gospel Train Am Coming*." In: *Up-To-Date Republican Campaign Songs*, page 3. Published by J. Burgess Brown "(Leader of the Celebrated Bald-Headed Glee Club), [Indianapolis, IN.]." 1908. [8" × 11"]. B/w photos of William H. Taft and John Sherman. B/w drawing of American Flag — "We'll rally 'round the flag, boys." Verse. "Written and compiled for the State Central Committee." [Crew/WHT-66].

• **AmPM-403 OWEN**, Robert Dale (State House, 1835–1838 & 1851; U.S. House, 1843–1847; U.S. Minister to the Two Sicilies, 1853–1858)

403.1 *'Tis Home Where'er The Heart Is*. w. "From the *Drama Of Pocahontas*." m. Hon. Robert Dale Owen. a. John H. Hewitt. Published by F.D. Benteen, Baltimore, MD. 1844. Non-pictorial geometric designs. 4pp. Pages 1 and 4: Blank.

• **AmPM-404 PACKARD**, Jasper (U.S. House, 1869–1875)

404.1 *Captain Grant*. w. No composer indicated. m. "Air — *Captain Jenks*." In: *Tilden And Hendricks' Reform Songs (For The Centennial Campaign Of 1876)*, page 33. Published by The National Democratic Committee, Box 3637, New York, NY. 1876. [3⅞" × 5¹⁵⁄₁₆"]. Gn/bk litho of Samuel J. Tilden and Thomas A. Hendricks, geometric design border. 40pp. [M-203]. [Crew/SJT-21].

404.2 Tilden And The Colored Vote. w. No composer indicated. m. "Air—*Ise De Happiest Darkey Out.*" In: *Tilden And Hendricks' Reform Songs (For The Centennial Campaign Of 1876)*, page 17. Published by The National Democratic Committee, Box 3637, New York, NY. 1876. [3⅞" × 5$^{15}/_{16}$"]. Gn/bk litho of Samuel J. Tilden and Thomas A. Hendricks, geometric design border. 40pp. [M-203]. [Crew/SJT-21].

• **AmPM-405** **PEITZ**. (Candidate, 1908)

405.1 The Hoosier Boom De-Aye. w. No composer indicated. m. "Tune—*Ta-Ra-Ra-Ra Boom-De-Aye.*" In: *Up-To-Date Republican Campaign Songs*, page 3. Published by J. Burgess Brown "(Leader of the Celebrated Bald-Headed Glee Club), [Indianapolis, IN.]." 1908. [8" × 11"]. B/w photos of William H. Taft and John Sherman. B/w drawing of American Flag—"We'll rally 'round the flag, boys." Verse. "Written and compiled for the State Central Committee." [Crew/WHT-66].

• **AmPM-406** **POFFIT**, George H. (State House, 1831–1832 & 1836–1838; U.S. House, 1839–1843)

406.1 Go And No Go (Or Dan's Scowl At Ty's Serving Men). w. "By the Author of *Van's Mews* [John H. Warland]." m. "Tune—*Dame Durden.*" Long narrative titled "Argument" followed by "Dramatis Person_. Wise, Ty's vanguard. Cabe [Caleb] another in the guard, who doesn't stop running till he reaches China. Poffe, [Proffit] the rear-guard, who runs to South America and back. Wick, P.M.G. David the Henshaw Fowl, Ex-Secretary of the Navy, and k-navy exmanager of the Commonwealth Bank, Spence, [Spencer] the evil-genius of the administration. Ike, [Isaac Hill] the blank wrapping-paper-and-twine contractor for all the old Tories and all the new territories, etc. Porte, [Porter] Ex-Secretary of War. Seth, the hissing gentleman, one of David's pets and appointees. Bobby the Ranting Owl, a well known custom-house rat and legislative Ranter also a pet of David." In: *The National Clay Melodist (A Collection Of Popular And Patriotic Songs, Second Edition, Enlarged And Improved)*, page 76. Published by Benj. Adams, No. 54 Court Street, Boston, MA. 1844. [3" × 5¼"]. Inside title page: B/w litho of Henry Clay's home—"O'er Ashland's lawns the skies are bright, From West to East The radiance streams and glows, The land beneath its beams gay beats the heart with joy, Hurrah! Hurrah! Hip! Hurrah!" 108pp. [M-050?]. [Crew/HC-13].

• **AmPM-407** **PORTER**, Albert Gallitan (U.S. House, 1859–1863; Governor, 1881–1885; U.S. Ambassador to Italy, 1889–1892)

407.1 Porter's Invitation To The Boys (As Bennie Beat Blue Jeans). w. No composer indicated. m. "Tune—*Walker In.*" In: *Music For The Campaign (A Collection Of Original And Selected Songs, Adapted to Familiar Tunes For Use at Campaign Meetings, For 1880)*, page 7. Published by The Indianapolis Sentinel as a newspaper supplement, Indianapolis, IN. 1880. [7¾" × 10⅝"]. B/w lithos of Winfield Scott Hancock and William H. English. "This Collection of fifty one first-class Campaign Songs will be sent to any address, postage paid as follows: 25 for 30 cts.; 50 for 60 cts.; 100 for $1.00. Address Sentinel Company, Indianapolis, Ind." 8pp. Foldover. [Crew/WSH-11].

• **AmPM-408** **PRATT**, Daniel Darwin (State House, 1851 & 1853; U.S. Senate, 1869–1875; U.S. Commissioner of Internal Revenue, 1875–1876)

408.1 Go! Grant, Go! w. No author indicated. m. "Tune—*Old Black Joe.*" [1876]. [4$^{11}/_{16}$" × 8¼"]. Non-pictorial. 2pp. Page 2: Blank. [Crew SJT-17].

• **AmPM-408A** **QUAYLE**, J. Danforth (U.S. House, 1977–1981; U.S. Senate; 1981–1989; Vice President; 1989–1993) [ALSO SEE: DOC/PSM-GB]

408A.1 Ballad Of Dan Quayle. w. William K. Tong. m. "Sung to the tune of *Ballad Of Jed Clampett* from the *Beverly Hillbillies.*" Published online at <http:// www.bootnewt.envy.nu/dqballad.htm>.

408A.1A The Ballad Of Jeb Bush. w. Alan C. Bessey. m. "Sung to the tune of *Ballad Of Jed Clampett* from the Beverly Hillbillies." Published online at <http:// www.geocities.com/wmktong/bootnewt/balladjeb.htm>. [ca. 2000].

408A.2 Battle Hymn Of The Republicans. w. No composer indicated. m. Tune—*Battle Hymn Of The Republic.* N/c photos of George Bush. Ronald Reagan, Willie Horton, peacemaker missile, clear-cut forest, Dick Armey, Bill Archer, Pete Wilson, H. Ross Perot and George W. Bush. "The Washington press corps serenaded president-elect George Bush on his campaign plane with the first verse and refrain of this hymn in 1988. We added a few more stanzas." Published online by PoliticsOL.com at <http://www.presi dentialelection2000.com/battle_hymn_of_the_repub licans.html>. 2000.

408A.3 Bill 'N' Dan's Draft Dodgin' Rag. w. Bill Strauss and Elaina Newport. On CD: *Fools On The Hill.* Published by Capitol Steps Productions, 1505 King Street, Alexandria, VA. #CSCD-1011. 1992. CD Cover: N/c Capitol building.

408A.4 Bush And Gorby. w. No composer indicated. m. "Parody of *Love And Marriage* by Frank Sinatra." Lyrics published by *The Bob Rivers Show* with Bob, Spike & Joe and Twisted Tunes online at <http:// www.twistedradio.com/player/lyrics.asp?songID=558>. [199-].

408A.5 Dan Quayle. w. Edward Goldstein. m. "Parody of Wang Chung's *Betrayal.*" Published online at <http://www.bagelfather.com/funstuff/parody/parody7.htm>. [199-].

408A.6 Dan Quayle. w. No composer indicated. m. "Parody of *Rag Doll* by Aerosmith." Lyrics published by *The Bob Rivers Show* with Bob, Spike & Joe and Twisted Tunes online at <http://www.twistedradio.com/player/lyrics.asp?songID=841>. [1992?].

408A.7 The Dan Quayle Song Book. w. William K. Tong. "Could anyone seriously vote to put this 'patatoehead' in the Oval Office?" Published online at <http://www.bootnewt.envy.nu/hydesong.htm>. Songs include:

408A.7A Danny Doll. w. Bill Strauss and Elaina Newport. On CD: *Stand By Your Dan.* Published by Capitol Steps Productions, 1505 King Street, Alexandria, VA. 1989. CD cover: N/c drawing of George Bush and Dan Quayle.

408A.8 Danny Q. w. William K. Tong. m. "Sung to the tune of *Suzy Q* by Creedence Clearwater Revival." Published online at <http://www.bootnewt.envy.nu/danny-q.htm>.

408A.9 Election Impossible. w. S.T.G. m. "*Mission Impossible 2 Theme*, originally by Limp Bizkit." "It does not follow exactly to River of Dreams because I cut out a verse or two in the middle." Published online at <http://www.amiright.com/parody/2000s/limpbizkit2.shml>. [ca. 2000].

408A.10 Every Breath Bush Takes. w. No composer indicated. m. "Parody of *Every Breath You Take* by The Police." Lyrics published by *The Bob Rivers Show* with Bob, Spike & Joe and Twisted Tunes online at <http://www.twistedradio.com/player/lyrics.asp?songID=858>. [1992?].

408A.11 George Bush Rap. w. Kurt Williams. m. No tune indicated. Published online at <http://ucolick.org/~williams/bushrap.txt>. [1992]

408A.12 Grand Old Party. w. William K. Tong. m. "Sung to the tune of *Garden Party* by Rick Nelson." In: *The Sting The Right Wing Song Book* at <http://www.geocities.com/wmktong/bootnewt/goparty.htm>.

408A.13 Help Republicans Fail. w. William K. Tong. m. "Sung to the tune of *The Ballad Of Gilligan's Isle*." In: *The Sting The Right Wing Song Book* at <http://www.geocities.com/wmktong/bootnewt/repfail.htm>.

408A.14 Impeachment. w. Amanda Marlowe. m. "To the tune of *I'm A Believer* by Neil Diamond (IIRC), Monkees version." Published online at <http://groups.google.com/groups?oi=djq&ic=1&selm=an_392667274>.

408A.15 No JFK. w. Michael Pacholek. m. "*Y.M.C.A.*, based on a performance by The Village People." "After three years of watching George W. Bush's stupidities and sanctimony, I'm beginning to think America owes Dan Quayle an apology. Because, after 40 years, everyone [is] 'no Jack Kennedy.' The closest we've come to JFK is Bill Clinton. Except the press was nicer to JFK. Then, the reporters really were liberal, even if the editorial pages weren't." Published online at <http://www.amiright.com/parody/70s/thevillagepeople16.shtml>. 2003.

408A.16 Q-U-A-Y-L-E. w.m. Joseph Erdelyi, Jr. Copyright by Erdelyi Music Publishing Co., 358 W. 51st Street, New York, NY. 1988. Non-pictorial. "Dedicated to the memory of my parents, Joseph Sr. and Maria Toth, who came to America through Ellis Island from Austria-Hungary in 1896 and 1898." "Campaign song for Dan Quayle 1988 Republican Candidate for Vice President of the United States." 2pp. Page 2: Blank. [Crew/GB-3].

408A.17 Quayle Calypso. w. William K. Tong. m. "Sung to the tune of *Day O* by Harry Belafonte." "A call-and-response song parody done in calypso style." Published online at <http://www.bootnewt.envy.nu/dqcalyps.htm>.

408A.18 Ross Can't Get No Satisfaction. w. Paul Silhan. m. "Sung to *Satisfaction* by The Rolling Stones." On: Cassette: *Brother Lib's Traveling Salvation Show*. Lyrics published at <http://www.paulsilhan.com/bl-13.htm>. 1995.

408A.19 Stand By Your Dan. w. Bill Strauss and Elaina Newport. On CD: *Stand By Your Dan*. Published by Capitol Steps Productions, 1505 King Street, Alexandria, VA. 1989. CD cover: N/c drawing of George Bush and Dan Quayle.

408A.20 Talk Like A Dan. w. Bill Strauss and Elaina Newport. On CD: *Georgie On My Mind*. Published by Capitol Steps Productions, 1505 King Street, Alexandria, VA. 1990. CD cover: N/c drawing of George Bush.

408A.21 You're A Mean One, Mr. Bush. w. Michael Pacholek. m. "*You're A Mean One, Mr. Grinch,* based on the performance by Doctor Seuss." "I know Christmas is over, but this one is not dependent upon time of year." Published online at <http://www.amiright.com/parody/60s/doctorseuss0.shtml>. 2004.

• **AmPM-409 RALSTON,** Samuel Moffett (School Board, Lebanon, 1908-1911; Governor, 1913-1917; U.S. Senator, 1923-1925)

409.1 Hoosier State (You're Just One Century Old) (Centennial Marching Song). w. Earl E. Crooke. m. Eugene E. Noel. Copyright 1916 by Warner C. Williams, Indianapolis, Ind. R/w/b litho of crossed American flags, state seal, Governor Jonathan Jennings—"Governor 1816." Bl/w photo of Samuel Ralston—"Governor 1916." "Indiana Centennial Souvenir 1816-1916, Containing the Song *Hoosier State*. 6pp. Page 2: List of Committee members. Page 5: Popular songs for singing. Page 6: Events program for Centennial.

409.2 Indianapolis (A Booster Song For The Capitol of Indiana). w.m. Stella Hall Millikan. Published by S.H. Millikan, 632 Occidental Building, Indianapolis, IN. 1916. Bl/w photos of Jonathan Jennings, "Governor, 1816" and Samuel Ralston, "Governor, 1916." R/w/b crossed American flags, state map of Indiana as background. "Dedicated to Indianapolis, No Mean City." 6pp. Page 2: At top of music—"Dedicated to Indianapolis, No Mean City and written in Honor of the Hundredth Anniversary of the admission of the Hoosier State to the U.S.A." Page 6: Blank.

• **AmPM-410 SELF.** (Candidate, 1908)

410.1 The Hoosier Boom De-Aye. w. No composer indicated. m. "Tune—*Ta-Ra-Ra-Ra Boom-De-Aye.*" In: *Up-To-Date Republican Campaign Songs*, page 3. Published by J. Burgess Brown "(Leader of the Celebrated Bald-Headed Glee Club), [Indianapolis, IN.]." 1908. [8" × 11"]. B/w photos of William H. Taft and John Sherman. B/w drawing of American Flag—"We'll rally 'round the flag, boys." Verse. "Written and compiled for the State Central Committee." [Crew/WHT-66].

• **AmPM-411 SCHORTMEIER,** Frederick E. (Candidate, 1924)

411.1 Rally The Standard Of "Abe" Lincoln. w. Mrs. S.R. Artma "(Composer of *Guess, One Who Cares For Me, The Organ And The Choir*)." m. Roy L. Burtch. Published by Halcyon Publishing Company, No. 307 East North Street, Indianapolis, IN. 1924. Br/w photos of "Calvin Coolidge," "Charles G. Dawes," "Abraham Lincoln" and "Ed Jackson" [Republican nominee for Governor of Indiana], geometric design border. "American Campaign March Song." 4pp. + Insert letter. Page 4: Biographies of candidates and other Republicans from Indiana, including "Ed Jackson, F. Harold Van Orman, Frederick E. Schortmeier, Lewis S. Bohman, Ben H. Urbahns, Arthur L. Gillam, F.M. Thompson, Willard R. Gimmill, Judge Willoughby, E.A. Dausman, Noble Sherwood, Mrs. Edward F.

White." Insert — Page 1: Letter from composer to Republican State Committee. Page 2: Advertising.

• **AmPM-412 SHERWOOD**, Noble (Superintendent of Schools, Jonesboro, 1906–1907; Candidate, 1924)

412.1 Rally The Standard Of "Abe" Lincoln. w. Mrs. S.R. Artma "(Composer of *Guess, One Who Cares For Me, The Organ And The Choir*)." m. Roy L. Burtch. Published by Halcyon Publishing Company, No. 307 East North Street, Indianapolis, IN. 1924. Br/w photos of "Calvin Coolidge," "Charles G. Dawes," "Abraham Lincoln" and "Ed Jackson" [Republican nominee for Governor of Indiana], geometric design border. "American Campaign March Song." 4pp. + Insert letter. Page 4: Biographies of candidates and other Republicans from Indiana, including "Ed Jackson, F. Harold Van Orman, Frederick E. Schortmeier, Lewis S. Bohman, Ben H. Urbahns, Arthur L. Gillam, F.M. Thompson, Willard R. Gimmill, Judge Willoughby, E.A. Dausman, Noble Sherwood, Mrs. Edward F. White." Insert — Page 1: Letter from composer to Republican State Committee. Page 2: Advertising.

• **AmPM-413 SCHRICKER**, Henry Frederick (State Senate; 1932; Lt. Governor, 1937–1941; Governor, 1941–1945 & 1949–1953; Candidate for U.S. Senate, 1944 & 1952)

413.1 We Can Win With Roosevelt. w.m. Daniel P. O'Donnell. Published by Indiana Democratic State Central Committee, Fred Bays, State Chairman. 1940. B/w photos of "President Franklin D. Roosevelt" and "Vice-President Henry A. Wallace," Capitol building. B/w drawing of two flags. 6pp. Page 2: Campaign advertising for "Lieut. Gov. Henry Schricker" and "Senator Minton." Page 6: State Democratic ticket.

• **AmPM-414 SIMS**, Fred A. (Candidate, 1908)

414.1 The Hoosier Boom De-Aye. w. No composer indicated. m. "Tune — *Ta-Ra-Ra-Ra Boom-De-Aye.*" In: *Up-To-Date Republican Campaign Songs*, page 3. Published by J. Burgess Brown "(Leader of the Celebrated Bald-Headed Glee Club), [Indianapolis, IN.]." 1908. [8" × 11"]. B/w photos of William H. Taft and John Sherman. B/w drawing of American Flag — "We'll rally 'round the flag, boys." Verse. "Written and compiled for the State Central Committee." [Crew/WHT-66].

• **AmPM-415 SMITH**, Caleb Blood (State House, 1833–1937 & 1840–1841; U.S. House, 1843–1849; U.S. Secretary of the Interior, 1861–1862; U.S. District Court Judge, 1863–1864)

415.1 Fourth Of July (Song). w.m. No composer or tune indicated. No publisher indicated. [ca. 1862]. [Approx. 4¾" 8¾"]. Non-pictorial geometric design border. "Gotten up expressly for those who have an appreciative mind." 2pp. Page 2: Blank. [WFU].

415.2 Sic Semper. w. "By A Virginian." m. No tune indicated. No publisher indicated. [1861–1862]. [Approx. 6" × 9½"]. Non-pictorial geometric design border. 2pp. Page 2: Blank. [AMC].

415.3 The White House. w. G.R. Edeson. m. "Air — *Root, Hog, Or Die!*" Published by H. De Marsan, 54 Chatham Street, New York, NY. [1861–1862]. B/w litho border of minstrels, geometric designs. 2pp. Page 2: Blank. [AMC].

• **AmPM-416 STEPHENS**, George L. (Candidate for County Assessor, Porter County, 1934)

416.1 Roosevelt We Hand The Flag To You! w. William Foster. m. Edna May Foster. Published by Calumet Music Publishers, Gary, IN. 1934. R/w/b eagle, trees, geometric designs. Bl/w photo of Franklin D. Roosevelt. 6pp. Page 2: Advertisement for Carroll Holly for Sheriff. Page 6: Advertisements for various office seekers including "George L. Stephens, Democratic Candidate for County Assessor, Porter County, I Advocate a duplicate of your assessment sheet for you. Help Me win!"

• **AmPM-417 STONER**, Ezra (Candidate for County Auditor, Porter County, 1934)

417.1 Roosevelt We Hand The Flag To You! w. William Foster. m. Edna May Foster. Published by Calumet Music Publishers, Gary, IN. 1934. R/w/b eagle, trees, geometric designs. Bl/w photo of Franklin D. Roosevelt. 6pp. Page 2: Advertisement for Carroll Holly for Sheriff. Page 6: Advertisements for various office seekers including "Ezra Stoner, Democratic Candidate for County Auditor, Porter County, Honesty, Courtesy, Qualified. Vote For Ezra Stoner." B/w photo of Ezra Stoner.

• **AmPM-418 STOTSENBURG**, Evan B. (State Attorney General, 1915–1917; Delegate to Democratic National Convention from Indiana, 1924 & 1932)

418.1 Till Over The Top We Go. w.m. Roy L. Burtch "(Composer of *When The Bugle Calls, Peace On Earth And Liberty, Think Of Me, Tell Me, The Organ And The Choir, Bye Bye Baby Dear*)." Published by The Halcyon Publishing Company, Indianapolis, IN. 1918. Drawing of soldier — "U.S. Marine," machine gun. "The Song Our Allies, Lodges and Glee Clubs are Singing." "State Campaign Song — Democratic State Committee, Denison Hotel, Indianapolis, Ind." "Extra copies of this March Song mailed free on request." 4pp. Page 4: Photos of Woodrow Wilson and 13 State Democratic candidates. "The Party with a Purpose." Text on 11 reasons to vote Democratic. [Crew/WW-121].

• **AmPM-419 TAGGART**, Thomas (County Auditor, Marion County, 1886–1894; Mayor, Indianapolis, 1895–1901; Democratic National Committee, 1900–1916; U.S. Senate, 1916)

419.1 The Cuckoos. w. No composer indicated. m. "Tune — *Billy Magee McGaw.*" In: *The Rough Rider (Republican Campaign Song Book)*, page 8. c. J. Burgess Brown. Published by J. Burgess Brown, Indianapolis, IN. 1900. [6" × 9"]. Br/bk non-pictorial. "ROUGH ON DemocRATS." 28pp. Page 3: B/w litho of William McKinley. Page 28: "Republican National Ticket — 1900. [Crew/WM-330].

419.2 Ship Ahoy. w.m. Jim C. Madden. In: *America First (Republican Campaign Song Book)*, page 10. Published for The Republican National Committee, No. 19 West 44th Street, New York, NY., by Weldon Company, No. 119 Walnut Street, Philadelphia, PA. 1920. [6" × 9"]. Br/bk photos of "Warren Harding — For President" and "Calvin Coolidge — For Vice President." 20pp. [M-411]. [Crew/WGH-23].

419.3 Three Crows. w. No composer indicated. m. "Tune — *Billy McGee McGraw.*" In: *Up-To-Date Republican Campaign Songs*, page 5. Published by J. Burgess Brown (Leader of the Celebrated Bald-Headed

Glee Club), [Indianapolis, IN.]. 1908. [8" × 11"]. B/w photos of William H. Taft and John Sherman. B/w drawing of American Flag—"We'll rally 'round the flag, boys." Verse. "Written and compiled for the State Central Committee." [Crew/WHT-66].

419.4 The White House Gate (Solo and Chorus). w.m. Logan S. Porter. In: *Roosevelt Campaign Songster 1904 (For Male Voices)*, page 26. c. Logan S. Porter. Published by The Home Music Company, Logansport, IN. 1904. [6" × 9"]. Be/bk photos of Theodore Roosevelt and Charles Fairbanks. Be/bk drawing of a star, geometric designs. "Single Copy 15 cts—$1.60 per Dozen." 36pp. [M-391]. [Crew/TR-356].

- **AmPM-420 TAYLOR**, William L. (State Attorney General, 1899)

420.1 Our Candidates. w. No composer indicated. m. "Tune—*Boom De-Ay*." In: *The Rough Rider (Republican Campaign Song Book)*, page 6. c. J. Burgess Brown. Published by J. Burgess Brown, Indianapolis, IN. 1900. [6" × 9"]. Br/bk non-pictorial. "ROUGH ON DemocRATS." 28pp. Page 3: B/w litho of William McKinley. Page 28: "Republican National Ticket—1900. [Crew/WM-330].

- **AmPM-421 THOMPSON**, F.M. (Circuit Prosecuting Attorney, 1894–1906?; Circuit Judge, 1906; Candidate, 1924)

421.1 Rally The Standard Of "Abe" Lincoln. w. Mrs. S.R. Artma "(Composer of *Guess, One Who Cares For Me, The Organ And The Choir*)." m. Roy L. Burtch. Published by Halcyon Publishing Company, No. 307 East North Street, Indianapolis, IN. 1924. Br/w photos of "Calvin Coolidge," "Charles G. Dawes," "Abraham Lincoln" and "Ed Jackson" [Republican nominee for Governor of Indiana], geometric design border. "American Campaign March Song." 4pp. + Insert letter. Page 4: Biographies of candidates and other Republicans from Indiana, including "Ed Jackson, F. Harold Van Orman, Frederick E. Schortmeier, Lewis S. Bohman, Ben H. Urbahns, Arthur L. Gillam, F.M. Thompson, Willard R. Gimmill, Judge Willoughby, E.A. Dausman, Noble Sherwood, Mrs. Edward F. White." Insert—Page 1: Letter from composer to Republican State Committee. Page 2: Advertising.

- **AmPM-422 THORNTON**, Michael Charles (State Senator, 1907–1913; State Senate, 1915–1917)

422.1 Angel Of Comfort (God Bless Her, to Pa). w.m. Senator M.C. Thornton. a. William Rahuer. Published by M.C. Thornton Publishing, Elsby Building, New Albany, IN. Copyright 1921 by M.C. Thornton.

422.2 Butterfly Nell. w.m. Senator M.C. Thornton "(Composer of *Will You Say To My Dear Mammy, Mother's Kiss, Angel Of Comfort*, etc.)." a. Clifford E. Slider. Published by M.C. Thornton, 314 Elsby Bldg., New Albany, IN. 1921. Y/pl/w drawing off pretty girl with butterfly wings. 6pp. Page 2: Blank. Page 6: Advertising.

422.3 I Like My President. w.m. Hon. M.C. Thornton. a. Earl Edwards. Published by Hon. M.C. Thornton, No. 207 Elsby Building, New Albany, IN. 1943. Bl/w non-pictorial line border. "Introduced by Mary Pat Melcher and Bette Wolf at Manzanita Tribes President's Ball with immediate success." 4pp.

422.4 Mother's Kiss. w.m. Senator M.C. Thornton.

422.5 The Sentinel Of The Marne. w.m. Senator M.C. Thornton "(Composer of *Will You Say To My Dear Mammy*)." a. Wm. Rehnor [sp?] and Erma Lyons. Published by M.C. Thornton Publishing, Elsby Building, New Albany, IN. 1919. Bl/w/gd drawing of a soldier in silhouette guarding the Marne River, grave sites in the foreground. "Sung by Louise C. Blanchard." 4pp. Page 4: Advertising.

422.6 The Sentinel's Song. w.m. Senator M.C. Thornton "(Composer of *Will You Say To My Dear Mammy*)." Published by M.C. Thornton, New Albany, IN. 1919. Bl/gd/w drawing of a lone soldier guarding a grave beside the waves. "Sung by Louise Blanchard." 4pp. Page 4: Advertising.

422.7 Will You Say To My Dear Mammy. w.m. Senator M.C. Thornton "(Composer of *Will You Say To My Dear Mammy*)." a. Wm. Rahner. Published by M.C. Thornton Publishing, Elsby Building, New Albany, IN. 1918. O/w/bl drawing of woman and daughter looking at a photograph of husband on the wall. 4pp. Page 4: Blank.

- **AmPM-423 TOWNSEND**, Maurice Clifford (Superintendent of Schools; Blackford County; State House, 1923; Lt. Governor, 1933–1937; Governor, 1937–1941)

423.1 Roosevelt We Hand The Flag To You! w. William Foster. m. Edna May Foster. Published by Calumet Music Publishers, Gary, IN. 1934. R/w/b eagle, trees, geometric designs. Bl/w photo of Franklin D. Roosevelt. 6pp. Page 2: Advertisement and song for M. Clifford Townsend, Democratic Candidate for Governor of Indiana. Page 6: Advertisement for Carroll Holly for Sheriff.

423.2 Roosevelt We Hand The Flag To You! w. William Foster. m. Edna May Foster. Published by Democratic Boosters of Indiana, Gary, IN. 1936. Drawing of Franklin D. Roosevelt, star, shield. 6pp. Page 2: Photo of "M. Clifford Townsend, Democratic candidate for Governor." "You are for Roosevelt! Then Vote for those who are for Roosevelt." Page 6: Photo of "Carroll Holley, Sheriff." "Re-Elect."

- **AmPM-424 URBAHNS**, Ben H. (County Treasurer, Porter County, 1910–1914; Deputy State Treasurer, 1917–1924?)

424.1 Rally The Standard Of "Abe" Lincoln. w. Mrs. S.R. Artma "(Composer of *Guess, One Who Cares For Me, The Organ And The Choir*)." m. Roy L. Burtch. Published by Halcyon Publishing Company, No. 307 East North Street, Indianapolis, IN. 1924. Br/w photos of "Calvin Coolidge," "Charles G. Dawes," "Abraham Lincoln" and "Ed Jackson" [Republican nominee for Governor of Indiana], geometric design border. "American Campaign March Song." 4pp. + Insert letter. Page 4: Biographies of candidates and other Republicans from Indiana, including "Ed Jackson, F. Harold Van Orman, Frederick E. Schortmeier, Lewis S. Bohman, Ben H. Urbahns, Arthur L. Gillam, F.M. Thompson, Willard R. Gimmill, Judge Willoughby, E.A. Dausman, Noble Sherwood, Mrs. Edward F. White." Insert—Page 1: Letter from composer to Republican State Committee. Page 2: Advertising.

- **AmPM-425 VAN ORMAN**, F. Harold (State Senate, 1920–1924?)

425.1 Rally The Standard Of "Abe" Lincoln. w. Mrs. S.R. Artma "(Composer of *Guess, One Who Cares For Me, The Organ And The Choir*)." m. Roy L. Burtch. Published by Halcyon Publishing Company, No. 307 East North Street, Indianapolis, IN. 1924. Br/w photos of "Calvin Coolidge," "Charles G. Dawes," "Abraham Lincoln" and "Ed Jackson" [Republican nominee for Governor of Indiana], geometric design border. "American Campaign March Song." 4pp. + Insert letter. Page 4: Biographies of candidates and other Republicans from Indiana, including "Ed Jackson, F. Harold Van Orman, Frederick E. Schortmeier, Lewis S. Bohman, Ben H. Urbahns, Arthur L. Gillam, F.M. Thompson, Willard R. Gimmill, Judge Willoughby, E.A. Dausman, Noble Sherwood, Mrs. Edward F. White." Insert — Page 1: Letter from composer to Republican State Committee. Page 2: Advertising.

• **AmPM-426 VAN NUYS**, Frederick (State Senate, 1913–1916; U.S. Senate, 1933–1944)

426.1 Daisies Won't Tell. w. No composer indicated. m. No publisher indicated. [ca. 1938]. [6¼" × 9½"]. B/w drawing of "U.S. Senator Fred Van Nuys" as the center of a daisy. 4pp. Pages 2 and 3: Advertising for Dr. Cliff Townsend's Soothing Syrup. B/w photo of Senator Van Nuys before taking the syrup — "Grouchy" and after — Smiling. Page 4: Music.

• **AmPM-427 VORHEES**, Daniel Wolsey (District Attorney, 1858–1861; U.S. House, 1861–1866 & 1869–1873; U.S. Senate, 1877–1897)

427.1 Campaign Barbers. w. No composer indicated. m. "Arr. By Tariff Reform." In: *Red Hot Democratic Campaign Songs For 1888*, page 2. e. John Bunyon Herbert. Published by The S. Brainard's Sons Company, Chicago, IL. 1888. [5⅜" × 7$\frac{7}{16}$"]. R/bk geometric designs. 36pp. [M-294]. [Crew/GC-141].

427.2 The Last Days Of Ulysses. w. No composer indicated. m. "Air — *Put Me In My Little Bed.*" In: *The Sun's Greeley Campaign Songster*, page 22. c. Amos J. Cummings. Published from *The Sun* Office, New York, NY. 1872. [4⅛" × 6½"]. Be/bk litho of Horace Greeley, wreath. "He shines for all." 64pp. [Crew/HG-5].

427.3 Lines To A Copperhead. w. Enarc. m. No tune indicated. No publisher indicated. [ca. 1863]. Non-pictorial. "An editor in Southern Illinois, in reply to a Union editor who had called him a Copperhead, replied — 'Yes, sir, we are a Copperhead, and so are Vallandigham and Dan Voorhees Copperheads, and we and the glory in it! What are you going to do about it?' To them, and like all men, these lines were addressed by a western soldier, while lying wounded in a hospital in Collierville, Tenn." 2pp. Page 2: Blank. [AMC].

427.4 Oh, Forney, I Am Tired Now. w. No composer indicated. m. "Air — *Put Me In My Little Bed.*" In: *Greeley Campaign Songster*, page 67. "Respectfully dedicated to the Greeley Clubs of the Country." Published by Halpin & McClure, Chicago, IL. 1872. [4" × 5$\frac{11}{16}$"]. Pl/bk litho of Horace Greeley, geometric design border. "Chicago: Western News Company, Wholesale Agents." 72pp. [M-187]. [Crew/HG-21].

427.5 The Old White Hat. w. No composer indicated. m. "Air — *When This Old Hat Was New.*" In: *National Republican Grant And Wilson Campaign Song-Book*, page 42. From the *Chattanooga Herald*. Published by The Union Republican Congressional Committee, Washington, DC. 1872. [3$\frac{13}{16}$" × 8$\frac{9}{16}$"]. Be/bk litho of Ulysses S. Grant. "We'll Sing a Song for U.S. Grant." 100pp. [M-182]. [Crew/USG-110].

427.6 Political Barber Shop. w. R. Campaign. m. Notation. "Male Voices." In: *True Blue Republican Campaign Songs For 1888*, page 8. Published by S. Brainard's Sons, Nos. 145 and 147 Wabash Avenue, Chicago, IL. 1888. [5⅜" × 7½"]. Bl/bk non-pictorial geometric designs. 36pp. [M-269, 270]. [Crew/BFH-32].

427.7 The Stronghold Of Fraud Rocking In. w. No composer indicated. m. "Air — *Put Me In My Little Bed.*" "The last day of Useless before he was Laid out by H.G. and the People." In: *The Farmer Of Chappaqua Songster, Containing A Great Number Of The Best Campaign Songs That The Unanimous And Enthusiastic Nomination Of The Hon. Horace Greeley For President Has Produced*, page 56. Published by Robert M. De Wit, Publisher, No. 33 Rose Street, New York, NY. 1872. [4¼" × 6¼"]. R/w/bl/y litho caricature of Horace Greeley. 102pp.

427.8 Witches' Scene From MacGreeley (Which is Seen to be a Fact). w.m. No composer or tune indicated. From the "*New York Standard.*" In: *National Republican Grant And Wilson Campaign Song-Book*, page 34. From the *New York Standard*. Published by The Union Republican Congressional Committee, Washington, DC. 1872. [3$\frac{13}{16}$" × 8$\frac{9}{16}$"]. Be/bk litho of Ulysses S. Grant. "We'll Sing a Song for U.S. Grant." 100pp. [M-182]. [Crew/USG-110].

• **AmPM-428 WALLACE**, Lewis (State Senate, 1856; Governor, New Mexico Territory, 1878–1881; U.S. Minister to Turkey, 1881–1885)

428.1 Chariot Race (Or Ben Hur March). m. E.T. Paull. Published by E.T. Paull, [V-1: 20 East 17th Street] [V-2: 243 West 42nd Street], New York, NY. 1894. N/c litho of a Roman chariot race, classical busts. "Respectfully inscribed to Gen. Lew Wallace, Author of Ben Hur." "Played by Sousa's Band." 8pp. Pages 2 and 8: Blank.

428.2 Native Hoosier. w. Grace Patterson Lopez-Dias. m. Mae Doelling Schmidt. Published by Clayton F. Summy Company, Chicago, IL. 1940. R/w/b drawing of the State of Indiana with a list of famous Hoosiers — "James Whitcomb Riley, Thomas Marshall, Gene Stratton Porter, Wendell L. Willkie, John T. McCutcheon, George Ade, General Lew Wallace, Booth Tarkington, Meredith Nicholson, Claude Wickard, William Lowe Bryan, Paul McNutt, Kenesaw Mountain Landis, ad-infinitum." 6pp. Page 2: Blank. Page 6: Advertising. [Crew/WLW-61].

428.3 The Stolen Stars Or Good Old Father Washington. w. Gen. Lew Wallace. m.a. R. Hastings. Published by A.C. Peters & Bro., Cincinnati, OH. 1863. B/w litho of shield with stars and stripes. 6pp. [Crew/GW-586].

428.4 Year Of Jubilee Or Kingdom Has Come. w.m. Sambo. Published by H.M. Higgins, 117 Randolph Street, Chicago, IL. 1862. B/w non-pictorial geometric designs. 6pp.

• **AmPM-429 WATSON**, James Eli (U.S. House,

1895-1897 & 1899-1909; Candidate for Governor, 1908; U.S. Senate, 1916-1933)

429.1 *The Hoosier Boom De-Aye*. w. No composer indicated. m. "Tune—*Ta-Ra-Ra-Ra Boom-De-Aye*." In: *Up-To-Date Republican Campaign Songs*, page 3. Published by J. Burgess Brown "(Leader of the Celebrated Bald-Headed Glee Club), [Indianapolis, IN]." 1908. [8" × 11"]. B/w photos of William H. Taft and John Sherman. B/w drawing of American Flag— "We'll rally 'round the flag, boys." Verse. "Written and compiled for the State Central Committee." [Crew/WHT-66].

429.2 *The Republican Camp*. w. No composer indicated. m. "Tune—*In The Morning By The Bright Light*." In: *Up-To-Date Republican Campaign Songs*, page 3. Published by J. Burgess Brown "(Leader of the Celebrated Bald-Headed Glee Club), [Indianapolis, IN]." 1908. [8" × 11"]. B/w photos of William H. Taft and John Sherman. B/w drawing of American Flag— "We'll rally 'round the flag, boys." Verse. "Written and compiled for the State Central Committee." [Crew/WHT-66].

429.3 *Republican Train*. w. No composer indicated. m. "Tune—*The Gospel Train Am Coming*." In: *Up-To-Date Republican Campaign Songs*, page 3. Published by J. Burgess Brown "(Leader of the Celebrated Bald-Headed Glee Club), [Indianapolis, IN]." 1908. [8" × 11"]. B/w photos of William H. Taft and John Sherman. B/w drawing of American Flag—"We'll rally 'round the flag, boys." Verse. "Written and compiled for the State Central Committee." [Crew/WHT-66].

429.4 *We'll Win With Watson*. w. No composer indicated. m. "Tune—*Every Day Will Be Sunday Bye And Bye*." In: *Up-To-Date Republican Campaign Songs*, page 3. Published by J. Burgess Brown "(Leader of the Celebrated Bald-Headed Glee Club), [Indianapolis, IN.]." 1908. [8" × 11"]. B/w photos of William H. Taft and John Sherman. B/w drawing of American Flag— "We'll rally 'round the flag, boys." Verse. "Written and compiled for the State Central Committee." [Crew/WHT-66].

- **AmPM-430 WHITE**, Joseph Livingston (U.S. House, 1841-1843)

430.1 *Order Of Exercises* (At the Meeting of the Democratic Clay Club of the 10th Ward, City of New York) [Songster]. "Published in behalf of the Ladies of the ward." [1844]. [6" × 9½"]. Y/bk engraving of Henry Clay, star, two women, eagle. "Justice to Harry, the Star of the West." "Held at the Apollo Saloon, 410 Broadway on Tuesday evening, April 23, for the reception of a beautiful & appropriate banner painted by C.E. Weir, to be presented to the Club by the Hon. Joseph L. White. The President of the Club, N.C. Bradford, Esq., will take the Chair at a quarter before 8 o'clock. William Wood, Esq., will preside at the piano. Music by the Band." 4pp.

- **AmPM-431 WICKENS**, Hugh (Candidate for Appellate Court, 1918)

431.1 *Till Over The Top We Go*. w.m. Roy L. Burtch "(Composer of *When The Bugle Calls, Peace On Earth And Liberty, Think Of Me, Tell Me, The Organ And The Choir, Bye Bye Baby Dear*)." Published by The Halcyon Publishing Company, Indianapolis, IN. 1918. Drawing of soldier—"U.S. Marine," machine gun. "The Song Our Allies, Lodges and Glee Clubs are Singing." "State Campaign Song—Democratic State Committee, Denison Hotel, Indianapolis, Ind." "Extra copies of this March Song mailed free on request." 4pp. Page 4: Photos of Woodrow Wilson and 13 State Democratic candidates. "The Party with a Purpose." Text on 11 reasons to vote Democratic. [Crew/WW-121].

- **AmPM-432 WILLKIE**, Wendell Lewis (Candidate for President, 1940) [ALSO SEE: DOC/PSM-WLW]

432.1 *(Americans) We Want Willkie* (In The Presidential Chair). w.m. C. Mader" (Band Director, 131st U.S. Inf., A.E.F.)." a. Fred Huffer. Copyright 1940 by Carl Mader, Forest Park, IL. [8½" × 11"]. 4pp. Page 4: Blank. [Crew/WLW-71].

432.1A *The Battle Hymn Of The Republicans*. w. Sidney m. "Happy" Rowe. m. *Battle Hymn Of The Republic*. Published by Sidney M. Rowe, Johnson City, TN. [1940]. B/w photos of "Wendell Willkie" and "Sidney M. 'Happy' Rowe, Speaker, entertainer and now engaged in Personnel work in Tennessee. As sung by him at the 'McNeill for Governor' Republican Rally in North Carolina." B/w reproduction of two bars of music from the song. 4pp. Pages 2 and 4: Blank.

432.2 *But He Wouldn't Say Yes!* w. No composer indicated. m. "Air—*I Can't Say No*." In: *Dealers Choice or Back-To-Back Biting*, page 15. Published by the Albany Legislative Correspondent's Association of New York State, Albany, NY. 1944. [8" × 11¾"]. N/c drawing of Franklin Roosevelt, Thomas Dewey, "Chiang," "Winnie" and "Joe" playing cards—"Featuring the World's Most Exciting Egomaniacs in a Marvelous Musical of Messianic and Mystery: Showing Sinners, Sycophants, Suckers, and Sleuths Saving Civilization with Sound; or Find the Joker!" "Dealt Off the Bottom of a Hot Deck—In Three Acts at Ten Eyck, Albany, March 9, 1944." [Crew/FDR-364].

432.3 *Dance Of The Liberal Republicans*. w.m. Gerald Gardner. In: *These Are The Songs That Were* [Song Book], page 10. e. Gerald Gardner "(Writer *Of Who's In Charge Here?, News-Reals*, and *That Was The Week That Was*)." Published by Edwin H. Morris and Company, No. 31 West 54th Street, New York, NY. 10019. 1965. B/w photo of Lyndon B. Johnson, Hubert Humphrey, Everett Dirksen, others. R/w/bk cover. List of contents. 36pp. Pages 8, 23 and 25: Photos of politicians. [Crew/LBJ-6].

432.4 *Hold That Hanley!* w. No composer indicated. m. "Air—*MacNamara's Band*." In: *Gone With The Winner*, page 13. Published by Albany Legislative Correspondents' Association of New York State, Albany, NY. March 20, 1941. [9" × 11⅙"]. R/w/bl/y drawing of Franklin Roosevelt and Wendell Willkie riding "A Bicycle Built For Two" labeled—"Roosevelt-Willkie Axis." Wheels—"New Deal" and "Lend Lease Bill." "Or 'Back in the Lap of God.' A Hoosier-Hyde Park Honeymoon Hit, Staring the G. Oomph P.'s Lost Leader and the King of Krum Elbow in 'Lucky Partners.' Says F.D.R.—'He's My Man.' Says the Republican Party—'Once a New Dealer, Sometimes a Double-Dealer.' Says the Public—'Willkie's the Life of the Party, But What Party?" "Served Piping Hot at Hotel Ten Eyck, Albany, New York, Thursday Night, March 20, 1941, at 7:30 o'clock." [Crew/FDR-394].

432.5 Mutual 'Shun Society. w. No composer indicated. m. "Air — *The Last Time I Saw Paris.*" In: *Gone With The Winner*, page 8. Published by Albany Legislative Correspondents' Association of New York State, Albany, NY. March 20, 1941. [9" × 11¹⁄₁₆"]. R/w/bl/y drawing of Franklin Roosevelt and Wendell Willkie riding "A Bicycle Built For Two" labeled — "Roosevelt-Willkie Axis." Wheels — "New Deal" and "Lend Lease Bill." "Or 'Back in the Lap of God.' A Hoosier-Hyde Park Honeymoon Hit, Staring the G. Oomph P.'s Lost Leader and the King of Krum Elbow in 'Lucky Partners.' Says F.D.R. — 'He's My Man.' Says the Republican Party — 'Once a New Dealer, Sometimes a Double- Dealer.' Says the Public — 'Willkie's the Life of the Party, But What Party?" "Served Piping Hot at Hotel Ten Eyck, Albany, New York, Thursday Night, March 20, 1941, at 7:30 o'clock." [Crew/FDR-394].

432.6 Pattern For Politics. w. No composer indicated. m. "Air — *The Man On The Flying Trapeze, Little Sir Echo* and *God Bless America.*" In: *Gone With The Winner*, page 14. Published by Albany Legislative Correspondents' Association of New York State, Albany, NY. March 20, 1941. [9" × 11¹⁄₁₆"]. R/w/bl/y drawing of Franklin Roosevelt and Wendell Willkie riding "A Bicycle Built For Two" labeled — "Roosevelt-Willkie Axis." Wheels — "New Deal" and "Lend Lease Bill." "Or 'Back in the Lap of God.' A Hoosier-Hyde Park Honeymoon Hit, Staring the G. Oomph P's Lost Leader and the King of Krum Elbow in 'Lucky Partners.' Says F.D.R. — 'He's My Man.' Says the Republican Party — 'Once a New Dealer, Sometimes a Double- Dealer.' Says the Public — 'Willkie's the Life of the Party, But What Party?" "Served Piping Hot at Hotel Ten Eyck, Albany, New York, Thursday Night, March 20, 1941, at 7:30 o'clock." [Crew/FDR-394].

432.7 Right Is Might (With Honest People). w.m. Franklin E. Parker. Published by Sprague-Coleman, New York, NY. 1940. 6pp. + a 2pp insert titled "A Divine Challenge to Dictatorship." Page 6: Blank. [Crew/WLW-73].

432.8 Thank God! We've Found The Man. w.m. Robert Crawford. 78 rpm record. Sprague-Coleman, 62 West 45th Street, New York, NY. #76466/76467. Performed by Robert Crawford and The Scarletiers. [1940]. Side B: *The Star Spangled Banner* performed by Robert Crawford and The Scarletiers.

432.9 They Knew What They Wanted. w. No composer indicated. m. "Air — *One, Two, Three Kick.*" In: *Gone With The Winner*, page 14. Published by Albany Legislative Correspondents' Association of New York State, Albany, NY. March 20, 1941. [9" × 11¹⁄₁₆"]. R/w/bl/y drawing of Franklin Roosevelt and Wendell Willkie riding "A Bicycle Built For Two" labeled — "Roosevelt-Willkie Axis." Wheels — "New Deal" and "Lend Lease Bill." "Or 'Back in the Lap of God.' A Hoosier-Hyde Park Honeymoon Hit, Staring the G. Oomph P.'s Lost Leader and the King of Krum Elbow in 'Lucky Partners.' Says F.D.R. — 'He's My Man.' Says the Republican Party — 'Once a New Dealer, Sometimes a Double- Dealer.' Says the Public — 'Willkie's the Life of the Party, But What Party?" "Served Piping Hot at Hotel Ten Eyck, Albany, New York, Thursday Night, March 20, 1941, at 7:30 o'clock." [Crew/FDR-394].

432.9A We Want Willkie (A Republican Campaign Song). m. W.C. Tichenor. Published by W.C. Tichenor, Waynesville, OH. 1940. Non-pictorial. "Single copies of this song with piano accompaniment, 35 cents, 10 copies $3.00, 25 copies, $7.00, 50 copies, #11.00, 100 copies, $20.00, qualities mat be sent by mail C.O.D. if preferred, A splendid rousing band arrangement, for 32 pieces, 75 cents, leaflets or cards with the words of the song only, by mail 5 cts. Each, 100 copies $2.00. These are useful where the audiences sing. Live agents wanted. Send all orders to W.C. Tichenor, Waynesville, Ohio." 4pp. Page 4: Advertising.

432.10 Wendell's The Works. w. No composer indicated. m. "Air — *When I Was A Lad* from *H.M.S. Pinafore.*" In: *Gone With The Winner*, page 7. Published by Albany Legislative Correspondents' Association of New York State, Albany, NY. March 20, 1941. [9" × 11¹⁄₁₆"]. R/w/bl/y drawing of Franklin Roosevelt and Wendell Willkie riding "A Bicycle Built For Two" labeled — "Roosevelt-Willkie Axis." Wheels — "New Deal" and "Lend Lease Bill." "Or 'Back in the Lap of God.' A Hoosier-Hyde Park Honeymoon Hit, Staring the G. Oomph P.'s Lost Leader and the King of Krum Elbow in 'Lucky Partners.' Says F.D.R. — 'He's My Man.' Says the Republican Party — 'Once a New Dealer, Sometimes a Double-Dealer.' Says the Public — 'Willkie's the Life of the Party, But What Party?" "Served Piping Hot at Hotel Ten Eyck, Albany, New York, Thursday Night, March 20, 1941, at 7:30 o'clock." [Crew/FDR-394].

432.11 Who All Is Goin' My Way? w. No composer indicated. m. No tune indicated. In: *Dealers Choice or Back-To-Back Biting*, page 14. Published by the Albany Legislative Correspondent's Association of New York State, Albany, NY. 1944. [8" × 11¾"]. N/c drawing of Franklin Roosevelt, Thomas Dewey, "Chiang," "Winnie" and "Joe" playing cards — "Featuring the World's Most Exciting Egomaniacs in a Marvelous Musical of Messianic and Mystery: Showing Sinners, Sycophants, Suckers, and Sleuths Saving Civilization with Sound; or Find the Joker!" "Dealt Off the Bottom of a Hot Deck — In Three Acts at Ten Eyck, Albany, March 9, 1944." [Crew/FDR-364].

432.12 A Willkie For President Clubs Song. w. Bess Evangeline Murch. m. "Tune — *Let Me Call You Sweetheart.*" Published by Bess Evangeline Murch, Hotel Tuller, Detroit, MI. [1940]. [4¼" × 9¼"]. Non-pictorial. 2pp. Page 2: Blank. [Crew/WLW-72].

432.13 The Willkie Song. w.m. Rosalin Wells. [1940]. Photo of Wendell Willkie. [Crew/WLW-74].

• **AmPM-433 WILLOUGHBY.** (State House, 1895–1899; Circuit Court Judge, 1912–1918; State Supreme Court, 1918–1924?)

433.1 Rally The Standard Of "Abe" Lincoln. w. Mrs. S.R. Artma "(Composer of *Guess, One Who Cares For Me, The Organ And The Choir*)." m. Roy L. Burtch. Published by Halcyon Publishing Company, No. 307 East North Street, Indianapolis, IN. 1924. Br/w photos of "Calvin Coolidge," "Charles G. Dawes," "Abraham Lincoln" and "Ed Jackson" [Republican nominee for Governor of Indiana], geometric design border. "American Campaign March Song." 4pp. + Insert letter. Page 4: Biographies of candidates and other Republicans from Indiana, including "Ed Jackson, F. Harold Van Orman, Frederick E. Schortmeier, Lewis S. Bohman, Ben H. Urbahns, Arthur L. Gillam, F.M. Thompson, Willard R. Gimmill, Judge Willoughby, E.A. Dausman, Noble Sherwood, Mrs. Edward F. White." Insert — Page 1: Letter from composer to Republican State Committee. Page 2: Advertising.

• **AmPM-434 ZOLLARS**, Allen (State House, 1869; State Superior Court Judge, 1877; Delegate, Democratic National Convention, 1880; State Supreme Court, 1883–1889)

434.1 The Winning Ticket. w. No composer indicated. m. "Air — *When Johnny Comes Marching Home*." In: *Democratic Song Book For The Campaign Of 1888*, page 3. c. John R. East. Published by John R. East, Bloomington, IN. 1888. [4¼" × 5¹³⁄₁₆"]. Bl/bl litho of Grover Cleveland and Allen Thurman. "Price 10 cents, postage prepaid, Liberal Discounts to Dealers." 20pp. [Crew/GC-140].

• **AmPM-435 MISCELLANEOUS MUSIC**

435.1 The Capital City (Waltz). m. J. Markus H. Winteringer. Published by The Winteringer Music Co., Limited, Pittsburgh, PA. 1907. Bl/w photos of various Indianapolis scenes including the State House. "Expressly written and dedicated to the citizens of the Capital City, Indianapolis, Indiana, also to the Mothers, Wives and Fair Daughters, also all newspapers and press publications, secret societies, musical societies and all firms and corporations of Indianapolis, Chamber of Commerce, commercial and social, medical, dental, political, legal, and all government employees of Indianapolis." "Composed for the Piano." B/w photo of J. Markus H. Winteringer. 6pp. Page 6: Blank.

435.2 Indiana's Home Rule Song. w.m. Roy L. Burtch.

435.3 Official Centennial March. m. John E. Porter. Published by J.E. Porter Music Pub. Co., Indianapolis, IN. 1916. B/w photo of the Capitol at Indianapolis. R/w/bl/o drawings of flags, shields eagle. "1816–1916." 6pp. Page 2: At title — "Respectfully dedicated to the State of Indiana." "J.E. Porter, Composer of *Sleep, Baby, Sleep, The Old Homestead On The Hill, Coast To Coast March*." Page 6: Blank.

435.4 Our Pride March Two-Step. m. Walter E. Fox. a. William A. Young. Published by W.E. Fox, Ft. Wayne, IN. 1901. B/w photo of unidentified man. Ma/w cover. 6pp. Pages 2 and 6: Blank.

IOWA

• **AmPM-436 ALLISON**, William Boyd (U.S. House, 1863–1871; U.S. Senate, 1873–1908)

436.1 Allison March. w. Tacitus Hussey. m. Frederick Phinney "(Grand Master Iowa State Band)." a. T.B. Boyer. Published by Frederick Phinney, Des Moines, IA. 1896. B/w photo of "Wm. B. Allison." "Respectfully inscribed and dedicated to Hon. Wm. B. Allison." "Published for Band and Orchestra. B/w photo of the Iowa State Band. "As played by the celebrated Iowa State Band, and enthusiastically received at the Republican Convention, Des Moines, Iowa, March 11, 1896." [Crew/MISC-194].

436.2 Git On Board. w. J.W. Matthews. m. Notation. "Old Melody." "For Male Voices." In: *True Blue Republican Campaign Songs For 1896*, page 19. c. J.B. Herbert. Published by The S. Brainard's Sons Company, Chicago, IL. 1896. [5⅜" × 6⅞"]. R/w/b drawing of crossed flags, wreath, ribbons. Bl/w photo of "Hon. Wm. McKinley." "Protection." 36pp. [M-328]. [Crew/WM-169].

436.3 The Jacket Of Blue. w. H. Thayer, Nashua, Iowa. m. "Tune — *Villikins And His Dinah*." In: *1888 Campaign Songs*, page 1. No publisher indicated [presumed Thayer]. 1888. [5⅜" × 8½"]. Non-pictorial black line border. Other page 1 song — *Our Ben's Raisin.'* 2pp. Page 2: Blank. [Crew/BFH-122].

436.4 Republican National Convention March. m. Al G. Mark. Published by Mark Bros. Music Publishing Company, No. 3940 Page Avenue, St. Louis, MO. 1896. R/w/b drawings of William McKinley, Levi P. Morton, Thomas Reed, Wm. Allison and "?" [question mark] on flag background, shields. "Dedicated to the City of St. Louis, June 1896." 8pp. Page 2: B/w photos of "Prominent Republicans and Gentlemen who were instrumental in securing the Republican National Convention for St. Louis — Sam M. Kennard, President Business Men's League; Chas. H. Sampson, Chairman Convention Committee; Hon. Chauncey Ives Filley, Chairman Reception Committee; Frank Gaienne, Gen'l. Mgr., St. Louis Exposition; L.S. W. Wall; Chas. F. Wenneker." Page 7: B/w photos of "Merchant's League Club — Wm. H. Hobbs, Vice-President; Louis F. Zipp, Treasurer; Hon. J.A. Talty, President; Theo. D. Kalbfell, Chair., Republican Central Committee; Morris Langsdorf, Sec." Page 8: Blank. [Crew/WM-1].

• **AmPM-437 BELKNAP**, William Worth (State House, 1857–1858; U.S. Secretary of War, 1869–1876)

437.1 Captain Grant. w. No composer indicated. m. "Air — *Captain Jenks*." In: *Tilden And Hendricks' Reform Songs (For The Centennial Campaign Of 1876)*, page 33. Published by The National Democratic Committee, Box 3637, New York, NY. 1876. [3⅞" × 5¹⁵⁄₁₆"]. Gn/bk litho of Samuel J. Tilden and Thomas A. Hendricks, geometric design border. 40pp. [M-203]. [Crew/SJT-21].

437.2 The Gathering. w. No composer indicated. m. "Air—*The Coming Of The Clans.*" In: *Tilden And Hendricks' Reform Songs (For The Centennial Campaign Of 1876)*, page 13. Published by The National Democratic Committee, Box 3637, New York, NY. 1876. [3⅞" × 5¹⁵⁄₁₆"]. Gn/bk litho of Samuel J. Tilden and Thomas A. Hendricks, geometric design border. 40pp. [M-203]. [Crew/SJT-21].

437.3 Glory, Hallelujah. w. No composer indicated. m. "Air—*The John Brown Chorus.*" In: *Tilden And Hendricks' Reform Songs (For The Centennial Campaign Of 1876)*, page 7. Published by The National Democratic Committee, Box 3637, New York, NY. 1876. [3⅞" × 5¹⁵⁄₁₆"]. Gn/bk litho of Samuel J. Tilden and Thomas A. Hendricks, geometric design border. 40pp. [M-203]. [Crew/SJT-21].

437.4 Go! Grant, Go! w. No composer indicated. m. "Tune—*Old Black Joe.*" [1876]. [4¹¹⁄₁₆" × 8¼"]. Non-pictorial. 2pp. Page 2: Blank. [Crew SJT-17].

437.5 Hancock's Solid Ranks. w. No composer indicated. m. "Air—*Tramp, Tramp, Tramp.*" In: *Hancock And English Campaign Songster*, page 30. Published by New York Popular Publishing Company, A.J. Dick, Manager, No. 32 Beekman Street, New York, NY. 1880. Be/bk litho of Winfield Scott Hancock. "Containing the Largest and Most Complete Collection of Songs, All Written to the Most Popular Airs of the Day." "The Most Popular Edition Of Hancock And English Campaign Songster." 68pp. Page 68: Be/bk litho of William H. English. [M-217]. [Crew/WSH-41].

437.6 Hark! How Sweet Those Organs Play! w. No composer indicated. m. "Air—*Hieland Laddie, Bonnie Laddie!*" In: *Tilden And Hendricks' Reform Songs (For The Centennial Campaign Of 1876)*, page 8. Published by The National Democratic Committee, Box 3637, New York, NY. 1876. [3⅞" × 5¹⁵⁄₁₆"]. Gn/bk litho of Samuel J. Tilden and Thomas A. Hendricks, geometric design border. 40pp. [M-203]. [Crew/SJT-21].

437.7 Och! Is It Myself Yez Want To Sing? w. No composer indicated. m. "Air—*Old Irish Song.*" In: *Tilden And Hendricks' Reform Songs (For The Centennial Campaign Of 1876)*, page 35. Published by The National Democratic Committee, Box 3637, New York, NY. 1876. [3⅞" × 5¹⁵⁄₁₆"]. Gn/bk litho of Samuel J. Tilden and Thomas A. Hendricks, geometric design border. 40pp. [M-203]. [Crew/SJT-21].

437.8 Our New Uncle Sam. w. No composer indicated. m. "Air—*Uncle Sam.*" In: *Tilden And Hendricks' Reform Songs (For The Centennial Campaign Of 1876)*, page 14. Published by The National Democratic Committee, Box 3637, New York, NY. 1876. [3⅞" × 5¹⁵⁄₁₆"]. Gn/bk litho of Samuel J. Tilden and Thomas A. Hendricks, geometric design border. 40pp. [M-203]. [Crew/SJT-21].

437.9 See The People Turning Out. w.m. No composers indicated. "Sung by the Hutchinson Family." In: *Hayes & Wheeler Campaign Songster*, page 6. Published by John Church & Company, Cincinnati, OH. 1876. [4" × 5⅝"]. Bl/w litho of Rutherford Hayes and William A. Wheeler. "Including Biographical Sketches & Constitution for Campaign Clubs." 52pp. Page 3: Title—*Hayes & Wheeler Campaign Carols*. [M-194]. [Crew/RBH-4].

437.10 Tilden And Hendricks' Democratic Centennial Campaign March (With Radical Accompaniments). m. A. Lutz. Published by St. Louis Music Publishing Company, No. 9 North 15th Street, St. Louis, MO. Copyright 1876 by R. Staples. B/w litho of political caricatures including marching rats poking fun at Republican scandals—Benjamin Butler—"Loyal Mashtub." James G. Blaine—"Maine stock jobber $60,000." John A. Logan—"Our Darling." Ulysses S. Grant—"Let Us Have (a) Peace." Rutherford B. Hayes—"The Cooped Chickens." 8pp. Page 2: Blank. Page 3 Title: ***Democratic Centinial*** [sic] ***March***. Page 8: More drawings. List of Republican scandals: Ben Butler as a frog—"Brother-In-Law Casey and the New Orleans Custom House;" James G. Blaine—"A Bird Who Has Lost its Plumage;" "We Heartily Endorse Bab, Belknap & Blaine and Oppose Further Investigation;" "Godless S. Orth;" "Schneck and the Emma Mine." [Crew/SJT-7].

437.11 Tilden And Reform. w. No composer indicated. m. "Air—*The Wearing Of The Green.*" In: *Tilden And Hendricks' Reform Songs (For The Centennial Campaign Of 1876)*, page 3. Published by The National Democratic Committee, Box 3637, New York, NY. 1876. [3⅞" × 5¹⁵⁄₁₆"]. Gn/bk litho of Samuel J. Tilden and Thomas A. Hendricks, geometric design border. 40pp. [M-203]. [Crew/SJT-21].

437.12 When Hancock's At The White House. w. No composer indicated. m. James Bland, "Air—*In The Morning By The Bright Light.*" In: *Hancock And English Campaign Songster*, page 6. Published by New York Popular Publishing Company, A.J. Dick, Manager, No. 32 Beekman Street, New York, NY. 1880. Be/bk litho of Winfield Scott Hancock. "Containing the Largest and Most Complete Collection of Songs, All Written to the Most Popular Airs of the Day." "The Most Popular Edition Of Hancock And English Campaign Songster." 68pp. Page 68: Be/bk litho of William H. English. [M-217]. [Crew/WSH-41].

437.13 When We Went 'Lectioneering. w. No composer indicated. m. "Air—*Evacuation Day.*" In: *Tilden And Hendricks' Reform Songs (For The Centennial Campaign Of 1876)*, page 20. Published by The National Democratic Committee, Box 3637, New York, NY. 1876. [3⅞" × 5¹⁵⁄₁₆"]. Gn/bk litho of Samuel J. Tilden and Thomas A. Hendricks, geometric design border. 40pp. [M-203]. [Crew/SJT-21].

• **AmPM-438 BOIES**, Horace (State Assembly, New York, 1855; Governor, Iowa, 1890–1894).

438.1 An Auspicious Occasion. w. No composer indicated. m. "Tune—*Odd Fellows' Hall.*" In: *Republican Campaign Parodies And Songs* [Songster], page 13. Published by Betts and Burnett, South Butler, Wayne County, NY. 1896. [7¾" × 5½"]. Be/bk non-pictorial. "McKinley and Hobart." "1896." 28pp. [M-340]. [Crew/WM-67].

438.2 Boy Bryan's Epitaph. w. No composer indicated. m. "Tune—*Upidee.*" In: *Republican Campaign Parodies And Songs* [Songster], page 12. Published by Betts and Burnett, South Butler, Wayne County, NY. 1896. [7¾" × 5½"]. Be/bk non-pictorial. "McKinley and Hobart." "1896." 28pp. [M-340]. [Crew/WM-67].

438.3 Bryan Walked Off With The Coveted Prize.

w. No composer indicated. m. "Tune — *The Band Played On.*" In: *Republican Campaign Parodies And Songs* [Songster], page 5. Published by Betts and Burnett, South Butler, Wayne County, NY. 1896. [7¾" × 5½"]. Be/bk non-pictorial. "McKinley and Hobart." "1896." 28pp. [M-340]. [Crew/WM-67].

438.4 Exit Old Party. w. No composer indicated. m. "Tune — *Good-by, My Lover, Good-by.*" In: *Republican Campaign Parodies And Songs* [Songster], page 22. Published by Betts and Burnett, South Butler, Wayne County, NY. 1896. [7¾" × 5½"]. Be/bk non-pictorial. "McKinley and Hobart." "1896." 28pp. [M-340]. [Crew/WM-67].

• **AmPM-439 CUMMINS**, Albert Baird (State House, 1888–1890; Republican National Committee 1896–1900; Governor, 1902–1908; U.S. Senate, 1908–1926)

439.1 He Didn't Mean It. w. Gerald Grey. m. J.A. Parks. In: *Parks' Democratic Campaign Songs* (For Male Voices), page 31. Published by The J.A. Parks Company, York, NE. 1912. [7" × 9½"]. Gn/bl non-pictorial geometric designs. 36pp. [M-399]. [Crew/WW-178].

439.2 A Worried Look. w. Gerald Grey. m. J.A. Parks. In: *Parks' Democratic Campaign Songs* (For Male Voices), page 28. Published by The J.A. Parks Company, York, NE. 1912. [7" × 9½"]. Gn/bl non-pictorial geometric designs. 36pp. [M-399]. [Crew/WW-178].

• **AmPM-439A DRAKE**, Francis Marion (Governor, 1896–1898)

439A.1 This Is A Nation (La Grande Marche Militaire). w.m. Stephe. S. Bonbright, Op. 60 "(*Author Of Sherman Of Shiloh Grand March, Legal Triumph Grand March, First Brigade Grand March, Kentucky Grand March, Veterans Grand Review Grand March, La Grande Marche Des Gymnastes, Listen To The Evening Chimes Nocturne, In Remembrance Waltzes, Wildwood Fairy Waltzes, Royal Chimes Polka, Tiny Tempest Galop, Peek A Boo Waltz, Etc., Etc.*)." Published by Geo. W. Gale & Co., 174 Race Street, Emery Arcade, Cincinnati, OH. 1884. B/w litho of "Main Building, Drake University, "Genl. F.M. Drake" — "Very Kindly Yours, F.M. Drake." "To one of Iowa's efficient officers during the war and most generous benefactors during peace, Genl. F.M. Drake." 8pp. Pages 2, 7 and 8: Blank. Page 3: At top of music — "In the scale of National greatness Liberty is Mistress, but Culture is Queen."

• **AmPM-440 FILLEY**, Chauncey Ives (Mayor, St. Louis, 1863–1864)

440.1 Republican National Convention March. m. Al G. Mark. Published by Mark Bros. Music Publishing Company, No. 3940 Page Avenue, St. Louis, MO. 1896. R/w/b drawings of William McKinley, Levi P. Morton, Thomas Reed, Wm. Allison and "?" on flag background, shields. "Dedicated to the City of St. Louis, June 1896." 8pp. Page 2: B/w photos of "Prominent Republicans and Gentlemen who were instrumental in securing the Republican National Convention for St. Louis — Sam M. Kennard, President Business Men's League; Chas. H. Sampson, Chairman Convention Committee; Hon. Chauncey Ives Filley, Chairman Reception Committee; Frank Gaienne, Gen'l. Mgr., St. Louis Exposition; L.S. W. Wall; Chas. F. Wenneker." Page 7: B/w photos of "Merchant's League Club — Wm. H. Hobbs, Vice-President; Louis F. Zipp, Treasurer; Hon. J.A. Talty, President; Theo. D. Kalbfell, Chair., Republican Central Committee; Morris Langsdorf, Sec." Page 8: Blank. [Crew/WM-1].

• **AmPM-441 GRIMES**, James Wilson (Territorial House, 1838–1839 & 1843–1844; Governor, 1854–1858; U.S. Senate, 1859–1869)

441.1 The Political Grimes. w. No composer indicated. m. "Air — *Old Grimes Is Dead.*" In: *Fillmore And Donelson Songs For The Campaign*, page 33. Published by Robert M. De Witt, Nos. 160 and 162 Nassau Street, New York, NY. November 4, 1856. [4¾" × 7⅛"]. Bl/bk litho of George Washington — "July 4, 1776," wreath, geometric design border. "This is the only authorized edition containing Duganne's Songs. Price 6 cts. each, $4 per 100. Discount to trade." Long quote from George Washington's "Farewell Address." 40pp. [M-101, 102]. [Crew/MF-10].

441.2 Seven Men! Seven Men! w. No composer indicated. m. "Air — *Maryland, My Maryland.*" In: *The Grant Campaign Songster, Containing All The Most Popular Original Songs, Ballads And Recitations That Will Be Most Sung During This Presidential Campaign, Adapted To Very Popular And Well-Known Airs And Choruses*, page 10. Published by Robert M. Dewitt, Publisher, No. 13 Frankfort Street, New York, NY. 1868. [4¼" × 5¾"]. [V-1: Be/bk] [V-2: Gn/bk] litho of Ulysses S. Grant. 76pp. [M-155]. [Crew/USG-75].

• **AmPM-442 HARKIN**, Thomas Richard (U.S. House, 1975–1985; U.S. Senate, 1985–Present)

442.1 Sixteen Scandals. w. Michael Pacholek. m. "*Sixteen Candles*, based on a performance by Johnny Maestro & The Crests." Published online at <http://www.amiright.com/parody/misc/johnnymaestrothecrests.shtml>. [ca. 2003].

• **AmPM-443 HIGGINS**, Thomas J., Jr. (General Assembly, 1973–1976)

443.1 Battle Hymn Of The Republic. 45 rpm record. #H-1. Performed by Thomas J. Higgins, Jr. Larry Sochterman, Organist. "Tom Higgins is your candidate for The Assembly 3 A.D."

• **AmPM-443x HOOVER**, Herbert Clark (U.S. Food Administration, 1917–1918; Secretary of Commerce, 1921–1929; President, 1929–1933) [SEE: DOC/PSM-HCH]

• **AmPM-444 HOPKINS**, Harry Lloyd (U.S. Secretary of Commerce, 1938–1940)

444.1 He's Got Them On The List. w. No composer indicated. m. "Tune — *I've Got A Little List.*" In: *Again And Again And Again Or All At Sea*, page 13. Published by Albany Legislative Correspondents' Association of New York State, Albany, NY. 1945. [8¾" × 11"]. N/c drawing of Franklin Roosevelt as pirate, Thomas Dewey as "Black Tom," Henry Wallace, Sidney Hillman, others on ship — "Union Ship C.I.O.-P.A.C." "Black Tom" Dewey walking plank. "Featuring Political Craft and Cunning and Contortions; Also Summoned by Subpoena, or Hit-Toddy and the Shady Lady, the Indestructible Dame Known as Lu-Lu; Together with Mystical Midsummer Mummery of '46, in a Roaring and Raucous and Revealing Racing Scene

Entitled 'Hoots and Straddles.'" "All Done with Music, Magic, and Mirrors — In Three Acts at Hotel Ten Eyck, Albany, March 15, 1945." [Crew/FDR-371].

444.2 We're All For F.D.R. w. No composer indicated. m. "Tune — *By The Beautiful Sea.*" In: *Again And Again And Again Or All At Sea,* page 9. Published by Albany Legislative Correspondents' Association of New York State, Albany, NY. 1945. [8¾" × 11"]. N/c drawing of Franklin Roosevelt as pirate, Thomas Dewey as "Black Tom," Henry Wallace, Sidney Hillman, others on ship — "Union Ship C.I.O.-P.A.C." "Black Tom" Dewey walking plank. "Featuring Political Craft and Cunning and Contortions; Also Summoned by Subpoena, or Hit-Toddy and the Shady Lady, the Indestructible Dame Known as Lu-Lu; Together with Mystical Midsummer Mummery of '46, in a Roaring and Raucous and Revealing Racing Scene Entitled 'Hoots and Straddles.'" "All Done with Music, Magic, and Mirrors — In Three Acts at Hotel Ten Eyck, Albany, March 15, 1945." [Crew/FDR-371].

• **AmPM-445 KASSON**, John Adam (U.S. House, 1863–1867, 1873–1877 & 1881–1884; State House, 1868–1872; U.S. Ambassador to Austria-Hungary, 1877–1881; U.S. Ambassador to Germany, 1884)

445.1 Constitutional Centennial March. m. Fred T. Baker. Published by F.A. North & Company, Publishers, No. 1308 Chestnut Street, Philadelphia, PA. 1887. B/w lithos of "James Madison," "President Grover Cleveland," "General Geo. Washington," "Alex. Hamilton," "Hampton L. Carson, Secretary, Constitutional Centennial Committee," "Col. A. Louden Snowden, Marshall, Industrial Parade, Phila., Sept. 15th, 1887," "Amos R. Little, Chairman Executive Committee, Constitutional Centennial Committee," "John A. Kasson, President, Constitutional Centennial Committee." "In Commemoration of the One Hundredth Anniversary of the Adoption of the Constitution of the U.S., Sept. 15th, 16th and 17th." "1787–1887." 4pp. Page 4: Advertising. [Crew/GC-7].

445.2 Iowa. w. L. May Wheeler. m. "Air — *Once For All.*" "'We will have homes on all the hill-tops, and no saloons in the valleys,' said Senator [sic] Kasson at the Republican Convention, June 27, 1883.'" In: *Booklet Of Song: A Collection Of Suffrage And Temperance Melodies (No. 1),* page 32. c. L. May Wheeler. Published by Co-operative Printing Company, Minneapolis, Minnesota. 1884. [6½" × 4½"]. Non-pictorial geometric designs, flora, fauna. 54pp. [Crew/S-1884–1].

• **AmPM-446 LANE**, Gordon (City Council, Fort Madison, 1956–1957; Mayor, Fort Madison, 1970–1973 & 1976)

446.1 Fort Madison — Out Town. w.m. Marie Hilpert. a. Amy Jean Lampe. No publisher indicated. Copyright by Marie Hilpert and Amy Jean Lampe, Ft. Madison, IA. 52627. B/w watercolor of skyline of Ft. Madison, water. 4pp. Page 2: At top of music — Dedicated to Mayor Gordon Lane, 1976."

• **AmPM-447 SHAW**, Leslie Mortimer (Governor, 1898; U.S. Secretary of the Treasury, 1902–1907)

447.1 Shaw, Our Standard Bearer. m. "*Battle Cry Of Freedom.*" In: *1899 Campaign Songs,* page 2. Issued by Iowa Republican State Central Committee, H.O. Weaver, Chairman. [Des Moines, IA]. [5¾" × 6⅜"]. B/w non-pictorial floral designs. "Everybody Sing." 4pp. Page 4: Blank. [Crew/WM-344].

• **AmPM-448 SHERMAN**, Buren Robinson (State Court Judge, 1865; State Auditor, 1875–1881; Governor, 1882–1886)

448.1 Gov. Sherman's March. m. Dora Stuart Van Gilder. Published by John Church & Co., 66 West Fourth Street, Cincinnati, OH. 1883. B/w litho of Buren Sherman, geometric design frame. "To Buren R. Sherman." 6pp. Page 6: Blank.

448.2 Sherman Of Shiloh Grand March. m. Stephe S. Bonbright, Op. 3. Published by F.W. Helmick, 189 Elm Street, Cincinnati, OH. 1881. B/w litho of "The New Capitol of Iowa, First to be Occupied by Gov. Sherman," geometric design border. "To Hon. Buren R. Sherman, 'The Hero of Shiloh,' Des Moines." "As played by the Third Regiment Band, I.N.G." 6pp. Page 6: Advertising.

• **AmPM-449 STONE**, William M. (Judge, 1857; Governor, 1864–1868; State House, 1878–1879)

449.1 The Soldier's Battle Prayer (Song). w. Col. J.L. Geddes, "8th Iowa Infantry Vet. Volls. Author of *Brave Old Flag.*" m. B.A. Whaples. Published by Wm. A. Pond & Co., 547 Broadway, New York, NY. 1865. B/w non-pictorial geometric designs. "Respectfully dedicated to His Excellency Col. Wm. Stone, Governor of Iowa." 6pp. Pages 2 and 6: Blank.

• **AmPM-450 THURSTON**, Lloyd (State Senate, 1920–1924; U.S. House, 1925–1939)

450.1 Father Of The Land We Love. w.m. George M. Cohan. Published by the United States George Washington Bicentennial Commission, Washington, DC. Copyright 1931 by Sol Bloom. N/c litho of a James Montgomery Flagg painting of George Washington. "Written for the American People by George M. Cohan to Commemorate the Two Hundredth Anniversary of the Birth of George Washington." "Painting contributed by James Montgomery Flagg." Counter Stamp: "From Lloyd Thurston, Congressman, 5th Congressional District, Iowa." 4pp. 6pp. Page 2: Narrative — "The Story of Washington." Page 6: N/a painting of George Washington.

• **AmPM-451 VALENTINE**, John (Democratic Candidate for Governor, 1940)

451.1 Valentine For Governor. w.m. Ethel Kemis. Published by McDermott Publishing Co., Sioux City, IA. 1940. B/w non-pictorial geometric designs. 4pp. Page 4: Blank.

• **AmPM-451A WALLACE**, Henry Agard (U.S. Secretary of Agriculture, 1833–1940; Vice President, 1941–1945; U.S. Secretary of Commerce, 1945–1946; Progressive Party Candidate for President, 1848) [ALSO SEE: DOC/PSM-FDR & HAW]

451A.1 Clear It With Sidney. w. No composer indicated. m. "Tune — *Bellbottom Trousers.*" In: *Again And Again And Again Or All At Sea,* page 10. Published by Albany Legislative Correspondents' Association of New York State, Albany, NY. 1945. [8¾" × 11"]. N/c drawing of Franklin Roosevelt as pirate, Thomas Dewey as "Black Tom," Henry Wallace, Sidney Hillman, others on ship — "Union Ship C.I.O.-P.A.C." "Black Tom" Dewey walking plank. "Featuring Political Craft and Cunning and Contortions; Also

Summoned by Subpoena, or Hit-Toddy and the Shady Lady, the Indestructible Dame Known as Lu-Lu; Together with Mystical Midsummer Mummery of '46, in a Roaring and Raucous and Revealing Racing Scene Entitled 'Hoots and Straddles.'" "All Done with Music, Magic, and Mirrors — In Three Acts at Hotel Ten Eyck, Albany, March 15, 1945." [Crew/FDR-371].

451A.2 Far Away Bosses. w. No composer indicated. m. "Tune—*Far Away Places*." Sung by "Henry Wallace." In: *Alice In Blunderland Or Through The Rooking Class* [Program and Songbook], page 7 Published by The Legislative Correspondents' Association of New York State, Albany, NY. 1949. [8⅝" × 11"]. N/c drawings of Harry Truman, Thomas Dewey, Franklin Roosevelt, Henry Wallace, Harold Stassen, Alben Barkley, Robert Taft, Earl Warren, other politicians. "A Scintillating Satire of Sadistic Surprises and Surprising Successes Featuring a Dramatic Disclosure of How Tom Did Not Go Down to D.C. in Slips; Together with a Give-Away-Nothing Radio Broadcast and Epic Melodrama of the Indian Wars Entitled 'When the Cat's Away the Mice Will Play.'" "Done With Music and Mirrors — Particularly Mirrors in Three Acts at Hotel Ten Eyck, Albany, March 12, 1949." [Crew/HST-20].

451A.3 He's Got Them On The List. w. No composer indicated. m. "Tune—*I've Got A Little List*." In: *Again And Again And Again Or All At Sea*, page 13. Published by Albany Legislative Correspondents' Association of New York State, Albany, NY. 1945. [8¾" × 11"]. N/c drawing of Franklin Roosevelt as pirate, Thomas Dewey as "Black Tom," Henry Wallace, Sidney Hillman, others on ship — "Union Ship C.I.O.-P.A.C." "Black Tom" Dewey walking plank. "Featuring Political Craft and Cunning and Contortions; Also Summoned by Subpoena, or Hit-Toddy and the Shady Lady, the Indestructible Dame Known as Lu-Lu; Together with Mystical Midsummer Mummery of '46, in a Roaring and Raucous and Revealing Racing Scene Entitled 'Hoots and Straddles.'" "All Done with Music, Magic, and Mirrors — In Three Acts at Hotel Ten Eyck, Albany, March 15, 1945." [Crew/FDR-371].

451A.4 I Can Pass On My Troubles. w. No composer indicated. m. "Tune—*I've Got The Sun In The Morning*." In: *Visions And Revisions*, page 8. Published by The Albany Legislative Correspondents' Association, Albany, NY. March 6, 1947. [8½" × 11"]. R/w/gn/y/bk drawing of Thomas "Dewey" as Santa Claus, sign — "Santa's Workshop," other New York politicians. "Revealing in Rhapsodic Revelry of Song and Stunt How a Political Scrooge Became a Political Saint; or, What Happened When Many Paws Raided the Wonderful Workshop of Santa Claus Dewey; Together with Other Strange and Silly Scenes." "Hotel Ten Eyck, Albany, March 6, 1947." 24pp. [Crew/TED-34].

451A.5 I've Got A Ballot. w. E.Y. Harburg. m. "Tune—*I've Got A Six-Pence*." [1948]. Original not located. Lyric sheet published in *Election Songs Of The United States*. Sung by Oscar Brand; Accompanied on Guitar and Banjo by Billy Faier; Notes by Irwin Silber. 33⅓ rpm LP. Produced by Folkways Records FH 5280. Scholastic Records, Englewood Cliffs, NJ. 1963.

451A.6 Jesse Jones. w. No composer indicated. m. "Tune—*Casey Jones*." In: *Again And Again And Again Or All At Sea*, page 7. Published by Albany Legislative Correspondents' Association of New York State, Albany, NY. 1945. [8¾" × 11"]. N/c drawing of Franklin Roosevelt as pirate, Thomas Dewey as "Black Tom," Henry Wallace, Sidney Hillman, others on ship — "Union Ship C.I.O.-P.A.C." "Black Tom" Dewey walking plank. "Featuring Political Craft and Cunning and Contortions; Also Summoned by Subpoena, or Hit-Toddy and the Shady Lady, the Indestructible Dame Known as Lu-Lu; Together with Mystical Midsummer Mummery of '46, in a Roaring and Raucous and Revealing Racing Scene Entitled 'Hoots and Straddles.'" "All Done with Music, Magic, and Mirrors — In Three Acts at Hotel Ten Eyck, Albany, March 15, 1945." [Crew/FDR-371].

451A.7 Keep A Growin'. w.m. Alan Lomax. In: *People's Songs*, December, 1948, Vol. III, No. 11, page 3. Published by Peoples Songs, Inc., 126 West 21st St., New York, NY. 1948. [8¼" × 10¼"]. B/w geometric design cover. 12pp. [Crew/HAW-12].

451A.8 The People's Songs For '48. Published by UOPWA [?]. [1948]. [8½" × 11"]. Non-pictorial. 2pp. Page 1: Songs—**Battle Hymn Of '48** {451A.8–1}and **Henry Wallace Is The Man** {451A.8–2}. Page 2: Blank. [Crew/HAW-11].

• **AmPM-452 WEAVER**, James Baird (District Attorney, 1866–1870; Assessor of Internal Revenue, Iowa, 1867–1873; U.S. House, 1879–1881 & 1885–1889; Candidate for President, 1888 & 1892; Mayor, Colfax, 1901–1903) [ALSO SEE: DOC/PSM-JBW]

452.1 [Here The Voice Of Freedom Calling]. w. P.R. Crosby. m. "Tune—*Battle Cry Of Freedom*." In: *Po Crosby's Campaign Songs*, page 4. Published by P.R. Crosby, Verne, Saginaw County, MI. [1892]. [3⅞" × 5⅝"]. Be/bk geometric designs. 16pp. [Crew/JBW-12].

452.2 New People's Party Songster. w. Theo. P. Stelle. m. Popular tunes. Published by Theo. P. Stelle, Mt. Vernon, IL. [ca. 1894]. 36pp. [Crew/JBW-13].

452.3 Po Crosby's Campaign Songs. w. P.R. Crosby. Published by P.R. Crosby, Verne, Saginaw County, MI. [1892]. [3⅞" × 5⅝"]. Be/bk geometric designs. 16pp. [Crew/JBW-12].

452.4 [Shall The Two Old Parties]. w. P.R. Crosby. m. "Tune—*Glory, Glory How The Freemen Sang*." In: *Po Crosby's Campaign Songs*, page 6. Published by P.R. Crosby, Verne, Saginaw County, MI. [1892]. [3⅞" × 5⅝"]. Be/bk geometric designs. 16pp. [Crew/JBW-12].

452.5 [Ye Factions Stale And Old]. w. P.R. Crosby. m. "Tune—*America*." In: *Po Crosby's Campaign Songs*, page 10. Published by P.R. Crosby, Verne, Saginaw County, MI. [1892]. [3⅞" × 5⅝"]. Be/bk geometric designs. 16pp. [Crew/JBW-12].

• **AmPM-453 WILSON**, James (State House, 1867–1873; U.S. House, 1873–1877 & 1883–1885; State Railroad Commission, 1882–1888; U.S. Secretary of Agriculture, 1897–1913)

453.1 The Cabinet Grand March. m. Hans S. Line, Op. 64. Published by National Music Company, Nos. 215–221 Wabash Avenue, Chicago, IL. 1897. R/w cover. B/w photo of William McKinley and eight Cabinet members. "Dedicated to Hon. Lyman J. Gage." 6pp. Page 6: Advertising. [Crew/WM-15].

KANSAS

- **AmPM-454 BRINKLEY**, J.R. (Candidate for Governor, 1930 & 1932)
454.1 He's The Man. w.m. Maudie Butler Shreffler. Published by The Vosberg Publishing Co., Milford, KS. 1932. B/w photo of "Dr. J.R. Brinkley." Bl/w cover design. 6pp. Page 6: Advertising.

- **AmPM-455 CAPPER**, Arthur (Publisher; President of the Board of Regents, Kansas Agricultural College, 1910–1913; Governor, 1915–1919; U.S. Senate, 1919–1949)
455.1 America My Country (The New National Anthem). w. Jens K. Grondahl. m. E.F. Maetzold. Published by The Red Wing Printing Co., Red Wing, MN. 1917. R/w/b litho of a shield, geometric designs. "Long paragraph on the song — *"America, My Country* is said to be the greatest patriotic song-poem of the war..." 4pp. Page 4: Testimonial signed by officers of the National Editorial Association. List of Governors who had "written letters commending the nation-wide use of this song" including "Gov. Capper of Kansas."

- **AmPM-456 CHAIN**, John M. (Candidate for County Treasurer, Wichita, 1913)
456.1 Pawnee Dear. w.m. Terry Sherman. Published for the Palace Theatre, Wichita. Copyright 1913 by Forster Music Publishing, Chicago, IL. Gn/w/bk geometric designs. 8pp. Page 1–8: Advertising for various local businesses and politicians. Pages 3, 5 and 7: Music. Page 2: Political — B/w photo of and advertising for J.B. Fishback for re-election to Clerk of Court (Republican); B/w photo of and advertising for John M. Chain for County Treasurer (Republican); Advertising for Ross McCormick for re-election as County Attorney (Democrat). Page 4: Political — B/w photo and advertising for I.F. Sarver for re-election for Sheriff (Republican); B/w photo of and advertising for Jas. N. Miller, Candidate for Register of Deeds (Republican); Advertising for Paul Dean, Candidate for Register of Deeds (Democrat).

- **AmPM-456A CURTIS**, Charles (Prosecuting Attorney, Shawnee County, 1885–1889; U.S. House, 1893–1907; U.S. Senate, 1907–1913 & 1915–1929; Vice President, 1929–1933) [ALSO SEE: DOC/PSM-HCH]
456A.1 Hoover And Curtis [Song Sheet]. w. Gene Hanford, "Westfield, NJ." m. "Set to good old tunes we can all sing." Published by Gene Hanford, Westfield, NJ. 1928 [9" × 12"]. Bl/w non-pictorial. "Written especially for this campaign." "$1.25 per 100; $7.50 per 1,000." "1928–1928." 2pp. Page 2: Blank. [Crew/HCH-41].
456A.1 Hoover And Curtis Campaign Song Of Cumberland County. w. Helen Hall Bucher. m. "Tune — *Yankee Doodle*." Published by Helen Hall Bucher, Highland Terrace, Boiling Springs, PA. [1928]. [3½" × 5¾"]. B/w photo of Herbert Hoover. 4pp. Page 4: Blank. [Crew/HCH-72].
456A.3 Hoover-Curtis (Rhode Island Campaign Song). w.m. Ada Holding Miller and Ruth Tripp. Published for The Woman's Republican Club of Rhode Island. 1928. Bl/w stars and geometric designs. 4pp. Page 2: "Dedicated to Leona Curtis Knight." Page 4: Blank. [Crew/HCH-58].
456A.4 Vote For Hoover. w. N.B. Herrell. m. Vanna G. Patterson. Copyright 1928 by H.B. Herrell. B/w photo by Underwood & Underwood of "Herbert C. Hoover." B/w drawings of shield, elephant, floral and geometric designs. 4pp. Page 4: B/w photos by Harris & Ewing of "Herbert C. Hoover" and "Charles Curtis." B/w drawings of elephant, shield, eagle, stars. [Crew/HCH-65].
456A.5 We're For Hoover (Song). w.m. Lawrence Stoddard Graebling. Copyright 1928 by Lawrence Stoddard Graebling, P.O. Box 1907, Washington, DC. [6¾" × 10¾"]. B/w photos of "Herbert Hoover For President" and "Charles Curtis For Vice President." B/w drawing of an elephant — "Get off and Push," geometric designs. "The Republican Party Standard Bearers." 4pp. Page 4: Blank. [Crew/HCH-49].
456A.6 (We're For) Hoover And Curtis. w.m. Albert Gould and Tom Shane. Published by M. Witmark and Sons, New York, NY. 1928. B/w photos of Herbert Hoover inscribed "Cordially Yours" [facsimile handwriting], and Charles Curtis inscribed "Cordially Yours" [facsimile handwriting]. R/w/b drawings of Puritan, Indian, Capitol building. 6pp. Pages 2 and 6: Advertising. Page 3: "Respectfully Dedicated to the Hon. Charles Curtis, Republican Nominee for Vice-President of the U.S. by the Curtis for Vice-President Club of New York." [Crew/HCH-1].
456A.7 Your Cause And Mine. w. William Oliver McIndoo. m. Charles L. Johnson. Published by McIndoo Publishing Company, Kansas City, MO. 1928. Photos of Herbert Hoover and Charles Curtis. Drawings of eagle, barge, farm. [Crew/HCH-26].

- **AmPM-457 DEAN**, Paul (Candidate for Register of Deeds, 1913)
457.1 Pawnee Dear. w.m. Terry Sherman. Published for the Palace Theatre, Wichita. Copyright 1913 by Forster Music Publishing, Chicago, IL. Gn/w/bk geometric designs. 8pp. Page 1–8: Advertising for various local businesses and politicians. Pages 3, 5 and 7: Music. Page 2: Political — B/w photo of and Advertising for J.B. Fishback for re-election to Clerk of Court (Republican); B/w photo of and Advertising for John M. Chain for County Treasurer (Republican); Advertising for Ross McCormick for re-election as County Attorney (Democrat). Page 4: Political — B/w photo and Advertising for I.F. Sarver for re-election for Sheriff (Republican); B/w photo of and Advertising for Jas. N. Miller, Candidate for Register of Deeds (Republican); Advertising for Paul Dean, Candidate for Register of Deeds (Democrat).

- **AmPM-458 DOLE**, Robert Joseph (State House, 1951–1953; County Attorney, Russell County 1953–1961; U.S. House, 1961–1969; U.S. Senate, 1969–1996; Republican Candidate for Vice President, 1976; Republican Candidate for President, 1996) [SEE: DOC/PSM-GRF]

458.1 Battle Hymn Of The Republicans. w. No composer indicated. m. Tune—*Battle Hymn Of The Republic.* N/c photos of George Bush. Ronald Reagan, Willie Horton, peacemaker missile, clear-cut forest, Dick Armey, Bill Archer, Pete Wilson, H. Ross Perot and George W. Bush. "The Washington press corps serenaded president-elect George Bush on his campaign plane with the first verse and refrain of this hymn in 1988. We added a few more stanzas." Published online by PoliticsOL.com at <http://www.presidentialelection2000.com/battle_hymn_of_the_republicans.html>. 2000.

458.2 Bill Clinton Rhapsody. w. Tom Stevens. m. *"Another Bohemian Rhapsody,* originally by Queen." Published online at <http://www.amiright.com/parody/70s/queen14.shtml>. [ca. 2000].

458.3 Bob Dole Picked Jack. w. Paul Silhan. m. "Sung to *My Boyfriend's Back* by The Angels." On: Cassette: *Running On Empty.* Lyrics published at <http://www.paulsilhan.com/roe-3.htm>. [ca. 1996].

458.4 Bob Dole's Millennial Moment. w. Bill Strauss and Elaina Newport. On CD: *It's Not Over 'Til The First Lady Sings.* Published by Capitol Steps Productions, 1505 King Street, Alexandria, VA. 2000. CD Cover: Gn/bl/y drawing of George Bush and George W. Bush as Seuss characters.

458.5 The Clintonian So-Slick Blues. w. Paul Silhan. m. "Sung to Bob (Zimmerman) Dylan's *Subterranean Homesick Blues."* "As heard on Rush's radio Show." Lyrics published online at <http://www.paulsilhan.com/dylan.htm>. 1996.

458.6 Dole Fan. w. No composer indicated. m. "Parody of *Soul Man* by Sam & Dave." Lyrics published by *The Bob Rivers Show* with Bob, Spike & Joe and Twisted Tunes online at <http://www.twistedradio.com/player/lyrics.asp?songID=849>. [ca. 1996].

458.7 Dole Man. w. William K. Tong. m. "Sung to the tune of *Soul Man* by Sam & Dave." Published online at <http://www.bootnewt.envy.nu/doleman.htm>.

458.8 Dole's A Loser. w. Tim Weber. m. No tune indicated [Lennon & McCartney]. Published at <htpp://www.geocities.com/WallStreet.4240/Lyrics.html>. [ca. 1996].

458.9 G.O.P. Is Running This Town. w. William K. Tong. m. "Sung to the tune of *Santa Claus Is Coming To Town."* In: *The Sting The Right Wing Song Book* at <http://www.geocities.com/wmktong/bootnewt/thistown.htm>.

458.10 Hard Line Robert Dole. w. William K. Tong. m. "Sung to the tune of *Old Time Rock & Roll* by Bob Seger." In: *The Sting The Right Wing Song Book* at <http://www.geocities.com/wmktong/bootnewt/hardline.htm>.

458.11 Help Republicans Fail. w. William K. Tong. m. "Sung to the tune of *The Ballad Of Gilligan's Isle."* In: *The Sting The Right Wing Song Book* at <http://www.geocities.com/wmktong/bootnewt/repfail.htm>.

458.12 I Can't Vote For That (No Can Do). w. William K. Tong. m. "Sung to the tune of *I Can't Go For that* (No Can Do) by Daryl Hall & John Oats." In: *The Sting The Right Wing Song Book* at <http://www.geocities.com/wmktong/bootnewt/nocando.htm>.

458.13 I Love DC. w. William Ross. m. "To the tune of *I Love L.A.* by Randy Newman." Lyrics and sound file published online at <http://www.seanet.com/-billr/ilovedc.htm>. 1996.

458.14 I Saw Al Gore Kissing David Boise. w. MedicManager. m. Tune—*"I Saw Mommy Kissing Santa Claus,* by Traditional." Published online at <http://www.amiright.com/parody/misc/traditional8.shml>. [ca. 2000].

458.15 Jack Kemp, Supply Sider. w. William Ross. m. "To the tune of *The Witchdoctor* by David Seville and the Chipmunks." Lyrics and sound file published online at <http://www.seanet.com/billr/kemp.htm>. 1996.

458.16 Just Vote For Me. w. Angela Kuo "(axk23@psu.edu)." m. "To the tune of *Under The Sea* from *The Little Mermaid."* "Well, it's less than a month to go and with the recent presidential and vice-presidential debates, I thought it might be appropriate to post this [song]. Right now I am still undecided which candidate I will vote for. Somehow I doubt much will happen in the next month to change that. But I will vote anyway. At least it gives me the right to complain." Published online at <http://geocities.com/Hollywood/5082/vote.html>. 1996.

458.17 Lirty Dies: The Kesidntial Prandidates. w. Bill Strauss and Elaina Newport. Published by The Capitol Steps online at <http://capsteps.com/lirty/prandidates.html>. [ca. 1992].

458.18 Nine Little Leaders. w. William K. Tong. m. "Sung to the tune of *Nine Little Reindeers* by Gene Autry." In: *The Sting The Right Wing Song Book* at <http://www.geocities.com/wmktong/bootnewt/9litlead.htm>.

458.19 On The Dole Again! w. Bill Strauss and Elaina Newport. On CD: *First Lady And The Tramp.* Published by Capitol Steps Productions, 1505 King Street, Alexandria, VA. 1999. CD Cover: Gn/bl/y drawing of George Bush and George W. Bush as Seuss characters.

458.20 Robert Dole's Speeches. w. William K. Tong. m. "Sung to the tune of *Rock & Roll Music* by Chuck Berry." In: *The Sting The Right Wing Song Book* at <http://www.geocities.com/wmktong/bootnewt/speeches.htm>.

458.21 Speaker Of The House. w. William Ross. m. "To the tune of *Leader Of The Pack."* "Sung in a female voice impersonating Arianna Huffington." Lyrics and sound file published online at <http://www.seanet.com/-billr/speaker.htm>. 1996.

458.22 "There's No One There" v. **"Someone Who's Older"** or **"Excuse Me, How Do I Write In 'Colin Powell?'"** w. Keith H. Peterson. m. "Berlin's *You're Just In Love."* Published online at <http://mysite.verizon.net/vze1qld3/id50.html>. [ca. 1992].

458.23 The Viagra Song. w. Alan Friedman and Southern Discomfort. m. *"Venus* originally by Frankie Avalon." Published at <http://amiright.com/parody/60s/rollingstones.shtml>.

458.24 We Gotta Get You A Ballot. w. Weird O'l Yankee Vic. m. *"We Gotta Get You A Woman,* originally by Todd Rundgren." "G.W. Bush Sings." Published online at <http://www.amiright.com/parody/70s/toddrundgren0.shtml>. [ca. 2000].

458.25 We Like That Old Time Robert Dole. w.

Bill Strauss and Elaina Newport. On CD: *Sixteen Scandals*. Published by Capitol Steps Productions, 1505 King Street, Alexandria, VA. 1997. CD Cover: Gn/bl/y drawing of George Bush and George W. Bush as Seuss characters.

458.26 When I'm Sixty-Five. w. William K. Tong. m. Sung to the tune of *When I'm Sixty-Four* by the Beatles." In: *The Sting The Right Wing Song Book* at <http://www.geocities.com/wmktong/bootnewt/whenim65.htm>.

458.27 Willy's Little Helper (Ode To Bob Dole). w. "Bubba." m. Tune—*Mother's Little Helper* originally by Rolling Stones." "An Ode to Viagra." Published at <http://amiright.com/parody/60s/rollingstones.shtml>.

458.28 You're A Mean One, Mr. Bush. w. Michael Pacholek. m. "*You're A Mean One, Mr. Grinch,* based on the performance by Doctor Seuss." "I know Christmas is over, but this one is not dependent upon time of year." Published online at <http://www.amiright.com/parody/60s/doctorseuss0.shtml>. 2004.

• **AmPM-458x EISENHOWER**, Dwight David (President, 1953–1961) [SEE: DOC/PSM-DDE]

• **AmPM-459 FISHBACK**, J.B. (Clerk of Court, Wichita, 1913)

459.1 Pawnee Dear. w.m. Terry Sherman. Published for the Palace Theatre, Wichita. Copyright 1913 by Forster Music Publishing, Chicago, IL. Gn/w/bk geometric designs. 8pp. Page 1–8: Advertising for various local businesses and politicians. Pages 3, 5 and 7: Music. Page 2: Political — B/w photo of and Advertising for J.B. Fishback for re-election to Clerk of Court (Republican); B/w photo of and Advertising for John M. Chain for County Treasurer (Republican); Advertising for Ross McCormick for re-election as County Attorney (Democrat). Page 4: Political — B/w photo and Advertising for I.F. Sarver for re-election for Sheriff (Republican); B/w photo of and Advertising for Jas. N. Miller, Candidate for Register of Deeds (Republican); Advertising for Paul Dean, Candidate for Register of Deeds (Democrat).

GEARY, John White (Governor, Kansas Territory, 1856–1857) [See: Pennsylvania]

• **AmPM-460 HELVERING**, Guy Tresillian (U.S. House, 1913–1919; Mayor, Salina, 1926; State Democratic Chairman, 1930–1934)

460.1 Calling For Roosevelt. w.m. Hank Barnes. a. Harold G. Rhoades. a. Len Fleming. Published by Anderson Printing, No. 105 West 4th Street, Topeka, KS. 1932. Pl/w geometric designs. 6pp. Page 4: "Sponsored by Harry H. Woodring, Gov. of Kansas, Guy T. Helvering, Chair. Demo. State Central Cmte., Chas. E. Miller, Chair. Leavenworth Cnty." Page 6: "Featured by The Purple & White Minstrels."

• **AmPM-461 HUXMAN**, Walter Augustus (Governor, 1937–1939; Judge of U.S. Court of Appeals, 1939–1957)

461.1 Kansas My Home And You. w.m. John Rogers. Published by John Rogers, Quenemo, Topeka, KS. 1938. B/w photo of "Walter A. Huxman." B/w geometric designs. 6pp. Pages 2 and 6: Blank. Page 3: At top of music — "Dedicated to a great governor of a great state."

• **AmPM-462 INGALLS**, John James (State Senate, 1862; U.S. Senate, 1873–1891)

462.1 Campaign Barbers. w. No composer indicated. m. "Arr. By Tariff Reform." In: *Red Hot Democratic Campaign Songs For 1888*, page 2. e. John Bunyon Herbert. Published by The S. Brainard's Sons Company, Chicago, IL. 1888. [5⅜" × 7 7/16"]. R/bk geometric designs. 36pp. [M-294]. [Crew/GC-141].

462.2 The Harrison Badges. w. J.L. Shinn, Vilas, Kansas, 1890. m. "Airs — *Charming Young Widow, Sing To Me Rolin, Old Oaken Bucket.*" "Inscribed to Kansas Ben." In: *Third Edition Of The Alliance And Labor Songster, A Collection Of Labor And Comic Songs For Use Of Alliances, Debating Clubs, Political Gatherings*, page 48. Published by R. & L. Vincent, Printers, Winfield, KS. 1890. [4¾" × 7½"]. 66pp.

462.3 We've Got Him On The List. w. No composer indicated. "Arr. by Tariff Reform." In: *Red Hot Democratic Campaign Songs For 1888*. page 16. e. John Bunyon Herbert. Published by The S. Brainard's Sons Company, Chicago, IL. 1888. [5⅜" × 7 7/16"]. R/bk geometric designs. 36pp. [M-294]. [Crew/GC-141].

• **AmPM-464 LANDON**, Alfred Mossman (Governor, 1933–1937; Candidate for President, 1936) [ALSO SEE: DOC/PSM-AML]

464.1 Alf Landon Sign. w. Mary Bush Lang. m. "*Auld Lang Syne.*" In: *Landing With Landon (Landon And Knox Campaign Songs 1936)*, page 12. Published by Mary Lang, No. 90 Nowell Road, Melrose Highlands, MA. 1936. [4" × 9"]. Non-pictorial. "Compliments of Massachusetts Republican State Committee." "Landon-Knox-Lyrics 1936." 12pp. [M-422]. [Crew/AML-15].

464.2 America Sings For Americanism. 1936. [6" × 8½"]. Litho of an elephant labeled "G.O.P., sunflower labeled "Landon and Knox." "Songs of the Rhode Island Young Republicans." 4pp. [Crew/AML-38].

464.3 [The Brain Trust]. w. No composer indicated. m. "Air — *I'm Forever Blowing Bubbles.*" In: *Campaign Songs For The Liberty Quartette*, page 4. Published for The Liberty Quartette, Utica, NY. [1936]. [4¼" × 8 11/16"]. Bk/br litho of four men singing, eagle. 18pp. [Crew/AML-36].

464.4 Campaign Songs For The Liberty Quartette. Published for The Liberty Quartette, Utica, NY. [1936]. [4¼" × 8 11/16"]. Bk/br litho of four men singing, eagle. 18pp. [Crew/AML-36].

464.5 [Come Along And Get You Ready For Some Grand And Glorious Fun]. w. No composer indicated. m. "Air — *There'll Be A Hot Time In The Old Town Tonight.*" In: *Campaign Songs For The Liberty Quartette*, page 13. Published for The Liberty Quartette, Utica, NY. [1936]. [4¼" × 8 11/16"]. Bk/br litho of four men singing, eagle. 18pp. [Crew/AML-36].

464.6 Community Songs For Landon Meeting. w. No composers indicated. m. Popular tunes. Published by The Volunteers, 17th Floor Tribune Building, 435 N. Michigan Street, Chicago, IL. 1936. [4" × 9"]. Be/bk non-pictorial. Community Songs For Landon Meeting, Chicago Stadium, October 9, 1936." 4pp. [Crew/AML-40].

464.7 For Landon's Marching On. w. Mary Bush Lang. m. "*John Brown's Body.*" In: *Landing With Landon (Landon And Knox Campaign Songs 1936)*, page 7. Published by Mary Lang, No. 90 Nowell Road, Melrose Highlands, MA. 1936. [4" × 9"]. Non-pictorial.

"Compliments of Massachusetts Republican State Committee." "Landon-Knox-Lyrics 1936." 12pp. [M-422]. [Crew/AML-15].

464.8 [Four Years We Have Drifted And Wandered]. w. No composer indicated. m. "Air—*My Bonnie Lies Over The Ocean.*" In: *Campaign Songs For The Liberty Quartette*, page 6. Published for The Liberty Quartette, Utica, NY. [1936]. [4¼" × 8$\frac{11}{16}$"]. Bk/br litho of four men singing, eagle. 18pp. [Crew/AML-36].

464.9 Good-Bye N.R.A.! w. Mary Bush Lang. m. "*Good-Bye Dolly Gray.*" In: *Landing With Landon (Landon And Knox Campaign Songs 1936)*, page 7. Published by Mary Lang, No. 90 Nowell Road, Melrose Highlands, MA. 1936. [4" × 9"]. Non-pictorial. "Compliments of Massachusetts Republican State Committee." "Landon-Knox-Lyrics 1936." 12pp. [M-422]. [Crew/AML-15].

464.10 G.O.P. w. Mary Bush Lang. m. "*Tammany.*" In: *Landing With Landon (Landon And Knox Campaign Songs 1936)*, page 3. Published by Mary Lang, No. 90 Nowell Road, Melrose Highlands, MA. 1936. [4" × 9"]. Non-pictorial. "Compliments of Massachusetts Republican State Committee." "Landon-Knox-Lyrics 1936." 12pp. [M-422]. [Crew/AML-15].

464.11 He'll Be Sittin' In The White House. w. James J. McAlvany, Jr. m. "Tune—*She'll Be Comin' 'Round The Mountain When She Comes.*" In: *Community Songs For Landon Meeting*, page 3. Published by The Voluneteers, 17th Floor Tribune Building, 435 N. Michigan Street, Chicago, IL. 1936. [4" × 9"]. Be/bk non-pictorial. Community Songs For Landon Meeting, Chicago Stadium, October 9, 1936." 4pp. [Crew/AML-40].

464.12 [Hiram Said To Aunt Miranda]. w. No composer indicated. m. "Air—*Put On Your Old Gray Bonnet.*" In: *Campaign Songs For The Liberty Quartette*, page 12. Published for The Liberty Quartette, Utica, NY. [1936]. [4¼" × 8$\frac{11}{16}$"]. Bk/br litho of four men singing, eagle. 18pp. [Crew/AML-36].

464.13 Horse And Buggy Ways. w. Mary Bush Lang. m. "*Jingle Bells.*" In: *Landing With Landon (Landon And Knox Campaign Songs 1936)*, page 6. Published by Mary Lang, No. 90 Nowell Road, Melrose Highlands, MA. 1936. [4" × 9"]. Non-pictorial. "Compliments of Massachusetts Republican State Committee." "Landon-Knox-Lyrics 1936." 12pp. [M-422]. [Crew/ AML-15].

464.14 I'm A New Dealer Donkey. w. Mary Bush Lang. m. "*Solomon Levy.*" In: *Landing With Landon (Landon And Knox Campaign Songs 1936)*, page 3. Published by Mary Lang, No. 90 Nowell Road, Melrose Highlands, MA. 1936. [4" × 9"]. Non-pictorial. "Compliments of Massachusetts Republican State Committee." "Landon-Knox-Lyrics 1936." 12pp. [M-422]. [Crew/AML-15].

464.15 [In 1932 They Made A Platform] (Solo). w. No composer indicated. m. "Air—*Carolina Moon.*" In: *Campaign Songs For The Liberty Quartette*, page 1. Published for The Liberty Quartette, Utica, NY. [1936]. [4¼" × 8$\frac{11}{16}$"]. Bk/br litho of four men singing, eagle. 18pp. [Crew/AML-36].

464.16 [It Was In The Balmy Springtime Back In 1933]. w. No composer indicated. m. "Air—*Nellie Gray.*" In: *Campaign Songs For The Liberty Quartette*, page 14. Published for The Liberty Quartette, Utica, NY. [1936]. [4¼" × 8$\frac{11}{16}$"]. Bk/br litho of four men singing, eagle. 18pp. [Crew/AML-36].

464.17 It Will Soon Be Voting Time. w. Mary Bush Lang. m. "*In The Good Old Summer Time.*" In: *Landing With Landon (Landon And Knox Campaign Songs 1936)*, page 11. Published by Mary Lang, No. 90 Nowell Road, Melrose Highlands, MA. 1936. [4" × 9"]. Non-pictorial. "Compliments of Massachusetts Republican State Committee." "Landon-Knox-Lyrics 1936." 12pp. [M-422]. [Crew/AML-15].

464.18 [I've A Word To Say To You, Franklin D.]. w. No composer indicated. m. "Air—*Sweet Marie.*" In: *Campaign Songs For The Liberty Quartette*, page 11. Published for The Liberty Quartette, Utica, NY. [1936]. [4¼" × 8$\frac{11}{16}$"]. Bk/br litho of four men singing, eagle. 18pp. [Crew/AML-36].

464.18A Landon And Knox. w. No composer indicated. m. "Tune—*Land Of Mine.*" In: *Kent County Woman's Republican Club Song Sheet*, page 4. [1936]. [5$\frac{3}{16}$" × 10$\frac{7}{16}$"]. B/w litho of Abraham Lincoln. "Let us have a Singing, Smiling United Membership." 4pp.

464.19 Landing With Landon. w. Mary Bush Lang. m. "*Marching Through Georgia.*" In: *Landing With Landon (Landon And Knox Campaign Songs 1936)*, page 7. Published by Mary Lang, No. 90 Nowell Road, Melrose Highlands, MA. 1936. [4" × 9"]. Non-pictorial. "Compliments of Massachusetts Republican State Committee." "Landon-Knox-Lyrics 1936." 12pp. [M-422]. [Crew/AML-15].

464.20 Landon, Landon Here The People's Call! {464.20-1}. w. Mary Bush Lang. m. "*Funiculi, Funicula.*" In: *Landing With Landon (Landon And Knox Campaign Songs 1936)*, page 10. Published by Mary Lang, No. 90 Nowell Road, Melrose Highlands, MA. 1936. [4" × 9"]. Non-pictorial. "Compliments of Massachusetts Republican State Committee." "Landon-Knox-Lyrics 1936." 12pp. [M-422]. [Crew/AML-15].

A Landon Lyric {464.20-2}. [Crew/AML-39].

464.21 Our Bet's On You. w.m. Mary Durham Barker. Published by G.W. Durham. 1936. B/w photo by Harris & Ewing of Alf Landon. 4pp. Page 4: Blank. [Crew/AML-34].

464.22 Let's All Sing Landon Campaign Songs. Published by Dudley Field Malon Rally, Dreamland Auditorium, Post & Steiner Sts., San Francisco, CA. October 22, 1936. Small litho of Pan. List of songs. 4pp. [Crew/AML-35].

464.23 Listen Here, Listen Here. w. Mary Bush Lang. m. "*Over There.*" In: *Landing With Landon (Landon And Knox Campaign Songs 1936)*, page 3. Published by Mary Lang, No. 90 Nowell Road, Melrose Highlands, MA. 1936. [4" × 9"]. Non-pictorial. "Compliments of Massachusetts Republican State Committee." "Landon-Knox-Lyrics 1936." 12pp. [M-422]. [Crew/AML-15].

464.24 Mister Donley Had A Deal. w. Mary Bush Lang. m. "*Old MacDonald Had A Farm.*" In: *Landing With Landon (Landon And Knox Campaign Songs 1936)*, page 8. Published by Mary Lang, No. 90 Nowell Road, Melrose Highlands, MA. 1936. [4" × 9"]. Non-pictorial. "Compliments of Massachusetts Republican State Committee." "Landon-Knox-Lyrics 1936." 12pp. [M-422]. [Crew/AML-15].

464.25 [The Nation Of Our Fathers Is Assailed By Foes Within]. w. No composer indicated. m. "Air—*Battle Hymn Of The Republic.*" In: *Campaign Songs For The Liberty Quartette*, page 8. Published for The Liberty Quartette, Utica, NY. [1936]. [4¼" × 8 11/16"]. Bk/br litho of four men singing, eagle. 18pp. [Crew/AML-36].

464.26 [O Come, Come Away]. w. No composer indicated. m. "Tune—*O Come, Come Away.*" In: *Kent County Woman's Republican Club Song Sheet*, page 4. [1936]. [5 3/16" × 10 7/16"]. B/w litho of Abraham Lincoln. "Let us have a Singing, Smiling United Membership." 4pp.

464.27 [O Franklin D, O Franklin D.]. w. No composer indicated. m. "Air—*Genevieve.*" In: *Campaign Songs For The Liberty Quartette*, page 3. Published for The Liberty Quartette, Utica, NY. [1936]. [4¼" × 8 11/16"]. Bk/br litho of four men singing, eagle. 18pp. [Crew/AML-36].

464.28 [O Give Me A Home Where No Brain Trusters Roam]. w. No composer indicated. m. "Air—*Home On The Range.*" In: *Campaign Songs For The Liberty Quartette*, page 5. Published for The Liberty Quartette, Utica, NY. [1936]. [4¼" × 8 11/16"]. Bk/br litho of four men singing, eagle. 18pp. [Crew/AML-36].

464.29 [O Listen While We Sing About The Billions Spent]. w. No composer indicated. m. "Air—*Jingle Bells.*" In: *Campaign Songs For The Liberty Quartette*, page 10. Published for The Liberty Quartette, Utica, NY. [1936]. [4¼" × 8 11/16"]. Bk/br litho of four men singing, eagle. 18pp. [Crew/AML-36].

464.30 [O The New Dealers' Plan Wouldn't Stand On The Shelf]. w. No composer indicated. m. "Air—*My Grandfather's Clock.*" In: *Campaign Songs For The Liberty Quartette*, page 16. Published for The Liberty Quartette, Utica, NY. [1936]. [4¼" × 8 11/16"]. Bk/br litho of four men singing, eagle. 18pp. [Crew/AML-36].

464.31 Oh! Alf Landon. w. Mary Bush Lang. m. "*Oh! Susanna.*" In: *Landing With Landon (Landon And Knox Campaign Songs 1936)*, page 2. Published by Mary Lang, No. 90 Nowell Road, Melrose Highlands, MA. 1936. [4" × 9"]. Non-pictorial. "Compliments of Massachusetts Republican State Committee." "Landon-Knox-Lyrics 1936." 12pp. [M-422]. [Crew/AML-15].

464.32 On The Good Ship G.O.P. w. Mary Bush Lang. m. "*On A Sunny Afternoon.*" In: *Landing With Landon (Landon And Knox Campaign Songs 1936)*, page 11. Published by Mary Lang, No. 90 Nowell Road, Melrose Highlands, MA. 1936. [4" × 9"]. Non-pictorial. "Compliments of Massachusetts Republican State Committee." "Landon-Knox-Lyrics 1936." 12pp. [M-422]. [Crew/AML-15].

464.33 Our Landon. w.m. No composer or tune indicated. In: *Community Songs For Landon Meeting*, page 4. Published by The Voluneteers, 17th Floor Tribune Building, 435 N. Michigan Street, Chicago, IL. 1936. [4" × 9"]. Be/bk non-pictorial. Community Songs For Landon Meeting, Chicago Stadium, October 9, 1936." 4pp. [Crew/AML-40].

464.34 [Out In Kansas, Prairie Kansas]. w. No composer indicated. m. "Air—*Clementine.*" In: *Campaign Songs For The Liberty Quartette*, page 9. Published for The Liberty Quartette, Utica, NY. [1936]. [4¼" × 8 11/16"]. Bk/br litho of four men singing, eagle. 18pp. [Crew/AML-36].

464.35 [Over The Top We're Going, Girls]. w. No composer indicated. m. "Tune—*Marching Through Georgia.*" In: *Kent County Woman's Republican Club Song Sheet*, page 3. [1936]. [5 3/16" × 10 7/16"]. B/w litho of Abraham Lincoln. "Let us have a Singing, Smiling United Membership." 4pp.

464.36 Pack Up Your Troubles. w. No composer indicated. m. "Tune—*Pack Up Your Troubles In An Old Kit Bag.*" In: *Kent County Woman's Republican Club Song Sheet*, page 4. [1936]. [5 3/16" × 10 7/16"]. B/w litho of Abraham Lincoln. "Let us have a Singing, Smiling United Membership." 4pp.

464.37 Rock's Big Candy Mountain. w. Noel E. Parmentel, Jr. and Marshall J. Dodge. In: *Folk Songs For Conservatives*, page 25. Published by Unicorn Press, Inc., No. 790 Madison Avenue, New York, NY. 10021. 1964. [5" × 8⅜"]. Bl/w drawings of Barry Goldwater, Bill Buckley, Ray Cohn, eagle. List of contents. "Sung by Noel E. Parmentel, Jr. and His Unbleached Muslims, Greatest Political Satirists Since Cohn and Schine." "Right Wing Hootenanny." 36pp. [Crew/BMG-13].

464.38 Safe To Land With Landon. w. Mary Bush Lang. m. "*School Days.*" In: *Landing With Landon (Landon And Knox Campaign Songs 1936)*, page 9. Published by Mary Lang, No. 90 Nowell Road, Melrose Highlands, MA. 1936. [4" × 9"]. Non-pictorial. "Compliments of Massachusetts Republican State Committee." "Landon-Knox-Lyrics 1936." 12pp. [M-422]. [Crew/AML-15].

464.39 Shake Off Your Troubles With A Landon Vote. w. Mary Bush Lang. m. "*Pack Up Your Troubles In Your Old Kit Bag.*" In: *Landing With Landon (Landon And Knox Campaign Songs 1936)*, page 2. Published by Mary Lang, No. 90 Nowell Road, Melrose Highlands, MA. 1936. [4" × 9"]. Non-pictorial. "Compliments of Massachusetts Republican State Committee." "Landon-Knox-Lyrics 1936." 12pp. [M-422]. [Crew/AML-15].

464.40 Songs For Volunteers. Published by Music Division, Tribune Tower. [1936]. [8½" × 11"]. B/w non-pictorial. 34pp. [Crew/AML-37].

464.41 A Sure, Safe Trail. w. Mary Bush Lang. m. "*There's A Long, Long Trail.*" In: *Landing With Landon (Landon And Knox Campaign Songs 1936)*, page 12. Published by Mary Lang, No. 90 Nowell Road, Melrose Highlands, MA. 1936. [4" × 9"]. Non-pictorial. "Compliments of Massachusetts Republican State Committee." "Landon-Knox-Lyrics 1936." 12pp. [M-422]. [Crew/AML-15].

464.42 [There'll Be Smiles]. w. No composer indicated. m. "Tune—*Smiles.*" In: *Kent County Woman's Republican Club Song Sheet*, page 4. [1936]. [5 3/16" × 10 7/16"]. B/w litho of Abraham Lincoln. "Let us have a Singing, Smiling United Membership." 4pp.

464.43 There Are Deals. w. Mary Bush Lang. m. "*Smiles.*" In: *Landing With Landon (Landon And Knox Campaign Songs 1936)*, page 7. Published by Mary Lang, No. 90 Nowell Road, Melrose Highlands, MA. 1936. [4" × 9"]. Non-pictorial. "Compliments of

Massachusetts Republican State Committee." "Landon-Knox-Lyrics 1936." 12pp. [M-422]. [Crew/AML-15].

464.44 Troubles. w. Mary Bush Lang. m. "*Comrades.*" In: *Landing With Landon (Landon And Knox Campaign Songs 1936)*, page 10. Published by Mary Lang, No. 90 Nowell Road, Melrose Highlands, MA. 1936. [4" × 9"]. Non-pictorial. "Compliments of Massachusetts Republican State Committee." "Landon-Knox-Lyrics 1936." 12pp. [M-422]. [Crew/AML-15].

464.45 The Volunteers (Our Campaign Hymn). w. James J. McAlvany, Jr. m. "Sung to the Old Hymn tune *Cutler.*" In: *Community Songs For Landon Meeting*, page 3. Published by The Voluneteers, 17th Floor Tribune Building, 435 N. Michigan Street, Chicago, IL. 1936. [4" x 9"]. Be/bk non-pictorial. Community Songs For Landon Meeting, Chicago Stadium, October 9, 1936." 4pp. [Crew/AML-40].

464.46 [The Washington Bunch Is A Funny Bunch]. w. No composer indicated. m. "Air—*When Johnny Comes Marching Home.*" In: *Campaign Songs For The Liberty Quartette*, page 7. Published for The Liberty Quartette, Utica, NY. [1936]. [4¼" × 8$^{11}/_{16}$"]. Bk/br litho of four men singing, eagle. 18pp. [Crew/AML-36].

464.47 We Greet You! w. No composer indicated. m. "Tune—*Jingle Bells.*" In: *Kent County Woman's Republican Club Song Sheet*, page 4. [1936]. [5$^{3}/_{16}$" × 10$^{7}/_{16}$"]. B/w litho of Abraham Lincoln. "Let us have a Singing, Smiling United Membership." 4pp.

464.48 We Want Landon! w. Mary Bush Lang. m. "*Old Black Joe.*" In: *Landing With Landon (Landon And Knox Campaign Songs 1936)*, page 2. Published by Mary Lang, No. 90 Nowell Road, Melrose Highlands, MA. 1936. [4" × 9"]. Non-pictorial. "Compliments of Massachusetts Republican State Committee." "Landon-Knox-Lyrics 1936." 12pp. [M-422]. [Crew/AML-15].

464.49 [We Women Call For Landon]. w. No composer indicated. m. "Tune—*Land Of Mine.*" In: *Kent County Woman's Republican Club Song Sheet*, page 4. [1936]. [5$^{3}/_{16}$" × 10$^{7}/_{16}$"]. B/w litho of Abraham Lincoln. "Let us have a Singing, Smiling United Membership." 4pp.

464.50 [When The Call To Arms Was Sounded]. w. No composer indicated. m. "Air—*Far Above Cayuga's Waters.*" In: *Campaign Songs For The Liberty Quartette*, page 2. Published for The Liberty Quartette, Utica, NY. [1936]. [4¼" × 8$^{11}/_{16}$"]. Bk/br litho of four men singing, eagle. 18pp. [Crew/AML-36].

464.51 Who All Is Goin' My Way? w. No composer indicated. m. No tune indicated. In: *Dealers Choice Or Back-To-Back Biting*, page 14. Published by the Albany Legislative Correspondent's Association of New York State, Albany, NY. 1944. [8" × 11¾"]. N/c drawing of Franklin Roosevelt, Thomas Dewey, "Chiang," "Winnie" and "Joe" playing cards—"Featuring the World's Most Exciting Egomaniacs in a Marvelous Musical of Messianic and Mystery: Showing Sinners, Sycophants, Suckers, and Sleuths Saving Civilization with Sound; or Find the Joker!" "Dealt Off the Bottom of a Hot Deck—In Three Acts at Ten Eyck, Albany, March 9, 1944." [Crew/FDR-364].

464.53 You'll Have A Brand New Bonnet. w. Mary Bush Lang. m. "*Put On Your Old Gray Bonnet.*" In: *Landing With Landon (Landon And Knox Campaign Songs 1936)*, page 5. Published by Mary Lang, No. 90 Nowell Road, Melrose Highlands, MA. 1936. [4" × 9"]. Non-pictorial. "Compliments of Massachusetts Republican State Committee." "Landon-Knox-Lyrics 1936." 12pp. [M-422]. [Crew/AML-15].

• **AmPM-465 LEASE**, Mary Elizabeth '(Ellen)' (Populist, Agrarian and Political Reformer and Temperance Advocate)

465.1 We'll All Be Happy Then. w.m. J.A. Parks. In: *Park's Republican Campaign Songs (For Male Voices)*, page 16. e. James Asher Parks. Published by The J.A. Parks Company, York, NE. 1900. Gn/bk non-pictorial. "Respectfully inscribed to Gen. Chas. F. Manderson." 40pp. [M-371]. [Crew/WM-106].

465.2 When The Votes Are Counted. w.m. J.A. Parks. In: *Park's Republican Campaign Songs (For Male Voices)*, page 26. e. James Asher Parks. Published by The J.A. Parks Company, York, NE. 1900. Gn/bk non-pictorial. "Respectfully inscribed to Gen. Chas. F. Manderson." 40pp. [M-371]. [Crew/WM-106].

• **AmPM-466 LEWELLING**, Lorenzo Dow (Governor, 1893–1895; State Senate, 1896)

466.1 When The Votes Are Counted. w.m. J.A. Parks. In: *Park's Republican Campaign Songs (For Male Voices)*, page 26. e. James Asher Parks. Published by The J.A. Parks Company, York, NE. 1900. Gn/bk non-pictorial. "Respectfully inscribed to Gen. Chas. F. Manderson." 40pp. [M-371]. [Crew/WM-106].

• **AmPM-467 MANDERSON**, Charles Frederick (County Attorney, Stark County; 1865?–1869?; City Attorney, Omaha, 1870s; U. S. Senate, 1883–1895)

467.1 When The Votes Are Counted. w.m. J.A. Parks. In: *Park's Republican Campaign Songs (For Male Voices)*, page 26. e. James Asher Parks. Published by The J.A. Parks Company, York, NE. 1900. Gn/bk non-pictorial. "Respectfully inscribed to Gen. Chas. F. Manderson." 40pp. [M-371]. [Crew/WM-106].]

• **AmPM-468 MARTIN**, John Alexander (State Senate, 1859; Mayor, Atchison, 1865; Governor, 1885–1889)

468.1 Governor Martin's March. m. H.M. Wright. Published by Whitney & Holmes Organ Co., Quincy, IL. 1885. Non-pictorial geometric designs. 6pp. Pages 2 and 6: Blank.

• **AmPM-469 MCCORMICK**, Ross (County Attorney, Wichita, 1913)

469.1 Pawnee Dear. w.m. Terry Sherman. Published for the Palace Theatre, Wichita. Copyright 1913 by Forster Music Publishing, Chicago, IL. Gn/w/bk geometric designs. 8pp. Page 1–8: Advertising for various local businesses and politicians. Pages 3, 5 and 7: Music. Page 2: Political—B/w photo of and advertising for J.B. Fishback for re-election to Clerk of Court (Republican); B/w photo of and Advertising for John M. Chain for County Treasurer (Republican); Advertising for Ross McCormick for re-election as County Attorney (Democrat). Page 4: Political—B/w photo and Advertising for I.F. Sarver for re-election for Sheriff (Republican); B/w photo of and Advertising for Jas. N. Miller, Candidate for Register of Deeds

(Republican); Advertising for Paul Dean, Candidate for Register of Deeds (Democrat).

MEDARY, Samuel (Governor, Kansas Territory, 1858–1860) [See: Kansas]

• **AmPM-470 MILLER**, Charles E. (Delegate to Democratic National Convention from Kansas, 1940)

470.1 Calling For Roosevelt. w.m. Hank Barnes. a. Harold G. Rhoades. a. Len Fleming. Published by Anderson Printing, No. 105 West 4th Street, Topeka, KS. 1932. Pl/w geometric designs. 6pp. Page 4: "Sponsored by Harry H. Woodring, Gov. of Kansas, Guy T. Helvering, Chair. Demo. State Central Cmte., Chas. E. Miller, Chair. Leavenworth Cnty." Page 6: "Featured by The Purple & White Minstrels."

• **AmPM-471 MILLER**, James N. (Candidate for Register of Deeds, 1913)

471.1 Pawnee Dear. w.m. Terry Sherman. Published for the Palace Theatre, Wichita. Copyright 1913 by Forster Music Publishing, Chicago, IL. Gn/w/bk geometric designs. 8pp. Page 1–8: Advertising for various local businesses and politicians. Pages 3, 5 and 7: Music. Page 2: Political — B/w photo of and advertising for J.B. Fishback for re-election to Clerk of Court (Republican); B/w photo of and Advertising for John M. Chain for County Treasurer (Republican); Advertising for Ross McCormick for re-election as County Attorney (Democrat). Page 4: Political — B/w photo and Advertising for I.F. Sarver for re-election for Sheriff (Republican); B/w photo of and Advertising for Jas. N. Miller, Candidate for Register of Deeds (Republican); Advertising for Paul Dean, Candidate for Register of Deeds (Democrat).

MOORE, Ely (Indian Agent, Kansas, 1853; Register of the U.S. Land Office, Lecompton, Kansas, 1855–1860) [See: New York]

• **AmPM-472 NORTON**, Gail (State Attorney General, 1991–1999; U.S. Secretary of the Interior, 2001–Present)

472.1 Talking Cabinet Blues. w. Dave Lippman. m. No tune indicated. Published online at <http://www.davelippman.com/Cabinet.html>. N/c photo of Dave Lippman. [ca. 2001].

• **AmPM-472A PEFFER**, William Alfred (State Senate 1874–1876; Presidential Elector, 1880; U.S. Senate, 1891–1897; Candidate for Governor, 1898)

472A.1 The Train Rolled On. w. Wilson Imbrie Davenny. m. "Adapted to *The Band Played On.*" In: *Old Glory Songster*, page 10. c. Wilson Imbrie Davenny. Published by the National Music Company, Chicago, IL. 1896. [4⅜" × 5 15/16"]. R/w/b flag design. "Containing the Latest Campaign Ballads." 20pp. [Crew/WM-174].

• **AmPM-473 PLUMB**, Preston B. (State House, 1862 & 1867–1868; U.S. Senate, 1877–1891)

473.1 The Harrison Badges. w. J.L. Shinn, Vilas, Kansas, 1890. m. "Airs — *Charming Young Widow, Sing To Me Rolin, Old Oaken Bucket.*" "Inscribed to Kansas Ben." In: *The Alliance And Labor Songster (Third Edition), A Collection Of Labor And Comic Songs For Use Of Alliances, Debating Clubs, Political Gatherings*, page 48. Published by R. & L. Vincent, Printers, Winfield, KS. 1890. [4¾" × 7½"]. 66pp.

• **AmPM-474 ROBINSON**, Charles Lawrence (State Assembly, California, 1851–1852; Governor, Kansas, 1861–1863; State Senate, Kansas, 1873)

474.1 Governor Robinson's Polka. m. Andrew Whitney "(Author of The *Rollstone, Fitchburg Polka*, &c.)." Published by Andrew Whitney, 132 Main Street, Fitchburg, MA. 1856. B/w tinted litho by L.H. Bradford & Co. of Charles Robinson. "As Played by the Fitchburg Cornet Band." "Composed for the Piano Forte and respectfully dedicated to his friend, Charles Robinson, first Governor of the State of Kansas." 6pp. Page 2: Blank. Page 6: Advertising.

• **AmPM-475 ROSS**, Edmund Gibson (Publisher; State Constitutional Convention, 1859–1861; U.S. Senate, 1866–1871; Candidate for Governor, 1880; Territorial Governor, New Mexico, 1885–1889)

475.1 Seven Men! Seven Men! w. No composer indicated. m. "Air — *Maryland, My Maryland.*" In: *The Grant Campaign Songster, Containing All The Most Popular Original Songs, Ballads And Recitations That Will Be Most Sung During This Presidential Campaign, Adapted To Very Popular And Well-Known Airs And Choruses*, page 10. Published by Robert M. Dewitt, Publisher, No. 13 Frankfort Street, New York, NY. 1868. [4¼" × 5¾"]. [V-1: Be/bk] [V-2: Gn/bk] litho of Ulysses S. Grant. 76pp. [M-155]. [Crew/USG-75].

• **AmPM-476 SARVER**, I.F. (Sheriff, Wichita County, 1913)

476.1 Pawnee Dear. w.m. Terry Sherman. Published for the Palace Theatre, Wichita. Copyright 1913 by Forster Music Publishing, Chicago, IL. Gn/w/bk geometric designs. 8pp. Page 1–8: Advertising for various local businesses and politicians. Pages 3, 5 and 7: Music. Page 2: Political — B/w photo of and advertising for J.B. Fishback for re-election to Clerk of Court (Republican). B/w photo of and Advertising for John M. Chain for County Treasurer (Republican). Advertising for Ross McCormick for re-election as County Attorney (Democrat). Page 4: Political — B/w photo and Advertising for I.F. Sarver for re-election for Sheriff (Republican); B/w photo of and Advertising for Jas. N. Miller, Candidate for Register of Deeds (Republican); Advertising for Paul Dean, Candidate for Register of Deeds (Democrat).

• **AmPM-477 SHANNON**, Wilson (Prosecuting Attorney, Belmont County, 1833–1835; State Prosecuting Attorney, 1835; Governor, 1838–1840 & 1842–1844; U.S. Ambassador to Mexico, 1844–1845; U.S. House, 1853–1855; Governor, Kansas, 1855–1856) [Also See: Ohio]

477.1 Campaign Song. w. E.W. Locke. m. "Air — *Old Dan Tucker.*" In: *The Freeman's Glee Book, A Collection Of Songs, Odes, Glees And Ballads With Music, Original And Selected, Harmonized And Arranged For Each. Published Under The Auspices Of The Central Fremont And Dayton Glee Club Of The City Of New York, And Dedicated To All, Who, Cherishing Republican Liberty Consider Freedom Worth A Song*, page 42. Published by Miller, Orton & Mulligan, No. 25 Park Row, New York, NY. [and Auburn, NY]. 1856. [4 15/16" × 6"]. Pk/bk litho of man on mountain peak, music sheets, geometric designs. 112pp. [Crew/JCF-16].

477.2 Down With Douglass, Pierce And Shannon. w. No composer indicated. m. No tune indicated. In: *Fremont Glees* [Song Sheet]. [1856]. [9¾" × 15½"].

Non-pictorial cloth. "As Sung by the Centerville Republican Club." 2pp. Page 2: Blank. [Crew/JCF-38].

477.3 The Friends Of Old Buchan. w. No composer indicated. m. No composer indicated. In: *The Fremont Songster*, page 6. Published by [V-1: H.S. Riggs & Company, Publishers, No. 4 Cortland Street] [V-2: P.J. Cozans, No. 107 Nassau Street], New York, NY. 1856. [V-1: 3⅝" × 5¾"] [V-2: 3½" × 5⅝"]. Be/bk litho of wreath, John C. Fremont. "With a current likeness of John C. Fremont, The People's Candidate for the Presidency." 40pp. [M-094, 095]. [Crew/JCF-45].

477.4 The Gudgeon Of Democracy And Southron Ark. w. No composer indicated. m. "Air—*The Cruel Troopers Riding By*." In: *The Republican Campaign Songster, A Collection Of Lyrics, Original And Selected, Specifically Prepared For The Friends Of Freedom In The Campaign Of Fifty-Six*, page 6. Published by Miller, Orton & Mulligan, No. 25 Park Row, New York, NY. 1856. [3 13/16" × 6"]. Be/bk litho of "Colonel John C. Fremont" facing to viewer's left, black line border. 112pp. Pages 2, 111 and 112: Blank. Pages 109–110: Contents. [M-097]. [Crew/JCF-24].

477.5 [Rouse Ye, Freemen, From Your Slumbers] (Campaign Song). w. E.W. Locke. m. "Air—*Old Dan Tucker*." In: *The Fremont Songster*, page 46. Published by [V-1: H.S. Riggs & Company, Publishers, No. 4 Cortland Street] [V-2: P.J. Cozans, No. 107 Nassau Street], New York, NY. 1856. [V-1: 3⅝" × 5¾"] [V-2: 3½" × 5⅝"]. Be/bk litho of wreath, John C. Fremont. "With a current likeness of John C. Fremont, The People's Candidate for the Presidency." 40pp. [M-094, 095]. [Crew/JCF-45].

477.6 Song. w. No composer indicated. m. "Air—*Sparkling And Bright*." In: *Fremont Songs For The People (Original And Selected)*, page 44. c. Thomas Drew "(Editor of *The Massachusetts Spy*)." Published by John P. Jewett & Company, Boston, MA. Copyright 1856 by Thomas Drew. [3⅝" × 5½"]. B/w litho of "J.C. Fremont." "The Campaign of 1856." 68pp. [Crew/JCF-18].

477.7 Those Noble Old Statesmen. w. No composer indicated. m. "Air—*Araby's Daughter*." In: *The Fremont Songster*, page 18. Published by [V-1: H.S. Riggs & Company, Publishers, No. 4 Cortland Street] [V-2: P.J. Cozans, No. 107 Nassau Street], New York, NY. 1856. [V-1: 3⅝" × 5¾"] [V-2: 3½" × 5⅝"]. Be/bk litho of wreath, John C. Fremont. "With a current likeness of John C. Fremont, The People's Candidate for the Presidency." 40pp. [M-094, 095]. [Crew/JCF-45].

477.8 'Tis Time That Freemen Raise A Hand. w. No composer indicated. m. "Air—*Yankee Doodle*." In: *The Fremont Campaign Songster*, page 20. Published by Frost & Dory, Publishers, No. 140–142 Vine Street, Cincinnati, OH. 1856. [3½" × 5½"]. B/w litho of John C. Fremont. 32pp. Page 2: "To the Fremont Clubs and the Republican Party throughout the Union, this little volume is Respectfully Dedicated by the Publishers." [M-093]. [Crew/JCF-42].

477.9 What Has Caused This Great Commotion. w. No composer indicated. m. No composer indicated. In: *The Fremont Songster*, page 8. Published by [V-1: H.S. Riggs & Company, Publishers, No. 4 Cortland Street] [V-2: P.J. Cozans, No. 107 Nassau Street], New York, NY. 1856. [V-1: 3⅝" × 5¾"] [V-2: 3½" × 5⅝"]. Be/bk litho of wreath, John C. Fremont. "With a current likeness of John C. Fremont, The People's Candidate for the Presidency." 40pp. [M-094, 095]. [Crew/JCF-45].

• **AmPM-478 ST. JOHN**, John Pierce (State Senate, 1873; Governor, 1879–1883; Prohibition Candidate for President, 1884) [ALSO SEE: DOC/PSM-JSJ]

478.1 Allow Me A Vote Of Thanks. w. J.M. Whyte and W.A.W. m. J.M. Whyte. In: Published in: *Silver Tones, A New Temperance And Prohibition Song Book Containing The Most Popular Songs Sung By The Silver Lake Quartette, For Use In W.C.T.U., Temperance, And Prohibition Party Work, Religious Meetings, Entertainments, Evenings Of Song, Etc.*, page 94. Published by W.A. Williams, Publisher, Warnock, Ohio. Edited by Rev. C.H. Mead, G.E. Chambers, and Rev. W.A. Williams. Copyright: 1892 (Book). 1888 by J.G. Dailey (Song). [5 11/16" × 8"]. Be/bk geometric design border. 132pp.

478.2 Campaign Song No. 1. w. George H. Leithead. m. "Air—*Hoist Up The Flag*." No publisher indicated. [5" × 7½"]. Non-pictorial. "1884." "Copyright secured August 18th, 1884." 2pp. Page 2: Blank. [AMC].

478.3 A Democratic Toast. w. No composer indicated. m. "Arr. By Tariff Reform." In: *Red Hot Democratic Campaign Songs For 1888*, page 6. e. John Bunyon Herbert. Published by The S. Brainard's Sons Company, Chicago, IL. 1888. [5⅜" × 7 7/16"]. R/bk geometric designs. 36pp. [M-294]. [Crew/GC-141].

478.4 Prohibition And St. John (For God, And Home, And Native Land). w. J.W. Barnes. m. F.J. Fuller, Op. 22. Published by F.J. Fuller, Bradford, PA. 1884. Non-pictorial geometric designs. "Two Musical Gems." Other title—*Father And Son*." 4pp. Page 4: Blank. [Crew/JSJ-7].

478.5 Vote The Ticket Straight. w.m. W.A. Williams. In: *Silver Tones, A New Temperance And Prohibition Song Book Containing The Most Popular Songs Sung By The Silver Lake Quartette, For Use In W.C.T.U., Temperance, And Prohibition Party Work, Religious Meetings, Entertainments, Evenings Of Song, Etc.*, page 62. Published by W.A. Williams, Publisher, Warnock, Ohio. Edited by Rev. C.H. Mead, G.E. Chambers, and Rev. W.A. Williams. Copyright:1892 (Book). 1888 by J.G. Dailey (Song). [5 11/16" × 8"]. Be/bk geometric design border. 132pp.

STANTON, Frederick Perry (Governor, Kansas Territory, 1858–1861) [See: Tennessee]

• **AmPM-479 STRINGFELLOW**, Benjamin F. (State House, Missouri, 1840s; State Attorney General, Missouri, 1845–1849; Platte County Self-Defense Association, Kansas, 1854; Territorial Representative, Kansas, 1855)

479.1 Buck Shooting. w. No composer indicated. m. "Air—*Will They Miss Me*." In: *The Republican Campaign Songster, A Collection Of Lyrics, Original And Selected, Specifically Prepared For The Friends Of Freedom In The Campaign Of Fifty-Six*, page 67. Published by Miller, Orton & Mulligan, No. 25 Park Row, New York, NY. 1856. [3 13/16" × 6"]. Be/bk litho of "Colonel John C. Fremont" facing to viewer's left, black line border. 112pp. [M-097]. [Crew/JCF-24].

479.2 Freedom And Fremont. w.m. No composer or tune indicated. In: *The Fremont Songster*, page 43. Published by [V-1: H.S. Riggs & Company, Publishers, No. 4 Cortland Street] [V-2: P.J. Cozans, No. 107 Nassau Street], New York, NY. 1856. [V-1: 3⅝" × 5¾"] [V-2: 3½" × 5⅝"]. Be/bk litho of wreath, John C. Fremont. "With a current likeness of John C. Fremont, The People's Candidate for the Presidency." 40pp. [M-094, 095]. [Crew/JCF-45].

479.3 The Republican Ball. w. James A. Boone. m. "Air — *Rosin The Bow.*" In: *The Republican Campaign Songster, A Collection Of Lyrics, Original And Selected, Specifically Prepared For The Friends Of Freedom In The Campaign Of Fifty-Six*, page 90. Published by Miller, Orton & Mulligan, No. 25 Park Row, New York, NY. 1856. [3¹³⁄₁₆" × 6"]. Be/bk litho of "Colonel John C. Fremont" facing to viewer's left, black line border. 112pp. [M-097]. [Crew/JCF-24].

479.4 The Retrospect. w. No composer indicated. m. "Air — *The Old Oaken Bucket.*" In: *The Republican Campaign Songster, A Collection Of Lyrics, Original And Selected, Specifically Prepared For The Friends Of Freedom In The Campaign Of Fifty-Six*, page 9. Published by Miller, Orton & Mulligan, No. 25 Park Row, New York, NY. 1856. [3¹³⁄₁₆" × 6"]. Be/bk litho of "Colonel John C. Fremont" facing to viewer's left, black line border. 112pp. [M-097]. [Crew/JCF-24].

479.5 Song For The Times (On The State of the Union). w. Judson. m. "Tune — *Axes To Grind.*" In: *Hutchinson's Republican Songster For 1860*, page 30. e. John W. Hutchinson "(of the Hutchinson Family Singers)." Published by O. Hutchinson, Publisher, No. 272 Greenwich Street, New York, NY. 1860. B/w floral design border. "Lincoln and Liberty." 76pp. [M-110]. [Crew/AL-317].

TABOR, Horace Austin Warner (State House, Kansas, 1856–1857 [See: Colorado]
WAITE, Davis Hanson (State Legislature, Kansas, 1879) [See: Colorado]
WALKER, Robert James (Governor of Kansas, 1857) [See: Mississippi]
• AmPM-480 WOODRING Harry H. (Governor, 1931–1933)
480.1 Calling For Roosevelt. w.m. Hank Barnes. a. Harold G. Rhoades. a. Len Fleming. Published by Anderson Printing, No. 105 West 4th Street, Topeka, KS. 1932. Pl/w geometric designs. 6pp. Page 4: "Sponsored by Harry H. Woodring, Gov. of Kansas, Guy T. Helvering, Chair. Demo. State Central Cmte., Chas. E. Miller, Chair. Leavenworth Cnty." Page 6: "Featured by The Purple & White Minstrels."
• AmPM-480A MISCELLANEOUS MUSIC
480A.1 Kansas City. m. S.L. Tyler. Published by W.H. Boner & Co., 1102 Chestnut Street, Philadelphia, PA. 1886. B/w litho of various state capitol buildings: "Madison, Wis., Harrisburg, Pa., Hartford, Conn., Columbus, O., Lansing, Mich., Washington, D.C., St. Paul, Minn., Richmond Va., Sacramento, Cal., Albany, NY., Boston, Mass., Montgomery, Ala." "The Capitol Collection." 8pp. Page 2: Blank. Page 3: At top of music — "To my Brother, C.A. Tyler." Page 8: Advertising.
480A.2 Topeka. w.m. H.W. Jones. Published by The Mills Co., Topeka, KS. [ca. 1912]. B/w photo of State House building at Topeka, downtown. O/w/bk floral drawings. 4pp. Page 4: B/w photo of a building — "The Shopping Center of Kansas, The Mills Dry Goods Company, Kansas Avenue at Ninth Street, Topeka, Kansas."

KENTUCKY

• AmPM-480B BARKLEY, Alben William (Prosecuting Attorney, McCracken County, 1905–1909; Judge, McCracken County, 1909–1913; U.S. House, 1913–1927; U.S. Senate, 1927–1949 & 1955–1956; Vice President, 1949–1953) [SEE: DOC/PSM-HST]
• AmPM-481 BECK, James Burnie (U.S. House, 1867–1875; U.S. Senate, 1877–1890)
481.1 Concerning The War We Are In. w. W.A. Croffut. m. "Air — *Meg Maguire.*" "As sung by Senator Thurman, basso; Senator Hill, tenor; Senator Beck, soprano; Accompanied by Eaton with Trombone, and Proctor Knott with piccolo." In: *Bourbon Ballads*, page 2. Published in the *New York Tribune*, Extra No. 52, September, 1879. Non-pictorial newspaper supplement. "Songs for the Stump." 4pp. [Crew/MISC-226]. [AMC].
• AmPM-482 BENJAMIN, Judah Philip (State House, 1842–1844; U.S. Senate, 1853–1861; Confederate Attorney General, 1861; Acting Confederate Secretary of War, 1861; Confederate Secretary of War; 1861–1862; Confederate Secretary of State 1862–1865)
482.1 Advice To The Rebels. w. No composer indicated. m. "Air — *Dan Tucker.*" In: *Beadle's Dime Knapsack Songster: Containing The Choicest Patriotic Songs, Together With Many New And Original Ones, Set To Old Melodies*, page 70. Published by Beadle and Company, No. 141 William Street, New York, NY. 1862. [3¾" × 5¾"]. Litho of coin — "One Dime, United States of America." 74pp. [Crew/GBM-78].
482.2 Secessia Land. w. No composer indicated. m. "Air — *Promised Land.*" Published by A.W. Auner, Song Publisher, Auner's Printing Office, 110 North Tenth Street, above Arch, Philadelphia, PA. [1862–1864]. B/w litho border. 2pp. Page 2: Blank. [AMC].
BIRNEY, James Gillespie (General Assembly, Kentucky, 1816; State House, Alabama, 1819; American Colonization Society, 1832–1833; Vice President,

American Anti-Slavery Society, 1835; Candidate for President, 1840 & 1844) [See: Alabama]

• **AmPM-483 BLACKBURN**, Joseph Clay Stiles (State House, 1871–1875; U.S. House, 1875–1885; U.S. Senate, 1885–1897 & 1901–1907; Governor, Canal Zone, 1907–1909)

483.1 An Auspicious Occasion. w. No composer indicated. m. "Tune—*Odd Fellows' Hall.*" In: *Republican Campaign Parodies And Songs* [Songster], page 13. Published by Betts and Burnett, South Butler, Wayne County, NY. 1896. [7¾" × 5½"]. Be/bk non-pictorial. "McKinley and Hobart." "1896." 28pp. [M-340]. [Crew/WM-67].

483.2 Bryan Walked Off With The Coveted Prize. w. No composer indicated. m. "Tune—*The Band Played On.*" In: *Republican Campaign Parodies And Songs* [Songster], page 5. Published by Betts and Burnett, South Butler, Wayne County, NY. 1896. [7¾" × 5½"]. Be/bk non-pictorial. "McKinley and Hobart." "1896." 28pp. [M-340]. [Crew/WM-67].

483.3 Campaign Barbers. w. No composer indicated. m. "Arr. By Tariff Reform." In: *Red Hot Democratic Campaign Songs For 1888*, page 2. e. John Bunyon Herbert. Published by The S. Brainard's Sons Company, Chicago, IL. 1888. [5⅜" × 7⁷⁄₁₆"]. R/bk geometric designs. 36pp. [M-294]. [Crew/GC-141].

483.4 Exit Old Party. w. No composer indicated. m. "Tune—*Good-By, My Lover, Good-By.*" In: *Republican Campaign Parodies And Songs* [Songster], page 20. Published by Betts and Burnett, South Butler, Wayne County, NY. 1896. [7¾" × 5½"]. Be/bk non-pictorial. "McKinley and Hobart." "1896." 28pp. [M-340]. [Crew/WM-67].

• **AmPM-484 BLAIR**, Francis J. (Member, Kitchen Cabinet of Andrew Jackson, 1820s; Founder, *Washington Globe* (1830) & *Congressional Globe* [*Congressional Record*])

484.1 Clearing The Kitchen And White House (A Song For The Fourth of March, 1841). w. No composer indicated. m. "Tune—*Young Lochinvar.*" In: *The Tippecanoe Campaign Of 1840*, page 61. Published by A.B. Norton, Mount Vernon, OH. 1888. [5½" × 7½"]. Bl/gd book. 496pp. Pages 1–382: Text. Pages 383–485: "Tippecanoe Songs of the Log Cabin Boys and Girls of 1840." [M-276]. [Crew/WHH-96].

484.2 The Dutchman. w. No composer indicated. m. "Air—*The Poachers.*" In: *A Miniature Of Martin Van Buren (With A Selection Of The Best And Most Popular Tippecanoe Songs)*, page 49. 1840. [3½" × 6½"]. [V-1: Br/bk] [V-2: Gn/bk] [V-3: Y/bk] litho of man, chain around neck. Van Buren quote. "Amos Kendall's Veracity—Tom Benton's Honesty—Francis Blair's Beauty." "What is wanting cant be numbered [sic]." 58pp. [M-016]. [Crew/WHH-88].

484.3 Jackson's Lament. w. No composer indicated. m. No tune indicated. In: *A Miniature Of Martin Van Buren (With A Selection Of The Best And Most Popular Tippecanoe Songs)*, page 51. 1840. [3½" × 6½"]. [V-1: Br/bk] [V-2: Gn/bk] [V-3: Y/bk] litho of man, chain around neck. Van Buren quote. "Amos Kendall's Veracity—Tom Benton's Honesty—Francis Blair's Beauty." "What is wanting cant be numbered [sic]." 58pp. [M-016]. [Crew/WHH-88].

484.4 John C. Calhoun, My Jo. w. No composer indicated. w. "The Milford Bard." m. "Tune—*John Anderson, My Jo.*" In: *A Miniature Of Martin Van Buren (With A Selection Of The Best And Most Popular Tippecanoe Songs)*, page 32. 1840. [3½" × 6½"]. [V-1: Br/bk] [V-2: Gn/bk] [V-3: Y/bk] litho of man, chain around neck. Van Buren quote. "Amos Kendall's Veracity—Tom Benton's Honesty—Francis Blair's Beauty." "What is wanting cant be numbered [sic]." 58pp. [M-016]. [Crew/WHH-88].

484.5 Keep The Ball Rolling. w. No composer indicated. m. Notation. In: *The Log Cabin*, page 4, Vol. 1, No. 26, Oct. 24, 1840. Published by Horace Greeley & Company, New York, NY. 1840. Non-pictorial. [Crew/WHH-91].

484.6 King Andrew (Glee). w. No composer indicated. m. "Tune—*Dame Durden.*" Published by S.H. Parker, No. 141 Washington Street, Boston, MA. August, 1834. Non-pictorial. "As Sung at the Salem Whig Festival." 4pp. Pages 1 and 4: Blank. [Crew/AJK-7].

484.7 King Andrew. w. No composer indicated. m. "Tune—*Dame Durden.*" In: *A Miniature Of Martin Van Buren (With A Selection Of The Best And Most Popular Tippecanoe Songs)*, page 46. 1840. [3½" × 6½"]. [V-1: Br/bk] [V-2: Gn/bk] [V-3: Y/bk] litho of man, chain around neck. Van Buren quote. "Amos Kendall's Veracity—Tom Benton's Honesty—Francis Blair's Beauty." "What is wanting cant be numbered [sic]." 58pp. [M-016]. [Crew/WHH-88].

484.8 King Martin's Soliloquy (A Modern Democratic Melody). w. No composer indicated. m. "Air—*It Is Not On The Battle Field.*" In: *Harrison Melodies (Original And Selected)*, page 19. Published by Weeks, Jordan & Co., Boston, MA. 1840. [3³⁄₁₆" × 6"]. B/w litho of William Henry Harrison. "Published under the direction of the Boston Harrison Club." 76pp. Page 5: "To William Henry Harrison of Ohio, the gallant soldier, the enlightened statesman, the consistent Republican, and the Honest man..." [M-001, 002, 003]. [Crew/WHH-86].

484.9 King Matty And Blair. w. No composer indicated. m. "Tune—*Lord Lovell And Nancy Bell.*" In: *A Miniature Of Martin Van Buren (With A Selection Of The Best And Most Popular Tippecanoe Songs)*, page 32. 1840. [3½" × 6½"]. [V-1: Br/bk] [V-2: Gn/bk] [V-3: Y/bk] litho of man, chain around neck. Van Buren quote. "Amos Kendall's Veracity—Tom Benton's Honesty—Francis Blair's Beauty." "What is wanting cant be numbered [sic]." 58pp. [M-016]. [Crew/WHH-88].

484.10 The Last Cabinet Council. w. No composer indicated. m. "Tune—*There's Nae Luck About The House.*" "A Very Pathetic and musical appeal to the Dear People, by an Ex-Post Master General." In: *Tippecanoe Song-Book (A Collection Of Log Cabin And Patriotic Melodies)*, page 45. Published by Marshall, Williams & Butler, Philadelphia, PA. 1840. White on black litho of log cabin, plow, flags, eagle. 180pp. [M-024]. [Crew/WHH-61].

484.11 The Last Cabinet Council. w. No composer indicated. m. "Air—*There's Nae Luck About The House.*" In: *The Log Cabin & Hard Cider Melodies, A Collection Of Popular And Patriotic Songs*, page 30. Published by Charles Adams, No. 23 Tremont Street, Boston, MA. 1840. [3¾" × 6"]. [V-1: Pk/bk] [V-2:

Gn/bk] litho of William Henry Harrison. "The Freeman's glittering Sword be Blest, For ever blest the Freeman's Lyre." 78pp. Pages 2 and 77: Blank. Page 3: Inside title page. B/w litho of log cabin. "Respectfully Dedicated to the Friends of Harrison and Tyler." Page 78: Advertising. [M-012]. [Crew/WHH-68].

484.12 The Locofoco Exit, On The Fourth Of March, 1841. w. No composer indicated. m. "Tune—*I See Them On Their Winding Way.*" In: *Songs For The People (Or Tippecanoe Melodies)* [Songster], page 33. "Dedicated to the Democratic Whig Young Men of the City and County of New York." Published for the Authors by James P. Giffing, No. 56 Gold Street, New York, NY. 1840. [3¾" × 6"]. Litho of William Henry Harrison, log cabin, flag. "Original and Selected." 76pp. [M-019]. [Crew/WHH-63].

484.13 The Lounger's Lament. w. No composer indicated. m. No tune indicated. In: *Whig Songs For 1844* [Songster], page 14. Published by Greeley & McElrath, New York, NY. 1844. [5⅞" × 9³⁄₁₆"]. Nonpictorial. 16pp. Page 16: "Odes and Poems." [M-061]. [Crew/HC-35].

484.14 The Lounger's Lament. w. No composer indicated. m. "Tune—*The Exile Of Erin.*" In: *The Clay Minstrel Or National Songster*, page 282. c. John Stockton Littell. Published by Greeley & M'Elrath, Tribune Building, New York, NY. 1844. [3⅛" × 4⅞"]. Nonpictorial. 396pp. [Crew/HC-18].

484.15 The Lounger's Lament. w. No composer indicated. m. "Air—*Exile Of Erin.*" In: *The Log Cabin & Hard Cider Melodies, A Collection Of Popular And Patriotic Songs*, page 42. Published by Charles Adams, No. 23 Tremont Street, Boston, MA. 1840. [3¾" × 6"]. [V-1: Pk/bk] [V-2: Gn/bk] litho of William Henry Harrison. "The Freeman's glittering Sword be Blest, For ever blest the Freeman's Lyre." 78pp. Pages 2 and 77: Blank. Page 3: Inside title page. B/w litho of log cabin. "Respectfully Dedicated to the Friends of Harrison and Tyler." Page 78: Advertising. [M-012]. [Crew/WHH-68].

484.16 A Miniature Of Martin Van Buren. w.m. No composer or tune indicated. In: *A Miniature Of Martin Van Buren (With A Selection Of The Best And Most Popular Tippecanoe Songs)*, page 3. 1840. [3½" × 6½"]. [V-1: Br/bk] [V-2: Gn/bk] [V-3: Y/bk] litho of man, chain around neck. Van Buren quote. "Amos Kendall's Veracity—Tom Benton's Honesty—Francis Blair's Beauty." "What is wanting cant be numbered [sic]." 58pp. [M-016]. [Crew/WHH-88].

484.17 Oh! Oh! Where Shall I Fly To. w. No composer indicated. m. "Tune—*Thou, thou, reign'st In this Bosom.*" In: *A Miniature Of Martin Van Buren (With A Selection Of The Best And Most Popular Tippecanoe Songs)*, page 28. 1840. [3½" × 6½"]. [V-1: Br/bk] [V-2: Gn/bk] [V-3: Y/bk] litho of man, chain around neck. Van Buren quote. "Amos Kendall's Veracity—Tom Benton's Honesty—Francis Blair's Beauty." "What is wanting cant be numbered [sic]." 58pp. [M-016]. [Crew/WHH-88].

484.18 Old Tippecanoe Come Out Of The West. w. No composer indicated. m. "Tune—*Young Lochinvar.*" In: *Tippecanoe Song-Book (A Collection Of Log Cabin And Patriotic Melodies)*, page 58. Published by Marshall, Williams & Butler, Philadelphia, PA. 1840. White on black litho of log cabin, plow, flags, eagle. 180pp. [M-024]. [Crew/WHH-61].

484.19 The Second Polk Song. w. No composer indicated. m. "Tune—*Lucy Long.*" In: *The National Clay Minstrel*, page 10. Published by [V-1: George Hood, No. 15 North 6th Street, Philadelphia, PA] [V-2: James Fisher, No. 71 Court Street, Boston, MA]. 1843. [3" × 4½"]. Y/bk litho of raccoon sitting on fence, black border. 68pp. Pages 2 and 67: Blank. Pages 65–66: Contents. [Crew/HC-10].

484.20 Seymour's Consent. w. No composer indicated. m. "Tune—*Am O Not Fondly Thine Own.*" In: *The Grant And Colfax Republican Songster, Containing Campaign Songs, Ballads And Choruses. Adapted To The Most Popular And Stirring Tunes*, page 55. Published by R.M. Dewitt, Publisher, No. 13 Frankfort Street, New York, NY. 1868. [4" × 6³⁄₁₆"]. R/w/b litho of flag. Advertising. 100pp. [M-150]. [Crew/USG-63].

484.21 A Song For The Martin, 1841. w. No composer indicated. m. "Air—*My Heart's In The Highlands.*" In: *Harrison Melodies (Original And Selected)*, page 16. Published by Weeks, Jordan & Co., Boston, MA. 1840. [3⁹⁄₁₆" × 6"]. B/w litho of William Henry Harrison. "Published under the direction of the Boston Harrison Club." 76pp. [M-001, 002, 003]. [Crew/WHH-86].

484.22 Tanners' Chorus. w. No composer indicated. m. "Air—*Tippecanoe And Tyler, Too!*" In: *The Grant And Colfax Republican Songster, Containing Campaign Songs, Ballads And Choruses. Adapted To The Most Popular And Stirring Tunes*, page 4. Published by R.M. Dewitt, Publisher, No. 13 Frankfort Street, New York, NY. 1868. [4" × 6³⁄₁₆"]. R/w/b litho of flag. Advertising. 100pp. [M-150]. [Crew/USG-63].

484.23 Ye Whigs Of Columbia. w. No composer indicated. m. "Tune—*Lochiel's Warning.*" In: *Tippecanoe Song-Book (A Collection Of Log Cabin And Patriotic Melodies)*, page 83. Published by Marshall, Williams & Butler, Philadelphia, PA. 1840. White on black litho of log cabin, plow, flags, eagle. 180pp. [M-024]. [Crew/WHH-61].

484.24 Young Men's National Convention. w. No composer indicated. m. No tune indicated. In: *The Tippecanoe Campaign Of 1840*, page 74. Published by A.B. Norton, Mount Vernon, OH. 1888. [5½" × 7½"]. Bl/gd book. 496pp. Pages 1–382: Text. Pages 383–485: "Tippecanoe Songs of the Log Cabin Boys and Girls of 1840." [M-276]. [Crew/WHH-96].

• **AmPM-485 BLAIR**, J.H. (Sheriff, Bell County, 1931–1932)

485.1 Which Side Are You On? w. Florence Reece, Harlan, Ky., 1931. m. "Old hymn tune." In: *Songs For Wallace*, page 10. Published by People's Song, Inc. for the National Office of The Progressive Party, No. 39 Park Avenue, New York, NY. 1948. [8⅜" × 10¼"]. B/w drawing of Henry A. Wallace, farm. 12pp. [M-428]. [Crew/HAW-3].

485.2 Which Side Are You On? w. Florence Reece. m. No tune indicated. [ca. 1931]. [TPL, p. 66].

BLAIR, Montgomery (State Court Judge, Kentucky, 1843–1849) [See: Maryland]

• **AmPM-486 BOYD**, Linn (State House, 1827–1832; U.S. House, 1835–1837 & 1839–1855)

486.1 Hurrah For Old Tip. w. No composer indicated. m. No tune indicated. In: *The Tippecanoe Campaign Of 1840*, page 15. Published by A.B. Norton, Mount Vernon, OH. 1888. [5½" × 7½"]. Bl/gd book. 496pp. Pages 1–382: Text. Pages 383–485: "Tippecanoe Songs of the Log Cabin Boys and Girls of 1840." [M-276]. [Crew/WHH-96].

486.2 Hurrah Song. w. No composer indicated. m. No tune indicated. In: *The Tippecanoe Campaign Of 1840*, page 53. Published by A.B. Norton, Mount Vernon, OH. 1888. [5½" × 7½"]. Bl/gd book. 496pp. Pages 1–382: Text. Pages 383–485: "Tippecanoe Songs of the Log Cabin Boys and Girls of 1840." [M-276]. [Crew/WHH-96].

486.3 The Hurrah Song. w.m. No composer or tune indicated. In: *The Log Cabin & Hard Cider Melodies, A Collection Of Popular And Patriotic Songs*, page 24. Published by Charles Adams, No. 23 Tremont Street, Boston, MA. 1840. [3¾" × 6"]. [V-1: Pk/bk] [V-2: Gn/bk] litho of William Henry Harrison. "The Freeman's glittering Sword be Blest, For ever blest the Freeman's Lyre." 78pp. Pages 2 and 77: Blank. Page 3: Inside title page. £/w litho of log cabin. "Respectfully Dedicated to the Friends of Harrison and Tyler." Page 78: Advertising. [M-012]. [Crew/WHH-68].

486.4 The Last Cabinet Council. w. No composer indicated. m. "Tune — *There's Nae Luck About The House.*" "A Very Pathetic and musical appeal to the Dear People, by an Ex-Post Master General." In: *Tippecanoe Song-Book (A Collection Of Log Cabin And Patriotic Melodies)*, page 45. Published by Marshall, Williams & Butler, Philadelphia, PA. 1840. White on black litho of log cabin, plow, flags, eagle. 180pp. [M-024]. [Crew/WHH-61].

486.5 The Last Cabinet Council. w. No composer indicated. m. "Air — *There's Nae Luck About The House.*" In: *The Harrison And Log Cabin Song Book*, page 35. Published by I.N. Whiting, Columbus, OH. 1840. [3½" × 5½"]. Bl/bk hard cover book with litho of log cabin, flag, eagle. 124pp. [M-008]. [Crew/WHH-76].

486.6 The Last Cabinet Council. w. No composer indicated. m. "Air — *There's Nae Luck About The House.*" In: *The Log Cabin & Hard Cider Melodies, A Collection Of Popular And Patriotic Songs*, page 30. Published by Charles Adams, No. 23 Tremont Street, Boston, MA. 1840. [3¾" × 6"]. [V-1: Pk/bk] [V-2: Gn/bk] litho of William Henry Harrison. "The Freeman's glittering Sword be Blest, For ever blest the Freeman's Lyre." 78pp. [M-012]. [Crew/WHH-68].

486.7 Old Tip's The Boy. w. No composer indicated. m. "Air — *The Hurrah Song.*" In: *A Miniature Of Martin Van Buren (With A Selection Of The Best And Most Popular Tippecanoe Songs)*, page 43. 1840. [3½" × 6½"]. [V-1: Br/bk] [V-2: Gn/bk] [V-3: Y/bk] litho of man, chain around neck. Van Buren quote. "Amos Kendall's Veracity — Tom Benton's Honesty — Francis Blair's Beauty." "What is wanting cant be numbered [sic]." 58pp. [M-016]. [Crew/WHH-88].

• **AmPM-486A BRECKENRIDGE**, John Cabell (State House, 1849; U.S. House, 1851–1855; Vice President, 1856; Candidate for President in 1860; U.S. Senate, 1861; Confederate Secretary of War, 1861–1865) [ALSO SEE: DOC/PSM-JB & JCB]

486A.1 The Bachelor Candidate. w. No composer indicated. m. "Air — *The Campbells Are Coming.*" In: *Fremont Songs For The People (Original And Selected)*, page 43. c. Thomas Drew "(Editor of *The Massachusetts Spy*)." Published by John P. Jewett & Company, Boston, MA. Copyright 1856 by Thomas Drew. [3⅜" × 5½"]. B/w litho of "J.C. Fremont." "The Campaign of 1856." 68pp. [Crew/JCF-18].

486A.2 The Bachelor Candidate. w. No composer indicated. m. "Air — *Rory O'More.*" Published by Andrews, Printer, No. 38 Chatham Street, New York, NY. [1856]. B/w penny song sheet with litho border of geometric designs. "Andrews, Printer, No. 38 Chatham Street, N.Y. Dealer in Songs, Games, Toy Books, Mottos, Verses, Valentines, &c." 2pp. Page 2: Blank. [Crew/JCF-59].

486A.3 The Baltimore Convention. w. B. m. "Tune — *Tip And Ty.*" In: *The Wide Awake Vocalist (Or Rail Splitters' Song Book)*, page 26. Published by E.A. Daggett, No. 333 Broadway, New York, NY. 1860. Non-pictorial geometric design border. "Words and Music for the Republican Campaign of 1860, Embracing a Great Variety of Songs, Solos, Duets and Choruses Arranged for Piano or melodeon; The best collection of Words and Music ever published for a campaign, Every Club and Family should have copies, so as to join in the choruses; The Ladies are invited to join in the choruses at the meetings." 68pp. [M-116]. [Crew/AL-59].

486A.4 The Bay State Hurrah. w.m. No composer or tune indicated. In: *Fremont Songs For The People (Original And Selected)*, page 37. c. Thomas Drew "(Editor of *The Massachusetts Spy*)." Published by John P. Jewett & Company, Boston, MA. Copyright 1856 by Thomas Drew. [3⅜" × 5½"]. B/w litho of "J.C. Fremont." "The Campaign of 1856." 68pp. [Crew/JCF-18].

486A.5 Buchanan And John Breckenridge. w.m. Stephen Foster. On CD: *Presidential Campaign Songs, 1789–1996*. Smithsonian Folkways Recording #SFW CD 45051. Arranged and performed by Oscar Brand. 1999.

486A.6 Buck Shooting. w. No composer indicated. m. "Air — *Will They Miss Me.*" In: *The Republican Campaign Songster, A Collection Of Lyrics, Original And Selected, Specifically Prepared For The Friends Of Freedom In The Campaign Of Fifty-Six*, page 67. Published by Miller, Orton & Mulligan, No. 25 Park Row, New York, NY. 1856. [3¹⁵⁄₁₆" × 6"]. Be/bk litho of "Colonel John C. Fremont" facing to viewer's left, black line border. 112pp. [M-097]. [Crew/JCF-24].

486A.7 Clear The Track! w. No composer indicated. m. "Music — *Begone, Dull Care!*" Published in the *New York Weekly Times, And National Democrat*, July 26, 1856. [VBL, p. 334].

486A.8 [Come Join Our Throng, Ye Patriots True] (A Rallying Song). w. No composer indicated. m. "Air — *Dan Tucker.*" In: *The Democratic Campaign Songster, No. #1*, page 35. Published by American Publishing House, No. 60 West Fourth Street, Cincinnati, OH. 1860. [3⅞" × 5¹⁵⁄₁₆"]. Pk/bk litho of "Stephen A. Douglas," black line border. At top of cover — "No. 1, Price 10 Cents." 52pp. [M-118]. [Crew/SAD-12].

486A.9 A Dirge For H.G. w. No composer indicated. m. "Air — *Not For Joseph.*" From the "*Springfield*

Republican." In: *National Republican Grant And Wilson Campaign Song-Book,* page 80. Published by The Union Republican Congressional Committee, Washington, DC. 1872. [3¹³⁄₁₆" × 8⁹⁄₁₆"]. Be/bk litho of Ulysses S. Grant. "We'll Sing a Song for U.S. Grant." 100pp. [M-182]. [Crew/USG-110].

486A.10 Douglas And His Dinah (Song or Duet, and Chorus for Male Voices). w. No composer indicated. m.a. A. Cull. In: *The Wide Awake Vocalist (Or Rail Splitters' Song Book),* page 52. Published by E.A. Daggett, No. 333 Broadway, New York, NY. 1860. Non-pictorial geometric design border. "Words and Music for the Republican Campaign of 1860, Embracing a Great Variety of Songs, Solos, Duets and Choruses Arranged for Piano or melodeon; The best collection of Words and Music ever published for a campaign, Every Club and Family should have copies, so as to join in the choruses; The Ladies are invited to join in the choruses at the meetings." 68pp. [M-116]. [Crew/AL-59].

486A.11 The Douglas Cause Is Growing. w. No composer indicated. m. "Air—*Free And Easy.*" In: *The Democratic Campaign Songster: Douglas & Johnson Melodies,* page 35. Published by P.J. Cozans, Publisher, New York, NY. [1860]. [3⅞" × 6"]. Y/bk litho of an eagle with ribbon—"Douglas & Johnson," train, ships, monument—"Liberty" sitting on rock base—"The Constitution." 40pp. [M-117]. [Crew/SAD-5].

486A.12 Douglas Going Home (National Song). w. No composer indicated. m. "Air—*Few Days.*" In: *The Democratic Campaign Songster: Douglas & Johnson Melodies,* page 24. Published by P.J. Cozans, Publisher, New York, NY. [1860]. [3⅞" × 6"]. Y/bk litho of an eagle with ribbon—"Douglas & Johnson," train, ships, monument—"Liberty" sitting on rock base—"The Constitution." 40pp. [M-117]. [Crew/SAD-5].

486A.13 Douglas Our Choice. w. No composer indicated. m. "Tune—*Old Dan Tucker.*" In: *The Democratic Campaign Songster, No. #1,* page 25. Published by American Publishing House, No. 60 West Fourth Street, Cincinnati, OH. 1860. [3⅞" × 5¹¹⁄₁₆"]. Pk/bk litho of "Stephen A. Douglas," black line border. At top of cover—"No. 1, Price 10 Cents." 52pp. [M-118]. [Crew/SAD-12].

486A.14 Douglas Shall Be President. w. No composer indicated. m. "Air—*Yankee Doodle.*" In: *The Democratic Campaign Songster, No. #1,* page 39. Published by American Publishing House, No. 60 West Fourth Street, Cincinnati, OH. 1860. [3⅞" × 5¹¹⁄₁₆"]. Pk/bk litho of "Stephen A. Douglas," black line border. At top of cover—"No. 1, Price 10 Cents." 52pp. [M-118]. [Crew/SAD-12].

486A.15 Douglas's Going Home. w. No composer indicated. m. "Air—*Yankee Doodle.*" In: *The Democratic Campaign Songster, No. #1,* page 39. Published by American Publishing House, No. 60 West Fourth Street, Cincinnati, OH. 1860. [3⅞" × 5¹¹⁄₁₆"]. Pk/bk litho of "Stephen A. Douglas," black line border. At top of cover—"No. 1, Price 10 Cents." 52pp. [M-118]. [Crew/SAD-12].

486A.16 For Freedom And Fremont (The Hurrah Song). w. No composer indicated. m. Air—*The Hurrah Song.* In: *Fremont Songs For The People (Original And Selected),* page 24. c. Thomas Drew "(Editor of *The Massachusetts Spy*)." Published by John P. Jewett & Company, Boston, MA. Copyright 1856 by Thomas Drew. [3⅝" × 5½"]. B/w litho of "J.C. Fremont." "The Campaign of 1856." 68pp. [Crew/JCF-18].

486A.17 For Fremont And Freedom. w. No composer indicated. m. "Air—*Rory O'More.*" In: *The Republican Campaign Songster, A Collection Of Lyrics, Original And Selected, Specifically Prepared For The Friends Of Freedom In The Campaign Of Fifty-Six,* page 20. Published by Miller, Orton & Mulligan, No. 25 Park Row, New York, NY. 1856. [3¹³⁄₁₆" × 6"]. Be/bk litho of "Colonel John C. Fremont" facing to viewer's left, black line border. 112pp. [M-097]. [Crew/JCF-24].

486A.18 Fremont And Freedom. w. No composer indicated. m. "Air—*Right Over Wrong.*" In: *Fremont Songs For The People (Original And Selected),* page 18. c. Thomas Drew "(Editor of *The Massachusetts Spy*)." Published by John P. Jewett & Company, Boston, MA. Copyright 1856 by Thomas Drew. [3⅝" × 5½"]. B/w litho of "J.C. Fremont." "The Campaign of 1856." 68pp. [Crew/JCF-18].

486A.19 Get Out Of The Way, 'Ten-Cent Jimmy.' w.m. No composer or tune indicated. In: *Fremont Songs For The People (Original And Selected),* page 52. c. Thomas Drew "(Editor of *The Massachusetts Spy*)." Published by John P. Jewett & Company, Boston, MA. Copyright 1856 by Thomas Drew. [3⅝" × 5½"]. B/w litho of "J.C. Fremont." "The Campaign of 1856." 68pp. [Crew/JCF-18].

486A.20 Hail! The Little Giant, Hail! w. No composer indicated. m. "Tune—*Hail Columbia.*" In: *The Democratic Campaign Songster, No. #1,* page 16. Published by American Publishing House, No. 60 West Fourth Street, Cincinnati, OH. 1860. [3⅞" × 5¹¹⁄₁₆"]. Pk/bk litho of "Stephen A. Douglas," black line border. At top of cover—"No. 1, Price 10 Cents." 52pp. [M-118]. [Crew/SAD-12].

486A.21 Hurrah Song For Fremont. w. No composer indicated. m. "Air—*Lucy Neal.*" In: *The Fremont Campaign Songster,* page 8. Published by Frost & Dory, Publishers, No. 140–142 Vine Street, Cincinnati, OH. 1856. [3½" × 5½"]. B/w litho of John C. Fremont. 32pp. Page 2: "To the Fremont Clubs and the Republican Party throughout the Union, this little volume is Respectfully Dedicated by the Publishers." [M-093]. [Crew/JCF-42].

486A.22 A Jolly Good Crew We'll Have. w. W.S. Sanford. m. "Air—*Little More Cider.*" In: *Connecticut Wide-Awake Songster,* page 71. e. John W. Hutchinson "(of Hutchinson Family Singers)" and Benjamin Jepson. Published by O. Hutchinson, Publisher, No. 272 Greenwich Street, New York, NY. 1860. [4" × 6"]. Bl/bk non-pictorial line border. "Lincoln and liberty." 76pp. Pages 2, 75 and 76: Advertising. Pages 5 and 6: Contents. Pages 7 to 10: Republican platform. [M-109]. [Crew/AL-175].

486A.23 The Lincoln Wedge. w. No composer indicated. m. "Air—*Maggie Lauder.*" "Respectfully dedicated to Gen. Clark of the Burlington, Vermont, *Times.*" In: *The Great Republican Campaigns Of 1860 And 1896,* page 180. e. Osborn H. Oldroyd. Published by Laird & Lee, Chicago, IL. 1896. [5⁵⁄₁₆" × 7⁷⁄₁₆"]. Gn/r/bk photos of Abraham Lincoln, William McKinley and Garrett Hobart. "Sound Money, Protection, Prosperity." 208pp. [Crew/AL-574].

486A.24 Nail Up The Flag. w. Dr. W.R. Fahnestock. m. No tune indicated. B/w wood cut of a man atop a flag pole nailing a flag to the pole. "For the *Democrat*." "Dedicated to the Wheatland Glee Club." In: *The Democrat*, October 8th, 1856, Lancaster, PA.

486A.25 Ode To Abraham. w.m. No composers or tune indicated. In: *Songs For The Union*, page 8. "Printed for the Union Congressional Committee by John A. Gray & Geen, New York," NY. [ca. 1861]. Non-pictorial. 8pp. [AMC].

486A.26 [Oh, Douglas! The Choice Of The People] (Campaign Song). w. Miss R.H. m. No tune indicated. In: *The Democratic Campaign Songster: Douglas & Johnson Melodies*, page 14. Published by P.J. Cozans, Publisher, New York, NY. [1860]. [3⅞" × 6"]. Y/bk litho of an eagle with ribbon—"Douglas & Johnson," train, ships, monument—"Liberty" sitting on rock base—"The Constitution." 40pp. [M-117]. [Crew/SAD-5].

486A.27 [Oh Greeley, I Leave The Course] (Campaign Song). w. Col. George S. Hickox. m. "Air—*Oh, Carry Me Till I Die*." "Dedicated to the Douglas and Johnson Club, of Olean." In: *The Democratic Campaign Songster: Douglas & Johnson Melodies*, page 21. Published by P.J. Cozans, Publisher, New York, NY. [1860]. [3⅞" × 6"]. Y/bk litho of an eagle with ribbon—"Douglas & Johnson," train, ships, monument—"Liberty" sitting on rock base—"The Constitution." 40pp. [M-117]. [Crew/SAD-5].

486A.28 Old Uncle Abe. w. No composer indicated. m. "Air—*My Old Kentucky Home*." In: *The Democratic Campaign Songster: Douglas & Johnson Melodies*, page 30. Published by P.J. Cozans, Publisher, New York, NY. [1860]. [3⅞" × 6"]. Y/bk litho of an eagle with ribbon—"Douglas & Johnson," train, ships, monument—"Liberty" sitting on rock base—"The Constitution." 40pp. [M-117]. [Crew/SAD-5].

486A.29 The People Had Five Candidates (Or The Medley Crew). w. No composer indicated. m.a. Henry Tucker. In: *The Wide Awake Vocalist (Or Rail Splitters' Song Book)*, page 42. Published by E.A. Daggett, No. 333 Broadway, New York, NY. 1860. Non-pictorial geometric design border. "Words and Music for the Republican Campaign of 1860, Embracing a Great Variety of Songs, Solos, Duets and Choruses Arranged for Piano or melodeon; The best collection of Words and Music ever published for a campaign, Every Club and Family should have copies, so as to join in the choruses; The Ladies are invited to join in the choruses at the meetings." 68pp. [M-116]. [Crew/AL-59].

Presidential Aspirants. w. No composer indicated. m. "Air—*Ho! For the White House*." Published in the New York Herald, August 30, 1860. [VBL, p. 342].

486A.30 The Presidential Track. w. No composer indicated. m. "Air—*Old Dan Tucker*." In: *Fillmore And Donelson Songs For The Campaign* (Songster), page 35. Published by Robert M. De Witt, Nos. 160 and 162 Nassau Street, New York, NY. November 4, 1856. [4¾" × 7⅛"]. Bl/bk litho of George Washington—"July 4, 1776," wreath, geometric design border. "This is the only authorized edition containing Duganne's Songs. Price 6 cts. each, $4 per 100. Discount to trade." Long quote from George Washington's "Farewell Address." 40pp. Page 3: "Union and Peace." [M-101, 102]. [Crew/MF-10].

486A.31 The Rail Splitters. w. No composer indicated. m. "Air—*Uncle Ned*." In: *The Great Republican Campaigns Of 1860 And 1896*, page 164. e. Osborn H. Oldroyd. Published by Laird & Lee, Chicago, IL. 1896. [5 5/16" × 7 7/16"]. Gn/r/bk photos of Abraham Lincoln, William McKinley and Garrett Hobart. "Sound Money, Protection, Prosperity." 208pp. [Crew/AL-574].

486A.32 Rally For Breckenridge And Lane. w. No composer indicated. m. "Air—*The Low Back'd Car*." Published by H. De Marsan, Publisher, No. 60 Chatham Street, New York, NY. [1860]. R/w/b hand-colored penny song sheet with litho order of cherubs, sailor, Miss Liberty, geometric designs. 2pp. Page 2: Blank. [Crew/JCB-7]. [AMC].

486A.33 Rally For Douglas. w. No composer indicated. m. "Air—*Washing Day*." In: *The Democratic Campaign Songster: Douglas & Johnson Melodies*, page 34. Published by P.J. Cozans, Publisher, New York, NY. [1860]. [3⅞" × 6"]. Y/bk litho of an eagle with ribbon—"Douglas & Johnson," train, ships, monument—"Liberty" sitting on rock base—"The Constitution." 40pp. [M-117]. [Crew/SAD-5].

486A.34 A Song Of The Campaign. w. No composer indicated. m. "Air—*Wait For The Wagon*." In: *Republican Song Book*, page 55. c. Thomas Drew "(Late Editor of *The Massachusetts Spy*)." Published by Thayer and Eldridge, Boston, MA. 1860. [3⅞" × 5⅞"]. Br/bk litho of beardless Abraham Lincoln, vignettes of young Lincoln chopping rails, polling raft. 68pp. [M-108]. [Crew/AL-8].

486A.35 Song Of The Office Holder. w. No composer indicated. m. "Air—*A Few Days*." In: *Republican Song Book*, page 9. c. Thomas Drew "(Late Editor of *The Massachusetts Spy*)." Published by Thayer and Eldridge, Boston, MA. 1860. [3⅞" × 5⅞"]. Br/bk litho of beardless Abraham Lincoln, vignettes of young Lincoln chopping rails, polling raft. 68pp. [M-108]. [Crew/AL-8].

486A.36 Stand By The Flag. w.m. No composer or tune indicated. In: *The Democratic Campaign Songster: Douglas & Johnson Melodies*, page 10. Published by P.J. Cozans, Publisher, New York, NY. [1860]. [3⅞" × 6"]. Y/bk litho of an eagle with ribbon—"Douglas & Johnson," train, ships, monument—"Liberty" sitting on rock base—"The Constitution." 40pp. [M-117]. [Crew/SAD-5].

486A.37 They Will Miss You At Home. w.m. No composer or tune indicated. In: *The Democratic Campaign Songster: Douglas & Johnson Melodies*, page 30. Published by P.J. Cozans, Publisher, New York, NY. [1860]. [3⅞" × 6"]. Y/bk litho of an eagle with ribbon—"Douglas & Johnson," train, ships, monument—"Liberty" sitting on rock base—"The Constitution." 40pp. [M-117]. [Crew/SAD-5].

486A.38 Uncle Abe And Johnny Breck. w. No composer indicated. m. "Air—*Robin Ruff*." In: *The Democratic Campaign Songster: Douglas & Johnson Melodies*, page 29. Published by P.J. Cozans, Publisher, New York, NY. [1860]. [3⅞" × 6"]. Y/bk litho of an eagle with ribbon—"Douglas & Johnson," train, ships, monument — "Liberty" sitting on rock base — "The Constitution." 40pp. [M-117]. [Crew/SAD-5].

486A.39 Vive La Honest Abe (A Wide-Awake Song). w. C.L. Russell. m. "Air — *Vive La Companie*." In: *Connecticut Wide-Awake Songster*, page 29. e. John W. Hutchinson "(of Hutchinson Family Singers)" and Benjamin Jepson. Published by O. Hutchinson, Publisher, No. 272 Greenwich Street, New York, NY. 1860. [4" × 6"]. Bl/bk non-pictorial line border. "Lincoln and liberty." 76pp. Pages 2, 75 and 76: Advertising. Pages 5 and 6: Contents. Pages 7 to 10: Republican platform. [M-109]. [Crew/AL-175].

486A.40 Vote For Bell Of Tennessee. w. No composer indicated. m. "Air — *Harlem National Union Glee Club No. 1*." Published in the *New York Herald*, 1960. [VBL, p. 343].

• **AmPM-487 BRECKINRIDGE**, Robert Jefferson, Jr. (Confederate Congress, 1862–1864; Common Pleas Court, 1876)

487.1 Farewell Enchanting Hope. w. S.E.H. m. Felix Lessing. Published by Geo. Dunn & Co., Richmond, VA. and Julian A. Selby, Columbia, SC. [ca. 1863]. Non-pictorial geometric designs. "The Confederate States classical series of song and ballad music, No. 1." "Dedicated to Mrs. Robt. Breckinridge, of Kentucky. 4pp. Page 4: Blank. [H-4352].

• **AmPM-488 BRISTOW**, Benjamin Helm (State Senate, 1863–1865; U.S. District Attorney for Kentucky, 1866–1870; U.S. Secretary of the Treasury, 1874–1876)

488.1 Hark! How Sweet Those Organs Play! w. No composer indicated. m. "Air — *Hieland Laddie, Bonnie Laddie!*" In: *Tilden And Hendricks' Reform Songs (For The Centennial Campaign Of 1876)*, page 8. Published by The National Democratic Committee, Box 3637, New York, NY. 1876. [3⅞" × 5¹⁵⁄₁₆"]. Gn/bk litho of Samuel J. Tilden and Thomas A. Hendricks, geometric design border. 40pp. [M-203]. [Crew/SJT-21].

488.2 Hayes. w. No composer indicated. m. "Air — *Life On The Ocean Wave*." In: *Hayes & Wheeler Campaign Song Book (For The Centennial Year)*, page 37. Published by the American News Company, Nos. 117, 119, 121, 123 Nassau Street, New York, NY. 1876. [3⅞" × 6¹⁄₁₆"]. Y/bk litho of Rutherford B. Hayes and William A. Wheeler, liberty cap, geometric designs. 74pp. [M-193]. [Crew/RBH-11].

• **AmPM-489 BUCKNER**, Simon Bolivar (Governor, 1887–1891; Candidate for Vice President, 1896)

489.1 Wanamaker's Session Song. w. Samuel R. Wanamaker. m. "Air — *Wait For The Wagon*." Published by Samuel R. Wanamaker, Provision Dealer, 619 Federal Street, above Sixth, Philadelphia, PA. [186-]. Non-pictorial. "Samuel R. Wanamaker, Provision Dealer, 619 Federal Street, above Sixth, Philadelphia, Dealer in Butter, Eggs, Lard, Hams, Dried Beef, Fresh and Salt Beef, Mutton, Pork, Veal, Fruits and Vegetables, &c. All Orders sent to the Store promptly filled and delivered." 2pp. Page 2: Blank. [AMC].

• **AmPM-490 BUTLER**, William Orlando (State House; 1817–1818; U.S. House, 1839–1843; Candidate for Vice President, 1848) [ALSO SEE: DOC/PSM-LC]

490.1 A Song For Cass And Butler. w. No composer indicated. m. No tune indicated. Published in the *Daily Union*, October 18, 1848. [VBL, p. 323].

490.2 The Taylor Polka. w. No composer indicated. m. "Tune — *The Jim Crow Polka*." In: *Taylor And Fillmore Songster, An Original Collection Of New Whig Songs For The Campaign Of 1848*, page 17. Published by Turner & Fisher, New York, NY. 1848. [2¾" × 4⅜"]. [V-1: Pk/bk] [V-2: Bl/bk] litho of Zachary Taylor. 34pp. [M-074, 075]. [Crew/ZT-56].

• **AmPM-491 CARLISLE**, John Griffin (State Senate, 1866; Lt. Governor, 1871–1875; U.S. House, 1877–1890; U.S. Senate, 1890–1893; U.S. Secretary of the Treasury, 1893–1897)

491.1 The Betters In Our Block. w. Frank N. Scott. In: *P.T. Schultz & Co's Blaine And Logan Bugle Call*, page 8. Published by P.T. Schultz & Company, No. 172 Race Street, Cincinnati, OH. 1881. [1884 Edition]. [5⅞" × 7⅝"]. Bk/gn litho of James G. Blaine and John A. Logan, flags and eagle, geometric design border. 36pp. Page 36: Advertising. [M-245]. [Crew/JGB-67].

491.2 The Bradbury Schottische. m. Dayton Vreeland. Published by F.G. Smith, 109 & 111 Broadway, Paterson, NJ. 1897. B/w geometric designs. "Dedicated to H.N. Lakeham." 4pp. Page 4: Advertising for Bradbury pianos with photo of "Famous Patrons of Bradbury Pianos" including: "U.S. Grant, J.A. Garfield, C.A. Arthur, Benj. Harrison, R.B. Hayes, Grover Cleveland, Stanley Mathews, J.M Rusk, Benj. Tracy, Levi Morton, Thos. B. Reed, J.W. Noble, William Windom, John G. Carlisle, C.C. McCabe, A.H. Colquitt [and] Walter Q. Gresham." [Crew/MISC-142]

491.3 Exit Old Party. w. No composer indicated. m. "Tune — *Good-By, My Lover, Good-by*." In: *Republican Campaign Parodies And Songs* [Songster], page 22. Published by Betts and Burnett, South Butler, Wayne County, NY. 1896. [7¾" × 5½"]. Be/bk non-pictorial. "McKinley and Hobart." "1896." 28pp. [M-340]. [Crew/WM-67].

491.4 Political Barber Shop. w.m. No composer or tune indicated. "Male Voices." In: *True Blue Republican Campaign Songs For 1896*, page 12. c. J.B. Herbert. Published by The S. Brainard's Sons Company, Chicago, IL. 1896. [5⅜" × 6⅞"]. R/w/b drawing of crossed flags, wreath, ribbons. Bl/w photo of "Hon. Wm. McKinley." "Protection." 36pp. [M-328]. [Crew/WM-169].

491.5 The Popocratic Circus. w. H.L. Frisbie. m. J.F. Kinsey. In: *The Golden Glory! (Republican Songster For 1896)*, page 4. Published by Echo Music Company, Lafayette, IN. 1896. [5⅜" × 7¾"]. Bl/w litho of William "McKinley" and Garret "Hobart." R/w/b geometric designs. 26pp. [M-327]. [Crew/WM-279].

491.6 A Thousand Dollars A Minute (Solo or Quartet). w. J.W. Matthews. m. J.B. Herbert. "For Male Voices." In: *True Blue Republican Campaign Songs For 1896*, page 16. c. J.B. Herbert. Published by The S. Brainard's Sons Company, Chicago, IL. 1896. [5⅜" × 6⅞"]. R/w/b drawing of crossed flags, wreath, ribbons. Bl/w photo of "Hon. Wm. McKinley." "Protection." 36pp. [M-328]. [Crew/WM-169].

491.7 Young Tip's Broom. w. No composer indicated. m. "Air—*Buy A Broom.*" In: *The Harrison Log-Cabin Song Book Of 1840*, page 11. e. O.C. Hooper. Published by A.H. Smythe, Columbus, OH. 1888. [4$^{15}/_{16}$" × 5¾"]. Y/bk litho of log cabin—"1840—1888." "Revised for the Campaign of 1888, with Numerous New Songs to Patriotic Airs." [V-2: "Music Edition"]. 68pp. [M-272, 273]. [Crew/BFH-23].

• **AmPM-492 CASEY,** Samuel Lewis (State Legislature; U.S. House, 1862–1863; Delegate, Republican National Convention, 1868 & 1872)

492.1 As A Matter Of Course. w.m. No composer or tune indicated. In: *The Sun's Greeley Campaign Songster*, page 35. c. Amos J. Cumming. Published from *The Sun* Office, New York, NY. 1872. [4⅛" × 6½"]. Be/bk litho of Horace Greeley, wreath. "He shines for all." 64pp. [Crew/HG-5].

492.2 Grant's Family Ring. w.m. No composer or tune indicated. In: *The Sun's Greeley Campaign Songster*, page 12. c. Amos J. Cumming. Published from *The Sun* Office, New York, NY. 1872. [4⅛" × 6½"]. Be/bk litho of Horace Greeley, wreath. "He shines for all." 64pp. [Crew/HG-5].

492.3 Greeley And Gratz Campaign Song. w.m. No composer indicated. m. Air—*The John Brown Chorus.*" In: *The Sun's Greeley Campaign Songster*, page 47. c. Amos J. Cumming. Published from *The Sun* Office, New York, NY. 1872. [4⅛" × 6½"]. Be/bk litho of Horace Greeley, wreath. "He shines for all." 64pp. [Crew/HG-5].

492.4 The White Chapeau. w. E.F. m. "Air—*Wearing Of The Green.*" "Brooklyn, N.Y." In: *The Sun's Greeley Campaign Songster*, page 31. c. Amos J. Cumming. Published from *The Sun* Office, New York, NY. 1872. [4⅛" × 6½"]. Be/bk litho of Horace Greeley, wreath. "He shines for all." 64pp. [Crew/HG-5].

• **AmPM-493 CHANDLER,** Albert Benjamin "Happy" (State Senate, 1930–1931; Lt. Governor, 1931–1935; Governor, 1935–1939 & 1955–1959; U.S. Senate, 1939–1945)

493.1 Come Back To Your Kentucky {493.1–1}. w.m. H.I. Miranda. 45 rpm record. Miranda Records, 105 York Street, Lexington, KY. #666/#1275–45–666. Performed by A.B. Happy Chandler and the Cecil Jones Studio Orchestra under the direction of Johnny Edmonson Side B: ***Roses In December*** {493.1–2}. Performed by A.B. Chandler. [196-]. Album sleeve: B/w photo of Happy Chandler.

493.2 Kentucky Colonel Song. w.m. Buck Ram and Irving Mills. Published by Mills Music, Inc. Music Publishers, 1619 Broadway, New York, NY. 1939. Green photo of Albert Chandler; floral and geometric design background. "Dedicated to the Commander-In-Chief of the Honorable Order if Kentucky Colonels, Governor Albert B. Chandler." 6pp. Pages 2 and 6: Advertising.

• **AmPM-494 CHAO,** Elaine (Federal Maritime Commission, 1988; Deputy Secretary of the U.S. Department of Transportation, 1989–1991; Peace Corps Director, 1991–1992; U.S. Secretary of Labor, 2001–Present)

494.1 Talking Cabinet Blues. w. Dave Lippman. m. No tune indicated. Published online at <http://www.davelippman.com/Cabinet.html>. N/c photo of Dave Lippman. [ca. 2001].

• **AmPM-495 CLAY,** Cassius Marcellus (State House, 1835–1837, U.S. Minister to Russia, 1861–1862 & 1863–1869)

495.1 Dixie Unionized. w. A.W. Muzzy, "A member of the Guards, of Panama, New York." m. Dan D. Emmett. Published for the author by Firth Pond & Co., 547 Broadway, New York, NY. 1861. Non-pictorial. "Respectfully dedicated to Cassius M. Clay's Washington Guards." 6pp. Pages 2 and 6: Blank. Page 3: Facsimile letter from L.H. Sigourney to the composer praising the song's lyrics. Page 5: At the bottom of the music—Facsimile letters from the New York Commercial Advertiser, Professor McCoy, Secretary of the Washington Clay Guards, and from the Hon. W.C. Parsons, of New York, praising the music.

495.2 For Abe Shall Have The Belt. w. "S." m.a. Henry Tucker. In: *The Wide Awake Vocalist (Or Rail Splitters' Song Book)*, page 30. Published by E.A. Daggett, No. 333 Broadway, New York, NY. 1860. Non-pictorial geometric design border. "Words and Music for the Republican Campaign of 1860, Embracing a Great Variety of Songs, Solos, Duets and Choruses Arranged for Piano or melodeon; The best collection of Words and Music ever published for a campaign, Every Club and Family should have copies, so as to join in the choruses; The Ladies are invited to join in the choruses at the meetings." 68pp. [M-116]. [Crew/AL-59].

495.3 Freedom's Battle-Call. w. George W. Bungay. m. No tune indicated. "Respectfully dedicated to Cassius M. Clay." In: *The Wide Awake Vocalist (Or Rail Splitters' Song Book)*, page 56. Published by E.A. Daggett, No. 333 Broadway, New York, NY. 1860. Non-pictorial geometric design border. "Words and Music for the Republican Campaign of 1860, Embracing a Great Variety of Songs, Solos, Duets and Choruses Arranged for Piano or melodeon; The best collection of Words and Music ever published for a campaign, Every Club and Family should have copies, so as to join in the choruses; The Ladies are invited to join in the choruses at the meetings." 68pp. [M-116]. [Crew/AL-59].

495.4 [Our Good Old Uncle Sam Is Sick] (A Campaign Song). w.m. No composer or tune indicated. In: *The Republican Campaign Songster No. #1*, page 30. Published by American Publishing House, No. 60 West Fourth Street, Cincinnati, OH. [1860]. [3¾" × 5¾"]. B/w litho of Abraham Lincoln. 48pp. [?]. [M-113]. [Crew/AL-298].

495.5 The White House. w. G.R. Edeson. m. "Air—*Root, Hog, Or Die!*" Published by H. De Marsan, 54 Chatham Street, New York, NY. [1861–1862]. B/w litho border of minstrels, geometric designs. 2pp. Page 2: Blank. [AMC].

• **AmPM-496 CLAY,** Henry (State House, 1803 & 1808–1809; U.S. Senate, 1806–1807, 1810–1811, 1831–1842 & 1849–1852; Candidate for President, 1824, 1932 & 1844; U.S. House, 1811–1814, 1815–1821 & 1823–1825; U.S. Secretary of State, 1825–1829) [ALSO SEE: DOC/PSM-HC]

496.1 Advance Whigs. w. No composer indicated. m. "Tune—*Boatman's Dance.*" B/w litho of a man plowing, White House, large 'OK' symbol. In: *The National Clay Minstrel*, page 22. Published by [V-1:

George Hood, No. 15 North 6th Street, Philadelphia, PA] [V-2: James Fisher, No. 71 Court Street, Boston, MA]. 1843. [3" × 4½"]. Y/bk litho of raccoon sitting on fence, black border. 68pp. [Crew/HC-10].

496.2 All Hail To The Chief! w. E.M. M'Graw. m. "Tune—*Mellow Horn*." In: *The National Clay Melodist (A Collection Of Popular And Patriotic Songs, Second Edition, Enlarged And Improved)*, page 31. Published by Benj. Adams, No. 54 Court Street, Boston, MA. 1844. [3" × 5¼"]. Inside title page: B/w litho of Henry Clay's home—"O'er Ashland's lawns the skies are bright, From West to East The radiance streams and glows, The land beneath its beams gay beats the heart with joy, Hurrah! Hurrah! Hip! Hurrah!" 108pp. [M-050?]. [Crew/HC-13].

496.3 Appeal To Freemen. w. No composer indicated. m. "Tune—*Bruce's Address*." In: *The National Clay Minstrel (And True Whig's Pocket Companion For The Presidential Canvass Of 1844)*, page 104. Published by [V-1: George Hood, No. 15 North 6th Street, Philadelphia, PA] [V-2: James Fisher, No. 71 Court Street, Boston, MA]. 1843. [3¼" × 5⅛"]. Y/bk litho of raccoon—"That Coon" and flag—"Henry Clay," log cabin. "New and Improved Edition." 128pp. [Crew/HC-11].

496.4 As The Stream From The Mountain (A Clay Song). w. Jno. Diston Fairbairn, Esqr. m. James M. Deems. Published by James M. Deems, Baltimore, MD. 1844. Non-pictorial geometric designs. 4pp. Page 4: Blank. [AMC].

496.5 At Linden, When Van's Sun Was Low. w. No composer indicated. m. "Tune—*Hoenlinden*." "Written for the *Clay Melodist*." B/w litho of five raccoons with instruments—"That Same Old Tune Coon Concert." In: *The National Clay Melodist (A Collection Of Popular And Patriotic Songs, Second Edition, Enlarged And Improved)*, page 46. Published by Benj. Adams, No. 54 Court Street, Boston, MA. 1844. [3" × 5¼"]. Inside title page: B/w litho of Henry Clay's home—"O'er Ashland's lawns the skies are bright, From West to East The radiance streams and glows, The land beneath its beams gay beats the heart with joy, Hurrah! Hurrah! Hip! Hurrah!" 108pp. [M-050?]. [Crew/HC-13].

496.6 Away, Away For Harry Clay. w. No composer indicated. m. "Tune—*Away, Away At Early Day*." "Sung at the great Connecticut Mass Gathering, at Hartford, on Washington's birth day." In: *The National Clay Melodist (A Collection Of Popular And Patriotic Songs, Second Edition, Enlarged And Improved)*, page 92. Published by Benj. Adams, No. 54 Court Street, Boston, MA. 1844. [3" × 5¼"]. Inside title page: B/w litho of Henry Clay's home—"O'er Ashland's lawns the skies are bright, From West to East The radiance streams and glows, The land beneath its beams gay beats the heart with joy, Hurrah! Hurrah! Hip! Hurrah!" 108pp. [M-050?]. [Crew/HC-13].

496.7 Away To The Battle! w. No composer indicated. m. "Tune—*The Campbells Are Coming*." In: *The National Clay Melodist (A Collection Of Popular And Patriotic Songs, Second Edition, Enlarged And Improved)*, page 12. Published by Benj. Adams, No. 54 Court Street, Boston, MA. 1844. [3" × 5¼"]. Inside title page: B/w litho of Henry Clay's home—"O'er Ashland's lawns the skies are bright, From West to East The radiance streams and glows, The land beneath its beams gay beats the heart with joy, Hurrah! Hurrah! Hip! Hurrah!" 108pp. [M-050?]. [Crew/HC-13].

496.8 Away With Traitor Tyler. w. No composer indicated. m. "Tune—*Away With Melancholy*." "Written for the Choir of the National Clay Club." In: *The National Clay Minstrel*, page 16. Published by [V-1: George Hood, No. 15 North 6th Street, Philadelphia, PA] [V-2: James Fisher, No. 71 Court Street, Boston, MA]. 1843. [3" × 4½"]. Y/bk litho of raccoon sitting on fence, black border. 68pp. [Crew/HC-10].

496.9 Beggar's Petition. w. No composer indicated. m. "Tune—*All On Hobbies*." "A very pathetic and musical appeal to the Dear People, by an Ex-Postmaster General." In: *Tippecanoe Song-Book (A Collection Of Log Cabin And Patriotic Melodies)*, page 14. Published by Marshall, Williams & Butler, Philadelphia, PA. 1840. White on black litho of log cabin, plow, flags, eagle. 180pp. [M-024]. [Crew/WHH-61].

496.10 [Begone Tyler John] (Song 11). w. W.A. m. "Tune—*Begone Dull Care*." In: *Original Clay Songs: Humorous And Sentimental, Designed To Inculcate Just Political Sentiments, To Suit The Present Political Crisis, And To Advocate The Claims Of Henry Clay To The Highest Honors His Country Can Bestow*, page 16. w. W.A. Philomath, Union Co., Ind. Published by Philomath, Cincinnati, OH. 1842. [4¼" × 6"]. Be/bk litho of an eagle, U.S. Flag. "The eagle soars above the throng; And listen's [sic] to fair Freedom's song, Hails the merry roundelay, Claps his glad wings and hails the day." 20pp. Page 20: Be/bk litho of four men—"Tyler Expounding the Constitution! The effect of 'treading in the footsteps.'" [M-057]. [Crew/HC-104].

496.11 A Blast From The Bugle. w. Hon. Francis James. m. "Tune—*Star Spangled Banner*." In: *The National Clay Melodist (A Collection Of Popular And Patriotic Songs, Second Edition, Enlarged And Improved)*, page 8. "Some time since, the Richmond Enquirer, in commenting on a published letter written by Henry Clay to some of his political friends, styled it is derision—'A blast from the Bugle,' and affected to consider it a summons which the Whigs of the Union would not venture to disobey." Published by Benj. Adams, No. 54 Court Street, Boston, MA. 1844. [3" × 5¼"]. Inside title page: B/w litho of Henry Clay's home—"O'er Ashland's lawns the skies are bright, From West to East The radiance streams and glows, The land beneath its beams gay beats the heart with joy, Hurrah! Hurrah! Hip! Hurrah!" 108pp. [M-050?]. [Crew/HC-13].

496.12 The Blue Hen's Chickens. w. J.A. Allderdice, "of Wilmington, Del." m. "Tune—*Old Dan Tucker*." B/w litho of a setting hen. "Delaware." In: *The National Clay Minstrel*, page 12. Published by [V-1: George Hood, No. 15 North 6th Street, Philadelphia, PA] [V-2: James Fisher, No. 71 Court Street, Boston, MA]. 1843. [3" × 4½"]. Y/bk litho of raccoon sitting on fence, black border. 68pp. [Crew/HC-10].

496.13 The Bold Kentucky Boy. w. No composer indicated. m. "Tune—*The Highland Minstrel Boy*." In: *The National Clay Minstrel (And True Whig's Pocket Companion For The Presidential Canvass Of 1844)*, page

105. Published by [V-1: George Hood, No. 15 North 6th Street, Philadelphia, PA] [V-2: James Fisher, No. 71 Court Street, Boston, MA]. 1843. [3¼" × 5⅛"]. Y/bk litho of raccoon—"That Coon" and flag—"Henry Clay," log cabin. "New and Improved Edition." 128pp. [Crew/HC-11].

496.14 The Bonnie Clay Flag. w. John H. Warland. m. No tune indicated. "Set to music and copyright by C.S. Keith." "Inscribed to the Boston Clay Club, No. 1." B/w litho of crown with a flag inscribed "Ashland." In: *The National Clay Melodist (A Collection Of Popular And Patriotic Songs, Second Edition, Enlarged And Improved)*, page 5. Published by Benj. Adams, No. 54 Court Street, Boston, MA. 1844. [3" × 5¼"]. Inside title page: B/w litho of Henry Clay's home—"O'er Ashland's lawns the skies are bright, From West to East The radiance streams and glows, The land beneath its beams gay beats the heart with joy, Hurrah! Hurrah! Hip! Hurrah!" 108pp. [M-050?]. [Crew/HC-13].

496.15 Buena Vista. w.m. No composer or tune indicated. In: *The Patriot's Songster*, page 13. Published by Mumford & Company, Cincinnati, OH. 1862. [3½" × 6"]. Non-pictorial. 48pp. [Son Henry Clay, Jr. Killed at Buena Vista].

496.16 [The Campaign Commences Most Nobly] (Campaign Song). w. No composer indicated. m. "Air—*Rosin The Bow*." In: *Hutchinson's Republican Songster For 1860*, page 68. e. John W. Hutchinson "(of the Hutchinson Family Singers)." Published by O. Hutchinson, Publisher, No. 272 Greenwich Street, New York, NY. 1860. B/w floral design border. "Lincoln and Liberty." 76pp. [M-110]. [Crew/AL-317].

496.17 A Catch. w. No composer indicated. m. "Tune—*Here's A Health To All Good Lasses*." B/w litho of an eagle. In: *The National Clay Minstrel*, page 25. Published by [V-1: George Hood, No. 15 North 6th Street, Philadelphia, PA] [V-2: James Fisher, No. 71 Court Street, Boston, MA]. 1843. [3" × 4½"]. Y/bk litho of raccoon sitting on fence, black border. 68pp. [Crew/HC-10].

496.18 The Chief Of The West. w. No composer indicated. m. "Tune—*The Spring Time Of The Year Is Coming*." "Written for the *National Clay Minstrel*." In: *The National Clay Minstrel (And True Whig's Pocket Companion For The Presidential Canvass Of 1844)*, page 81. Published by [V-1: George Hood, No. 15 North 6th Street, Philadelphia, PA] [V-2: James Fisher, No. 71 Court Street, Boston, MA]. 1843. [3¼" × 5⅛"]. Y/bk litho of raccoon—"That Coon" and flag—"Henry Clay," log cabin. "New and Improved Edition." 128pp. Page 10: Dedication—"To the National Clay Club this work is respectfully dedicated by the Publisher." [Crew/HC-11].

496.19 Clay And Frelinghuysen. w. J. Greiner. m. "Tune—*Old Dan Tucker*." In: *The National Clay Minstrel*, page 1. Published by [V-1: George Hood, No. 15 North 6th Street, Philadelphia, PA] [V-2: James Fisher, No. 71 Court Street, Boston, MA]. 1843. [3" × 4½"]. Y/bk litho of raccoon sitting on fence, black border. 68pp. [Crew/HC-10].

496.20 Clay And Frelinghuysen. w. No composer indicated. m. "Music—*Old Dan Tucker*." On 33⅓ rpm LP: *Sing Along With Millard Fillmore*. Life Records #RB 360 T2/#61 P3. "The Life Album of Presidential Campaign Songs."

496.21 Clay And Frelinghuysen. w. No composer indicated. m. "Tune—*Lucy Neal*." In: *The National Clay Minstrel*, page 31. Published by [V-1: George Hood, No. 15 North 6th Street, Philadelphia, PA] [V-2: James Fisher, No. 71 Court Street, Boston, MA]. 1843. [3" × 4½"]. Y/bk litho of raccoon sitting on fence, black border. 68pp. [Crew/HC-10].

496.22 The Clay Diggins (Song 10). w. W.A. m. "Tune—*Gee Ho Dobbin*." In: *Original Clay Songs: Humorous And Sentimental, Designed To Inculcate Just Political Sentiments, To Suit The Present Political Crisis, And To Advocate The Claims Of Henry Clay To The Highest Honors His Country Can Bestow*, page 14. w. W.A. Philomath, Union Co., Ind. Published by Philomath, Cincinnati, OH. 1842. [4¼" × 6"]. Be/bk litho of an eagle, U.S. Flag. "The eagle soars above the throng; And listen's [sic] to fair Freedom's song, Hails the merry roundelay, Claps his glad wings and hails the day." 20pp. Page 20: Be/bk litho of four men—"Tyler Expounding the Constitution! The effect of 'treading in the footsteps.'" [M-057]. [CrewHC-104].

496.23 The Clay Flag. w. No composer indicated. m. "Tune—*The Soldier's Gratitude*." "Written for the *National Clay Minstrel*." In: *The National Clay Minstrel (And True Whig's Pocket Companion For The Presidential Canvass Of 1844)*, page 76. Published by [V-1: George Hood, No. 15 North 6th Street, Philadelphia, PA] [V-2: James Fisher, No. 71 Court Street, Boston, MA]. 1843. [3¼" × 5⅛"]. Y/bk litho of raccoon—"That Coon" and flag—"Henry Clay," log cabin. "New and Improved Edition." 128pp. [Crew/HC-11].

496.24 The Clay Gathering. w. No composer indicated. m. "Tune—*The Macgregor's Gathering*." "Written for the *National Clay Minstrel*." In: *The National Clay Minstrel (And True Whig's Pocket Companion For The Presidential Canvass Of 1844)*, page 83. Published by [V-1: George Hood, No. 15 North 6th Street, Philadelphia, PA] [V-2: James Fisher, No. 71 Court Street, Boston, MA]. 1843. [3¼" × 5⅛"]. Y/bk litho of raccoon—"That Coon" and flag—"Henry Clay," log cabin. "New and Improved Edition." 128pp. [Crew/HC-11].

496.25 The Clay Girl's Song. w. No composer indicated. m. "Tune—*Old Rosin The Bow*." In: *The National Clay Melodist (A Collection Of Popular And Patriotic Songs, Second Edition, Enlarged And Improved)*, page 81. Published by Benj. Adams, No. 54 Court Street, Boston, MA. 1844. [3" × 5¼"]. Inside title page: B/w litho of Henry Clay's home—"O'er Ashland's lawns the skies are bright, From West to East The radiance streams and glows, The land beneath its beams gay beats the heart with joy, Hurrah! Hurrah! Hip! Hurrah!" 108pp. [M-050?]. [Crew/HC-13].

496.26 Clay, Our Nation's Glory. w. No composer indicated. m. "Tune—*March To The Battle Field*." "Written for the *National Clay Minstrel*." In: *The National Clay Minstrel (And True Whig's Pocket Companion For The Presidential Canvass Of 1844)*, page 82. Published by [V-1: George Hood, No. 15 North 6th Street, Philadelphia, PA] [V-2: James Fisher, No. 71 Court Street, Boston, MA]. 1843. [3¼" × 5⅛"]. Y/bk litho of raccoon—"That Coon" and flag—"Henry

Clay," log cabin. "New and Improved Edition." 128pp. [Crew/HC-11].

496.27 The Clay Rally Cry. w. No composer indicated. m. "Tune—*All The Blue Bonnets.*" In: *The National Clay Minstrel (And True Whig's Pocket Companion For The Presidential Canvass Of 1844)*, page 62. Published by [V-1: George Hood, No. 15 North 6th Street, Philadelphia, PA] [V-2: James Fisher, No. 71 Court Street, Boston, MA]. 1843. [3¼" × 5⅛"]. Y/bk litho of raccoon—"That Coon" and flag—"Henry Clay," log cabin. "New and Improved Edition." 128pp. [Crew/HC-11].

496.28 The Clay Ship. w. "B." Luther Leland. m. "Tune—*Soldier's Dream.*" "Written for the *National Clay Minstrel.*" In: *The National Clay Minstrel (And True Whig's Pocket Companion For The Presidential Canvass Of 1844)*, page 73. Published by [V-1: George Hood, No. 15 North 6th Street, Philadelphia, PA] [V-2: James Fisher, No. 71 Court Street, Boston, MA]. 1843. [3¼" × 5⅛"]. Y/bk litho of raccoon—"That Coon" and flag—"Henry Clay," log cabin. "New and Improved Edition." 128pp. [Crew/HC-11].

496.29 Clear The Way For Harry Clay. w. No composer indicated. m. "Tune—*What Has Caused This Great Commotion?*" In: *The National Clay Minstrel*, page 50. Published by [V-1: George Hood, No. 15 North 6th Street, Philadelphia, PA] [V-2: James Fisher, No. 71 Court Street, Boston, MA]. 1843. [3" × 4½"]. Y/bk litho of raccoon sitting on fence, black border. 68pp. [Crew/HC-10].

496.30 Cling To The Union. w. No composer indicated. m. "Air—*Wait For The Wagon.*" Published by Johnson, Song Publisher, No. 7 N. Tenth Street, [Philadelphia, PA]. [1850–1860]. B/w non-pictorial geometric design litho border." 2pp. Page 2: Blank. [AMC].

496.31 Come, All Hands, Ahoy! w. No composer indicated. m. "Tune—*Great Way Off At Sea.*" In: *The National Clay Melodist (A Collection Of Popular And Patriotic Songs, Second Edition, Enlarged And Improved)*, page 44. Published by Benj. Adams, No. 54 Court Street, Boston, MA. 1844. [3" × 5¼"]. Inside title page: B/w litho of Henry Clay's home—"O'er Ashland's lawns the skies are bright, From West to East The radiance streams and glows, The land beneath its beams gay beats the heart with joy, Hurrah! Hurrah! Hip! Hurrah!" 108pp. [M-050?]. [Crew/HC-13].

496.32 Come All Ye Bold Lads Of Old Forty. w. No composer indicated. m. "Tune—*'Rosin The Bow.*" In: *The National Clay Melodist (A Collection Of Popular And Patriotic Songs, Second Edition, Enlarged And Improved)*, page 50. Published by Benj. Adams, No. 54 Court Street, Boston, MA. 1844. [3" × 5¼"]. Inside title page: B/w litho of Henry Clay's home—"O'er Ashland's lawns the skies are bright, From West to East The radiance streams and glows, The land beneath its beams gay beats the heart with joy, Hurrah! Hurrah! Hip! Hurrah!" 108pp. [M-050?]. [Crew/HC-13].

496.33 [Come All Ye Good Hearted Whigs] (Whig Song). w. No composer indicated. m. "Tune—*Yankee Doodle.*" In: *The National Clay Almanac, 1845*, page 31. B/w litho of a raccoon. Published by Desilver & Muir, No. 18 South Fourth Street, Philadelphia, PA. 1844. [6¹³⁄₁₆" × 7⅞"]. B/w litho of Henry Clay, ship—"Commerce," plow, crops—"Agriculture." [Crew/HC-89].

496.34 Come All Ye Good Men Of The Nation (A Clay Song). w. No composer indicated. m. "Air—*Rosin The Bow.*" In: *The National Clay Minstrel (And True Whig's Pocket Companion For The Presidential Canvass Of 1844)*, page 21. Published by [V-1: George Hood, No. 15 North 6th Street, Philadelphia, PA] [V-2: James Fisher, No. 71 Court Street, Boston, MA]. 1843. [3¼" × 5⅛"]. Y/bk litho of raccoon—"That Coon" and flag—"Henry Clay," log cabin. "New and Improved Edition." 128pp. [Crew/HC-11].

496.35 Come All Ye Men Who Push The Plow (A Popular Clay Song). w. No composer indicated. m. "Air—*Auld Lang Syne.*" In: *The National Clay Minstrel (And True Whig's Pocket Companion For The Presidential Canvass Of 1844)*, page 21. Published by [V-1: George Hood, No. 15 North 6th Street, Philadelphia, PA] [V-2: James Fisher, No. 71 Court Street, Boston, MA]. 1843. [3¼" × 5⅛"]. Y/bk litho of raccoon—"That Coon" and flag—"Henry Clay," log cabin. "New and Improved Edition." 128pp. [Crew/HC-11].

496.36 [Come All You Whigs And Democrats] (Song 4). w. W.A. m. "Tune—*The Hunters Of Kentucky.*" In: *Original Clay Songs: Humorous And Sentimental, Designed To Inculcate Just Political Sentiments, To Suit The Present Political Crisis, And To Advocate The Claims Of Henry Clay To The Highest Honors His Country Can Bestow*, page 7. w. W.A. Philomath, Union Co., Ind. Published by Philomath, Cincinnati, OH. 1842. [4¼" × 6"]. Be/bk litho of an eagle, U.S. Flag. "The eagle soars above the throng; And listen's [sic] to fair Freedom's song, Hails the merry roundelay, Claps his glad wings and hails the day." 20pp. [M-057]. [CrewHC-104].

496.37 Come Friends, Gather 'Round. w. No composer indicated. m. "Tune—*Lucy Neal.*" In: *The National Clay Minstrel*, page 20. Published by [V-1: George Hood, No. 15 North 6th Street, Philadelphia, PA] [V-2: James Fisher, No. 71 Court Street, Boston, MA]. 1843. [3" × 4½"]. Y/bk litho of raccoon sitting on fence, black border. 68pp. [Crew/HC-10].

496.38 Come One, Come All (Hurrah Song). w. No composer indicated. m. "Tune—*Old Tip's The Boy.*" In: *The National Clay Melodist (A Collection Of Popular And Patriotic Songs, Second Edition, Enlarged And Improved)*, page 90. Published by Benj. Adams, No. 54 Court Street, Boston, MA. 1844. [3" × 5¼"]. Inside title page: B/w litho of Henry Clay's home—"O'er Ashland's lawns the skies are bright, From West to East The radiance streams and glows, The land beneath its beams gay beats the heart with joy, Hurrah! Hurrah! Hip! Hurrah!" 108pp. [M-050?]. [Crew/HC-13].

496.39 [Come Rouse Ye Honest Whigs All] (Song 9). w. W.A. m. "Tune—*The Swiss Boy.*" In: *Original Clay Songs: Humorous And Sentimental, Designed To Inculcate Just Political Sentiments, To Suit The Present Political Crisis, And To Advocate The Claims Of Henry Clay To The Highest Honors His Country Can Bestow*, page 13. w. W.A. Philomath, Union Co., Ind. Published by Philomath, Cincinnati, OH. 1842. [4¼" × 6"]. Be/bk litho of an eagle, U.S. Flag. "The eagle soars above the throng; And listen's [sic] to fair Freedom's song, Hails the merry roundelay, Claps his glad wings and hails the day." 20pp. Page 20: Be/bk litho of four men — "Tyler Expounding the Constitution! The effect of 'treading in the footsteps.'" [M-057]. [CrewHC-104].

496.40 Come, Sons Of Men Who Made The Tea. w. No composer indicated. m. "Air — *Who'll Be King But Charlie?*" In: *The National Clay Melodist (A Collection Of Popular And Patriotic Songs, Second Edition, Enlarged And Improved)*, page 35. Published by Benj. Adams, No. 54 Court Street, Boston, MA. 1844. [3" × 5¼"]. Inside title page: B/w litho of Henry Clay's home — "O'er Ashland's lawns the skies are bright, From West to East The radiance streams and glows, The land beneath its beams gay beats the heart with joy, Hurrah! Hurrah! Hip! Hurrah!" 108pp. [M-050?]. [Crew/HC-13].

496.41 Convention Song. w. No composer indicated. m. "Tune — *Take Heed! Whisper Low!*" "Written for the Choir of the National Clay Club of Phila. And sung by them with unbounded applause at Baltimore." In: *The National Clay Minstrel*, page 8. Published by [V-1: George Hood, No. 15 North 6th Street, Philadelphia, PA] [V-2: James Fisher, No. 71 Court Street, Boston, MA]. 1843. [3" × 4½"]. Y/bk litho of raccoon sitting on fence, black border. 68pp. [Crew/HC-10].

496.42 The Coon Song. w. No composer indicated. m. "Tune — *Jim Dandy O Caroline*." "Written for the *National Clay Minstrel*." B/w litho of a raccoon labeled "That Coon" atop a log cabin with a flag labeled "Henry Clay." In: *The National Clay Minstrel*, page 61. Published by [V-1: George Hood, No. 15 North 6th Street, Philadelphia, PA] [V-2: James Fisher, No. 71 Court Street, Boston, MA]. 1843. [3" × 4½"]. Y/bk litho of raccoon sitting on fence, black border. 68pp. [Crew/HC-10].

496.43 The Coon Song. w. J. Greiner. m. "Tune — *Ole Dan Tucker*." "Sung at the great Mass Convention at Columbus, Ohio, Feb. 22, 1844." In: *The National Clay Melodist (A Collection Of Popular And Patriotic Songs, Second Edition, Enlarged And Improved)*, page 102. Published by Benj. Adams, No. 54 Court Street, Boston, MA. 1844. [3" × 5¼"]. Inside title page: B/w litho of Henry Clay's home — "O'er Ashland's lawns the skies are bright, From West to East The radiance streams and glows, The land beneath its beams gay beats the heart with joy, Hurrah! Hurrah! Hip! Hurrah!" 108pp. [M-050?]. [Crew/HC-13].

496.44 The Poor Lighterman's Song. w. New York Plebeian. m. "Air — *Lucy Neal*." Published in *Coldwater Sentinel*, page 1, Friday Morning, October 15, 1844, Coldwater, MI.

496.45 The Dawn Of Brighter Days. w. No composer indicated. m. Tune — *Carrier Dove*." In: *The National Clay Melodist (A Collection Of Popular And Patriotic Songs, Second Edition, Enlarged And Improved)*, page 66. Published by Benj. Adams, No. 54 Court Street, Boston, MA. 1844. [3" × 5¼"]. Inside title page: B/w litho of Henry Clay's home — "O'er Ashland's lawns the skies are bright, From West to East The radiance streams and glows, The land beneath its beams gay beats the heart with joy, Hurrah! Hurrah! Hip! Hurrah!" 108pp. [M-050?]. [Crew/HC-13].

496.46 The Days When We Went Canvassing. w. No composer indicated. m. "Air — *The Days When We Went Gypsying*." In: *The National Clay Minstrel*, page 53. Published by [V-1: George Hood, No. 15 North 6th Street, Philadelphia, PA] [V-2: James Fisher, No. 71 Court Street, Boston, MA]. 1843. [3" × 4½"]. Y/bk litho of raccoon sitting on fence, black border. 68pp. [Crew/HC-10].

496.47 The Dayton Gathering. w.m. No composer or tune indicated. In: *The National Clay Almanac, 1845*, page 21. Published by Desilver & Muir, No. 18 South Fourth Street, Philadelphia, PA. 1844. 36pp. [6¹³⁄₁₆" × 7⅞"]. B/w litho of Henry Clay, ship — "Commerce," plow, crops — "Agriculture." 36pp. [Crew/HC-89].

496.48 De Possum's Tree. w. No composer indicated. m. "Air — *Dance To De Boatman*." In: *The National Clay Minstrel (And True Whig's Pocket Companion For The Presidential Canvass Of 1844)*, page 19. Published by [V-1: George Hood, No. 15 North 6th Street, Philadelphia, PA] [V-2: James Fisher, No. 71 Court Street, Boston, MA]. 1843. [3¼" × 5⅛"]. Y/bk litho of raccoon — "That Coon" and flag — "Henry Clay," log cabin. "New and Improved Edition." 128pp. [Crew/HC-11].

496.49 Deeds Of Clay. w. No composer indicated. m. "Tune — *The Bonny Boat*." In: *The National Clay Minstrel (And True Whig's Pocket Companion For The Presidential Canvass Of 1844)*, page 38. Published by [V-1: George Hood, No. 15 North 6th Street, Philadelphia, PA] [V-2: James Fisher, No. 71 Court Street, Boston, MA]. 1843. [3¼" × 5⅛"]. Y/bk litho of raccoon — "That Coon" and flag — "Henry Clay," log cabin. "New and Improved Edition." 128pp. Page 10: Dedication — "To the National Clay Club this work is respectfully dedicated by the Publisher." [Crew/HC-11].

496.50 Demagogue Van (Orator Puff). w. No composer indicated. m. No tune indicated. "Written for the Clay Melodist." B/w litho of Martin Van Buren riding a horse backwards saying — "Gee up Dobbin" and "Stop Dobbin." In: *The National Clay Melodist (A Collection Of Popular And Patriotic Songs, Second Edition, Enlarged And Improved)*, page 33. Published by Benj. Adams, No. 54 Court Street, Boston, MA. 1844. [3" × 5¼"]. Inside title page: B/w litho of Henry Clay's home — "O'er Ashland's lawns the skies are bright, From West to East The radiance streams and glows, The land beneath its beams gay beats the heart with joy, Hurrah! Hurrah! Hip! Hurrah!" 108pp. [M-050?]. [Crew/HC-13].

496.51 Did You Ever Hear Of The Farmer? w. No composer indicated. m. "Tune — *'Tis My Delight*." "An Old Song Altered." In: *The National Clay Melodist (A Collection Of Popular And Patriotic Songs, Second Edition, Enlarged And Improved)*, page 85. Published by Benj. Adams, No. 54 Court Street, Boston, MA. 1844. [3" × 5¼"]. Inside title page: B/w litho of Henry Clay's home — "O'er Ashland's lawns the skies are bright, From West to East The radiance streams and glows, The land beneath its beams gay beats the heart with joy, Hurrah! Hurrah! Hip! Hurrah!" 108pp. [M-050?]. [Crew/HC-13].

496.52 The Dutchman. w. No composer indicated.

m. "Tune—*The Poachers.*" In: *A Miniature Of Martin Van Buren (With A Selection Of The Best And Most Popular Tippecanoe Songs)*, page 49. 1840. [3½" × 6½"]. [V-1: Br/bk] [V-2: Gn/bk] [V-3: Y/bk] litho of man, chain around neck. Van Buren quote. "Amos Kendall's Veracity—Tom Benton's Honesty—Francis Blair's Beauty." "What is wanting cant be numbered [sic]." 58pp. [M-016]. [Crew/WHH-88].

496.53 The Farmer Of Kentucky. w. No composer indicated. m. "Tune—*The Hunter's Of Kentucky.*" "Written for the *Clay Minstrel.*" In: *The National Clay Minstrel (And True Whig's Pocket Companion For The Presidential Canvass Of 1844)*, page 70. Published by [V-1: George Hood, No. 15 North 6th Street, Philadelphia, PA] [V-2: James Fisher, No. 71 Court Street, Boston, MA]. 1843. [3¼" × 5⅛"]. Y/bk litho of raccoon—"That Coon" and flag—"Henry Clay," log cabin. "New and Improved Edition." 128pp. [Crew/HC-11].

496.54 The Farmer Of Tippecanoe. w. No composer indicated. m. "Tune—*The Campbells Are Coming.*" "Couldn't get a sweetheart to please her mind." In: *The Log Cabin & Hard Cider Melodies, A Collection Of Popular And Patriotic Songs*, page 54. Published by Charles Adams, No. 23 Tremont Street, Boston, MA. 1840. [3¾" × 6"]. [V-1: Pk/bk] [V-2: Gn/bk] litho of William Henry Harrison. "The Freeman's glittering Sword be Blest, For ever blest the Freeman's Lyre." 78pp. Pages 2 and 77: Blank. Page 3: Inside title page. B/w litho of log cabin. "Respectfully Dedicated to the Friends of Harrison and Tyler." Page 78: Advertising. [M-012]. [Crew/WHH-68].

496.55 The Fighting Captain. w. F.B. Graham, Esq. m. "Tune—*It Will Never Do To Give It Up So Soon.*" B/w litho of a ship with banner reading "Don't Give Up The Ship." In: *The National Clay Minstrel*, page 24. Published by [V-1: George Hood, No. 15 North 6th Street, Philadelphia, PA] [V-2: James Fisher, No. 71 Court Street, Boston, MA]. 1843. [3" × 4½"]. Y/bk litho of raccoon sitting on fence, black border. 68pp. [Crew/HC-10].

496.56 A Fine Old Gentleman. w. No composer indicated. m. "Air—*The Fine Old English Gentleman.*" In: *The Great Republican Campaigns Of 1860 And 1896*, page 168. e. Osborn H. Oldroyd. Published by Laird & Lee, Chicago, IL. 1896. [5⁵⁄₁₆" × 7⁷⁄₁₆"]. Gn/r/bk photos of Abraham Lincoln, William McKinley and Garrett Hobart. "Sound Money, Protection, Prosperity." 208pp. [Crew/AL-574].

496.57 The First Polk Song. w. No composer indicated. m. "Tune—*Old Dan Tucker.*" In: *The National Clay Minstrel*, page 26. Published by [V-1: George Hood, No. 15 North 6th Street, Philadelphia, PA] [V-2: James Fisher, No. 71 Court Street, Boston, MA]. 1843. [3" × 4½"]. Y/bk litho of raccoon sitting on fence. 68pp. [Crew/HC-10].

496.58 Fling Forth The Clay Banner. w. No composer indicated. m. "Tune—*The Star Spangled Banner.*" In: *The National Clay Minstrel*, page 28. Published by [V-1: George Hood, No. 15 North 6th Street, Philadelphia, PA] [V-2: James Fisher, No. 71 Court Street, Boston, MA]. 1843. [3" × 4½"]. Y/bk litho of raccoon sitting on fence, black border. 68pp. [Crew/HC-10].

496.59 [Friends Of Freedom, Hear The Story] (Song). w. No composer indicated. m. "Air—*Dixey's Land.*" In: *Hutchinson's Republican Songster For 1860*, page 66. e. John W. Hutchinson "(of the Hutchinson Family Singers)." Published by O. Hutchinson, Publisher, No. 272 Greenwich Street, New York, NY. 1860. B/w floral design border. "Lincoln and Liberty." 76pp. [M-110]. [Crew/AL-317].

496.60 [Friends Of The Union] (Song). w. No composer indicated. m. "Air—*Dixey's Land.*" In: *The Democratic Campaign Songster: Douglas & Johnson Melodies*, page 18. Published by P.J. Cozans, Publisher, New York, NY. [1860]. [3⅞" × 6"]. Y/bk litho of an eagle with ribbon—"Douglas & Johnson," train, ships, monument—"Liberty" sitting on rock base—"The Constitution." 40pp. [M-117]. [Crew/SAD-5].

496.61 The Gallant Whigs Have Drawn The Sword. w.m. No composer or tune indicated. In: *The National Clay Melodist (A Collection Of Popular And Patriotic Songs, Second Edition, Enlarged And Improved)*, page 55. Published by Benj. Adams, No. 54 Court Street, Boston, MA. 1844. [3" × 5¼"]. Inside title page: B/w litho of Henry Clay's home—"O'er Ashland's lawns the skies are bright, From West to East The radiance streams and glows, The land beneath its beams gay beats the heart with joy, Hurrah! Hurrah! Hip! Hurrah!" 108pp. [M-050?]. [Crew/HC-13].

496.62 Gallant Young Whigs. w. No composer indicated. m. "Tune—*Soldier's Return.*" In: *The National Clay Minstrel (And True Whig's Pocket Companion For The Presidential Canvass Of 1844)*, page 103. Published by [V-1: George Hood, No. 15 North 6th Street, Philadelphia, PA] [V-2: James Fisher, No. 71 Court Street, Boston, MA]. 1843. [3¼" × 5⅛"]. Y/bk litho of raccoon—"That Coon" and flag—"Henry Clay," log cabin. "New and Improved Edition." 128pp. [Crew/HC-11].

496.63 The Gathering Of The States (Or Who'll Be Chief But Harry?). w. "By a Gentleman of Philadelphia." m. "Air—*Who'll Be King But Charlie?* "Written expressly for the *National Clay Minstrel.*" In: *The National Clay Minstrel (And True Whig's Pocket Companion For The Presidential Canvass Of 1844)*, page 11. Published by [V-1: George Hood, No. 15 North 6th Street, Philadelphia, PA] [V-2: James Fisher, No. 71 Court Street, Boston, MA]. 1843. [3¼" × 5⅛"]. Y/bk litho of raccoon—"That Coon" and flag—"Henry Clay," log cabin. "New and Improved Edition." 128pp. [Crew/HC-11].

496.64A Get Along Harry, You're Bound To Win. w. No composer indicated. m. "Tune—*Gee Up Dobbin.*" In: *The Clay Minstrel Or National Songster*, page 201. c. John Stockton Littell. Published by Greeley & M'Elrath, Tribune Building, New York, NY. 1844. [3⅛" × 4⅞"]. Non-pictorial. 396pp. [Crew/HC-18].

496.64 Get Off The Track. w. Jesse Hutchinson. m. "Air—*Dan Tucker.*" In: *The Liberty Minstrel*, page 144. e. George W. Clark. Published by George W. Clark, New York, NY. 1844. [4⅝" × 6¾"]. Non-pictorial songbook with gold leaf title. "And Sold by Wm. Harned, 22 Spruce St., New York and Baltimore and Marsh, Boston, Mass." 230pp. [Crew/JBR-1].

496.65 Glorious Harry Clay. w. No composer indicated. m. "Tune—*The Hurrah Song.*" B/w litho of a raccoon." In: *The National Clay Minstrel (And True Whig's Pocket Companion For The Presidential Canvass Of 1844)*, page 58. Published by [V-1: George Hood, No. 15 North 6th Street, Philadelphia, PA] [V-2: James Fisher, No. 71 Court Street, Boston, MA]. 1843. [3¼" × 5⅛"]. Y/bk litho of raccoon—"That Coon" and flag—"Henry Clay," log cabin. "New and Improved Edition." 128pp. [Crew/HC-11].

496.65A Greeley. w.m. No composer or tune indicated. In: *The Farmer Of Chappaqua Songster, Containing A Great Number Of The Best Campaign Songs That The Unanimous And Enthusiastic Nomination Of The Hon. Horace Greeley For President Has Produced*, page 72. Published by Robert M. De Wit, Publisher, No. 33 Rose Street, New York, NY. 1872. [4¼" × 6¼"]. R/w/bl/y litho caricature of Horace Greeley. 102pp.

496.66 Great Harry Clay. w. Mr. Vorhees. m. "Air—*Away Up Salt River.*" In: *The National Clay Minstrel (And True Whig's Pocket Companion For The Presidential Canvass Of 1844)*, page 16. Published by [V-1: George Hood, No. 15 North 6th Street, Philadelphia, PA] [V-2: James Fisher, No. 71 Court Street, Boston, MA]. 1843. [3¼" × 5⅛"]. Y/bk litho of raccoon—"That Coon" and flag—"Henry Clay," log cabin. "New and Improved Edition." 128pp. [Crew/HC-11].

496.67 Greeley's Old White Coat. w.m. No composer or tune indicated. In: *The Sun's Greeley Campaign Songster*, page 27. c. Amos J. Cumming. Published from *The Sun* Office, New York, NY. 1872. [4⅛" × 6½"]. Be/bk litho of Horace Greeley, wreath. "He shines for all." 64pp. [Crew/HG-5].

496.68 Hark! From The Broad And Noble West. w. No composer indicated [John H. Warland]. m. "Tune—*All's Well.*" In: *The National Clay Minstrel (And True Whig's Pocket Companion For The Presidential Canvass Of 1844)*, page 63. Published by [V-1: George Hood, No. 15 North 6th Street, Philadelphia, PA] [V-2: James Fisher, No. 71 Court Street, Boston, MA]. 1843. [3¼" × 5⅛"]. Y/bk litho of raccoon—"That Coon" and flag—"Henry Clay," log cabin. "New and Improved Edition." 128pp. [Crew/HC-11].

496.69 Harry Clay When A Boy. w. No composer indicated. m. "Tune—*Harry Bluff.*" In: *The National Clay Melodist (A Collection Of Popular And Patriotic Songs, Second Edition, Enlarged And Improved)*, page 103. Published by Benj. Adams, No. 54 Court Street, Boston, MA. 1844. [3" × 5¼"]. Inside title page: B/w litho of Henry Clay's home—"O'er Ashland's lawns the skies are bright, From West to East The radiance streams and glows, The land beneath its beams gay beats the heart with joy, Hurrah! Hurrah! Hip! Hurrah!" 108pp. [M-050?]. [Crew/HC-13].

496.70 Harry Clay's Raisin. w. No composer indicated. m. "Air—*Old Tip's Raisin.*" In: *The National Clay Minstrel*, page 54. Published by [V-1: George Hood, No. 15 North 6th Street, Philadelphia, PA] [V-2: James Fisher, No. 71 Court Street, Boston, MA]. 1843. [3" × 4½"]. Y/bk litho of raccoon sitting on fence, black border. 68pp. [Crew/HC-10].

496.71 Harry Of Kentucky. w. No composer indicated. m. "Tune—*'Tis My Delight Of A Shiny Night.*" In: *The National Clay Minstrel*, page 40. Published by [V-1: George Hood, No. 15 North 6th Street, Philadelphia, PA] [V-2: James Fisher, No. 71 Court Street, Boston, MA]. 1843. [3" × 4½"]. Y/bk litho of raccoon sitting on fence, black border. 68pp. [Crew/HC-10].

496.72 Harry Of Kentucky, Ho! Ieroe! w. No composer indicated. m. "Tune—*Hail To The Chief Who In Triumph Advances.*" In: *The National Clay Minstrel (And True Whig's Pocket Companion For The Presidential Canvass Of 1844)*, page 52. Published by [V-1: George Hood, No. 15 North 6th Street, Philadelphia, PA] [V-2: James Fisher, No. 71 Court Street, Boston, MA]. 1843. [3¼" × 5⅛"]. Y/bk litho of raccoon—"That Coon" and flag—"Henry Clay," log cabin. "New and Improved Edition." 128pp. [Crew/HC-11].

496.73 Harry Of Kentucky, Oh. w. F. Buckingham Graham. m. "Tune—*Green Grow The Rushes, Oh!*" In: *The National Clay Melodist (A Collection Of Popular And Patriotic Songs, Second Edition, Enlarged And Improved)*, page 100. Published by Benj. Adams, No. 54 Court Street, Boston, MA. 1844. [3" × 5¼"]. Inside title page: B/w litho of Henry Clay's home—"O'er Ashland's lawns the skies are bright, From West to East The radiance streams and glows, The land beneath its beams gay beats the heart with joy, Hurrah! Hurrah! Hip! Hurrah!" 108pp. [M-050?]. [Crew/HC-13].

496.74 Harry Of The West (A Song). w. Jesse Hutchinson, Jr. m. John W. Hutchinson. Published by C. Holt, Jr., No. 156 Fulton Street, New York, NY. 1848. Non-pictorial geometric designs. "Written & Sung on the Occasion of the Reception of Henry Clay in the City of New York, March 7th, 1848, by the Hutchinson Family." 4pp. Page 4: Blank. [Crew/HC-125].

496.75 Harry Of The West. w. Charles Collins, Esq. m. Oliver Shaw. Published by Oliver Shaw, No. 70 Westminster Street, Providence, RI. 1844. Non-pictorial geometric designs. "Music Composed & Respectfully Dedicated to the Rhode Island Clay Clubs." 4pp. Pages 1 and 4: Blank. [Crew/HC-121].

496.76 Harry Of The West. w. No composer indicated. m. "Tune—*The Star Spangled Banner.*" "Written for the *National Clay Minstrel.*" In: *The National Clay Minstrel (And True Whig's Pocket Companion For The Presidential Canvass Of 1844)*, page 75. Published by [V-1: George Hood, No. 15 North 6th Street, Philadelphia, PA] [V-2: James Fisher, No. 71 Court Street, Boston, MA]. 1843. [3¼" × 5⅛"]. Y/bk litho of raccoon—"That Coon" and flag—"Henry Clay," log cabin. "New and Improved Edition." 128pp. [Crew/HC-11].

496.77 Harry, The Honest And True. w. No composer indicated. m. "Tune—*Rosin The Beau.*" In: *The National Clay Minstrel*, page 37. Published by [V-1: George Hood, No. 15 North 6th Street, Philadelphia, PA] [V-2: James Fisher, No. 71 Court Street, Boston, MA]. 1843. [3" × 4½"]. Y/bk litho of raccoon sitting on fence, black border. 68pp. [Crew/HC-10].

496.78 Harry The True And The Jersey Blue. w. F. Buckingham Graham. m. "Tune—*What Has Caused This Great Commotion.*" In: *The National Clay Minstrel*, page 9. Published by [V-1: George Hood, No. 15 North 6th Street, Philadelphia, PA] [V-2: James

Fisher, No. 71 Court Street, Boston, MA]. 1843. [3" × 4½"]. Y/bk litho of raccoon sitting on fence, black border. 68pp. [Crew/HC-10].

496.79 Henry Clay And Frelinghuysen. w.m. No composer or tune indicated. In: *The National Clay Almanac, 1845*, page 30. Published by Desilver & Muir, No. 18 South Fourth Street, Philadelphia, PA. 1844. [6¹³⁄₁₆" × 7⅞"]. B/w litho of Henry Clay, ship—"Commerce," plow, crops—"Agriculture." 36pp. [Crew/HC-89].

496.80 Henry Clay At The Helm. w. "B." Luther Leland. m. "Tune—*Soldier's Dream*." B/w litho of Henry Clay guiding the rudder on a ship inscribed "U.S., two sinking ships in the background with flags labeled "J.C.C. [John C. Calhoun] and "MVB." In: *The National Clay Melodist (A Collection Of Popular And Patriotic Songs, Second Edition, Enlarged And Improved)*, page 89. Published by Benj. Adams, No. 54 Court Street, Boston, MA. 1844. [3" × 5¼"]. Inside title page: B/w litho of Henry Clay's home—"O'er Ashland's lawns the skies are bright, From West to East The radiance streams and glows, The land beneath its beams gay beats the heart with joy, Hurrah! Hurrah! Hip! Hurrah!" 108pp. [M-050?]. [Crew/HC-13].

496.81 The Henry Clay Waltzes. m. Dr. Charles Glasier. Published by A. Foit, 196 Chestnut Street, Philadelphia, PA. 1844. Non-pictorial geometric designs. "Composed, arranged for the Piano Forte and Most Respectfully dedicated to his friend E. King, Esqr." 8pp. Page 8: Blank. [Crew/HC-123].

496.82 Henry Clay's Alabama March. m. Amand P. Pfister. Published by Firth & Hall, No. 1 Franklin Square, New York, NY. 1847. Non-pictorial. "Composed and Respectfully Inscribed to Miss Sarah Frances Thoinlen [?] of Eutaw, Alabama." 4pp. Page 4: Blank. [Crew/HC-124].

496.83 Henry Clay's Grand March. m. Dr. John C. Bartlett. Published by Oliver Ditson, No. 135 Washington Street, Boston, MA. 1844. Non-pictorial. "Composed for the Piano Forte." 2pp. [Crew/HC-125].

496.84 Henry Clay's Quick Step. w.m. No composers indicated. No publisher indicated. [1844]. Non-pictorial. 2pp. Page 2: Blank. [Crew/HC-122]

496.85 Henry Clay's Remonstrance. w. No composer indicated. m. "To the tune of *I Won't Be A Nun*." Published in the *U.S. Telegraph*, July 2, 1828. [VBL, p. 241].

496.86 [Here's A Health To The Workingman's Friend]. w. No composer indicated. m. *Hurrah For The Bonnets Of Blue*. Published in the *Daily National Intelligencer, July 28*, 1832. [VBL, p. 246].

496.87 Here's A Health To Our Own Harry Clay. w. No composer indicated. m. "Tune—*Hurrah For The Bonnets O Blue*." In: *The National Clay Minstrel (And True Whig's Pocket Companion For The Presidential Canvass Of 1844)*, page 62. Published by [V-1: George Hood, No. 15 North 6th Street, Philadelphia, PA] [V-2: James Fisher, No. 71 Court Street, Boston, MA]. 1843. [3¼" × 5⅛"]. Y/bk litho of raccoon—"That Coon" and flag—"Henry Clay," log cabin. "New and Improved Edition." 128pp. [Crew/HC-11].

496.88 Here's A Health To The Free Born. w. Alonzo Lewis, Esq. "of Lynn, Mass." m. "Tune—*Young Lochinvar*." "Written for the Young Men's National Convention, at Baltimore, May 4, 1840." In: *Tippecanoe Song-Book (A Collection Of Log Cabin And Patriotic Melodies)*, page 153. Published by Marshall, Williams & Butler, Philadelphia, PA. 1840. White on black litho of log cabin, plow, flags, eagle. 180pp. [M-024]. [Crew/WHH-61].

496.89 Ho! Why Dost Thou Shiver And Shake, Harry Clay? w. No composer indicated. m. "Air—*Gaffar Gray*." Published in the *Washington Globe*, September 12, 1832. [VBL, p. 247].

496.90 Honest Farmer Boy. w. No composer indicated. m. "Tune—*My Old Aunt Sally*." "Written for the *National Clay Minstrel*." In: *The National Clay Minstrel (And True Whig's Pocket Companion For The Presidential Canvass Of 1844)*, page 106. Published by [V-1: George Hood, No. 15 North 6th Street, Philadelphia, PA] [V-2: James Fisher, No. 71 Court Street, Boston, MA]. 1843. [3¼" × 5⅛"]. Y/bk litho of raccoon—"That Coon" and flag—"Henry Clay," log cabin. "New and Improved Edition." 128pp. [Crew/HC-11].

496.91 How Many Clay Men Are There? w. No composer indicated. m. "Air—*Rosin The Bow*." "Dedicated to the Clay Club of Salem, N.J." In: *The National Clay Minstrel (And True Whig's Pocket Companion For The Presidential Canvass Of 1844)*, page 35. Published by [V-1: George Hood, No. 15 North 6th Street, Philadelphia, PA] [V-2: James Fisher, No. 71 Court Street, Boston, MA]. 1843. [3¼" × 5⅛"]. Y/bk litho of raccoon—"That Coon" and flag—"Henry Clay," log cabin. "New and Improved Edition." 128pp. [Crew/HC-11].

496.92 Hurrah For The Clay. w. "Written by a Gentleman of Philadelphia." m. "Air—*How Happy's The Soldier*." In: *The National Clay Minstrel (And True Whig's Pocket Companion For The Presidential Canvass Of 1844)*, page 25. Published by [V-1: George Hood, No. 15 North 6th Street, Philadelphia, PA] [V-2: James Fisher, No. 71 Court Street, Boston, MA]. 1843. [3¼" × 5⅛"]. Y/bk litho of raccoon—"That Coon" and flag—"Henry Clay," log cabin. "New and Improved Edition." 128pp. [Crew/HC-11].

496.93 Hurrah Song. w.m. No composer or tune indicated. In: *The National Clay Minstrel*, page 21. Published by [V-1: George Hood, No. 15 North 6th Street, Philadelphia, PA] [V-2: James Fisher, No. 71 Court Street, Boston, MA]. 1843. [3" × 4½"]. Y/bk litho of raccoon sitting on fence, black border. 68pp. Pages 2 and 67: Blank. Pages 65–66: Contents. [Crew/HC-10].

496.94 I Won't Go For Van (A Song For Honest Locos). w. No composer indicated. m. "*I Won't Be A Nun*." "Written for the *Clay Melodist*." B/w litho of a man with a whip forcing people into a megaphone inscribed "Loco Foco Gathering 1844" and captioned—"Putting an extinguisher upon the Locos." In: *The National Clay Melodist (A Collection Of Popular And Patriotic Songs, Second Edition, Enlarged And Improved)*, page 82. Published by Benj. Adams, No. 54 Court Street, Boston, MA. 1844. [3" × 5¼"]. Inside title page: B/w litho of Henry Clay's home—"O'er Ashland's lawns the skies are bright, From West to

East The radiance streams and glows, The land beneath its beams gay beats the heart with joy, Hurrah! Hurrah! Hip! Hurrah!" 108pp. [M-050?]. [Crew/HC-13].

496.94 I'm Afloat! w. No composer indicated. m. No composer indicated. In: *The Fremont Songster*, page 4. Published by [V-1: H.S. Riggs & Company, Publishers, No. 4 Cortland Street] [V-2: P.J. Cozans, No. 107 Nassau Street], New York, NY. 1856. [V-1: 3⅝" × 5¾"] [V-2: 3½" × 5⅝"]. Be/bk litho of wreath, John C. Fremont. "With a current likeness of John C. Fremont, The People's Candidate for the Presidency." 40pp. [M-094, 095]. [Crew/JCF-45].

496.95 An Invitation To The Log Cabin Boys To Old Tippecanoe's Raisin.' w. No composer indicated. m. "Tune—*The Good Old Days Of Adam And Eve.*" "As sung by The Buckeye Blacksmith." In: *Tippecanoe Club Songster*, page 27. Published by [V-1: Turner & Fisher, No. 15 North Sixth Street, Philadelphia, PA] [V-2: H.A. Turner, Baltimore, MD]. 1841. [3" × 4⁷⁄₁₆"]. Hand Colored engraving of William Henry Harrison, log cabin. 68pp. [M-021, 022]. [Crew/WHH-18].

496.96 [It Is Now Pretty Clear] (Song 3). w. W.A. m. "Tune—*Landlady Of France.*" In: *Original Clay Songs: Humorous And Sentimental, Designed To Inculcate Just Political Sentiments, To Suit The Present Political Crisis, And To Advocate The Claims Of Henry Clay To The Highest Honors His Country Can Bestow*, page 6. w. W.A. Philomath, Union Co., Ind. Published by Philomath, Cincinnati, OH. 1842. [4¼" × 6"]. Be/bk litho of an eagle, U.S. Flag. "The eagle soars above the throng; And listen's [sic] to fair Freedom's song, Hails the merry roundelay, Claps his glad wings and hails the day." 20pp. Page 20: Be/bk litho of four men—"Tyler Expounding the Constitution! The effect of 'treading in the footsteps.'" [M-057]. [CrewHC-104].

496.97 Jimmie Polk Of Tennessee. w. J. Greiner. m. "Tune—*Dandy Jim Of Caroline.*" In: *The National Clay Minstrel*, page 2. Published by [V-1: George Hood, No. 15 North 6th Street, Philadelphia, PA] [V-2: James Fisher, No. 71 Court Street, Boston, MA]. 1843. [3" × 4½"]. Y/bk litho of raccoon sitting on fence, black border. 68pp. [Crew/HC-10].

496.98 John A. Dix's Revenge. w. No composer indicated. m. "A Ballad by the Former Governor, Entitled *Somebody Else Is Getting; It Where I Got Mine.*" In: *The Red Book, Containing Portraits And Biographies Of Some Persons More Or Less Prominent Public Life Written Entirely Without Respect To The Libel Laws, In A Studious Effort To Conceal Everything But The Truth; Some Songs Built Upon The Same Principle, And Other Important (?) Material Entirely Unfit To Print*, page 16. Published by Legislative Correspondents' Association of the State of New York, Albany, NY. 1913. [5" × 7¼"]. R/w/bk hardback book with drawing of State House, seal of New York, geometric designs. 90pp.

496.99 John C. Calhoun My Jo. w. No composer indicated. m. "Tune—*John Anderson my Jo.*" In: *Log Cabin Song Book* (A Collection of Popular and Patriotic Songs), page 40. Published at *The Log Cabin* office, No. 30 Ann-Street, New York, NY. 1840. [4⅞" × 7"]. [V-1: Br/bk] [V-2: Y/bk] litho of log cabin, cider barrel, farmer with plow, flag—"Harrison and Tyler," geometric design border. "The Freeman's glittering Sword be Blest, For ever blest the Freeman's Lyre" Page 3: B/w litho of "Major-General William Henry Harrison, of Ohio," facsimile signature. 74pp. [M-020]. [Crew/WHH-56].

496.100 Johnny The Broker. w. No composer indicated. m. *John Anderson, My Jo.* Published in the *Richmond Inquirer*, Richmond, VA., September20, 1828. [VBL, p. 240].

496.101 The Kentuckian Broom Girl. w. John H. Warland. m. No tune indicated. "Written for the *Clay Melodist.*" In: *The National Clay Melodist (A Collection Of Popular And Patriotic Songs, Second Edition, Enlarged And Improved)*, page 52. Published by Benj. Adams, No. 54 Court Street, Boston, MA. 1844. [3" × 5¼"]. Inside title page: B/w litho of Henry Clay's home—"O'er Ashland's lawns the skies are bright, From West to East The radiance streams and glows, The land beneath its beams gay beats the heart with joy, Hurrah! Hurrah! Hip! Hurrah!" 108pp. [M-050?]. [Crew/HC-13].

496.102 Kentucky Central March And Quick Step. m. William Ratel. Published by George Willig, 171 Chesnut Street, Philadelphia, PA. 1844. Non-pictorial geometric designs. "As performed at the great Whig barbeque on Boyle County, by the Amateur Band Composed expressly for the occasion by William Ratel." 4pp. [AMC].

496.103 [Kentucky Is Coming Oh Ho, Oh Ho!] (Song 8). w. W.A. m. "Tune—*The Campbells Are Coming.*" In: *Original Clay Songs: Humorous And Sentimental, Designed To Inculcate Just Political Sentiments, To Suit The Present Political Crisis, And To Advocate The Claims Of Henry Clay To The Highest Honors His Country Can Bestow*, page 12. w. W.A. Philomath, Union Co., Ind. Published by Philomath, Cincinnati, OH. 1842. [4¼" × 6"]. Be/bk litho of an eagle, U.S. Flag. "The eagle soars above the throng; And listen's [sic] to fair Freedom's song, Hails the merry roundelay, Claps his glad wings and hails the day." 20pp. Page 20: Be/bk litho of four men—"Tyler Expounding the Constitution! The effect of 'treading in the footsteps.'" [M-057]. [CrewHC-104].

496.104 Kentucky O! w. No composer indicated. m. "Tune—*On Yonder Rock Reclining.*" "Written for the Choir of the National Clay Club." In: *The National Clay Minstrel*, page 29. Published by [V-1: George Hood, No. 15 North 6th Street, Philadelphia, PA] [V-2: James Fisher, No. 71 Court Street, Boston, MA]. 1843. [3" × 4½"]. Y/bk litho of raccoon sitting on fence, black border. 68pp. [Crew/HC-10].

496.105 The Knight Of The Box. w.m. No composer or tune indicated. In: *Greeley Campaign Songster*, page 18. Published by Halpin & McClure, Chicago, IL. 1872. [4" × 5¹⁵⁄₁₆"]. Pl/bk litho of Horace Greeley, geometric design border. "Chicago: Western News Company, Wholesale Agents." 72pp. [M-187]. [Crew/HG-21].

496.106 Ladies, Come Weave A New Banner. w. No composer indicated. m. "Tune—*Old Rosin The Bow.*" In: *The National Clay Minstrel (And True Whig's Pocket Companion For The Presidential Canvass Of 1844)*, page 58. Published by [V-1: George Hood, No. 15 North 6th Street, Philadelphia, PA] [V-2: James Fisher, No. 71 Court Street, Boston, MA]. 1843. [3¼"

× 5⅛"]. Y/bk litho of raccoon—"That Coon" and flag—"Henry Clay," log cabin. "New and Improved Edition." 128pp. [Crew/HC-11].

496.107 The Ladies' Whig Song. w. No composer indicated. m. "Tune—*Rosin The Beau*." In: *The National Clay Minstrel*, page 39. Published by [V-1: George Hood, No. 15 North 6th Street, Philadelphia, PA] [V-2: James Fisher, No. 71 Court Street, Boston, MA]. 1843. [3" × 4½"]. Y/bk litho of raccoon sitting on fence, black border. 68pp. [Crew/HC-10].

496.108 Leave Vain Regrets. w. No composer indicated. m. "Tune—*Auld Lang Syne*." In: *The National Clay Minstrel*, page 35. Published by [V-1: George Hood, No. 15 North 6th Street, Philadelphia, PA] [V-2: James Fisher, No. 71 Court Street, Boston, MA]. 1843. [3" × 4½"]. Y/bk litho of raccoon sitting on fence, black border. 68pp. [Crew/HC-10].

496.109 Leave Vain Regrets For Errors Past. w. No composer indicated. m. Tune—*The American Star*." In: *The National Clay Melodist (A Collection Of Popular And Patriotic Songs, Second Edition, Enlarged And Improved)*, page 73. Published by Benj. Adams, No. 54 Court Street, Boston, MA. 1844. [3" × 5¼"]. Inside title page: B/w litho of Henry Clay's home—"O'er Ashland's lawns the skies are bright, From West to East The radiance streams and glows, The land beneath its beams gay beats the heart with joy, Hurrah! Hurrah! Hip! Hurrah!" 108pp. [M-050?]. [Crew/HC-13].

496.110 [Life Let Us Cherish] (Song 5). w. W.A. m. "Tune—*Life Let Us Cherish*." In: *Original Clay Songs: Humorous And Sentimental, Designed To Inculcate Just Political Sentiments, To Suit The Present Political Crisis, And To Advocate The Claims Of Henry Clay To The Highest Honors His Country Can Bestow*, page 9. w. W.A. Philomath, Union Co., Ind. Published by Philomath, Cincinnati, OH. 1842. [4¼" × 6"]. Be/bk litho of an eagle, U.S. Flag. "The eagle soars above the throng; And listen's [sic] to fair Freedom's song, Hails the merry roundelay, Claps his glad wings and hails the day." 20pp. Page 20: Be/bk litho of four men—"Tyler Expounding the Constitution! The effect of 'treading in the footsteps.'" [M-057]. [CrewHC-104].

496.111 Lincoln's Picture. w. John Quod, Jr. m. No tune indicated. In: *The Democratic Campaign Songster: Douglas & Johnson Melodies*, page 22."Written in behalf of several leading Republicans, and respectfully submitted to the party, by John Quod, Jr." Published by P.J. Cozans, Publisher, New York, NY. [1860]. [3⅞" × 6"]. Y/bk litho of an eagle with ribbon—"Douglas & Johnson," train, ships, monument—"Liberty" sitting on rock base—"The Constitution." 40pp. [M-117]. [Crew/SAD-5].

496.112 The Little Red Fox. w. No composer indicated. m. "Tune—*Old Dan Tucker*." In: *The National Clay Melodist (A Collection Of Popular And Patriotic Songs, Second Edition, Enlarged And Improved)*, page 38. Published by Benj. Adams, No. 54 Court Street, Boston, MA. 1844. [3" × 5¼"]. Inside title page: B/w litho of Henry Clay's home—"O'er Ashland's lawns the skies are bright, From West to East The radiance streams and glows, The land beneath its beams gay beats the heart with joy, Hurrah! Hurrah! Hip! Hurrah!" 108pp. [M-050?]. [Crew/HC-13].

496.112 The Lynn Clay Club Glee. w. John H. Warland. m. No tune indicated. B/w litho "Reduced from Dodge's view of Ashland." "Written for the *Clay Melodist*." In: *The National Clay Melodist (A Collection Of Popular And Patriotic Songs, Second Edition, Enlarged And Improved)*, page 26. Published by Benj. Adams, No. 54 Court Street, Boston, MA. 1844. [3" × 5¼"]. Inside title page: B/w litho of Henry Clay's home—"O'er Ashland's lawns the skies are bright, From West to East The radiance streams and glows, The land beneath its beams gay beats the heart with joy, Hurrah! Hurrah! Hip! Hurrah!" 108pp. [M-050?]. [Crew/HC-13].

496.113 March, Freemen, March. w. No composer indicated. m. "Tune—*Dance, Boatman, Dance*." In: *Scott And Graham Melodies (Being A Collection Of Campaign Songs For 1852)*, page 26. Published by Huestis & Cozans, Nos. 104 and 106 Nassau Street, New York, NY. 1852. [3¹³⁄₁₆" × 6⁵⁄₁₆"]. B/w litho of Winfield Scott, geometric design border. "As sung by the Whig Clubs throughout the United States." 76pp. [M-086]. [Crew/WS-15].

496.114 The Moon Was Shining Silver Bright (A Whig Song). w. J. Greenier. m. "Tune—*Old Dan Tucker*." In: *The National Clay Minstrel (And True Whig's Pocket Companion For The Presidential Canvass Of 1844)*, page 44. Published by [V-1: George Hood, No. 15 North 6th Street, Philadelphia, PA] [V-2: James Fisher, No. 71 Court Street, Boston, MA]. 1843. [3¼" × 5⅛"]. Y/bk litho of raccoon—"That Coon" and flag—"Henry Clay," log cabin. "New and Improved Edition." 128pp. [Crew/HC-11].

496.115 A New Song. w. No composer indicated. m. "Tune—*Old Rosin The Bow*." In: *The National Clay Minstrel*, page 18. Published by [V-1: George Hood, No. 15 North 6th Street, Philadelphia, PA] [V-2: James Fisher, No. 71 Court Street, Boston, MA]. 1843. [3" × 4½"]. Y/bk litho of raccoon sitting on fence, black border. 68pp. [Crew/HC-10].

496.116 Now He's In Dutch. w. No composer indicated. m. "Air—*It Was The Dutch*." In: *The Red Book, Containing Portraits And Biographies Of Some Persons More Or Less Prominent Public Life Written Entirely Without Respect To The Libel Laws, In A Studious Effort To Conceal Everything But The Truth; Some Songs Built Upon The Same Principle, And Other Important (?) Material Entirely Unfit To Print*, page 20. Published by Legislative Correspondents' Association of the State of New York, Albany, NY. 1913. [5" × 7¼"]. R/w/bk hardback book with drawing of State House, seal of New York, geometric designs. 90pp.

496.117 Oh Dear, What Will Become Of Them? w. No composer indicated. m. "Tune—*Oh Dear, What Can The Matter Be?*" In: *The National Clay Melodist (A Collection Of Popular And Patriotic Songs, Second Edition, Enlarged And Improved)*, page 93. Published by Benj. Adams, No. 54 Court Street, Boston, MA. 1844. [3" × 5¼"]. Inside title page: B/w litho of Henry Clay's home—"O'er Ashland's lawns the skies are bright, From West to East The radiance streams and glows, The land beneath its beams gay beats the heart with joy, Hurrah! Hurrah! Hip! Hurrah!" 108pp. [M-050?]. [Crew/HC-13].

496.118 Oh, Henry Clay Will Be The Man. w. No

composer indicated. m. "Tune—*Nancy Dawson.*" In: *The National Clay Minstrel,* page 35. Published by [V-1: George Hood, No. 15 North 6th Street, Philadelphia, PA] [V-2: James Fisher, No. 71 Court Street, Boston, MA]. 1843. [3" × 4½"]. Y/bk litho of raccoon sitting on fence, black border. 68pp. [Crew/HC-10].

496.119 Old Abe And His Fights. w. No composer indicated. m. "Air—*Roger De Coverly.*" In: *The Great Republican Campaigns Of 1860 And 1896,* page 175. e. Osborn H. Oldroyd. Published by Laird & Lee, Chicago, IL. 1896. [5⁵⁄₁₆" × 7⁷⁄₁₆"]. Gn/r/bk photos of Abraham Lincoln, William McKinley and Garrett Hobart. "Sound Money, Protection, Prosperity." 208pp. [Crew/AL-574].

496.120 Old Abe And His Fights. w. No composer indicated. m. "Air—*Roger De Coverly.*" Published in the *New York Herald,* August 30, 1860. [VBL, p. 343].

496.121 Old Abe The Rail Splitter. w.m. No composer indicated. m. "Tune—*The Star Spangled Banner.*" In: *The Republican Campaign Songster No. #1,* page 17. Published by American Publishing House, No. 60 West Fourth Street, Cincinnati, OH. [1860]. [3¾" × 5¾"]. B/w litho of Abraham Lincoln. 48pp. [?]. [M-113]. [Crew/AL-298].

496.122 Old Tariff Harry. w. No composer indicated. m. "Tune—*Good Old Days Of Adam And Eve.*" In: *The National Clay Minstrel (And True Whig's Pocket Companion For The Presidential Canvass Of 1844),* page 71. Published by [V-1: George Hood, No. 15 North 6th Street, Philadelphia, PA] [V-2: James Fisher, No. 71 Court Street, Boston, MA]. 1843. [3¼" × 5⅛"]. Y/bk litho of raccoon—"That Coon" and flag—"Henry Clay," log cabin. "New and Improved Edition." 128pp. [Crew/HC-11].

496.123 Old Tippecanoe (A Patriotic Song). w.m. "A Pennsylvanian." Published by L.D. Meignen & Company, Publishers and Importers of Music, Musical Instruments, Italian Strings, &c., No. 217 Chesnut Street, Philadelphia, PA. 1840. B/w litho by C.S. Duval of nine vignettes of William Henry Harrison's military career, log cabin scene, cannons, William Henry Harrison, crossed flags. Description of each vignette. "Baltimore Convention." "Written, to be sung at Baltimore during the Young Men's Whig Convention and most respectfully inscribed to the Young Ladies of this Monumental City." 4pp. Page 4: Blank. [Crew/WHH-79].

496.124 Old Tippecanoe's Raisin.' m.a. Thomas Carr. Published by G.E. Blake, No. 13 South 5th Street, Philadelphia, PA. 1840. B/w litho by Sinclair's Litho. of men, cabin, horse, oxen team, flag. "Respectfully inscribed to all true Republicans in the United States." "Blake's Log Cabin Music." 6pp. Pages 2 and 6: Blank. Page 3: B/w litho of log cabin, flag inscribed "Tippecanoe." "Sung with Volcanic effect by the Buckeye Blacksmith." "Dedicated to the friends of Liberty & Reform." [Crew/WHH-47(F)].

496.125 The Old Whig Cause. w.m. No composer or tune indicated. In: *The National Clay Melodist (A Collection Of Popular And Patriotic Songs, Second Edition, Enlarged And Improved),* page 97. Published by Benj. Adams, No. 54 Court Street, Boston, MA. 1844. [3" × 5¼"]. Inside title page: B/w litho of Henry Clay's home—"O'er Ashland's lawns the skies are bright, From West to East The radiance streams and glows, The land beneath its beams gay beats the heart with joy, Hurrah! Hurrah! Hip! Hurrah!" 108pp. [M-050?]. [Crew/HC-13].

496.126 Once More, And At Our Country's Call. w.m. No composer or tune indicated. In: *The National Clay Melodist (A Collection Of Popular And Patriotic Songs, Second Edition, Enlarged And Improved),* page 48. Published by Benj. Adams, No. 54 Court Street, Boston, MA. 1844. [3" × 5¼"]. Inside title page: B/w litho of Henry Clay's home—"O'er Ashland's lawns the skies are bright, From West to East The radiance streams and glows, The land beneath its beams gay beats the heart with joy, Hurrah! Hurrah! Hip! Hurrah!" 108pp. [M-050?]. [Crew/HC-13].

496.127 Onward! w. No composer indicated. m. "Tune—*Rory O'More.*" "Written for the *National Clay Minstrel.*" In: *The National Clay Minstrel (And True Whig's Pocket Companion For The Presidential Canvass Of 1844),* page 98. Published by [V-1: George Hood, No. 15 North 6th Street, Philadelphia, PA] [V-2: James Fisher, No. 71 Court Street, Boston, MA]. 1843. [3¼" × 5⅛"]. Y/bk litho of raccoon—"That Coon" and flag—"Henry Clay," log cabin. "New and Improved Edition." 128pp. Page 10: Dedication—"To the National Clay Club this work is respectfully dedicated by the Publisher." [Crew/HC-11].

496.128 The Orator's Coming. w. No composer indicated. m. "Tune—*The Campbells Are Coming.*" "Written for the *National Clay Minstrel.*" B/w litho of a raccoon labeled "That Coon" atop a log cabin with a flag labeled "Henry Clay." In: *The National Clay Minstrel,* back cover. Published by [V-1: George Hood, No. 15 North 6th Street, Philadelphia, PA] [V-2: James Fisher, No. 71 Court Street, Boston, MA]. 1843. [3" × 4½"]. Y/bk litho of raccoon sitting on fence, black border. 68pp. [Crew/HC-10].

496.129 Order Of Performance At The Whig Celebration, July 4, 1834. 1834. [Approx. 9" × 12"]. Non-pictorial. 4pp. Pages 1 and 4: Blank. Page 2: *Ode, For 4th July, 1834.* m. "Air, *Adams And Liberty.*" Page 3: "Order of Performance" incl. "*Original Ode*" (page 3) and *Hymn.* [Crew/HC-127].

496.130 Our Candidate. w. No composer indicated. m. "Tune—*Hurrah, Hurrah.*" In: *The National Clay Minstrel (And True Whig's Pocket Companion For The Presidential Canvass Of 1844),* page 60. Published by [V-1: George Hood, No. 15 North 6th Street, Philadelphia, PA] [V-2: James Fisher, No. 71 Court Street, Boston, MA]. 1843. [3¼" × 5⅛"]. Y/bk litho of raccoon—"That Coon" and flag—"Henry Clay," log cabin. "New and Improved Edition." 128pp. [Crew/HC-11].

496.131 Our Glorious Constitution. w. Townsend Haines. m. "Tune—*Tullochgorum.*" In: *The National Clay Melodist (A Collection Of Popular And Patriotic Songs, Second Edition, Enlarged And Improved),* page 41. Published by Benj. Adams, No. 54 Court Street, Boston, MA. 1844. [3" × 5¼"]. Inside title page: B/w litho of Henry Clay's home—"O'er Ashland's lawns the skies are bright, From West to East The radiance streams and glows, The land beneath its beams gay beats the heart with joy, Hurrah! Hurrah! Hip! Hurrah!" 108pp. [M-050?]. [Crew/HC-13].

496.132 Paging One Pitcher. w. No composer indicated. m. "Air — *I Wonder What's Become Of Sally.*" In: *Gone With The Winner*, page 9. Published by Albany Legislative Correspondents' Association of New York State, Albany, NY. March 20, 1941. [9" × 11¹⁄₁₆"]. R/w/bl/y drawing of Franklin Roosevelt and Wendell Willkie riding "A Bicycle Built For Two" labeled — "Roosevelt-Willkie Axis." Wheels — "New Deal" and "Lend Lease Bill." "Or 'Back in the Lap of God.' A Hoosier-Hyde Park Honeymoon Hit, Staring the G. Oomph P.'s Lost Leader and the King of Krum Elbow in 'Lucky Partners.' Says F.D.R. — 'He's My Man.' Says the Republican Party — 'Once a New Dealer, Sometimes a Double- Dealer.' Says the Public — 'Willkie's the Life of the Party, But What Party?" "Served Piping Hot at Hotel Ten Eyck, Albany, New York, Thursday Night, March 20, 1941, at 7:30 o'clock. [Crew/FDR-394].

496.133 A Peep At Washington. w. "Composed and Sung by Mr. Rice, in Washington, D.C., during the session of Congress, 1850." m. "Tune — *Susannah.*" In: *Dan Rice's Great American Humorist Song Book*, page 23. 1866. [4⅛" × 5¾"]. Br/bk drawing of an actor. "Containing Original and Selected Songs, Carefully Revised & Corrected." 34pp.

496.134 Pennsylvania Song. w. No composer indicated. m. "Tune — *Rosin The Beau.*" B/w litho of Pennsylvania seal. In: *The National Clay Minstrel*, page 27. Published by [V-1: George Hood, No. 15 North 6th Street, Philadelphia, PA] [V-2: James Fisher, No. 71 Court Street, Boston, MA]. 1843. [3" × 4½"]. Y/bk litho of raccoon sitting on fence, black border. 68pp. [Crew/HC-10].

496.135 The People's Own. w.m. No composer or tune indicated. In: *The National Clay Melodist (A Collection Of Popular And Patriotic Songs, Second Edition, Enlarged And Improved)*, page 99. Published by Benj. Adams, No. 54 Court Street, Boston, MA. 1844. [3" × 5¼"]. Inside title page: B/w litho of Henry Clay's home — "O'er Ashland's lawns the skies are bright, From West to East The radiance streams and glows, The land beneath its beams gay beats the heart with joy, Hurrah! Hurrah! Hip! Hurrah!" 108pp. [M-050?]. [Crew/HC-13].

496.136 A Political Catch. w. No composer indicated. m. "Tune — *The Little Tailor Boy.*" In: *The National Clay Minstrel*, page 11. Published by [V-1: George Hood, No. 15 North 6th Street, Philadelphia, PA] [V-2: James Fisher, No. 71 Court Street, Boston, MA]. 1843. [3" × 4½"]. Y/bk litho of raccoon sitting on fence, black border. 68pp. [Crew/HC-10].

496.137 The Political Grimes. w. No composer indicated. m. "Air — *Old Grimes Is Dead.*" In: *Fillmore And Donelson Songs For The Campaign* (Songster), page 33. Published by Robert M. De Witt, Nos. 160 and 162 Nassau Street, New York, NY. November 4, 1856. [4¾" × 7⅛"]. Bl/bk litho of George Washington — "July 4, 1776," wreath, geometric design border. "This is the only authorized edition containing Duganne's Songs. Price 6 cts. each, $4 per 100. Discount to trade." Long quote from George Washington's "Farewell Address." 40pp. [M-101, 102]. [Crew/MF-10].

496.138 Presidential Cotillion. w.m. No composer or tune indicated. Published in the *New York Statesman*, September 24, 1824. [VBL, p. 226].

496.139 Remember The Day. w. No composer indicated. m. "Air — *Remember The Day When Erin's Proud Glory.*" In: *Tippecanoe Song-Book (A Collection Of Log Cabin And Patriotic Melodies)*, page 170. Published by Marshall, Williams & Butler, Philadelphia, PA. 1840. White on black litho of log cabin, plow, flags, eagle. 180pp. [M-024]. [Crew/WHH-61].

496.140 Republicans To The Rescue. w. Dr. Ethel Hurd. m. "Tune — *Battle Hymn Of The Republic.*" In: *Republican Campaign Songs*, page 19. Published by Republican State Committee Headquarters, Topeka, Kansas. 1920. [5⁷⁄₁₆" × 7³⁄₁₆"]. Be/bk photos of "Warren G. Harding" and "Calvin Coolidge" — "Our Country Needs Them." "Sing and Smile on to Victory." 24pp. [Crew/WGH-63].

496.141 Rouse, Ye Whigs, To Your Duty. w. No composer indicated. m. "Tune — *Thou Reign'st In This Bosom.*" "Written for the *Clay Melodist*. Dedicated to the Lowell Clay Clubs." In: *The National Clay Melodist (A Collection Of Popular And Patriotic Songs, Second Edition, Enlarged And Improved)*, page 79. Published by Benj. Adams, No. 54 Court Street, Boston, MA. 1844. [3" × 5¼"]. Inside title page: B/w litho of Henry Clay's home — "O'er Ashland's lawns the skies are bright, From West to East The radiance streams and glows, The land beneath its beams gay beats the heart with joy, Hurrah! Hurrah! Hip! Hurrah!" 108pp. [M-050?]. [Crew/HC-13].

496.142 The Rousing Song. w. John H. Warland. m. "Tune — *Draw The Sword, Scotland.*" "Written for the *Clay Melodist*. Dedicated to the Lowell Clay Clubs." In: *The National Clay Melodist (A Collection Of Popular And Patriotic Songs, Second Edition, Enlarged And Improved)*, page 13. Published by Benj. Adams, No. 54 Court Street, Boston, MA. 1844. [3" × 5¼"]. Inside title page: B/w litho of Henry Clay's home — "O'er Ashland's lawns the skies are bright, From West to East The radiance streams and glows, The land beneath its beams gay beats the heart with joy, Hurrah! Hurrah! Hip! Hurrah!" 108pp. [M-050?]. [Crew/HC-13].

496.143 The Rubber; Or Mat's Third And Last Game. w. No composer indicated. m. "Tune — *Miss Bailey.*" In: *The National Clay Minstrel (And True Whig's Pocket Companion For The Presidential Canvass Of 1844)*, page 46. Published by [V-1: George Hood, No. 15 North 6th Street, Philadelphia, PA] [V-2: James Fisher, No. 71 Court Street, Boston, MA]. 1843. [3¼" × 5⅛"]. Y/bk litho of raccoon — "That Coon" and flag — "Henry Clay," log cabin. "New and Improved Edition." 128pp. [Crew/HC-11].

496.144 The Senator (Quadrille). w. No composer indicated. m. No tune indicated. In: *The Ashland Quadrilles.* m. W.C. Peters. Published by Peters & Company, Cincinnati, OH. 1844. B/w litho of Henry Clay. Br/w geometric border. "Selected and Arranged for the Pianoforte and Respectfully dedicated to the Friends of the Hon. Henry Clay." "Peters & Company's Collection of Musical Publications for the Pianoforte, Guitar, &c., &c., Containing Songs, Duetts [sic], Rondos, Variations, Quadrilles, Marches, Waltzes, &c." 8pp. Page 2: Blank. Page 3: **The Mill**

Boy {496.144-1}. Page 4: ***The Farmer*** {496.144-2}. Page 5: ***The Senator*** {496.144-3}. Page 6: ***The Patriot*** {496.144-4}. Page 7: ***The Kentucky Gentleman*** {496.144-5}. Page 8: Catalog of music.

496.145 ***That Same Old Coon*** (A New Comic Whig Song). w. "The Milford Bard." m. "Tune—*Sittin On A Rail*." [7¾" × 13¼"]. B/w litho of a crow on its back and a raccoon speaking "Why Don't You Crow." "A New Comic Whig Song written for 1844 by the Milford Bard by Particular Desire." 2pp. Page 2: Blank. [Crew/HC-120].

496.146 ***Saint Louis Clay Club Song***. w. No composer indicated. m. "Tune—*Rosin The Beau*." "Respectfully dedicated to the Clay Club of St. Louis." In: *The National Clay Minstrel (And True Whig's Pocket Companion For The Presidential Canvass Of 1844)*, page 94. Published by [V-1: George Hood, No. 15 North 6th Street, Philadelphia, PA] [V-2: James Fisher, No. 71 Court Street, Boston, MA]. 1843. [3¼" × 5⅛"]. Y/bk litho of raccoon—"That Coon" and flag—"Henry Clay," log cabin. "New and Improved Edition." 128pp. [Crew/HC-11].

496.147 ***Salt River***. w. F.B. Graham, Esq. m. "Tune—*In Good Old Colony Times*." "Written for the Choir attached to the Philade. National Clay Club." B/w litho of man on horse with bugle. In: *The National Clay Minstrel*, page 17. Published by [V-1: George Hood, No. 15 North 6th Street, Philadelphia, PA] [V-2: James Fisher, No. 71 Court Street, Boston, MA]. 1843. [3" × 4½"]. Y/bk litho of raccoon sitting on fence, black border. 68pp. [Crew/HC-10].

496.148 ***The Same Old Coon***. w. Rev. W. Brownlow. m. No tune indicated. B/w litho of a raccoon standing over a dead crow saying—"Why don't you crow?" In: *The National Clay Melodist (A Collection Of Popular And Patriotic Songs, Second Edition, Enlarged And Improved)*, page 64. Published by Benj. Adams, No. 54 Court Street, Boston, MA. 1844. [3" × 5¼"]. Inside title page: B/w litho of Henry Clay's home—"O'er Ashland's lawns the skies are bright, From West to East The radiance streams and glows, The land beneath its beams gay beats the heart with joy, Hurrah! Hurrah! Hip! Hurrah!" 108pp. [M-050?]. [Crew/HC-13].

496.149 ***The Same Old Tune***. w. No composer indicated. "Tune—*'Vive La Companie*." In: *The National Clay Melodist (A Collection Of Popular And Patriotic Songs, Second Edition, Enlarged And Improved)*, page 87. Published by Benj. Adams, No. 54 Court Street, Boston, MA. 1844. [3" × 5¼"]. Inside title page: B/w litho of Henry Clay's home—"O'er Ashland's lawns the skies are bright, From West to East The radiance streams and glows, The land beneath its beams gay beats the heart with joy, Hurrah! Hurrah! Hip! Hurrah!" 108pp. [M-050?]. [Crew/HC-13].

496.150 ***A Settin' In The Chair***. w. No composer indicated. m. "Tune—*Sittin' On A Rail*." In: *The National Clay Minstrel (And True Whig's Pocket Companion For The Presidential Canvass Of 1844)*, page 92. Published by [V-1: George Hood, No. 15 North 6th Street, Philadelphia, PA] [V-2: James Fisher, No. 71 Court Street, Boston, MA]. 1843. [3¼" × 5⅛"]. Y/bk litho of raccoon—"That Coon" and flag—"Henry Clay," log cabin. "New and Improved Edition." 128pp. [Crew/HC-11].

496.151 ***The Ship Columbia***. w. F.B. Graham. m. "Air—*Hail To The Chief*." In: *The National Clay Minstrel*, page 58. "Written for the National Clay Minstrel." B/w litho of a man on a flagpole, flag inscribed "Henry Clay." Published by [V-1: George Hood, No. 15 North 6th Street, Philadelphia, PA] [V-2: James Fisher, No. 71 Court Street, Boston, MA]. 1843. [3" × 4½"]. Y/bk litho of raccoon sitting on fence, black border. 68pp. Crew/HC-10].

496.152 *[Should True Born Patriots Be Forgot]* (Song 2). w. W.A. Philomath. m. "Tune—*Auld Lang Syne*." In: *Original Clay Songs: Humorous And Sentimental, Designed To Inculcate Just Political Sentiments, To Suit The Present Political Crisis, And To Advocate The Claims Of Henry Clay To The Highest Honors His Country Can Bestow*, page 5. w. W.A. Philomath, Union Co., Ind. Published by Philomath, Cincinnati, OH. 1842. [4¼" × 6"]. Be/bk litho of an eagle, U.S. Flag. "The eagle soars above the throng; And listen's [sic] to fair Freedom's song, Hails the merry roundelay, Claps his glad wings and hails the day." 20pp. Page 20: Be/bk litho of four men—"Tyler Expounding the Constitution! The effect of 'treading in the footsteps.'" [M-057]. [CrewHC-104].

496.153 ***A Sittin' On A Tree***. w. Rev. W. Brownlow. m. "Tune—*Sittin' On A Rail*." In: *The National Clay Minstrel (And True Whig's Pocket Companion For The Presidential Canvass Of 1844)*, page 43. Published by [V-1: George Hood, No. 15 North 6th Street, Philadelphia, PA] [V-2: James Fisher, No. 71 Court Street, Boston, MA]. 1843. [3¼" × 5⅛"]. Y/bk litho of raccoon—"That Coon" and flag—"Henry Clay," log cabin. "New and Improved Edition." 128pp. [Crew/HC-11].

496.154 ***The Siege Of Fort Meigs***. w. No composer indicated. m. "The music adapted from the popular air, *Oh 'Twas My Delight Of A Shiny Night, In The Season Of The Year*." In: *Songs For The People (Or Tippecanoe Melodies)* [Songster], page 55. "Dedicated to the Democratic Whig Young Men of the City and County of New York." Published for the Authors by James P. Giffing, No. 56 Gold Street, New York, NY. 1840. [3¾" × 6"]. Litho of William Henry Harrison, log cabin, flag. "Original and Selected." 76pp. [M-019]. [Crew/WHH-63].

496.155 ***A Song For Cass And Butler***. w. No composer indicated. m. No tune indicated. Published in the *Daily Union*, October 18, 1848. [VBL, p. 323].

496.156 ***Song For The Young Men's Convention*** (To Meet At Baltimore In May Next). w. No composer indicated. m. "Tune—*Pibroch Of Donnel Dhu*." In: *The National Clay Melodist (A Collection Of Popular And Patriotic Songs, Second Edition, Enlarged And Improved)*, page 83. Published by Benj. Adams, No. 54 Court Street, Boston, MA. 1844. [3" × 5¼"]. Inside title page: B/w litho of Henry Clay's home—"O'er Ashland's lawns the skies are bright, From West to East The radiance streams and glows, The land beneath its beams gay beats the heart with joy, Hurrah! Hurrah! Hip! Hurrah!" 108pp. [M-050?]. [Crew/HC-13].

496.157 ***Song Of The Campaign***. w. No composer indicated. m. "Tune—*Uncle Ned*." In: *The Republican Campaign Songster No. #1*, page 19. Published by American Publishing House, No. 60 West Fourth Street, Cincinnati, OH. [1860]. [3¾" × 5¾"]. B/w litho of Abraham Lincoln. 48pp. [?]. [M-113]. [Crew/AL-298].

496.158 Song Of The Pauper. w. No composer indicated. m. "Tune — *Up Salt River.*" "As sung by the late P.M.G." In: *Songs For The People (Or Tippecanoe Melodies)* [Songster], page 46. "Dedicated to the Democratic Whig Young Men of the City and County of New York." Published for the Authors by James P. Giffing, No. 56 Gold Street, New York, NY. 1840. [3¾" × 6"]. Litho of William Henry Harrison, log cabin, flag. "Original and Selected." 76pp. [M-019]. [Crew/WHH-63].

496.159 Song Of The Whig. w. No composer indicated. m. "Tune — *Remember The Day When Erin's Proud Glory.*" In: *Log Cabin Song Book (A Collection Of Popular And Patriotic Songs)*, page 16. Published at *The Log Cabin* office, No. 30 Ann-Street, New York, NY. 1840. [4⅞" × 7"]. [V-1: Br/bk] [V-2: Y/bk] litho of log cabin, cider barrel, farmer with plow, flag — "Harrison and Tyler," geometric design border. "The Freeman's glittering Sword be Blest, For ever blest the Freeman's Lyre" Page 3: B/w litho of "Major-General William Henry Harrison, of Ohio," facsimile signature. 74pp. [M-020]. [Crew/WHH-56].

496.160 Song Of The Young Whigs. w. No composer indicated. m. "Air — *What Fairy-Like Music.*" In: *The National Clay Minstrel*, page 60. Published by [V-1: George Hood, No. 15 North 6th Street, Philadelphia, PA] [V-2: James Fisher, No. 71 Court Street, Boston, MA]. 1843. [3" × 4½"]. Y/bk litho of raccoon sitting on fence, black border. 68pp. [Crew/HC-10].

496.161 Splittin Ob De Rail. w.m. No composer or tune indicated. In: *The Republican Campaign Songster No. #1*, page 20. Published by American Publishing House, No. 60 West Fourth Street, Cincinnati, OH. [1860]. [3¾" × 5¾"]. B/w litho of Abraham Lincoln. 48pp. [?]. [M-113]. [Crew/AL-298].

496.162 The Star Of Ashland. w.m. No composer or tune indicated. In: *The National Clay Minstrel (And True Whig's Pocket Companion For The Presidential Canvass Of 1844)*, page 74. Published by [V-1: George Hood, No. 15 North 6th Street, Philadelphia, PA] [V-2: James Fisher, No. 71 Court Street, Boston, MA]. 1843. [3¼" × 5⅛"]. Y/bk litho of raccoon — "That Coon" and flag — "Henry Clay," log cabin. "New and Improved Edition." 128pp. [Crew/HC-11].

496.163 The Star Of The West. w. No composer indicated. m. "Tune — *Meeting Of The Waters.*" In: *The National Clay Melodist (A Collection Of Popular And Patriotic Songs, Second Edition, Enlarged And Improved)*, page 43. Published by Benj. Adams, No. 54 Court Street, Boston, MA. 1844. [3" × 5¼"]. Inside title page: B/w litho of Henry Clay's home — "O'er Ashland's lawns the skies are bright, From West to East The radiance streams and glows, The land beneath its beams gay beats the heart with joy, Hurrah! Hurrah! Hip! Hurrah!" 108pp. [M-050?]. [Crew/HC-13].

496.164 The Tars Will Man Their Gallant Ship. w. No composer indicated. m. "Tune — *Washing Day.*" "Written for the *National Clay Minstrel.*" In: *The National Clay Minstrel (And True Whig's Pocket Companion For The Presidential Canvass Of 1844)*, page 99. Published by [V-1: George Hood, No. 15 North 6th Street, Philadelphia, PA] [V-2: James Fisher, No. 71 Court Street, Boston, MA]. 1843. [3¼" × 5⅛"]. Y/bk litho of raccoon — "That Coon" and flag — "Henry Clay," log cabin. "New and Improved Edition." 128pp [Crew/HC-11].

496.165 That Brave Old Coon. w. No composer indicated. m. "Tune — *The American Star.*" B/w litho of John Tyler sitting in the presidential chair while a raccoon gnaws at the chair's leg." In: *The National Clay Melodist (A Collection Of Popular And Patriotic Songs, Second Edition, Enlarged And Improved)*, page 71. Published by Benj. Adams, No. 54 Court Street, Boston, MA. 1844. [3" × 5¼"]. Inside title page: B/w litho of Henry Clay's home — "O'er Ashland's lawns the skies are bright, From West to East The radiance streams and glows, The land beneath its beams gay beats the heart with joy, Hurrah! Hurrah! Hip! Hurrah!" 108pp. [M-050?]. [Crew/HC-13].

496.166 That Same Old 'Koon. w. No composer indicated. m. "Tune — *Woodland Mary.*" B/w litho of a raccoon." In: *The National Clay Minstrel (And True Whig's Pocket Companion For The Presidential Canvass Of 1844)*, page 56. Published by [V-1: George Hood, No. 15 North 6th Street, Philadelphia, PA] [V-2: James Fisher, No. 71 Court Street, Boston, MA]. 1843. [3¼" × 5⅛"]. Y/bk litho of raccoon — "That Coon" and flag — "Henry Clay," log cabin. "New and Improved Edition." 128pp. [Crew/HC-11].

496.167 Then He'll Blow, Blow, Blow. w. No composer indicated. m. "Air—*Then He'd Row, Row, Row.*" In: *The Red Book, Containing Portraits And Biographies Of Some Persons More Or Less Prominent Public Life Written Entirely Without Respect To The Libel Laws, In A Studious Effort To Conceal Everything But The Truth; Some Songs Built Upon The Same Principle, And Other Important (?) Material Entirely Unfit To Print*, page 26. Published by Legislative Correspondents' Association of the State of New York, Albany, NY. 1913. [5" × 7¼"]. R/w/bk hardback book with drawing of State House, seal of New York, geometric designs. 90pp.

496.168 [There's A Winding Trail Through Our History]. w. Mrs. W.W. Remington. m. "To the tune of *The Barefoot Trail.*" In: *Patriotic Songs*, page 5. Published by The Republican Woman's Club of Minneapolis, Minneapolis, MN. 1920. [3$\frac{11}{16}$" × 6"]. Bl/bl drawing of elephant. "Republican Campaign 1920." 8pp. Page 2: "Republican Standard Bearers For President — Warren G. Harding of Ohio, For Vice-President Calvin Coolidge of Massachusetts." "America First." [Crew/WGH-47].

496.169 Tippecanoe's Rasin'. w. No composer indicated. m. "Tune — *The Good Old Times Of Adam And Eve.*" In: *Tippecanoe Song-Book (A Collection Of Log Cabin And Patriotic Melodies)*, page 77. Published by Marshall, Williams & Butler, Philadelphia, PA. 1840. White on black litho of log cabin, plow, flags, eagle. 180pp. [M-024]. [Crew/WHH-61].

496.170 To Abe Lincoln. w.m. No composer or tune indicated. In: *The Republican Campaign Songster No. #1*, page 10. Published by American Publishing House, No. 60 West Fourth Street, Cincinnati, OH. [1860]. [3¾" × 5¾"]. B/w litho of Abraham Lincoln. 48pp. [?]. [M-113]. [Crew/AL-298].

496.171 True Harry Of Kentucky, Oh. w. No composer indicated. m. "Air—*Green Grow The Rushes Oh.*" In: *The National Clay Minstrel (And True Whig's Pocket Companion For The Presidential Canvass Of 1844)*, page 28. Published by [V-1: George Hood, No. 15 North 6th Street, Philadelphia, PA] [V-2: James Fisher, No. 71 Court Street, Boston, MA]. 1843. [3¼" × 5⅛"]. Y/bk litho of raccoon—"That Coon" and flag—"Henry Clay," log cabin. "New and Improved Edition." 128pp. [Crew/HC-11].

496.172 Uncle Sam's Talk To His Man, John. w. John H. Warland, Esq., "late editor of the Claremont, N.H. *Eagle*." m. "Air—*Malbrook* or *L,A,W, Law.*" "Sung at a Whig Dinner at the Maverick House, Boston, on the glorious Fourth." In: *The National Clay Minstrel (And True Whig's Pocket Companion For The Presidential Canvass Of 1844)*, page 32. Published by [V-1: George Hood, No. 15 North 6th Street, Philadelphia, PA] [V-2: James Fisher, No. 71 Court Street, Boston, MA]. 1843. [3¼" × 5⅛"]. Y/bk litho of raccoon—"That Coon" and flag—"Henry Clay," log cabin. "New and Improved Edition." 128pp [Crew/HC-11].

496.173 The Union Course. w. No composer indicated. m. "Air—*Jordan Is A Hard Road To Travel.*" In: *Fillmore And Donelson Songs For The Campaign*, page 26. Published by Robert M. De Witt, Nos. 160 and 162 Nassau Street, New York, NY. November 4, 1856. [4¾" × 7⅛"]. Bl/bk litho of George Washington—"July 4, 1776," wreath, geometric design border. "This is the only authorized edition containing Duganne's Songs. Price 6 cts. each, $4 per 100. Discount to trade." Long quote from George Washington's "Farewell Address." 40pp. [M-101, 102]. [Crew/MF-10].

496.174 The Union For Ever For Me. w.m. No composer or tune indicated. Published by H. De Marsan, 54 Chatham Street, New York, NY. B/w litho border of military and naval war scenes. H. De Marsan, Publisher, Songs, Ballads, Toy Books, paper dolls, small playing cards, motto verses, &c." 2pp. Page 2: Blank. [AMC].

496.175 The Union Wagon. w. No composer indicated. m. "Air—*Wait For The Wagon.*" In: *Fillmore And Donelson Songs For The Campaign*, page 12. Published by Robert M. De Witt, Nos. 160 and 162 Nassau Street, New York, NY. November 4, 1856. [4¾" × 7⅛"]. Bl/bk litho of George Washington—"July 4, 1776," wreath, geometric design border. "This is the only authorized edition containing Duganne's Songs. Price 6 cts. each, $4 per 100. Discount to trade." Long quote from George Washington's "Farewell Address." 40pp. [M-101, 102]. [Crew/MF-10].

496.176 Van's Mews, Or Uncle Sam's Talk To His Brindled Cat. w. John H. Warland. m. No tune indicated. "Thrice the brindled cat hath mewed—Macbeth." "Written for the *Clay Melodist.*" In: *The National Clay Melodist (A Collection Of Popular And Patriotic Songs, Second Edition, Enlarged And Improved)*, page 56. Published by Benj. Adams, No. 54 Court Street, Boston, MA. 1844. [3" × 5¼"]. Inside title page: B/w litho of Henry Clay's home—"O'er Ashland's lawns the skies are bright, From West to East The radiance streams and glows, The land beneath its beams gay beats the heart with joy, Hurrah! Hurrah! Hip! Hurrah!" 108pp. [M-050?]. [Crew/HC-13].

496.177 Vermont Whig Song. w. "That Same Old Whig." m. No tune indicated. No publisher indicated. [1844]. B/w litho of a raccoon, geometric design border. 2pp. Page 2: Blank. [Crew/HC-128]. [AMC].

496.178 The Vermonter's Song At Baltimore. w. No composer indicated. m. "Tune—*Old Dan Tucker.*" In: *The National Clay Minstrel*, page 6. Published by [V-1: George Hood, No. 15 North 6th Street, Philadelphia, PA] [V-2: James Fisher, No. 71 Court Street, Boston, MA]. 1843. [3" × 4½"]. Y/bk litho of raccoon sitting on fence, black border. 68pp. [Crew/HC-10].

496.179 Voice Of The People. w. No composer indicated. m. "Tune—*A Life On The Ocean Wave.*" In: *The National Clay Minstrel*, page 49. Published by [V-1: George Hood, No. 15 North 6th Street, Philadelphia, PA] [V-2: James Fisher, No. 71 Court Street, Boston, MA]. 1843. [3" × 4½"]. Y/bk litho of raccoon sitting on fence, black border. 68pp. [Crew/HC-10].

496.180 Wake Up Whigs, All Come Along For Harry Clay. w. No composer indicated. m. "Tune—*The Cravovienne.*" "Written for the *National Clay Minstrel.*" In: *The National Clay Minstrel (And True Whig's Pocket Companion For The Presidential Canvass Of 1844)*, page 96. Published by [V-1: George Hood, No. 15 North 6th Street, Philadelphia, PA] [V-2: James Fisher, No. 71 Court Street, Boston, MA]. 1843. [3¼" × 5⅛"]. Y/bk litho of raccoon—"That Coon" and flag—"Henry Clay," log cabin. "New and Improved Edition." 128pp. [Crew/HC-11].

496.181 We Are Met Again Like Jolly Boys. w. By a Downeaster." m. "Tune—*Ole Dan Tucker.*" In: *The National Clay Melodist (A Collection Of Popular And Patriotic Songs, Second Edition, Enlarged And Improved)*, page 95. Published by Benj. Adams, No. 54 Court Street, Boston, MA. 1844. [3" × 5¼"]. Inside title page: B/w litho of Henry Clay's home—"O'er Ashland's lawns the skies are bright, From West to East The radiance streams and glows, The land beneath its beams gay beats the heart with joy, Hurrah! Hurrah! Hip! Hurrah!" 108pp. [M-050?]. [Crew/HC-13].

496.182 We Ask Not Material Glory. w.m. No composer or tune indicated. In: *The Liberty Minstrel*, page 94. e. George W. Clark. Published by George W. Clark, New York, NY. 1844. [4⅝" × 6¾"]. Non-pictorial songbook with gold leaf title. "And Sold by Wm. Harned, 22 Spruce St., New York and Baltimore and Marsh, Boston, Mass." 230pp. [Crew/JBR-1].

496.183 Welcome The Strain. w. No composer indicated. m. "Tune—*Hail To The Chief.*" In: *The National Clay Melodist (A Collection Of Popular And Patriotic Songs, Second Edition, Enlarged And Improved)*, page 27. Published by Benj. Adams, No. 54 Court Street, Boston, MA. 1844. [3" × 5¼"]. Inside title page: B/w litho of Henry Clay's home—"O'er Ashland's lawns the skies are bright, From West to East The radiance streams and glows, The land beneath its beams gay beats the heart with joy, Hurrah! Hurrah! Hip! Hurrah!" 108pp. [M-050?]. [Crew/HC-13].

496.184 When This Old Hat Was New. w.m. No composer or tune indicated. In: *The Log Cabin & Hard Cider Melodies, A Collection Of Popular And Patriotic*

Songs, page 47. Published by Charles Adams, No. 23 Tremont Street, Boston, MA. 1840. [3¾" × 6"]. [V-1: Pk/bk] [V-2: Gn/bk] litho of William Henry Harrison. "The Freeman's glittering Sword be Blest, For ever blest the Freeman's Lyre." 78pp. [M-012]. [Crew/WHH-68].

496.185 When We Met In Convention. w. No composer indicated. m. "Air—*Tis My Delight Of A Shiny Night.*" In: *Fillmore And Donelson Songs For The Campaign* (Songster), page 21. Published by Robert M. De Witt, Nos. 160 and 162 Nassau Street, New York, NY. November 4, 1856. [4¾" × 7⅛"]. Bl/bk litho of George Washington—"July 4, 1776," wreath, geometric design border. "This is the only authorized edition containing Duganne's Songs. Price 6 cts. each, $4 per 100. Discount to trade." Long quote from George Washington's "Farewell Address." 40pp. [M-101, 102]. [Crew/MF-10].

496.186 Whig Battle Cry. w. No composer indicated. m. "Tune—*The Campbells Are Coming.*" "Written for the *National Clay Minstrel.*" B/w litho of a sailor on a mast with a flag that reads 'Henry Clay.'" In: *The National Clay Minstrel (And True Whig's Pocket Companion For The Presidential Canvass Of 1844)*, page 87. Published by [V-1: George Hood, No. 15 North 6th Street, Philadelphia, PA] [V-2: James Fisher, No. 71 Court Street, Boston, MA]. 1843. [3¼" × 5⅛"]. Y/bk litho of raccoon—"That Coon" and flag—"Henry Clay," log cabin. "New and Improved Edition." 128pp. [Crew/HC-11].

496.187 The Whig Chief. w. No composer indicated. m. "Tune—*Hail To The Chief.*" In: *The National Clay Minstrel (And True Whig's Pocket Companion For The Presidential Canvass Of 1844)*, page 72. Published by [V-1: George Hood, No. 15 North 6th Street, Philadelphia, PA] [V-2: James Fisher, No. 71 Court Street, Boston, MA]. 1843. [3¼" × 5⅛"]. Y/bk litho of raccoon—"That Coon" and flag—"Henry Clay," log cabin. "New and Improved Edition." 128pp. [Crew/HC-11].

496.188 Whig Girls Of 1840. w. No composer indicated. m. "Tune—*Dan Tucker.*" In: *The National Clay Minstrel*, page 44. Published by [V-1: George Hood, No. 15 North 6th Street, Philadelphia, PA] [V-2: James Fisher, No. 71 Court Street, Boston, MA]. 1843. [3" × 4½"]. Y/bk litho of raccoon sitting on fence, black border. 68pp. [Crew/HC-10].

496.189 Whig Glee. w.m. No composer or tune indicated. In: *The National Clay Minstrel*, page 52. Published by [V-1: George Hood, No. 15 North 6th Street, Philadelphia, PA] [V-2: James Fisher, No. 71 Court Street, Boston, MA]. 1843. [3" × 4½"]. Y/bk litho of raccoon sitting on fence, black border. 68pp. [Crew/HC-10].

496.190 Whig Quodlibet. w.m. No composer or tune indicated. B/w litho of two raccoons. In: *The National Clay Minstrel*, page 22. Published by [V-1: George Hood, No. 15 North 6th Street, Philadelphia, PA] [V-2: James Fisher, No. 71 Court Street, Boston, MA]. 1843. [3" × 4½"]. Y/bk litho of raccoon sitting on fence, black border. 68pp. [Crew/HC-10].

496.191 Whig Rally Song. w. F.B. Graham. m. "Air—*Scots Wha Ha'e Wallace Bled.*" "Written for the *National Clay Minstrel.*" In: *The National Clay Minstrel (And True Whig's Pocket Companion For The Presidential Canvass Of 1844)*, page 15. Published by [V-1: George Hood, No. 15 North 6th Street, Philadelphia, PA] [V-2: James Fisher, No. 71 Court Street, Boston, MA]. 1843. [3¼" × 5⅛"]. Y/bk litho of raccoon—"That Coon" and flag—"Henry Clay," log cabin. "New and Improved Edition." 128pp. [Crew/HC-11].

496.192 The Whig Rifle. w. No composer indicated. m. "Tune—*Old Rosin, The Beau.*" "Written for the *National Clay Minstrel.*" In: *The National Clay Minstrel (And True Whig's Pocket Companion For The Presidential Canvass Of 1844)*, page 79. Published by [V-1: George Hood, No. 15 North 6th Street, Philadelphia, PA] [V-2: James Fisher, No. 71 Court Street, Boston, MA]. 1843. [3¼" × 5⅛"]. Y/bk litho of raccoon—"That Coon" and flag—"Henry Clay," log cabin. "New and Improved Edition." 128pp. [Crew/HC-11].

496.193 Whig Song. w. No composer indicated. m. "Tune—*Willie Brew'd A Peck O' Maut.*" "Written for the Choir of the National Clay Club." In: *The National Clay Minstrel*, page30. Published by [V-1: George Hood, No. 15 North 6th Street, Philadelphia, PA] [V-2: James Fisher, No. 71 Court Street, Boston, MA]. 1843. [3" × 4½"]. Y/bk litho of raccoon sitting on fence, black border. 68pp. [Crew/HC-10].

496.194 Whig Song. w. No composer indicated. m. "Tune—*Roy's Wife Of Aldivalloch.*" In: *The National Clay Minstrel (And True Whig's Pocket Companion For The Presidential Canvass Of 1844)*, page 36. Published by [V-1: George Hood, No. 15 North 6th Street, Philadelphia, PA] [V-2: James Fisher, No. 71 Court Street, Boston, MA]. 1843. [3¼" × 5⅛"]. Y/bk litho of raccoon—"That Coon" and flag—"Henry Clay," log cabin. "New and Improved Edition." 128pp. [Crew/HC-11].

496.195 Whigs, Who Ne'er From Contest Fled. w. No composer indicated. m. "Tune—*Bruce's Address.*" In: *The National Clay Melodist (A Collection Of Popular And Patriotic Songs, Second Edition, Enlarged And Improved)*, page 73. Published by Benj. Adams, No. 54 Court Street, Boston, MA. 1844. [3" × 5¼"]. Inside title page: B/w litho of Henry Clay's home—"O'er Ashland's lawns the skies are bright, From West to East The radiance streams and glows, The land beneath its beams gay beats the heart with joy, Hurrah! Hurrah! Hip! Hurrah!" 108pp. [M-050?]. [Crew/HC-13].

496.196 The White House. w. G.R. Edeson. m. "Air—*Root, Hog, Or Die!*" Published by H. De Marsan, 54 Chatham Street, New York, NY. [1861–1862]. B/w litho border of minstrels, geometric designs. 2pp. Page 2: Blank. [AMC].

496.197 The White-Plumed Knight. w. Mrs. M. Jennie Porter. m. "Air—*Bonnie Blue Flag.*" In: *Blaine And Logan Campaign Song-Book*, page 35. e. Prof. F. Widdows. Published by The Republican National Committee, New York, NY. 1884. [4⅜" × 5¹¹⁄₁₆"]. [V-1: Bk/y] [V-2: Pk/bk] litho of James G. Blaine and John A. Logan. "From the School—House to the Cabinet, From the Cabin to the Senate." 52pp. [M-251]. [Crew/JGB-32].

496.198 Wide-Awake Club Song. w. No composer indicated. m. "Air—*A Wet Sheet And A Flowing Sea.*" In: *Connecticut Wide-Awake Songster*, page 70. e. John

W. Hutchinson "(of Hutchinson Family Singers)" and Benjamin Jepson. Published by O. Hutchinson, Publisher, No. 272 Greenwich Street, New York, NY. 1860. [4" × 6"]. Bl/bk non-pictorial line border. "Lincoln and liberty." 76pp. [M-109]. [Crew/AL-175].

496.199 *The Workingman's Song.* w. No composer indicated. m. "Tune—*There's Nae Luck About The House;* or *The Washing Day.*" In: *The National Clay Minstrel*, page 46. Published by [V-1: George Hood, No. 15 North 6th Street, Philadelphia, PA] [V-2: James Fisher, No. 71 Court Street, Boston, MA]. 1843. [3" × 4½"]. Y/bk litho of raccoon sitting on fence, black border. 68pp. [Crew/HC-10].

- **AmPM-497 CRITTENDEN**, John Jordan (Attorney General, Illinois Territory, 1809–1810; State House, 1811–1817, 1825 & 1829–1832; U.S. Senate, 1817–1819, 1842–1848 & 1855–1861; U.S. District Attorney, 1827–1829; U.S. Attorney General, 1841 & 1850–1853; Governor, 1848–1850; U.S. House, 1861–1863)

497.1 *Liberty's Revillé.* w. W.S. Hurlocke, M.D. m. Jas. W. Porter. Published by I.D. Wright, Washington, DC. 1861. Non-pictorial geometric designs. "Respectfully Inscribed to Hon. J.J. Crittenden of Kentucky." 6pp. Pages 2 and 6: Blank. [LL/JH].

497.2 *The Union Wagon.* w. No composer indicated. m. "Air—*Wait For The Wagon.*" In: *Fillmore And Donelson Songs For The Campaign* (Songster), page 12. Published by Robert M. De Witt, Nos. 160 and 162 Nassau Street, New York, NY. November 4, 1856. [4¾" × 7⅛"]. Bl/bk litho of George Washington—"July 4, 1776," wreath, geometric design border. "This is the only authorized edition containing Duganne's Songs. Price 6 cts. each, $4 per 100. Discount to trade." Long quote from George Washington's "Farewell Address." 40pp. [M-101, 102]. [Crew/MF-10].

EDWARDS, Ninian (State House, Kentucky, 1796–1797; Judge of the General Court, Kentucky, 1803; Judge, Circuit Court, Kentucky, 1804; Judge, Court of Appeals, Kentucky, 1806; State Supreme Court, Kentucky, 1808) [See: Illinois]

- **AmPM-498 GRAINGER**, Charles F. (Mayor, Louisville, 1901–1905)

498.1 *Jockey Club March* (Or Two Step). m. A. Liberati. a. August Damm. Published by Sig. A. Liberati, 148 East 86th Street, New York City, NY. 1903. B/w photo of A. Liberati. Gn/w litho of horses, floral and geometric designs. 6pp. Pages 2 and 6: Blank. Page 3: At top of music—"Dedicated to Mayor Chas. F. Granger."

- **AmPM-499 GRAVES**, William Jordan (State House, 1834 & 1843; U.S. House, 1835–1841)

499.1 *Murder Of Cilley.* w.m. No composer or tune indicated. No publisher indicated. [ca. 1838]. [Approx. 5½" × 9"]. Non-pictorial geometric designs. Followed on page 1 by "Gossip Chat," a paragraph of nonsense comic narrative. 2pp. Page 2: Blank. [AMC].

GRUNDY, Felix (State House, Kentucky, 1800–1805; State Supreme Court, Kentucky, 1806–1807) [See: Tennessee]

- **AmPM-500 HARDIN**, John J. (Prosecuting Attorney, Morgan County, 1832; State House, 1836–1842; U.S. House, 1843–1845)

500.1 *Buena Vista.* w.m. No composer or tune indicated. In: *The Patriot's Songster*, page 13. Published by Mumford & Company, Cincinnati, OH. 1862. [3½" × 6"]. Non-pictorial. 48pp.

- **AmPM-501 HELM**, John Larue (State House, 1826; State Senate, 1844; Lt. Governor, 1848–1850; Governor, 1850–1851 & 1867)

501.1 *Louisville Grand March.* m. John A. Metcalfe. Published by F.W. Ratcliffe, Louisville, KY. 1851. B/w non-pictorial geometric designs. "Composed & arranged for the Ladies Musical Library and dedicated to Governor Helm of Ky." 4pp. Pages 1 and 4: Blank.

- **AmPM-502 HOLT**, Joseph (U.S. Postmaster General, 1859–1860; U.S. Secretary of War, 1861)

502.1 *The Land Of Washington* (Quartette & Chorus). w.m. J.H. McNaughton. Published by Oliver Ditson & Co., No. 277 Washington Street, Boston, MA. B/w non-pictorial geometric designs. "To Hon. Joseph Holt, Kentucky." 6pp. Pages 2 and 6: Blank.

- **AmPM-503 KENDALL**, Amos (U.S. Postmaster General, 1835–1840)

503.1 *All Round My 'At I Vers A Veeping Villow.* w.m. No composer or tune indicated. "A Song to be Sung at Van Buren's Indignation meetings." In: *Songs For The People (Or Tippecanoe Melodies)* [Songster], page 27. "Dedicated to the Democratic Whig Young Men of the City and County of New York." Published for the Authors by James P. Giffing, No. 56 Gold Street, New York, NY. 1840. [3¾" × 6"]. Litho of William Henry Harrison, log cabin, flag. "Original and Selected." 76pp. [M-019]. [Crew/WHH-63].

503.2 *Amos Kendall's Lament* (A Comic Whig Song). w. G.A. Harington and B.F. Copeland, Esq. m. Geo. O. Farmer. Published by Geo. P. Reed's, No. 17 Tremont Row, Boston, MA. 1840. B/w Thayer litho of "Amos Kendall" at his desk. "Sung with great applause at the Whig Conventions at Roxbury, Randolph, Quincy & other places." [Crew/WHH-137].

503.3 *The Baby Walker.* w.m. No composer indicated. m. "Tune—*Lullaby.*" In: *A Miniature Of Martin Van Buren (With A Selection Of The Best And Most Popular Tippecanoe Songs)*, page 30. 1840. [3½" × 6½"]. [V-1: Br/bk] [V-2: Gn/bk] [V-3: Y/bk] litho of man, chain around neck. Van Buren quote. "Amos Kendall's Veracity—Tom Benton's Honesty—Francis Blair's Beauty." "What is wanting cant be numbered [sic]." 58pp. [M-016]. [Crew/WHH-88].

503.4 *The Banner Of Tippecanoe.* w. No composer indicated. m. "Air—*American Star.*" In: *Tippecanoe Song-Book (A Collection Of Log Cabin And Patriotic Melodies)*, page 174. Published by Marshall, Williams & Butler, Philadelphia, PA. 1840. White on black litho of log cabin, plow, flags, eagle. 180pp. [M-024]. [Crew/WHH-61].

503.5 *The Beggar's Petition.* w. No composer indicated. m. "Tune—*All On Hobbies.*" "A Very Pathetic and musical appeal to the Dear People, by an Ex-Post Master General." In: *Tippecanoe Song-Book (A Collection Of Log Cabin And Patriotic Melodies)*, page 14. Published by Marshall, Williams & Butler, Philadelphia, PA. 1840. White on black litho of log cabin, plow, flags, eagle. 180pp. [M-024]. [Crew/WHH-61].

503.6 *Clay And Frelinghuysen.* w. J. Greiner. m. "Air—*Old Dan Tucker.*" In: *Incidents In The Campaign Of 1844*, page 13. c. James T. Hathaway. Published by

J.T. Hathaway, No. 287 Crown Street, New Haven, CT. 1905. [5" × 7"]. Bl/gy non-pictorial geometric design border. "Printed for private distribution among old friends." "Here's to you, Harry Clay—Old Song." 68pp. [Crew/ HC-119]. & [Crew/HC-10, p. 1]

503.7 Clearing The Kitchen And White House (A Song For The Fourth of March, 1841). w. No composer indicated. m. "Tune—*Young Lochinvar.*" In: *The Tippecanoe Campaign Of 1840*, page 61. Published by A.B. Norton, Mount Vernon, OH. 1888. [5½" × 7½"]. Bl/gd book. 496pp. Pages 1–382: Text. Pages 383–485: "Tippecanoe Songs of the Log Cabin Boys and Girls of 1840." [M-276]. [Crew/WHH-96].

503.8 The Defaulter's Farewell. w. No composer indicated. m. "Tune—*The Bride's Farewell.*" In: *Songs For The People (Or Tippecanoe Melodies)* [Songster], page 66. Published for the Authors by James P. Giffing, No. 56 Gold Street, New York, NY. 1840. [3¾" × 6"]. Litho of William Henry Harrison, log cabin, flag. "Original and Selected." 76pp. [M-019]. [Crew/WHH-63].

503.9 A Democratic Harrison Song. w. No composer indicated. m. "Tune—*Landlady Of France.*" In: *Tippecanoe Club Songster*, page 54. Published by [V-1: Turner & Fisher, No. 15 North Sixth Street, Philadelphia, PA] [V-2: H.A. Turner, Baltimore, MD]. 1841. [3" × 4⁷⁄₁₆"]. Hand Colored engraving of William Henry Harrison, log cabin. 68pp. [M-021, 022]. [Crew/WHH-18].

503.10 The Dutchman. w. No composer indicated. m. "Tune—*The Poachers.*" In: *A Miniature Of Martin Van Buren (With A Selection Of The Best And Most Popular Tippecanoe Songs)*, page 49. 1840. [3½" × 6½"]. [V-1: Br/bk] [V-2: Gn/bk] [V-3: Y/bk] litho of man, chain around neck. Van Buren quote. "Amos Kendal's Veracity—Tom Benton's Honesty—Francis Blair's Beauty." "What is wanting cant be numbered [sic]." 58pp. [M-016]. [Crew/WHH-88].

503.11 The Farmer Of North Bend. Published by Charles T. Geslain, No. 357 Broadway, New York, NY. 1840. B/w litho of a log cabin, horse and buggy, steamboat. "The Patriot's Home." "A Very Popular Whig Song Respectfully Dedicated to the Log Cabin Association the United States by the Publisher." "Pr. 50 cts." 6pp. Pages 2 and 6: Blank. [Crew/WHH-9].

503.12 Harrison Song. w. No composer indicated. m. "Tune—*Hunters Of Kentucky.*" "Prepared and sung at the raising of the Log Cabin at Wareham, by John Maxim, a Laboring man, in Carver." In: *Log Cabin Minstrel (Or Tippecanoe Songster)*, page 41. c. "A Member of the Roxbury Whig Association." Published at the *Patriot And Democrat* Office, Roxbury, [MA]. 1840. [4½" × 6¾"]. [V-1:Y/bk] [V-2: Bl/bk] litho of William Henry Harrison, geometric design border. "Old Tip's the boy to swing the flail. Hurrah! Hurrah! Hurrah!" 64pp. Page 3: Title page—"Containing a Selection of Songs Original and Selected Many of them Written Expressly for this Work, Compiled, Published and Arranged by a member of the Roxbury Democratic Whig Association and Respectfully Dedicated to the Log Cabin Boys of the U.S." [M-013]. [Crew/WHH-71].

503.13 Here's To Van Buren, The Chief Of Our Land. w. No composer indicated. m. "Tune—*Here's To The Maiden Of Blushing Fifteen.*" In: *Songs For The People (Or Tippecanoe Melodies)* [Songster], page 24. "Dedicated to the Democratic Whig Young Men of the City and County of New York." Published for the Authors by James P. Giffing, No. 56 Gold Street, New York, NY. 1840. [3¾" × 6"]. Litho of William Henry Harrison, log cabin, flag. "Original and Selected." 76pp. [M-019]. [Crew/WHH-63].

503.14 The Hero Of Fort Meigs. w. J.H. Watts, Esq. m. "Tune—*Auld Lang Syne.*" In: *Tippecanoe Song-Book (A Collection Of Log Cabin And Patriotic Melodies)*, page 62. Published by Marshall, Williams & Butler, Philadelphia, PA. 1840. White on black litho of log cabin, plow, flags, eagle. 180pp. [M-024]. [Crew/WHH-61].

503.15 The Hero Of Tippecanoe. w. No composer indicated. m. "Tune—*When The Banner Of Freedom.*" In: *Tippecanoe Song-Book (A Collection Of Log Cabin And Patriotic Melodies)*, page 68. Published by Marshall, Williams & Butler, Philadelphia, PA. 1840. White on black litho of log cabin, plow, flags, eagle. 180pp. [M-024]. [Crew/WHH-61].

503.16 Hurrah For The Man We Love. w. No composer indicated. m. "Air—*Vive L'Amor.*" [1864]. [7⅜" × 14¼"]. Non-pictorial. "A McClellan and Union Mass Meeting will be held at Cooper Institute on the beginning of the 17th inst. at which Hon. Amos Kendall, General Jackson's Postmaster General, and President of the 'Conservative Union National Committee' will preside and a large number of our most prominent citizens and military gentlemen have accepted invitations to act as vice-presidents. The exercises will consist of Addresses by eminent speakers interspersed with Patriotic and McClellan songs, by a Glee Club and the whole audience... Old men are especially invited to attend and welcome the venerable Mr. Kendall, and all such will be furnished with tickets admitting them to talk before seven o'clock by sending their names to R.F. Stevens, 105 East 49th Street, by mail or otherwise. The following letter from the Hon. Amos Kendall speaks for itself—Washington, March 24, 1864; Dr. R.F. Stevens, 105 East 49th Street, My Dear Sir: Your letter, informing me that the 17th inst. had been fixed upon for the McClellan Demonstration, came to hand this morning. If the friends of McClellan and the Country, in New York, think it would further the cause for me to preside, you are at liberty to make the announcement. I am losing my patience reading Gen. McClellan's report. The injustice to him, and the atrocious wrong to his noble army and the country, are enough to make the blood of honest and patriotic men boil within them—Yours truly, Amos Kendall." "At the close of this song, a McClellan and Union Flag Raising will take place, with the air *Star Spangled Banner.*" [Crew/GBM-62].

503.17 Hurrah For The Man We Love. w. No composer indicated. m. "Air—*Vive L'Amour.*" In: *McClellan And Liberty* [Song Sheet]. Published by Frank McElroy, No. 113 Nassau Street, New York, NY. 1864. [7" × 17"]. Non-pictorial. "Stand by the Union and I'll Stand by you." "The Work before us; To suppress the Rebellion, To preserve the Union, To maintain the sovereignty of the People!" "Let us apply ourselves to the duty of uniting all the conservative elements of the country, in the effort to place in the Presidential Chair a man who will revere the Constitution as his highest political authority — Such a man is George B. McClellan." "The following is from a recent letter of the Hon. Amos Kendall: I am losing my patience in reading Gen. McClellan's report. The injustice to him, and the atrocious wrong to his noble army and the country, are enough to make the blood of honest and patriotic men boil within them." 2pp. [Crew/GBM-61].

503.18 Jackson's Lament. w. No composer indicated. m. No tune indicated. In: *A Miniature Of Martin Van Buren (With A Selection Of The Best And Most Popular Tippecanoe Songs)*, page 51. 1840. [3½" × 6½"]. [V-1: Br/bk] [V-2: Gn/bk] [V-3: Y/bk] litho of man, chain around neck. Van Buren quote. "Amos Kendall's Veracity — Tom Benton's Honesty — Francis Blair's Beauty." "What is wanting cant be numbered [sic]." 58pp. [M-016]. [Crew/WHH-88].

503.19 John C. Calhoun My Jo. w. No composer indicated. m. "Tune — *John Anderson My Jo*." In: *Log Cabin Song Book (A Collection Of Popular And Patriotic Songs)*, page 40. Published at *The Log Cabin* office, No. 30 Ann-Street, New York, NY. 1840. [4⅞" × 7"]. [V-1: Br/bk] [V-2: Y/bk] litho of log cabin, cider barrel, farmer with plow, flag — "Harrison and Tyler," geometric design border. "The Freeman's glittering Sword be Blest, For ever blest the Freeman's Lyre" Page 3: B/w litho of "Major-General William Henry Harrison, of Ohio," facsimile signature. 74pp. [M-020]. [Crew/WHH-56].

503.20 Keep The Ball Rolling. w. No composer indicated. m. No tune indicated. In: *The Log Cabin*, page 4, Vol. 1, No. 26, Oct. 24, 1840. Published by Horace Greeley & Company, New York, NY. 1840. Non-pictorial. [Crew/WHH-91].

503.21 Kendall's Petition. w. No composer indicated. m. "A Parody on *Pity The Sorrows Of A Poor Old Man*." In: *Songs For The People (Or Tippecanoe Melodies)* [Songster], page 63. Published for the Authors by James P. Giffing, No. 56 Gold Street, New York, NY. 1840. [3¾" × 6"]. Litho of William Henry Harrison, log cabin, flag "Original and Selected." 76pp. [M-019]. [Crew/WHH-63].

503.22 King Andrew. w. No composer indicated. m. "Tune — *Dame Durden*." In: *A Miniature Of Martin Van Buren (With A Selection Of The Best And Most Popular Tippecanoe Songs)*, page 46. 1840. [3½" × 6½"]. [V-1: Br/bk] [V-2: Gn/bk] [V-3: Y/bk] litho of man, chain around neck. Van Buren quote. "Amos Kendall's Veracity — Tom Benton's Honesty — Francis Blair's Beauty." "What is wanting cant be numbered [sic]." 58pp. [M-016]. [Crew/WHH-88].

503.23 King Martin's Soliloquy (A Modern Democratic Melody). w. No composer indicated. m. "Air — *It Is Not On The Battle Field*." In: *Harrison Melodies (Original And Selected)*, page 19. Published by Weeks, Jordan & Co., Boston, MA. 1840. [3⁹⁄₁₆" × 6"]. B/w litho of William Henry Harrison. "Published under the direction of the Boston Harrison Club." 76pp. Page 5: "To William Henry Harrison of Ohio, the gallant soldier, the enlightened statesman, the consistent Republican, and the Honest man..." [M-001, 002, 003]. [Crew/WHH-86].

503.24 Lines Supposed To Be Written On The Twelfth Of November, 1840. w. No composer indicated. m. "Air — *Farewell, Farewell To Thee, Araby's Daughter*." In: *Harrison Melodies (Original And Selected)*, page 14. Published by Weeks, Jordan & Co., Boston, MA. 1840. [3⁹⁄₁₆" × 6"]. B/w litho of William Henry Harrison. "Published under the direction of the Boston Harrison Club." 76pp. [M-001, 002, 003]. [Crew/WHH-86].

503.25 The Locofoco Exit, On The Fourth Of March, 1841. w. No composer indicated. m. "Tune — *I See Them On Their Winding Way*." In: *Songs For The People (Or Tippecanoe Melodies)* [Songster], page 33. "Dedicated to the Democratic Whig Young Men of the City and County of New York." Published for the Authors by James P. Giffing, No. 56 Gold Street, New York, NY. 1840. [3¾" × 6"]. Litho of William Henry Harrison, log cabin, flag. "Original and Selected." 76pp. [M-019]. [Crew/WHH-63].

503.26 Martin Van Buren To John M. Niles. w. No composer indicated. m. "Air — *Come Rest In this Bosom*." In: *Harrison Melodies (Original And Selected)*, page 17. Published by Weeks, Jordan & Co., Boston, MA. 1840. [3⁹⁄₁₆" × 6"]. B/w litho of William Henry Harrison. "Published under the direction of the Boston Harrison Club." 76pp. [M-001, 002, 003]. [Crew/WHH-86].

503.27 Matty's Soliloquy After Retirement From Office. w.m. No composer or tune indicated. In: *Harrison Melodies (Original And Selected)*, page 23. Published by Weeks, Jordan & Co., Boston, MA. 1840. [3⁹⁄₁₆" × 6"]. B/w litho of William Henry Harrison. "Published under the direction of the Boston Harrison Club." 76pp. Page 5: "To William Henry Harrison of Ohio, the gallant soldier, the enlightened statesman, the consistent Republican, and the Honest man..." [M-001, 002, 003]. [Crew/WHH-86].

593.28 The Mill Boy Of The Slashes. w. Dr. Darlington. m. "Tune— *Green Grove* [sic] *The Rushes, O*." In: *The Kentucky Minstrel And Jersey Warbler* [Song Book], page 28. Published by Robinson & Peterson, No. 98 Chestnut Street, Philadelphia, PA. 1844. [2⅞" × 4⁹⁄₁₆"]. Y/bk litho of Henry Clay and Theodore Frelinghuysen. 68pp. Page 3: "Being a Choice Selection of Coon Melodies." Page 68: Y/bk litho of Henry Clay and Theodore Frelinghuysen. [M-045]. [Crew/HC-17].

503.29 A Miniature Of Martin Van Buren. w.m. No composer or tune indicated. In: *A Miniature Of Martin Van Buren (With A Selection Of The Best And Most Popular Tippecanoe Songs)*, page 3. 1840. [3½" × 6½"]. [V-1: Br/bk] [V-2: Gn/bk] [V-3: Y/bk] litho of man, chain around neck. Van Buren quote. "Amos Kendall's Veracity — Tom Benton's Honesty — Francis Blair's Beauty." "What is wanting cant be numbered [sic]." 58pp. [M-016]. [Crew/WHH-88].

503.30 Mr. Van Buren's Farewell To The Palace. w.m. No composers or tune indicated. No publisher indicated. [1840]. [Approx. 5" × 12"]. Non-pictorial. 2pp. Page 2: Blank. [Crew/MVB-19]. [AMC].

503.31 Oh! Oh! Where Shall I Fly To. w.m. No composer indicated. m. "Tune — *Thou, Thou Reihn'st In The Bosom*." In: *A Miniature Of Martin Van Buren (With A Selection Of The Best And Most Popular*

Tippecanoe Songs), page 28. 1840. [3½" × 6½"]. [V-1: Br/bk] [V-2: Gn/bk] [V-3: Y/bk] litho of man, chain around neck. Van Buren quote. "Amos Kendall's Veracity — Tom Benton's Honesty — Francis Blair's Beauty." "What is wanting cant be numbered [sic]." 58pp. [M-016]. [Crew/WHH-88].

503.32 Old Tippecanoe Come Out Of The West. w. No composer indicated. m. "Tune — *Young Lochinvar*." In: *Tippecanoe Song-Book (A Collection Of Log Cabin And Patriotic Melodies)*, page 58. Published by Marshall, Williams & Butler, Philadelphia, PA. 1840. White on black litho of log cabin, plow, flags, eagle. 180pp. [M-024]. [Crew/WHH-61].

503.33 Parody On The Flail Song. w. No composer indicated. m. "Air — *Derry Down*." In: *Log Cabin Minstrel (Or Tippecanoe Songster)*, page 9. c. "A Member of the Roxbury Whig Association." Published at the *Patriot And Democrat* Office, Roxbury, [MA]. 1840. [4½" × 6¾"]. [V-1:Y/bk] [V-2: Bl/bk] litho of William Henry Harrison, geometric design border. "Old Tip's the boy to swing the flail. Hurrah! Hurrah! Hurrah!" 64pp. Page 3: Title page — "Containing a Selection of Songs Original and Selected Many of them Written Expressly for this Work, Compiled, Published and Arranged by a member of the Roxbury Democratic Whig Association and Respectfully Dedicated to the Log Cabin Boys of the U.S." [M-013]. [Crew/WHH-71].

503.34 A Political Catch. w. No composer indicated. m. "Tune — *The Little Tailor Boy*." In: *The National Clay Minstrel*, page 11. Published by [V-1: George Hood, No. 15 North 6th Street, Philadelphia, PA] [V-2: James Fisher, No. 71 Court Street, Boston, MA]. 1843. [3" × 4½"]. Y/bk litho of raccoon sitting on fence, black border. 68pp. Pages 2 and 67: Blank. Pages 65–66: Contents. [Crew/HC-10].

503.35 Song For Jim Crow. w. No composer indicated. m. "Tune — *Tell Chapman He Must Crow*." In: *The Tippecanoe Campaign Of 1840*, page 13. Published by A.B. Norton, Mount Vernon, OH. 1888. [5½" × 7½"]. Bl/gd book. 496pp. Pages 1–382: Text. Pages 383–485: "Tippecanoe Songs of the Log Cabin Boys and Girls of 1840." [M-276]. [Crew/WHH-96].

503.36 A Song For The Martin, 1841. w. No composer indicated. m. "Air — *My Heart's In The Highlands*." In: *Harrison Melodies (Original And Selected)*, page 16. Published by Weeks, Jordan & Co., Boston, MA. 1840. [3⁵⁄₁₆" × 6"]. B/w litho of William Henry Harrison. "Published under the direction of the Boston Harrison Club." 76pp. Page 5: "To William Henry Harrison of Ohio, the gallant soldier, the enlightened statesman, the consistent Republican, and the Honest man..." [M-001, 002, 003]. [Crew/WHH-86].

503.37 The Spirit Of Destiny. w. No composer indicated. m. "Air — *Thimble's Scolding Wife Lay Dead*." In: *Harrison Melodies (Original And Selected)*, page 20. Published by Weeks, Jordan & Co., Boston, MA. 1840. [3⁵⁄₁₆" × 6"]. B/w litho of William Henry Harrison. "Published under the direction of the Boston Harrison Club." 76pp. Page 5: "To William Henry Harrison of Ohio, the gallant soldier, the enlightened statesman, the consistent Republican, and the Honest man..." [M-001, 002, 003]. [Crew/WHH-86].

503.38 The Spoilsmen. w.m. No composer or tune indicated. In: *Songs For The People (Or Tippecanoe Melodies)* [Songster], page 31. "Dedicated to the Democratic Whig Young Men of the City and County of New York." Published for the Authors by James P. Giffing, No. 56 Gold Street, New York, NY. 1840. [3¾" × 6"]. Litho of William Henry Harrison, log cabin, flag. "Original and Selected." 76pp. [M-019]. [Crew/WHH-63].

503.39 The Treasury Chest. w. No composer indicated. m. "Tune — *The Mistletoe Bough*." "A Very Pathetic and musical appeal to the Dear People, by an Ex-Post Master General." In: *Tippecanoe Song-Book (A Collection Of Log Cabin And Patriotic Melodies)*, page 99. Published by Marshall, Williams & Butler, Philadelphia, PA. 1840. White on black litho of log cabin, plow, flags, eagle. 180pp. [M-024]. [Crew/WHH-61].

503.40 Van And The Farmer. w. No composer indicated. m. "Air — *The King And The Countryman*." In: *Harrison Melodies (Original And Selected)*, page 45. Published by Weeks, Jordan & Co., Boston, MA. 1840. [3⁵⁄₁₆" × 6"]. B/w litho of William Henry Harrison. "Published under the direction of the Boston Harrison Club." 76pp. Page 5: "To William Henry Harrison of Ohio, the gallant soldier, the enlightened statesman, the consistent Republican, and the Honest man..." [M-001, 002, 003]. [Crew/WHH-86].

503.41 Van And The Farmer. w. No composer indicated. m. "Tune — *King And The Countryman*." In: *The Log Cabin & Hard Cider Melodies, A Collection Of Popular And Patriotic Songs*, page 22. Published by Charles Adams, No. 23 Tremont Street, Boston, MA. 1840. [3¾" × 6"]. [V-1: Pk/bk] [V-2: Gn/bk] litho of William Henry Harrison. "The Freeman's glittering Sword be Blest, For ever blest the Freeman's Lyre." 78pp. Pages 2 and 77: Blank. Page 3: Inside title page. B/w litho of log cabin. "Respectfully Dedicated to the Friends of Harrison and Tyler." Page 78: Advertising. [M-012]. [Crew/WHH-68].

503.42 Van Can't Come It. w.m. No composer or tune indicated. In: *The National Clay Melodist (A Collection Of Popular And Patriotic Songs, Second Edition, Enlarged And Improved)*, page 75. Published by Benj. Adams, No. 54 Court Street, Boston, MA. 1844. [3" × 5¼"]. Inside title page: B/w litho of Henry Clay's home — "O'er Ashland's lawns the skies are bright, From West to East The radiance streams and glows, The land beneath its beams gay beats the heart with joy, Hurrah! Hurrah! Hip! Hurrah!" 108pp. [M-050?]. [Crew/HC-13].

503.43 We've Walloped Them So (A Favorite Patriotic Ballad). w. "By a member of the Fifth Ward Club." Published by Atwill, No. 201 Broadway, New York, NY. 1840. Non-pictorial. "A Favorite Patriotic Ballad as sung by the Tippecanoe Glee Club, with great applause. Written, Arranged and Dedicated, to the Tippecanoe Associations." 4pp. Page 4: Blank. [Crew/WHH-98].

503.44 Ye Whigs Of Columbia. w. No composer indicated. m. "Tune — *Lochiel's Warning*." In: *Tippecanoe Song-Book (A Collection Of Log Cabin And Patriotic Melodies)*, page 83. Published by Marshall, Williams & Butler, Philadelphia, PA. 1840. White on black litho of log cabin, plow, flags, eagle. 180pp. [M-024]. [Crew/WHH-61].

503.45 Young Men's National Convention. w.m. No composer or tune indicated. In: *The Tippecanoe Campaign Of 1840*, page 74. Published by A.B. Norton, Mount Vernon, OH. 1888. [5½" × 7½"]. Bl/gd book. 496pp. Pages 1–382: Text. Pages 383–485: "Tippecanoe Songs of the Log Cabin Boys and Girls of 1840." [M-276]. [Crew/WHH-96].

• **AmPM-504 KNOTT**, James Proctor (State House, Missouri, 1857; State Attorney General, Missouri, 1859–1860; U.S. House, Kentucky, 1867–1871 & 1875–1883; Governor, Kentucky, 1883–1887)

504.1 Concerning The War We Are In. w. W.A. Croffut. m. "Air—*Meg Maguire*." "As sung by Senator Thurman, basso; Senator Hill, tenor; Senator Beck, soprano; Accompanied by Eaton with Trombone, and Proctor Knott with piccolo." In: *Bourbon Ballads*, page 2. Published in the *New York Tribune*, Extra No. 52, September, 1879. Non-pictorial newspaper supplement. "Songs for the Stump." 4pp. [Crew/MISC-226]. [AMC].

504.2 The Presidential Racecourse. w. No composer indicated. m. "Tune—*Camptown Races*." "From the *Graphic*." In: *Hayes & Wheeler Song Book*, page 40. Published by The Union Republican Congressional Committee, Washington, DC. 1876. [5¾" × 9¼"]. Br/bk litho of Rutherford B. Hayes and William A. Wheeler, shield, geometric design border. "I'll be on hand again shortly." [V-1: "Series I" under title on cover] [V-2: Series not indicated on cover]. 52pp. [M-196, 197]. [Crew/RBH-20].

LYON, Matthew (State House, Kentucky, 1802; U.S. House, Kentucky, 1803–1811) [See: Vermont]

• **AmPM-504A JOHNSON**, Richard Mentor (State House, 1804–1807, 1819 & 1841–1842; U.S. House, 1807–1819 & 1829–1837; U.S. Senate, 1819–1829; Vice President, 1837–1841) [ALSO SEE: DOC-/PSM-MVB].

504A.1 The Abortive Van Buren Convention. w. No composer indicated. m. "Tune—*Pretty Betty Martin, Tiptoe Fine, Couldn't Get A Sweetheart To Please Her Mind*." In: *Tippecanoe Song-Book (A Collection Of Log Cabin And Patriotic Melodies)*, page 43. Published by Marshall, Williams & Butler, Philadelphia, PA. 1840. White on black litho of log cabin, plow, flags, eagle. 180pp. [M-024]. [Crew/WHH-61].

504A.2 All Round My 'At I Vers A Veeping Villow. w.m. No composer or tune indicated. "A Song to be Sung at Van Buren's Indignation meetings." In: *Songs For The People (Or Tippecanoe Melodies)* [Songster], page 27. "Dedicated to the Democratic Whig Young Men of the City and County of New York." Published for the Authors by James P. Giffing, No. 56 Gold Street, New York, NY. 1840. [3¾" × 6"]. Litho of William Henry Harrison, log cabin, flag. "Original and Selected." 76pp. [M-019]. [Crew/WHH-63].

504A.3 A Buckeye Song. w. No composer indicated. m. "Tune—*Yankee Doodle*." In: *Tippecanoe Club Songster*, page 49. Published by [V-1: Turner & Fisher, No. 15 North Sixth Street, Philadelphia, PA] [V-2: H.A. Turner, Baltimore, MD]. 1841. [3" × 4⁷⁄₁₆"]. Hand Colored engraving of William Henry Harrison, log cabin. 68pp. [M-021, 022]. [Crew/WHH-18].

504A.4 Clare De Kitchen. w. No composer indicated. m. No tune indicated. In: *The Clay Minstrel Or National Songster*, page 273. c. John Stockton Littell. Published by Greeley & M'Elrath, Tribune Building, New York, NY. 1844. [3⅛" × 4⅞"]. Non-pictorial. 396pp. [Crew/HC-18].

504A.5 The Clay Diggins (Song 10). w. W.A. Philomath. m. "Tune—*Gee Ho Dobbin*." In: *Original Clay Songs: Humorous And Sentimental, Designed To Inculcate Just Political Sentiments, To Suit The Present Political Crisis, And To Advocate The Claims Of Henry Clay To The Highest Honors His Country Can Bestow*, page 14. w. W.A. Philomath, Union Co., Ind. Published by Philomath, Cincinnati, OH. 1842. [4¼" × 6"]. Be/bk litho of an eagle, U.S. Flag. "The eagle soars above the throng; And listen's [sic] to fair Freedom's song, Hails the merry roundelay, Claps his glad wings and hails the day." 20pp. Page 20: Be/bk litho of four men—"Tyler Expounding the Constitution! The effect of 'treading in the footsteps.'" [M-057]. [CrewHC-104].

504A.6 [Come All Ye Good Hearted Whigs] (Whig Song). w. No composer indicated. m. "Tune—*Yankee Doodle*." In: *The National Clay Almanac, 1845*, page 31. B/w litho of a raccoon. Published by Desilver & Muir, No. 18 South Fourth Street, Philadelphia, PA. 1844. [6¹³⁄₁₆" × 7⅞"]. B/w litho of Henry Clay, ship—"Commerce," plow, crops—"Agriculture." [Crew/HC-89].

504A.7 Come All Ye Good Men Of The Nation (A Clay Song). w. No composer indicated. m. "Air—*Rosin The Bow*." In: *The National Clay Minstrel (And True Whig's Pocket Companion For The Presidential Canvass Of 1844)*, page 21. Published by [V-1: George Hood, No. 15 North 6th Street, Philadelphia, PA] [V-2: James Fisher, No. 71 Court Street, Boston, MA]. 1843. [3¼" × 5⅛"]. Y/bk litho of raccoon—"That Coon" and flag—"Henry Clay," log cabin. "New and Improved Edition." 128pp. [Crew/HC-11].

504A.8 The Coon Song. w. No composer indicated. m. "Tune—*Jim Dandy Of Caroline*." In: *The Clay Minstrel Or National Songster*, page 355. c. John Stockton Littell. Published by Greeley & M'Elrath, Tribune Building, New York, NY. 1844. [3⅛" × 4⅞"]. Non-pictorial. 396pp. [Crew/HC-18].

504A.9 Get Out Of The Way! w. No composer indicated. m. "Tune—*Old Dan Tucker*." In: *The Clay Minstrel Or National Songster*, page 175. c. John Stockton Littell. Published by Greeley & M'Elrath, Tribune Building, New York, NY. 1844. [3⅛" × 4⅞"]. Non-pictorial. 396pp. [Crew/HC-18].

504A.10 The Grand Backing-Out. w. John H. Warland. m. "Tune—*The Hunters Of Kentucky*." B/w litho of a hunter shooting a raccoon—"Don't fire, Captain Scott, I'll Come Down." In: *The National Clay Melodist (A Collection Of Popular And Patriotic Songs, Second Edition, Enlarged And Improved)*, page 20. Published by Benj. Adams, No. 54 Court Street, Boston, MA. 1844. [3" × 5¼"]. Inside title page: B/w litho of Henry Clay's home—"O'er Ashland's lawns the skies are bright, From West to East The radiance streams and glows, The land beneath its beams gay beats the heart with joy, Hurrah! Hurrah! Hip! Hurrah!" 108pp. [M-050?]. [Crew/HC-13].

504A.11 If E'er I Should Wish To Get Married. w. "A Lady." m. "Tune—*Rosin The Bow*." "If The Ladies, Heaven bless them! Could vote, the election of Mr. Clay would be carried by acclamation! Their influence was powerfully felt in 1840, and their appreciation of eloquence, patriotism and genius, will prompt them to a warm support of 'Harry of the West.' Of this the following excellent song is proof." In: *The Clay Minstrel Or National Songster*, page 261. c. John Stockton Littell. Published by Greeley & M'Elrath, Tribune Building, New York, NY. 1844. [3⅛" × 4⅞"]. Non-pictorial. 396pp. [Crew/HC-18].

504A.12 *Irish Song On General Harrison.* w. No composer indicated. m. "Air — *Sprig Of Shillalah.*" In: *The Log Cabin & Hard Cider Melodies, A Collection Of Popular And Patriotic Songs*, page 43. Published by Charles Adams, No. 23 Tremont Street, Boston, MA. 1840. [3¾" × 6"]. [V-1: Pk/bk] [V-2: Gn/bk] litho of William Henry Harrison. "The Freeman's glittering Sword be Blest, For ever blest the Freeman's Lyre." 78pp. Pages 2 and 77: Blank. Page 3: Inside title page. B/w litho of log cabin. "Respectfully Dedicated to the Friends of Harrison and Tyler." Page 78: Advertising. [M-012]. [Crew/WHH-68].

504A.13 *Jimmie Polk Of Tennessee.* w. J. Greiner. m. "Tune — *Dandy Jim Of Caroline.*" In: *The National Clay Minstrel*, page 2. Published by [V-1: George Hood, No. 15 North 6th Street, Philadelphia, PA] [V-2: James Fisher, No. 71 Court Street, Boston, MA]. 1843. [3" × 4½"]. Y/bk litho of raccoon sitting on fence, black border. 68pp. Pages 2 and 67: Blank. Pages 65–66: Contents. [Crew/HC-10].

504A.14 *Kilkenny Cats.* w. No composer indicated. m. "Tune — *Old Dan Tucker.*" In: *The National Clay Minstrel*, page 12. Published by [V-1: George Hood, No. 15 North 6th Street, Philadelphia, PA] [V-2: James Fisher, No. 71 Court Street, Boston, MA]. 1843. [3" × 4½"]. Y/bk litho of raccoon sitting on fence, black border. 68pp. Pages 2 and 67: Blank. Pages 65–66: Contents. [Crew/HC-10].

504A.15 *The Ladies' Whig Song.* w. No composer indicated. m. "Tune — *Rosin The Beau.*" In: *The National Clay Minstrel*, page 39. Published by [V-1: George Hood, No. 15 North 6th Street, Philadelphia, PA] [V-2: James Fisher, No. 71 Court Street, Boston, MA]. 1843. [3" × 4½"]. Y/bk litho of raccoon sitting on fence, black border. 68pp. Pages 2 and 67: Blank. Pages 65–66: Contents. [Crew/HC-10].

504A.16 *The Lounger's Lament.* w. No composer indicated. m. "Air — *Exile Of Erin.*" In: *The Log Cabin & Hard Cider Melodies, A Collection Of Popular And Patriotic Songs*, page 42. Published by Charles Adams, No. 23 Tremont Street, Boston, MA. 1840. [3¾" × 6"]. [V-1: Pk/bk] [V-2: Gn/bk] litho of William Henry Harrison. "The Freeman's glittering Sword be Blest, For ever blest the Freeman's Lyre." 78pp. [M-012]. [Crew/WHH-68].

504A.17 *The Lounger's Lament.* w. No composer indicated. m. "Tune — *The Exile Of Erin.*" In: *The Clay Minstrel Or National Songster*, page 282. c. John Stockton Littell. Published by Greeley & M'Elrath, Tribune Building, New York, NY. 1844. [3⅛" × 4⅞"]. Non-pictorial. 396pp. [Crew/HC-18].

504A.18 *The Moon Was Shining Silver Bright* (A Whig Song). w. J. Greiner. m. "Tune — *Old Dan Tucker.*" In: *The National Clay Minstrel (And True Whig's Pocket Companion For The Presidential Canvass Of 1844)*, page 44. Published by [V-1: George Hood, No. 15 North 6th Street, Philadelphia, PA] [V-2: James Fisher, No. 71 Court Street, Boston, MA]. 1843. [3¼" × 5⅛"]. Y/bk litho of raccoon — "That Coon" and flag — "Henry Clay," log cabin. "New and Improved Edition." 128pp. Page 10: Dedication — "To the National Clay Club this work is respectfully dedicated by the Publisher." [Crew/HC-11].

504A.19 *A New Song.* w. No composer indicated. m. "Tune — *Old Rosin The Bow.*" In: *The National Clay Minstrel*, page 18. Published by [V-1: George Hood, No. 15 North 6th Street, Philadelphia, PA] [V-2: James Fisher, No. 71 Court Street, Boston, MA]. 1843. [3" × 4½"]. Y/bk litho of raccoon sitting on fence, black border. 68pp. [Crew/HC-10].

504A.20 *Patrick O'Rourke's Huzza.* w. No composer indicated. m. "Air — *Sprig Of Shilellah.*" In: *Tippecanoe Song-Book (A Collection Of Log Cabin And Patriotic Melodies)*, page 168. Published by Marshall, Williams & Butler, Philadelphia, PA. 1840. White on black litho of log cabin, plow, flags, eagle. 180pp. [M-024]. [Crew/WHH-61].

504A.21 *Patriotic Exultation on Lyon's Release From The Federal Bastille, in Vergennes.* w. No composer indicated. m. "Tune — *Black Sloven.*" Published in the *Centinel of Freedom*, March 5, 1799. "Sung at Bennington, the third of Release, Feb. 12, 1799. [VBL, p. 151].

504A.22 *Rouse, Ye Whigs, To Your Duty.* w. No composer indicated. m. "Tune — *Thou Reign'st In This Bosom.*" "Written for the *Clay Melodist.* Dedicated to the Lowell Clay Clubs." In: *The National Clay Melodist (A Collection Of Popular And Patriotic Songs, Second Edition, Enlarged And Improved)*, page 79. Published by Benj. Adams, No. 54 Court Street, Boston, MA. 1844. [3" × 5¼"]. Inside title page: B/w litho of Henry Clay's home — "O'er Ashland's lawns the skies are bright, From West to East The radiance streams and glows, The land beneath its beams gay beats the heart with joy, Hurrah! Hurrah! Hip! Hurrah!" 108pp. [M-050?]. [Crew/HC-13].

504A.23 *The Rubber; Or Mat's Last Game.* w.m. No composer indicated. "Tune — *Miss Bailey.*" In: *The Clay Minstrel Or National Songster*, page 347. c. John Stockton Littell. Published by Greeley & M'Elrath, Tribune Building, New York, NY. 1844. [3⅛" × 4⅞"]. Non-pictorial. 396pp. [Crew/HC-18].

504A.24 *The Rubber; Or Mat's Third And Last Game.* w. No composer indicated. m. "Tune — *Miss Bailey.*" In: *The National Clay Minstrel (And True Whig's Pocket Companion For The Presidential Canvass Of 1844)*, page 46. Published by [V-1: George Hood, No. 15 North 6th Street, Philadelphia, PA] [V-2: James Fisher, No. 71 Court Street, Boston, MA]. 1843. [3¼" × 5⅛"]. Y/bk litho of raccoon — "That Coon" and flag — "Henry Clay," log cabin. "New and Improved Edition." 128pp. [Crew/HC-11].

504A.25 *Salt River.* w. F.B. Graham, Esq. m. "Tune — *In Good Old Colony Times.*" "Written for the Choir attached to the Philade. National Clay Club." B/w litho of man on horse with bugle. In: *The National Clay Minstrel*, page 17. Published by [V-1: George Hood, No. 15 North 6th Street, Philadelphia, PA] [V-2: James Fisher, No. 71 Court Street, Boston, MA]. 1843. [3" × 4½"]. Y/bk litho of raccoon sitting on fence, black border. 68pp. [Crew/HC-10].

504A.26 The Second Polk Song. w. No composer indicated. m. "Tune—*Lucy Long.*" In: *The National Clay Minstrel*, page 10. Published by [V-1: George Hood, No. 15 North 6th Street, Philadelphia, PA] [V-2: James Fisher, No. 71 Court Street, Boston, MA]. 1843. [3" × 4½"]. Y/bk litho of raccoon sitting on fence, black border. 68pp. Pages 2 and 67: Blank. Pages 65–66: Contents. [Crew/HC-10].

504A.27 The Standard Floats! w.m. No composer indicated. "Tune—*Old Aunt Sally.*" In: *The Clay Minstrel Or National Songster*, page 331. c. John Stockton Littell. Published by Greeley & M'Elrath, Tribune Building, New York, NY. 1844. [3⅛" × 4⅞"]. Non-pictorial. 396pp. [Crew/HC-18].

504A.28 That Same Old Coon (A New Comic Whig Song). w. "The Milford Bard." m. "Tune—*Sittin On A Rail.*" [7¾" × 13¼"]. B/w litho of a crow on its back and a raccoon speaking "Why Don't You Crow." "A New Comic Whig Song written for 1844 by the Milford Bard by Particular Desire." 2pp. Page 2: Blank. [Crew/HC-120].

504A.29 The Van Buren Convention. w. No composer indicated. m. "Tune—*Pretty Betty Martin, Tip-Toe Fine.*" "Couldn't get a sweetheart to please her mind." In: *The Log Cabin & Hard Cider Melodies, A Collection Of Popular And Patriotic Songs*, page 53. Published by Charles Adams, No. 23 Tremont Street, Boston, MA. 1840. [3¾" × 6"]. [V-1: Pk/bk] [V-2: Gn/bk] litho of William Henry Harrison. "The Freeman's glittering Sword be Blest, For ever blest the Freeman's Lyre." 78pp. Pages 2 and 77: Blank. Page 3: Inside title page. B/w litho of log cabin. "Respectfully Dedicated to the Friends of Harrison and Tyler." Page 78: Advertising. [M-012]. [Crew/WHH-68].

504A.30 Vermont Whig Song. w. "That Same Old Whig." m. No tune indicated. No publisher indicated. [1844]. B/w litho of a raccoon, geometric design border. 2pp. Page 2: Blank. [Crew/HC-128]. [AMC].

504A.31 Whig Song. w.m. No composer or tune indicated. In: *Incidents In The Campaign Of 1844*, page 16. c. James T. Hathaway. Published by J.T. Hathaway, No. 287 Crown Street, New Haven, CT. 1905. [5" × 7"]. Bl/gy non-pictorial geometric design border. "Printed for private distribution among old friends." "*Here's To You, Harry Clay*—Old Song." 68pp. [Crew/HC-119].

• **AmPM-505 MARSHALL**, Humphrey (U.S. House, 1849–1852 & 1855–1859; U.S. Minister to China, Confederate Congress, 186?–?)

505.1 Buena Vista. w.m. No composer or tune indicated. In: *The Patriot's Songster*, page 13. Published by Mumford & Company, Cincinnati, OH. 1862. [3½" × 6"]. Non-pictorial. 48pp.

• **AmPM-506 MATHEWSON**, J.O. (Mayor of Ashland, 1906–1910)

506.1 Teddy In The Jungles (Grand March Heroique) (Descriptive). m. Joe W. Phillips. 1909. Photos of "Mayor of Ashland, KY., J.O. Mathewson, Shriner, State Commander R.S. Moses, Knights Templar, Louisville, Ky., Joe Wm. Phillips." Drawing of a boat, sun. "Dirinost Dramatizations to Louisville, Ky., June 9, 1909, Shrine Souvenir Imperial Council of the United States of America, Music Inspirations." "A Toast To T.R. In Africa—When your camp-fire is low in the midnight tropics, where lion, tiger and elephant about your moss-cot frolics, where night-birds, piercing notes through the jungle rings accompanying queer sounding croaks and bleats and rasping of wings, when all else of your camps are in the land of dreams, ar'nt you wistfully 'a'thrill for more sociable themes? [sic]." "Response to Louisville's eruption (1909) of divertissement with the Mystic Shrine." 8pp.

• **AmPM-507 MCCONNELL**, Addison Mitchell (Deputy Assistant U.S. Attorney, 1974–1975; Judge-Executive, Jefferson County, 1978–1985; U.S. Senate, 1985–Present)

507.1 Georgy Bush's Smarmy Jerks Club Band. w. Bo 'Ice' Bielefeldt. m. "*Sergeant Pepper's Lonely Hearts Club Band* by Beatles." Published online by Amiright.com at <http://www.amiright.com/parody/misc/beatles1.shtml>. [ca. 2002].

• **AmPM-508 MOREHEAD**, Charles Slaughter (State House, 1828–1829, 1838–1842, 1844 & 1853; State Attorney General, 1830–1835; U.S. House, 1847–1851; Governor, 1855–1859)

508.1 The Slow, Passing Bell (Solo and Quartette). w. Mrs. Emily M. Pratt. m. W.J. Landram. Published by Millet & Son, No. 329 Broadway, New York, NY. 1855. Non-pictorial. "As Sung by the National Vocalists." "NOTE: As a testimony of respect to the memory of Washington, the Boats in Passing Mount Vernon toll their Bells." "To the Hon. Charles Morehead of Kentucky and the Friends of the American Union." 6pp. Pages 2 and 6: Blank.

• **AmPM-509 MORROW**, Edwin Proch (District Attorney, Eastern District of Kentucky, 1910–1915; Governor, 1919–1923)

509.1 Morrow's The Man. w.m. Harry T. Myers. Published by The Zoeller Music Co., Republic Building, Louisville, KY. 1919. Br/w photo of Edwin Morrow, black line border. 4pp. Page 2: At top of Music—"The Campaign Song of the Day written especially for the Republican State Campaign Committee." Page 4: Advertising.

• **AmPM-510 MORTON**, Thurston B. (U.S. House, 1947–1953; U.S. Senate, 1957–1969; Chairman of Republican National Committee, 1959–1961)

510.1 The Good Times Train. w. Johnny Lehmann. m. Jimmie Driftwood. Copyright 1960 by Worden Music Co., Inc. In: *Welcome GOP To The Jumbo Jamboree Uline Arena, April 4, 1960, Washington, DC.* [Program], page 4. R/w/b elephant. 4pp. Page 3 and 4: Elected dignitaries in attendance — Senators Thurston Morton, Barry Goldwater, and Everett M. Dirksen; Congressmen William Miller and Charles Halleck.

SHELBY, Isaac (Governor, Kentucky, 1792–1796 & 1812–1816) [See: North Carolina]

• **AmPM-511 SISCO**, Gene (Magistrate, Martin County, ca. 1970s)

511.1 Tell Jimmy Daddy Tried {511.1–1}. w.m. Gene Sisco and G. Perine. 45 rpm. Published by S-E-Y Enterprises, Inc. #SEY-101–45. Performed by Gene Sisco. B-Side: ***Champion Of Fools*** {511.1–2}. w.m. Gene Sisco. Sleeve: "The record is dedicated to all the truck drivers of America."

• **AmPM-512 SMITH**, Walter B. (County Attorney, Bell County, 1931–1932)

512.1 Welcome The Traveler Home. w. James Garland. m. No tune indicated. [1831–1932]. [TPL, p. 78].

• **AmPM-513** SPEED, John (Judge, Farmington [Louisville], 1820)

513.1 The Birthday Of Washington. w. "From the *National Intelligencer*. m. A.P. Heinrich. In: *The Dawning Of Music In Kentucky, Or The Pleasures Of Harmony In The Solitudes Of Nature. Opera Prima*, page 85. Published by Bacon & Hart and A.P. Heinrich, Kentucky. 1820. It is with great regret that A.P. Heinrich has to publish the following music without inserting the name of the author of the poetry. He can only add that from repeated inquiries at the office of the *National Intelligencer* he could not gain the desired information. The composer trust that the melody throughout will be found smooth and flowing and well adapted for the flute and violin. Should the piano forte accompaniment prove difficult, the same is left ad libitum. The music composed with an accompaniment for the piano forte at the request of the Hon. Judge Speed of Farmington (Louisville), to whom and to an indulgent public it is most respectfully presented by their devoted fellow citizen, A.P. Heinrich." 269pp. [W-3588].

• **AmPM-514** UNDERWOOD, John Cox (City Council, Bowling Green; Mayor, Bowling Green, 1871–1872; Lt. Governor, 1875–1979)

514.1 The Governor's March. m. Hubbard T. Smith. Published by The Hubsmith Company, cor. 11th and "F" Streets N.W., Washington, DC. 1895. Bl/w geometric designs. "To Governor John C. Underwood." 8pp. Pages 2 and 8: Blank.

• **AmPM-515** WATTERSON, Henry (Publisher; U.S. House, 1876–1977)

515.1 An Auspicious Occasion. w. No composer indicated. m. "Tune — *Odd Fellows' Hall*." In: *Republican Campaign Parodies And Songs* [Songster], page 13. Published by Betts and Burnett, South Butler, Wayne County, NY. 1896. [7¾" × 5½"]. Be/bk non-pictorial. "McKinley and Hobart." "1896." 28pp. [M-340]. [Crew/WM-67].

515.2 [Oh Grover Played A Free Trade Tune]. w. No composer indicated. m. "Air — *O, Susannah*." Republican Campaign Songs, page 4. Published by the Bath Republican Glee Club, Bath, ME. 1888. [3⅓" × 7½"]. B/w litho of eagle. "To James G. Blaine." 4pp. [Foldout]. [Crew/JGB-50].

515.3 [One Night As I Lay On My Pillow]. w. No composer indicated. m. "Air — *My Bonnie Lies Over The Ocean*." B/w drawing of Taft walking to Chicago. In: *Gridiron Nights*, page 306. Published by Frederick A. Stokes Company, Publishers, New York, NY. Copyright 1915 by Arthur Wallace Dunn. [7½" × 10½"]. B/gd imprinting of comedy mask, lamps, floral designs. 406pp.

515.4 'Tis Fine To Be A President. w. E.J. Seymour. m. No tune indicated. In: *Harrison And Reid Campaign Song Book*, page 6. w. E.J. Seymour. m. Popular Airs. [1892]. [3⅞" × 5⅛"]. Bl/gn non-pictorial, stars, geometric designs. 36pp. Pages 2 and 35: Blank. Page 36: Advertising for this songbook. [M-316]. [Crew/BFH-35].

• **AmPM-516** WICKLIFFE, Charles Anderson (State House, 1812–1813, 1822–1823 and 1833–1835, U.S. House, 1823–1833 & 1861–1863; Lt. Governor, 1836–1839; Governor, 1839–1840; U.S. Postmaster General, 1841–1845)

516.1 Tilden And The Colored Vote. w. No composer indicated. m. "Air — *Ise de Happiest Darkey Out*." In: *Tilden And Hendricks' Reform Songs (For The Centennial Campaign Of 1876)*, page 17. Published by The National Democratic Committee, Box 3637, New York, NY. 1876. [3⅞" × 5¹⁵⁄₁₆"]. Gn/bk litho of Samuel J. Tilden and Thomas A. Hendricks, geometric design border. 40pp. [M-203]. [Crew/SJT-21].

516.2 The Treasury Chest. w. No composer indicated. m. "Tune — *The Mistletoe Bough*." In: *The Clay Minstrel Or National Songster*, page 302. c. John Stockton Littell. Published by Greeley & M'Elrath, Tribune Building, New York, NY. 1844. [3⅛" × 4⅞"]. Non-pictorial. 396pp. [Crew/HC-18].

• **AmPM-517** MISCELLANEOUS MUSIC

517.1 High Sheriff Of Hazard. w. Tom Paxton. m. No tune indicated. "Copyright Cherry Lane Music Co., Inc." Lyrics and sound file published online at <http://www.mudcat.org/kids/@displaysong.cfm?SongID=2645>. [199-].

LOUISIANA

• **AmPM-518** ALLEN, Henry Watkins (State House, Texas, 1853; Governor, Louisiana, 1864–1865)

518.1 The Wandering Refugee. w. "Beautiful Song and Chorus by Will S. Hays. m. "Brilliante Variations by" Charles Grobe. Published by Louis Tripp, Harmony Hall, Louisville, KY. B/w litho of a young girl in tattered clothier and barefoot. "New Edition with additional words by W.B. Wood, M.D., Franklin, LA." "To Mrs. Robt. W. Hays." "Tho' I wander far away, Lonely o'er life's stormy sea, Who will shed one gentle tear, For a wandering refugee." 1865. 6pp. Pages 2 and 6: Blank. Page 3: "Inscribed to the memory of the lamented Ex-Gov. Allen."

518.2 The Wandering Refugee. w. Will S. Hays. Published by Louis Tripp, Harmony Hall, Louisville, KY. 1865. B/w non-pictorial geometric designs. "To Mrs. Belle Hays." "Charming Collection of Music Composed for Piano." List of other titles in the series. 6pp. Pages 2 and 6: Blank. Page 5: At top of "Additional Verses"—"Inscribed to the memory of the lamented Ex-Gov. Allen. St. Mary, July 1866."

• **AmPM-519 DAVIS**, James Huston (Clerk of Criminal Court, Shreveport, 1928–1938; Commissioner of Public Safety, Shreveport, 1938–1942; State Public Service Commissioner, 1942–1944; Governor, 1944–1948 & 1960–1964)

519.1 The BMI Number 18 Folio. Published by Southern Music Publishing Co., Inc., 1619 Broadway, New York 19, NY. [ca. 1940]. Non-pictorial geometric designs. "Contains the best songs of Jimmie Rodgers, Carson J. Robinson, Jimmie Davis, The Carter Family, Bradley Kincade, and many others."

519.2 The Door Is Always Open. 33⅓ rpm LP. Decca Records #DL 8729. Performed by Jimmy Davis.

519.3 Favorites As Sung By Jimmy Davis. Published by Jimmie Davis Music Co., P.O. Box 2626, Baton Rouge, LA. 70821. 1968. N/c photo of Jimmie Davis. Gd/r/bk/w cover. 28pp. Davis composed songs include: ***I Wouldn't Take Nothin' For My Journey*** {519.3–1}(with Charles Goodman); ***Someone To Care***; ***One More Valley*** {519.3–2} (with Dottie Rambo); ***So Many Reasons*** {519.3–3}(with David Reece).

519.4 Four Star Folio: (Cavalcade Of Melodies Of Today And Yesterday). Published by Southern Music Publishing Co., Inc., 1619 Broadway, New York 19, NY. [ca. 1940]. Photos of four county music stars including "Jimmie Davis, Jimmie Rodgers, Montana Slim, The Carter Family." "*It Makes No Difference Now.*"

519.5 God's Last Alter Call. 33⅓ rpm LP. MCA Records #MCA-323. Performed by Jimmie Davis. Includes song by Jimmie Davis: ***Draw Me Near*** {519.5–1} (Arranged by Jimmie Davis); ***Mama Would Pray*** {519.5–2}(Ernie Goff, Jerry Simms and Jimmie Davis); ***Lord, Is There Room In Your Mansion For Me*** {519.3–3} (Wanda Ballman and Jimmie Davis); and ***Lighthouse Shine On Me*** {519.3–4} (A.T. Watts and Jimmie Davis). Album cover: N/c photo of Jimmie Davis. 1973.

519.6 Golden Hits. 33⅓ rpm green vinyl LP. Plantation Records #PLP-524. Performed by Jimmie Davis. 1977.

519.7 Hail Him With A Song. 33⅓ rpm LP. Decca Records #DL 8786. Performed by Jimmie Davis.

519.8 Highway Too Heaven. 33⅓ rpm Album. Decca Records #DL-4432. [ca. 1960s]. Performed by Jimmie Davis. Songs included by Jimmie Davis: ***Will You Be Saved?*** {519.8–1} (Jimmie Davis and Larry Goss); ***White Robes*** {519.8–2} (Jimmie Davis and B.A. Mercer); ***At The Cross*** {519.8–3} (Arranged by Jimmie Davis); ***He's Holding My Hand*** {519.8–4} (Jimmie Davis and Bill Harmon); ***Softly And Tenderly*** {519.8–5} (Arranged by Jimmie Davis); and ***Where We'll Never Grow Old*** {519.8–6} (Arranged by Jimmie Davis).

519.9 How Great Thy Art. 33⅓ rpm LP. Decca Records #DL 4322/74322. Performed by Jimmy Davis. Album cover: Photo of clouds.

519.10 Hymn Time. 33⅓ rpm LP. Decca Records #DL 8572. Performed by Jimmy Davis.

519.11 It Makes No Difference Now. w.m. Jimmie Davis "(Writer of *Nobody's Darlin' But Mine*)" and Floyd Tillman. Published by Southern Music Pub. Co., 1619 Broadway, New York, NY. 1939. Gn/w photo of "Wilf Carter." Gn/w geometric designs. List of records where song was published. 4pp. Page 4: Advertising.

519.12 I Wouldn't Take Nothin' For My Journey. w.m. Charles Goodman and Jimmie Davis. 1964.

519.13 Jimmy Davis' Favorite Sacred Songs. Published by Jimmie Davis Music Corp., Shreveport, LA. 1953. B/w photo of Jimmie Davis. Bl/w/bl/gy drawing of church. Davis composed songs include: ***Someone To Care*** {519.13–1}; ***That Great Milky Way*** {519.13–2} (with Jim Davis); ***When I Prayed Last Night*** {519.13–3}; ***When We All Get Together Up There*** {519.13–4} (with Johnny Roberts); ***The River Of Ages Ago*** {519.13–5} (with Raymond E. Hall); ***Lord, I'm Coming; Let Jesus Lead The Way*** {519.13–6} (with Johnny Roberts); ***When It's Round Up Time In Heaven*** {519.13–7}.

519.14 Jimmy Davis Folio Of Favorite Songs. Published by Jimmie Davis Music Corp., 1619 Broadway, New York, NY. 1948. Bl/w photos of Jimmie Davis, pelican, flower. O/w/bk cover. Bl/w drawing of the State of Louisiana, seal. "My best to you all, Sincerely Jimmie Davis, Gov. of Louisiana [facsimile handwriting]." 32pp. Davis composed songs include: ***When It's Round-Up Time In Heaven*** {519.14–1}; ***I'm Hurt Too Much To Cry*** {519.14–2}; ***There's A New Moon Over My Shoulder*** {519.14–3} (with Ekko Ehelan and Lee Blastic); ***You Won't Be Satisfied That Way*** {519.14–4} (with Lloyd Ellis); ***All Aboard For Louisiana*** {519.14–5} (with Charles Mitchell); ***You Are My Sunshine*** {519.14–6} (with Charles Mitchell); ***It Makes No Difference Now*** {519.14–7} (with Floyd Tillman); ***Bang Bang, My Mary*** {519.14–8} (with Stuart Hamblen); ***Golden Girls*** {519.14–9}; ***Sweethearts Or Strangers*** {519.14–10} (with Lou Wayne).

519.15 Jimmy Davis Song Folio. Published by Southern Music Publishing Co., Inc., 1619 Broadway, New York, NY. Copyright 1942 by Peer International Corp. B/w photos of Jimmie Davis. Pl/bk/w cover of wood rail frame. 64pp. Davis composed songs include: ***The Answer to 'Nobody's Darling But Mine'*** {519.15–1}; ***Sweethearts Or Strangers*** {519.15–2} (with Lou Wayne); ***It Makes No Difference Now*** {519.15–3} (with Floyd Tillman); ***Worried Mind*** {519.15–4} (with Ted Daffan); ***Nobody's Darling But Mine*** {519.15–5}; ***Prairie Of Love*** {519.15–6}; ***Sweetheart Of West Texas*** {519.15–7} (with Bonnie Dodd); ***When It's Round-Up Time In Heaven*** {519.15–8}; ***Some Must Win, Some Must Lose*** {519.15–9} (with Lou Wayne); ***Don't Say Goodbye If You Love Me*** {519.15–10} (with Bonnie Dodd); ***You Are My Sunshine*** {519.15–11} (with Charles Mitchell); ***You Don't Love Me Anymore Little Darling*** {519.15–12} (with Charles Mitchell and Hoke Rice); ***That's Why I'm Nobody's Darling*** {519.15–13}; ***Why Do You Treat Me Like Dirt Under Your Feet*** {519.15–14} (with Charles Mitchell); ***Two More Years And I'll Be Free*** {519.15–15} (with Floyd Tillman); ***In My Cabin Tonight*** {519.15–16}; ***You're My Darling*** {519.15–17}; ***Walls Of White*** {519.15–18} (with Lou Wayne); ***There's An Old Fashion House On A Hillside*** {519.15–19} (with Walter Lane); ***I'll Come Back Dear If You're Still In Love With Me*** {519.15–20} (with Buddy Jones); ***New Worried Man***

{519.15-21} (with Ted Daffan); *Did You* {519.15-22} (with Hoke Rice); *I Hung My Head And Cried* {519.15-23} (with Clif Bruner); *I Told You So!* {519.15-24} (with Rex Griffin); *I'm Knocking At Your Door Again* {519.15-25}.

519.16 *Just Forgive And Forget* {527.1-1}. w.m. Jimmie Davis. 78 rpm record. Decca #61815/5415A. Performed by Jimmie Davis. [1940s-1950s]. Side B: *Sweetheart Of West Texas* {527.1-2} by Jimmie Davis.

519.17 *The Love I Have For You* {519.17-1}. w.m. Jimmie Davis and Dinky Ard. 78 rpm record. Decca #68099/5889B. Performed by Jimmie Davis with Charles Mitchell's Orchestra. [1940s-1950s]. Side A: *You're My Darling* {519.17-2} by Jimmie Davis.

519.18 *Near The Cross*. 33⅓ rpm LP. Decca Records #DL 8174. Performed by Jimmy Davis.

519.19 *Nearer The Cross*. 33⅓ rpm LP. Decca Records #DL 8174. Performed by Jimmie Davis with the Anita Kerr Singers. [ca. 1960s]. Song written by Jimmie Davis include: *Near The Cross* {519.19-1} (Wilbur Jones, Jimmie Davis and Ira Stanphill); *To My Mansion In The Sky* {519.19-2} (Jimmie Davis and Jim Davis); *Why Didn't You Tell Me* {519.19-3} (Jimmie Davis and Frankie Bailes); and *Somewhere There's A Friend* {519.19-4} (Jimmie Davis).

519.20 *No One Stands Alone*. 33⅓ rpm LP. Vocalion Record #VL 73676. Performed by Jimmie Davis. [ca. 196-]. Davis composed songs include: *Someone To Care* {519.20-1} (Jimmie Davis); *When I Prayed Last Night* {519.20-2} (Jimmie Davis); *I Know What He Meant* {519.20-3} (Jimmie Davis); *When We All Get Together Up There* {510.20-4} (Jimmie Davis and Jim Davis); *Lord, I'm Coming Home* {519.20-5} (Arranged by Jimmie Davis); *The Great Milky Way* {519.20-6} (Jimmie Davis and Jim Davis).

519.21 *Nobody's Darling* (But Mine). w.m. Jimmie Davis. Published by Jenkins Music Company, Publishers, Kansas City, MO. 1935. Ma/w photo of "Judy, Anne and Zeke Canova. "Featured by Judy, Anne and Zeke Canova, Whiteman Our." Ma/w drawing of a couple silhouetted against a mountain, lake and tree. 6pp. Page 5: Arrangement for "Trio with Bass." Page 6: Advertising.

519.22 *One More Valley*. w.m. Dottie Rambo and Jimmie Davis. 1966. B/w non-pictorial.

519.23 *So Many Reasons*. w.m. David Reece and Jimmie Davis. Published by Jimmie Davis Music Company, Inc., 836 Rutherford Street, Shreveport, LA. 1964. Non-pictorial geometric designs. 4pp. Page 2: Blank. Page 4: Advertising.

519.24 *Someone To Care*. w.m. Jimmie Davis. Published by Jimmie Davis Music Co., Inc., 836 Rutherford Street, Shreveport, LA. 1952. Gn/w non-pictorial geometric design. "A Song of Comfort and Consolation." 4pp. Page 2: "Recorded by Jimmie Davis, Decca; The Speer Family, Bullet." Page 4: Advertising.

519.25 *Someone To Care*. 33⅓ rpm LP. Decca Records #DL 4037/74037. Performed by Jimmy Davis. Album cover: Photo of Jimmie Davis, church window.

519.26 *Someone Watching Over You*. 33⅓ rpm LP. Decca Records #DL 4186/74186. Performed by Jimmy Davis with The Plainsmen. Album cover: Photo of praying hands.

519.27 *Songs Of Consolation*. 33⅓ rpm Album. Decca Records DL-75199. 1970. Songs performed by Jimmy Davis. Davis written songs include: *The Three Nails* {519.27-1} (Jimmie Davis and Lewis Harrah); *He's So Precious To Me* {519.27-2} (Arranged by Jimmie Davis); *I Believe* {19.27-3} (Gerald Williams and Jimmie Davis); *Sheltered In The Arms Of God* {519.27-4} (Jimmie Davis and Dottie Rambo); *Shake The Nail-Scarred Hands Of Jesus* {519.27-5} (Charles Adams and Jimmie Davis); *Today I'm Giving You Away* {519.27-6} (Jimmie Davis); and *A Day Without Prayer* {519.27-7} (Lorine Emberton and Jimmie Davis).

519.28 *Songs Of Faith*. 33⅓ rpm LP. Decca Records #DL 4220/74322. Performed by Jimmy Davis. Album cover: Photo of Jimmie Davis, church window.

519.29 *Songs Of Jimmie Davis*. [Folio]. Published by Southern Music Publishing Co., Inc., 1619 Broadway, New York 19, NY. 1938. Pl/w photo of Jimmie Davis with his guitar. Y/br cover. "Writer of *Nobody's Darling* and 49 Other Songs." 64pp. Songs by Davis include: *Nobody's Darling But Mine* {519.29-1}; *Lonely Hobo* {519.29-2}; *The Answer To Nobody's Darling But Mine* {519.29-3}; *That's Why I'm Nobody's Darling* {519.29-4}; *In My Cabin Tonight* {519.29-5}; *Cowboy's Home Sweet Home* {519.29-6}; *Jellyroll Blues* {519.29-7}; *Bury Me In Old Kentucky* {519.29-8}; *Arabella Blues* {519.29-9}; *Alla En El Rancho Grande* {519.29-10} (arranged by Donald Reep); *Bear Cat Mama From Horner's Corners* {519.29-11}; *It's All Coming Home To You* {519.29-12}; *Yo-Yo Mama* {519.29-13}; *Shirt-Tail Blues* {519.29-14}; *Prairie Of Love* {519.29-15}; *Would You* {519.29-16}; *Hold 'Er Newt* {519.29-17}; *Graveyard Blues* {519.29-18}; *Get On Board, Aunt Susan* {519.29-19}; *Sweetheart Of West Texas* {519.29-20} (with Bonnie Dodd); *Home In Carolin'* {519.29-21}; *Alimony Blues* {519.29-22}; *She's A Hum-Dinger* {519.29-23}; *Organ Grinder Blues* {519.29-24}; *Jealous Lover* {519.29-25}; *Shotgun Wedding* {519.29-26}; *I'll Get Mine Bye And Bye* {519.29-27}; *Davis*; *Salty Dog* {519.29-28}; *The Davis Limited* {519.29-29}; *High-Geared Daddy* {519.29-30}; *Come On Over To My House* {519.29-31}; *Just Forgive And Forget* {519.29-32}; *Don't Say Goodbye If You Love Me* {519.29-33} (with Bonnie Dodd); *Sewing Machine Blues* {519.29-34}; *High Behind Blues* {519.29-35}; *Gambler's Return* {519.29-36}; *Down At The Old Church* {519.29-37}; *Red Nightgown Blues* {519.29-38}; *I Want Her Tailor-Made* {519.29-39}; *I Wonder If She's Blue* {519.29-40}; *Saturday Night Stroll* {519.29-41}; *When It's Round Up Time In Heaven* {519.29-42}; *Wild And Reckless Hobo* {519.29-43} (with Jones); *Honkey Tonk Blues* {519.29-44}; *You'll Be Comin' Back Some Day* {519.29-45}; *Pi-Rootin' Around*; *Midnight Blues*; *Home Wreckin' Blues* {519.29-46} (with Ed Schaffer).

519.30 *Songs Of The Soil* (All Star Hillbilly Folio). Published by Gordon Music Company, 1651 Cosmo Street, Hollywood, CA. 19441. B/w photos of country singers: "Jimmie Davis, Roy Rogers, Zeke Manners, Smiley Brunette, Roy Acuff, Tex Ritter." Bl/bk/w drawing of guitar. "Featuring Six Select Stars." 48pp. Pages 26 and 27: B/w photo of Jimmie Davis and

"Scenes Jimmie Davis' Columbia Production *Riding Through Nevada*."
519.31 *Suppertime*. 33⅓ rpm LP. Decca Records #DL 2953/78953. Performed by Jimmy Davis. Album cover: Photo of Jimmie Davis.
519.31 *Sweet Hour Of Prayer*. 33⅓ rpm LP. Decca Records #DL 4087/74087. Performed by Jimmy Davis. Album cover: Photo of Jimmie Davis.
519.33 *There's A New Moon Over My Shoulder*. w.m. Jimmie Davis, Ekko Whelan and Lee Blastic. Published by Southern Music Pub. Co., 1619 Broadway, New York, NY. 1944. [V-1: Bl/w photo of "Tex Ritter"] [V-2" Gn/w photo of "Dave Wakely"]. V-1: Bl/w] [V-2: Gn/w] geometric and musical designs. 4pp. Page 4: Advertising.
519.34 *There's No Other Like My Saviour*. w.m. Jimmie Davis and Anna Allen. Published by Vern Music Co., 843 Delaware Street, Shreveport, LA. 1957. Pl/w non-pictorial geometric design. 4pp. Page 4: Advertising.
519.35 *There's Nothing My God Can't Do*. w.m. Dottie Rambo and Jimmie Davis. Published by Jimmie Davis Music Company, Inc., 836 Ratchford Street, Shreveport, LA. 1961. Gn/w non-pictorial.
519.36 *These Hands Of Clay*. w.m. Jimmie Davis. Published by Vern Music Co., 843 Delaware Street, Shreveport, LA. 1958. Non-pictorial geometric design. 4pp. Page 4: Advertising.
519.37 *To My Mansion In The Sky*. w.m. Jimmie Davis and Jim Davis. Published by Jimmie Davis Music Corp., 843 Delaware Street, Shreveport, LA. 1954. Non-pictorial. 4pp. Page 4: Advertising.
519.38 *Travel Me Home*. w.m. Zeno Goss and Jimmie Davis. Published by Jimmie Davis Music Company, Inc., 843 Delaware Street, Shreveport, LA. 1958. Non-pictorial geometric design. 4pp. Page 4: Advertising.
519.39 *What A Day That Will Be*. w.m. Jim Hall. Published by Ben Speer Music, P.O. Box 9201, Nashville 4, TN. Bl/w photo of Jimmie Davis. "Recorded on Decca Records by The Honorable Jimmie Davis, Governor of Louisiana." 4pp. Page 4: Advertising.
519.40 *What Good Will It Do*. w.m. Frank Luther "(Writer of *Barnacle Bill The Sailor*)." Published by Leeds Music Corp., 1393 6th Avenue, New York, NY. 1939. Ma/w photo of Jimmie Davis on horseback— "Sincerely Yours Jimmie Davis [facsimile handwriting], Decca Recording Star." 4pp. Page 4: Advertising.
519.41 *When I Prayed Last*. w.m. Jimmie Davis. Published by Jimmie Davis Music Corp., 1619 Broadway, New York, NY. 1953. Non-pictorial geometric design. 4pp.
519.42 *When It's Roundup Time In Heaven* {519.42–1}. w.m. Jimmie Davis. 78 rpm record. Decca #C9495/5090A. Performed by Jimmie Davis. [1940s-1950s]. Side B: *Nobody's Darlin' But Mine* {519.42–2} by Jimmie Davis.
519.43 *White Robes*. w.m. B.A. Mercer and Jimmie Davis. Published by Jimmie Davis Music Company, Inc., 836 Rutherford Street, Shreveport, LA. 1964. Non-pictorial geometric design. 4pp. Page 4: Advertising.
519.44 *Worried Mind*. w.m. Jimmie Davis and Ted Daffan. Published by Allan & Co., Ltd., Melbourne, Australia and Southern Music Publishing Company, New York, NY. Copyright 1941 by Peer International Corp. Bl/w photo of "Smoky Dawson." Bl/w drawing of a cowboy playing a guitar, another on a bucking bronco, home. 4pp. Page 4: Advertising.
519.45 *You Are My Sunshine*. w.m. Jimmy Davis and Charles Mitchell. Published by Southern Music Publishing Co., Inc., 1619 Broadway, New York 19, NY. Copyright 1940 by Peer International Corp. Bl/w photo of "Jimmie Davis." Bl/w music notes, geometric designs. "Featured by Jimmie Davis." 4pp. Page 4: Advertising.
519.46 *You Are My Sunshine*. w.m. Jimmy Davis and Charles Mitchell. Published by Southern Music Publishing Co., Inc., 1619 Broadway, New York 19, NY. Copyright 1940 by Southern Music Publishing Co. R/w photo of "Jimmie Davis." R/w geometric designs. List of stars that have recorded the song. 4pp. Page 4: Advertising.
519.47 *You Are My Sunshine*. w. Jimmie Davis and Charles Mitchell. m. Sound file provided. "Copyright 1940 and 1977 by Peer International Corp. Jimmie Davis was a gospel singer who later served two terms as governor of Louisiana..." Lyrics and sound file published online at <http://www.mudcat.org/kids/@displaysong.cfm?SongID=8008>. [199-].
519.48 *You Are My Sunshine*. 33⅓ rpm LP. Decca Records #DL 8896/78896. Performed by Jimmy Davis.

• **AmPM-519A   DROWN**, Charles W. (Civil Sheriff, Orleans Parish, 1888)
519A.1 *Continental Guards March*. m. J.C. Chandler. a. Richard Gerber "Four Hand Arrangement." Published by White-Smith Music Publishing Co., Boston. MA. 1894. B/w litho of members of the Continental guard including: Captain Charles W. Drown, Lieut. R.H. Keen, Lieut. R.H. Hackney, Lieut. Thos. O'Connor and Surgeon Wm. Hincks. B/w lithos of soldiers, military equipment, backpack—"1854–1894." 8pp. Page 8: Advertising.

• **AmPM-520   DUKE**, David (National Director of the Knights of the Ku Klux Klan, 1974; State House, 1989)
520.1 *Duking It Out*. w.m. Martin A. Childs. Cassette tape. Chance Records #36621. Side 2: Every Man A King. w.m. Huey Long and Castro Carazo. 1991.
520.2 *Matt Gets Arrested While Hitch-Hiking In The Same Louisiana County In Which A Member Of The Klu Klux Klan Was Elected To The State Legislature*. Sprawl. On CD: *The King Of Parking*. Rastaman Work Ethic Production #CD 01. Rastaman Work Ethic Production, P.O.B. 2011, Rice University, Houston, Texas. 1990. [Crew/K-110R]
520.3 *Put Up Your Duke*. w. Bill Strauss and Elaina Newport. On CD: *Shamlet*. Published by Capitol Steps Productions, 1505 King Street, Alexandria, VA. 1988. CD Cover: N/c drawing of shield.
520.4 *The Search For A Likely Candidate*. w.m. Henry and Bobbie Shaffner. Published as a photocopy by Henry and Bobbie Shaffner and Saul Broudy, Bala Cynwyd, PA. 1991. [8½" × 11"]. Non-pictorial. 2pp. Page 2: Blank.
520.5 *[Teddy The Red Nosed Senator]*. w. No composer indicated. m. "Sung to the tune of *Rudolph, The*

Red Nosed Reindeer." "Here's one from the Bob Rivers and Twisted Radio Album, *I Am Santa Claus* that we are spinning at our college station, WTTU…" Published online at <http://catweasel.org/Site1/Digests.H9312140.php>. 1993.

520.6 Theme To The David Duke Show. w. Douglas Butcher. m. "*Identical Cousins* (Theme To T*he Patty Duke Show*), based on the performance by Sidney Ramin and Robert Wells." "In the spirit of that show where identical cousins couldn't be more different, we find one man changing identities who always remains disturbingly the same." Published online at <http://www.amiright.com/parody/60s/sidneyraminandrobertwells9.shtml>. [ca. 1990].

• **AmPM-521** **EDWARDS**, Edwin Washington (City Council, Crowley, 1954–1962; State Senate, 1964–1965; U.S. House, 1965–1972; Governor, 1972–1980, 1984–1988, 1992–1996. State Supreme Court, 1980)

521.1 Ballad Of Edwin Edwards. w.m. Bennie Rizzo, Jr. 33⅓ rpm 6⅞" record. E.W.E. Records, #NR14671-1. 1983. Performed by Easy Waters. "Recorded at Soundtrax Recording Studio, Baton Rouge, Louisiana." "Official Edwin Edwards Campaign Song." Side 2: *Movin On Towards New Orleans.* w.m. Bennie Rizzo, Jr. Performed by Easy Waters. "Special thanks to Pasty Powell, Jimmy George, Johnny Jambalaya, Catheryn Dusenberry."

• **AmPM-521A** **FITZMORRIS**, James E. "Jimmy" (City Council, New Orleans, 1954–1966; Candidate for Mayor, New Orleans, 1965; Lt. Governor, 1972–1980; Candidate for Governor, 1969)

521A.1 The Ballad Of Jimmy Fitz. w.m. R.M. Howes, "M.D., Ph.D." 45 rpm vinyl 6⅞" record. Renaissance Records, Inc. #DRP 3534/R.R. 151 1979. Performed by Doc Randolph. Side 2: Same.

• **AmPM-522** **FLOWER**, Walter (Mayor, New Orleans, 1896–1900)

522.1 The Flower March. m. Laurence Dubuclet. Published by Louis Grunwald Co., Ltd., 715 Canal Street, New Orleans, LA. 1896. B/w drawing of "Walter Flower." Bl/w geometric designs. "Respectfully Dedicated to The Hon. Walter Flower, Mayor of the City of N.O." "Latest Two-Step." 6. Pages 2 and 6: Blank.

• **AmPM-522A** **GARRISON**, Earling Carothers "Jim" (Assistant District Attorney, 1954–1968; District Attorney, New Orleans, 1962–1973)

522A.1 Overture. w. No composer indicated. m. "*Yellow Rose Of Texas.*" In: *The Capitol Correspondents Present The 1967 Gridiron Show*, page 2. Published by Capitol Correspondents Assn. [Baton Rouge, LA]. 1967. [5½" × 8½"]. Bl/bk/w drawing of John McKeithen on a stepladder wearing angel wings preparing to fly. 20pp.

522A.2 Three-Dollar Bill. w. No composer indicated. m. "*If You Knew Susie.*" In: *The Capitol Correspondents Present The 1967 Gridiron Show*, page 19. Published by Capitol Correspondents Assn. [Baton Rouge, LA]. 1967. [5½" × 8½"]. Bl/bk/w drawing of John McKeithen on a stepladder wearing angel wings preparing to fly. 20pp.

• **AmPM-522B** **GRAVOLET**, Edward W. (State House, 1948–1960)

522B.1 Overture. w. No composer indicated. m. "*Yellow Rose Of Texas.*" In: *The Capitol Correspondents Present The 1967 Gridiron Show*, page 2. Published by Capitol Correspondents Assn. [Baton Rouge, LA]. 1967. [5½" × 8½"]. Bl/bk/w drawing of John McKeithen on a stepladder wearing angel wings preparing to fly. 20pp.

• **AmPM-523** **JONES**, Sam Huston (Governor, 1940–1944)

523.1 How Do You Do Sam Jones. 1940.

• **AmPM-524** **KELLOGG**, William Pitt (Chief Justice of the Supreme Court of the Territory of Nebraska, 1861; Collector of the Port of New Orleans, 1865–1868; U.S. Senate, Louisiana, 1868–1872 & 1877–1883; Governor, 1873–1877; U.S. House, Louisiana, 1883–1885)

524.1 Tilden And The Colored Vote. w. No composer indicated. m. "Air — *Ise De Happiest Darkey Out.*" In: *Tilden And Hendricks' Reform Songs (For The Centennial Campaign Of 1876)*, page 17. Published by The National Democratic Committee, Box 3637, New York, NY. 1876. [3⅞" × 5¹⁵⁄₁₆"]. Gn/bk litho of Samuel J. Tilden and Thomas A. Hendricks, geometric design border. 40pp. [M-203]. [Crew/SJT-21].

• **AmPM-525** **LECHE**, Richard Webster (Governor, 1936–1939; Democratic Party State Chairman, 1937)

525.1 Louisiana's Goin' Places (Come Along!). w.m. Paul English. No publisher indicated. 1936. Y/bk/ bl/gn drawing of Louisiana with a b/w photo of a crowd inside. Y/bk photos of "Earl K. Long, Lieutenant Governor," "Richard W. Leche, Governor of Louisiana," and "Robert S. Maestri, Mayor of New Orleans." "The official Louisiana State PEP Song." 4pp. Page 4: Listing of all state officials in Louisiana.

525.2 Onward & Forward With Leche. w. Paul English "(Writer of *Share The Wealth, Louisiana's Goin' Places, Colonel Bob*)." m. N.J. Clesi (Writer of the famous song hit *I'm Sorry I Made You Cry*)." No composer indicated. Copyright 1936 by Paul English. Br/w photo of Richard Leche. Bl/w/y photos of Louisiana scenes, airplane. "The Official Administration March Song." 4pp. Page 4: Advertising.

• **AmPM-526** **LIVINGSTON**, Robert Linligthgow, Jr. (Assistant U.S. Attorney, 1970–1973; Chief Special Prosecutor, Orleans Parish, 1974–1975; Chief Prosecutor, State Attorney General's Office, 1975–1976; U.S. House, 1977–1999)

526.1 Republican Clowns. w. H.R. Yeager. m. "Sung to the tune of *Send In The Clowns.*" Published online at <http://www.geocities.com/CapitolHill/Congress/3950>. 1998.

• **AmPM-527** **LONG**, Earl (Lt. Governor, 1936–1939; Governor, 1939–1940, 1948–1952 & 1956–1960)

527.1 Louisiana's Goin' Places (Come Along!). w.m. Paul English. No publisher indicated. 1936. Y/bk/ bl/gn drawing of Louisiana with a b/w photo of a crowd inside. Y/bk photos of "Earl K. Long, Lieutenant Governor," Richard W. Leche, Governor of Louisiana," and "Robert S. Maestri, Mayor of New Orleans." "The official Louisiana State PEP Song." 4pp. Page 4: Listing of all state officials in Louisiana.

• **AmPM-528** **LONG**, Huey Pierce (State Public Service Commission, 1918–1928; Governor, 1928–1932; U.S. Senate, 1932–1935)

528.1 *Appreciation*. w. L.H. Poole. m. George C. Stout. Copyright by Geo. C. Stout and L.H. Poole, Baton Rouge, LA. 1931. [10⅜" × 15½"]. R/be/bk drawing of the Louisiana State Capitol building, house — "Night Schools for the older people," books — "Free schools for all children." "Dedicated to Governor Huey P. Long." "Paved Highways and Free Bridges." "Help for the old Confederate veterans they were paid their $212.00 each and their pension was raised to $60.00 per month; New four year farmers road program; Millions of dollars in increased sums of money to save schools of state; Repealed tobacco tax; State medical school; Home for epileptics; Thousands of insane treated humanely who formerly lived in straight jackets and jail cells; Port of New Orleans rescued from financial distress — its charges reduced and sprinkler system installed that lowers insurance rate from $1.04 to 29cts. per $1000.00 on property and cargo; charity hospital death rates reduced 300 per cent living salaries for higher court jurists; New Orleans $3,500,000 overdraft debt paid city placed on cash basis and given $700,000 per year for street improvements; Airport and lakefront improvement and sea wall for New Orleans; Natural gas for New Orleans and Jefferson and St. Bernard parishes; Curbing of carbon black menace." 4pp. [Crew/MISC-164].

***528.2 Every Man A King*.** w.m. Huey P. Long and Castro Carazo. Published by Rainbow Music Co., 799 Seventh Avenue, New York, NY. 1935. B/w photo of Huey Long — Best wishes Huey P. Long [facsimile handwriting]." Bl/w/bk drawings of castle, ship, geometric designs. 6pp. Page 6: Advertising.

***528.3 Every Man A King*.** w.m. Huey P. Long and Castro Carazo. No publisher indicated. Copyright 1935 by National Book Co., Inc., New Orleans, LA. Bk/w/gd/r of a crown, rays of light emanating from the crown. Music begins on page 1. 4pp.

***528.4 Follow Long*.** w.m. Chris Yarich and Frank Arena. [1935]. R/w/bl/gn drawing of a road through the countryside into a rising sun. Music starts on page 1.

528.5 Franklin, Can You Spare A Job? w. No composer indicated. m. "Air — *Brother, Can You Spare A Dime*." In: *Foam Sweet Foam*, page 12. Published by Albany Legislative Correspondents' Association, Albany, NY. 1933. [8" × 11¾"]. N/c drawing by Jerry Costello of Franklin D. Roosevelt, Al Smith and other politicians riding a bottle of beer — "The Lager Limited." "A Rollicking Review Rotating on Resurrection of Bouncing Beverages, Tipsily Tapped at Ten Eyck Hotel Rathskeller, Albany, New York, the evening of Thursday, February 23, 1933, at Seven-Thirty o'clock." 20pp. [Crew/FDR-277].

***528.6 Kingfish*.** w.m. Carmel Green. Published by Carmel Green, 2400 Market Street, Fort Worth, TX. 1935. Bl/w drawing of a fish with a crown, geometric designs. 6pp. Pages 2 and 6: Blank.

***528.7 Kingfish*.** w.m. Randy Newman. On LP: *Good Old Boys*. Warner Bros. Records #MS 2193. Performed by Randy Newman. Lyrics on Album cover reverse. 1974.

***528.8 Share The Wealth*.** w. Paul English. [1935?]. [Copy not located].

***528.9 So Long Huey Long*.** w.m. Clarence Williams. Published by Clarence Williams Music Pub. Co., Inc., 145 West 45th Street, New York, NY. 1935. B/w nonpictorial geometric design, black border. 6pp. Pages 2 and 6: Advertising.

***528.10 Touchdown For LSU*.** w.m. Huey P. Long and Castro Carazo. Published by M. Witmark & Sons, New York, NY. 1935. Y/pl photo of a tower on the campus of Louisiana State University. 6pp. Pages 2 and 6: Advertising.

528.11 Welcome Song To Huey Long (Our U.S. Senator). w.m. Tom McNelly. a. Joseph Garrow. Published by Tom McNelly, Music Publishers, New Orleans, LA. 1931. Photo of Huey Long. Drawings of the "Louisiana State Capitol" building and the "U.S. Capitol" building, geometric designs. 8pp. Page 8: Blank.

• **AmPM-528A LONG**, Russell Billiu (U.S. Senate, 1948–1987)

***528A.1 Hello, Dere Lyndon*.** w. No composer indicated. m. "*Hello Dolly*." In: *The Capitol Correspondents Present The 1967 Gridiron Show*, page 12. Published by Capitol Correspondents Assn. [Baton Rouge, LA]. 1967. [5½" × 8½"]. Bl/bk/w drawing of John McKeithen on a stepladder wearing angel wings preparing to fly. 20pp.

• **AmPM-529 MAESTRI**, Robert Sidney (Mayor, New Orleans, 1936–1946)

***529.1 Colonel Bob*.** w. Paul English. [1936?]. Mayor Robt. S. Maestri's Official Song. [Copy not located].

529.2 Louisiana's Goin' Places (Come Along!). w.m. Paul English. No publisher indicated. 1936. Y/bk/bl/gn drawing of Louisiana with a b/w photo of a crowd inside. Y/bk photos of "Earl K. Long, Lieutenant Governor," Richard W. Leche, Governor of Louisiana," and "Robert S. Maestri, Mayor of New Orleans." "The official Louisiana State PEP Song." 4pp. Page 4: Listing of all state officials in Louisiana.

• **AmPM-529A MCKEITHEN**, John Julian (State, 1949–1952; Candidate for Lt. Governor, 1952; Governor, 1964–1972; Independent Candidate for U.S. Senator, 1972)

***529A.1 Back To Cabl*.** w. No composer indicated. m. "*I'm Going Back To Dixie*." In: *The Capitol Correspondents Present The 1967 Gridiron Show*, page 12. Published by Capitol Correspondents Assn., [Baton Rouge, LA]. 1967. [5½" × 8½"]. Bl/bk/w drawing of John McKeithen on a stepladder wearing angel wings preparing to fly. 20pp.

***529A.2 Coonastrodome Needza Name*.** w. No composer indicated. m. "*Home On The Range*." In: *The Capitol Correspondents Present The 1967 Gridiron Show*, page 16. Published by Capitol Correspondents Assn., [Baton Rouge, LA]. 1967. [5½" × 8½"]. Bl/bk/w drawing of John McKeithen on a stepladder wearing angel wings preparing to fly. 20pp.

***529A.3 A Federal Case*.** w. No composer indicated. m. "H.M.S. Pinafore." In: *The Capitol Correspondents Present The 1967 Gridiron Show*, page 12. Published by Capitol Correspondents Assn., [Baton Rouge, LA]. 1967. [5½" × 8½"]. Bl/bk/w drawing of John McKeithen on a stepladder wearing angel wings preparing to fly.

***529A.4 Finale*.** w. No composer indicated. m. "*Bat-*

tle Hymn Of The Republic." In: *The Capitol Correspondents Present The 1967 Gridiron Show*, page 19. Published by Capitol Correspondents Assn., [Baton Rouge, LA]. 1967. [5½" × 8½"]. Bl/bk/w drawing of John McKeithen on a stepladder wearing angel wings preparing to fly. 20pp.

529A.5 Give Me Your Hand. w. No composer indicated. m. "From *Don Giovanni.*" In: *The Capitol Correspondents Present The 1967 Gridiron Show*, page 8. Published by Capitol Correspondents Assn., [Baton Rouge, LA]. 1967. [5½" × 8½"]. Bl/bk/w drawing of John McKeithen on a stepladder wearing angel wings preparing to fly. 20pp.

529A.6 Implementation Time. w. No composer indicated. m. "*I've Been Working On The Railroad.*" In: *The Capitol Correspondents Present The 1967 Gridiron Show*, page 4. Published by Capitol Correspondents Assn., [Baton Rouge, LA]. 1967. [5½" × 8½"]. Bl/bk/w drawing of John McKeithen on a stepladder wearing angel wings preparing to fly. 20pp.

529A.6A Louisiana. w.m. John J. McKeithen. 45 rpm 7" vinyl record. #119/LH3568. "State of Louisiana Governor John J. McKeithen Campaign Song." Side 2: *Campaign Song for Eddie J. Ste. Marie.* [1960–1970].

529A.7 Monster Rally. w. No composer indicated. m. "*The Wheel Of Hurt.*" In: *The Capitol Correspondents Present The 1967 Gridiron Show*, page 15. Published by Capitol Correspondents Assn., [Baton Rouge, LA]. 1967. [5½" × 8½"]. Bl/bk/w drawing of John McKeithen on a stepladder wearing angel wings preparing to fly. 20pp.

529A.8 My Lord, Its That Witch Again. w. No composer indicated. m. "*Bill Bailey, Won't You Please Come Home.*" In: *The Capitol Correspondents Present The 1967 Gridiron Show*, page 2. Published by Capitol Correspondents Assn., [Baton Rouge, LA]. 1967. [5½" × 8½"]. Bl/bk/w drawing of John McKeithen on a stepladder wearing angel wings preparing to fly. 20pp.

529A.9 My Second Act. w. No composer indicated. m. "*Top Of Old Smoky.*" In: *The Capitol Correspondents Present The 1967 Gridiron Show*, page 9. Published by Capitol Correspondents Assn., [Baton Rouge, LA]. 1967. [5½" × 8½"]. Bl/bk/w drawing of John McKeithen on a stepladder wearing angel wings preparing to fly. 20pp.

529A.10 Overture. w. No composer indicated. m. "*Yellow Rose Of Texas.*" In: *The Capitol Correspondents Present The 1967 Gridiron Show*, page 2. Published by Capitol Correspondents Assn., [Baton Rouge, LA]. 1967. [5½" × 8½"]. Bl/bk/w drawing of man on a ladder. 20pp.

529A.11 Political Has-Beens. w. No composer indicated. m. "*This Old Man Went Rolling Home.*" In: *The Capitol Correspondents Present The 1967 Gridiron Show*, page 14. Published by Capitol Correspondents Assn., [Baton Rouge, LA]. 1967. [5½" × 8½"]. Bl/bk/w drawing of man on a ladder. 20pp.

529A.12 Smothers Mother. w. No composer indicated. m. "*John Henry.*" In: *The Capitol Correspondents Present The 1967 Gridiron Show*, page 18. Published by Capitol Correspondents Assn., [Baton Rouge, LA]. 1967. [5½" × 8½"]. Bl/bk/w drawing of man on a ladder. 20pp.

529A.13 Survival Song. w. No composer indicated. m. "*Winchester Cathedral.*" In: *The Capitol Correspondents Present The 1967 Gridiron Show*, page 8. Published by Capitol Correspondents Assn., [Baton Rouge, LA]. 1967. [5½" × 8½"]. Bl/bk/w drawing of John McKeithen on a stepladder wearing angel wings preparing to fly. 20pp.

529A.14 Up Your Assessment. w. No composer indicated. m. "*Toreador* from *Carmen.*" In: *The Capitol Correspondents Present The 1967 Gridiron Show*, page 6. Published by Capitol Correspondents Assn., [Baton Rouge, LA]. 1967. [5½" × 8½"]. Bl/bk/w drawing of John McKeithen on a stepladder wearing angel wings preparing to fly. 20pp.

• **AmPM-530 NICHOLLS**, Francis Tillou (Governor, 1877–1880 & 1888–1892; State Supreme Court, 1892–1911)

530.1 Govr. Francis T. Nicholls's Triumphal March. m. Hubert Rolling "of New Orleans, Op. 25." No publisher indicated. 1877. Sepia photograph of Francis Nicholls attached. B/w litho of hands shaking—"United We Stand, Divided We Fall." 8pp. Page 2: Blank.

• **AmPM-530A O'CONNOR**, Thomas, Jr. (Fire Chief, New Orleans, 1891–1911)

530A.1 Continental Guards March. m. J.C. Chandler. a. Richard Gerber "Four Hand Arrangement." Published by White-Smith Music Publishing Co., Boston. MA. 1894. B/w litho of members of the Continental guard including: Captain Charles W. Drown, Lieut. R.H. Keen, Lieut. R.H. Hackney, Lieut. Thos. O'Conner and Surgeon Wm. Hincks. B/w lithos of soldiers, military equipment, backpack—"1854–1894." 8pp. Page 8: Advertising.

• **AmPM-530B PELTIER**, Harvey, Jr. (State Senate, 1970's)

530B.1 Peltier Campaign Song. 45 rpm vinyl record. w.m. L.J. Foret. R&R Records, 317 E. Main Street, Houma, LA. Label reads—"Re-Elect Senator Harvey Peltier, Jr." "Lafourche-Terrebonne-Assumption-St Mary Parishes." Side 2, non-political song *Elle Est Pas La Plus Jolie.* [ca. 197-].

• **AmPM-531 ROMAN**, Andre B. (Governor, 1831–1835 & 1839–1843)

531.1 Grande Marche Triomphale de la Legion De La Louisisne. m. G.P. Mamouvrier, "de la Nouville Orléans." Published by George Willig, 171 Chesnut Street, Philadelphia, PA. 1838. Litho of oak leaves. "Composée et respectueusement présenté au Gouberneur A.B. Roman, Commandant en chef des Armies de Pétat de la Louisiane." 8pp. Pages 2 and 8: Blank.

• **AmPM-532 SCHIRO**, Victor Hugo. (City Council, New Orleans, 1954–1961; Mayor, New Orleans, 1961–1970)

532.1 Hey, Look Me Over. w. Carolyn Leigh. m. Cy Coleman. Published by the Schiro Campaign. Copyright 1960 by Carolyn Leigh and Cy Coleman. [7¼" × 10⁷⁄₁₆"]. B/w photo of Victor H. Schiro walking. "Vote the Schiro Ticket." "*Hey Look Me Over* from the new musical *Wildcat.*" 2pp.

• **AmPM-533 SOULÉ**, Pierre (State Senate, 1846; U.S. Senate, 1847 & 1849–1853, U.S. Minister to Spain, 1853–1855)

533.1 The Presidential Track. w. No composer indicated. m. "Air — *Old Dan Tucker*." In: *Fillmore And Donelson Songs For The Campaign* (Songster), page 35. Published by Robert M. De Witt, Nos. 160 and 162 Nassau Street, New York, NY. November 4, 1856. [4¾" × 7⅛"]. Bl/bk litho of George Washington — "July 4, 1776," wreath, geometric design border. "This is the only authorized edition containing Duganne's Songs. Price 6 cts. each, $4 per 100. Discount to trade." Long quote from George Washington's "Farewell Address." 40pp. [M-101, 102]. [Crew/MF-10].

- **AmPM-533A STE. MARIE**, Eddie J. (Candidate for Parrish Sheriff, LaFource Parrish, ca. 1960–1970)

533A.1 Campaign Song for Eddie J. Ste. Marie. 45 rpm 7" vinyl record. #119/LH3568. Side 1: *Louisiana*. w.m. John J. McKeithen. [1960–1970].

- **AmPM-534 WARMOUTH**, Henry Clay (Delegate to Republican National Convention from Louisiana, 1868, 1900 & 1912; Governor, 1868–1872)

534.1 Tilden And The Colored Vote. w. No composer indicated. m. "Air — *Ise De Happiest Darkey Out*." In: *Tilden And Hendricks' Reform Songs (For The Centennial Campaign Of 1876)*, page 17. Published by The National Democratic Committee, Box 3637, New York, NY. 1876. [3⅞" × 5⅚"]. Gn/bk litho of Samuel J. Tilden and Thomas A. Hendricks, geometric design border. 40pp. [M-203]. [Crew/SJT-21].

- **AmPM-535 WILLIS**, Edwin Edward (State Senate, 1948–1949; Delegate to Democratic National Convention, 1956; U.S. House, 1949–1969)

535.1 Overture. w. No composer indicated. m. "*Yellow Rose Of Texas*." In: *The Capitol Correspondents Present The 1967 Gridiron Show*, page 2. Published by Capitol Correspondents Assn. [Baton Rouge, LA]. 1967. [5½" × 8½"]. Bl/bk/w drawing of John McKeithen on a stepladder wearing angel wings preparing to fly. 20pp.

- **AmPM-535A WOMACK**, Lantz (State House, 1956–1976)

535A.1 Overture. w. No composer indicated. m. "*Yellow Rose Of Texas*." In: *The Capitol Correspondents Present The 1967 Gridiron Show*, page 2. Published by Capitol Correspondents Assn. [Baton Rouge, LA]. 1967. [5½" × 8½"]. Bl/bk/w drawing of man on a ladder. 20pp.

- **AmPM-535B MISCELLANEOUS MUSIC**

535B.1 Y.M.D.A. Waltz. m. W.P. Published by Louis Grunewald, 127 Canal Street, New Orleans, LA. 1888. R/w drawing of a Rooster crowing. "Dedicated to the Members of the Y.M.D.A. [Young Men's Democratic Association] of New Orleans in Remembrance of their patriotic Deed on the 17th of April, 1888." 6pp. Pages 2 and 6: Blank.

MAINE

- **AmPM-536 BISHOP**. (Candidate for Governor, 1920)

536.1 Democracy (Campaign Song). w.m. Edward P. Favor "(Writer of *Jingles, Valley Of Visions*, &c.)." Copyright 1920 by Edward P. Favor, Richmond, ME. Non-pictorial manuscript. 4pp. Pages 3 and 4: Additional verse added so the song could be adapted for the Bishop campaign for Governor of Maine.

- **AmPM-537 BLAINE**, James Gillespie (State House, 1859–1862; U.S. House, 1863–1876; U.S. Senate, 1876–1881; U.S. Secretary of State, 1881 & 1889–1892; Candidate for President, 1884)

537.1 After The Voting Is Through. w. "By Demo." m. "Tune — *Over The Garden Wall*." In: *Cleveland & Hendricks Songster*, page 10. Copyright 1884 by E.Y. Landis. R/w/bl/gn/br drawing of Grover Cleveland, Thomas Hendricks, George "Washington," Thomas "Jefferson," Andrew "Jackson," ribbons, geometric designs. 64pp. [M-230]. [Crew/GC-46].

537.2 All They Want's An Office To Fill. w. Dan Yell. m. "Tune — *Pop Goes The Weasel*." In: *Cleveland & Hendricks Songster*, page 34. Copyright 1884 by E.Y. Landis. R/w/bl/gn/br drawing of Grover Cleveland, Thomas Hendricks, George "Washington," Thomas "Jefferson," Andrew "Jackson," ribbons, geometric designs. 64pp. [M-230]. [Crew/GC-46].

537.3 American Crow. w. No composer indicated. m. Notation. "Male Voices." In: *True Blue Republican Campaign Songs For 1892*, page 12. Published by [V-1: Oliver Ditson Company, Boston, MA] [V-2: The S. Brainard's Son's Company, Chicago, IL]. 1892. [5⅜" × 7¼"]. Bl/bk litho of Benjamin F. Harrison, eagle, flag, geometric designs. 36pp. [M-307]. [Crew/BFH-47].

537.4 American Workman's Battle Song. w. Mrs. M. Jennie Porter. m. "Air — *The Marseilles Hymn*." In: *Blaine And Logan Campaign Song-Book*, page 17. e. Prof. F. Widdows. Published by The Republican National Committee, New York, NY. 1884. [4⅜" × 5⅚"]. [V-1: Bk/y] [V-2: Pk/bk] litho of James G. Blaine and John A. Logan. "From the School — House to the Cabinet, From the Cabin to the Senate." 52pp. [M-251]. [Crew/JGB-32].

537.5 Answer To Fred Harris's 'Who Wears The Next Presidential Shoes?' w. J.W.B. Siders. m. No tune indicated. In: *Blaine And Logan Campaign Songster*, page 8. Published by American News Company, New York, NY. 1884. 36pp. [M-249]. [Crew/JGB-84].

537.6 Are The Democrats Hungry? w. No composer indicated. m. Notation. In: *The People's Songs For Blaine & Logan*, page 26. Published by Acme Publishing Bureau, J.C.O. Redington, General Manager, No. 252 Broadway, New York, NY. Copyright 1884 by J.C.O. Redington. [4⅞" × 6⅝"]. B/w litho of James G. Blaine. "Adopted by the General Republican Committees in New York City and elsewhere." "Adapted for every Voice in the Glorious Land of Freedom. All the Nation may Sing." "Come, join that Columbia's blessings increase, All Singing for Liberty, Glory and Peace." "Acme Songs." 32pp. [M-246]. [Crew/JGB-45].

537.7 [Arise! Ye Brave, Your Country Calls You] (Rallying Song). w. No composer indicated. m. "Air—*The Marseillaise.*" In: *P.T. Schultz & Co's Blaine And Logan Bugle Call*, page 23. Published by P.T. Schultz & Company, No. 172 Race Street, Cincinnati, OH. 1881. [1884 Edition]. [5⅞" × 7⅝"]. Bk/gn litho of James G. Blaine and John A. Logan, flags and eagle, geometric design border. 36pp. [M-245]. [Crew/JGB-67].

537.8 Away To The Polls. w. No composer indicated. m. "Air—*O Come, Come Away.*" In: *Blaine And Logan Songster*, page 7. Published by Thomas Hunter, Philadelphia, PA. 1884. [5½" × 7¼"]. N/c litho of Abraham Lincoln and James Garfield—"Our Martyred Presidents." Br/w litho of James G. Blaine—"Our Next President," and John A. Logan—"Our Next Vice-President," George Washington, Ulysses S. Grant. 68pp [M-237]. [Crew/JGB-35].

537.9 The Banner Of Blaine And Logan. w. No composer indicated. m. "Air—*Flag Of The Constellation.*" In: *Blaine And Logan Campaign Songster*, page 40. Published by John Church & Company, Cincinnati, OH. 1884. [4⅞" × 5¹³⁄₁₆"]. Y/bk non-pictorial geometric design border. "Including Biographical Sketches & Constitution for Campaign Clubs." 52pp. [M-233?]. [Crew/JGB-29].

537.10 The Banner Of Protection. w. A. De Leur. m. "Tune—*Marching Through Georgia.*" In: *Republican Club Campaign Song Book For 1888*, page 24. a. Thomas Byron. Published by Protection Publication Company, South Central Street, Chicago, IL. 1888. [6⅛" × 8⅞"]. Be/bk litho of Benjamin F. Harrison—"For President" and Levi P. Morton—"For Vice-President," eagle, flags, geometric designs. "Thirty Rousing Songs Written to Popular Airs." 36pp. [M-257]. [Crew/BFH-20].

537.11 The Battle (Marching Song). w.m. R.E.D. a. Prof. F.L. Morley. Published by George S. Deer, Wabash Avenue, Chicago, IL. 1884. B/w litho of a "Ballot Box" located under a large cupola which is topped with an eagle holding a ribbon inscribed "E Pluribus Unum," crowd of men carrying "Blaine" ballots. 6pp. Pages 2 and 6: Blank. [Crew/JGB-107].

537.12 The Battle Cry. w. J.W.B. Siders. m. "Air—*Battle Cry Of Freedom.*" In: *Blaine And Logan Campaign Songster*, page 10. Published by American News Company, New York, NY. 1884. 36pp. [M-249]. [Crew/JGB-84].

537.13 Battle Cry Of Freedom. w. No composer indicated. m. *Battle Cry Of Freedom.* B/w litho of "Maj.-Gen. John A. Logan." In: *The Good Old Songs We Used To Sing, ('61 to '65)* [Song Book], page 23. Published by O.H. Oldroyd, Lincoln Homestead, Springfield, IL. [ca. 1880]. [5¹¹⁄₁₆" × 8⅝"]. Ma/bl litho from "Photo from Life—1864—General Ulysses S. Grant." 36pp. [Crew/JGB-100].

537.14 Battle Cry Of Freemen. w. No composer indicated. m. "Air—*Battle Cry Of Freedom.*" In: *Blaine And Logan Campaign Songster*, page 36. Published by John Church & Company, Cincinnati, OH. 1884. [4⅞" × 5¹³⁄₁₆"]. Y/bk non-pictorial geometric design border. "Including Biographical Sketches & Constitution for Campaign Clubs." 52pp. [M-233?]. [Crew/JGB-29].

537.15 Ben And Levi. w. No composer indicated. m. "Air—*Solomon And Levi.*" In: *Democratic Song Book For The Campaign Of 1888*, page 8. c. John R. East. Published by John R. East, Bloomington, IN. 1888. [4¼" × 5¹³⁄₁₆"]. Bl/bl litho of Grover Cleveland and Allen Thurman. "Price 10 cents, postage prepaid, Liberal Discounts to Dealers." 20pp. [Crew/GC-140].

537.16 The Betters In Our Block. w. Frank N. Scott. m. "Air—*Babies In Our Block.*" In: *P.T. Schultz & Co's Blaine And Logan Bugle Call*, page 8. Published by P.T. Schultz & Company, No. 172 Race Street, Cincinnati, OH. 1881. [1884 Edition]. [5⅞" × 7⅝"]. Bk/gn litho of James G. Blaine and John A. Logan, flags and eagle, geometric design border. 36pp. [M-245]. [Crew/JGB-67].

537.17 The Big I. w. W. Gray. m. Air—*What Has Caused This Great Commotion.* In: *Republican Club Campaign Song Book For 1888*, page 12. a. Thomas Byron. Published by Protection Publication Company, South Central Street, Chicago, IL. 1888. [6⅛" × 8⅞"]. Be/bk litho of Benjamin F. Harrison—"For President" and Levi P. Morton—"For Vice-President," eagle, flags, geometric designs. "Thirty Rousing Songs Written to Popular Airs." 36pp. [M-257]. [Crew/BFH-20].

537.18 Blaine And Logan (A Campaign Song). w. Fred Layton. w. "Air—*The Star Spangled Banner.*" In: *Blaine And Logan Campaign Songster*, page 17. Published by American News Company, New York, NY. 1884. 36pp. [M-249]. [Crew/JGB-84].

537.19 Blaine And Logan Rallying Song. w.m. Chas. B. Morrell. Published by Geo. D. Newhall Co., Cincinnati, OH. 1884. B/w geometric design and line border. "Republican Campaign Songs." "The Newest, Sprightliest and the Best." List of other songs in the series. [Crew/JGB-101].

537.20 Blaine And Logan Song. w. N.B. Milliken. m. "Air—*John Brown.*" In: *Blaine And Logan Campaign Song-Book*, page 18. e. Prof. F. Widdows. Published by The Republican National Committee, New York, NY. 1884. [4⅜" × 5¹¹⁄₁₆"]. [V-1: Bk/y] [V-2: Pk/bk] litho of James G. Blaine and John A. Logan. "From the School—House to the Cabinet, From the Cabin to the Senate." 52pp. [M-251]. [Crew/JGB-32].

537.21 Blaine And Logan, Too. w.m. No composers indicated. m. Notation. In: *Blaine And Logan Campaign Songster*, page 21. Published by John Church & Company, Cincinnati, OH. 1884. [4⅞" × 5¹³⁄₁₆"]. Y/bk non-pictorial geometric design border. "Including Biographical Sketches & Constitution for Campaign Clubs." 52pp. [M-233?]. [Crew/JGB-29].

537.22 Blaine And Victory. w. No composer indicated. m. "Air—*Silver Threads, etc.*" In: *Beulah's Blaine*

And Logan Original Campaign Song Book 1884, page 9. Printed and Published by Birnie Paper Company, Springfield, MA. 1884. [4" × 5¾"]. Gy/bk litho of James G. Blaine and John A. Logan, eagle, flags, shield, line border. 36pp. [M-232]. [Crew/JGB-41].

537.23 Blaine And Victory. w. Capt. P. Kelly. m. "Air—*Wearing Of The Green*." In: *Blaine And Logan Campaign Song-Book*, page 34. e. Prof. F. Widdows. Published by The Republican National Committee, New York, NY. 1884. [4⅜" × 5$^{11}/_{16}$"]. [V-1: Bk/y] [V-2: Pk/bk] litho of James G. Blaine and John A. Logan. "From the School—House to the Cabinet, From the Cabin to the Senate." 52pp. [M-251]. [Crew/JGB-32].

537.24 The Blaine Army. w. No composer indicated. m. "Tune—*Auld Lang Syne*." In: *The People's Songs For Blaine & Logan*, page 28. Published by Acme Publishing Bureau, J.C.O. Redington, General Manager, No. 252 Broadway, New York, NY. Copyright 1884 by J.C.O. Redington. [4⅞" × 6⅝"]. B/w litho of James G. Blaine. "Adopted by the General Republican Committees in New York City and elsewhere." "Adapted for every Voice in the Glorious Land of Freedom. All the Nation may Sing." "Come, join that Columbia's blessings increase, All Singing for Liberty, Glory and Peace." "Acme Songs." 32pp. [M-246]. [Crew/JGB-45].

537.25 Blaine At The White House Door. w. "By Demo." m. "Tune—*Old Joe*." In: *Cleveland & Hendricks Songster*, page 19. Copyright 1884 by E.Y. Landis. R/w/bl/gn/br drawing of Grover Cleveland, Thomas Hendricks, George "Washington," Thomas "Jefferson," Andrew "Jackson," ribbons, geometric designs. 64pp. [M-230]. [Crew/GC-46].

537.26 Blaine, Blaine, Blaine Of Maine. m. Ray. Published by John Church & Co., Cincinnati, OH. 1884. "John Church & Co's Collection of the Latest and Most Popular Brass & Reed Band Music arranged to suit any band from 8 to 20 performers. Full parts set for band]. [Crew/JGB-109].

537.27 Blaine From Maine. w.m. Malcolm S. Gordon. In: *Blaine And Logan Campaign Songster*, page 4. Published by John Church & Company, Cincinnati, OH. 1884. [4⅞" × 5$^{13}/_{16}$"]. Y/bk non-pictorial geometric design border. "Including Biographical Sketches & Constitution for Campaign Clubs." 52pp. [M-233?]. [Crew/JGB-29].

537.28 Blaine Goes Marching On. m. Wm. Howard Doane. Published by Geo. D. Newhall Co., Cincinnati, OH. 1884. B/w geometric design and line border. "Republican Campaign Songs." "The Newest, Sprightliest and the Best." List of other songs in the series. [Crew/JGB-101].

537.29 Blaine Is Our Man. w. No composer indicated. m. "Air—*Oh! Come, Come Away*." In: *Blaine And Logan Campaign Songster*, page 18. Published by John Church & Company, Cincinnati, OH. 1884. [4⅞" × 5$^{13}/_{16}$"]. Y/bk non-pictorial geometric design border. "Including Biographical Sketches & Constitution for Campaign Clubs." 52pp. [M-233?]. [Crew/JGB-29].

537.30 Blaine Is The Man. w.m. No composers indicated. m. Notation. In: *Blaine And Logan Campaign Songster*, page 14. Published by John Church & Company, Cincinnati, OH. 1884. [4⅞" × 5$^{13}/_{16}$"]. Y/bk non-pictorial geometric design border. "Including Biographical Sketches & Constitution for Campaign Clubs." 52pp. [M-233?]. [Crew/JGB-29].

537.31 Blaine J. Of Maine. w. No composer indicated. m. "Tune—*O Come, Come Away*." In: *Cleveland & Hendricks Songster*, page 31. Copyright 1884 by E.Y. Landis. R/w/bl/gn/br drawing of Grover Cleveland, Thomas Hendricks, George "Washington," Thomas "Jefferson," Andrew "Jackson," ribbons, geometric designs. 64pp. [M-230]. [Crew/GC-46].

537.32 Blaine, Logan, Victory (Song And Chorus). w.m. J.M. Jolley. Published by John Church & Co., No. 66 West Fourth Street, Cincinnati, OH. 1884. Non-pictorial. 8pp. Pages 7 and 8: Advertising. [Crew/JGB-102].

537.33 Blaine's Boom. w. No composer indicated. m. "Air—*Cradle's Empty—Baby's Gone*." In: *Beulah's Blaine And Logan Original Campaign Song Book 1884*, page 23. Printed and Published by Birnie Paper Company, Springfield, MA. 1884. [4" × 5¾"]. Gy/bk litho of James G. Blaine and John A. Logan, eagle, flags, shield, line border. 36pp. [M-232]. [Crew/JGB-41].

537.34 Blaine's Rallying Song. w. No composer indicated. m. "Air—*Marching Through Georgia*." In: *Blaine And Logan Campaign Songster*, page 42. Published by John Church & Company, Cincinnati, OH. 1884. [4⅞" × 5$^{13}/_{16}$"]. Y/bk non-pictorial geometric design border. "Including Biographical Sketches & Constitution for Campaign Clubs." 52pp. [M-233?]. [Crew/JGB-29].

537.35 Blaine's The People's Choice. w. J.W.B. Siders. m. "Air—*Hail Jerusalem Morn*." In: *Blaine And Logan Campaign Songster*, page 9. Published by American News Company, New York, NY. 1884. 36pp. [M-249]. [Crew/JGB-84].

537.36 Blow The Bugle Call Again. w. Mose M. Bigue. m. No tune indicated. "Written for the Mississippi Republican Association." In: *Blaine And Logan Campaign Song-Book*, page 26. e. Prof. F. Widdows. Published by The Republican National Committee, New York, NY. 1884. [4⅜" × 5$^{11}/_{16}$"]. [V-1: Bk/y] [V-2: Pk/bk] litho of James G. Blaine and John A. Logan. "From the School—House to the Cabinet, From the Cabin to the Senate." 52pp. [M-251]. [Crew/JGB-32].

537.37 Bound To Vote Down Wrong. w. No composer indicated. m. "Air—*Clear The Way*." In: *National Greenback Labor Songster*, page 45. c. B.M. Lawrence, M.D. Published by D.M. Bennett, Liberal and Scientific Publishing House, No. 141 8th Street, New York, NY. 1878. [3¾" × 6¼"]. Gn/bk litho of arm with hammer. 52pp. Page 3: "Containing Original, Practical, Patriotic, Progressive and Stirring Songs, Adapted to the Most Popular Airs in addition to which will be found choice and humorous readings, including 'The Bankers and I Are Out,' 'Men and Monkeys,' 'What We Want,' &c."

537.38 Boys In Blue. w. J.W.B. Siders. w. "Air—*Hold The Fort*." In: *Blaine And Logan Campaign Songster*, page 15. Published by American News Company, New York, NY. 1884. 36pp. [M-249]. [Crew/JGB-84].

537.39 Boys In Blue. w. Peter Maithre. m. "Air—

Hold The Fort." In: *Blaine And Logan Campaign Song-Book*, page 16. e. Prof. F. Widdows. Published by The Republican National Committee, New York, NY. 1884. [4⅜" × 5$^{11}/_{16}$"]. [V-1: Bk/y] [V-2: Pk/bk] litho of James G. Blaine and John A. Logan. "From the School — House to the Cabinet, From the Cabin to the Senate." 52pp. [M-251]. [Crew/JGB-32].

537.40 Brave Hancock Is The Man (A Campaign Song And Chorus). w. Colonel T.G. Morrison "(Formerly of the 12th and 66th Regts., Ind. Inf.)." m. William B. Richardson. Published by John Church & Company, No. 66 West 4th Street, Cincinnati, OH. 1880. B/w litho of Winfield S. Hancock, star border. "Democratic Campaign Music." List of other songs in series. 6pp. Page 6: Blank. [Crew/WSH-19].

537.41 Brave Hosts Are Coming. w. No composer indicated. m. "Air — *Tramp, Tramp, Tramp.*" In: *Beulah's Blaine And Logan Original Campaign Song Book 1884*, page 29. Printed and Published by Birnie Paper Company, Springfield, MA. 1884. [4" × 5¾"]. Gy/bk litho of James G. Blaine and John A. Logan, eagle, flags, shield, line border. 36pp. [M-232]. [Crew/JGB-41].

537.42 Bring Out Your Campaign Banners. w. "By Demo." m. "Tune — *Marching Through Georgia.*" In: *Cleveland & Hendricks Songster*, page 45. Copyright 1884 by E.Y. Landis. R/w/bl/gn/br drawing of Grover Cleveland, Thomas Hendricks, George "Washington," Thomas "Jefferson," Andrew "Jackson," ribbons, geometric designs. 64pp. [M-230]. [Crew/GC-46].

537.43 Bring The Starry Banner Boys. w.m. A.T. Gorham, Oliver Ditson & Co., 451 Washington Street, Boston, MA. 1884. Non-pictorial geometric designs. "Dedicated to The Grand Old Party." "Blaine And Logan Rallying Song." 6pp. Pages 2 and 6: Blank. [Crew/JAG-108].

537.44 [Bring Your Honest Hearts, My Boys] (Rallying Song). w. No composer indicated. "Air — *Marching Through Georgia.*" In: *P.T. Schultz & Co's Blaine And Logan Bugle Call*, page 20. Published by P.T. Schultz & Company, No. 172 Race Street, Cincinnati, OH. 1881. [1884 Edition]. [5⅞" × 7⅝"]. Bk/gn litho of James G. Blaine and John A. Logan, flags and eagle, geometric design border. 36pp. [M-245]. [Crew/JGB-67].

537.45 By Jingo! w. "N.Y. Sun." m. J.B. Herbert. "Male Voices." In: *True Blue Republican Campaign Songs For 1896*, page 2. c. J.B. Herbert. Published by The S. Brainard's Sons Company, Chicago, IL. 1896. [5⅜" × 6⅞"]. R/w/b drawing of crossed flags, wreath, ribbons. Bl/w photo of "Hon. Wm. McKinley." "Protection." 36pp. [M-328]. [Crew/WM-169].

537.46 Campaign Barbers. w. No composer indicated. m. "Arr. By Tariff Reform." In: *Red Hot Democratic Campaign Songs For 1888*, page 2. e. John Bunyon Herbert. Published by The S. Brainard's Sons Company, Chicago, IL. 1888. [5⅜" × 7$^{7}/_{16}$"]. R/bk geometric designs. 36pp. [M-294]. [Crew/GC-141].

537.47 Campaign Medley. w. Geo. M. White. m. William E. Chandler. Published by Russell Brothers, No. 126 Tremont Street, Boston, MA. B/w lithos of James G. Blaine and John A. Logan, lyre, wreath. "Russell's Musical Library." "Campaign Songs, 1884." 4pp. Page 2: "Respectfully dedicated to Mrs. Nancy Bourbon, in grateful memory of the happy union consummated at Chicago, July 11th, 1884." [Crew/JGB-104].

537.48 Campaign Song No. 1. w. George H. Leithead. m. "Air — *Hoist Up The Flag.*" No publisher indicated. [5" × 7½"]. Non-pictorial. "1884." "Copyright secured August 18th, 1884." 2pp. Page 2: Blank.

537.49 Chalk It Down. w. "By Demo." m. "Tune — *Bobbin' Round.*" In: *Cleveland & Hendricks Songster*, page 20. Copyright 1884 by E.Y. Landis. R/w/bl/gn/br drawing of Grover Cleveland, Thomas Hendricks, George "Washington," Thomas "Jefferson," Andrew "Jackson," ribbons, geometric designs. 64pp. [M-230]. [Crew/GC-46].

537.50 Champions Of Liberty. w. No composer indicated. m. "Air — *America.*" In: *Blaine And Logan Songster*, page 3. Published by Thomas Hunter, Philadelphia, PA. 1884. [5½" × 7¼"]. N/c litho of Abraham Lincoln and James Garfield — "Our Martyred Presidents." Br/w litho of James G. Blaine — "Our Next President," and John A. Logan — "Our Next Vice-President," George Washington, Ulysses S. Grant. 68pp [M-237]. [Crew/JGB-35].

537.51 Cheer, Freemen, Cheer! w. No composers indicated. m. "Air — *Marseilles Hymn.*" In: *Blaine And Logan Campaign Songster*, page 23. Published by John Church & Company, Cincinnati, OH. 1884. [4⅞" × 5$^{13}/_{16}$"]. Y/bk non-pictorial geometric design border. "Including Biographical Sketches & Constitution for Campaign Clubs." 52pp. [M-233?]. [Crew/JGB-29].

537.52 Choice Of The Fearless Free. w. No composers indicated. m. "Air — *America.*" In: *Blaine And Logan Campaign Songster*, page 22. Published by John Church & Company, Cincinnati, OH. 1884. [4⅞" × 5$^{13}/_{16}$"]. Y/bk non-pictorial geometric design border. "Including Biographical Sketches & Constitution for Campaign Clubs." 52pp. [M-233?]. [Crew/JGB-29].

537.53 Cleveland Will Be Beaten. w. No composer indicated. m. "Air — *There's Music In The Air, Boys.*" In: *Beulah's Blaine And Logan Original Campaign Song Book 1884*, page 4. Printed and Published by Birnie Paper Company, Springfield, MA. 1884. [4" × 5¾"]. Gy/bk litho of James G. Blaine and John A. Logan, eagle, flags, shield, line border. 36pp. [M-232]. [Crew/JGB-41].

537.54 Climbing Jacob's Ladder. w. J.W.B. Siders. w. No tune indicated. In: *Blaine And Logan Campaign Songster*, page 22. Published by American News Company, New York, NY. 1884. 36pp. [M-249]. [Crew/JGB-84].

537.55 Come Gather Round. w. No composer indicated. m. "Air — *Auld Lang Syne.*" In: *Blaine And Logan Campaign Songster*, page 28. Published by John Church & Company, Cincinnati, OH. 1884. [4⅞" × 5$^{13}/_{16}$"]. Y/bk non-pictorial geometric design border. "Including Biographical Sketches & Constitution for Campaign Clubs." 52pp. [M-233?]. [Crew/JGB-29].

537.56 Come March With The Union Blues. w. No composer indicated. m. "Air — *Life On The Ocean Wave.*" In: *Blaine And Logan Songster*, page 8. Published by Thomas Hunter, Philadelphia, PA. 1884. [5½" × 7¼"]. N/c litho of Abraham Lincoln and James Garfield — "Our Martyred Presidents." Br/w litho of James G. Blaine — "Our Next President," and John A.

Logan — "Our Next Vice-President," George Washington, Ulysses S. Grant. 68pp [M-237]. [Crew/JGB-35].

537.57 Come Rally For Blaine And For Logan. w. M.S. Gordon. m. "Air — *Old Rosin The Bow.*" In: *Blaine And Logan Campaign Songster*, page 3. Published by John Church & Company, Cincinnati, OH. 1884. [4⅞" × 5¹³⁄₁₆"]. Y/bk non-pictorial geometric design border. "Including Biographical Sketches & Constitution for Campaign Clubs." 52pp. [M-233?]. [Crew/JGB-29].

537.58 Come, Wake Up, Voters. w. No composer indicated. m. "Air — *The Girl I Left Behind Me.*" In: *Blaine And Logan Campaign Song-Book*, page 33. e. Prof. F. Widdows. Published by The Republican National Committee, New York, NY. 1884. [4⅜" × 5¹⁄₁₆"]. [V-1: Bk/y] [V-2: Pk/bk] litho of James G. Blaine and John A. Logan. "From the School — House to the Cabinet, From the Cabin to the Senate." 52pp. [M-251]. [Crew/JGB-32].

537.59 Come, Ye Freemen! w. No composer indicated. m. "Air — *Hail, Columbia.*" In: *Blaine And Logan Campaign Songster*, page 19. Published by John Church & Company, Cincinnati, OH. 1884. [4⅞" × 5¹³⁄₁₆"]. Y/bk non-pictorial geometric design border. "Including Biographical Sketches & Constitution for Campaign Clubs." 52pp. [M-233?]. [Crew/JGB-29].

537.60 The Democratic Leaders. w. No composer indicated. m. "Tune — *Yankee Doodle.*" In: *Cleveland & Hendricks Songster*, page 32. Copyright 1884 by E.Y. Landis. R/w/bl/gn/br drawing of Grover Cleveland, Thomas Hendricks, George "Washington," Thomas "Jefferson," Andrew "Jackson," ribbons, geometric designs. 64pp. [M-230]. [Crew/GC-46].

537.61 Dinna Ye Hear The Slogan? w. Prof. F. Widdows. m. "Air — *Johnny Comes Marching Home.*" In: *Blaine And Logan Campaign Song-Book*, page 11. e. Prof. F. Widdows. Published by The Republican National Committee, New York, NY. 1884. [4⅜" × 5¹⁄₁₆"]. [V-1: Bk/y] [V-2: Pk/bk] litho of James G. Blaine and John A. Logan. "From the School — House to the Cabinet, From the Cabin to the Senate." 52pp. [M-251]. [Crew/JGB-32].

537.62 Do You See Our Banner Floating. w. No composer indicated. m. "Air — *Comin' Through The Rye.*" In: *Blaine And Logan Campaign Songster*, page 27. Published by John Church & Company, Cincinnati, OH. 1884. [4⅞" × 5¹³⁄₁₆"]. Y/bk non-pictorial geometric design border. "Including Biographical Sketches & Constitution for Campaign Clubs." 52pp. [M-233?]. [Crew/JGB-29].

537.63 Du-Da. w. No composer indicated. m. "Tune — *Camptown Races.*" In: *Red Hot Democratic Campaign Songs For 1892*, page 24. c. John Bunyon Herbert. Published by The S. Brainard's Sons Company, Chicago, IL. 1892. [5½" × 7¼"]. R/bk litho of Grover Cleveland on a banner, Capitol building, marchers, geometric design border. 36pp. [M-299]. [Crew/GC-82].

537.64 Early In The Morning. w. John H. Sarchet. m. Arnold von Schilling. Published by Geo. D. Newhall Co., Cincinnati, OH. 1884. B/w geometric design and line border. "Republican Campaign Songs." "The Newest, Sprightliest and the Best." List of other songs in the series. 4pp. Page 4: Advertising. [Crew/JGB-101]. [AMC].

537.65 Election Is Certain For Blaine. w. No composer indicated. m. Notation. In: *The People's Songs For Blaine & Logan*, page 14. Published by Acme Publishing Bureau, J.C.O. Redington, General Manager, No. 252 Broadway, New York, NY. Copyright 1884 by J.C.O. Redington. [4⅞" × 6⅝"]. B/w litho of James G. Blaine. "Adopted by the General Republican Committees in New York City and elsewhere." "Adapted for every Voice in the Glorious Land of Freedom. All the Nation may Sing." "Come, join that Columbia's blessings increase, All Singing for Liberty, Glory and Peace." "Acme Songs." 32pp. [M-246]. [Crew/JGB-45].

537.66 Fatherland, America. w. No composer indicated. m. "Air — *Maryland, My Maryland.*" In: *Tilden And Hendricks' Reform Songs (For The Centennial Campaign Of 1876)*, page 30. Published by The National Democratic Committee, Box 3637, New York, NY. 1876. [3⅞" × 5¹³⁄₁₆"]. Gn/bk litho of Samuel J. Tilden and Thomas A. Hendricks, geometric design border. 40pp. [M-203]. [Crew/SJT-21].

537.67 Fellow-Workers, Would You Know? w. J.G.W. m. "Tune — *Tramp, Tramp.*" In: *Young Republican Campaign Song Book*, page 55. c. Henry Camp. Published by the Brooklyn Young Republican Club, Brooklyn, NY. 1888. [4⅜" × 6½"]. R/w/b litho of a U.S. flag. "Campaign 1888." 100pp. Page 100: B/w lithos of Benjamin Harrison and Levi Morton. [M-258, 259]. [Crew/BFH-53].

537.68 Fling Out Your Broad Banner. w. No composer indicated. m. Notation. In: *The People's Songs For Blaine & Logan*, page 20. Published by Acme Publishing Bureau, J.C.O. Redington, General Manager, No. 252 Broadway, New York, NY. Copyright 1884 by J.C.O. Redington. [4⅞" × 6⅝"]. B/w litho of James G. Blaine. "Adopted by the General Republican Committees in New York City and elsewhere." "Adapted for every Voice in the Glorious Land of Freedom. All the Nation may Sing." "Come, join that Columbia's blessings increase, All Singing for Liberty, Glory and Peace." "Acme Songs." 32pp. [M-246]. [Crew/JGB-45].

537.69 For Blaine And Logan Still. w. No composer indicated. m. "Air — *Gay And Happy.*" In: *Blaine And Logan Campaign Song-Book*, page 22. e. Prof. F. Widdows. Published by The Republican National Committee, New York, NY. 1884. [4⅜" × 5¹⁄₁₆"]. [V-1: Bk/y] [V-2: Pk/bk] litho of James G. Blaine and John A. Logan. "From the School — House to the Cabinet, From the Cabin to the Senate." 52pp. [M-251]. [Crew/JGB-32].

537.70 For Blaine My Boys Hurrah! w. No composer indicated. m. "Air — *The Bonnie Blue Flag.*" In: *Blaine And Logan Campaign Songster*, page 29. Published by John Church & Company, Cincinnati, OH. 1884. [4⅞" × 5¹³⁄₁₆"]. Y/bk non-pictorial geometric design border. "Including Biographical Sketches & Constitution for Campaign Clubs." 52pp. [M-233?]. [Crew/JGB-29].

537.71 For Pity's Sake, Don't Breathe It (For Goodness Sake Be Mum) (Sparkling Topical Song). w.m. Monroe H. Rosenfeld. Published by Hitchcock's

Music Store, Sun Building, 166 Nassau Street, Opp. City Hall, New York, NY. 1884. B/w non-pictorial geometric designs. "The Great Hit of the Hour." 6pp. Page 2: Blank. Page 6: Advertising.

537.72 For Victory Again. w. No composer indicated. m. "Air—*Marching Through Georgia.*" In: *Blaine And Logan Songster*, page 20. Published by Thomas Hunter, Philadelphia, PA. 1884. [5½" × 7¼"]. N/c litho of Abraham Lincoln and James Garfield—"Our Martyred Presidents." Br/w litho of James G. Blaine—"Our Next President," and John A. Logan—"Our Next Vice-President," George Washington, Ulysses S. Grant. 68pp [M-237]. [Crew/JGB-35].

537.73 Forward, March! Republicans! (Drum Obbligato). w.m. George Findet. Published by Geo. D. Newhall Co., Cincinnati, OH. 1884. B/w geometric design and line border. "Republican Campaign Songs." "The Newest, Sprightliest and the Best." List of other songs in the series. [Crew/JGB-101].

537.74 Forward! See The White Plumes Waving! w. Frank P. Cleary, M.D. m. "Air—*Tramp, Tramp, The Boys Are Marching.*" In: *Blaine And Logan Campaign Song-Book*, page 15. e. Prof. F. Widdows. Published by The Republican National Committee, New York, NY. 1884. [4⅜" × 5¹¹⁄₁₆"]. [V-1: Bk/y] [V-2: Pk/bk] litho of James G. Blaine and John A. Logan. "From the School—House to the Cabinet, From the Cabin to the Senate." 52pp. [M-251]. [Crew/JGB-32].

537.75 Freeman's Shout For Freedom's Heroes. w. A. Wood. m. "Air—*Old Folks At Home.*" In: *Blaine And Logan Campaign Song-Book*, page 25. e. Prof. F. Widdows. Published by The Republican National Committee, New York, NY. 1884. [4⅜" × 5¹¹⁄₁₆"]. [V-1: Bk/y] [V-2: Pk/bk] litho of James G. Blaine and John A. Logan. "From the School—House to the Cabinet, From the Cabin to the Senate." 52pp. [M-251]. [Crew/JGB-32].

537.76 General Logan And The Fifteenth Army Corps. w. Capt. R.W. Burt, "76th Ohio V.V.I." m. "Tune—*The Kingdom Am A Comin.*" Published by Charles Magnus, No. 12 Frankfort Street, New York, NY. [ca. 1863]. [5" × 8"]. Non-pictorial bl/w geometric design border. Lines note paper. "Ten illustrated Songs on Notepaper, mailed to any Address on receipt of 50 cts." 2pp. Page 2: Blank. [Crew/JGB-112].

537.77 Give Us Blaine. m. W.L. Blumenschein. Published by Geo. D. Newhall Co., Cincinnati, OH. 1884. B/w geometric design and line border. "Republican Campaign Songs." "The Newest, Sprightliest and the Best." List of other songs in the series. [Crew/JGB-101].

537.78 Glory, Hallelujah! w. No composer indicated. m. "Tune—*John Brown.*" In: *Facts And Songs For The People*, page 17. Published by C.E. Bolton, Cleveland, OH. 1884. [5" × 7⅛"]. R/w/bl drawing of Miss Liberty, flag, scroll—"Vox populi, Vox Dei, 1884." 54pp. Pages 2 and 53: Advertising. Page 3: B/w photo of "Hon. James G. Blaine." Page 4: Photo of "Gen. John A. Logan." Page 5: Title—*Facts & Songs For The People Prepared Specially For Use In The Blaine And Logan Campaign.* [M-239]. [Crew/JGB-65].

537.79 Glory, Hallelujah! (Our Blaine & Logan Lead). w. No composer indicated. m. Tune—*Glory Hallelujah.* In: *The People's Songs For Blaine & Logan*, page 15. Published by Acme Publishing Bureau, J.C.O. Redington, General Manager, No. 252 Broadway, New York, NY. Copyright 1884 by J.C.O. Redington. [4⅞" × 6⅝"]. B/w litho of James G. Blaine. "Adopted by the General Republican Committees in New York City and elsewhere." "Adapted for every Voice in the Glorious Land of Freedom. All the Nation may Sing." "Come, join that Columbia's blessings increase, All Singing for Liberty, Glory and Peace." "Acme Songs." 32pp. [M-246]. [Crew/JGB-45].

537.80 Good-Bye Cleveland, Good-Bye. w. J.W.B. Siders. m. "Air—*Good-Bye, My Lover, Good-bye.*" In: *Blaine And Logan Campaign Songster*, page 25. Published by American News Company, New York, NY. 1884. 36pp. [M-249]. [Crew/JGB-84].

537.81 Good Bye, Old Grover, Good Bye. w. A.A. Rowley. m. "Air—*Good-Bye, My Lover, Good-Bye.*" In: *Republican Campaign Songs*, page 2. w. A.A. Rowley "(Beloit, Kas.)." Published by The Western News Company, Chicago, IL. 1888. [5¼" × 7½"]. B/w litho of "The Author, in '63, 17th Illinois Cav." "Original, Pointed and Spicy ... Set to Old Familiar Tunes, Suitable for Glee Clubs and Marching Clubs." "Look at it and you will buy it." 36pp. Page 3: Index. "Composed for the Campaign of 1888 and Set to Old Familiar Airs, Suitable for Glee Clubs and Campaign Clubs." "Respectfully Dedicated to my Comrades of the Civil War, who still vote the way they fought—A.A. Rowley, Beloit, Kan." [M-283]. [Crew/BFH-64].

537.82 Good-Bye, White House, Good Bye. w. C.E. Morris. m. "Air—*Good-Bye My Lover, Good-Bye.*" In: *Acme Songs, Republican Glee Book, And Cartridge Box Of Truth* (Campaign of 1888), page 33. Published by The Acme Publishing Bureau, J.C.O. Redington, General Manager, No. 35 University Avenue, Syracuse, NY. Copyright 1888 by J.C.O. Redington. [5⅝" × 6¹³⁄₁₆"]. Gy/bk lithos of eagle, shield, tent, flag, soldiers, Uncle Sam. "With Music and 20 Illustrations by Nast and others." "Price 10 cents." "Only Book Prepared by Soldiers, The Only Illustrated Campaign Glee Book Ever Printed." "With Music and 20 Illustrations." "Illustrated by Nast and Others." "A Filled Pocket Haversack of Loyalty, Glory, Song, Fun and Facts for Every Individual, Whether Singer or Not." 68pp. [M-255]. [Crew/BFH-25].

537.83 Grover's Lament. w. No composer indicated. m. "Tune—*Swing Low, Sweet Chariot.*" In: *Young Republican Campaign Song Book*, page 40. c. Henry Camp. Published by the Brooklyn Young Republican Club, Brooklyn, NY. 1888. [4⅜" × 6½"]. R/w/b litho of a U.S. flag. "Campaign 1888." 100pp. Page 100: B/w lithos of Benjamin Harrison and Levi Morton. [M-258, 259]. [Crew/BFH-53].

537.84 Gwine To Git Dar. w.m. No composer or tune indicated. In: *The Harrison Log-Cabin Song Book Of 1840*, page 54. e. O.C. Hooper. Published by A.H. Smythe, Columbus, OH. 1888. [4¹⁵⁄₁₆" × 5¾"]. Y/bk litho of log cabin—"1840—1888." "Revised for the Campaign of 1888, with Numerous New Songs to Patriotic Airs." [V-2: "Music Edition"]. 68pp. [M-272, 273]. [Crew/BFH-23].

537.85 Hail To The Plumed Knight! And Logan! w. Col. Thad. K. Preuss. m. "Air—*Columbia, The Gem Of The Ocean.*" In: *Blaine And Logan Campaign*

Song-Book, page 8. e. Prof. F. Widdows. Published by The Republican National Committee, New York, NY. 1884. [4⅜" × 5¹¹⁄₁₆"]. [V-1: Bk/y] [V-2: Pk/bk] litho of James G. Blaine and John A. Logan. "From the School — House to the Cabinet, From the Cabin to the Senate." 52pp. [M-251]. [Crew/JGB-32].

537.86 Hayes. w. No composer indicated. m. "Air — *Life On The Ocean Wave*." In: *Hayes & Wheeler Campaign Song Book (For The Centennial Year)*, page 37. Published by the American News Company, Nos. 117, 119, 121, 123 Nassau Street, New York, NY. 1876. [3⅞" × 6⅝"]. Y/bk litho of Rutherford B. Hayes and William A. Wheeler, liberty cap, geometric designs. 74pp. [M-193]. [Crew/RBH-11].

537.87 Hear! Hear The Shout. w. No composer indicated. m. "Air — *Tramp, Tramp, Tramp*." In: *Blaine And Logan Campaign Songster*, page 17. Published by John Church & Company, Cincinnati, OH. 1884. [4⅞" × 5¹³⁄₁₆"]. Y/bk non-pictorial geometric design border. "Including Biographical Sketches & Constitution for Campaign Clubs." 52pp. [M-233?]. [Crew/JGB-29].

537.88 Here The Joyful Song. w. No composer indicated. m. "Air — *Battle Cry Of Freedom*." In: *Blaine And Logan Songster*, page 16. Published by Thomas Hunter, Philadelphia, PA. 1884. [5½" × 7¼"]. N/c litho of Abraham Lincoln and James Garfield — "Our Martyred Presidents." Br/w litho of James G. Blaine — "Our Next President," and John A. Logan — "Our Next Vice-President," George Washington, Ulysses S. Grant. 68pp [M-237]. [Crew/JGB-35].

537.89 Hold The Fort For Blaine And Logan. w. No composer indicated. m. "Air — *Hold The Fort*." In: *Blaine And Logan Campaign Songster*, page 30. Published by John Church & Company, Cincinnati, OH. 1884. [4⅞" × 5¹³⁄₁₆"]. Y/bk non-pictorial geometric design border. "Including Biographical Sketches & Constitution for Campaign Clubs." 52pp. [M-233?]. [Crew/JGB-29].

537.90 Hold The Helm. w. Mouse-in-the-Corner. m. "Air — *Hold The Fort*." In: *Blaine And Logan Campaign Song-Book*, page 12. e. Prof. F. Widdows. Published by The Republican National Committee, New York, NY. 1884. [4⅜" × 5¹¹⁄₁₆"]. [V-1: Bk/y] [V-2: Pk/bk] litho of James G. Blaine and John A. Logan. "From the School — House to the Cabinet, From the Cabin to the Senate." 52pp. [M-251]. [Crew/JGB-32].

537.91 How Bright To-night. w. No composer indicated. m. "Air — *Flag Of Constellation*." In: *Blaine And Logan Campaign Songster*, page 37. Published by John Church & Company, Cincinnati, OH. 1884. [4⅞" × 5¹³⁄₁₆"]. Y/bk non-pictorial geometric design border. "Including Biographical Sketches & Constitution for Campaign Clubs." 52pp. [M-233?]. [Crew/JGB-29].

537.92 Hurrah! Boys, Hurrah! w. C.L.S. m. "Air — *Come, Come Away*." In: *P.T. Schultz & Co's Blaine And Logan Bugle Call*, page 9. Published by P.T. Schultz & Company, No. 172 Race Street, Cincinnati, OH. 1881. [1884 Edition]. [5⅞" × 7⅝"]. Bk/gn litho of James G. Blaine and John A. Logan, flags and eagle, geometric design border. 36pp. [M-245]. [Crew/JGB-67].

537.93 Hurrah For Blaine And Logan. w. F.N.S. m. "Music — *Soldier's Farewell*." In: *P.T. Schultz & Co's Blaine And Logan Bugle Call*, page 6. Published by P.T. Schultz & Company, No. 172 Race Street, Cincinnati, OH. 1881. [1884 Edition]. [5⅞" × 7⅝"]. Bk/gn litho of James G. Blaine and John A. Logan, flags and eagle, geometric design border. 36pp. [M-245]. [Crew/JGB-67].

537.94 Hurrah For James G. Blaine. w. No composer indicated. m. "Tune — *Come Now, My Merry, Happy Boy*." In: *The People's Songs For Blaine & Logan*, page 19. Published by Acme Publishing Bureau, J.C.O. Redington, General Manager, No. 252 Broadway, New York, NY. Copyright 1884 by J.C.O. Redington. [4⅞" × 6⅝"]. B/w litho of James G. Blaine. "Adopted by the General Republican Committees in New York City and elsewhere." "Adapted for every Voice in the Glorious Land of Freedom. All the Nation may Sing." "Come, join that Columbia's blessings increase, All Singing for Liberty, Glory and Peace." "Acme Songs." 32pp. [M-246]. [Crew/JGB-45].

537.95 Hurrah For The Plumed Knight. w. C.L.S. m. "Air — *A Life On The Ocean Wave*." In: *P.T. Schultz & Co's Blaine And Logan Bugle Call*, page 17. Published by P.T. Schultz & Company, No. 172 Race Street, Cincinnati, OH. 1881. [1884 Edition]. [5⅞" × 7⅝"]. Bk/gn litho of James G. Blaine and John A. Logan, flags and eagle, geometric design border. 36pp. [M-245]. [Crew/JGB-67].

537.96 Hurrah! Hurrah! w. No composer indicated. m. Notation. In: *Blaine And Logan Campaign Songster*, page 12. Published by John Church & Company, Cincinnati, OH. 1884. [4⅞" × 5¹³⁄₁₆"]. Y/bk non-pictorial geometric design border. "Including Biographical Sketches & Constitution for Campaign Clubs." 52pp. [M-233?]. [Crew/JGB-29].

537.97 In A Few Days. w. No composer indicated. m. "Music — *Mary Blane*." On 33⅓ rpm LP: *Sing Along With Millard Fillmore*. Life Records #RB 360 T2/#61 P3. "The Life Album of Presidential Campaign Songs." 1964.

537.98 In November. w. J.W.B. Siders. m. "Air — *In The Morning By The Bright Light*." In: *Blaine And Logan Campaign Songster*, page 23. Published by American News Company, New York, NY. 1884. 36pp. [M-249]. [Crew/JGB-84].

537.99 In Praise Of Blaine Of Maine. w. No composer indicated. "Air — *When Johnny Comes Marching Home*." In: *Blaine And Logan Campaign Song-Book*, page 31. e. Prof. F. Widdows. Published by The Republican National Committee, New York, NY. 1884. [4⅜" × 5¹¹⁄₁₆"]. [V-1: Bk/y] [V-2: Pk/bk] litho of James G. Blaine and John A. Logan. "From the School — House to the Cabinet, From the Cabin to the Senate." 52pp. [M-251]. [Crew/JGB-32].

537.100 In The Morning At The White House. w. J.E. Miller. m. "Air — *In The Morning by The Bright Light*." In: *Blaine And Logan Campaign Song-Book*, page 19. e. Prof. F. Widdows. Published by The Republican National Committee, New York, NY. 1884. [4⅜" × 5¹¹⁄₁₆"]. [V-1: Bk/y] [V-2: Pk/bk] litho of James G. Blaine and John A. Logan. "From the School — House to the Cabinet, From the Cabin to the Senate." 52pp. [M-251]. [Crew/JGB-32].

537.101 The Irishman's Greeting To The Ticket. w.

A. Wood. m. "Air—*Rory O'More.*" In: *Blaine And Logan Campaign Song-Book*, page 14. e. Prof. F. Widdows. Published by The Republican National Committee, New York, NY. 1884. [4⅜" × 5¹¹⁄₁₆"]. [V-1: Bk/y] [V-2: Pk/bk] litho of James G. Blaine and John A. Logan. "From the School—House to the Cabinet, From the Cabin to the Senate." 52pp. [M-251]. [Crew/JGB-32].

537.102 Jimmy B. w. "By Demo." m. "Tune—*Baby Mine.*" In: *Cleveland & Hendricks Songster*, page 27. Copyright 1884 by E.Y. Landis. R/w/bl/gn/br drawing of Grover Cleveland, Thomas Hendricks, George "Washington," Thomas "Jefferson," Andrew "Jackson," ribbons, geometric designs. 64pp. [M-230]. [Crew/GC-46].

537.103 Jimmy Blaine. w. "By Demo." m. "Tune—*Nelly Bly.*" In: *Cleveland & Hendricks Songster*, page 5. Copyright 1884 by E.Y. Landis. R/w/bl/gn/br drawing of Grover Cleveland, Thomas Hendricks, George "Washington," Thomas "Jefferson," Andrew "Jackson," ribbons, geometric designs. 64pp. [M-230]. [Crew/GC-46].

537.104 Labor's Hosts. w. No composer indicated. m. "Air—*Maxwelton's Braes Are Bonnie.*" In: *Beulah's Blaine And Logan Original Campaign Song Book 1884*, page 31. Printed and Published by Birnie Paper Company, Springfield, MA. 1884. [4" × 5¾"]. Gy/bk litho of James G. Blaine and John A. Logan, eagle, flags, shield, line border. 36pp. [M-232]. [Crew/JGB-41].

537.105 Led By Blaine And Logan. w. Dr. Frank P. Cleary. m. "Air—*Marching Through Georgia.*" In: *Blaine And Logan Campaign Song-Book*, page 36. e. Prof. F. Widdows. Published by The Republican National Committee, New York, NY. 1884. [4⅜" × 5¹¹⁄₁₆"]. [V-1: Bk/y] [V-2: Pk/bk] litho of James G. Blaine and John A. Logan. "From the School—House to the Cabinet, From the Cabin to the Senate." 52pp. [M-251]. [Crew/JGB-32].

537.106 A Life In The White House Halls. w. Dan Yell. m. "Tune—*Life On The Ocean Wave.*" In: *Cleveland & Hendricks Songster*, page 36. Copyright 1884 by E.Y. Landis. R/w/bl/gn/br drawing of Grover Cleveland, Thomas Hendricks, George "Washington," Thomas "Jefferson," Andrew "Jackson," ribbons, geometric designs. 64pp. [M-230]. [Crew/GC-46].

537.107 Logan's Grand March. m. John Mack. Published by White, Smith & Co., Chicago, IL. 1884. B/w litho of John A. Logan. "Respectfully Dedicated to Gen. John A. Logan," geometric design border. 6pp. Page 2: Blank. Page 6: Advertising. [Crew/JGB-103].

537.108 Loyal And True. w. No composer indicated. m. "Tune—*Sweet Bye And Bye.*" In: *Blaine And Logan Songster*, page 43. Published by Thomas Hunter, Philadelphia, PA. 1884. [5½" × 7¼"]. N/c litho of Abraham Lincoln and James Garfield—"Our Martyred Presidents." Br/w litho of James G. Blaine—"Our Next President," and John A. Logan—"Our Next Vice-President," George Washington, Ulysses S. Grant. 68pp [M-237]. [Crew/JGB-35].

537.109 The Man From Maine (Campaign Song). w. I.F. Felton. m. F. Fanciulli. Published by Wm. A. Pond & Co., No. 25 Union Square, New York, NY. 1884. B/w litho of James G, Blaine in a knight's armor with arms and legs labeled—"Power, Right, victory, Patriotism, firmness, strength;" snake labeled Democratic Camps." "Dedicated to the Party, that has never been buried." "A Tattoo." 6pp. Pages 2 and 6: Blank. [Crew/JGB-106].

537.110 March Of The Plumed Knight. w. Chas. B. Morrell. m. Wm. Howard Doane. "For Male Voices." Published by Geo. D. Newhall Co., Cincinnati, OH. 1884. B/w geometric design and line border. "Republican Campaign Songs." "The Newest, Sprightliest and the Best." List of other songs in the series. [Crew/JGB-101].

537.111 March To Victory. w. "Words published in the *N.Y. Tribune.*" m. William E. Chandler. Published by Russell Brothers, No. 126 Tremont Street, Boston, MA. B/w lithos of James G. Blaine and John A. Logan, lyre, wreath. "Russell's Musical Library." "Campaign Songs, 1884." 4pp. Page 2: "To the Knights of the White Plume." [Crew/JGB-104].

537.112 Marching To The White House. w. Frank N. Scott. m. No tune indicated. In: *P.T. Schultz & Co's Blaine And Logan Bugle Call*, page 21. Published by P.T. Schultz & Company, No. 172 Race Street, Cincinnati, OH. 1881. [1884 Edition]. [5⅞" × 7⅝"]. Bk/gn litho of James G. Blaine and John A. Logan, flags and eagle, geometric design border. 36pp. [M-245]. [Crew/JGB-67].

537.113 Marching To Victory. w. J.K. Tyler. m. "Air—*Marching Through Georgia.*" In: *Blaine And Logan Campaign Song-Book*, page 43. e. Prof. F. Widdows. Published by The Republican National Committee, New York, NY. 1884. [4⅜" × 5¹¹⁄₁₆"]. [V-1: Bk/y] [V-2: Pk/bk] litho of James G. Blaine and John A. Logan. "From the School—House to the Cabinet, From the Cabin to the Senate." 52pp. [M-251]. [Crew/JGB-32].

537.114 McKinley And Hobart. w. No composer indicated. m. "Air—*When Summer Comes Again.*" In: *McKinley And Hobart Song Book*, page 12. c.w.a. G.E. Treadway. Published by G.E. Treadway, Pittsburgh, PA. 1896. [5" × 6⅝"]. R/w/b litho of William McKinley and Garret Hobart, flag design. "Now used by the celebrated Tariff Club Quartette of Pittsburgh, Pa." 28pp. [M-349]. [Crew/WM-256].

537.115 McKinley's Dinner Pail. w. C.B.R. m. C.W. Bennett. In: *The Golden Glory! (Republican Songster For 1896)*, page 8. Published by Echo Music Company, Lafayette, IN. 1896. [5⁵⁄₁₆" × 7¾"]. Bl/w litho of William "McKinley" and Garret "Hobart." R/w/b geometric designs. 26pp. [M-327]. [Crew/WM-279].

537.116 The Mugwumps Met Him On The Way. w. No composer indicated. m. "Arr. By Tariff Reform to the *John Brown* tune." In: *Red Hot Democratic Campaign Songs For 1888*, page 8. e. John Bunyon Herbert. Published by The S. Brainard's Sons Company, Chicago, IL. 1888. [5⅜" × 7⁷⁄₁₆"]. R/bk geometric designs. 36pp. [M-294]. [Crew/GC-141].

537.117 The New Head And The Old Tail. w.m. No composer or tune indicated. In: *Blaine And Logan Campaign Songster*, page 24. Published by American News Company, New York, NY. 1884. 36pp. [M-249]. [Crew/JGB-84].

537.118 North, South, East And West For Blaine. w. No composer indicated. m. "Tune—*Tramp, Tramp, Tramp.*" In: *The People's Songs For Blaine & Logan*, page 10. Published by Acme Publishing Bureau, J.C.O. Redington, General Manager, No. 252 Broadway, New York, NY. Copyright 1884 by J.C.O. Redington. [4⅞" × 6⅝"]. B/w litho of James G. Blaine. "Adopted by the General Republican Committees in New York City and elsewhere." "Adapted for every Voice in the Glorious Land of Freedom. All the Nation may Sing." "Come, join that Columbia's blessings increase, All Singing for Liberty, Glory and Peace." "Acme Songs." 32pp. [M-246]. [Crew/JGB-45].

537.119 Not For Blaine. w. "By Demo." m. "Tune—*Not For Joe.*" In: *Cleveland & Hendricks Songster*, page 4. Copyright 1884 by E.Y. Landis. R/w/bl/gn/br drawing of Grover Cleveland, Thomas Hendricks, George "Washington," Thomas "Jefferson," Andrew "Jackson," ribbons, geometric designs. 64pp. [M-230]. [Crew/GC-46].

537.120 Now Blaine's Got Back. w. C.C. McBride, "Editor of the Elizabeth (N.J.) *Journal.*" m. "Tune—*Marching Through Georgia.*" In: *The Republican League Campaign Song Book*, page 5. c. Professor J.M. Hager. Published by the Republican League of the United States, No. 202 Fifth Avenue, New York, NY. 1888. [4" × 5⅞"]. Bk/gy litho of Benjamin F. Harrison and Levi P. Morton, flags, Capitol building. 36pp. [M-265]. [Crew/BFH-58].

537.121 Now, Three Times Three. w.m. No composers indicated. m. Notation. In: *Blaine And Logan Campaign Songster*, page 35. Published by John Church & Company, Cincinnati, OH. 1884. [4⅞" × 5¹³⁄₁₆"]. Y/bk non-pictorial geometric design border. "Including Biographical Sketches & Constitution for Campaign Clubs." 52pp. [M-233?]. [Crew/JGB-29].

537.122 O Bring Out Your Banners! w.m. No composer or tune indicated. In: *Blaine And Logan Songster*, page 19. Published by Thomas Hunter, Philadelphia, PA. 1884. [5½" × 7¼"]. N/c litho of Abraham Lincoln and James Garfield—"Our Martyred Presidents." Br/w litho of James G. Blaine—"Our Next President," and John A. Logan—"Our Next Vice-President," George Washington, Ulysses S. Grant. 68pp [M-237]. [Crew/JGB-35].

537.123 O, The Crow, The Beautiful Crow. m. "Air — O, *The Snow, The Beautiful Snow.*" "As sung by the Blaine men, Conklingites, Morton men and other defeated Republican leaders." In: *Illustrated Campaign Song And Joke*, page 26. Published by The American News Company, New York, NY. [4¾" × 7½"]. 1876. Y/bk litho of Samuel J. Tilden, geometric design border. 50pp. [?]. Page 5: Title—*The Illustrated Campaign Tilden Song And Joke Book*. [Crew/SJT-8].

537.124 Oh, Blaine, It Is Of Thee. w. No composer indicated. m. "Air—*My Country, 'Tis Of Thee.*" In: *Beulah's Blaine And Logan Original Campaign Song Book 1884*, page 3. Printed and Published by Birnie Paper Company, Springfield, MA. 1884. [4" × 5¾"]. Gy/bk litho of James G. Blaine and John A. Logan, eagle, flags, shield, line border. 36pp. [M-232]. [Crew/JGB-41].

537.125 Old Loyalty's Campaign Song. w. Chaplain Lozier. m. "Air—*Little Old Log Cabin.*" In: *Harrison And Reid Campaign Songster*, page 36. Published by The John Church Company, No. 74 West 4th Street, Cincinnati, OH. 1892. [4⅛" × 5¾"]. Be/bk non-pictorial geometric design border. "Including Biographical Sketches & Constitution for Campaign Clubs." 52pp. [M-305]. [Crew/BFH-49].

537.126 One Trial More. w. C.L.S. m. "Air—*Upidee.*" In: *P.T. Schultz & Co's Blaine And Logan Bugle Call*, page 31. Published by P.T. Schultz & Company, No. 172 Race Street, Cincinnati, OH. 1881. [1884 Edition]. [5⅞" × 7⅝"]. Bk/gn litho of James G. Blaine and John A. Logan, flags and eagle, geometric design border. 36pp. [M-245]. [Crew/JGB-67].

537.127 The Other Candidate. w. "After Puck." m. F.G.F. In: *Red Hot Democratic Campaign Songs For 1888*, page 12. e. John Bunyon Herbert. Published by The S. Brainard's Sons Company, Chicago, IL. 1888. [5⅜" × 7⁷⁄₁₆"]. R/bk geometric designs. 36pp. [M-294]. [Crew/GC-141].

537.128 Our Candidate. w. No composer indicated. m. "Air—*Then Let The Hurricane Roar.*" In: *Beulah's Blaine And Logan Original Campaign Song Book 1884*, page 5. Printed and Published by Birnie Paper Company, Springfield, MA. 1884. [4" × 5¾"]. Gy/bk litho of James G. Blaine and John A. Logan, eagle, flags, shield, line border. 36pp. [M-232]. [Crew/JGB-41].

537.129 Our Candidates. w. No composer indicated. m. "Tune—*Johnny Comes Marching Home.*" In: *Facts And Songs For The People*, page 17. Published by C.E. Bolton, Cleveland, OH. 1884. [5" × 7⅛"]. R/w/bl drawing of Miss Liberty, flag, scroll—"Vox populi, Vox Dei, 1884." 54pp. Pages 2 and 53: Advertising. Page 3: B/w photo of "Hon. James G. Blaine." Page 4: Photo of "Gen. John A. Logan." Page 5: Title—*Facts & Songs For The People Prepared Specially For Use In The Blaine And Logan Campaign*. [M-239]. [Crew/JGB-65].

537.130 Our Candidates. w. No composer indicated. m. "Tune—*Hold The Fort.*" In: *Blaine And Logan Songster*, page 45. Published by Thomas Hunter, Philadelphia, PA. 1884. [5½" × 7¼"]. N/c litho of Abraham Lincoln and James Garfield—"Our Martyred Presidents." Br/w litho of James G. Blaine—"Our Next President," and John A. Logan—"Our Next Vice-President," George Washington, Ulysses S. Grant. 68pp [M-237]. [Crew/JGB-35].

537.131 Our Choice. w. No composer indicated. m. "Air—*Maxwelton's Braes Are Bonnie.*" In: *Beulah's Blaine And Logan Original Campaign Song Book 1884*, page 6. Printed and Published by Birnie Paper Company, Springfield, MA. 1884. [4" × 5¾"]. Gy/bk litho of James G. Blaine and John A. Logan, eagle, flags, shield, line border. 36pp. [M-232]. [Crew/JGB-41].

537.131 Our Chosen Leader. w. No composer indicated. m. "Air—*The Battle Cry Of Freedom.*" In: *Blaine And Logan Campaign Song-Book*, page 9. e. Prof. F. Widdows. Published by The Republican National Committee, New York, NY. 1884. [4⅜" × 5¹¹⁄₁₆"]. [V-1: Bk/y] [V-2: Pk/bk] litho of James G. Blaine and John A. Logan. "From the School—House to the Cabinet, From the Cabin to the Senate." 52pp. [M-251]. [Crew/JGB-32].

537.132 Our Good Old Democrats. w. "By Demo." m. "Tune—*King Of The Cannibal Islands.*" In: *Cleveland & Hendricks Songster*, page 12. Copyright 1884 by E.Y. Landis. R/w/bl/gn/br drawing of Grover Cleveland, Thomas Hendricks, George "Washington,"

Thomas "Jefferson," Andrew "Jackson," ribbons, geometric designs. 64pp. [M-230]. [Crew/GC-46].

537.133 Our Jim Is Coming (Rallying Song). w.m. John H. Sarchet. Published by Geo. D. Newhall Co., Cincinnati, OH. 1884. B/w geometric design and line border. "Republican Campaign Songs." "The Newest, Sprightliest and the Best." List of other songs in the series. [Crew/JGB-101].

537.134 Our Jimmy's Train. w.m. John H. Sarchet. Published by Geo. D. Newhall Co., Cincinnati, OH. 1884. B/w geometric design and line border. "Republican Campaign Songs." "The Newest, Sprightliest and the Best." List of other songs in the series. [Crew/JGB-101].

537.135 Our Leader Blaine. w. Mrs. M. Jennie Porter. m. "Air—*From Greenland's Icy Mountains.*" "Mrs. M.J. Porter, the writer of the above and other songs with her signature, is a native Georgian, and the daughter of a Confederate soldier." In: *Blaine And Logan Campaign Song-Book*, page 13. e. Prof. F. Widdows. Published by The Republican National Committee, New York, NY. 1884. [4⅜" × 5¹³⁄₁₆"]. [V-1: Bk/y] [V-2: Pk/bk] litho of James G. Blaine and John A. Logan. "From the School—House to the Cabinet, From the Cabin to the Senate." 52pp. [M-251]. [Crew/JGB-32].

537.136 Our Leaders. w. No composer indicated. m. "Tune—*Maryland, My Maryland.*" In: *Blaine And Logan Songster*, page 47. Published by Thomas Hunter, Philadelphia, PA. 1884. [5½" × 7¼"]. N/c litho of Abraham Lincoln and James Garfield—"Our Martyred Presidents." Br/w litho of James G. Blaine—"Our Next President," and John A. Logan—"Our Next Vice-President," George Washington, Ulysses S. Grant. 68pp [M-237]. [Crew/JGB-35].

537.137 Our New Uncle Sam. w. No composer indicated. m. "Air—*Uncle Sam.*" In: *Tilden And Hendricks' Reform Songs (For The Centennial Campaign Of 1876)*, page 14. Published by The National Democratic Committee, Box 3637, New York, NY. 1876. [3⅞" × 5¹⁵⁄₁₆"]. Gn/bk litho of Samuel J. Tilden and Thomas A. Hendricks, geometric design border. 40pp. [M-203]. [Crew/SJT-21].

537.138 Our Next President. w. No composer indicated. m. "Tune—*Johnny Comes Marching Home.*" In: *Blaine And Logan Songster*, page 59. Published by Thomas Hunter, Philadelphia, PA. 1884. [5½" × 7¼"]. N/c litho of Abraham Lincoln and James Garfield—"Our Martyred Presidents." Br/w litho of James G. Blaine—"Our Next President," and John A. Logan—"Our Next Vice-President," George Washington, Ulysses S. Grant. 68pp [M-237]. [Crew/JGB-35].

537.139 Our Nominations. w. Frank N. Scott. m. "Air—*The One Horse Chaise.*" In: *P.T. Schultz & Co's Blaine And Logan Bugle Call*, page 13. Published by P.T. Schultz & Company, No. 172 Race Street, Cincinnati, OH. 1881. [1884 Edition]. [5⅞" × 7⅝"]. Bk/gn litho of James G. Blaine and John A. Logan, flags and eagle, geometric design border. 36pp. [M-245]. [Crew/JGB-67].

537.140 Our Nominee. w. "By Demo." m. "Tune—*Hurrah, Hurrah, Hurrah!*" In: *Cleveland & Hendricks Songster*, page 58. Copyright 1884 by E.Y. Landis. R/w/bl/gn/br drawing of Grover Cleveland, Thomas Hendricks, George "Washington," Thomas "Jefferson," Andrew "Jackson," ribbons, geometric designs. 64pp. [M-230]. [Crew/GC-46].

537.141 Over The Left. w. "By Demo." m. "Tune—*Sweet Kitty Clover.*" In: *Cleveland & Hendricks Songster*, page 50. Copyright 1884 by E.Y. Landis. R/w/bl/gn/br drawing of Grover Cleveland, Thomas Hendricks, George "Washington," Thomas "Jefferson," Andrew "Jackson," ribbons, geometric designs. 64pp. [M-230]. [Crew/GC-46].

537.142 Paddy Speaks. w. No composer indicated. m. "Air—*The Wearing Of The Green.*" In: *Beulah's Blaine And Logan Original Campaign Song Book 1884*, page 12. Printed and Published by Birnie Paper Company, Springfield, MA. 1884. [4" × 5¾"]. Gy/bk litho of James G. Blaine and John A. Logan, eagle, flags, shield, line border. 36pp. [M-232]. [Crew/JGB-41].

537.143 Peace, Order And Stability. w. No composer indicated. m. "Air—*Yankee Doodle.*" In: *Blaine And Logan Songster*, page 10. Published by Thomas Hunter, Philadelphia, PA. 1884. [5½" × 7¼"]. N/c litho of Abraham Lincoln and James Garfield—"Our Martyred Presidents." Br/w litho of James G. Blaine—"Our Next President," and John A. Logan—"Our Next Vice-President," George Washington, Ulysses S. Grant. 68pp [M-237]. [Crew/JGB-35].

537.144 The People Are Shouting. w. No composer indicated. m. "Air—*The Campbells Are Coming.*" In: *Blaine And Logan Campaign Songster*, page 9. Published by John Church & Company, Cincinnati, OH. 1884. [4⅞" × 5¹³⁄₁₆"]. Y/bk non-pictorial geometric design border. "Including Biographical Sketches & Constitution for Campaign Clubs." 52pp. [M-233?]. [Crew/JGB-29].

537.145 The Plumed Knight. w. No composer indicated. m. "Tune—*Battle Cry Of Freedom.*" In: *Facts And Songs For The People*, page 16. Published by C.E. Bolton, Cleveland, OH. 1884. [5" × 7⅛"]. R/w/bl drawing of Miss Liberty, flag, scroll—"Vox populi, Vox Dei, 1884." 54pp. Pages 2 and 53: Advertising. Page 3: B/w photo of "Hon. James G. Blaine." Page 4: Photo of "Gen. John A. Logan." Page 5: Title—*Facts & Songs For The People Prepared Specially For Use In The Blaine And Logan Campaign.* [M-239]. [Crew/JGB-65].

537.146 The Plumed Knight. w. No composer indicated. m. "Air—*Miselto* [sic] *Bough.*" In: *Beulah's Blaine And Logan Original Campaign Song Book 1884*, page 22. Printed and Published by Birnie Paper Company, Springfield, MA. 1884. [4" × 5¾"]. Gy/bk litho of James G. Blaine and John A. Logan, eagle, flags, shield, line border. 36pp. [M-232]. [Crew/JGB-41].

537.147 The Plumed Knight Band. w. No composer indicated. m. Notation. In: *Blaine And Logan Campaign Songster*, page 9. Published by John Church & Company, Cincinnati, OH. 1884. [4⅞" × 5¹³⁄₁₆"]. Y/bk non-pictorial geometric design border. "Including Biographical Sketches & Constitution for Campaign Clubs." 52pp. [M-233?]. [Crew/JGB-29].

537.148 The Plumed Knight Of Maine (Song & Chorus). w.m. D.O.S. Lowell. Published by John Church & Co., No. 66 West Fourth Street, Cincinnati, OH 1884. B/w litho of a feather. 6pp. Pages 2 and 6: Blank. [Crew/JGB-111].

537.149 The Plumed Knight's Dream. w. No composer indicated. m. "Air—*Mother Kissed Me In My Dreams.*" In: *Beulah's Blaine And Logan Original Campaign Song Book 1884*, page 11. Printed and Published by Birnie Paper Company, Springfield, MA. 1884. [4" × 5¾"]. Gy/bk litho of James G. Blaine and John A. Logan, eagle, flags, shield, line border. 36pp. [M-232]. [Crew/JGB-41].

537.150 The Presidential Racecourse. w. No composer indicated. m. "Air—*Camptown Races.*" In: *Blaine And Logan Campaign Songster*, page 5. Published by John Church & Company, Cincinnati, OH. 1884. [4⅞" × 5¹³⁄₁₆"]. Y/bk non-pictorial geometric design border. "Including Biographical Sketches & Constitution for Campaign Clubs." 52pp. [M-233?]. [Crew/JGB-29].

537.151 The 'Pubs Are Out Drumming. w. "By Demo." m. "Tune—*The Campbells Are Comin.*" In: *Cleveland & Hendricks Songster*, page 39. Copyright 1884 by E.Y. Landis. R/w/bl/gn/br drawing of Grover Cleveland, Thomas Hendricks, George "Washington," Thomas "Jefferson," Andrew "Jackson," ribbons, geometric designs. 64pp. [M-230]. [Crew/GC-46].

537.152 Put Him Through. w. No composer indicated. m. Notation. In: *Blaine And Logan Campaign Songster*, page 6. Published by John Church & Company, Cincinnati, OH. 1884. [4⅞" × 5¹³⁄₁₆"]. Y/bk non-pictorial geometric design border. "Including Biographical Sketches & Constitution for Campaign Clubs." 52pp. [M-233?]. [Crew/JGB-29].

537.153 The Rally (Song). w.m. Grace Appleton. a. D. King. Published by Wm. A. Pond & Co., No. 25 Union Square, New York, NY. 1884. Non-pictorial geometric designs. "Song For The Blaine Campaign." 6pp. [?]. [Crew/JGB-105].

537.154 Rally! Freemen, Rally! w. Frank N. Scott. m. "Music—*Scots Wha Hae.*" In: *P.T. Schultz & Co's Blaine And Logan Bugle Call*, page 22. Published by P.T. Schultz & Company, No. 172 Race Street, Cincinnati, OH. 1881. [1884 Edition]. [5⅞" × 7⅝"]. Bk/gn litho of James G. Blaine and John A. Logan, flags and eagle, geometric design border. 36pp. [M-245]. [Crew/JGB-67].

537.155 Rally On Colors. w. C.A. Murch. m. J.B. Herbert. In: *Echo Republican Campaign Songs For 1908*, page 22. c. Dr. J.B. Herbert. Published by The Echo Music Company, Publishers, No. 358 Dearborn Street, Chicago, IL. 1908. [6⅞" × 10"]. B/w drawing of "Wm. H. Taft—For President," and "Jas. S. Sherman—For Vice-President," shield, eagle, black line border. "Republican Candidates." "For Male Voices." 36pp. [M-395]. [Crew/WHT-29].

537.156 Rally, Rally, Republicans, Rally. w. No composer indicated. m. Notation. In: *The People's Songs For Blaine & Logan*, page 3. Published by Acme Publishing Bureau, J.C.O. Redington, General Manager, No. 252 Broadway, New York, NY. Copyright 1884 by J.C.O. Redington. [4⅞" × 6⅝"]. B/w litho of James G. Blaine. "Adopted by the General Republican Committees in New York City and elsewhere." "Adapted for every Voice in the Glorious Land of Freedom. All the Nation may Sing." "Come, join that Columbia's blessings increase, All Singing for Liberty, Glory and Peace." "Acme Songs." 32pp. [M-246]. [Crew/JGB-45].

537.157 Rallying Song, 1884. w. J.H. Coggswell. m. "Air—*Marching Through Georgia.*" In: *Blaine And Logan Campaign Song-Book*, page 5. e. Prof. F. Widdows. Published by The Republican National Committee, New York, NY. 1884. [4⅜" × 5¹¹⁄₁₆"]. [V-1: Bk/y] [V-2: Pk/bk] litho of James G. Blaine and John A. Logan. "From the School—House to the Cabinet, From the Cabin to the Senate." 52pp. [M-251]. [Crew/JGB-32].

537.158 The Republican Convention. w. "By Demo." m. "Tune—*Little Tailor Boy.*" In: *Cleveland & Hendricks Songster*, page 8. Copyright 1884 by E.Y. Landis. R/w/bl/gn/br drawing of Grover Cleveland, Thomas Hendricks, George "Washington," Thomas "Jefferson," Andrew "Jackson," ribbons, geometric designs. 64pp. [M-230]. [Crew/GC-46].

537.159 The Republican Slogan. w. Dr. H.A. Dobson. m. "Air—*Yankee Doodle.*" In: *Blaine And Logan Campaign Song-Book*, page 27. e. Prof. F. Widdows. Published by The Republican National Committee, New York, NY. 1884. [4⅜" × 5¹¹⁄₁₆"]. [V-1: Bk/y] [V-2: Pk/bk] litho of James G. Blaine and John A. Logan. "From the School—House to the Cabinet, From the Cabin to the Senate." 52pp. [M-251]. [Crew/JGB-32].

537.160 Republican Watchword. w. Prof. F. Widdows. w. No tune indicated. "Let us have a Peace." In: *Blaine And Logan Campaign Song-Book*, page 21. e. Prof. F. Widdows. Published by The Republican National Committee, New York, NY. 1884. [4⅜" × 5¹¹⁄₁₆"]. [V-1: Bk/y] [V-2: Pk/bk] litho of James G. Blaine and John A. Logan. "From the School—House to the Cabinet, From the Cabin to the Senate." 52pp. [M-251]. [Crew/JGB-32].

537.161 Republicans To The Rescue. w. Dr. Ethel Hurd. m. "Tune—*Battle Hymn Of The Republic.*" In: *Republican Campaign Songs*, page 19. Published by Republican State Committee Headquarters, Topeka, Kansas. 1920. [5⁷⁄₁₆" × 7¹³⁄₁₆"]. Be/bk photos of "Warren G. Harding" and "Calvin Coolidge"—"Our Country Needs Them." "Sing and Smile on to Victory." 24pp. [Crew/WGH-63].

537.162 The Right Is Marching On. w. No composer indicated. m. "Air—*Glory Hallelujah.*" In: *Blaine And Logan Campaign Songster*, page 32. Published by John Church & Company, Cincinnati, OH. 1884. [4⅞" × 5¹³⁄₁₆"]. Y/bk non-pictorial geometric design border. "Including Biographical Sketches & Constitution for Campaign Clubs." 52pp. [M-233?]. [Crew/JGB-29].

537.163 Ring The Bells Of Freedom! w. H.E. Peterson. m. "Air—*Tramp! Tramp! Tramp! The Boys Are Marching!*" In: *Blaine And Logan Campaign Song-Book*, page 44. e. Prof. F. Widdows. Published by The Republican National Committee, New York, NY. 1884. [4⅜" × 5¹¹⁄₁₆"]. [V-1: Bk/y] [V-2: Pk/bk] litho of James G. Blaine and John A. Logan. "From the School—House to the Cabinet, From the Cabin to the Senate." 52pp. [M-251]. [Crew/JGB-32].

537.164 Serenade. w. J.W.B. Siders. w. No composer indicated. In: *Blaine And Logan Campaign Songster*, page 12. Published by American News Company, New York, NY. 1884. 36pp. [M-249]. [Crew/JGB-84].

537.165 The Ship Of State. w. J.W.B. Siders. m.

"Air—*Sail On, My Bark.*" In: *Blaine And Logan Campaign Songster*, page 13. Published by American News Company, New York, NY. 1884. 36pp. [M-249]. [Crew/JGB-84].

537.166 Shout The Battle Cry. m. W.L. Blumenschein. Published by Geo. D. Newhall Co., Cincinnati, OH. 1884. B/w geometric design and line border. "Republican Campaign Songs." "The Newest, Sprightliest and the Best." List of other songs in the series. [Crew/JGB-101].

537.167 Shouting For Blaine And Logan. w. No composer indicated. m. "Air—*Battle Cry Of Freedom.*" In: *Blaine And Logan Campaign Songster*, page 16. Published by John Church & Company, Cincinnati, OH. 1884. [4⅞" × 5 13/16"]. Y/bk non-pictorial geometric design border. "Including Biographical Sketches & Constitution for Campaign Clubs." 52pp. [M-233?]. [Crew/JGB-29].

537.168 Shouting The Cry Of Blaine And Logan. w. Frank N. Scott. m. No tune indicated. In: *P.T. Schultz & Co's Blaine And Logan Bugle Call*, page 17. Published by P.T. Schultz & Company, No. 172 Race Street, Cincinnati, OH. 1881. [1884 Edition]. [5⅞" × 7⅝"]. Bk/gn litho of James G. Blaine and John A. Logan, flags and eagle, geometric design border. 36pp. [M-245]. [Crew/JGB-67].

537.169 Singing For Blaine And Logan. w. No composer indicated. m. "Air—*Battle Cry Of Freedom.*" In: *Blaine And Logan Songster*, page 18. Published by Thomas Hunter, Philadelphia, PA. 1884. [5½" × 7¼"]. N/c litho of Abraham Lincoln and James Garfield—"Our Martyred Presidents." Br/w litho of James G. Blaine—"Our Next President," and John A. Logan—"Our Next Vice-President," George Washington, Ulysses S. Grant. 68pp [M-237]. [Crew/JGB-35].

537.170 Solid Is Our Party. w. "By Demo." m. "Tune—*Captain Jenks.*" In: *Cleveland & Hendricks Songster*, page 12. Copyright 1884 by E.Y. Landis. R/w/bl/gn/br drawing of Grover Cleveland, Thomas Hendricks, George "Washington," Thomas "Jefferson," Andrew "Jackson," ribbons, geometric designs. 64pp. [M-230]. [Crew/GC-46].

537.171 Song For Blaine. w. No composer interested. m. "Air—*Tramp, Tramp, Tramp.*" In: *Blaine And Logan Campaign Song-Book*, page 4. e. Prof. F. Widdows. Published by The Republican National Committee, New York, NY. 1884. [4⅜" × 5 11/16"]. [V-1: Bk/y] [V-2: Pk/bk] litho of James G. Blaine and John A. Logan. "From the School—House to the Cabinet, From the Cabin to the Senate." 52pp. [M-251]. [Crew/JGB-32].

537.172 Song Of Eighty-Four. m. William E. Chandler. Published by Russell Brothers, No. 126 Tremont Street, Boston, MA. B/w lithos of James G. Blaine and John A. Logan, lyre, wreath. "Russell's Musical Library." "Campaign Songs, 1884." [Crew/JGB-104].

537.173 Song Of The Loyal Legions. w. No composer indicated. m. "Air—*Tramp! Tramp!*" In: *Blaine And Logan Songster*, page 17. Published by Thomas Hunter, Philadelphia, PA. 1884. [5½" × 7¼"]. N/c litho of Abraham Lincoln and James Garfield—"Our Martyred Presidents." Br/w litho of James G. Blaine—"Our Next President," and John A. Logan—"Our Next Vice-President," George Washington, Ulysses S. Grant. 68pp [M-237]. [Crew/JGB-35].

537.174 The South Is Coming. w. No composer indicated. m. "Air—*Star Spangled Banner.*" In: *P.T. Schultz & Co's Blaine And Logan Bugle Call*, page 24. Published by P.T. Schultz & Company, No. 172 Race Street, Cincinnati, OH. 1881. [1884 Edition]. [5⅞" × 7⅝"]. Bk/gn litho of James G. Blaine and John A. Logan, flags and eagle, geometric design border. 36pp. [M-245]. [Crew/JGB-67].

537.175 Stand By The Grand Old Party. w.m. John H. Sarchet. Published by Geo. D. Newhall Co., Cincinnati, OH. 1884. B/w geometric design and line border. "Republican Campaign Songs." "The Newest, Sprightliest and the Best." List of other songs in the series. [Crew/JGB-101].

537.176 Stand, Comrades, Stand. w. C.L.S. m. "Air—*The Marseillaise.*" In: *P.T. Schultz & Co's Blaine And Logan Bugle Call*, page 23. Published by P.T. Schultz & Company, No. 172 Race Street, Cincinnati, OH. 1881. [1884 Edition]. [5⅞" × 7⅝"]. Bk/gn litho of James G. Blaine and John A. Logan, flags and eagle, geometric design border. 36pp. [M-245]. [Crew/JGB-67].

537.177 [A Statesman For Our Leader Is What We Want Today]. w. No composer indicated. m. "Air—*Marching Through Georgia.*" In: *P.T. Schultz & Co's Blaine And Logan Bugle Call*, page 15. Published by P.T. Schultz & Company, No. 172 Race Street, Cincinnati, OH. 1881. [1884 Edition]. [5⅞" × 7⅝"]. Bk/gn litho of James G. Blaine and John A. Logan, flags and eagle, geometric design border. 36pp. [M-245]. [Crew/JGB-67].

537.178 Still We Lead The Nation (Rallying Song). w.m. Chas. B. Morrell, M.D. Published by Geo. D. Newhall Co., Cincinnati, OH. 1884. B/w geometric design and line border. "Republican Campaign Songs." "The Newest, Sprightliest and the Best." List of other songs in the series. [Crew/JGB-101].

537.179 A Struggle For Victory. w. No composer indicated. m. "Tune—*Marching Through Georgia.*" In: *Facts And Songs For The People*, page 16. Published by C.E. Bolton, Cleveland, OH. 1884. [5" × 7⅛"]. R/w/bl drawing of Miss Liberty, flag, scroll—"Vox populi, Vox Dei, 1884." 54pp. Pages 2 and 53: Advertising. Page 3: B/w photo of "Hon. James G. Blaine." Page 4: Photo of "Gen. John A. Logan." Page 5: Title—*Facts & Songs For The People Prepared Specially For Use In The Blaine And Logan Campaign.* [M-239]. [Crew/JGB-65].

537.180 That Man Jimmy Blaine. w. "By Demo." m. "Tune—*Widow Malone.*" In: *Cleveland & Hendricks Songster*, page 3. Copyright 1884 by E.Y. Landis. R/w/bl/gn/br drawing of Grover Cleveland, Thomas Hendricks, George "Washington," Thomas "Jefferson," Andrew "Jackson," ribbons, geometric designs. 64pp. [M-230]. [Crew/GC-46].

537.181 There They Stand. w. No composer indicated. m. "Air—*Hail, Columbia.*" In: *Blaine And Logan Campaign Songster*, page 24. Published by John Church & Company, Cincinnati, OH. 1884. [4⅞" × 5 13/16"]. Y/bk non-pictorial geometric design border. "Including Biographical Sketches & Constitution for Campaign Clubs." 52pp. [M-233?]. [Crew/JGB-29].

537.182 There's Vict'ry In The Air. w. H.E. Gordon. m. "Air—*Tramp, Tramp, Tramp.*" In: *Blaine And Logan Campaign Song-Book*, page 46. e. Prof. F. Widdows. Published by The Republican National Committee, New York, NY. 1884. [4⅜" × 5 11/16"]. [V-1: Bk/y] [V-2: Pk/bk] litho of James G. Blaine and John A. Logan. "From the School—House to the Cabinet, From the Cabin to the Senate." 52pp. [M-251]. [Crew/JGB-32].

537.183 Three Times Three For Blaine. w. J.S. Ellis. m. "Air—*Bonnie Blue Flag.*" In: *Blaine And Logan Campaign Song-Book*, page 30. e. Prof. F. Widdows. Published by The Republican National Committee, New York, NY. 1884. [4⅜" × 5 11/16"]. [V-1: Bk/y] [V-2: Pk/bk] litho of James G. Blaine and John A. Logan. "From the School—House to the Cabinet, From the Cabin to the Senate." 52pp. [M-251]. [Crew/ JGB-32].

537.184 The Tidal Wave. w. S.N. Holmes. m. "Tune—*Tippecanoe And Tyler, Too*—1840." In: *The Republican Campaign Song Book, With Music, 1892*, page 54. e. Samuel Newall Holmes. Published by Samuel Newall Holmes, Syracuse, NY. 1892. Be/bk non-pictorial. "Composed and especially prepared by Judge S.N. Holmes of Syracuse, N.Y." "Headquarters: Syracuse, N.Y." "Price twenty-five cents." 60pp. [M-308]. [Crew/BFH-107].

537.185 Tilden And Reform. w. No composer indicated. m. "Air—*The Wearing Of The Green.*" In: *Tilden And Hendricks' Reform Songs (For The Centennial Campaign Of 1876)*, page 3. Published by The National Democratic Committee, Box 3637, New York, NY. 1876. [3⅞" × 5 15/16"]. Gn/bk litho of Samuel J. Tilden and Thomas A. Hendricks, geometric design border. 40pp. [M-203]. [Crew/SJT-21].

537.186 Tippecanoe And Morton, Too! w. No composer indicated. m. "Tune—*Tippecanoe And Tyler Too.*" m. Notation. In: *Young Republican Campaign Song Book*, page 8. c. Henry Camp. Published by the Brooklyn Young Republican Club, Brooklyn, NY. 1888. [4⅜" × 6½"]. R/w/b litho of a U.S. flag. "Campaign 1888." 100pp. Page 100: B/w lithos of Benjamin Harrison and Levi Morton. [M-258, 259]. [Crew/ BFH-53].

537.187 Tippecanoe And Morton, Too! w. William Gray. m. "Tune—*Tippecanoe And Tyler Too.*" Notation. In: *The Republican League Campaign Song Book*, page 3. c. Professor J.M. Hager. Published by the Republican League of the United States, No. 202 Fifth Avenue, New York, NY. 1888. [4" × 5⅞"]. Bk/gy litho of Benjamin F. Harrison and Levi P. Morton, flags, Capitol building. 36pp. [M-265]. [Crew/BFH-58].

537.188 'Tis For Blaine And Logan. w.m. Chas. B. Morrell Published by Geo. D. Newhall Co., Cincinnati, OH. 1884. B/w geometric design and line border. "Republican Campaign Songs." "The Newest, Sprightliest and the Best." List of other songs in the series. [Crew/JGB-101].

537.189 The Toiler's Golden Day. w. No composer indicated. m. "Air—*Wearing Of The Green.*" In: *Blaine And Logan Campaign Song-Book*, page 40. e. Prof. F. Widdows. Published by The Republican National Committee, New York, NY. 1884. [4⅜" × 5 11/16"]. [V-1: Bk/y] [V-2: Pk/bk] litho of James G. Blaine and John A. Logan. "From the School—House to the Cabinet, From the Cabin to the Senate." 52pp. [M-251]. [Crew/JGB-32].

537.190 Tramp, Tramp. w. Frank N. Scott. m. Air—*Tramp, Tramp, Tramp.* In: *P.T. Schultz & Co's Blaine And Logan Bugle Call*, page 24. Published by P.T. Schultz & Company, No. 172 Race Street, Cincinnati, OH. 1881. [1884 Edition]. [5⅞" × 7⅝"]. Bk/gn litho of James G. Blaine and John A. Logan, flags and eagle, geometric design border. 36pp. [M-245]. [Crew/JGB-67].

537.191 Treason's Fate. w. S.N. Holmes. m. "Tune—*A Thousand Years*, &c." In: *The Republican Campaign Song Book, With Music, 1892*, page 15. e. Samuel Newall Holmes. Published by Samuel Newall Holmes, Syracuse, NY. 1892. Be/bk non-pictorial. "Composed and especially prepared by Judge S.N. Holmes of Syracuse, N.Y." "Headquarters: Syracuse, N.Y." "Price twenty-five cents." 60pp. [M-308]. [Crew/BFH-107].

537.192 Uncle Ben. w. Sam Booth. m. "Air—*Auld Lang Syne.*" In: *Harrison And Reid Campaign Songster*, page 5. Published by The John Church Company, No. 74 West 4th Street, Cincinnati, OH. 1892. [4⅛" × 5¾"]. Be/bk non-pictorial geometric design border. "Including Biographical Sketches & Constitution for Campaign Clubs." 52pp. [M-305]. [Crew/BFH-49].

537.193 Uncle Sam's A Coming. w. No composer indicated. m. "Air—*Babylon Is Fallen.*" In: *Tilden And Hendricks' Reform Songs (For The Centennial Campaign Of 1876)*, page 19. Published by The National Democratic Committee, Box 3637, New York, NY. 1876. [3⅞" × 5 15/16"]. Gn/bk litho of Samuel J. Tilden and Thomas A. Hendricks, geometric design border. 40pp. [M-203]. [Crew/SJT-21].

537.194 Uncle Sam's Choice Of Blaine And Logan. w. No composer indicated. m. Notation. In: *The People's Songs For Blaine & Logan*, page 7. Published by Acme Publishing Bureau, J.C.O. Redington, General Manager, No. 252 Broadway, New York, NY. Copyright 1884 by J.C.O. Redington. [4⅞" × 6⅝"]. B/w litho of James G. Blaine. "Adopted by the General Republican Committees in New York City and elsewhere." "Adapted for every Voice in the Glorious Land of Freedom. All the Nation may Sing." "Come, join that Columbia's blessings increase, All Singing for Liberty, Glory and Peace." "Acme Songs." 32pp. [M-246]. [Crew/JGB-45].

537.195 The Union, The Hope Of The Free. w.m. No composers indicated. m. Notation. In: *Blaine And Logan Campaign Songster*, page 26. Published by John Church & Company, Cincinnati, OH. 1884. [4⅞" × 5 13/16"]. Y/bk non-pictorial geometric design border. "Including Biographical Sketches & Constitution for Campaign Clubs." 52pp. [M-233?]. [Crew/JGB-29].

537.196 Upidee! w. J.W.B. Siders. m. No tune indicated. In: *Blaine And Logan Campaign Songster*, page 5. Published by American News Company, New York, NY. 1884. 36pp. [M-249]. [Crew/JGB-84].

537.197 The Vacant Chair. w. No composer indicated. m. *The Vacant Chair*. In: *War Songs*, page 12. Published by Woolson Spice Company, Toledo, OH. [ca. 1884]. [4¾" × 6⅞"]. N/c litho of war scene, company logos for "Lion Coffee" and "Woolson Spice Co." "Dedicated to the G.A.R., The Woman's Relief Corps and The Sons of Volunteers." 36pp. [Crew/JGB-112].

537.198 Victory Rests With You. w. No composer indicated. m. "Air—*Hold The Fort.*" In: *Blaine And Logan Songster,* page 15. Published by Thomas Hunter, Philadelphia, PA. 1884. [5½" × 7¼"]. N/c litho of Abraham Lincoln and James Garfield—"Our Martyred Presidents." Br/w litho of James G. Blaine—"Our Next President," and John A. Logan—"Our Next Vice-President," George Washington, Ulysses S. Grant. 68pp [M-237]. [Crew/JGB-35].

537.199 Wait. w. H.E. Gordon. m. "Air—*Wait Till The Clouds Roll By.*" In: *Blaine And Logan Campaign Song-Book,* page 42. e. Prof. F. Widdows. Published by The Republican National Committee, New York, NY. 1884. [4⅜" × 5¹¹⁄₁₆"]. [V-1: Bk/y] [V-2: Pk/bk] litho of James G. Blaine and John A. Logan. "From the School—House to the Cabinet, From the Cabin to the Senate." 52pp. [M-251]. [Crew/JGB-32].

537.200 Wait Till The Votes Are Counted! (Drum Obbligato). w.m. John H. Sarchet. Published by Geo. D. Newhall Co., Cincinnati, OH. 1884. B/w geometric design and line border. "Republican Campaign Songs." "The Newest, Sprightliest and the Best." List of other songs in the series. 4pp. Page 4: Advertising. [Crew/JGB-101]. [AMC].

537.201 Wake Up Freemen Wake. w. "By Demo." m. "Tune—*Boatman Dance.*" In: *Cleveland & Hendricks Songster,* page 7. Copyright 1884 by E.Y. Landis. R/w/bl/gn/br drawing of Grover Cleveland, Thomas Hendricks, George "Washington," Thomas "Jefferson," Andrew "Jackson," ribbons, geometric designs. 64pp. [M-230]. [Crew/GC-46].

537.202 Wake Up, Republicans (Campaign Song). w. J.L. Feeney. m. "Air—*Wake Up, America.*" In: *Hughes And Fairbanks Campaign Song Book,* page 4. c. James L. Feeney. Published by William H. Delaney, Song Publisher, No. 117 Park Row, New York, NY. Copyright 1916 by William W. DeLaney. [8" × 11"]. R/w/b flags, shield. Bl/w photos of "Charles Evans Hughes" and "Charles Warren Fairbanks." "Preparedness, Protection, Prosperity." R/w/b drawing of flags, shield, geometric designs. 20pp. [M-407]. [Crew/CEH-1].

537.203 We Are Followers Of Blaine And Logan. w. No composer indicated. m. "Air—*Old Dan Tucker.*" In: *Beulah's Blaine And Logan Original Campaign Song Book 1884,* page 16. Printed and Published by Birnie Paper Company, Springfield, MA. 1884. [4" × 5¾"]. Gy/bk litho of James G. Blaine and John A. Logan, eagle, flags, shield, line border. 36pp. [M-232]. [Crew/JGB-41].

537.204 We Remember The Days, etc. w. No composer indicated. m. "Air—*Tenting To-Night, etc.*" In: *Beulah's Blaine And Logan Original Campaign Song Book 1884,* page 13. Printed and Published by Birnie Paper Company, Springfield, MA. 1884. [4" × 5¾"]. Gy/bk litho of James G. Blaine and John A. Logan, eagle, flags, shield, line border. 36pp. [M-232]. [Crew/JGB-41].

537.205 Welcome To Blaine. w. No composer indicated. m. "Air—*America.*" In: *P.T. Schultz & Co's Blaine And Logan Bugle Call,* page 5. Published by P.T. Schultz & Company, No. 172 Race Street, Cincinnati, OH. 1881. [1884 Edition]. [5⅞" × 7⅝"]. Bk/gn litho of James G. Blaine and John A. Logan, flags and eagle, geometric design border. 36pp. [M-245]. [Crew/JGB-67].

537.206 We'll Carry O-HI-O! w. J.W.B. Siders. m. "Air—*Aunt Jemimah.*" In: *Blaine And Logan Campaign Songster,* page 6. Published by American News Company, New York, NY. 1884. 36pp. [M-249]. [Crew/JGB-84].

537.207 We'll Run 'Em In! w. Prof. F. Widdows. m. "Air—*Genevieve Guards Duet.*" In: *Blaine And Logan Campaign Song-Book,* page 3. e. Prof. F. Widdows. Published by The Republican National Committee, New York, NY. 1884. [4⅜" × 5¹¹⁄₁₆"]. [V-1: Bk/y] [V-2: Pk/bk] litho of James G. Blaine and John A. Logan. "From the School—House to the Cabinet, From the Cabin to the Senate." 52pp. [M-251]. [Crew/JGB-32].

537.208 We'll Stand By Garfield's Friend. w.m. John H. Sarchet. Published by Geo. D. Newhall Co., Cincinnati, OH. 1884. B/w geometric design and line border. "Republican Campaign Songs." "The Newest, Sprightliest and the Best." List of other songs in the series. [Crew/JGB-101].

537.209 We'll Vote The Straight Ticket. w. No composer indicated. m. "Air—*We're Going To The Cotton Fields.*" In: *Blaine And Logan Songster,* page 10. Published by Thomas Hunter, Philadelphia, PA. 1884. [5½" × 7¼"]. N/c litho of Abraham Lincoln and James Garfield—"Our Martyred Presidents." Br/w litho of James G. Blaine—"Our Next President," and John A. Logan—"Our Next Vice-President," George Washington, Ulysses S. Grant. 68pp [M-237]. [Crew/JGB-35].

537.210 We've Got Him On The List. w. No composer indicated. m. "Arr. by Tariff Reform." In: *Red Hot Democratic Campaign Songs For 1888,* page 16. e. John Bunyon Herbert. Published by The S. Brainard's Sons Company, Chicago, IL. 1888. [5⅜" × 7⁷⁄₁₆"]. R/bk geometric designs. 36pp. Pages 2, 31 and 32: Advertising. Page 3: Contents. [M-294]. [Crew/GC-141].

537.211 What Means This Raising Of Banners. w. No composer indicated. m. "Air—*The Red, White And Blue.*" In: *Beulah's Blaine And Logan Original Campaign Song Book 1884,* page 14. Printed and Published by Birnie Paper Company, Springfield, MA. 1884. [4" × 5¾"]. Gy/bk litho of James G. Blaine and John A. Logan, eagle, flags, shield, line border. 36pp. [M-232]. [Crew/JGB-41].

537.212 When Blaine Takes The Helm. w. No composer indicated. m. "Air—*When Johnny Comes Marching Home.*" In: *Beulah's Blaine And Logan Original Campaign Song Book 1884,* page 32. Printed and Published by Birnie Paper Company, Springfield, MA. 1884. [4" × 5¾"]. Gy/bk litho of James G. Blaine and John A. Logan, eagle, flags, shield, line border. 36pp. [M-232]. [Crew/JGB-41].

537.213 When Election Day Is Over. w. J.W.B. Siders. m. "Air—*Glory, Glory, Hallelujah!*" In: *Blaine And Logan Campaign Songster,* page 4. Published by American News Company, New York, NY. 1884. 36pp. [M-249]. [Crew/JGB-84].

537.214 When Voting Day Shall Come. w. No composer indicated. m. "Air—*When Johnny Comes Marching Home.*" In: *Blaine And Logan Campaign Song-Book,* page 41. e. Prof. F. Widdows. Published by The Republican National Committee, New York, NY. 1884. [4⅜" × 5¹⁵⁄₁₆"]. [V-1: Bk/y] [V-2: Pk/bk] litho of James G. Blaine and John A. Logan. "From the School—House to the Cabinet, From the Cabin to the Senate." 52pp. [M-251]. [Crew/JGB-32].

537.215 When We Went 'Lectioneering. w. No composer indicated. m. "Air—*Evacuation Day.*" In: *Tilden And Hendricks' Reform Songs (For The Centennial Campaign Of 1876),* page 20. Published by The National Democratic Committee, Box 3637, New York, NY. 1876. [3⅞" × 5¹⁵⁄₁₆"]. Gn/bk litho of Samuel J. Tilden and Thomas A. Hendricks, geometric design border. 40pp. [M-203]. [Crew/SJT-21].

537.216 The White House Broom. w. "By Demo." m. "Tune—*Clar De Katchin.*" In: *Cleveland & Hendricks Songster,* page 18. Copyright 1884 by E.Y. Landis. R/w/bl/gn/br drawing of Grover Cleveland, Thomas Hendricks, George "Washington," Thomas "Jefferson," Andrew "Jackson," ribbons, geometric designs. 64pp. [M-230]. [Crew/GC-46].

537.217 The White House Wasn't Made For You. w. No composer indicated. m. "Air—*When Johnny Comes Marching Home.*" In: *Beulah's Blaine And Logan Original Campaign Song Book 1884,* page 20. Printed and Published by Birnie Paper Company, Springfield, MA. 1884. [4" × 5¾"]. Gy/bk litho of James G. Blaine and John A. Logan, eagle, flags, shield, line border. 36pp. [M-232]. [Crew/JGB-41].

537.218 The White Plume And The Tramp (A Campaign Song). w.m. REX. Published by F.H. Chandler, No. 172 Montague Street, Brooklyn, NY. 1884. Non-pictorial geometric designs. 6pp. Pages 2 and 6: Blank. [Crew/JGB-110].

537.219 The White-Plumed Knight. w. Mrs. M. Jennie Porter. m. "Air—*Bonnie Blue Flag.*" In: *Blaine And Logan Campaign Song-Book,* page 35. e. Prof. F. Widdows. Published by The Republican National Committee, New York, NY. 1884. [4⅜" × 5¹⁵⁄₁₆"]. [V-1: Bk/y] [V-2: Pk/bk] litho of James G. Blaine and John A. Logan. "From the School—House to the Cabinet, From the Cabin to the Senate." 52pp. [M-251]. [Crew/JGB-32].

537.220 Why Are The Democrats Sorrowing So? w. No composer indicated. m. Notation. In: *The People's Songs For Blaine & Logan,* page 20. Published by Acme Publishing Bureau, J.C.O. Redington, General Manager, No. 252 Broadway, New York, NY. Copyright 1884 by J.C.O. Redington. [4⅞" × 6⅝"]. B/w litho of James G. Blaine. "Adopted by the General Republican Committees in New York City and elsewhere." "Adapted for every Voice in the Glorious Land of Freedom. All the Nation may Sing." "Come, join that Columbia's blessings increase, All Singing for Liberty, Glory and Peace." "Acme Songs." 32pp. [M-246]. [Crew/JGB-45].

537.221 With Blaine And Jack We'll Clear The Track (Song & Chorus). w.m. W.B. Richardson. John Church & Co., No. 66 W. Fourth Street, Cincinnati, OH. 1884. Non-pictorial geometric designs. 6pp. Pages 2 and 6: Blank. [Crew/JGB-113].

537.222 Work For Blaine And Logan. w. Michigander. m.a. F. Widdows. In: *Blaine And Logan Campaign Song-Book,* page 10. e. Prof. F. Widdows. Published by The Republican National Committee, New York, NY. 1884. [4⅜" × 5¹⁵⁄₁₆"]. [V-1: Bk/y] [V-2: Pk/bk] litho of James G. Blaine and John A. Logan. "From the School—House to the Cabinet, From the Cabin to the Senate." 52pp. [M-251]. [Crew/JGB-32].

537.223 The Workingman's Campaign Song. w. Frank P. Cleary, M.D. m. "Air—*Away Down South In Dixie.*" In: *Blaine And Logan Campaign Song-Book,* page 24. e. Prof. F. Widdows. Published by The Republican National Committee, New York, NY. 1884. [4⅜" × 5¹⁵⁄₁₆"]. [V-1: Bk/y] [V-2: Pk/bk] litho of James G. Blaine and John A. Logan. "From the School—House to the Cabinet, From the Cabin to the Senate." 52pp. [M-251]. [Crew/JGB-32].

537.224 Yankee Doodle At Chicago. w. No composer indicated. m. "Tune—*Yankee Doodle.*" In: *Blaine And Logan Songster,* page 46. Published by Thomas Hunter, Philadelphia, PA. 1884. [5½" × 7¼"]. N/c litho of Abraham Lincoln and James Garfield—"Our Martyred Presidents." Br/w litho of James G. Blaine—"Our Next President," and John A. Logan—"Our Next Vice-President," George Washington, Ulysses S. Grant. 68pp [M-237]. [Crew/JGB-35].

537.225 Yankee Doodle At St. Louis. w. No composer indicated. m. "Tune—*Yankee Doodle.*" In: *Republican Campaign Parodies And Songs* [Songster], page 14. Published by Betts and Burnett, South Butler, Wayne County, NY. 1896. [7¾" × 5½"]. Be/bk non-pictorial. "McKinley and Hobart." "1896." 28pp. [M-340]. [Crew/WM-67].

• **AmPM-538 BURLEIGH,** Edwin Chick (State Land Agent, 1876–1878; Assistant Clerk in the State House, 1878; Clerk in the Office of the State Treasurer, 1880–1884; State Treasurer 1884–1888; Governor, 1889–1892; U.S. House, 1897–1911; U.S. Senate, 1913–1916)

538.1 Gov. Burleigh's March. m. W.G. Brooks. Published by F. Trifet, Publisher, No. 36 Bromfield Street, Boston, MA. Copyright 1889. [Edition ca. 1896]. Non-pictorial geometric and floral designs. Published as an issue of the "*Boston Weekly Journal Of Sheet Music.*" 6pp. Page 2: Inside title—**Governor Burleigh's Reception March.** Page 6: Advertising.

538.2 Gov. Burleigh's Reception March. m. W.G. Brooks. In: *43 Marches And Two-Steps,* page 70. Published by F. Trifet, Publisher, 36 Bromfield Street, Boston, MA. [1896]. 132pp.

538.3 Gov. Burleigh's Reception March. m. W.G. Brooks. In: *42 Marches And Quicksteps.* Published by F. Trifet, Publisher, 36 Bromfield Street, Boston, MA. [1896]. 132pp.

538.4 [The Fishermen Are Coming]. w. No composer indicated. m. "Air—*I'll Have A Sheepskin Too.*" *Republican Campaign Songs,* page 2. Published by the Bath Republican Glee Club, Bath, ME. 1888. [3⅓" × 7½"]. B/w litho of eagle. "To James G. Blaine." 4pp. [Foldout]. [Crew/JGB-50].

• **AmPM-539 CURTIS,** Oakley Chester (Mayor, Portland, 1911–1914; Governor, 1915–1917)

539.1 Democratic Success (March & Two Step). Leon Douglas. Published by Leon Douglas Music Pub., Augusta, ME. 1914. B/w photo of "Oakley C. Curtis." B/w geometric designs. 6pp. Page 6: Blank.

• **AmPM-540 DINGLEY,** Nelson, Jr. (State

House, 1862–1865, 1868 & 1873, Governor, 1874; U.S. House, 1881–1899)

540.1 How They Missed It, Boys! w. W.G. Thomas. m. Logan S. Porter. In: *McKinley Campaign Songster For 1900 (For Male Voices)*, page 14. e. W.G. Thomas. Published by The Home Music Company, Logansport, IN. 1900. Gn/bk litho of "William McKinley for President" and "Theo. Roosevelt For Vice President," eagle, flags, shield. "Send cash with order." "All orders will be promptly filled if accompanied by cash." "Single copy 15 cts. $.50 per dozen." "Note: Our McKinley Campaign Songster No. 2, Entirely Different from this will be issued September 10th. Same Price." 36pp. [M-373]. [Crew/WM-275].

540.2 Loop The Loop. w. No composer indicated. m. "Tune — *Down On The Farm*." In: *Campaign Songs* [Song Sheet], page 8. w. Edwin A. Hartshorn. m. Popular tunes. Printed by McAuliffe & Booth, Printers, New York, NY. 1904. [5³⁄₁₆" × 8½"]. Non-pictorial. "Seventh Edition" "1904–1904." 8pp. [M-388]. [Crew/TR-161].

• **AmPM-541 DOW**, Neal (Mayor, Portland, 1851 & 1855; State House, 1858–1859; Candidate for President, 1880) [ALSO SEE: DOC/PSM-ND]

541.1 Don't Mix Your Liquor Boys. w. No composer indicated. m. "*Low-Backed Car* or *Wait For The Wagon.*" Published by Andrews, Printer, 38 Chatham Street, New York, NY. [185-]. B/w non-pictorial geometric design border. "Andrews, Printer, 38 Chatham St., N.Y., Dealer in Songs, Games Books, Toy Motto Verses, &c., Wholesale and Retain." 2pp. Page 2: Blank. [AMC].

• **AmPM-542 FAIRFIELD**, John (U.S. House, 1835–1838; Governor, 1939–1843; U.S. Senate, 1843–1847)

542.1 Boundary March And Quick Step. m. E.L. White. Published by C. Bradlee, 135 Washington Street, Boston, MA. [1839–1843]. Non-pictorial geometric designs. "Respectfully Dedicated to Gov. Fairfield and the Defenders of the Territory of Maine." 4pp. Page 4: Blank.

542.2 Gov. Fairfield's Quick Step. m. H.F. Williams. Published by C. Bradlee, 135 Washington Street, Boston, MA. [1839–1843]. Non-pictorial geometric designs. "Composed and Respectfully Dedicated to his Excellency." 4pp. Pages 1 and 4: Blank.

542.3 The Grand North Eastern Boundary March. m. Charles M. King. Published by Firth & Hall, 1 Franklin Square, New York, NY. 1839. B/w litho of an eagle holding an American flag in its mouth. "Respectfully Inscribed to His Excellency Governor Fairfield (Governor of the State of Maine.)" "Pr. 25c nett." 6pp. [?].

• **AmPM-543 FESSENDEN**, William Pitt (State House, 1832, 1840, 1845–1846 & 1853–1854; U.S. House, 1841–1843; U.S. Senate, 1854–1864 & 1865–1869; Secretary of the Treasury, 1864–1865)

543.1 Seven Men! Seven Men! w. No composer indicated. m. "Air — *Maryland, My Maryland.*" In: *The Grant Campaign Songster, Containing All The Most Popular Original Songs, Ballads And Recitations That Will Be Most Sung During This Presidential Campaign, Adapted To Very Popular And Well-Known Airs And Choruses*, page 10. Published by Robert M. Dewitt, Publisher, No. 13 Frankfort Street, New York, NY. 1868. [4¼" × 5¾"]. [V-1: Be/bk] [V-2: Gn/bk] litho of Ulysses S. Grant. 76pp. [M-155]. [Crew/USG-75].

• **AmPM-543A HAMLIN**, Hannibal (State House, 1836–1840 & 1847; U.S. House, 1843–1847; U.S. Senate, 1848–1857, 1857–1861 & 1869–1881; Governor, 1857; Vice President, 1861–1865; U.S. Minister to Spain, 1881–1882) [SEE: DOC/PSM-AL]

543A.1 The Baltimore Convention. w. B. m. "Tune — *Tip And Ty.*" In: *The Wide Awake Vocalist (Or Rail Splitters' Song Book)*, page 26. Published by E.A. Daggett, No. 333 Broadway, New York, NY. 1860. Non-pictorial geometric design border. "Words and Music for the Republican Campaign of 1860, Embracing a Great Variety of Songs, Solos, Duets and Choruses Arranged for Piano or melodeon; The best collection of Words and Music ever published for a campaign, Every Club and Family should have copies, so as to join in the choruses; The Ladies are invited to join in the choruses at the meetings." 68pp. [M-116]. [Crew/AL-59].

543A.2 The Banner Of Freedom. w. No composer indicated. m. "Air — *Star Spangled Banner.*" In: *The Republican Campaign Songster For 1860*, page 27. c. W.H. Burleigh. Published by [V-1 and V-2: H. Dayton, No. 36 Howard Street, New York, NY] [V-3: McNally & Company, No. 81 Dearborn Street, Chicago, IL]. 1860. [V-1: Gn/bk] [V-2: Y/bk] [V-3: Be/bk] [V-4: Bl/bk]. "Price 10 cents." [3¹³⁄₁₆" × 6"]. 72pp. [M-104]. [Crew/AL-57].

543A.3 Banner Of Freedom. w.m. No composer or tune indicated. In: *Republican Song Book*, page 51. c. Thomas Drew "(Late Editor of *The Massachusetts Spy*)." Published by Thayer and Eldridge, Boston, MA. 1860. [3⅞" × 5⅞"]. Br/bk litho of beardless Abraham Lincoln, vignettes of young Lincoln chopping rails, polling raft. 68pp. [M-108]. [Crew/AL-8].

543A.4 [The Campaign Commences Most Nobly] (Campaign Song). w. No composer indicated. m. "Air — *Rosin The Bow.*" In: *Hutchinson's Republican Songster For 1860*, page 68. e. John W. Hutchinson "(of the Hutchinson Family Singers)." Published by O. Hutchinson, Publisher, No. 272 Greenwich Street, New York, NY. 1860. B/w floral design border. "Lincoln and Liberty." 76pp. [M-110]. [Crew/AL-317].

543A.5 Cheer, Boys, Cheer. w. No composer indicated. m. "Air — *Cheer, Boys, Cheer.*" "Respectfully dedicated to Hon. Horace Greeley." In: *The Wide Awake Vocalist (Or Rail Splitters' Song Book)*, page 63. Published by E.A. Daggett, No. 333 Broadway, New York, NY. 1860. Non-pictorial geometric design border. "Words and Music for the Republican Campaign of 1860, Embracing a Great Variety of Songs, Solos, Duets and Choruses Arranged for Piano or melodeon; The best collection of Words and Music ever published for a campaign, Every Club and Family should have copies, so as to join in the choruses; The Ladies are invited to join in the choruses at the meetings." 68pp. Page 2: Index. Page 67: Blank. Page 68: Advertising for Horace Waters publications. [M-116]. [Crew/AL-59].

543A.6 [Come, All Ye Good Republicans] (Campaign Song). w. No composer indicated. m. "Tune — *Wait For The Wagon.*" In: *Republican Song Book*, page

28. c. Thomas Drew "(Late Editor of *The Massachusetts Spy*)." Published by Thayer and Eldridge, Boston, MA. 1860. [3⅞" × 5⅞"]. Br/bk litho of beardless Abraham Lincoln, vignettes of young Lincoln chopping rails, polling raft. 68pp. [M-108]. [Crew/AL-8].

543A.7 Come, Freemen, Come Rally. w.m. No composer or tune indicated. In: *The Wide Awake Vocalist (Or Rail Splitters' Song Book)*, page 9. Published by E.A. Daggett, No. 333 Broadway, New York, NY. 1860. Non-pictorial geometric design border. "Words and Music for the Republican Campaign of 1860, Embracing a Great Variety of Songs, Solos, Duets and Choruses Arranged for Piano or melodeon; The best collection of Words and Music ever published for a campaign, Every Club and Family should have copies, so as to join in the choruses; The Ladies are invited to join in the choruses at the meetings." 68pp. [M-116]. [Crew/AL-59].

543A.8 Douglas. w.m. No composer or tune indicated. In: *The Democratic Campaign Songster: Douglas & Johnson Melodies,* page 23. Published by P.J. Cozans, Publisher, New York, NY. [1860]. [3⅞" × 6"]. Y/bk litho of an eagle with ribbon—"Douglas & Johnson," train, ships, monument—"Liberty" sitting on rock base—"The Constitution." 40pp. [M-117]. [Crew/SAD-5].

543A.9 Flag Of The Brave. w.m. No composer or tune indicated. In: *Connecticut Wide-Awake Songster*, page 17. e. John W. Hutchinson "(of Hutchinson Family Singers)" and Benjamin Jepson. Published by O. Hutchinson, Publisher, No. 272 Greenwich Street, New York, NY. 1860. [4" × 6"]. Bl/bk non-pictorial line border. "Lincoln and liberty." 76pp. Pages 2, 75 and 76: Advertising. Pages 5 and 6: Contents. Pages 7 to 10: Republican platform. [M-109]. [Crew/AL-175].

543A.10 For Abe Shall Have The Belt. w. S. m.a. Henry Tucker. In: *The Wide Awake Vocalist (Or Rail Splitters' Song Book)*, page 30. Published by E.A. Daggett, No. 333 Broadway, New York, NY. 1860. Non-pictorial geometric design border. "Words and Music for the Republican Campaign of 1860, Embracing a Great Variety of Songs, Solos, Duets and Choruses Arranged for Piano or melodeon; The best collection of Words and Music ever published for a campaign, Every Club and Family should have copies, so as to join in the choruses; The Ladies are invited to join in the choruses at the meetings." 68pp. [M-116]. [Crew/AL-59].

543A.11 Freedom Through The Land. w.m. No composer indicated. m. "Tune—*Old Granite State.*" In: *The Republican Campaign Songster No. #1*, page 14. Published by American Publishing House, No. 60 West Fourth Street, Cincinnati, OH. [1860]. [3¾" × 5¾"]. B/w litho of Abraham Lincoln. 48[?]pp. [M-113]. [Crew/AL-298].

543A.12 The Freeman's Union. w.m. No composer or tune indicated. In: *Republican Song Book*, page 50. c. Thomas Drew "(Late Editor of *The Massachusetts Spy*)." Published by Thayer and Eldridge, Boston, MA. 1860. [3⅞" × 5⅞"]. Br/bk litho of beardless Abraham Lincoln, vignettes of young Lincoln chopping rails, polling raft. 68pp. [M-108]. [Crew/AL-8].

543A.13 The Gathering Republican Army. w. No composer indicated. m. "Air—*Vilikins And His Dinah.*" In: *Connecticut Wide-Awake Songster*, page 30. e. John W. Hutchinson "(of Hutchinson Family Singers)" and Benjamin Jepson. Published by O. Hutchinson, Publisher, No. 272 Greenwich Street, New York, NY. 1860. [4" × 6"]. Bl/bk non-pictorial line border. "Lincoln and liberty." 76pp. Pages 2, 75 and 76: Advertising. Pages 5 and 6: Contents. Pages 7 to 10: Republican platform. [M-109]. [Crew/AL-175].

543A.14 Give Us Abe And Hamlin Too. w. Mrs. L.L. Deming. m. "Air—*A Wet Sheet And A Flowing Sea.*" In: *The Great Republican Campaigns Of 1860 And 1896*, page 170. e. Osborn H. Oldroyd. Published by Laird & Lee, Chicago, IL. 1896. [5 5/16" × 7 7/16"]. Gn/r/bk photos of Abraham Lincoln, William McKinley and Garrett Hobart. "Sound Money, Protection, Prosperity." 208pp. [Crew/AL-574].

543A.15 The Grand Rally. w.m. No composer or tune indicated. In: *Connecticut Wide-Awake Songster*, page 21. e. John W. Hutchinson "(of Hutchinson Family Singers)" and Benjamin Jepson. Published by O. Hutchinson, Publisher, No. 272 Greenwich Street, New York, NY. 1860. [4" × 6"]. Bl/bk non-pictorial line border. "Lincoln and Liberty." 76pp. Pages 2, 75 and 76: Advertising. Pages 5 and 6: Contents. Pages 7 to 10: Republican platform. [M-109]. [Crew/AL-175].

543A.16 Hamlin From The Pilgrim Land. w. No composer indicated. m. "Tune—*Lu Lu Is Our Darling Pride.*" In: *The Wide Awake Vocalist (Or Rail Splitters' Song Book)*, page 25. Published by E.A. Daggett, No. 333 Broadway, New York, NY. 1860. Non-pictorial geometric design border. "Words and Music for the Republican Campaign of 1860, Embracing a Great Variety of Songs, Solos, Duets and Choruses Arranged for Piano or melodeon; The best collection of Words and Music ever published for a campaign, Every Club and Family should have copies, so as to join in the choruses; The Ladies are invited to join in the choruses at the meetings." 68pp. [M-116]. [Crew/AL-59].

543A.17 Have You Heard From Chicago? w. No composer indicated. m. "Air—*Star Spangled Banner.*" In: *The Wide Awake Vocalist (Or Rail Splitters' Song Book)*, page 59. Published by E.A. Daggett, No. 333 Broadway, New York, NY. 1860. Non-pictorial geometric design border. "Words and Music for the Republican Campaign of 1860, Embracing a Great Variety of Songs, Solos, Duets and Choruses Arranged for Piano or melodeon; The best collection of Words and Music ever published for a campaign, Every Club and Family should have copies, so as to join in the choruses; The Ladies are invited to join in the choruses at the meetings." 68pp. [M-116]. [Crew/AL-59].

543A.18 Hi, Rally! Ho, Rally! w. J.B. Marsh. m. "Air—*Nelly Bly.*" "Written for and sung at the Ratification Meeting in White Hall, New Castle, Pa., May 22, 1860." In: *The Wide Awake Vocalist (Or Rail Splitters' Song Book)*, page 40. Published by E.A. Daggett, No. 333 Broadway, New York, NY. 1860. Non-pictorial geometric design border. "Words and Music for the Republican Campaign of 1860, Embracing a Great Variety of Songs, Solos, Duets and Choruses Arranged for Piano or melodeon; The best collection of Words and Music ever published for a campaign, Every Club and Family should have copies, so as to join in the choruses; The Ladies are invited to join in the choruses at the meetings." 68pp. [M-116]. [Crew/AL-59].

543A.19 Hurrah For Abe Lincoln! w. No composer indicated. m. "Tune—*Boatman Dance.*" In: *Connecticut Wide-Awake Songster*, page 12. e. John W. Hutchinson "(of Hutchinson Family Singers)" and Benjamin Jepson. Published by O. Hutchinson, Publisher, No. 272 Greenwich Street, New York, NY. 1860. [4" × 6"]. Bl/bk non-pictorial line border. "Lincoln and liberty." 76pp. Pages 2, 75 and 76: Advertising. Pages 5 and 6: Contents. Pages 7 to 10: Republican platform. [M-109]. [Crew/AL-175].

543A.20 Hurrah For Lincoln. w.m. No composer or tune indicated. In: *The Republican Campaign Songster For 1860*, page 45. c. W.H. Burleigh. Published by [V-1 and V-2: H. Dayton, No. 36 Howard Street, New York, NY] [V-3: McNally & Company, No. 81 Dearborn Street, Chicago, IL]. 1860. [V-1: Gn/bk] [V-2: Y/bk] [V-3: Be/bk] [V-4: Bl/bk]. "Price 10 cents." [3¹⁵⁄₁₆" × 6"]. 72pp. [M-104]. [Crew/AL-57].

543A.21 A Jolly Good Crew We'll Have. w. W.S. Sanford. m. "Air—*Little More Cider.*" In: *Connecticut Wide-Awake Songster*, page 71. e. John W. Hutchinson "(of Hutchinson Family Singers)" and Benjamin Jepson. Published by O. Hutchinson, Publisher, No. 272 Greenwich Street, New York, NY. 1860. [4" × 6"]. Bl/bk non-pictorial line border. "Lincoln and liberty." 76pp. Pages 2, 75 and 76: Advertising. Pages 5 and 6: Contents. Pages 7 to 10: Republican platform. [M-109]. [Crew/AL-175].

543A.22 Last Hope Of Buchanan. w. No composer indicated. m. "Air—*Last Rose Of Summer.*" In: *Fremont Songs For The People (Original and Selected)*, page 41. c. Thomas Drew "(Editor of *The Massachusetts Spy*)." Published by John P. Jewett & Company, Boston, MA. Copyright 1856 by Thomas Drew. [3⅜" × 5½"]. B/w litho of "J.C. Fremont." "The Campaign of 1856." 68pp. [Crew/JCF-18].

543A.23 Lincoln And Hamlin (A Campaign Song). w. Samuel Copp, "A Veteran." m. No tune indicated. "The following Campaign Song was written by Samuel Copp, Esq., aged 75 years, for the Lincoln and Hamlin Club of Stonington, Conn., a place rendered memorable by the gallant repulse of a naval attack by the British, on the 9th, 10th, 11th, and 12th of Aug., 1814, in which four days' contest Mr. Copp took part. The original song is furnished to us by the author's friend, Samuel C. Brewster, Esq." In: *Connecticut Wide-Awake Songster*, page 24. e. John W. Hutchinson "(of Hutchinson Family Singers)" and Benjamin Jepson. Published by O. Hutchinson, Publisher, No. 272 Greenwich Street, New York, NY. 1860. [4" × 6"]. Bl/bk non-pictorial line border. "Lincoln and liberty." 76pp. Pages 2, 75 and 76: Advertising. Pages 5 and 6: Contents. Pages 7 to 10: Republican platform. [M-109]. [Crew/AL-175].

543A.24 Lincoln & Hamlin. w. No composer indicated. m. "Tune—*Nelly Gray.*" [1860]. B/w non-pictorial line border. "People's Campaign Song, No. 2." 2pp. Page 2: Blank. [Penny Song Sheet]. [Crew/AL-523].

543A.25 Lincoln And Hamlin. w.m. No composer or tune indicated. In: *Republican Song Book*, page 18 c. Thomas Drew "(Late Editor of *The Massachusetts Spy*)." Published by Thayer and Eldridge, Boston, MA. 1860. [3⅞" × 5⅞"]. Br/bk litho of beardless Abraham Lincoln, vignettes of young Lincoln chopping rails, polling raft. 68pp. [M-108]. [Crew/AL-8].

543A.26 Lincoln And Hamlin—God Bless Them! w. No composer indicated. m. "Air—*Columbia The Gen Of The Ocean.*" In: *The Great Republican Campaigns Of 1860 And 1896*, page 162. e. Osborn H. Oldroyd. Published by Laird & Lee, Chicago, IL. 1896. [5⁵⁄₁₆" × 7⅞₁₆"]. Gn/r/bk photos of Abraham Lincoln, William McKinley and Garrett Hobart. "Sound Money, Protection, Prosperity." 208pp. [Crew/AL-574].

543A.27 Lincoln And Hamlin The True. w. No composer indicated. m. "Air—*The Red, White And Blue.*" In: *The Wide Awake Vocalist (Or Rail Splitters' Song Book)*, page 36. Published by E.A. Daggett, No. 333 Broadway, New York, NY. 1860. Non-pictorial geometric design border. "Words and Music for the Republican Campaign of 1860, Embracing a Great Variety of Songs, Solos, Duets and Choruses Arranged for Piano or melodeon; The best collection of Words and Music ever published for a campaign, Every Club and Family should have copies, so as to join in the choruses; The Ladies are invited to join in the choruses at the meetings." 68pp. [M-116]. [Crew/AL-59].

543A.28 The Lincoln Banner. w.m. No tune or composer indicated. In: *Republican Song Book*, page 60. c. Thomas Drew "(Late Editor of *The Massachusetts Spy*)." Published by Thayer and Eldridge, Boston, MA. 1860. [3⅞" × 5⅞"]. Br/bk litho of beardless Abraham Lincoln, vignettes of young Lincoln chopping rails, polling raft. 68pp. [M-108]. [Crew/AL-8].

543A.29 The Lincoln Boys. w.m. No composer or tune indicated. In: *The Wide Awake Vocalist (Or Rail Splitters' Song Book)*, page 64. Published by E.A. Daggett, No. 333 Broadway, New York, NY. 1860. Non-pictorial geometric design border. "Words and Music for the Republican Campaign of 1860, Embracing a Great Variety of Songs, Solos, Duets and Choruses Arranged for Piano or melodeon; The best collection of Words and Music ever published for a campaign, Every Club and Family should have copies, so as to join in the choruses; The Ladies are invited to join in the choruses at the meetings." 68pp. Page 2: Index. Page 67: Blank. Page 68: Advertising for Horace Waters publications. [M-116]. [Crew/AL-59].

543A.30 Lincoln Going To Washington. w. S.C.M. m. "Air—*Jimmy, Crack Corn.*" In: *Connecticut Wide-Awake Songster*, page 22. e. John W. Hutchinson "(of Hutchinson Family Singers)" and Benjamin Jepson. Published by O. Hutchinson, Publisher, No. 272 Greenwich Street, New York, NY. 1860. [4" × 6"]. Bl/bk non-pictorial line border. "Lincoln and liberty." 76pp. Pages 2, 75 and 76: Advertising. Pages 5 and 6: Contents. Pages 7 to 10: Republican platform. [M-109]. [Crew/AL-175].

543A.31 Lincoln, The Pride Of The Nation. w. No composer indicated. m. "Air—*The Red, White, And Blue.*" In: *Connecticut Wide-Awake Songster*, page 46. e. John W. Hutchinson "(of Hutchinson Family Singers)" and Benjamin Jepson. Published by O. Hutchinson, Publisher, No. 272 Greenwich Street, New York, NY. 1860. [4" × 6"]. Bl/bk non-pictorial line border. "Lincoln and liberty." 76pp. Pages 2, 75 and 76: Advertising. Pages 5 and 6: Contents. Pages 7 to 10: Republican platform. [M-109]. [Crew/AL-175].

543A.32 Lincoln's Nomination. w. K.A.M. m. "Air — *Yankee Doodle.*" In: *Connecticut Wide-Awake Songster*, page 31. e. John W. Hutchinson "(of Hutchinson Family Singers)" and Benjamin Jepson. Published by O. Hutchinson, Publisher, No. 272 Greenwich Street, New York, NY. 1860. [4" × 6"]. Bl/bk non-pictorial line border. "Lincoln and liberty." 76pp. Pages 2, 75 and 76: Advertising. Pages 5 and 6: Contents. Pages 7 to 10: Republican platform. [M-109]. [Crew/AL-175].

543A.33 Our Country's Call. w. No composer indicated. m. "Tune — *Hail Columbia.*" In: *Connecticut Wide-Awake Songster*, page 20. e. John W. Hutchinson "(of Hutchinson Family Singers)" and Benjamin Jepson. Published by O. Hutchinson, Publisher, No. 272 Greenwich Street, New York, NY. 1860. [4" × 6"]. Bl/bk non-pictorial line border. "Lincoln and liberty." 76pp. Pages 2, 75 and 76: Advertising. Pages 5 and 6: Contents. Pages 7 to 10: Republican platform. [M-109]. [Crew/AL-175].

543A.34 [Our Good Old Uncle Sam Is Sick] (A Campaign Song). w.m. No composer or tune indicated. In: *The Republican Campaign Songster No. #1*, page 30. Published by American Publishing House, No. 60 West Fourth Street, Cincinnati, OH. [1860]. [3¾" × 5¾"]. B/w litho of Abraham Lincoln. 48[?]pp. [M-113]. [Crew/AL-298].

543A.35 The People's Candidate. w. No composer indicated. m. "Air — *A Wet Sheet And A Flowing Sea.*" In: *The Republican Campaign Songster For 1860*, page 46. c. W.H. Burleigh. Published by [V-1 and V-2: H. Dayton, No. 36 Howard Street, New York, NY] [V-3: McNally & Company, No. 81 Dearborn Street, Chicago, IL]. 1860. [V-1: Gn/bk] [V-2: Y/bk] [V-3: Be/bk] [V-4: Bl/bk]. "Price 10 cents." [3¹³⁄₁₆" × 6"]. 72pp. [M-104]. [Crew/AL-57].

543A.36 Republicans! The Nation Calls You (Mixed Quartette and Chorus). w. G.W. Bungay. m.a. A. Cull. In: *The Wide Awake Vocalist (Or Rail Splitters' Song Book)*, page 48. Published by E.A. Daggett, No. 333 Broadway, New York, NY. 1860. Non-pictorial geometric design border. "Words and Music for the Republican Campaign of 1860, Embracing a Great Variety of Songs, Solos, Duets and Choruses Arranged for Piano or melodeon; The best collection of Words and Music ever published for a campaign, Every Club and Family should have copies, so as to join in the choruses; The Ladies are invited to join in the choruses at the meetings." 68pp. [M-116]. [Crew/AL-59].

543A.37 The Rising Tide. w.m. No composer or tune indicated. "Sung at the great Republican gathering at Erie, Pa., September, 12, 1860." In: *The Great Republican Campaigns Of 1860 And 1896*, page 174. e. Osborn H. Oldroyd. Published by Laird & Lee, Chicago, IL. 1896. [5⁵⁄₁₆" × 7⁷⁄₁₆"]. Gn/r/bk photos of Abraham Lincoln, William McKinley and Garrett Hobart. "Sound Money, Protection, Prosperity." 208pp. [Crew/AL-574].

543A.38 Roll On The Ball. w. No composer indicated. m. "Air — *Rosin The Bow.*" In: *The Republican Campaign Songster For 1860*, page 55. c. W.H. Burleigh. Published by [V-1 and V-2: H. Dayton, No. 36 Howard Street, New York, NY] [V-3: McNally & Company, No. 81 Dearborn Street, Chicago, IL]. 1860. [V-1: Gn/bk] [V-2: Y/bk] [V-3: Be/bk] [V-4: Bl/bk]. "Price 10 cents." [3¹³⁄₁₆" × 6"]. 72pp. [M-104]. [Crew/AL-57].

543A.39 Roll On The Republican Ball. w. No composer indicated. m. "Air — *Rosin The Bow.*" In: *The Wide Awake Vocalist (Or Rail Splitters' Song Book)*, page 7. Published by E.A. Daggett, No. 333 Broadway, New York, NY. 1860. Non-pictorial geometric design border. "Words and Music for the Republican Campaign of 1860, Embracing a Great Variety of Songs, Solos, Duets and Choruses Arranged for Piano or melodeon; The best collection of Words and Music ever published for a campaign, Every Club and Family should have copies, so as to join in the choruses; The Ladies are invited to join in the choruses at the meetings." 68pp. [M-116]. [Crew/AL-59].

543A.40 Shout For The Prairie King (Quartette or Chorus foe Male or Mixed Voices). w. G.W. Bungay. m.a. A. Cull. "Respectfully dedicated to the Young Men's Republican Union Club, of New York City." In: *The Wide Awake Vocalist (Or Rail Splitters' Song Book)*, page 12. Published by E.A. Daggett, No. 333 Broadway, New York, NY. 1860. Non-pictorial geometric design border. "Words and Music for the Republican Campaign of 1860, Embracing a Great Variety of Songs, Solos, Duets and Choruses Arranged for Piano or melodeon; The best collection of Words and Music ever published for a campaign, Every Club and Family should have copies, so as to join in the choruses; The Ladies are invited to join in the choruses at the meetings." 68pp. [M-116]. [Crew/AL-59].

543A.41 Song For The People. w.m. No composer or tune indicated. Published by Andrews, Printer, 38 Chatham Street, New York, NY. [1856]. [Approx. 6" × 10"]. B/w non-pictorial geometric design litho border. "Andrews, Printer, 38 Chatham Street, N.Y., Songs, Games, Toy Books, Motto Verses, &c., Wholesale and Retail." 2pp. Page 2: Blank. [AMC].

543A.42 Strike For The Right. w. E.W. Locke. m. No tune indicated. In: *The Republican Campaign Songster For 1860*, page 26. c. W.H. Burleigh. Published by [V-1 and V-2: H. Dayton, No. 36 Howard Street, New York, NY] [V-3: McNally & Company, No. 81 Dearborn Street, Chicago, IL]. 1860. [V-1: Gn/bk] [V-2: Y/bk] [V-3: Be/bk] [V-4: Bl/bk]. "Price 10 cents." [3¹³⁄₁₆" × 6"]. 72pp. [M-104]. [Crew/AL-57].

543A.43 Strike For The Right. w.m. No tune or composer indicated. "Sung at the Ratification Convention at Warsaw, Ill., July 2, 1860." In: *Republican Song Book*, page 59. c. Thomas Drew "(Late Editor of *The Massachusetts Spy*)." Published by Thayer and Eldridge, Boston, MA. 1860. [3⅞" × 5⅞"]. Br/bk litho of beardless Abraham Lincoln, vignettes of young Lincoln chopping rails, polling raft. 68pp. [M-108]. [Crew/AL-8].

543A.44 Strike For The Right. w.m. No tune or composer indicated. In: *Connecticut Wide-Awake Songster*, page 10. e. John W. Hutchinson "(of Hutchinson Family Singers)" and Benjamin Jepson. Published by O. Hutchinson, Publisher, No. 272 Greenwich Street, New York, NY. 1860. [4" × 6"]. Bl/bk non-pictorial line border. "Lincoln and liberty." 76pp. Pages 2, 75 and 76: Advertising. Pages 5 and 6: Contents. Pages 7 to 10: Republican platform. [M-109]. [Crew/AL-175].

543A.45 [Take Down The Harp Of The Last Campaign] (A Campaign Song). w. No composer indicated. m. "Air — *The Harp That Once In Tara's Halls.*" In: *Republican Song Book*, page 46. c. Thomas Drew "(Late Editor of *The Massachusetts Spy*)." Published by Thayer and Eldridge, Boston, MA. 1860. [3⅞" × 5⅞"]. Br/bk litho of beardless Abraham Lincoln, vignettes of young Lincoln chopping rails, polling raft. 68pp. [M-108]. [Crew/AL-8].

543A.46 [The War Drums Are Beating] (Rallying Song). w.m. No composer or tune indicated. In: *Hutchinson's Republican Songster For 1860*, page 47. e. John W. Hutchinson "(of the Hutchinson Family Singers)." Published by O. Hutchinson, Publisher, No. 272 Greenwich Street, New York, NY. 1860. B/w floral design border. "Lincoln and Liberty." 76pp. [M-110]. [Crew/AL-317].

543A.47 We Will Vote For Old Abe Lincoln. w. No composer indicated. m. "Air — *The Old Granite State.*" In: *The Wide Awake Vocalist (Or Rail Splitters' Song Book)*, page 54. Published by E.A. Daggett, No. 333 Broadway, New York, NY. 1860. Non-pictorial geometric design border. "Words and Music for the Republican Campaign of 1860, Embracing a Great Variety of Songs, Solos, Duets and Choruses Arranged for Piano or melodeon; The best collection of Words and Music ever published for a campaign, Every Club and Family should have copies, so as to join in the choruses; The Ladies are invited to join in the choruses at the meetings." 68pp. [M-116]. [Crew/AL-59].

543A.48 We'll Send Buchanan Home. w. No composer indicated. m. "Air — *Few Days.*" In: *Connecticut Wide-Awake Songster*, page 62. e. John W. Hutchinson "(of Hutchinson Family Singers)" and Benjamin Jepson. Published by O. Hutchinson, Publisher, No. 272 Greenwich Street, New York, NY. 1860. [4" × 6"]. Bl/bk non-pictorial line border. "Lincoln and Liberty." 76pp. Pages 2, 75 and 76: Advertising. Pages 5 and 6: Contents. Pages 7 to 10: Republican platform. [M-109]. [Crew/AL-175].

543A.49 The Western Star. w. No composer indicated. m. "Air — *Gaily The Troubadour.*" In: *The Republican Campaign Songster For 1860*, page 37. c. W.H. Burleigh. Published by [V-1 and V-2: H. Dayton, No. 36 Howard Street, New York, NY] [V-3: McNally & Company, No. 81 Dearborn Street, Chicago, IL]. 1860. [V-1: Gn/bk] [V-2: Y/bk] [V-3: Be/bk] [V-4: Bl/bk]. "Price 10 cents." [3¹³⁄₁₆" × 6"]. 72pp. [M-104]. [Crew/ AL-57].

543A.50 Western Star! Give It Three Cheers. w. No composer indicated. "Air — *Gaily The Troubadour.*" In: *The Wide Awake Vocalist (Or Rail Splitters' Song Book)*, page 16. Published by E.A. Daggett, No. 333 Broadway, New York, NY. 1860. Non-pictorial geometric design border. "Words and Music for the Republican Campaign of 1860, Embracing a Great Variety of Songs, Solos, Duets and Choruses Arranged for Piano or melodeon; The best collection of Words and Music ever published for a campaign, Every Club and Family should have copies, so as to join in the choruses; The Ladies are invited to join in the choruses at the meetings." 68pp. [M-116]. [Crew/AL-59].

543A.51 Where Are They? w. No composer indicated. m. "Tune — *Where, Oh Where Are The Hebrew Children?*" In: *Republican Song Book*, page 28. c. Thomas Drew "(Late Editor of *The Massachusetts Spy*)." Published by Thayer and Eldridge, Boston, MA. 1860. [3⅞" × 5⅞"]. Br/bk litho of beardless Abraham Lincoln, vignettes of young Lincoln chopping rails, polling raft. 68pp. [M-108]. [Crew/AL-8].

543A.52 Where, Oh! Where Is Jimmy Buchanan? w. No composer indicated. m. "Air — *Where, Oh Where Are The Hebrew Children?* In: *The Wide Awake Vocalist (Or Rail Splitters' Song Book)*, page 40. Published by E.A. Daggett, No. 333 Broadway, New York, NY. 1860. Non-pictorial geometric design border. "Words and Music for the Republican Campaign of 1860, Embracing a Great Variety of Songs, Solos, Duets and Choruses Arranged for Piano or melodeon; The best collection of Words and Music ever published for a campaign, Every Club and Family should have copies, so as to join in the choruses; The Ladies are invited to join in the choruses at the meetings." 68pp. [M-116]. [Crew/AL-59].

543A.53 Wide Awake (Campaign Song). w. No composer indicated. m. "Tune — *A Wet Sheet And A Flowing Sea.*" In: *Republican Song Book*, page 27. c. Thomas Drew "(Late Editor of *The Massachusetts Spy*)." Published by Thayer and Eldridge, Boston, MA. 1860. [3⅞" × 5⅞"]. Br/bk litho of beardless Abraham Lincoln, vignettes of young Lincoln chopping rails, polling raft. 68pp. [M-108]. [Crew/AL-8].

543A.54 Wide-Awake Club Song. w. No composer indicated. m. "Air — *A Wet Sheet And A Flowing Sea.*" In: *Connecticut Wide-Awake Songster*, page 70. e. John W. Hutchinson "(of Hutchinson Family Singers)" and Benjamin Jepson. Published by O. Hutchinson, Publisher, No. 272 Greenwich Street, New York, NY. 1860. [4" × 6"]. Bl/bk non-pictorial line border. "Lincoln and Liberty." 76pp. Pages 2, 75 and 76: Advertising. Pages 5 and 6: Contents. Pages 7 to 10: Republican platform. [M-109]. [Crew/AL-175].

• **AmPM-544 HOLMES**, John (Massachusetts General Court, 1802, 1803, & 1812; State Senate, Massachusetts, 1813 & 1814; U.S. House, Massachusetts, 1817–1820; U.S. Senate, Maine, 1820–1827 & 1829–1833; State House, Maine, 1836–1837; U.S. Attorney for Maine, 1841–1843)

544.1 Harrison Song. w. Hon. John Holmes, "of Maine." m. "Air — *Yankee Doodle.*" "Read by [Holmes] from the balcony of the State House, Augusta, on the 24th of June, 1840." In: *Log Cabin Minstrel (Or Tippecanoe Songster)*, page 13. c. "A Member of the Roxbury Whig Association." Published at the *Patriot And Democrat* Office, Roxbury, [MA]. 1840. [4½" × 6¾"]. [V-1:Y/bk] [V-2: Bl/bk] litho of William Henry Harrison, geometric design border. "Old Tip's the boy to swing the flail. Hurrah! Hurrah! Hurrah!" 64pp. Page 3: Title page — "Containing a Selection of Songs Original and Selected Many of them Written Expressly for this Work, Compiled, Published and Arranged by a member of the Roxbury Democratic Whig Association and Respectfully Dedicated to the Log Cabin Boys of the U.S." [M-013]. [Crew/WHH-71].

544.2 The Log Cabin Song. w. No composer indicated. m. "Tune — *Yankee Doodle.*" "Before the adjournment of the Convention at Augusta, the Hon. John Holmes of Thomaston, offered and read the following song." In: *Tippecanoe Song-Book (A Collection Of Log Cabin And Patriotic Melodies)*, page 71. Published by Marshall, Williams & Butler, Philadelphia, PA. 1840. White on black litho of log cabin, plow, flags, eagle. 180pp. [M-024]. [Crew/WHH-61].

• **AmPM-545 KENT,** Edward (Mayor, Bangor, 1836–1837; Governor, 1838–1839 & 1841–1842; State Supreme Court, 1859–1873)

545.1 Governor Kent's March. m. Benjamin Wyman, "Teacher of Music at the Teacher's Seminary, Gorham." No publisher indicated. [1838–1842]. Non-pictorial. "Composed and Arranged for the Piano Forte and Respectfully Inscribed to Edward Kent, Esq." 4pp. Pages 1 and 4: Blank.

545.2 Old Tippecanoe. w. No composer indicated. m. "Tune — *Roast Beef.*" "Sung by R.R. Kendall of Freeport at a Whig Convention of the Fourth in Lincoln Co., Maine." In: *The Log Cabin*, page 4, Vol. 1, No. 12, July 18, 1840. Published by Horace Greeley & Company, New York, NY. 1840. Non-pictorial. [Crew/WHH-91].

545.3 Tip And Tye (A Favorite Patriotic Ballad). w. No composer indicated. a. "A member of the Fifth Ward Glee Club." Copyright 1840 by Thomas Birch. Non-pictorial. "As sung at the Tippecanoe Associations with great applause, Arranged with an Accompaniment for the Piano Forte by a Member of the Fifth Ward Club." 4pp. Page 4: Blank. [Crew/WHH-75].

• **AmPM-546 MUSKIE,** Edmund Sixtus (Board of Adjustment, Waterville, 1948–1955; City Solicitor, Waterville, 1954; State House, 1947–1951; Governor, 1955–1959; U.S. Senate, 1959–1980; Candidate for Vice President, 1968; U.S. Secretary of State, 1980–1981) [ALSO SEE: DOC/PSM-LBJ & HHH]

546.1 Mr. Democrat. w. Peter Quinto, S. Spilmon and M. Vallo. m. Vincent Chiarelli. 45 rpm vinyl record. Published by Vincent Records, 1528 Broadway, Rockford, IL. #VR-105/ZTSC-121836. Performed by Pete Quinto and the Dave Remington Quartet. 1968.

• **AmPM-547 REED,** Thomas Bracket (State House, 1868–1869; State Senate, 1870; State Attorney General, 1870–1872; City Solicitor, Portland, 1874–1877; U.S. House, 1866–1899)

547.1 The Bradbury Schottische. m. Dayton Vreeland. Published by F.G. Smith, 109 & 111 Broadway, Paterson, NJ. 1897. B/w geometric designs. "Dedicated to H.N. Lakeham." 4pp. Page 4: Advertising for Bradbury pianos with photo of "Famous Patrons of Bradbury Pianos" including: "U.S. Grant, J.A. Garfield, C.A. Arthur, Benj. Harrison, R.B. Hayes, Grover Cleveland, Stanley Mathews, J.M Rusk, Benj. Tracy, Levi Morton, Thos. B. Reed, J.W. Noble, William Windom, John G. Carlisle, C.C. McCabe, A.H. Colquitt [and] Walter Q. Gresham." [Crew/MISC-142].

547.2 Git On Board. w. J.W. Matthews. m. Notation. "Old Melody." "For Male Voices." In: *True Blue Republican Campaign Songs For 1896*, page 19. c. J.B. Herbert. Published by The S. Brainard's Sons Company, Chicago, IL. 1896. [5⅜" × 6⅞"]. R/w/b drawing of crossed flags, wreath, ribbons. Bl/w photo of "Hon. Wm. McKinley." "Protection." 36pp. [M-328]. [Crew/WM-169].

547.3 Harrison Will Hold The Job. w. E.J. Seymour. m. "Air — *When McGinnis Gets A Job.*" In: *Harrison And Reid Campaign Song Book*, page 13. w. E.J. Seymour. m. Popular Airs. [1892]. [3⅞" × 5⅛"]. Bl/gn non-pictorial, stars, geometric designs. 36pp. Pages 2 and 35: Blank. Page 36: Advertising for this songbook. [M-316]. [Crew/BFH-35].

547.4 My Boyhood's Happy Home Way Down In Maine. w. Albert Edwin Fowler "(Author of *Pictures In The Album, Forgive Me For Our Baby's Sake, Just Another Broken Heart*, etc.)." Published by Albert E. Fowler, Newburyport, MA. 1900. Gn/bl/w drawing of an old home, pine wreath. "A Beautiful Ballad for the Home." "Respectfully inscribed to Maine's favorite son Hon. Thomas Bracket Reed." 6pp. Pages 2 and 6: Blank.

547.5 Our Leader Two Step March. m. Gilbert Ashton. Published by The B.F. Wood Music Co., Boston, MA. 1896. B/w photo of Thomas B. Reed — facsimile signature. 1896. 8pp. Page 2: Blank. Page 3: At top of music — "Respectfully Dedicated to Hon. Thomas B. Reed." Page 8: Advertising.

547.6 Reed's Grand March. m. Clement Ryder. Published by Clement Ryder, No. 55 Hawthorne Street, Chelsea MA. 1896. B/w photo of Thomas Reed. B/w geometric designs. "To Thomas B. Reed." "Pianoforte." [Crew/MISC-193].

547.7 Reed Song (For The St. Louis Convention). w. Sophia P. Snow. m. Prof. Arthur Turner. Published by Sophia P. Snow. 1896. B/w photo of Thomas Reed. R/w floral and geometric designs. [Crew/MISC-189].

547.8 Republican National Convention March. m. Al G. Mark. Published by Mark Bros. Music Publishing Company, No. 3940 Page Avenue, St. Louis, MO. 1896. R/w/b drawings of William McKinley, Levi P. Morton, Thomas Reed, Wm. Allison and "?" [question mark] on flag background, shields. "Dedicated to the City of St. Louis, June 1896." 8pp. Page 2: B/w photos of "Prominent Republicans and Gentlemen who were instrumental in securing the Republican National Convention for St. Louis — Sam M. Kennard, President Business Men's League; Chas. H. Sampson, Chairman Convention Committee; Hon. Chauncey Ives Filley, Chairman Reception Committee; Frank Gaienne, Gen'l. Mgr., St. Louis Exposition; L.S. W. Wall; Chas. F. Wenneker." Page 7: B/w photos of "Merchant's League Club — Wm. H. Hobbs, Vice-President; Louis F. Zipp, Treasurer; Hon. J.A. Talty, President; Theo. D. Kalbfell, Chair., Republican Central Committee; Morris Langsdorf, Sec." Page 8: Blank. [Crew/WM-1]

547.9 Tom Reed Campaign Songs. Published by T.J. Hampton, No. 110 North Broadway, Los Angeles, CA. 1896. Gn/bk litho of Thomas B. Reed, geometric designs. [5⅞" × 8¾"]. "Souvenir." 28pp. Inside advertising, patriotic and pro-McKinley songs. [M-348].

547.10 What An Alteration. w. W.A.P. In: *Republican Campaign Songs (As Sung By The Marquette Club Quartette)*, page 5. Published by the Marquette Club of Chicago, Dearborn Avenue and Maple Street, Chicago, IL. 1888. [3½" × 6¼"]. Be/bl geometric design border. "W.A. Paulson, 1st Bass; R.J. Wherry, 1st Tenor; M.O. Naramore, 2nd Bass; O.B. Knight, 2nd Tenor." "Music and Instructions Cheerfully Furnished on Application." 28pp. [Crew/BFH-129].

547.11 You Can't Vote In Our Crowd. w. Herbert N. Casson. m. No tune indicated. In: *Labor Songs*, page 10. c. Herbert N. Casson. Published by Lynn Labor Press, 153 Oxford Street, Lynn, MA. [189-]. [3¾" × 5¾"]. Gn/bk geometric designs. 36pp. [Crew/ SLP-3]

• **AmPM-548** RICE, William (Mayor, Bath, 1856–1858, 1873–1875)

548.1 Guide Me. w.m. William Rice. a. Thomas P.I. Magoun. Published by Thomas P.I. Magoun, Bath, ME. 1882. Non-pictorial. "Composed by the Late Hon. Wm. Rice." 4pp. Page 4: Blank.

• **AmPM-549** SAUERWEIN, Peter G. (Collector of Internal Revenue, Baltimore, 1861?–1865?)

549.1 To Sauerwein. w. "By A Member of the Baltimore Corn Exchange." m. "Air—*Maryland, My Maryland*." No publisher indicated. Published in Baltimore, June, 1862. [Approx. 5⅞" × 9⅝"]. Non-pictorial. 2pp. Page 2: Blank. [WFU].

• **AmPM-550** SEWELL, Arthur (Candidate for Vice President, 1896) [ALSO SEE: DOC/PSM-WJB]

550.1 Bryan And Sewell Grand March. m. Noles. In: *42 Selections For Organ And Piano*. Published by F. Trifet, Publisher, 36 Bromfield Street, Boston, MA. [1896]. [Crew/WJB-103].

550.2 Exit Old Party. w. No composer indicated. m. "Tune—*Good-By, My Lover, Good-By*." In: *Republican Campaign Parodies And Songs* [Songster], page 22. Published by Betts and Burnett, South Butler, Wayne County, NY. 1896. [7¾" × 5½"]. Be/bk non-pictorial. "McKinley and Hobart." "1896." 28pp. [M-340]. [Crew/WM-67].

• **AmPM-551** SMITH, Margaret Chase (U.S. House, 1940–1949; U.S. Senate; 1949–1973)

551.1 Dance Of The Liberal Republicans. w.m. Gerald Gardner. In: *These Are The Songs That Were* [Song Book], page 10. e. Gerald Gardner (Writer *Of Who's In Charge Here?, News-Reals*, and *That Was The Week That Was*). Published by Edwin H. Morris and Company, No. 31 West 54th Street, New York, NY. 10019. 1965. B/w photo of Lyndon B. Johnson, Hubert Humphrey, Everett Dirksen, others. R/w/bk cover. List of contents. 36pp. Pages 8, 23 and 25: Photos of politicians. [Crew/LBJ-6].

• **AmPM-552** WILLIAMS, Reuel (State House, 1822–1826 & 1829–1832; State Senate, 1827–1828; State Commissioner of Public Buildings, 1831; U.S. Senate, 1837–1843)

552.1 When This Old Hat Was New. w.m. No composer or tune indicated. In: *The Log Cabin & Hard Cider Melodies, A Collection Of Popular And Patriotic Songs*, page 47. Published by Charles Adams, No. 23 Tremont Street, Boston, MA. 1840. [3¾" × 6"]. [V-1: Pk/bk] [V-2: Gn/bk] litho of William Henry Harrison. "The Freeman's glittering Sword be Blest, For ever blest the Freeman's Lyre." 78pp. Pages 2 and 77: Blank. Page 3: Inside title page. B/w litho of log cabin. "Respectfully Dedicated to the Friends of Harrison and Tyler." Page 78: Advertising. [M-012]. [Crew/ WHH-68].

552.2 When This Old Hat Was New. w.m. No composer or tune indicated. In: *The Clay Minstrel Or National Songster*, page 326. c. John Stockton Littell. Published by Greeley & M'Elrath, Tribune Building, New York, NY. 1844. [3⅛" × 4⅞"]. Non-pictorial. 396pp. [Crew/HC-18].

552.3 When This Old Hat Was New. w.m. No composer or tune indicated. In: *Whig Songs For 1844* [Songster], page 9. Published by Greeley & McElrath, New York, NY. 1844. [5⅞" × 9³⁄₁₆"]. Non-pictorial. 16pp. Page 16: "Odes and Poems." [M-061]. [Crew/ HC-35].

• **AmPM-553** YOUNG, Charles H. (Enforcement Candidate for Sheriff, ca. 1900)

553.1 Drive Out Rum Vote For Young. No composers indicated. No publisher indicated. [ca. 1900]. [7¼" × 12¼"]. B/w photo of Charles Young. "Rev. C.H. Young, Enforcement Candidate for Sheriff of Sagadahoc County, Maine." 2pp. Page 2: Blank.

• **AmPM-554** MISCELLANEOUS MUSIC

554.1 The Maine Capitol March. m. R.P. Chase. Published by Jean M. Missud, Salem, MA. 1897. Gn/w litho of the Maine State House building, geometric designs. "1797–1897." "Dedicated to the Hundredth Anniversary of the City of Augusta." 6pp. Page 6: Advertising.

MARYLAND

• **AmPM-554A** AGNEW, Spiro Theodore (County Executive, Baltimore County, 1962–1966; Governor, Maryland 1966–1969; Vice President, 1969–1973) [SEE: DOC/PSM-RMN]

554A.1 Convention '72. w.m. N. Canel and N. Kousaloos. 45rpm record. Mainstream Records, MRL 5525/ZT8P 224228. Performed by The Delegates. 1972.

54A.2 Having A Time. w. No composer indicated. m. "Tune—*Bidin' My Time*." As sung by Gerald "Ford." In: *Thoroughly Mad-ern Malcolm or He Didn't Need A Course In Forensics To Become A Famous Public Speaker*, page 12. Published by the New York State Legislative Correspondents' Association, Albany, NY. 1974. N/w photo of Malcolm Wilson as Alfred E. Newman—"What—Me Governor?" "Featuring the New York Correspondents' Association, March 16. 1974." 32pp.

554A.3 The Ribald Rebel's Song (Fight For Liberation). w. No composer indicated. m. *Tramp Tramp*. Lyrics and sound file published online at <http://www.mudcat.org/kids/@displaysong.cfm?SongID= 6892>. [199-].

***554A.4 [Teddy The Red Nosed Senator]*. w. No composer indicated. m. "Sung to the tune of *Rudolph, The Red Nosed Reindeer*." "Here's one from the Bob Rivers and Twisted Radio Album, *I Am Santa Claus* that we are spinning at our college station, WTTU..." Published online at <http://catweasel.org/Site1/Digests.H9312140.php>. 1993.

• **AmPM-555 BLAIR**, Montgomery (State Court Judge, Kentucky, 1843–1849; U.S. Postmaster General, 1861–1864; State House, Maryland, 1878; Candidate for U.S. House, Maryland, 1882)

555.1 Cabinet Pictures. w.m. No composer or tune indicated. In: *Copperhead Minstrel, (A Choice Collection Of Democratic Poems & Songs)*, page 24. Published by Feeks and Bancker, Wholesale Agents, No. 24 Ann Street, New York. 1863. [4¾" × 7¼"]. O/bk non-pictorial. "For the use of Political Clubs and the Social Circle." "Price 25 cents." 64pp. [M-133] [Crew/GBM-64].

555.2 Fourth Of July (Song). w.m. No composer or tune indicated. No publisher indicated. [ca. 1862]. [Approx. 4¾" 8¾"]. Non-pictorial geometric design border. "Gotten up expressly for those who have an appreciative mind." 2pp. Page 2: Blank. [WFU].

555.3 Sic Semper. w. "By A Virginian." m. No tune indicated. No publisher indicated. [1861–1862]. [Approx. 6" × 9½"]. Non-pictorial geometric design border. 2pp. Page 2: Blank. [AMC].

555.4 The White House. w. G.R. Edeson. m. "Air—*Root, Hog, Or Die!*" Published by H. De Marsan, 54 Chatham Street, New York, NY. [1861–1862]. B/w litho border of minstrels, geometric designs. 2pp. Page 2: Blank. [AMC].

• **AmPM-556 BROENING**, William Frederick (State House, 1902; Mayor, Baltimore, 1919–1923 & 1927–1931)

556.1 We Want Preston (Campaign Song). w. Henry Creamer "(Writer of *Strut Miss Lizzie, Dear Old Southland, Way Down Yonder In New Orleans*)." m. Anabel Anderson. No publisher indicated. [ca. 1919]. [Cover missing]. 6pp. Page 2: At top of music— "Dedicated to Hon. James Preston." Page 6: Blank.

• **AmPM-557 BRADFORD**, Augustus Williamson (Governor, 1862–1866)

557.1 Maryland, My Maryland! w. No composer indicated. m. "Air—*My Normandy*." Published by Charles Magnus, No. 12 Frankfort Street, New York, NY. [ca. 1863]. [Approx. 6¼" × 9½"]. H/c litho of a young girl. "500 Illustrated ballads, lithographed and printed by Charles Magnus." 2pp. Page 2: Blank. [AMC].

• **AmPM-558 BROWN**, George William (Mayor, Baltimore, 1860–1861; Municipal Judge, 1872)

558.1 Fiat Justitia. w. H. Rebel. m. No tune indicated. Published at Baltimore, MD. 1862. Non-pictorial. 2pp. Page 2: Blank. [WFU].

558.2 The Gallant Mayor Brown (Song). w. No composer indicated. m. "Air—*Roseas* [sic] *Dream*." No publisher indicated. [ca. 1861]. [Approx. 4¾" × 13"]. Litho of a man with a top hat, geometric design border. 2pp. Page 2: Blank. [WFU].

558.3 God Will Repay. w. H. Rebel. m. No tune indicated. No Publisher indicated. Published at Baltimore, 1862. [Approx. 3¾" × 9"]. R/w litho of the scales of justice, line border. "Privately Printed." 2pp. Page 2: Blank. [WFU].

558.4 God Will Repay. w. H. Rebel. m. No tune indicated. Published at Baltimore, MD. 1862. B/w litho of scales of justice., geometric design border. 2pp. Page 2: Blank. [AMC].

558.5 Mayor Brown. w. No composer indicated. m. "Air—*Rosseau's Dream*." No publisher indicated [probably in Baltimore]. [Approx. 6¼" × 10¼"]. B/w geometric design border. 2pp. Page 2: Blank. [AMC].

558.6 Right Must Prevail. w. H. Rebel. m. No composer or tune indicated. No publisher indicated. Published in Baltimore, MD. 1862. R/w litho of the scales of justice. "Privately Printed." 2pp. Page 2: Blank. [AMC] [WFU].

• **AmPM-559 CARROLL**, Charles (of Carrollton) (Revolutionary Convention of Maryland, 1775; Continental Commissioner to Canada, 1776; Board of War 1776–1777; Continental Congress, 1776–1778; Signer of the Declaration of Independence, 1776; State Senate 1777–1800; U.S. Senate, 1789–1792)

559.1 The Carrollton March. m. A. Clifton. Published by John Cole, Baltimore, MD. July 1, 1828. Non-pictorial geometric designs. "Performed at the ceremony of commencing the Baltimore & Ohio Railroad, on the Fourth of July, 1828." "Dedicated by permission to the Hon Charles Carroll of Carrollton." 4pp. Pages 1 and 4: Blank. [LL/JH].

559.2 The Declaration Of Independence Of The United States Of North America, July 4, 1776. w. From the Declaration of Independence. m. John E. Wilson. Published by John E. Wilson, Baltimore, MD. 1863. B/w litho of the interior of Independence Hall. "Arranged and adapted for Vocal and Instrumental Music as the Great National Chant." 4pp. [?]. Page 4: Facsimile signatures of all signers.

559.3 Maryland. w. No composer indicated. m. "Air—*My Normandy*." No publisher indicated. [ca. 1861]. [Approx. 4" × 13"?]. [V-1: B/w] [V-2: Y/r] litho of the Maryland state seal, geometric design border. 2pp. Page 2: Blank. [WFU].

559.4 Maryland! My Maryland! w. [V-1: No composer indicated] [V-2: James R. Randall, of Baltimore, MD]. m. "Air—*My Normandy*." No publisher indicated. [ca. 1861]. [Approx. 6½" × 7¼"]. Non-pictorial geometric design border. 2pp. Page 2: Blank. [WFU].

559.5 Old Independence Hall. w. A. Fletcher Stayman. m. Francis Weiland. Published by Stayman & Brothers, No. 210 Chesnut Street, Philadelphia, PA. 1855. Non-pictorial. "Respectfully dedicated to the Memory of the Signers of the Declaration of Independence." "Fac Simile of their signatures" including John Adams, Sam Adams, Elbridge Gerry, Thomas Jefferson. 8pp. Pages 2 and 8: Blank. [Crew/MISC-34].

• **AmPM-560 CHASE**, Samuel (General Assembly, 1764–1784; Continental Congress, 1774–1778; Signer of the Declaration of Independence, 1776;

Criminal Court Judge, Baltimore, 1788; Judge, State General Court, 1791; U.S. Supreme Court, 1796–1811)

560.1 Beauties Of Anglo-Federalism, Displayed (Or State Tricks Developed). w. No composer indicated. m. "Tune—*Moderation And Alteration*." In: *The Republican Harmonist (Being A Select Collection Of Republican, Patriotic, And Sentimental Songs, Odes, Sonnets, &c, American And European: Some Of Which Are Original, And Most Of The Others Now Come For The First Time From An American Press)*, page 29. c. D.E. [Daniel Ebsworth] "(A Citizen of the World)." Printed "for the People," Boston, MA. 1801. Non-pictorial. 152pp. [Crew/TJ-10].

560.2 The Declaration Of Independence Of The United States Of North America, July 4, 1776. w. From the Declaration of Independence. m. John E. Wilson. Published by John E. Wilson, Baltimore, MD. 1863. B/w litho of the interior of Independence Hall. "Arranged and adapted for Vocal and Instrumental Music as the Great National Chant." 4pp. [?]. Page 4: Facsimile signatures of all signers.

560.3 The Duke's Retreat To Braintree. w. No composer indicated. m. "Tune—*I Follow'd Him To Glasgow Town*." In: *The Republican Harmonist (Being A Select Collection Of Republican, Patriotic, And Sentimental Songs, Odes, Sonnets, &c, American And European: Some Of Which Are Original, And Most Of The Others Now Come For The First Time From An American Press)*, page 13. c. D.E. [Daniel Ebsworth] "(A Citizen of the World)." Printed "for the People," Boston, MA. 1801. Non-pictorial. 152pp. [Crew/TJ-10].

560.4 The Duke's Retreat To Braintree. w. No composer indicated. m. *Yankee Doodle.* Published in *The American Republican Harmonist.* 1803. [VBL, p. 166].

560.5 Old Independence Hall. w. A. Fletcher Stayman. m. Francis Weiland. Published by Stayman & Brothers, No. 210 Chesnut Street, Philadelphia, PA. 1855. Non-pictorial. "Respectfully dedicated to the Memory of the Signers of the Declaration of Independence." "Fac Simile of their signatures" including John Adams, Sam Adams, Elbridge Gerry, Thomas Jefferson. 8pp. Pages 2 and 8: Blank. [Crew/MISC-34].

560.6 The Presidential Wagon. w. No composer indicated. m. "Air—*Wait For The Wagon*." In: *The Grant Songster*, page 39. Published by Haney & Co., Publishers, 119 Nassau Street, New York, NY. 1867. [4⅛" × 6⅜"]. Gd/bk drawing of "Ulysses S. Grant," White House. 64pp. [Crew/USG-32].

560.7 The Retrospect: Or A Touch On The Tories. w. No composer indicated. m. "Tune—*Pretty Work For Twelve Dollars A Day*." In: *The Republican Harmonist (Being A Select Collection Of Republican, Patriotic, And Sentimental Songs, Odes, Sonnets, &c, American And European: Some Of Which Are Original, And Most Of The Others Now Come For The First Time From An American Press)*, page 20. c. D.E. [Daniel Ebsworth] "(A Citizen of the World)." Printed "for the People," Boston, MA. 1801. Non-pictorial. 152pp. [Crew/TJ-10].

• **AmPM-561** CILLEY, Jonathan (State House, 1831–1836; U.S. House, 1837–1838)

561.1 Murder Of Cilley. w.m. No composer or tune indicated. No publisher indicated. [ca. 1838]. [Approx. 5½" × 9"]. Non-pictorial geometric designs. Followed on page 1 by "Gossip Chat," a paragraph of nonsense comic narrative. 2pp. Page 2: Blank. [AMC].

• **AmPM-562** CONTEE, John (House of Delegates, 1858–1860; Delegate to Democratic National Convention, 1860)

562.1 Some Love To Ride (A Much Admired Hunting Song; in Answer to *Some Love To Roam*). w. F.P. Radcliffe, Esqre. m. C. Meineke Published by John Cole, Baltimore, MD. [ca. 1850s]. B/w litho by Endicott of people riding horses in the countryside. "Composed and Respectfully Dedicated to Col. John Contee of Prince Georges by C. Meineke." 6pp. Page 2: Blank.

• **AmPM-563** DAVIS, Henry Winter (U.S. House, 1855–1861 & 1863–1865)

563.1 States' Rights Song. w. No composer indicated. m. "Air—*The Grocery Store*." No publisher indicated. [ca. 1861]. [Approx. 6¼" × 9½"]. Non-pictorial geometric design border. 2pp. Page 2: Blank. [WFU].

• **AmPM-564** GARY, James Albert (Republican National Committee, 1880–1896; Republican State Chairman, 1883; U.S. Postmaster General, 1897–1898)

564.1 The Cabinet Grand March. m. Hans S. Line, Op. 64. Published by National Music Company, Nos. 215–221 Wabash Avenue, Chicago, IL. 1897. R/w cover. B/w photo of William McKinley and eight Cabinet members. "Dedicated to Hon. Lyman J. Gage." 6pp. Page 6: Advertising. [Crew/WM-15].

• **AmPM-565** GLENDENING, Parris (City Council, Hyattsville, 1973; Prince George's County Council, 1974–1982; Prince George's County Executive, 1982–1994 Governor, 1995–2003)

565.1 Gunnery Sgt. Glendening Can't Unlock The Gun. w. Doug from Upland. m. "Song parody—*Green Berets*." "This is one of the funniest stories ever. The governor demonstrates the new lock and makes a fool of himself by trying to undue it 54 times. Turn on the idiot alert." Published online by FreeRepublic.com at <http://www.freerepublic.com/forum/a38dc5f950ac8.htm>. 2000.

• **AmPM-566** GORDON, Josiah H. (State's Attorney, Allegany County, 1851–1857; House of Delegates, 1859–1861; Circuit Court Judge, 1883–1887?)

566.1 Fiat Justitia. w. H. Rebel. m. No tune indicated. Published at Baltimore, MD. 1862. Non-pictorial. 2pp. Page 2: Blank. [WFU].

566.2 God Will Repay. w. H. Rebel. m. No tune indicated. No Publisher indicated. Published at Baltimore, 1862. [Approx. 3¾" × 9"]. R/w litho of the scales of justice, line border. "Privately Printed." 2pp. Page 2: Blank. [WFU].

566.3 God Will Repay. w. H. Rebel. m. No tune indicated. Published at Baltimore, MD. 1862. B/w litho of scales of justice, geometric design border. 2pp. Page 2: Blank. [AMC].

• **AmPM-567** GORMAN, Arthur Pue (State House, 1869–1873; State Senate, 1875–1881; U.S. Senate, 1881–1889 & 1903–1906)

567.1 Loop The Loop. w. No composer indicated. m. "Tune—*Down On The Farm*." In: *Campaign Songs* [Song Sheet], page 8. w. Edwin A. Hartshorn. m. Popular tunes. Printed by McAuliffe & Booth, Printers, New York, NY. 1904. [5³⁄₁₆" × 8½"]. Non-pictorial.

"Seventh Edition." "1904–1904." 8pp. [M-388]. [Crew/TR-161].

567.2 Other Arrangements. w.m. J.A. Parks. In: *Park's Republican Songs Campaign Of 1904 (For Male Voices)* [Song Book], page 3. Published by J.A. Parks Company, York, NE. 1904. [6 15/16" × 9¾"]. Br/br non-pictorial geometric design border. 40pp. [M-390]. [Crew/TR-157].

567.3 We'll All Be Happy Then. w.m. J.A. Parks. In: *Park's Republican Songs Campaign Of 1904 (For Male Voices)* [Song Book], page 4. Published by J.A. Parks Company, York, NE. 1904. [6 15/16" × 9¾"]. Br/br non-pictorial geometric design border. 40pp. [M-390]. [Crew/TR-157].

567.4 We'll Try To Get Along. w.m. J.A. Parks. In: *Park's Republican Songs Campaign Of 1904 (For Male Voices)* [Song Book], page 26. Published by J.A. Parks Company, York, NE. 1904. [6 15/16" × 9¾"]. Br/br non-pictorial geometric design border. 40pp. [M-390]. [Crew/TR-157].

567.5 The White House Gate (Solo and Chorus). w.m. Logan S. Porter. In: *Roosevelt Campaign Songster 1904 (For Male Voices)*, page 26. c. Logan S. Porter. Published by The Home Music Company, Logansport, IN. 1904. [6" × 9"]. Be/bk photos of Theodore Roosevelt and Charles Fairbanks. Be/bk drawing of a star, geometric designs. "Single Copy 15 cts—$1.60 per Dozen." 36pp. [M-391]. [Crew/TR-356].

HARPER, Robert Goodloe [State Senate, 181-; U.S. Senate, 1816) [See: South Carolina]

• **AmPM-568 HARRISON**, William G. (State House, 1861)

568.1 Virginia's Knocking Around. w.m. No composers or tune indicated. Published in Baltimore, MD. March 30, 1862. Non-pictorial. 2pp. Page 2: Blank. [AMC].

• **AmPM-569 HICKS**, Thomas Holliday (State House, 1829–1830, 1836; Governor, 1858–1862; U.S. Senate, 1862–1865)

569.1 Appeal To The South (Song). w.m. No composer or tune indicated. No publisher indicated. [1861–1862]. [Approx. 5" × 10"]. B/w litho of ships, cargo including a box labeled "Ednes Print," geometric design border. 2pp. Page 2: Blank. [WFU].

569.2 Audax Omnia Perpeti Gens Lincolna Ruit Per Vetitum Nefas. w.m. No composers or tune indicated. No publisher indicated. [1861–1862]. B/w non-pictorial geometric design border. 2pp. Page 2: Blank. [AMC].

569.3 Da Vis! w. "Quien Sabe?" m. No tune indicated. No publisher indicated. Published in Baltimore, MD. February 10, 1862. B/w litho of a flag with the Maryland state seal. 2pp. Page 2: Blank. [AMC].

569.4 Every Dog Has His Day (A Comic Song on the Times). w. Walter W. Warren. m. "Air—*Joe Bowers.*" No publisher indicated. [1861–1862]. [Approx. 6" × 9"]. Non-pictorial geometric design border. "Composed by Walter W. Warren Expressly for Jacob K. Search, & Sung by him at Thomas Opera House." 2pp. Page 2: Blank.

569.5 Gov. Hicks. w. No composer indicated. m. "Air—*Money Musk.*" Published in the South. [1861–1862]. [4½" × 7½"]. Pk/bk non-pictorial geometric design border. 2pp. Page 2: Blank.

569.4 Hicks The Pirate. w. No composer indicated. m. "Air—*The Rose Tree.*" Published by H. De Marsan, 38 & 50 Chatham Street, New York, NY. [ca. 1861]. BH/c litho border. "H. De Marsan, Publisher of Songs and Ballads Paper Dolls Toy Books &c." 2pp. Page 2: Blank. [AMC].

569.5 Jeff Davis In The White House. w. No composer indicated. m. "Air—*Ye Parliaments Of England.*" No publisher indicated. [ca. 1862]. [4⅝" × 12½"]. Litho of a house, geometric design litho border. 2pp. Page 2: Blank. [WFU].

569.6 Jeff Davis In The White House. w. "By a Lady, Daughter of one our Defenders." m. "Air—*Ye Parliaments Of England.*" No publisher indicated. [ca. 1862]. [4½" × 8¾"]. Geometric design litho border. 2pp. Page 2: Blank. [WFU].

569.7 Maryland, My Maryland! w. No composer indicated. m. "Air—*My Normandy.*" Published by Charles Magnus, No. 12 Frankfort Street, New York, NY. [ca. 1863]. [Approx. 6¼" × 9½"]. H/c litho of a young girl. "500 Illustrated ballads, lithographed and printed by Charles Magnus." 2pp. Page 2: Blank. [AMC]. [VBL, p. 361].

569.8 Mayor Brown. w. No composer indicated. m. "Air—*Rosseau's Dream.*" No publisher indicated [probably in Baltimore]. [Approx. 6¼" × 10¼"]. B/w geometric design border. 2pp. Page 2: Blank. [AMC].

569.9 States' Rights Song. w. No composer indicated. m. "Air—*The Grocery Store.*" No publisher indicated. [ca. 1861]. [Approx. 4⅝" × 8¼"]. Non-pictorial geometric design border. 2pp. Page 2: Blank. [WFU].

• **AmPM-570 HOWARD**, Charles (Commissioner of Police, Baltimore, 1861)

570.1 Da Vis! w. "Quien Sabe?" m. No tune indicated. No publisher indicated. Published in Baltimore, MD. February 10, 1862. B/w litho of a flag with the Maryland state seal. 2pp. Page 2: Blank. [AMC].

570.2 Maryland. w. No composer indicated. m. "Air—*My Normandy.*" No publisher indicated. [ca. 1861]. [Approx. 4" × 13"?]. [V-1: B/w] [V-2: Y/r] litho of the Maryland state seal, geometric design border. 2pp. Page 2: Blank. [WFU].

570.3 Maryland! My Maryland! w. [V-1: No composer indicated] [V-2: James R. Randall, of Baltimore, MD]. m. "Air—*My Normandy.*" No publisher indicated. [ca. 1861]. [Approx. 6½" × 7¼"]. Non-pictorial geometric design border. 2pp. Page 2: Blank. [WFU].

570.4 Virginia's Knocking Around. w.m. No composers or tune indicated. Published in Baltimore, MD. March 30, 1862. Non-pictorial. 2pp. Page 2: Blank. [AMC].

• **AmPM-571 HOWARD**, George (Governor, 1831–1833)

571.1 Governor Howard's Grand March. m. Henry Dielman. Published by George Willig, Jr., 149 Market Street, Baltimore, MD. [1831–1833]. Non-pictorial. "Composed for the Piano Forte." 4pp. Pages 1 and 4: Blank.

• **AmPM-572 JACKSON**, Howard W. (Mayor, Baltimore, 1923–1927, 1931–1943)

572.1 We Want Preston (Campaign Song). w. Henry Creamer "(Writer of *Strut Miss Lizzie, Dear Old South-*

land, Way Down Yonder In New Orleans)." m. Anabel Anderson. No publisher indicated. [ca. 1919]. [Cover missing]. 6pp. Page 2: At top of music—"Dedicated to Hon. James Preston." Page 6: Blank.

- **AmPM-573 JOHNSON**, Bradley Tyler (State's Attorney, Frederick County, 1851; Candidate for State Comptroller, 1857, Chairman of the Democratic State Central Committee, 1859–1860; State Senate, Virginia, 1877–1879; President of the Maryland Electoral College, 1884)

573.1 Jeff Davis Is Getting Tired Of The War. w. No composer indicated. m. "Air—*Maryland, My Maryland*." [186-]. B/w litho of two women, geometric design border. [186-]. 2pp. Page 2: Blank. [Crew/JD-80]. [AMC].

- **AmPM-574 KANE**, George Proctor (Collector, Port of Baltimore, 1849; Marshal of Police, Baltimore, 1861; Mayor, Baltimore, 1877–1878)

574.1 God Will Repay. w. H. Rebel. m. No tune indicated. No Publisher indicated. Published at Baltimore, 1862. [Approx. 3¾" x 9"]. R/w litho of the scales of justice, line border. "Privately Printed." 2pp. Page 2: Blank. [WFU].

574.2 God Will Repay. w. H. Rebel. m. No tune indicated. Published at Baltimore, MD. 1862. B/w litho of scales of justice, geometric design border. 2pp. Page 2: Blank. [AMC].

574.3 Marshal Kane (Song). w. No composer indicated. No Publisher indicated. [1861–1862]. [4½" x 11"]. Litho vignette of man, woman under tree, geometric design border. 2pp. Page 2: Blank. [WFU].

574.4 Oh Jeff! Why Don't You Come? w. No composer indicated. m. "Air—*Willie We Have Missed You*." No publisher indicated [probably Baltimore]. [Approx. 5¾" x 9½"]. Non-pictorial geometric design border. 2pp. Page 2: Blank. [WFU].

574.5 Right Must Prevail. w. H. Rebel. m. No composer or tune indicated. No publisher indicated. Published in Baltimore, MD. 1862. R/w litho of the scales of justice. "Privately Printed." 2pp. Page 2: Blank. [AMC] [WFU].

574.6 There's Life In The Old Land Yet! w. Jas. R. Randall, "of Baltimore (Author of *Maryland, My Maryland*)." m. No tune indicated. No publisher indicated [probably Baltimore]. [1961–1862]. [Approx. 3⅞" x 10¾"]. Y/bk litho of Lady justice with scales and sword, black line border. 2pp. Page 2: Blank. [WFU].

574.7 There's Life In The Old Land Yet! w. No composer indicated. m. No tune indicated. No publisher indicated [probably Baltimore]. [1961–1862]. [Approx. 5¼" x 9¾"]. Y/bk non-pictorial. 2pp. Page 2: Blank. [WFU].

574.8 Virginia's Knocking Around. w.m. No composers or tune indicated. Published in Baltimore, MD. March 30, 1862. Non-pictorial. 2pp. Page 2: Blank. [AMC].

- **AmPM-575 KENNEDY**, John Pendleton (State House, 1821–1823 & 1846; U.S. House, 1838–1839 & 1841–1845; U.S. Secretary of the Navy, 1852–1853)

575.1 The Kennedy Grand March. m. A.H. Durocher "of Baltimore." Published by James L. Hewitt & Co., 239 Broadway, Baltimore, MD. 1842. Non-pictorial. "Composed for the Piano Forte." "Respectfully Dedicated to the Honble. J.P. Kennedy By his friend A.H. Durocher." 4pp. Pages 1 and 4: Blank. [LL, JH].

- **AmPM-576 KRONMILLER**, John (City Council, Baltimore, 1905–1907; U.S. House, 1909–1911; Board of Supervisors of Election, Baltimore, 1914–1916)

576.1 Taft And Sherman Campaign Songster. 1908. [4½" x 6"]. Bl/w photos of "Wm. H. Taft" and "James S. Sherman." Drawing of eagle, flags, shield. "26 Original Songs Set to Familiar and Popular Airs." "1908." 32pp. Pages 2 and 31: Blank. Page 32: R/w eagle, ballot marked "X." Pro-Taft quotes. Counterstamped: "For Congress, Third Congressional District, John Kronmiller, Republican X." [M-397]. [Crew/WHT-1].

- **AmPM-577 LATROBE**, Ferdinand Claiborne (State House, 1868; Mayor, Baltimore, 1875–1877, 1878–1881, 1883–1885, 1887–1889 & 1891–1895)

577.1 Sequi-Centennial March. m. P. Baraldi. Published by George Willig & Co., Baltimore, MD. 1880. Non-pictorial geometric designs. "To Ferdinand C. Latrobe, Mayor of Baltimore." "Composed for the Piano." 6pp. Pages 2 and 6: Blank. [LL/JH].

- **AmPM-578 LAWSON**, Thomas W. (Candidate for U.S. Senate, 1918)

578.1 The Copper King March And Two Step. m. Charles Emons George. Published by A.H. Goetting, Springfield, MA. 1905. B/w photo of Thomas W. Watson. Bl/w floral and geometric designs. "Dedicated to Thos. W. Watson."

- **AmPM-578A LEVERING**, Joshua (Candidate for President, 1896) [SEE: DOC/PSM-JL]

- **AmPM-579 LLOYD**, Henry (State Senate, 1882–1884; Governor, 1885–1888; Circuit Judge, 1892–1908)

579.1 The Eidelweil Waltzes. m. G. Kettlewell. Published by Otto Sutro & Co., Publishers, Baltimore, MD. 1888. B/w photo of Henry Lloyd and his staff in military uniforms. B/w litho of Maryland State seal, quill and ink, document, swords. "Respectfully dedicated to Hon. Henry Lloyd, Governor of Maryland and the Members of his Staff." 8pp. Page 2: "These waltzes are issued as a compliment to the National Guard of Maryland which at this time reflects more credit to the state than at any period in its history, and to this result the efforts of Governor Lloyd and the Members of his Staff have contributed to a Greater extent than any other influence." Page 8: Blank. [LL/JH].

- **AmPM-580 LOWE**, Enoch Louis (State House, 1845; Governor, 1851–1854)

580.1 Governor's Quick March. m. Henry Dielman, Mus. Doc. Published by G. Willig, Jr., Baltimore, MD. [1851]. Non-pictorial geometric designs. "Composed & Respectfully dedicated (by permission) to his Excellency, Enoch Louis Lowe, of Maryland." 4pp. Pages 1 and 4: Blank.

580.2 Jeff Davis Is Getting Tired Of The War. w. No composer indicated. m. "Air—*Maryland, My Maryland*." [186-]. B/w litho of two women, geometric design border. [186-]. 2pp. Page 2: Blank. [Crew/JD-80]. [AMC].

- **AmPM-581 MAHONEY**, George P. (Candi-

date for Governor, 1950, 1954; 1962 & 1966; Candidate for U.S. Senate, 1952, 1956, 1958 & 1968)
  581.1 *He's Ma' Honey, Mahoney* (My Own). w.m. Ben Kriger and Jack Sherr. No publisher indicated. 1950. [7" × 9"]. B/w photo of George Mahoney. "Vote for George P. Mahoney for Governor, September 11, 1950." 4pp.
• **AmPM-582 MANDELL**, Marvin (State House, 1952–1969; Democratic Party State Chairman, 1968–1969; Governor, 1969–1977 & 1979)
  582.1 *Governor Marvin Mandel.* w.m. Mervin Conn, ASCAP. No publisher indicated. 1971. [8½" × 11"]. Non-pictorial. 2pp. Page 2: Blank.
• **AmPM-583 MCCURRY**, Mike (Director of Communications, Democratic National Committee, 1988–1990; White House Press Secretary, 1995–1998)
  583.1 *Spinball Wizard.* w. Paul Silhan. m. "Sung to *Pinball Wizard* by The Who." On: Cassette: *Spinball Wizard*. "As heard on Rush's Radio Show." Lyrics published at <http://www.paulsilhan.com/spinball.htm>. 1997.
• **AmPM-584 MERRYMAN**, John (State Legislator, 1861; State Treasurer, 1870–1872)
  584.1 *John Merryman.* w. No composer indicated. m. "Air—*Old Dan Tucker*." Published as a penny song sheet (Probably in Baltimore). [ca. 1861]. [4⅞" × 7¾"]. Pk/bk non-pictorial geometric design border. 2pp. Page 2: Blank. [Crew/JD-47].
  584.2 *There's Life In The Old Land Yet!* w. Jas. R. Randall, "of Baltimore (Author of *Maryland, My Maryland*)." m. No tune indicated. No publisher indicated [probably Baltimore]. [1961–1862]. [Approx. 3⅞" × 10¾"]. Y/bk litho of Lady justice with scales and sword, black line border. 2pp. Page 2: Blank. [WFU].
  584.3 *There's Life In The Old Land Yet!* w. No composer indicated. m. No tune indicated. No publisher indicated [probably Baltimore]. [1961–1862]. [Approx. 5¼" × 9¾"]. Y/bk non-pictorial. 2pp. Page 2: Blank. [WFU].
• **AmPM-585 NICHOLSON**, Joseph Hopper (State House, 1796–1798; U.S. House, 1799–1806; State Court of Appeals, 1806–1817)
  585.1 *Poor Jude, Or The Death Of The Judiciary.* w. No composer indicated. m. "An AmPMified Parody of the celebrated Song *Cock-Robin*." Published in the *Washington Federalist*, December 8, 1802. [VBL, p. 173].
• **AmPM-585A O'MALLEY**, Martin (Assistant State's Attorney, Baltimore, 1988–1990; City Council, Baltimore, 1991–1999; Mayor, Baltimore, 1999–Present)
  585A.1 *The Battle Of Baltimore.* m. Martin O'Malley. a. Jared Denhard. Performed live by O'Malley's March and the Baltimore Symphony Orchestra, September 25th, 2003. Also on CD *O'Malley's March LIVE*.
  585A.2 *The Boys March At Dawn* {585A.2–1}. CD. Performed by O'Malley's March. #CD3. 2002. Including songs by Martin O'Malley: *Breastplate Of St. Patrick* {585A.2–2}.
  585A.3 *Celtic Fury* {585A.3–1}. CD. Performed by O'Malley's March. #CD1. 1997. Including songs by Martin O'Malley: *Farewell Clonbur* {585A.3–2}; *The Great O-Neill* {585A.3–3}; *Leaving Home Once More* {585A.3–4}.

  585A.4 *O'Malley's March LIVE*. CD Performed by O'Malley's March. #CD4. 2004.
  585A.5 *Wait For Me* {585A.5–1}. CD. Performed by O'Malley's March. 2000. #OMM 2000. Including songs by Martin O'Malley: *Native People* {585A.5–2}; *Wait For Me* {585A.5–3}; *South Baltimore Lullaby* {585A.5–4}; and *Song For Justice* {585A.5–5}.
• **AmPM-586 PACA**, William (Provincial Assembly, 1771–1774; Continental Congress, 1774–1779; Signer of the Declaration of Independence, 1776; State Senate, 1777–1779; Chief Judge of the Superior Court of Maryland, 1778–1780; Chief Justice, Court of Appeals in Prize and Admiralty Cases, 1780–1782; Governor, 1782–1785; Judge of the United States Court for Maryland, 1789–1799)
  586.1 *The Declaration Of Independence Of The United States Of North America, July 4, 1776.* w. From the Declaration of Independence. m. John E. Wilson. Published by John E. Wilson, Baltimore, MD. 1863. B/w litho of the interior of Independence Hall. "Arranged and adapted for Vocal and Instrumental Music as the Great National Chant." 4pp. [?]. Page 4: Facsimile signatures of all signers.
  586.2 *Old Independence Hall.* w. A. Fletcher Stayman. m. Francis Weiland. Published by Stayman & Brothers, No. 210 Chesnut Street, Philadelphia, PA. 1855. Non-pictorial. "Respectfully dedicated to the Memory of the Signers of the Declaration of Independence." "Fac Simile of their signatures" including John Adams, Sam Adams, Elbridge Gerry, Thomas Jefferson. 8pp. Pages 2 and 8: Blank. [Crew/MISC-34].
• **AmPM-587 PEARCE**, James Alfred (State House, 1831; U.S. House, 1835–1839 & 1841–1843; U.S. Senate, 1843–1862)
  586.3 *Union March.* m. Hans Krummacher. Published by Henry McCaffrey, No. 207 Baltimore Street, Baltimore, MD. N/w litho by A. Hoen & Co. of woman, eagle, doves within a frame of flowers. "To the Hon. J. Alfred Pearce." 6pp. Pages 2 and 6: Blank.
• **AmPM-588 PRESTON**, James H. (State House, 1890–1894; Mayor, Baltimore, 1911–1919)
  588.1 *Baltimore, Our Baltimore.* w. Folger McKinsey, "The 'Benztown Bard.'" m. Emma Hemberger. Published by G. Fred Krantz Music Co., 100 N. Charles St., cor Fayette St., Baltimore, MD. 1916. [7⅞" × 10⅜"]. Gd/bk/w lithos of the Baltimore City flag and seal of the City. "Unison Song for Schools 5c net." "Mixed Voices 12c." 4pp. Page 4: Narrative "Having conceived the idea of a Municipal Anthem for the City of Baltimore, the Mayor, the Honorable James H. Preston, offered a prize of $250.00 in gold for the best original poem on 'Baltimore' and a similar prize for the best musical-setting of the prize winning poem..."
  588.2 *We Want Preston* (Campaign Song). w. Henry Creamer "(Writer of *Strut Miss Lizzie*, *Dear Old Southland*, *Way Down Yonder In New Orleans*)." m. Anabel Anderson. No publisher indicated. [ca. 1919]. [Cover missing]. 6pp. Page 2: At top of music—"Dedicated to Hon. James Preston." Page 6: Blank.
• **AmPM-589 PRICE**, William (State Senate, ca. 186-)
  589.1 *William Price.* w. No composer indicated. m. "Air—*John Todd*." No publisher indicated [Maryland]. [ca. 1861]. [Approx. 4¼" × 18"]. Be/bk non-pictorial

line border. Note on the music—"Member of the Maryland 'State' Senate, and the author of the infamous 'Treason Bill.'" 2pp. Page 2: Blank. [AMC] [WFU].
- **AmPM-590   ROPES**, Archer (City Counselor, Baltimore, 1849–1852)
590.1 The Maryland Cadets' Quick Step. m. A.F. Knight. Published by Henry Prentiss, 33 Court Street, Boston, MA. [1830–1840]. Non-pictorial geometric designs. "Respectfully dedicated to Capt. Archer Ropes and the Officers and Members of the Prize Banner Corps, by the Boston Independent Company of Cadets. "Arranged for the Piano Forte." 6pp. Pages 2 and 6: Blank. [LL, JH].
- **AmPM-591   SCOTT**, Harkins (State Legislator, 1861)
591.1 Fiat Justitia. w. H. Rebel. m. No tune indicated. Published at Baltimore, MD. 1862. Non-pictorial. 2pp. Page 2: Blank. [WFU].
591.2 God Will Repay. w. H. Rebel. m. No tune indicated. No Publisher indicated. Published at Baltimore, 1862. [Approx. 3¾" × 9"]. R/w litho of the scales of justice, line border. "Privately Printed." 2pp. Page 2: Blank. [WFU].
591.3 God Will Repay. w. H. Rebel. m. No tune indicated. Published at Baltimore, MD. 1862. B/w litho of scales of justice, geometric design border. 2pp. Page 2: Blank. [AMC].
591.4 Hurrah For Jeff Davis. w. No composer indicated. m. "Tune—*Gum Tree Canoe*." No publisher indicated. [ca. 1862]. [Approx. 5" × 9½"]. Bl/bl geometric design border, line under title. 2pp. Page 2: Blank. [Crew/JD-97]. [WFU].
591.5 Right Must Prevail. w. H. Rebel. m. No composer or tune indicated. No publisher indicated. Published in Baltimore, MD. 1862. R/w litho of the scales of justice. "Privately Printed." 2pp. Page 2: Blank. [AMC] [WFU].
- **AmPM-592   SHRIVER**, Robert Sargent, Jr. (Director, Peace Corp, 1961–1966; U.S. Ambassador to France, 1968–1970; Democratic Candidate for Vice President, 1972) [ALSO SEE: DOC/PSM-GSM]
592.1 Convention '72. w.m. N. Canel and N. Kousaloos. 45 rpm record. Mainstream Records, MRL 5525/ZT8P 224228. Performed by The Delegates. 1972.
592.2 A Few Short Years Ago. From CD: *American Way*. Performed by Dimpled Chad & The Disenfranchised. Lyrics published at <http:/dimpledchad.net>. [ca. 2000].
592.3 I Run For Gov'nor, Maria. w. Michael Pacholek. m. Tune—"*Take A Letter Maria* originally by R.B. Greaves." Published online at <http://www.amiright.com/parody/60s/rbgreaves0.shtml>. 2003
592.4 The Peace Corps Goes Rolling Along. w. Milton M. Schwartz. m. *As The Caissons Go Rolling Along*. In: *Sing Along With Jack* [Song Sheet], page 1. [1963]. [8½" × 11"]. Non-pictorial. 2pp. Page 2: "These lyrics are reproduced from the book *Sing Along With Jack* with permission of Bonny Publishing Corporation." [Crew/JFK-76].
592.5 Vive La Dynasty. w. Milton M. Schwartz. m. No tune indicated. In: *Sing Along With Jack* [Song Sheet], page 1. [1963]. [8½" × 11"]. Non-pictorial. 2pp. Page 2: "These lyrics are reproduced from the book *Sing Along With Jack* with permission of Bonny Publishing Corporation." [Crew/JFK-76].
- **AmPM-593   STEUART**, William (Mayor, Baltimore, 1831–1832)
593.1 Colonel Steuart's Quick Step. m. H.N. Giles. Published and sold by T. Carr, Music Store, Baltimore, MD. [1820?]. Non-pictorial. "The Armonica, No. 1." 4pp. Pages 1 and 4: Blank.
593.2 Colonel Wm. Steuart's March And Quickstep. m. "Composed By a Lady." Published by John Cole, Baltimore, MD. [1825]. Non-pictorial geometric designs. 4pp. Pages 1 and 4: Blank.
- **AmPM-593A   STONE**, Thomas, (State Senate, 1779–1783; Continental Congress, 1775–1776, 1778, & 1784; Signer of the Declaration of Independence, 1776)
593A.1 The Declaration Of Independence Of The United States Of North America, July 4, 1776. w. From the Declaration of Independence. m. John E. Wilson. Published by John E. Wilson, Baltimore, MD. 1863. B/w litho of the interior of Independence Hall. "Arranged and adapted for Vocal and Instrumental Music as the Great National Chant." 4pp. [?]. Page 4: Facsimile signatures of all signers.
593A.2 Old Independence Hall. w. A. Fletcher Stayman. m. Francis Weiland. Published by Stayman & Brothers, No. 210 Chesnut Street, Philadelphia, PA. 1855. Non-pictorial. "Respectfully dedicated to the Memory of the Signers of the Declaration of Independence." "Fac Simile of their signatures" including John Adams, Sam Adams, Elbridge Gerry, Thomas Jefferson. 8pp. Pages 2 and 8: Blank. [Crew/MISC-34].
- **AmPM-594   TANEY**, Roger Brooke (State House, 1799–1800; State Senate, 1816–1821; U.S. Attorney General, 1831–1833; U.S. Secretary of the Treasury, 1833–1836; U.S. Supreme Court, 1836–1864)
594.1 Chief Justice Taney (Song). w. No composer indicated. m. "Air—*The Days Of Absence*." No publisher indicated. [186-]. B/w litho of a man with hat in his hand. 2pp. Page 2: Blank. [AMC].
594.2 King Andrew (Glee). m. "Tune—*Dame Durden*." Published by S.H. Parker, No. 141 Washington Street, Boston, MA. August, 1834. Non-pictorial. "As Sung at the Salem Whig Festival." 4pp. Pages 1 and 4: Blank. [Crew/AJK-7].
594.3 King Andrew. m. "Tune—*Dame Durden*." In: *A Miniature Of Martin Van Buren (With A Selection Of The Best And Most Popular Tippecanoe Songs)*, page 46. 1840. [3½" × 6½"]. [V-1: Br/bk] [V-2: Gn/bk] [V-3: Y/bk] litho of man, chain around neck. Van Buren quote. "Amos Kendal's Veracity—Tom Benton's Honesty—Francis Blair's Beauty." "What is wanting cant be numbered [sic]." 58pp. [M-016]. [Crew/WHH-88].
594.4 We Have A Man Whom Freedom Hails. w. F.A. Haney, "Madison, Wis." m. No composer or tune indicated. In: *The Wide Awake Vocalist (Or Rail Splitters' Song Book)*, page 61. Published by E.A. Daggett, No. 333 Broadway, New York, NY. 1860. Non-pictorial geometric design border. "Words and Music for the Republican Campaign of 1860, Embracing a Great Variety of Songs, Solos, Duets and Choruses Arranged for Piano or melodeon; The best collection

of Words and Music ever published for a campaign, Every Club and Family should have copies, so as to join in the choruses; The Ladies are invited to join in the choruses at the meetings." 68pp. Page 2: Index. Page 67: Blank. Page 68: Advertising for Horace Waters publications. [M-116]. [Crew/AL-59].
• **AmPM-595   THOMPSON.** (City Register, Baltimore, ca. 1863)
595.1 Trip Toniacara Falls. w. "By one who went along." m. No tune indicated. [1863–1865]. Non-pictorial geometric design border. 2pp. Page 2: Blank. [AMC].
• **AmPM-596   WALLIS,** Severn Teackle (State House, 1861)
596.1 Fiat Justitia. w. H. Rebel. m. No tune indicated. Published at Baltimore, MD. 1862. Non-pictorial. 2pp. Page 2: Blank. [WFU].
596.2 God Will Repay. w. H. Rebel. m. No tune indicated. No Publisher indicated. Published at Baltimore, 1862. [Approx. 3¾" × 9"]. R/w litho of the scales of justice, line border. "Privately Printed." 2pp. Page 2: Blank. [WFU].
596.3 God Will Repay. w. H. Rebel. m. No tune indicated. Published at Baltimore, MD. 1862. B/w litho of scales of justice, geometric design border. 2pp. Page 2: Blank. [AMC].
596.4 Right Must Prevail. w. H. Rebel. m. No tune indicated. No publisher indicated. Published in Baltimore, MD. 1862. R/w litho of the scales of justice. "Privately Printed." 2pp. Page 2: Blank. [AMC] [WFU].
596.5 Virginia's Knocking Around. w.m. No composers or tune indicated. Published in Baltimore, MD. March 30, 1862. Non-pictorial. 2pp. Page 2: Blank. [AMC].
• **AmPM-597   WARFIELD,** Edwin (State Senate, 1882–1886; Governor, 1904–1908)
597.1 Annapolis Capitol Gavotte (A Colonial Dance). m. W. Perlitz, Op. 106. Published by W. Purlitz, Eastport, MD. 1905. B/w photos of W. Perlitz and the "Maryland State Capitol, Annapolis, MD." B/w geometric designs. "Respectfully Dedicated to His Excellency Governor Edwin Warfield." 6pp. Pages 2 and 6: Blank. [LL/JH].
• **AmPM-598   WINDER,** Levin (State House, 1789–1793, 1806–1809; Presidential Elector, 1792; Governor, 1812–1816)
598.1 General Winder's March. m. No composer indicated. Published by John Cole, 123 Market Street, Baltimore, MD. 1824. 2pp. Page 2: Blank. [W-2948].
• **AmPM-599   MISCELLANEOUS MUSIC**
599.1 Trip Toniacara Falls. w. "By one who went along." m. No tune indicated. [1863–1865]. Non-pictorial geometric design border. 2pp. Page 2: Blank. [Baltimore City Council]. [AMC].

MASSACHUSETTS

• **AmPM-599x   ADAMS,** John (Delegate, Continental Congress, 1774–1778; Signer, Declaration of Independence, 1776; U.S. Minister to Netherlands, 1781–1788; U.S. Minister to Great Britain, 1785–1788; Vice President, 1789–1797; President, 1797–1801) [SEE: DOC/PSM-JA]
• **AmPM-599xx   ADAMS,** John Quincy (U.S. Minister to the Netherlands, 1794–1797; U.S. Minister to Prussia, 1797–1801; State Senator, 1802; U.S. Senator, 1803–1808; U.S. Minister to Russia, 1809–1814; Chief Negotiator, Treaty of Ghent, 1814; U.S. Minister to Great Britain, 1815–1817; U.S. Secretary of State, 1817–1825; President, 1825–1829) [SEE: DOC/PSM-JQA]
• **AmPM-600   ADAMS,** Samuel (General Court, 1765–1774; Continental Congress, 1774–1782; Signer of the Declaration of Independence, 1776; State Senate, 1781; Lt. Governor, 1789–1794; Governor, 1794–1797)
600.1 The Declaration Of Independence Of The United States Of North America, July 4, 1776. w. From the Declaration of Independence. m. John E. Wilson. Published by John E. Wilson, Baltimore, MD. 1863. B/w litho of the interior of Independence Hall. "Arranged and adapted for Vocal and Instrumental Music as the Great National Chant." 4pp. [?]. Page 4: Facsimile signatures of all signers.
600.2 Old Independence Hall. w. A. Fletcher Stayman. m. Francis Weiland. Published by Stayman & Brothers, No. 210 Chesnut Street, Philadelphia, PA. 1855. Non-pictorial. "Respectfully dedicated to the Memory of the Signers of the Declaration of Independence." "Fac Simile of their signatures" including John Adams, Sam Adams, Elbridge Gerry, Thomas Jefferson. 8pp. Pages 2 and 8: Blank. [Crew/MISC-34].
• **AmPM-601   ALLEN,** Samuel Clesson, (State House, 1806–1810; State Senate, 1812–1815 & 1831; U.S. House, 1817–1829); Governor's Executive Council, 1829–1830)
601.1 When This Old Hat Was New. w.m. No composer or tune indicated. In: *The Log Cabin & Hard Cider Melodies, A Collection Of Popular And Patriotic Songs,* page 47. Published by Charles Adams, No. 23 Tremont Street, Boston, MA. 1840. [3¾" × 6"]. [V-1: Pk/bk] [V-2: Gn/bk] litho of William Henry Harrison. "The Freeman's glittering Sword be Blest, For ever blest the Freeman's Lyre." 78pp. Pages 2 and 77: Blank. Page 3: Inside title page. B/w litho of log cabin. "Respectfully Dedicated to the Friends of Harrison and Tyler." Page 78: Advertising. [M-012]. [Crew/WHH-68].
601.2 When This Old Hat Was New. w. No composer indicated. In: *Whig Songs For 1844* [Songster], page 9. Published by Greeley & McElrath, New York,

NY. 1844. [5⅞" × 9³⁄₁₆"]. Non-pictorial. 16pp. Page 16: "Odes and Poems." [M-061]. [Crew/HC-35].

• **AmPM-603** AMES, Oakes (State Executive Council, 1860; U.S. House, 1863–1873)

603.1 Captain Grant. w. No composer indicated. m. "Air — *Captain Jenks*." In: *Tilden And Hendricks' Reform Songs (For The Centennial Campaign Of 1876)*, page 33. Published by The National Democratic Committee, Box 3637, New York, NY. 1876. [3⅞" × 5¹⁵⁄₁₆"]. Gn/bk litho of Samuel J. Tilden and Thomas A. Hendricks, geometric design border. 40pp. [M-203]. [Crew/SJT-21].

603.2 Hancock's Solid Ranks. w. No composer indicated. m. "Air — *Tramp, Tramp, Tramp*." In: *Hancock And English Campaign Songster*, page 30. Published by New York Popular Publishing Company, A.J. Dick, Manager, No. 32 Beekman Street, New York, NY. 1880. Be/bk litho of Winfield Scott Hancock. "Containing the Largest and Most Complete Collection of Songs, All Written to the Most Popular Airs of the Day." "The Most Popular Edition Of Hancock And English Campaign Songster." 68pp. Page 68: Be/bk litho of William H. English. [M-217]. [Crew/WSH-41].

603.3 The Hickory Wagon. m. "Tune — *Wait For The Wagon*." In: *Music For The Campaign (A Collection Of Original And Selected Songs, Adapted To Familiar Tunes For Use At Campaign Meetings, For 1880)*, page 4. Published by The *Indianapolis Sentinel* as a newspaper supplement, Indianapolis, IN. 1880. [7¾" × 10⅝"]. B/w lithos of Winfield Scott Hancock and William H. English. "This Collection of fifty one first-class Campaign Songs will be sent to any address, postage paid as follows: 25 for 30 cts.; 50 for 60 cts.; 100 for $1.00. Address Sentinel Company, Indianapolis, Ind." 8pp. Foldover. [Crew/WSH-11].

• **AmPM-604** ANDREW, John A. (State House 1858; Governor, 1861–1866)

604.1 Governor Andrew's Funeral March. m. John S. Porter. Published by Oliver Ditson & Co., 277 Washington Street, Boston, MA. 1867. B/w litho by John H. Bufford's Lith., 34 Chauncy St., [Boston], of John A. Andrew. 6pp. Pages 2 and 6: Blank.

• **AmPM-605** ANTHONY, Susan B. (Teacher; Agent for Anti-Slavery Society, 1856–1861; Temperance Activist; Women's Rights Activist; Publisher of *The Revolution*, 1868–1870)

605.1 Female Suffrage (Song And Chorus). w. R.A. Cohen. m. "Air by the Celebrated Prof. A.J. Phelps, of the Harmoneon Vocalists." a. "With Symphonies, Accompaniments, &c. by George H. Briggs." Published by P.L. Huyett & Son, No. 8 Fourth Street, St. Joseph, MO. 1867. B/w litho vine frame. "Dedicated to Lucy Stone, Susan B. Anthony, Elizabeth Cady Stanton, George Francis Train, And the Advocates of Female Suffrage." 6pp. Page 2: Blank. Page 6: Advertisement. [Crew/S-1867-1].

605.2 The Mother Of Us All (An Opera). w. Gertrude Stein. m. Virgil Thompson. 33⅓ rpm LP. Published by New World Records, #NW 288. Copyright 1977 by Recorded Anthology of America Music, Inc. 2 Vols. Album cover: Drawing of "Susan B." "The Santa Fe Opera, John Crosby General Director; Conducted by Raymond Leppard." Includes a 32 page libretto.

605.3 Political Millennium (In Posse). w. S.N. Holmes. m. "Tune — *Common Meter*." In: *The Republican Campaign Song Book, With Music, 1892*, page 52. e. Samuel Newall Holmes. Published by Samuel Newall Holmes, Syracuse, NY. 1892. Be/bk non-pictorial. "Composed and especially prepared by Judge S.N. Holmes of Syracuse, N.Y." "Headquarters: Syracuse, N.Y." "Price twenty-five cents." 60pp. [M-308]. [Crew/BFH-107].

605.4 The Suffrage Flag. w. William P. Adkinson ("By Permission"). m. "Air — *Bonnie Blue Flag*." "Dedicated to Elizabeth Cady Stanton, Lucy Stone, Susan B. Anthony, Mary A. Livermore and other pioneer women in the Woman Suffrage Movement." In: *Booklet Of Song: A Collection Of Suffrage And Temperance Melodies (No. 1)*, page 17. c. L. May Wheeler. Published by Co-operative Printing Company, Minneapolis, Minnesota. 1884. [6½" × 4½"]. Non-pictorial geometric designs, flora, fauna. 54pp. [Crew/S-1884-1].

605.5 We'll Show You When We Come To Vote (The Great Woman's Suffrage) (Song & Chorus). w.m. Frank Howard "(Author of *Only A Poor Little Beggar, Out In The Starlight I'm Waiting For Thee, Drunkard's Home, Fairy Of The Vail, I'm Happy Little Ned, Grape Vine Swing In The Dell*)." Published by W.W. Witney's Palace of Music, Toledo, OH. 1869. B/w litho of women lined up to vote, wall signs reading — "Vote for Susan B. Anthony for President," "For Vice President Mrs. Geo. F. Train," "For Governor of N.Y. Elizabeth Cady Stanton," "For Governor of Mass. Lucy Stone," "Down with Male Rule." "To Mrs. J.M. Ashley." [Crew/S-1869-5].

• **AmPM-606** ASHLEY, Charles S. (Common Council, New Bedford, 1884; Alderman, New Bedford, 1887–1888; Mayor, New Bedford, 1891–1892, 1897–1905, 1907, 1910–1914, 1917–1921 and 1927–1936; School Committee, New Bedford, 1923–1924)

606.1 Charles S. Ashley (Golden Anniversary Song). w.m. Clarence 'Tony' Senna. Published by Ashley Party, New Bedford, MA. Copyright 1934 by Clarence 'Tony' Senna. B/w drawing of Charles S. Ashley — 50th Anniversary 1884–1934." 6pp. Pages 2 and 6: Blank.

• **AmPM-607** BACON, John (State House, 1780, 1783–1784, 1786, 1789–1791 & 1793; State Senate, 1781–1782, 1794–1796, 1798 & 1803–1806; U.S. House, 1801–1803; State Supreme Court, 1809)

607.1 Poor Jude, Or The Death Of The Judiciary. w. No composer indicated. m. "An AmPMified Parody of the celebrated Song *Cock-Robin*." Published in the *Washington Federalist*, December 8, 1802. [VBL, p. 173].

• **AmPM-608** BANCROFT, George (Collector, Port of Boston, 1838; U.S. Secretary of the Navy, 1845–1846; U.S. Minister to Great Britain, 1846–1849; U.S. Minister to Prussia, 1867–1871; U.S. Minister to Germany, 1871–1874)

608.1 The Lounger's Lament. w. No composer indicated. m. "Air — *Exile Of Erin*." In: *Harrison Melodies (Original And Selected)*, page 63. Published by Weeks, Jordan & Co., Boston, MA. 1840. [3³⁄₁₆" × 6"]. B/w litho of William Henry Harrison. "Published under the direction of the Boston Harrison Club." 76pp. Page 5: "To William Henry Harrison of Ohio, the gallant soldier, the enlightened statesman, the consistent Republican, and the Honest man..." [M-001, 002, 003]. [Crew/WHH-86].

608.2 *A Miniature Of Martin Van Buren*. w.m. No composer or tune indicated. In: *A Miniature Of Martin Van Buren (With A Selection Of The Best And Most Popular Tippecanoe Songs)*, page 3. 1840. [3½" × 6½"]. [V-1: Br/bk] [V-2: Gn/bk] [V-3: Y/bk] litho of man, chain around neck. Van Buren quote. "Amos Kendall's Veracity — Tom Benton's Honesty — Francis Blair's Beauty." "What is wanting cant be numbered [sic]." 58pp. [M-016]. [Crew/WHH-88].

608.3 *Parody On The Flail Song*. w. No composer indicated. m. "Air — *Derry Down*." In: *Log Cabin Minstrel (or Tippecanoe Songster)*, page 9. c. "A Member of the Roxbury Whig Association." Published at the *Patriot And Democrat* Office, Roxbury, [MA]. 1840. [4½" × 6¾"]. [V-1:Y/bk] [V-2: Bl/bk] litho of William Henry Harrison, geometric design border. "Old Tip's the boy to swing the flail. Hurrah! Hurrah! Hurrah!" 64pp. Page 3: Title page — "Containing a Selection of Songs Original and Selected Many of them Written Expressly for this Work, Compiled, Published and Arranged by a member of the Roxbury Democratic Whig Association and Respectfully Dedicated to the Log Cabin Boys of the U.S." [M-013]. [Crew/WHH-71].

• **AmPM-609** BANKS, Nathaniel Prentice (State House, 1849–1852; U.S. House, 1853–1857, 1865–1873, 1875–1879 & 1889–1891; Governor, 1858–1861; State Senate, 1874) [ALSO SEE: DOC/PSM-NB]

609.1 *The Final Victory* (Ballad No. 3). w. A. Anderson. m. "Air — *Johnny Fill Up The Bowl*." Published by A. Anderson, 420 South Tenth Street, Philadelphia, PA. 1864. [Approx. 6" × 9½"]. B/w non-pictorial geometric design border. "See numbers one and two." "A. Anderson, 420 South Tenth Street, Philadelphia, Where all Ballads bearing his name may be had; also all the most Popular Songs of the times, Wholesale and Retail." 2pp. Page 2: Blank. [AMC].

609.2 *The Greeley Pill*. w. No composer indicated. m. "Air — *The Mistletoe Bough*." "Mixed at Cincinnati and taken to Baltimore." "Sung by the Union Glee Club at a Grant Republican rally at Cooper Institute." Published in the *New York Times*, September 26, 1872. [VBL, p. 456].

609.3 *Hurrah! For The Union!* w.m. No composer or tune indicated. No publisher indicated. [186-]. Approx. 5¾" × 10"]. B/w litho of a globe, titled "America," floating in water, American flag planted at the North Pole, geometric design border. 2pp. Page 2: Blank. [AMC].

609.3 *Marshal Kane* (Song). w. No composer indicated. No Publisher indicated. [1861–1862]. [4½" × 11"]. B/w litho vignette of man, woman under tree, geometric design border. 2pp. Page 2: Blank. [WFU].

609.4 *McClellan's Address To His Army*. w. No composer indicated. m. "Air — *Bruce's Address*." In: *Beadle's Dime Knapsack Songster: Containing The Choicest Patriotic Songs, Together with many New And Original Ones, Set to Old Melodies*, page 18. Published by Beadle and Company, No. 141 William Street, New York, NY. 1862. [3¾" × 5¾"]. Litho of coin — "One Dime, United States of America." 74pp. [Crew/GBM-78].

609.5 *My God! What Is All This For?* w. No composer indicated. m. "Air — *Rosseau's Dream*." No publisher indicated. [1861–1862]. [V-1: B/w geometric design border] [V-2: Pk/bk line border]. "The above is the dying words of a Federal soldier on the Battle field of Manassas, 1861." 2pp. Page 2: Blank. [V-1: AMC] [V-2: WFU].

609.6 *Hurrah! For Fremont The Brave* (To The Republicans Of The Union). m. Annie Page. Published by L. Carleton, No. 58 North 8th Street, Philadelphia, PA. 1856. Non-pictorial geometric designs. "To the Hon. N.P. Banks." "Here's A Health To Freemont [sic]." "Campaign Song No. 1." 6pp. Pages 2 and 6: Blank. [Crew/JCF-56].

609.7 *Our General's Grand March*. m. C.S. Grafulla. Published by E.A. Daggett, New York, NY. 1861. N/c litho [horizontal format] of Union generals, including "Scott, Butler, McClellan, Sprague, Prentiss, Tyler, Burnside, Hunter, Blenker, M'Dowell, Anderson, M'Call, Woll, Rosecrans, Lander, Dix, Curtis, Stone, Heintzelman, Banks, and Fremont. 8pp. Pages 2 and 8: Blank. Page 3: Title — *Our General's Quickstep*. "As Performed by the 7th Reg. National Guard Band." [Crew/WS-14].

609.8 *Quamdiu Yendem Abutere Patientiae Nostra? Ad Quen Finem Sese Jactabit Audacia?* (Come gentle muse, Give me Your Aid). w. "B." m. No tune indicated. No publisher indicated. Published in Baltimore, June 30, 1861. B/w geometric design border. 2pp. Page 2: Blank. [AMC].

609.9 *Rebellion's Weak Back*. w.m. F. Wilmarth. Published by Russell & Patee, Boston, MA. [ca. 1862]. Non-pictorial geometric designs. "As sung by Billy Morris at Morris Bros., Pell and Trowbridge." [AMC].

609.10 *Richmond Is A Hard Road To Travel* (Or The New Jordan). w. No composer indicated. m. *Jordan Is A Hard Road To Travel*. No publisher indicated. [ca. 1862]. "Respectfully Dedicated to Gen. Ambrose E. Burnside." "As sung with enthusiastic applause in all the Northern States." 2pp. Page 2: Blank. [AMC].

609.11 *Sing A Song Of Greenbacks*. w.m. No composer or tune indicated. In: *Democratic Presidential Campaign Songster (No. 1)*, page 66. Published by J.F. Feeks, No. 26 Ann Street, New York, NY. 1864. [3¾" × 5½"]. Y/bk litho of George B. McClellan, chain link frame. "McClellan & Pendleton." "Original Campaign Songs, Choruses, &c." 74pp. [M-135, 136]. [Crew/GBM-23].

609.12 *Song*. w. No composer indicated. m. "Tune — *Happy Land Of Canaan*." No publisher indicated. [ca. 1863]. [Approx. 4½" × 13"]. Y/bl non pictorial. 2pp. Page 2: Blank. [WFU].

609.13 *Welcome 'Jeff' To Baltimore*. w. No composer indicated. m. "Air — *Annie Of The Vale*." No composer indicated. [1861–1862]. [Approx. 4½" × 9"]. Y/bk litho of a monument, black line border. 2pp. Page 2: Blank. [WFU].

• **AmPM-610** BATES, John Lewis (State House, 1894–1899; Lt. Governor, 1900–1903; Governor, 1903–1905)

610.1 *Massachusetts Song* (Unison, Solo, or Chorus). w.m. Edward J. Cox. Published by E.J. Cox, Newtonville, MA. 1904. B/w photo of the Massachusetts capitol building. Bl/w drawing of the Bunker Hill

Monument. "Respectfully Dedicated by Permission to His Excellency The Governor Hon. John L. Bates." 6pp. Page 6: Blank.

• **AmPM-611 BIRD**, Charles Sumner (Candidate for Governor, 1912 & 1913)

611.1 Everybody Sing Please [Song Booklet]. Published by the Massachusetts State Committee Progressive Party, No. 70 Devonshire Street, [Boston, MA]. [1912]. [6" × 9⁵⁄₁₆"]. B/w photos of "Progressive Party Standard Bearers — Theodore Roosevelt for President, Hiram Johnson for Vice President, Charles Sumner Bird of Walpole for Governor, Daniel Cosgrove of Lowell for Lieut. Governor." "The power is the people's and only the people's — Roosevelt." "Patriotism and prayers should march hand in hand — Lincoln." 4pp.

• **AmPM-612 BOUTWELL**, George S. (State House, 1842–1844 & 1847–1850; Governor, 1851–1852; U.S. House, 1863–1869; U.S. Secretary of the Treasury, 1869–1873; U.S. Senate, 1873–1877)

612.1 Governor Boutwell's Grand March. m. Jos. W. Turner. Published by Oliver Ditson, 115 Washington Street, Boston, MA. [1851–1852]. Non-pictorial geometric designs. "Composed and respectfully dedicated to his Excellency George S. Boutwell." 4pp. Pages 1 and 4: Blank.

612.2 Our Wagon. m. "Air — *Red, White And Blue.*" In: *The Grant Songster (For The Campaign Of 1868)*, page 7. Published by Root & Cady, No. 67 Washington Street, Chicago, IL. 1868. [4¾" × 6⅜"]. O/bk litho of Ulysses S. Grant. "A Collection of Campaign Songs for 1868." 48pp. Page 48: Advertising for Grant Campaign music. [M-158, 159]. [Crew/USG-113].

• **AmPM-613 BOWDOIN**, James (State General Court, 1753–1774; State Governing Council, 1775–1777; State Constitutional Convention, 1779; Governor, 1785–1787)

613.1 Choro Grando. w. No composer indicated. m. No composer indicated. In: *The American Musical Miscellany, A Collection Of The Newest And Most Appoved* [Sic] *Songs, Set To Music*, page 123. Printed by Andrew Wright for Daniel Wright & Company, Northampton, MA. 1798. 300pp. [S/U, p. 16].

• **AmPM-614 BRADFORD**, William (Governor, Plymouth Colony, 1621–1633, 1635–1636, 1637–1638, 1639–1644 & 1645–1657)

614.1 Our Mayflower (The Thanksgiving Song). w.m. Marie Rich Rockwood. Published by Mayflower Music, Stockbridge, MA. 1953. Pl/w drawing of the ship Mayflower. "Dedicated to The Society of Mayflower Descendants." 8pp. Page 2: Facsimile letter from the Mayflower Society in Connecticut. Page 3: At bottom of music — "Marie Rich Rockwood [facsimile signature] — Descendant of Governor William Bradford who came on The Mayflower in 1620." Page 7: Facsimile letter from Governor Christian Herter of Massachusetts to Mrs. Rockwood. Page 8: Publisher's address.

• **AmPM-615 BRIMMER**, Martin (Mayor, Boston, 1843)

615.1 Brimmer's Quick Step. m. S. Knaebel. Published by Chas. H. Keith, 67 & 69 Court Street, Boston, MA. 1843. Non-pictorial geometric designs. "As performed by the Boston Brass Band at their concerts." "And respectfully dedicated by permission to the Hon. Martin Brimmer, Mayor of Boston." 4pp.

• **AmPM-616 BROOKS**, John (Mass. General Court, 1785–1786; Governor, 1816–1823)

616.1 Govr. Brook's Grand March. m. G. Graupner. Published by G. Graupner, No. 6 Franklin Street, Boston, MA. [1820]. Non-pictorial geometric designs. "Composed and dedicated to Miss Swan and young Ladies at her Academy, Medford." 4pp. Pages 1 and 4: Blank. [W-3200].

616.2 Governor Brooks' Favorite Scotch March. m. No composer indicated. Published by Geo. Willig, 171 Chesnut Street, Philadelphia, PA. [1819–1823]. Non-pictorial. 2pp. Page 2: Blank.

616.3 Governor Brooks' Favorite Scotch March. m. No composer indicated. Published by Graupner & Co., Boston, MA. [1817?]. Non-pictorial. "Arranged for the Piano Forte." 4pp. Pages 1 and 4: Blank. Page 3: *A Favorite Polish Waltz.* [W-3173].

616.4 Governor Brooks' Favorite Scotch March. m. No composer indicated. Published by Graupner & Co., Boston, MA. [182-]. Non-pictorial. "Arranged for the Piano Forte." "Sold for G.G. by John Ashton, No. 197 Washington Street, Boston, MA." 4pp. Pages 1 and 4: Blank. Page 3: *A Favorite Polish Waltz.* [W-3173B].

616.5 Governor Brooks' Favorite Scotch March. m. No composer indicated. Published by A. Bacon, No. 11 South 4th Street, Philadelphia, PA. [1817–1822]. Non-pictorial geometric designs. 4pp. Pages 1 and 4: Blank. Page 3: *Panharmonicon* and *Tyrolese Waltz.* [W-3174].

616.6 Governor Brooks' Favorite Scotch March. m. No composer indicated. In: *Massachusetts Collection Of Martial Musick [Sic], Containing A Plain, Easy & Concise Introduction To The Grounds Of Martial Musick [Sic], Laid Down In The Most Comprehensive Manner, Together With A Large Collection Of The Most Approved Beats, Marches, Airs, &c., Introducing The Principal Part Of The Duties Of The Camp, The Evolutions For The Musicians, And Their Signals, A Great Part Of Which Was Never Before Published, Designed Principally For The Benefit Of The Militia Of The United States*, page 28. Published by Alvan Robinson, Jr., Exeter, NH. 1820. [W-7521].

• **AmPM-617 BUNDY**, McGeorge (Special Assistant for National Security Affairs, 1961–1966, President, Ford Foundation, 1966–1979)

617.1 Cool Goldwater. w. Noel E. Parmentel, Jr. and Marshall J. Dodge. In: *Folk Songs For Conservatives*, page 11. Published by Unicorn Press, Inc., No. 790 Madison Avenue, New York, NY. 10021. 1964. [5" × 8⅜"]. Bl/w drawings of Barry Goldwater, Bill Buckley, Ray Cohn, eagle. List of contents. "Sung by Noel E. Parmentel, Jr. and His Unbleached Muslims, Greatest Political Satirists Since Cohn and Schine." "Right Wing Hootenanny." 36pp. [Crew/BMG-13].

617.2 I'm Called Little Caroline. w. Milton M. Schwartz. m. "Tune — *I'm Called Little Buttercup.*" In: *Sing Along With Jack* [Song Book], page 10. Published by Pocket Books, Inc., New York, NY. Copyright 1963 by Bonny Publishing Corporation. [9" × 11⅞"]. R/w/bk drawing of sheet music *Vive La Dynasty*, silhouette of John F. Kennedy in chair with conductor's baton, caricature of Kennedy family. "Hit Songs from the New Frontier." 36pp. Page 3: "Illustrations by David Gantz." Page 36: Drawing of John F. Kennedy in chair with baton. Song titles. [Crew/JFK-17].

• **AmPM-618 BURLINGAME**, Anson (State Senate, 1852; U.S. House, 1855–1861; Ambassador to China, 1861–1867)

618.1 The Artful Dodger. w. No composer indicated. m. "Air—*The Frog He Would A Wooing Go.*" In: *The Freeman's Glee Book, A Collection Of Songs, Odes, Glees And Ballads With Music, Original And Selected, Harmonized And Arranged For Each. Published Under The Auspices Of The Central Fremont And Dayton Glee Club Of The City Of New York, And Dedicated To All, Who, Cherishing Republican Liberty Consider Freedom Worth A Song*, page 8. Published by Miller, Orton & Mulligan, No. 25 Park Row, New York, NY. [and Auburn, NY]. 1856. [4 15/16" × 6"]. Pk/bk litho of man on mountain peak, music sheets, geometric designs. 112pp. [Crew/JCF-16].

618.2 Brooks' Canada Song. w. No composer indicated. m. "Air—*The Washing Day.*" In: *The Freeman's Glee Book, A Collection Of Songs, Odes, Glees And Ballads With Music, Original And Selected, Harmonized And Arranged For Each. Published Under The Auspices Of The Central Fremont And Dayton Glee Club Of The City Of New York, And Dedicated To All, Who, Cherishing Republican Liberty Consider Freedom Worth A Song*, page 60. Published by Miller, Orton & Mulligan, No. 25 Park Row, New York, NY. [and Auburn, NY]. 1856. [4 15/16" × 6"]. Pk/bk litho of man on mountain peak, music sheets, geometric designs. 112pp. [Crew/JCF-16].

• **AmPM-619 BUTLER**, Benjamin Franklin (State House, 1853; State Senate, 1859; U.S. House, 1867–1875 & 1877–1879; Governor, 1883–1884; Candidate for President, 1884) [ALSO SEE: DOC/PSM-BFB]

619.1 The Battle Of Big Bethel. w.m. No composers or tune indicated. No publisher indicated. [ca. 1862]. [3½" × 11¾"]. Non-pictorial geometric design border. 2pp. Page 2: Blank. [WFU].

619.2 Beauregard's Bells. w. No composer indicated. m. "Air—*Picayune Butler's Coming, Coming.*" No publisher indicated. [186-]. [Approx. 16" × 5½"]. Non-pictorial geometric design border. 2pp. Page 2: Blank. [AMC].

619.3 Behold The Man! w. No composer indicated. m. "Air—*A Little More Cider Too.*" In: *The Republican Campaign Songster, A Collection Of Lyrics, Original And Selected, Specifically Prepared For The Friends Of Freedom In The Campaign Of Fifty-Six*, page 105. Published by Miller, Orton & Mulligan, No. 25 Park Row, New York, NY. 1856. [3 13/16" × 6"]. Be/bk litho of "Colonel John C. Fremont" facing to viewer's left, black line border. 112pp. Pages 2, 111 and 112: Blank. Pages 109–110: Contents. [M-097]. [Crew/JCF-24].

619.4 Ben Butler In New Orleans. w. No composer indicated. m. "Air—*Yankee Doodle.*" In: *Beadle's Dime Knapsack Songster: Containing The Choicest Patriotic Songs, Together With Many New And Original Ones, Set To Old Melodies*, page 29. Published by Beadle and Company, No. 141 William Street, New York, NY. 1862. [3¾" × 5¾"]. Litho of coin—"One Dime, United States of America." 74pp. [Crew/GBM-78].

619.5 Ben Butler Is Our Candidate. w. P. Richards. m. Thomas Coates. Copyright 1884 by P. Richards. Non-pictorial geometric designs. 4pp. Page 4: Blank. [Crew/BFB-27].

619.6 Ben Butler Leads The Way! (A Patriotic Song And Chorus). Published by Ward, Chase & Co., Importing Dealers, Broadway, New York, NY. 1884. Non-pictorial geometric designs. 4pp. Page 4: Blank. [Crew/BFB-26].

619.7 The Betters In Our Block. w. Frank N. Scott. In: *P.T. Schultz & Co's Blaine And Logan Bugle Call*, page 8. Published by P.T. Schultz & Company, No. 172 Race Street, Cincinnati, OH. 1881. [1884 Edition]. [5⅞" × 7⅝"]. Bk/gn litho of James G. Blaine and John A. Logan, flags and eagle, geometric design border. 36pp. Page 36: Advertising. [M-245]. [Crew/JGB-67].

619.8 The Broker's Stamp Act Lament. w.m. No composer or tune indicated. No publisher indicated. [July, 1862. [Approx. 3½" × 7½"]. Y/bk non-pictorial black line border, line under title. 2pp. Page 2: Blank. [WFU]. [AMC].

619.9 The Broom. w.m. No composer or tune indicated. In: *Republican Song Book*, page 44. c. Thomas Drew "(Late Editor of *The Massachusetts Spy*)." Published by Thayer and Eldridge, Boston, MA. 1860. [3⅞" × 5⅞"]. Br/bk litho of beardless Abraham Lincoln, vignettes of young Lincoln chopping rails, polling raft. 68pp. [M-108]. [Crew/AL-8].

619.10 Butler, The Beast. w. "By the Ladies of New Orleans." m. "Air—*Rory O'More.*" In: *Beadle's Dime Knapsack Songster: Containing The Choicest Patriotic Songs, Together With Many New And Original Ones, Set To Old Melodies*, page 14. Published by Beadle and Company, No. 141 William Street, New York, NY. 1862. [3¾" × 5¾"]. Litho of coin—"One Dime, United States of America." 74pp. [Crew/GBM-78].

610.11 Campaign Song No. 1. w. George H. Leithead. m. "Air—*Hoist Up The Flag.*" No publisher indicated. [5" × 7½"]. Non-pictorial. "1884." "Copyright secured August 18th, 1884." 2pp. Page 2: Blank. [AMC].

619.12 The Carte-De-Visite Album. w. No composer indicated. m. "Air—*Chanting Benny.*" Published by H. De Marsan, 60 Chatham Street, New York, NY. [1861–1865]. [Approx. 6" × 9"]. B/w litho border of theatrical-type people, lion's head, geometric designs. "A Comic Song written for Tony Pastor." 2pp. Page 2: Blank. [AMC].

619.13 Cleveland's Farewell (Song). w.m. J.A. Adams. Published by John Church & Company, No. 66 West 4th Street, Cincinnati, OH. 1884. Non-pictorial. "As Sung by the Great Campaign Singer, J.A. Adams." "Oh! Patriots True and Boys in Blue, Farewell Farewell, A Last Adieu, I now must bid Good Bye of you, Farewell Farewell, A Last Adieu, You Fought for Country, Truth and Right and I opposed with all my Might, and now I must crawl out of Sight, Farewell Farewell, A Last Adieu." 6pp. Pages 2 and 6: Blank. [Crew/JGB-36].

619.14 Confederate Flag Red, White And Blue. w. J.S. Privatt. m. No tune indicated. No publisher indicated. [1861–1862]. B/w non-pictorial geometric design border. "Composed and sung by J.S. Prevatt, Co. E. 6th Ga. Reg." 2pp. Page 2: Blank. [AMC].

619.15 Dedicated To The She Rebels Of Baltimore. w. No composer indicated. m. "Air—*Yankee Doodle.*" No publisher indicated. [ca. 1862]. [Approx. 4¾" × 10½"]. B/w non-pictorial geometric design border. 2pp. Page 2: Blank. [AMC].

619.16 Democratic Horses. w. Frank N. Scott. In: *P.T. Schultz & Co's Blaine And Logan Bugle Call,* page 25. Published by P.T. Schultz & Company, No. 172 Race Street, Cincinnati, OH. 1881. [1884 Edition]. [5⅞" × 7⅝"]. Bk/gn litho of James G. Blaine and John A. Logan, flags and eagle, geometric design border. 36pp. Page 36: Advertising. [M-245]. [Crew/JGB-67].

619.17 Fable Or Fact. w. Krys. m. "Air—*A Watcher Pale And Fearful.*" In: *The People's Songs For Blaine & Logan,* page 23. Published by Acme Publishing Bureau, J.C.O. Redington, General Manager, No. 252 Broadway, New York, NY. Copyright 1884 by J.C.O. Redington. [4⅞" × 6⅝"]. B/w litho of James G. Blaine. "Adopted by the General Republican Committees in New York City and elsewhere." "Adapted for every Voice in the Glorious Land of Freedom. All the Nation may Sing." "Come, join that Columbia's blessings increase, All Singing for Liberty, Glory and Peace." "Acme Songs." 32pp. [M-246]. [Crew/JGB-45].

619.18 For Pity's Sake, Don't Breathe It (For Goodness Sake Be Mum) (Sparkling Topical Song). w.m. Monroe H. Rosenfeld. Published by Hitchcock's Music Store, Sun Building, 166 Nassau Street, Opp. City Hall, New York, NY. 1884. B/w non-pictorial geometric designs. "The Great Hit of the Hour." 6pp. Page 2: Blank. Page 6: Advertising.

619.19 General Butler. w. No composer indicated. m. "Tune—*Yankee Doodle.*" No publisher indicated. [1861–1862]. Litho of a house, geometric design border. 2pp. Page 2: Blank. [Crew/BFB-29]. [WFU].

619.20 Good As Wheat (March and Song). w.m. "Old Rye." Published by D.P. Faulds, No. 70 Main Street, Louisville, KY. [ca. 1880]. B/w litho of farmer cutting wheat, Ben Butler and other politicos watching. "Respectfully dedicated to the Farmers of the United States." [Crew/BFB-23].

619.21 The Hat Of Chappaqua. w.m. No composer or tune indicated. In: *The Sun's Greeley Campaign Songster,* page 28. c. Amos J. Cumming. Published from *The Sun* Office, New York, NY. 1872. [4⅛" × 6½"]. Be/bk litho of Horace Greeley, wreath. "He shines for all." 64pp. [Crew/HG-5].

619.22 Hiram's Menagerie. w. No composer indicated. m. "Air—*Battle Cry Of Freedom.*" In: *The Sun's Greeley Campaign Songster,* page 15. c. Amos J. Cumming. Published from *The Sun* Office, New York, NY. 1872. [4⅛" × 6½"]. Be/bk litho of Horace Greeley, wreath. "He shines for all." 64pp. [Crew/HG-5].

619.23 Hold On Abraham (Uncle Sam's Boys Are Coming Right Along) (Song and Chorus). w.m. B. Bradbury "(Author of *Marching Along, The Dear Old Flag, Flag Of Our Union,* &c., &c.)." Published by William A. Pond & Co., No. 547 Broadway, New York, NY. 1862. B/w non-pictorial. "Being a response of Uncle Sam's Boys to the Call for 'Three Hundred Thousand More.'" "Sung with Immense success by Wood's Minstrels." "To the President of the United States." 6pp. Page 6: Blank. [Crew/AL-46].

619.24 Hurrah For Jeff Davis. w. No composer indicated. m. "Tune—*Gum Tree Canoe.*" No publisher indicated. [ca. 1862]. [Approx. 5" × 9½"]. Bl/bl geometric design border, line under title. 2pp. Page 2: Blank. [Crew/JD-97]. [WFU].

619.25 Inflation Galop! m. W. Stuckenholz. Published by Wm. A. Pond & Company, No. 547 Broadway, New York, NY. 1874. B/w litho [horizontal format] from a cartoon by W.H. Sheldon of Ulysses S. Grant, Ben Butler, Oliver P. Morton and Matthew Hale Carpenter blowing up large balloon labeled "Inflation" "$400,000,000" and "$44,000,000 Legalized." 6pp. [Crew/USG-15].

619.26 Marshal Kane (Song). w. No composer indicated. No Publisher indicated. [1861–1862]. [4½" × 11"]. B/w litho vignette of man, woman under tree, geometric design border. 2pp. Page 2: Blank. [WFU].

619.27 My God! What Is All This For? w. No composer indicated. m. "Air—*Rosseau's Dream.*" No publisher indicated. [1861–1862]. [V-1: B/w geometric design border] [V-2: Pk/bk line border]. "The above is the dying words of a Federal soldier on the Battle field of Manassas, 1861." 2pp. Page 2: Blank. [V-1: AMC] [V-2: WFU].

619.28 The New Skedaddle Song. w.m. No composer or tune indicated. Published by H. De Marsan, 54 Chatham Street, New York, NY. [186-]. [Approx. 5½" × 9"]. B/w litho border of Black minstrel characters, cherubs. "The music of this song can be obtained of Root & Cady Music Publishers, 95 Clark Street, Chicago." 2pp. Page 2: Blank. [AMC].

619.29 No Time For Side Shows. w.m. No composer or tune indicated. In: *Acme Songs, Republican Glee Book, And Cartridge Box Of Truth* (Campaign of 1888), page 42. Published by The Acme Publishing Bureau, J.C.O. Redington, General Manager, No. 35 University Avenue, Syracuse, NY. Copyright 1888 by J.C.O. Redington. [5⅜" × 6¹³⁄₁₆"]. Gy/bk lithos of eagle, shield, tent, flag, soldiers, Uncle Sam. "With Music and 20 Illustrations by Nast and others." "Price 10 cents." "Only Book Prepared by Soldiers, The Only Illustrated Campaign Glee Book Ever Printed." "With Music and 20 Illustrations." "Illustrated by Nast and Others." "A Filled Pocket Haversack of Loyalty, Glory, Song, Fun and Facts for Every Individual, Whether Singer or Not." 68pp. [M-255]. [Crew/BFH-25].

619.30 Oh Jeff! Why Don't You Come? w. No composer indicated. m. "Air—*Willie We Have Missed You.*" No publisher indicated [probably Baltimore]. [Approx. 5¾" × 9½"]. Litho geometric design border. 2pp. Page 2: Blank. [WFU].

619.31 Oh No, Ben! (Republican Campaign Song). w.m. Edward H. Phelps. Published by Edward H. Phelps, Springfield, MA. 1878. Non-pictorial. 2pp. "Price 5 Cents, 35 Copies for $1.00; 200 Copies for $2.00." Page 2: Blank. [Crew/BFB-28]. [AMC].

619.32 Old Shoddy. w.m. No composer or tune indicated. In: *Copperhead Minstrel (A Choice Collection Of Democratic Poems & Songs),* page 26. Published by Feeks and Bancker, Wholesale Agents, No. 24 Ann Street, New York. 1863. [4¾" × 7¼"]. O/bk non-pictorial. "For the use of Political Clubs and the Social Circle." "Price 25 cents." 64pp. [M-133] [Crew/GBM-64].

619.33 The Old Union Wagon. w. Robert M. Hart. m. "Air—*Wait For The Wagon*." In: *Patriotic Song Book For The G.A.R., For The Use Of The G.A.R. In their Post-Meeting, Reunions, Camp-Fires, Installation Exercises, Fourth Of July Celebrations, And Memorial Service*, page 76. Published by Orwell Blake, Des Moines, IA. 1883. [5¹⁵⁄₁₆" × 9⁵⁄₁₆"]. R/gd litho of a G.A.R. badge. 116pp.

619.34 Our Wagon. m. "Air—*Red, White And Blue*." In: *The Grant Songster (For The Campaign Of 1868)*, page 7. Published by Root & Cady, No. 67 Washington Street, Chicago, IL. 1868. [4¾" × 6⅜"]. O/bk litho of Ulysses S. Grant. "A Collection of Campaign Songs for 1868." 48pp. Page 48: Advertising for Grant Campaign music. [M-158, 159]. [Crew/USG-113].

619.35 Picaynue Butler. w. No composer indicated. m. "Tune—*All On Hobbies*." [ca. 1861]. [Approx. 3¾" × 8"]. Litho of man with club, snake. 2pp. Page 2: Blank. [WFU].

619.36 Quamdiu Yendem Abutere Patientiae Nostra? Ad Quen Finem Sese Jactabit Audacia? (Come gentle muse, Give me Your Aid). w. "B." m. No tune indicated. No publisher indicated. Published in Baltimore, June 30, 1861. B/w geometric design border. 2pp. Page 2: Blank. [AMC].

619.37 Radical Campaign Song. w. Hon. B.F. Whittemore. m. "Air—*Marching On*." No publisher indicated. [ca. 1868]. [Approx. 4" × 12"]. Non-pictorial. 2pp. Page 2: Blank.

619.38 Rally For Cleaveland [sic] ***And Hendricks***. w. A.S. Barry. m. M. Barry. Published by I.L.A. Brodersen & Co., No. 137 and 139 Post Street, San Francisco, CA. 1884. Non-pictorial geometric design border. "Respectfully dedicated to the Cleveland Hundred of San Jose." 6pp. Pages 2 and 6: Blank. [Crew/GC-187].

619.39 The Rebel's Retort (Song). w. No composer indicated. m. "Air—*Cocachelunk*." No publisher indicated. [ca. 1861]. [Approx. 4⅝" × 9½"]. Litho of mill house, trees, geometric design border. 2pp. Page 2: Blank. [WFU].

619.40 The Right Men In The Right Place (Topical Song and Refrain). w.m. E.F. Morse. Published by Charles D. Blake & Co., 488 Washington Street, Boston, MA. 1887. Non-pictorial geometric designs. 6pp. Pages 2 and 6: Advertising. [AMC].

619.41 Seymour's Now The People's Choice. w. No composer indicated. m. "Air—*When Johnny Comes Marching Home*." In: *Seymour Campaign Songster*, page 21. Published by Pattee & Hubbard, Democratic State Committee Rooms, World Building, No. 37 Park Row, New York, NY. 1868. [4" × 5¼"]. Gn/bk litho of Horatio Seymour and Francis Blair. "In the spirit of George Washington and the Patriots of the Revolution, Let us take the steps to re-inaugurate our Government, to start it once again on its course to greatness and prosperity—Horatio Seymour." 38pp. [M-173]. [Crew/HS-8].

619.43 The Shoddy Brigadier. w.m. No composer or tune indicated. In: *Copperhead Minstrel (A Choice Collection Of Democratic Poems & Songs)*, page 38. Published by Feeks and Bancker, Wholesale Agents, No. 24 Ann Street, New York. 1863. [4¾" × 7¼"]. O/bk non-pictorial. "For the use of Political Clubs and the Social Circle." "Price 25 cents." 64pp. [M-133] [Crew/GBM-64].

619.44 Southern Red, White And Blue. w.m. No composer or tune indicated. No publisher indicated. [1861–1862]. Non-illustrated. 2pp. Page 2: Blank. [AMC].

619.45 Three Cheers For Abe And Andy (A Song For The Times). w.m. Chas. B. Brigham. Published by H.M. Higgins, No. 117 Randolph Street, Chicago, IL. 1964. Non-pictorial geometric designs. "Inscribed to Capt. H.G. Brigham, 107 N.Y. Vol." 6pp. Pages 2 and 6: Blank. [Crew/AL-540].

619.46 Three Cheers For Bonny Ben (Campaign Song And Chorus). w.m. Frank Drayton. Published by James C. Beckel, No. 914 Sansome Street, Philadelphia, PA. 1884. B/w litho of Benjamin Butler in oval and geometric frame. "To John W. Bardsley, Esq., Germantown, Pa." 4pp. Page 4: Blank. [Crew/BFB-25].

619.47 Tilden And Hendricks' Democratic Centennial Campaign March (With Radical Accompaniments). m. A. Lutz. Published by St. Louis Music Publishing Company, No. 9 North 15th Street, St. Louis, MO. Copyright 1876 by R. Staples. B/w litho of political caricatures including marching rats poking fun at Republican scandals—Benjamin Butler—"Loyal Mashtub." James G. Blaine—"Maine stock jobber $60,000." John A. Logan—"Our Darling." Ulysses S. Grant—"Let Us Have (a) Peace." Rutherford B. Hayes—"The Cooped Chickens." 8pp. Page 2: Blank. Page 3 Title: ***Democratic Centinial*** [sic] ***March***. Page 8: More drawings. List of Republican scandals: Ben Butler as a frog—"Brother-In-Law Casey and the New Orleans Custom House;" James G. Blaine—"A Bird Who Has Lost its Plumage;" "We Heartily Endorse Bab, Belknap & Blaine and Oppose Further Investigation;" "Godless S. Orth;" "Schneck and the Emma Mine;" &c. [Crew/SJT-7].

619.48 Tilden And Reform. w. No composer indicated. m. "Air—*The Wearing Of The Green*." In: *Tilden And Hendricks' Reform Songs (For The Centennial Campaign Of 1876)*, page 3. Published by The National Democratic Committee, Box 3637, New York, NY. 1876. [3⅞" × 5¹⁵⁄₁₆"]. Gn/bk litho of Samuel J. Tilden and Thomas A. Hendricks, geometric design border. 40pp. [M-203]. [Crew/SJT-21].

619.49 Uncle Ben. w. No composer indicated. m. Notation. In: *The People's Songs For Blaine & Logan*, page 28. Published by Acme Publishing Bureau, J.C.O. Redington, General Manager, No. 252 Broadway, New York, NY. Copyright 1884 by J.C.O. Redington. [4⅞" × 6⅝"]. B/w litho of James G. Blaine. "Adopted by the General Republican Committees in New York City and elsewhere." "Adapted for every Voice in the Glorious Land of Freedom. All the Nation may Sing." "Come, join that Columbia's blessings increase, All Singing for Liberty, Glory and Peace." "Acme Songs." 32pp. [M-246]. [Crew/JGB-45].

619.50 Uncle Ben (A Campaign Song For Massachusetts For 1882). w. Geo. Russell Jackson. m. W.H. Lawrence. Published by W.A. Evans & Bro., Publishers, No. 50 Broomfield Street, Boston, MA. 1882. B/w floral and geometric designs. 6pp. Page 2: Blank. Page 6: Advertising. [Crew/BFB-24].

619.51 Uncle Sam's Currency. w. No composer indicated. m. "Air—*King And Countrymen.*" In: *Democratic Presidential Campaign Songster (No. 1)*, page 57. Published by J.F. Feeks, No. 26 Ann Street, New York, NY. 1864. [3¾" × 5½"]. Y/bk litho of George B. McClellan, chain link frame. "McClellan & Pendleton." "Original Campaign Songs, Choruses, &c." 74pp. [M-135, 136]. [Crew/GBM-23].

619.52 Upside Down! (Humorous Song) w.m. Arranger: Howard Paul. Published by Wm. A. Pond & Co., 25 Union Square, Broadway Side, New York, NY. 1866. B/w litho of a Sol Smith Russell—"Sung with great Success by Sol Smith Russell." "Popular Comic Songs." 4pp. Page 4: Advertising.

619.53 The Very Latest From Butler. w.m. No composer or tune indicated. No publisher indicated. [ca. 1862]. [4½" × 10"?]. Y/bk litho of man posting a sign with song title, black line border. 2pp. Page 2: Blank. [WFU].

619.54 Virginia's Knocking Around. w.m. No composers or tune indicated. Published in Baltimore, MD. March 30, 1862. Non-pictorial. 2pp. Page 2: Blank. [AMC].

619.55 A Voice From A Rebel. w. No composer indicated. m. "Air—*Cocachelunk.*" No publisher indicated. [ca. 1862]. [5" × 7⅜"]. Geometric design litho border. 2pp. Page 2: Blank.

619.56 Ye Doleful Lament Of A Dismal Office-Holder. w. No composer indicated. m. "Air—*Dear Father, Come Home.*" In: *The Sun's Greeley Campaign Songster*, page 43. c. Amos J. Cumming. Published from *The Sun* Office, New York, NY. 1872. [4⅛" × 6½"]. Be/bk litho of Horace Greeley, wreath. "He shines for all." 64pp. [Crew/HG-5].

• **AmPM-620** CARABINE, John (Judge)

620.1 Work, Work, Work. w. Judge John Carabine, Springfield, MA. m. "Tune—*Tramp, Tramp, Tramp.*" In: *Townsend Convention Song Book*, page 3. Published by the Townsend National Recovery Plan for the Cleveland, Ohio, Convention, 1936. Copyright 1936 by Frank Dryer. [4⅜" × 8¼"]. Be/r geometric design border, Townsend Plan logos. 34pp.

• **AmPM-621** CARD, Andrew H., Jr. (State House, 1975–1983; Assistant to the President and Deputy Chief of Staff, 1988–1992; U.S. Secretary of Transportation, 1992–1993; White House Chief of Staff, 2000–Present)

621.1 The Bush Mess Song. w. William Tong. m. "*The Christmas Song*, originally by Nat King Cole." Published online at <http://www.amiright.com/parody/misc/natkingcole0.shtml>. [ca. 2000].

621.2 Bush's White House Is For Sale. w. William Tong. m. "*A Whiter Shade Of Pale*, originally by Procol Harum." Published online at <http://www.amiright.com/parody/70s/procolharum0.shtml>. [2001].

• **AmPM-622** COOLIDGE, Arthur W. (Lt. Governor, 1950; Candidate for Governor, 1950)

622.1 Our March. m. Herman Henry. No publisher indicated. Distributed by Herman Henry, Cambridge MA. Copyright 1948 by Herman Henry. R/w/b stripes. "Arranged for Full military Band and Full Symphonic Orchestra by Gustav Strube." "Dedicated to The Honorable Arthur W. Coolidge, Lieutenant Governor of the Commonwealth of Massachusetts." "Piano Solo, Price One Dollar." 6pp. Page 6: Blank.

• **AmPM-622x** COOLIDGE, Calvin (City Council, Northampton, 1899; City Solicitor, Northampton, 1900–1901; Clerk of Courts, Northampton, 1904; State House, 1907–1908; Mayor, Northampton, 1910–1911; State Senate, 1912–1915; Lt. Governor, 1916–1918; Governor, 1919–1920; Vice President, 1921–1923; President, 1923–1929) [SEE: DOC/PSM-BFB]

• **AmPM-623** COSGROVE, Daniel (Candidate for Lt. Governor, 1912)

623.1 Everybody Sing Please [Song Booklet]. Published by the Massachusetts State Committee Progressive Party, No. 70 Devonshire Street, [Boston, MA]. [1912]. [6" × 9⁵⁄₁₆"]. B/w photos of "Progressive Party Standard Bearers—Theodore Roosevelt for President, Hiram Johnson for Vice President, Charles Sumner Bird of Walpole for Governor, Daniel Cosgrove of Lowell for Lieut. Governor." "The power is the people's and only the people's—Roosevelt." "Patriotism and prayers should march hand in hand—Lincoln." 4pp.

• **AmPM-624** CURLEY, James W. (Common Council, Boston, 1900–1901; State House, 1902–1903; Alderman, Boston, 1904–1909; City Council, Boston, 1910–1911; U.S. House, 1911–1914 & 1943–1947; Mayor, 1914–1918, 1922–1926, 1930–1934 & 1946–1950; Governor, 1935–1937)

624.1 America I Love You. w. Edgar Leslie. m. Archie Gottler. Published by [V-1: Kalmar & Puck, 152 West 54th Street] [V-2: Kalmar, Puck & Abrahams, 1570 Broadway], New York, NY. 1915. R/w/b drawings by Al. Barbelle of patriotic scenes: farming, Pilgrims, covered wagons, skyscraper, Statue of Liberty, Liberty Bell, Boston Tea Party. Bl/w photo of James Curley—"I consider *America, I Love You* The greatest popular song of its kind ever written, signed; James W. Curley [script], Mayor City of Boston." 6pp. Page 6: Advertising.

624.2 Dear Old Boston. w. Joshua H. Jones, Jr. m. Jack Caddigan and Chick Story. Published by Ward and Jones, 66 Myrtle Street, Boston, MA. 1923. Bl/w photos of City Hall and state capitol building. N/c [tinted] photo of James Curley. R/e/b drawing of Bunker Hill Monument, skyscraper. "Respectfully Dedicated to The Hon. James M. Curley, Mayor of Boston." 6pp. Page 2: Blank. Page 6: Advertising.

624.3 For The Good Of The People March And Two Step (Pro Bono Publico). m. Chick Story. B/w photo of James Curley, facsimile signature. Published by O.E. Story, Music Publishers, Boston, MA. 1914. B;/w floral and geometric designs. 6pp. Page 2: At top of music—"Dedicated to His Honor, James M. Curley, Mayor of Boston." Page 6: Advertising.

624.4 Let's All Do Something (Uncle Sammy Wants Us Now). w. Andrew B. Sterling. m. Arthur Lange. Published by Jos. Morris Music Co., 145 West 45th Street, New York, NY. [1917]. Br/be photo of "Hon. James J. [sic] Curley, Mayor of Boston," floral designs. "This song accepted by His Honor James J. [sic] Curley, Mayor of Boston, Mass. As the best of all Patriotic Songs."

• **AmPM-625** CUSHING, Caleb (State House, 1825,1833–1834, 1845–1846 & 1850; State Senate, 1827 U.S. House, 1835–1843; U.S. Commissioner to

China, 1843–1845; Mayor, Newburyport, 1851–1852; State Supreme Court, 1852; U.S. Attorney General, 1853–1857; U.S. Minister to Spain, 1874–1877)

625.1 National Cement. w. George W. Bungay. m. No tune indicated. In: *The Republican Campaign Songster For 1860,* page 48. c. W.H. Burleigh. Published by [V-1 and V-2: H. Dayton, No. 36 Howard Street, New York, NY] [V-3: McNally & Company, No. 81 Dearborn Street, Chicago, IL]. 1860. [V-1: Gn/bk] [V-2: Y/bk] [V-3: Be/bk] [V-4: Bl/bk]. "Price 10 cents." [3¹³⁄₁₆" × 6"]. 72pp. [M-104]. [Crew/AL-57].

625.2 Our Country (A Patriotic Song). w. Hon. Geo, Lunt. m. I.B. Woodbury. Published by Oliver Ditson, 115 Washington Street, Boston, MA. [ca. 1847]. B/w litho of soldiers on horseback, marching. "Respectfully Inscribed to Col. Caleb Cushing of Massachusetts." 6pp. Pages 2 and 6: Blank. [LL/JH].

625.3 The President's Conscience. w. W.A. m. "Tune—*The West Countryman.*" In: *Original Clay Songs: Humorous And Sentimental, Designed To Inculcate Just Political Sentiments, To Suit The Present Political Crisis, And To Advocate The Claims Of Henry Clay To The Highest Honors His Country Can Bestow,* page 3. w. W.A. Philomath, Union Co., Ind. Published by Philomath, Cincinnati, OH. 1842. [4¼" × 6"]. Be/bk litho of an eagle, U.S. Flag. "The eagle soars above the throng; And listen's [sic] to fair Freedom's song, Hails the merry roundelay, Claps his glad wings and hails the day." 20pp. Page 20: Be/bk litho of four men—"Tyler Expounding the Constitution! The effect of 'treading in the footsteps.'" [M-057]. [CrewHC-104].

625.4 The Republican Ball. w. James A. Boone. m. "Air—*Rosin The Bow.*" In: *The Republican Campaign Songster, A Collection Of Lyrics, Original And Selected, Specifically Prepared For The Friends Of Freedom In The Campaign Of Fifty-Six,* page 90. Published by Miller, Orton & Mulligan, No. 25 Park Row, New York, NY. 1856. [3¹³⁄₁₆" × 6"]. Be/bk litho of "Colonel John C. Fremont" facing to viewer's left, black line border. 112pp. [M-097]. [Crew/JCF-24].

• **AmPM-626** DAVIS, John (U.S. House, 1825–1834; Governor, 1834–1835 & 1841–1843; U.S. Senate, 1835–1841 & 1845–1853)

626.1 The Dayton Gathering. w.m. No composer or tune indicated. In: *The National Clay Almanac, 1845,* page 21. Published by Desilver & Muir, No. 18 South Fourth Street, Philadelphia, PA. 1844. 36pp. [6³⁄₁₆" × 7⅞"]. B/w litho of Henry Clay, ship—"Commerce," plow, crops—"Agriculture." 36pp. [Crew/HC-89].

626.2 Gov: Davis' Quick Step. m. George Hews. Published by C. Bradlee, Washington Street, Boston, MA. 1834. Non-pictorial geometric designs. "Composed for the Piano Forte." 4pp. Pages 1 and 4: Blank.

• **AmPM-627** DAWES, Thomas Jr. (State House, ca. 1780s; State Senate, ca. 1780s; State Constitutional Conventions, 1780, 1789 & 1820, State Supreme Court, 1792–1803; Judge of the Municipal Court, Boston, 1803–1823)

627.1 [Now Let Rich Music Sound]. w. Thomas Dawes, Jr. m. "To the foregoing Tune [page 130]." "Written by Thomas Dawes, Jr., Esquire, and sung at the entertainment given on Bunker Hill by the Proprietors of Charles River Bridge, at the opening of the same." In: *The American Musical Miscellany, A Collection Of The Newest And Most Appoved [sic] Songs, Set to Music,* page 134. Printed by Andrew Wright for Daniel Wright & Company, Northampton, MA. 1798. 300pp. [S/U, p. 16].

• **AmPM-628** DEARBORN, Henry (U.S. Marshal for the District of Maine, 1789; U.S. House, 1793–1797; U.S. Secretary of War, 1801–1809; Collector, Port of Boston, 1809–1812; U.S. Minister Plenipotentiary to Portugal, 1822–1824)

628.1 A New Song (On the Causes — Beginnings, Events — End — and Consequence of the Late War with Great Britain). w. Silas Ballou, "Richmond, New-Hampshire." m. "Tune—*The Girl I Left Behind Me.*" No publisher indicated. B/w engraving of an eagle. 2pp. Page 2: Blank.

• **AmPM-629** DOUGLAS, William L. (State House, 1884–1885; State Senate, 1887; Mayor, Brockton, 1890; Governor, 1905–1906)

629.1 Governor Douglas March. m. Wilhelm E. Hauff. Published by The Crown Publishing Co., Armonk, NY. Copyright 1904 by Mrs. Emilie A. Hauff. B/w photo of the capitol building. R/w geometric designs. 8pp. Pages 2 and 8: Blank. Page 3: At top of music—"Dedicated to Mr. W.L. Douglas."

629.2 Governor Douglas March. m. Carl F. Burrell. a. T. Francis Burke. Published by Clif Edson, Music Publisher, Brockton, MA. 1915. B/w photo of William Douglas. Gn/w geometric designs. "Dedicated to Hon. W.L. Douglas." 6pp. Page 6: Blank.

• **AmPM-630** DUKAKIS, Michael Stanley (State House, 1963–1970; Governor, 1975–1979, 1983–91; Candidate for President, 1988) [SEE: DOC/PSM-MSD]

630.1 Bush And Cheney. w. Stuart Schimler. m. "*When Johnny Comes Marching Home,* originally published by Patrick Gilmore." "Election song for Bush and Cheney—was originally about Hayes and Wheeler..." Published online at <http://amiright.com/parody/misc/publishedpatrickgilmore0.shml>. [ca. 2002].

630.2 Dukakis Victory Song. w.m. No composer indicated. Cassette Tape. Published by Keynote Associates, One Montgomery Avenue, Bala Cynwyd, PA. Tape #CM1398. 1988. Cassette cover: B/w photo of Michael Dukakis.

630.3 Howard Dean's Leading In Taxachusetts. w. Michael McVey. m. "*Massachusetts,* based on a performance by The Bee Gees." "As for the other 49 states, well, does the name McGovern ring a bell?" Published online at <http://www.amiright.com/parody/70s/thebeegees23.shml>. 2003.

630.4 Jesse Jackson. w. No composer indicated. m. "Parody of *Foxey Lady* by Jimmy Hendrix." Lyrics published by *The Bob Rivers Show* with Bob, Spike & Joe and Twisted Tunes online at <http://www.twistedradio.com/player/lyrics.asp?songID=539>. [199-].

630.5 J.F. Kerryville. w. Kelly S. Solid. m. "*Margaritaville,* based on a performance by Jimmy Buffet." Published online at <http://amiright.com/parody/70s/jimmybuffet14.shtml. [2004].

• **AmPM-631** EUSTIS, William (State General Court, 1788–1794; U.S. House, 1801–1805 & 1820–1823; U.S. Secretary of War, 1809–1813; Governor, 1823–1825)

631.1 Governor Eustis's March. m. P.A. von Hagen. Published by S. Wetherbee, Boston, MA. [1824?]. Non-pictorial. "Arranged for the Piano Forte." 2pp. Page 2: Blank. [W-3290]

631.2 Governor Eustis's Quick Step. m. P.A. von Hagen. Published by S. Wetherbee, Boston, MA. [1824?]. Non-pictorial. 2pp. Page 2: Blank. [W-3291].

631.3 Welcome Lafayette (A Favorite Song). m. Joseph Wilson "(Organist At the Rev. Doct. Porter's Church, Roxbury)" Published by G. Graupner, No. 6 Franklin Street, Boston, MA. [ca. 1824]. Non-pictorial. "Composed and dedicated to Govr. Eustis." 4pp. Pages 1 and 4: Blank. [W-10019].

• **AmPM-632 EVERETT**, Alexander Hill (U.S. Charge d'Affaires, Netherlands, 1818–1824; U.S. Minister to Spain, 1825–1829; State House, 1830–1835; U.S. Commissioner to China, 1845–1847)

632.1 A Song For The Martin, 1840. w. No composer indicated. m. "Air—*My Heart's In The Highlands.*" In: *Harrison Melodies (Original And Selected)*, page 16. Published by Weeks, Jordan & Co., Boston, MA. 1840. [3⁹⁄₁₆" × 6"]. B/w litho of William Henry Harrison. "Published under the direction of the Boston Harrison Club." 76pp. Page 5: "To William Henry Harrison of Ohio, the gallant soldier, the enlightened statesman, the consistent Republican, and the Honest man..." [M-001, 002, 003]. [Crew/WHH-86].

632.2 When This Old Hat Was New. w.m. No composer or tune indicated. In: *The Log Cabin & Hard Cider Melodies, A Collection Of Popular And Patriotic Songs*, page 47. Published by Charles Adams, No. 23 Tremont Street, Boston, MA. 1840. [3¾" × 6"]. [V-1: Pk/bk] [V-2: Gn/bk] litho of William Henry Harrison. "The Freeman's glittering Sword be Blest, For ever blest the Freeman's Lyre." 78pp. Pages 2 and 77: Blank. Page 3: Inside title page. B/w litho of log cabin. "Respectfully Dedicated to the Friends of Harrison and Tyler." Page 78: Advertising. [M-012]. [Crew/WHH-68].

632.3 When This Old Hat Was New. w.m. No composer or tune indicated. In: *The Clay Minstrel Or National Songster*, page 326. c. John Stockton Littell. Published by Greeley & M'Elrath, Tribune Building, New York, NY. 1844. [3⅛" × 4⅞"]. Non-pictorial. 396pp. [Crew/HC-18].

632.4 When This Old Hat Was New. w. No composer indicated. In: *Whig Songs For 1844* [Songster], page 9. Published by Greeley & McElrath, New York, NY. 1844. [5⅞" × 9⁵⁄₁₆"]. Non-pictorial. 16pp. Page 16: "Odes and Poems." [M-061]. [Crew/HC-35].

• **AmPM-633 EVERETT**, Edward (U.S. House 1825–1835; Governor, 1836–1840; U.S. Secretary of State, 1852–1853; U.S. Senate, 1853–1854; Candidate for Vice President, 1860) [SEE: DOC/PSM-JBL]

633.1 [The Campaign Opens Brightly] (Campaign Song). w. No composer indicated. m. "Air—*Benny Haven.*" Published in the *Louisville Daily Courier*, August 16, 1860. Lyrics published online at <http://lincoln.lib.niu.edu/498R/danielle/Breckinridge-CampSong.html>.

633.2 Douglas. w.m. No composer or tune indicated. In: *The Democratic Campaign Songster: Douglas & Johnson Melodies*, page 23. Published by P.J. Cozans, Publisher, New York, NY. [1860]. [3⅞" × 6"]. Y/bk litho of an eagle with ribbon—"Douglas & Johnson," train, ships, monument—"Liberty" sitting on rock base—"The Constitution." 40pp. [M-117]. [Crew/SAD-5].

633.3 National Cement. w. George W. Bungay. m. No tune indicated. In: *The Republican Campaign Songster For 1860*, page 48. c. W.H. Burleigh. Published by [V-1 and V-2: H. Dayton, No. 36 Howard Street, New York, NY] [V-3: McNally & Company, No. 81 Dearborn Street, Chicago, IL]. 1860. [V-1: Gn/bk] [V-2: Y/bk] [V-3: Be/bk] [V-4: Bl/bk]. "Price 10 cents." [3¹³⁄₁₆" × 6"]. 72pp. [M-104]. [Crew/AL-57].

633.4 A Song Of The Campaign. w. No composer indicated. m. "Air—*Wait For The Wagon.*" In: *Republican Song Book*, page 55. c. Thomas Drew "(Late Editor of *The Massachusetts Spy*)." Published by Thayer and Eldridge, Boston, MA. 1860. [3⅞" × 5⅞"]. Br/bk litho of beardless Abraham Lincoln, vignettes of young Lincoln chopping rails, polling raft. 68pp. [M-108]. [Crew/AL-8].

633.5 Song Of The Office Holder. w. No composer indicated. m. "Air—*A Few Days.*" In: *Republican Song Book*, page 8. c. Thomas Drew "(Late Editor of *The Massachusetts Spy*)." Published by Thayer and Eldridge, Boston, MA. 1860. [3⅞" × 5⅞"]. Br/bk litho of beardless Abraham Lincoln, vignettes of young Lincoln chopping rails, polling raft. 68pp. [M-108]. [Crew/AL-8].

• **AmPM-634 FITZGERALD**, John Francis (Common Council, Boston, 1892, State Senate, 1893–1894; U.S. House, 1895–1901 & 1919; Mayor, Boston, 1906–1907 & 1910–1914)

634.1 I'm Going Back To Boston (Song). w.m. F. Winthrop Wheeler "(Composer of *Hearts Of Old New England*)." Published by Lotus Publishing Co., Boston, MA. 1912. Bl/gn/w drawing of Boston skyline, man in automobile, pretty girl in vignette. "To the Hon. John F. Fitzgerald, Mayor of Boston, This song is Respectfully Dedicated." 6pp. Page 2: Blank. Page 6: Advertising.

634.2 John F. Fitzgerald March. m. Jos. M. Daly "(Composer of *Miss Liberty, Yankee Tar*, etc.)." Published by Jos. M. Daly, 218 Tremont Street, Boston, MA. 1909. B/w photo of John Fitzgerald. R/w cover. 6pp. Page 6: Advertising.

• **AmPM-635 FOX**, Gustavus, V. (Assistant Secretary of the Navy, 1861–1866)

635.1 Miantonomoh Galop. m. Heinrich Furstnow. Published by Wm. Pond & Co., New York, NY. 1867. [10¼" × 13½"]. B/w lithograph of ironclad naval ship.

• **AmPM-636 GAGE**, Thomas (Governor, Massachusetts Bay Colony, 1774)

636.1 The Burning Of Charlestown. w. [Joel Barlow]. m. No tune indicated. Published in the Rivington's *Gazetteer*, 1775. [SBAR, p. 74].

636.2 Loyal York. w.m. No composers or tune indicated. No publisher indicated, 1775. [SBAR, p. 95].

636.3 Maryland Resolves. w. No composer indicated. m. "*Abbot Of Canterbury* or *Wilkes' Wriggle*. Published in the *Rivington's Gazette*, 1774. "You, no doubt, have seen the resolves of certain magnates, naming themselves as a Provisional Congress! I will not say these worthies are under the influence of the moon, or are proper subjects for confinement, but one of their resolves is exactly circulated for the meridian of the inquisition, and the other smell furiously of Bedlam. I gladly contribute my humble mite to ridicule the folly, ingratitude, and violence of our deluded patriots." [SBAR, p. 70].

636.4 *A Proclamation*. w. No composer indicated. m. No tune indicated. Published in the *Virginia Gazette*, 1774. "Friendly Warning." [SBAR, p. 65].

636.5 *A Song*. w. No composer indicated. m. No tune indicated. Published in the *Connecticut Gazette*. 1776. [SBAR, p 118].

- **AmPM-636A GARDNER**, Henry J. (Common Council, Boston, 1850 & 1854; Governor, 1855–1858)

636A.1 *Know Nothing Polka*. m. John P. Ordway. Published by J.P. Ordway, Ordway Hall, Washington Street, Boston, MA. 1855. B/w litho by L.H. Bradford & Co. of Henry J. Gardner, geometric design border. "Music Composed and Respectfully Dedicated to His Excellency, Henry J. Gardner, Governor of Massachusetts." "As danced by Pike and Pell of Ordway's Aeolians." 6pp. Pages 2 and 6: Blank.

- **AmPM-637 GARRISON**, William Lloyd (Publisher of *The Liberator*, 1831; Abolitionist; Founder of the Anti-Slavery Society, 1833)

637.1 *Brooks' Canada Song*. w. No composer indicated. m. "Air—*The Washing Day*." In: *The Freeman's Glee Book, A Collection Of Songs, Odes, Glees And Ballads With Music, Original And Selected, Harmonized And Arranged For Each. Published Under The Auspices Of The Central Fremont And Dayton Glee Club Of The City Of New York, And Dedicated To All, Who, Cherishing Republican Liberty Consider Freedom Worth A Song*, page 60. Published by Miller, Orton & Mulligan, No. 25 Park Row, New York, NY. [and Auburn, NY]. 1856. [4⅕⁶" × 6"]. Pk/bk litho of man on mountain peak, music sheets, geometric designs. 112pp. [Crew/JCF-16].

637.2 *Thirty-First Anniversary Of The American Anti-Slavery Society* [Song Sheet]. Published by the Anti-Slavery Printing Office, 21 Spruce Street, 2d floor. 1864. Non-pictorial geometric design border. "At the Church of the Puritans, Tuesday, May 10th, 1864." Four songs: *[O Thou]* {637.2–1}. w. Theodore Tilton. m. *L.M. Rothwell*; *[God Made All His Creatures Free]* {637.2–2}. w. James Montgomery. m. *7s—Nuremburg*; *[Out Of The Dark The Circling Sphere]* {637.2–3}. w. Samuel Longfellow. m. *L.M.—Duke Street*; and *[Thy Kingdom Come!]* {637.2–4}. w. Harriet Martineau. m. *S.M.—Silver Street*. At bottom of the page—"The Americans Anti-Slavery Society will hold another public meeting, at the Cooper Institute, on Wednesday Evening, May 11, at 8 o'clock. Speakers—William Lloyd Garrison, Wendell Phillips, George Thompson. To defray expenses, tickets of admission will be sold at the doors—for 10 cents. The business meetings of the Society will be held in the Lecture Room of the Church of the Puritans, on Tuesday evening at 7½ o'clock, and on Wednesday morning at 10 o'clock." [AMC].

637.3 *Twenty-Fifth Anniversary Manhattan Single Tax Club, Oct. 12, 1912* [Song Sheet]. Published by Manhattan Single Tax Club, 47 W. 42nd Street, New York NY. 1912. Bl/w photos of "Leo Tolstoy, Henry George, Dr. Edward McGlynn, Wm. Lloyd Garrison, Ernest H. Crosby, Wm. T. Croasdale, Tom L. Johnson [and] Thomas G. Sherman." "This association of poverty with progress is the great enigma of our times. It is the riddle which the Sphinx of Fate puts to our civilization, and which not to answer is to be destroyed. *Progress And Poverty*, page 10." 4pp. Page 2: Song—**The Land Song** {637.3.1}. m. "Air, *Marching Through Georgia*." Page 3: Song—**Our Message** {637.3.2}. w. Grace Isabel Colburn. m. "Music of the *Battle Hymn Of The Republic*." Page 4: Narratives on "Our Object" and "Tariffometry."

637.4 *Will You Ever Give The Colored Race A Show?* (An Appeal To Congress). w.m. Robert P. Jackson. Copyright 1898? by Robert P. Jackson, 3143 Dearborn Street, Chicago, IL. B/w photos of Abraham "Lincoln—The Shackles Fell 1863," Charles "Sumner—The Original Champion of the Slaves 1856," William "McKinley—Prosperity 1896." Photo of Robert P. Jackson. Drawing of soldiers marching labeled "The U.S. 25th Inft. Colored Soldiers, the first called on to fight to free Cuba," "white laborers going to work" at a factory labeled "Prosperity & at peace with all nations," "Negroes waiting" behind a "Color Line." 6pp. Page 2: Narrative on "The Negro In The Field Of Labor." Page 6: Blank. [Crew/WM-341]

- **AmPM-637A GERRY**, Elbridge (Colonial House, 1772–1775; Signer, Declaration of Independence, 1776; Continental Congress, 1776–1781 & 1782–1785; U.S. House, 1789–1793; Governor, 1810–1811; Vice President, 1813–1814) [SEE: DOC/PSM-JMD]

637A.1 *American Spirit*. w.m. No composer or tune indicated. In: *The Columbian Songster, Being A Large Collection Of Fashionable Songs, For Gentlemen & Ladies In A Series Of Numbers*, Song IV, page 10. Printed by Nathaniel Heaton, Jur., [Wrentham, MA]. 1799. [3½" × 5¾"]. Hard cover. 196pp. [S/U, p. 79].

637A.2 *The Declaration Of Independence Of The United States Of North America, July 4, 1776*. w. From the Declaration of Independence. m. John E. Wilson. Published by John E. Wilson, Baltimore, MD. 1863. B/w litho of the interior of Independence Hall. "Arranged and adapted for Vocal and Instrumental Music as the Great National Chant." 4pp. [?]. Page 4: Facsimile signatures of all signers.

637A.3 *A New Song* (On Commodore Perry's Victory). w. No composer indicated. m. "Tune—*The Constellation*." In: *The American Naval And Patriotic Songster: As Sung At Various Places Of Amusement, In Honor Of The American Naval And Military Heroes; Together With A Variety Of The Sentimental And Other Songs*, page 47. No publisher indicated. Published in Baltimore, 1841. [3" × 4⅜"]. Non-pictorial leather hand bound. Gold title on spine—*Naval Songs*. 328pp. [Crew/AJK-60].

637A.4 *New Verses To An Old Tune*. w. No composer indicated. m. *Yankee Doodle*. Published in the *Commercial Advertiser*, June 29, 1798. [VBL, p. 141].

637A.5 *Old Independence Hall*. w. A. Fletcher Stayman. m. Francis Weiland. Published by Stayman & Brothers, No. 210 Chesnut Street, Philadelphia, PA. 1855. Non-pictorial. "Respectfully dedicated to the Memory of the Signers of the Declaration of Independence." "Fac Simile of their signatures" including John Adams, Sam Adams, Elbridge Gerry, Thomas Jefferson. 8pp. Pages 2 and 8: Blank. [Crew/MISC-34].

637A.6 The Same Old Coon. w. Robert E.H. Levering. m. "Air — *Long Tail Blue*." Published at Lancaster, OH. September 7, 1842. [18" × 5½"]. Bk/pk litho on silk of a raccoon, geometric design border. "Well, Judge, what do you think of the next Campaign?" "I could at one time calculate political results, but who can tell the influence of the d — n-d 'Whig Songs.'" "Why does a certain criminal put the Democrats on the rack? Because it is a Rack Coon!" 2pp. Page 2: Blank. [Crew/HC-90].

- **AmPM-638** GLYNN, Martin H. (U.S. House, 1899–1901; State Comptroller, 1907–08; Lt. Governor, 1913; Governor, 1913–1915)

638.1 When Massachusetts Heads The Line. w.m. James E. Fitzgerald. Published by James E. Fitzgerald, Boston, MA. 1914. B/w photo of "Governor David. I. Walsh." Bl/w ribbon inscribed Ense Petit Placidam Sub Libertate Quietem." "Massachusetts led in Revolutioney [sic] times: The first man killed in the Civil War was a Massachusetts man: The first man killed at Vera Cruz, Mexico, was a Massachusetts man." "Governor Martin H. Glynn, of New York, addressing the members of the Massachusetts Legislature, in the spring of 1914 said — 'The Country expects Massachusetts to lead the way.'" "Dedicated to His Excellency Governor Davis I. Walsh." 4pp. Page 4: Blank.

- **AmPM-638A** GOETTING, August Henry (Assistant State Quartermaster General, 1890; Assistant State Adjutant General, 1894, 1895 & 1896; Governor's Council, 1909–1913; Candidate for Lt. Governor,1893)

638A.1 Col. Goetting's Grand March. m. Frederick E. White, Op. 12. Published by White, Smith Music Publishing Co., Boston, MA. 1890. B/w photo of Col. Goetting. "Dedicated to Col. A.H. Goetting of the Governor's Staff of Mass." 6pp. Page 6: Advertising.

- **AmPM-639** GOVE, Wesley A. (Candidate for Board of Selectmen, Winthorp, 1908)

639.1 This Dear Little Town Of Ours (Song). w. David Benshimol. m. D.L. White. No publisher indicated. Copyright 1908 by White-Smith Music Publishing Co., Boston, MA. B/w photos of "Wesley A. Gove," "Brendon J. Keenan," and "William Sanby" — "Candidates for the Board of Selectmen for 1908." B/w photo of town waterfront. Bl/w drawing of a sail boat. "Expressly written and dedicated to the Winthrop Town Government Association." "Souvenir of the concert held at Crest Hall, Winthrop, Feb. 19, 1908." 6pp. Pages 2 and 6: Blank.

- **AmPM-640** GREENHALGE Frederick Thomas (Common Council, Lowell, 1868–1869; School Board, Lowell, 1871–1873; Mayor, Lowell, 1880–1881; State House, 1885; U.S. House, 1889–1891; Governor, 1894–1896)

640.1 Governor Greenhalge March. m. A. Mirault. Published by Merwin Music Co, 110 Boylston Street, Boston, MA. 1894. B/w geometric designs. "Respectfully Dedicated to Hon. F.T. Greenhalge." 6pp. Page 2: Blank. Page 6: Advertising.

- **AmPM-641** GUILD, Curtis, Jr. (State House, 1881; Lt. Governor, 1903–1906; Governor, 1906–1909; U.S. Ambassador to Russia, 1911–1913).

641.1 Hearts Of Old New England. (Song). w.m. F. Winthorp Wheeler "(Composer of *I'm Going Back To Boston*)." Published by Lotus Publishing Co., Boston, MA. 1912. Y/w/bl drawing of a soldier and woman embracing, ship at sea. "To the Hon. Curtis Guild, Jr., U.S. Ambassador to Russia and former Governor of Massachusetts, this Song is Respectfully Dedicated." 6pp. Page 2: Blank. Page 6: Advertising.

- **AmPM-642** HANCOCK, John (Selectman, Boston, ca. 1760; Provincial Legislature, 1766–1772; Provincial Congress, 1774; Continental Congress, 1775–1778 & 1785–1786; Signer, Declaration of Independence, 1776; Governor, 1780–1785 & 1787–1793)

642.1 Adam's Fall (The Trip To Cambridge). w. No composer indicated. m. *Yankee Doodle*. [1775–1780]. 2pp. Page 2: Blank. [VBL, p. 60].

642.2 American Liberty (Or the Sovereign Right of Thinking) (A New Song). w. No composer indicated. m. "Tune — *Nancy Dawson*." Published by the *Newark Centinel Of Freedom*, August 14, 1798. [VBL, p. 150].

642.3 Bunker's Hill, A New Song. w. No composer indicated. m. *Yankee Doodle*. [1775]. 2pp. Page 2: Blank. [VBL, p. 57].

642.4 A Campaign Carol. w. No composer indicated. m. "Air — *The Star Spangled Banner*." In: *The Hancock And English Democratic Campaign Song Book*, page 26. Published by W.R. Swane & Company, No. 174 Race Street, Cincinnati, OH. 1880. [4⅛" × 6"]. B/w litho of "Winfield S. Hancock" and "W.H. English," eagle, shield, flags. 34pp. [M-216]. [Crew/WSH-39].

642.5 Castle Island Song. w. No composer indicated. m. No tune indicated. Published as a broadside, March, 1770. "A New song much in vogue among the friends to arbitary[sic] power, and the soldiery at Castle Island, where it was composed, since the troops have evacuated the town of Boston." 2pp. Page 2: Blank. [SBAR, p. 51].

642.6 Castle Island Song. w. No composer indicated. m. *Derry Down*. Lyrics and sound file published online at <http://www.mudcat.org/kids/@displaysong.cfm?SongID=1113>. [199-].

642.7 Choro Grando. w. No composer indicated. m. No composer indicated. In: *The American Musical Miscellany, A Collection Of The Newest And Most Appoved [sic] Songs, Set to Music*, page 123. Printed by Andrew Wright for Daniel Wright & Company, Northampton, MA. 1798. 300pp. [S/U, p. 16].

642.8 The Declaration Of Independence (A Poem: Accompanied By Odes, Songs, &c. Adapted To The Day). w. "By a citizen of Boston [George Richards]." Published at Boston [by Isaiah Thomas and E.T. Andrews] Faust's Statue, No. 45 Newbury Street. 1793. 24pp. "Dedicated to John Hancock." [S/U, p. 104].

642.9 The Declaration Of Independence Of The United States Of North America, July 4, 1776. w. From the Declaration of Independence. m. John E. Wilson. Published by John E. Wilson, Baltimore, MD. 1863. B/w litho of the interior of Independence Hall. "Arranged and adapted for Vocal and Instrumental Music as the Great National Chant." 4pp. [?]. Page 4: Facsimile signatures of all signers.

642.10 Dr. Rogerson's Anthem (Sacred To The Memory Of His Excellency John Hancock, Esq., Late Governor And Commander In Chief Of The Commonwealth Of Massachusetts). "For sale [published] by Isaiah Thomas and E.T. Andrews Faust's Statue, No. 45 Newbury Street, Boston" [MA]. October, 1793. Arranged for "guittar with piano forte accompaniment." [S/U, p. 113].

642.11 Expedition To Rhode Island. w. No composer indicated. m. [*Yankee Doodle*]. Published in Rivington's *Royal Gazette*, New York, NY. October 3, 1778. [SBAR, p. 231].

642.12 Gov. Hancock's March. w. No composer indicated. In. *Bacon's Complete Preceptor For The Clarinet, With A Selection Of Airs, Marches, &c.*, page 20. Published by A. Bacon, Music Seller And Publisher, No. 11 South 4th Street, Philadelphia, PA. [1818?]. 30pp. [W-411].

642.13 Home Of The Free. w. No composer indicated. m. No tune indicated. In: *The Free Soil Minstrel*, page 13. c. George W. Clark. Published by Martyn & Ely, No. 162 Nassau Street, New York, NY. 1848. [4¾" × 7¼"]. Br/br non-pictorial geometric designs on hardback cover. 228pp. [M-079].

642.14 Independence. w. No composer indicated. m. "Parody on an ode published in the *Town And Country Magazine* [1774]." In: *Freeman's Journal or New Hampshire Gazette*, June [?], 1776. [SBAR, p. 139].

642.15 Maryland Resolves. w. No composer indicated. m. "*Abbot Of Canterbury* or *Wilkes' Wriggle*. Published in the *Rivington's Gazette*, 1774. "You, no doubt, have seen the resolves of certain magnates, naming themselves as a Provisional Congress! I will not say these worthies are under the influence of the moon, or are proper subjects for confinement, but one of their resolves is exactly circulated for the meridian of the inquisition, and the other smell furiously of Bedlam. I gladly contribute my humble mite to ridicule the folly, ingratitude, and violence of our deluded patriots." [SBAR, p. 72].

642.16 A New Song. w. "Lately Compos'd on Castle Island." m. *Derry Down*. 'At present said to be in much Vogue among the Caledonians." In: *Boston Gazette*, March 26, 1770. [VBL, p. 39].

642.17 A New Song. w. No composer indicated. m. "To the tune of the *British Grenadier*." No publisher indicated. [177-]. Non-pictorial. 2pp. Page 2: Blank. [AMC].

642.18 Old Independence Hall. w. A. Fletcher Stayman. m. Francis Weiland. Published by Stayman & Brothers, No. 210 Chesnut Street, Philadelphia, PA. 1855. Non-pictorial. "Respectfully dedicated to the Memory of the Signers of the Declaration of Independence." "Fac Simile of their signatures" including John Adams, Sam Adams, Elbridge Gerry, Thomas Jefferson. 8pp. Pages 2 and 8: Blank. [Crew/MISC-34].

642.19 Our Standard Bearer. w. No composer indicated. m. "Air—*America*." In: *The National Democratic Campaign Songster*, page 8. Printed by The Courier Printing Company, Syracuse, NY. Copyright 1880 by G.N. Harding. [3¾" × 5⅝"]. B/w litho of Winfield S. Hancock and William H. English, eagle, flag. Winfield S. Hancock quote. "1880 Hancock & English." 52pp. [M-218]. [Crew/WSH-2].

642.20 A Song (Composed By The British Soldiers, After The Fight At Bunker Hill, June 17, 1775). w.m. No composers or tune indicated. No publisher indicated. [1775]. B/w woodblock print of soldiers in camp. 2pp. Page 2: Blank. [AMC].

642.21 A Song. w. No composer indicated. m. No tune indicated. Published in the *Connecticut Gazette*. 1776. [SBAR, p 118].

642.22 A Song About Charleston. w. "Written by a soldier of the Royal Army." m. Tune — "*Watery God*." Published as a broadside. 1780. [SBAR, p. 293].

642.23 Sonnet For The Fourteenth of October, 1793. w. Hans Gram, "Organist of Brattle Street Church in Boston." m. Graun. No publisher indicated. [1793]. "When were entombed the Remains of his Excellency John Hancock, Esq., late Governor and Commander in Chief of the Commonwealth of Massachusetts. The music taken from an oratorio by the famous Graun, of Berlin." 4pp. [S/U, p. 405].

642.24 Trip To Cambridge. w. No composer indicated. m. "*Yankee Doodle*." No publisher indicated. [1775]. [SBAR, p. 99].

642.25 The Trumpet Of Freedom. m. No composer indicated. m. No tune indicated. In: *The Liberty Minstrel*, page 157. e. George W. Clark. Published by George W. Clark, New York, NY. 1844. [4⅜" × 6¾"]. Non-pictorial songbook with gold leaf title. "And Sold by Wm. Harned, 22 Spruce St., New York and Baltimore and Marsh, Boston, Mass." 230pp. [Crew/JBR-1].

642.26 Washington (A Favorite New Song in the American Camp). w. [Jonathan Mitchell Sewell]. m. Air — *British Grenadier*. "Printed and sold next to the Bell-Tavern, in Danvers," [MA]. [1776]. [4⅜" × 10⅝"]. B/w woodblock of George Washington and General Artemas Ward. "Cash paid for rags." 2pp. Page 2: Blank. [VBL, p. 63]. [Crew/GW-23].

642.27 Yankee Doodle's Expedition To Rhode Island. w. "Written at Philadelphia." m. *Yankee Doodle*. In: Rivington's *Royal Gazette*,[N.Y.], October 3, 1778. [VBL, p. 79].

642.28 Yankee Song. w. No composer indicated. m. *Yankee Doodle*. Published in the *Massachusetts Centinel*, March 5, 1788. [VBL, p. 106].

• **AmPM-643** HANLEY, Dr. James F. (Candidate for State Senate, 1915)

643.1 Our Candidate March (March For Piano). m. Lawrence B. O'Connor. Published by Premier Music Co., Boston, MA. [1915]. B/w photo of James F. Hanley. R/w geometric designs. "For the best interests of the people." "Dedicated to James F. (Dr.) Hanley." "For Senator — Wards 18–19–22." 6pp. Pages 2 and 6: Blank.

• **AmPM-644** HART, Thomas Norton (Mayor, Boston, 1889–1890 & 1900–1902)

644.1 Hart's Reform Administration. w. Edward Fitzwilliam. m. "Air, *Yankee Doodle*." In: *20th Century Municipal Campaign Songs & Poems*, page 8. No publisher indicated. Copyright 1901 by Edward Fitzwilliam. [6" × 9"]. Br/bk geometric design border. "Unlike what in secret mysteriously delves, These poems need no preface, the speak for themselves." 12pp.

• **AmPM-645** HENSHAW, David (State Senate, 1826; State House, 1839; U.S. Secretary of the Navy, 1843–1844)

645.1 Go And No Go (Or Dan's Scowl At Ty's Serving Men). w. "By the Author of Van's Mews [John H. Warland]." m. "Tune—*Dame Durden.*" Long narrative titled "Argument" followed by "Dramatis Person_. Wise, Ty's vanguard. Cabe [Caleb] another in the guard, who doesn't stop running till he reaches China. Poffe, [Proffit] the rear-guard, who runs to South America and back. Wick, P.M.G. David the Henshaw Fowl, Ex-Secretary of the Navy, and k-navy ex-manager of the Commonwealth Bank, Spence, [Spencer] the evil-genius of the administration. Ike, [Isaac Hill] the blank wrapping-paper-and-twine contractor for all the old Tories and all the new territories, etc. Porte, [Porter] Ex-Secretary of War. Seth, the hissing gentleman, one of David's pets and appointees. Bobby the Ranting Owl, a well known custom-house rat and legislative Ranter also a pet of David." In: *The National Clay Melodist (A Collection Of Popular And Patriotic Songs, Second Edition, Enlarged And Improved)*, page 76. Published by Benj. Adams, No. 54 Court Street, Boston, MA. 1844. [3" × 5¼"]. Inside title page: B/w litho of Henry Clay's home—"O'er Ashland's lawns the skies are bright, From West to East The radiance streams and glows, The land beneath its beams gay beats the heart with joy, Hurrah! Hurrah! Hip! Hurrah!" 108pp. [M-050?]. [Crew/HC-13].

645.2 The Treasury Chest. w. No composer indicated. m. "Tune—*The Mistletoe Bough.*" In: *The Clay Minstrel Or National Songster*, page 302. c. John Stockton Littell. Published by Greeley & M'Elrath, Tribune Building, New York, NY. 1844. [3⅛" × 4⅞"]. Nonpictorial. 396pp. [Crew/HC-18].

645.3 Yankee Doodle — New Version. w. No composer indicated. m. Tune—*Yankee Doodle.* In: *Log Cabin Minstrel (Or Tippecanoe Songster)*, page 50. c. "A Member of the Roxbury Whig Association." Published at the *Patriot And Democrat* Office, Roxbury, [MA]. 1840. [4½" × 6¾"]. [V-1:Y/bk] [V-2: Bl/bk] litho of William Henry Harrison, geometric design border. "Old Tip's the boy to swing the flail. Hurrah! Hurrah! Hurrah!" 64pp. Page 3: Title page—"Containing a Selection of Songs Original and Selected Many of them Written Expressly for this Work, Compiled, Published and Arranged by a member of the Roxbury Democratic Whig Association and Respectfully Dedicated to the Log Cabin Boys of the U.S." [M-013]. [Crew/WHH-71].

• **AmPM-646 HERTER**, Christian Archibald (State House, 1931–1943; U.S. House, 1943–1953; Governor, 1953–1957)

646.1 Our Governor's March. w. Ruth L. Seanor. m. Hon. Vincent Mottola. Published by The Music of Tomorrow Publishing Co., 715 Old South Building, Boston, MA. 1954. Bl/w photo of "Governor Christian Herter." 6pp. Page 2: Blank. Page 6: Advertising.

646.2 Our Mayflower (The Thanksgiving Song). w.m. Marie Rich Rockwood. Published by Mayflower Music, Stockbridge, MA. 1953. Pl/w drawing of the ship Mayflower. "Dedicated to The Society of Mayflower Descendants." 8pp. Page 2: Facsimile letter from the Mayflower Society in Connecticut. Page 3: At bottom of music—Marie Rich Rockwood [facsimile signature]—Descendant of Governor William Bradford who came on The Mayflower in 1620." Page 7: Facsimile letter from Governor Christian Herter of Massachusetts to Mrs. Rockwood. Page 8: Publisher address.

• **AmPM-646A HESS-MAHAN**, Ted (Candidate for Alderman, West Newton, 2003).

646A.1 Ted Hess-Mahan For Alderman Campaign Theme Song. w. Bridget Hess-Mahan, "Also known as the artist formerly known as Bridget." m. "To the tune of *SpongeBob Squarepants Theme Song.*" Lyrics published online at <http://www.tedhess-mahan.com/theme_song.htm>. 2003.

HOLMES, John (Massachusetts General Court, 1802, 1803, & 1812; State Senate, Massachusetts, 1813 & 1814; U.S. House, Massachusetts, 1817–1820) [See: Maine]

• **AmPM-647 HUTCHINSON**, Thomas (Selectman, Boston, 1737; Provincial Legislature, 1737-?; Speaker, State house, 1746; Probate Court Judge, Suffolk County, 1752; Chief Justice of the Superior Court of Judicature, 1760; Lt. Governor; Royal Governor, Massachusetts, 1771–1774)

647.1 Taxation Of America. w. Peter St. John. m. No tune indicated. No publisher indicated. [177–]. [SABR, p. 1].

• **AmPM-648 KEENAN**, Brendon J. (Candidate for Board of Selectmen, Winthorp, 1908)

648.1 This Dear Little Town Of Ours (Song). w. David Benshimol. m. D.L. White. No publisher indicated. Copyright 1908 by White-Smith Music Publishing Co., Boston, MA. B/w photos of "Wesley A. Gove," "Brendon J. Keenan," and "William Sanby"—"Candidates for the Board of Selectmen for 1908." B/w photo of town waterfront. Bl/w drawing of a sail boat. "Expressly written and dedicated to the Winthrop Town Government Association." "Souvenir of the concert held at Crest Hall, Winthrop, Feb. 19, 1908." 6pp. Pages 2 and 6: Blank.

• **AmPM-649 KENNEDY**, Edward Moore (Assistant District Attorney, Suffolk County, 1961; U.S. Senate, 1962–Present)

649.1 Bill Clinton Got Run Over By A Taxi. w. Billy Florio. m. "*Grandma Got Run Over By A Reindeer*, originally by Elmo & Patsy." Published online at <http://amiright.com/parody/80s/elmoandpatsy0.shml>. [ca. 2001].

649.2 Boyz On The Hill. w. "Antic the Fearless." m. Tune—"*Boyz In The Hood* originally by Dynamite Hack." Published online at <http://www.amiright.com/parody/2000s/dynamitehack0.shtml>. 2003

649.3 Chappaquidick. w. Kev O'Keefe. m. Tune—"*The River* originally by Bruce Springsteen." "This is my first attempt at parody." Published online at <http://www.amiright.com/parody/80s/brucespringsteen4/shtml>. 2003

649.4 Convention '72. w.m. N. Canel and N. Kousaloos. 45 rpm record. Mainstream Records, MRL 5525/ZT8P 224228. Performed by The Delegates. 1972.

649.5 Chubby Ted. w. David Chrenko. m. "*Happy Jack,* based on a performance by The Who." "This is simply a modern fairy tale. Any resemblance to a U.S.

Senator, living or dead, is purely coincidental." Published online at <http://www.amiright.com/parody/60s/thewho35.shtml>. 2003.

649.6 I Killed A Girl. w. Mad Hoopster. m. *I Kissed A Girl* originally by Jill Sobule." Published online at <http://www.amiright.com/parody/90s/jillsobule0.shtml>. [ca. 2002].

649.7 Kennedy The Letch. w. No composer indicated. m. "Parody of *Henry The VIII, I Am* by Herman's Hermits." Lyrics published by *The Bob Rivers Show* with Bob, Spike & Joe and Twisted Tunes online at <http://www.twistedradio.com/player/lyrics.asp?songID=686>. [199-].

649.7A Kennedy The Blank. w. A Room Full of Monkeys. m. "*Henry The Eighth*, based on a performance by Herman's Hermits." Published online at <http://www.amiright.com/parody/60s/hermanshermits52.shtml>. 2004.

649.8 Kerry's A Dork. w. Malcolm Higgins. m. Tune — "*Cherry Hill Park*, based on the performance by Billy Joe Royal. Published online at <http://www.amiright.com/parody/misc/billyjoeroyal0.shtml>. [ca. 2003].

649.9 Mary Jo, Mary Jo. 45 rpm vinyl record. New England Novelty Recording, 1143 Chamberlain Highway, Kensington, Conn. Record No. # 92–71. Performed by The Whisper." [186-].

649.10 New Hampshire Primary Marching Cadence. w. Guy DiRito. m. "*Military Cadence (Sound Off)*, based on a performance by Traditional." "This song is done to the traditional military cadence beat. Practice marching as you sound off to this." Published online at <http://www.amiright.com/parody/misc/traditional430.shtml>. 2004.

649.11 [Oh, My Darling Mary Jo]. w. John Biggert. m. Tune — *Oh, My Darling Clementine*. Published by John Biggert, No. 1875 DuPont Avenue, Memphis, TN. 38127. [ca. 196-]. [2¼" × 3⅞"]. Obv: B/w photo of "Teddy Kennedy" — "Wanted For Murder or President?" Rev: Song. "*Oh, My Darling Clementine* was never like this." Prices for bulk purchase of cards. [Crew/MISC-175].

649.12 Old Ted. w. Paul Shaklin. On CD: *This Land Was Your Land*. Published by Narodniki Records. CD Cover: N/c drawing of Bill Clinton in a Superman-like suit with money and dollar sign. See: <www.paulShaklin.com>. 2001.

649.13 People Who Tried (Political). w. Malcolm Higgins. m. Tune — "*People Who Died*, based on a performance by Jim Carroll." Published online at <http://www.amiright.com/parody/misc/jimcarroll0.shtml>. [ca. 2003].

649.14 Spinball Wizard. w. Paul Silhan. m. "Sung to *Pinball Wizard* by The Who." On: Cassette: *Spinball Wizard*. "As heard on Rush's Radio Show." Lyrics published at <http://www.paulsilhan.com/spinball.htm>. 1997.

649.15 Ted Kennedy Song. w. No composer indicated. m. *Irish Washerwoman*. "A reasonable candidate for a Songs-In-The-Worst-Taste-Workshop. From Michael Cooney's singing." Lyrics and sound file published online at <http://www.mudcat.org/kids/@displaysong.cfm?SongID=5703>. [199-].

649.16 [Teddy The Red Nosed Senator]. w. No composer indicated. m. "Sung to the tune of *Rudolph, The Red Nosed Reindeer*." "Here's one from the Bob Rivers and Twisted Radio Album, *I Am Santa Claus* that we are spinning at our college station, WTTU..." Published online at <http://catweasel.org/Site1/Digests.H9312140.php>. 1993. Also at <http://forwardgarden.com/forward/1382.html>.

649.16A They Shall Not Pass. w. Keith H. Peterson. m. "*The Marines' Hymn*." Published online at <http://mysite.verizon.net/vzelq1d3/id11.html>. [ca. 1972].

649.17 Vive La Dynasty. w. Milton M. Schwartz. m. "Tune — *Vive L' Amour Ago*." In: *Sing Along With Jack* [Song Book], page 6. Published by Pocket Books, Inc., New York, NY. Copyright 1963 by Bonny Publishing Corporation. [9" × 11⅞"]. R/w/bk drawing of sheet music *Vive La Dynasty*, silhouette of John F. Kennedy in chair with conductor's baton, caricature of Kennedy family. "Hit Songs from the New Frontier." 36pp. Page 3: "Illustrations by David Gantz." Page 36: Drawing of John F. Kennedy in chair with baton. Song titles. [Crew/JFK-17].

649.18 You Don't Mess With Jesse And Win. w. Paul Silhan. m. "Sung to *You Don't Mess Around With Jim* by Jim Croce." On: Cassette: *Spinball Wizard*. "As heard on Rush's Radio Show." Lyrics published at <http://www.paulsilhan.com/jesse.htm>. 1997.

• **AmPM-649x KENNEDY**, John Fitzgerald (U.S. House, 1947–1953; U.S. Senate, 1953–1960, President, 1961–1963) [SEE: DOC/PSM-JFK]

• **AmPM-650 KERRY**, John Forbes (District Attorney, Middlesex County, 1977–1982; Lt. Governor, 1982–1984; U.S. Senate, 1985–Present; Candidate for President, 2004)

650.1 All You Democrats. w. Adam Bernstein. m. "*Mr. Tambourine Man*, based on a performance by Bob Dylan." Published online at <http://www.amiright.com/parody/60s/bobdylan17.shtml>. [ca. 2003].

650.2 Andrew J. And John Kerry. w. Royce Miller. m. "*Ebony And Ivory*, based on a performance by Paul McCartney/Stevie Wonder." "This came about from watching 'Fox and Friends' 2½-and seeing Mancow hold up a $20 bill and say 'doesn't he look like John Kerry.'" Published online at <http://www.amiright.com/parody/80s/paulmccartneysteviewonder0.shtml>. 2004.

650.3 Another John Kerry Done Somebody Wrong Song. w. Michael McVey. m. "*Somebody Done Somebody Wrong Song*, based on a performance by B.J. Thomas." Published online at <http://www.amiright.com/parody/70s/bjthomas11.shtml>. [2004].

650.4 Antagonist Congress. w. ParodyKeet. m. "*American Woman*, based on a performance by Guess Who." "I may have set this tune to words before but I'm on a political roll in the name of dumping our present Kaiser." Published online at <http://amiright.com/parody/70s/guesswho5.shtml>. 2003.

650.5 The Ballad Of The War Protestors. w. Michael Pacholek. m. "*The Ballad Of John And Yoko* originally by The Beatles." "'Finks' is the plural of 'fink,' not somebody's name. 'The wife,' like the President, and his reasons for going to war, is fictional — in each case, unfortunately. And if I keep writing this stuff, well, all three Dixie Chicks are married, so I guess I'm stuck. For Now." Published online at <http://www.amiright.com/parody/60s/thebeatles102.shtml>. [ca. 2003].

650.6 The Ballad Of Wesley Clark. w. Mac195. m. "*The Ballad Of Davy Crockett,* based on a performance by The Kentucky Headhunters." Published online at <http://amiright.com/parody/misc/thekentuckyheadhunters0.shtml>. [2004].

650.7 Bonesmen, Kerry And Shrubbie. w. Coral Snake. m. "*The Living Daylights,* based on a performance by James Bond Movie Theme." "Midi available at: <http://midis.jamesbond-online.com>." Published online at <http://amiright.com/parody/90s/jamesbondmovietheme0.shtml>. [ca. 2004].

650.8 Born To Run (John and Theresa Kerry Version). w. Mac195. m. Tune—"*Born To Run,* based on a performance by Bruce Springsteen." Published online at <http://amiright.com/parody/70s/brucespringsteen6.shtml>. [2004].

650.9 Bush And Kerry. w. Lionel Mertens. m. "*Jack and Diane,* based on the performance by John Cougar Melencamp." Published online at <http://www.amiright.com/parody/80s/johncougarmelencamp0.shtml>. 2004

650.10 Conner Gets Killed And Kerry Don't Care. w. Michael McVey. m. "*Jimmy Crack Corn And I Don't Care,* based on a performance by Traditional." "I try to be fair to both sides of the political divide and loyal to neither, but the murder of Laci and Conner Peterson, and the way liberal politicians including John Kerry blatantly put politics over people, compassion and justice in the aftermath, was so far over the line I have no choice but to take the gloves off..." Published online at <http://www.amiright.com/parody/misc/traditional453.shtml>. 2004.

650.11 Dashing Through The States. w. John Jenkins. m. Tune —"*Jingle Bells,* based on the performance by Traditional." "The Democratic field of presidential candidates has been reduced from 10 to 7 with more candidates expected to withdraw this week. Will the selection process eventually narrow down to two candidates in a replay of the Super Bowl with the upstart from Carolina going against the veteran from Massachusetts?" Published online at <http://www.amiright.com/parody/misc/traditional437.shtml>. 2004.

650.12 Dean On Me. w. "Guy DiRito". m. Tune—"*Lean On Me,* based on a performance by Bill Withers." "See? I can make fun of liberals, too! But is that what I'm really doing here? Howard's freak-out shows what we Democrats knew all along: This guy is much further to the right than most people realize!" Published online at <http://www.amiright.com/parody/70s/billwithers7.shtml>. 2004.

650.13 Democrat Plans. w. Royce Miller. m. "*Truck Dirvin' Man,* based on a performance by Rick Nelson." Published online at <http://www.amiright.com/parody/60s/ricknelson1.shtml>. [ca. 2003].

650.14 The Democratic Presidential Candidate Show. w. Laurence Dunne. m. "*The Muppet Show* by The Muppets." "I'm not a Republican by and certainly I'm not a Dubya fan, as my Bush parodies will attest <http://www.amiright.com/parody/60s/thebradybunchtvshow0.shtml>." Published online at <http://amiright.com/parody/70s/muppets0.shtml>. [ca. 2003].

650.15 Democratic Schemin.' w. Billy Slim. m. "*California Dreamin,'* based on a performance by The Mamas and the Papas." "This is another John Kerry bash parody. I love writing these!=D." Published online at <http://www.amiright.com/parody/60s/themamasandthepapas10.shtml>. 2004.

650.16 The Democrats, Man. w. ColdRedRain. m. "*Candy Man Can,* based on a performance by Nikka Costa." Published online at <http://www.amiright.com/parody/misc/nikkacosta0.shtml>. 2004.

650.17 Don't Let Me Get Me—John Kerry. w. DDT_keepsmehappy. m. "*Don't Let Me Get Me,* based on a performance by Pink." Published online at <http://www.amiright.com/parody/2000s/pink48.shtml>. 2004.

650.18 Dummy Knows Nothing (He Needs Dick Cheyney [sic]. w. Bush League. m. "*Money For Nothing (And The Chicks For Free),* based on a performance by Dire Straits." "An experiment trying to use as much of the original song's rhymes, etc. as possible... Believe me, if Kerry actually had a heartbeat, I'd find material to use against him too." Published online at <http://www.amiright.com/parody/80s/direstraights30.shtml>. 2004.

650.19 Edwards, Dean And Kerry. w. Mac195. m. "*Lawyers, Guns And Money,* based on a performance by Warren Zevon." Published online at <http://www.amiright.com/parody/70s/warrenzevon10.shtml>. [ca. 2003].

650.20 Election City. w. Michael Pacholek. m. "*Atlantic City,* based on a performance by Bruce Springsteen." "For the record, it was Pierre Ambroise Francois Choderios de LaClos (1741–1803), author of *Dangerous Liaisons,* who said, Revenge is a dish best served cold.' Not an old Klingon proverb, as Gene Roddenberry (or Quinton Tarantino) would have us believe. And while governing should not be, politics is often all about revenge. Burr..." Published online at <http://www.amiright.com/parody/80s/brucespringsteen22.shtml>. [ca. 2003].

650.21 Eye Of The Tiger (Howard Dean Version). w. Mac195. m. Tune—"*Eye Of The Tiger,* based on a performance by Survivor." Published online at <http://amiright.com/parody/80s/survivor11.shtml>. [2004].

650.22 Fell Off Their Bikes (Bush, Kerry). w. Phil Nelson. m. "*Come Sail Away,* based on a performance by Styx." "About both of their recent accidents." Published online at <http://www.amiright.com/parody/70s/styx20.shtml>. 2004.

650.23 50 States Dean Will Freak Out In. w. Adam Bernstein. m. "*50 Ways To Leave Your Lover,* based on a performance by Paul Simon." "Great link to Dean Freak Out MP3 below." Published online at <http://amiright.com/parody/70s/paulsimon38.shtml>. [ca. 2004].

650.23A The Flop. w. Ralph Paterno. m. "Parody of the 1950s song *At The Hop.*" "It playfully and accurately details President Bush flip flips." Published online by Politicalsong.net at <http://www.politicalsong.net>. 2004.

650.24 Green Party Man. w. Charlie Decker. m. "*Street Fighting Man,* based on a performance by Rolling Stones." "Although I am a Democrat politically, I sympathize with the Green Party, even if only to keep Dems honest." Published online at <http://www.amiright.com/parody/60s/rollingstones34.shtml>. [ca. 2003].

650.25 Head Just Like A Rock. w. Michael Pacholek. m. "*Loves Me Like A Rock* originally by Paul Simon." "Yeah, I know, Kerry's still gotta get through the primaries against those heavyweights Howard Dean, John Edwards, and Joe Lie-berman. If Lieberman is a Democrat, then I'm the center fielder for the Yankees. But Kerry vs. Bush? That debate will make Bartlet vs. Richie (On *The West Wing*) look like Ali v. Frazier!" Published online at <http://www.amiright.com/parody/70s/paulsimon15.shtml>. 2003

650.26 Howard Dean. w. Arcade Junkie. m. "*Let It Be,* based on a performance by The Beatles." "It's a good thing Howard Dean is out of the race. No shouting involved!" Published online at <http://www.amiright.com/parody/70s/thebeatles24.shtml>. [2004].

650.27 Howard Dean. w. Chris Bodily TM. m. "*Killer Queen,* based on a performance by Queen." "A sad ode to Howard Dean ailing at the polls... If I can't vote for him, I'll vote for ALF for President." Published online at <http://www.amiright.com/parody/70s/queen163.shtml>. [2004].

650.28 I'm A Little Bit Insane. w. "Guy DiRito." m. "*If I Only Had A Brain,* based on a performance by Wizard of Oz." "Our boy has calmed down quite a bit after Iowa now that the meds have kicked back in." Published online at <http://amiright.com/parody/misc/wizardofoz2.shtml. 2004.

650.29 In-No-vem-ber-You-Will-Be-Mine / Kerry. w. Jaw W. m. "*867–5309/Jenny,* based on the performance by Tommy Tutone." "I can't wait until these two debate: Linguistic master vs. Texas hold'em poker allusions." Published online at <http://www.amiright.com/parody/80s/tommytutone4.shtml>. 2004.

650.30 J.F. Kerryville. w. Kelly S. Solid. m. "*Margaritaville,* based on a performance by Jimmy Buffet." Published online at <http://amiright.com/parody/70s/jimmybuffet14.shtml>. [2004].

650.31 John Kerry. w. Michael Florio. m. "*Yesterday,* based on a performance by Beatles." "Anyone realize how Kerry didn't start to actually try to win until he was named the democratic presidential nominee? That and, he's really scary ... heres his song [sic]." Published online at <http://www.amiright.com/parody/60s/beatles184.shtml>. [2004].

650.32 John Kerry. w. BigG. m. "*Prince Charming,* based on a performance by Metallica." Published online at <http://www.amiright.com/parody/90s/metallica29.shtml>. 2004.

650.33 John Kerry. w. Phil Nelson. m. "*Zombie,* based on a performance by The Cranberries." "Ever notice how much John Kerry looks like a zombie?" Published online at <http://www.amiright.com/parody/90s/thecranberries6.shtml>. 2004.

650.34 John Kerry Is Evil. w. Billy Slim. m. "*I Think I'm Paranoid,* based on a performance by Garbage." "Now, this is the first parody I had ever written where I'm being mean. And I love it! B-) John Kerry will be the worst choice for President and I'm opposed to him. It's the damn truth! He'll ruin this country, more that it already is. God, I'm such a hippy at heart." Published online at <http://www.amiright.com/parody/90s/garbage6.shtml>. 2004.

650.35 Kerry. w. Johnny D. m. "*Sherry,* based on a performance by Frankie Valli and the Four Seasons. "I'm not saying I'll vote for Kerry or Bush or Nader or Lyndon LaRouche... It's just that politicians are always fair game on Amiright ... heh heh heh..." Published online at <http://www.amiright.com/parody/60s/frankievalliandthefourseasons2.shtml>. [2004].

650.36 Kerry. w. Dave Rackmales. m. "Sung to the tune of *Carey* by Joni Mitchell." "Spread The Word Through Song and Music! Songs For Dean, Songs to get elected by." N/c photo of Howard Dean. Lyrics published online at <http://songsfordean.com/so/lyrics/somethingtosee.php>. 2004.

650.37 Kerry Fans. w. Victor Fernando Magana. m. "*Carrie Anne,* based on the performance by The Hollies. "A tribute to the new Democratic front-runner for 2004 (as of January 26)." Published online at <http://www.amiright.com/parody/60s/thehollies8.shtml>. 2004.

650.38 Kerry, Kerry (A Progressive's Lament). w. Ravyn Rant. m. "*Momma Mia,* based on a performance by Abba." "I started this right after Super Tuesday, when the Democratic candidate was announced months before the convention." Published online at <http://www.amiright.com/parody/70s/abba61.shtml>. [2004].

650.39 Kerry Man! w. John A. Barry. m. "*Carrie Anne* originally by The Hollies." Published online at <http://www.amiright.com/parody/60s/hollies1.shtml>.

650.40 Kerry Man. w. Guy DiRito. m. "*Carrie Anne,* originally by The Hollies." Published online at <http://www.amiright.com/parody/60s/thehollies4.shtml>.

650.41 The Kerry Pokey. w. Royce Miller. m. "*The Hokey Pokey,* based on a performance by Ram Trio. "This was written for the ski crowd, a long time ago, something about slippery slopes made me think of Kerry." Published online at <http://www.amiright.com/parody/misc/ramtrio0.shtml>. [2004].

650.42 Kerry, That's Great. w. Malcolm Higgins. m. "*Carry That Weight,* based on a performance by The Beatles." Published online at <http://www.amiright.com/parody/60s/thebeatles631.shtml>. [2004].

650.43 Kerry's A Dork. w. Malcolm Higgins. m. "*Cherry Hill Park,* based on the performance by Billy Joe Royal. Published online at <http://www.amiright.com/parody/misc/billyjoeroyal0.shtml>. [ca. 2003].

650.44 Kerry's On A Wayward Run. w. Malcolm Higgins. m. "*Carry On Wayward Son,* based on a performance by Kansas." "To the 'war hero' kerry ... yeah right." Published online at <http://www.amiright.com/parody/70s/kansas27.shtml>. [2004].

650.45 Let's Send John K. To The Moon. w. Guy DiRito. m. "*Everyone's Gone To The Moon,* based on a performance by Jonathan King. Published online at <http://www.amiright.com/parody/60s/jonathanking1.shtml>. [2004].

650.46 Lieberman Bites The Dust. w. Steve Kalafut. m. "*Another One Bites The Dust,* based on the performance by Queen." "Joe Lieberman withdraws from the campaign to win his party's presidential nomination." Published online at <http://www.amiright.com/parody/80s/queen47.shtml>. 2004.

650.47 L-T Kerry Purple Heart Grab Man. w. Guy DiRito. m. "*SGT Pepper's Lonely Hearts Club Band*, based on the performance by The Beatles." "John Kerry blasted George Bush a few months ago concerning his Air National Guard service record. Now it seems it's Kerry's turn in the barrel..." Published online at <http://www.Amiright.com/parody/60s/thebeatles656.shtml>. 2004.

650.47A Marryin' Libertarians. w. John A. Barry. "*Marian The Librarian* (From *The Music Man*), base4d on the performance by Robert Preston." "From The Bu'shit Man my unfinished parody of *The Music Man*. This is an extended take on the original, combined with the part of *Gary, Indiana*." Published online at <http://amiright.com/parody/misc/robertpreston0/shtml>. 2004.

650.48 New Hampshire Primary Marching Cadence. w. Guy DiRito. m. "*Military Cadence (Sound Off)*, based on a performance by Traditional." "This song is done to the traditional military cadence beat. Practice marching as you sound off to this." Published online at <http://www.amiright.com/parody/misc/traditional430.shtml>. 2004.

650.49 No JFK. w. Michael Pacholek. m. "*YMCA*, based on a performance by The Village People." "After three years of watching George W. Bush's stupidities and sanctimony, I'm beginning to think America owes Dan Quayle an apology. Because, after 40 years, everyone [is] 'no Jack Kennedy.' The closest we've come to JFK is Bill Clinton. Except the press was nicer to JFK. Then, the reporters really were liberal, even if the editorial pages weren't." Published online at <http://www.amiright.com/parody/70s/thevillagepeople16.shtml>. 2003.

650.49A Oh, Teresa. w. John A. Barry. m. "*Mona Lisa*, based on the performance by Nat King Cole." Published online at <http://www.amiright.com/parody/misc/natkingcole27.shtml>. 2004.

650.50 Pal Wesley Clark. w. Michael Pacholek. m. "*Palisades Park*, based on the performance by Freddy Cannon." "I should have written this weeks ago. The flavor of the month has melted. Not that this was an endorsement anyway." "And now Clark's fade is well underway. Maybe Kerry will appoint him Secretary of Defense, After all, Clark shouldn't have trouble getting his fellow Republicans to confirm him in the Senate." Published online at <http://www.amiright.com/parody/60s/freddycannon0.shtml>. 2003.

650.50A Political Spin. w. Ralph Paterno. m. "No tune indicated. "Political Songs for trying times." Published online by Politicalsong.net at <http://www.politicalsong.net/political_spin>. 2004.

650.51 Return Of Nader. w. Phil Nelson. m. "*Eye Of The Tiger*, based on a performance by Survivor." "Ralph Nader's Running Again." Published online at <http://www.amiright.com/parody/80s/survivor.shtml>. 2004.

650.52 Richard Clarke, Shut Up. w. William Tong. m. "*Start Me Up*, based on a performance by The Rolling Stones. "Dubya and his administration unravels as they are unable to refute the testimony of former security official Richard Clarke, who blasts the Bushies for being obsessed with Iraq, while being negligent and unprepared against terrorism, leading to the September 11 attacks. As sung by a desperate Dubya Bush, about to lose his 'wartime president' credentials." Published online at <http://www.amiright.com/parody/80s/therollingstones2.shtml>. [2004].

650.53 Scary Kerry? w. Charlie Decker. m. "*Maybe Katie*, based on a performance by Barenaked Ladies." "Is Kerry really all that scary? Well, now that he's got the Democratic nomination locked up, if you're a Democrat: Get over it!" Published online at <http://www.amiright.com/parody/2000s/barenakedladies18.shtml>. 2004.

650.54 Simply Indefensible. w. Michael Pacholek. m. "*Simply Irresistible*, based on a performance by Robert Palmer." "Robert Palmer didn't live to see the end of the Bush Maladministration. I'm sorry to hear that." Published online at <http://amiright.com/parody/80s/robertpalmer14.shtml>. [2004].

650.55 The Smarms Of Kerry. w. Malcolm Higgins. m. "*The Arms Of Mary*, based on a performance by Chilliwack." Published online at <http://www.amiright.com/parody/70s/chilliwack0.shtml>. [2004].

650.56 Some Wail Away. w. Malcolm Higgins. m. "*Come Sail Away*, based on a performance by Styx." "Written of yourse [sic] by the ultimate lefty ... me." Published online at <http://www.amiright.com/parody/misc/styx0.shtml>. [ca. 2003].

650.57 Springtime For Lefties & John Kerry. w. Tim K. m. "*Springtime For Hitler*, based on a performance by Mel Brooks." "I'm feeling political today. Democrats, don't take this personally. Life would be boring without some opposition." Published online at <http://www.amiright.com/parody/90s/melbrooks0.shtml>. 2004.

650.58 (Theme From) Bush Kerry. w. Kimba T. Dogg. m. "*(Theme From) Green Acres*, based on a performance by Vic Mizzy." Published online at <http://www.amiright.com/parody/60s/vicmizzy1.shtml>. [2004].

650.59 They're Coming To Take Dean Away, Ha-Ha! w. Michael Pacholek. m. Tune —"*They're Coming To Take Me Away,. Ha-Ha!*, based on the performance by Napoleon XIV." Published online at <http://www.amiright.com/parody/60s/napoleonxiv2.shtml>. 2004.

650.60 30 Months Of Proof He's Bananas. w. Michael Pacholek. m. "*30,000 Pounds Of Bananas*, based on a performance by Harry Chapin." "It's actually been 32 months since the Great Pretender took office..." Published by Amiright.com at <http://www.amiright.com/parody/70s/harrychapin10.shtml>. [ca. 2003].

650.61 33.3% Sure (I Won't Lose It In '04). w. Mike Armstrong. m. "*99.9% Sure* (I've Never Been Here Before) originally by Brian McComas." "Yea, so, this is a really cool country song — idea just kind of hit me while I was listening to it, hopefully you like it. With questions surrounding the '04 election, the fact that the presidency is up in the air is what I'm trying to convey." Published online at <http://www.amiright.com/parody/2000s/brianmccomas0.shtml>. [ca. 2003].

650.61A This Land (Will Surely Vote For Me). w. Greg & Evan Speridellis. m. Woody Guthrie and Adrienne Speridellis. "Parody on Woody Guthrie's This Land." Published at <www.JibJab.com>. Atom Films starring George Bush and John Kerry."

650.62 To Kerry With Love. w. Michael McVey. m. "*To Sir With Love,* based on a performance by Lulu. Published online at <http://www.amiright.com/parody/60s/lulu3.shtml>. [2004].

650.63 Total Eclipse Of Gephardt. w. John Jenkins. m. "*Total Eclipse Of The Heart,* based on a performance by Bonnie Tyler." "Dick Gephardt's presidential campaign came to a sudden conclusion after his distant fourth place finish in the Iowa caucuses, which was especially disappointing since he won Iowa in his 1988 campaign." Published online at <http://amiright.com/parody/80s/bonnietyler12.shtml>. [2004].

650.64 Versus Kerry. w. Floyd's Garage. m. "*Voices Carry,* based on a performance by 'Til Tuesday." Published online at <http://www.amiright.com/parody/80s/tiltuesday1.shtml>. [2004].

650.65 Vote. w. Moscowman. m. "*Vogue,* based on a performance by Madonna." "The Election is coming in November, voters reading the magazines and think what's their decision on the upcoming election." Published online at <http://amiright.com/parody/90s/thekinks3.shtml>. [2004].

650.66 Vote Lover. w. Mac195. m. "*Art Lover,* based on a performance by The Kinks." Published online at <http://amiright.com/parody/80s/madonna19.shtml>. [2004].

650.67 We Want Howard Dean. w.m. Denny Zartman. m. No tune indicated. "Spread The Word Through Song and Music! Songs For Dean, Songs to get elected by." N/c photo of Howard Dean. Lyrics and sound file published online at <http://songsfordean.com/so/lyrics/somethingtosee.php>. 2004.

650.68 Yell Like Howard Dean. w. John Jenkins. m. "*Yellow Submarine,* based on the performance by The Beatles." "As the race for the Democratic presidential nomination approaches the first two voter tests, the Iowa caucus and the New Hampshire primary (both in January), Dr. Howard Dean is combining his fire breathing campaign rhetoric and his unique internet appeal to lead the polls in both states. Will he stay there?" Published online at <http://amiright.com/parody/60s/thebeatles415.shml>. [ca. 2004].

650.69 You're A Long Shot, Senator Kerry. w. John Jenkins. m. Tune — "*It's A Long Way To Tipperary* originally by Jack Judge and Harry Williams." Published online at <http://www.amiright.com/parody/2000s/threedoorsdown0.shtml>. 2004.

KING, Rufus (State House, 1783–1785; Continental Congress, 1784–1787) [See: New York].

• **AmPM-651 KNOWLTON**, George W., Jr. (Selectman, Worcester; Candidate for State Senator, 1932?)

651.1 Hello Voters (We're Glad To See You Know) (Fox-Trot). w.m. Charles D. Bourcier. a. Fred W. Clement. Published by John Worley Company, 166 Terrace Street, Roxbury, MA. 1932. B/w drawing of a sample ballot — Public Office, Vote for Two: Mr. Candidate X, Mr. Candidate X." 6pp. Page 2: Blank. Page 3: At top of music — "Dedicated to Mr. And Mrs. R.D. Voter." Page 6: "Voters, Remember September 20th, Vote at the Primaries, For Senator, 4th Worcester District — George W. Knowlton, Jr."

• **AmPM-652 KNOX**, Henry (U.S. Secretary of War, 1785–1794)

652.1 Gen. Knox's March. m. No composer indicated. In: *The Instrumental Assistant, Containing Instructions For The Violin, German Flute, Clarionett, Bass Viol And Hautboy. Compiled From Late European Publications. Also A Selection Of Favourite Airs, Marches &c. Progressively Arranged And Adapted For The Use Of Learners*, page 52. m. Samuel Holyoke, A.M. Printed at Exeter, New Hampshire [sic], by H. Ranlet, and sold at his book-store. Sold also by most of the booksellers in the United States. 1800. [S/U, p.209].

652.2 Genl. Knox's March {652.2–1}. m. No composer indicated. Published by J.G. Osbourn's Music Saloon, No. 30 South 4th Street, Philadelphia, PA. [ca. 1840]. Non-pictorial geometric designs. Preceded on page 1 by **Genl. Gates Grand March**{652.2–2}. 2pp. Page 2: Blank.

652.3 On Gen. Waynes Taking Stoney Point. m. No composer indicated. w. No composer indicated. m. "Tune — *One Night As Ned Slept Into Bed.*" In: *Liberty Songs,* page 6. No publisher indicated. 8pp. [ca. 178–]. 8pp. [S/U, p. 228].

• **AmPM-653 LASELL**, John W. (Selectman, Northbridge, 1925–1932; Candidate for U.S. House, 1932)

653.1 Hello Voters (We're Glad To See You Know) (Fox-Trot). w.m. Charles D. Bourcier. a. Fred W. Clement. Published by John Worley Company, 166 Terrace Street, Roxbury, MA. 1932. B/w drawing of a sample ballot — Public Office, Vote for Two: Mr. Candidate X, Mr. Candidate X." 6pp. Page 2: Blank. Page 3: At top of music — "Dedicated to Mr. And Mrs. R.D. Voter." Page 6: B/w photo of John Lasell. "Voters, Remember November 8th, Vote at the Election for Representative 7th Worcester District — John W. Lasell, Northbridge."

• **AmPM-654 LAWRENCE**, Abbott (Common Council, Boston, 1831; U.S. House, 1835–1837 & 1839–1840; U.S. Minister to Great Britain, 1849–1852)

654.1 Lawrence Quick Step. m. A. Kurek. a. Knaebel. Published by Charles Keith, 67 & 69 Court Street, Boston, MA. 1839. B/w litho of the "Encampment at Barnstable, Sept. 1839." "Respectfully Dedicated to S. Abbott Lawrence and the members of the New England Guards." 4pp. Page 4: Blank.

• **AmPM-655 LESLIE**, Harry Guyer (State House, 1923–1927, Governor, 1929–1933)

655.1 'Round My Indiana Home. w. J. Will Callahan. m. Joe Dunn. Published by Chappell-Harms Inc., New York, NY. 1931. [Cover on examination copy missing]. 6pp. Page 2: [?]. Page 2: At top of music — "Dedicated by Permission to Honorable Harry G. Leslie, Governor of Indiana.

• **AmPM-656 LINCOLN**, Benjamin (Magistrate, Provincial Legislature, Provincial Congress, Lt. Governor, 1788–1789)

656.1 About Savannah. w. No composer indicated. m. No tune indicated. No publisher indicated. 1779. [SBAR, p. 268].

656.2 Choro Grando. w. No composer indicated. m. No composer indicated. In: *The American Musical Miscellany, A Collection Of The Newest And Most Appoved* [Sic] *Songs, Set To Music*, page 123. Printed by Andrew Wright for Daniel Wright & Company, Northampton, MA. 1798. 300pp. [S/U, p. 16].

656.3 A New Song. w. No composer indicated. m. *Doodle Doo.* Published in Rivington's *Gazette*, 1779. "A new song to an old tune, written by a Yankee, and sung to the tune of Doodle doo." [SBAR, p. 275].

656.4 A Song About Charleston. w. Written by a soldier of the Royal Army. m. Tune — *Watery God.* Published as a broadside. 1780. [SBAR, p. 293].

• **AmPM-657** LINCOLN, Levi (State Senate, 1812–1813 & 1844–1845; State House, 1814–1822; Lt. Governor, 1823; Governor, 1825–1834; U.S. House, 1834–1841; Mayor, Worcester, 1848)

657.1 Governor Lincoln's Grand March. m. James Hewitt. Published by James L. Hewitt & Co., At Their Music Store, No. 36 Market Street, Boston, MA., and No. 129 Broadway, New York, NY. [1826–1829]. Non-pictorial. "As performed by the Brigade Band at the inauguration of his Excellency." "Composed & respectfully Dedicated to Miss Corna. Hall." 4pp. Pages 1 and 4: Blank.

657.2 Governor Lincoln's March And Quickstep Massachusetts. m. Miss Exxxxxxxx Lxxxxx. Published for the Author by C. Bradlee, No. 164 Washington Street, Boston, MA. [1827–1834]. Non-pictorial geometric designs. 2pp. Page 2: *Quick Step.*

• **AmPM-658** LIVERMORE, Mary Ashton (Agent, U.S. Sanitary Commission, 1961–1865; Suffragist; Organized Chicago Woman Suffrage Convention, 1868; Publisher, *The Agitator*; Editor of *The Woman's Journal*, 1870)

658.1 Daughters Of Freedom! The Ballot Be Yours (Solo Or Quartet). w. George Cooper. m. Edwin Christie. Published by Oliver Ditson & Co., 277 Washington Street, Boston, Massachusetts. 1871. B/w non-pictorial geometric designs. "To Mrs. Mary Livermore." 6pp. Pages 2 and 6: Blank. Pages 2–5 music. [Crew/S-1871-1]

658.2 Political Millennium (In Posse). w. S.N. Holmes. m. "Tune — Common Meter." In: *The Republican Campaign Song Book, With Music, 1892*, page 52. e. Samuel Newall Holmes. Published by Samuel Newall Holmes, Syracuse, NY. 1892. Be/bk non-pictorial. "Composed and especially prepared by Judge S.N. Holmes of Syracuse, N.Y." "Headquarters: Syracuse, N.Y." "Price twenty-five cents." 60pp. [M-308]. [Crew/BFH-107].

658.3 The Suffrage Flag. w. William P. Adkinson "(By Permission)." m. "Air — *Bonnie Blue Flag.*" "Dedicated to Elizabeth Cady Stanton, Lucy Stone, Susan B. Anthony, Mary A. Livermore and other pioneer women in the Woman Suffrage Movement." In: *Booklet Of Song: A Collection Of Suffrage And Temperance Melodies (No. 1)*, page 17. c. L. May Wheeler. Published by Co-operative Printing Company, Minneapolis, Minnesota. 1884. [6½" × 4½"]. Non-pictorial geometric designs, flora, fauna. 54pp. [Crew/S-1884-1].

• **AmPM-659** LODGE, Henry Cabot (State House, 1880–1881; U.S. House, 1887–1893; U.S. Senate, 1893–1924)

659.1 Coxey Doodle. w. H.L.S. m. "Tune — *Yankee Doodle.*" In: *America First (Republican Campaign Song Book)*, page 16. Published for The Republican National Committee, No. 19 West 44th Street, New York, NY., by Weldon Company, No. 119 Walnut Street, Philadelphia, PA. 1920. [6" × 9"]. Br/bk photos of "Warren Harding — For President" and "Calvin Coolidge — For Vice President." 20pp. [M-411]. [Crew/WGH-23].

• **AmPM-660** LODGE, Henry Cabot, Jr. (State House, 1933–1936; U.S. Senate, 1937–1944 & 1947–1953; U.S. Representative to the United Nations, 1953–1960; Candidate for Vice President, 1960; U.S. Ambassador to Republic of Vietnam, 1963–1964 & 1965–1967; U. S. Ambassador at Large, 1967–1968; U.S. Ambassador to Germany, 1968–1969; U.S. Special Envoy to the Vatican, 1970–1977)

660.1 Cool Goldwater. w. Noel E. Parmentel, Jr. and Marshall J. Dodge. In: *Folk Songs For Conservatives*, page 11. Published by Unicorn Press, Inc., No. 790 Madison Avenue, New York, NY. 10021. 1964. [5" × 8⅜"]. Bl/w drawings of Barry Goldwater, Bill Buckley, Ray Cohn, eagle. List of contents. "Sung by Noel E. Parmentel, Jr. and His Unbleached Muslims, Greatest Political Satirists Since Cohn and Schine." "Right Wing Hootenanny." 36pp. [Crew/BMG-13].

660.2 [Hurrah For Kennedy Trala]. w. No composer indicated. m. *Solomon Levi.* In: *Untitled John F. Kennedy Song Sheet*, page 1. 1952. Non-pictorial. 2pp.

660.3 Yellow Rose Of Saigon. w. Tom Bowen. m. *Yellow Rose Of Texas.* "From The Longest Year by Bowen and Fish." Lyrics and sound file published online at <http://www.mudcat.org/kids/@displaysong.cfm?SongID=7996>. [199-].

• **AmPM-661** LONG, John Davis (State House, 1875; Lt. Governor, 1879–1880; Governor, 1880–1883; U.S. House, 1883–1889; U.S. Secretary of the Navy, 1897–1902)

661.1 The Cabinet Grand March. m. Hans S. Line, Op. 64. Published by National Music Company, Nos. 215–221 Wabash Avenue, Chicago, IL. 1897. R/w cover. B/w photo of William McKinley and eight Cabinet members. "Dedicated to Hon. Lyman J. Gage." 6pp. Page 6: Advertising. [Crew/WM-15].

• **AmPM-662** LUNT, George (U.S. District Attorney, 1850–1853; Delegate to Democratic National Convention, 1864)

662.1 Our Country (A Patriotic Song). w. Hon. Geo. Lunt. m. I.B. Woodbury. Published by Oliver Ditson, 115 Washington Street, Boston, MA. [ca. 1847]. B/w litho of soldiers on horseback, marching. "Respectfully Inscribed to Col. Caleb Cushing of Massachusetts." 6pp. Pages 2 and 6: Blank. [LL/JH].

• **AmPM-663** LYNCH, Stephen F. (State House, 1995–1996; State Senate, 1997–2001; U.S. House, 2001–Present)

663.1 Cead Mile Failte! [Song Book]. Published by Ironworkers Local 7, Union Hall, South Boston, MA. 1999. [5⅜" × 8½"]. B/w photo of Senator Stephen F. Lynch and Vice President Al Gore. Gn/w drawing of a shamrock. "1999 Senator Stephen F. Lynch's St. Patrick's Day Breakfast." 24pp. Pages 2, 4, 22, 23 and 24: Blank. Page 3: Index. [Crew/BC-11].

• **AmPM-664** MARTIN, Joseph William, Jr. (State House, 1912–1914; State Senate, 1915–1917; U.S.

House, 1925–1967; Chairman of the Republican National Committee, 1940–1942)

664.1 *Always True To Fashion*. w. No composer indicated. m. "Tune—*Always True To You In My Fashion*." "Quartette—Stassen, Taft, Warren and Martin." In: *Alice In Blunderland Or Through The Rooking Class* [Program and Songbook], page 6. Published by The Legislative Correspondents' Association of New York State, Albany, NY. 1949. [8⅝" × 11"]. N/c drawings of Harry Truman, Thomas Dewey, Franklin Roosevelt, Henry Wallace, Harold Stassen, Alben Barkley, Robert Taft, Earl Warren, other politicians. "A Scintillating Satire of Sadistic Surprises and Surprising Successes Featuring a Dramatic Disclosure of How Tom Did Not Go Down to D.C. in Slips; Together with a Give-Away-Nothing Radio Broadcast and Epic Melodrama of the Indian Wars Entitled 'When the Cat's Away the Mice Will Play.'" "Done With Music and Mirrors—Particularly Mirrors in Three Acts at Hotel Ten Eyck, Albany, March 12, 1949." [Crew/HST-20].

- **AmPM-665** MCCALL, Samuel Walker (State House, 1888–1889 & 1892; U.S. House, 1893–1913; Governor, 1916–1918)

665.1 *Massachusetts* (You're The Cradle of Liberty). w. Miles J. O'Brien. m. Melvin Stepper. Published by Modern Music Co., Music Publishers, Boston, MA. 1917. B/w photo of Samuel McCall. Bl/w shields, stripes. "Respectfully Dedicated to His Excellency, Samuel W. McCall." 4pp. Page 4: Advertising.

665.2 *My America*. w.m. Frank Peer Beal. Published by The Boston Music Company, 26 & 28 West Street Boston, MA. Copyright 1917 by Frank Beal. [8¾" × 10½"]. Bl/w litho of American flag, stars, geometric designs. "Endorsed by the Governors of New Hampshire, Connecticut & Massachusetts. Sung on the floor of the House of Congress, April 4, 1917." "All benefits from the sale of this publication are to be donated to the American Red Cross." List of Arrangements available." 4pp. Page 2: Endorsements by "H.M. Keyes, Governor of New Hampshire," "Samuel W. McCall, Governor of Massachusetts," and "Marcus H. Holcomb, Governor of Connecticut," and "F.H. Gallinger, United States Senator." Page 4: Bl/e geometric design.

- **AmPM-666** MORSE, Elijah Adams (State House, 1876; State Senate, 1886–1887; U.S. House, 1889–1897)

666.1 *Morse's Grand March*. m. Everett B. Beal. Published by J.Q. Beal & Son, Rockland, MA. 1892. B/w litho of Elijah A. Morse. "To the Hon. Elijah A. Morse, M.C." 8pp. Pages 2 and 8: Blank.

- **AmPM-667** MORTON, Marcus (Clerk of the State Senate, 1811–1812; U.S. House, 1817–1821; Lt. Governor, 1824; State Supreme Bench, 1825–1839; Governor, 1840–1844; State House, 1858; Superior Court, Suffolk County, 1858; Superior Bench, 1859, State Supreme Court, 1869–1872)

667.1 *Gov. Morton's Grand March*. m. J. Friedheim. Published by Henry Prentiss, No. 35 Court Street (Opposite the new Court House), Boston, MA. 1889. R/w/bk litho of military equipment, flag. "Composed & Arranged for the Piano Forte." "Respectfully dedicated to his Excellency, Marcus Morton. 4pp. Page 4: Blank. [LL/JH].

667.2 *Governor Morton's Grand March*. m. Adam Kurek, "Polish Exile." Published by Chas. H. Keith, 67 & 69 Court Street, Boston, MA. 1843. B/w litho by Sharp's litho. of Marcus Morton. "Arranged for the Piano Forte by J.R. Garcia, and Respectfully Dedicated by Permission to His Excellency Gov. Morton by the Publisher." 6pp. Page 6: Blank.

667.3 *Green's Quick Step*. m. F.L. Raymond. Published by Henry Prentiss, No. 33 Court Street, Boston, MA. Be/bk litho of a coin? engraved with a seated Miss Liberty, stars and the date "1840," geometric border designs. "Composed, arranged and respectfully dedicated to Col. C.C. Greene, Aid de Camp to His Excellency Marcus Morton, Governor of Massachusetts." 4pp. Page 4: Blank. [LL/JH].

667.4 *Lines Supposed To Be Written On The Twelfth Of November, 1840*. w. No composer indicated. m. "Air—*Farewell, Farewell To Thee, Araby's Daughter*." In: *Harrison Melodies (Original And Selected)*, page 14. Published by Weeks, Jordan & Co., Boston, MA. 1840. [3⁵⁄₁₆" × 6"]. B/w litho of William Henry Harrison. "Published under the direction of the Boston Harrison Club." 76pp. Page 5: "To William Henry Harrison of Ohio, the gallant soldier, the enlightened statesman, the consistent Republican, and the Honest man..." [M-001, 002, 003]. [Crew/WHH-86].

667.5 *The Log Cabin And Hard Cider Song*. w. No composer indicated. m. "Tune—*The Hunters Of Kentucky*." From the "*Boston Atlas*." In: *Log Cabin Minstrel (Or Tippecanoe Songster)*, page 18. c. "A Member of the Roxbury Whig Association." Published at the *Patriot And Democrat* Office, Roxbury, [MA]. 1840. [4½" × 6¾"]. [V-1:Y/bk] [V-2: Bl/bk] litho of William Henry Harrison, geometric design border. "Old Tip's the boy to swing the flail. Hurrah! Hurrah! Hurrah!" 64pp. Page 3: Title page—"Containing a Selection of Songs Original and Selected Many of them Written Expressly for this Work, Compiled, Published and Arranged by a member of the Roxbury Democratic Whig Association and Respectfully Dedicated to the Log Cabin Boys of the U.S." [M-013]. [Crew/ WHH-71].

667.6 *Yankee Doodle—New Version*. w. No composer indicated. m. Tune—*Yankee Doodle*. In: *Log Cabin Minstrel (Or Tippecanoe Songster)*, page 50. c. "A Member of the Roxbury Whig Association." Published at the *Patriot And Democrat* Office, Roxbury, [MA]. 1840. [4½" × 6¾"]. [V-1:Y/bk] [V-2: Bl/bk] litho of William Henry Harrison, geometric design border. "Old Tip's the boy to swing the flail. Hurrah! Hurrah! Hurrah!" 64pp. Page 3: Title page—"Containing a Selection of Songs Original and Selected Many of them Written Expressly for this Work, Compiled, Published and Arranged by a member of the Roxbury Democratic Whig Association and Respectfully Dedicated to the Log Cabin Boys of the U.S." [M-013]. [Crew/WHH-71].

- **AmPM-668** MOTTOLA, Vincent (Candidate for U.S. House, 1942)

668.1 *Our Governor's March*. w. Ruth L. Seanor. m. Hon. Vincent Mottola. Published by The Music of Tomorrow Publishing Co., 715 Old South Building, Boston, MA. 1954. Bl/w photo of "Governor Christian Herter." 6pp. Page 2: Blank. Page 6: Advertising.

- **AmPM-669 O'BRIEN**, Lawrence Francis (U.S. Postmaster General, 1965–1968; Chairman of the National Democratic Party, 1968–1969 & 1970–1972; NBA Commissioner, 1974–1984)

669.1 Larry O'Brien. w.m. Charles Tobias. Published by Toby Music Corp. [1965-1968]. [8½" × 11"]. Bl/b mimeograph. 2pp. Page 2: Blank. [From a "Testimonial Banquet" for O'Brien].

- **AmPM-669A O'BRIEN**, Walter F. (Communist Candidate for Mayor, Boston, 1949)

669A.1 M.T.A. w. Jacqueline Steiner. m. Bess Lomax Hawes. Published online at <http://users2.evl.net/~smyth/linernotes/thesongs/MTA.htm>. Recorded by The Kingston Trio.

- **AmPM-670 O'HARA**, Michael S. (Mayor, Worcester, 1924–1931)

670.1 The Heart Of The Commonwealth (Song). w. William P. Cantwell. m. Ernest H. Johnson. Published by Johnson & Cantwell Publishing Co., Worcester, MA. 1930. Bl/w photos of "Mayor Michael J. O'Hara" and "City Hall." "Dedicated to the City of Worcester, Massachusetts." Bl/w geometric design border. 6pp. Page 6: Blank.

- **AmPM-671 OLNEY**, Richard (State House, 1902; Board of Selectmen, Leicester, 1902–1903; Candidate for Lt. Governor, 1903; State Minimum Wage Commission, 1911; Delegate, Democratic National Convention, 1912; U.S. House, 1915–1921; World War Foreign Debt Commission, 1923–1925?; State Parole Board, 1932–1937; State Commission of the Necessaries of Life, 1938–1939)

671.1 Exit Old Party. w. No composer indicated. m. "Tune — *Good-By, My Lover, Good-By.*" In: *Republican Campaign Parodies And Songs* [Songster], page 22. Published by Betts and Burnett, South Butler, Wayne County, NY. 1896. [7¾" × 5½"]. Be/bk non-pictorial. "McKinley and Hobart." "1896." 28pp. [M-340]. [Crew/WM-67].

- **AmPM-672 O'NEILL**, Thomas Phillip, Jr. (State House, 1936–1952; School Committee, Cambridge, 1946–1947; U.S. House, 1953–1987)

672.1 California Girls. w. John Jenkins. m. "*California Girls*, based on the performance by Beach Boys." The last four leaders of the Democratic Party in the House of Representatives have been Tip O'Neill (Massachusetts, 1977–87), Jim Wright (Texas, 87–89), Tom Foley (Washington, 89–94), and Dick Gephardt (Missouri, 94–2002)..." Published online at <http://amiright.com/parody/60s/beachboys17.shml>. [2003].

672.2 That Leftist Tart From San Francisco. w. John Jenkins. m. Tune — "*I Left My Heart In San Francisco* originally by Tony Bennett." "A duet with the last two lines of each verse (after the introduction) sung by Nancy Pelosi and the balance sung by an anonymous Democrat Congressman." Published online at <http://www.amiright.com/parody/60s/tonybennett2.shml>. [ca. 2003].

672.3 Tip O. w. Bill Strauss and Elaina Newport. On Cassette: *The Capitol Steps Live*. 1984. Cassette Cover: B/w photo of the Capitol building with the Capitol Steps in foreground.

672.4 We're In Such A Fixie! m. "Sung to the tune of *Dixie.*" "Every great cause has always had a song to lift and inspire, something to rally 'round before a conflict. The Civil War had opposing 'great causes' that produced two memorial songs, *The Battle Hymn Of The Republic* and *Dixie*. Since the goings-on in Washington these days all too often resemble the Civil War, we thought that these great songs should be revived and revised a bit — as up-to-date calls to arms for supply-siders and big spenders. Take your pick, and tune up your vocal chords." Published by Dots Okay, Inc., Annandale, VA. 1982. [9½" × 3¼"]. Published with a boxed cloth "Reganomics Doll" with song sheet insert. 2pp. Obv: *The Battle Hymn Of The Republicans*. Rev: Song — *We're In Such A Fixie!* [Crew/RR-31].

- **AmPM-673 OTIS**, Harrison Gray (State House, 1796 & 1802–1804; U.S. House, 1797–1801; State Senate, 1805–1816; U.S. Senate, 1817–1822; Mayor, Boston, 1829–1832)

673.1 Grand Centennial March. m. Ch: Zeuner. Published by C. Bradlee, 164 Washington Street, Boston, MA. 1830. B/w litho of the "State House From the Mall, Boston." "As performed by the Boston Bands. Composed and respectfully dedicated to the Hon. Harrison Gray Otis, Mayor of Boston." 4pp. Page 4: Blank. [LL, JH].

673.2 Grand Centennial March. m. Charles Zeuner. Published and sold by G. Willig, Jr., Baltimore, MD. [1831]. Non-pictorial geometric designs. Composed and dedicated to the Hon. Harrison Gray Otis. 4pp. Pages 1 and 4: Blank.

673.3 Otis's Quick Step. a. Ch. Zeuner. Published by C. Bradlee, Washington Street, Boston, MA. 1831. Non-pictorial geometric designs. "As performed by the Boston Bands." 2pp. Page 2: Blank.

- **AmPM-674 OTIS**, James, Jr. (Advocate General of the Vice Admiralty Court, 1756–1761; State Assembly, 1761–1766 & 1771; Stamp-Act Congress, 1765)

674.1 Jemmibullero (A Fragment of an Ode of Orpheus). w. Peter Minin, Esq. "Freely translated from the original Tongue, and adapted to British Music." In: *Boston Evening-Post*, May 13, 1765. [VBL, p. 25].

674.2 Jimmicumjunto (An Ode for the New Year 1768). m. "Henry Scratch'em, Esq., Director General of the Ordinance, and Surveyor and Controller of the Fire-Works." In: *Boston Evening-Post*, January 11, 1768. [VBL, p. 25].

674.3 The Liberty Song. In: *Bickerstaf's Boston Almanac For The Year Of Our Lord 1779, Being The Second Year After Leap Year*. Printed by Mein and Flemming, and sold by John Mein, at the London Book-Store, North side of King Street, Boston, MA. 1769. B/w woodblock of "The Hon. James Otis, Jun, Esq." on the cover.

- **AmPM-675 PAIGE**, Calvin De Witt (State House, 1878–1879; U.S. House, 1913–1925)

675.1 It's A Grand Old Flag To Fight For (March Song). w. John H.G. Fraser. m. Duncan E. MacPherson. Published by MacPherson & Fraser, Room 12, No. 164A Tremont Street, Boston, MA. 1918. R/w/b silhouette drawing of soldiers, facsimile letter — "The White House, Washington, 12 February, 1918, Hon. Calvin D. Paige, House of Representatives, My Dear Mr. Paige: May I not thank you for your courtesy in bringing to my attention the song *Its A Grand Old Flag To Fight For* by Mr. Fraser and Mr. MacPherson? It is very delightful to see such assurances of patriotic feeling. Cordially and sincerely yours, (Signed) Woodrow Wilson [facsimile signature]." B/w photo of Sergt. George "Duddy" Conners—"Successfully introduced by George Conners of Camp Devens." 4pp. Page 4: Advertising.

• **AmPM-676 PAINE**, Robert Treat (General Assembly; Continental Congress, 1774–1778; Signer of the Declaration of Independence, 1776; State Attorney General, 1780–1790; State Supreme Court, 1790–1804)

676.1 Adams And Liberty. w. R.T. Paine, Esq., "in 1798." m. No tune indicated. In: *Boston Musical Miscellany (Volume II)*, page 195. Published by J.T. Buckingham, No. 5 Marlbough Street, Boston, MA. 1815. [4" × 6½"]. Be/bk hardback cover with litho of musical instruments, geometric design border. 228pp. [W-954]. [Crew/JA-21].

676.2 Adams And Liberty. w.m. T. Paine. In: *The American Musical Miscellany, A Collection Of The Newest And Most Appoved* [Sic] *Songs, Set To Music*, page 211. Printed by Andrew Wright for Daniel Wright & Company, Northampton, MA. 1798. 300pp. [S/U, p. 16].

676.3 The Declaration Of Independence Of The United States Of North America, July 4, 1776. w. From the Declaration of Independence. m. John E. Wilson. Published by John E. Wilson, Baltimore, MD. 1863. B/w litho of the interior of Independence Hall. "Arranged and adapted for Vocal and Instrumental Music as the Great National Chant." 4pp. [?]. Page 4: Facsimile signatures of all signers.

676.4 Liberty Tree. w. Robert Treat Payne [sic]. m. No tune indicated. In: *The Southern Warbler, A New Collection Of Patriotic, National, Naval, Martial, Professional, Convivial, Humorous, Pathetic, Sentimental, Old, And New Songs*, p. 27. Published by Babcock & Company, Charleston, SC. 1845. [3⅝" × 6⅞"]. Gold imprinting of a lyre, music page, instruments and eagle on brown hard cover. 330pp.

676.5 Old Independence Hall. w. A. Fletcher Stayman. m. Francis Weiland. Published by Stayman & Brothers, No. 210 Chesnut Street, Philadelphia, PA. 1855. Non-pictorial. "Respectfully dedicated to the Memory of the Signers of the Declaration of Independence." "Fac Simile of their signatures" including John Adams, Sam Adams, Elbridge Gerry, Thomas Jefferson. 8pp. Pages 2 and 8: Blank. [Crew/MISC-34].

• **AmPM-677 PAINE**, Thomas (Patriot; Writer of *Common Sense*)

677.1 Boston Patriotic Song. w. Thomas Paine, A.M. m. "Tune—*Anacreon In Heaven*." In: *The Columbian Songster, Being A Large Collection Of Fashionable Songs, For Gentlemen & Ladies In A Series Of Numbers*, Song LXIV, page 31. Printed by Nathaniel Heaton, Jur., [Wrentham, MA]. 1799. [3½" × 5¾"]. Hard cover. 196pp. [S/U, p. 79].

677.2 Liberty Tree. w. Thomas Paine. m. No tune indicated. Published in the *Pennsylvania Magazine*, July 1775. [SBAR, p. 18].

677.3 Liberty Tree. w. Thomas Paine. m. "Tune—*In A Mouldering Cave*." In: *The Republican Harmonist (Being A Select Collection Of Republican, Patriotic, And Sentimental Songs, Odes, Sonnets, &c, American And European: Some Of Which Are Original, And Most Of The Others Now Come For The First Time From An American Press)*, page 68. c. D.E. [Daniel Ebsworth] "(A Citizen of the World)." Printed "for the People," Boston, MA. 1801. Non-pictorial. 152pp. [Crew/TJ-10].

677.4 Justice To Paine. w. No composer indicated. m. "Air—*Thou Reign'st*." In: *Programme—The Birthday Of Thomas Paine!* No publisher indicated. [18??]. Non-pictorial. "Published by The Friends of Mental Liberty and Free Government propose to commemorate the 133d anniversary of the birthday of the author-hero of the Revolution, Thomas Paine, by a free lecture, By Horace Seaver, upon his revolutionary services. At Mercantile Hall, Sumner St., on Sunday, Jan. 30th, Commencing at 7½ o'clock P.M." "Admittance Free." 2pp. Page 2: Blank. [AMC].

677.5 Lines Supposed To Be Written On The Twelfth Of November, 1840. w. No composer indicated. m. "Air—*Farewell, Farewell To Thee, Araby's Daughter*." In: *Harrison Melodies (Original And Selected)*, page 14. Published by Weeks, Jordan & Co., Boston, MA. 1840. [3⁵⁄₁₆" × 6"]. B/w litho of William Henry Harrison. "Published under the direction of the Boston Harrison Club." 76pp. Page 5: "To William Henry Harrison of Ohio, the gallant soldier, the enlightened statesman, the consistent Republican, and the Honest man..." [M-001, 002, 003]. [Crew/WHH-86].

677.6 Notes From Tom Paine. m. Norman Dello Joio. Performed by The Goldman Band, Richard Franko Goldman, Conducting and The dePaur Chorus, Harriet Wingreen, Pianist; Leonard dePaur, Conducting. On LP: *A Bicentennial Celebration (200 Years Of American Music)*. Columbia Masterworks M-33838. [ca. 1976]. Album cover: Drawing of a brass band.

677.7 Paine's Ode To America. w. Thomas Payne. m. "Air—*Rule Britannia*." In: *Programme—The Birthday Of Thomas Paine!* No publisher indicated. [18??]. Non-pictorial. "Published by The Friends of Mental Liberty and Free Government propose to commemorate the 133d anniversary of the birthday of the author-hero of the Revolution, Thomas Paine, by a free lecture, By Horace Seaver, upon his revolutionary services. At Mercantile Hall, Sumner St., on Sunday, Jan. 30th, Commencing at 7½ o'clock p.m." "Admittance Free." 2pp. Page 2: Blank. [AMC].

677.8 There's Nothing Like The Truth. w.m. No composer or tune indicated. Published by George Warren (Aged 12 years) with Josiah Warren's Amateur Printing Apparatus. 1839. Bl/bk non-pictorial. "Songs sung at the celebration of Paine's birth day, in New Harmony, Jan. 29, 1839." Followed on page 1 by **677.9 The Sweets Of Liberty**. 2pp. Page 2: Blank. [AMC].

• **AmPM-678 PHILBAN**, Philip Joseph (Special Counsel, U.S. Senate Committee, 1934–1936; Referee, U.S. Department of Labor, 1936–1937; Advisory Board, Massachusetts Unemployment Compensation Commission, 1937–1940; Finance Committee, Clinton; 1935; U.S. House, 1943–1971)

678.1 We'll Never Get Our Fill With Philbin. w.m. John Redmond (ASCAP). No publisher indicated. Copyright Novelty Music, 1650 Broadway, New York, NY. R/w photo of Philip Philbin. "Congressman

Philip J. Philbin." 4pp. Page 2: At top of music — "Dedicated to Congressman Philip J. Philbin at the request of his many friends and admirers." Page 4: Newspaper headlines about Philbin. Quote by Philbin.

- AmPM-679   PHILLIPS, Wendell (Abolitionist; President of the Anti-Slavery Society, 1865)

679.1 The Bill-Poster's Dream (Or Cross Readings). w. No composer indicated. m. "Air — *The Captain With His Whiskers.*" Published by H. De Marsan, Publisher, 54 Chatham Street, New York, NY. [ca. 1859]. [Approx. 6" × 9½"]. B/w litho border of four characters intertwined with star-studded ribbon, floral and geometric designs. 2pp. Page 2: Blank.

679.2 De Nigger On De Fence. w. No composer indicated. m. "Tune — *All Round My Hat.*" In: *Copperhead Minstrel* (A Choice Collection of Democratic Poems & Songs), page 38. Published by Feeks and Bancker, Wholesale Agents, No. 24 Ann Street, New York. 1863. [4¾" × 7¼"]. O/bk non-pictorial. "For the use of Political Clubs and the Social Circle." "Price 25 cents." 64pp. [M-133] [Crew/GBM-64].

679.3 A Hundred Years Hence. w. Tony Pastor. m. No tune indicated. Published by Charles Magnus, 12 Franklin Street, New York, NY. [1863–1864]. N/c lithos of an Indian with a American flag inscribed "For The Union," and a litho of a bull and man chopping a tree titled "Indiana." 2pp. Page 2: Blank. [AMC].

679.4 The Last Wendell Phillips. w. No composer indicated. m. "Tune — *The Last Rose Of Summer.*" In: *Copperhead Minstrel (A Choice Collection Of Democratic Poems & Songs)*, page 52. Published by Feeks and Bancker, Wholesale Agents, No. 24 Ann Street, New York. 1863. [4¾" × 7¼"]. O/bk non-pictorial. "For the use of Political Clubs and the Social Circle." "Price 25 cents." 64pp. [M-133] [Crew/GBM-64].

679.5 Lesh Us Have Peash! w. No composer indicated. m. "Air — *Old Dan Tucker.*" "Verses from a Radical Campaign Song, as sung by Simpson after one of his One-Horse Acts." In: *Seymour Campaign Songster*, page 18. Published by Pattee & Hubbard, Democratic State Committee Rooms, World Building, No. 37 Park Row, New York, NY. 1868. [4" × 5¼"]. Gn/bk litho of Horatio Seymour and Francis Blair. "In the spirit of George Washington and the Patriots of the Revolution, Let us take the steps to re-inaugurate our Government, to start it once again on its course to greatness and prosperity — Horatio Seymour." 38pp. [M-173]. [Crew/HS-8].

679.6 Sing A Song Of Greenbacks. w.m. No composer or tune indicated. In: *Democratic Presidential Campaign Songster (No. 1)*, page 66. Published by J.F. Feeks, No. 26 Ann Street, New York, NY. 1864. [3¾" × 5½"]. Y/bk litho of George B. McClellan, chain link frame. "McClellan & Pendleton." "Original Campaign Songs, Choruses, &c." 74pp. [M-135, 136]. [Crew/GBM-23].

679.7 Song Of The Contraband. w. No composer indicated. m. "Air — *Lucy Long.*" In: *Democratic Presidential Campaign Songster (No. 1)*, page 24. Published by J.F. Feeks, No. 26 Ann Street, New York, NY. 1864. [3¾" × 5½"]. Y/bk litho of George B. McClellan, chain link frame. "McClellan & Pendleton." "Original Campaign Songs, Choruses, &c." 74pp. [M-135, M-136]. [Crew/GBM-23].

679.8 Thirty-First Anniversary Of The American Anti-Slavery Society [Song Sheet]. Published by the Anti-Slavery Printing Office, 21 Spruce Street, 2d floor. 1864. Non-pictorial geometric design border. "At the Church of the Puritans, Tuesday, May 10th, 1864." Four songs: *[O Thou]* {679.8–1}. w. Theodore Tilton. m. *L.M. Rothwell*; *[God Made All His Creatures Free]* {679.8–2}. w. James Montgomery. m. *7s — Nuremburg*; *[Out Of The Dark The Circling Sphere]* {679.8–3}. w. Samuel Longfellow. m. *L.M. — Duke Street*; and *[Thy Kingdom Come!]* {679.8–4}. w. Harriet Martineau. m. *S.M. — Silver Street.* At bottom of the page — "The Americans Anti-Slavery Society will hold another public meeting, at the Cooper Institute, on Wednesday Evening, May 11, at 8 o'clock. Speakers — William Lloyd Garrison, Wendell Phillips, George Thompson. To defray expenses, tickets of admission will be sold at the doors — for 10 cents. The business meetings of the Society will be held in the Lecture Room of the Church of the Puritans, on Tuesday evening at 7½ o'clock, and on Wednesday morning at 10 o'clock." [AMC].

679.9 Union Emotions. w. John C. Cross. m. "Air — *Glory Hallelujah.*" Published by H. De Marsan, Publisher, 54 Chatham Street, New York, NY. [1861–1865]. B/w litho border. 2pp. Page 2: Blank. [AMC].

679.10 Sherman's March. w. Michael Fee. m. "*Ginger Blue.*" Published by H. De Marsan, Dealer in Songs Toy-Books &c., 54 Chatham Street, New York, NY. [1863–1865]. B/w non-pictorial geometric design border. 2pp. Page 2: Blank. [AMC].

679.11 The Veto Galop! m. "Make Peace." Published by McCarrell & Mininger, No. 91 West Jefferson Street, Louisville, KY. 1866. B/w litho by Bennett, Donaldson & Elmes of "Andy" Johnson holding a document inscribed "Veto" and riding a horse named "Constitution" men labeled "Dead Ducks," including "W. Phillips," "Wade," "Stevens, "Fr. Douglass," "Freedmans Bureau;" Crowd cheering — "Hurrah for Andy," "See the Lame Ducks." Litho of building in the background — "Forney & Co., Dealers in Game." 6pp. Pages 2 and 6: Blank. [Crew/AJN-17].

- AmPM-680   PICKERING, Timothy (Selectman and Assessor, Salem, 1772–1777; Committee on State of Rights of Colonists, 1773; Committee of Correspondence and Safety, 1774–1775; State Legislature, 1776; Board of War, 1777; U.S. Postmaster General 1791–1795, U.S. Secretary of War, 1795; U.S. Secretary of State, 1795–1800; State Court of Common Pleas and General Sessions, 1802; U.S. Senate, 1803–1811; State Executive Council, 1812–1813; U.S. House, 1813–1817)

680.1 The American State Coach. w.m. Daniel Ebsworth & C.W. "Altered from a late English Publication." In: *The Republican Harmonist (Being A Select Collection Of Republican, Patriotic, And Sentimental Songs, Odes, Sonnets, &c, American And European: Some Of Which Are Original, And Most Of The Others Now Come For The First Time From An American Press)*, page 93. c. D.E. [Daniel Ebsworth] "(A Citizen of the World)." Printed "for the People," Boston, MA. 1801. Non-pictorial. 152pp. [Crew/TJ-10].

680.2 Beauties Of Anglo-Federalism, Displayed (Or State Tricks Developed). w. No composer indicated. m. "Tune—*Moderation And Alteration.*" In: *The Republican Harmonist (Being A Select Collection Of Republican, Patriotic, And Sentimental Songs, Odes, Sonnets, &c, American And European: Some Of Which Are Original, And Most Of The Others Now Come For The First Time From An American Press)*, page 29. c. D.E. [Daniel Ebsworth] "(A Citizen of the World)." Printed "for the People," Boston, MA. 1801. Non-pictorial. 152pp. [Crew/TJ-10].

680.3 *The Duke's Retreat To Braintree.* w. No composer indicated. m. "Tune—*I Follow'd Him To Glasgow Town.*" In: *The Republican Harmonist (Being A Select Collection Of Republican, Patriotic, And Sentimental Songs, Odes, Sonnets, &c, American And European: Some Of Which Are Original, And Most Of The Others Now Come For The First Time From An American Press)*, page 13. c. D.E. [Daniel Ebsworth] "(A Citizen of the World)." Printed "for the People," Boston, MA. 1801. Non-pictorial. 152pp. [Crew/TJ-10].

680.4 *The Duke's Retreat To Braintree.* w. No composer indicated. m. *Yankee Doodle.* Published in *The American Republican Harmonist.* 1803. [VBL, p. 166].

680.5 *The Retrospect: Or A Touch On The Tories.* w. No composer indicated. m. "Tune—*Pretty Work For Twelve Dollars A Day.*" In: *The Republican Harmonist (Being A Select Collection Of Republican, Patriotic, And Sentimental Songs, Odes, Sonnets, &c, American And European: Some Of Which Are Original, And Most Of The Others Now Come For The First Time From An American Press)*, page 20. c. D.E. [Daniel Ebsworth] "(A Citizen of the World)." Printed "for the People," Boston, MA. 1801. Non-pictorial. 152pp. [Crew/TJ-10].

• **AmPM-681** POORE, Benjamin Perley (Attaché of the American Legation at Brussels, 1841–1848; Clerk of the Committee of the U.S. Senate on Printing Records, 1850s; Journalist; Author)

681.1 *The Wheelbarrow Polka.* w.m. "A Barrel Apples." Published by Oliver Ditson, No. 115 Washington Street, Boston, MA. 1856. B/w litho by J.H. Bufford's Litho. [Attributed to Winslow Homer] of Major Ben. Perley Poore pushing a wheelbarrow loaded with an apple barrel to Boston after losing a wager on the 1856 election between James Buchanan and John C. Fremont. Narrative on event—"Major Ben. Perley Poore of Newbury, made a bet with Col. Robert I. Burbank of Boston, on the Presidential vote in Massachusetts. The bet doomed the loser to wheel a barrel of apples from his house to the house of the winner. The Colonel won the bet, and the Major started the next morning for Newbury (36 miles from Boston) with the apples (notwithstanding the Col. had promptly released him from the conditions of the bet) and arrived at the Tremont House the third day at 2½ o'clock—where in the presence of at least 30,000 enthusiastic spectators the most interesting ceremonies took place between the parties." "Composed and Dedicated to Major Ben. Perley Poore." 6pp. Pages 2 and 6: Blank. [Crew/JB-12]. [LL, JH].

• **AmPM-682** RAWLE, William (U.S. Attorney for Pennsylvania, 1791–1800)

682.1 *American Liberty* (Or The Sovereign Right of Thinking) (A New Song). w. No composer indicated.

m. "Tune—*Nancy Dawson.*" Published in the Newark Centinel of Freedom, August 14, 1798. [VBL, 150].

• **AmPM-683** REVERE, Christian M. Paul (Sons of Liberty; Boston Tea Party, 1973; Courier for the Boston Committee of Correspondence and the Massachusetts Committee of Safety, 1870s)

683.1 *Biggest Ride Since Paul Revere* (The Ballad of John Glenn). m. Fred Hellerman (ASCAP) and Fran Minkoff (ASCAP). Published by Amrita Music, Inc., 200 West 57th Street, and Paris Music, Inc., 1650 Broadway, New York, NY. 1962. Bl/w photo of John Glenn. Bl/w drawing of a rocket. "Recorded by The Neighbors on M.G.M. Records." 4pp. Page 4: Bl/w drawing of a rocket.

683.2 *Garbage.* w. Bill Steele. m. Sound file provided. "Copyright 1969, The Rainbow Collection, Ltd. (BMI)." Published online by Mudcat Café at <http://mudcat.org/@displaysong.cfm?SongID=2175>. [199-].

683.3 *Lirty Dies: Maddam And Yubble-Doo.* w.m. The Capitol Steps. Published by The Capitol Steps online at < http://capsteps.com/lirty/maddam.html>. 2003

683.4 *Paul Revere* (Won't You Ride For Us Again). w. Joe Goodwin, "Writer of *Liberty Bell.*" m. Halsey K. Mohr. 1918. N/c drawing of Paul Revere on horseback, riding through town.

683.5 *Paul Revere Galop.* m. E.N. Catlin, "Musical Director of the Eastern Museum." Published by G.D. Russell & Company, 126 Tremont Street, Boston, MA. 1876. B/w non-pictorial geometric designs. 6pp. Pages 2 and 6: Blank. [AMC].

683.6 *Paul Revere's Ride* (March Two-Step Galop). m. E.T. Paull. Published by E.T. Paull Music Co., 243 West 42nd Street, New York, NY. 1905. [V-1: Pre-1919 size] [V-2: Post 1919 size]. N/w litho of Paul Revere on horseback riding through a village. "Respectfully inscribed to the Daughters of the American Revolution." 6pp. Page 6: Advertising.

683.7 *Paul Revere's Ride* (Galop Brillante). m. Webb Miller. Published by John Church & Co., 66 West Fourth Street, Cincinnati, OH. 1884. B/w litho of Paul Revere on horseback, North Church in the background. "As Arranged and Played by Major Neven's Celebrated Band." 10pp. Page 10: Blank. [AMC].

• **AmPM-684** ROBINSON, George Dexter (State House, 1874; State Senate, 1876; U.S. House, 1877–1884; Governor, 1884–1887)

684.1 *Governor Robinson's March.* m. J. Thomas Baldwin. a. L. Knight. Published by Oliver Ditson & Co., 452 Washington Street, Boston, MA. 1883. B/w litho by J.H. Bufford's Sons of George Robinson. "As played with great success by Baldwin's Boston Cadet Band." 6pp. Pages 2 and 6: Blank.

684.2 *Gov. Robinson's March.* m. Chas. D. Blake. Published by White-Smith & Co., 316 Washington Street, Boston, MA. 1883. B/w litho of three characters from the opera "Beggar Student (Der Bettelstudent), Comic Opera by C. Millöcker." 6pp. Pages 2 and 6: Blank. Page 3: Music—*Gov. Robinson's March* by Chas. D. Blake.

• **AmPM-684A** ROMNEY, Mitt (Candidate for U.S. Senate, 1994; Governor, 2003–Present)

684A.1 We're So Sorry, Gov'nor Romney. w. Johnny D. m. Tune—"*Uncle Albert/Admiral Halsey,* based on the performance by Paul McCarthney." "This coming Monday, May 17th, barring any last minute judicial stays, my home state of Massachusetts will become the only state in America to issue marriage licenses to gay and lesbian couples. Our Governor, Mitt Romney, has been fighting this every step of the way. "Jumping the broom" is the old fashion folk-expression for getting married." Published online at <http://www.amiright.com/parody/70s/paulmccartney43.shml>. 2004.

• **AmPM-685** ROSTOW, Walt Whitman (Deputy Special Assistant for National Security Affairs, 1960; Counselor to the State Department, 1961)

685.1 Cool Goldwater. w. Noel E. Parmentel, Jr. and Marshall J. Dodge. In: *Folk Songs For Conservatives,* page 11. Published by Unicorn Press, Inc., No. 790 Madison Avenue, New York, NY. 10021. 1964. [5" × 8⅜"]. Bl/w drawings of Barry Goldwater, Bill Buckley, Ray Cohn, eagle. List of contents. "Sung by Noel E. Parmentel, Jr. and His Unbleached Muslims, Greatest Political Satirists Since Cohn and Schine." "Right Wing Hootenanny." 36pp. [Crew/BMG-13].

• **AmPM-686** RUSSELL, William Eustis (Mayor, Cambridge 1884–1887; Governor, 1891–1894)

686.1 Columbia My Country (American Anthem). w.m. George M. Vickers "(Composer of *Guard The Flag, God Bless Our Land,* &c.)." [ca. 1893]. Bl/w litho of Miss Columbia, two women, steamboat. "The New Patriotic Song Approved by People from New England to Alaska." "The sentiment of this song will, I am sure, be indorsed by every true American—William McKinley; Full of Patriotic sentiment, well expressed—Governor Wm. E. Russell, Massachusetts; It is patriotic in sentiment and the music is charming, Governor J.M. Stone, Mississippi; It is a patriotic gem and will probably remain one of the patriotic songs of our country—Governor Elisha P. Ferry, Washington; I trust it may be welcomed by an appreciative public with the favour it deserves—Gen. Lyman E. Knapp, Alaska; I regard such music as a important part of the education of the young people of the land—Hon. John Wanamaker, and representative Americans in all parts of the United States." 4pp. Page 2: Facsimile letter releasing copyright. Page 4: Blank.

• **AmPM-687** SANBY, William (Candidate for Board of Selectmen, Winthorp, 1908)

687.1 This Dear Little Town Of Ours (Song). w. David Benshimol. m. D.L. White. No publisher indicated. Copyright 1908 by White-Smith Music Publishing Co., Boston, MA. B/w photos of "Wesley A. Gove," "Brendon J. Keenan," and "William Sanby"—"Candidates for the Board of Selectmen for 1908." B/w photo of town waterfront. Bl/w drawing of a sail boat. "Expressly written and dedicated to the Winthrop Town Government Association." "Souvenir of the concert held at Crest Hall, Winthrop, Feb. 19, 1908." 6pp. Pages 2 and 6: Blank.

• **AmPM-688** STONE, Lucy (Abolitionist; Suffragist; Founder, American Woman Suffrage Association, 1869)

688.1 A Dirge For H.G. w. No composer indicated. m. "Air—*Not For Joseph.*" From the "*Springfield Republican.*" In: *National Republican Grant And Wilson Campaign Song-Book,* page 80. Published by The Union Republican Congressional Committee, Washington, DC. 1872. [3³⁄₁₆" × 8⅜"]. Be/bk litho of Ulysses S. Grant. "We'll Sing a Song for U.S. Grant." 100pp. [M-182]. [Crew/USG-110].

688.2 Female Suffrage (Song And Chorus). w. R.A. Cohen. m. "Air by the Celebrated Prof. A.J. Phelps, of the Harmoneon Vocalists." a. "With Symphonies, Accompaniments, &c. by George H. Briggs." Published by P.L. Huyett & Son, No. 8 Fourth Street, St. Joseph, MO. 1867. B/w litho vine frame. "Dedicated to Lucy Stone, Susan B. Anthony, Elizabeth Cady Stanton, George Francis Train, And the Advocates of Female Suffrage." 6pp. Page 2: Blank. Page 6: Advertisement. [Crew/S-1867–1].

688.3 Political Millennium (In Posse). w. S.N. Holmes. m. "Tune—*Common Meter.*" In: *The Republican Campaign Song Book, With Music, 1892,* page 52. e. Samuel Newall Holmes. Published by Samuel Newall Holmes, Syracuse, NY. 1892. Be/bk non-pictorial. "Composed and especially prepared by Judge S.N. Holmes of Syracuse, N.Y." "Headquarters: Syracuse, N.Y." "Price twenty-five cents." 60pp. [M-308]. [Crew/BFH-107].

688.4 The Suffrage Flag. w. William P. Adkinson ("By Permission"). m. "Air—*Bonnie Blue Flag.*" "Dedicated to Elizabeth Cady Stanton, Lucy Stone, Susan B. Anthony, Mary A. Livermore and other pioneer women in the Woman Suffrage Movement." In: *Booklet Of Song: A Collection Of Suffrage And Temperance Melodies (No. 1),* page 17. c. L. May Wheeler. Published by Co-operative Printing Company, Minneapolis, Minnesota. 1884. [6½" × 4½"]. Non-pictorial geometric designs, flora, fauna. 54pp. [Crew/S-1884–1].

688.5 We'll Show You When We Come To Vote (The Great Woman's Suffrage) (Song & Chorus). w.m. Frank Howard "(Author of *Only A Poor Little Beggar, Out In The Starlight I'm Waiting For Thee, Drunkard's Home, Fairy Of The Vail, I'm Happy Little Ned, Grape Vine Swing In The Dell*)." Published by W.W. Witney's Palace of Music, Toledo, OH. 1869. B/w litho of women lined up to vote, wall signs reading—"Vote for Susan B. Anthony for President," "For Vice President Mrs. Geo. F. Train," "For Governor of N.Y. Elizabeth Cady Stanton," "For Governor of Mass. Lucy Stone," "Down with Male Rule." "To Mrs. J.M. Ashley."

• **AmPM-689** STRONG, Caleb (Revolutionary Committee on Safety, Northampton, 17—; Governor, 1800–1807 & 1812–1816)

689.1 Governor Strong's March. m. No composer indicated. In: *Gentleman's Pocket Companion, Being A Collection Of The Most Favorite Marches, Airs, Songs, Rondos, & Adapted As Duettinos For Two German Flutes Or Flute And Violin, No. 1,* page 28. a. Frederick Granger. Printed and sold by G. Graupner at his Musical Repository, No. 59 Maiden Lane, New York, NY. [1802–1803]. Non-pictorial geometric designs. 32pp. [W-3191]. [[LL/JH]].

689.2 Governor Strong's March. m. No composer indicated. Published and sold by G. Graupner at his Music Store, No. 6 Franklin Street, Boston, MA. [1813]. Non-pictorial. 2pp. Page 2: Blank. [W-3175]

689.3 Governor Strong's March. m. Wattles. In:

The Instrumental Preceptor, Comprising Instructions For The Clarinet, Hautboy, Flute And Bassoon, With A Variety Of The Most Celebrated Airs, Marches, Minutes, Songs, Rondos, Trios, &c., page 57. c. William Whiteley. Printed by Seward & Williams, No. 36 Genesse Street, Utica, NY. 1816. 72pp. [W-9885].

689.4 *Governor Strong's March*. Published and sold by G. Graupner at his Music Store, No. 6 Franklin Street, Boston, MA. "Sold for G.G., by John Ashton, No. 197 Washington Street." [182-]. Non-pictorial. 2pp. Page 2: Blank. [W-3175A].

689.5 *Governor Strong's New March*. a. J. Hewitt. Printed and sold at J. Hewitt's Musical Repository & Library, No. 58½ Newbury Street, Boston, MA. [1813?]. Non-pictorial. "Arranged for the Piano Forte." 2pp. Page 2: Blank. [LL/JH].

• **AmPM-690 SULLIVAN, James** (King's Council, York County, 17 –; Provincial State Congress, 1774–1775; General Court [State Legislature], 1775–1776; State Supreme Court, 1776–1782; State Attorney General, 1790–1807; Governor, 1807–1808)

690.1 *Gov. Sullivan's March*. m. U.K. Hill. [1807-1808]. Non-pictorial. 2pp. Page 2: Blank. [W-3834].

690.2 *Gov. Sullivan's March*. m. No composer indicated. In: *Martial Music: A Collection Of Marches Harmonized For Field Bands On Various Keys, Such As Are The Most Familiar And Easy To Perform On The Clarinet, Oboe, Bassoon &c. Also A Number Of Easy Lessons For Young Practitioners*, page 27. Published by Daniel Steele, Bookseller, Court Street, Albany, NY. 1807. Printed by Manning & Loring, Boston, MA. 44pp. [W-6660].

• **AmPM-691 SUMNER, Charles** (Founder of the Free Soil Party, 1848; Candidate for U.S. House, 1848; U.S. Senator, 1851–1874)

691.1 *Charles Sumner*. w. No composer indicated. m. "Air – *The Harp That Once Through Tara's Halls*." "Lines suggested by observing the vacant chair of Senator Sumner, on a recent visit to the Capitol." In: *The Republican Campaign Songster, A Collection Of Lyrics, Original And Selected, Specifically Prepared For The Friends Of Freedom In The Campaign Of Fifty-Six*, page 88. Published by Miller, Orton & Mulligan, No. 25 Park Row, New York, NY. 1856. [3¹³⁄₁₆" × 6"]. Be/bk litho of "Colonel John C. Fremont" facing to viewer's left, black line border. 112pp. [M-097]. [Crew/JCF-24].

691.2 *Charles Sumner Funeral March*. m. E. Mack. Published by Lee & Walker, 922 Chestnut Street, Philadelphia, PA. 1874. B/w litho by Thos. Sinclair & Son, Philadelphia, of Charles Sumner, black geometric border, facsimile signature. 6pp. Page 2: Blank. Page 3: At top of music – "In Memoriam. 'There is a Reaper, whose name is Death, And with his sickle keen, He reaps the bearded grain at a breath, And the flowers that grow between – Longfellow.'" Page 6: Advertising.

691.3 *Charles Sumner Funeral March*. m. J.W. Turner. Published by Oliver Ditson & Co., 277 Washington Street, Boston, MA. 1874. B/w litho by J.H. Bufford's Sons, Boston, of Charles Sumner, black border. "In Memoriam." 6pp. Pages 2 and 6: Blank.

691.4 *A Dangerous Man*. w.m. No composer or tune indicated. "Mr. Sumner says Grant is a bold, bad, dangerous man. – *Newspaper*." In: *National Republican Grant And Wilson Campaign Song-Book*, page 14. Published by The Union Republican Congressional Committee, Washington, DC. 1872. [3¹³⁄₁₆" × 8⅝"]. Be/bk litho of Ulysses S. Grant. "We'll Sing a Song for U.S. Grant." 100pp. [M-182]. [Crew/USG-110].

691.5 *The Dawn Of Peace*. w.m. Samuel Jarden, Baltimore, Maryland. 1866. Non-pictorial geometric designs. "Respectfully Dedicated to President Johnson." 6pp. Pages 2 and 6: Blank. [Crew/AJN-27].

691.6 *De Nigger On De Fence*. w. No composer indicated. m. "Tune – *All Round My Hat*." In: *Copperhead Minstrel* (A Choice Collection of Democratic Poems & Songs), page 38. Published by Feeks and Bancker, Wholesale Agents, No. 24 Ann Street, New York. 1863. [4¾" × 7¼"]. O/bk non-pictorial. "For the use of Political Clubs and the Social Circle." "Price 25 cents." 64pp. [M-133] [Crew/GBM-64].

691.7 *De Nigger On De Fence*. w. No composer indicated. m. "Air – *All Round my Hat*." No publisher indicated. [ca. 1864]. H/c litho of two Black men. 2pp. Page 2: Blank. [AMC].

691.8 *For Abe Shall Have The Belt*. w. "S." m.a. Henry Tucker. In: *The Wide Awake Vocalist (Or Rail Splitters' Song Book)*, page 30. Published by E.A. Daggett, No. 333 Broadway, New York, NY. 1860. Non-pictorial geometric design border. "Words and Music for the Republican Campaign of 1860, Embracing a Great Variety of Songs, Solos, Duets and Choruses Arranged for Piano or melodeon; The best collection of Words and Music ever published for a campaign, Every Club and Family should have copies, so as to join in the choruses; The Ladies are invited to join in the choruses at the meetings." 68pp. [M-116]. [Crew/AL-59].

691.9 *A Fourth Of July Ode For The Freemen Of Fifty-Six*. m. "Air – *Scots Wha Hae*." In: *The Republican Campaign Songster, A Collection Of Lyrics, Original And Selected, Specifically Prepared For The Friends Of Freedom In The Campaign Of Fifty-Six*, page 13. Published by Miller, Orton & Mulligan, No. 25 Park Row, New York, NY. 1856. [3¹³⁄₁₆" × 6"]. Be/bk litho of "Colonel John C. Fremont" facing to viewer's left, black line border. 112pp. Pages 2, 111 and 112: Blank. Pages 109–110: Contents. [M-097]. [Crew/JCF-24].

691.10 *Free Soil Waltzes*. m. M.A.C. Published by Stephen W. Marsh, Piano Forte Maker and Music Store Dealer, No. 371 Washington Street, Boston, MA. 1848. Gd/bk/w litho of sunburst design. "Arranged for the Piano Forte." "Respectfully dedicated to Charles Sumner, Esq." "Price 25 cts. nett [sic]." 8pp. Pages 2 and 8: Blank. [Crew/MVB-11]. [LL/JH].

691.11 *Freedom's Call*. w. J.J.H. m. "Air – *Ellen Bayne*." In: *Connecticut Wide-Awake Songster*, page 33. e. John W. Hutchinson "(of Hutchinson Family Singers)" and Benjamin Jepson. Published by O. Hutchinson, Publisher, No. 272 Greenwich Street, New York, NY. 1860. [4" × 6"]. Bl/bk non-pictorial line border. "Lincoln and liberty." 76pp. Pages 2, 75 and 76: Advertising. Pages 5 and 6: Contents. Pages 7 to 10: Republican platform. [M-109]. [Crew/AL-175].

691.12 *Fremont And Dayton*. w. No composer indicated. m. "Air – *Yankee Doodle*." In: *The Freeman's Glee Book, A Collection Of Songs, Odes, Glees And Bal-*

lads With Music, Original And Selected, Harmonized And Arranged For Each. Published Under The Auspices Of The Central Fremont And Dayton Glee Club Of The City Of New York, And Dedicated To All, Who, Cherishing Republican Liberty Consider Freedom Worth A Song, page 70. Published by Miller, Orton & Mulligan, No. 25 Park Row, New York, NY. [and Auburn, NY]. 1856. [4¹⁵⁄₁₆" × 6"]. Pk/bk litho of man on mountain peak, music sheets, geometric designs. 112pp. [Crew/JCF-16].

691.13 Gen Lee, Is Pretty Good Looking (But He Can't Come To Maryland). w. No composer indicated. m. "Air—*Oh, Carry Me Back To Old Virginia*." No publisher indicated. [1862–1863]. [Approx. 6" × 9½"]. B/w litho of a military man, geometric design border. 2pp. Page 2: Blank. [AMC].

691.14 [Grant Is The Man Will Surely Win] (Campaign Song). w. No composer indicated. m. "Air—*Old Tip's The Boy*." In: *National Republican Grant And Wilson Campaign Song-Book*, page 29. Published by The Union Republican Congressional Committee, Washington, DC. 1872. [3¹³⁄₁₆" × 8⁵⁄₁₆"]. Be/bk litho of Ulysses S. Grant. "We'll Sing a Song for U.S. Grant." 100pp. [M-182]. [Crew/USG-110].

691.15 Grant's Victory. w. Mrs. Jennie M. Cutter. m. "Air—*Marching Through Georgia*." In: *Grant And Wilson Campaign Songster*, page 14. Published by Frank Eastman, Book and Job Printer, No. 509 Clay Street, San Francisco, CA. [4¼" × 5⅝"]. 1872. Bk/bl geometric design border. 40pp. [Crew/USG-69].

691.16 The Greeley Pill. w. No composer indicated. m. "Air—*The Mistletoe Bough*." "Mixed at Cincinnati and taken to Baltimore." "Sung by the Union Glee Club at a Grant Republican rally at Cooper Institute." Published in the *New York Times*, September 26, 1872. [VBL, p. 456].

691.17 The Gudgeon Of Democracy And The Southern Ark. w. No composer indicated. m. "Air—*The Cruel Troopers Riding By*." In: *The Republican Campaign Songster, A Collection Of Lyrics, Original And Selected, Specifically Prepared For The Friends Of Freedom In The Campaign Of Fifty-Six*, page 7. Published by Miller, Orton & Mulligan, No. 25 Park Row, New York, NY. 1856. [3¹³⁄₁₆" × 6"]. Be/bk litho of "Colonel John C. Fremont" facing to viewer's left, black line border. 112pp. [M-097]. [Crew/JCF-24].

691.18 Hurrah For The Man We Love. "Air—*Vive L'Amour*." In: *McClellan And Liberty* [Song Sheet]. Published by Frank McElroy, No. 113 Nassau Street, New York, NY. 1864. [7" × 17"]. Non-pictorial. "Stand by the Union and I'll Stand by you." "The Work before us; To suppress the Rebellion, To preserve the Union, To maintain the sovereignty of the People!" "Let us apply ourselves to the duty of uniting all the conservative elements of the country, in the effort to place in the Presidential Chair a man who will revere the Constitution as his highest political authority—Such a man is George B. McClellan." "The following is ... from a recent letter of the Hon. Amos Kendall: I am losing my patience in reading Gen. McClellan's report. The injustice to him, and the atrocious wrong to his noble army and the country, are enough to make the blood of honest and patriotic men boil within them." 2pp. [Crew/GBM-61].

691.19 I Go Straight Ulysses. w. No composer indicated. m. "Air—*How Are You, Horace Greeley*." "Columbia S.C., July, 1872." In: *National Republican Grant And Wilson Campaign Song-Book*, page 87. Published by The Union Republican Congressional Committee, Washington, DC. 1872. [3¹³⁄₁₆" × 8⁵⁄₁₆"]. Be/bk litho of Ulysses S. Grant. "We'll Sing a Song for U.S. Grant." 100pp. [M-182]. [Crew/USG-110].

691.20 Impeachment Song. w.m. L.A. Dochez. Published in New York, NY. 1868. Non-pictorial. 4pp. Page 4: Blank. [Crew/AJN-14].

691.21 John Brown's Entrance Into Hell. w.m. Non-pictorial. No composers or tune indicated. No publisher indicated. [ca. 1861–1865]. 2pp. Page 2: Blank. [AMC].

691.22 March Funebre. m. A.E. Warren. Published by Oliver Ditson & Co., 277 Washington Street, Boston, MA. 1874. B/w litho by J.H. Bufford's Sons, Boston, of Charles Sumner, black border. "In Memoriam."

691.23 March Sumner. m. Ophelia Watts Jackson. Published by Ophelia Watts Jackson, Kansas City, MO. 1929. B/w photo of "Charles Sumner School." Bl/w geometric designs. 6pp. Pages 2 and 6: Blank. Page 3: At top of music—"Affectionately dedicated to the girls and boys of the Public Schools of Greater Kansas City."

691.24 My God! What Is All This For? w. No composer indicated. m. "Air—*Rosseau's Dream*." No publisher indicated. [1861–1862]. [V-1: B/w geometric design border] [V-2: Pk/bk line border]. "The above is the dying words of a Federal soldier on the Battle field of Manassas, 1861." 2pp. Page 2: Blank. [V-1: AMC] [V-2: WFU].

691.25 Niggers In Convention (Sumner's Speech). w.m. No composer or tune indicated. No publisher indicated. [186-]. Non-pictorial black line border. 2pp. Page 2: Blank. [AMC].

691.26 Oh! Abraham Resign! w. "A New Contributor." m. No tune indicated. No publisher indicated. [ca. 1861]. [Approx. 6" × 10"]. Gn/bk non-pictorial. 2pp. Page 2: Blank. [WFU].

691.27 Old Men's Grant Meeting. w. No composer indicated. m. "Air—*Bennie Havens, O!*" In: *National Republican Grant And Wilson Campaign Song-Book*, page 39. From the *New York Standard*. Published by The Union Republican Congressional Committee, Washington, DC. 1872. [3¹³⁄₁₆" × 8⁵⁄₁₆"]. Be/bk litho of Ulysses S. Grant. "We'll Sing a Song for U.S. Grant." 100pp. [M-182]. [Crew/USG-110].

691.28 The Old White Hat. w. No composer indicated. m. "Air—*When This Old Hat Was New*." In: *National Republican Grant And Wilson Campaign Song-Book*, page 42. From the *Chattanooga Herald*. Published by The Union Republican Congressional Committee, Washington, DC. 1872. [3¹³⁄₁₆" × 8⁵⁄₁₆"]. Be/bk litho of Ulysses S. Grant. "We'll Sing a Song for U.S. Grant." 100pp. [M-182]. [Crew/USG-110].

691.29 Patent Chivalry. w. No composer indicated. m. "Air—*A Highland Lad My Love Was Born*." In: *Fremont Songs For The People (Original And Selected)*, page 39. c. Thomas Drew "(Editor of *The Massachusetts Spy*)." Published by John P. Jewett & Company, Boston, MA. Copyright 1856 by Thomas Drew. [3⅝"

× 5½"]. B/w litho of "J.C. Fremont." "The Campaign of 1856." 68pp. [Crew/JCF-18].

691.30 The People's Candidate. w. No composer indicated. m. "Air—*A Wet Sheet And A Flowing Sea.*" In: *The Republican Campaign Songster For 1860*, page 46. c. W.H. Burleigh. Published by [V-1 and V-2: H. Dayton, No. 36 Howard Street, New York, NY] [V-3: McNally & Company, No. 81 Dearborn Street, Chicago, IL]. 1860. [V-1: Gn/bk] [V-2: Y/bk] [V-3: Be/bk] [V-4: Bl/bk]. "Price 10 cents." [3$^{13}/_{16}$" × 6"]. 72pp. [M-104]. [Crew/AL-57].

691.31 The President's Ball. w. No composer indicated. m. "Air—*Lannegan's Ball.*" Published by H. De Marsan, 54 Chatham Street, New York, NY. [1860–1862]. [Approx. 6" × 9"]. B/w litho border of theatrical-type figures, leaves, lion's head, stars. "Sung by Joe English." 2pp. Page 2: Blank. [AMC].

691.32 Rally Round The Standard. w. N.G. Sawyer. m. No tune indicated. In: *Grant And Wilson Campaign Songster*, page 26. Published by Frank Eastman, Book and Job Printer, No. 509 Clay Street, San Francisco, CA. [4¼" × 5⅝"]. 1872. Bk/bl geometric design border. 40pp. [Crew/USG-69].

691.33 The Sale Of Kansas. m. No composer indicated. m. "Air—*Villikens And His Dinah.*" In: *Fillmore And Donelson Songs For The Campaign* (Songster), page 23. Published by Robert M. De Witt, Nos. 160 and 162 Nassau Street, New York, NY. November 4, 1856. [4¾" × 7⅛"]. Bl/bk litho of George Washington—"July 4, 1776," wreath, geometric design border. "This is the only authorized edition containing Duganne's Songs. Price 6 cts. each, $4 per 100. Discount to trade." Long quote from George Washington's "Farewell Address." 40pp. [M-101, 102]. [Crew/MF-10].

691.34 So Come Along And Swell Out The Tune. w. No composer indicated. m. "Air—*So Come Along.*" In: *National Republican Grant And Wilson Campaign Song-Book*, page 18. Published by The Union Republican Congressional Committee, Washington, DC. 1872. [3$^{13}/_{16}$" × 8$^{9}/_{16}$"]. Be/bk litho of Ulysses S. Grant. "We'll Sing a Song for U.S. Grant." 100pp. [M-182]. [Crew/USG-110].

691.35 Strike Together. w. No composer indicated. m. "Air—*Men Of Labor.*" "Forget, forgive, unite—Whittier." In: *The Freeman's Glee Book, A Collection Of Songs, Odes, Glees And Ballads With Music, Original And Selected, Harmonized And Arranged For Each. Published Under The Auspices Of The Central Fremont And Dayton Glee Club Of The City Of New York, And Dedicated To All, Who, Cherishing Republican Liberty Consider Freedom Worth A Song*, page 79. Published by Miller, Orton & Mulligan, No. 25 Park Row, New York, NY. [and Auburn, NY]. 1856. [4$^{15}/_{16}$" × 6"]. Pk/bk litho of man on mountain peak, music sheets, geometric designs. 112pp. [Crew/JCF-16].

691.36 Sumner's Funeral March. m. Frederic H. Pease. Published by A.H. Brown, Jackson, MI. 1874. B/w litho of Charles Sumner, black border. 6pp. Page 2: Advertising. Page 6: Blank.

691.37 Sumner's Funeral March. m. J.W. Turner. Published by G.D. Russell & Co., 126 Tremont Street, Boston, MA. 1874. B/w non-pictorial geometric designs, line black border. "To The Memory Of Hon. Charles Sumner." 6pp. Pages 2 and 6: Blank.

691.38 Sumner With His Whiskers. w. Bob Hart. m. "Tune—*Captain With His Whiskers.*" No publisher indicated, probably Philadelphia. [1861–1862]. [Approx. 6" × 9"]. Non-pictorial geometric designs. "Bob Hart's Latest! Sung Nightly at the Academy of Music." 2pp. Page 2: Blank. [AMC].

691.39 Take Of [sic] ***Your Coats, Boys.*** w. No composer indicated. . "Air—*The Other Side Of Jordan.*" In: *The Wide Awake Vocalist (Or Rail Splitters' Song Book)*, page 55. Published by E.A. Daggett, No. 333 Broadway, New York, NY. 1860. Non-pictorial geometric design border. "Words and Music for the Republican Campaign of 1860, Embracing a Great Variety of Songs, Solos, Duets and Choruses Arranged for Piano or melodeon; The best collection of Words and Music ever published for a campaign, Every Club and Family should have copies, so as to join in the choruses; The Ladies are invited to join in the choruses at the meetings." 68pp. [M-116]. [Crew/AL-59].

691.40 To Our New Friend, The Old Democrat, H.G. w. No composer indicated. m. "Air—*The Groves Of Blarney.*" From the "*New York Times*, July 23, 1872." In: *National Republican Grant And Wilson Campaign Song-Book*, page 47. Published by The Union Republican Congressional Committee, Washington, DC. 1872. [3$^{13}/_{16}$" × 8$^{9}/_{16}$"]. Be/bk litho of Ulysses S. Grant. "We'll Sing a Song for U.S. Grant." 100pp. [M-182]. [Crew/USG-110].

691.41 Treason's Fate. w. S.N. Holmes. m. "Tune—*A Thousand Years*, &c." In: *The Republican Campaign Song Book, With Music, 1892*, page 15. e. Samuel Newall Holmes. Published by Samuel Newall Holmes, Syracuse, NY. 1892. Be/bk non-pictorial. "Composed and especially prepared by Judge S.N. Holmes of Syracuse, N.Y." "Headquarters: Syracuse, N.Y." "Price twenty-five cents." 60pp. [M-308]. [Crew/BFH-107].

691.42 Uncle Sam Consumpted! (What Will Cure Him?) (A National Song). w. No composer indicated. m. "Tune—*Yankee Doodle.*" Published by Mills, Printer. [18—]. Non-pictorial border. "Every body should use Anker's Pulmonic Tar Drops. The cure Coughs, Colds, Hoarseness and Bad Breath, so disagreeable to every one with whom its possessor comes in contact. They cost but Ten Cents A Package. Give them a trial. For sale by all Druggists and Confectioneries. N.B. Be cautious to ask for Anker's Pulmonic Tar Drops, and pay no more than 10 cents for a package." 2pp. Page 2: Blank. [AMC].

691.43 The Veto Galop! m. "Make Peace." Published by McCarrell & Mininger, No. 91 West Jefferson Street, Louisville, KY. 1866. B/w litho by Bennett, Donaldson & Elmes of "Andy" Johnson holding a document inscribed "Veto" and riding a horse named "Constitution," men labeled "Dead Ducks," including "W. Phillips," "Wade," "Stevens, "Fr. Douglass," "Freedmans Bureau;" Crowd cheering—"Hurrah for Andy," "See the Lame Ducks." Litho of building in the background—"Forney & Co., Dealers in Game." 6pp. Pages 2 and 6: Blank. [Crew/AJN-17].

691.44 Virginia's Knocking Around. w.m. No composers or tune indicated. Published in Baltimore, MD. March 30, 1862. Non-pictorial. 2pp. Page 2: Blank. [AMC].

691.45 Viva La Companie. w. No composer or tune

indicated. In: *Grant And Wilson Campaign Songster*, page 16. Published by Frank Eastman, Book and Job Printer, No. 509 Clay Street, San Francisco, CA. [4¼" × 5⅝"]. 1872. Bk/bl geometric design border. 40pp. [Crew/USG-69].

691.46 We Can Hoe The Rows. w. No composer indicated. m. "Air—*Kingdom Coming.*" From the *Missouri Democrat.* In: *National Republican Grant And Wilson Campaign Song-Book*, page 45. Published by The Union Republican Congressional Committee, Washington, DC. 1872. [3¹³⁄₁₆" × 8⁵⁄₁₆"]. Be/bk litho of Ulysses S. Grant. "We'll Sing a Song for U.S. Grant." 100pp. [M-182]. [Crew/USG-110].

691.47 We'll Vote For General G. w. No composer indicated. m. "Air—*Little Brown Jug.*" In: *National Republican Grant And Wilson Campaign Song-Book*, page 79. Published by The Union Republican Congressional Committee, Washington, DC. 1872. [3¹³⁄₁₆" × 8⁵⁄₁₆"]. Be/bk litho of Ulysses S. Grant. "We'll Sing a Song for U.S. Grant." 100pp. [M-182]. [Crew/USG-110].

691.48 The White House. w. G.R. Edeson. m. "Air—*Root, Hog, Or Die!*" Published by H. De Marsan, 54 Chatham Street, New York, NY. [1861–1862]. B/w litho border of minstrels, geometric designs. 2pp. Page 2: Blank. [AMC].

691.49 Wide-Awake Club Song. w. No composer indicated. m. "Air—*A Wet Sheet And A Flowing Sea.*" In: *Connecticut Wide-Awake Songster*, page 70. e. John W. Hutchinson "(of Hutchinson Family Singers)" and Benjamin Jepson. Published by O. Hutchinson, Publisher, No. 272 Greenwich Street, New York, NY. 1860. [4" × 6"]. Bl/bk non-pictorial line border. "Lincoln and liberty." 76pp. [M-109]. [Crew/AL-175].

691.50 Will You Ever Give The Colored Race A Show? (An Appeal To Congress). w.m. Robert P. Jackson. Copyright 1898? by Robert P. Jackson, 3143 Dearborn Street, Chicago, IL. B/w photos of Abraham "Lincoln—The Shackles Fell 1863," Charles "Sumner—The Original Champion of the Slaves 1856," William "McKinley—Prosperity 1896." Photo of Robert P. Jackson. Drawing of soldiers marching labeled "The U.S. 25th Inft. Colored Soldiers, the first called on to fight to free Cuba," "white laborers going to work" at a factory labeled "Prosperity & at peace with all nations," "Negroes waiting" behind a "Color Line." 6pp. Page 2: Narrative on "The Negro In The Field Of Labor." Page 6: Blank. [Crew/WM-341]

691.51 Wilson And Grant. w. N.G. Sawyer. m. "Tune—*Whip-Poor-Will's Call.*" In: *Grant And Wilson Campaign Songster*, page 15. Published by Frank Eastman, Book and Job Printer, No. 509 Clay Street, San Francisco, CA. [4¼" × 5⅝"]. 1872. Bk/bl geometric design border. 40pp. [Crew/USG-69].

691.52 Wilson And Grant. w.m. No composer or tune indicated. In: *National Republican Grant And Wilson Campaign Song-Book*, page 26. Published by The Union Republican Congressional Committee, Washington, DC. 1872. [3¹³⁄₁₆" × 8⁵⁄₁₆"]. Be/bk litho of Ulysses S. Grant. "We'll Sing a Song for U.S. Grant." 100pp. [M-182]. [Crew/USG-110].

691.53 Witches' Scene From MacGreeley (Which is Seen to be a Fact). w.m. No composer or tune indicated. From the "*New York Standard.*" In: *National Republican Grant And Wilson Campaign Song-Book*, page 34. From the "*New York Standard.*" Published by The Union Republican Congressional Committee, Washington, DC. 1872. [3¹³⁄₁₆" × 8⁵⁄₁₆"]. Be/bk litho of Ulysses S. Grant. "We'll Sing a Song for U.S. Grant." 100pp. [M-182]. [Crew/USG-110].

691.54 Yan-Kee-Dom! (Or The Times). w. No composer indicated. m. "Air—*Times And Fashion.*" Published by Harrison's Book Store, Post Office Avenue, Second Street. [185-]. [Approx. 6" × 10"]. Non-pictorial geometric design border. "As sung by Dick Watkins at all the principal Concerts in the City." [AMC].

• **AmPM-692 TALBOT**, Thomas (State House, 1861–1864; Governor's Council, 1864–1869; Lt. Governor, 1872–1874; Governor, 1874–1875 & 1879–1880)

692.1 Gov. Talbot's Grand March. m. Chas. D. Blake "(Author of *Clayton's Grand March, Shepherd's Evening Song*, &c.)." Published by White, Smith & Company, 516 Washington Street, Boston, MA. 1878. B/w litho of Thomas Talbot. "To his Excellency." 6pp. Page 6: Blank.

692.2 Oh No, Ben! (Republican Campaign Song). w.m. Edward H. Phelps. Published by Edward H. Phelps, Springfield, MA. 1878. Non-pictorial. 2pp. "Price 5 Cents, 35 Copies for $1.00; 200 Copies for $2.00." Page 2: Blank. [Crew/BFB-28]. [AMC].

• **AmPM-693 TOBIN**, Maurice J. (State House, 1926–1928; School Committee, Boston, 1931–1937; Mayor, Boston, 1938–1944; Governor, 1945–1947; U.S. Secretary of Labor, 1948–1953)

693.1 Danny-Me-Lamb. w.m. Jack Conley. Published by Regal Publications, 1260 North King Street, West Hollywood, CA. 1945. Gn/w drawing of a sailor waving good-bye to woman, soldiers in parade in the background. "Dedicated to Brother Elk Governor Maurice J. Tobin." 6pp. Page 6: Advertising.

• **AmPM-694 TRASH**, Eliphalet (Mayor, Springfield, 1856)

694.1 Springfield City Hall Polka. m. G.F. Robbins. Published by Henry Tolman, 153 Washington Street, Boston, MA. 1856. B/w litho of the Springfield, Massachusetts, City Hall. "As played by the Springfield Brass Band at the Dedication, Jan. 1st, 1856." "Composed & arranged for the Piano Forte by G.F. Robbins and respectfully dedicated to Mayor Eliphalet Trash." 6pp. Pages 2 and 6: Blank.

• **AmPM-695 TSONGAS**, Paul Efthemios (Peace Corps Volunteer, 1962–1964 & 1967–1968; State Deputy Assistant Attorney General, 1969–1971; City Councilor, Lowell, 1969–1972; County Commissioner, Middlesex County, 1973–1974; U.S. House, 1975-January 3, 1979; U.S. Senate, 1979–1985; Candidate for Democratic Presidential nomination, 1992)

695.1 The Tsounds Of Tsongas. w. Bill Strauss and Elaina Newport. On CD: *Fools On The Hill.* Published by Capitol Steps Productions, 1505 King Street, Alexandria, VA. #CSCD-1011. 1992. CD Cover: N/c Capitol building.

• **AmPM-696 WALSH**, David Ignatius (State House, 1900–1901; Lt. Governor, 1913; Governor, 1914–1915; U.S. Senate, 1919–1925 & 1926–1947)

696.1 When Massachusetts Heads The Line. w.m. James E. Fitzgerald. Published by James E. Fitzgerald,

Boston, MA. 1914. B/w photo of "Governor David. I. Walsh." Bl/w ribbon inscribed Ense Petit Placidam Sub Libertate Quietem." "Massachusetts led in Revolutionery [sic] times: The first man killed in the Civil War was a Massachusetts man: The first man killed at Vera Cruz, Mexico, was a Massachusetts and: Governor Martin H. Glynn, of New York, addressing the members of the Massachusetts Legislature, in the spring of 1914 said — 'The Country expects Massachusetts to lead the way.'" "Dedicated to His Excellency Governor Davis I. Walsh." 4pp. Page 4: Blank.

• AmPM-697 WANAMAKER, John (U.S. Postmaster General, 1889–1893)

697.1 Columbia My Country (American Anthem). w.m. George M. Vickers "(Composer of *Guard The Flag, God Bless Our Land*, &c)." [ca. 1893]. Bl/w litho of Miss Columbia, two women, steamboat. "The New Patriotic Song Approved by People from New England to Alaska." "The sentiment of this song will, I am sure, be indorsed by every true American — William McKinley; Full of Patriotic sentiment, well expressed — Governor Wm. E. Russell, Massachusetts; It is patriotic in sentiment and the music is charming, Governor J.M. Stone, Mississippi; It is a patriotic gem and will probably remain one of the patriotic songs of our country — Governor Elisha P. Ferry, Washington; I trust it may be welcomed by an appreciative public with the favour it deserves — Gen. Lyman E. Knapp, Alaska; I regard such music as a important part of the education of the young people of the land — Hon. John Wanamaker, and representative Americans in all parts of the United States." 4pp. Page 2: Facsimile letter releasing copyright. Page 4: Blank.

697.2 Der Leedle Shop Of Ben And Levi. w. No composer indicated. m. Notation. "Male Voices." In: *Red Hot Democratic Campaign Songs For 1892*, page 6. c. John Bunyon Herbert. Published by The S. Brainard's Sons Company, Chicago, IL. 1892. [5½" × 7¼"]. R/bk litho of Grover Cleveland on a banner, Capitol building, marchers, geometric design border. 36pp. [M-299]. [Crew/GC-82].

697.3 He's Talking Thro' His Hat. w.m. W.R. Williams. Published by Will Rossiter, 204 Dearborn Street, Chicago, IL. 1891. Bl/w non-pictorial. "A Great Comic Song." "Just Tell Them I Said So!" List of other titles available form publisher. 6pp. Page 2: Blank. Page 6: Advertising.

697.4 Where Are The Old Folks (Song And Chorus). w. Fanny Crosby. m. John R. Sweeney. Published by Jno. P. Dougherty, 530 Market Street, Chester, PA. 1882. B/w non-pictorial geometric designs. "To my friend, Jno. Wanamaker, Esq. 6pp.

• AmPM-698 WARD, Artemas (Chief Justice of the Court of Common Pleas, Worcester County, 1776–1777; State Executive Council, 1777–1779; State House, 1779–1785, Continental Congress, 1780–1781; U.S. House, 1791–1795)

698.1 The Bill-Poster's Dream (Or Cross Readings). w. No composer indicated. m. "Air — *The Captain With His Whiskers*." Published by H. De Marsan, Publisher, 54 Chatham Street, New York, NY. [ca. 1859]. [Approx. 6" × 9½"]. B/w litho border of four characters intertwined with star-studded ribbon, floral and geometric designs. 2pp. Page 2: Blank. [AMC].

698.2 Washington (A Favorite New Song in the American Camp). w. [Jonathan Mitchell]. m. "British Grenadier. [1776?]. B/w woodblock of George Washington, Artemas Ward. "Printed and sold next the Bell-Tavern, Danvers." "Cash paid for rags." 2pp. Page 2: Blank. [VBL, p. 63].

• AmPM-699 WEBSTER, Daniel (U.S. House, New Hampshire, 1813–1817 & Massachusetts, 1823–1827; U.S. Senate, Massachusetts, 1827–1841 & 1845–1850; U.S. Secretary of State, 1841–1843 & 1850–1852) [ALSO SEE: DOC/PSM-DW]

699.1 All Along The Line (Labor-Song With Chorus In Marching Time). w.m. N. Graver. Published by Willis Woodward & Co., New York, NY. 1884. Non-pictorial geometric and floral designs. Quotations from Longfellow and Daniel Webster — "Labor is one of the great elements of society." 6pp. Page 2: "Dedicated to Mr. Edward Sellew." Page 6: Blank. [Crew/DW-37].

699.2 Beggar's Petition. w. No composer indicated. m. "Tune — *All On Hobbies*." "A very pathetic and musical appeal to the Dear People, by an Ex-Postmaster General." In: *Tippecanoe Song-Book (A Collection Of Log Cabin And Patriotic Melodies)*, page 14. Published by Marshall, Williams & Butler, Philadelphia, PA. 1840. White on black litho of log cabin, plow, flags, eagle. 180pp. [M-024]. [Crew/WHH-61].

699.3 Bunker-Hill Battle (A Song for June 17, 1843). w.m. No composer or tune indicated. No publisher indicated. [1843]. Non-pictorial. 2pp. Page 2: Blank. [AMC].

699.4 Cling To The Union. w. No composer indicated. m. "Air — *Wait For The Wagon*." Published by Johnson, Song Publisher, No. 7 N. Tenth Street, [Philadelphia, PA]. [1850–1860]. B/w non-pictorial geometric design litho border." 2pp. Page 2: Blank. [AMC].

699.5 Doctor Greeley (A Campaign Song). w. George Alfred Townsend. m. "Air — *The Umbareller*." "Whoo-hoop For Horace!" "Baltimore, Md., May 11, 1872." In: *The Sun's Greeley Campaign Songster*, page 4. c. Amos J. Cumming. Published from *The Sun* Office, New York, NY. 1872. [4⅛" × 6½"]. Be/bk litho of Horace Greeley, wreath. "He shines for all." 64pp. [Crew/HG-5].

699.6 Empire Song (The Old Granite State). w. "By the President of the Club." m. *The Old Granite State*. [1852]. B/w litho of an eagle holding a ribbon inscribed "E Pluribus Unum," geometric design border. 2pp. Page 2: Blank.

699.7 Heads We Win — Tails You Lose. w. No composer indicated. m. "Air — *Dearest May*." "The delightful game suggested by Millard Fillmore to the South, in his celebrated Albany Speech." "By permission of O. Ditson." In: *The Freeman's Glee Book, A Collection Of Songs, Odes, Glees And Ballads With Music, Original And Selected, Harmonized And Arranged For Each. Published Under The Auspices Of The Central Fremont And Dayton Glee Club Of The City Of New York, And Dedicated To All, Who, Cherishing Republican Liberty Consider Freedom Worth A Song*, page 52. Published by Miller, Orton & Mulligan, No. 25 Park Row, New York, NY. [and Auburn, NY]. 1856. [4¹⁵⁄₁₆" × 6"]. Pk/bk litho of man on mountain peak, music sheets, geometric designs. 112pp. [Crew/JCF-16].

699.8 Here's A Health To The Free Born. w. Alonzo Lewis, Esq., "of Lynn, Mass." m. "Tune—*Young Lochinvar.*" "Written for the Young Men's National Convention, at Baltimore, May 4, 1840." In: *Tippecanoe Song-Book (A Collection Of Log Cabin And Patriotic Melodies)*, page 153. Published by Marshall, Williams & Butler, Philadelphia, PA. 1840. White on black litho of log cabin, plow, flags, eagle. 180pp. [M-024]. [Crew/WHH-61].

699.9 The Knight Of The Box. w.m. No composer or tune indicated. In: *Greeley Campaign Songster*, page 18. Published by Halpin & McClure, Chicago, IL. 1872. [4" × 5 11/16"]. Pl/bk litho of Horace Greeley, geometric design border. "Chicago: Western News Company, Wholesale Agents." 72pp. [M-187]. [Crew/HG-21].

699.10 The Last Rebel Yell. w. George Alfred Townsend. m. No tune indicated. "Whoo-hoop For Horace!" In: *The Sun's Greeley Campaign Songster*, page 3. c. Amos J. Cumming. Published from *The Sun* Office, New York, NY. 1872. [4⅛" × 6½"]. Be/bk litho of Horace Greeley, wreath. "He shines for all." 64pp. [Crew/HG-5].

699.11 Liberty And Union. w. C.B. Barr. m. J.T. Wamelink. Published by Wamelink & Barr, Pittsburgh, PA. 1864. B/w litho of an arch labeled "Liberty"—"Union"—"Law"—"Independence," eagle, crossed flags, Miss Liberty, globe. Long quote by Daniel Webster ending—"...Liberty & Union, now and forever, one and inseparable." 8pp. Pages 2 and 8: Blank. [Crew/DW-39]

699.12 Lincoln's Picture. w. John Quod, Jr. m. No tune indicated. In: *The Democratic Campaign Songster: Douglas & Johnson Melodies*, page 22."Written in behalf of several leading Republicans, and respectfully submitted to the party, by John Quod, Jr." Published by P.J. Cozans, Publisher, New York, NY. [1860]. [3⅞" × 6"]. Y/bk litho of an eagle with ribbon—"Douglas & Johnson," train, ships, monument—"Liberty" sitting on rock base—"The Constitution." 40pp. [M-117]. [Crew/SAD-5].

699.13 My Cigar. w. "By a Virginia Merchant." m. No tune indicated. Published by L. Deming, wholesale and retail, North Hanover Street, 2d door from Federal Street, Boston, MA. [ca. 1840]. B/w litho of an Indian holding a tobacco leaf and standing next to a barrel marked "Best Virginia." Followed on page 1 by another song—Journeyman Tailor." 2pp. Page 2: Blank. [AMC].

699.14 My Heart's In New England. w. No composer indicated. m. "Air—*I Think Of Old Ireland.*" In: *Beadle's Dime Knapsack Songster: Containing The Choicest Patriotic Songs, Together With Many New And Original Ones, Set To Old Melodies*, page 69. Published by Beadle and Company, No. 141 William Street, New York, NY. 1862. [3¾" × 5¾"]. Litho of coin—"One Dime, United States of America." 74pp. [Crew/GBM-78].

699.15 The North Is Discovered! w. No composer indicated. m. "Air—*The Star Spangled Banner.*" In: *The Republican Campaign Songster, A Collection Of Lyrics, Original And Selected, Specifically Prepared For The Friends Of Freedom In The Campaign Of Fifty-Six*, page 3. Published by Miller, Orton & Mulligan, No. 25 Park Row, New York, NY. 1856. [3 13/16" × 6"]. Be/bk litho of "Colonel John C. Fremont" facing to viewer's left, black line border. 112pp. [M-097]. [Crew/JCF-24].

699.16 Old Abe And His Fights. w. No composer indicated. m. "Air—*Roger De Coverly.*" In: *The Great Republican Campaigns Of 1860 And 1896*, page 175. e. Osborn H. Oldroyd. Published by Laird & Lee, Chicago, IL. 1896. [5 5/16" × 7 7/16"]. Gn/r/bk photos of Abraham Lincoln, William McKinley and Garrett Hobart. "Sound Money, Protection, Prosperity." 208pp. [Crew/AL-574].

699.17 Old Abe And His Fights. w. No composer indicated. m. "Air—*Roger De Coverly.*" Published in the *New York Herald*, August 30, 1860. [VBL, p. 343].

699.18 The President's Conscience. w. W.A. m. "Tune—*The West Countryman.*" In: *Original Clay Songs: Humorous And Sentimental, Designed To Inculcate Just Political Sentiments, To Suit The Present Political Crisis, And To Advocate The Claims Of Henry Clay To The Highest Honors His Country Can Bestow*, page 3. w. W.A. Philomath, Union Co., Ind. Published by Philomath, Cincinnati, OH. 1842. [4¼" × 6"]. Be/bk litho of an eagle, U.S. Flag. "The eagle soars above the throng; And listen's [sic] to fair Freedom's song, Hails the merry roundelay, Claps his glad wings and hails the day." 20pp. Page 20: Be/bk litho of four men—"Tyler Expounding the Constitution! The effect of 'treading in the footsteps.'" [M-057]. [CrewHC-104].

699.19 Song Of The Pauper. w. No composer indicated. m. "Tune—*Up Salt River.*" "As sung by the late P.M.G." In: *Songs For The People (Or Tippecanoe Melodies)* [Songster], page 46. "Dedicated to the Democratic Whig Young Men of the City and County of New York." Published for the Authors by James P. Giffing, No. 56 Gold Street, New York, NY. 1840. [3¾" × 6"]. Litho of William Henry Harrison, log cabin, flag. "Original and Selected." 76pp. [M-019]. [Crew/WHH-63].

699.20 The Statesman's Dirge. w. Rev. Chas. W. Denison. m. Mrs. Mary A. Denison. Published by E.H. Wade, No. 197 Washington Street, Boston, MA. [ca. 1861]. B/w litho by Tappan & Bradford's of Daniel Webster, flags, urn, geometric design border. "Arranged for the Piano-Forte, and dedicated to the Family and Friends of Daniel Webster." [Crew/DW-38].

699.21 [There's A Winding Trail Through Our History]. w. Mrs. W.W. Remington. m. "To the tune of *The Barefoot Trail.*" In: *Patriotic Songs*, page 5. Published by The Republican Woman's Club of Minneapolis, Minneapolis, MN. 1920. [3 11/16" × 6"]. Bl/bl drawing of elephant. "Republican Campaign 1920." 8pp. Page 2: "Republican Standard Bearers For President—Warren G. Harding of Ohio, For Vice-President Calvin Coolidge of Massachusetts." "America First." [Crew/WGH-47].

699.22 A Trader's Lyric. w.m. No composer or tune indicated. In: *Copperhead Minstrel* "(A Choice Collection of Democratic Poems & Songs)," page 6. Published by Feeks and Bancker, Wholesale Agents, No. 24 Ann Street, New York. 1863. [4¾" × 7¼"]. O/bk non-pictorial. "For the use of Political Clubs and the Social Circle." "Price 25 cents." 64pp. [M-133] [Crew/GBM-64].

699.23 The Union For Ever For Me. w.m. No composer or tune indicated. Published by H. De Marsan, 54 Chatham Street, New York, NY. B/w litho border of military and naval war scenes. H. De Marsan, Publisher, Songs, Ballads, Toy Books, paper dolls, small playing cards, motto verses, &c." 2pp. Page 2: Blank. [AMC].

699.24 Union Of The Whigs. w. No composer indicated. m. "Air—*The Shamrock.*" "Sung at the opening of the Dorchester Whig Association." In: *Log Cabin Minstrel (Or Tippecanoe Songster)*, page 6. c. "A Member of the Roxbury Whig Association." Published at the *Patriot And Democrat* Office, Roxbury, [MA]. 1840. [4½" × 6¾"]. [V-1:Y/bk] [V-2: Bl/bk] litho of William Henry Harrison, geometric design border. "Old Tip's the boy to swing the flail. Hurrah! Hurrah! Hurrah!" 64pp. Page 3: Title page—"Containing a Selection of Songs Original and Selected Many of them Written Expressly for this Work, Compiled, Published and Arranged by a member of the Roxbury Democratic Whig Association and Respectfully Dedicated to the Log Cabin Boys of the U.S." [M-013]. [Crew/WHH-71].

699.25 The Union Wagon. w. No composer indicated. m. "Air—*Wait For The Wagon.*" In: *Fillmore And Donelson Songs For The Campaign* (Songster), page 12. Published by Robert M. De Witt, Nos. 160 and 162 Nassau Street, New York, NY. November 4, 1856. [4¾" × 7⅛"]. Bl/bk litho of George Washington—"July 4, 1776," wreath, geometric design border. "This is the only authorized edition containing Duganne's Songs. Price 6 cts. each, $4 per 100. Discount to trade." Long quote from George Washington's "Farewell Address." 40pp. Page 3: "Union and Peace." [M-101, 102]. [Crew/MF-10].

699.26 Webster's Quick Step. Published by F.D. Benteen, Baltimore, MD. [ca. 184-]. Non-pictorial geometric designs. "Evenings At Home, A Collection of Popular & Admired Airs arranged as Duetts for two performers on the Piano Forte." List of titles in the series. [Crew/DW-40].

699.27 Webster's Funeral March. m. L.V. Beethoven. Published by Oliver Ditson Company, Boston, MA. [ca. 1900]. B/w non-pictorial geometric design border. "Choice Instrumental Music." List of other titles in the series. [Crew/DW-41].

699.28 What's His Name? w.m. No composer or tune indicated. In: *The Sun's Greeley Campaign Songster*, page 5. c. Amos J. Cumming. Published from *The Sun* Office, New York, NY. 1872. [4⅛" × 6½"]. Be/bk litho of Horace Greeley, wreath. "He shines for all." 64pp. [Crew/HG-5].

699.29 When We Met In Convention. w. No composer indicated. m. "Air—*Tis My Delight Of A Shiny Night.*" In: *Fillmore And Donelson Songs For The Campaign* (Songster), page 21. Published by Robert M. De Witt, Nos. 160 and 162 Nassau Street, New York, NY. November 4, 1856. [4¾" × 7⅛"]. Bl/bk litho of George Washington—"July 4, 1776," wreath, geometric design border. "This is the only authorized edition containing Duganne's Songs. Price 6 cts. each, $4 per 100. Discount to trade." Long quote from George Washington's "Farewell Address." 40pp. [M-101, 102]. [Crew/MF-10].

• **AmPM-700 WELD**, William Floyd (Candidate for State Attorney General, 1978; U.S. District Attorney, 1981–1986; Governor, 1991–1997)

700.1 Battle Hymn Of The Republicans. w. No composer indicated. m. Tune—*Battle Hymn Of The Republic.* N/c photos of George Bush. Ronald Reagan, Willie Horton, peacemaker missile, clear-cut forest, Dick Armey, Bill Archer, Pete Wilson, H. Ross Perot and George W. Bush. "The Washington press corps serenaded president-elect George Bush on his campaign plane with the first verse and refrain of this hymn in 1988. We added a few more stanzas." Published online by PoliticsOL.com at <http://www.presidentialelection2000.com/battle_hymn_of_the_republicans.html>. 2000.

• **AmPM-700A WILSON**, Henry (State House, 1841–1842; State Senate, 1844–1846 & 1850–1852; U.S. Senate, 1855–1873; Vice-President, 1873–1875) [ALSO SEE: DOC/PSM-USG]

700A.1 The Brave And The True. m. J.W.S. m. "Air—*Red, White And Blue.*" From the "*Louisville Commercial.*" In: *National Republican Grant And Wilson Campaign Song-Book*, page 65. Published by The Union Republican Congressional Committee, Washington, DC. 1872. [$3\frac{13}{16}$" × $8\frac{9}{16}$"]. Be/bk litho of Ulysses S. Grant. "We'll Sing a Song for U.S. Grant." 100pp. [M-182]. [Crew/USG-110].

700A.2 Campaign Version Of 'John Brown.' w. No composer indicated. m. Air—*John Brown.* In: *National Republican Grant And Wilson Campaign Song-Book*, page 6. Published by The Union Republican Congressional Committee, Washington, DC. 1872. [$3\frac{13}{16}$" × $8\frac{9}{16}$"]. Be/bk litho of Ulysses S. Grant. "We'll Sing a Song for U.S. Grant." 100pp. [M-182]. [Crew/USG-110].

700A.3 Chappaqua. w.m. No composer or tune indicated. In: *Grant And Wilson Campaign Songster*, page 22. Published by Frank Eastman, Book and Job Printer, No. 509 Clay Street, San Francisco, CA. [4¼" × 5⅝"]. 1872. Bk/bl geometric design border. 40pp. [Crew/USG-69].

700A.4 The Colored Voter's Song. w. No composer indicated. m. "Air—*Tramp, Tramp, Tramp.*" In: *National Republican Grant And Wilson Campaign Song-Book*, page 22. Published by The Union Republican Congressional Committee, Washington, DC. 1872. [$3\frac{13}{16}$" × $8\frac{9}{16}$"]. Be/bk litho of Ulysses S. Grant. "We'll Sing a Song for U.S. Grant." 100pp. [M-182]. [Crew/USG-110].

700A.5 Fling Out The Banner. m. No composer indicated. m. "Air—*Uncle Sam's Farm.*" In: *National Republican Grant And Wilson Campaign Song-Book*, page 69. Published by The Union Republican Congressional Committee, Washington, DC. 1872. [$3\frac{13}{16}$" × $8\frac{9}{16}$"]. Be/bk litho of Ulysses S. Grant. "We'll Sing a Song for U.S. Grant." 100pp. [M-182]. [Crew/USG-110].

700A.6 [From North To South, From East To West] (Campaign Song). w. No composer indicated. m. "Air—*The Days When We Went Gypsying.*" In: *National Republican Grant And Wilson Campaign Song-Book*, page 35. From the *New York Standard.* Published by The Union Republican Congressional Committee, Washington, DC. 1872. [$3\frac{13}{16}$" × $8\frac{9}{16}$"]. Be/bk litho of

Ulysses S. Grant. "We'll Sing a Song for U.S. Grant." 100pp. [M-182]. [Crew/USG-110].

700A.7 Grant And Wilson. w. No composer indicated. m. "Air—*Yankee Doodle.*" In: *National Republican Grant And Wilson Campaign Song-Book,* page 1. Published by The Union Republican Congressional Committee, Washington, DC. 1872. [3 13/16" × 8 9/16"]. Be/bk litho of Ulysses S. Grant. "We'll Sing a Song for U.S. Grant." 100pp. [M-182]. [Crew/USG-110].

700A.8 Grant And Wilson. w. No composer indicated. m. "Air—*Red, White And Blue.*" From the "*Syracuse Journal.*" In: *National Republican Grant And Wilson Campaign Song-Book,* page 58. Published by The Union Republican Congressional Committee, Washington, DC. 1872. [3 13/16" × 8 9/16"]. Be/bk litho of Ulysses S. Grant. "We'll Sing a Song for U.S. Grant." 100pp. [M-182]. [Crew/USG-110].

700A.9 Grant, Wilson And Success. w. No composer indicated. m. "Air—*Auld Lang Syne.*" In: *National Republican Grant And Wilson Campaign Song-Book,* page 75. Published by The Union Republican Congressional Committee, Washington, DC. 1872. [3 13/16" × 8 9/16"]. Be/bk litho of Ulysses S. Grant. "We'll Sing a Song for U.S. Grant." 100pp. [M-182]. [Crew/USG-110].

700A.10 Grant's What's The Matter. w.m. No composer or tune indicated. In: *National Republican Grant And Wilson Campaign Song-Book,* page 16. Published by The Union Republican Congressional Committee, Washington, DC. 1872. [3 13/16" × 8 9/16"]. Be/bk litho of Ulysses S. Grant. "We'll Sing a Song for U.S. Grant." 100pp. [M-182]. [Crew/USG-110].

700A.11 A Hero In War, And A Statesman In Peace! w. N.G. Sawyer. m. "Air—*Grave Of Bonaparte.*" In: *Grant And Wilson Campaign Songster,* page 27. Published by Frank Eastman, Book and Job Printer, No. 509 Clay Street, San Francisco, CA. [4¼" × 5⅝"]. 1872. Bk/bl geometric design border. 40pp. [Crew/USG-69].

700A.12 Hon. Henry Wilson. w. N.G. Sawyer. m. "Air—*Whip-Poor-Will's Call.*" In: *Grant And Wilson Campaign Songster,* page 30. Published by Frank Eastman, Book and Job Printer, No. 509 Clay Street, San Francisco, CA. [4¼" × 5⅝"]. 1872. Bk/bl geometric design border. 40pp. [Crew/USG-69].

700A.13 Horatia! w. No composer indicated. m. "Air—*Now Moses.*" In: *Grant And Wilson Campaign Songster,* page 21. Published by Frank Eastman, Book and Job Printer, No. 509 Clay Street, San Francisco, CA. [4¼" × 5⅝"]. 1872. Bk/bl geometric design border. 40pp. [Crew/USG-69].

700A.14 Hunkidori. w. No composer indicated. m. "Air—*Hunkidori, I Oh!*" In: *National Republican Grant And Wilson Campaign Song-Book,* page 73. Published by The Union Republican Congressional Committee, Washington, DC. 1872. [3 13/16" × 8 9/16"]. Be/bk litho of Ulysses S. Grant. "We'll Sing a Song for U.S. Grant." 100pp. [M-182]. [Crew/USG-110].

700A.15 Hurrah For General Grant. w. Sam Booth. m. No tune indicated. In: *Grant And Wilson Campaign Songster,* page 4. Published by Frank Eastman, Book and Job Printer, No. 509 Clay Street, San Francisco, CA. [4¼" × 5⅝"]. 1872. Bk/bl geometric design border. 40pp. [Crew/USG-69].

700A.16 Hurrah For The Man We Love. "Air—*Vive L'Amour.*" In: *McClellan And Liberty* [Song Sheet]. Published by Frank McElroy, No. 113 Nassau Street, New York, NY. 1864. [7" × 17"]. Non-pictorial. "Stand by the Union and I'll Stand by you." "The Work before us; To suppress the Rebellion, To preserve the Union, To maintain the sovereignty of the People!" "Let us apply ourselves to the duty of uniting all the conservative elements of the country, in the effort to place in the Presidential Chair a man who will revere the Constitution as his highest political authority—Such a man is George B. McClellan." "The following is ... from a recent letter of the Hon. Amos Kendall: I am losing my patience in reading Gen. McClellan's report. The injustice to him, and the atrocious wrong to his noble army and the country, are enough to make the blood of honest and patriotic men boil within them." 2pp. [Crew/GBM-61].

700A.17 Hurrah For U.S. Grant! w. Col. H. Orndorff. m. No tune indicated. In: *Grant And Wilson Campaign Songster,* page 18. Published by Frank Eastman, Book and Job Printer, No. 509 Clay Street, San Francisco, CA. [4¼" × 5⅝"]. 1872. Bk/bl geometric design border. 40pp. [Crew/USG-69].

700A.18 Hurrah Song. w. N.G. Sawyer. m. No tune indicated. In: *Grant And Wilson Campaign Songster,* page 33. Published by Frank Eastman, Book and Job Printer, No. 509 Clay Street, San Francisco, CA. [4¼" × 5⅝"]. 1872. Bk/bl geometric design border. 40pp. [Crew/USG-69].

700A.19 [In Early Days Our Fathers Wore] (A Campaign Song). w. No composer indicated. m. "Air—*Yankee Doodle.*" In: *National Republican Grant And Wilson Campaign Song-Book,* page 4. Published by The Union Republican Congressional Committee, Washington, DC. 1872. [3 13/16" × 8 9/16"]. Be/bk litho of Ulysses S. Grant. "We'll Sing a Song for U.S. Grant." 100pp. [M-182]. [Crew/USG-110].

700A.20 [Let It Resound The Land Around] (Campaign Song). w. No composer indicated. m. "Air—*Sparkling And Bright.*" From the "*Sandwich Gazette.*" In: *National Republican Grant And Wilson Campaign Song-Book,* page 78. Published by The Union Republican Congressional Committee, Washington, DC. 1872. [3 13/16" × 8 9/16"]. Be/bk litho of Ulysses S. Grant. "We'll Sing a Song for U.S. Grant." 100pp. [M-182]. [Crew/USG-110].

700A.21 The Men Of Leather. w. Sam Booth. m. No tune indicated. In: *Grant And Wilson Campaign Songster,* page 7. Published by Frank Eastman, Book and Job Printer, No. 509 Clay Street, San Francisco, CA. [4¼" × 5⅝"]. 1872. Bk/bl geometric design border. 40pp. [Crew/USG-69].

700A.22 [My Friends, I Guess You All Have Heard] (Campaign Song). w. No composer indicated. m. "Air—*Never Mind The Weather So The Wind Don't Blow.*" In: *National Republican Grant And Wilson Campaign Song-Book,* page 7. Published by The Union Republican Congressional Committee, Washington, DC. 1872. [3 13/16" × 8 9/16"]. Be/bk litho of Ulysses S. Grant. "We'll Sing a Song for U.S. Grant." 100pp. [M-182]. [Crew/USG-110].

700A.23 No Slave Beneath That Starry Flag. w. Rev. George Lansing Taylor. m. Mrs. Parkhurst "(Author of *The New Emancipation Song, Little Joe, The Contraband, Sweet Home Of My Early Days, Art Thou Thinking Of Me In My Absence*)." Published by Horace Waters, No. 481 Broadway, New York, NY. 1864. B/w geometric design frame. "To the Hon. Henry Wilson, Senator from Massachusetts, to whose distinguished ability, integrity, and firmness for the right, in this and many other instances, humanity and the future are so much indebted, this song is, by his special permission, most respectfully dedicated by the Author." 6pp. Page 2: "The conference committee (of the Senate and the House of Representatives) inserted one very important amendment in the (conscription) bill, when it was before them. Senator Wilson announced to them his firm resolution that no slave should serve the government for one moment 'as a slave' and it was provided that the drafted or enlisted slave shall be free the instant that he enters the service." Page 6: Advertising. Miscellaneous Music.

700A.24 Not For Horace. w. C.B. Parker. m. "Air—*Not For Joseph*." In: *National Republican Grant And Wilson Campaign Song-Book*, page 28. Published by The Union Republican Congressional Committee, Washington, DC. 1872. [$3\frac{13}{16}$" × $8\frac{9}{16}$"]. Be/bk litho of Ulysses S. Grant. "We'll Sing a Song for U.S. Grant." 100pp. [M-182]. [Crew/USG-110].

700A.25 [Now Put The Ball In Motion] (Campaign Song). w. No composer indicated. m. Kinkel. "Air—*Soldier's Farewell*." In: *National Republican Grant And Wilson Campaign Song-Book*, page 18. Published by The Union Republican Congressional Committee, Washington, DC. 1872. [$3\frac{13}{16}$" × $8\frac{9}{16}$"]. Be/bk litho of Ulysses S. Grant. "We'll Sing a Song for U.S. Grant." 100pp. [M-182]. [Crew/USG-110].

700A.26 [O'er All The Land We Hear The Cry] (Campaign Song). w. No composer indicated. m. "Air—*Maryland, My Maryland*." "Columbia S.C., July, 1872." In: *National Republican Grant And Wilson Campaign Song-Book*, page 86. Published by The Union Republican Congressional Committee, Washington, DC. 1872. [$3\frac{13}{16}$" × $8\frac{9}{16}$"]. Be/bk litho of Ulysses S. Grant. "We'll Sing a Song for U.S. Grant." 100pp. [M-182]. [Crew/USG-110].

700A.27 Our Wagon. m. "Air—*Red, White And Blue*." In: *The Grant Songster (For The Campaign Of 1868)*, page 7. Published by Root & Cady, No. 67 Washington Street, Chicago, IL. 1868. [4¾" × 6⅜"]. O/bk litho of Ulysses S. Grant. "A Collection of Campaign Songs for 1868." 48pp. Page 48: Advertising for Grant Campaign music. [M-158, 159]. [Crew/USG-113].

700A.28 Stand Up For Grant And Wilson. w. No composer indicated. m. "Air—*Marching Through Georgia*." In: *Grant And Wilson Campaign Songster*, page 3. Published by Frank Eastman, Book and Job Printer, No. 509 Clay Street, San Francisco, CA. [4¼" × 5⅝"]. 1872. Bk/bl geometric design border. 40pp. [Crew/USG-69].

700A.29 Sumner With His Whiskers. w. Bob Hart. m. "Tune—*Captain With His Whiskers*." No publisher indicated, probably Philadelphia. [1861– 1862]. [Approx. 6" × 9"]. Non-pictorial geometric designs. "Bob Hart's Latest! Sung Nightly at the Academy of Music." 2pp. Page 2: Blank. [AMC].

700A.30 Viva La Companie. w.m. No composer or tune indicated. In: *Grant And Wilson Campaign Songster*, page 16. Published by Frank Eastman, Book and Job Printer, No. 509 Clay Street, San Francisco, CA. [4¼" × 5⅝"]. 1872. Bk/bl geometric design border. 40pp. [Crew/USG-69].

700A.31 [We've Another Contest Coming] (Campaign Song). w. No composer indicated. m. "Air—*Marching Through Georgia*." In: *National Republican Grant And Wilson Campaign Song-Book*, page 46. Published by The Union Republican Congressional Committee, Washington, DC. 1872. [$3\frac{13}{16}$" × $8\frac{9}{16}$"]. Be/bk litho of Ulysses S. Grant. "We'll Sing a Song for U.S. Grant." 100pp. [M-182]. [Crew/USG-110].

700A.32 What I Know About Beet. w. No composer indicated. m. "Air—*Little Brown Jug*." In: *National Republican Grant And Wilson Campaign Song-Book*, page 17. Published by The Union Republican Congressional Committee, Washington, DC. 1872. [$3\frac{13}{16}$" × $8\frac{9}{16}$"]. Be/bk litho of Ulysses S. Grant. "We'll Sing a Song for U.S. Grant." 100pp. [M-182]. [Crew/USG-110].

700A.33 Wilson And Grant. w. N.G. Sawyer. m. "Air—*Whip-Poor-Will's Call*." In: *Grant And Wilson Campaign Songster*, page 15. Published by Frank Eastman, Book and Job Printer, No. 509 Clay Street, San Francisco, CA. [4¼" × 5⅝"]. 1872. Bk/bl geometric design border. 40pp. [Crew/USG-69].

700A.34 Wilson And Grant. w. No composer or tune indicated. In: *National Republican Grant And Wilson Campaign Song-Book*, page 26. Published by The Union Republican Congressional Committee, Washington, DC. 1872. [$3\frac{13}{16}$" × $8\frac{9}{16}$"]. Be/bk litho of Ulysses S. Grant. "We'll Sing a Song for U.S. Grant." 100pp. [M-182]. [Crew/USG-110].

700A.35 Young Men's Grant Meeting. w. No composer indicated. m. "Air—*Bennie Havens, O!*" In: *National Republican Grant And Wilson Campaign Song-Book*, page 41. From the *New York Standard*. Published by The Union Republican Congressional Committee, Washington, DC. 1872. [$3\frac{13}{16}$" × $8\frac{9}{16}$"]. Be/bk litho of Ulysses S. Grant. "We'll Sing a Song for U.S. Grant." 100pp. [M-182]. [Crew/USG-110].

• **AmPM-700B WINTHROP**, Robert Charles (State House, 1835–1840; U.S. House, 1840–1842 & 1842–1850; U.S. Senate, 1850–1851)

700B.1 American Reunion (A Song Of Patriotism And Peace). w.m. George W. Putnam. Published by Louis P. Goullaud, 108 Tremont Street, Boston, MA. 1882. B/w litho of two graves side-by-side at Gettysburg—"A Lieut. Colonel in the Confederate Army Aged 28 years, Fell at the Battle of Gettysburg, July, 1863" and "A Major in the Union Army, Aged 27 years, Fell at the Battle of Gettysburg, July 1863." "All silent and still the Blue and Gray are sleeping side by side." 8pp. Page 2: "To the friends of Peace, Liberty and union throughout the nation. The song Inspired by the Oration of Hon. Rob't C. Winthrop at Yorktown, Va., Oct. 19, 1881" Testimonials. Page 8: Blank. [LL/JH].

700B.2 A Peep At Washington. w. "Composed and Sung by Mr. Rice, in Washington, D.C., during the session of Congress, 1850." m. "Tune—*Susannah*." In: *Dan Rice's Great American Humorist Song Book*, page 23. 1866. [4⅛" × 5¾"]. Br/bk drawing of an actor.

"Containing Original and Selected Songs, Carefully Revised & Corrected." 34pp.

- **AmPM-701 MISCELLANEOUS MUSIC**

701.1 Boston. m. S.L. Tyler. Published by W.H. Boner & Co., 1102 Chestnut Street, Philadelphia, PA. 1886. B/w litho of various state capitol buildings: "Madison, Wis., Harrisburg, Pa., Hartford, Conn., Columbus, O., Lansing, Mich., Washington, D.C., St. Paul, Minn., Richmond Va., Sacramento, Cal., Albany, NY., Boston, Mass., Montgomery, Ala." "The Capitol Collection." 8pp. Page 2: Blank. Page 3: At top of music—"To my Brother, C.A. Tyler." Page 8: Advertising.

701.2 Boston Light Infantry Quick Step No. 1 & No. 2. m. William C. Glynn. Published by H. Prentiss, 33 Court Street, Boston, MA. 1844. N/c litho by Bouvé & Sharp of two soldiers standing under an elaborately decorated gate. Gate decorated with cherubs, shields, tigers, dolphins, floral and geometric designs. View of the State capitol dome in the background. 8pp. Pages 2 and 8: Blank. Page 3: "2 Quick Steps For The Piano Forte dedicated to the Boston Light Infantry."

701.3 The Boston March Two-Step. m. R.E. Hildreth. Published by G.W. Setchell, 633 Washington Street, Boston, MA. Gd/gn/bl/w drawing of a view of the State House dome through a window. 6pp. Page 2: Blank. Page 6: Advertising.

701.4 Brocktonian March Two-Step. m. Sylvester B. Grant. Published by Old Colony Piano Co., 4 Main Street, Brockton, MA. 1896. Bl/w photo of Brockton's "New City Hall." "Respectfully dedicated to the City of Brockton." "For Piano-Forte." 6pp. Pages 2 and 6: Advertising.

701.5 Cochituate Grand Quick Step. m. Geo. Schnapp. Published by Stephen W. Marsh, Piano Forte maker & Music Dealer, No. 371 Washington Street, Boston, MA. 1849. B/w litho by J.H. Bufford & Co. of a park scene. "Composed for the celebration of the introduction of water into the City of Boston, Oct. 25th, 1848, and Respectfully dedicated to the Mayor, Alderman & Common Council." 8pp. Pages 2 and 8: Blank.

701.6 Farewell Song Sung At The Close Of The Legislature. w. Phineas Stowe, "Chaplain of the House." m. "Tune—*America*." No publisher indicated. "Printed by Wright & Potter, Printers, 4 Spring Lane, cor. Devonshire Street, Boston." April 30, 1862. [5⅚" × 8½"]. Non-pictorial geometric designs. 2pp. Page 2: Blank.

701.7 The Governor's Day March. m. Sylvester B. Grant. Published by Old Colony Piano Co., 4 Main Street, Brockton, MA. 1906. B/w photo of the Massachusetts Capitol building. Bl/w columns, geometric designs. "For Piano." "Souvenir—Brockton—Fair 1906." 6pp. Page 2: Blank. Page 6: Advertising.

701.8 New England Guards Quick Step. m. Chas. Zeuner. Published by C. Bradlee, Boston, MA. 1835. B/w litho by Pendleton's of troops in front of the Massachusetts State House building. 4pp. Page 4: Blank.

701.9 On The Road To Boston Or The Durham Election. No composers indicated. No publisher indicated. [ca. 1850s]. [7¼" × 11¼"]. Non-pictorial geometric design border. 2pp. Page 2: Blank.

701.10 The State Street Quick Step. m. Oliver Shaw. Published in New York City, NY. 1842. B/w litho of State Street and the State House. "First performed at Mass. Temperance Celebration." 4pp. Pages 1 and 4: Blank.

701.11 A Toast To Springfield. w.m. William B. Bell. a. Bert Green. Published by the Springfield Centennial Committee, Springfield, MA. 1952. B/w photo of the Springfield City Hall complex. Gn/w music notes. "Centennial Edition." 4pp. Page 4: Blank.

MICHIGAN

- **AmPM-702 ABRAHAM**, Spencer (Chairman of the Michigan Republican Party, 1983–1991; Co-Chairman, National Republican Congressional Committee, 1990–1992; U.S. Senate, 1995–2001; U.S. Secretary of Energy, 2001–Present)

702.1 Talking Cabinet Blues. w. Dave Lippman. m. No tune indicated. Published online at <http://www.davelippman.com/Cabinet.html>. N/c photo of Dave Lippman. [ca. 2001].

- **AmPM-703 ALGER**, Russell Alexander (Governor, 1884–1886; U.S. Secretary of War, 1897–1899; U.S. Senate, 1902–1907)

703.1 The Cabinet Grand March. m. Hans S. Line, Op. 64. Published by National Music Company, Nos. 215–221 Wabash Avenue, Chicago, IL. 1897. R/w cover. B/w photo of William McKinley and eight Cabinet members. "Dedicated to Hon. Lyman J. Gage." 6pp. Page 6: Advertising. [Crew/WM-15].

703.2 General Alger's March. m. Harry R. Williams. Published by Detroit Music Company, Publishers and Importers, 184 & 186 Woodward Avenue, Detroit, MI. 1888. B/w litho by Bufford Co. of General Alger. "Dedicated by permission to General Russell A. Alger." 8pp. Pages 2, 7 and 8: Blank.

- **AmPM-704 BAGLEY**, John Judson (Commissioners of the Metropolitan Police Force, Detroit, 1865 1871; Chairman of the Republican State Central Committee, 1868–1869; Governor, 1873–1877)

704.1 A Comrade's Greeting. m. William H. Marston. Published by Roe Stephens, 113 Woodward Avenue, Detroit, MI. 1876. Litho by Practical Litho's of Detroit of "John J. Bagley," geometric design frame "Respectfully Dedicated to John J. Bagley, Governor of Michigan, A True Friend to the Boys in Blue."

- **AmPM-705 BALDWIN**, Henry Porter (State

Senate, 1861–1862; Governor, 1869–1873; U.S. Senate, 1879–1881)
705.1 *Governor's Grand March*. m. R.T. Yarndley. Published by R.T. Yarndley, Detroit, MI. 1869. B/w litho of Henry Baldwin. "Respectfully Dedicated to Governor Baldwin of Mich." 10pp. Pages 2, 9 and 10: Blank. [LL/JH].
• **AmPM-706** BAUM, William B. (Mayor, Saginaw, 1898)
706.1 *Saginaw Carnival March*. m. Alfred W. Norris "(Composer of *20th Century Woman, Fair Detective, Krinolin March Two-Steps*)." Published by A.W. Norris, 202 Genesee Avenue, Saginaw, MI. 1898. B/w photos of "Wm. B. Baum, Mayor," D.E. Prall, Treas., Capt. A.L. Button, Thos. A. Downs, Pres., M.W. Tanner, Sec'y." O/w/bk drawings of clowns, geometric designs. "Respectfully dedicated to State Fair and Carnival Committee." 6pp. Page 6: Advertising.
• **AmPM-707** BLISS, Aaron Thomas (State Senate, 1882; U.S. House, 1889–1891; Governor, 1900–1904)
707.1 *We Are For Bliss* (Campaign Song). m. Harry H. Zickel. 1900. B/w photo of Aaron T. Bliss R/w/b drawing of Bliss riding elephant inscribed "G.O.P." on the road to The Capitol, cheering crowd, individuals with hats and shirts inscribed "Young Soldier," "Old Soldier," "Farmer," "Business Man," "Clerk," "Working Man." Flags and pennants inscribed "Sound Money," "Full Dinner Pail," "Expansion of Trade," "Protection," "Equal Taxation." 4pp. Page 4: Bl/w drawing of William McKinley and Theodore Roosevelt—"Let Well Enough Alone."
• **AmPM-708** BONIOR, David Edward (State House, 1973–1977; U.S. House, 1977–2003)
708.1 *The Little First Lady With Megalomania*. w. Paul Silhan. m. "Sung to *The Little Old Lady From Pasadena* by Jan & Dean." On: Cassette: *Lie-A-lot*. Lyrics published at <http://www.paulsilhan.com/lal-1.htm>. 1995.
708.2 *They Want Newt So Bad*. w. Paul Silhan. m. "Sung to Bob (Zimmerman) Dylan's *I Want You So Bad*." "As heard on Rush's radio Show." Lyrics published online at <http://www.paulsilhan.com/dylan3.htm>. 1996.
• **AmPM-709** BROWN, Prentiss Marsh (Prosecuting Attorney, Mackinac County, 1914–1926; City Attorney, St. Ignace, 1916–1928; U.S. House, 1933–1936; U.S. Senate, 1936–1943; Administrator in the Office of Price Administration, 1943)
709.1 *Our Nation's On A Ration*. w. Bill Tinker. m. Ted Wardman and Larry Turner. Published by Success Music Company, 32 South River Street, Aurora, IL. 1943. R/w/b/ American flag, geometric design border. 4pp. Page 4: Advertising.
• **AmPM-710** BRUCKER, Wilbur M. (Prosecuting Attorney, Saginaw County, 1922–1926; State Attorney General, 1928–1930; Governor, 1930–1932; U.S. Secretary of the Army, 1955–1961)
710.1 *The Army Goes Marching Along*. w.m. H.W. Arberg. "Based upon *The Cason Song* by Brig. Gen. E.L. Gruber." Published by Broadcast Music Inc., 589 Fifth Avenue, New York 17, NY. 1956. N/c photo of the U.S. Capitol building, Army color guard. 8pp. Page 2: Narrative on the song by "Wilber M. Brucker, Secretary of the Army, November, 1956." Page 7: Blank. Page 8: Eagle.
• **AmPM-711** BURNS, Frances E. (Delegate, Democratic National Convention, 1920)
711.1 *Frances E. Burns March*. 1898.
• **AmPM-712** CAMPAU, Louis (Founder, Grand Rapids, 1826; Village Trustee, Grand Rapids, 1838–1839)
712.1 *Grand Rapids*. w. Julia A. Moore. m. "Air—*Lucy Long*." In: *The Sentimental Song Book*, page 23. Published by Julia A. Moore, Grand Rapids, MI. 1876. [4⅛" × 5¹³⁄₁₆"]. Gn/bk non-pictorial back line border. "Centennial, 1876." 62pp.
• **AmPM-713** CASS, Lewis (State House, 1806; U.S. Marshal, 1807–1812; Territorial Governor, 1813–1831; U.S. Secretary of War, 1831–1836; U.S. Senate, 1845–1848 & 1849–1857; U.S. Secretary of State, 1857–1860)
713.1 *The Boat Horn*. w. General William O. Butler. m. C.H. Thornbecke. In: *The Cass And Butler Almanac For 1849*. Published by John B. Perry, No. 198 Market Street, Philadelphia, PA. [1848]. Be/bk litho of Lewis Cass. "Compiled by the Democratic Committee of Publication of the City and County of Philadelphia." [Crew/LC-5].
713.2 *Cling To The Union*. w. No composer indicated. m. "Air—*Wait For The Wagon*." Published by Johnson, Song Publisher, No. 7 N. Tenth Street, [Philadelphia, PA]. [1850–1860]. B/w non-pictorial geometric design litho border." 2pp. Page 2: Blank. [AMC].
713.3 *[Come All Ye Good Hearted Whigs]* (Whig Song). w. No composer indicated. m. "Tune—*Yankee Doodle*." In: *The National Clay Almanac, 1845*, page 31. B/w litho of a raccoon. Published by Desilver & Muir, No. 18 South Fourth Street, Philadelphia, PA. 1844. [6³⁄₁₆" × 7⅞"]. B/w litho of Henry Clay, ship—"Commerce," plow, crops—"Agriculture." [Crew/HC-89].
713.4 *Come All Ye Men Who Push The Plow* (A Popular Clay Song). w. No composer indicated. m. "Air—*Auld Lang Syne*." In: *The National Clay Minstrel (And True Whig's Pocket Companion For The Presidential Canvass Of 1844)*, page 21. Published by [V-1: George Hood, No. 15 North 6th Street, Philadelphia, PA] [V-2: James Fisher, No. 71 Court Street, Boston, MA]. 1843. [3¼" × 5⅛"]. Y/bk litho of raccoon—"That Coon" and flag—"Henry Clay," log cabin. "New and Improved Edition." 128pp. Page 10: Dedication—"To the National Clay Club this work is respectfully dedicated by the Publisher." [Crew/HC-11].
713.5 *The Coon Song*. w. No composer indicated. m. "Tune—*Jim Dandy Of Caroline*." "Written for the *National Clay Minstrel*." B/w litho of a raccoon labeled "That Coon" atop a log cabin with a flag labeled "Henry Clay." In: *The National Clay Minstrel*, page 61. Published by [V-1: George Hood, No. 15 North 6th Street, Philadelphia, PA] [V-2: James Fisher, No. 71 Court Street, Boston, MA]. 1843. [3" × 4½"]. Y/bk litho of raccoon sitting on fence, black border. 68pp. [Crew/HC-10].
713.6 *The Coon Song*. w. No composer indicated. m. "Tune—*Jim Dandy Of Caroline*." In: *The Clay Minstrel Or National Songster*, page 355. c. John Stockton Littell. Published by Greeley & M'Elrath, Tribune

Building, New York, NY. 1844. [3⅛" × 4⅞"]. Non-pictorial. 396pp. [Crew/HC-18].

713.7 Empire Song (The Old Granite State). w. "By the President of the Club." m. *The Old Granite State.* [1852]. B/w litho of an eagle holding a ribbon inscribed "E Pluribus Unum," geometric design border. 2pp. Page 2: Blank.

713.8 The Fainting General. w. No composer indicated. m. "Air—*Dolly Day.*" No publisher indicated. [ca. 1852]. Non-pictorial. 2pp. Page 2: Blank. [Crew/FP-13] [AMC].

713.9 The First Polk Song. w. No composer indicated. m. "Tune—*Old Dan Tucker.*" In: *The National Clay Minstrel,* page 26. Published by [V-1: George Hood, No. 15 North 6th Street, Philadelphia, PA] [V-2: James Fisher, No. 71 Court Street, Boston, MA]. 1843. [3" × 4½"]. Y/bk litho of raccoon sitting on fence, black border. 68pp. [Crew/HC-10].

713.10 The Four Years' Race. w. No composer indicated. m. "Air—*Few Days.*" In: *The Freeman's Glee Book, A Collection Of Songs, Odes, Glees And Ballads With Music, Original And Selected, Harmonized And Arranged For Each. Published Under The Auspices Of The Central Fremont And Dayton Glee Club Of The City Of New York, And Dedicated To All, Who, Cherishing Republican Liberty Consider Freedom Worth A Song,* page 40. Published by Miller, Orton & Mulligan, No. 25 Park Row, New York, NY. [and Auburn, NY]. 1856. [4¹⁵⁄₁₆" × 6"]. Pk/bk litho of man on mountain peak, music sheets, geometric designs. 112pp. [Crew/JCF-16].

713.11 Free Soil Rally. w. Jesse Hutchinson, Jr. m. "Tune—*Hurrah Song.*" In: *Free Soil Songs,* page 1. w. Messrs. Hutchinson, Jewell, Bates and Foster, of Massachusetts. 1848. [8½" × 13⅜"]. Non-pictorial. "Composed and sung at the Buffalo Convention, August 9, and 10, 1848." "Printed by R.A. Maynard & Co., Printers Republic Office, Buffalo." 2pp. Page 2: Blank. [Crew/MVB-13].

713.12 The Free Soiler's Song. w.m. No composer or tune indicated. In: *The Free Soil Minstrel,* page 49. c. George W. Clark. Published by Martyn & Ely, No. 162 Nassau Street, New York, NY. 1848. [4¾" × 7¼"]. Br/br non-pictorial geometric designs on hardback cover. 228pp. [M-079].

713.13 General Cass Grand March. m. J.A. Getze. Published by George Willig, 171 Chestnut Street, Philadelphia, PA. 1842. Non-pictorial geometric designs. "Composed for the Piano Forte and Respectfully dedicated to Genl. Lewis Cass." 4pp. Page 4: Blank. [AMC].

713.14 Get Out Of The Way. w. No composer indicated. m. "Tune—*Ole Dan Tucker.*" In: *Whig Songs For 1844* [Songster], page 2. Published by Greeley & McElrath, New York, NY. 1844. [5⅞" × 9³⁄₁₆"]. Non-pictorial. 16pp. Page 16: "Odes and Poems." [M-061]. [Crew/HC-35].

713.15 Harmonious Coons. w. No composer indicated. m. *Dame Durden.* Published in the *Richmond Enquirer,* Richmond, VA., September 22, 1848. [VBL, p. 322

713.16 Here's To You General Scott. w.m. No composer or tune indicated. In: *Scott And Graham Melodies (Being A Collection Of Campaign Songs For 1852),* page 8. Published by Huestis & Cozans, Nos. 104 and 106 Nassau Street, New York, NY. 1852. [3¹³⁄₁₆" × 6⁵⁄₁₆"]. B/w litho of Winfield Scott, geometric design border. "As sung by the Whig Clubs throughout the United States." 76pp. [M-086]. [Crew/WS-15].

713.17 The Hero Of Chippewa. w. No composer indicated. m. "Tune—*Lucy Neal.*" In: *Scott And Graham Melodies (Being A Collection Of Campaign Songs For 1852),* page 28. Published by Huestis & Cozans, Nos. 104 and 106 Nassau Street, New York, NY. 1852. [3¹³⁄₁₆" × 6⁵⁄₁₆"]. B/w litho of Winfield Scott, geometric design border. "As sung by the Whig Clubs throughout the United States." 76pp. [M-086]. [Crew/WS-15].

713.18 The Hero With Never A Scar. w. No composer indicated. m. "Tune—*The Low-Back'd Car.*" In: *Scott And Graham Melodies, (Being A Collection Of Campaign Songs For 1852),* page 34. Published by Huestis & Cozans, Nos. 104 and 106 Nassau Street, New York, NY. 1852. [3¹³⁄₁₆" × 6⁵⁄₁₆"]. B/w litho of Winfield Scott, geometric design border. "As sung by the Whig Clubs throughout the United States." 76pp. [M-086]. [Crew/WS-15].

713.19 If You'd Like To Know, Just Ask Arista! w. Isaac Wayne Olwine, Esq., "late editor of the *Philadelphia Bee.*" m. "Tune—*The Polka.*" In: *Taylor And Fillmore Songster, An Original Collection Of New Whig Songs For The Campaign Of 1848,* page 6. Published by Turner & Fisher, New York, NY. 1848. [2¾" × 4⅜"]. [V-1: Pk/bk] [V-2: Bl/bk] litho of Zachary Taylor. 34pp. [M-074, 075]. [Crew/ZT-56].

713.20 Jimmie Polk Of Tennessee. w. J. Greiner. m. "Tune—*Dandy Jim Of Caroline.*" In: *The National Clay Minstrel,* page 2. Published by [V-1: George Hood, No. 15 North 6th Street, Philadelphia, PA] [V-2: James Fisher, No. 71 Court Street, Boston, MA]. 1843. [3" × 4½"]. Y/bk litho of raccoon sitting on fence, black border. 68pp. Pages 2 and 67: Blank. Pages 65–66: Contents. [Crew/HC-10].

713.21 Kilkenny Cats. w. No composer indicated. m. "Tune—*Old Dan Tucker.*" In: *The National Clay Minstrel,* page 12. Published by [V-1: George Hood, No. 15 North 6th Street, Philadelphia, PA] [V-2: James Fisher, No. 71 Court Street, Boston, MA]. 1843. [3" × 4½"]. Y/bk litho of raccoon sitting on fence, black border. 68pp. Pages 2 and 67: Blank. Pages 65–66: Contents. [Crew/HC-10].

713.22 King Andrew. m. "Tune—*Dame Durden.*" In: *A Miniature Of Martin Van Buren (With A Selection Of The Best And Most Popular Tippecanoe Songs),* page 46. 1840. [3½" × 6½"]. [V-1: Br/bk] [V-2: Gn/bk] [V-3: Y/bk] litho of man, chain around neck. Van Buren quote. "Amos Kendall's Veracity—Tom Benton's Honesty—Francis Blair's Beauty." "What is wanting cant be numbered [sic]." 58pp. [M-016]. [Crew/WHH-88].

713.23 Last Hope Of Buchanan. w. No composer indicated. m. "Air—*Last Rose Of Summer.*" In: *Fremont Songs For The People (Original And Selected),* page 41. c. Thomas Drew "(Editor of *The Massachusetts Spy*)." Published by John P. Jewett & Company, Boston, MA. Copyright 1856 by Thomas Drew. [3⅝" × 5½"]. B/w litho of "J.C. Fremont." "The Campaign of 1856." 68pp. [Crew/JCF-18].

713.24 A Little More Grape, Captain Bragg. w. Isaac Wayne Olwine, Esq. m. "Tune—*Old Dan Tucker.*" In: *Taylor And Fillmore Songster, An Original Collection Of New Whig Songs For The Campaign Of 1848*, page 32. Published by Turner & Fisher, New York, NY. 1848. [2¾" × 4⅜"]. [V-1: Pk/bk] [V-2: Bl/bk] litho of Zachary Taylor. 34pp. [M-074, 075]. [Crew/ZT-56].

713.25 The Loco Foco National Convention. w. J. Covert. m. "Tune—*Camptown Races.*" In: *Scott And Graham Melodies, Being A Collection Of Campaign Songs For 1852*, page 22. Published by Huestis & Cozans, Nos. 104 and 106 Nassau Street, New York, NY. 1852. [3^13/16" × 6^1/16"]. B/w litho of Winfield Scott, geometric design border. "As sung by the Whig Clubs throughout the United States." 76pp. [M-086]. [Crew/WS-15].

713.26 Matty Van. w. No composer indicated. m. "Tune—*Lucy Long.*" In: *Whig Songs For 1844* [Songster], page 2. Published by Greeley & McElrath, New York, NY. 1844. [5⅞" × 9^3/16"]. Non-pictorial. 16pp. Page 16: "Odes and Poems." [M-061]. [Crew/HC-35].

713.27 The Moon Was Shining Silver Bright (A Whig Song). w. J. Grenier. m. "Tune—*Old Dan Tucker.*" In: *The National Clay Minstrel (And True Whig's Pocket Companion For The Presidential Canvass Of 1844)*, page 44. Published by [V-1: George Hood, No. 15 North 6th Street, Philadelphia, PA] [V-2: James Fisher, No. 71 Court Street, Boston, MA]. 1843. [3¼" × 5⅛"]. Y/bk litho of raccoon—"That Coon" and flag—"Henry Clay," log cabin. "New and Improved Edition." 128pp. Page 10: Dedication—"To the National Clay Club this work is respectfully dedicated by the Publisher." [Crew/HC-11].

713.28 National Cement. w. George W. Bungay. m. No tune indicated. In: *The Republican Campaign Songster For 1860*, page 48. c. W.H. Burleigh. Published by [V-1 and V-2: H. Dayton, No. 36 Howard Street, New York, NY] [V-3: McNally & Company, No. 81 Dearborn Street, Chicago, IL]. 1860. [V-1: Gn/bk] [V-2: Y/bk] [V-3: Be/bk] [V-4: Bl/bk]. "Price 10 cents." [3^13/16" × 6"]. 72pp. [M-104]. [Crew/AL-57].

713.29 A New Song. w. No composer indicated. m. "Tune—*Old Rosin The Bow.*" In: *The National Clay Minstrel*, page 18. Published by [V-1: George Hood, No. 15 North 6th Street, Philadelphia, PA] [V-2: James Fisher, No. 71 Court Street, Boston, MA]. 1843. [3" × 4½"]. Y/bk litho of raccoon sitting on fence, black border. 68pp. Pages 2 and 67: Blank. Pages 65–66: Contents. [Crew/HC-10].

713.30 Old Abe And The Fire-Eaters. w. R. Colby. m. "Air—*Dearest May.*" In: *The Republican Campaign Songster For 1860*, page 39. c. W.H. Burleigh. Published by [V-1 and V-2: H. Dayton, No. 36 Howard Street, New York, NY] [V-3: McNally & Company, No. 81 Dearborn Street, Chicago, IL]. 1860. [V-1: Gn/bk] [V-2: Y/bk] [V-3: Be/bk] [V-4: Bl/bk]. "Price 10 cents." [3^13/16" × 6"]. 72pp. [M-104]. [Crew/AL-57].

713.31 Old Abe's Preliminary Visit To The White House. w. No composer indicated. m. "Tune—*The King And Countryman.*" In: *Republican Song Book*, page 810 c. Thomas Drew "(Late Editor of *The Massachusetts Spy*)." Published by Thayer and Eldridge, Boston, MA. 1860. [3⅞" × 5⅞"]. Br/bk litho of beardless Abraham Lincoln, vignettes of young Lincoln chopping rails, polling raft. 68pp. [M-108]. [Crew/AL-8].

713.32 Old Abe's Preliminary Visit To The White House. w. No composer indicated. m. "Air—*Villikins And His Dinah.*" In: *The Great Republican Campaigns Of 1860 And 1896*, page 151. e. Osborn H. Oldroyd. Published by Laird & Lee, Chicago, IL. 1896. [5^5/16" × 7^7/16"]. Gn/r/bk photos of Abraham Lincoln, William McKinley and Garrett Hobart. "Sound Money, Protection, Prosperity." 208pp. [Crew/AL-574].

713.33 Old Rough And Ready. w. No composer indicated. m. "Tune—*Rosin The Bow.*" In: *Taylor And Fillmore Songster, An Original Collection Of New Whig Songs For The Campaign Of 1848*, page 7. Published by Turner & Fisher, New York, NY. 1848. [2¾" × 4⅜"]. [V-1: Pk/bk] [V-2: Bl/bk] litho of Zachary Taylor. 34pp. [M-074, 075]. [Crew/ZT-56].

713.34 One Day Just At Set Of Sun. w. No composer indicated. m. "Tune—*Get Along Home My Yeller Gals.*" In: *The Clay Minstrel Or National Songster*, page 340. c. John Stockton Littell. Published by Greeley & M'Elrath, Tribune Building, New York, NY. 1844. [3⅛" × 4⅞"]. Non-pictorial. 396pp. [Crew/HC-18].

713.35 A Peep At Washington. w. "Composed and Sung by Mr. Rice, in Washington, D.C., during the session of Congress, 1850." m. "Tune—*Susannah.*" In: *Dan Rice's Great American Humorist Song Book*, page 23. 1866. [4⅛" × 5¾"]. Br/bk drawing of an actor. "Containing Original and Selected Songs, Carefully Revised & Corrected." 34pp.

713.36 Pierce's Lament. w. No composer indicated. m. "Tune—*Oh, Boys, Carry Me 'Long.*" In: *Scott And Graham Melodies, Being A Collection Of Campaign Songs For 1852*, page 35. Published by Huestis & Cozans, Nos. 104 and 106 Nassau Street, New York, NY. 1852. [3^13/16" × 6^1/16"]. B/w litho of Winfield Scott, geometric design border. "As sung by the Whig Clubs throughout the United States." 76pp. [M-086]. [Crew/WS-15].

713.37 The Presidential Chair (Or The Lament Of Buchanan). w. No composer indicated. m. "Tune—*The Old Arm Chair.*" In: *Scott And Graham Melodies, Being A Collection Of Campaign Songs For 1852*, page 61. Published by Huestis & Cozans, Nos. 104 and 106 Nassau Street, New York, NY. 1852. [3^13/16" × 6^1/16"]. B/w litho of Winfield Scott, geometric design border. "As sung by the Whig Clubs throughout the United States." 76pp. [M-086]. [Crew/WS-15].

713.38 The Rubber; Or Mat's Third And Last Game. w. No composer indicated. m. "Tune—*Miss Bailey.*" In: *The National Clay Minstrel (And True Whig's Pocket Companion For The Presidential Canvass Of 1844)*, page 46. Published by [V-1: George Hood, No. 15 North 6th Street, Philadelphia, PA] [V-2: James Fisher, No. 71 Court Street, Boston, MA]. 1843. [3¼" × 5⅛"]. Y/bk litho of raccoon—"That Coon" and flag—"Henry Clay," log cabin. "New and Improved Edition." 128pp. Page 10: Dedication—"To the National Clay Club this work is respectfully dedicated by the Publisher." [Crew/HC-11].

713.39 Salt River Chorus. w. No composer indicated. a. G.W.C. m. "Air—*Cheer Up, My Lively Lads.*" In: *The Free Soil Minstrel*, page 19. c. George W. Clark.

Published by Martyn & Ely, No. 162 Nassau Street, New York, NY. 1848. [4¾" × 7¼"]. Br/br non-pictorial geometric designs on hardback cover. 228pp. [M-079].

713.40 Slavery Embarkation. w. No composer indicated. m. "Air—*Fisherman's Bark.*" In: *Fremont Songs For The People (Original And Selected)*, page 48. c. Thomas Drew "(Editor of *The Massachusetts Spy*)." Published by John P. Jewett & Company, Boston, MA. Copyright 1856 by Thomas Drew. [3⅝" × 5½"]. B/w litho of "J.C. Fremont." "The Campaign of 1856." 68pp. [Crew/JCF-18].

713.41 A Song For Cass And Butler. w. No composer indicated. m. No tune indicated. Published in the *Daily Union*, October 18, 1848. [VBL, p. 323].

713.42 Song Of The Office Holder. w. No composer indicated. m. "Air—*A Few Days.*" In: *Republican Song Book*, page 8. c. Thomas Drew "(Late Editor of *The Massachusetts Spy*)." Published by Thayer and Eldridge, Boston, MA. 1860. [3⅞" × 5⅞"]. Br/bk litho of beardless Abraham Lincoln, vignettes of young Lincoln chopping rails, polling raft. 68pp. [M-108]. [Crew/AL-8].

713.43 The Rubber; Or Mat's Last Game. w. No composer indicated. m. "Tune—*Miss Bailey.*" In: *The Clay Minstrel Or National Songster*, page 347. c. John Stockton Littell. Published by Greeley & M'Elrath, Tribune Building, New York, NY. 1844. [3⅛" × 4⅞"]. Non-pictorial. 396pp. [Crew/HC-18].

713.44 The Second Polk Song. w. No composer indicated. m. "Tune—*Lucy Long.*" In: *The National Clay Minstrel*, page 10. Published by [V-1: George Hood, No. 15 North 6th Street, Philadelphia, PA] [V-2: James Fisher, No. 71 Court Street, Boston, MA]. 1843. [3" × 4½"]. Y/bk litho of raccoon sitting on fence, black border. 68pp. Pages 2 and 67: Blank. Pages 65–66: Contents. [Crew/HC-10].

713.45 The Standard Floats! w. No composer indicated. m. "Tune—*Old Aunt Sally.*" In: *The Clay Minstrel Or National Songster*, page 331. c. John Stockton Littell. Published by Greeley & M'Elrath, Tribune Building, New York, NY. 1844. [3⅛" × 4⅞"]. Non-pictorial. 396pp. [Crew/HC-18].

713.46 The Taylor Polka. w. No composer indicated. m. "Tune—*The Jim Crow Polka.*" In: *Taylor And Fillmore Songster, An Original Collection Of New Whig Songs For The Campaign Of 1848*, page 17. Published by Turner & Fisher, New York, NY. 1848. [2¾" × 4⅜"]. [V-1: Pk/bk] [V-2: Bl/bk] litho of Zachary Taylor. 34pp. [M-074, 075]. [Crew/ZT-56].

713.47 That Same Old Coon (A New Comic Whig Song). w. "The Milford Bard." m. "Tune -*Sittin On A Rail.*" [7¾" × 13¼"]. B/w litho of a crow on its back and a raccoon speaking "Why Don't You Crow." "A New Comic Whig Song written for 1844 by the Milford Bard by Particular Desire." 2pp. Page 2: Blank. [Crew/HC-120].

713.48 Three Cheers For Gallant Zach. w. Isaac Wayne Olwine, Esq. m. "Tune—*Ole Dan Tucker.*" In: *Taylor And Fillmore Songster, An Original Collection Of New Whig Songs For The Campaign Of 1848*, page 22. Published by Turner & Fisher, New York, NY. 1848. [2¾" × 4⅜"]. [V-1: Pk/bk] [V-2: Bl/bk] litho of Zachary Taylor. 34pp. [M-074, 075]. [Crew/ZT-56].

713.49 Whig Song. w. No composer indicated. m. "No tune indicated. In: *Incidents In The Campaign Of 1844*, page 16. c. James T. Hathaway. Published by J.T. Hathaway, No. 287 Crown Street, New Haven, CT. 1905. [5" × 7"]. Bl/gy non-pictorial geometric design border. "Printed for private distribution among old friends." "*Here's To You, Harry Clay*—Old Song." 68pp. [Crew/ HC-119].

• **AmPM-714 CAVANAGH**, Jerome (Mayor, Detroit, 1965)

714.1 Mayor Of Our Town. w.m. Raymond J. Meurer. a. Donn Preston. No publisher indicated. Copyright 1965 by Raymond J. Meurer, Detroit, MI. B/w photo within a four-leaf clover design of Jerome P. Cavanagh. Gn/w clovers. 4pp. Page 4: "Autographs."

• **AmPM-714A CHANDLER**, Zachariah (Candidate for Governor, 1852; U.S. Senate, 1857–1875 & 1879; U.S. Secretary of the Interior, 1875–1877; Chairman, Republican National Executive Committee, 1868–1876)

714A.1 O Stand Fast, Dear Native Land. w. J.E. Rankin, D.D. m. "Music — German." "Dedicated to the Stalwart, Loyal Brave and Consistent." In: *My Country 'Tis Of Thee Sweet Land Of Liberty Of Thee I Sing (Republican Campaign Song Book 1880)*, page 34. c. L. Fayette Sykes. Published by The Republican Central Campaign Club of New York, Headquarters, Coleman House, No. 1169 Broadway, New York, NY. 1880. [5¹³⁄₁₆" × 9⅛"]. Gn/bk non-pictorial geometric designs. "For President Gen'l. James A. Garfield of Ohio, For Vice-President Gen'l. Chester A. Arthur of New York." 52pp. [M-211, 212]. [Crew/JAG-41].

• **AmPM-715 CLARK**, Richard J. (City Council, Novi, 1995–1997; Mayor, Novi, 1999–Present)

715.1 Like A Relative Unknown. w. "Forty-Niner." m. "*Like A Rolling Stone* by Bob Dylan." Published online at <http://www.amiright.com/parody/60s/bob-dylan0.shml>. [ca. 2000].

COPELAND, Royal Samuel [See: New York]

• **AmPM-716 COUGHLIN**, Father Charles Edward (Founder, National Union for Social Justice, 1934)

716.1 Father Coughlin Came Along. w.m. Kenyon Scott. Published by Scott, Eisner Co., Inc., Music Publishers, 1587 Madison Avenue, New York, NY. 1935. Bl/w photo of Father Coughlin. Bl/w geometric design border. "Dedicated to the members of the National Union for Social Justice." 6pp. Page 6: Narrative titles "Father Coughlin's Sixteen Points."

716.2 The Golden Call. w. "Poetically adapted from the book *Golden Hour Of The Little Flower* by Rev. Fr. Chas. E. Coughlin." m. "Musical setting by Rev. Fr. John de Dep, O.F.M., Director of Music to the Shrine of the Little Flower." No publisher indicated. [ca. 1931]. Drawing of Jesus on a cross on the Shrine of the Little Flower, Shrine labeled "Charity," sun's rays. "The original theme song of the *Golden Hour Of The Little Flower* as introduced by the Rev. Fr. Chas. E. Coughlin at the 'Shrine of the Little Flower,' Detroit (Royal Oak), Michigan." Page 3: At top of music — "As sung by Muriel Magerl Kyle on the *Golden Hour Of The Little Flower* on the Radio."

716.3 Little Flower. w.m. Edward McGuire, Frank Donovan and George Carpenter. Published by Harms,

Inc., New York, NY. 1934. Bl/w photo of Father Coughlin. Bl/bk drawing of church steeple. "Dedicated to Rev. Chas. E. Coughlin, The Shrine of the Little Flower." 6pp. Pages 2 and 6: Advertising.

716.4 Shepherd Of The Air. w.m. Clarence Gaskill. Published by Olman Music Corp., 745 7th Avenue, New York, NY. 1933. Bl/w/bk silhouette drawing of Father Caughlin at a microphone, doves, clouds. "Respectfully Dedicated to Father Rev. Charles E. Coughlin, Pastor of the Shrine of the Little Flower." 4pp. Page 4: Advertising.

716.5 Two Sacred Songs. w.m. Rev. Fr. Chas. E. Coughlin, Pastor Shrine of The Little Flower, and Rev. Fr. John de Deo, O.F.M., Musical Director of the Golden Hour of The Little Flower and Duns Scotus College. Published by The Golden Hour Music Publishers, Detroit, MI. 1931. Be/br drawing of a cross, rays, window frame, geometric designs. 16pp. Pages 2–4 and 13–16: Blank. Pages 2–3 and 13–14: Onion skin. Page 5: Title page for ***The Golden Call*** {716.5–1}. Poetically adapted from the book *Golden Hour Of The Little Flower* by Rev. Fr. Chas. E. Coughlin." "Musical setting by Rev. Fr. John de Dep, O.F.M., Director of Music to the Shrine of the Little Flower." "The original theme song of the *Golden Hour Of The Little Flower* as introduced by the Rev. Fr. Chas. E. Coughlin at the 'Shrine of the Little Flower,' Detroit (Royal Oak), Michigan." Page 6: At top of music—"As sung by Muriel Magerl Kyle on the *Golden Hour Of The Little Flower* on the Radio." Page 9: Title page for ***Behold The Man*** (Ecce Homo) {716.5–2}. B/w drawing of Jesus. "Poem suggested by Rev. Fr. Chas. E. Coughlin, Pastor, Shrine of the Little Flower." "Music by Rev. Fr. John de Deo, O.F.M., Musical Director of the Shrine of The Little Flower and Duns Scotus College. "Introduced with great success by Frederick Jencks during the *Golden Hour Of The Little Flower*, at the dedication Services of the Shrine of the Little Flower, Detroit (Royal Oak), Michigan."

• **AmPM-717 CRARY**, Isaac Edwin (Delegate, State Constitutional Convention, 1835 & 1850; U.S. House, 1837–1841; Board of Regents, University of Michigan, 1837–1843; State House, 1842–1846; State Board of Education, 1850–1854)

717.1 A Buckeye Song. w. No composer indicated. m. "Tune—*Yankee Doodle.*" In: *Tippecanoe Club Songster*, page 49. Published by [V-1: Turner & Fisher, No. 15 North Sixth Street, Philadelphia, PA] [V-2: H.A. Turner, Baltimore, MD]. 1841. [3" × 4⁷⁄₁₆"]. Hand Colored engraving of William Henry Harrison, log cabin. 68pp. [M-021, 022]. [Crew/WHH-18].

• **AmPM-717A DENBY**, Edwin (State House, 1903; U.S. House, 1905–1911; U.S. Secretary of the Navy, 1921–1924)

717A.1 Legion Girl. w.m. Roy T. Burke. No publisher indicated. Copyright [ca. 1929] by Roy T. Burke. Bl/w "Illustration Drawn by Jane A. Johnston, Art Student of the Federal Schools, Minneapolis, Minn.," of a girl. "The Foreign Legion's $100,000 Prize Ballad." Lyrics and Music by Roy T. Burke, Ex-Editor-in-Chief of the Devil-Dogs, United States Marine." "Composer's Dedication—To the finest Soldier I ever Knew, The Late Edwin Denby, Ex-Secretary of Navy, who resigned his Congressional Seat for the Honor of Enlisting in the U.S. Marines During the World War." 8pp. Pages 2,3 7 and 8: Advertising.

717A.2 Way Down Yonder In The White House. w. No composer indicated. m. "Tune—*Way Down Yonder In The Corn Field.*" In: *Lincoln—La Follette Songster*, page 5. Published by Warren H. Eddy, No. 205 North Flower Street, Los Angeles, CA. [4" × 7"]. [1924]. Bl/bk drawing of Abraham Lincoln. Bl/bk photo of Robert M. La Follette. 20pp. Page 20: Bl/bk photo of "Burton K. Wheeler." [Crew/RML-4].

• **AmPM-718 DICKINSON**, Donald McDonald (Chairman National Democratic Party, 1880–1885; U.S. Postmaster General, 1888–1889)

718.1 The College League. w. E.J. Seymour. m. "Air—*Marching Through Georgia.*" In: *Harrison And Reid Campaign Song Book*, page 30. w. E.J. Seymour. m. Popular Airs. [1892]. [3⅞" × 5⅛"]. Bl/gn non-pictorial, stars, geometric designs. 36pp. Pages 2 and 35: Blank. Page 36: Advertising for this songbook. [M-316]. [Crew/BFH-35].

718.2 Glory! Glory! Hallelujah. w. E.J. Seymour. m. Air—*Glory Hallelujah.* In: *Harrison And Reid Campaign Song Book*, page 27. w. E.J. Seymour. m. Popular Airs. [1892]. [3⅞" × 5⅛"]. Bl/gn non-pictorial, stars, geometric designs. 36pp. Pages 2 and 35: Blank. Page 36: Advertising for this songbook. [M-316]. [Crew/BFH-35].

718.3 Oh! What A Difference In November. w. E.J. Seymour. m. "Air—*Oh! What A Difference In The Morning.*" In: *Harrison And Reid Campaign Song Book*, page 18. w. E.J. Seymour. m. Popular Airs. [1892]. [3⅞" × 5⅛"]. Bl/gn non-pictorial, stars, geometric designs. 36pp. Pages 2 and 35: Blank. Page 36: Advertising for this songbook. [M-316]. [Crew/BFH-35].

718.4 The Two Chairmen. w. E.J. Seymour. In: *Harrison And Reid Campaign Song Book*, page 24. w. E.J. Seymour. m. Popular Airs. [1892]. [3⅞" × 5⅛"]. Bl/gn non-pictorial, stars, geometric designs. 36pp. Pages 2 and 35: Blank. Page 36: Advertising for this songbook. [M-316]. [Crew/BFH-35].

• **AmPM-719 FERRIS**, Woodbridge Nathan (Governor, 1913–1916; U.S. Senate, 1923–1928)

719.1 America Can Count On Me. w.m. Wm. Wakefield. Published by Wm. Wakefield, Detroit, MI. 1916. B/w photo of Woodbridge N. Ferris [facsimile signature]. R/w/b flag, shield, geometric designs. "Dedicated by permission to His Excellency Hon. Woodbridge N. Ferris, Governor of Michigan." "Song of Allegiance." 6pp. Page 6: Advertising.

719.2 W.N. Big Chief (An Indian Frolic). m. Louis D. Green "(Composer of *Crimson And Gold March, Water Power City March*)." Published by Louis D. Gerin, Big Rapids, MI. 1915. B/w photo of "Governor W.N. Ferris." Ma/w drawings of Indians. 6pp. Pages 2 and 6: Blank. Page 3: At top of music—"Respectfully Dedicated to Hon. W.N. Ferris, The Good Grey Governor."

719.3 The Wolverine State March. m. Lida Browning White. Published by The Crescent Publishing Company, 818 Monroe Street, Gary, IN. 1913. B/w photo of "Governor Ferris." R/w/br/gn flowers. "Dedicated to Governor Woodbridge N. Ferris." 8pp. Page 8: Advertising.

• **AmPM-719A FITZGERALD**, Frank D.

(Michigan Secretary of State, 1930–1934, Governor, 1935–1936 & 1939)

719A.1 [Fitzgerald For Governor Of Our State]. w. No composer indicated. m. "Tune—*Michigan, My Michigan.*" In: *Kent County Woman's Republican Club Song Sheet*, page 2. [1936]. [5 3/16" × 10 7/16"]. B/w litho of Abraham Lincoln. "Let us have a Singing, Smiling United Membership." 4pp.

719A.2 How D'ye Do? w. No composer indicated. m. No tune indicated. In: *Kent County Woman's Republican Club Song Sheet*, page 2. [1936]. [5 3/16" × 10 7/16"]. B/w litho of Abraham Lincoln. "Let us have a Singing, Smiling United Membership." 4pp.

719A.3 Landon And Knox. w. No composer indicated. m. "Tune—*Land Of Mine.*" In: *Kent County Woman's Republican Club Song Sheet*, page 4. [1936]. [5 3/16" × 10 7/16"]. B/w litho of Abraham Lincoln. "Let us have a Singing, Smiling United Membership." 4pp.

719A.4 On Fitzgerald. w. No composer indicated. m. "Tune—*On Wisconsin.*" In: *Kent County Woman's Republican Club Song Sheet*, page 2. [1936]. [5 3/16" × 10 7/16"]. B/w litho of Abraham Lincoln. "Let us have a Singing, Smiling United Membership." 4pp.

719A.5 'Till We Meet Again. w. No composer indicated. m. No tune indicated. In: *Kent County Woman's Republican Club Song Sheet*, page 3. [1936]. [5 3/16" × 10 7/16"]. B/w litho of Abraham Lincoln. "Let us have a Singing, Smiling United Membership." 4pp.

719A.6 [We Are Kent County Workers]. w. No composer indicated. m. "Tune—*Old Grey Bonnet.*" In: *Kent County Woman's Republican Club Song Sheet*, page 3. [1936]. [5 3/16" × 10 7/16"]. B/w litho of Abraham Lincoln. "Let us have a Singing, Smiling United Membership." 4pp.

• **AmPM-719Ax FORD**, Gerald Rudolph, Jr. (U.S. House, 1949–1973; Vice President, 1974–1974; President, 1974–1977) [SEE: DOC/PSM-GRF]

• **AmPM-720 GREEN**, Fred Warren (Treasurer, Michigan Republican Party, 1915–1919; Governor, 1927–1930)

720.1 March Commander. m. Joe Greenfield. Published by Land & Hess Music Co., Escanba, MI. 1929. B/w photo of Fred Green. "Dedicated to the Honorable Fred W. Green, Governor of Michigan and National Commander of the Spanish American War Veterans Association, War-Time 1st Lieutenant & Brigadier General of Michigan National Guards." 6pp. Pages 2 and 6: Blank.

• **AmPM-721 GRIFFIN**, Robert Paul (U.S. House, 1957–1966; U.S. Senate; 1966–1979)

721.1 Youth And Experience. w. Auld & Brown. No publisher indicated. [ca. 1972]. [8" × 9½"]. Non-pictorial lead sheet. 2pp. Page 2: Blank.

• **AmPM-722 LAPHAM**, Smith (Founder, Rockford, 1843; Postmaster, Rockford, 1848)

722.1 The Early Days Of Rockford. w. Julia A. Moore. m. "Air—*Lucy Long.*" In: *The Sentimental Song Book*, page 22. Published by Julia A. Moore, Grand Rapids, MI. 1876. [4⅛" × 5 13/16"]. Gn/bk non-pictorial back line border. "Centennial, 1876." 62pp.

• **AmPM-723 MAPES**, Carl Edgar (Assistant Prosecuting Attorney, Kent County, 1900–1904; State House, 1905–1907; State Senate, 1909–1913; U.S. House, 1913–1939)

723.1 Landon And Knox. w. No composer indicated. m. "Tune—*Land Of Mine.*" In: *Kent County Woman's Republican Club Song Sheet*, page 4. [1936]. [5 3/16" × 10 7/16"]. B/w litho of Abraham Lincoln. "Let us have a Singing, Smiling United Membership." 4pp.

• **AmPM-723A MCCLELLAND**, Robert (State House, 1837, 1839 & 1943; Mayor, Monroe, 1841; U.S. House, 1843–1849; Governor, 1851–1853; U.S. Secretary of the Interior, 1853–1857)

723A.1 The McClelland Schottische. m. James L. Hambaugh. Published by H.M. Higgins, 117 Randolph Street, Chicago, IL. 1862. Non-pictorial geometric designs. 6pp. Pages 2 and 6: Blank.

• **AmPM-724 MCMILLIAN**, James (Commissioner, Parks Board, Detroit; Board of Estimate, Detroit; U.S. Senator, 1889–1902)

724.1 Senator James McMillian's Grand March. m. Harry R. Williams. Published by Detroit Music Company, 184 & 186 Woodward Avenue, Detroit, MI. 1889. B/w litho by Bufford Co. of James McMillian. "Dedicated by permission to Hon. James McMillian." 8pp. Pages 2, 7 and 8: Blank.

• **AmPM-725 MITCHELL**, John Newton (U.S. Attorney General, 1969–1972)

725.1 Convention '72. w.m. N. Canel and N. Kousaloos. 45 rpm record. Mainstream Records, MRL 5525/ZT8P 224228. Performed by The Delegates. 1972.

725.2 Down At The Old Watergate. w. Congressman William L. Hungate, Democrat, Missouri. Copyright 1973 by Popdraw, Inc., No. 165 West 46th Street, New York, NY. "Recorded by Perception Records, 165 West 46th Street, New York, NY." In: *Poor Richard's Watergate*, page 8. e. Roy Kammerman. Published by Price/Stern/Sloan, Publishers, Los Angeles, CA. 1973. [5¼" × 6¾"]. Bl/w photo of Richard Nixon. 68pp.

725.3 Haldeman, Ehrlichman, Mitchell And Dean. w. Bob Warren. m. "Sung by The Creep." Mr. G. Records, G-826, ca. 1973. Transcribed by ahs@nevada.edu." Published online at <http://php.indiana-edu/~jbmorris/LYRICS/hemd.html>. [ca. 1973].

725.4 I'm So Lonesome Tonight. w. No composer indicated. m. "Tune—*Are You Lonesome Tonight.*" In: *Thoroughly Mad-ern Malcolm Or He Didn't Need A Course In Forensics To Become A Famous Public Speaker*, page 13. Published by the New York State Legislative Correspondents' Association, Albany, NY. 1974. N/w photo of Malcolm Wilson as Alfred E. Newman—"What—Me Governor?" "Featuring the New York Correspondents' Association, March 16. 1974." 32pp.

725.5 Watergate Bug. w. David Arkin. m. "Tune—*Tam Pearce.*" In: *Sing Out! The Folk Song Magazine, Volume 22, Number 3, 1973*, page 23. Published by *Sing Out!*, No. 595 Broadway, New York, NY. 1979. [7" × 10"]. [Crew/RMN-43].

725.6 Watergate Rag. w. Millea Kenin. m. "Tune—*Wish I Could Shimmy Like My Sister Kate.*" In: *Sing Out! The Folk Song Magazine, Volume 22, Number 3, 1973*, page 22. Published by *Sing Out!*, No. 595 Broadway, New York, NY. 1979. [7" × 10"]. [Crew/RMN-43].

• **AmPM-726 PINGREE**, Hazen S. (Mayor, Detroit, 1890–1997; Governor, 1897–1901)

726.1 The Governor's March Two Step. m. Ella

Cleveland-Keiller. Published by Ella Cleveland-Keiller, 25 East Columbia Street, Detroit, MI. 1896. B/w photo of Hazen Pingree. Bl/w drawings of Michigan's Capitol building, floral and geometric designs. "Respectfully dedicated to America's only Governor-Mayor Hon Hazen S. Pingree." "Played by all the Prominent Band and Orchestras in America." 6pp. Page 6: Advertising.

726.2 Pingree March. m. Ida Thorpe Barton. Published by Whitney-Marvin Music Co., Publishers, Detroit, MI. Copyright 1895 by G.D. Bouton. B/w litho of Hazen Pingree. Br/w/bk litho of "Municipal Lighting" tower, "Municipal Potato," gas meter — "Gas 80¢ per m.," trolley car — "Three Cent Fare." "Dedicated to Hon. Hazen S. Pingree, Mayor, Detroit, Michigan." "Published for Band and Orchestra by Willard Bryant, Detroit, Mich." 6pp. Page 6: Advertising.

726.3 Pingree Memorial March (In Memory Of Governor Pingree). m. C.A. Grimm. Published by C.W. Marvin Publishing Company, Detroit, MI. 1901. B/w photo of Hazen Pingree. B/w drawing of palm branches, geometric designs. "Played at the Funeral of Ex-Governor Pingree by 150 Musicians." 8pp. Pages 2, 7 and 8: Blank.

- **AmPM-727 RABAUT**, Louis Charles (Delegate, Democratic National Convention, 1836–1940; U.S. House, 1935–1947 & 1949–1961)

727.1 All Over. w.m. Louis C. Rabaut, "Member of Congress, 14th District, Michigan." A. Lindsay McPhail. Copyright 1943 by Louis C. Rabaut. B/w drawings by B. Henk of military scenes — fighting, family, troops marching, tank, etc. 4pp.

- **AmPM-728 ROMNEY**, George Wilcken (President of American Motors, 1954–1962; Governor, 1963–1969; U.S. Secretary of Housing and Urban Development, 1969–1973)

728.1 Dance Of The Liberal Republicans. w.m. Gerald Gardner. In: *These Are The Songs That Were*, page 10. e. Gerald Gardner "(Writer *Of Who's In Charge Here?*, *News-Reals*, and *That Was The Week That Was*)." Published by Edwin H. Morris and Company, No. 31 West 54th Street, New York, NY. 10019. 1965. B/w photo of Lyndon B. Johnson, Hubert Humphrey, Everett Dirksen, others. R/w/bk cover. List of contents. 36pp. Pages 8, 23 and 25: Photos of politicians. [Crew/LBJ-6].

728.2 If You Want Romney. w. J.B. Ritch II. m. B.G. DeSylvia. No publisher indicated. [1966]. [8½" × 14"]. Non-pictorial photocopy-type. 2pp. Page 2: Blank.

728.3 Keep Michigan On The Move (Keep Romney). w. Walker Graham. m. Jimmy Clark. Published for the Romney Campaign for Governor. Copyright 1964 by Walker Graham and Jimmy Clark, 2501 Iroquois Avenue, Detroit 14, MI. B/w photo of George Romney. Facsimile handwriting — "For a greater Michigan, George Romney." Bl/w/bk printing. "A sprightly Campaign song for Michigan's hard-working Governor." 4pp. Page 4: Campaign narrative. B/w photo of George Romney.

- **AmPM-729 SMITH**, John W. (State Senate; Mayor, Detroit, 1924–1927 & 1933–1934)

729.1 Johnny For Mayor. w. Richard W. Pascoe. m. H. O'Reilly Clint. Published by the John W. Smith Campaign Com., Detroit, MI. [1926–1933]. B/w photo of John Smith. B/w geometric designs. 6pp. Page 6: B/w photo of "H. O'Reilly Clint and The Wolverine Quartet, Detroit's Favorite Entertainers." "Featured with Tremendous Success by H. O'Reilly Clint and The Wolverine Quartet, Detroit's Favorite Entertainers."

729.2 Johnny Smith. w. Raymond B. Egan. m. William Ortmann and Richard Whiting. Published by the John W. Smith Campaign Committee, Detroit, MI. [ca. 1930]. Br/w photo of John W. Smith. B/w drawings of "Newsboy," "soldier," "State Senator," and "Postmaster," Detroit skyline. "Dedicated to our friend — John W. Smith." 6pp. Page 2: Blank. Page 6: "Win With Smith."

729.3 Pride Of The Wolverines March. m. John Philip Sousa. Published by Sam Fox Pub. Co., Cleveland, OH. 1926. Gn/o/bk drawing of a wolverine, sun. 6pp. Page 2: At top of music — "Written especially for and dedicated to The Honorable John W. Smith, Mayor and the people of Detroit." Page 6: Advertising.

- **AmPM-730 STOCKMAN**, David Alan (Executive Director, U.S. House Republican Conference, 1972–1975; U.S. House, 1977–1981; Director, Office of Management and Budget, 1981–1985)

730.1 The Battle Hymn Of The Republicans. m. "Sung to the tune of *The Battle Hymn Of The Republic*." Published by Dots Okay, Inc., Annandale, VA. 1982. [9½" × 3¼"]. Published with a boxed cloth "Reganomics Doll" with song sheet insert. 2pp. Obv: *The Battle Hymn Of The Republicans* {730.1-1}. Rev: Song — *We're In Such A Fixie!* {730.1-2} [Crew/RR-31].

- **AmPM-731 TRIPP**, H.D. (State Senate, 1943–1950)

731.1 No Less Precious. w.m. Senator H.D. Tripp, Allegan, Michigan. a. Fred Douglas. No publisher indicated. 1959. B/w photo of a little girl. Pl/w stars. "Cover design by Mahlon Read." 4pp. Page 4: Narrative on "The Allegan County Story for Retarded Children."

- **AmPM-732 VANDENBERG**, Arthur (Publisher, Grand Rapids, 1912–1928; U.S. Senate, 1928–1951)

732.1 Always True To Fashion. w. No composer indicated. m. "Tune — *Always True To You In My Fashion*." "Quartette — Stassen, Taft, Warren and Martin." In: *Alice In Blunderland Or Through The Rooking Class* [Program and Songbook], page 6. Published by The Legislative Correspondents' Association of New York State, Albany, NY. 1949. [8⅜" × 11"]. N/c drawings of Harry Truman, Thomas Dewey, Franklin Roosevelt, Henry Wallace, Harold Stassen, Alben Barkley, Robert Taft, Earl Warren, other politicians. "A Scintillating Satire of Sadistic Surprises and Surprising Successes Featuring a Dramatic Disclosure of How Tom Did Not Go Down to D.C. in Slips; Together with a Give-Away-Nothing Radio Broadcast and Epic Melodrama of the Indian Wars Entitled 'When the Cat's Away the Mice Will Play.'" "Done With Music and Mirrors — Particularly Mirrors in Three Acts at Hotel Ten Eyck, Albany, March 12, 1949." [Crew/HST-20].

732.2 How Are Things With You? w. No composer

indicated. m. "Tune—*How Are Things In Glocca Morra?*" In: *Visions And Revisions*, page 18. Published by The Albany Legislative Correspondents' Association, Albany, NY. March 6, 1947. [8½" × 11"]. R/w/gn/y/bk drawing of Thomas "Dewey" as Santa Claus, sign—"Santa's Workshop," other New York politicians. "Revealing in Rhapsodic Revelry of Song and Stunt How a Political Scrooge Became a Political Saint; or, What Happened When Many Paws Raided the Wonderful Workshop of Santa Claus Dewey; Together with Other Strange and Silly Scenes." "Hotel Ten Eyck, Albany, March 6, 1947." 24pp. [Crew/TED-34].

732.3 I Can Pass On My Troubles. w. No composer indicated. m. "Tune—*I've Got The Sun In The Morning*." In: *Visions And Revisions*, page 8. Published by The Albany Legislative Correspondents' Association, Albany, NY. March 6, 1947. [8½" × 11"]. R/w/ gn/y/bk drawing of Thomas "Dewey" as Santa Claus, sign—"Santa's Workshop," other New York politicians. "Revealing in Rhapsodic Revelry of Song and Stunt How a Political Scrooge Became a Political Saint; or, What Happened When Many Paws Raided the Wonderful Workshop of Santa Claus Dewey; Together with Other Strange and Silly Scenes." "Hotel Ten Eyck, Albany, March 6, 1947." 24pp. [Crew/TED-34].

723.4 Keep 'Em Pure. w. No composer indicated. m. "Air—*If I Had Rhythm In My Nursery Rhymes*." In: *Tory, Tory Hallelujah*, page 9. Published by Albany Legislative Correspondents' Association, Albany, NY. 1936. [8" × 11¾"]. N/c drawing of Franklin D. Roosevelt, other politicians dressed as Revolutionary soldiers in battle scene—"A Dashing Delirious Drama, Lampooning Loyalists and Liberty Leaguers, Daggering Despots, Dictators and Dummy Donkey-Drivers to music by Red-Coats and Lyrics by Turn-Coats, the Combat Being Played Against a Spangled Back-Drop." "Furiously Fought at Ten Eyck Hotel, Albany, New York, The Evening of Thursday, March 12, 1936, at Seven-Thirty o'clock." [Crew/FDR-325].

732.4A Stalling Stanzas. w. No composer indicated. m. "Air—*The Little Man Who Wasn't There* and *I'm Bidin' My Time.*" "Sung by Hanley and Lehman." In: *So You Won't Talk, A Rollicking Rhapsody Ribbing Strong Silent Statesmen With Twelve Year Itch, Twitting Third Termites And Starring The G.O.P. White House Hopeful In 'Mr. Myth Goes To Washington.' Plus That Pari-Muted Phantasy, 'Three Million Men On A Horse,'* page 12. Published by The Legislative Correspondents' Association of New York, Albany, NY. 1942. [7¾" × 10½"]. N/c drawing of two Veiled brides labeled "Democratic Presidential Nominee" and "Republican Presidential Nominee" and a donkey and elephant dressed as grooms standing on the street at "1940" Convention Corner." Drawing titled "Blind Dates." "Daringly Unreeled at Hotel Ten Eyck, Albany, New York, on the evening of Thursday, February 29th, 1940, at seven-thirty o'clock."16pp.

732.5 They Knew What They Wanted. w. No composer indicated. m. "Air—*One, Two, Three Kick*." In: *Gone With The Winner*, page 14. Published by Albany Legislative Correspondents' Association of New York State, Albany, NY. March 20, 1941. [9" × 11⁶⁄₁₆"]. R/w/bl/y drawing of Franklin Roosevelt and Wendell Willkie riding "A Bicycle Built For Two" labeled—"Roosevelt-Willkie Axis." Wheels—"New Deal" and "Lend Lease Bill." "Or 'Back in the Lap of God.' A Hoosier-Hyde Park Honeymoon Hit, Staring the G. Oomph P.'s Lost Leader and the King of Krum Elbow in 'Lucky Partners.' Says F.D.R.—'He's My Man.' Says the Republican Party—'Once a New Dealer, Sometimes a Double- Dealer.' Says the Public—'Willkie's the Life of the Party, But What Party?" "Served Piping Hot at Hotel Ten Eyck, Albany, New York, Thursday Night, March 20, 1941, at 7:30 o'clock." [Crew/FDR-394].

732.6 Wanted: A Winner. w. No composer indicated. m. "Air—*Stout-Hearted Men*." In: *Gone With The Winner*, page 6. Published by Albany Legislative Correspondents' Association of New York State, Albany, NY. March 20, 1941. [9" × 11⁶⁄₁₆"]. R/w/bl/y drawing of Franklin Roosevelt and Wendell Willkie riding "A Bicycle Built For Two" labeled—"Roosevelt-Willkie Axis." Wheels—"New Deal" and "Lend Lease Bill." "Or 'Back in the Lap of God.' A Hoosier-Hyde Park Honeymoon Hit, Staring the G. Oomph P.'s Lost Leader and the King of Krum Elbow in 'Lucky Partners.' Says F.D.R.—'He's My Man.' Says the Republican Party—'Once a New Dealer, Sometimes a Double-Dealer.' Says the Public—'Willkie's the Life of the Party, But What Party?" "Served Piping Hot at Hotel Ten Eyck, Albany, New York, Thursday Night, March 20, 1941, at 7:30 o'clock." [Crew/FDR-394].

732.7 Who Will It Be?— I Hope! w. No composer indicated. m. "Tune—*Who Do You Love, I Hope*." In: *Visions And Revisions*, page 7. Published by The Albany Legislative Correspondents' Association, Albany, NY. March 6, 1947. [8½" × 11"]. R/w/gn/y/bk drawing of Thomas "Dewey" as Santa Claus, sign—"Santa's Workshop," other New York politicians. "Revealing in Rhapsodic Revelry of Song and Stunt How a Political Scrooge Became a Political Saint; or, What Happened When Many Paws Raided the Wonderful Workshop of Santa Claus Dewey; Together with Other Strange and Silly Scenes." "Hotel Ten Eyck, Albany, March 6, 1947." 24pp. [Crew/TED-34].

• **AmPM-733 WARNER**, Fred Malthy (State Senate, 1895–1898; Michigan Secretary of State, 1901–1904; Governor, 1905–1911)

733.1 Administration March & Two-Step. m. Julius Wuerthner. Published by Julius Wuerthner, Manchester, MI. 1908. B/w photo of Julius Wuerthner. B/w drawings of the Michigan capitol dome, eagle. R/w/b American flag, shield. "Respectfully dedicated to Fred M. Warner, Governor of Michigan." 6pp. Page 6: Blank.

• **AmPM-734 WOLCOTT**, Thomas (Sheriff, Flint, 1936–1937)

734.1 Battle Of Bull's [sic] ***Run***. w. No composer indicated. m. No tune indicated. [1937]. [TPL, p. 96].

• **AmPM-735 YOUNG**, Coleman Alexander (State Senate, 1965–1973; Democratic National Committee, 1969–1981; Delegate to Democratic National Convention, 1972, 1980 & 1996; Mayor, Detroit, 1974–1993)

735.1 Who Would Have Thought It. w.m. Various. 33⅓ rpm LP. Published by Temp-Tee Bar-B-Q, 4505 Livernois, Detroit, MI. [197-]. Record #AR 4838.

Songs and speeches. "Dedicated to Mayor Coleman Young, Detroit's First Black Mayor."
• **AmPM-736 MISCELLANEOUS MUSIC**
736.1 Detroit-Washington March. m. Carry Baxter Jennings. Published by Carrie B. Jennings, Howard City, MI. 1923. Bl/w drawings of U.S. Capitol building, Detroit skyline with municipal building. 6pp. Page 2: At top of music—"In pleasant recollection of the trip from Detroit, Michigan, to Washington, D.C. in company with the Michigan delegation organized by W.C. Hollands, Past Grand Patron O.E.S., to attend the seventeenth Triennial Assembly of the General Chapter in November, 1923." Page 6: Advertising.

736.2 Lansing. m. S.L. Tyler. Published by W.H. Boner & Co., 1102 Chestnut Street, Philadelphia, PA. 1886. B/w litho of various state capitol buildings: "Madison, Wis., Harrisburg, Pa., Hartford, Conn., Columbus, O., Lansing, Mich., Washington, D.C., St. Paul, Minn., Richmond Va., Sacramento, Cal., Albany, NY., Boston, Mass., Montgomery, Ala." "The Capitol Collection." 8pp. Page 2: Blank. Page 3: At top of music—"To my Brother, C.A. Tyler." Page 8: Advertising.

MINNESOTA

• **AmPM-737 BALL**, Joseph Hurst (U.S. Senate, 1940–1949).
737.1 How Are Things With You? w. No composer indicated. m. "Tune—*How Are Things In Glocca Morra?*" In: *Visions And Revisions*, page 18. Published by The Albany Legislative Correspondents' Association, Albany, NY. March 6, 1947. [8½" × 11"]. R/w/gn/y/bk drawing of Thomas "Dewey" as Santa Claus, sign—"Santa's Workshop," other New York politicians. "Revealing in Rhapsodic Revelry of Song and Stunt How a Political Scrooge Became a Political Saint; or, What Happened When Many Paws Raided the Wonderful Workshop of Santa Claus Dewey; Together with Other Strange and Silly Scenes." "Hotel Ten Eyck, Albany, March 6, 1947." 24pp. [Crew/TED-34].
• **AmPM-738 BENSON**, Elmer Austin (State Commissioner of Securities, 1933; State Commissioner of Banks, 1933–1935; U.S. Senate, 1935–1936, Governor, 1937–1939)
738.1 Roosevelt-Benson. Published by The Minnesota Negro Democratic League. 1936. [7½" × 10¼"]. Pk/bk drawing of globe labeled "The World Sings Peace, Yes Peace." 2nd Series October 13th, 1936, Williams Advertising Political Review." "Re-Elect Franklin D. Roosevelt President of the United States. Election Tuesday, Nov. 3rd, Forester Hall, 4th Ave. W. and 1st St." 4pp. Page 2: Advertising. Page 3: Music. Page 4: Blank. [Crew/FDR-447].
• **AmPM-739 BERGER**, Warren Earl (Assistant U.S. Attorney General, 1953; US Court of Appeals, 1955; Chief Justice U.S. Supreme Court, 1969–1986).
739.1 Bye Bye Burger. w. Bill Strauss and Elaina Newport. On Cassette: *Thank God I'm A Contra Boy*. Published by Capitol Steps Productions, 1505 King Street, Alexandria, VA. 1986. Cassette Cover: Capitol building.
• **AmPM-740 BURNQUIST**, Joseph Alfred Arner (State House, 1909–1911; Lt. Governor, 1913–1915; Governor, 1915–1921; State Attorney General, 1939–1955)

740.1 America My Country (The New National Anthem). w. Jens K. Grondahl. m. E.F. Maetzold. Published by The Red Wing Printing Co., Red Wing, MN. 1917. R/w/b litho of a shield, geometric designs. "Long paragraph on the song—"*America, My Country* is said to be the greatest patriotic song-poem of the war..." 4pp. Page 4: Testimonial signed by officers of the National Editorial Association. List of Governors who had "written letters commending the nation-wide use of this song" including "Gov. Burnquist of Minnesota."
• **AmPM-740A COLEMAN**, Norm (State Solicitor General; Mayor, St. Paul, 1993–1998; U.S. Senate, 2003–Present)
740A.1 Hey! Mr. Tennesse [sic] *Man* (Ode to Harold Ford Jr.). w. New York Republican. m. "Suggest to play lefty Bob Dylan mp3 along with it: To the tune of *Mr. Tambourine Man*." "I don't seriously believe that dem centrist Harold Ford jr. would switch. Nor do I think he's conservative. But there may be hope. Look at how Norm Coleman and even David Horowitz had their awakenings. I hope that Mr. Ford reads JC Watts' book. Anyway ... here is an excerpt of my song parody up to the harmonica instrumental." Published online at <http://www.freerepublic.com/focus/news/790095/posts>. 2002.
• **AmPM-741 DONNELLY**, Ignatius (Lt. Governor, 1859–1863; U.S. House, 1863–1869; State Senate, 1874–1878)
741.1 Keep The Ball A-Rolling (Song and Chorus). w.m. Ossian E. Dodge. Published by Root & Cady, No. 67 Washington Street, Chicago, IL. 1868. Nonpictorial geometric lines. "Dedicated to the 'Little Grant' of Minnesota, Hon. Ignatius Donnelly." 6pp. Page 6: Blank.
• **AmPM-742 HOLTON**, J.A. (State Commissioner of Agriculture, 194-)
742.1 Mississippi (That Grand Old State Of Mine). w.m. R. Roy Coats, "Director 'Ole Miss Band;' Writer of *Down Where The Sweet Magnolia Blooms*, etc." Published by R. Roy Coats, University, MS. 1930. [Edi-

tion ca. 194-]. B/w photo of Dennis Murphree. Br/w/gn/r drawing of a train, flowers, tree. 6pp. Page 2: Narrative on the "History of the 'Know Mississippi Better' Train." "Written Specially for and Dedicated to Ex-Governor Dennis Murphree and The Know Mississippi Better Train." Page 6: B/w photos of J.C. Holton, Com. Of Agriculture, Member of Executive Committee; W.F. Bond, State Supt. Of Education, Member of Executive Committee; Dennis Murphree, Ex-Governor, Mississippi, General Chairman; Dr. Felix Underwood, State Health Officer, Member of Executive Committee, L.A. Wilson, Editor of Richton Dispatch, Advance Agent; Dr. Frank Dunn, State Sec'y. of Christian Church Program Director." Narrative on the train.

- **AmPM-742A HUMPHREY**, Hubert Horatio, Jr., (Mayor, Minneapolis, 1945–1948; U.S. Senate, 1949–1964; Vice President; 1965–1969 & 1971–1978; Candidate for President, 1968) [SEE: DOC/PSM-LBJ & HHH]

742A.1 Beware: Here Come Friends. w.m. Richard Kohler and Barbara Dane, 1968. In: *The Vietnam Songbook*, page 100. c. Barbara Dane and Irwin Silber. Published by The Guardian, No. 32 West 22nd Street, New York, NY. Copyright 1969 by Barbara Dane and Irwin Silber. [7" × 10"]. B/w photo of a protest march. O/y/r/bk cover. 228pp.

742A.2 Burn, Baby, Burn. w.m. Jimmy Collier. "I made up this song while the riot in Watts was going on..." In: *Freedom Is A Constant Struggle, Songs of the Freedom Movement*, page 188. c. Guy and Candie Carawan. Published by Oak Publications, New York, NY. 1968. 224pp.

742A.3 Here Comes The Prez {742A.3–1}. w.m. Leonard Seus. 45rpm record. Abby Records#AGI-10014. Performed by Stanley Morgan's World Famous Ink Spots. "Arranged and conducted by Leonard Seus." Followed on side 1 by: *When Humphrey Wins This Year* {742A.3–2}. w.m. Leonard Seus. Side 2: *Hubert Humphrey Speaks Out* with Hubert Humphrey. 1968.

742A.4 Honor Our Commitment. w.m. Jacqueline Sharpe. Copyright 1966 by Marks Music. "This has been one of the stock phrases used by Johnson and Rusk (Humphrey too, I believe) to justify our war against Vietnam." In: *The Vietnam Songbook*, page 52. c. Barbara Dane and Irwin Silber. Published by The Guardian, No. 32 West 22nd Street, New York, NY. Copyright 1969 by Barbara Dane and Irwin Silber. [7" × 10"]. B/w photo of a protest march. O/y/r/bk cover. 228pp.

742A.5 Hubert Humphrey—The President For You And Me. w. Joe Glazer. m. "Tune—*Davy Crockett*." In: *Sing And Win With Hubert Humphrey*, page 1. [1960]. [8½" × 13"]. B/w photo of Hubert H. Humphrey in front of a poster of Franklin D. Roosevelt. "These songs (except for one) were made up by Joe Glazer for the next President of the United States, Hubert Humphrey. *The President For You And Me* was written by Wisconsin's wonderful Lt. Governor and strong Humphrey supporter, Phileo Nash." 2pp. Page 2: Blank. [Crew/HHH-4].

742A.6 The Humphrey-Johnson Tap Routine. w.m. Hank Levine. On LP: *Washington Is For The Birds*. 33⅓rpm LP. Reprise Records # RS-6212. [196-]. Album cover: N/c drawings of Lyndon and Lady Bird Johnson. "The Authentic voices of Lady Bird Johnson, L.B.J. and People like That."

742A.7 I'm Gonna Vote For Hubert Humphrey. w. Joe Glazer. m. "Tune—*Give Me That Old Time Religion*." In: *Sing And Win With Hubert Humphrey*, page 1. [1960]. [8½" × 13"]. B/w photo of Hubert H. Humphrey in front of a poster of Franklin D. Roosevelt. "These songs (except for one) were made up by Joe Glazer for the next President of the United States, Hubert Humphrey. *The President For You And Me* was written by Wisconsin's wonderful Lt. Governor and strong Humphrey supporter, Phileo Nash." 2pp. Page 2: Blank. [Crew/HHH-4].

742A.8 The Man From Minnesota. w. Joe Glazer. m. "Tune—*Yellow Rose Of Texas*." In: *Sing And Win With Hubert Humphrey*, page 1. [1960]. [8½" × 13"]. B/w photo of Hubert H. Humphrey in front of a poster of Franklin D. Roosevelt. "These songs (except for one) were made up by Joe Glazer for the next President of the United States, Hubert Humphrey. *The President For You And Me* was written by Wisconsin's wonderful Lt. Governor and strong Humphrey supporter, Phileo Nash." 2pp. Page 2: Blank. [Crew/HHH-4].

742A.9 Ride On That Humphrey Train. w. Joe Glazer. m. "Tune—*Crawdad Song*." In: *Sing And Win With Hubert Humphrey*, page 1. [1960]. [8½" × 13"]. B/w photo of Hubert H. Humphrey in front of a poster of Franklin D. Roosevelt. "These songs (except for one) were made up by Joe Glazer for the next President of the United States, Hubert Humphrey. *The President For You And Me* was written by Wisconsin's wonderful Lt. Governor and strong Humphrey supporter, Phileo Nash." 2pp. Page 2: Blank. [Crew/HHH-4].

742A.10 The Sea Bees. w. Wayne Lalor and Bob Addie. m. Barnee Breeskin (ASCAP). Non-pictorial. [9½" × 12½"]. Handwritten dedication—"Dedicated to the Vice President and Mrs. Humphrey—the most wonderful friends we have—Barnee." 10pp. Odd numbered pages music. Even numbered pages blank. [Crew/HHH-7].

742A.11 The Search For A Likely Candidate. w.m. Henry and Bobbie Shaffner. Published as a photocopy by Henry and Bobbie Shaffner and Saul Broudy, Bala Cynwyd, PA. 1991. [8½" × 11"]. Non-pictorial. 2pp. Page 2: Blank.

742A.12 We Shall Not Be Moved. w. Joe Glazer. m. "Tune—Old Gospel Song *I Shall Not Be Moved*." In: *Sing And Win With Hubert Humphrey*, page 1. [1960]. [8½" × 13"]. B/w photo of Hubert H. Humphrey in front of a poster of Franklin D. Roosevelt. "These songs (except for one) were made up by Joe Glazer for the next President of the United States, Hubert Humphrey. *The President For You And Me* was written by Wisconsin's wonderful Lt. Governor and strong Humphrey supporter, Phileo Nash." 2pp. Page 2: Blank. [Crew/HHH-4].

742A.13 What Ever Became Of Hubert Humphrey? w.m. Tom Lehrer. On 33⅓rpm LP: *That Was The Year That Was*. Reprise Records #6179. Performed by Tom Lehrer. 1965.

- **AmPM-743 JOHNSON**, Charles W. (City

Clerk, Minneapolis; Candidate for County Treasurer, Hennepin County, 1904)

743.1 *It's Up To You And Me*. w. Charles W. Johnson. m. "Melody — *There's Music In The Air*." Published in Minneapolis, MN. [1904]. [2⅞" × 5½"]. B/w photo of Charles W. Johnson. Long narrative on "Charles W. Johnson's Record, Republican Candidate For County Treasurer of Hennepin County." 2pp. Page 2: Teddy Roosevelt song — *Roosevelt's Call To Duty*. [Crew/TR-390].

- **AmPM-744 JOHNSON**, John A. (Governor, 1905–1909)

744.1 *Governor John A. Johnson Grand March*. m. A. Lageratrom. Published by A. Lagerstrom, Cannon Falls, MN. 1909. Pk/w/gn litho of flowers. "In Memory of Our Beloved Governor John A. Johnson." 6pp. Pages 22 and 6: Blank.

744.2 *In Memoriam*. m. Dr. R. Lagerstrom. Published by St. Peter Music Company, St. Peter, MN. 1909. B/w photo of John Johnson. B/w litho of drape, palm branches, flowers, geometric designs. "Dedicated to the Memory of Gov. John A. Johnson." 8pp. Page 8: Blank.

- **AmPM-745 LADUKE**, Winona (Candidate for Vice President, 2000)

745.1 *Sing We Sing* [Song Book]. Published online by Radio IUMA at <http://www.artists2.iuma.com/IUMA/Bands/Sing_We_Sing/lyrics-0.html>. 2000. Eleven songs. "Click this link to purchase *Sing We Sing* for $10+$5 shipping and handling. All profits generated from the sale of *Sing We Sing* will be donated to Green Party causes and the Vote Nader 2004 Campaign." Gn/w photo of a "Vote Nader & LaDuke" campaign button. [Crew/MISC-198].

- **AmPM-746 LINDBERGH**, Charles Augustus (U.S. House, 1907–1917; Candidate for Governor, 1918)

746.1 *Freedom For All Forever*. 1918.

- **AmPM-747 MCCARTHY**, Eugene (U.S. House, 1949–1959; U.S. Senate, 1959–1971; Candidate for President, 1868) [ALSO SEE: DOC/PSM-MISC]

747.1 *Eugene McCarthy For President* (If You Love Your Country) {747.1–1}. w.m. Peter, Paul & Mary. 45 rpm record. Pepamar Music Corp. #ZTSP 140676/7. Performed by Peter, Paul & Mary. [1968]. Side B: *If You Love Your Country* (Song and Speech Excerpts) {747.1–2}. Performed by Peter, Paul & Mary & Eugene McCarthy.

747.2 *Hitler Ain't Dead*. w.m. Bill Frederick. Copyright 1968 by Futura Music Publishers. "This isn't a personal attack on the president … It's a political attack on the imperialist system, of which Hitler and LBJ (or Eugene McCarthy) are two sides of the same coin." In: *The Vietnam Songbook*, page 102. c. Barbara Dane and Irwin Silber. Published by The Guardian, No. 32 West 22nd Street, New York, NY. Copyright 1969 by Barbara Dane and Irwin Silber. [7" × 10"]. B/w photo of a protest march. O/y/r/bk cover. 228pp.

747.3 *Lyndon Johnson Told The Nation*. w.m. Tom Paxton, 1965. In: *The Vietnam Songbook*, page 35. c. Barbara Dane and Irwin Silber. Published by The Guardian, No. 32 West 22nd Street, New York, NY. Copyright 1969 by Barbara Dane and Irwin Silber. [7" × 10"]. B/w photo of a protest march. O/y/r/bk cover. 228pp.

MEDARY, Samuel (Governor, Minnesota Territory, 1857–1858) [See: Kansas]

- **AmPM-748 MILLER**, Stephen (Governor 1864–1866)

748.1 *I'm Thinking, Mother Dear Tonight*. w. Gov. S. Miller, "of Minnesota." m. H.C. Orth. Published by W.R. Smith, 135 North Eighth Street, Philadelphia, PA. 1866. B/w geometric designs.

- **AmPM-748A MONDALE**, Walter Frederick "Fritz" (State Attorney General, 1960–1964; U.S. Senate, 1964–1976; Vice President, 1977–1981; Candidate for President, 1984; Ambassador to Japan, 1993–1996) [SEE: DOC/PSM-JEC & WFM]

748A.1 *The Wreck Of The Walter Fritz Mondale*. w. Bill Strauss and Elaina Newport. On Cassette: *The Capitol Steps Live*. Published by Capitol Steps Productions, 1505 King Street, Alexandria, VA. 1985. Cassette Cover: NB/w photo of The Capitol, the Capitol Steps group in foreground.

- **AmPM-749 NASH**, Phileo (Lt. Governor, 1960)

749.1 *The President For You And Me*. w. Phileo Nash. In: *Sing And Win With Hubert Humphrey* [Song Sheet]. m. Popular Airs. [1960]. [8½" × 13"]. B/w photo of Hubert H. Humphrey in front of a poster of Franklin D. Roosevelt. "These songs (except for one) were made up by Joe Glazer for the next President of the United States, Hubert Humphrey. *The President For You And Me* was written by Wisconsin's wonderful Lt. Governor and strong Humphrey supporter, Phileo Nash." 2pp. Page 2: Blank. [Crew/HHH-4].

749.2 *Sing And Win With Hubert Humphrey* [Song Sheet]. w. Joe Glazer. m. Popular Airs. [1960]. [8½" × 13"]. B/w photo of Hubert H. Humphrey in front of a poster of Franklin D. Roosevelt. "These songs (except for one) were made up by Joe Glazer for the next President of the United States, Hubert Humphrey. *The President For You And Me* was written by Wisconsin's wonderful Lt. Governor and strong Humphrey supporter, Phileo Nash." 2pp. Page 2: Blank. [Crew/HHH-4].

- **AmPM-750 NOLAN**, Richard Michael (State House, 1969–1973; U.S. House, 1975–1981)

750.1 *Congressman Nolan He Is Our Friend*. w.m. Larry Long. 33⅓ rpm 6¾" vinyl record. Grassroots Publications #CN2-B. 1979. Performed by Larry Long. "For bookings 900 S Broadway, Sauk Rapids, MN. 56379. Side 2: *Matthias Dahl — The Fiddle-Maker*. Record sleeve: B/w photo of Rick Nolan, narrative on loss of family farms.

- **AmPM-751 PERPICH**, Rudy (School Board, Hibbing, 1955–1962; State Legislature, 1962–1970; Lt. Governor, 1971–1976; Governor, 1976–1979 & 1983–1991)

751.1 *The Rudy Perpich Quickstep, A Revenue Developer*. w.m. Al Blair. Published by Northcountry Publishing Co., Alexandria, MN. 1988. [8½" × 11"]. Y/bk drawing of Rudy Perpich waving a Minnesota pennant and holding a sign reading "Explore Minnesota, mile post reading "Minnesota U.S.A. 5,923 Miles," an Oriental-looking man on a camel. 8pp. Page 2: Copyright information. Page 7: Advertising. Page 8: Publisher data.

• **AmPM-752 STASSEN, Harold** (Governor, 1939–1943)

752.1 Always True To Fashion. w. No composer indicated. m. "Tune—*Always True To You In My Fashion.*" "Quartette — Stassen, Taft, Warren and Martin." In: *Alice In Blunderland Or Through The Rooking Class* [Program and Songbook], page 6. Published by The Legislative Correspondents' Association of New York State, Albany, NY. 1949. [8⅝" × 11"]. N/c drawings of Harry Truman, Thomas Dewey, Franklin Roosevelt, Henry Wallace, Harold Stassen, Alben Barkley, Robert Taft, Earl Warren, other politicians. "A Scintillating Satire of Sadistic Surprises and Surprising Successes Featuring a Dramatic Disclosure of How Tom Did Not Go Down to D.C. in Slips; Together with a Give-Away-Nothing Radio Broadcast and Epic Melodrama of the Indian Wars Entitled 'When the Cat's Away the Mice Will Play.'" "Done With Music and Mirrors—Particularly Mirrors in Three Acts at Hotel Ten Eyck, Albany, March 12, 1949." [Crew/HST-20].

752.2 Dance Of The Liberal Republicans. w.m. Gerald Gardner. In: *These Are The Songs That Were* [Song Book], page 10. e. Gerald Gardner (Writer Of *Who's In Charge Here?*, *News-Reals*, and *That Was The Week That Was*). Published by Edwin H. Morris and Company, No. 31 West 54th Street, New York, NY. 10019. 1965. B/w photo of Lyndon B. Johnson, Hubert Humphrey, Everett Dirksen, others. R/w/bk cover. List of contents. 36pp. Pages 8, 23 and 25: Photos of politicians. [Crew/LBJ-6].

752.3 I Can Pass On My Troubles. w. No composer indicated. m. "Tune—*I've Got The Sun In The Morning.*" In: *Visions And Revisions*, page 8. Published by The Albany Legislative Correspondents' Association, Albany, NY. March 6, 1947. [8½" × 11"]. R/w/gn/y/bk drawing of Thomas "Dewey" as Santa Claus, sign—"Santa's Workshop," other New York politicians. "Revealing in Rhapsodic Revelry of Song and Stunt How a Political Scrooge Became a Political Saint; or, What Happened When Many Paws Raided the Wonderful Workshop of Santa Claus Dewey; Together with Other Strange and Silly Scenes." "Hotel Ten Eyck, Albany, March 6, 1947." 24pp. [Crew/TED-34].

752.4 Minnesota Young Republican League Presents 1939 State Convention [Program and Song Sheet]. Published by The Young Republicans of Minnesota. 1939. [6¼" × 9⅛"]. Bl drawing of an elephant. 12pp. Pages 2 11 and 12: Blank. Page 5: B/w photo of "Harold E. Stassen, Governor of Minnesota."

752.5 Rock's Big Candy Mountain. w. Noel E. Parmentel, Jr. and Marshall J. Dodge. In: *Folk Songs For Conservatives*, page 25. Published by Unicorn Press, Inc., No. 790 Madison Avenue, New York, NY. 10021. 1964. [5" × 8⅜"]. Bl/w drawings of Barry Goldwater, Bill Buckley, Ray Cohn, eagle. List of contents. "Sung by Noel E. Parmentel, Jr. and His Unbleached Muslims, Greatest Political Satirists Since Cohn and Schine." "Right Wing Hootenanny." 36pp. [Crew/BMG-13].

752.6 [Sound Off]. w. No composer indicated. m. "Tune—*Sound Off.*" In: *Eisenhower Song Book*, page 8. [1952]. [5" × 9"]. R/w/b non-pictorial lines. 13pp. 24pp. Ten songs written to popular tunes. [M-430]. [Crew/DDE-23].

752.7 Who Will It Be?— I Hope! w. No composer indicated. m. "Tune—*Who Do You Love, I Hope.*" In: *Visions And Revisions*, page 7. Published by The Albany Legislative Correspondents' Association, Albany, NY. March 6, 1947. [8½" × 11"]. R/w/gn/y/bk drawing of Thomas "Dewey" as Santa Claus, sign—"Santa's Workshop," other New York politicians. "Revealing in Rhapsodic Revelry of Song and Stunt How a Political Scrooge Became a Political Saint; or, What Happened When Many Paws Raided the Wonderful Workshop of Santa Claus Dewey; Together with Other Strange and Silly Scenes." "Hotel Ten Eyck, Albany, March 6, 1947." 24pp. [Crew/TED-34].

• **AmPM-753 TOWNE, Charles Arnett** (Judge Advocate General, Minnesota, 1893–1895; U.S. House, Minnesota, U.S. Senate, Minnesota, 1900–1901; U.S. House, New York, 1905–1907)

753.1 Other Arrangements. w.m. J.A. Parks. In: *Park's Republican Songs Campaign Of 1904 (For Male Voices)*, page 3. Published by J.A. Parks Company, York, NE. 1904. [6¹⁵⁄₁₆" × 9¾"]. Br/br non-pictorial geometric design border. 40pp. [M-390]. [Crew/TR-157].

753.2 We'll Try To Get Along. w.m. J.A. Parks. In: *Park's Republican Songs Campaign Of 1904 (For Male Voices)*, page 26. Published by J.A. Parks Company, York, NE. 1904. [6¹⁵⁄₁₆" × 9¾"]. Br/br non-pictorial geometric design border. 40pp. [M-390]. [Crew/TR-157].

753.3 We've Waited, Billy, Waited Long For You. w. Stephen Laskey. m. "Tune—*I've Waited, Honey, Waited Long For You.*" In: *McKinley & Roosevelt Campaign 1900* [Song Book], page 16. Published for the Wholesale Dry Goods Republican Club, No. 350 Broadway by C.G. Burgoyne, New York, NY. 1900. [4¾" × 7"]. Y/bk litho of William McKinley and Theodore Roosevelt, eagle, shield. "Meetings daily from 12 Noon until 2 p.m." "A bird that can sing and won't must be made to sing." 20pp. [M-376]. [Crew/WM-84].

• **AmPM-754 VAN LEAR, Thomas** (Socialist Labor Candidate for Governor, 1902; Mayor, Minneapolis, 1917–1919)

754.1 The Marseillaise. Published on the reverse of an admission ticket to "International Socialist Press Picnic, Riverview Big Picnic Grove, Sunday, June 17th, 1917. [2¹⁵⁄₁₆" × 4½"]. Obv: "Speakers: Thomas Van Lear, Socialist Mayor of Minneapolis, John C. Kennedy, Wm. E. Rodriguez, Seymour Stedman, Robert B. Howe." "For A World Democracy."

• **AmPM-755 VENTURA, Jesse** [Born: James George Janos] (Mayor, Brooklyn Park, 1991–1995; Governor, 1999–2003)

755.1 The Body Rules {755.1–1}. w.m. Mark Orion. 33⅓ rpm 11⅞" picture record. Manufactured and Distributed by Twin/Tone Records, 2541 Nicollet Ave., South Minneapolis, MN. #TTR 8442. Copyright 1984 by White Dog Songs, Inc. "Written and Produced by Mark Orion; Engineered by Paul Stark." Side 1: N/c photo in vinyl of "Jesse (The Body) Ventura" with guitar. "This is dedicated to the U.S. Seals who died in Vietnam and Grenada." "Photography by Arndt-Berthiaume; Weapons by T. Simon." Side 2: ***Showdown With Mr. V.*** {755.1–2}. N/c photo in vinyl of Jesse Venture in military garb with weapons.

755.2 Instant Clinton. w. Tom Smith. m. *"Where The Hell Is Bill?* by Camper Van Beethoven." "This mid-80s demented classis ... is a perfect forum for riffing on the Clinton Administration." "Published online at <http://www. tomsmithonline.com/lyrics/instantclinton.htm>. 1999.

755.3 Jesse The Body vs. Saddam I Am. w. Bill Strauss and Elaina Newport. On CD: *First Lady And The Tramp.* Published by Capitol Steps Productions, 1505 King Street, Alexandria, VA. 1999. CD Cover: Gn/bl/y drawing of George Bush and George W. Bush as Seuss characters.

755.4 Thoughts On Minnesota's 1998 Election. w. S. Ellis Dickerson. m. No tune indicated. "No tune supplied, more's the pity. It will work to *Mountains Of Mourne* (or to Gilbert and Sullivan's *Tit-Willow.*" Lyrics published online at <http://www.mudcat.org/kids/@displaysong.cfm?SongID=7291>. 1999.

• **AmPM-756 VOLSTEAD,** Andrew John (Board of Education, Granite Falls, 1880s; City Attorney, Granite Falls, 1880s; Prosecuting Attorney, Yellow Medicine County, 1886–1902; Mayor, Granite Falls, 1900–1902; U.S. House, 1903–1923)

756.1 The Farmer's Prayer. w. No composer indicated. m. "Sung to the tune *After The Ball.*" In: *Democratic Song Book,* page 5. Published by Charles W. Stewart, No. 439 Arlington Place, Chicago, IL. July 21, 1928. [3¾" × 6⅛"]. Non-pictorial geometric design border. "Dedicated to sane government and honest administration with 'Life, Liberty and The Pursuit of Happiness' without blue laws or fool laws. The most damnable tyranny is the tyranny of small things. 'Give me the writing of a nation's songs and I care not who writes its laws.' The best way to cure a fool of his folly — to Laugh him out of it." "Sing Brother Sing!" 6pp. Various Christian and anti-prohibition sayings throughout — "Would Christ have joined the Ku Klux Klan or the Anti-Saloon League?, &c." [M-418]. [Crew/AES-70].

756.2 Fetters Of Gold. w. No composer indicated. m. "Can be sung to the tune of *Better Than Gold* by Chas. K. Harris." In: *Democratic Song Book,* page 3. Published by Charles W. Stewart, No. 439 Arlington Place, Chicago, IL. July 21, 1928. [3¾" × 6⅛"]. Non-pictorial geometric design border. "Dedicated to sane government and honest administration with 'Life, Liberty and The Pursuit of Happiness' without blue laws or fool laws. The most damnable tyranny is the tyranny of small things. 'Give me the writing of a nation's songs and I care not who writes its laws.' The best way to cure a fool of his folly — to Laugh him out of it." "Sing Brother Sing!" 6pp. Various Christian and anti-prohibition sayings throughout — "Would Christ have joined the Ku Klux Klan or the Anti-Saloon League?, &c." [M-418]. [Crew/AES-70].

756.3 I Want To Run When You Run (Plaintive Paean of Party Patriots Hopeful of Hopping on Big Smith Band-wagon this Fall). w. No composer indicated. m. "Air — *Let Me Call You Sweetheart.*" In: *Old Hokum Week,* page 13. Published by The Albany Legislative Correspondents' Association of New York State, Albany, NY. 1926. N/c drawing by Fred O. Seibel of Statue of Liberty with Beer, Al Smith, Coolidge, other politicians. "A Rousing Reunion of Ravenous and Rampant Republican Rajahs, Rallying Round Resolution to Raid and Ravish, Recapture and Replenish, and Reeking with Hungry Hordes, Head-Hunters, Hughes and Hydro and Hewitt-Hutchinson Hocus Pocus, Plus a Peek Into the Puppet-Shows and Pow-Wows of Pap-Greedy, Picket-Fence Plum-Seekers." "Held Somewhere Near Geneseo, N.Y. Train leaves Ten Eyck Hotel for Rural Rendezvous at Seven-thirty o'clock the evening of Thursday, March, Twenty-fifth, 1926." [Crew/AES-68].

756.4 Mansion Memories. w. No composer indicated. m. "Air — *After The Ball.*" In: *Al S. In Wonderland,* page 10. Published by The Albany Legislative Correspondents' Association of New York State, Albany, NY. 1924. [8½" × 10½"]. N/c drawing by Fred O. Seibel of Statue of Liberty with Beer, "Al Smith," Calvin "Coolidge" as a dragon, other politicians. "A Jocose Junket in Phantom Pullmans to that Roisterous Realm, where Hectic Hopes, Hocus-Pocus Harmonies, Folly, Froth and Flim Flam Blend Blithely with Becalmed Booms, Budget Butchers, Bubbles, Blunders and Barters." "Departing from at Ten Eyck Hotel Terminal, Albany, NY., at 7 o'clock, Eastern Time, on the evening of Thursday, March, 27, 1924." [Crew/AES-67].

756.5 Oily Blues. w. A.A. Granger. m. Raymond Francis. Published by Granger and Francis, Suite 3, No. 107 West University Avenue, Champaign, IL. 1928. R/w/bl/gy drawing by Hugh Leslie of the U.S. Capitol dome resting in "Oily Blues" water, oil dripping on the Statue of Liberty, donkey kicking elephant out of Capitol dome, "teapot" tied to elephant's tail. 4pp. Page 4: Arrangement for Quartet. [Crew/AES-18].

756.5A Volstead Vaporings. w. No composer indicated. m. "Air — *Sidewalks Of New York.*" In: *The Public Frutilities Of 1923,* page 10. Published by The Albany Legislative Correspondents' Association of New York State, Albany, NY. 1923. [8" × 10¾"]. N/c drawing by Fred O. Seibel of Al Smith and Jimmy Walker at the seashore trying to hold back waves of "Traction Lobby," "Electric Light Trust," Water Power Ring," and "GOP Bloc of 81." "A ribald revue, redolent of guff, gestures, gold-bricks, hydrohokum, horse-cars, trackless telephones, transit thugs, synthetic budgets, five-cent fare fiascos, black-jacks, blue noses, monkey wrenches and the 'M.M.M.' (Machold's Minute Men.) "At Ten Eyck, Albany, NY., April, 5, 1923."

756.6 When I Leave The Chair Behind (In Which 'Al' Proclaims Himself Weary of the Game and Admits His Preference for the Golf-Stick to the Veto-Power Pen). m. "Air — *When I Leave The World Behind.*" In: *Statutes And Statuettes,* page 11. Published by Albany Legislative Correspondents' Association, Albany, NY. 1925. N/c drawing by Fred O. Seibel of "Venus De-Milo Smith," other politicians as historical figures. "A Private Presentation of Immortal Images and Matchless Masterpieces From the 1925 Legislative Louvre Frivolously Fashioned in Political Pigments and Capitoline Colors and Featuring Etchers and Fetchers, Chisels and Fizzles, Hues and Hewitts, G.O.P. Gargoyles, Democratic Dorics, Prohibition Pastels, Lowman Landscapes and McGinnies Models, Combined with a Superficial Squint into the Gallery of Gee-

Gaws, Freaks and Flim Flam." "Viewed at Ten Eyck Hotel, Albany, N.Y., on the Evening of March 12, 1925, Seven o'clock." 20pp. [Crew/AES-17].

- **AmPM-757 WINDOM**, William (U.S. House, 1859–1869; U.S. Senate, 1870–1883; U.S. Secretary of the Treasury, 1881 & 1889–1891)

757.1 The Bradbury Schottische. m. Dayton Vreeland. Published by F.G. Smith, 109 & 111 Broadway, Paterson, NJ. 1897. B/w geometric designs. "Dedicated to H.N. Lakeham." 4pp. Page 4: Advertising for Bradbury pianos with photo of "Famous Patrons of Bradbury Pianos" including: "U.S. Grant, J.A. Garfield, C.A. Arthur, Benj. Harrison, R.B. Hayes, Grover Cleveland, Stanley Mathews, J.M Rusk, Benj. Tracy, Levi Morton, Thos. B. Reed, J.W. Noble, William Windom, John G. Carlisle, C.C. McCabe, A.H. Colquitt [and] Walter Q. Gresham." [Crew/MISC-142].

- **AmPM-758 MISCELLANEOUS MUSIC**

758.1 The Senator From Minnesota (Opening Scene III — Act II). w. Ira Gershwin. m. George Gershwin. In: *Of Thee I Sing*, page 140. Published by Warner Bros. Music, 488 Madison Avenue, New York, NY. 10022. 1932. [Edition ca. 197-]. Br/be non-pictorial. Score. "The Pulitzer Prize Musical Sam H. Harris presents *Of Thee I Sing*; Book by George Kaufman and Morrie Ryskind; Directed by George Kaufman; Dances and Ensemble by George Hale." 206pp.

758.2 St. Paul. m. S.L. Tyler. Published by W.H. Boner & Co., 1102 Chestnut Street, Philadelphia, PA. 1886. B/w litho of various state capitol buildings: "Madison, Wis., Harrisburg, Pa., Hartford, Conn., Columbus, O., Lansing, Mich., Washington, D.C., St. Paul, Minn., Richmond Va., Sacramento, Cal., Albany, NY., Boston, Mass., Montgomery, Ala." "The Capitol Collection." 8pp. Page 2: Blank. Page 3: At top of music — "To my Brother, C.A. Tyler." Page 8: Advertising.

MISSISSIPPI

- **AmPM-759 BARBER or BARBOUR**, Haley (Republican Nominee for U.S. Senate, 1982; Director of the White House Office of Political Affairs; National Republican Party Chairman, 1993–1997; Governor, 2004–Present)

759.1 Aren't They Loathsome, The Right? w. William K. Tong. m. Sung to the tune of *Are You Lonesome Tonight* by Elvis Presley." In: *The Sting The Right Wing Song Book* at <http://www.geocities.com/wmktong/bootnewt/loaright.htm> and at <http://amiright.com/parody/miosc/elvispresley5.shtml>.

- **AmPM-760 BARNETT**, Ross Robert (Delegate, Democratic National Convention, 1960; Governor, 1960–1964)

760.1 Ballad For Bill Moore. w. Don West. m. *You've Got To Walk That Lonesome Valley.* "Bill Moore was journeying to present his personal plea for civil rights to Governor Ross Barnett." In: *We Shall Overcome, Song Of The Southern Freedom Movement*, page 104. Compiled by Guy and Candie Carawan for The Student Non-Violent Coordinating Committee. Published by Oak Publications, 165 W. 46th Street, New York, NY. [ca. 1968]. [5½" × 8½"]. Bl/bk photo of marchers. 112pp.

760.2 Get On Board, Little Children. w. Sam Block and Willie Peacock. m. Traditional. In: *We Shall Overcome, Song Of The Southern Freedom Movement*, page 84. Compiled by Guy and Candie Carawan for The Student Non-Violent Coordinating Committee. Published by Oak Publications, 165 W. 46th Street, New York, NY. [ca. 1968]. [5½" × 8½"]. Bl/bk photo of marchers. 112pp.

760.2A Go Mississippi. w.m. Houston Davis. 45 rpm 6⅞" vinyl record. "Governor Ross R. Barnett Campaign Souvenir 1959 Campaign Songs #133–658. Performed by Jerry Lane Orchestra. "Complimentary — Not For Sale."

760.2B Roll With Ross. w.m. Houston Davis. 45 rpm 6⅞" vinyl record. "Governor Ross R. Barnett Campaign Souvenir 1959 Campaign Songs #133–658. Performed by Jerry Lane Orchestra. "Complimentary — Not For Sale." Followed by: *Little Carroll's Last Stand.*

760.3 Which Side Are You On? w. "Original by Mrs. Florence Reece. New words by James Farmer (CORE)." In: *We Shall Overcome, Song Of The Southern Freedom Movement*, page 43. Compiled by Guy and Candie Carawan for The Student Non-Violent Coordinating Committee. Published by Oak Publications, 165 W. 46th Street, New York, NY. [ca. 1968]. [5½" × 8½"]. Bl/bk photo of marchers. 112pp.

- **AmPM-761 BILBO**, Theodore Gilmore (State Senate, 1908–1912; Lt. Governor, 1912–1916; Governor, 1916–1920 & 1928–1932; U.S. Senate, 1935–1947)

761.1 Listen, Mr. Bilbo. w. Bob and Adrienne Claiborne. m. "Traditional." a. Waldemar Hille. In: *The People's Song Book*, 105. e. Waldemar Hille. Published by Boni & Gaer, Inc., New York, NY. 1948. [7" × 10½"]. R/w/b music notes and keyboard. "Forward by Alan Lomax; Preface by B.A. Botkin." 128pp. [Crew/AL-490].

- **AmPM-762 BOND**, W.F. (State Superintendent Of Education, 194-)

762.1 Mississippi (That Grand Old State Of Mine). w.m. R. Roy Coats, "Director 'Ole Miss Band;' Writer of *Down Where The Sweet Magnolia Blooms*, etc." Published by R. Roy Coats, University, MS. 1930. [Edition ca. 194-]. B/w photo of Dennis Murphree. Br/w/gn/r drawing of a train, flowers, tree. 6pp. Page

2: Narrative on the "History of the 'Know Mississippi Better' Train." "Written Specially for and Dedicated to Ex-Governor Dennis Murphree and The Know Mississippi Better Train." Page 6: B/w photos of J.C. Holton, Com. Of Agriculture, Member of Executive Committee; W.F. Bond, State Supt. Of Education, Member of Executive Committee; Dennis Murphree, Ex-Governor, Mississippi, General Chairman; Dr. Felix Underwood, State Health Officer, Member of Executive Committee, L.A. Wilson, Editor of Richton Dispatch, Advance Agent; Dr. Frank Dunn, State Sec'y. of Christian Church Program Director." Narrative on the train.
  • **AmPM-762x** DAVIS, Jefferson (U. S. Senate, 1847–1851 & 1857–1861; U.S. Secretary of War, 1853–1857; President of the Confederacy, 1861–1865) [SEE: DOC/PSM-JD]
  • **AmPM-763** DAVIS, Joseph Roberts (State Legislature, 1860; Delegate, Democratic National Convention, 1860)
763.1 Madison Rifles March. m. Adolphus Brown. Published by A.E. Blackmar & Bro., New Orleans, LA. and Blackmar & Bro Vicksburg, MS. 1861. "To the Hon. Jos. R. Davis, Capitan of the Madison Rifles." 6pp. Page 6: Blank. [H-3624].
  • **AmPM-764** FOOTE, Henry S. (U.S. Senate, 1847–1852; Governor, 1852–1854; Confederate Congress, Tennessee)
764.1 Freedom's Flag (Patriotic Song). w. Robert Jones. m. Mathias Keller. Published by M. Keller & J. Neff, North 9th Street, above Arch, Philadelphia, PA. 1850. B/w litho by P.S. Duval's Steam Litho. Press, Philadelphia, of woman holding an American flag with a lighthouse and sailing ship in the background. "Written and Respectfully Dedicated to Senator Foote." 6pp. Pages 2 and 6: Blank.
764.2 A Peep At Washington. w. "Composed and Sung by Mr. Rice, in Washington, D.C., during the session of Congress, 1850." m. "*Tune—Susannah*." In: *Dan Rice's Great American Humorist Song Book*, page 23. 1866. [4⅛" × 5¾"]. Br/bk drawing of an actor. "Containing Original and Selected Songs, Carefully Revised & Corrected." 34pp.
  • **AmPM-764A** GARTEN, J. Carroll (Lt. Governor, 1956–1960 & 1964–1966; Candidate for Governor, 1959)
764A.1 Little Carroll's Last Stand. w.m. Houston Davis. 45 rpm 6⅞" vinyl record. "Governor Ross R. Barnett Campaign Souvenir 1959 Campaign Songs #133–658. Performed by Jerry Lane Orchestra. "Complimentary — Not For Sale." Followed by: *Roll With Ross*.
  GWIN, William McKendree (U.S. Marshal, Mississippi, 1833; U.S. House, Mississippi, 1841–1843) [See: California]
  HOLLAND, Josiah Gilbert (Superintendent of Public Schools, Vicksburg, Mississippi, ca. 1845–1846) [See: New York].
  • **AmPM-765** HURST, Eugene H. (State House, 1963)
765.1 Ballad Of Herbert Lee. w. Ernie Marrs and Guy Carawan. m. Traditional Irish. In: *We Shall Overcome, Song Of The Southern Freedom Movement*, page 96. Compiled by Guy and Candie Carawan for The Student Non-Violent Coordinating Committee. Published by Oak Publications, 165 W. 46th Street, New York, NY. [ca. 1968]. [5½" × 8½"]. Bl/bk photo of marchers. 112pp.
765.2 We'll Never Turn Back. w. Bertha Gober. m. Traditional. "Herbert Lee ... was shot to death by State Representative Eugene Hurst." In: *We Shall Overcome, Song Of The Southern Freedom Movement*, page 93. Compiled by Guy and Candie Carawan for The Student Non-Violent Coordinating Committee. Published by Oak Publications, 165 W. 46th Street, New York, NY. [ca. 1968]. [5½" × 8½"]. Bl/bk photo of marchers. 112pp.
  • **AmPM-766** LOTT, Chester Trent (U.S. House, 1973–1989; U.S. Senate, 1989–Present)
766.1 Apartheid Lover. w. Teri Nadershahi. m. "*Part Time Lover* originally by Stevie Wonder." "Doctor, this is Trent. I need to borrow your 'jaws of life' To get both feet out of my mouth..." Published online at <http://www.amiright.com/parody/80s/steviewonder1.shml>. [ca. 2002].
766.2 Ballad Of Three Very Thin Men. w. "Zimmy Fallinout." m. "*Ballad Of A Thin Man* originally by Bob Dylan." Published online at <http://www.amiright.com/parody/60s/bobdylan8.shml>. [ca. 2000].
766.3 Chester. w. Malcolm Pacholek. m. "*Pressure*, based on the performance by Billy Joel." "I tried to turn A Boy Named Sue by Johnny Cash into a boy named Trent, but it didn't work out. Then I heard Pressure on the radio, and remembered that Trent is Lott's middle name, and that his real first name is Chester ... and the parody wrote itself in about five minutes." Published online at <http://www.amiright.com/parody/80s/billyjoel28.shml>. [ca. 2002].
766.4 Daddy Told Me Powell's The One. w. Skisics Surus, "skisics@yahoo.com." m. "Sung to the tune of *Mama Told Me Not To Come* by Three Dog Night." "As sung by Dubya Bush." Published online at <http://www.geocities.com/wmktong/bootnewt/daddytoldme.htm>. [ca. 2000].
766.5 The Dennis Hastert Blue. w. Kneton Ngo. m. "*Where Everybody Knows Your Name* originally by Gary Portnoy and Judy Hart Angelo." Published online at <http://www.amiright.com/parody/80s/garyportnoyandjudyhartangelo0.shml>. [ca. 2002].
766.6 Ebony And Ivory. w. Mark Hoolihan. m. "*Ebony And Ivory*, based on a performance by Stevie Wonder and Paul McCartney." "In honor of Trent Lott's recent racist comments." at <http://www.amiright.com/parody/80s/steviewonderandpaulmccartney0.shml>. [ca. 2002].
766.7 The Entertainer. w. Skisics Surus. m. "*The Entertainer*, originally by Billy Joel." Published online at <http://www.amiright.com/parody/70s/billyjoel3.shtml>. [ca. 2000].
766.8 Fallin' Fumblin' Trippin'. w. Skisics Surus, "skisics@yahoo.com." m. "Sung to the tune of *Lovin' Touchin' Squeezin'* by Journey." "As sung by Trent Lott and Dennis Hastert." Published online at <http://www.geocities.com/wmktong/bootnewt/fallfumb.htm>. [ca. 2000].
766.9 Fiasco. w. William Tong. m. "*El Paso*, originally by Marty Robbins." Published online at <http://

www.amiright.com/parody/70s/martyrobbins0.shtml>. [ca. 2001].

766.10 Fristy The Surgeon. w. Madeleine Begun Kane. m. "Feel free to sing along to *Frosty The Snowman* by Steve Nelson & Jack Rollins." "Trent Lott got his own song parody and a satirical poem too. Now it's his successor's turn." Published online at <http://www.raisingkane.com/first.html>. [ca. 2002.

766.11 Gingrich The White-Hared Speaker. w. William K. Tong. m. "*Rudolph The Red-Nosed Reindeer*, based on a performance by Gene Autry." Published online at <http://www.amiright.com/parody/misc/geneautry14.shtml>. [ca. 1996].

766.12 Go Give Lott A Shove. w. William K. Tong. m. Sung to the tune of *Lotta Love* by Nicolette Larson." [V-1: In: *The Sting The Right Wing Song Book* at <http://www.geocities.com/wmktong/bootnewt/lottshov.htm>. N/c photo of Trent Lott—"Believe it; or Don't! Hi, I'm Trent Lott and I like my white sheets starched extra stiff... Just like my white shirts. That way it keeps the eye-holes from fraying and the pointy hood from drooping over." "Senator Trent Lott (Republican-Mississippi) is a member of the CCC (the Council for Concerned Citizens); an offshoot of the KKK!—Believe it!"] [V-2: "Written originally in 1999, and still appropriate for today, as the returning Senate Majority Leader Trent Lott puts his foot in his mouth again by praising the 1948 segregationist platform of Strom Thurman, who ran for president that year as an [sic] Dixiecrat independent." Published online at <http://www.amiright.com/parody/70s/nicolettelarson0.shml>. [V-1: 1999] [V-2: ca. 2002].

766.13 I Love DC. w. William Ross. m. "To the tune of *I Love L.A.* by Randy Newman." Lyrics and sound file published online at <http://www.seanet.com/-billr/ilovedc.htm>. 1996.

766.14 Instant Clinton. w. Tom Smith. m. "*Where The Hell is Bill?* by Camper Van Beethoven." "This mid-80s demented classis ... is a perfect forum for riffing on the Clinton Administration." "Published online at <http://www.tomsmithonline.com/lyrics/instantclinton.htm>. 1999.

766.15 Lenator Sott. w. Bill Strauss and Elaina Newport. On CD: *Between Iraq And A Hard Place*. Published by Capitol Steps Productions, 1505 King Street, Alexandria, VA. 2003. CD Cover: N/c drawing of a U.N. vehicle.

766.16 Living In A Liberal World. w. "Rice Cube and Walt Daddy." m. "*Material Girl* by Madonna." Published online at <http://www.amiright.com/parody/80s/madonna6.shml>. [ca. 2002].

766.17 Lott Hangs On. w. William K. Tong. m. "*Let's Hang On* by The Four Seasons." "Satire about returning[?] Senate Majority Leader Trent Lott (R-MS), whose praise of Strom Thurmond's 1948 segregationist presidential campaign has ignited a political firestorm." Published online at <http://www.amiright.com/parody/60s/thefourseasons2.shml>. [ca. 2002].

766.18 Ode To Trent Lott. w. Mike Juergens. m. "*Ode To Billie Joe* originally by Bobbie Gentry." Published online at <http://www.amiright.com/parody/60s/bobdylan8.shml>. [ca. 2002].

766.19 Oust Mr. Trent Lott. w. William K. Tong. m. "Sung to the tune of *Up On The House Top*." "Satire about returning Senate Majority Leader Trent Lott (R-MS), whose praise of Strom Thurmond's 1948 segregationist presidential campaign has ignited a political firestorm." Published online at <http://www.bootnewt.envy.nu/oustmrtrentlott.htm> and at <http://www.amiright.com/parody/misc/traditional131.shml>. [ca. 2002]. N/c photo of Trent Lott—"Believe it; or Don't! Hi, I'm Trent Lott and I like my white sheets starched extra stiff... Just like my white shirts. That way it keeps the eye-holes from fraying and the pointy hood from drooping over." "Senator Trent Lott (Republican-Mississippi) is a member of the CCC (the Council for Concerned Citizens); an offshoot of the KKK!— Believe it!"

766.20 Racist's Song. w. Alvin Dover and Bill Tong. m. "*The Christmas Song* originally by Nat King Cole." Published online at <http://www.amiright.com/parody/misc/natkingcole3.shml>. [ca. 2002].

766.21 The Rantings Of Trent Lott. w. Madeleine Begun Kane. m. "To be sung to *The Sidewalks Of New York*, by Chas. B. Lawlor and James W. Blake." Published online at <http://www.raisingkane.com/lott.html>. 2003.

766.22 Send Their Green, Green Asses Home. w. Darrell Decker. m. "*Green Grass Of Home*, based on the performance by Tom Jones." Published online at <http://amiright.com/parody/70s/tomjones0.shml>. [2001].

766.23 Should Lott Resign. w. "Leo." m. "*Auld Lang Syne* originally by Traditional." "The Republican leader in the U.S. Senate, Senator Trent Lott from Mississippi, is now in very hot water after some remarks that praised Senator Strom Thurmond's segregationist policies during the latter's 1948 presidential run. It seems to be that both conservative and liberals are calling for his resignation for the leadership, despite multiple apologies." Published online at <http://www.amiright.com/parody/misc/traditional128.shml>. [ca. 2002].

766.24 Speaker Of The House. w. "Bubba." m. "*Leader Of The Pack* originally by Shangri-La's." Published online at <http://www.amiright.com/parody/60s/ shangrilas0.shml>. [ca. 2002].

766.25 Tradition. w. Mark Hoolihan. m. "*Tradition*, based on the performance by *Fiddler On The Roof* cast." "In honor of Trent Lott's recent racist comments." Published online at <http://www.amiright.com/parody/60s/fiddlerontheroofcast0.shtml>. [ca. 2002].

766.26 Trent Lott's Ass Is Blowin' Lots Of Wind. w. "Sassy And Boot Newt." m. "Sung to the tune of *Blowin' In The Wind* by Bob Dylan." "Satire about Senator Trent Lott (R-MS), whose recently stepped down as Senate Majority Leader." Published online at <http://www.bootnewt.envy.nu/lottsass.htm>. [ca. 2002].

766.27 Trent Lott'A White Christmas. w. Richard Cairo and Lover Dudley." m. "*White Christmas* originally by Bing Crosby." "It's the holidays!" Published online at <http://www.amiright.com/parody/misc/bingcrosby11.shml>. [ca. 2002].

- **AmPM-767 MCRAE**, John Jones (State House, 1848–1850; U.S. Senate, 1851–1852; Governor, 1854–1858; U.S. House, 1858–1861; Confederate Congress, 1862–1864)

767.1 Gov. McRae's Grand Waltz. m. E.H. Kent. Published by Henry Tolman, 153 Washington Street, opposite The old South Church, Boston, MA. 1854. B/w litho of a river scene, sailboats, homes. "To His Ex. John J. McRae of Mississippi." "The Pascagoula Melodies." 4pp. Page 4: Blank. [LL/JH].

• **AmPM-768 MURPHREE**, Herron Dennis (State House, 1912–1924; Lt. Governor, 1923–1927 & 1931–1943; Governor, 1927–1828 & 1943–1944)

768.1 Mississippi (That Grand Old State Of Mine). w.m. R. Roy Coats, "Director 'Ole Miss Band;' Writer of *Down Where The Sweet Magnolia Blooms*, etc." Published by R. Roy Coats, University, MS. 1930. [Edition ca. 194-]. B/w photo of Dennis Murphree. Br/w/gn/r drawing of a train, flowers, tree. 6pp. Page 2: Narrative on the "History of the 'Know Mississippi Better' Train." "Written Specially for and Dedicated to Ex-Governor Dennis Murphree and The Know Mississippi Better Train." Page 6: B/w photos of J.C. Holton, Com. Of Agriculture, Member of Executive Committee; W.F. Bond, State Supt. Of Education, Member of Executive Committee; Dennis Murphree, Ex-Governor, Mississippi, General Chairman; Dr. Felix Underwood, State Health Officer, Member of Executive Committee, L.A. Wilson, Editor of Richton Dispatch, Advance Agent; Dr. Frank Dunn, State Sec'y. of Christian Church Program Director." Narrative on the train.

• **AmPM-768A PHILLIPS**, Rubel (State Public Service Commission; Candidate for Governor, 1963)

768A.1 [Rubel, Rubel]. w. No composer indicated. m. "Sung to the tune of the folk song *Ruben, Ruben.*" "Music and the Rubel Phillips Campaign." Lyrics published online at <http://www.msys.net/cress/ballots2/phillips.htm>.

• **AmPM-769 QUITMAN**, John A. (Governor, 1835–1836 & 1850–1851)

769.1 Gen. Quitman's Grand March. m. Edwd. O. Eaton, "of Natchez." Published by Beck & Lawton, SE Cor. 7th & Chesnut, Philadelphia, PA. 1858. B/w litho of Gen. Quitman. "Composed and respectfully inscribed to Gen John A. Quitman of Misspi." Facsimile letter: "Mr. Edwd. O. Eaton, Dear Sir, Please accept many thanks for the beautiful march which you have done me the honor to inscribe to me and with every wish for your future success, believe me to be ever yours, John A. Quitman." 6pp. Page 6: Blank.

• **AmPM-770 RANKIN**, John Elliott (Prosecuting Attorney, Lee County, 1911–1915; U.S. House, 1921–1953)

770.1 DDT. w. No composer indicated. m. "*Bury Me Not On The Lone Parie* [sic]." In: *National Youth Lobby* [Program with Songs], page 27. Published by The Young Progressive Citizens of America. 1947. [8½" × 11"]. B/w drawing of man, the Capitol. "Jobs! Peace! Freedom!" "Hear Henry Wallace Keynote the National Youth Lobby." "Sponsored by Y.P.C.A. in Washington, D.C., on June 15 and 16, 1947." 30pp. Pages 25 to 27: Songs. [Crew/HAW-9].

770.2 Listen, Mr. Rankin. w. Bob and Adtienne Clairborne. m. Tune—"*Listen, Mr. Bilbo* or *Listen, Mr. Bigot.*" *Songs For Wallace*, page 6. Published by People's Songs, Inc. for the National Office of The Progressive Party, No. 39 Park Avenue, New York, NY.

1948. [8⅜" × 10¼"]. B/w drawing of Henry A. Wallace, farm. 12pp. [M-428]. [Crew/HAW-3].

• **AmPM-771 SINGLETON**, Otho Robards (State House, 1846–1847; State Senate, 1848–1854; U.S. House, 1853–1855, 1857–1861, & 1875–1887; Confederate Congress, 1861–1865)

771.1 Confederates Grand March. m. Wm. H. Hartwell. Published by A.E. Blackmar & Bro., 74 Camp Street, New Orleans, LA. [ca. 1862]. R/w/b litho of the Confederate stars and bars flag. "To Capt. O.R. Singleton of the Confederates, Madison Co., Miss." [H-3390].

• **AmPM-772 SLIDELL**, John (State House; U.S. District Attorney, 1829–1833; U.S. House, 1843–1845; U.S. Senate, 1853–1861; Confederate Commissioner to Great Britain, 1861–1865)

772.1 Abraham's Daughter No. 2. Published by H. De Marsan, Publisher, No. 54 Chatham Street, New York, NY. [ca. 1863]. [9½" × 6¹³⁄₁₆"]. B/w border litho of flags, soldier, slave. 2pp. Page 2: Blank. [Crew/AL-521].

772.2 Any Other Man (Or John Bull). w. Walter W. Warren. m. No tune indicated. Published by H. De Marsan, Publisher, 54 Chatham Street, New York, NY. [ca. 1863]. B/w litho border. 2pp. Page 2: Blank. [AMC].

772.3 Confederate Flag Red, White And Blue. w. J.S. Privatt. m. No tune indicated. No publisher indicated. [1861–1862]. B/w non-pictorial geometric design border. "Composed and sung by J.S. Prevatt, Co. E. 6th Ga. Reg." 2pp. Page 2: Blank. [AMC].

772.4 Dixie. Where Is My Dixie? w. Ned Buntline. m. No tune indicated. Published by A.W. Auner, Song Publisher, Auner's Printing Office, 110 North Tenth Street, above Arch, Philadelphia, PA. [1861–1863]. B/w non-pictorial geometric design border. [AMC].

772.5 Jeff Davis (Or The King Of The Southern Dominions). w. No composer indicated. m. "Air— *The King Of The Cannibal Island.*" Published by H. De Marsan, Publisher, No. 54 Chatham Street, New York, NY. [1863?]. [6¾" × 9¾"]. B/w penny song sheet with litho border of caricatures of musicians, Black man and children, jesters. 2pp. Page 2: Blank. [Crew/JD-52].

772.6 Jeff Davis (Or The King Of The Southern Dominion). m. "Air— *The King Of The Cannibal Island.*" Published by J. Wrigley, Publisher, No. 27 Chatham Street, New York, NY. [186-]. [6" × 9"]. R/w/b hand colored star and stripe border. "No. 799." "J. Wrigley, Publisher of Songs, Ballads, and Toy Books, Conversation, Age, and Small Playing Cards, Alphabet Wood Blocks, Valentines, Motto Verses, and Cut Motto Paper, &c." 2pp. Page 2: Blank.

772.7 Jeff Davis' Last Proclamation To His Council. w. No composer indicated. m. "Air— *The Girl I Left Behind Me.*" [186-]. Non-pictorial geometric design border. 2pp. Page 2: Blank.

772.8 John Bull (Or Any Other Man). w. No composer indicated [Walter W. Warren]. m. No tune indicated. Published by Johnson, Song Publisher, &c., 7 North 10th Street, Philadelphia, PA. [ca. 1863]. B/w litho border. "Send for Johnson's New Catalogue." 2pp. Page 2: Blank. [AMC].

772.9 Long Live McClellan. w. No composer indicated. m. "Air—*Happy Land Of Canaan.*" No publisher indicated. [1862–1864]. B/w litho border. 2pp. Page 2: Blank. [AMC].

772.10 Mason & Slidell Quick Step. w.m. H.N. Hempatead. Published by C.D. Benson [1861], "Respectfully dedicated to Messrs. Mason & Slidell, out [sic] Southern ministers to England, forcibly taken from the British steamer Trent." 6pp. [H-3646].

772.11 Ode To Mason And Slidell. w. H. Webster Canterbury m. "Air—*Twenty Years Ago.*" In: *New Patriotic Songs* [Song Sheet], page 1. [1860]. [12⅞" × 14½"]. B/w litho of Abraham Lincoln and George Washington, "Price only five cents a sheet." 2pp. Page 2: Blank. [Crew/AL-508].

772.12 Our Country Right Or Wrong. w. Thomas A. Becket. m. "Tune—*Few Days.*" Published by Weaver & Royal, Printer, Harrisburg, PA. [1862–1863]. B/w non-pictorial geometric design border. "Tho's a'Becket, author of *Columbia The Gem Of The Ocean, Pennsylvania Battle Cry,* &c., &c. Sung nightly at Sanford's Opera House." 2pp. Page 2: Blank. [AMC].

772.13 Overtures From Richmond. w. Francis J. Child. m. "*Liliburloro* by Henry Purcell, c. 1686." In: *No More Booze! And After Ribtickling, Knee Stomping, Gut Busting, High Stepping, Side Splitting, Tow Tapping, Fantastically Funny! Folk Songs For Guitar*, page 54. c.a. Jerry Silverman. Published by G. Shirmer, New York, NY. 1978. Pl/o/bk/w geometric designs. 68pp. [Crew/WM-257].

772.14 Patent Chivalry. w. No composer indicated. m. "Air—*A Highland Lad My Love Was Born.*" In: *Fremont Songs For The People (Original And Selected)*, page 39. c. Thomas Drew "(Editor of *The Massachusetts Spy*)." Published by John P. Jewett & Company, Boston, MA. Copyright 1856 by Thomas Drew. [3⅜" × 5½"]. B/w litho of "J.C. Fremont." "The Campaign of 1856." 68pp. [Crew/JCF-18].

772.15 The People Are A-Coming. w. No composer indicated. m. No composer indicated. In: *The Republican Campaign Songster For 1860*, page 29. c. W.H. Burleigh. Published by [V-1 and V-2: H. Dayton, No. 36 Howard Street, New York, NY] [V-3: McNally & Company, No. 81 Dearborn Street, Chicago, IL]. 1860. [V-1: Gn/bk] [V-2: Y/bk] [V-3: Be/bk] [V-4: Bl/bk]. "Price 10 cents." [3¹³⁄₁₆" × 6"]. 72pp. [M-104]. [Crew/AL-57].

772.16 Secessia Land. w. No composer indicated. m. "Air—*Promised Land.*" Published by A.W. Auner, Song Publisher, Auner's Printing Office, 110 North Tenth Street, above Arch, Philadelphia, PA. [1862–1864]. B/w litho border. 2pp. Page 2: Blank. [AMC].

772.17 The Song Of The Democracy. w.m. No composer or tune indicated. In: *The Democratic Campaign Songster, No. #1*, page 5. Published by American Publishing House, No. 60 West Fourth Street, Cincinnati, OH. 1860. [3⅞" × 5⅟₁₆"]. Pk/bk litho of "Stephen A. Douglas," black line border. At top of cover—"No. 1, Price 10 Cents." 52pp. [M-118]. [Crew/SAD-12].

772.18 Southern Red, White And Blue. w. No composer indicated. m. No tune indicated. No publisher indicated. [1861–1862]. Non-illustrated. 2pp. Page 2: Blank. [AMC].

• **AmPM-773 SPEAKES,** Larry (Deputy White House Press Secretary, 1981–1987; White House Press Secretary, 2001?)

773.1 Mommar Said To His Men. w. Mark Graham. m. Sound file provided. Lyrics and sound file published online by Mudcat Café at <http://mudcat.org/@displaysong.cfm?SongID=4007>. [199-].

• **AmPM-774 SPENCER.** (Judge, Jackson, 1963)

774.1 [If You Ever Go To Jackson]. w. No composer indicated. m. "Tune—*Midnight Special.*" In: *We Shall Overcome, Song Of The Southern Freedom Movement*, page 56. Compiled by Guy and Candie Carawan for The Student Non-Violent Coordinating Committee. Published by Oak Publications, 165 W. 46th Street, New York, NY. [ca. 1968]. [5½" × 8½"]. Bl/bk photo of marchers. 112pp.

• **AmPM-775 STONE,** John M. (Governor, 1876–1882 & 1890–1896)

775.1 Columbia My Country (American Anthem). w.m. George M. Vickers "(Composer of *Guard The Flag, God Bless Our Land,* &c.)." [ca. 1893]. Bl/bk litho of Miss Columbia, two women, steamboat. "The New Patriotic Song Approved by People from New England to Alaska." "The sentiment of this song will, I am sure, be indorsed by every true American—William McKinley; Full of Patriotic sentiment, well expressed—Governor Wm. E. Russell, Massachusetts; It is patriotic in sentiment and the music is charming, Governor J.M. Stone, Mississippi; It is a patriotic gem and will probably remain one of the patriotic songs of our country—Governor Elisha P. Ferry, Washington; I trust it may be welcomed by an appreciative public with the favour it deserves—Gen. Lyman E. Knapp, Alaska; I regard such music as a important part of the education of the young people of the land—Hon. John Wanamaker, and representative Americans in all parts of the United States." 4pp. Page 2: Facsimile letter releasing copyright. Page 4: Blank.

• **AmPM-776 SULLIVAN,** Charles L. (Lt. Governor)

776.1 Charles Sullivan Campaign Souvenir Record. 45 rpm vinyl record. Globe, Nashville #SoN 00981. R/sl label with bk/r photo of Charles Sullivan. "Approved and paid for by Charles L. Sullivan." 1963. Side 1: A Personal Message to you from Charlie Sullivan. Side 2: Three campaign songs: *S-U-L-L-I-V-A-N* {776.1–1}. Performed by The Cee-Jays; *Sullivan's The One* {776.1–2}. Performed by The Mud Creek Three. *Sullivan's For Me In '63* {776.1–3}. Performed by The Sullivan Singers.

• **AmPM-777 WALKER,** Robert James (U.S. Senate, 1835–1845; U.S. Secretary of the Treasury, 1845–1849; Governor of Kansas, 1857; U.S. Financial Agent to Europe, 1863–1864)

777.1 Flag Of Our Sires (National Hymn). w. Hon. Robert J. Walker. m. J.N. Pychoeski. No publisher indicated. [ca. 1860]. B/w litho by Hatch & Co., New York, of woman with sword and American flag—"Patria spes ultima mundi." B/w geometric designs. 6pp. Pages 2 and 6: Blank. [LL/JH].

777.2 The Lament Of An 'O.P.A.' w. No composer indicated. m. No tune indicated. In: *The Republican Campaign Songster For 1860*, page 69. c. W.H. Burleigh. Published by [V-1 and V-2: H. Dayton, No.

36 Howard Street, New York, NY] [V-3: McNally & Company, No. 81 Dearborn Street, Chicago, IL]. 1860. [V-1: Gn/bk] [V-2: Y/bk] [V-3: Be/bk] [V-4: Bl/bk]. "Price 10 cents." [3$\frac{15}{16}$" × 6"]. 72pp. [M-104]. [Crew/AL-57].

777.3 Ladies, Come Weave A New Banner. w. No composer indicated. m. "Tune — *Old Rosin The Bow.*" In: *The National Clay Minstrel (And True Whig's Pocket Companion For The Presidential Canvass Of 1844)*, page 58. Published by [V-1: George Hood, No. 15 North 6th Street, Philadelphia, PA] [V-2: James Fisher, No. 71 Court Street, Boston, MA]. 1843. [3¼" × 5⅛"]. Y/bk litho of raccoon — "That Coon" and flag — "Henry Clay," log cabin. "New and Improved Edition." 128pp. Page 10: Dedication — "To the National Clay Club this work is respectfully dedicated by the Publisher." [Crew/HC-11].

• **AmPM-778 WILLIAMS**, John S. (U.S. House, 1893–1909; U.S. Senate, 1911–1923)

778.1 An Auspicious Occasion. w. No composer indicated. m. "Tune — *Odd Fellows' Hall.*" In: *Republican Campaign Parodies And Songs* [Songster], page 13. Published by Betts and Burnett, South Butler, Wayne County, NY. 1896. [7¾" × 5½"]. Be/bk non-pictorial. "McKinley and Hobart." "1896." 28pp. [M-340]. [Crew/WM-67].

778.2 The North American March. m. Marie Louka "(Composer of *The Rajah March And Two Step* and *A Silent Prayer Reverie*)." Published by H.A. Weymann and Son, 923 Market Street, Philadelphia, PA. 1904. R/e/bk drawings of Joe Cannon and John Williams on the front page of the newspaper The North American. Drawing titled "After-Dinner faces of 'Uncle Joe' Cannon, Speaker of the House and John Williams, Leader of the House Democrats." Four drawings of Indian Chiefs. "Its all here and it's all true." 6pp. Page 6: Advertising.

MISSOURI

• **AmPM-779 ASHCROFT**, John David (State Auditor, 1973–1975; State Attorney General, 1976–1985; Governor, 1985–1993; U.S. Senate, 1995–2001; U.S. Attorney General, 2001–Present)

779.1 A.G. Ashcroft Lies. w. William K. Tong. m. "Sung to the tune of *Bette Davis Eyes* by Kim Carnes." N/c photo of John Ashcroft. "Dedicated to that power-hungry zealot, Attorney-General (A.G.) John Ashcroft." Published at <http://www.bootnewt.envy.nu/agashcroft.htm>. 2001.

779.2 All Night Long. w. Alvin Dover, "alvindover@hotmail.com." m. "Sung to the tune of *All Night Long* by Lionel Richie." "As sung by Attorney General John Ashcroft." Published at <http://www.bootnewt.envy.nu/allnightlong.htm>. 2001.

779.3 American Lie. w. Mark Hoolihan. m. "*American Pie*, based on a performance by Don Mclean." "I wrote this after I saw the Justice Department explaining why it was OK for the, to ignore the constitutional rights of US citizens when they felt like it. Well I felt like writing this. Why ... because I can." Published online at <http://www.amiright.com/parody/70s/donmclean48.shtml>. Copyright 2004 by Boniface Bugle Productions.

779.4 Are We Still Free Now? w. Skisics Surus, skisics@yahoo.com. m. "Sung to the tune of *Who Can It Be Now* by Men At Work." Published at <http://www.bootnewt.envy.nu/arewestillfree.htm>. 2002.

779.5 Ashcroft. w. William K. Tong. m. "Sung to the tune of *Your Mama Don't Dance* by Loggins and Messina." B/w cartoon of two men talking, Poster on wall behind them with "Ashcroft's record — Antichoice, Anti-Gun Control, Anti-Affirmative Action, Anti-Miranda Ruling, Anti-Gay." One man says: "If he's confirmed, remember — no dancing in the streets — he's personally against dancing too." Published at <http://www.bootnewt.envy.nu/dontdance.htm>. 2001.

779.6 Ashcroft. w. William Tong. m. "*Angie*, originally by The Rolling Stones." "Dedicated to Attorney General Ashcroft." Published online at <http://amiright.com/parody/misc/therollingstones3.shml>. [ca. 2001].

779.7 The Ashcroft Follies (A Musical). w. Stephen C. Day. m. Popular tunes. Published at <http://www.poppolitics.com/articles/2002-07-03-ashcroftfollies.shtml>. 2002. Songs include: **God Bless John Ashcroft** {779.7–1}. m. "From the music *God Bless America* by Irving Berlin;" **It's Fun To Attorney General** {779.7–2}. m. "To the music of *Y.M.C.A.* by the Village People;" **John Ashcroft Is A Bulldog** {779.7–3}. m. "From *Joy To The World* by Three Dog Night;" **There's No Wing Like The Right Wing** {779.7–4}. m. "To The music of *There's No Business Like Show Business* by Irving Berlin;" **What Your Government Needs Is Love** {779.7–5}. m. "To the tune of *What The World Needs Is Love* by Burt Bachrach and Hal David;"

779.8 Ashcroft Is A Nervous Guy. w. William K. Tong. m. "Sung to the tune of *Angels We Have Heard On High.*" N/c photo of John Ashcroft. Published at <http://www.bootnewt.envy.nu/nervousguy.htm>. 2002.

779.9 Ashcroft Is A Nut. w. Alvin Dover, "alvindover@ hotmail.com." m. "Sung to the tune of *I Can't Go For That* (No Can Do) by Daryl Hall and John Oats." Published at <http://www.bootnewt.envy.nu/ashcroftnut.htm>. 2001.

779.10 Ashcroft Is Hunting You Down. w. William K. Tong. m. "Sung to the tune of "*Santa Claus Com-*

ing To Town." N/c photo of John Ashcroft. Published at <http://www.bootnewt.envy.nu/ashcrofthunt.htm>. 2001.

779.11 Ashcroft Lies. w. "Attmay." m. "Sung to the tune of *Walk On By* by Dionne Warwick." Published at <http://www.bootnewt.envy.nu/ashcroftlies.htm>. 2001.

779.12 Ashcroft, The New Darth Vader. w. William K. Tong. m. "Sung to the tune of *Rudolph The Red-Nosed Reindeer* by Gene Autry." N/c photos of John Ashcroft and Darth Vader. Published at <http://www.bootnewt.envy.nu/ashcroftvader.htm>. 2002.

779.13 Ashcroft's Army. w. John McCutcheon. m. No tune indicated. Published by the Centre for Political Song at http://polsong.gcal.ac.uk/songs/mccutcheon.html>. 2002.

779.14 Ashcroft's Favorite Things. w. Madeleine Begun Kane. Published online at <http://www.madkane.com/favoritethings.html>. "To be sung to the tune of *My Favorite Things* from *The Sound Of Music*. If you'd like to sing along, here's a midi link which opens a second window." 2002.

779.15 Ashcroft's Way. w. Alvin Dover, alvindover@hotmail.com. m. "Sung to the tune of *Nature's Way* by Spirit." "Dedicated to Attorney General John Ashcroft." Published at <http://www.bootnewt.envy.nu/ashcroftsway.htm>. 2001.

779.16 Ashcroft's Working Hard To Railroad. w. William K. Tong. m. "Sung to the tune of *I've Been Working On The Railroad*." B/w drawing of Ashcroft and Bush as Taliban — "We have met the enemy and they are us." Published at <http://www.bootnewt.envy.nu/ashcroftrr.htm>. 2002.

779.17 Axis Of Evil. w. William K. Tong. m. "Sung to the tune of *Evil Ways* by Santana." "As sung by President Dubya Bush." B/w drawing of George Bush as a gunslinger — "Go ahead, make my day Iran, Iraq N. Korea, Yemen, Lebanon, Syria, Somalia, China, Russia, Philippines, Malaysia, Saudi Arabia, Cuba, Tunisia, Libya, Pakistan... (To be continued)." Published at <http://www.bootnewt.envy.nu/axisofevil.htm>. 2002.

779.18 Bare Lady. w. William K. Tong. m. "Sung to the tune of *Lady* by Little River Band." "John Ashcroft the Prude orders cover-up ... of partially nude Lady Sprit of Justice statue!" B/w two-part cartoon of statue and Ashcroft saying "Would someone please cover up that embarrassment? and second part showing Ashcroft covered up with a blanket." Published at <http://www.bootnewt.envy.nu /bareLady.htm>. 2002.

779.19 Behind Blue Velvet. w. William K. Tong. m. "Sung to the tune of *Blue Velvet* by Bobby Vinton." N/c photos of John Ashcroft in front of partially nude Lady Justice statue — 'How many boobs are there really in this picture.'" N/c photo of Ashcroft and a calico cat — "In your guts, you know he's nuts." Published at <http://www.bootnewt.envy.nu/bluevelvet.htm>. 2002.

779.20 The Blue-Nosed Spy. w. William K. Tong. m. "Sung to the tune of *The Blue-Tailed Fly*." N/c photo of John Ashcroft — "Fascist John's Tip 'O The Day: When spying on your neighbor ... remember to act like they are your friends. And remember, snooping can be a fun experience for the whole family!" Published at <http://www.bootnewt.envy.nu/bluenosedspy.htm>. 2002.

779.21 The Bomber. w. William K. Tong. m. "Sung to the tune of *La Bamba* by Ritchie Valens." "Attorney General Ashcroft is now taking public flak for his hysterical handling of the arrest of the accused 'dirty bomber' suspect, Jose Padilla." Published at <http://www.bootnewt.envy.nu/thebomber.htm>. 2002.

779.22 Brother John's Patriot Salvation Show. w. William Tong. m. "*Brother Love's Traveling Salvation Show*, originally by Neil Diamond." "Satire inspired by Attorney General John Ashcroft's attempt to drum up failing public support for the unpopular Patriot Act, which has been condemned as unconstitutional via resolutions by Alaska, Hawaii, and Vermont and over 100 U.S. cities." Published online at <http://amiright.com/parody/70s/neildiamond27.shml>. [2003].

779.23 Calico Cats. w. William K. Tong. m. "Sung to the tune of *Crazy* by Patsy Cline." "Dedicated to the religious crackpot John AshKKKroft, Bush's Attorney General (A.G.)." Published at <http://www.bootnewt.envy.nu/crazy-ag.htm>. 2002.

779.24 Calico's Revenge. w. "Chookie." m. "Sung to the tune of the *Meow Mix* Cat Food jingle." "Opposing Attorney General John Ashcroft and his loathing of calico cats is the group known as C.A.L.I.C.O. (Citizens Against Looney Ideological unconstitutional Oligarchs), with this serenade." N/c photo/graphic by Chookie of John Ashcroft and a calico cat — "In your guts, you know he's nuts." Published at <http://www.bootnewt.envy.nu/calicosrevenge.htm>. 2002.

779.25 The Christ-What-A-Mess Song. w. Tom Smith. m. *The Christmas Song*. From "A Very Dubya Xmas." "Published online at <http://www.tomsmithonline.com/lyrics/very_dubya_xmas.htm>. 2002.

779.26 Crisco Kid. w. Ernest Stewart. m. "Sung to the tune of *Cisco Kid* by War." "A Republican Chicken Heart fantasy: The adventures of John "Crisco Kid" Ashcroft and sidekick G.W. 'Smirko' Bush on the war front in Afghanistan (yeah, right!)." N/c photo of John Ashcroft praying with a can of Crisco oil on his head — "The Anointed One." Published at <http://www.bootnewt.envy.nu/criscokid2.htm>. [ca. 2002].

779.27 Crisco Kid. w. William K. Tong. m. "Sung to the tune of *Cisco Kid* by War." "Former Senator John Ashcroft (now Attorney General), defeated for re-election by the ghost of the late Gov. Mel Carnahan, was known to anoint himself with Crisco oil in religious ceremonies." N/c photo of John Ashcroft praying with a can of Crisco oil on his head — "The Anointed One." Published at <http://www.bootnewt.envy.nu/criscokid.htm>. [ca. 2002].

779.28 C.R.A.B. (Cheney, Rumsfeld, Ashcroft & Bush). w. Todd Samusson. m. "No tune indicated. Published online by the Centre for Political Song at http://polsong.gcal.ac.uk/songs/samusson.html>. 2002.

779.29 Crazy A.G. w. Darrell Decker. m. "Sung to the tune of *Alley Cat* by Bobby Rydell." "Attorney General John Ashcroft fears calico cats, believing them agents of Satan." N/c photo of John Ashcroft and a calico cat — "In your guts, you know he's nuts." Published at <http://www.bootnewt.envy.nu/bluevelvet.htm>. 2002.

779.30 Creep. w. Sara Rose. m. "*Creep*, originally by Radiohead." Published online at <http://amiright.com/parody/90s/radiohead1.shml>. [ca. 2000].

779.31 Dirty Bomb. w. Alan Dover and William K. Tong. m. "Sung to the tune of *Cherry Bomb* by John Mellencamp." "As sung by Jose Padilla, the accused 'dirty bomber,' jailed indefinitely in a military prison." N/c photo of Jose Padilla—"Dirty, Dirty Bomber." Published at <http://www.bootnewt.envy.nu/dirtybomb.htm>. 2002.

779.32 Do What I Like. w. William Tong. m. "*My Life*, originally by Billy Joel." Published online at <http://www.amiright.com/parody/70s/billyjoel5.shtml>. [ca. 2001].

779.33 Don't Know Much (Version I). w. "The Diva." m. "Sung to the tune of *What A Wonderful World* by Sam Cook." Published at <http://www.bootnewt.envy.nu/jaworld1.htm>. 2001.

779.34 Don't Know Much (Version 2). w. "The Diva." m. "Sung to the tune of *What A Wonderful World* by Sam Cook." Published at <http://www.bootnewt.envy.nu/jaworld2.htm>. 2001.

779.35 Dubya's People. w. Alvin Dover and Bill Tong. m. "*Everyday People*, based on a performance by Sly & The Family Stone." Published online at <http://www.amiright.com/parody/2000s/ludacris16.shtml>. 2003.

779.36 Fun, Fun, Fun ('Til John Ashcroft Takes Our Freedom Away). w. Don Clinchy. m. "*Fun, Fun, Fun' Til Her Daddy Takes The T-Bird Away*, written by Brian Wilson and Mike Love, performed by The Beach Boys." Published by the Centre for Political Song online at <http://polsong.gcal.ac.uk/songs/beachboys.html> and at <http://www.georgybush.com/lyrics.html>. [ca. 2003].

779.36A George Bush Stole The Election. On CD: *Lying King.* Performed by Dick Bush and the Rummys. Published on CD by everyamericanvotes.com. Remastered by John Reynolds at Cool Blue Studios. 2004.

779.37 Georgeamaniac. w. T.J. Zmina. m. "*Animaniacs Theme*, originally by Theme Song." Published online at <http://www.amiright.com/parody/90s/themesong0.shtml>. [ca. 2001].

779.38 Georgy Bush's Smarmy Jerks Club Band. w. Bo 'Ice' Bielefeldt. m. "*Sergeant Pepper's Lonely Hearts Club Band* by Beatles." Published online by Amiright.com at <http://www.amiright.com/parody/misc/beatles1.shtml>. [ca. 2002].

779.39 Gonna Lock Down Democracy. w. William K. Tong. m. "Sung to the tune of *Rockin' Around The Christmas Tree* by Brenda Lee." "Sung by Attorney General John Ashcroft." NB/w cartoon of John Ashcroft dressed as a Mullah—"I can hold you 7 days without charges, I can listen to your conversations with your lawyer, I may not even let you have a lawyer, I can try you and convict you in secret, I can execute you without appeal, 'Mullah Ashcroft, the New Taliban.'" Published at <http://www.bootnewt.envy.nu/lockdown.htm>. 2001.

779.40 He Spies. w. William K. Tong. m. "Sung to the tune of *These Eyes* by The Guess Who." "Satire about Attorney General John Ashcroft, who wants to snoop on all citizens with impunity." N/c photo of John Ashcroft. Published at <http://www.bootnewt.envy.nu/hespies.htm>. 2002.

779.41 He Wants To Lynch Blacks, Gays, And Jews. w. "Attmay." m. "Sung to the tune of *I Only Want To Be With You* by Dusty Springfield." Published at <http://www.bootnewt.envy.nu/lynch.htm>. 2001.

779.42 He's Unwise. w. Alvin Dover, alvindover@hotmail.com. m. "Sung to the tune of *Edelweiss* from *The Sound Of Music* by Rogers & Hammerstein." "Dedicated to Attorney General John Ashcroft." Published at <http://www.bootnewt.envy.nu/hes-unwise.htm>. 2001.

779.43 Hey, Kid Crisco. w. Sara Rose, "ariel@runesofao.com." m. "Sung to the tune of *Hey Big Spender* by Shirley Bassey." Published at <http://www.bootnewt.envy.nu/heykidcrisco.htm>. 2001.

779.44 His Noose. w. William K. Tong. m. "Sung to the tune of *Footloose* by Kenny Loggins." "From an idea suggested by The Diva." Published at <http://www.bootnewt.envy.nu/hisnoose.htm>. [ca. 2001].

779.45 Hits The Spot, Spot, Spot. w. Alan Dover, "alvindover@hotmail.com." m. "Sung to the tune of *Hot, Hot, Hot* by Buster Poindexter." "Attorney General John Ashcroft reportedly leads public sing-alongs of his own patriotic songs at the Department of Justice, much to the dismay of many of his federal employees." "N/w photo of Ashcroft in an American flag dress holding a microphone in one hand and a dead eagle in the other." Published at <http://www.bootnewt.envy.nu/let-hisehosoar.htm>. 2002.

779.46 I Know Dubya Wants To Change The Laws. w. William K. Tong. m. "Sung to the tune of *I Saw Mommie Kissing Santa Clause* by Jimmy Boyd." Published at <http://www.bootnewt.envy.nu/knowdubya.htm>. 2001.

779.47 If You Bicker At All. w. William K. Tong. m. "Sung to the tune of *Another Brick In The Wall, Part 2* by Pink Floyd." "As sung by Attorney General John Ashcroft." N/c photo of John Ashcroft." Published at <http://www.bootnewt.envy.nu/ifyoubickeratall.htm>. [ca. 2002].

779.48 I'm A Dummy. w. Alvin Dover, "alvindover@hotmail.com." m. "Sung to the tune of *I Feel Pretty* from the musical, *West Side Story*." "As sung by President Bush." Published at <http://www.bootnewt.envy.nu/imadummy.htm>. 2002.

779.49 I'm In The White House Now. w. Sara Rose. m. "*I've Got My Mind Set On You*, originally by George Harrison." "Sung by the Shrub." Published online at <http://amiright.com/parody/80s/georgeharrison0.shml>. [ca. 2000].

779.50 Jackboot Snitching Morons. w. William K. Tong. m. "Sung to the tune of *Witchy Woman* by The Eagles." "Satire about the low-lifes who would volunteer to be snitches for Operation TIPS." N/c facsimile 'Uncle Sam Wants You' poster reading—"I'm Turning You In!! TIPS, Turn In Poor Suckers, Office of Homeland Security." Published at <http://www.bootnewt.envy.nu/snitchingmorons.htm>. 2002.

779.51 John Ashcroft Don't Dance. w. William Tong. m. "*Your Mama Don't Dance*, originally by Loggins & Messina." Published online at <http://amiright.com/parody/70s/logginsmessina0.shtml>. [ca. 2001].

779.52 John Ashcroft Is Coming To Town. w. Tom Smith. m. *Santa Claus Is Coming To Town*. From "A

Very Dubya Xmas." "Published online at <http://www.tomsmithonline.com/lyrics/very_dubya_xmas.htm>. 2002.

779.53 John Ashcroft Is Hunting You Down. w. William Tong. m. "*Santa Claus Is Coming To Town*, originally by Traditional." Published online at <http://www.amiright.com/parody/misc/traditional59.html>. [ca. 2002].

779.54 The John Ashcroft Song Book. w. Various. m. Popular tunes. Published online at <http://www.bootnewt.envy.nu/ashsongs.htm>. [2001–2003].

779.55 John Ashcroft's Kangaroo Courts. w. Skisics Surus, "skisics@yahoo.com." m. "Sung to the tune of *Magical Mystery Tour* by The Beatles." Published at <http://www.bootnewt.envy.nu/kangaroo-courts.htm>. 2002.

779.56 John, The Son Of A Preacher Man. w. William K. Tong. m. "Sung to the tune of *Son Of A Preacher Man* by Dusty Springfield." "Dedicated to the Crisco Kid, Attorney General John Ashcroft." N/c photo from a painting by Roberto Parada of John Ashcroft with a picture of Jesus and a bottle of Crisco oil. Published at <http://www.bootnewt.envy.nu/johntheson.htm>. 2002.

779.57 Johnny Ashcroft. w. William K. Tong. m. "Sung to the tune of *Johnny Angel* by Shelly Fabares." Published at <http://www.bootnewt.envy.nu/Johnny.htm>. 2001.

779.58 Johnny Don't. w. Alvin Dover, "alvindover@hotmail.com." m. "Sung to the tune of *Honey Don't* by The Beatles." "Dedicated to Attorney General John Ashcroft." Published at <http://www.bootnewt.envy.nu/johnnydont.htm>. 2001.

779.59 Johnny's No Good. w. William K. Tong. m. "Sung to the tune of *Johnny B. Goode* by Chuck Berry." "Dedicated to the Crisco Kid, Attorney General John AssKKKroft." N/c photo from a painting by Roberto Parada of John Ashcroft with a picture of Jesus and a bottle of Crisco oil. Published at <http://www.bootnewt.envy.nu/johnnysnogood.htm>. 2002.

779.60 Kooky. w. William K. Tong. m. "Sung to the tune of *Spooky* by The Classics IV." "Parody inspired by Regina Litman and her calico cat, Spooky." N/c photo of John Ashcroft and calico cat — "In your guts, you know he's nuts." Published at <http://www.bootnewt.envy.nu/kooky.htm>. 2002.

779.61 Let His Ego Soar. w. William K. Tong. m. "Sung to the tune of *Let The Eagle Soar* by John Ashcroft." "Attorney General John Ashcroft reportedly leads public sing-alongs of his own patriotic songs at the Department of Justice, much to the dismay of many of his federal employees." "As sung by disgusted Department of Justice employees forced to hear Ashcroft sing." N/w photo of Ashcroft in an American flag dress holding a microphone in one hand and a dead eagle in the other." Published at <http://www.bootnewt.envy.nu/let-hisehosoar.htm>. 2002.

779.62 Let's Take Back America. w. William K. Tong. m. "Sung to the tune of *Pink Houses* by John Mellencamp." "The great MIDI was sequenced by Ron Tilden." N/c photos of John Ashcroft and George Bush." Published at <http://www.bootnewt.envy.nu/takebackamerica.htm>. 2002.

779.63 Let Those Iron Pokers Glow. w. "Daedalus." m. "Sung to the tune of the *Old Time Rock & Roll* by Bob Seger & The Silver Bullet Band." "As sung by Attorney General John Ashcroft." "Satire about Attorney General John Ashcroft's contemplated use of torture in interrogations." N/c photo of John Ashcroft. Published at <http://www.bootnewt.envy.nu/ironpokersglow. htm>. 2002.

779.64 Looney. w. Alvin Dover, "alvindover@hotmail.com." m. "Sung to the tune of *Money* by The Beatles." Published at <http://www.bootnewt.envy.nu/looney.htm>. 2001.

779.64A Mean John Ashcroft. w. 2LD4U. m. "*Bent Cold Sidewalk,* based on the performance by Tangerine Dream." "And now ... a parody for all you Tangerine Dream fans out there!" Published online at <http://www.amiright.com/parody/70s/tangerinedream0.shtml>. 2004.

779.64B Mean John Ashcroft, Part 2. w. 2LD4U. m. "*Bent Cold Sidewalk,* based on the performance by Tangerine Dream." Published online at <http://www.amiright.com/parody/70s/tangerinedream1.shtml>. 2004.

779.65 The Meanie In The Pillory w. Skisics Surus, skisics@yahoo.com. m. "Sung to the tune of *The Minstrel In The Gallery* by Jethro Tull." Published at <http://www.bootnewt.envy.nu/meanie.htm>. 2001.

779.66 Messed Up Fool Begs. w. Skisics Surus, "skisics@yahoo.com." m. "Sung to the tune of *Death on Two Legs* by Queen." "Dedicated to John Ashcroft." Published at <http://www.bootnewt.envy.nu/messed up.htm>. 2001.

779.67 Monsters. w. Skisics Surus, "skisics@yahoo.com." m. "Sung to the tune of *Monster* by Steppenwolf." Published at <http://www.bootnewt.envy.nu/monsters.htm>. 2001.

779.68 My Front Pages. w. Michael Pacholek. m. "*My Back Pages,* based on a performance by Bob Dylan." "Check out the front page of the November 3, 2004 edition of the New York Post: 'Oh, S —!' The narrator is Our Fearless Appointed Leader With a Purpose, a.k.a. George of the Bungle, Oilfinger, the Spinning heel, Jay Jay the Jet Plane, the Presi-dunce, the Pretz-ident, the Wayward Son, the President-Select, the President-defective, President Stem Cell, the White House Squatter, the Demanded-in-Thief, or, as Bill Maher calls him, Drinky McDumbass. My favorite? I didn't think this one up, but "Third Reich From The Son!" Published online at <http://www.amiright.com/parody/60s/bobdylan41.shtml>. [ca. 2003].

779.69 The New So Long It's Been [Good] To Know You. w. Joel Landy and Stephen L. Suffet. m. "Original words and music by Woodie Guthrie." Published by the Centre For Political Song online at <http://polsong.ac.uk/songs/guthrie.htm>. 2001, 2002 & 2003.

779.70 New Secret Police Running Our Homeland. w. Alvin Dover and Bill Tong. m. "*Sgt. Pepper's Lonely Hearts Club Band,* originally by The Beatles." Published online at <http://www.amiright.com/parody/70s/thebeatles2.shtml>. [ca. 2002].

779.71 No Rights w. Skisics Surus, "skisics@yahoo.com." m. "Sung to the tune of *My Life* by Billy Joel." Published at <http://www.bootnewt.envy.nu/norights.htm>. 2002.

779.72 Obnoxious Right Wing Nazi Pig Dog From Missouri. w. "Attmay." m. "Sung to the tune of *Boogie-Woogie Bugle Boy* by The Andrews Sisters." Published at <http://www.bootnewt.envy.nu/nazipigdog.htm>. 2001.

779.73 Our Hearts Are Black. w. Alvin Dover, "alvindover@hotmail.com." m. "Sung to the tune of *Baby's In Black* by The Beatles." N/c photos of George Bush and John Ashcroft. Published at <http://www.bootnewt.envy.nu/heartsblack.htm>. 2001.

779.74 Our Rights Are Dead, John Ashcroft. w. William K. Tong. m. "Sung to the tune of *Tom Dooley* by The Kingston Trio." "Inspired by Alan Dover's version of this parody, *Teach Me My Rights, John Ashcroft.*" N/c photo from a painting by Roberto Parada of John Ashcroft with a picture of Jesus and a bottle of Crisco oil. Published at <http://www.bootnewt.envy.nu/ourrights.htm>. 2001.

779.75 P-A-T-R-I-O-T-A-C-T. w. Michael McVey. m. "*D-I-V-O-R-C-E*, based on a performance by Tammy Wynette." "If you're dead, remember that in Chicago you vote for the Democrats, and in Missouri they vote for you. Otherwise, Ashcroft would be just another Senator." Published online at <http://www.amiright.com/parody/70s/tammywynette2.shml>. 2003.

779.76 Prying Eyes. w. William K. Tong. m. "Sung to the tune of *Private Eyes* by Daryl Hall and John Oats." "A satirical version of a near-future AmeriKKKa under Bush's fascist TIPS* surveillance — *TIPS: Terrorism Information & Processing System, Bush's proposed neighborhood snoop program." Published at <http://www.bootnewt.envy.nu/pryingeyes.htm>. 2002.

779.77 The Right Wing Tricksters Came To Town. w. William Tong. m. "*The Night They Drove Old Dixie Down*, originally by Joan Baez. Published online at <http://www.amiright.com/parody/70s/joanbaez0.shtml>. [ca. 20010.

779.78 Shred The Constitution. w. Alvin Dover, "alvindover@hotmail.com." m. "Sung to the tune of *Ball Of Confusion* by The Temptations." Published at <http://www.bootnewt.envy.nu/shredconstitution.htm>. 2001.

779.79 Sixteen Scandals. w. Michael Pacholek. m. "*Sixteen Candles*, based on a performance by Johnny Maestro & The Crests." Published online at <http://www.amiright.com/parody/misc/johnnymaestrothecrests.shtml>. [ca. 2003].

779.80 Spinning Fool. w. William Tong. m. "*Spinning Wheel*, originally by Blood, Sweat and Tears." Published online at <http://www.amiright.com/parody/70s/bloodsweattears0.shtml>. [ca. 2001].

779.81 Spying Days Are Here Again (The Patriot Act Song). w. Madeleine Begun Kane. Published online at <http://www.madkane.com/spy.html>. "John Ashcroft's been running around on a 'Patriot' tour, trying to drum up support for some bigger and better infringements of our privacy rights. So naturally I had to write the old songwriter a song. Feel free to sing *Spying Days Are Here Again* a/k/a The Patriot Act Song to *Happy Days Are Here Again*, by Jack Yellen and Milton Ager, using this midi link which opens a second window." 2003.

779.82 Stubborn Man. w. William K. Tong. m. "Sung to the tune of *Southern Man* by Neil Young." B/w cartoon of John Ashcroft in a Klansman's robe. N/c photos of John Ashcroft and a calico cat — In your guts, you know he's nuts." Published at <http://www.bootnewt.envy.nu/stubbornman.htm>. 2002.

779.83 Subterranean Homesick Blues. w. Skisics Surus. m. Tune — "*Subterranean Homesick Blues*, originally by Bob Dylan." Published online at <http://amiright.com/parody/60s/bobdylan5.shml>. [ca. 2001].

779.84 Super Duper Tuesday. w. ParodyKeet. m. "*If I Were A Rich Man*, based on a performance by Tevye, star of *Fiddler On The Roof.*" Published online at <http://amiright.com/parody/misc/tevyestaroffidlerontheroof0.shtml>. 2003.

779.85 Talking Cabinet Blues. w. Dave Lippman. m. No tune indicated. Published online at <http://www.davelippman.com/Cabinet.html>. N/c photo of Dave Lippman. [ca. 2001].

779.86 Teach Me My Rights, John Ashcroft. w. Alvin Dover, "alvindover@hotmail.com." m. "Sung to the tune of *Tom Dooley* by The Kingston Trio." N/c photo from a painting by Roberto Parada of John Ashcroft with a picture of Jesus and a bottle of Crisco oil. Published at <http://www.bootnewt.envy.nu/myrights.htm>. 2001.

779.87 They're Beginning To Look A Lot Like Nazis. w. Darrell Decker. m. "Sung to the tune of *It's Beginning To Look A Lot Like Christmas*." N/c photo of George Bush in Nazi uniform — "Ein Volk, ein Reich, ein Führer!" Published at <http://www.bootnewt.envy.nu/lookalotlike.htm>. 2001.

779.88 Truth. 33⅓ rpm LP. American Artists Custom Records, POB 4501, Springfield, MO. #AAS-1149-LP. [1973–1975]. Album cover: N/w photo of John Ashcroft and Max Bacon. — "Volume One, Edition One, Ashcroft & Bacon." Songs include: **Why Me Lord** {779.88–1}; **Reach Out Jesus** {779.88–2}; **Jesus Hold My Hand** {779.88–3}; **The Broken Vessel** {779.88–4}; **King Jesus** {779.88–5}; **Unseen Hand** {779.88–6}; **Didn't He Shine** {779.88–7}; **I Find No Fault In Him** {779.88–8}; **More About Jesus** {779.88–9}; **We've Come This Far By Him** {779.88–10}; **Come Holy Spirit** {779.88–11}; and **Jesus Is Lord Of All** {779.88–12}.

779.89 We Know That They're Mean. w. William K. Tong. m. "Sung to the tune of *If You Know What I Mean* by Neil Diamond." Published at <http://www.bootnewt.envy.nu/theyremean.htm>. 2002.

779.90 We'll Resist You. w. Sara Rose, "ariel@runesofao.com." m. "Sung to the tune of *We Will Rock You* by Queen." Published at <http://www.bootnewt.envy.nu/resistyou.htm>. 2001.

779.91 Wreck Of The Ol' Constitution. w. William K. Tong. m. "Sung to the tune of *Wreck Of The Old 97* — also known as *MTA* by the Kingston Trio." "Satire about John Ashcroft's Justice Department campaign against Oregon's assisted suicide statute." N/c photo from a painting by Roberto Parada of John Ashcroft with a picture of Jesus and a bottle of Crisco oil. Published at <http://www.bootnewt.envy.nu/wreckold.htm>. 2001.

779.92 You Can't Hide From Pryin' Eyes. w.

William K. Tong. m. "Sung to the tune of *Lyin' Eyes* by The Eagles." "Satirical vision of near-future AmeriKKKa under Bush's fascist, paranoid TIPS surveillance." Published at <http://www.bootnewt.envy.nu/hidefrompryineyes.htm>. 2002.

779.93 *You Must Be Nice To W*. w. William K. Tong. m. "Sung to the tune of *Nice To Be With You* by Gallery." "Sung by Attorney General Ashcroft." Published at <http://www.bootnewt.envy.nu/niceto-w.htm>. 2002.

779.94 *You Will Be Watched Covertly*. w. William K. Tong. m. "Sung to the tune of *Someone To Watch Over Me* by Frank Sinatra [sic]." "John Ashcroft sings the praises of the proposed Terrorism Information & Protection System (TIPS)." Published at <http://www.bootnewt.envy.nu/youwillbewatched.htm>. 2002.

779.95 *Yellow Bush Of Texas*. w. Madeleine Begun Kane. Published online at <http://www.madkane.com/yellow.html>. "Feel free to sing *Yellow Bush Of Texas* to *Yellow Rose Of Texas* using this midi link which opens a second window." 2003.

779.96 *You Can't Worry, Shrub*. w. William Tong. m. "*You Can't Hurry Love*, originally by The Supremes." Published online at <http:// www.amiright.com/parody/misc/thesupremes1.shtml>. [ca. 2001].

• **AmPM-780** ATCHISON, David Rice (State House 1834 & 1838; Circuit Court Judge, Platte County, 1841; U.S. Senate, 1843–1855)

780.1 *Freedom And Fremont*. w.m. No composer or tune indicated. In: *The Fremont Songster*, page 43. Published by [V-1: H.S. Riggs & Company, Publishers, No. 4 Cortland Street] [V-2: P.J. Cozans, No. 107 Nassau Street], New York, NY. 1856. [V-1: 3⅜" × 5¾"] [V-2: 3½" × 5⅝"]. Be/bk litho of wreath, John C. Fremont. "With a current likeness of John C. Fremont, The People's Candidate for the Presidency." 40pp. [M-094, 095]. [Crew/JCF-45].

780.2 *The Retrospect*. w. No composer indicated. m. "Air—*The Old Oaken Bucket*." In: *The Republican Campaign Songster, A Collection Of Lyrics, Original And Selected, Specifically Prepared For The Friends Of Freedom In The Campaign Of Fifty-Six*, page 9. Published by Miller, Orton & Mulligan, No. 25 Park Row, New York, NY. 1856. [3¹³⁄₁₆" × 6"]. Be/bk litho of "Colonel John C. Fremont" facing to viewer's left, black line border. 112pp. [M-097]. [Crew/JCF-24].

780.3 *Song For The Times* (On The State of the Union). w. Judson. m. "Tune—*Axes To Grind*." In: *Hutchinson's Republican Songster For 1860*, page 30. e. John W. Hutchinson "(of the Hutchinson Family Singers)." Published by O. Hutchinson, Publisher, No. 272 Greenwich Street, New York, NY. 1860. B/w floral design border. "Lincoln and Liberty." 76pp. [M-110]. [Crew/AL-317].

780.4 *What Has Caused This Great Commotion*. w. No composer indicated. m. No composer indicated. In: *The Fremont Songster*, page 8. Published by [V-1: H.S. Riggs & Company, Publishers, No. 4 Cortland Street] [V-2: P.J. Cozans, No. 107 Nassau Street], New York, NY. 1856. [V-1: 3⅜" × 5¾"] [V-2: 3½" × 5⅝"]. Be/bk litho of wreath, John C. Fremont. "With a current likeness of John C. Fremont, The People's Candidate for the Presidency." 40pp. [M-094, 095]. [Crew/JCF-45].

• **AmPM-780A** BACON, Max E. (State House, 1970–1972; Magistrate Judge, Greene County, 1975–1976; Circuit Judge, 1977–1988; Associate Circuit Judge, Greene County, ?–Present)

780A.1 *Truth*. 33⅓ rpm LP. American Artists Custom Records, POB 4501, Springfield, MO. #AAS-1149-LP. [1973–1975]. Album cover: N/w photo of John Ashcroft and Max Bacon.—"Volume One, Edition One, Ashcroft & Bacon." Songs include: ***Why Me Lord*** {780A.1–1}; ***Reach Out Jesus*** {780A.1–2}; ***Jesus Hold My Hand*** {780A.1–3}; ***The Broken Vessel*** {780A.1–4}; ***King Jesus*** {780A.1–5}; ***Unseen Hand*** {780A.1–6}; ***Didn't He Shine*** {780A.1–7}; ***I Find No Fault In Him*** {780A.1–8}; ***More About Jesus*** {780A.1–9}; ***We've Come This Far By Him*** {780A.1–10}; ***Come Holy Spirit*** {780A.1–11}; and ***Jesus Is Lord Of All*** {780A.1–12}.

• **AmPM-781** BATES, Edward (Prosecuting Attorney, 1818; State's Attorney, 1820; State House, 1822 & 1834; U.S. District Attorney, 1821–1826; U.S. House, 1827–1829; State Senate, 1830; Judge, St. Louis, 1853–1856; U.S. Attorney General, 1861–1864)

781.1 *Cabinet Pictures*. w. No composer indicated. In: *Copperhead Minstrel (A Choice Collection Of Democratic Poems & Songs)*, page 24. Published by Feeks and Bancker, Wholesale Agents, No. 24 Ann Street, New York. 1863. [4¾" × 7¼"]. O/bk non-pictorial. "For the use of Political Clubs and the Social Circle." "Price 25 cents." 64pp. [M-133] [Crew/GBM-64].

781.2 *Fourth Of July* (Song). w.m. No composer or tune indicated. No publisher indicated. [ca. 1862]. [Approx. 4¾" × 8¾"]. Non-pictorial geometric design border. "Gotten up expressly for those who have an appreciative mind." 2pp. Page 2: Blank. [WFU].

781.3 *Old Abe And Old Nick*. w. No composer indicated. m. "Tune—*Lord Lovel*." In: *Copperhead Minstrel (A Choice Collection Of Democratic Poems & Songs)*, page 34. Published by Feeks and Bancker, Wholesale Agents, No. 24 Ann Street, New York. 1863. [4¾" × 7¼"]. O/bk non-pictorial. "For the use of Political Clubs and the Social Circle." "Price 25 cents." 64pp. [M-133] [Crew/GBM-64].

781.4 *The People's Nominee*. w. Karl Kriton. m. "Tune—*Boatman Dance*." In: *Connecticut Wide-Awake Songster*, page 15. e. John W. Hutchinson "(of Hutchinson Family Singers)" and Benjamin Jepson. Published by O. Hutchinson, Publisher, No. 272 Greenwich Street, New York, NY. 1860. [4" × 6"]. Bl/bk non-pictorial line border. "Lincoln and liberty." 76pp. Pages 2, 75 and 76: Advertising. Pages 5 and 6: Contents. Pages 7 to 10: Republican platform. [M-109]. [Crew/AL-175].

781.5 *The People's Nominee*. w. Karl Kriton. m. "Tune—*Nelly Bly*." In: *Hutchinson's Republican Songster For 1860*, page 15. e. John W. Hutchinson "(of the Hutchinson Family Singers)." Published by O. Hutchinson, Publisher, No. 272 Greenwich Street, New York, NY. 1860. B/w floral design border. "Lincoln and Liberty." 76pp. [M-110]. [Crew/AL-317].

781.6 *The Senator's Lament*. w. No composer indicated. m. "Air—*Robinson Crusoe*." In: *Republican Song Book*, page 58. c. Thomas Drew "(Late Editor of *The Massachusetts Spy*)." Published by Thayer and Eldridge, Boston, MA. 1860. [3⅞" × 5⅞"]. Br/bk litho of beardless Abraham Lincoln, vignettes of young Lincoln chopping rails, polling raft. 68pp. [M-108]. [Crew/AL-8].

781.7 Sic Semper. w. "By A Virginian." m. No tune indicated. No publisher indicated. [1861–1862]. [Approx. 6" × 9½"]. Non-pictorial geometric design border. 2pp. Page 2: Blank. [AMC].

781.8 Splittin' Ob The Rail. w. No composer indicated. m. "Air — *Sittin' On A Rail*." In: *The Wide Awake Vocalist (Or Rail Splitters' Song Book)*, page 33. Published by E.A. Daggett, No. 333 Broadway, New York, NY. 1860. Non-pictorial geometric design border. "Words and Music for the Republican Campaign of 1860, Embracing a Great Variety of Songs, Solos, Duets and Choruses Arranged for Piano or melodeon; The best collection of Words and Music ever published for a campaign, Every Club and Family should have copies, so as to join in the choruses; The Ladies are invited to join in the choruses at the meetings." 68pp. [M-116]. [Crew/AL-59].

781.9 The White House. w. G.R. Edeson. m. "Air — *Root, Hog, Or Die!*" Published by H. De Marsan, 54 Chatham Street, New York, NY. [1861–1862]. B/w litho border of minstrels, geometric designs. 2pp. Page 2: Blank. [AMC].

- **AmPM-782 BENTON, Thomas Hart** (U.S. Senate, 1821–1851; U.S. House, 1853–1855)

782.1 Agricultural Song. w.m. No composer or tune indicated. "Written expressly for the Barn Meeting, Jamaica Plains, Roxbury, May, 1840." In: *Log Cabin Minstrel (Or Tippecanoe Songster)*, page 11. c. "A Member of the Roxbury Whig Association." Published at the *Patriot And Democrat* Office, Roxbury, [MA]. 1840. [4½" × 6¾"]. [V-1:Y/bk] [V-2: Bl/bk] litho of William Henry Harrison, geometric design border. "Old Tip's the boy to swing the flail. Hurrah! Hurrah! Hurrah!" 64pp. Page 3: Title page — "Containing a Selection of Songs Original and Selected Many of them Written Expressly for this Work, Compiled, Published and Arranged by a member of the Roxbury Democratic Whig Association and Respectfully Dedicated to the Log Cabin Boys of the U.S." [M-013]. [Crew/WHH-71].

782.2 All Round My 'At I Vers A Veeping Villow. w.m. No composer or tune indicated. "A Song to be Sung at Van Buren's Indignation meetings." In: *Songs For The People (Or Tippecanoe Melodies)* [Songster], page 27. "Dedicated to the Democratic Whig Young Men of the City and County of New York." Published for the Authors by James P. Giffing, No. 56 Gold Street, New York, NY. 1840. [3¾" × 6"]. Litho of William Henry Harrison, log cabin, flag. "Original and Selected." 76pp. [M-019]. [Crew/WHH-63].

782.3 Clare De Kitchen. w. No composer indicated. m. No tune indicated. In: *The Clay Minstrel Or National Songster*, page 273. c. John Stockton Littell. Published by Greeley & M'Elrath, Tribune Building, New York, NY. 1844. [3⅛" × 4⅞"]. Non-pictorial. 396pp. [Crew/HC-18].

782.4 Clearing The Kitchen And White House (A Song For The Fourth of March, 1841). w. No composer indicated. m. "Tune — *Young Lochinvar*." In: *The Tippecanoe Campaign Of 1840*, page 61. Published by A.B. Norton, Mount Vernon, OH. 1888. [5½" × 7½"]. Bl/gd book. 496pp. Pages 1–382: Text. Pages 383–485: "Tippecanoe Songs of the Log Cabin Boys and Girls of 1840." [M-276]. [Crew/WHH-96].

782.5 Come One And All! w.m. No composer indicated. m. "Tune — *Old Tip's The Boy Gals*." In: *The Clay Minstrel Or National Songster*, page 342. c. John Stockton Littell. Published by Greeley & M'Elrath, Tribune Building, New York, NY. 1844. [3⅛" × 4⅞"]. Non-pictorial. 396pp. [Crew/HC-18].

782.6 Come One, Come All (Hurrah Song). w. No composer indicated. m. "Tune — *Old Tip's The Boy*." In: *The National Clay Melodist (A Collection Of Popular And Patriotic Songs, Second Edition, Enlarged And Improved)*, page 90. Published by Benj. Adams, No. 54 Court Street, Boston, MA. 1844. [3" × 5¼"]. Inside title page: B/w litho of Henry Clay's home — "O'er Ashland's lawns the skies are bright, From West to East The radiance streams and glows, The land beneath its beams gay beats the heart with joy, Hurrah! Hurrah! Hip! Hurrah!" 108pp. [M-050?]. [Crew/HC-13].

782.7 [Come Rouse Ye Honest Whigs All] (Song 9). w. W.A. Philomath. m. "Tune — *The Swiss Boy*." In: *Original Clay Songs: Humorous And Sentimental, Designed To Inculcate Just Political Sentiments, To Suit The Present Political Crisis, And To Advocate The Claims Of Henry Clay To The Highest Honors His Country Can Bestow*, page 13. w. W.A. Philomath, Union Co., Ind. Published by Philomath, Cincinnati, OH. 1842. [4¼" × 6"]. Be/bk litho of an eagle, U.S. Flag. "The eagle soars above the throng; And listen's [sic] to fair Freedom's song, Hails the merry roundelay, Claps his glad wings and hails the day." 20pp. Page 20: Be/bk litho of four men — "Tyler Expounding the Constitution! The effect of 'treading in the footsteps.'" [M-057]. [CrewHC-104].

782.8 Currency Song. w. No composer indicated. m. "Tune — *Hunters Of Kentucky*." In: *Songs For The People (Or Tippecanoe Melodies)* [Songster], page 62. "Dedicated to the Democratic Whig Young Men of the City and County of New York." Published for the Authors by James P. Giffing, No. 56 Gold Street, New York, NY. 1840. [3¾" × 6"]. Litho of William Henry Harrison, log cabin, flag. "Original and Selected." 76pp. [M-019]. [Crew/WHH-63].

782.9 The Dispersion Of The Spoilers. w.m. No composer indicated. m. "Tune — *The Star Spangled Banner*." In: *The Clay Minstrel Or National Songster*, page 334. c. John Stockton Littell. Published by Greeley & M'Elrath, Tribune Building, New York, NY. 1844. [3⅛" × 4⅞"]. Non-pictorial. 396pp. [Crew/HC-18].

782.10 Fisherman's Song. w. No composer indicated. m. "Air — *Buy A Broom*." In: *Harrison Melodies (Original And Selected)*, page 17. Published by Weeks, Jordan & Co., Boston, MA. 1840. [3³⁄₁₆" × 6"]. B/w litho of William Henry Harrison. "Published under the direction of the Boston Harrison Club." 76pp. Page 5: "To William Henry Harrison of Ohio, the gallant soldier, the enlightened statesman, the consistent Republican, and the Honest man..." [M-001, 002, 003]. [Crew/WHH-86].

782.11 Freedom And Fremont. w. No composer indicated. m. "Air — *Yankee Doodle*." In: *The Freeman's*

Glee Book, A Collection Of Songs, Odes, Glees And Ballads With Music, Original And Selected, Harmonized And Arranged For Each. Published Under The Auspices Of The Central Fremont And Dayton Glee Club Of The City Of New York, And Dedicated To All, Who, Cherishing Republican Liberty Consider Freedom Worth A Song, page 82. Published by Miller, Orton & Mulligan, No. 25 Park Row, New York, NY. [and Auburn, NY]. 1856. [4 15/16" × 6"]. Pk/bk litho of man on mountain peak, music sheets, geometric designs. 112pp. [Crew/JCF-16].

782.12 Fremont And Dayton. w. No composer indicated. m. "Air—*O, What Has Caused This Great Commotion*." In: *Fremont Songs For The People (Original And Selected)*, page 22. c. Thomas Drew "(Editor of *The Massachusetts Spy*)." Published by John P. Jewett & Company, Boston, MA. Copyright 1856 by Thomas Drew. [3⅝" × 5½"]. B/w litho of "J.C. Fremont." "The Campaign of 1856." 68pp. [Crew/JCF-18].

782.13 Gathering Song. w. No composer indicated. m. "Tune—*Come, Haste To The Wedding*." "Yale College, 1840." In: *The Log Cabin & Hard Cider Melodies, A Collection Of Popular And Patriotic Songs*, page 67. Published by Charles Adams, No. 23 Tremont Street, Boston, MA. 1840. [3¾" × 6"]. [V-1: Pk/bk] [V-2: Gn/bk] litho of William Henry Harrison. "The Freeman's glittering Sword be Blest, For ever blest the Freeman's Lyre." 78pp. Pages 2 and 77: Blank. Page 3: Inside title page. B/w litho of log cabin. "Respectfully Dedicated to the Friends of Harrison and Tyler." Page 78: Advertising. [M-012]. [Crew/WHH-68].

782.14 Give 'Em Jesse And Fremont. w. No composer indicated. m. "Air—*Jessie, The Flower Of Dumblane*." "From the *N.Y. Evening Mirror*." In: *The Republican Campaign Songster, A Collection Of Lyrics, Original And Selected, Specifically Prepared For The Friends Of Freedom In The Campaign Of Fifty-Six*, page 38. Published by Miller, Orton & Mulligan, No. 25 Park Row, New York, NY. 1856. [3 13/16" × 6"]. Be/bk litho of "Colonel John C. Fremont" facing to viewer's left, black line border. 112pp. [M-097]. [Crew/JCF-24].

782.15 Harrison. w. No composer indicated. m. "Air—*Yankee Doodle*." In: *The Log Cabin & Hard Cider Melodies, A Collection Of Popular And Patriotic Songs*, page 40. Published by Charles Adams, No. 23 Tremont Street, Boston, MA. 1840. [3¾" × 6"]. [V-1: Pk/bk] [V-2: Gn/bk] litho of William Henry Harrison. "The Freeman's glittering Sword be Blest, For ever blest the Freeman's Lyre." 78pp. Pages 2 and 77: Blank. Page 3: Inside title page. B/w litho of log cabin. "Respectfully Dedicated to the Friends of Harrison and Tyler." Page 78: Advertising. [M-012]. [Crew/WHH-68].

782.16 Harrison Song. w. Hon. John Holmes, "of Maine." m. "Air—*Yankee Doodle*." "Read by [Holmes] from the balcony of the State House, Augusta, on the 24th of June, 1840." In: *Log Cabin Minstrel (or Tippecanoe Songster)*, page 13. c. "A Member of the Roxbury Whig Association." Published at the *Patriot And Democrat* Office, Roxbury, [MA]. 1840. [4½" × 6¾"]. [V-1:Y/bk] [V-2: Bl/bk] litho of William Henry Harrison, geometric design border. "Old Tip's the boy to swing the flail. Hurrah! Hurrah! Hurrah!" 64pp. Page 3: Title page—"Containing a Selection of Songs Original and Selected Many of them Written Expressly for this Work, Compiled, Published and Arranged by a member of the Roxbury Democratic Whig Association and Respectfully Dedicated to the Log Cabin Boys of the U.S." [M-013]. [Crew/WHH-71].

782.17 Harry Of Kentucky. w. No composer indicated. m. "Tune—*'Tis My Delight Of A Shiny Night*." In: *The Clay Minstrel Or National Songster*, page 160. c. John Stockton Littell. Published by Greeley & M'Elrath, Tribune Building, New York, NY. 1844. [3⅛" × 4⅞"]. Non-pictorial. 396pp. [Crew/HC-18].

782.18 Harry Of Kentucky, Oh. w. F. Buckingham Graham. m. "Tune—*Green Grow The Rushes, Oh!*" In: *The National Clay Melodist (A Collection Of Popular And Patriotic Songs, Second Edition, Enlarged And Improved)*, page 100. Published by Benj. Adams, No. 54 Court Street, Boston, MA. 1844. [3" × 5¼"]. Inside title page: B/w litho of Henry Clay's home—"O'er Ashland's lawns the skies are bright, From West to East The radiance streams and glows, The land beneath its beams gay beats the heart with joy, Hurrah! Hurrah! Hip! Hurrah!" 108pp. [M-050?]. [Crew/HC-13].

782.19 The Hero Of Fort Meigs. w. J.H. Watts, Esq. m. "Tune—*Auld Lang Syne*." In: *Tippecanoe Song-Book (A Collection Of Log Cabin And Patriotic Melodies)*, page 62. Published by Marshall, Williams & Butler, Philadelphia, PA. 1840. White on black litho of log cabin, plow, flags, eagle. 180pp. [M-024]. [Crew/WHH-61].

782.20 If E'er I Should Wish To Get Married. w. "A Lady." m. "Tune—*Rosin The Bow*." "If The Ladies, Heaven bless them! Could vote, the election of Mr. Clay would be carried by acclamation! Their influence was powerfully felt in 1840, and their appreciation of eloquence, patriotism and genius, will prompt them to a warm support of 'Harry of the West.' Of this the following excellent song is proof." In: *The Clay Minstrel Or National Songster*, page 261. c. John Stockton Littell. Published by Greeley & M'Elrath, Tribune Building, New York, NY. 1844. [3⅛" × 4⅞"]. Non-pictorial. 396pp. [Crew/HC-18].

782.21 Jackson's Lament. w. No composer indicated. In: *A Miniature Of Martin Van Buren (With A Selection Of The Best And Most Popular Tippecanoe Songs)*, page 51. 1840. [3½" × 6½"]. [V-1: Br/bk] [V-2: Gn/bk] [V-3: Y/bk] litho of man, chain around neck. Van Buren quote. "Amos Kendall's Veracity—Tom Benton's Honesty—Francis Blair's Beauty." "What is wanting cant be numbered [sic]." 58pp. [M-016]. [Crew/WHH-88].

782.22 John C. Calhoun My Jo. w. No composer indicated. m. "Tune—*John Anderson my Jo*." In: *Log Cabin Song Book (A Collection Of Popular And Patriotic Songs)*, page 40. Published at *The Log Cabin* office, No. 30 Ann-Street, New York, NY. 1840. [4⅞" × 7"]. [V-1: Br/bk] [V-2: Y/bk] litho of log cabin, cider barrel, farmer with plow, flag—"Harrison and Tyler," geometric design border. "The Freeman's glittering Sword be Blest, For ever blest the Freeman's Lyre" Page 3: B/w litho of "Major-General William Henry Harrison, of Ohio," facsimile signature. 74pp. [M-020]. [Crew/WHH-56].

782.23 John Fremont's Coming. w. No composer indicated. m. "Air—*Old Dan Tucker.*" In: *Fremont Songs For The People (Original And Selected)*, page 16. c. Thomas Drew "(Editor of *The Massachusetts Spy*)." Published by John P. Jewett & Company, Boston, MA. Copyright 1856 by Thomas Drew. [3⅝" × 5½"]. B/w litho of "J.C. Fremont." "The Campaign of 1856." 68pp. [Crew/JCF-18].

782.24 King Martin's Soliloquy (A Modern Democratic Melody). w. No composer indicated. m. "Air—*It Is Not On The Battle Field.*" In: *Harrison Melodies (Original And Selected)*, page 19. Published by Weeks, Jordan & Co., Boston, MA. 1840. [3⁹⁄₁₆" × 6"]. B/w litho of William Henry Harrison. "Published under the direction of the Boston Harrison Club." 76pp. Page 5: "To William Henry Harrison of Ohio, the gallant soldier, the enlightened statesman, the consistent Republican, and the Honest man..." [M-001, 002, 003]. [Crew/WHH-86].

782.25 Ladies, Come Weave A New Banner. w. No composer indicated. m. "Tune—*Old Rosin The Bow.*" In: *The National Clay Minstrel (And True Whig's Pocket Companion For The Presidential Canvass Of 1844)*, page 58. Published by [V-1: George Hood, No. 15 North 6th Street, Philadelphia, PA] [V-2: James Fisher, No. 71 Court Street, Boston, MA]. 1843. [3¼" × 5⅛"]. Y/bk litho of raccoon—"That Coon" and flag—"Henry Clay," log cabin. "New and Improved Edition." 128pp. Page 10: Dedication—"To the National Clay Club this work is respectfully dedicated by the Publisher." [Crew/HC-11].

782.26 The Ladies' Whig Song. w. No composer indicated. m. "Tune—*Rosin The Beau.*" In: *The National Clay Minstrel*, page 39. Published by [V-1: George Hood, No. 15 North 6th Street, Philadelphia, PA] [V-2: James Fisher, No. 71 Court Street, Boston, MA]. 1843. [3" × 4½"]. Y/bk litho of raccoon sitting on fence, black border. 68pp. Pages 2 and 67: Blank. Pages 65–66: Contents. [Crew/HC-10].

782.27 Lines Supposed To Be Written On The Twelfth Of November, 1840. w. No composer indicated. m. "Air—*Farewell, Farewell To Thee, Araby's Daughter.*" In: *Harrison Melodies (Original And Selected)*, page 14. Published by Weeks, Jordan & Co., Boston, MA. 1840. [3⁹⁄₁₆" × 6"]. B/w litho of William Henry Harrison. "Published under the direction of the Boston Harrison Club." 76pp. Page 5: "To William Henry Harrison of Ohio, the gallant soldier, the enlightened statesman, the consistent Republican, and the Honest man..." [M-001, 002, 003]. [Crew/WHH-86].

782.28 The Log Cabin And Hard Cider Song. w. No composer indicated. m. "Tune—*The Hunters Of Kentucky.*" From the "*Boston Atlas.*" In: *Log Cabin Minstrel (Or Tippecanoe Songster)*, page 18. c. "A Member of the Roxbury Whig Association." Published at the *Patriot And Democrat* Office, Roxbury, [MA]. 1840. [4½" × 6¾"]. [V-1:Y/bk] [V-2: Bl/bk] litho of William Henry Harrison, geometric design border. "Old Tip's the boy to swing the flail. Hurrah! Hurrah! Hurrah!" 64pp. Page 3: Title page—"Containing a Selection of Songs Original and Selected Many of them Written Expressly for this Work, Compiled, Published and Arranged by a member of the Roxbury Democratic Whig Association and Respectfully Dedicated to the Log Cabin Boys of the U.S." [M-013]. [Crew/WHH-71].

782.29 The Log Cabin Song. w. No composer indicated. m. "Tune—*Yankee Doodle.*" "Before the adjournment of the Convention at Augusta, the Hon. John Holmes of Thomaston, offered and read the following song." In: *Tippecanoe Song-Book (A Collection Of Log Cabin And Patriotic Melodies)*, page 71. Published by Marshall, Williams & Butler, Philadelphia, PA. 1840. White on black litho of log cabin, plow, flags, eagle. 180pp. [M-024]. [Crew/WHH-61].

782.30 The Lounger's Lament. w. No composer indicated. m. "Air—*Exile Of Erin.*" In: *The Log Cabin & Hard Cider Melodies, A Collection Of Popular And Patriotic Songs*, page 42. Published by Charles Adams, No. 23 Tremont Street, Boston, MA. 1840. [3¾" × 6"]. [V-1: Pk/bk] [V-2: Gn/bk] litho of William Henry Harrison. "The Freeman's glittering Sword be Blest, For ever blest the Freeman's Lyre." 78pp. [M-012]. [Crew/WHH-68].

782.31 The Lounger's Lament. w.m. No composer or tune indicated. In: *Whig Songs For 1844* [Songster], page 14. Published by Greeley & McElrath, New York, NY. 1844. [5⅞" × 9⁵⁄₁₆"]. Non-pictorial. 16pp. Page 16: "Odes and Poems." [M-061]. [Crew/HC-35].

782.32 March! March! Van Buren Collar Men. w. No composer indicated. m. "Tune—*All The Blue Bonnets Are Over The Border.*" In: *Songs For The People (Or Tippecanoe Melodies)* [Songster], page 51. Published for the Authors by James P. Giffing, No. 56 Gold Street, New York, NY. 1840. [3¾" × 6"]. Litho of William Henry Harrison, log cabin, flag. "Original and Selected." 76pp. [M-019]. [Crew/WHH-63].

782.33 Martin Van Buren To John M. Niles. w. No composer indicated. m. "Air—*Come Rest In This Bosom.*" In: *Harrison Melodies (Original And Selected)*, page 17. Published by Weeks, Jordan & Co., Boston, MA. 1840. [3⁹⁄₁₆" × 6"]. B/w litho of William Henry Harrison. "Published under the direction of the Boston Harrison Club." 76pp. Page 5: "To William Henry Harrison of Ohio, the gallant soldier, the enlightened statesman, the consistent Republican, and the Honest man..." [M-001, 002, 003]. [Crew/WHH-86].

782.34 McKinley Leads. w.m. D.E. Bryer. In: *McKinley Campaign Songster For 1900 (For Male Voices)*, page 28. e. W.G. Thomas. Published by The Home Music Company, Logansport, IN. 1900. Gn/bk litho of "William McKinley for President" and "Theo. Roosevelt For Vice President," eagle, flags, shield. "Send cash with order." "All orders will be promptly filled if accompanied by cash." "Single copy 15 cts. $.50 per dozen." "Note: Our McKinley Campaign Songster No. 2, Entirely Different from this will be issued September 10th. Same Price." 36pp. [M-373]. [Crew/WM-275].

782.35 A Miniature Of Martin Van Buren. w.m. No composer or tune indicated. In: *A Miniature Of Martin Van Buren (With A Selection Of The Best And Most Popular Tippecanoe Songs)*, page 3. 1840. [3½" × 6½"]. [V-1: Br/bk] [V-2: Gn/bk] [V-3: Y/bk] litho of man, chain around neck. Van Buren quote. "Amos Kendall's Veracity—Tom Benton's Honesty—Francis Blair's Beauty." "What is wanting cant be numbered [sic]." 58pp. [M-016]. [Crew/WHH-88].

782.36 O! Van Buren! w. N.E.B. m. "Tune—*The Hunter's Of Kentucky.*" In: *Tippecanoe Song-Book (A Collection Of Log Cabin And Patriotic Melodies)*, page 135. Published by Marshall, Williams & Butler, Philadelphia, PA. 1840. White on black litho of log cabin, plow, flags, eagle. 180pp. [M-024]. [Crew/ WHH-61].

782.37 Oh! Oh! Where Shall I Fly To. w. No composer indicated. m. "Tune—*Thou, Thou, Reign'st In This Bosom.*" In: *A Miniature Of Martin Van Buren (With A Selection Of The Best And Most Popular Tippecanoe Songs)*, page 28. 1840. [3½" × 6½"]. [V-1: Br/bk] [V-2: Gn/bk] [V-3: Y/bk] litho of man, chain around neck. Van Buren quote. "Amos Kendall's Veracity—Tom Benton's Honesty—Francis Blair's Beauty." "What is wanting cant be numbered [sic]." 58pp. [M-016]. [Crew/WHH-88].

782.38 Old Tippecanoe (A Patriotic Song). w.m. "A Pennsylvanian." Published by L.D. Meignen & Company, Publishers and Importers of Music, Musical Instruments, Italian Strings, &c., No. 217 Chesnut Street, Philadelphia, PA. 1840. B/w litho by C.S. Duval of nine vignettes of William Henry Harrison's military career, log cabin scene, cannons, William Henry Harrison, crossed flags. Description of each vignette. "Baltimore Convention." "Written, to be sung at Baltimore during the Young Men's Whig Convention and most respectfully inscribed to the Young Ladies of this Monumental City." 4pp. Page 4: Blank. [Crew/WHH-79].

782.39 Old Tippecanoe. w. No composer indicated. m. "Tune—*Roast Beef.*" "Sung by R.R. Kendall of Freeport at a Whig Convention of the Fourth in Lincoln Co., Maine." In: *The Log Cabin*, page 4, Vol. 1, No. 12, July 18, 1840. Published by Horace Greeley & Company, New York, NY. 1840. Non-pictorial. [Crew/WHH-91(A)].

782.40 Old Tippecanoe Come Out Of The West. w. No composer indicated. m. "Tune—*Young Lochinvar.*" In: *Tippecanoe Song-Book (A Collection Of Log Cabin And Patriotic Melodies)*, page 58. Published by Marshall, Williams & Butler, Philadelphia, PA. 1840. White on black litho of log cabin, plow, flags, eagle. 180pp. [M-024]. [Crew/WHH-61].

782.41 A Parody On Up Salt River. w. No composer indicated. m. "Tune—*All On Hobbies.*" In: *Songs For The People (Or Tippecanoe Melodies)* [Songster], page 37. "Dedicated to the Democratic Whig Young Men of the City and County of New York." Published for the Authors by James P. Giffing, No. 56 Gold Street, New York, NY. 1840. [3¾" × 6"]. Litho of William Henry Harrison, log cabin, flag. "Original and Selected." 76pp. [M-019]. [Crew/WHH-63].

782.42 The People Are Coming. w. No composer indicated. m. "Tune—*The Star Spangled Banner.*" In: *The Clay Minstrel Or National Songster*, page 247. c. John Stockton Littell. Published by Greeley & M'Elrath, Tribune Building, New York, NY. 1844. [3⅛" × 4⅞"]. Non-pictorial. 396pp. [Crew/HC-18].

782.43 The People's Rally. w. No composer indicated. m. "Tune—*The Campbells Are Coming.*" In: *The Clay Minstrel Or National Songster*, page 233. c. John Stockton Littell. Published by Greeley & M'Elrath, Tribune Building, New York, NY. 1844. [3⅛" × 4⅞"]. Non-pictorial. 396pp. [Crew/HC-18].

782.44 Polk Is A Used Up Joke. w.m. No composers or tune indicated. [1844]. Non-pictorial geometric design border. 2pp. Page 2: Blank.

782.45 Quamdiu Yendem Abutere Patientiae Nostra? Ad Quen Finem Sese Jactabit Audacia? (Come gentle Muse, Give Me Your Aid). w. "B." m. No tune indicated. No publisher indicated. Published in Baltimore, June 30, 1861. B/w geometric design border. 2pp. Page 2: Blank. [AMC].

782.46 The Retrospect. w. No composer indicated. m. "Air—*The Old Oaken Bucket.*" In: *The Republican Campaign Songster, A Collection Of Lyrics, Original And Selected, Specifically Prepared For The Friends Of Freedom In The Campaign Of Fifty-Six*, page 9. Published by Miller, Orton & Mulligan, No. 25 Park Row, New York, NY. 1856. [3¹³⁄₁₆" × 6"]. Be/bk litho of "Colonel John C. Fremont" facing to viewer's left, black line border. 112pp. [M-097]. [Crew/JCF-24].

782.47 The Rubber; Or Mat's Third And Last Game. w. No composer indicated. m. "Tune—*Miss Bailey.*" In: *The National Clay Minstrel (And True Whig's Pocket Companion For The Presidential Canvass Of 1844)*, page 46. Published by [V-1: George Hood, No. 15 North 6th Street, Philadelphia, PA] [V-2: James Fisher, No. 71 Court Street, Boston, MA]. 1843. [3¼" × 5⅛"]. Y/bk litho of raccoon—"That Coon" and flag—"Henry Clay," log cabin. "New and Improved Edition." 128pp. Page 10: Dedication—"To the National Clay Club this work is respectfully dedicated by the Publisher." [Crew/HC-11].

782.48 Song. w. No composer indicated. m. "Tune—*Rosin The Bow.*" In: *The Tippecanoe Campaign Of 1840*, page 100. Published by A.B. Norton, Mount Vernon, OH. 1888. [5½" × 7½"]. Bl/gd book. 496pp. Pages 1–382: Text. Pages 383–485: "Tippecanoe Songs of the Log Cabin Boys and Girls of 1840." [M-276]. [Crew/WHH-96].

782.49 Song. w. No composer indicated. w. No tune indicated. "I was well; I wished to be better; I took Tom Benton's humbug, and here I lie,—J.C.C." In: *Log Cabin Minstrel* (or *Tippecanoe Songster*), page 15. c. "A Member of the Roxbury Whig Association." Published at the *Patriot And Democrat* Office, Roxbury, [MA]. 1840. [4½" × 6¾"]. [V-1: Y/bk] [V-2: Bl/bk] litho of William Henry Harrison, geometric design border. "Old Tip's the boy to swing the flail. Hurrah! Hurrah! Hurrah!" 64pp. Page 3: Title page—"Containing a Selection of Songs Original and Selected Many of them Written Expressly for this Work, Compiled, Published and Arranged by a member of the Roxbury Democratic Whig Association and Respectfully Dedicated to the Log Cabin Boys of the U.S." [M-013]. [Crew/WHH-71].

782.50 Song And Chorus. w. No composer indicated. m. "Air—*Old Tip's The Boy.*" In: *The National Clay Minstrel*, page 56. Published by [V-1: George Hood, No. 15 North 6th Street, Philadelphia, PA] [V-2: James Fisher, No. 71 Court Street, Boston, MA]. 1843. [3" × 4½"]. Y/bk litho of raccoon sitting on fence, black border. 68pp. Pages 2 and 67: Blank. Pages 65–66: Contents. [Crew/HC-10].

782.51 The Spoilsmen. w.m. No composer or tune indicated. In: *Songs For The People (Or Tippecanoe Melodies)* [Songster], page 31. "Dedicated to the Democratic Whig Young Men of the City and County of New York." Published for the Authors by James P. Giffing, No. 56 Gold Street, New York, NY. 1840. [3¾" × 6"]. Litho of William Henry Harrison, log cabin, flag. "Original and Selected." 76pp. [M-019]. [Crew/WHH-63].

782.52 The Taylor Polka. w. No composer indicated. m. "Tune—*The Jim Crow Polka.*" In: *Taylor And Fillmore Songster, An Original Collection Of New Whig Songs For The Campaign Of 1848*, page 17. Published by Turner & Fisher, New York, NY. 1848. [2¾" × 4⅜"]. [V-1: Pk/bk] [V-2: Bl/bk] litho of Zachary Taylor. 34pp. [M-074, 075]. [Crew/ZT-56].

782.53 A Tory Hymn. w. No composer indicated. m. "Tune—*Funeral Thought.*" From the "*Boston Currier.*" In: *Log Cabin Minstrel (Or Tippecanoe Songster)*, page 27. c. "A Member of the Roxbury Whig Association." Published at the *Patriot And Democrat* Office, Roxbury, [MA]. 1840. [4½" × 6¾"]. [V-1: Y/bk] [V-2: Bl/bk] litho of William Henry Harrison, geometric design border. "Old Tip's the boy to swing the flail. Hurrah! Hurrah! Hurrah!" 64pp. Page 3: Title page—"Containing a Selection of Songs Original and Selected Many of them Written Expressly for this Work, Compiled, Published and Arranged by a member of the Roxbury Democratic Whig Association and Respectfully Dedicated to the Log Cabin Boys of the U.S." [M-013]. [Crew/WHH-71].

782.54 True Harry Of Kentucky, Oh. w. No composer indicated. m. "Air—*Green Grow The Rushes Oh.*" In: *The National Clay Minstrel (And True Whig's Pocket Companion For The Presidential Canvass Of 1844)*, page 28. Published by [V-1: George Hood, No. 15 North 6th Street, Philadelphia, PA] [V-2: James Fisher, No. 71 Court Street, Boston, MA]. 1843. [3¼" × 5⅛"]. Y/bk litho of raccoon—"That Coon" and flag—"Henry Clay," log cabin. "New and Improved Edition." 128pp. Page 10: Dedication—"To the National Clay Club this work is respectfully dedicated by the Publisher." [Crew/HC-11].

782.55 Union Of The Whigs. w. No composer indicated. m. "Air—*The Shamrock.*" "Sung at the opening of the Dorchester Whig Association." In: *Log Cabin Minstrel (or Tippecanoe Songster)*, page 6. c. "A Member of the Roxbury Whig Association." Published at the *Patriot And Democrat* Office, Roxbury, [MA]. 1840. [4½" × 6¾"]. [V-1: Y/bk] [V-2: Bl/bk] litho of William Henry Harrison, geometric design border. "Old Tip's the boy to swing the flail. Hurrah! Hurrah!" 64pp. Page 3: Title page—"Containing a Selection of Songs Original and Selected Many of them Written Expressly for this Work, Compiled, Published and Arranged by a member of the Roxbury Democratic Whig Association and Respectfully Dedicated to the Log Cabin Boys of the U.S." [M-013]. [Crew/WHH-71].

782.56 Up Salt River (A New Whig Song). w. G.B.W. "of Toledo, Ohio." m. "Tune—*All On Hobbies.*" "Respectfully dedicated to the Toledo Tippecanoe Club." In: *The Log Cabin & Hard Cider Melodies, A Collection Of Popular And Patriotic Songs*, page 65. Published by Charles Adams, No. 23 Tremont Street, Boston, MA. 1840. [3¾" × 6"]. [V-1: Pk/bk] [V-2: Gn/bk] litho of William Henry Harrison. "The Freeman's glittering Sword be Blest, For ever blest the Freeman's Lyre." 78pp. Pages 2 and 77: Blank. Page 3: Inside title page. B/w litho of log cabin. "Respectfully Dedicated to the Friends of Harrison and Tyler." Page 78: Advertising. [M-012]. [Crew/WHH-68].

782.57 Van Can't Come It. w.m. No composer or tune indicated. In: *The National Clay Melodist (A Collection Of Popular And Patriotic Songs, Second Edition, Enlarged And Improved)*, page 75. Published by Benj. Adams, No. 54 Court Street, Boston, MA. 1844. [3" × 5¼"]. Inside title page: B/w litho of Henry Clay's home—"O'er Ashland's lawns the skies are bright, From West to East The radiance streams and glows, The land beneath its beams gay beats the heart with joy, Hurrah! Hurrah! Hip! Hurrah!" 108pp. [M-050?]. [Crew/HC-13].

782.58 We've Walloped Them So (A Favorite Patriotic Ballad). w. "By a member of the Fifth Ward Club." Published by Atwill, No. 201 Broadway, New York, NY. 1840. Non-pictorial. "A Favorite Patriotic Ballad as sung by the Tippecanoe Glee Club, with great applause. Written, Arranged and Dedicated, to the Tippecanoe Associations." 4pp. Page 4: Blank. [Crew/WHH-98].

782.59 What Sam Tells The People. w. No composer indicated. m. "Air—*Dandy Jim.*" In: *Fillmore And Donelson Songs For The Campaign* (Songster). Published by Robert M. De Witt, Nos. 160 and 162 Nassau Street, New York, NY. November 4, 1856. [4¾" × 7⅛"]. Bl/bk litho of George Washington—"July 4, 1776," wreath, geometric design border. "This is the only authorized edition containing Duganne's Songs. Price 6 cts. each, $4 per 100. Discount to trade." Long quote from George Washington's "Farewell Address." 40pp. Page 3: "Union and Peace" [M-101, 102]. [Crew/MF-10]. [VBL, p. 334].

782.60 Whig Rallying Song. w. No composer indicated. m. "Tune—*The Campbells Are Coming.*" In: *Tippecanoe Song-Book (A Collection Of Log Cabin And Patriotic Melodies)*, page 23. Published by Marshall, Williams & Butler, Philadelphia, PA. 1840. White on black litho of log cabin, plow, flags, eagle. 180pp. [M-024]. [Crew/WHH-61].

782.61 Whig Rallying Song. w. No composer indicated. m. "Tune—*The Campbells Are Coming.*" In: *The Log Cabin & Hard Cider Melodies, A Collection Of Popular And Patriotic Songs*, page 57. Published by Charles Adams, No. 23 Tremont Street, Boston, MA. 1840. [3¾" × 6"]. [V-1: Pk/bk] [V-2: Gn/bk] litho of William Henry Harrison. "The Freeman's glittering Sword be Blest, For ever blest the Freeman's Lyre." 78pp. Pages 2 and 77: Blank. Page 3: Inside title page. B/w litho of log cabin. "Respectfully Dedicated to the Friends of Harrison and Tyler." Page 78: Advertising. [M-012]. [Crew/WHH-68].

- **AmPM-783 BLAIR**, Francis Preston, Sr. (State House 1852–1856 & 1870; U.S. House, 1857–1859, 1860, 1861–1864; Democratic Candidate for Vice President, 1868; U.S. Senate, 1871–1873; State Insurance Commissioner, 1874) [ALSO SEE: DOC/PSM-HS]

783.1 A Campaign Rattler. w.m. No composer or tune indicated. "Music of the Song published in the *Radical Drum Call.*" In: *The Grant And Colfax Republican Songster, Containing Campaign Songs, Ballads And*

Choruses. Adapted To The Most Popular And Stirring Tunes, page 16. Published by R.M. Dewitt, Publisher, No. 13 Frankfort Street, New York, NY. 1868. [4" × 6³⁄₁₆"]. R/w/b litho of flag. Advertising. 100pp. [M-150]. [Crew/USG-63].

783.2 Campaign Song. w. Isaac F. Bosworth. m. "Air—*Uncle Ned.*" In: *Seymour Campaign Songster*, page 27. Published by Pattee & Hubbard, Democratic State Committee Rooms, World Building, No. 37 Park Row, New York, NY. 1868. [4" × 5¼"]. Gn/bk litho of Horatio Seymour and Francis Blair. "In the spirit of George Washington and the Patriots of the Revolution, Let us take the steps to re-inaugurate our Government, to start it once again on its course to greatness and prosperity—Horatio Seymour." 38pp. [M-173]. [Crew/HS-8].

783.3 Confederate Notes. w. No composer indicated. m. "Air—*Oh, Cruel Was The Captain.*" In: *The Grant And Colfax Republican Songster, Containing Campaign Songs, Ballads And Choruses. Adapted To The Most Popular And Stirring Tunes*, page 49. Published by R.M. Dewitt, Publisher, No. 13 Frankfort Street, New York, NY. 1868. [4" × 6³⁄₁₆"]. R/w/b litho of flag. Advertising. 100pp. [M-150]. [Crew/USG-63].

783.4 Democratic Campaign Appeal. w. E.S. Riley. m. "Music arranged by Edward Spott. Adapted to *Maryland O My Maryland.*" In: *Seymour Campaign Songster*, page 23. Published by Pattee & Hubbard, Democratic State Committee Rooms, World Building, No. 37 Park Row, New York, NY. 1868. [4" × 5¼"]. Gn/bk litho of Horatio Seymour and Francis Blair. "In the spirit of George Washington and the Patriots of the Revolution, Let us take the steps to re-inaugurate our Government, to start it once again on its course to greatness and prosperity—Horatio Seymour." 38pp. [M-173]. [Crew/HS-8].

783.5 Gineral Boom Of The C.S.A. w. No composer indicated. m. "Air—*Captain Jenks.*" In: *The Grant And Colfax Republican Songster, Containing Campaign Songs, Ballads And Choruses. Adapted To The Most Popular And Stirring Tunes*, page 3. Published by R.M. Dewitt, Publisher, No. 13 Frankfort Street, New York, NY. 1868. [4" × 6³⁄₁₆"]. R/w/b litho of flag. Advertising. 100pp. [M-150]. [Crew/USG-63].

783.6 Horatio's Wedding. w. No composer indicated. m. "Air—*A Frog He Would A Wooing Go.*" In: *The Grant And Colfax Republican Songster, Containing Campaign Songs, Ballads And Choruses. Adapted To The Most Popular And Stirring Tunes*, page 96. Published by R.M. Dewitt, Publisher, No. 13 Frankfort Street, New York, NY. 1868. [4" × 6³⁄₁₆"]. R/w/b litho of flag. Advertising. 100pp. [M-150]. [Crew/USG-63].

783.7 I Go Straight Ulysses. w. No composer indicated. m. "Air—*How Are You, Horace Greeley.*" "Columbia S.C., July, 1872." In: *National Republican Grant And Wilson Campaign Song-Book*, page 87. Published by The Union Republican Congressional Committee, Washington, DC. 1872. [3¹³⁄₁₆" × 8³⁄₁₆"]. Be/bk litho of Ulysses S. Grant. "We'll Sing a Song for U.S. Grant." 100pp. [M-182]. [Crew/USG-110].

783.8 Lesh Us Have Peash! w. No composer indicated. m. "Air—*Old Dan Tucker.*" "Verses from a Radical Campaign Song, as sung by Simpson after one of his One-Horse Acts." In: *Seymour Campaign Songster*, page 18. Published by Pattee & Hubbard, Democratic State Committee Rooms, World Building, No. 37 Park Row, New York, NY. 1868. [4" × 5¼"]. Gn/bk litho of Horatio Seymour and Francis Blair. "In the spirit of George Washington and the Patriots of the Revolution, Let us take the steps to re-inaugurate our Government, to start it once again on its course to greatness and prosperity—Horatio Seymour." 38pp. [M-173]. [Crew/HS-8].

783.9 Not For Horace. w. C.B. Parker. m. "Air—*Not For Joseph.*" In: *National Republican Grant And Wilson Campaign Song-Book*, page 28. Published by The Union Republican Congressional Committee, Washington, DC. 1872. [3¹³⁄₁₆" × 8³⁄₁₆"]. Be/bk litho of Ulysses S. Grant. "We'll Sing a Song for U.S. Grant." 100pp. [M-182]. [Crew/USG-110].

783.10 November, Sixty-Eight. w. No composer indicated. m. "Air—*Wearing Of The Green.*" In: *Seymour Campaign Songster*, page 31. Published by Pattee & Hubbard, Democratic State Committee Rooms, World Building, No. 37 Park Row, New York, NY. 1868. [4" × 5¼"]. Gn/bk litho of Horatio Seymour and Francis Blair. "In the spirit of George Washington and the Patriots of the Revolution, Let us take the steps to re-inaugurate our Government, to start it once again on its course to greatness and prosperity—Horatio Seymour." 38pp. [M-173]. [Crew/HS-8].

783.11 Old Abe And Old Nick. w. No composer indicated. m. "Tune—*Lord Lovel.*" In: *Copperhead Minstrel (A Choice Collection Of Democratic Poems & Songs)*, page 34. Published by Feeks and Bancker, Wholesale Agents, No. 24 Ann Street, New York. 1863. [4¾" × 7¼"]. O/bk non-pictorial. "For the use of Political Clubs and the Social Circle." "Price 25 cents." 64pp. [M-133] [Crew/GBM-64].

783.12 The Old White Hat. w. No composer indicated. m. "Air—*When This Old Hat Was New.*" In: *National Republican Grant And Wilson Campaign Song-Book*, page 42. From the *Chattanooga Herald*. Published by The Union Republican Congressional Committee, Washington, DC. 1872. [3¹³⁄₁₆" × 8³⁄₁₆"]. Be/bk litho of Ulysses S. Grant. "We'll Sing a Song for U.S. Grant." 100pp. [M-182]. [Crew/USG-110].

783.13 The Political Code. w. No composer indicated. m. "Air—*Cocachelunk.*" In: *The Grant Songster*, page 48. Published by Haney & Co., Publishers, 119 Nassau Street, New York, NY. 1867. [4⅛" × 6⅜"]. Gd/bk drawing of "Ulysses S. Grant," White House. 64pp. [Crew/USG-32].

783.14 Rally For Seymour And Blair. w. No composer indicated. m. No tune indicated. In: *Seymour Campaign Songster*, page 21. Published by Pattee & Hubbard, Democratic State Committee Rooms, World Building, No. 37 Park Row, New York, NY. 1868. [4" × 5¼"]. Gn/bk litho of Horatio Seymour and Francis Blair. "In the spirit of George Washington and the Patriots of the Revolution, Let us take the steps to re-inaugurate our Government, to start it once again on its course to greatness and prosperity—Horatio Seymour." 38pp. [M-173]. [Crew/HS-8].

783.15 Seymour And Blair. w. No composer indicated. m. "Air—*Columbia, The Gem Of The Ocean.*" In: *Seymour Campaign Songster*, page 14. Published by Pattee & Hubbard, Democratic State Committee

Rooms, World Building, No. 37 Park Row, New York, NY. 1868. [4" × 5¼"]. Gn/bk litho of Horatio Seymour and Francis Blair. "In the spirit of George Washington and the Patriots of the Revolution, Let us take the steps to re-inaugurate our Government, to start it once again on its course to greatness and prosperity — Horatio Seymour." 38pp. [M-173]. [Crew/HS-8].

783.16 The Song Of The Democracy. w.m. No composer or tune indicated. In: *The Democratic Campaign Songster, No. #1,* page 5. Published by American Publishing House, No. 60 West Fourth Street, Cincinnati, OH. 1860. [3⅞" × 5¹¹⁄₁₆"]. Pk/bk litho of "Stephen A. Douglas," black line border. At top of cover — "No. 1, Price 10 Cents." 52pp. [M-118]. [Crew/SAD-12].

783.17 Trip Toniacara Falls. w. "By one who went along." m. No tune indicated. [1863–1865]. Non-pictorial geometric design border. 2pp. Page 2: Blank. [AMC].

783.18 Union. w. No composer indicated. m. "Air — *We'll Be Gay And Happy* In: *Seymour Campaign Songster,* page 16. Published by Pattee & Hubbard, Democratic State Committee Rooms, World Building, No. 37 Park Row, New York, NY. 1868. [4" × 5¼"]. Gn/bk litho of Horatio Seymour and Francis Blair. "In the spirit of George Washington and the Patriots of the Revolution, Let us take the steps to re-inaugurate our Government, to start it once again on its course to greatness and prosperity — Horatio Seymour." 38pp. [M-173]. [Crew/HS-8].

783.19 U.S. Race (Republican Campaign Song With Chorus). w.m. J. William Pope "(Author of *Allegheny: An Indian's Lament, Wake From Thy Slumbers, Leave Me Alone In My Sorrow,* etc)." Published by C.C. Mellor, No. 81 Wood Street, Pittsburgh, PA. 1868. R/w non-pictorial geometric designs. "Dedicated to the Oakland Glee Club." 4pp. [Crew/USG-291]. [AMC].

783.20 Wilson And Grant. w. Sam Booth. m. "Tune — *Bonnie Dundee.*" In: *Grant And Wilson Campaign Songster,* page 2. Published by Frank Eastman, Book and Job Printer, No. 509 Clay Street, San Francisco, CA. [4¼" × 5⅝"]. 1872. Bk/bl geometric design border. 40pp. [Crew/USG-69].

783.21 Witches' Scene From MacGreeley (Which is Seen to be a Fact). w.m. No composer or tune indicated. From the "*New York Standard.*" In: *National Republican Grant And Wilson Campaign Song-Book,* page 34. From the *New York Standard.* Published by The Union Republican Congressional Committee, Washington, DC. 1872. [3¹³⁄₁₆" × 8⁹⁄₁₆"]. Be/bk litho of Ulysses S. Grant. "We'll Sing a Song for U.S. Grant." 100pp. [M-182]. [Crew/USG-110].

BLAIR, Montgomery (District Attorney; Mayor, St. Louis; Judge) [See: Maryland]

• **AmPM-784 BLAND**, Richard Parks (Treasurer, Carson County, Nevada, 1860–1865; U.S. House, Missouri, 1873–1895 & 1897–1899)

784.1 An Auspicious Occasion. w. No composer indicated. m. "Tune — *Odd Fellows' Hall.*" In: *Republican Campaign Parodies And Songs* [Songster], page 13. Published by Betts and Burnett, South Butler, Wayne County, NY. 1896. [7¾" × 5½"]. Be/bk non-pictorial. "McKinley and Hobart." "1896." 28pp. [M-340]. [Crew/WM-67].

784.2 Bland Waileth Over The Silver Bill. w. No composer indicated. m. "Tune — *Baby Mine.*" In: *True Blue Republican Campaign Songs For 1892,* page 31. Published by [V-1: Oliver Ditson Company, Boston, MA] [V-2: The S. Brainard's Son's Company, Chicago, IL]. 1892. [5⅜" × 7¼"]. Bl/bk litho of Benjamin F. Harrison, eagle, flag, geometric designs. 36pp. [M-307]. [Crew/BFH-47].

784.3 Boy Bryan's Epitaph. w. No composer indicated. m. "Tune — *Upidee.*" In: *Republican Campaign Parodies And Songs* [Songster], page 12. Published by Betts and Burnett, South Butler, Wayne County, NY. 1896. [7¾" × 5½"]. Be/bk non-pictorial. "McKinley and Hobart." "1896." 28pp. [M-340]. [Crew/WM-67].

784.4 Bryan Walked Off With The Coveted Prize. w. No composer indicated. m. "Tune — *The Band Played On.*" In: *Republican Campaign Parodies And Songs* [Songster], page 5. Published by Betts and Burnett, South Butler, Wayne County, NY. 1896. [7¾" × 5½"]. Be/bk non-pictorial. "McKinley and Hobart." "1896." 28pp. [M-340]. [Crew/WM-67].

784.5 If Only Gab Could Win. w. AW.C. Vaughn. m. No tune indicated. In: *Republican Victory Campaign Songs,* page 28. c. F.F. Gilbert. Published by Home Music Company, No. 41 East Randolph Street, Chicago, IL. [5⅜" × 7¾"]. 1896. B/w photo of William McKinley. R/w/b drawing of U.S. Flags. 36pp. Page 2: Advertising for the City of Idaho Falls, Idaho. Page 3: Advertising for Keystone Remedy Company. Page 4: Advertising for campaign music. Page 5: Title page. "As sung The Wagner and Leading Quartettes." Page 6 and 35: Advertising for "America Cycle Mfg. Co." Page 31: Advertising for campaign books. Page 32: Advertising. Page 33: Advertising for "Uncle Sam's Tobacco Cure." Page 34: Advertising for "McKinley X-Ray Puzzle." Page 36: Advertising for "Wheeler & Wilson Mfg. Co." Bicycles. [Crew/WM-251]

784.6 Lochinvar Bryan. w. A.T. Garrett. m. "Arranged by F.F. Gilbert. m. "Air — *Good-Bye, My Lover, Good-Bye.*" In: *Republican Victory Campaign Songs,* page 7. c. F.F. Gilbert. Published by Home Music Company, No. 41 East Randolph Street, Chicago, IL. [5⅜" × 7¾"]. 1896. B/w photo of William McKinley. R/w/b drawing of U.S. Flags. 36pp. Page 2: Advertising for the City of Idaho Falls, Idaho. Page 3: Advertising for Keystone Remedy Company. Page 4: Advertising for campaign music. Page 5: Title page. "As sung The Wagner and Leading Quartettes." Page 6 and 35: Advertising for "America Cycle Mfg. Co." Page 31: Advertising for campaign books. Page 32: Advertising. Page 33: Advertising for "Uncle Sam's Tobacco Cure." Page 34: Advertising for "McKinley X-Ray Puzzle." Page 36: Advertising for "Wheeler & Wilson Mfg. Co." Bicycles. [Crew/WM-251]

784.7 The New Dollar. w. E.J. Seymour. m. Tune — *The New Bully.*" In: *Campaign Songs, 1896* [Song Sheet]. Published by Wholesale Dry Goods Republican Club, New York, NY. 1896. [12" × 18¼"]. Non-pictorial. 2pp. [Six songs per page]. [Crew/WM-128].

• **AmPM-785 BROOKS**, John A. (Candidate for Vice President, 1888) [SEE:DOC/PSM-CBF]

785.1 Presidential Ball. w. A.A. Rowley. m. "Air — *Dance By The Light Of The Moon.*" In: *Republican Campaign Songs,* page 23. Published by The Western News Company, Chicago, IL. 1888. [5¼" × 7½"]. B/w litho of "The Author, in '63, 17th Illinois Cav." "Original, Pointed and Spicy ... Set to Old Familiar Tunes, Suitable for Glee Clubs and Marching Clubs." "Look at it and you will buy it." 36pp. Page 2, 35 and 36: Blank. Page 3: Index. "Composed for the Campaign of 1888 and Set to Old Familiar Airs, Suitable for Glee Clubs and Campaign Clubs." "Respectfully Dedicated to my Comrades of the Civil War, who still vote the way they fought—A.A. Rowley, Beloit, Kan." [M-283]. [Crew/BFH-64].

• **AmPM-786 BROWN**, Benjamin Gratz (State House, 1852–1858; U.S. Senate, 1863–1867; Governor, 1871–1873; Candidate for Vice President, 1872) [SEE: DOC/PSM-HG]

786.1 As A Matter Of Course. w.m. No composer or tune indicated. In: *The Sun's Greeley Campaign Songster*, page 35. c. Amos J. Cumming. Published from *The Sun* Office, New York, NY. 1872. [4⅛" × 6½"]. Be/bk litho of Horace Greeley, wreath. "He shines for all." 64pp. [Crew/HG-5].

786.2 Axe Grinding. w.m. No composer or tune indicated. In: *National Republican Grant And Wilson Campaign Song-Book*, page 11. Published by The Union Republican Congressional Committee, Washington, DC. 1872. [$3\frac{13}{16}$" × $8\frac{9}{16}$"]. Be/bk litho of Ulysses S. Grant. "We'll Sing a Song for U.S. Grant." 100pp. [M-182]. [Crew/USG-110].

786.3 Beware! w. No composer indicated. m. "Air—*I Know A Maiden*." In: *Grant And Wilson Campaign Songster*, page 11. Published by Frank Eastman, Book and Job Printer, No. 509 Clay Street, San Francisco, CA. [4¼" × 5⅝"]. 1872. Bk/bl geometric design border. 40pp. [Crew/USG-69].

786.4 Bound To Sweep The Nation (Horace and Gratz). w. No composer indicated. m. "Air—*Sparkling And Bright*." In: *Greeley Campaign Songster*, page 24. "Respectfully dedicated to the Greeley Clubs of the Country." Published by Halpin & McClure, Chicago, IL. 1872. [4" × $5\frac{11}{16}$"]. Pl/bk litho of Horace Greeley, geometric design border. "Chicago: Western News Company, Wholesale Agents." 72pp. [M-187]. [Crew/HG-21].

786.5 The Child's Inquiry. w. No composer indicated. m. "Air—*Auld Lang Syne*." In: *National Republican Grant And Wilson Campaign Song-Book*, page 85. Published by The Union Republican Congressional Committee, Washington, DC. 1872. [$3\frac{13}{16}$" × $8\frac{9}{16}$"]. Be/bk litho of Ulysses S. Grant. "We'll Sing a Song for U.S. Grant." 100pp. [M-182]. [Crew/USG-110].

786.6 Come Greeleyites, Stand To Your Guns. w. No composer indicated. m. "Air—*The Low-Backed Car*." In: *Greeley Campaign Songster*, page 69. "Respectfully dedicated to the Greeley Clubs of the Country." Published by Halpin & McClure, Chicago, IL. 1872. [4" × $5\frac{11}{16}$"]. Pl/bk litho of Horace Greeley, geometric design border. "Chicago: Western News Company, Wholesale Agents." 72pp. [M-187]. [Crew/HG-21].

786.7 [Everywhere, Everywhere] (Campaign Song). w. No composer indicated. m. "Air—*Nelly Bligh*." In: *National Republican Grant And Wilson Campaign Song-Book*, page 63. Published by The Union Republican Congressional Committee, Washington, DC. 1872. [$3\frac{13}{16}$" × $8\frac{9}{16}$"]. Be/bk litho of Ulysses S. Grant. "We'll Sing a Song for U.S. Grant." 100pp. [M-182]. [Crew/USG-110].

786.8 [From North To South, From East To West] (Campaign Song). w. No composer indicated. m. "Air—*The Days When We Went Gypsying*." In: *National Republican Grant And Wilson Campaign Song-Book*, page 35. From the *New York Standard*. Published by The Union Republican Congressional Committee, Washington, DC. 1872. [$3\frac{13}{16}$" × $8\frac{9}{16}$"]. Be/bk litho of Ulysses S. Grant. "We'll Sing a Song for U.S. Grant." 100pp. [M-182]. [Crew/USG-110].

786.9 Going To Vote For Greeley. w. No composer indicated. m. "Air—*Don't Be Angry With Me, Darling*." In: *The Farmer Of Chappaqua Songster, Containing A Great Number Of The Best Campaign Songs That The Unanimous And Enthusiastic Nomination Of The Hon. Horace Greeley For President Has Produced*, page 23. Published by Robert M. De Wit, Publisher, No. 33 Rose Street, New York, NY. 1872. [4¼" × 6¼"]. R/w/bl/y litho caricature of Horace Greeley. 102pp.

786.10 The Good Time Coming. w.m. No composer or tune indicated. In: *The Sun's Greeley Campaign Songster*, page 23. c. Amos J. Cumming. Published from *The Sun* Office, New York, NY. 1872. [4⅛" × 6½"]. Be/bk litho of Horace Greeley, wreath. "He shines for all." 64pp. [Crew/HG-5].

786.11 Grant's Victory. w. Mrs. Jennie M. Cutter. m. "Air—*Marching Through Georgia*." In: *Grant And Wilson Campaign Songster*, page 14. Published by Frank Eastman, Book and Job Printer, No. 509 Clay Street, San Francisco, CA. [4¼" × 5⅝"]. 1872. Bk/bl geometric design border. 40pp. [Crew/USG-69].

786.12 Greeley And Brown Campaign Song. w.m. No composer or tune indicated. In: *The Sun's Greeley Campaign Songster*, page 24. c. Amos J. Cumming. Published from *The Sun* Office, New York, NY. 1872. [4⅛" × 6½"]. Be/bk litho of Horace Greeley, wreath. "He shines for all." 64pp. [Crew/HG-5].

786.13 Greeley And Gratz Brown. w. No composer indicated. m. "Air—*Glory Hallelujah*." "An Imitation of the Famous Dutch song, as Sung by the celebrated Star Campaign, Gus Williams, throughout the Union." In: *The Farmer Of Chappaqua Songster, Containing A Great Number Of The Best Campaign Songs That The Unanimous And Enthusiastic Nomination Of The Hon. Horace Greeley For President Has Produced*, page 29. Published by Robert M. De Wit, Publisher, No. 33 Rose Street, New York, NY. 1872. [4¼" × 6¼"]. R/w/bl/y litho caricature of Horace Greeley. 102pp.

786.14 Greeley And Gratz Campaign Song. w. No composer indicated. m. "Air—*Not For Joseph*." In: *The Sun's Greeley Campaign Songster*, page 56. c. Amos J. Cumming. Published from *The Sun* Office, New York, NY. 1872. [4⅛" × 6½"]. Be/bk litho of Horace Greeley, wreath. "He shines for all." 64pp. [Crew/HG-5].

786.15 Greeley And Gratz Campaign Song. w.m. No composer indicated. m. "Air—*When This Cruel War Is Over*." In: *The Sun's Greeley Campaign Songster*, page 32. c. Amos J. Cumming. Published from *The Sun* Office, New York, NY. 1872. [4⅛" × 6½"]. Be/bk litho of Horace Greeley, wreath. "He shines for all." 64pp. [Crew/HG-5].

786.16 Greeley And Gratz Campaign Song. w.m.

No composer indicated. m. "Air—*The Red, White, And Blue.*" In: *The Sun's Greeley Campaign Songster*, page 21. c. Amos J. Cumming. Published from *The Sun* Office, New York, NY. 1872. [4⅛" × 6½"]. Be/bk litho of Horace Greeley, wreath. "He shines for all." 64pp. [Crew/HG-5].

786.17 Greeley's Defeat. w. No composer indicated. m. "Air—*Yankee Doodle.*" In: *Grant And Wilson Campaign Songster*, page 22. Published by Frank Eastman, Book and Job Printer, No. 509 Clay Street, San Francisco, CA. [4¼" × 5⅝"]. 1872. Bk/bl geometric design border. 40pp. [Crew/USG-69].

786.18 Greeley, Greeley, Hallelujah. w. No composer indicated. m. "Air—*Glory Hallelujah.*" In: *The Farmer Of Chappaqua Songster, Containing A Great Number Of The Best Campaign Songs That The Unanimous And Enthusiastic Nomination Of The Hon. Horace Greeley For President Has Produced*, page 74. Published by Robert M. De Wit, Publisher, No. 33 Rose Street, New York, NY. 1872. [4¼" × 6¼"]. R/w/bl/y litho caricature of Horace Greeley. 102pp.

786.19 Horace Greeley's Pardy [sic]. w. No composer indicated. m. "Air—*Mygel Snyder's Pardy.*" "An Imitation of the Famous Dutch song, as Sung by the celebrated Star Campaign, Gus Williams, throughout the Union." In: *The Farmer Of Chappaqua Songster, Containing A Great Number Of The Best Campaign Songs That The Unanimous And Enthusiastic Nomination Of The Hon. Horace Greeley For President Has Produced*, page 34. Published by Robert M. De Wit, Publisher, No. 33 Rose Street, New York, NY. 1872. [4¼" × 6¼"]. R/w/bl/y litho caricature of Horace Greeley. 102pp.

786.20 Hunkidori. w. No composer indicated. m. "Air—*Hunkidori, I Oh!*" In: *National Republican Grant And Wilson Campaign Song-Book*, page 73. Published by The Union Republican Congressional Committee, Washington, DC. 1872. [$3\frac{13}{16}$" × $8\frac{9}{16}$"]. Be/bk litho of Ulysses S. Grant. "We'll Sing a Song for U.S. Grant." 100pp. [M-182]. [Crew/USG-110].

786.21 Hurrah For Horace Greeley And Benjamin Gratz Brown! w.m. No composer or tune indicated. In: *The Sun's Greeley Campaign Songster*, page 52. c. Amos J. Cumming. Published from *The Sun* Office, New York, NY. 1872. [4⅛" × 6½"]. Be/bk litho of Horace Greeley, wreath. "He shines for all." 64pp. [Crew/HG-5].

786.22 [In Early Days Our Fathers Wore] (A Campaign Song). w. No composer indicated. m. "Air—*Yankee Doodle.*" In: *National Republican Grant And Wilson Campaign Song-Book*, page 4. Published by The Union Republican Congressional Committee, Washington, DC. 1872. [$3\frac{13}{16}$" × $8\frac{9}{16}$"]. Be/bk litho of Ulysses S. Grant. "We'll Sing a Song for U.S. Grant." 100pp. [M-182]. [Crew/USG-110].

786.23 Ku-Klux Song. w. No composer indicated. m. "Air—*Dixie.*" In: *National Republican Grant And Wilson Campaign Song-Book*, page 77. Published by The Union Republican Congressional Committee, Washington, DC. 1872. [$3\frac{13}{16}$" × $8\frac{9}{16}$"]. Be/bk litho of Ulysses S. Grant. "We'll Sing a Song for U.S. Grant." 100pp. [M-182]. [Crew/USG-110].

786.24 [Let It Resound The Land Around] (Campaign Song). w. No composer indicated. m. "Air—*Sparkling And Bright.*" From the "*Sandwich Gazette.*" In: *National Republican Grant And Wilson Campaign Song-Book*, page 78. Published by The Union Republican Congressional Committee, Washington, DC. 1872. [$3\frac{13}{16}$" × $8\frac{9}{16}$"]. Be/bk litho of Ulysses S. Grant. "We'll Sing a Song for U.S. Grant." 100pp. [M-182]. [Crew/USG-110].

786.25 [The Lib'ral Game Is A Game Of Brag] (Campaign Song). m. A. Downing. m. "Air—*Nelly Bly.*" In: *National Republican Grant And Wilson Campaign Song-Book*, page 51. Published by The Union Republican Congressional Committee, Washington, DC. 1872. [$3\frac{13}{16}$" × $8\frac{9}{16}$"]. Be/bk litho of Ulysses S. Grant. "We'll Sing a Song for U.S. Grant." 100pp. [M-182]. [Crew/USG-110].

786.26 [My Friends, I Guess You All Have Heard] (Campaign Song). w. No composer indicated. m. "Air—*Never Mind The Weather So The Wind Don't Blow.*" In: *National Republican Grant And Wilson Campaign Song-Book*, page 7. Published by The Union Republican Congressional Committee, Washington, DC. 1872. [$3\frac{13}{16}$" × $8\frac{9}{16}$"]. Be/bk litho of Ulysses S. Grant. "We'll Sing a Song for U.S. Grant." 100pp. [M-182]. [Crew/USG-110].

786.27 The New Departure. w. N.G. Sawyer. m. "Air—*Whip-Poor-Will's Call.*" In: *Grant And Wilson Campaign Songster*, page 28. Published by Frank Eastman, Book and Job Printer, No. 509 Clay Street, San Francisco, CA. [4¼" × 5⅝"]. 1872. Bk/bl geometric design border. 40pp. [Crew/USG-69].

786.28 Not For Horace. w. C.B. Parker. m. "Air—*Not For Joseph.*" In: *National Republican Grant And Wilson Campaign Song-Book*, page 28. Published by The Union Republican Congressional Committee, Washington, DC. 1872. [$3\frac{13}{16}$" × $8\frac{9}{16}$"]. Be/bk litho of Ulysses S. Grant. "We'll Sing a Song for U.S. Grant." 100pp. [M-182]. [Crew/USG-110].

786.29 Now This Cruel War Is Over. w. Charles G. Hayes. m. "Air—*Beautiful River.*" In: *Greeley Campaign Songster*, page 24. "Respectfully dedicated to the Greeley Clubs of the Country." Published by Halpin & McClure, Chicago, IL. 1872. [4" × $5\frac{11}{16}$"]. Pl/bk litho of Horace Greeley, geometric design border. "Chicago: Western News Company, Wholesale Agents." 72pp. [M-187]. [Crew/HG-21].

786.30 Oh! Poor Hiram Ulysses. w.m. No composer indicated. m. "Air—*Oh Poor Robinson Crusoe.*" In: *The Sun's Greeley Campaign Songster*, page 18. c. Amos J. Cumming. Published from *The Sun* Office, New York, NY. 1872. [4⅛" × 6½"]. Be/bk litho of Horace Greeley, wreath. "He shines for all." 64pp. [Crew/HG-5].

786.31 Old White Hat. w.m. No composer or tune indicated. In: *The Sun's Greeley Campaign Songster*, page 39. c. Amos J. Cumming. Published from *The Sun* Office, New York, NY. 1872. [4⅛" × 6½"]. Be/bk litho of Horace Greeley, wreath. "He shines for all." 64pp. [Crew/HG-5].

786.32 The Old White Hat. w. No composer indicated. m. "Air—*When This Old Hat Was New.*" In: *National Republican Grant And Wilson Campaign Song-Book*, page 42. From the *Chattanooga Herald*. Published by The Union Republican Congressional Committee, Washington, DC. 1872. [$3\frac{13}{16}$" × $8\frac{9}{16}$"].

Be/bk litho of Ulysses S. Grant. "We'll Sing a Song for U.S. Grant." 100pp. [M-182]. [Crew/USG-110].

786.33 Our Grant Leads The Battle. w. No composer indicated. m. "Air — *Wait For The Wagon.*" In: *National Republican Grant And Wilson Campaign Song-Book*, page 19. Published by The Union Republican Congressional Committee, Washington, DC. 1872. [3 13/16" × 8 5/16"]. Be/bk litho of Ulysses S. Grant. "We'll Sing a Song for U.S. Grant." 100pp. [M-182]. [Crew/USG-110].

786.34 Peter Von Blixen's Campaign Song. w. No composer indicated. m. "Air — *Hoist Up The Flag.*" In: *The Farmer Of Chappaqua Songster, Containing A Great Number Of The Best Campaign Songs That The Unanimous And Enthusiastic Nomination Of The Hon. Horace Greeley For President Has Produced*, page 52. Published by Robert M. De Wit, Publisher, No. 33 Rose Street, New York, NY. 1872. [4 1/4" × 6 1/4"]. R/w/bl/y litho caricature of Horace Greeley. 102pp.

786.35 [Say Union Boys, Have You Seen Old Greeley] (A Campaign Song). w. No composer indicated. m. "Air — *Kingdom Coming.*" "Written for the *Marietta Register*, by the Muskingum Township Union Band." In: *National Republican Grant And Wilson Campaign Song-Book*, page 27. Published by The Union Republican Congressional Committee, Washington, DC. 1872. [3 13/16" × 8 5/16"]. Be/bk litho of Ulysses S. Grant. "We'll Sing a Song for U.S. Grant." 100pp. [M-182]. [Crew/USG-110].

786.36 The Southern Rally For Greeley And Brown. w.m. No composer or tune indicated. In: *Greeley Campaign Songster*, page 16. Published by Halpin & McClure, Chicago, IL. 1872. [4" × 5 1/16"]. Pl/bk litho of Horace Greeley, geometric design border. "Chicago: Western News Company, Wholesale Agents." 72pp. [M-187]. [Crew/HG-21].

786.37 Swift The Ball Is Rolling On. w.m. No composer indicated. m. "Air — *Tippecanoe And Tyler, Too.*" In: *Greeley Campaign Songster*, page 20. Published by Halpin & McClure, Chicago, IL. 1872. [4" × 5 1/16"]. Pl/bk litho of Horace Greeley, geometric design border. "Chicago: Western News Company, Wholesale Agents." 72pp. [M-187]. [Crew/HG-21].

786.38 That's Where They Make The Mistake. w. No composer indicated. m. "Air — *That's Where You Make The Mistake.*" In: *The Farmer Of Chappaqua Songster, Containing A Great Number Of The Best Campaign Songs That The Unanimous And Enthusiastic Nomination Of The Hon. Horace Greeley For President Has Produced*, page 55. Published by Robert M. De Wit, Publisher, No. 33 Rose Street, New York, NY. 1872. [4 1/4" × 6 1/4"]. R/w/bl/y litho caricature of Horace Greeley. 102pp.

786.39 A Wall. w. No composer indicated. m. "Air — *Three Black Crows.*" In: *National Republican Grant And Wilson Campaign Song-Book*, page 76. Published by The Union Republican Congressional Committee, Washington, DC. 1872. [3 13/16" × 8 5/16"]. Be/bk litho of Ulysses S. Grant. "We'll Sing a Song for U.S. Grant." 100pp. [M-182]. [Crew/USG-110].

786.40 We Are Coming, Father Greeley. w. Lewis Herbert. m. "Air — *Wait For The Wagon.*" In: *Greeley Campaign Songster*, page 53. "Respectfully dedicated to the Greeley Clubs of the Country." Published by Halpin & McClure, Chicago, IL. 1872. [4" × 5 1/16"]. Pl/bk litho of Horace Greeley, geometric design border. "Chicago: Western News Company, Wholesale Agents." 72pp. [M-187]. [Crew/HG-21].

786.41 We Shall Solid Go For Grant. w. No composer indicated. m. "Air — *Suit Yourself.*" In: *National Republican Grant And Wilson Campaign Song-Book*, page 38. From the *New York Standard*. Published by The Union Republican Congressional Committee, Washington, DC. 1872. [3 13/16" × 8 5/16"]. Be/bk litho of Ulysses S. Grant. "We'll Sing a Song for U.S. Grant." 100pp. [M-182]. [Crew/USG-110].

786.42 We'll Vote For General G. w. No composer indicated. m. "Air — *Little Brown Jug.*" In: *National Republican Grant And Wilson Campaign Song-Book*, page 79. Published by The Union Republican Congressional Committee, Washington, DC. 1872. [3 13/16" × 8 5/16"]. Be/bk litho of Ulysses S. Grant. "We'll Sing a Song for U.S. Grant." 100pp. [M-182]. [Crew/USG-110].

786.43 What I Know About Beet. w. No composer indicated. m. "Air — *Little Brown Jug.*" In: *National Republican Grant And Wilson Campaign Song-Book*, page 17. Published by The Union Republican Congressional Committee, Washington, DC. 1872. [3 13/16" × 8 5/16"]. Be/bk litho of Ulysses S. Grant. "We'll Sing a Song for U.S. Grant." 100pp. [M-182]. [Crew/USG-110].

786.44 Wilson And Grant. w. N.G. Sawyer. m. "Air — *Whip-Poor-Will's Call.*" In: *Grant And Wilson Campaign Songster*, page 15. Published by Frank Eastman, Book and Job Printer, No. 509 Clay Street, San Francisco, CA. [4 1/4" × 5 5/8"]. 1872. Bk/bl geometric design border. 40pp. [Crew/USG-69].

786.45 Wilson And Grant. w. No composer or tune indicated. In: *National Republican Grant And Wilson Campaign Song-Book*, page 26. Published by The Union Republican Congressional Committee, Washington, DC. 1872. [3 13/16" × 8 5/16"]. Be/bk litho of Ulysses S. Grant. "We'll Sing a Song for U.S. Grant." 100pp. [M-182]. [Crew/USG-110].

• **AmPM-787 CARNAHAN**, Melvin Eugene (Municipal Judge, Rolla, 1960–1962; State House, 1963–1967; State Treasurer, 1981–1985; Lt. Governor, 1989–1993; Governor, 1993–2000; Candidate for U.S. Senate, 2000)

787.1 Ashcroft. w. William Tong. m. "*Angie*, originally by The Rolling Stones." "Dedicated to Attorney General Ashcroft." Published online at <http://amiright.com/parody/misc/therollingstones3.shml>. [ca. 2001].

787.2 Crisco Kid. m. "Sung to the tune of *Cisco Kid* by War." "Former Senator John Ashcroft (now Attorney General), defeated for re-election by the ghost of the late Gov. Mel Carnahan, was known to anoint himself with Crisco oil in religious ceremonies." N/c photo of John Ashcroft praying with a can of Crisco oil on his head — "The Anointed One." Published at <http://www.bootnewt.envy.nu/criscokid.htm>. [ca. 2002].

• **AmPM-788 CASE**, Theodore Spencer (Alderman, Kansas City, 1860; Quartermaster-General of Missouri; Postmaster, Kansas City, 1873–1885)

788.1 Lincoln (In Memoriam) [sic]. w. William P.

Fox. m. Francis Wolcott. Published by John Church, Jr., No. 66 West Fourth Street, Cincinnati, OH. 1865. Non-pictorial black line border. "The words written and dedicated to Col. Theo. S. Case, Qr. M. Genl. of Mo." 6pp. [Crew/AL-274].

• **AmPM-789 CLARK**, James Beauchamp "Champ" (State House, 1889–1891; U.S. Representative, 1893–1895 & 1897–1921; Speaker of the U.S. House of Representatives) [ALSO SEE: DOC/PSM-MISC]

789.1 [Bring Back The G.O.P.'s Of Childhood]. w. I.E. Henry. m. "Tune—*Bring Back Those Wonderful Days*." In: *Republican Campaign Songs*, page 6. Published by Republican State Committee Headquarters, Topeka, Kansas. 1920. [$5\frac{7}{16}$" × $7\frac{13}{16}$"]. Be/bk photos of "Warren G. Harding" and "Calvin Coolidge"—"Our Country Needs Them." "Sing and Smile on to Victory." 24pp. [Crew/WGH-63].

789.2 Bring Your Houn'. w.m. Norman Pruitt. Original publication not located. 1912. Published, with lyric sheet, in *Winners & Losers, Campaign Songs From The Critical Elections In American History, Volume 2—1896–1976*. Sung with notes by Peter Janovsky. $33\frac{1}{3}$ rpm LP. Folkways Records FSS 37261. 1980.

789.3 Columbia Victorious! (The Battle Cry Of America). w. Maurice Freeman. m. Ralph Garren. No publisher indicated. Copyright 1917 by Freeman & Garren. B/w non-pictorial. "Dedicated to our boys across the sea." "Champ Clark—a truly Democratic American—says: 'Having heard the *Columbia Victorious* song, I believe it to be expressive of the spirit of America's entrance into the war and think it will prove a popular marching song.'" 4pp. Page 4: Blank.

789.4 Do Your Bit Help Send A Kit (For Our Boys In France). w.m. G.F. Bickford. Published by Our Boys In France Tobacco Fund, No. 25 West 44th Street, New York, NY. 1917. R/w/b drawing of a soldier and a sailor smoking. "Soldier's and Sailor's Official Tobacco Song." "SOS—Send Over Smokes." "Endorsed by the Secretaries of the Army and Navy." "Other endorsements Alton B. Parker, The American Red Cross, Cardinal Gibbons, Speaker Champ Clark, Rabbi Wise, Lyman Abbott, Gertrude Atherton, Governor Whitman and the entire nation." "Theodore Roosevelt says—I wish you all possible success in your admirable effort to get our boys in France tobacco." 4pp. Page 4: Narrative: "Gun Smoke Everywhere—But Not a Whiff of Tobacco Smoke to Cheer a Fellow Up." [Crew/TR-292].

789.5 They Gotta Quit Kickin' My Dawg Around. w.m. No composers indicated [Webb M. Oungst. m. Cy Perkins]. Published as a post card by Lewis Publishing Company, Pittsburgh, PA. [ca. 1918]. Y/w/br drawing by Herbert Johnson of man rolling up sleeve to fight a dog wearing a cost labeled—Common People," and an old dog labeled "Popular Government," White House in the background. Drawing titled—"Come On, Gol Darn Ye!" Rev: Post card space for address and message. [Crew/MISC-221].

• **AmPM-790 DAVIS**, Webster (Mayor of Kansas City, 1894–1895)

790.1 [Bill McKinley In The Chair]. w. H.D. Tutewiler. m. "To the tune *Bull Frog On The Bank*." In: *The March Of The Flag Songbook*, page 20. Published by H.D. Tutewiler, No. 133 West Market Street, Indianapolis, IN. 1900. [5" × $7\frac{5}{8}$"]. Be/bk litho of flag. "The Only Republican Campaign Songs for 1900 Having the Authorized Endorsement [sic] of Both National Republican Committees." 28pp. [M-374]. [Crew/WM-155].

• **AmPM-791 DYER**, David Patterson (Prosecuting Attorney, Missouri, 1860; State House, 1862–1865; U.S. House, 1869–1871)

791.1 Carve That Possum. w. No composer indicated. In: *Democratic Campaign Songs* [Song Book], page 4. w. No composer indicated. m. "Popular Airs." Published in Madison County, Alabama. [1876]. [$3\frac{5}{8}$" × $6\frac{9}{16}$"]. Non-pictorial geometric design border. 4pp. [M-2–1]. [Crew/ SJT-11].

791.2 Go! Grant, Go! w. No composer indicated. m. "Tune—*Old Black Joe*." [1876]. [$4\frac{11}{16}$" × $8\frac{1}{4}$"]. Non-pictorial. 2pp. Page 2: Blank. [Crew SJT-17].

• **AmPM-792 EAGLETON**, Thomas Francis (Circuit Attorney, St. Louis, 1956; State Attorney General, 1960–1964; Lt. Governor, 1964–1968; U.S. Senate, 1968–1987)

792.1 Convention '72. w.m. N. Canel and N. Kousaloos. 45 rpm record. Mainstream Records, MRL 5525/ ZT8P 224228. Performed by The Delegates. 1972.

• **AmPM-793 FILLEY**, Chauncey Ives (Delegate, Republican National Convention, 1860. 1868–1892Chair,am Republican State Committee, 1876; Republican National Committee, 1876–1892; Mayor, St. Louis, 1863–1864)

793.1 Republican National Convention March. m. Al G. Mark. Published by Mark Bros. Music Publishing Company, No. 3940 Page Avenue, St. Louis, MO. 1896. R/w/b drawings of William McKinley, Levi P. Morton, Thomas Reed, Wm. Allison and "?" [question mark] on flag background, shields. "Dedicated to the City of St. Louis, June 1896." 8pp. Page 2: B/w photos of "Prominent Republicans and Gentlemen who were instrumental in securing the Republican National Convention for St. Louis—Sam M. Kennard, President Business Men's League; Chas. H. Sampson, Chairman Convention Committee; Hon. Chauncey Ives Filley, Chairman Reception Committee; Frank Gaienne, Gen'l. Mgr., St. Louis Exposition; L.S. W. Wall; Chas. F. Wenneker." Page 7: B/w photos of "Merchant's League Club—Wm. H. Hobbs, Vice-President; Louis F. Zipp, Treasurer; Hon. J.A. Talty, President; Theo. D. Kalbfell, Chair., Republican Central Committee; Morris Langsdorf, Sec." Page 8: Blank. [Crew/WM-1].

• **AmPM-794 FRANCIS**, David Rowland (Mayor, St. Louis, 1885–1989; Governor, 1889–1893; U.S. Secretary of the Interior, 1896–1997; U.S. Ambassador to Russia, 1916–1917)

794.1 Greetings To The President (Louisiana Purchase Exposition, 1904). w.m. Dr. George A. Carreras, St. Louis, Mo. Published by Ev. E. Carreras, Printer and Binder, 509 North Third Street, St. Louis, MO. 1904. B/w photos of "Hon. David R. Francis," "Festival Hall & Cascades," "Administration Building," "Missouri State Capitol," and "Government Building." "Respectfully Dedicated to Hon. David Rowland Francis, President, Louisiana Purchase Exposition." 8pp. Pages 2, 6, 7 and 8: Blank.

794.2 Inauguration March. m. Prof. W.C. Nordmann. Published by Washington Music Company, Washington, MO. 1890. B/w litho of D.R. Franci, geometric and floral design border. "Dedicated to Gov. D.R. Francis, of Missouri, As Played at His Inauguration; January 14th, 1889." 8pp. Pages 2 and 8: Blank.

- AmPM-795 GAIENNIE, Frank (Board of Police Commissioners, St. Louis, 1885–1888)

795.1 Republican National Convention March. m. Al G. Mark. Published by Mark Bros. Music Publishing Company, No. 3940 Page Avenue, St. Louis, MO. 1896. R/w/b drawings of William McKinley, Levi P. Morton, Thomas Reed, Wm. Allison and "?" [question mark] on flag background, shields. "Dedicated to the City of St. Louis, June 1896." 8pp. Page 2: B/w photos of "Prominent Republicans and Gentlemen who were instrumental in securing the Republican National Convention for St. Louis — Sam M. Kennard, President Business Men's League; Chas. H. Sampson, Chairman Convention Committee; Hon. Chauncey Ives Filley, Chairman Reception Committee; Frank Gaienne, Gen'l. Mgr., St. Louis Exposition; L.S. W. Wall; Chas. F. Wenneker." Page 7: B/w photos of "Merchant's League Club — Wm. H. Hobbs, Vice-President; Louis F. Zipp, Treasurer; Hon. J.A. Talty, President; Theo. D. Kalbfell, Chair., Republican Central Committee; Morris Langsdorf, Sec." Page 8: Blank. [Crew/WM-1].

- AmPM-796 GEPHARDT, Richard Andrew (Democratic Committeeman, St. Louis, 1968–1971; Alderman, St. Louis, 1971–1976; U.S. House, 1977–Present)

796.1 All You Democrats. w. Adam Bernstein. m. "*Mr. Tambourine Man,* based on a performance by Bob Dylan." Published online at <http://www.amiright.com/parody/60s/bobdylan17.shtml>. [ca. 2003].

796.2 California Girls. w. John Jenkins. m. "*California Girls,* based on the performance by Beach Boys." The last four leaders of the Democratic Party in the House of Representatives have been Tip O'Neill (Massachusetts, 1977–87), Jim Wright (Texas, 87–89), Tom Foley (Washington, 89–94), and Dick Gephardt (Missouri, 94–2002)..." Published online at <http://amiright.com/parody/60s/beachboys17.shtml>. [2003].

796.3 Democrat Plans. w. Royce Miller. m. "*Truck Dirvin' Man,* based on a performance by Rick Nelson." Published online at <http://www.amiright.com/parody/60s/ricknelson1.shtml>. [ca. 2003].

796.4 The Democratic Presidential Candidate Show. w. Laurence Dunne. m. "*The Muppet Show* by The Muppets." "I'm not a Republican by and certainly I'm not a Dubya fan, as my Bush parodies will attest <http://www.amiright.com/parody/60s/thebradybunchtvshow0.shtml>." Published online at <http://amiright.com/parody/70s/muppets0.shtml>. [ca. 2003].

796.5 Don't You Vote For Gephardt. w. Bubba. m. "*Don't Go Breakin' My Heart,* based on a performance by Elton John and Kiki Dee." "The Campaign trail, that is. Oy, oy, Joe, another one bites the dust." Published online at <http://www.amiright.com/parody/70s/eltonjohnkikidee0.shtml>. [ca. 2003].

796.6 Election City. w. Michael Pacholek. m. "*Atlantic City,* based on a performance by Bruce Springsteen." "For the record, it was Pierre Ambroise Francois Choderios de LaClos (1741–1803), author of *Dangerous Liaisons,* who said, Revenge is a dish best served cold.' Not an old Klingon proverb, as Gene Roddenberry (or Quinton Tarantino) would have us believe. And while governing should not be, politics is often all about revenge. Burr ..." Published online at <http://www.amiright.com/parody/80s/brucespringsteen22.shtml>. [ca. 2003].

796.7 Fifty Guys Runnin' 'Gainst Dubya. w. Charlie Decker. m. "*Fifty Ways To Leave Your Lover,* based on the performance by Paul Simon." Published online at <http://amiright.com/parody/70s/paulsimon28.shml>. [2003].

796.8 Goodbye Congressman Gephardt. w. Kev O'Keefe. m. Tune — "*Rainbow In The Dark* originally by Dio." "It seems this term will be Dich [sic] Gebhardt's, as he has no plans to run again ... he's too busy eyeing the presidency, like every democrat & their moms it seems." Published online at <http://www.amiright.com/parody/70s/dio0.shtml>.

796.9 If You'd Voted For Gephardt. w. Guy DiRito. m. "*If I Only Had A Heart,* based on a performance by Wizard Of Oz." Published online at <http://amiright.com/parody/misc/wizardofoz4.shtml>. 2003.

796.10 I'm A Dick. w. Spaff.com. m. "*Bitch,* based on a performance by Meredith Brooks." Published online at <http://amiright.com/parody/90s/meredithbrooks5.shtml>. 2003.

796.11 New Hampshire Primary Marching Cadence. w. Guy DiRito. m. "*Military Cadence (Sound Off),* based on a performance by Traditional." "This song is done to the traditional military cadence beat. Practice marching as you sound off to this." Published online at <http://www.amiright.com/parody/misc/traditional430.shtml>. 2004.

796.12 The Little First Lady With Megalomania. w. Paul Silhan. m. "Sung to *The Little Old Lady From Pasadena* by Jan & Dean." On: Cassette: *Lie-A-lot.* Lyrics published at <http://www.paulsilhan.com/lal-1.htm>. 1995.

796.13 '04 Elections Are Coming. w. KAH & Ana. m. "*Santa Clause Is Coming To Town,* based on a performance by Traditional." "For the Holidays, our AP Gov teacher gave us an assignment to write some holiday song political song parodies ... and here's what we came up with. Enjoy!" Published online at <http://amiright.com/parody/misc/traditional387.shtml>. 2003.

796.14 Pal Wesley Clark. w. Michael Pacholek. m. "*Palisades Park,* based on the performance by Freddy Cannon." "I should have written this weeks ago. The flavor of the month has melted. Not that this was an endorsement anyway." "And now Clark's fade is well underway. Maybe Kerry will appoint him Secretary of Defense, After all, Clark shouldn't have trouble getting his fellow Republicans to confirm him in the Senate." Published online at <http://www.amiright.com/parody/60s/freddycannon0.shtml>. 2003.

796.15 Season On The Trail. w. Michael Pacholek. m. "*Season's In The Sun,* based on a performance by Terry Jacks." "The Campaign trail, that is. Oy, oy, Joe, another one bites the dust." Published online at

<http://www.amiright.com/parody/70s/terryjacks5.shtml>. [ca. 2004].

796.16 That Leftist Tart From San Francisco. w. John Jenkins. m. Tune — "*I Left My Heart In San Francisco* originally by Tony Bennett." "A duet with the last two lines of each verse (after the introduction) sung by Nancy Pelosi and the balance sung by an anonymous Democrat Congressman." Published online at <http://www.amiright.com/parody/60s/tonybennett2.shml>. [ca. 2003].

796.17 Total Eclipse Of Gephardt. w. John Jenkins. m. Tune — "*Total Eclipse Of The Heart,* based on a performance by Bonnie Tyler." "Dick Gephardt's presidential campaign came to a sudden conclusion after his distant fourth place finish in the Iowa caucuses, which was especially disappointing since he won Iowa in his 1988 campaign." Published online at <http://amiright.com/parody/80s/bonnietyler12.shtml>. [2004].

796.18 We Want Howard Dean. w.m. Denny Zartman. m. No tune indicated. "Spread The Word Through Song and Music! Songs For Dean, Songs to get elected by." N/c photo of Howard Dean. Lyrics and sound file published online at <http://songsfordean.com/so/lyrics/somethingtosee.php>. 2004.

796.19 Yell Like Howard Dean. w. John Jenkins. m. "*Yellow Submarine,* based on the performance by The Beatles." "As the race for the Democratic presidential nomination approaches the first two voter tests, the Iowa caucus and the New Hampshire primary (both in January), Dr. Howard Dean is combining his fire breathing campaign rhetoric and his unique internet appeal to lead the polls in both states. Will he stay there?" Published online at <http://amiright.com/parody/60s/thebeatles415.shml>. [ca. 2004].

• **AmPM-797   HADLEY,** Herbert S. (Governor, 1909–1913)

797.1 Governor Hadley's March. m. Myrna Kent-Kelly. Published by Johannes Goetze, Moberly, MO. [1909–1913]. B/w photo of Herbert Hadley. Gn/w geometric designs. 6pp. Pages 2 and 6: Blank.

• **AmPM-798   HANNEGAN,** Robert Emmet (Delegate to Democratic National Convention, 1940; Chairman of Democratic National Committee, 1944–1947; U.S. Postmaster General, 1945–1947)

798.1 Clear It With Sidney. w. No composer indicated. m. "Tune — *Bellbottom Trousers.*" In: *Again And Again And Again Or All At Sea,* page 10. Published by Albany Legislative Correspondents' Association of New York State, Albany, NY. 1945. [8¾" × 11"]. N/c drawing of Franklin Roosevelt as pirate, Thomas Dewey as "Black Tom," Henry Wallace, Sidney Hillman, others on ship — "Union Ship C.I.O.-P.A.C." "Black Tom" Dewey walking plank. "Featuring Political Craft and Cunning and Contortions; Also Summoned by Subpoena, or Hit-Toddy and the Shady Lady, the Indestructible Dame Known as Lu-Lu; Together with Mystical Midsummer Mummery of '46, in a Roaring and Raucous and Revealing Racing Scene Entitled 'Hoots and Straddles.'" "All Done with Music, Magic, and Mirrors — In Three Acts at Hotel Ten Eyck, Albany, March 15, 1945." [Crew/FDR-371].

798.2 Use Your Ballot. w. Louise Jeffers. m. No tune indicated. In: *Songs For A New Party,* page 12. Copyright 1948 by People's Songs. [3½" × 7"]. Non-pictorial. "Music for these songs in *Songs For Wallace.*" "Permission for use on television, newsreel, radio, &c., can easily be obtained from People's Songs by calling WA 9–2356 (NYC)." 16pp. [M-429]. [Crew/HAW-5].

• **AmPM-799   HENDERSON,** John Brooks (State House, 1848–1850 & 1856–1858; U.S. Senate, 1862–1869; Special United States Attorney, St. Louis, 1875; Commissioner to Treat with Hostile Tribes of Indians, 1877)

799.1 Seven Men! Seven Men! w. No composer indicated. m. "Air — *Maryland, My Maryland.*" In: *The Grant Campaign Songster, Containing All The Most Popular Original Songs, Ballads And Recitations That Will Be Most Sung During This Presidential Campaign, Adapted To Very Popular And Well-Known Airs And Choruses,* page 10. Published by Robert M. Dewitt, Publisher, No. 13 Frankfort Street, New York, NY. 1868. [4¼" × 5¾"]. [V-1: Be/bk] [V-2: Gn/bk] litho of Ulysses S. Grant. 76pp. [M-155]. [Crew/USG-75].

• **AmPM-800   HOLDEN,** Bob (State Treasurer, 1990s; Governor, 2001–Present)

800.1 Concealed. w.m. Jeff Parnell "@ www.jeffparnell.com." On CD: *Great Words.* Published by Junglecat Productions/Jeff Parnell, P.O. Box 388, Rogersville, MO. 65742. 2003.

800.2 We Can't Keep Holden On. w.m. Jeff Parnell "@ www.jeffparnell.com." On CD: *Great Words.* Published by Junglecat Productions/Jeff Parnell, P.O. Box 388, Rogersville, MO. 65742. 2003.

• **AmPM-801   HUNGATE,** William Leonard (Prosecuting Attorney, Lincoln County, 1958–1964; U.S. House, 1964–1977; U.S. District Court Judge, Missouri, 1979)

801.1 Down At The Old Watergate. w. Congressman William L. Hungate, "Democrat, Missouri." Copyright 1973 by Popdraw, Inc., No. 165 West 46th Street, New York, NY. "Recorded by Perception Records, 165 West 46th Street, New York, NY." In: *Poor Richard's Watergate,* page 8. e. Roy Kammerman. Published by Price/Stern/Sloan, Publishers, Los Angeles, CA. 1973. [5¼" × 6¾"]. Bl/w photo of Richard Nixon. 68pp.

• **AmPM-801A   INGRAM,** William B., Jr. (Mayor, Memphis, 1963–1967)

801A.1 My Memphis Baby. w.m. Harry Godwin and Narvin Kimball. Copyright 1966 by Rayster Music Pub. Co., 1650 Broadway, New York, NY. Bk/be drawing of a steam boat, cotton ball. "Special Dedication Edition, Beale Street Memphis on the Mississippi." "All proceeds from the sale of this edition will be donated to the Beale Street Elks Christmas Fund." 4pp. Page 2: Letter from Mayor William Ingram designating the song as "the official song for the Beale Street Designation Program." Page 4: Blank.

KNOTT, James Proctor (State House, Missouri, 1857; State Attorney General, Missouri, 1859–1860) [See: Kentucky]

• **AmPM-802   LEUPOLD,** Julius (Founder, Hermann, 1836; Board of Trustees, Hermann, 1839; Clerk, Hermann, 1841)

802.1 Miss Lucy Long. m. J.C. Viereck, Op. 73. Published by A. Foit, 196 Chesnut Street, Philadelphia, PA. 1842. B/w non-pictorial designs. "With Introduction and Variations Composed for the Piano Forte and Dedicated to Julius Leupold, Esqr., Founder of the German Settlement in Hermann, Mo. By J.C. Viereck, Member of said Settlement." 8pp. Page 8: Blank.

- AmPM-803   MELEN, Victor (Mayor, St. Louis, 1925–1933)

803.1 Hello Lindy. w.m. Larry Conley and Dave Silverman. Published by Larry Conley, Inc., Music Published, Shubert Rialto Theatre Blvd., St. Louis, MO. 1927. B/w photo of Charles A. Lindbergh, *Sprit Of St. Louis* airplane. "The Official Spirit of St. Louis Welcome Song." "Dedicated to Capt. Chas. A. Lindbergh America's flying hero, as a tribute to his successful Trans-Atlantic non-stop flight New York to Paris, May 20–21, 1927." "It is a pleasure to endorse this meritorious Song ... Sincerely, Victor J. Melen, Mayor, City of St. Louis" [facsimile handwriting]. 6pp. Page2: Blank. Page 3: At top of music — "A Tribute to Captain Charles A. Lindbergh." Page 6: Advertising.

- AmPM-804   MOREHOUSE, Albert P. (Governor, 1887–1889)

804.1 Ewing Brooks. w. No composer indicated. m. "An adaptation of *Charles Guiteau*." "From *Ozark Folksongs* by Randolph. Collected from Myrtle Devore, Arkansas, 1930." Lyrics and sound file published online at <http://www.mudcat.org/kids/@displaysong.cfm?SongID=1873>. 1996.

- AmPM-805   NOBLE, John Willock (U.S. District Attorney, 1867–1870; U.S. Secretary of the Interior, 1889–1893)

805.1 The Bradbury Schottische. m. Dayton Vreeland. Published by F.G. Smith, 109 & 111 Broadway, Paterson, NJ. 1897. B/w geometric designs. "Dedicated to H.N. Lakeham." 4pp. Page 4: Advertising for Bradbury pianos with photo of "Famous Patrons of Bradbury Pianos" including: "U.S. Grant, J.A. Garfield, C.A. Arthur, Benj. Harrison, R.B. Hayes, Grover Cleveland, Stanley Mathews, J.M Rusk, Benj. Tracy, Levi Morton, Thos. B. Reed, J.W. Noble, William Windom, John G. Carlisle, C.C. McCabe, A.H. Colquitt [and] Walter Q. Gresham." [Crew/MISC-142].

- AmPM-806   O'NEIL, Paul H. (Deputy Director of Office of Management and Budget, 1974–1977; U.S. Secretary of the Treasury, 2001–2003).

806.1 Ashcroft The New Darth Vader. w. William Tong. m. "*Rudolph The Red Nosed Reindeer*, based on the performance by Gene Autry." "Dedicated to Attorney General John Ashcroft." Published online at <http://amiright.com/parody/misc/geneautry4.shml>. [2003].

- AmPM-807   PARNELL, Jeff (Candidate for U.S. House, 2004)

807.1 Concealed. w.m. Jeff Parnell "@ www.jeffparnell.com." On CD: *Great Words*. Published by Junglecat Productions/Jeff Parnell, P.O. Box 388, Rogersville, MO. 65742. 2003.

807.2 We Can't Keep Holden On. w.m. Jeff Parnell "@ www.jeffparnell.com." On CD: *Great Words*. Published by Junglecat Productions/Jeff Parnell, P.O. Box 388, Rogersville, MO. 65742. 2003.

- AmPM-808   PHELPS, John S. (Governor, 1877–1881)

808.1 Gov. J.S. Phelps Grand March. m. S.T. Bravoula. Published by Balmer & Weber, Publishers, St. Louis, MO. 1877. B/w litho by G. Hamilton & Co. "From photo by Charles W. Scholler" of James Phelps, geometric designs. "Respectfully dedicated to Gov. J.S. Phelps, Mo." 6pp. Pages 2 and 6: Blank.

- AmPM-809   POLK, Trusten (Governor, 1857; U.S. Senate, 1857–1862)

809.1 Governor Polk's March. m. W.W. Rossington. Published by Balmer & Weber, 56 Fourth Street, St. Louis, MO. 1856. B/w tinted litho by Sarony, Major & Knapp of Trusten Polk. "Composed and respectfully inscribed to Trusten Polk, Esq., Governor of Missouri." 8pp. [?]. Page 2: Blank.

- AmPM-810   PRICE, Sterling (State House, 1840–1844; U.S. House, 1845–1846; Governor, 1853–1857; State Bank Commissioner, 1857–1861; Delegate, Missouri Confederate State Convention, 1861)

810.1 Agricultural Song. w.m. No composer or tune indicated. "Written expressly for the Barn Meeting, Jamaica Plains, Roxbury, May, 1840." In: *Log Cabin Minstrel (Or Tippecanoe Songster)*, page 11. c. "A Member of the Roxbury Whig Association." Published at the *Patriot And Democrat* Office, Roxbury, [MA]. 1840. [4½" × 6¾"]. [V-1:Y/bk] [V-2: Bl/bk] litho of William Henry Harrison, geometric design border. "Old Tip's the boy to swing the flail. Hurrah! Hurrah! Hurrah!" 64pp. Page 3: Title page — "Containing a Selection of Songs Original and Selected Many of them Written Expressly for this Work, Compiled, Published and Arranged by a member of the Roxbury Democratic Whig Association and Respectfully Dedicated to the Log Cabin Boys of the U.S." [M-013]. [Crew/WHH-71].

810.2 The Aristocracy Of Democracy. w. "An Old Democrat, 1798." m. "Tune — *John Anderson, My Jo*." "The Following song was written by an Old Democrat of 1798, an original Jackson man, but not an admirer of such modern or patent democracy as is professed by 'Nor-a-single-drop-of-democratic-blood' Buchanan, or 'As-long-as-the-federal-flag-waved-in-New-Jersey-I-was-proud-to-rally-under-it' Garret D. Wall." In: *The Clay Minstrel Or National Songster*, page 224. c. John Stockton Littell. Published by Greeley & M'Elrath, Tribune Building, New York, NY. 1844. [3⅛" × 4⅞"]. Non-pictorial. 396pp. [Crew/HC-18].

810.3 Good Advice! w. W.C. m. No tune indicated. No publisher indicated. [ca. 1861–1862]. B/w geometric design border. 2pp. Page 2: Blank. [AMC].

810.4 Harrison Song. w. Hon. John Holmes, "of Maine." m. "Air — *Yankee Doodle*." "Read by [Holmes] from the balcony of the State House, Augusta, on the 24th of June, 1840." In: *Log Cabin Minstrel (Or Tippecanoe Songster)*, page 13. c. "A Member of the Roxbury Whig Association." Published at the *Patriot And Democrat* Office, Roxbury, [MA]. 1840. [4½" × 6¾"]. [V-1:Y/bk] [V-2: Bl/bk] litho of William Henry Harrison, geometric design border. "Old Tip's the boy to swing the flail. Hurrah! Hurrah! Hurrah!" 64pp. Page 3: Title page — "Containing a Selection of Songs Original and Selected Many of them Written Expressly for this Work, Compiled, Published and Arranged by a member of the Roxbury Democratic Whig Association and Respectfully Dedicated to the Log Cabin Boys of the U.S." [M-013]. [Crew/WHH-71].

810.5 Harrison Song. w. No composer indicated. m. "Tune—*Bruce's Address.*" In: *Log Cabin Minstrel (Or Tippecanoe Songster)*, page 27. c. "A Member of the Roxbury Whig Association." Published at the *Patriot And Democrat* Office, Roxbury, [MA]. 1840. [4½" × 6¾"]. [V-1:Y/bk] [V-2: Bl/bk] litho of William Henry Harrison, geometric design border. "Old Tip's the boy to swing the flail. Hurrah! Hurrah! Hurrah!" 64pp. Page 3: Title page—"Containing a Selection of Songs Original and Selected Many of them Written Expressly for this Work, Compiled, Published and Arranged by a member of the Roxbury Democratic Whig Association and Respectfully Dedicated to the Log Cabin Boys of the U.S." [M-013]. [Crew/WHH-71].

810.6 The Log Cabin Song. w. No composer indicated. m. "Tune—*Yankee Doodle.*" "Before the adjournment of the Convention at Augusta, the Hon. John Holmes of Thomaston, offered and read the following song." In: *Tippecanoe Song-Book (A Collection Of Log Cabin And Patriotic Melodies)*, page 71. Published by Marshall, Williams & Butler, Philadelphia, PA. 1840. White on black litho of log cabin, plow, flags, eagle. 180pp. [M-024]. [Crew/WHH-61].

810.7 The New Skedaddle Song. w. No composer indicated. m. No tune indicated. In: *Beadle's Dime Song Book.* Published by Beadle and Company, No. 141 William Street, New York, NY. 1864. [3¾" × 5¾"]. [VBL, p. 368].

810.8 O! Who Does Not See In This Heart-Cheering Ray. w. No composer indicated. m. "Tune—*Star Spangled Banner.*" In: *Tippecanoe Song-Book (A Collection Of Log Cabin And Patriotic Melodies)*, page 37. Published by Marshall, Williams & Butler, Philadelphia, PA. 1840. White on black litho of log cabin, plow, flags, eagle. 180pp. [M-024]. [Crew/WHH-61].

810.9 Old Tip's The Boy. w. No composer indicated. m. "Air—*The Hurrah Song.*" In: *A Miniature Of Martin Van Buren (With A Selection Of The Best And Most Popular Tippecanoe Songs)*, page 43. 1840. [3½" × 6½"]. Br/bk] [V-2: Gn/bk] [V-3: Y/bk] litho of man, chain around neck. Van Buren quote. "Amos Kendall's Veracity—Tom Benton's Honesty—Francis Blair's Beauty." "What is wanting cant be numbered [sic]." 58pp. [M-016]. [Crew/WHH-88].

810.10 Van Buren's Lament. w. No composer indicated. m. "Tune—*O No, I'll Never Mention Her.*" In: *Tippecanoe Song-Book (A Collection Of Log Cabin And Patriotic Melodies)*, page 53. Published by Marshall, Williams & Butler, Philadelphia, PA. 1840. White on black litho of log cabin, plow, flags, eagle. 180pp. [M-024]. [Crew/WHH-61].

810.11 The Whig Rally. w. No composer indicated. m. "Tune—*Bruce's Address.*" In: *Tippecanoe Club Songster*, page 33. Published by [V-1: Turner & Fisher, No. 15 North Sixth Street, Philadelphia, PA] [V-2: H.A. Turner, Baltimore, MD]. 1841. [3" × 4⅞"]. Hand Colored engraving of William Henry Harrison, log cabin. 68pp. [M-021, 022]. [Crew/WHH-18].

810.12 Ye Who Fought With Washington. w. No composer indicated. m. "Tune—*Bruce's Address.*" In: *Tippecanoe Song-Book (A Collection Of Log Cabin And Patriotic Melodies)*, page 79. Published by Marshall, Williams & Butler, Philadelphia, PA. 1840. White on black litho of log cabin, plow, flags, eagle. 180pp. [M-024]. [Crew/WHH-61].

• **AmPM-811 REED**, James Byron (Mayor, Kansas City, 1900–1904; U.S. Senate, 1911–1929) [ALSO SEE: DOC/PSM-MISC]

811.1 Welcome Song To Huey Long. (Our U.S. Senator). w.m. Tom McNelly. a. Joseph Garrow. Published by Tom McNelly, Music Publishers, New Orleans, LA. 1931. Photo of Huey Long. Drawings of the "Louisiana State Capitol" building and the "U.S. Capitol" building, geometric designs. 8pp. Page 8: Blank.

RUFFIN, Thomas (Circuit Attorney, Missouri, 1844–1848) [See: North Carolina]

• **AmPM-812 SCHURZ**, Carl [Karl] (U.S. Senate, 1869–1875; U.S. Secretary of the Interior, 1877–1881)

812.1 Campaign Song. w. No composer indicated. m. "Air—*Never Mind The Weather So The Wind Don't Blow.*" In: *National Republican Grant And Wilson Campaign Song-Book*, page 7. Published by The Union Republican Congressional Committee, Washington, DC. 1872. [3¹³⁄₁₆" × 8⁵⁄₁₆"]. Be/bk litho of Ulysses S. Grant. "We'll Sing a Song for U.S. Grant." 100pp. [M-182]. [Crew/USG-110].

812.2 Campaign Version Of 'John Brown.' w. No composer indicated. m. Air—*John Brown.* In: *National Republican Grant And Wilson Campaign Song-Book*, page 6. Published by The Union Republican Congressional Committee, Washington, DC. 1872. [3¹³⁄₁₆" × 8⁵⁄₁₆"]. Be/bk litho of Ulysses S. Grant. "We'll Sing a Song for U.S. Grant." 100pp. [M-182]. [Crew/USG-110].

812.3 Chap-Chap-Paw-Quah. m. No composer indicated. m. "Air—*Little Brown Jug.*" From the "*Louisville Commercial.*" In: *National Republican Grant And Wilson Campaign Song-Book*, page 64. Published by The Union Republican Congressional Committee, Washington, DC. 1872. [3¹³⁄₁₆" × 8⁵⁄₁₆"]. Be/bk litho of Ulysses S. Grant. "We'll Sing a Song for U.S. Grant." 100pp. [M-182]. [Crew/USG-110].

812.4 The Child's Inquiry. w. No composer indicated. m. "Air—*Auld Lang Syne.*" In: *National Republican Grant And Wilson Campaign Song-Book*, page 85. Published by The Union Republican Congressional Committee, Washington, DC. 1872. [3¹³⁄₁₆" × 8⁵⁄₁₆"]. Be/bk litho of Ulysses S. Grant. "We'll Sing a Song for U.S. Grant." 100pp. [M-182]. [Crew/USG-110].

812.5 Fatherland, America. w. No composer indicated. m. "Air—*Maryland, My Maryland.*" In: *Tilden And Hendricks' Reform Songs (For The Centennial Campaign Of 1876)*, page 30. Published by The National Democratic Committee, Box 3637, New York, NY. 1876. [3⅞" × 5¹⁵⁄₁₆"]. Gn/bk litho of Samuel J. Tilden and Thomas A. Hendricks, geometric design border. 40pp. [M-203]. [Crew/SJT-21].

812.6 Fling Out The Banner. m. No composer indicated. m. "Air—*Uncle Sam's Farm.*" In: *National Republican Grant And Wilson Campaign Song-Book*, page 69. Published by The Union Republican Congressional Committee, Washington, DC. 1872. [3¹³⁄₁₆" × 8⁵⁄₁₆"]. Be/bk litho of Ulysses S. Grant. "We'll Sing a

Song for U.S. Grant." 100pp. [M-182]. [Crew/USG-110].

812.7 From Cincinnati To The White House. w.m. No composer or tune indicated. In: *The Sun's Greeley Campaign Songster*, page 61. c. Amos J. Cumming. Published from *The Sun* Office, New York, NY. 1872. [4⅛" × 6½"]. Be/bk litho of Horace Greeley, wreath. "He shines for all." 64pp. [Crew/HG-5].

812.8 The Great Coming Contest (Song and Chorus for the Campaign of 1868). w. P.M. Sutton. m. Alfred von Rochow "(Author of *I Wonder If She Cares For Me*)." Published by Balmer & Weber, No. 206 North Fifth Street, Street, Louis, MO. 1868. B/w litho by Scharr and Brother of flags, flowers. "To Gen. Carl Schurz." 8pp. Pages 2 and 8: Blank. [Crew/USG-85].

812.9 The Greeley Pill. w. No composer indicated. m. "Air—*The Mistletoe Bough*." "Mixed at Cincinnati and taken to Baltimore." "Sung by the Union Glee Club at a Grant Republican rally at Cooper Institute." Published in the *New York Times*, September 26, 1872. [VBL, p. 456].

812.10 The Hat Of Chappaqua. w.m. No composer or tune indicated. In: *The Sun's Greeley Campaign Songster*, page 28. c. Amos J. Cumming. Published from *The Sun* Office, New York, NY. 1872. [4⅛" × 6½"]. Be/bk litho of Horace Greeley, wreath. "He shines for all." 64pp. [Crew/HG-5].

812.11 H.G.'s Inquiry. w. No composer indicated. m. "Air—*Tell Me, Ye Winged Winds*." In: *National Republican Grant And Wilson Campaign Song-Book*, page 81. Published by The Union Republican Congressional Committee, Washington, DC. 1872. [$3\frac{13}{16}$" × $8\frac{3}{16}$"]. Be/bk litho of Ulysses S. Grant. "We'll Sing a Song for U.S. Grant." 100pp. [M-182]. [Crew/USG-110].

812.12 Inflation Galop! m. W. Stuckenholz. Published by Wm. A. Pond & Company, No. 547 Broadway, New York, NY. 1874. B/w litho [horizontal format] from a cartoon by W.H. Sheldon of Ulysses S. Grant, Ben Butler, Oliver P. Morton, Carl Schurz, and Matthew Hale Carpenter blowing up large balloon labeled "Inflation," "$400,000,000" and "$44,000,000 Legalized." 6pp. [Crew/USG-15]. [VBL, p. 458].

812.13 The Liberal's Victory (March Quickstep). m. Justin Juch. Published by F.P. Kinney, New York, NY. 1872. Non-pictorial. "To Senator Karl Schurz."

812.14 [A Little Bird Sat On A Linden Tree] (Campaign Song). w.m. No composer or tune indicated. In: *National Republican Grant And Wilson Campaign Song-Book*, page 10. Published by The Union Republican Congressional Committee, Washington, DC. 1872. [$3\frac{13}{16}$" × $8\frac{3}{16}$"]. Be/bk litho of Ulysses S. Grant. "We'll Sing a Song for U.S. Grant." 100pp. [M-182]. [Crew/USG-110].

812.15 O! What Makes Grant So Fearfully Frown? (Song and Chorus). w.m. The Saint Paul Greeley Club. Published by Weide & Ross, St. Paul, MN. [1872]. B/w engraving of Horace Greeley, geometric design border. "Composed and Sung by the St. Paul Greeley Club and Respectfully Dedicated by them to Horace Greeley." 4pp. Page 4: Advertising. [Crew/HG-3].

812.16 Old Men's Grant Meeting. w. No composer indicated. m. "Air—*Bennie Havens, O!*" In: *National Republican Grant And Wilson Campaign Song-Book*, page 39. From the *New York Standard*. Published by The Union Republican Congressional Committee, Washington, DC. 1872. [$3\frac{13}{16}$" × $8\frac{3}{16}$"]. Be/bk litho of Ulysses S. Grant. "We'll Sing a Song for U.S. Grant." 100pp. [M-182]. [Crew/USG-110].

812.17 Rally Round The Standard. w. N.G. Sawyer. m. No tune indicated. In: *Grant And Wilson Campaign Songster*, page 26. Published by Frank Eastman, Book and Job Printer, No. 509 Clay Street, San Francisco, CA. [4¼" × 5⅝"]. 1872. Bk/bl geometric design border. 40pp. [Crew/USG-69].

812.18 Schurz, Schirtz, Or Schootz. w.m. No composer or tune indicated. In: *The World's Peace Jubilee And Back Bay Bawl*, page 23. Published by New England News Company, No. 41 Court Street, Boston, MA. 1872. 36pp. [4¼" × 6½"]. Y/bl caricature of Horace Greeley holding sheet music to the song *I Want To Be President*, Ulysses S. Grant, dog labeled—"Democracy." "I want to be President and in the White House stand, The nation on my shoulders her fortunes in my hand."

812.19 So Come Along And Swell Out The Tune. w. No composer indicated. m. "Air—*So Come Along*." In: *National Republican Grant And Wilson Campaign Song-Book*, page 18. Published by The Union Republican Congressional Committee, Washington, DC. 1872. [$3\frac{13}{16}$" × $8\frac{3}{16}$"]. Be/bk litho of Ulysses S. Grant. "We'll Sing a Song for U.S. Grant." 100pp. [M-182]. [Crew/USG-110].

812.20 The Stately Statesman. w. No composer indicated. m. "Air—*The Minstrel Boy*." In: *National Republican Grant And Wilson Campaign Song-Book*, page 2. Published by The Union Republican Congressional Committee, Washington, DC. 1872. [$3\frac{13}{16}$" × $8\frac{3}{16}$"]. Be/bk litho of Ulysses S. Grant. "We'll Sing a Song for U.S. Grant." 100pp. [M-182]. [Crew/USG-110].

812.21 Viva La Companie. w. No composer or tune indicated. In: *Grant And Wilson Campaign Songster*, page 16. Published by Frank Eastman, Book and Job Printer, No. 509 Clay Street, San Francisco, CA. [4¼" × 5⅝"]. 1872. Bk/bl geometric design border. 40pp. [Crew/USG-69].

812.22 Wilson And Grant. w. No composer or tune indicated. In: *National Republican Grant And Wilson Campaign Song-Book*, page 26. Published by The Union Republican Congressional Committee, Washington, DC. 1872. [$3\frac{13}{16}$" × $8\frac{3}{16}$"]. Be/bk litho of Ulysses S. Grant. "We'll Sing a Song for U.S. Grant." 100pp. [M-182]. [Crew/USG-110].

812.23 Wilson And Grant. w. Sam Booth. m. "Tune—*Bonnie Dundee*." In: *Grant And Wilson Campaign Songster*, page 2. Published by Frank Eastman, Book and Job Printer, No. 509 Clay Street, San Francisco, CA. [4¼" × 5⅝"]. 1872. Bk/bl geometric design border. 40pp. [Crew/USG-69].

812.24 Wilson And Grant. w. N.G. Sawyer. m. "Tune—*Whip-Poor-Will's Call*." In: *Grant And Wilson Campaign Songster*, page 15. Published by Frank Eastman, Book and Job Printer, No. 509 Clay Street, San Francisco, CA. [4¼" × 5⅝"]. 1872. Bk/bl geometric design border. 40pp. [Crew/USG-69].

812.25 Witches' Scene From MacGreeley (Which is Seen to be a Fact). w.m. No composer or tune indicated. From the "*New York Standard*." In: *National Republican Grant And Wilson Campaign Song-Book*, page 34. From the *New York Standard*. Published by The Union Republican Congressional Committee, Washington, DC. 1872. [3¹³⁄₁₆" × 8⅜"]. Be/bk litho of Ulysses S. Grant. "We'll Sing a Song for U.S. Grant." 100pp. [M-182]. [Crew/USG-110].

STRINGFELLOW, Benjamin F. (State House, Missouri, 1840s; State Attorney General, Missouri, 1845–1849) [See: Kansas]

- **AmPM-813 TALTY**, John A. (Judge, Court of Criminal Correction, 1890–1891; Circuit Judge, 1896–1899?)

813.1 Republican National Convention March. m. Al G. Mark. Published by Mark Bros. Music Publishing Company, No. 3940 Page Avenue, St. Louis, MO. 1896. R/w/b drawings of William McKinley, Levi P. Morton, Thomas Reed, Wm. Allison and "?" [question mark] on flag background, shields. "Dedicated to the City of St. Louis, June 1896." 8pp. Page 2: B/w photos of "Prominent Republicans and Gentlemen who were instrumental in securing the Republican National Convention for St. Louis — Sam M. Kennard, President Business Men's League; Chas. H. Sampson, Chairman Convention Committee; Hon. Chauncey Ives Filley, Chairman Reception Committee; Frank Gaienne, Gen'l. Mgr., St. Louis Exposition; L.S. W. Wall; Chas. F. Wenneker." Page 7: B/w photos of "Merchant's League Club — Wm. H. Hobbs, Vice-President; Louis F. Zipp, Treasurer; Hon. J.A. Talty, President; Theo. D. Kalbfell, Chair., Republican Central Committee; Morris Langsdorf, Sec." Page 8: Blank. [Crew/WM-1].

- **AmPM-814 TAYLOR**, Maxwell Davenport (Ambassador to South Vietnam, 1964–1965; he was Special Consultant to the President and Chairman of the Foreign Intelligence Advisory Board, 1965–1969)

814.1 Yellow Rose Of Saigon. w. Tom Bowen. m. *Yellow Rose Of Texas*. "*From The Longest Year* by Bowen and Fish." Lyrics and sound file published online at <http://www.mudcat.org/kids/@displaysong.cfm?SongID= 7996>. [199-].

- **AmPM-815 THOMAS**, Clarence (Assistant U.S. Attorney General, 1974–1977; Senate Legislative Assistant, 1979–1981; Assistant U.S. Secretary of Education, 1981–1982; Chairman, U.S. Equal Employment Opportunity Commission, 1982–1990; U.S. Court of Appeals, 1990–1991; U.S. Supreme Court, 1991–Present)

815.1 Babs Boxer. w. "Laz." m. *The Boxer* by Simon & Garfunkel. Published by FreeRepublic.com at <http://www.freerepublic.com/forum/a373bfb5b2bf1.htm>. [199-].

815.2 The Boxer (Barbara, lie, lie, lie). w. "Doug from Upland." m. *The Boxer* by Simon & Garfunkel. Published by FreeRepublic.com at <http://www.freerepublic.com/forum/a36365032755e.htm>. 1998.

815.3 Condoleeza Rice. w. Bruno the Elder. m. "*Wouldn't It Be Nice*, originally by The Beach Boys." "This one is about African American Republicans or OREOS are they are sometimes known as." Published online at <http://www.amiright.com/parody/misc/thebeachboys5.shtml>. [ca. 2001].

815.4 Diff'rent Votes. w. Attmay. m. "Sung to the tune of the theme from *Diff'rent Strokes*." Published online at <http://www.geocities.com/wmktong/bootnewt/diffvotes.htm>. [ca. 2000].

815.5 I Got No Thrill (From Anita Hill). w. No composer indicated. m. "Parody of *Blueberry Hill* by Fats Domino." Lyrics published by *The Bob Rivers Show* with Bob, Spike & Joe and Twisted Tunes online at <http://www.twistedradio.com/player/lyrics.asp?songID=662>. [199-].

815.6 To Hell With Vote Machines. w. William Tong. m. Tune — "*Yellow Submarine*, originally by The Beatles." Published online at <http://amiright.com/parody/misc/thebeatles7.shml>. [ca. 2000].

- **AmPM-816 THOMPSON**, Meriwether "Jeff" (City Engineer, St. Joseph, ca. 1847; Mayor, St. Joseph, ca. 1860)

816.1 Dis-Union Dixie Land. w. No composer indicated. m. Air — *Dixie*. Published by J.W. DuBree, Printer, No. 1169 South Eleventh Street, Philadelphia, PA. [1860–1861]. Non-pictorial. "J.W. DuBree, Song Publisher, Card and Job Printer, No. 1169 South Eleventh Street, Philadelphia." "Union." "Badges, Letter and Note Paper, Envelopes, Shields, Stars, Flags, all sizes, Cockades, and Rosettes. Songs of all kinds for the Union, Wholesale & Retail." 2pp. Page 2: Blank. [AMC].

816.2 The New Red, White & Blue. w. Genl. M. Jeff Thompson. m. Theod. Von La Hache. Published by A.E. Blackmar & Bro., New Orleans, LA. And Moody & Kuner, Vicksburg, MS. [ca. 1865]. "Blackmar & Bro's Selection of favorite polkas, schottisches, waltzes, dances, &c." 4pp. Page 4: Blank.

- **AmPM-816x TRUMAN**, Harry S (Judge, Jackson County, 1922–1924 & 1926–1934; U.S. Senate, 1935–1945; Vice President, 1945; President, 1945–1953) [SEE: DOC/PSM-HST]

- **AmPM-817 WELLS**, Rolla (Mayor, St. Louis, 1902)

817.1 New St. Louis (Or the Louisiana Purchase Exposition March Two-Step). m. Bert Morgan "(Author of *My Sweetheart Went Down With The Maine* and other popular compositions)." Published by M.P. Koch Co., St. Louis, MO. 1902. B/w photos of "David R. Francis, President Louisiana Purchase Exposition" and "Hon. Rolla Wells, Mayor of St. Louis." R/w/b drawing of an allegorical symbol of three women, geometric designs. "A good thing, Push it along!" "Dedicated to the New St. Louis and the promoters and patrons of the Louisiana Purchase Exposition to be held at St. Louis, U.S.A., 1904." 6pp. Page 6: Blank. [LL/JH].

- **AmPM-818 ZIEGENHEIM**, Henry (Mayor, St. Louis, 1897–1901)

818.1 Uncle Henry's March. m. Louis Retter. Published by Louis Retter Music Co., St. Louis, MO. [1898]. Bl/w photo of Henry Ziegenheim. R/w/b flag, drawings of St. Louis building. "Dedicated to Hon. Henry Zeihenheim, Mayor, St. Louis." Published for "Piano," Band," and "Orchestra."

- **AmPM-819 MISCELLANEOUS MUSIC**

819.1 Hush A Bye, Ma Baby (The Missouri Waltz). Published by Forster, Chicago, IL. 1943. Gd/bl/w drawing of the state seal, outline of the state, stars. "Souvenir Edition." "The Official State Song of Missouri." Back cover — "On June 1949, the 65th General Assembly of legend and history — steeped Missouri adopted the *Missouri Waltz* as the state's official song ... [it] has taken it's officially honored place beside the state's Gold Seal, Tricolor, Bluebird and Hawthorne."

MONTANA

- **AmPM-820 CARTER**, Thomas Henry (U.S. House, 1889–1891; U.S. Senate, 1895–1901 & 1905–1911)
820.1 Harrison Will Hold The Job. w. E.J. Seymour. m. "Air — *When McGinnis Gets A Job.*" In: *Harrison And Reid Campaign Song Book*, page 13. w. E.J. Seymour. m. Popular Airs. [1892]. [3⅞" × 5⅛"]. Bl/gn non-pictorial, stars, geometric designs. 36pp. Pages 2 and 35: Blank. Page 36: Advertising for this songbook. [M-316]. [Crew/BFH-35].
820.2 University Club Banquet [Song Book]. Published by The University Club, Washington, DC. 1911. Bk/br/w drawing of buildings, grapes, glasses, geometric designs. 30pp. Page 3: "The Seventh Annual Banquet, the New Willard Hotel, Monday, February 27, 1911, 7:00 p.m." Page 5: Menu. Pages 6 to 10: Drawings of Senator Thomas Carter, William H. Taft, Ambassador Bryce, Senator Depew and Hon. Morton Littleton.

- **AmPM-821 FORD**, Samuel Clarence (State Attorney General, 1917–1921; State Supreme Court, 1929–1933; Governor, 1941–1949)
821.1 Montana. w. Chas. C. Cohan. m. Joseph E. Howard. Published for Montana Children's Home & Hospital, Inc., and Shodair Crippled Children's Hospital, 840 Helena Avenue, Helena, MT. 1910. [Edition ca. 194-]. Bl/w drawing of "Shodair Hospital, mountains. "Official State Song of Montana." "13th Edition." 4pp. Page 2: At top of music — Official State Song adopted by Gov. Edwin L. Norris, 1910." Page 3: At top of music — "Adopted as the official song of the State of Montana by the 29th Legislative Assembly of Montana and approved by Governor Sam C. Ford, February 20, 1945."

- **AmPM-822 GALEN**, Albert J. (State Attorney General, 1910)
822.1 Montana. w. Chas. C. Cohan "(Author of *The Runaway Princess*)." m. Joseph E. Howard "(*The Time, Place And Girl, The Land Of Nod, A Prince Of Tonight, The Goddess Of Liberty, Miss Nobody from Starland, I Wonder Who's Kissing Her Now*)." Published for Montana Children's Home Society, Helena, MT. 1910. Bl/w drawing of State Seal, covered wagon, geometric designs. "Official Approved as the State Song of Montana by Governor Edwin L. Norris, Secretary of State A.N. Yoder, Attorney General Albert J. Galen; Approved and Adopted by Montana University Athletes; Approved for State Militia by Adjutant General Phil Greenan." "Dedicated to Mrs. E. Creighton Largey." "Song featured in *Goddess Of Liberty*." 4pp. Page 2: At top of music — Official State Song adopted by Gov. Edwin L. Norris, 1910." Page 3: At top of music — "Official State Song Adopted by Gov. Edwin L. Norris."

- **AmPM-823 GREENAN**, Phil (State Adjutant General, 1910)
823.1 Montana. w. Chas. C. Cohan "(Author of *The Runaway Princess*)." m. Joseph E. Howard "(*The Time, Place And Girl, The Land Of Nod, A Prince Of Tonight, The Goddess Of Liberty, Miss Nobody From Starland, I Wonder Who's Kissing Her Now*)." Published for Montana Children's Home Society, Helena, MT. 1910. Bl/w drawing of State Seal, covered wagon, geometric designs. "Official Approved as the State Song of Montana by Governor Edwin L. Norris, Secretary of State A.N. Yoder, Attorney General Albert J. Galen; Approved and Adopted by Montana University Athletes; Approved for State Militia by Adjutant General Phil Greenan." "Dedicated to Mrs. E. Creighton Largey." "Song featured in *Goddess Of Liberty*." 4pp. Page 2: At top of music — Official State Song adopted by Gov. Edwin L. Norris, 1910." Page 3: At top of music — "Official State Song Adopted by Gov. Edwin L. Norris."

- **AmPM-824 GUERIN**, John (Chief of Police, Great Falls, 1898)
824.1 When Teddy Comes Marching Home. w.m. Joe Hayden. Published by Will Rossiter, No. 56 5th Avenue, Chicago, IL. 1898. Drawing of Theodore Roosevelt and Rough Riders, cheering crowd, border of stars. "Dedicated to John Guerin (My old partner), Chief of Police, Great Falls, Mont." [Crew/TR-166].

- **AmPM-825 NORRIS**, Edwin L. (Governor, 1908–1913)
825.1 Montana. w. Chas. C. Cohan. m. Joseph E. Howard. Published for Montana Children's Home & Hospital, Inc., and Shodair Crippled Children's Hospital, 840 Helena Avenue, Helena, MT. 1910 [Edition ca. 194-]. Bl/w drawing of "Shodair Hospital, mountains. "Official State Song of Montana." "13th Edition." 4pp. Page 2: At top of music — Official State Song adopted by Gov. Edwin L. Norris, 1910." Page 3: At top of music — "Adopted as the official song of the State of Montana by the 29th Legislative Assembly of Montana and approved by Governor Sam C. Ford, February 20, 1945."
825.2 Montana. w. Chas. C. Cohan "(Author of *The Runaway Princess*)." m. Joseph E. Howard "(*The Time, Place And Girl, The Land Of Nod, A Prince Of Tonight, The Goddess Of Liberty, Miss Nobody From Starland, I Wonder Who's Kissing Her Now*)." Published for Montana Children's Home Society, Helena, MT. 1910. Bl/w drawing of State Seal, covered wagon, geometric designs. "Official Approved as the State Song of Montana by Governor Edwin L. Norris, Secretary of State A.N. Yoder, Attorney General Albert J. Galen; Approved and Adopted by Montana University Athletes; Approved for State Militia by Adjutant General Phil Greenan." "Dedicated to Mrs. E. Creighton Largey." "Song featured in *Goddess Of Liberty*." 4pp. Page 2: At top of music — Official State Song adopted by Gov. Edwin L. Norris, 1910." Page 3: At top of music — "Official State Song Adopted by Gov. Edwin L. Norris."

- **AmPM-826 MANSFIELD**, Michael Joseph (U.S. House, 1943–1953; U.S. Senate, 1953–1977)
826.1 Elegy {826.1-1}. w. Sen. Mike Mansfield. On page 4 of: ***America America*** {826.1-2}. w.m. Frank

Murman. Published by Airy Music Company, R.D. 4, Box 62, Mountain Top, PA. 18707. 1964. [6⅛" × 9⅜"]. Bl/w photo of "John Fitzgerald Kennedy." "In Memoriam." "As recorded by Frank Murman on Mur-E-Cord Records." 4pp. Page 4: *Elegy* by Sen. Mike Mansfield. Quote from John F. Kennedy's Inaugural speech.

• **AmPM-827 WALSH**, Thomas James (U.S. Senate, 1913-1933)
827.1 Welcome Song To Huey Long. (Our U.S. Senator). w.m. Tom McNelly. a. Joseph Garrow. Published by Tom McNelly, Music Publishers, New Orleans, LA. 1931. Photo of Huey Long. Drawings of the "Louisiana State Capitol" building and the "U.S. Capitol" building, geometric designs. 8pp. Page 8: Blank.
827.2 Montana. w. Chas. C. Cohan "(Author of *The Runaway Princess*)." m. Joseph E. Howard "(*The Time, Place And Girl, The Land Of Nod, A Prince Of Tonight, The Goddess Of Liberty, Miss Nobody From Starland, I Wonder Who's Kissing Her Now*)." Published for Montana Children's Home Society, Helena, MT. 1910. Bl/w drawing of State Seal, covered wagon, geometric designs. "Official Approved as the State Song of Montana by Governor Edwin L. Norris, Secretary of State A.N. Yoder, Attorney General Albert J. Galen; Approved and Adopted by Montana University Athletes; Approved for State Militia by Adjutant General Phil Greenan." "Dedicated to Mrs. E. Creighton Largey." "Song featured in *Goddess Of Liberty*." 4pp. Page 2: At top of music — Official State Song adopted by Gov. Edwin L. Norris, 1910." Page 3: At top of music — "Official State Song Adopted by Gov. Edwin L. Norris."

• **AmPM-828 WHEELER**, Burton Kendall (State House, 1910-1912; U.S. District Attorney for Montana, 1913-1918; U.S. Senate, 1923-1947; Candidate for Vice President, 1924) [ALSO SEE: DOC-/PSN-RML]
828.1 Oh Uncle Sam, Dear Uncle Sam. w. No composer indicated. m. "Tune — *Evangeline*." In: *Lincoln — La Follette Songster*, page 10. Published by Warren H. Eddy, No. 205 North Flower Street, Los Angeles, CA. [4" × 7"]. [1924]. Bl/bk drawing of Abraham Lincoln. Bl/bk photo of Robert M. La Follette. 20pp. Page 20: Bl/bk photo of "Burton K. Wheeler." [Crew/RML-4].
828.2 Welcome Song To Huey Long. (Our U.S. Senator). w.m. Tom McNelly. a. Joseph Garrow. Published by Tom McNelly, Music Publishers, New Orleans, LA. 1931. Photo of Huey Long. Drawings of the "Louisiana State Capitol" building and the "U.S. Capitol" building, geometric designs. 8pp. Page 8: Blank.

• **AmPM-829 YODER**, A.N. (Montana Secretary of State, 1910)
829.1 Montana. w. Chas. C. Cohan "(Author of *The Runaway Princess*)." m. Joseph E. Howard "(*The Time, Place And Girl, The Land Of Nod, A Prince Of Tonight, The Goddess Of Liberty, Miss Nobody from Starland, I Wonder Who's Kissing Her Now*)." Published for Montana Children's Home Society, Helena, MT. 1910. Bl/w drawing of State Seal, covered wagon, geometric designs. "Official Approved as the State Song of Montana by Governor Edwin L. Norris, Secretary of State A.N. Yoder, Attorney General Albert J. Galen; Approved and Adopted by Montana University Athletes; Approved for State Militia by Adjutant General Phil Greenan." "Dedicated to Mrs. E. Creighton Largey." "Song featured in *Goddess Of Liberty*." 4pp. Page 2: At top of music — Official State Song adopted by Gov. Edwin L. Norris, 1910." Page 3: At top of music — "Official State Song Adopted by Gov. Edwin L. Norris."

NEBRASKA

• **AmPM-839 ALLEN**, William Vincent (District Court Judge, 1891-1893, 1899 & 1917-1924; U.S. Senate, 1893-1899 & 1899-1901)
839.1 Parks' Democratic Campaign Songs (For Male Voices). w.m. J.A. Parks. Published by The J.A. Parks Company, York, NE. 1900. Gn/bk non-pictorial. "Respectfully inscribed to Hon. Wm. V. Allen." 40pp. [M-385].
839.2 The Second Battle. w.m. J.A. Parks. In: *Park's Republican Campaign Songs (For Male Voices)*, page 28. e. James Asher Parks. Published by The J.A. Parks Company, York, NE. 1900. Gn/bk non-pictorial. "Respectfully inscribed to Gen. Chas. F. Manderson." 40pp. [M-371]. [Crew/WM-106].
839.3 Three Bills. w.m. J.A. Parks. In: *Park's Republican Campaign Songs (For Male Voices)*, page 3. e. James Asher Parks. Published by The J.A. Parks Company, York, NE. 1900. Gn/bk non-pictorial. "Respectfully inscribed to Gen. Chas. F. Manderson." 40pp. [M-371]. [Crew/WM-106].

• **AmPM-840 BRYAN**, Charles W. (Governor, 1923-1925 & 1931-1935; Candidate for Vice President, 1924) [ALSO SEE: DOC/PSM-JWD]
840.1 Davis And Bryan (Democratic Campaign Song). w.m. Mrs. W.D. O'Bannon. a. S.L. Amick. Published by Mrs. W.D. O'Bannon, No. 614 West Broadway, Sedalia, MO. 1924. B/w non-pictorial geometric designs and border. "Respectfully Dedicated to John W. Davis, Chas. W. Bryan and the Democratic Party of the United States of America." "Copies may be obtained by addressing Ms. W.D. O'Bannon, No. 614 West Broadway, Sedalia, Mo." 4pp. Page 4: Blank. [Crew/JWD-1].

• **AmPM-841 BRYAN**, William Jennings (U.S.

House, 1891–1895; Candidate for President, 1896, 1900, 1908; U.S. Secretary of State, 1913–1915) [ALSO SEE: DOC/PSM-WJB]

841.1 [About A Man To You We'll Sing]. w. H.D. Tutewiler. m. "To the tune *Just Foolin,' My Baby.*" In: *The March Of The Flag Songbook*, 16. Published by H.D. Tutewiler, No. 133 West Market Street, Indianapolis, IN. 1900. [5" × 7⅝"]. Be/bk litho of flag. "The Only Republican Campaign Songs for 1900 Having the Authorized Endorsement [sic] of Both National Republican Committees." 28pp. [M-374]. [Crew/WM-155].

841.2 All The Votes Look Alike To Me (The Popocrat's Pathetic Appeal). w. Stephen R. Royce. m. "Tune—*All Coons Look Alike To Me.*" "For the Wholesale Dry Goods Republican Club, September 20, 1900." In: *McKinley & Roosevelt Campaign 1900,* page 14. Published for the Wholesale Dry Goods Republican Club, No. 350 Broadway by C.G. Burgoyne, New York, NY. 1900. [4¾" × 7"]. Y/bk litho of William McKinley and Theodore Roosevelt, eagle, shield. "Meetings daily from 12 Noon until 2 p.m." "A bird that can sing and won't must be made to sing." 20pp. [M-376]. [Crew/WM-84].

841.3 Another Song. w. Hugh A. McCord. m. "Tune—*Marching Through Georgia.*" In: *McCord's Republican Club Songs (Campaign Of 1900)*, page 1. e. Hugh A. McCord. Published and for Sale by McCord & McCord, Emporia, KS. 1900. [4$\frac{3}{16}$" × 6$\frac{13}{16}$"]. Bl/w litho of William "McKinley" and Theodore "Roosevelt," "Prosperity" and "Protection," geometric border. "Price 10 Cents; $1.00 per Dozen." 22pp. [Crew/WM-347].

841.4 [At The Democrat Convention]. w. H.D. Tutewiler. m. "To the tune *Just Break The News To Mother.*" In: *The March Of The Flag Songbook*, 17. Published by H.D. Tutewiler, No. 133 West Market Street, Indianapolis, IN. 1900. [5" × 7⅝"]. Be/bk litho of flag. "The Only Republican Campaign Songs for 1900 Having the Authorized Endorsement [sic] of Both National Republican Committees." 28pp. [M-374]. [Crew/WM-155].

841.5 An Auspicious Occasion. w. No composer indicated. m. "Tune—*Odd Fellows' Hall.*" In: *Republican Campaign Parodies And Songs* [Songster], page 13. Published by Betts and Burnett, South Butler, Wayne County, NY. 1896. [7¾" × 5½"]. Be/bk non-pictorial. "McKinley and Hobart." "1896." 28pp. [M-340]. [Crew/WM-67].

841.6 The Band Played On. w. W.G. Thomas. m. Logan S. Porter. m. Notation. In: *McKinley Campaign Songster For 1900 (For Male Voices)*, page 4. e. W.G. Thomas. Published by The Home Music Company, Logansport, IN. 1900. Gn/bk litho of "William McKinley for President" and "Theo. Roosevelt For Vice President," eagle, flags, shield. "Send cash with order." "All orders will be promptly filled if accompanied by cash." "Single copy 15 cts. $.50 per dozen." "Note: Our McKinley Campaign Songster No. 2, Entirely Different from this will be issued September 10th. Same Price." 36pp. [M-373]. [Crew/WM-275].

841.7 Banks On The Wabash. m. "Music—*On The Banks Of The Wabash.*" In: *Bryan Electors (Pithy Pointers For The Campaign Of 1908)* [Song Book], page 3. Published by Holt County Democrat, O'Neill, NB. 1908. [6$\frac{1}{16}$" × 8⅛"]. Gn/bk/r drawing of "William Jennings Bryan—Our Next President." 16pp. [Crew/WJB-100].

841.8 Barney Google (Fox Trot). w.m. Billy Rose and Con Conrad. Published by Jerome H. Remick & Co., New York, NY. 1923. N/c litho of Barney Google riding his mule "Spark Plug." "By permission of DeBeck, creator of Barney Google." 6pp. Page 6: Advertising.

841.9 [Bill McKinley In The Chair]. w. H.D. Tutewiler. m. "To the tune *Bull Frog On The Bank.*" In: *The March Of The Flag Songbook*, page 20. Published by H.D. Tutewiler, No. 133 West Market Street, Indianapolis, IN. 1900. [5" × 7⅝"]. Be/bk litho of flag. "The Only Republican Campaign Songs for 1900 Having the Authorized Endorsement [sic] of Both National Republican Committees." 28pp. [M-374]. [Crew/WM-155].

841.10 Billy B__! w.m. J.A. Parks. m. Notation. In: *Park's Republican Campaign Songs (For Male Voices)*, page 3. e. James Asher Parks. Published by The J.A. Parks Company, York, NE. 1900. Gn/bk non-pictorial. "Respectfully inscribed to Gen. Chas. F. Manderson." 40pp. [M-371]. [Crew/WM-106].

841.11 Blue Water Line. w. No composer indicated. m. No tune indicated. "Recorded by Kingston Trio." Published online by Mudcat Café at <http://mudcat.org/@displaysong.cfm?SongID=752>. 1997.

841.12 Boy Bryan's Epitaph. w. No composer indicated. m. "Tune—*Upidee.*" In: *Republican Campaign Parodies And Songs* [Songster], page 12. Published by Betts and Burnett, South Butler, Wayne County, NY. 1896. [7¾" × 5½"]. Be/bk non-pictorial. "McKinley and Hobart." "1896." 28pp. [M-340]. [Crew/WM-67].

841.13 [Bring The Same Old Bugle Boys]. w. H.D. Tutewiler. m. "To the tune *Marching Through Georgia.*" In: *The March Of The Flag Songbook*, 9. Published by H.D. Tutewiler, No. 133 West Market Street, Indianapolis, IN. 1900. [5" × 7⅝"]. Be/bk litho of flag. "The Only Republican Campaign Songs for 1900 Having the Authorized Endorsement [sic] of Both National Republican Committees." 28pp. [M-374]. [Crew/WM-155].

841.14 Bryan And No More Bonds. w. B.M. Lawrence. m. "Air—*Rally Round The Flag.*" In: *Bryan Free Silver Song Book*, page 16. e. B.M. Lawrence, M.D. Published by Dr. B.M. Lawrence, Mansur Block, Indianapolis, IN. [2$\frac{15}{16}$" × 5½"]. [1896]. B/w litho of an American Flag, geometric design border. "Campaign Songs." "Price 5 cents; 50 cts. Per doz., $2.50 per 100, $25 per $1,000." 16pp. [Crew/WJB-55].

841.15 Bryan And Sewell Grand March. m. Noles. In: *42 Selections For Organ And Piano.* Published by F. Trifet, Publisher, 36 Bromfield Street, Boston, MA. [1896]. [Crew/WJB-103].

841.16 Bryan And Silver (Campaign Songs). c. Edith Darlings. 1896. [6" × 7¼"]. Bl/w photo of William Jennings Bryan. "Liberty—Prosperity." "Price Ten Cents." "For sale by all news dealers." List of contents. [Crew/WJB-102].

841.17 Bryan And Sixteen To One. w. B.M. Lawrence. m. "Air—*Star Spangled Banner.*" In: *Bryan Free*

Silver Song Book, page 8. e. B.M. Lawrence, M.D. Published by Dr. B.M. Lawrence, Mansur Block, Indianapolis, IN. [2⁹⁄₁₆" × 5½"]. [1896]. B/w litho of an American Flag, geometric design border. "Campaign Songs." "Price 5 cents; 50 cts. Per doz., $2.50 per 100, $25 per $1,000." 16pp. [Crew/WJB-55].

841.18 Bryan And Stevenson (Campaign Rallying Song). w.m. Sep. Winner. Published in an unknown newspaper of the time. 1900. [7½" × 11¼"]. B/w photo of "Sep. Winner." Long article on his life. Additional lyrics to the song. Musical notation. [Crew/WJB-98].

841.18A Bryan By Acclamation. w. D.K. Crockett. m. Miss Edith M. Cook. Published by D.K. Crockett, Murry, MO. Copyright 1900 by L. Stone. Bl/w photo of William Jennings Bryan. R/w/b geometric designs. "The Latest Campaign Song." 4pp. Page 4: Blank.

841.19 Bryan, Come Home. w. Hugh A. McCord. m. "Tune—*Father, Come Home*." In: *McCord's Republican Club Songs (Campaign Of 1900)*, page 10. e. Hugh A. McCord. Published and for Sale by McCord & McCord, Emporia, KS. 1900. [4⁵⁄₁₆" × 6¹³⁄₁₆"]. Bl/w litho of William "McKinley" and Theodore "Roosevelt," "Prosperity" and "Protection," geometric border. "Price 10 Cents; $1.00 per Dozen." 22pp. [Crew/WM-347].

841.20 Bryan Electors (Pithy Pointers For The Campaign Of 1908) [Song Book]. Published by Holt County Democrat, O'Neill, NB. 1908. [6⅙" × 8⅛"]. Gn/bk/r drawing of "William Jennings Bryan — Our Next President." 16pp. [Crew/WJB-100].

841.21 Bryan Faithful. w. Hugh A. McCord. m. "Tune—*Old Dog Tray*." In: *McCord's Republican Club Songs (Campaign Of 1900)*, page 8. e. Hugh A. McCord. Published and for Sale by McCord & McCord, Emporia, KS. 1900. [4⁵⁄₁₆" × 6¹³⁄₁₆"]. Bl/w litho of William "McKinley" and Theodore "Roosevelt," "Prosperity" and "Protection," geometric border. "Price 10 Cents; $1.00 per Dozen." 22pp. [Crew/WM-347].

841.22 Bryan Walked Off With The Coveted Prize. w. No composer indicated. m. "Tune—*The Band Played On*." In: *Republican Campaign Parodies And Songs* [Songster], page 5. Published by Betts and Burnett, South Butler, Wayne County, NY. 1896. [7¾" × 5½"]. Be/bk non-pictorial. "McKinley and Hobart." "1896." 28pp. [M-340]. [Crew/WM-67].

841.23 Bryan's Dirge. w. [Original] W.L. Douglass, "Co. A., 1892." ["Rehashed"] W.C. Engel, "Co. A, 1900." m. "Tune—*The Man That Broke The Bank At Monte Carlo*." In: *Company A Boys In Blue* (Campaign Songs), page 6. w. "Members of Company A." m. Popular Tunes. Published in Rochester, NY. [1900]. [4" × 6"]. Pl/bk non-pictorial. "Prosperity and the Flag." "Campaign Songs 1880–1900." 16pp [Crew/WM-328].

841.24 Bryan's Free Silver Two-Step March. m. Ray. T. Maston. Published by Isaac Doles, Indianapolis, IN. 1896. B/w photo of William Jennings Bryan, geometric design border. "Respectfully dedicated to Hon. W.J. Bryan. 6pp. Page 6: Advertising. [Crew/WJB-99].

841.25 Bryan's Mule. w. No composer indicated. m. "Tune—*Old Thompson's Mule*." In: *Up-To-Date Republican Campaign Songs*, page 2. Published by J. Burgess Brown "(Leader of the Celebrated Bald-Headed Glee Club), [Indianapolis, IN]." 1908. [8" × 11"]. B/w photos of William H. Taft and John Sherman. B/w drawing of American Flag—"We'll rally 'round the flag, boys." Verse. "Written and compiled for the State Central Committee." [Crew/WHT-66].

841.26 Bryan's Speech At Chicago. w. B.M. Lawrence. m. "Air—*Old Folks At Home*." In: *Bryan Free Silver Song Book*, page 3. e. B.M. Lawrence, M.D. Published by Dr. B.M. Lawrence, Mansur Block, Indianapolis, IN. [2⁹⁄₁₆" × 5½"]. [1896]. B/w litho of an American Flag, geometric design border. "Campaign Songs." "Price 5 cents; 50 cts. Per doz., $2.50 per 100, $25 per $1,000." 16pp. [Crew/WJB-55].

841.27 Can't Beat McKinley. w. Sam Booth. m. "Air adapted from *The Tattooed Man*." In: *California Republican Campaign Songster*, page 21. c. Sam Booth. Published by Republican State Central Committee, San Francisco, CA. 1900. [5½" × 7¹¹⁄₁₆"]. R/w/b lithos of "William McKinley — For President," and "Theodore Roosevelt — For Vice-President." "More McKinley and More Prosperity." 34pp. [Crew/WM-329].

841.28 Coining The Silvery Southern Moon. w. No composer indicated. m. "Tune—*Alabama Coon*." In: *Republican Campaign Parodies And Songs* [Songster], page 19. Published by Betts and Burnett, South Butler, Wayne County, NY. 1896. [7¾" × 5½"]. Be/bk non-pictorial. "McKinley and Hobart." "1896." 28pp. [M-340]. [Crew/WM-67].

841.29 A Corker. w. No composer indicated. m. Geo. B. Chase. In: *Echo Republican Campaign Songs For 1908*, page 29. c. Dr. J.B. Herbert. Published by The Echo Music Company, Publishers, No. 358 Dearborn Street, Chicago, IL. 1908. [6⅞" × 10"]. B/w drawing of "Wm. H. Taft — For President," and "Jas. S. Sherman — For Vice-President," shield, eagle, black line border. "Republican Candidates." "For Male Voices." 36pp. [M-395]. [Crew/WHT-29].

841.30 Crime Of Seventy-Three. w. B.M. Lawrence. m. "Air — *Oh! Susannah*." In: *Bryan Free Silver Song Book*, page 5. e. B.M. Lawrence, M.D. Published by Dr. B.M. Lawrence, Mansur Block, Indianapolis, IN. [2⁹⁄₁₆" × 5½"]. [1896]. B/w litho of an American Flag, geometric design border. "Campaign Songs." "Price 5 cents; 50 cts. Per doz., $2.50 per 100, $25 per $1,000." 16pp. [Crew/WJB-55].

841.31 The Crown Of Thorns. w. No composer indicated. m. "Tune—*The Marseillaise*." In: *Republican Campaign Parodies And Songs* [Songster], page 8. Published by Betts and Burnett, South Butler, Wayne County, NY. 1896. [7¾" × 5½"]. Be/bk non-pictorial. "McKinley and Hobart." "1896." 28pp. [M-340]. [Crew/WM-67].

841.32 The Cuckoos. w. No composer indicated. m. "Tune—*Billy Magee McGaw*." In: *The Rough Rider (Republican Campaign Song Book)*, page 8. c. J. Burgess Brown. Published by J. Burgess Brown, Indianapolis, IN. 1900. [6" × 9"]. Br/bk non-pictorial. "ROUGH ON DemocRATS." 28pp. Page 3: B/w litho of William McKinley. Page 28: "Republican National Ticket—1900. [Crew/WM-330].

841.33 Dare To Be A Bryanite. w. P.P. Bliss and J.J. Daniels. m. "Tune—*Dare To Be A Daniel*." In: *The Battle Cry, Campaign Songs For 1928, The Home In Ac-*

tion Against The Saloon, Page 15. Published by Dry Republicans and Dry Democrats, Minneapolis, MN. 1928. [5¾" × 8½"]. Br/bk non-pictorial geometric design border. The Motto of the United States — In God We Trust; The Motto of the W.C.T.U. — For God and Home Native Land; The Motto of the Anti-Saloon League — The Church in Action Against the Saloon." 32pp.

841.34 Dave Hill And William Bryan. w. No composer indicated. m. "Tune — *I Don't Want To Play In Your Yard.*" In: *Republican Campaign Parodies And Songs* [Songster], page 20. Published by Betts and Burnett, South Butler, Wayne County, NY. 1896. [7¾" × 5½"]. Be/bk non-pictorial. "McKinley and Hobart." "1896." 28pp. [M-340]. [Crew/WM-67].

841.35 De Saltee Ribber (Humming Chorus with Obligato). w. Logan S. Porter. m. S.C. Foster. a. W.T. Giffe. In: *Roosevelt Campaign Songster 1904 (For Male Voices)*, page 2. c. Logan S. Porter. Published by The Home Music Company, Logansport, IN. 1904. [6" × 9"]. Be/bk photos of Theodore Roosevelt and Charles Fairbanks. Be/bk drawing of a star, geometric designs. "Single Copy 15 cts — $1.60 per Dozen." 36pp. [M-391]. [Crew/TR-356].

841.36 Democratic National Hymn (La Paz Para Piano y Canto). w.m. Professor B.N. Silva. Published by Prof. B.N. Silva, San Luis, CO. 1915. Be/br photos of Woodrow Wilson and William Jennings Bryan. Be/br geometric designs. "Respectfully dedicated to the first official Congress and the Leaders of the Democratic Party of the U.S.A." 4pp. Page 4: Blank. [Crew/WW-219].

841.37 The Democratic-Populistic-Silver Plated Kid. w. No composer indicated. m. "Tune — *Solomon Levy.*" In: *The Rough Rider (Republican Campaign Song Book)*, page 12. c. J. Burgess Brown. Published by J. Burgess Brown, Indianapolis, IN. 1900. [6" × 9"]. Br/bk non-pictorial. "ROUGH ON DemocRATS." 28pp. Page 3: B/w litho of William McKinley. Page 28: "Republican National Ticket — 1900. [Crew/WM-330].

841.38 A Dollar For You. w. B.M. Lawrence. m. "Air — *Irish Washerwoman.*" In: *Bryan Free Silver Song Book*, page 6. e. B.M. Lawrence, M.D. Published by Dr. B.M. Lawrence, Mansur Block, Indianapolis, IN. [2⁹⁄₁₆" × 5½"]. [1896]. B/w litho of an American Flag, geometric design border. "Campaign Songs." "Price 5 cents; 50 cts. Per doz., $2.50 per 100, $25 per $1,000." 16pp. [Crew/WJB-55].

841.39 Don't Be A Fossil. w. C.A. Murch. m. J.B. Herbert. In: *Echo Republican Campaign Songs For 1908*, page 26. c. Dr. J.B. Herbert. Published by The Echo Music Company, Publishers, No. 358 Dearborn Street, Chicago, IL. 1908. [6⅞" × 10"]. B/w drawing of "Wm. H. Taft — For President," and "Jas. S. Sherman — For Vice-President," shield, eagle, black line border. "Republican Candidates." "For Male Voices." 36pp. [M-395]. [Crew/WHT-29].

841.40 Draw Up Your Belt. w. Dr. E.L. Smith, m. *Take It To The Lord In Prayer.* Handwritten manuscript on the stationary of the Martinsburg, West Virginia, Socialist Party Local, E.L. Smith, Secretary, 136 W. King Street, Martinsburg, WV. [ca. 1912]. [8½" × 17½"]. B/w photos of workers. R/w seal of the Socialist Party. 2pp. Page 2: Blank.

841.41 Dummy Rag-Time. w. J.A. Du Puv, "Co. A." m. "Tune — *On The Dummy Line.*" In: *Company A Boys In Blue* (Campaign Songs), page 5. w. "Members of Company A." m. Popular Tunes. Published in Rochester, NY. [1900]. [4" × 6"]. Pl/bk non-pictorial. "Prosperity and the Flag." "Campaign Songs 1880–1900." 16pp [Crew/WM-328].

841.42 Equal Rights For All. w. B.M. Lawrence. m. "Air — *Hold The Fort.*" In: *Bryan Free Silver Song Book*, page 7. e. w. B.M. Lawrence, M.D. Published by Dr. B.M. Lawrence, Mansur Block, Indianapolis, IN. [2⁹⁄₁₆" × 5½"]. [1896]. B/w litho of an American Flag, geometric design border. "Campaign Songs." "Price 5 cents; 50 cts. Per doz., $2.50 per 100, $25 per $1,000." 16pp. [Crew/WJB-55].

841.43 Exit Billy Bryan. w. C.A. Murch. m. J.B. Herbert. In: *Echo Republican Campaign Songs For 1908*, page 28. c. Dr. J.B. Herbert. Published by The Echo Music Company, Publishers, No. 358 Dearborn Street, Chicago, IL. 1908. [6⅞" × 10"]. B/w drawing of "Wm. H. Taft — For President," and "Jas. S. Sherman — For Vice-President," shield, eagle, black line border. "Republican Candidates." "For Male Voices." 36pp. [M-395]. [Crew/WHT-29].

841.44 Fairy Tales. w.m. No composer or tune indicated. In: *California Republican Campaign Songster*, page 12. c. Sam Booth. Published by Republican State Central Committee, San Francisco, CA. 1900. [5½" × 7¹¹⁄₁₆"]. R/w/b lithos of "William McKinley — For President," and "Theodore Roosevelt — For Vice-President." "More McKinley and More Prosperity." 34pp. [Crew/WM-329].

841.45 Free Silver Hymn. w. B.M. Lawrence. m. "Air — *Webb.*" In: *Bryan Free Silver Song Book*, page 15. e. B.M. Lawrence, M.D. Published by Dr. B.M. Lawrence, Mansur Block, Indianapolis, IN. [2⁹⁄₁₆" × 5½"]. [1896]. B/w litho of an American Flag, geometric design border. "Campaign Songs." "Price 5 cents; 50 cts. Per doz., $2.50 per 100, $25 per $1,000." 16pp. [Crew/WJB-55].

841.46 Freemen, Reclaim The Nation. w. B.M. Lawrence. m. "Air — *Marseillaise Hymn.*" In: *Bryan Free Silver Song Book*, page 14. e. B.M. Lawrence, M.D. Published by Dr. B.M. Lawrence, Mansur Block, Indianapolis, IN. [2⁹⁄₁₆" × 5½"]. [1896]. B/w litho of an American Flag, geometric design border. "Campaign Songs." "Price 5 cents; 50 cts. Per doz., $2.50 per 100, $25 per $1,000." 16pp. [Crew/WJB-55].

841.47 The Full Dinner Pail. w. Jack McInerney, "Co. A." m. "Tune — *Brown October Ale.*" In: *Company A Boys In Blue* (Campaign Songs), page 4. w. "Members of Company A." m. Popular Tunes. Published in Rochester, NY. [1900]. [4" × 6"]. Pl/bk non-pictorial. "Prosperity and the Flag." "Campaign Songs 1880–1900." 16pp [Crew/WM-328].

841.48 Go 'Long, Mule. w.m. Henry Creamer and Robert King. Published by Shapiro Bernstein & Co., Music Publishers, cor. Broadway & 47th Street, New York, NY. 1924. O/br/w drawing of a mule's head. Br/w photo of "Harwick's Ramblers." "The Dawgonedest Fool Song Ever!" "Four-Four Extra Verses In This Copy." "With Ukulele Accompaniment." 6pp. Page 6: Advertising.

841.49 Gold And McKinley For Me. w. E.G. Hanford. m. "Air—*Bring Back My Bonnie To Me*." In: *McKinley & Roosevelt Campaign 1900* [Song Book], page 3. Published for the Wholesale Dry Goods Republican Club, No. 350 Broadway by C.G. Burgoyne, New York, NY. 1900. [4¾" × 7"]. Y/bk litho of William McKinley and Theodore Roosevelt, eagle, shield. "Meetings daily from 12 Noon until 2 p.m." "A bird that can sing and won't must be made to sing." 20pp. [M-376]. [Crew/WM-84].

841.50 Gold Standard Must Go. w. B.M. Lawrence. m. "Air—*Red, White And Blue*." In: *Bryan Free Silver Song Book*, page 13. e. B.M. Lawrence, M.D. Published by Dr. B.M. Lawrence, Mansur Block, Indianapolis, IN. [2⅚" × 5½"]. [1896]. B/w litho of an American Flag, geometric design border. "Campaign Songs." "Price 5 cents; 50 cts. Per doz., $2.50 per 100, $25 per $1,000." 16pp. [Crew/WJB-55].

841.51 Good-Bye, Billy Bryan, Good-Bye. w. J.W.M. and Geo. B. Chase. m.a. Geo. B. Chase. In: *Republican Hot Shot (A Campaign Songster For 1900)*, page 7. e.a. George B. Chase and J.F. Kinsey. Published by Echo Music Company. 1900. [6" × 8¾"]. Bk/r lithos of William McKinley and Theodore Roosevelt. "Second Edition." 28pp. [M-365]. [Crew/WM-238].

841.52 Good Bye, Free Silver, Good Bye. w. Prof. J.A. Adams. m. "Tune—*Good Bye, My Lover, Good Bye*." In: *McKinley & Roosevelt Campaign 1900*, page 7. Published for the Wholesale Dry Goods Republican Club, No. 350 Broadway by C.G. Burgoyne, New York, NY. 1900. [4¾" × 7"]. Y/bk litho of William McKinley and Theodore Roosevelt, eagle, shield. "Meetings daily from 12 Noon until 2 p.m." "A bird that can sing and won't must be made to sing." 20pp. [M-376]. [Crew/WM-84].

841.53 Good-Bye, Hard Times. w. B.M. Lawrence. m. "Air—*A Thousand Years*." In: *Bryan Free Silver Song Book*, page 12. e. B.M. Lawrence, M.D. Published by Dr. B.M. Lawrence, Mansur Block, Indianapolis, IN. [2⅚" × 5½"]. [1896]. B/w litho of an American Flag, geometric design border. "Campaign Songs." "Price 5 cents; 50 cts. Per doz., $2.50 per 100, $25 per $1,000." 16pp. [Crew/WJB-55].

841.54 Good-Night, Bryan! w. W.G. Thomas. m. Notation. In: *McKinley Campaign Songster For 1900 (For Male Voices)*, page 23. e. W.G. Thomas. Published by The Home Music Company, Logansport, IN. 1900. Gn/bk litho of "William McKinley for President" and "Theo. Roosevelt For Vice President," eagle, flags, shield. "Send cash with order." "All orders will be promptly filled if accompanied by cash." "Single copy 15 cts. $.50 per dozen." "Note: Our McKinley Campaign Songster No. 2, Entirely Different from this will be issued September 10th. Same Price." 36pp. [M-373]. [Crew/WM-275].

841.55 Good Times Will Come Again. w. B.M. Lawrence. m. "Air—*John Brown*." In: *Bryan Free Silver Song Book*, page 11. e. B.M. Lawrence, M.D. Published by Dr. B.M. Lawrence, Mansur Block, Indianapolis, IN. [2⅚" × 5½"]. [1896]. B/w litho of an American Flag, geometric design border. "Campaign Songs." "Price 5 cents; 50 cts. Per doz., $2.50 per 100, $25 per $1,000." 16pp. [Crew/WJB-55].

841.56 A Gorgeous Prospect. w. No composer indicated. m. "Tune—*Tramp, Tramp, Tramp, The Boys Are Marching*." In: *Republican Campaign Parodies And Songs* [Songster], page 6. Published by Betts and Burnett, South Butler, Wayne County, NY. 1896. [7¾" × 5½"]. Be/bk non-pictorial. "McKinley and Hobart." "1896." 28pp. [M-340]. [Crew/WM-67].

841.57 Hard Times No More. w. W.C. Engel, "Co. A." m. "Tune—*Just Tell Them That You Saw Me*." In: *Company A Boys In Blue* (Campaign Songs), page 9. w. "Members of Company A." m. Popular Tunes. Published in Rochester, NY. [1900]. [4" × 6"]. Pl/bk non-pictorial. "Prosperity and the Flag." "Campaign Songs 1880–1900." 16pp [Crew/WM-328].

841.58 He's Dead! w.m. J.A. Parks. In: *Park's Republican Songs Campaign Of 1904 (For Male Voices)* [Song Book], page 6. Published by J.A. Parks Company, York, NE. 1904. [6¹⁵⁄₁₆" × 9¾"]. Br/br non-pictorial geometric design border. 40pp. [M-390]. [Crew/TR-157].

841.59 Hip! Hip! For McKinley And Teddy. w. T. Martin Towne. m. T. Martin Towne. In: *Republican Hot Shot (A Campaign Songster For 1900)*, page 22. e.a. George B. Chase and J.F. Kinsey. Published by Echo Music Company. 1900. [6" × 8¾"]. Bk/r lithos of William McKinley and Theodore Roosevelt. "Second Edition." 28pp. [M-365]. [Crew/WM-238].

841.60 His Raven Locks Are Hanging Down His Back. w. Stephen Laskey. m. "Tune—*Her Golden Hair, &c*." In: *McKinley & Roosevelt Campaign 1900*, page 8. Published for the Wholesale Dry Goods Republican Club, No. 350 Broadway by C.G. Burgoyne, New York, NY. 1900. [4¾" × 7"]. Y/bk litho of William McKinley and Theodore Roosevelt, eagle, shield. "Meetings daily from 12 Noon until 2 p.m." "A bird that can sing and won't must be made to sing." 20pp. [M-376]. [Crew/WM-84].

841.61 Holding Hands. w.m. J.A. Parks. In: *Park's Republican Songs Campaign Of 1904 (For Male Voices)* [Song Book], page 15. Published by J.A. Parks Company, York, NE. 1904. [6¹⁵⁄₁₆" × 9¾"]. Br/br non-pictorial geometric design border. 40pp. [M-390]. [Crew/TR-157].

841.62 Hoosier Voters. w. No composer indicated. m. "Tune—*Old Granite State*." In: *The Rough Rider (Republican Campaign Song Book)*, page 15. c. J. Burgess Brown. Published by J. Burgess Brown, Indianapolis, IN. 1900. [6" × 9"]. Br/bk non-pictorial. "ROUGH ON DemocRATS." 28pp. Page 3: B/w litho of William McKinley. Page 28: "Republican National Ticket—1900. [Crew/WM-330].

841.63 Hot Time. w. A.B. Sloan. m. Air—*Hot Time In The Old Town Tonight*. In: *McKinley & Roosevelt Campaign 1900* [Song Book], page 4. Published for the Wholesale Dry Goods Republican Club, No. 350 Broadway by C.G. Burgoyne, New York, NY. 1900. [4¾" × 7"]. Y/bk litho of William McKinley and Theodore Roosevelt, eagle, shield. "Meetings daily from 12 Noon until 2 p.m." "A bird that can sing and won't must be made to sing." 20pp. [M-376]. [Crew/WM-84].

841.64 A Hot Time In The Old Town Tonight. w. No composer indicated. m. Air—*A Hot Time In The Old Town Tonight*. In: *California Republican Campaign Songster*, page 13. c. Sam Booth. Published by Republican State Central Committee, San Francisco, CA. 1900. [5½" × 7¹¹⁄₁₆"]. R/w/b lithos of "William McKinley — For President," and "Theodore Roosevelt — For Vice-President." "More McKinley and More Prosperity." 34pp. [Crew/WM-329].

841.65 Hurrah! For Our McKinley. w.m. T. Martin Towne. "Inscribed to the Badger State McKinley Club." In: *Republican Hot Shot (A Campaign Songster For 1900)*, page 9. e.a. George B. Chase and J.F. Kinsey. Published by Echo Music Company. 1900. [6" × 8¾"]. Bk/r lithos of William McKinley and Theodore Roosevelt. "Second Edition." 28pp. [M-365]. [Crew/WM-238].

841.66 [I Am Sure With Me You'll All Agree]. w. H.D. Tutewiler. m. "To the tune *What Did Dugan Do To Him?*" In: *The March Of The Flag Songbook*, 7. Published by H.D. Tutewiler, No. 133 West Market Street, Indianapolis, IN. 1900. [5" × 7⅝"]. Be/bk litho of flag. "The Only Republican Campaign Songs for 1900 Having the Authorized Endorsement [sic] of Both National Republican Committees." 28pp. [M-374]. [Crew/WM-155].

841.67 [I Cannot See How A Ship Can Sail]. w. H.D. Tutewiler. m. "To the tune *I Guess That Will Hold 'Em For A While.*" In: *The March Of The Flag Songbook*, page 22. Published by H.D. Tutewiler, No. 133 West Market Street, Indianapolis, IN. 1900. [5" × 7⅝"]. Be/bk litho of flag. "The Only Republican Campaign Songs for 1900 Having the Authorized Endorsement [sic] of Both National Republican Committees." 28pp. [M-374]. [Crew/WM-155].

841.68 I Don't Believe He'll Do It. w.m. J.A. Parks. m. Notation. In: *Park's Republican Campaign Songs (For Male Voices)*, page 22. e. James Asher Parks. Published by The J.A. Parks Company, York, NE. 1900. Gn/bk non-pictorial. "Respectfully inscribed to Gen. Chas. F. Manderson." 40pp. [M-371]. [Crew/WM-106].

841.69 I Guess I'll Have To Telegraph My Baby. w. H.D. Tutewiler. m. No tune indicated. In: *The March Of The Flag Songbook*, page 25. Published by H.D. Tutewiler, No. 133 West Market Street, Indianapolis, IN. 1900. [5" × 7⅝"]. Be/bk litho of flag. "The Only Republican Campaign Songs for 1900 Having the Authorized Endorsement [sic] of Both National Republican Committees." 28pp. [M-374]. [Crew/WM-155].

841.70 I Wonder Why They Never Do It Now! w.m. J.A. Parks. In: *Park's Republican Songs Campaign Of 1904 (For Male Voices)* [Song Book], page 9. Published by J.A. Parks Company, York, NE. 1904. [6¹⁵⁄₁₆" × 9¾"]. Br/br non-pictorial geometric design border. 40pp. [M-390]. [Crew/TR-157].

841.71 In A Little While. w.m. J.A. Parks. In: *Park's Republican Campaign Songs (For Male Voices)*, page 34. e. James Asher Parks. Published by The J.A. Parks Company, York, NE. 1900. Gn/bk non-pictorial. "Respectfully inscribed to Gen. Chas. F. Manderson." 40pp. [M-371]. [Crew/WM-106].

841.72 Indiana's National Air. w. H.D. Tutewiler. m. "To the tune *Banks Of The Wabash.*" In: *The March Of The Flag Songbook*, 13. Published by H.D. Tutewiler, No. 133 West Market Street, Indianapolis, IN. 1900. [5" × 7⅝"]. Be/bk litho of flag. "The Only Republican Campaign Songs for 1900 Having the Authorized Endorsement [sic] of Both National Republican Committees." 28pp. [M-374]. [Crew/WM-155].

841.73 It Is Ever So Far Away. w. Sam Booth. m. "Air — *Ever So Far Away.*" In: *California Republican Campaign Songster*, page 25. c. Sam Booth. Published by Republican State Central Committee, San Francisco, CA. 1900. [5½" × 7¹¹⁄₁₆"]. R/w/b lithos of "William McKinley — For President," and "Theodore Roosevelt — For Vice-President." "More McKinley and More Prosperity." 34pp. [Crew/WM-329].

841.74 It Won't Go Down At All. w. No composer indicated. m. "Tune — *Forty-Nine Bottles.*" Published in *Sixteen Silver Songs*, Lincoln, NB. 1896. Published, with lyric sheet, in *Winners & Losers, Campaign Songs from The Critical Elections In American History, Volume 2—1896–1976*. Sung with notes by Peter Janovsky. 33⅓ rpm LP. Folkways Records FSS 37261. 1980.

841.75 I've Had All I Want In Mine. w.m. J.A. Parks. m. Notation. In: *Park's Republican Campaign Songs (For Male Voices)*, page 12. e. James Asher Parks. Published by The J.A. Parks Company, York, NE. 1900. Gn/bk non-pictorial. "Respectfully inscribed to Gen. Chas. F. Manderson." 40pp. [M-371]. [Crew/WM-106].

841.76 Just Because He Tells Such Awful Lies. w. Wm. C. Engel, "Co. A." m. "Tune — *Just Because She Made Them Goo Goo Eyes.*" In: *Company A Boys In Blue* (Campaign Songs), page 13. w. "Members of Company A." m. Popular Tunes. Published in Rochester, NY. [1900]. [4" × 6"]. Pl/bk non-pictorial. "Prosperity and the Flag." "Campaign Songs 1880–1900." 16pp [Crew/WM-328].

841.77 The Kicker. w. Logan S. Porter. m. W.G. Thomas. In: *McKinley Campaign Songster For 1900 (For Male Voices)*, page 1. e. W.G. Thomas. Published by The Home Music Company, Logansport, IN. 1900. Gn/bk litho of "William McKinley for President" and "Theo. Roosevelt For Vice President," eagle, flags, shield. "Send cash with order." "All orders will be promptly filled if accompanied by cash." "Single copy 15 cts. $.50 per dozen." "Note: Our McKinley Campaign Songster No. 2, Entirely Different from this will be issued September 10th. Same Price." 36pp. [M-373]. [Crew/WM-275].

841.78 Kurnel Bryan's Mule. w. No composer indicated. m. "Tune — *Old Thompson's Mule.*" In: *The Rough Rider (Republican Campaign Song Book)*, page 3. c. J. Burgess Brown. Published by J. Burgess Brown, Indianapolis, IN. 1900. [6" × 9"]. Br/bk non-pictorial. "ROUGH ON DemocRATS." 28pp. Page 3: B/w litho of William McKinley. Page 28: "Republican National Ticket — 1900. [Crew/WM-330].

841.79 Listen To My Tale Of Woe. w. A.B. Sloan, "186 W. 70th St.." m. No tune indicated. In: *McKinley & Roosevelt Campaign 1900*, page 6. Published for the Wholesale Dry Goods Republican Club, No. 350 Broadway by C.G. Burgoyne, New York, NY. 1900. [4¾" × 7"]. Y/bk litho of William McKinley and Theodore Roosevelt, eagle, shield. "Meetings daily from 12 Noon until 2 p.m." "A bird that can sing and won't must be made to sing." 20pp. [M-376]. [Crew/WM-84].

841.80 A Little Grey Matter. w.m. J.A. Parks. m.

Notation. In: *Park's Republican Campaign Songs (For Male Voices)*, page 24. e. James Asher Parks. Published by The J.A. Parks Company, York, NE. 1900. Gn/bk non-pictorial. "Respectfully inscribed to Gen. Chas. F. Manderson." 40pp. [M-371]. [Crew/WM-106].

841.81 Loyalty. w. No composer indicated. m. "Tune—*Little More Cider.*" In: *The Rough Rider (Republican Campaign Song Book)*, page 18. c. J. Burgess Brown. Published by J. Burgess Brown, Indianapolis, IN. 1900. [6" × 9"]. Br/bk non-pictorial. "ROUGH ON DemocRATS." 28pp. Page 3: B/w litho of William McKinley. Page 28: "Republican National Ticket—1900. [Crew/WM-330].

841.82 Mac Is Too Long In The Chair (Campaign Song for 1900). w. Rev. A.E. Hatch, "Shannon City, Iowa." m. "Air—*Johnny Has Gone To The Fair.*" In: *The Bryan Songster*, page 20. e. Leroy Miller. Published by News Printing House, Albia, IA. 1900. [5½" × 8¾"]. Gy/bk litho of William Jennings Bryan. "Price—Single Copy 25 Cents." 24pp. [M-383]. [Crew/WJB-69].

841.83 The Major And Rough Rider. w. R.J.P. m. Logan S. Porter. m. Notation. In: *McKinley Campaign Songster For 1900 (For Male Voices)*, page 22. e. W.G. Thomas. Published by The Home Music Company, Logansport, IN. 1900. Gn/bk litho of "William McKinley for President" and "Theo. Roosevelt For Vice President," eagle, flags, shield. "Send cash with order." "All orders will be promptly filled if accompanied by cash." "Single copy 15 cts. $.50 per dozen." "Note: Our McKinley Campaign Songster No. 2, Entirely Different from this will be issued September 10th. Same Price." 36pp. [M-373]. [Crew/WM-275].

841.84 The Man Who Served In Blue. w. No composer indicated. m. "Air—*Two Little Girls In Blue.*" In: *McKinley And Hobart Song Book*, page 18. c.w.a. G.E. Treadway. Published by G.E. Treadway, Pittsburgh, PA. 1896. [5" × 6⅝"]. R/w/b litho of William McKinley and Garret Hobart, flag design. "Now used by the celebrated Tariff Club Quartette of Pittsburgh, Pa." 28pp. [M-349]. [Crew/WM-256].

841.85 March On Victorious. w. B.M. Lawrence. m. "Air—*Marching Through Georgia.*" In: *Bryan Free Silver Song Book*, page 11. e. B.M. Lawrence, M.D. Published by Dr. B.M. Lawrence, Mansur Block, Indianapolis, IN. [2⁹⁄₁₆" × 5½"]. [1896]. B/w litho of an American Flag, geometric design border. "Campaign Songs." "Price 5 cents; 50 cts. Per doz., $2.50 per 100, $25 per $1,000." 16pp. [Crew/WJB-55].

841.86 Marchin' Wid De Yates Phalanx! w. C.C. Hassler. m. Geo. B. Chase. In: *Republican Hot Shot (A Campaign Songster For 1900)*, page 16. e.a. George B. Chase and J.F. Kinsey. Published by Echo Music Company. 1900. [6" × 8¾"]. Bk/r lithos of William McKinley and Theodore Roosevelt. "Second Edition." 28pp. [M-365]. [Crew/WM-238].

841.87 Marching To The Bugle Call. w. No composer indicated. m. "Tune—*Swinging In The Grape Vine Swing.*" In: *The Rough Rider (Republican Campaign Song Book)*, page 19. c. J. Burgess Brown. Published by J. Burgess Brown, Indianapolis, IN. 1900. [6" × 9"]. Br/bk non-pictorial. "ROUGH ON DemocRATS." 28pp. Page 3: B/w litho of William McKinley. Page 28: "Republican National Ticket—1900. [Crew/WM-330].

841.88 McKinley In The White House Chair. w. No composer indicated. m. "Air—*Climbing Up The Golden Stair.*" In: *McKinley And Hobart Song Book*, page 17. c.w.a. G.E. Treadway. Published by G.E. Treadway, Pittsburgh, PA. 1896. [5" × 6⅝"]. R/w/b litho of William McKinley and Garret Hobart, flag design. "Now used by the celebrated Tariff Club Quartette of Pittsburgh, Pa." 28pp. [M-349]. [Crew/WM-256].

841.89 [McKinley Is The Man]. w. H.D. Tutewiler. m. "To the tune *Syncopated Sandy.*" In: *The March Of The Flag Songbook*, 10. Published by H.D. Tutewiler, No. 133 West Market Street, Indianapolis, IN. 1900. [5" × 7⅝"]. Be/bk litho of flag. "The Only Republican Campaign Songs for 1900 Having the Authorized Endorsement [sic] of Both National Republican Committees." 28pp. [M-374]. [Crew/WM-155].

841.90 The McKinley Wagon. w. Logan S. Porter. m. Notation—"Old Tune." In: *McKinley Campaign Songster For 1900 (For Male Voices)*, page 32. e. W.G. Thomas. Published by The Home Music Company, Logansport, IN. 1900. Gn/bk litho of "William McKinley for President" and "Theo. Roosevelt For Vice President," eagle, flags, shield. "Send cash with order." "All orders will be promptly filled if accompanied by cash." "Single copy 15 cts. $.50 per dozen." "Note: Our McKinley Campaign Songster No. 2, Entirely Different from this will be issued September 10th. Same Price." 36pp. [M-373]. [Crew/WM-275].

841.91 McNally's Inside Pocket. w.m. J.A. Parks. In: *Park's Republican Campaign Songs (For Male Voices)*, page 30. e. James Asher Parks. Published by The J.A. Parks Company, York, NE. 1900. Gn/bk non-pictorial. "Respectfully inscribed to Gen. Chas. F. Manderson." 40pp. [M-371]. [Crew/WM-106].

841.92 McNally's Inside Pocket. w.m. J.A. Parks. In: *Park's Republican Songs Campaign Of 1904 (For Male Voices)* [Song Book], page 12. Published by J.A. Parks Company, York, NE. 1904. [6¹⁵⁄₁₆" × 9¾"]. Br/br non-pictorial geometric design border. 40pp. [M-390]. [Crew/TR-157].

841.93 Mr. Sheehan's Message. w. No composer indicated. m. "Tune—*Sweet Marie.*" In: *Republican Campaign Parodies And Songs* [Songster], page 4. Published by Betts and Burnett, South Butler, Wayne County, NY. 1896. [7¾" × 5½"]. Be/bk non-pictorial. "McKinley and Hobart." "1896." 28pp. [M-340]. [Crew/WM-67].

841.94 My Mortgaged Home. w. B.M. Lawrence. m. "Air—*Long, Long Ago.*" In: *Bryan Free Silver Song Book*, page 10. e. B.M. Lawrence, M.D. Published by Dr. B.M. Lawrence, Mansur Block, Indianapolis, IN. [2⁹⁄₁₆" × 5½"]. [1896]. B/w litho of an American Flag, geometric design border. "Campaign Songs." "Price 5 cents; 50 cts. Per doz., $2.50 per 100, $25 per $1,000." 16pp. [Crew/WJB-55].

841.95 My Old Kentucky Home (Revised). w. Logan S. Porter. m. S.C. Foster. a. W.T. Giffe. In: *Roosevelt Campaign Songster 1904 (For Male Voices)*, page 4. c. Logan S. Porter. Published by The Home Music Company, Logansport, IN. 1904. [6" × 9"]. Be/bk photos of Theodore Roosevelt and Charles Fairbanks. Be/bk drawing of a star, geometric designs. "Single Copy 15 cts—$1.60 per Dozen." 36pp. [M-391]. [Crew/TR-356].

841.96 The Nebraskan's Troubles. w. Hugh A. McCord. m. "Tune—*Tit Willow.*" In: *McCord's Republican Club Songs (Campaign Of 1900)*, page 3. e. Hugh A. McCord. Published and for Sale by McCord & McCord, Emporia, KS. 1900. [4¾₁₆" × 6¹³⁄₁₆"]. Bl/w litho of William "McKinley" and Theodore "Roosevelt," "Prosperity" and "Protection," geometric border. "Price 10 Cents; $1.00 per Dozen." 22pp. [Crew/WM-347].

841.97 No Crown Of Thorns, No Cross Of Gold. w. M.D. Pittman. m. Robert Beuchel. Original publication not located. 1896. Published, with lyric sheet, in *Winners & Losers, Campaign Songs from The Critical Elections In American History, Volume 2—1896–1976.* Sung with notes by Peter Janovsky. 33⅓ rpm LP. Folkways Records FSS 37261. 1980.

841.98 Not To Me. w. "The Bunch, Co. A." m. "Tune—*Good-Bye, My Lover, Good-Bye.*" In: *Company A Boys In Blue* (Campaign Songs), page 7. w. "Members of Company A." m. Popular Tunes. Published in Rochester, NY. [1900]. [4" × 6"]. Pl/bk non-pictorial. "Prosperity and the Flag." "Campaign Songs 1880–1900." 16pp [Crew/WM-328].

841.99 O, Jemima, Have You Heard The News? w.m. W.M. Grant. a. E.C. Dorsey. Published by H.N. Cockrell & Company, Music Publishers, Spokane, WA. 1895. B/w geometric designs. "The Great Silver Campaign Song?" "The Biggest Hit Of The Season." "Respectfully Dedicated to Hon. J.C. Sibley of Pennsylvania and the National Bi-metallic League, Washington, D.C." 6pp. Pages 2 and 6: Blank. [Crew/WJB-101].

841.100 [O, There Was A Man Four Years Ago]. w. H.D. Tutewiler. m. "To the tune *Listen To My Tale Of Woe.*" In: *The March Of The Flag Songbook*, 14. Published by H.D. Tutewiler, No. 133 West Market Street, Indianapolis, IN. 1900. [5" × 7⅝"]. Be/bk litho of flag. "The Only Republican Campaign Songs for 1900 Having the Authorized Endorsement [sic] of Both National Republican Committees." 28pp. [M-374]. [Crew/WM-155].

841.101 On Election Day (Negro Dialect). w.m. J.A. Parks. m. Notation. In: *Park's Republican Campaign Songs (For Male Voices)*, page 15. e. James Asher Parks. Published by The J.A. Parks Company, York, NE. 1900. Gn/bk non-pictorial. "Respectfully inscribed to Gen. Chas. F. Manderson." 40pp. [M-371]. [Crew/WM-106].

841.102 On Election Day (Negro Dialect). w.m. J.A. Parks. In: *Park's Republican Songs Campaign Of 1904 (For Male Voices)* [Song Book], page 7. Published by J.A. Parks Company, York, NE. 1904. [6¹⁵⁄₁₆" × 9¾"]. Br/br non-pictorial geometric design border. 40pp. [M-390]. [Crew/TR-157].

841.103 The Orator Boy. w. No composer indicated. m. "Tune—*The Streets Of Cairo.*" In: *Republican Campaign Parodies And Songs* [Songster], page 5. Published by Betts and Burnett, South Butler, Wayne County, NY. 1896. [7¾" × 5½"]. Be/bk non-pictorial. "McKinley and Hobart." "1896." 28pp. [M-340]. [Crew/WM-67].

841.104 Other Arrangements. w.m. J.A. Parks. In: *Park's Republican Songs Campaign Of 1904 (For Male Voices)* [Song Book], page 3. Published by J.A. Parks Company, York, NE. 1904. [6¹⁵⁄₁₆" × 9¾"]. Br/br non-pictorial geometric design border. 40pp. [M-390]. [Crew/TR-157].

841.105 Our Candidates. w. J.J. Kavanaugh. m. W.A. Sullenbarger. "Sung with Expression." In: *The National Democratic Song Book For 1900*, page 12. w. J.J. Kavanaugh. m. W.A. Sullenbarger. Published by The S. Brainard's Sons Company, Chicago, IL. Copyright 1900 by Kavanaugh and Sullenbarger. Be/bk photos of William J. Bryan and Adlai E. Stevenson. Be/bk geometric designs. "No. 1." 20pp. [M-382]. [Crew/WJB-8].

841.106 Our Candidates. w. No composer indicated. m. "Tune—*Menagerie.*" In: *Up-To-Date Republican Campaign Songs*, page 5. Published by J. Burgess Brown "(Leader of the Celebrated Bald-Headed Glee Club), [Indianapolis, IN]." 1908. [8" × 11"]. B/w photos of William H. Taft and John Sherman. B/w drawing of American Flag—"We'll rally 'round the flag, boys." Verse. "Written and compiled for the State Central Committee." [Crew/WHT-66].

841.107 Party Pals. w. No composer indicated. m. "Air—*I Just Couldn't Say Good-Bye.*" In: *Foam Sweet Foam*, page 77 Published by Albany Legislative Correspondents' Association, Albany, NY. 1933. [8" × 11¾"]. N/c drawing by Jerry Costello of Franklin D. Roosevelt, Al Smith and other politicians riding a bottle of beer—"The Lager Limited." "A Rollicking Review Rotating on Resurrection of Bouncing Beverages, Tipsily Tapped at Ten Eyck Hotel Rathskeller, Albany, New York, the evening of Thursday, February 23, 1933, at Seven-Thirty o'clock." 20pp. [Crew/FDR-277].

841.107A The People's President. w. Rev. L.G. Landenberger, "A Minister of The New Church." m. "Adapted from a German Air." Published by Balmer & Weber Music House Company, Publishers, St. Louis, MO. 1900. Bl/w photo of "Hon. Wm. Jennings Bryan." R/w/b geometric designs. "Dedication—To all who love the Declaration of Independence and believe that the Flag of our country means Freedom wherever it floats." "'The essence of uses is the Public Good. Every one who is delighted with the uses of his function for the sake of use, loves his country and fellow citizens; but he who is not delighted therewith for the sake of use, but only does it for the sake of himself, for honors and wealth, does not in his heart love his country.'—Swedenborg's Apocalypse Explained, No. 1226." 4pp. Page 4: Blank.

841.108 Poor Little Orator Boy. w. No composer indicated. m. "Tune—*Streets Of Cairo.*" Original publication not located. 1896. Published, with lyric sheet, in *Winners & Losers, Campaign Songs From The Critical Elections In American History, Volume 2—1896–1976.* Sung with notes by Peter Janovsky. 33⅓ rpm LP. Folkways Records FSS 37261. 1980.

841.109 The Presidential Pieman. w. C.A. Murch. m. J.B. Herbert. In: *Echo Republican Campaign Songs For 1908*, page 23. c. Dr. J.B. Herbert. Published by The Echo Music Company, Publishers, No. 358 Dearborn Street, Chicago, IL. 1908. [6⅞" × 10"]. B/w drawing of "Wm. H. Taft—For President," and "Jas. S. Sherman—For Vice-President," shield, eagle, black line border. "Republican Candidates." "For Male Voices." 36pp. [M-395]. [Crew/WHT-29].

841.110 Pull, Bryan, Pull. w. No composer indicated. m. "Air—*Pull For The Shore.*" B/w drawing of Bryan in a rowboat, White House in the background. In: *Gridiron Nights*, page 198. Published by Frederick A. Stokes Company, Publishers, New York, NY. Copyright 1915 by Arthur Wallace Dunn. [7½" × 10½"]. B/gd imprinting of comedy mask, lamps, floral designs. 406pp.

841.111 Rally Again. w. Hugh A. McCord. m. "Tune—*Rally Around The Flag, Boys.*" In: *McCord's Republican Club Songs (Campaign Of 1900)*, page 11. e. Hugh A. McCord. Published and for Sale by McCord & McCord, Emporia, KS. 1900. [4$\frac{9}{16}$" × 6$\frac{13}{16}$"]. Bl/w litho of William "McKinley" and Theodore "Roosevelt," "Prosperity" and "Protection," geometric border. "Price 10 Cents; $1.00 per Dozen." 22pp. [Crew/WM-347].

841.112 Refrigeration. w. F.H.M. m. "Tune—*There's Music In The Air.*" "For the Wholesale Dry Goods Republican Club, September 20, 1900." In: *McKinley & Roosevelt Campaign 1900*, page 9. Published for the Wholesale Dry Goods Republican Club, No. 350 Broadway by C.G. Burgoyne, New York, NY. 1900. [4¾" × 7"]. Y/bk litho of William McKinley and Theodore Roosevelt, eagle, shield. "Meetings daily from 12 Noon until 2 p.m." "A bird that can sing and won't must be made to sing." 20pp. [M-376]. [Crew/WM-84].

841.113 The Reign Of Prosperity. w. Wm. C. Engel, "Co. A." m. "Tune—*Mandy Lee.*" In: *Company A Boys In Blue* (Campaign Songs), page 11. w. "Members of Company A." m. Popular Tunes. Published in Rochester, NY. [1900]. [4" × 6"]. Pl/bk non-pictorial. "Prosperity and the Flag." "Campaign Songs 1880–1900." 16pp [Crew/WM-328].

841.114 Roosevelt Marching Song. w. W.T.G. m. W.T. Giffe. In: *McKinley Campaign Songster For 1900 (For Male Voices)*, page 31. e. W.G. Thomas. Published by The Home Music Company, Logansport, IN. 1900. Gn/bk litho of "William McKinley for President" and "Theo. Roosevelt For Vice President," eagle, flags, shield. "Send cash with order." "All orders will be promptly filled if accompanied by cash." "Single copy 15 cts. $.50 per dozen." "Note: Our McKinley Campaign Songster No. 2, Entirely Different from this will be issued September 10th. Same Price." 36pp. [M-373]. [Crew/WM-275].

841.115 Roosevelt's Shadow. w. No composer indicated. m. "Music—*When The Flowers Bloom In The Spring Time.*" In: *Bryan Electors (Pithy Pointers For The Campaign Of 1908)* [Song Book], page 7. Published by Holt County Democrat, O'Neill, NB. 1908. [6$\frac{1}{16}$" × 8⅛"]. Gn/bk/r drawing of "William Jennings Bryan—Our Next President." 16pp. [Crew/WJB-100].

841.116 The Second Battle. w.m. J.A. Parks. In: *Park's Republican Campaign Songs (For Male Voices)*, page 28. e. James Asher Parks. Published by The J.A. Parks Company, York, NE. 1900. Gn/bk non-pictorial. "Respectfully inscribed to Gen. Chas. F. Manderson." 40pp. [M-371]. [Crew/WM-106].

841.117 Sixteen To One Will Win. w. B.M. Lawrence. m. "Air—*Old Folks At Home.*" In: *Bryan Free Silver Song Book*, page 4. e. B.M. Lawrence, M.D. Published by Dr. B.M. Lawrence, Mansur Block, Indianapolis, IN. [2$\frac{9}{16}$" × 5½"]. [1896]. B/w litho of an American Flag, geometric design border. "Campaign Songs." "Price 5 cents; 50 cts. Per doz., $2.50 per 100, $25 per $1,000." 16pp. [Crew/WJB-55].

841.118 Snowed Under. w.m. J.A. Parks. In: *Park's Republican Campaign Songs (For Male Voices)*, page 31. e. James Asher Parks. Published by The J.A. Parks Company, York, NE. 1900. Gn/bk non-pictorial. "Respectfully inscribed to Gen. Chas. F. Manderson." 40pp. [M-371]. [Crew/WM-106].

841.119 The Strike That Wins. w. B.M. Lawrence. m. "Air—*Auld Lang Syne.*" In: *Bryan Free Silver Song Book*, page 9. e. B.M. Lawrence, M.D. Published by Dr. B.M. Lawrence, Mansur Block, Indianapolis, IN. [2$\frac{9}{16}$" × 5½"]. [1896]. B/w litho of an American Flag, geometric design border. "Campaign Songs." "Price 5 cents; 50 cts. Per doz., $2.50 per 100, $25 per $1,000." 16pp. [Crew/WJB-55].

841.120 Teddy's Boy Billy. w. No composer indicated. m. "Tune—*Waltz Me Around Again Willie.*" In: *Bryan Electors (Pithy Pointers For The Campaign Of 1908)* [Song Book], page 4. Published by Holt County Democrat, O'Neill, NB. 1908. [6$\frac{1}{16}$" × 8⅛"]. Gn/bk/r drawing of "William Jennings Bryan—Our Next President." 16pp. [Crew/WJB-100].

841.121 That Democrat Convention. w. Logan S. Porter. m. "Arr. From *Patience* by W.T. Giffe." In: *Roosevelt Campaign Songster 1904 (For Male Voices)*, page 10. c. Logan S. Porter. Published by The Home Music Company, Logansport, IN. 1904. [6" × 9"]. Be/bk photos of Theodore Roosevelt and Charles Fairbanks. Be/bk drawing of a star, geometric designs. "Single Copy 15 cts—$1.60 per Dozen." 36pp. [M-391]. [Crew/TR-356].

841.122 That Platform (Sirio Comic). w. J.J. Kavanaugh. m. W.A. Sullenbarger. In: *The National Democratic Song Book For 1900*, page 10. w. J.J. Kavanaugh. m. W.A. Sullenbarger. Published by The S. Brainard's Sons Company, Chicago, IL. Copyright 1900 by Kavanaugh and Sullenbarger. Be/bk photos of William J. Bryan and Adlai E. Stevenson. Be/bk geometric designs. "No. 1." 20pp. [M-382]. [Crew/WJB-8].

841.123 That Silver Song Was Wrong. w. Logan S. Porter. m. W.G. Thomas. m. Notation. In: *McKinley Campaign Songster For 1900 (For Male Voices)*, page 6. e. W.G. Thomas. Published by The Home Music Company, Logansport, IN. 1900. Gn/bk litho of "William McKinley for President" and "Theo. Roosevelt For Vice President," eagle, flags, shield. "Send cash with order." "All orders will be promptly filled if accompanied by cash." "Single copy 15 cts. $.50 per dozen." "Note: Our McKinley Campaign Songster No. 2, Entirely Different from this will be issued September 10th. Same Price." 36pp. [M-373]. [Crew/WM-275].

841.124 That Tired Feeling. w.m. J.A. Parks. m. Notation. In: *Park's Republican Campaign Songs (For Male Voices)*, page 14. e. James Asher Parks. Published by The J.A. Parks Company, York, NE. 1900. Gn/bk non-pictorial. "Respectfully inscribed to Gen. Chas. F. Manderson." 40pp. [M-371]. [Crew/WM-106].

841.125 That Tired Feeling. w.m. J.A. Parks. In: *Park's Republican Songs Campaign Of 1904 (For Male*

Voices) [Song Book], page 8. Published by J.A. Parks Company, York, NE. 1904. [6 15/16" × 9¾"]. Br/br non-pictorial geometric design border. 40pp. [M-390]. [Crew/TR-157].

841.126 That's What Worries The Dems. w. No composer indicated. m. "Arr. By H." In: *Echo Republican Campaign Songs For 1908*, page 31. c. Dr. J.B. Herbert. Published by The Echo Music Company, Publishers, No. 358 Dearborn Street, Chicago, IL. 1908. [6⅞" × 10"]. B/w drawing of "Wm. H. Taft—For President," and "Jas. S. Sherman—For Vice-President," shield, eagle, black line border. "Republican Candidates." "For Male Voices." 36pp. [M-395]. [Crew/WHT-29].

841.127 There Was Once A Man. w.m. J.A. Parks. In: *Park's Republican Songs Campaign Of 1904 (For Male Voices)* [Song Book], page 16. Published by J.A. Parks Company, York, NE. 1904. [6 15/16" × 9¾"]. Br/br non-pictorial geometric design border. 40pp. [M-390]. [Crew/TR-157].

841.128 There'll Be A Hot Time This Fall. w. Stephen R. Royce, "Author of *We Want You, McKinley*, the great campaign song of 1896." m. "Tune—*There'll Be A Hot Time In The Old Town Tonight.*" In: *McKinley & Roosevelt Campaign 1900,* page 15. Published for the Wholesale Dry Goods Republican Club, No. 350 Broadway by C.G. Burgoyne, New York, NY. 1900. [4¾" × 7"]. Y/bk litho of William McKinley and Theodore Roosevelt, eagle, shield. "Meetings daily from 12 Noon until 2 p.m." "A bird that can sing and won't must be made to sing." 20pp. [M-376]. [Crew/WM-84].

841.129 [There's Many A Democrat Today]. w. H.D. Tutewiler. m. "To the tune *Just Tell Them That You Saw Me.*" In: *The March Of The Flag Songbook*, 4. Published by H.D. Tutewiler, No. 133 West Market Street, Indianapolis, IN. 1900. [5" × 7⅝"]. Be/bk litho of flag. "The Only Republican Campaign Songs for 1900 Having the Authorized Endorsement [sic] of Both National Republican Committees." 28pp. [M-374]. [Crew/WM-155].

841.130 They Won't Be There. w. No composer indicated. m. Notation. In: *McKinley Campaign Songster For 1900 (For Male Voices)*, page 30. e. W.G. Thomas. Published by The Home Music Company, Logansport, IN. 1900. Gn/bk litho of "William McKinley for President" and "Theo. Roosevelt For Vice President," eagle, flags, shield. "Send cash with order." "All orders will be promptly filled if accompanied by cash." "Single copy 15 cts. $.50 per dozen." "Note: Our McKinley Campaign Songster No. 2, Entirely Different from this will be issued September 10th. Same Price." 36pp. [M-373]. [Crew/WM-275].

841.131 A Thousand Years. w.m. No composer or tune indicated. In: *Up-To-Date Republican Campaign Songs*, page 6. Published by J. Burgess Brown "(Leader of the Celebrated Bald-Headed Glee Club), [Indianapolis, IN]." 1908. [8" × 11"]. B/w photos of William H. Taft and John Sherman. B/w drawing of American Flag—"We'll rally 'round the flag, boys." Verse. "Written and compiled for the State Central Committee." [Crew/WHT-66].

841.132 Three Bills. w.m. J.A. Parks. m. Notation. In: *Park's Republican Campaign Songs (For Male Voices)*, page 18. e. James Asher Parks. Published by The J.A. Parks Company, York, NE. 1900. Gn/bk non-pictorial. "Respectfully inscribed to Gen. Chas. F. Manderson." 40pp. [M-371]. [Crew/WM-106].

841.133 Three Crows. w. No composer indicated. m. "Tune—*Billy McGee McGaw.*" In: *Up-To-Date Republican Campaign Songs*, page 5. Published by J. Burgess Brown "(Leader of the Celebrated Bald-Headed Glee Club), [Indianapolis, IN]." 1908. [8" × 11"]. B/w photos of William H. Taft and John Sherman. B/w drawing of American Flag—"We'll rally 'round the flag, boys." Verse. "Written and compiled for the State Central Committee." [Crew/WHT-66].

841.134 'Twas A Corker. w.m. Logan S. Porter. In: *Roosevelt Campaign Songster 1904 (For Male Voices)*, page 22. c. Logan S. Porter. Published by The Home Music Company, Logansport, IN. 1904. [6" × 9"]. Be/bk photos of Theodore Roosevelt and Charles Fairbanks. Be/bk drawing of a star, geometric designs. "Single Copy 15 cts—$1.60 per Dozen." 36pp. [M-391]. [Crew/TR-356].

841.135 We Haven't Changed Our Minds Since Then. w.m. J.A. Parks. m. Notation. In: *Park's Republican Campaign Songs (For Male Voices)*, page 4. e. James Asher Parks. Published by The J.A. Parks Company, York, NE. 1900. Gn/bk non-pictorial. "Respectfully inscribed to Gen. Chas. F. Manderson." 40pp. [M-371]. [Crew/WM-106].

841.136 We'll All Be Happy Then. w.m. J.A. Parks. In: *Park's Republican Songs Campaign Of 1904 (For Male Voices)* [Song Book], page 4. Published by J.A. Parks Company, York, NE. 1904. [6 15/16" × 9¾"]. Br/br non-pictorial geometric design border. 40pp. [M-390]. [Crew/TR-157].

841.137 We'll Try To Get Along. w.m. J.A. Parks. In: *Park's Republican Songs Campaign Of 1904 (For Male Voices)* [Song Book], page 26. Published by J.A. Parks Company, York, NE. 1904. [6 15/16" × 9¾"]. Br/br non-pictorial geometric design border. 40pp. [M-390]. [Crew/TR-157].

841.138 [We're For McKinley, He Is The Man] (Campaign Medley). w. No composer indicated. m. "Air—*Somebody Loves Me; School Play Ground;* and *You Can't Play In Our Yard.*" In: *McKinley And Hobart Song Book*, page 15. c.w.a. G.E. Treadway. Published by G.E. Treadway, Pittsburgh, PA. 1896. [5" × 6⅝"]. R/w/b litho of William McKinley and Garret Hobart, flag design. "Now used by the celebrated Tariff Club Quartette of Pittsburgh, Pa." 28pp. [M-349]. [Crew/WM-256].

841.139 We've A Smile. w. James Ball Nailor, "of the Glee Club." m. "Tune—*We've A Smile.*" In: *Harding Campaign Songs*, page 12. "Key of G." Published by The National Republican Committee, Will H. Hays, Chairman. [1920]. [3¾" × 6"]. Gy/bk non-pictorial. "As Sung by the Famous Republican Glee Club of Columbus, Ohio, Founded 1872, 100 Voices." 20pp. [Crew/WGH-31].

841.140 When Bryan Goes Marching Home. w. Hugh A. McCord. m. "Tune—*When Johnny Comes Marching Home.*" In: *McCord's Republican Club Songs (Campaign Of 1900)*, page 14. e. Hugh A. McCord. Published and for Sale by McCord & McCord, Emporia, KS. 1900. [4 5/16" × 6 13/16"]. Bl/w litho of William

"McKinley" and Theodore "Roosevelt," "Prosperity" and "Protection," geometric border. "Price 10 Cents; $1.00 per Dozen." 22pp. [Crew/WM-347].

841.141 When The Demmies Were In Power. w. Logan S. Porter. m. W.G. Thomas. In: *McKinley Campaign Songster For 1900 (For Male Voices)*, page 26. e. W.G. Thomas. Published by The Home Music Company, Logansport, IN. 1900. Gn/bk litho of "William McKinley for President" and "Theo. Roosevelt For Vice President," eagle, flags, shield. "Send cash with order." "All orders will be promptly filled if accompanied by cash." "Single copy 15 cts. $.50 per dozen." "Note: Our McKinley Campaign Songster No. 2, Entirely Different from this will be issued September 10th. Same Price." 36pp. [M-373]. [Crew/WM-275].

841.142 Where Do I Come In? w.m. J.A. Parks. m. Notation. In: *Park's Republican Campaign Songs (For Male Voices)*, page 20. e. James Asher Parks. Published by The J.A. Parks Company, York, NE. 1900. Gn/bk non-pictorial. "Respectfully inscribed to Gen. Chas. F. Manderson." 40pp. [M-371]. [Crew/WM-106].

841.143 Where The Chicken Got The Ax. w. No composer indicated. m. "Tune — *Wearing O' The Green.*" In: *Up-To-Date Republican Campaign Songs*, page 6. Published by J. Burgess Brown "(Leader of the Celebrated Bald-Headed Glee Club), [Indianapolis, IN]." 1908. [8" × 11"]. B/w photos of William H. Taft and John Sherman. B/w drawing of American Flag — "We'll rally 'round the flag, boys." Verse. "Written and compiled for the State Central Committee." [Crew/WHT-66].

841.144 The White House Gate (Solo and Chorus). w.m. Logan S. Porter. In: *Roosevelt Campaign Songster 1904 (For Male Voices)*, page 26. c. Logan S. Porter. Published by The Home Music Company, Logansport, IN. 1904. [6" × 9"]. Be/bk photos of Theodore Roosevelt and Charles Fairbanks. Be/bk drawing of a star, geometric designs. "Single Copy 15 cts — $1.60 per Dozen." 36pp. [M-391]. [Crew/TR-356].

841.145 Why Mr. McKinley, Whose President Are You? w. Stephen Laskey. m. "Tune — *My Hannah Lady.*" "For the Wholesale Dry Goods Republican Club, September 20, 1900." In: *McKinley & Roosevelt Campaign 1900*, page 10. Published for the Wholesale Dry Goods Republican Club, No. 350 Broadway by C.G. Burgoyne, New York, NY. 1900. [4¾" × 7"]. Y/bk litho of William McKinley and Theodore Roosevelt, eagle, shield. "Meetings daily from 12 Noon until 2 p.m." "A bird that can sing and won't must be made to sing." 20pp. [M-376]. [Crew/WM-84].

841.146 William Jennings Bryan. w. J.J. Daniels. m. "Tune — *Our Country Will Stay Dry.*" In: *The Battle Cry, Campaign Songs For 1928, The Home In Action Against The Saloon*, Page 15. Published by Dry Republicans and Dry Democrats, Minneapolis, MN. 1928. [5¾" × 8½"]. Br/bk non-pictorial geometric design border. The Motto of the United States — In God We Trust; The Motto of the W.C.T.U. — For God and Home Native Land; The Motto of the Anti-Saloon League — The Church in Action Against the Saloon." 32pp.

841.147 [We've Named A Ticket That's Bound To Win]. w. H.D. Tutewiler. m. 'To the tune *Billy McGee McGaw.*" In: *The March Of The Flag Songbook*, page 21. Published by H.D. Tutewiler, No. 133 West Market Street, Indianapolis, IN. 1900. [5" × 7⅜"]. Be/bk litho of flag. "The Only Republican Campaign Songs for 1900 Having the Authorized Endorsement [sic] of Both National Republican Committees." 28pp. [M-374]. [Crew/WM-155].

841.148 We've Waited, Billy, Waited Long For You. w. Stephen Laskey. m. "Tune — *I've Waited, Honey, Waited Long For You.*" "For the Wholesale Dry Goods Republican Club, September 20, 1900." In: *McKinley & Roosevelt Campaign 1900*, page 13. Published for the Wholesale Dry Goods Republican Club, No. 350 Broadway by C.G. Burgoyne, New York, NY. 1900. [4¾" × 7"]. Y/bk litho of William McKinley and Theodore Roosevelt, eagle, shield. "Meetings daily from 12 Noon until 2 p.m." "A bird that can sing and won't must be made to sing." 20pp. [M-376]. [Crew/WM-84].

841.149 [When Bill Bryan Talks About The Presidential Chair]. w. H.D. Tutewiler. m. 'To the tune *There'll Be A Hot Time In The Old Town Tonight.*" In: *The March Of The Flag Songbook*, 11. Published by H.D. Tutewiler, No. 133 West Market Street, Indianapolis, IN. 1900. [5" × 7⅜"]. Be/bk litho of flag. "The Only Republican Campaign Songs for 1900 Having the Authorized Endorsement [sic] of Both National Republican Committees." 28pp. [M-374]. [Crew/WM-155].

841.150 When Bryan Is At The Wheel. w. No composer indicated. m. "Music — *Why Don't You Try.*" In: *Bryan Electors (Pithy Pointers For The Campaign Of 1908)* [Song Book], page 5. Published by Holt County Democrat, O'Neill, NB. 1908. [6⅛" × 8⅛"]. Gn/bk/r drawing of "William Jennings Bryan — Our Next President." 16pp. [Crew/WJB-100].

841.151 When The Boys Begin To Vote. w.m. J.A. Parks. In: *Park's Republican Campaign Songs (For Male Voices)*, page 33. e. James Asher Parks. Published by The J.A. Parks Company, York, NE. 1900. Gn/bk non-pictorial. "Respectfully inscribed to Gen. Chas. F. Manderson." 40pp. [M-371]. [Crew/WM-106].

841.152 When The Votes Are Counted. w.m. J.A. Parks. In: *Park's Republican Campaign Songs (For Male Voices)*, page 26. e. James Asher Parks. Published by The J.A. Parks Company, York, NE. 1900. Gn/bk non-pictorial. "Respectfully inscribed to Gen. Chas. F. Manderson." 40pp. [M-371]. [Crew/WM-106].

841.153 While Darling Mother's Voting At The Polls. w.m. Willard Widney. In: *Under The Trigonometree (A Musical Extravaganza)*. Published by Theobold's and Ye College Shoppe, Chicago, IL. 1912. R/w/gn drawing of a dancing couple. "Given by the Class of 1915 of the Northwestern University. Book by Willard A. Widney. Lyrics by W.A. Widney, H.C. Greer, C.H. Boren and M. Wilcox. Music by W.A. Widney & Russel Morgan." 40pp.

841.154 The White House. w. No composer indicated. m. "Tune — *I'se Gwine Back To Dixie.*" In: *The Rough Rider (Republican Campaign Song Book)*, page 10. c. J. Burgess Brown. Published by J. Burgess Brown, Indianapolis, IN. 1900. [6" × 9"]. Br/bk non-pictorial. "ROUGH ON DemocRATS." 28pp. Page 3: B/w litho of William McKinley. Page 28: "Republican National Ticket — 1900. [Crew/WM-330].

841.155 The White House. w. No composer indicated. m. "Tune—*I'se Gwine Back To Dixie.*" In: *Up-To-Date Republican Campaign Songs,* page 2. Published by J. Burgess Brown "(Leader of the Celebrated Bald-Headed Glee Club), [Indianapolis, IN]." 1908. [8" × 11"]. B/w photos of William H. Taft and John Sherman. B/w drawing of American Flag—"We'll rally 'round the flag, boys." Verse. "Written and compiled for the State Central Committee." [Crew/WHT-66].

841.156 The Whole Thing. w. Hugh A. McCord. m. "Tune—*Charming Billy.*" In: *McCord's Republican Club Songs (Campaign Of 1900),* page 7. e. Hugh A. McCord. Published and for Sale by McCord & McCord, Emporia, KS. 1900. [4⅝" × 6¹³⁄₁₆"]. Bl/w litho of William "McKinley" and Theodore "Roosevelt," "Prosperity" and "Protection," geometric border. "Price 10 Cents; $1.00 per Dozen." 22pp. [Crew/WM-347].

841.157 William Jennings Bryan's Last Fight. w.m. McAfee. 78 rpm. Columbia #15039-D/140831. Columbia Phonograph Company, New York, NY. "Solo—Guitar and Violin Accomp." Performed by Vernon Dalhart, Tenor. [ca. 1925].

841.158 William McKinley. w. W.C. Engel, "Co. A." m. "Tune—*Solomon Levi.*" In: *Company A Boys In Blue* (Campaign Songs), page 8. w. "Members of Company A." m. Popular Tunes. Published in Rochester, NY. [1900]. [4" × 6"]. Pl/bk non-pictorial. "Prosperity and the Flag." "Campaign Songs 1880–1900." 16pp [Crew/WM-328].

841.159 Willie Boy. w. No composer indicated. m. "Tune—*Hush, Hush.*" In: *The Rough Rider (Republican Campaign Song Book),* page 16. c. J. Burgess Brown. Published by J. Burgess Brown, Indianapolis, IN. 1900. [6" × 9"]. Br/bk non-pictorial. "ROUGH ON DemocRATS." 28pp. Page 3: B/w litho of William McKinley. Page 28: "Republican National Ticket—1900. [Crew/WM-330].

841.160 The Woodchuck And The Coon. w. W.G. Thomas. m. Logan S. Porter. m. Notation. In: *McKinley Campaign Songster For 1900 (For Male Voices),* page 8. e. W.G. Thomas. Published by The Home Music Company, Logansport, IN. 1900. Gn/bk litho of "William McKinley for President" and "Theo. Roosevelt For Vice President," eagle, flags, shield. "Send cash with order." "All orders will be promptly filled if accompanied by cash." "Single copy 15 cts. $.50 per dozen." "Note: Our McKinley Campaign Songster No. 2, Entirely Different from this will be issued September 10th. Same Price." 36pp. [M-373]. [Crew/WM-275].

841.161 A Worried Look. w.m. J.A. Parks. m. Notation. In: *Park's Republican Campaign Songs (For Male Voices),* page 8. e. James Asher Parks. Published by The J.A. Parks Company, York, NE. 1900. Gn/bk non-pictorial. "Respectfully inscribed to Gen. Chas. F. Manderson." 40pp. [M-371]. [Crew/WM-106].

841.162 Yankee Doodle For McKinley. w.m. John Wilson. m. Notation. In: *National Campaigner (Marching Songs Republican Clubs)* [Song Book], page 28. Published by Dudley T. Limerick & Company, No. 4031 Locust Street, Philadelphia, PA. 1896. [6⅜" × 9¾"]. Non-pictorial. "The slogan: McKinley is Coming! O! ho! O! ho!" List of contents Long narrative on marching songs. 24pp. [M-336]. [Crew/WM-271].

841.163 Zion. w. No composer indicated. m. "Tune—*Other Side Of Jordan.*" In: *Up-To-Date Republican Campaign Songs,* page 5. Published by J. Burgess Brown "(Leader of the Celebrated Bald-Headed Glee Club), [Indianapolis, IN]." 1908. [8" × 11"]. B/w photos of William H. Taft and John Sherman. B/w drawing of American Flag—"We'll rally 'round the flag, boys." Verse. "Written and compiled for the State Central Committee." [Crew/WHT-66].

• **AmPM-842 BOYD,** James E. (State House, 1866; Mayor, Omaha, 1881–1883 & 1885–1887; Governor 1890–1893)

842.1 Governor Boyd's Grand Inaugural March. m. James Fairfield. Published by W.W. Mace & Co., Omaha, NB. 1891. B/w image of James Boyd "Drawn, Engraved and Printed by White-Smith Music Publishing Co., Boston." "Respectfully dedicated to the Hon. Jas. E. Boyd, Governor of Nebraska."

842.2 Governor Boyd's Grand March. m. F.M. Steinhauser. Published by Max Meyer & Bro. Co., Omaha, NB. 1891. B/w litho by Geo. H. Walker of James E. Boyd, American flags. "Dedicated to his many admirers." 6pp. Page 2: Blank. Page 6: Advertising.

KELLOGG, William Pitt (Chief Justice of the Supreme Court of the Territory of Nebraska, 1861) [See: Louisiana]

MAGOON, Charles E. Edward (U.S. Minister to Panama, 1905–1906; Provisional Governor, Cuba, 1908?) [See: U.S. Possessions]

• **AmPM-843 MANDERSON,** Charles Frederick (County Attorney, Stark County, 1865–1869; City Attorney, Omaha, 1870s; U.S. Senate, 1883–1885)

843.1 Park's Republican Campaign Songs (For Male Voices). e. James Asher Parks. Published by The J.A. Parks Company, York, NE. 1900. [7" × 9⁷⁄₁₆"]. Bl/bl non-pictorial, geometric design border. "Respectfully Inscribed to Gen. Chas. F. Manderson." 40pp. [M-371]. [Crew/WM-106].

843.2 When The Votes Are Counted. w.m. J.A. Parks. In: *Park's Republican Campaign Songs (For Male Voices),* page 26. e. James Asher Parks. Published by The J.A. Parks Company, York, NE. 1900. Gn/bk non-pictorial. "Respectfully inscribed to Gen. Chas. F. Manderson." 40pp. [M-371]. [Crew/WM-106].

• **AmPM-844 NORRIS,** George William (County Attorney, Furnas County; District Judge, Fourteenth District, 1895–1902; U.S. House, 1903–1913; U.S. Senate, 1913–1943)

844.1 Good Times-Roosevelt-Good Times! w. Loren H. Wittner. m. Bessie Latham Ginson and Ivan Eppinoff. Published by Latham Publishing House, Washington, DC. 1932. B/w photo of Ivan Eppinoff—"Featured by Ivan Eppinoff and his Orchestra." B/w drawing of American flag, geometric design border. 4pp. Page 4: Dedication—"Dedicated to Hon. George W. Norris, United States Senator, the Outstanding Progressive servant of the Common People, who said: "What the country needs is another Roosevelt." [Crew/FDR-468].

• **AmPM-845 SHELDON,** George L. (Governor, 1907–1909)

845.1 Our Governor March (March and Two-Step). m. Sig. A. Liberati. No publisher indicated. Copyright 1905 by A. Liberati. B/w photo of A. Liberati and his brass band — "Liberati's celebrated American fanfare detail as it appears when rendering this march." "With the compliments of the composer." B/w ribbon, geometric designs. 4pp. Page 2: At top of music — "Respectfully dedicated to His Excellency, Governor Sheldon, of Nebraska." Page 4: Blank.

• **AmPM-846 SORENSEN**, Theodore C. (Attorney, Federal Security Agency, 1951–1953; John Kennedy Senate Staff, 1953–61); Special Counsel to the President, 1961–1964; Candidate, New York State Senate, 1970)

846.1 I'm Called Little Caroline. w. Milton M. Schwartz. m. "Tune — *I'm Called Little Buttercup.*" In: *Sing Along With Jack* [Song Book], page 10. Published by Pocket Books, Inc., New York, NY. Copyright 1963 by Bonny Publishing Corporation. [9" × 11⅞"]. R/w/bk drawing of sheet music *Vive La Dynasty*, silhouette of John F. Kennedy in chair with conductor's baton, caricature of Kennedy family. "Hit Songs from the New Frontier." 36pp. Page 3: "Illustrations by David Gantz." Page 36: Drawing of John F. Kennedy in chair with baton. Song titles. [Crew/JFK-17].

846.2 Pennies For The White House. w.m. Gerald Gardner. In: *These Are The Songs That Were* [Song Book], page 26. e. Gerald Gardner (Writer *Of Who's In Charge Here?*, *News-Reals*, and *That Was The Week That Was*). Published by Edwin H. Morris and Company, No. 31 West 54th Street, New York, NY. 10019. 1965. B/w photo of Lyndon B. Johnson, Hubert Humphrey, Everett Dirksen, others. R/w/bk cover. List of contents. 36pp. Pages 8, 23 and 25: Photos of politicians. [Crew/LBJ-6].

• **AmPM-846A TALBOT**, A.H. (State Senate, 189-)

846A.1 Woodcraft. w.m. Horace Huron, "The Musical Funmaker of The Modern Woodmen of America, Author of *My Papa Was A Woodman*, *Brush The Frown Away* and other p[opular songs." Published by Horace Huron, Rock Island, IL. 1908. B/w photos of "C.W. Hawes, Head Clerk — The Grand Old Man of Woodcraft" and "A.R. Talbot, The Greatest Hustler in Fraternity." R/w/br/gn drawings of leaf, axes, geometric designs.6pp. Pages 2 and 6: Advertising.

• **AmPM-847 THURSTON**, John Mellen (City Council, Omaha, 1872–1874; City Attorney, Omaha, 1874–1877; State House, 1875–1877; U.S. Senate, 1895–1901; U.S. Commissioner to the St. Louis Exposition, 1901)

847.1 Song Of Protection (Prosperity and Patriotism). w. I.W. Miner. m. Jo F. Barton. Published by I.W. Miner, No. 422 South 15th Street, Omaha, NE. 1896. B/w photos of "Hon. Wm. McKinley of Ohio," "Hon. John M. Thurston, of Nebraska," "I.W. Miner" and "Jo Barton." "For the McKinley Campaign." "Dedicated to Hon. John M. Thurston, United States Senator, The McKinley Leader." "For sale by all music dealers." 6pp. Pages 2 and 6: Blank.

• **AmPM-848 TIPTON**, Thomas Weston (State House, 1845; Territorial Council, 1860; Assessor of Internal Revenue for Nebraska, 1865; U.S. Senate; 1867–1875)

848.1 Witches' Scene From MacGreeley (Which is Seen to be a Fact). w.m. No composer or tune indicated. From the "*New York Standard.*" In: *National Republican Grant And Wilson Campaign Song-Book*, page 34. From the *New York Standard*. Published by The Union Republican Congressional Committee, Washington, DC. 1872. [3¹³⁄₁₆" × 8⁵⁄₁₆"]. Be/bk litho of Ulysses S. Grant. "We'll Sing a Song for U.S. Grant." 100pp. [M-182]. [Crew/USG-110].

• **AmPM-849 MISCELLANEOUS MUSIC**

849.1 The Big O! w. EmiLoca. "*One More Day*, based on the performance by *Les Miserables*." "This is not what you think it is.... This is actually about the intense DISpleasure of living in my hometown of Omaha, Nebraska, especially when it's being mindlessly promoted during CWS season, from our cows up. WARNING: Some may find this unfunny. FYI, 'The Big O!' is our new nickname, commissioned by the City Council of Humiliation or something, Our mayor uses the term rather unwittingly." Published online at <http://amiright.com/parody/misc/lesmiserables0.shtml>. 2004.

849.2 Nebraska's Favorite Temperance Rallying Songs. c. Mrs. Frances Beveridge Heald, President Nebraska W.C.T.U. Published by Jason L. Claflin, University Place, Lincoln, NB. Copyright 1908 by Mrs. L.S. Corey, 2910 Vine Street, Lincoln, Nebr. [5¼" × 7¾"]. Gn/bk drawing of a large wave crashing into a city. Wave labeled — "Public Sentiment or the Temperance Wave, W.C.T.U., Prohibition Party, Anti-Saloon League, The Church, Republican Party, Democratic Party." 30pp.

849.3 Prairie Queen Polka. m. F.W. Hohmann. 1883. B/w litho of the "Nebraska State Capitol" building. "Respectfully dedicated to J.D. McFarland, Land Com. of the B. & M. R.R. at Lincoln, Neb."

NEVADA

BLAND, Richard Parks (Treasurer, Carson County, Nevada, 1860–1865) [See: Missouri]

• **AmPM-850 BOYLE**, Emmet Derby (Governor, 1915–1923)

850.1 America My Country (The New National Anthem). w. Jens K. Grondahl. m. E.F. Maetzold. Published by The Red Wing Printing Co., Red Wing, MN. 1917. R/w/b litho of a shield, geometric designs.

"Long paragraph on the song—"*America, My Country is said to be the greatest patriotic song-poem of the war...*" 4pp. Page 4: Testimonial signed by officers of the National Editorial Association. List of Governors who had "written letters commending the nation-wide use of this song" including "Gov. Boyle of Nevada."
- AmPM-851   MISCELLANEOUS MUSIC

851.1 Home Means Nevada. w.m. Bertha Raffetto. Published by Bertha Raffetto, Reno, NV. 1932. Gr/w drawing of mountains, trees, lake. "Nevada State Song by Act of Legislature, Feb. 6, 1933." 6pp. Page 2: "Dedicated to Nevada's Native Songs and Daughters." Page 6: Gn/w drawing of a deer, mountain, lake, trees.

NEW HAMPSHIRE

- AmPM-852   ADAMS, Sherman (State House, 1941–1944; U.S. House, 1945–1947; Governor, 1949–1953)

852.1 A Tribute To Sherman Adams. w. No composer indicated. m. "To the tune of *Old New Hampshire*." In: *A Tribute To Sherman Adams* [Song Book], page 1. No publisher indicated. [1949–1953]. [5½" × 8½"]. Non-pictorial geometric designs in the corners. "Written at the request of Joe Geisel." 4pp. Pages 2–4: Popular songs.

- AmPM-853   ATHERTON, Charles Gordon (State House, 1830, 1833–1835; U.S. House, 1837–1843; U.S. Senate, 1843–1849 & 1853)

853.1 The Huge Paw (A New Song To An Old Tune). w. No composer indicated. m. *Law*. "Respectfully dedicated to the Hon. Charles G. Atherton, of New Hampshire, the leading editor of the opposition in Massachusetts—the same one who ridiculed the 'huge paws' of the farmers. Hon. Mr. Atherton's letter to the *New Hampshire Patriot*, Dec. 1837." In: *Log Cabin Minstrel (Or Tippecanoe Songster)*, page 25. c. "A Member of the Roxbury Whig Association." Published at the *Patriot And Democrat* Office, Roxbury, [MA]. 1840. [4½" × 6¾"]. [V-1:Y/bk] [V-2: Bl/bk] litho of William Henry Harrison, geometric design border. "Old Tip's the boy to swing the flail. Hurrah! Hurrah! Hurrah!" 64pp. Page 3: Title page—"Containing a Selection of Songs Original and Selected Many of them Written Expressly for this Work, Compiled, Published and Arranged by a member of the Roxbury Democratic Whig Association and Respectfully Dedicated to the Log Cabin Boys of the U.S." [M-013]. [Crew/WHH-71].

- AmPM-854   BARTLETT, Josiah (Provincial Legislature, 1765, Justice of the Peace; Colonial Legislature, 1765–1775; Continental Congress, 1775–1776 & 1778; Signer of the Articles of Confederation, 1774; Signer, Declaration of Independence, 1776; Chief Justice, Court of Common Pleas, 1778; Superior Court, 1784–1788; President of New Hampshire, Governor, 1790–1792; Governor, 1792–1794)

854.1 The Declaration Of Independence Of The United States Of North America, July 4, 1776. w. From the Declaration of Independence. m. John E. Wilson. Published by John E. Wilson, Baltimore, MD. 1863. B/w litho of the interior of Independence Hall. "Arranged and adapted for Vocal and Instrumental Music as the Great National Chant." 4pp. [?]. Page 4: Facsimile signatures of all signers.

854.2 Old Independence Hall. w. A. Fletcher Stayman. m. Francis Weiland. Published by Stayman & Brothers, No. 210 Chesnut Street, Philadelphia, PA. 1855. Non-pictorial. "Respectfully dedicated to the Memory of the Signers of the Declaration of Independence." "Fac Simile of their signatures" including John Adams, Sam Adams, Elbridge Gerry, Thomas Jefferson. 8pp. Pages 2 and 8: Blank. [Crew/MISC-34].

- AmPM-855   BARTLETT, John Henry (Governor, 1919–1921)

855.1 New Hampshire Vacation Song. w. John Henry Bartlett, Ex-Governor of New Hampshire. m. Mollie Wren Whitman. Published by Mollie Wren Whitman, 179 Pleasant Street, Laconia, NH. Copyright 1934 by John Henry Bartlett. Gn/w drawing of the State of New Hampshire with towns and lakes located, Great seal of the State. "Vacation Song." 6pp. Page 6: Blank.

- AmPM-856   BECKWITH, Fred N. (Mayor, Dover)

856.1 The Fighting Mayor (March). w. Earl C. Daniels. m. L.O. Merrill. Published by Brown-Daniels Publishing Co., Dover, NH. 1919. Br/be photo of "Lieu. Fred. N. Beckwith." "Respectfully Dedicated to Ex-Mayor Fred. N. Beckwith, Dover, N.H." 6pp. Page 6: Advertising.

- AmPM-857   CUSHMAN, Samuel (County Treasurer, Portsmouth, 1823–1828; State House, 1833–1835; U.S. House, 1835–1839)

857.1 When This Old Hat Was New. w.m. No composer or tune indicated. In: *The Log Cabin & Hard Cider Melodies, A Collection Of Popular And Patriotic Songs*, page 47. Published by Charles Adams, No. 23 Tremont Street, Boston, MA. 1840. [3¾" × 6"]. [V-1: Pk/bk] [V-2: Gn/bk] litho of William Henry Harrison. "The Freeman's glittering Sword be Blest, For ever blest the Freeman's Lyre." 78pp. Pages 2 and 77: Blank. Page 3: Inside title page. B/w litho of log cabin. "Respectfully Dedicated to the Friends of Harrison and Tyler." Page 78: Advertising. [M-012]. [Crew/WHH-68].

857.2 When This Old Hat Was New. w.m. No composer or tune indicated. In: *The Clay Minstrel Or National Songster*, page 326. c. John Stockton Littell. Published by Greeley & M'Elrath, Tribune Building,

New York, NY. 1844. [3⅛" × 4⅞"]. Non-pictorial. 396pp. [Crew/HC-18].

857.3 When This Old Hat Was New. In: *Whig Songs For 1844* [Songster], page 9. Published by Greeley & McElrath, New York, NY. 1844. [5⅞" × 9³⁄₁₆"]. Non-pictorial. 16pp. Page 16: "Odes and Poems." [M-061]. [Crew/HC-35].

• **AmPM-858 DANA**, Charles A. (Assistant U.S. Secretary of War, 1864–1865)

858.1 Reunion March. m. Dr. H. Perabeau. Published by George Willig, No. 1 North Charles Street, Baltimore, MD. 1865. B/w geometric border. "To the Hon. C.A. Dana, Assistant Secretary of War." "Composed for the Piano." 6pp. Page 6: Blank.

858.2 To Our New Friend, The Old Democrat, H.G. w. No composer indicated. m. "Air — *The Groves Of Blarney.*" From the "*New York Times*, July 23, 1872." In: *National Republican Grant And Wilson Campaign Song-Book*, page 47. Published by The Union Republican Congressional Committee, Washington, DC. 1872. [3¹³⁄₁₆" × 8⁹⁄₁₆"]. Be/bk litho of Ulysses S. Grant. "We'll Sing a Song for U.S. Grant." 100pp. [M-182]. [Crew/USG-110].

• **AmPM-859 GALLINGER**, Jacob Harold (State Senate, 1878–1880; U.S. House, 1885–1889; U.S. Senate, 1891–1918)

859.1 My America. w.m. Frank Peer Beal. Published by The Boston Music Company, 26 & 28 West Street Boston, MA. Copyright 1917 by Frank Beal. [8¾" × 10½"]. Bl/w litho of American flag, stars, geometric designs. "Endorsed by the Governors of New Hampshire, Connecticut & Massachusetts. Sung on the floor of the House of Congress, April 4, 1917." "All benefits from the sale of this publication are to be donated to the American Red Cross." List of Arrangements available." 4pp. Page 2: Endorsements by "H.M. Keyes, Governor of New Hampshire," "Samuel W. McCall, Governor of Massachusetts," and "Marcus H. Holcomb, Governor of Connecticut," and "F.H. Gallinger, United States Senator." Page 4: Bl/e geometric design.

• **AmPM-860 HALE**, John Parker (State house, 1832 & 1846; U.S. Attorney, 1834–1841; U.S. House, 1843–1845; U.S. Senate, 1847–1853 & 1855–1865; Candidate for President, 1852; U.S. Minister to Spain, 1865–1869)

860.1 Let Us Speak Of A Man As We Find Him (Song And Chorus). w. Jas. Simmonds. m. J.R. Thomas. Published by H. Waters, 333 Broadway, New York, NY. 1854. Non-pictorial geometric designs. "To the Hon. John P. Hale." List of titles "By the same Composer" [Thomas]. 6pp. Pages 2 and 6: Blank. [LL/JH].

• **AmPM-861 HILL**, Isaac (State Senate, 1820–1822 & 1827; State House, 1826; Comptroller of the Treasury, 1829–1830; U.S. Senate, 1831–1836; Governor, 1836–1839; U.S. Subtreasurer, Boston, 1840–1841)

861.1 Go And No Go (Or Dan's Scowl At Ty's Serving Men). w. "By the Author of *Van's Mews* [John H. Warland]." m. "Tune — *Dame Durden.*" Long narrative titled "Argument" followed by "Dramatis Personæ. Wise, Ty's vanguard. Cabe [Caleb] another in the guard, who doesn't stop running till he reaches China. Poffe, [Proffit] the rear-guard, who runs to South America and back. Wick, P.M.G. David the Henshaw Fowl, Ex-Secretary of the Navy, and k-navy ex-manager of the Commonwealth Bank, Spence, [Spencer] the evil-genius of the administration. Ike, [Isaac Hill] the blank wrapping-paper-and-twine contractor for all the old Tories and all the new territories, etc. Porte, [Porter] Ex-Secretary of War. Seth, the hissing gentleman, one of David's pets and appointees. Bobby the Ranting Owl, a well known custom-house rat and legislative Ranter also a pet of David." In: *The National Clay Melodist (A Collection Of Popular And Patriotic Songs, Second Edition, Enlarged And Improved)*, page 76. Published by Benj. Adams, No. 54 Court Street, Boston, MA. 1844. [3" × 5¼"]. Inside title page: B/w litho of Henry Clay's home — "O'er Ashland's lawns the skies are bright, From West to East The radiance streams and glows, The land beneath its beams gay beats the heart with joy, Hurrah! Hurrah! Hip! Hurrah!" 108pp. [M-050?]. [Crew/HC-13].

861.2 King Andrew (Glee). w. No composer indicated. m. "Tune — *Dame Durden.*" Published by S.H. Parker, No. 141 Washington Street, Boston, MA. August, 1834. Non-pictorial. "As Sung at the Salem Whig Festival." 4pp. Pages 1 and 4: Blank. [Crew/AJK-7].

861.3 King Andrew. w. No composer indicated. m. "Air — *Dame Durden.*" In: *A Miniature Of Martin Van Buren (With A Selection Of The Best And Most Popular Tippecanoe Songs)*, page 46. 1840. [3½" × 6½"]. [V-1: Br/bk] [V-2: Gn/bk] [V-3: Y/bk] litho of man, chain around neck. Van Buren quote. "Amos Kendall's Veracity — Tom Benton's Honesty — Francis Blair's Beauty." "What is wanting cant be numbered [sic]." 58pp. [M-016]. [Crew/WHH-88].

861.4 The Lounger's Lament. w. No composer indicated. m. "Air — *Exile Of Erin.*" In: *Harrison Melodies (Original And Selected)*, page 63. Published by Weeks, Jordan & Co., Boston, MA. 1840. [3⁹⁄₁₆" × 6"]. B/w litho of William Henry Harrison. "Published under the direction of the Boston Harrison Club." 76pp. Page 5: "To William Henry Harrison of Ohio, the gallant soldier, the enlightened statesman, the consistent Republican, and the Honest man..." [M-001, 002, 003]. [Crew/WHH-86].

861.5 A Miniature Of Martin Van Buren. w.m. No composer or tune indicated. In: *A Miniature Of Martin Van Buren (With A Selection Of The Best And Most Popular Tippecanoe Songs)*, page 3. 1840. [3½" × 6½"]. [V-1: Br/bk] [V-2: Gn/bk] [V-3: Y/bk] litho of man, chain around neck. Van Buren quote. "Amos Kendall's Veracity — Tom Benton's Honesty — Francis Blair's Beauty." "What is wanting cant be numbered [sic]." 58pp. [M-016]. [Crew/WHH-88].

861.6 The Treasury Chest. w. No composer indicated. m. "Tune — *The Mistletoe Bough.*" "A Very Pathetic and musical appeal to the Dear People, by an Ex-Post Master General." In: *Tippecanoe Song-Book (A Collection Of Log Cabin And Patriotic Melodies)*, page 99. Published by Marshall, Williams & Butler, Philadelphia, PA. 1840. White on black litho of log cabin, plow, flags, eagle. 180pp. [M-024]. [Crew/WHH-61].

• **AmPM-862 HUBBARD**, Henry (Governor, 1842–1844)

862.1 When This Old Hat Was New. w.m. No composer or tune indicated. In: *The Log Cabin & Hard Cider Melodies, A Collection Of Popular And Patriotic Songs*, page 47. Published by Charles Adams, No. 23 Tremont Street, Boston, MA. 1840. [3¾" × 6"]. [V-1: Pk/bk] [V-2: Gn/bk] litho of William Henry Harrison. "The Freeman's glittering Sword be Blest, For ever blest the Freeman's Lyre." 78pp. Pages 2 and 77: Blank. Page 3: Inside title page. B/w litho of log cabin. "Respectfully Dedicated to the Friends of Harrison and Tyler." Page 78: Advertising. [M-012]. [Crew/WHH-68].

862.2 When This Old Hat Was New. w.m. No composer or tune indicated. In: *Whig Songs For 1844* [Songster], page 9. Published by Greeley & McElrath, New York, NY. 1844. [5⅞" × 9³⁄₁₆"]. Non-pictorial. 16pp. Page 16: "Odes and Poems." [M-061]. [Crew/ HC-35].

862.3 When This Old Hat Was New. w.m. No composer or tune indicated. In: *The Clay Minstrel Or National Songster*, page 326. c. John Stockton Littell. Published by Greeley & M'Elrath, Tribune Building, New York, NY. 1844. [3⅛" × 4⅞"]. Non-pictorial. 396pp. [Crew/HC-18].

• **AmPM-863 KEYES**, Henry Wilder (State House, 1891–1895; & 1915–1917; State Senate, 1903–1905; Governor, 1917–1919; U.S. Senate, 1919–1937)

863.1 My America. w.m. Frank Peer Beal. Published by The Boston Music Company, 26 & 28 West Street Boston, MA. Copyright 1917 by Frank Beal. [8¾" × 10½"]. Bl/w litho of American flag, stars, geometric designs. "Endorsed by the Governors of New Hampshire, Connecticut & Massachusetts. Sung on the floor of the House of Congress, April 4, 1917." "All benefits from the sale of this publication are to be donated to the American Red Cross." List of Arrangements available." 4pp. Page 2: Endorsements by "H.M. Keyes, Governor of New Hampshire," "Samuel W. McCall, Governor of Massachusetts," and "Marcus H. Holcomb, Governor of Connecticut," and "F.H. Gallinger, United States Senator." Page 4: Bl/e geometric design.

• **AmPM-864 KNOX**, William Franklin (Candidate for nomination for Governor, 1924; Candidate for Vice President, 1936; U.S. Secretary of the Navy, 1940–1944) [ALSO SEE: DOC/PSM-AML]

864.1 G.O.P. March. w.m. Gust Safstrom. Published by the De Montte Music Company, No. 855 East 75th Street, Chicago, IL. 1936. Bl/w photos of "Gov. Alf Landon — For President" and "Col. Frank Knox — For Vice-President." R/w/b drawing of an elephant, bass drum, eagle, crossed flags, silhouettes of George "Washington," Abraham "Lincoln." "Endorsed by the Illinois Republican State Central Committee, Perry B. McCullough, Chairman." "Sold to Help Finance the 1936 Campaign, Price 10 cents." 4pp. Page 4: Campaign advertising — "Opportunity and Landon-Knox." "Composer of record of President Franklin D. Roosevelt and Gov. Alf M. Landon." [AML-9].

864.2 [Hiram Said To Aunt Miranda]. w. No composer indicated. m. "Air — *Put On Your Old Gray Bonnet.*" In: *Campaign Songs For The Liberty Quartette*, page 12. Published for The Liberty Quartette, Utica, NY. [1936]. [4¼" × 8¹¹⁄₁₆"]. Bk/br litho of four men singing, eagle. 18pp. [Crew/AML-36].

864.3 It Will Soon Be Voting Time. w. Mary Bush Lang. m. "*In The Good Old Summer Time.*" In: *Landing With Landon (Landon And Knox Campaign Songs 1936)*, page 11. Published by Mary Lang, No. 90 Nowell Road, Melrose Highlands, MA. 1936. [4" × 9"]. Non-pictorial. "Compliments of Massachusetts Republican State Committee." "Landon-Knox-Lyrics 1936." 12pp. [M-422]. [Crew/AML-15].

864.4 Landon And Knox. w. No composer indicated. m. "Tune — *Land Of Mine.*" In: *Kent County Woman's Republican Club Song Sheet*, page 4. [1936]. [5³⁄₁₆" × 10⁷⁄₁₆"]. B/w litho of Abraham Lincoln. "Let us have a Singing, Smiling United Membership." 4pp.

864.5 Mister Donley Had A Deal. w. Mary Bush Lang. m. "*Old MacDonald Had A Farm.*" In: *Landing With Landon (Landon And Knox Campaign Songs 1936)*, page 8. Published by Mary Lang, No. 90 Nowell Road, Melrose Highlands, MA. 1936. [4" × 9"]. Non-pictorial. "Compliments of Massachusetts Republican State Committee." "Landon-Knox-Lyrics 1936." 12pp. [M-422]. [Crew/AML-15].

864.6 [O Come, Come Away]. w. No composer indicated. m. "Tune — *O Come, Come Away.*" In: *Kent County Woman's Republican Club Song Sheet*, page 4. [1936]. [5³⁄₁₆" × 10⁷⁄₁₆"]. B/w litho of Abraham Lincoln. "Let us have a Singing, Smiling United Membership." 4pp.

864.7 [O Give Me A Home Where No Brain Trusters Roam]. w. No composer indicated. m. "Air — *Home On The Range.*" In: *Campaign Songs For The Liberty Quartette*, page 5. Published for The Liberty Quartette, Utica, NY. [1936]. [4¼" × 8¹¹⁄₁₆"]. Bk/br litho of four men singing, eagle. 18pp. [Crew/AML-36].

864.8 [O Listen While We Sing About The Billions Spent]. w. No composer indicated. m. "Air — *Jingle Bells.*" In: *Campaign Songs For The Liberty Quartette*, page 10. Published for The Liberty Quartette, Utica, NY. [1936]. [4¼" × 8¹¹⁄₁₆"]. Bk/br litho of four men singing, eagle. 18pp. [Crew/AML-36].

864.9 [O The New Dealers' Plan Wouldn't Stand On The Shelf]. w. No composer indicated. m. "Air — *My Grandfather's Clock.*" In: *Campaign Songs For The Liberty Quartette*, page 16. Published for The Liberty Quartette, Utica, NY. [1936]. [4¼" × 8¹¹⁄₁₆"]. Bk/br litho of four men singing, eagle. 18pp. [Crew/AML-36].

864.10 Safe To Land With Landon. w. Mary Bush Lang. m. "*School Days.*" In: *Landing With Landon (Landon And Knox Campaign Songs 1936)*, page 9. Published by Mary Lang, No. 90 Nowell Road, Melrose Highlands, MA. 1936. [4" × 9"]. Non-pictorial. "Compliments of Massachusetts Republican State Committee." "Landon-Knox-Lyrics 1936." 12pp. [M-422]. [Crew/AML-15].

864.11 [The Washington Bunch Is A Funny Bunch]. w. No composer indicated. m. "Air — *When Johnny Comes Marching Home.*" In: *Campaign Songs For The Liberty Quartette*, page 7. Published for The Liberty Quartette, Utica, NY. [1936]. [4¼" × 8¹¹⁄₁₆"]. Bk/br litho of four men singing, eagle. 18pp. [Crew/AML-36].

864.12 We Greet You! w. No composer indicated. m. "Tune — *Jingle Bells.*" In: *Kent County Woman's Republican Club Song Sheet*, page 3. [1936]. [5³⁄₁₆" × 10⁷⁄₁₆"].

B/w litho of Abraham Lincoln. "Let us have a Singing, Smiling United Membership." 4pp.
- **AmPM-865   LAROUCHE**, Lyndon H., Jr. (U.S. Labor Party Candidate for President, 1976; Candidate for the Democratic Nomination for President, 1980, 1984, 1988, 1992, 1996 & 2000)

865.1 Swing On A Politician. w. Dave Aronson. m. Chorus from *Swing On A Star.* "I wrote this, about the less well-known candidates of the 1992 Presidential election..." Published online at <http://www.spealeasy.org/~dacearonson/personal/old/swingpol.html>. 1992.
- **AmPM-865x   PIERCE**, Franklin (State General Court, 1829–1833, U.S. House, 1833–1837; U.S. Senate, 1837–1842, President, 1853, 1857) [SEE: DOC/PSM-FP]
- **AmPM-866   QUINBY**, Henry B. (Governor, 1909–1911)

866.1 Governor Quinby's March. m. John M. Hubbard "(Composer of *Canney's March*)." Published by John M. Hubbard, Rochester, New Hampshire. 1909. B/w photo of "Governor Henry B. Quinby, Laconia, New Hampshire." R/w geometric designs. "Respectfully Dedicated to Hon. Henry B. Quinby, Governor of the State of New Hampshire, 1909–1910." 6pp. Page 6: Advertising.
- **AmPM-867   ROLLINS**, Frank W. (Governor, 1899–1901)

867.1 The Latch-String Is Out. w.m. J.W. Caverly "(Author of *The Dear Old Home, My Mother's Prayer,* etc., etc.)." Published by J.W. Caverly. Lynn, MA. 1904. Pl/w drawing of a home, well. Chickens. "Dedicated to Hon. Frank W. Rollins, Formerly Governor of New Hampshire and the Originator and founder of Old Home Week." "A Invitation Home." 6pp. Page 2: "Trade Mark" information by J.W. Caverly, The Blind Music Composer, 11 Vine Street, Lynn, Mass., U.S.A."
- **AmPM-868   SEWALL**, Jonathan M. (Register of Probate, Grafton County, 1774)

868.1 On Independence. w. Dr. Jonathan M. Seawall. m. No tune indicated. No publisher indicated. 1776. [SBAR, p. 139].
- **AmPM-868A   SOUTER**, David (Assistant State Attorney General, 1968–1971; Deputy State Attorney General, 1971–1976; State Attorney General, 1976–1978; State Superior Court, 1978–1983, State Supreme Court, 1983–1990, U.S. Court of Appeals, 1990; U.S. Supreme Court, 1990–Present)

868A.1 If You Knew Souter Like I Knew Souter. w. Bill Strauss and Elaina Newport. On CD: *Sheik, Rattle And Roll.* Published by Capitol Steps Productions, 1505 King Street, Alexandria, VA. 1990. CD Cover: Gn/r/w drawing of Roman rock and Roll guitarist.

868A.2 Won't The Courts Be Loverly? w. Lydia Theys. m. "*Wouldn't It Be Loverly?* originally by *My Fair Lady.*" "As Sung by Antonin Scalia." Published online at <http://amiright.com/parody/misc/myfairlady0.shml>. [ca. 2000].
- **AmPM-869   STEELE**, John H. (Governor, 1844–1846)

869.1 Incidents In The Life Of Pierce. w. No composer indicated. m. "Tune—*Northfield.*" Published in *The Signal,* October 23, 1852. [VBL, p. 329].
- **AmPM-870   STRAW**, Ezekiel A. (Governor, 1872–1874)

870.1 She's Not So Far Gone (But A Straw Can Redeem Her). w. Byron DeWolfe, "of Nashua." m. No tune indicated. In: *Campaign Songs For The N.H. Gubernatorial Campaign, Of 1872.* Published, Nashua, NH. February 24, 1872. [AML].

870.2 The New Departure (Or How My Wife Made Me Promise To Vote For Straw!). w. Byron DeWolfe, of Nashua. m. No tune indicated. In: *Campaign Songs For The N.H. Gubernatorial Campaign, Of 1872.* Published, Nashua, NH. February 24, 1872. [AML].
- **AmPM-871   SULLIVAN**, John (Continental Congress, 1774–1775 & 1780–1781; State Attorney General, 1782–1786; President of New Hampshire, 1786–1787 & 1789?; State House, 1788?; U.S. District Court Judge, 1789–1795)

871.1 Battle Of Trenton. w. No composer indicated. m. Probably *Fire Of Love.* No publisher indicated. [ca. 1776]. [SBAR, p. 150].

871.2 General Sullivan's Song. w. No composer indicated. m. No tune indicated. No publisher indicated. "Was sung before General Sullivan and a few gentlemen, at Portsmouth, New Hampshire, after the battle of Trenton." 1777. [SBAR, p. 165].
- **AmPM-872   SULLOWAY**, Cyrus Adams (State House, 1872–1873 & 1887–1893; U.S. House, 1895–1913 & 1915–1917)

872.1 Song Of 88. [1888]. [5" x 8"]? Non-pictorial broadside. 2pp. Page 2: Blank. [Crew/GC-64].
- **AmPM-873   THORNTON**, Matthew (State Assembly, 1758 & 1760–1761; Justice of the Peace; Provincial Congress, 1775; Committee of Safety, 1775; General Assembly, 1776 & 1783; Continental Congress, 1776 & 1777; Signer of the Declaration of Independence, 1776; Chief Justice of the Court of Common Pleas; Judge of the Superior Court, 1776–1782; State Senate, 1784; State Councilor, 1785)

873.1 The Declaration Of Independence Of The United States Of North America, July 4, 1776. w. From the Declaration of Independence. m. John E. Wilson. Published by John E. Wilson, Baltimore, MD. 1863. B/w litho of the interior of Independence Hall. "Arranged and adapted for Vocal and Instrumental Music as the Great National Chant." 4pp. [?]. Page 4: Facsimile signatures of all signers.

873.2 Old Independence Hall. w. A. Fletcher Stayman. m. Francis Weiland. Published by Stayman & Brothers, No. 210 Chesnut Street, Philadelphia, PA. 1855. Non-pictorial. "Respectfully dedicated to the Memory of the Signers of the Declaration of Independence." "Fac Simile of their signatures" including John Adams, Sam Adams, Elbridge Gerry, Thomas Jefferson. 8pp. Pages 2 and 8: Blank. [Crew/MISC-34].
- **AmPM-874   WESTON**, James A. (Governor, 1871–1872 & 1874–1875)

874.1 The New Departure (Or How My Wife Made Me Promise To Vote For Straw!). w. Byron DeWolfe, "of Nashua." m. No tune indicated. In: *Campaign Songs For The N.H. Gubernatorial Campaign, Of 1872.* Published, Nashua, NH. February 24, 1872. [AML].

WEBSTER, Daniel (U.S. House, New Hampshire, 1813–1817) [See: Massachusetts]
- **AmPM-875   WHEELER**, Katherine Wells (State Senate)

875.1 Five Reversible, Approved, Safe Means Of Contraception (Song For SB 175 Contraception Insurance Coverage). w. Katherine Wells Wheeler. m. "From *Mary Poppins*." "For June 8, 1999." Published online at <http://.www.katiewheeler.net/speeches/parodies/contraception.htm>. January 5, 1998.

875.2 Medical Necessity. w. Katherine Wells Wheeler. m. "To the tune of *Bare Necessities*." Published online at <http://.www.katiewheeler.net/speeches/parodies/medical_necessity.htm>. 1999.

875.3 Stop Spreading The Sludge. w. Katherine Wells Wheeler. m. "A parody to the tune of *New York, New York*." Spring 1997." Published online at <http://.www.katiewheeler.net/speeches/parodies/sludge_parody.htm>. 1997.

• **AmPM-876 WHIPPLE**, William (Provincial Congress at Exeter, 1775; Continental Congress, 1776–1779; Signer of the Declaration of Independence, 1776; State Assembly, 1780–1784; State Supreme Court, 1782; Financial Receiver for New Hampshire, 1782–1784)

876.1 The Declaration Of Independence Of The United States Of North America, July 4, 1776. w. From the Declaration of Independence. m. John E. Wilson. Published by John E. Wilson, Baltimore, MD. 1863. B/w litho of the interior of Independence Hall. "Arranged and adapted for Vocal and Instrumental Music as the Great National Chant." 4pp. [?]. Page 4: Facsimile signatures of all signers.

876.2 Old Independence Hall. w. A. Fletcher Stayman. m. Francis Weiland. Published by Stayman & Brothers, No. 210 Chesnut Street, Philadelphia, PA. 1855. Non-pictorial. "Respectfully dedicated to the Memory of the Signers of the Declaration of Independence." "Fac Simile of their signatures" including John Adams, Sam Adams, Elbridge Gerry, Thomas Jefferson. 8pp. Pages 2 and 3: Blank. [Crew/MISC-34].

• **AmPM-877 WINANT**, John G. (Governor, 1931–1935)

877.1 Our Governor March. m. Edward James Mills. Published by The Mills Music Publishing Co., 408 Manchester Street, Manchester, NH. 1925. B/w photo of John Winant. B/w geometric designs. "Respectfully Dedicated to Hon. John G. Winant, Governor of New Hampshire." 4pp. Page 4: Blank.

• **AmPM-878 WOODBURY**, Levi (Superior Court Judge, 1816; Governor, 1823–1824; State House, 1825; U.S. Senator, 1825–1831 & 1841–1845; Secretary of the Navy, 1831–1834; U.S. Secretary of the Treasury, 1834–1841; U.S. Supreme Court, 1843–1851)

878.1 Clearing The Kitchen And White House (A Song For The Fourth of March, 1841). w. No composer indicated. m. "Tune—*Young Lochinvar*." In: *The Tippecanoe Campaign Of 1840*, page 61. Published by A.B. Norton, Mount Vernon, OH. 1888. [5½" × 7½"]. Bl/gd book. 496pp. Pages 1–382: Text. Pages 383–485: "Tippecanoe Songs of the Log Cabin Boys and Girls of 1840." [M-276]. [Crew/WHH-96].

878.2 The Defaulter's Farewell. w. No composer indicated. m. "Tune—*The Bride's Farewell*." In: *Songs For The People (Or Tippecanoe Melodies)* [Songster], page 66. Published for the Authors by James P. Giffing, No. 56 Gold Street, New York, NY. 1840. [3¾" × 6"]. Litho of William Henry Harrison, log cabin, flag. "Original and Selected." 76pp. [M-019]. [Crew/WHH-63].

878.3 The Farmer Of North Bend. w. No composer indicated. Published by Charles T. Geslain, No. 357 Broadway, New York, NY. 1840. B/w litho of a log cabin, horse and buggy, steamboat. "The Patriot's Home." "A Very Popular Whig Song Respectfully Dedicated to the Log Cabin Association the United States by the Publisher." "Pr. 50 cts." 6pp. Pages 2 and 6: Blank. [Crew/WHH-9].

878.4 Harrison Song. w. No composer indicated. m. "Tune—*Hunters Of Kentucky*." "Prepared and sung at the raising of the Log Cabin at Wareham, by John Maxim, a Laboring man, in Carver." In: *Log Cabin Minstrel (or Tippecanoe Songster)*, page 41. c. "A Member of the Roxbury Whig Association." Published at the *Patriot And Democrat* Office, Roxbury, [MA]. 1840. [4½" × 6¾"]. [V-1:Y/bk] [V-2: Bl/bk] litho of William Henry Harrison, geometric design border. "Old Tip's the boy to swing the flail. Hurrah! Hurrah! Hurrah!" 64pp. Page 3: Title page—"Containing a Selection of Songs Original and Selected Many of them Written Expressly for this Work, Compiled, Published and Arranged by a member of the Roxbury Democratic Whig Association and Respectfully Dedicated to the Log Cabin Boys of the U.S." [M-013]. [Crew/WHH-71].

878.5 John And The Farmer. w. No composer indicated. m. "Tune—*The King And The Countryman*." In: *The Clay Minstrel Or National Songster*, page 295. c. John Stockton Littell. Published by Greeley & M'Elrath, Tribune Building, New York, NY. 1844. [3⅛" × 4⅞"]. Non-pictorial. 396pp. [Crew/HC-18].

878.6 The Last Cabinet Council. w. No composer indicated. m. "Air—*There's Nae Luck About The House*." In: *The Harrison And Log Cabin Song Book*, page 35. Published by I.N. Whiting, Columbus, OH. 1840. [3½" × 5½"]. Bl/bk hard cover book with litho of log cabin, flag, eagle. 124pp. [M-008]. [Crew/WHH-76].

878.7 The Last Cabinet Council. w. No composer indicated. m. "Air—*There's Nae Luck About The House*." In: *The Log Cabin & Hard Cider Melodies, A Collection Of Popular And Patriotic Songs*, page 30. Published by Charles Adams, No. 23 Tremont Street, Boston, MA. 1840. [3¾" × 6"]. [V-1: Pk/bk] [V-2: Gn/bk] litho of William Henry Harrison. "The Freeman's glittering Sword be Blest, For ever blest the Freeman's Lyre." 78pp. [M-012]. [Crew/WHH-68].

878.8 The Log Cabin And Hard Cider Song. w. No composer indicated. m. "Tune—*The Hunters Of Kentucky*." From the "*Boston Atlas*." In: *Log Cabin Minstrel (Or Tippecanoe Songster)*, page 18. c. "A Member of the Roxbury Whig Association." Published at the *Patriot And Democrat* Office, Roxbury, [MA]. 1840. [4½" × 6¾"]. [V-1:Y/bk] [V-2: Bl/bk] litho of William Henry Harrison, geometric design border. "Old Tip's the boy to swing the flail. Hurrah! Hurrah! Hurrah!" 64pp. Page 3: Title page—"Containing a Selection of Songs Original and Selected Many of them Written Expressly for this Work, Compiled, Published and Arranged by a member of the Roxbury Democratic Whig Association and Respectfully Dedicated to the Log Cabin Boys of the U.S." [M-013]. [Crew/WHH-71].

878.9 The Lounger's Lament. w. No composer or tune indicated. In: *Whig Songs For 1844* [Songster], page 14. Published by Greeley & McElrath, New York, NY. 1844. [5⅞" × 9 3/16"]. Non-pictorial. 16pp. Page 16: "Odes and Poems." [M-061]. [Crew/HC-35].

878.10 The Lounger's Lament. w. No composer indicated. m. "Tune — *The Exile Of Erin.*" In: *The Clay Minstrel Or National Songster*, page 282. c. John Stockton Littell. Published by Greeley & M'Elrath, Tribune Building, New York, NY. 1844. [3⅛" × 4⅞"]. Non-pictorial. 396pp. [Crew/HC-18].

878.11 The Lounger's Lament. w. No composer indicated. m. "Air — *Exile Of Erin.*" In: *The Log Cabin & Hard Cider Melodies, A Collection Of Popular And Patriotic Songs*, page 42. Published by Charles Adams, No. 23 Tremont Street, Boston, MA. 1840. [3¾" × 6"]. [V-1: Pk/bk] [V-2: Gn/bk] litho of William Henry Harrison. "The Freeman's glittering Sword be Blest, For ever blest the Freeman's Lyre." 78pp. Pages 2 and 77: Blank. Page 3: Inside title page. B/w litho of log cabin. "Respectfully Dedicated to the Friends of Harrison and Tyler." Page 78: Advertising. [M-012]. [Crew/WHH-68].

878.12 Mr. Van Buren's Farewell To The Palace. w.m. No composers or tune indicated. No publisher indicated. [1840]. [Approx. 5" × 12"]. Non-pictorial. 2pp. Page 2: Blank. [AMC]. [Crew/MVB-19].

878.13 Old Tippecanoe Come Out Of The West. w. No composer indicated. m. "Tune — *Young Lochinvar.*" In: *Tippecanoe Song-Book (A Collection Of Log Cabin And Patriotic Melodies)*, page 58. Published by Marshall, Williams & Butler, Philadelphia, PA. 1840. White on black litho of log cabin, plow, flags, eagle. 180pp. [M-024]. [Crew/WHH-61].

878.14 The Treasury Chest. w. No composer indicated. m. "Tune — *The Mistletoe Bough.*" "A Very Pathetic and musical appeal to the Dear People, by an Ex-Post Master General." In: *Tippecanoe Song-Book (A Collection Of Log Cabin And Patriotic Melodies)*, page 99. Published by Marshall, Williams & Butler, Philadelphia, PA. 1840. White on black litho of log cabin, plow, flags, eagle. 180pp. [M-024]. [Crew/ WHH-61].

878.15 Van And The Farmer. w. No composer indicated. m. "Tune — *King And The Countryman.*" In:

The Log Cabin & Hard Cider Melodies, A Collection Of Popular And Patriotic Songs, page 22. Published by Charles Adams, No. 23 Tremont Street, Boston, MA. 1840. [3¾" × 6"]. [V-1: Pk/bk] [V-2: Gn/bk] litho of William Henry Harrison. "The Freeman's glittering Sword be Blest, For ever blest the Freeman's Lyre." 78pp. Pages 2 and 77: Blank. Page 3: Inside title page. B/w litho of log cabin. "Respectfully Dedicated to the Friends of Harrison and Tyler." Page 78: Advertising. [M-012]. [Crew/WHH-68].

878.16 When This Old Hat Was New. w.m. No composer or tune indicated. In: *The Log Cabin & Hard Cider Melodies, A Collection Of Popular And Patriotic Songs*, page 47. Published by Charles Adams, No. 23 Tremont Street, Boston, MA. 1840. [3¾" × 6"]. [V-1: Pk/bk] [V-2: Gn/bk] litho of William Henry Harrison. "The Freeman's glittering Sword be Blest, For ever blest the Freeman's Lyre." 78pp. Pages 2 and 77: Blank. Page 3: Inside title page. B/w litho of log cabin. "Respectfully Dedicated to the Friends of Harrison and Tyler." Page 78: Advertising. [M-012]. [Crew/WHH-68].

878.17 When This Old Hat Was New. w.m. No composer or tune indicated. In: *The Clay Minstrel Or National Songster*, page 326. c. John Stockton Littell. Published by Greeley & M'Elrath, Tribune Building, New York, NY. 1844. [3⅛" × 4⅞"]. Non-pictorial. 396pp. [Crew/HC-18].

878.18 When This Old Hat Was New. w. No composer indicated. In: *Whig Songs For 1844* [Songster], page 9. Published by Greeley & McElrath, New York, NY. 1844. [5⅞" × 9 3/16"]. Non-pictorial. 16pp. Page 16: "Odes and Poems." [M-061]. [Crew/HC-35].

• **AmPM-879   MISCELLANEOUS MUSIC**

879.1 Campaign Song For 1859. w. "By The Same Old Coon." No publisher indicated. Published in Bradford, NH. Dec. 22, 1858. [7¾" × 9½"]. B/w geometric design border. 2pp. Page 2: Blank.

879.2 Campaign Songs For The N.H. Gubernatorial Campaign, Of 1872. w. Byron DeWolfe, of Nashua. Published, Nashua, NH. February 24, 1872.

879.3 To Arms (Patriotic Song, March And Two Step). w.m. Dick Eastman and Walt Jones. Published by The Eastman Music Co., Jefferson, NH. 1917. R/w non-pictorial. "Dedicated to the New Hampshire War Legislature of 1917."

NEW JERSEY

• **AmPM-880   AYCRIGG**, John Bancker (U.S. House, 1837–1839 & 1841–1843)

880.1 A Parody On Up Salt River. w. No composer indicated. m. "Tune — *All On Hobbies.*" In: *Songs For The People (Or Tippecanoe Melodies)* [Songster], page 37. "Dedicated to the Democratic Whig Young Men of the City and County of New York." Published for the Authors by James P. Giffing, No. 56 Gold Street, New York, NY. 1840. [3¾" × 6"]. Litho of William Henry Harrison, log cabin, flag. "Original and Selected." 76pp. [M-019]. [Crew/WHH-63].

880.2 Up Salt River (A New Whig Song). w. G.B.W. (Toledo, OH). m. "Tune — *All On Hobbies.*" Published by Firth & Hall, No. 1 Franklin Square, New York, NY. 1840. Non-pictorial. "Respectfully Dedicated to the Toledo Tippecanoe Club." "Pr. 25 c nett [sic]." 4pp. [Crew/ WHH-38].

880.3 Up Salt River (A New Whig Song). w. G.B.W.

"of Toledo, Ohio." m. "Tune—*All On Hobbies.*" "Respectfully dedicated to the Toledo Tippecanoe Club." In: *The Log Cabin & Hard Cider Melodies, A Collection Of Popular And Patriotic Songs*, page 65. Published by Charles Adams, No. 23 Tremont Street, Boston, MA. 1840. [3¾" × 6"]. [V-1: Pk/bk] [V-2: Gn/bk] litho of William Henry Harrison. "The Freeman's glittering Sword be Blest, For ever blest the Freeman's Lyre." 78pp. Pages 2 and 77: Blank. Page 3: Inside title page. B/w litho of log cabin. "Respectfully Dedicated to the Friends of Harrison and Tyler." Page 78: Advertising. [M-012]. [Crew/WHH-68].

• **AmPM-881 BARBER**, William Warren (Borough Council, Rumson, 1922; Mayor, Rumsom, 1923–1928; U.S. Senate, 1931–1937 & 1938–1943)
881.1 On Freedom's Shore. w. Gilbert Patten "(Author of the famous Frank Merriwell stories)." m. Everett Grieve. Published by Mills Music, Inc., Music Publishers, No. 1619 Broadway, New York, NY. 1936. R/w/b drawing by Robert Paterson of George Washington and Abraham Lincoln on flag background. 6pp. Pages 2 and 6: Blank. Page 3: "Dedicated to the Council Against Intolerance In America, Co-Chairmen George Gordon Battle, W. Warren Barbour and William Allen White. *On Freedom's Shore* is dedicated to the Independence Day Ceremony of the Council Against Intolerance In America, in which thousands of American communities has joined to make July Fourth a stirring re-affirmation of those basic principles of liberty and equality set forth in the Declaration of Independence upon which our Country is founded." [Crew/GW-296].

• **AmPM-882 BEATTY**, Daniel F. (Mayor, Washington, ca. 188-)
882.1 Beatty's Grand Welcome March. m. Ph. J. Lawrence, "of New York." No publisher indicated. [ca. 1880]. B/w litho of a "Night street scene in Washington, New Jersey" with buildings, including "Beatty's Pianos," marching band, carriages, representing the "Reception of Hon. Daniel F. Beatty Mayor of Washington New Jersey, the Famous Piano and Organ Manufacturer upon his return from Europe." B/w floral designs; musical instruments including guitar, harp, trumpet and drum. 6pp. Page 2: B/W litho of Beatty. Page 3: "Composed and Respectfully Dedicated to Hon. Daniel F. Beatty, the famous Piano and Organ Manufacturer as played at his grand Reception from Europe, in Washington, New Jersey." Page 6: Eight litho views of the interior and exterior of Beatty's manufacturing plant.

• **AmPM-883 BEDLE**, Joseph Dorsett (Governor, 1875–1878)
883.1 The New Jersey Grand Centennial March. m. H.F. Wagner, Op. 29. Published by W.H. Ewald & Bro., 136 Newark Avenue, Jersey City, NJ. 1876. B/w litho of the "New Jersey Building, Fairmont Park, Phila," American flags, seal of the State of New Jersey. "Respectfully dedicated to Gov. Jos. D. Bedle." 6pp. Pages 2 and 6: Blank. [LL/JH].

• **AmPM-884 BERGEN**, John (Candidate for State House, 1899)
884.1 How Can I Make A Dollar. German title: *Wie Kann Man Geld Verdienen?* (Campaign Song). w.m. Paul G. Zimmerman. Published by Paul G. Zimmerman, Morristown, NJ. 1899. B/w photos of "For President William Jennings Bryan," "For Vice-President Adlai E. Stevenson," and "For Congress Joshua S. Salmon." "For Assembly John Bergen, George Pierson [No photos]." "The 1900 Common Sense Campaign Song." "Respectfully Dedicated to Mrs. Mary B. Bryan." 4pp. [Crew/WJB-42].

• **AmPM-885 BISHOP**, James A. (Candidate for Freeholder, Bergan County, 1949)
885.1 We'll Change The Scene With Elmer Wene. w. Walter E. Brill. m. Frank T. Grasso. Published by Valemont Music Co., Montvale, NJ. 1949. Bl/w photo of Elmer Wene. R/w/b printing, stars. "The Campaign Song of Elmer H. Wene, Democratic Candidate for Governor of New Jersey." 4pp. + 2pp. insert. Page 4: Bergan County ticket including "Karl D. Van Wagner for State Senator, Lloyd S. Carr, David B. Foley, Patrick Tedesco, Robert Eichler, George B. Chelius, Jr., and Otto J. Stellato for General Assembly, Jacob Schneider, for Surrogate, and James A. Bishop and Francis E. Munley for Freeholders." "On Election Day Nov. 8, 1949."

• **AmPM-886 BRADLEY**, Bill (Professional Basketball Player 1967–1977; U.S. Senate, 1979–1997)
886.1 Indecision 2000. w. Gary S. O'Connor. m. Tune—"*Mack The Knife*, based on a performance by Bobby Darin." "I finally got to write my editorial on the Presidential Election of 2000. This is political fodder for your ears. The story of Al, Walker, Kathy, Hillary, Jessie and all the rest is set to the melody of Mack the Knife in this parody. By the way, this is not the Rush Limbaugh theme song, but it could be!" Published online at <http://www.amiright.com/parody/60s/bobbydarin2.shtml>. [ca. 2003].
886.2 Will To Live. w. "Al Gore." m. No tune indicated. [May be a poem]. In: *The Official George W. Bush Songbook.* Published by Bushwatch.com at <http://www.geocities.com/capitolHill/3750/busgsongs.htm>. [2000]. [Crew/GWB-23].
886.3 Won't You Go Home, Bill Bradley? w. Bill Strauss and Elaina Newport. On CD: *It's Not Over 'Til The First Lady Sings.* Published by Capitol Steps Productions, 1505 King Street, Alexandria, VA. 2000. CD Cover: Gn/bl/y drawing of George Bush and George W. Bush as Seuss characters.

BUTLER, Nicholas Murray (Board of Education, New Jersey, 1887–1895; President of Columbia University, 1901–1945; Delegate, Republican National Convention, 1888, 1904, 1912, 1916, 1924, 1928, & 1932; Republican Candidate for Vice-Presidency, 1912; Winner, Nobel Peace Prize, 1931] [See: New York]

• **AmPM-887 CARR**, Lloyd S. (Candidate for State House, 1949)
887.1 We'll Change The Scene With Elmer Wene. w. Walter E. Brill. m. Frank T. Grasso. Published by Valemont Music Co., Montvale, NJ. 1949. Bl/w photo of Elmer Wene. R/w/b printing, stars. "The Campaign Song of Elmer H. Wene, Democratic Candidate for Governor of New Jersey." 4pp. + 2pp. insert. Page 4: Bergan County ticket including "Karl D. Van Wagner for State Senator, Lloyd S. Carr, David B. Foley, Patrick Tedesco, Robert Eichler, George B. Chelius, Jr., and Otto J. Stellato for General Assembly, Jacob Schneider, for Surrogate, and James A. Bishop

and Francis E. Munley for Freeholders." "On Election Day Nov. 8, 1949."

• **AmPM-888 CATTELL**, Alexander Gilmore (General Assembly, 1840; Common Council, Philadelphia, 1848–1854; U.S., Senate, 1866–1871; U.S. Civil Service Commission, 1871–1873; U.S. Financial Agent, London, 1873–1874; Board of Tax Assessors, New Jersey, 1884–1891; State Board of Education, 1891–1894)

888.1 After The Election Is Over. w.m. No composer indicated. m. Air — *After The Opera Is Over.*" In: *The Sun's Greeley Campaign Songster*, page 10. c. Amos J. Cumming. Published from *The Sun* Office, New York, NY. 1872. [4⅛" × 6½"]. Be/bk litho of Horace Greeley, wreath. "He shines for all." 64pp. [Crew/HG-5].

888.2 Bryan Campaign Songster For 1900 (For Male Voices). e. Logan S. Porter. Published by Home Music Company, Logansport, IN. 1900. Pk/bk litho of William Jennings Bryan and Adlai E. Stevenson. 36pp. [M-386]. [Crew/WJB-71].

888.3 Carry The New To 'Lysses. w. No composer indicated. m. "Air — *Carry The News To Mary.*" In: *Greeley Campaign Songster*, page 40. "Respectfully dedicated to the Greeley Clubs of the Country." Published by Halpin & McClure, Chicago, IL. 1872. [4" × 5⅟₁₆"]. Pl/bk litho of Horace Greeley, geometric design border. "Chicago: Western News Company, Wholesale Agents." 72pp. [M-187]. [Crew/HG-21].

• **AmPM-889 CHELIUS**, Jr., George B. (Candidate for State House, 1949)

889.1 We'll Change The Scene With Elmer Wene. w. Walter E. Brill. m. Frank T. Grasso. Published by Valemont Music Co., Montvale, NJ. 1949. Bl/w photo of Elmer Wene. R/w/b printing, stars. "The Campaign Song of Elmer H. Wene, Democratic Candidate for Governor of New Jersey." 4pp. + 2pp. insert. Page 4: Bergan County ticket including "Karl D. Van Wagner for State Senator, Lloyd S. Carr, David B. Foley, Patrick Tedesco, Robert Eichler, George B. Chelius, Jr., and Otto J. Stellato for General Assembly, Jacob Schneider, for Surrogate, and James A. Bishop and Francis E. Munley for Freeholders." "On Election Day Nov. 8, 1949."

• **AmPM-890 COOPER**, William Raworth (State House, 1839–1841; U.S. House, 1839–1841)

890.1 A Parody On Up Salt River. w. No composer indicated. m. "Tune — *All On Hobbies.*" In: *Songs For The People (Or Tippecanoe Melodies)* [Songster], page 37. "Dedicated to the Democratic Whig Young Men of the City and County of New York." Published for the Authors by James P. Giffing, No. 56 Gold Street, New York, NY. 1840. [3¾" × 6"]. Litho of William Henry Harrison, log cabin, flag. "Original and Selected." 76pp. [M-019]. [Crew/WHH-63].

890.2 Up Salt River (A New Whig Song). w. G.B.W. (Toledo, OH). m. "Tune — *All On Hobbies.*" Published by Firth & Hall, No. 1 Franklin Square, New York, NY. 1840. Non-pictorial. "Respectfully Dedicated to the Toledo Tippecanoe Club." "Pr. 25 c nett [sic]." 4pp. [Crew/ WHH-38].

890.3 Up Salt River (A New Whig Song). w. G.B.W. "of Toledo, Ohio." m. "Tune — *All On Hobbies.*" "Respectfully dedicated to the Toledo Tippecanoe Club." In: *The Log Cabin & Hard Cider Melodies, A Collection Of Popular And Patriotic Songs*, page 65. Published by Charles Adams, No. 23 Tremont Street, Boston, MA. 1840. [3¾" × 6"]. [V-1: Pk/bk] [V-2: Gn/bk] litho of William Henry Harrison. "The Freeman's glittering Sword be Blest, For ever blest the Freeman's Lyre." 78pp. Pages 2 and 77: Blank. Page 3: Inside title page. B/w litho of log cabin. "Respectfully Dedicated to the Friends of Harrison and Tyler." Page 78: Advertising. [M-012]. [Crew/WHH-68].

• **AmPM-891 DAYTON**, Jonathan (State Assembly, 1786–1787 & 1790; Federal Constitutional Convention, 1787; Signer of the Constitution; 1789; Continental Congress, 1787–1788; State Council, 1790; U.S. House, 1791–1799; U.S. Senate, 1799–1805; State Assembly, 1814–1815)

891.1 The Legislative Pugilists. w. Francis Guy, "A Patriot Exile." m. "Tune — *The Night Before Larry Was Fetch'd.*" In: *The Republican Harmonist (Being A Select Collection Of Republican, Patriotic, And Sentimental Songs, Odes, Sonnets, &c, American And European: Some Of Which Are Original, And Most Of The Others Now Come For The First Time From An American Press)*, page 81. c. D.E. [Daniel Ebsworth] "(A Citizen of the World)." Printed "for the People," Boston, MA. 1801. Non-pictorial. 152pp. [Crew/TJ-10].

891.2 The Retrospect: Or A Touch On The Tories. w. No composer indicated. m. "Tune — *Pretty Work For Twelve Dollars A Day.*" In: *The Republican Harmonist (Being A Select Collection Of Republican, Patriotic, And Sentimental Songs, Odes, Sonnets, &c, American And European: Some Of Which Are Original, And Most Of The Others Now Come For The First Time From An American Press)*, page 20. c. D.E. [Daniel Ebsworth] "(A Citizen of the World)." Printed "for the People," Boston, MA. 1801. Non-pictorial. 152pp. [Crew/TJ-10].

• **AmPM-892 DAYTON**, William Lewis (State Council, 1837–1838; State Supreme Court, 1838–1841, U.S. Senate, 1842–1851; Republican Candidate for Vice President, 1856; State Attorney General, 1857–1861; U.S. Minister to France, 1861–1864) [ALSO SEE: DOC/PSM-JCF]

892.1 The Ballot Battle. w. No composer indicated. m. "Air — *Wait For The Wagon.*" In: *Fremont Songs For The People (Original And Selected)*, page 60. c. Thomas Drew "(Editor of *The Massachusetts Spy*)." Published by John P. Jewett & Company, Boston, MA. Copyright 1856 by Thomas Drew. [3⅝" × 5½"]. B/w litho of "J.C. Fremont." "The Campaign of 1856." 68pp. [Crew/JCF-18].

892.2 Buck, Buck Never Had Luck. w. A. Oakley Hall. m. "Air — *Tippecanoe And Tyler, Too.*" In: *The Republican Campaign Songster, A Collection Of Lyrics, Original And Selected, Specifically Prepared For The Friends Of Freedom In The Campaign Of Fifty-Six*, page 95. Published by Miller, Orton & Mulligan, No. 25 Park Row, New York, NY. 1856. [3⅛" × 6"]. Be/bk litho of "Colonel John C. Fremont" facing to viewer's left, black line border. 112pp. [M-097]. [Crew/JCF-24].

892.3 For Fremont And Freedom. w. No composer indicated. m. "Air — *Rory O'More.*" In: *The Republican Campaign Songster, A Collection Of Lyrics, Original And Selected, Specifically Prepared For The Friends Of Free-*

dom In The Campaign Of Fifty-Six, page 20. Published by Miller, Orton & Mulligan, No. 25 Park Row, New York, NY. 1856. [3¹³⁄₁₆" × 6"]. Be/bk litho of "Colonel John C. Fremont" facing to viewer's left, black line border. 112pp. [M-097]. [Crew/JCF-24].

892.4 Freedom's Dawn. w. No composer indicated. m. "Air—*The Morning Light Is Breaking*." In: *Freedom's Songs!* (For The Campaign Of 1856!). Published by Higgins & Bradley, No. 20 Washington Street, Boston, MA. 1856. B/w litho of John C. Fremont. "John C. Fremont, An Acrostic." Song sheet with four Fremont-related campaign songs. "Let Friends of freedom send in their orders early." 2pp. Page 2: Blank. [Crew/JCF-57].

892.5 Freedom's Song. w. No composer indicated. m. "Air—*The Morning Light Is Breaking*." In: *Freedom's Songs!* (For The Campaign Of 1856!). Published by Higgins & Bradley, No. 20 Washington Street, Boston, MA. 1856. B/w litho of John C. Fremont. "John C. Fremont, An Acrostic." Song sheet with four Fremont-related campaign songs. "Let Friends of freedom send in their orders early." 2pp. Page 2: Blank. [Crew/JCF-57].

892.6 The Freeman's Vow. w. No composer indicated. m. "Air—*Oh! Hard Times Come Again No More*." "By permission of the Author." In: *The Freeman's Glee Book, A Collection Of Songs, Odes, Glees And Ballads With Music, Original And Selected, Harmonized And Arranged For Each. Published Under The Auspices Of The Central Fremont And Dayton Glee Club Of The City Of New York, And Dedicated To All, Who, Cherishing Republican Liberty Consider Freedom Worth A Song*, page 100. Published by Miller, Orton & Mulligan, No. 25 Park Row, New York, NY. [and Auburn, NY]. 1856. [4¹⁵⁄₁₆" × 6"]. Pk/bk litho of man on mountain peak, music sheets, geometric designs. 112pp. [Crew/JCF-16].

892.7 Fremont And Dayton. w. No composer indicated. m. "Air—*O, What Has Caused This Great Commotion*." In: *Fremont Songs For The People (Original And Selected)*, page 22. c. Thomas Drew "(Editor of *The Massachusetts Spy*)." Published by John P. Jewett & Company, Boston, MA. Copyright 1856 by Thomas Drew. [3⅝" × 5½"]. B/w litho of "J.C. Fremont." "The Campaign of 1856." 68pp. [Crew/JCF-18].

892.8 Fremont And Dayton. w. No composer indicated. m. "Air—*Yankee Doodle*." In: *The Freeman's Glee Book, A Collection Of Songs, Odes, Glees And Ballads With Music, Original And Selected, Harmonized And Arranged For Each. Published Under The Auspices Of The Central Fremont And Dayton Glee Club Of The City Of New York, And Dedicated To All, Who, Cherishing Republican Liberty Consider Freedom Worth A Song*, page 70. Published by Miller, Orton & Mulligan, No. 25 Park Row, New York, NY. [and Auburn, NY]. 1856. [4¹⁵⁄₁₆" × 6"]. Pk/bk litho of man on mountain peak, music sheets, geometric designs. 112pp. [Crew/JCF-16].

892.9 Fremont And Dayton (Or Yankee Doodle Revised). w. No composer indicated. m. Air—*Yankee Doodle*. In: *Fremont Songs For The People (Original And Selected)*, page 54. c. Thomas Drew "(Editor of *The Massachusetts Spy*)." Published by John P. Jewett & Company, Boston, MA. Copyright 1856 by Thomas Drew. [3⅝" × 5½"]. B/w litho of "J.C. Fremont." "The Campaign of 1856." 68pp. [Crew/JCF-18].

892.10 Fremont And Freedom. w. No composer indicated. m. "Air—*Right Over Wrong*." In: *Fremont Songs For The People (Original And Selected)*, page 18. c. Thomas Drew "(Editor of *The Massachusetts Spy*)." Published by John P. Jewett & Company, Boston, MA. Copyright 1856 by Thomas Drew. [3⅝" × 5½"]. B/w litho of "J.C. Fremont." "The Campaign of 1856." 68pp. [Crew/JCF-18].

892.11 Fremont And Liberty. w. Joseph Gutman, Jr. m. No tune indicated. In: *The Republican Campaign Songster, A Collection Of Lyrics, Original And Selected, Specifically Prepared For The Friends Of Freedom In The Campaign Of Fifty-Six*, page 48. Published by Miller, Orton & Mulligan, No. 25 Park Row, New York, NY. 1856. [3¹³⁄₁₆" × 6"]. Be/bk litho of "Colonel John C. Fremont" facing to viewer's left, black line border. 112pp. [M-097]. [Crew/JCF-24].

892.12 Fremont Rally Song. w. No composer indicated. m. "Air—*Kinloch Of Kinloch*." In: *The Freeman's Glee Book, A Collection Of Songs, Odes, Glees And Ballads With Music, Original And Selected, Harmonized And Arranged For Each. Published Under The Auspices Of The Central Fremont And Dayton Glee Club Of The City Of New York, And Dedicated To All, Who, Cherishing Republican Liberty Consider Freedom Worth A Song*, page 58. Published by Miller, Orton & Mulligan, No. 25 Park Row, New York, NY. [and Auburn, NY]. 1856. [4¹⁵⁄₁₆" × 6"]. Pk/bk litho of man on mountain peak, music sheets, geometric designs. 112pp. [Crew/JCF-16].

892.13 Fremont, The Choice Of The Nation. w. No composer indicated. m. "Air—*The Red, White And Blue*." B/w litho of an American inscribed—"Freedom's Standard." In: *Fremont Songs For The People (Original And Selected)*, page 26 c. Thomas Drew "(Editor of *The Massachusetts Spy*)." Published by John P. Jewett & Company, Boston, MA. Copyright 1856 by Thomas Drew. [3⅝" × 5½"]. B/w litho of "J.C. Fremont." "The Campaign of 1856." 68pp. [Crew/ JCF-18].

892.14 Fremont's The Choice Of The Nation. w.m. No composer or tune indicated. "Sung first at the Brooklyn Ratification Meeting." In: *The Fremont Songster*, page 30. Published by [V-1: H.S. Riggs & Company, Publishers, No. 4 Cortland Street] [V-2: P.J. Cozans, No. 107 Nassau Street], New York, NY. 1856. [V-1: 3⅝" × 5¾"] [V-2: 3½" × 5⅝"]. Be/bk litho of wreath, John C. Fremont. "With a current likeness of John C. Fremont, The People's Candidate for the Presidency." 40pp. [M-094, 095]. [Crew/JCF-45].

892.15 Have You Heard Of One Fremont? w. No composer indicated. m. "Air—*Tippecanoe And Tyler, Too*." In: *The Freeman's Glee Book, A Collection Of Songs, Odes, Glees And Ballads With Music, Original And Selected, Harmonized And Arranged For Each. Published Under The Auspices Of The Central Fremont And Dayton Glee Club Of The City Of New York, And Dedicated To All, Who, Cherishing Republican Liberty Consider Freedom Worth A Song*, page 68. Published by Miller, Orton & Mulligan, No. 25 Park Row, New York, NY. [and Auburn, NY]. 1856. [4¹⁵⁄₁₆" × 6"]. Pk/bk litho of man on mountain peak, music sheets, geometric designs. 112pp. [Crew/JCF-16].

892.16 Jordan. w.m. No composer or tune indicated. In: *The Fremont Songster*, page 44. Published by [V-1: H.S. Riggs & Company, Publishers, No. 4 Cortland Street] [V-2: P.J. Cozans, No. 107 Nassau Street], New York, NY. 1856. [V-1: 3⅝" × 5¾"] [V-2: 3½" × 5⅝"]. Be/bk litho of wreath, John C. Fremont. "With a current likeness of John C. Fremont, The People's Candidate for the Presidency." 40pp. [M-094, 095]. [Crew/JCF-45].

892.17 The March Of Freedom. w. No composer indicated. m. "Air — *Old Dan Tucker.*" In: *The Republican Campaign Songster, A Collection Of Lyrics, Original And Selected, Specifically Prepared For The Friends Of Freedom In The Campaign Of Fifty-Six*, page 50. Published by Miller, Orton & Mulligan, No. 25 Park Row, New York, NY. 1856. [3¹³⁄₁₆" × 6"]. Be/bk litho of "Colonel John C. Fremont" facing to viewer's left, black line border. 112pp. [M-097]. [Crew/JCF-24].

892.18 The Nebraskaites Think. w. No composer indicated. m. "Air — *Jordan Is A Hard Road To Travel.*" "By permission of Oliver Ditson." In: *The Freeman's Glee Book, A Collection Of Songs, Odes, Glees And Ballads With Music, Original And Selected, Harmonized And Arranged For Each. Published Under The Auspices Of The Central Fremont And Dayton Glee Club Of The City Of New York, And Dedicated To All, Who, Cherishing Republican Liberty Consider Freedom Worth A Song*, page 44. Published by Miller, Orton & Mulligan, No. 25 Park Row, New York, NY. [and Auburn, NY]. 1856. [4⁵⁄₁₆" × 6"]. Pk/bk litho of man on mountain peak, music sheets, geometric designs. 112pp. [Crew/JCF-16].

892.18A [O, The Sunlight Of Freedom Shines Out Once Again]. In: *The True Issue* [A Cloth Bandanna/Songster]. Published by the Shawmut Chemical Printing Company, Boston, MA. [1856]. [10¼" × 10¾"]. Cloth bandanna printed with illustration of John C. Fremont. Narrative to either side. Three campaign songs. Rev: Blank. [Crew-JCF-12].

892.19 Oh Jemmy Buchan! w. No composer indicated. m. No composer indicated. In: *The Freeman's Glee Book, A Collection Of Songs, Odes, Glees And Ballads With Music, Original And Selected, Harmonized And Arranged For Each. Published Under The Auspices Of The Central Fremont And Dayton Glee Club Of The City Of New York, And Dedicated To All, Who, Cherishing Republican Liberty Consider Freedom Worth A Song*, page 62. Published by Miller, Orton & Mulligan, No. 25 Park Row, New York, NY. [and Auburn, NY]. 1856. [4⁵⁄₁₆" × 6"]. Pk/bk litho of man on mountain peak, music sheets, geometric designs. 112pp. [Crew/JCF-16].

892.20 Our Champions — Fremont And Dayton. w. No composer indicated. m. No tune indicated. In: *The Fremont Campaign Songster*, page 4. Published by Frost & Dory, Publishers, No. 140–142 Vine Street, Cincinnati, OH. 1856. [3½" × 5½"]. B/w litho of John C. Fremont. 32pp. Page 2: "To the Fremont Clubs and the Republican Party throughout the Union, this little volume is Respectfully Dedicated by the Publishers." [M-093]. [Crew/JCF-42].

892.21 Republican Song Of Freedom. w. No composer indicated. m. "Air — *E Pluribus Unum.*" In: *The Fremont Campaign Songster*, page 15. Published by Frost & Dory, Publishers, No. 140–142 Vine Street, Cincinnati, OH. 1856. [3½" × 5½"]. B/w litho of John C. Fremont. 32pp. Page 2: "To the Fremont Clubs and the Republican Party throughout the Union, this little volume is Respectfully Dedicated by the Publishers." [M-093]. [Crew/JCF-42].

892.22 [Sadly The Fugitive Weeps In His Cell]. w. No composer indicated. m. "Air — *Troubador.*" In: *The Fremont Campaign Songster*, page 19. Published by Frost & Dory, Publishers, No. 140–142 Vine Street, Cincinnati, OH. 1856. [3½" × 5½"]. B/w litho of John C. Fremont. 32pp. Page 2: "To the Fremont Clubs and the Republican Party throughout the Union, this little volume is Respectfully Dedicated by the Publishers." [M-093]. [Crew/JCF-42].

892.23 Song For Freedom. w.m. No composer or tune indicated. In: *The Republican Campaign Songster, A Collection Of Lyrics, Original And Selected, Specifically Prepared For The Friends Of Freedom In The Campaign Of Fifty-Six*, page 65. Published by Miller, Orton & Mulligan, No. 25 Park Row, New York, NY. 1856. [3¹³⁄₁₆" × 6"]. Be/bk litho of "Colonel John C. Fremont" facing to viewer's left, black line border. 112pp. [M-097]. [Crew/JCF-24].

892.24 Song For The People. w.m. No composer or tune indicated. Published by Andrews, Printer, 38 Chatham Street, New York, NY. [1856]. [Approx. 6" × 10"]. B/w non-pictorial geometric design litho border. "Andrews, Printer, 38 Chatham Street, N.Y., Songs, Games, Toy Books, Motto Verses, &c., Wholesale and Retail." 2pp. Page 2: Blank. [AMC].

892.25 The Song Of Fifty-Six. w. No composer indicated. m. "Air — *Oh! Hard Times Come Again No More.*" In: *The Republican Campaign Songster, A Collection Of Lyrics, Original And Selected, Specifically Prepared For The Friends Of Freedom In The Campaign Of Fifty-Six*, page 21. Published by Miller, Orton & Mulligan, No. 25 Park Row, New York, NY. 1856. [3¹³⁄₁₆" × 6"]. Be/bk litho of "Colonel John C. Fremont" facing to viewer's left, black line border. 112pp. [M-097]. [Crew/JCF-24].

892.26 [Take Down The Harp Of The Last Campaign] (A Campaign Song). w. No composer indicated. m. "Air — *The Harp That Once In Tara's Halls.*" In: *Republican Song Book*, page 46. c. Thomas Drew "(Late Editor of *The Massachusetts Spy*)." Published by Thayer and Eldridge, Boston, MA. 1860. [3⅞" × 5⅞"]. Br/bk litho of beardless Abraham Lincoln, vignettes of young Lincoln chopping rails, polling raft. 68pp. [M-108]. [Crew/AL-8].

892.27 'Tis Time That Freemen Raise A Hand. w. No composer indicated. m. "Air — *Yankee Doodle.*" In: *The Fremont Campaign Songster*, page 20. Published by Frost & Dory, Publishers, No. 140–142 Vine Street, Cincinnati, OH. 1856. [3½" × 5½"]. B/w litho of John C. Fremont. 32pp. Page 2: "To the Fremont Clubs and the Republican Party throughout the Union, this little volume is Respectfully Dedicated by the Publishers." [M-093]. [Crew/JCF-42].

892.28 The Toast. w. No composer indicated. m. "Air — *Vive La Companie.*" In: *The Freeman's Glee Book, A Collection Of Songs, Odes, Glees And Ballads With Music, Original And Selected, Harmonized And Arranged For Each. Published Under The Auspices Of

The Central Fremont And Dayton Glee Club Of The City Of New York, And Dedicated To All, Who, Cherishing Republican Liberty Consider Freedom Worth A Song, page 94. Published by Miller, Orton & Mulligan, No. 25 Park Row, New York, NY. [and Auburn, NY]. 1856. [4¹⁵⁄₁₆" × 6"]. Pk/bk litho of man on mountain peak, music sheets, geometric designs. 112pp. [Crew/JCF-16].

892.29 Volunteer Song. w. By A Lady. m. "Air—*Ole Dan Tucker*." In: *The Republican Campaign Songster, A Collection Of Lyrics, Original And Selected, Specifically Prepared For The Friends Of Freedom In The Campaign Of Fifty-Six*, page 75. Published by Miller, Orton & Mulligan, No. 25 Park Row, New York, NY. 1856. [3¹³⁄₁₆" × 6"]. Be/bk litho of "Colonel John C. Fremont" facing to viewer's left, black line border. 112pp. [M-097]. [Crew/JCF-24].

892.30 We're For Freedom Through This Land. w. No composer indicated. m. "Air—*The Old Granite State*." In: *The Freeman's Glee Book, A Collection Of Songs, Odes, Glees And Ballads With Music, Original And Selected, Harmonized And Arranged For Each. Published Under The Auspices Of The Central Fremont And Dayton Glee Club Of The City Of New York, And Dedicated To All, Who, Cherishing Republican Liberty Consider Freedom Worth A Song*, page 84. Published by Miller, Orton & Mulligan, No. 25 Park Row, New York, NY. [and Auburn, NY]. 1856. [4¹⁵⁄₁₆" × 6"]. Pk/bk litho of man on mountain peak, music sheets, geometric designs. 112pp. [Crew/JCF-16].

892.31 [What Has Caused This Great Commotion] (A Campaign Song). w. No composer indicated. m. "Air—*Oh! What Has Caused this Great Commotion?*" "From the *Boston Atlas*." In: *The Republican Campaign Songster, A Collection Of Lyrics, Original And Selected, Specifically Prepared For The Friends Of Freedom In The Campaign Of Fifty-Six*, page 40. Published by Miller, Orton & Mulligan, No. 25 Park Row, New York, NY. 1856. [3¹³⁄₁₆" × 6"]. Be/bk litho of "Colonel John C. Fremont" facing to viewer's left, black line border. 112pp. [M-097]. [Crew/JCF-24].

892.32 What Has Caused This Great Commotion (Concluded). w. No composer indicated. m. No composer indicated. In: *The Fremont Songster*, page 16. Published by [V-1: H.S. Riggs & Company, Publishers, No. 4 Cortland Street] [V-2: P.J. Cozans, No. 107 Nassau Street], New York, NY. 1856. [V-1: 3⅝" × 5¾"] [V-2: 3½" × 5⅝"]. Be/bk litho of wreath, John C. Fremont. "With a current likeness of John C. Fremont, The People's Candidate for the Presidency." 40pp. [M-094, 095]. [Crew/JCF-45].

892.33 [When Forth To The Battle The Bold Warrior Rode]. In: *The True Issue* [A Cloth Bandanna/Songster]. Published by the Shawmut Chemical Printing Company, Boston, MA. [1856]. [10¼" × 10¾"]. Cloth bandanna printed with illustration of John C. Fremont. Narrative to either side. Three campaign songs. Rev: Blank. [Crew-JCF-12].

• **AmPM-893 DICKERSON**, Philemon (State House, 1821–1822; U.S. House, 1833–1836 & 1839–1841; Governor, 1836–1837)

893.1 A Parody On Up Salt River. w. No composer indicated. m. "Tune—*All On Hobbies*." In: *Songs For The People (Or Tippecanoe Melodies)* [Songster], page 37. "Dedicated to the Democratic Whig Young Men of the City and County of New York." Published for the Authors by James P. Giffing, No. 56 Gold Street, New York, NY. 1840. [3¾" × 6"]. Litho of William Henry Harrison, log cabin, flag. "Original and Selected." 76pp. [M-019]. [Crew/WHH-63].

893.2 Up Salt River (A New Whig Song). w. G.B.W. (Toledo, OH). m. "Tune—*All On Hobbies*." Published by Firth & Hall, No. 1 Franklin Square, New York, NY. 1840. Non-pictorial. "Respectfully Dedicated to the Toledo Tippecanoe Club." "Pr. 25 c nett [sic]." 4pp. [Crew/ WHH-38].

893.3 Up Salt River (A New Whig Song). w. G.B.W. "of Toledo, Ohio." m. "Tune—*All On Hobbies*." Respectfully dedicated to the Toledo Tippecanoe Club." In: *The Log Cabin & Hard Cider Melodies, A Collection Of Popular And Patriotic Songs*, page 65. Published by Charles Adams, No. 23 Tremont Street, Boston, MA. 1840. [3¾" × 6"]. [V-1: Pk/bk] [V-2: Gn/bk] litho of William Henry Harrison. "The Freeman's glittering Sword be Blest, For ever blest the Freeman's Lyre." 78pp. [M-012]. [Crew/WHH-68].

• **AmPM-894 DILLON**, Clarence Douglas (Alternate Delegate, Republican National Convention, 1952; U.S. Ambassador to France, 1953–1957; U.S. Secretary of the Treasury, 1961–1965)

894.1 Cool Goldwater. w. Noel E. Parmentel, Jr. and Marshall J. Dodge. In: *Folk Songs For Conservatives*, page 11. Published by Unicorn Press, Inc., No. 790 Madison Avenue, New York, NY. 10021. 1964. [5" × 8⅜"]. Bl/w drawings of Barry Goldwater, Bill Buckley, Ray Cohn, eagle. List of contents. "Sung by Noel E. Parmentel, Jr. and His Unbleached Muslims, Greatest Political Satirists Since Cohn and Schine." "Right Wing Hootenanny." 36pp. [Crew/BMG-13].

894.2 I'm Called Little Caroline. w. Milton M. Schwartz. m. "Tune—*I'm Called Little Buttercup*." In: *Sing Along With Jack* [Song Book], page 10. Published by Pocket Books, Inc., New York, NY. Copyright 1963 by Bonny Publishing Corporation. [9" × 11⅞"]. R/w/bk drawing of sheet music *Vive La Dynasty*, silhouette of John F. Kennedy in chair with conductor's baton, caricature of Kennedy family. "Hit Songs from the New Frontier." 36pp. Page 3: "Illustrations by David Gantz." Page 36: Drawing of John F. Kennedy in chair with baton. Song titles. [Crew/JFK-17].

• **AmPM-895 DONNELLY**, Frederick W. (Mayor, Trenton, 1926?)

895.1 Dear Old Trenton. w.m. Albert Watson. Copyright 1926 by Albert Watson. Bl/y reproduction of Washington crossing the Delaware. "Dedicated to the City of Trenton, July, 1926, in Commemoration of the Sesqui-Centennial of the Battle of Trenton, Honorable Frederick W. Donnelly, Mayor." "Sung by William J. Flemming and James Newell with great success." 8pp. Pages 2, 7 and 8: Blank. [Crew/GW-704].

• **AmPM-896 EICHLER**, Robert (Candidate for State House, 1949)

896.1 We'll Change The Scene With Elmer Wene. w. Walter E. Brill. m. Frank T. Grasso. Published by Valemont Music Co., Montvale, NJ. 1949. Bl/w photo of Elmer Wene. R/w/b printing, stars. "The Campaign Song of Elmer H. Wene, Democratic Candidate for Governor of New Jersey." 4pp. + 2pp. insert. Page 4: Bergan County ticket including "Karl D. Van Wagner for State Senator, Lloyd S. Carr, David B. Foley, Patrick Tedesco, Robert Eichler, George B. Chelius, Jr., and Otto J. Stellato for General Assembly, Jacob Schneider, for Surrogate, and James A. Bishop and Francis E. Munley for Freeholders." "On Election Day Nov. 8, 1949."

• **AmPM-897** FISK, Clinton Bowen (Assistant Commissioner of Freedmen's Bureau, 1865; Board of Indian Commissioners, 1874; Candidate for Governor, 1886; Candidate for President, 1888) [ALSO SEE: DOC/PSM-CF]

897.1 A Democratic Toast. w. No composer indicated. m. "Arr. By Tariff Reform." In: *Red Hot Democratic Campaign Songs For 1888*, page 6. e. John Bunyon Herbert. Published by The S. Brainard's Sons Company, Chicago, IL. 1888. [5⅜" × 7⁷⁄₁₆"]. R/bk geometric designs. 36pp. [M-294]. [Crew/GC-141].

897.2 Presidential Ball. w. A.A. Rowley. m. "Air — *Dance By The Light Of The Moon*." In: *Republican Campaign Songs*, page 23. Published by The Western News Company, Chicago, IL. 1888. [5¼" × 7½"]. B/w litho of "The Author, in '63, 17th Illinois Cav." "Original, Pointed and Spicy ... Set to Old Familiar Tunes, Suitable for Glee Clubs and Marching Clubs." "Look at it and you will buy it." 36pp. Page 2, 35 and 36: Blank. Page 3: Index. "Composed for the Campaign of 1888 and Set to Old Familiar Airs, Suitable for Glee Clubs and Campaign Clubs." "Respectfully Dedicated to my Comrades of the Civil War, who still vote the way they fought — A.A. Rowley, Beloit, Kan." [M-283]. [Crew/BFH-64].

897.3 Prohibition Song. [ca. 1880s]. [4¼" × 6¹⁵⁄₁₆"]. Non-pictorial. 2pp. Page 2: Blank. [Crew/CBF-3].

• **AmPM-898** FLEISCHER, Ari (Press secretary to Congressman Norman Lent; Press Secretary for Senator Pete Dominici, 1989–1994; Press Secretary to the President, 2001–2003)

898.1 Ari, Ari. w. Madeleine Begun Kane. Published online at <http://www.madkane.com/ari.html>. "In honor of Ari Fleischer's resignation as Dubya's spokesman, I present my *Ari, Ari*, to be sung to *Monday, Monday* by John Phillips (The Mamas and the Papas). Feel free to use this midi link." [ca. 2003].

898.2 Ari Fleischer. w. William Tong. m. "*Albert Flasher*, originally by The Guess Who." Published online at <http://amiright.com/parody/70s/theguesswho1.shml>. [ca. 2001].

898.3 Ari The Snowman. w. Tom Smith. m. *Frosty The Snowman.* From "A Very Dubya Xmas." "Published online at <http://www.tomsmithonline.com/lyrics/very_dubya_xmas.htm>. 2002.

898.4 Flunkie Ari. w. William Tong. m. "*Brother Louie*, originally by Stories." "Dedicated to Bush Press Secretary Ari Fleischer." Published online at <http://www.amiright.com/parody/misc/stories0.html>. [ca. 2001].

898.5 La Dumbya. w. Alvin Dover. m. "*La Bamba*, originally by Ritchie Valens." Published online at <http://amiright.com/parody/misc/ritchievalens1.shml>. [ca. 2002].

898.6 New Secret Police Running Our Homeland. w. Alvin Dover and Bill Tong. m. "*Sgt. Pepper's Lonely Hearts Club Band*, originally by The Beatles." Published online at <http://www.amiright.com/parody/70s/thebeatles2.shtml>. [ca. 2002].

898.6A Shield Him From This. w. William Tong. m. "*Sealed With A Kiss*, originally by Brian Hyland." "As sung by Karl Rove to Ari Fleischer." Published online at <http://www.amiright.com/parody/60s/brianhymand0.shtml>. [ca. 2002].

898.7 Shred The Constitution. w. Alvin Dover. m. "*Ball Of Confusion*, originally by The Temptations." Published online at <http://www.amiright.com/parody/70s/thetemptations3.shtml>. [ca. 2002].

898.8 Subterranean Homesick Blues. w. Skisics Surus. m. "*Subterranean Homesick Blues*, originally by Bob Dylan." Published online at <http://amiright.com/parody/60s/bobdylan5.shml>. [ca. 2001].

• **AmPM-899** FOLEY, David B. (Candidate for State House, 1949)

899.1 We'll Change The Scene With Elmer Wene. w. Walter E. Brill. m. Frank T. Grasso. Published by Valemont Music Co., Montvale, NJ. 1949. Bl/w photo of Elmer Wene. R/w/b printing, stars. "The Campaign Song of Elmer H. Wene, Democratic Candidate for Governor of New Jersey." 4pp. + 2pp. insert. Page 4: Bergan County ticket including "Karl D. Van Wagner for State Senator, Lloyd S. Carr, David B. Foley, Patrick Tedesco, Robert Eichler, George B. Chelius, Jr., and Otto J. Stellato for General Assembly, Jacob Schneider, for Surrogate, and James A. Bishop and Francis E. Munley for Freeholders." "On Election Day Nov. 8, 1949."

• **AmPM-900** FORBES, Malcolm Stevenson, Jr. (Candidate for Republican nomination for President, 1996, 2000)

900.1 Grand Old Party. w. William K. Tong. m. "Sung to the tune of *Garden Party* by Rick Nelson." In: *The Sting The Right Wing Song Book* at <http://www.geocities.com/wmktong/bootnewt/goparty.htm>.

900.2 Nine Little Leaders. w. William K. Tong. m. "Sung to the tune of *Nine Little Reindeers* by Gene Autry." In: *The Sting The Right Wing Song Book* at <http://www.geocities.com/wmktong/bootnewt/9litlead.htm>.

900.3 Robert Dole's Speeches. w. William K. Tong. m. "Sung to the tune of *Rock & Roll Music* by Chuck Berry." In: *The Sting The Right Wing Song Book* at <http://www.geocities.com/wmktong/bootnewt/speeches.htm>.

• **AmPM-901** FRELINGHUYSEN, Joseph Sherman (State Senate, 1906–1912; U.S. Senate, 1917–1923)

901.1 Our Flag Old Glory (March Song-One Step). w.m. Paul G. Zimmerman, Publisher, Morristown, NJ. 1917. Non-pictorial geometric designs. "Respectfully Dedicated to Mr. Joseph S. Frelinghuysen, United States Senator of New Jersey (By Permission)." 4pp. Page 4: Blank.

• **AmPM-902** FRELINGHUYSEN, Theodore (State Attorney General, 1817–1829; U.S. Senate, 1829–1835; Mayor, Newark, 1837–1838; Candidate for Vice President, 1844) [ALSO SEE: DOC/PSM-HC]

902.1 Away With Traitor Tyler. w. No composer indicated. m. "Tune — *Away With Melancholy*." "Written for the Choir of the National Clay Club." In: *The National Clay Minstrel*, page 16. Published by [V-1: George Hood, No. 15 North 6th Street, Philadelphia, PA] [V-2: James Fisher, No. 71 Court Street, Boston, MA]. 1843. [3" × 4½"]. Y/bk litho of raccoon sitting on fence, black border. 68pp. Pages 2 and 67: Blank. Pages 65–66: Contents. [Crew/HC-10].

902.2 The Blue Hen's Chickens. w. J.A. Allderdice, "of Wilmington, Del." m. "Tune — *Old Dan Tucker.*" B/w litho of a setting hen. "Delaware." In: *The National Clay Minstrel*, page 12. Published by [V-1: George Hood, No. 15 North 6th Street, Philadelphia, PA] [V-2: James Fisher, No. 71 Court Street, Boston, MA]. 1843. [3" × 4½"]. Y/bk litho of raccoon sitting on fence, black border. 68pp. Pages 2 and 67: Blank. Pages 65–66: Contents. [Crew/HC-10].

902.3 Clay And Frelinghuysen. w. J. Greiner. m. "Tune — *Old Dan Tucker.*" In: *The National Clay Minstrel*, page 1. Published by [V-1: George Hood, No. 15 North 6th Street, Philadelphia, PA] [V-2: James Fisher, No. 71 Court Street, Boston, MA]. 1843. [3" × 4½"]. Y/bk litho of raccoon sitting on fence, black border. 68pp. Pages 2 and 67: Blank. Pages 65–66: Contents. [Crew/HC-10].

902.4 Clay And Frelinghuysen. w. No composer indicated. m. "Music — *Old Dan Tucker.*" On 33⅓ rpm LP: *Sing Along With Millard Fillmore.* Life Records #RB 360 T2/#61 P3. "The Life Album of Presidential Campaign Songs." 1964.

902.5 Clay And Frelinghuysen. w. No composer indicated. m. "Tune — *Lucy Neal.*" In: *The National Clay Minstrel*, page 31. Published by [V-1: George Hood, No. 15 North 6th Street, Philadelphia, PA] [V-2: James Fisher, No. 71 Court Street, Boston, MA]. 1843. [3" × 4½"]. Y/bk litho of raccoon sitting on fence, black border. 68pp. [Crew/HC-10].

902.6 Come Friends, Gather 'Round. w. No composer indicated. m. "Tune — *Lucy Neal.*" In: *The National Clay Minstrel*, page 20. Published by [V-1: George Hood, No. 15 North 6th Street, Philadelphia, PA] [V-2: James Fisher, No. 71 Court Street, Boston, MA]. 1843. [3" × 4½"]. Y/bk litho of raccoon sitting on fence, black border. 68pp. [Crew/HC-10].

902.7 The Fighting Captain. w. F.B. Graham, Esq. m. "Tune — *It Will Never Do To Give It Up So Soon.*" B/w litho of a ship with banner reading "Don't Give Up The Ship." In: *The National Clay Minstrel*, page 24. Published by [V-1: George Hood, No. 15 North 6th Street, Philadelphia, PA] [V-2: James Fisher, No. 71 Court Street, Boston, MA]. 1843. [3" × 4½"]. Y/bk litho of raccoon sitting on fence, black border. 68pp. [Crew/HC-10].

902.8 The First Polk Song. w. No composer indicated. m. "Tune — *Old Dan Tucker.*" In: *The National Clay Minstrel*, page 26. Published by [V-1: George Hood, No. 15 North 6th Street, Philadelphia, PA] [V-2: James Fisher, No. 71 Court Street, Boston, MA]. 1843. [3" × 4½"]. Y/bk litho of raccoon sitting on fence, black border. 68pp. Pages 2 and 67: Blank. Pages 65–66: Contents. [Crew/HC-10].

902.9 Harry The True And The Jersey Blue. w. F. Buckingham Graham. m. "Tune — *What Has Caused This Great Commotion.*" In: *The National Clay Minstrel*, page 9. Published by [V-1: George Hood, No. 15 North 6th Street, Philadelphia, PA] [V-2: James Fisher, No. 71 Court Street, Boston, MA]. 1843. [3" × 4½"]. Y/bk litho of raccoon sitting on fence, black border. 68pp. [Crew/HC-10].

902.10 Henry Clay And Frelinghuysen. w.m. No composer or tune indicated. In: *The National Clay Almanac, 1845*, page 30. Published by Desilver & Muir, No. 18 South Fourth Street, Philadelphia, PA. 1844. [6¹³⁄₁₆" × 7⅞"]. B/w litho of Henry Clay, ship — "Commerce," plow, crops — "Agriculture." [Crew/HC-89].

902.11 Hurrah Song. w.m. No composer or tune indicated. In: *The National Clay Minstrel*, page 21. Published by [V-1: George Hood, No. 15 North 6th Street, Philadelphia, PA] [V-2: James Fisher, No. 71 Court Street, Boston, MA]. 1843. [3" × 4½"]. Y/bk litho of raccoon sitting on fence, black border. 68pp. [Crew/HC-10].

902.12 Jimmie Polk Of Tennessee. w. J. Greiner. m. "Tune — *Dandy Jim Of Caroline.*" In: *The National Clay Minstrel*, page 2. Published by [V-1: George Hood, No. 15 North 6th Street, Philadelphia, PA] [V-2: James Fisher, No. 71 Court Street, Boston, MA]. 1843. [3" × 4½"]. Y/bk litho of raccoon sitting on fence, black border. 68pp. [Crew/HC-10].

902.13 Kilkenny Cats. w. No composer indicated. m. "Tune — *Old Dan Tucker.*" In: *The National Clay Minstrel*, page 12. Published by [V-1: George Hood, No. 15 North 6th Street, Philadelphia, PA] [V-2: James Fisher, No. 71 Court Street, Boston, MA]. 1843. [3" × 4½"]. Y/bk litho of raccoon sitting on fence, black border. 68pp. [Crew/HC-10].

902.14 A New Song. w. No composer indicated. m. "Tune — *Old Rosin The Bow.*" In: *The National Clay Minstrel*, page 18. Published by [V-1: George Hood, No. 15 North 6th Street, Philadelphia, PA] [V-2: James Fisher, No. 71 Court Street, Boston, MA]. 1843. [3" × 4½"]. Y/bk litho of raccoon sitting on fence, black border. 68pp. Pages 2 and 67: Blank. Pages 65–66: Contents. [Crew/HC-10].

902.15 Salt River. w. F.B. Graham, Esq. m. "Tune — *In Good Old Colony Times.*" "Written for the Choir attached to the Philade. National Clay Club." B/w litho of man on horse with bugle. In: *The National Clay Minstrel*, page 17. Published by [V-1: George Hood, No. 15 North 6th Street, Philadelphia, PA] [V-2: James Fisher, No. 71 Court Street, Boston, MA]. 1843. [3" × 4½"]. Y/bk litho of raccoon sitting on fence, black border. 68pp. [Crew/HC-10].

902.16 Song Of The Young Whigs. w. No composer indicated. m. "Air — *What Fairy-Like Music.*" In: *The National Clay Minstrel*, page 60. Published by [V-1: George Hood, No. 15 North 6th Street, Philadelphia, PA] [V-2: James Fisher, No. 71 Court Street, Boston, MA]. 1843. [3" × 4½"]. Y/bk litho of raccoon sitting on fence, black border. 68pp. [Crew/HC-10].

902.17 Vermont Whig Song. w. "That Same Old Whig." m. No tune indicated. No publisher indicated. [1844]. B/w litho of a raccoon, geometric design border. 2pp. Page 2: Blank. [Crew/HC-128]. [AMC].

902.18 The Vermonter's Song At Baltimore. w. No composer indicated. m. "Tune — *Old Dan Tucker.*" In: *The National Clay Minstrel*, page 6. Published by [V-1: George Hood, No. 15 North 6th Street, Philadelphia, PA] [V-2: James Fisher, No. 71 Court Street,

Boston, MA]. 1843. [3" × 4½"]. Y/bk litho of raccoon sitting on fence, black border. 68pp. [Crew/HC-10].

902.19 Whig Song. w. No composer indicated. m. "Tune — *Willie Brew'd A Peck O' Maut."* "Written for the Choir of the National Clay Club." In: *The National Clay Minstrel,* page30. Published by [V-1: George Hood, No. 15 North 6th Street, Philadelphia, PA] [V-2: James Fisher, No. 71 Court Street, Boston, MA]. 1843. [3" × 4½"]. Y/bk litho of raccoon sitting on fence, black border. 68pp. [Crew/HC-10].

• **AmPM-903** HAGUE, Frank (Mayor, Jersey City, 1917–1947; Vice-Chairman of Democratic National Committee, 1929)

903.1 Franklin, Can You Spare A Job? m. "Air — *Brother, Can You Spare A Dime."* In: *Foam Sweet Foam,* page 12. Published by Albany Legislative Correspondents' Association, Albany, NY. 1933. [8" × 11¾"]. N/c drawing by Jerry Costello of Franklin D. Roosevelt, Al Smith and other politicians riding a bottle of beer — "The Lager Limited." "A Rollicking Review Rotating on Resurrection of Bouncing Beverages, Tipsily Tapped at Ten Eyck Hotel Rathskeller, Albany, New York, the evening of Thursday, February 23, 1933, at Seven-Thirty o'clock." 20pp. [Crew/FDR-277].

903.2 We Are Democrats, Too. w. No composer indicated. m. "Tune — *I'm An Indian, Too."* In: *Alice In Blunderland Or Through The Rooking Class* [Program and Songbook], page 22. Published by The Legislative Correspondents' Association of New York State, Albany, NY. 1949. [8⅝" × 11"]. N/c drawings of Harry Truman, Thomas Dewey, Franklin Roosevelt, Henry Wallace, Harold Stassen, Alben Barkley, Robert Taft, Earl Warren, other politicians. "A Scintillating Satire of Sadistic Surprises and Surprising Successes Featuring a Dramatic Disclosure of How Tom Did Not Go Down to D.C. in Slips; Together with a Give-Away-Nothing Radio Broadcast and Epic Melodrama of the Indian Wars Entitled 'When the Cat's Away the Mice Will Play.'" "Done With Music and Mirrors — Particularly Mirrors in Three Acts at Hotel Ten Eyck, Albany, March 12, 1949." [Crew/HST-20].

903.3 We're For You Harry Truman. w. No composer indicated. m. "Tune — *Let Him Go, Let Him Tarry."* In: *Alice In Blunderland Or Through The Rooking Class* [Program and Songbook], page 10. Published by The Legislative Correspondents' Association of New York State, Albany, NY. 1949. [8⅝" × 11"]. N/c drawings of Harry Truman, Thomas Dewey, Franklin Roosevelt, Henry Wallace, Harold Stassen, Alben Barkley, Robert Taft, Earl Warren, other politicians. "A Scintillating Satire of Sadistic Surprises and Surprising Successes Featuring a Dramatic Disclosure of How Tom Did Not Go Down to D.C. in Slips; Together with a Give-Away-Nothing Radio Broadcast and Epic Melodrama of the Indian Wars Entitled 'When the Cat's Away the Mice Will Play.'" "Done With Music and Mirrors — Particularly Mirrors in Three Acts at Hotel Ten Eyck, Albany, March 12, 1949." [Crew/HST-20].

• **AmPM-904** HALSTEAD, William (Prosecuting Attorney, Hunterdon County, 1824–1829; U.S. House, 1837–1839 & 1841–1843)

904.1 Up Salt River (A New Whig Song). w. G.B.W. (Toledo, OH). m. "Tune — *All On Hobbies."* Published by Firth & Hall, No. 1 Franklin Square, New York, NY. 1840. Non-pictorial. "Respectfully Dedicated to the Toledo Tippecanoe Club." "Pr. 25 c nett [sic]." 4pp. [Crew/WHH-38].

904.2 Up Salt River (A New Whig Song). w. G.B.W. "of Toledo, Ohio." m. "Tune — *All On Hobbies."* "Respectfully dedicated to the Toledo Tippecanoe Club." In: *The Log Cabin & Hard Cider Melodies, A Collection Of Popular And Patriotic Songs,* page 65. Published by Charles Adams, No. 23 Tremont Street, Boston, MA. 1840. [3¾" × 6"]. [V-1: Pk/bk] [V-2: Gn/bk] litho of William Henry Harrison. "The Freeman's glittering Sword be Blest, For ever blest the Freeman's Lyre." 78pp. [M-012]. [Crew/WHH-68].

• **AmPM-905** HART, John (Provincial Assembly of New Jersey, 1761–1771; Judge, Hunterdon County, 1768–1775; New Jersey Provincial Congress, 1775–1776; Committee of Safety, 1775–1778; Continental Congress, 1776; Signer of the Declaration of Independence, 1776; General Assembly, 1776–1778)

905.1 The Declaration Of Independence Of The United States Of North America, July 4, 1776. w. From the Declaration of Independence. m. John E. Wilson. Published by John E. Wilson, Baltimore, MD. 1863. B/w litho of the interior of Independence Hall. "Arranged and adapted for Vocal and Instrumental Music as the Great National Chant." 4pp. [?]. Page 4: Facsimile signatures of all signers.

905.2 Old Independence Hall. w. A. Fletcher Stayman. m. Francis Weiland. Published by Stayman & Brothers, No. 210 Chesnut Street, Philadelphia, PA. 1855. Non-pictorial. "Respectfully dedicated to the Memory of the Signers of the Declaration of Independence." "Fac Simile of their signatures" including John Adams, Sam Adams, Elbridge Gerry, Thomas Jefferson. 8pp. Pages 2 and 8: Blank. [Crew/MISC-34].

• **AmPM-906** HARTLEY, Jr., Fred Allan (Library Commissioner, Kearny, 1923–1924; Police & Fire Commissioner, Kearney, 1934–1928; U.S. House, 1929–1949)

906.1 [Don't Vote For Dewey]. w. Bill Leader. m. "Sing to the tune of *Four Leaf Clover."* [1948]. 4½" × 6"]. R/w/b litho of clover leafs, geometric design border. 2pp. Page 2: Blank.

906.1A Eisenhower, Hold That Line. w.m. Lee Thornsby. On: *Grand Old Party Songs.* 33⅓ rpm 10" record. Published by Middlesex Trading Company, #G8-OL-7518. Performed by Eli Frantz and his Magic Guitar. [ca. 195-].

906.2 The Hartly Bill (Or The Bosses Solidarity Song), w. no composer indicated. m. "*John Brown's Body."* "Back in the 40's, the Taft-Hartley Bill, severely cutting back on many of the legal benefits unions had enjoyed since the mid-30s, was passed." "From the Person's Songbook, University of Chicago. 1848." Lyrics and sound file published online at <http://www.mudcat.org/kids/@ displaysong.cfm?SongID=6433>. [199-].

906.3 Have A Heart, Taft-Hartley, Have A Heart! w.m. Jack Lawrence. Published by Whale Music Corp., Six Saint Luke's Place, New York, NY. 1947. R/w/bk drawing of two men [politicians], holding out arms at arm's length against labor's heart. "When labor starts a-votin' then your fancy bill's all go up in smoke

... CIO Political Action Committee." 6pp. Page 6: Profile of Jack Lawrence.

906.4 Use Your Ballot. w. Louise Jeffers. m. No tune indicated. In: *Songs For A New Party*, page 12. Copyright 1948 by People's Songs. [3½" × 7"]. Non-pictorial. "Music for these songs in *Songs For Wallace*." "Permission for use on television, newsreel, radio, &c., can easily be obtained from People's Songs by calling WA 9-2356 (NYC)." 16pp. [M-429]. [Crew/HAW-5].

906.5 The Wallace Shout. w.m. Bryan M. French. *Songs For Wallace*, page 7. Published by People's Song, Inc. for the National Office of The Progressive Party, No. 39 Park Avenue, New York, NY. 1948. [8⅜" × 10¼"]. B/w drawing of Henry A. Wallace, farm. 12pp. [M-428]. [Crew/HAW-3].

• **AmPM-906A HOBART**, Garret Augustus (City Council, Paterson, 1871–1872; Council for Board of Freeholders, 1872; State House, 1872–1876; State Senate, 1876–1882; Vice-President, 1897–1899) [ALSO SEE: DOC/PSM-WM]

906A.1 After The Election. w. No composer indicated. m. "Air—*After The Ball*." In: *McKinley And Hobart Song Book*, page 19. c.w.a. G.E. Treadway. Published by G.E. Treadway, Pittsburgh, PA. 1896. [5" × 6⅝"]. R/w/b litho of William McKinley and Garret Hobart, flag design. "Now used by the celebrated Tariff Club Quartette of Pittsburgh, Pa." 28pp. [M-349]. [Crew/WM-256].

906A.2 All For McKinley And Hobart. w. No composer indicated. m. "Air—*Marching Through Georgia*." In: *McKinley And Hobart Song Book*, page 4. c.w.a. G.E. Treadway. Published by G.E. Treadway, Pittsburgh, PA. 1896. [5" × 6⅝"]. R/w/b litho of William McKinley and Garret Hobart, flag design. "Now used by the celebrated Tariff Club Quartette of Pittsburgh, Pa." 28pp. [M-349]. [Crew/WM-256].

906A.3 America—My Country 'Tis Of Thee. w.m. No composers indicated. No publisher indicated. [1896]. [5" × 8"]. B/w litho of American flag, geometric designs. "Republican Wigwam Opening! McKinley & Hobart Campaign Song." 2pp. Page 2: Blank. [Crew/WM-345].

906A.4 Coining The Silvery Southern Moon. w. No composer indicated. m. "Tune—*Alabama Coon*." In: *Republican Campaign Parodies And Songs* [Songster], page 19. Published by Betts and Burnett, South Butler, Wayne County, NY. 1896. [7¾" × 5½"]. Be/bk non-pictorial. "McKinley and Hobart." "1896." 28pp. [M-340]. [Crew/WM-67].

906A.5 The Dinner-Pail Brigade. w. Edwin Oliver, "a Laborer." m. "Air—*Little German Home Across The Sea*." In: *Republican Bugle Blasts, Rally Songs For The Campaign Of 1896*, page 10. Published by Norman G. Lenington, No. 308 Dearborn Street, Chicago, IL. 1896. [5½" × 8¾"]. Br/bk drawings of William McKinley and Garret Hobart. Advertising. 24pp. [M-335; Crew/WM-229].

906A.6 Good-Bye. w. No composer indicated. m. "Air—*Good-Bye, My Lover, Good-Bye*." In: *McKinley And Hobart Song Book*, page 10. c.w.a. G.E. Treadway. Published by G.E. Treadway, Pittsburgh, PA. 1896. [5" × 6⅝"]. R/w/b litho of William McKinley and Garret Hobart, flag design. "Now used by the celebrated Tariff Club Quartette of Pittsburgh, Pa." 28pp. [M-349]. [Crew/WM-256].

906A.7 Hurrah For McKinley And Hobart. w. Edwin Oliver. m. "College Air arr. by O.E.M." "Male Trio." In: *Republican Bugle Blasts, Rally Songs For The Campaign Of 1896*, page 7. Published by Norman G. Lenington, No. 308 Dearborn Street, Chicago, IL. 1896. [5½" × 8¾"]. Br/bk drawings of William McKinley and Garret Hobart. Advertising. 24pp. [M-335; Crew/WM-229].

906A.8 McKinley And Hobart. w. No composer indicated. m. "Air—*When Summer Comes Again*." In: *McKinley And Hobart Song Book*, page 12. c.w.a. G.E. Treadway. Published by G.E. Treadway, Pittsburgh, PA. 1896. [5" × 6⅝"]. R/w/b litho of William McKinley and Garret Hobart, flag design. "Now used by the celebrated Tariff Club Quartette of Pittsburgh, Pa." 28pp. [M-349]. [Crew/WM-256].

906A.9 McKinley And Hobart. m. Turner, Op. 356. In: *42 Marches And Quicksteps*. Published by F. Trifet, Publisher, 36 Bromfield Street, Boston, MA. [1896]. 132pp. [Crew/WM-360].

906A.10 McKinley & Hobart March And Two Step. m. Leon O. Underhill. Published by The Underhill Music Company, Rochester, NY. 1896. R/e non-pictorial. "The Latest." 6pp. Pages 2 and 6: Blank. [Crew/WM-350].

906A.11 McKinley Campaign Song. w. J.R. Nutting. m. "Melody: *John Brown*." 1896. [6⅛" × 11"]. Non-pictorial. "Written for the McKinley and Hobart Ratification Meeting at Davenport, Iowa, June 23, 1896." 2pp. Page 2: Blank. [Crew/WM-339].

906A.12 McKinley, Hobart And Protection. w. No composer indicated. m. "Air—*Marching Through Georgia*." In: *McKinley And Hobart Song Book*, page 23. c.w.a. G.E. Treadway. Published by G.E. Treadway, Pittsburgh, PA. 1896. [5" × 6⅝"]. R/w/b litho of William McKinley and Garret Hobart, flag design. "Now used by the celebrated Tariff Club Quartette of Pittsburgh, Pa." 28pp. [M-349]. [Crew/WM-256].

906A.13 McKinley, Protection And Gold. w. No composer indicated. m. "Tune—*Comrades*." "Money as sound as the Government itself and as untarnished as its honor—William McKinley." In: *Republican Campaign Parodies And Songs* [Songster], page 17. Published by Betts and Burnett, South Butler, Wayne County, NY. 1896. [7¾" × 5½"]. Be/bk non-pictorial. "McKinley and Hobart." "1896." 28pp. [M-340]. [Crew/WM-67].

906A.14 McKinley's Dinner Pail. w. C.B.R. m. C.W. Bennett. In: *The Golden Glory! (Republican Songster for 1896)*, page 8. Published by Echo Music Company, Lafayette, IN. 1896. [5⁵⁄₁₆" × 7¾"]. Bl/w litho of William "McKinley" and Garret "Hobart." R/w/b geometric designs. 26pp. [M-327]. [Crew/WM-279].

906A.15 The Peoples Choice (March and Two Step). m. Albert J. Robinson "(Bandmaster of Robinson's 29 Reg'mt Band of N.J.)." Published by Alberto Himan, No. 146 West 23rd Street, New York, NY. 1896. B/w photo of Garret A. Hobart, facsimile signature. "Respectfully dedicated to the Hon. Garret A. Hobart." [Crew/WM-332].

906A.16 Singing The Song Of Protection. w. No composer indicated. m. "Tune—*Shouting The Battle*

Cry Of Freedom." In: *Republican Campaign Parodies And Songs* [Songster], page 24. Published by Betts and Burnett, South Butler, Wayne County, NY. 1896. [7¾" × 5½"]. Be/bk non-pictorial. "McKinley and Hobart." "1896." 28pp. [M-340]. [Crew/WM-67].

906A.17 *Springing To The Call*. w. No composer indicated. m. "Tune — *The Battle Cry Of Freedom*." In: *Republican Campaign Parodies And Songs* [Songster], page 18. Published by Betts and Burnett, South Butler, Wayne County, NY. 1896. [7¾" × 5½"]. Be/bk non-pictorial. "McKinley and Hobart." "1896." 28pp. [M-340]. [Crew/WM-67].

906A.18 *Stand By McKinley*. w. John Wilson, "With energy." m. Tune — "*Upidee*." In: *National Campaigner (Marching Songs Republican Clubs)* [Song Book], page 20. Published by Dudley T. Limerick & Company, No. 4031 Locust Street, Philadelphia, PA. 1896. [6⅜" × 9¾"]. Non-pictorial. "The slogan: McKinley is Coming! O! ho! O! ho!" List of contents Long narrative on marching songs. 24pp. [M-336]. [Crew/WM-271].

906A.19 *Vote For McKinley And Hobart*. w. Edwin Oliver, "a Laborer." m. "Air — *When Johnny Comes Marching Home*." In: *Republican Bugle Blasts, Rally Songs For The Campaign Of 1896*, page 12. Published by Norman G. Lenington, No. 308 Dearborn Street, Chicago, IL. 1896. [5½" × 8¾"]. Br/bk drawings of William McKinley and Garret Hobart. Advertising. 24pp. [M-335; Crew/WM-229].

• **AmPM-907 HOFFMAN**, Harold G. Rep. (City Treasurer, South Amboy, 1920–1925; State House, 1923–1924; Mayor, South Amboy, 1925–1926; U.S. House, 1927–1931; Governor, 1935–1938)

907.1 *H-O-F-F-M-A-N*. w.m. Amos Harker. Published by the Hoffman Campaign, Paid for by B.L. Lamb. Copyright 1934 by Harry Engel, Inc., 1619 Broadway, New York, NY. 1934. Bl/w photos of Harold Hoffman and musical group "The Hoffman Four." "Introduced by the Hoffman Four." Bl/w drawing of the State House dome. 4pp. Page 4: Narrative on Harold Hoffman's career.

• **AmPM-908 HOPKINSON**, Francis (Collector of Customs, Salem, 1763; Provincial Council, New Jersey, 1774–1776; Continental Congress, 1776; Signer of the Declaration of Independence; 1776; Navy Board, Philadelphia, 1777; Treasurer of the Continental Loan Office, 1778; Judge of the Admiralty Court of Pennsylvania, 1779–1780 & 1787; U.S. District Court for the Eastern District of Pennsylvania, 1789–1791)

908.1 *American Independence*. w. Francis Hopkinson, Esq., "Author of the *Battle Of The Kegs*." In: *The New National Song Book, Containing Songs, Odes, And Other Poems On National Subjects Compiled From Various Sources*, page 16. Published by Leavitt and Allen, No. 379 Broadway, New York, NY. [1841]. [3½" × 5¼"]. Gd/br non-pictorial designs on hardback cover. Spine printed with title. 172pp. [Crew/GW-675].

908.2 *American Independence Established*. w. Francis Hopkinson, Esq. m. No tune indicated. In: *The Republican Harmonist (Being A Select Collection Of Republican, Patriotic, And Sentimental Songs, Odes, Sonnets, &c, American And European: Some Of Which Are Original, And Most Of The Others Now Come For The First Time From An American Press)*, page 69. c. D.E. [Daniel Ebsworth] "(A Citizen of the World)." Printed "for the People," Boston, MA. 1801. Non-pictorial. 152pp. [Crew/TJ-10].

908.3 *An Anthem From The 114th Psalm*. w.m. Francis Hopkinson. In: *A Volume Of Songs*, page 180. Self-published. [1759–1760]. [S/U, page 28].

908.4 *Battle Of The Kegs*. w. Francis Hopkinson, Esq. m. "Tune — *Mauggy Lauder*." In: *The Republican Harmonist (Being A Select Collection Of Republican, Patriotic, And Sentimental Songs, Odes, Sonnets, &c, American And European: Some Of Which Are Original, And Most Of The Others Now Come For The First Time From An American Press)*, page 69. c. D.E. [Daniel Ebsworth] "(A Citizen of the World)." Printed "for the People," Boston, MA. 1801. Non-pictorial. 152pp. [Crew/TJ-10].

908.5 *Battle Of The Kegs*. w. Francis Hopkinson. In: *The American Patriotic Songbook, A Collection Of Political, Descriptive, And Humorous Songs Of National Character And The Production Of American Poets Only, Interspersed With A Number Set To Music*, page 75. Published & Sold by W. M'Culloch, No. 306 Market Street, Philadelphia, PA. 1813. 108pp. Page 3: Title page — *American Patriotic Songbook, A Collection Of Political, Descriptive, And Humorous Songs Of National Character And The Production Of American Poets Only, Interspersed With A Number Set To Music*. "To Hull, and such heroes, a garland we raise, their valour in battle exultingly praise." [W-122].

908.6 *Battle Of The Kegs*. w. Francis Hopkinson. m. No tune indicated. In: *The New National Song Book, Containing Songs, Odes, And Other Poems On National Subjects Compiled From Various Sources*, page 150. Published by Leavitt and Allen, No. 379 Broadway, New York, NY. [1841]. [3½" × 5¼"]. Gd/br non-pictorial designs on hardback cover. Spine printed with title. 172pp.

908.7 *The Battle Of The Kegs*. w. Francis Hopkinson. m. *Yankee Doodle*. Lyrics and sound file published by Mudcat Café online at <http://www.mudcat.org/kids/@displaysong.cfm?SongID=5875>. [199-].

908.8 *The Declaration Of Independence Of The United States Of North America, July 4, 1776*. w. From the Declaration of Independence. m. John E. Wilson. Published by John E. Wilson, Baltimore, MD. 1863. B/w litho of the interior of Independence Hall. "Arranged and adapted for Vocal and Instrumental Music as the Great National Chant." 4pp. [?]. Page 4: Facsimile signatures of all signers.

908.9 *An Exercise Containing A Dialogue And Ode* (On the Accession of His Present Gracious Majesty, George III). [Dialogue] by Rev. Mr. Duehé. [Ode] by Francis Hopkinson. Printed by W. Dunlap, in Market Street, Philadelphia, [PA] 1762. 8pp. "Performed at the public commencement in the College of Philadelphia, May 18th, 1762." [S/U, p. 130].

908.10 *An Exercise Containing A Dialogue And Ode* (Sacred to the Memory of His late Gracious Majesty, George II). [Dialogue] by Rev. Dr. Smith. [Ode] by Francis Hopkinson. Printed by W. Dunlap, in Market Street, Philadelphia, [PA] 1761. 8pp. "Performed at the public commencement in the College of Philadelphia, May 20th, 1766."

908.11 The Garland. w.m. Francis Hopkinson, In: *A Volume Of Songs*, page 111. Self-published. [1759-1760]. [S/U, page 28].

908.12 [Give Me Thy Heart As I Give Mine] (A New Song). w.m. Francis Hopkinson. Published in *The Columbian Magazine*, page 490. August, 1789. [S/U, p. 165].

908.13 In Memory Of Mr. James Bremner (A Dirge). w.m. Francis Hopkinson. In: *Miscellaneous Writings*, v. III, page 184. ca. 1780. "Recitative and air." [S/U, p. 205].

908.14 My Days Have Been So Wonderous Free. w.m. Francis Hopkinson, In: *A Volume Of Songs*, page 63. Self-published. [1759-1760]. [S/U, page 282].

908.15 An Ode Designed For A Public Commencement In The College Of Philadelphia. w.m. Francis Hopkinson. In: *Miscellaneous Essays*, v. III, page 89.

908.16 Ode From Ossian's Poems. w.m. Francis Hopkinson. [179-] or [1803-1807]. Sold at Carr's Music Store, Baltimore, MD. "The music composed by The Honourable Francis Hopkinson." 6pp. [S/U, p. 311] [W-4290].

908.17 An Ode Set To Music On Mrs. B — s Birthday. w.m. Francis Hopkinson. In: *Occasional Poems, Miscellaneous Essays*, v. III, page 89. [S/U. p. 312].

908.18 Oh Come to Mason Borough's Grove. w.m. Francis Hopkinson, In: *A Volume Of Songs*, page 163. Self-published. [1759-1760]. [S/U, p. 28].

908.19 Old Independence Hall. w. A. Fletcher Stayman. m. Francis Weiland. Published by Stayman & Brothers, No. 210 Chesnut Street, Philadelphia, PA. 1855. Non-pictorial. "Respectfully dedicated to the Memory of the Signers of the Declaration of Independence." "Fac Simile of their signatures" including John Adams, Sam Adams, Elbridge Gerry, Thomas Jefferson. 8pp. Pages 2 and 8: Blank. [Crew/MISC-34].

908.20 The Raising (A New Song For Federal Mechanics). w. Francis Hopkinson. m. No tune indicated. Published in the *Pennsylvania Gazette*, February 6, 1788. [VBL, p. 106].

908.21 Seven Songs For Harpsichord. w.m. Francis Hopkinson. [November 20, 1788]. 11pp. "To His Excellency George Washington, Esquire." [S/U. page 403].

908.22 The Temple Of Minerva. w.m. Francis Hopkinson. Published in *Freeman's Journal*, Philadelphia, December 19, 1781. "An oratorio entertainment performed in Nov. 1781, by a company of gentlemen and ladies in the hotel of the minister of France in presence of his Excellency George Washington and his Lady." [S/U, p. 424].

908.23 Three Rondos (For the Piano Forte or Harpsichord). m. William Brown. Printed and sold by the Author, Philadelphia, PA. 1787. "Composed and humbly dedicated to the Honourable Francis Hopkinson." "Price Two Dollars." 8pp.

908.24 A Toast. w.m. Francis Hopkinson. In: *Brother Soldiers All Hail! (A Favorite New Patriotic Song In Honor Of Washington,* page 4. Printed & sold at B. Carr's Musical Repository, Philadelphia, J. Carr's Baltimore & J. Hewitt's, New York, NY. [1799]. [Crew/GW-11]. [S/U, p. 50].

908.25 The 23rd Psalm. w.m. Francis Hopkinson, In: *A Volume Of Songs*, page 179. Self-published. [1759-1760]. [S/U, p. 28].

908.26 With Pleasure Have I Past My Days. w.m. Francis Hopkinson, In: *A Volume Of Songs*, page 169. Self-published. [1759-1760]. [S/U. page 28].

HOPKINSON, Joseph (State Assembly, 18??) [See: Pennsylvania]

• **AmPM-909   KING**, Warren C. King (Republican Candidate for Governor, ca. 1919)

909.1 We'll March Into Trenton With King. No composer indicated. Published by King League State Headquarters, Bergen Square, Jersey City, N.J." [ca. 1920]. Bl/w photo of Warren C. King. Bl/w geometric and floral designs. "Play and Sing this Lively March Song." "Warren C. King, Candidate for the Republican Nomination for Governor of New Jersey." 4pp. Page 4: Platform for Warren King. "Hon. Charles A. Bloomfield, President, Metuchen, N.J."

• **AmPM-909A   KRAJEWSKI**, Henry B. (Candidate for President, 1952 & 1956; Candidate for Governor, 1953, 1957 & 1961; Candidate for U.S. Senate, 1954). [SEE: DOC/PSM-HK]

• **AmPM-910   KRUEGER.** (Judge, Newark, 1896)

910.1 The Judge Grand March. m. Wenham Smith. Published by Wm. E. Ashmall & Co., New York, NY. 1896. B/w photo of Judge Kruegar. Ma/w geometric designs. "Composed and dedicated to the Honorable Judge Krueger." "Played by Sousas Band at Manhattan Beach." "By the same Composer for piano, *Bertha Gavotte Moderne, Lilian Valse Caprise, Ziegner Tanz Gipsy Dance.*" 8pp. Page 2: At top of music — To the Honorable Judge Krueger, Newark, NJ." Page 8: Blank.

• **AmPM-911   LAUTENBERG**, Frank Raleigh (Commissioner of the Port Authority of New York and New Jersey, 1978-1982; U.S. Senate, 1982-2001 & 2003-Present)

911.1 Suin' For The Win. w. Madeleine Begun Kane. m. "To be sung to *Blowin' In The Wind* by Bob Dylan." "I'm relieved that the U.S. Supreme Court did the right thing in the Lautenberg ballot case. But memories of Election 2000 remain so painfully vivid, that I believe the legal wrangling by the GOP and Doug Forrester has only just begun." Published online at <http://www.raisingkane.com/sue.html>. 2003.

• **AmPM-912   MAXWELL**, John Patterson Bryan (U.S. House, 1837-1839 & 1841-1843)

912.1 A Parody On Up Salt River. w. No composer indicated. m. "Tune — *All On Hobbies.*" In: *Songs For The People (Or Tippecanoe Melodies)* [Songster], page 37. "Dedicated to the Democratic Whig Young Men of the City and County of New York." Published for the Authors by James P. Giffing, No. 56 Gold Street, New York, NY. 1840. [3¾" × 6"]. Litho of William Henry Harrison, log cabin, flag. "Original and Selected." 76pp. [M-019]. [Crew/WHH-63].

912.2 Up Salt River (A New Whig Song). w. G.B.W. (Toledo, OH). m. "Tune — *All On Hobbies.*" Published by Firth & Hall, No. 1 Franklin Square, New York, NY. 1840. Non-pictorial. "Respectfully Dedicated to the Toledo Tippecanoe Club." "Pr. 25 c nett [sic]." 4pp. [Crew/ WHH-38].

912.3 Up Salt River (A New Whig Song). w. G.B.W. "of Toledo, Ohio." m. "Tune — *All On Hobbies.*" "Respectfully dedicated to the Toledo Tippecanoe Club."

In: *The Log Cabin & Hard Cider Melodies, A Collection Of Popular And Patriotic Songs*, page 65. Published by Charles Adams, No. 23 Tremont Street, Boston, MA. 1840. [3¾" × 6"]. [V-1: Pk/bk] [V-2: Gn/bk] litho of William Henry Harrison. "The Freeman's glittering Sword be Blest, For ever blest the Freeman's Lyre." 78pp. Pages 2 and 77: Blank. Page 3: Inside title page. B/w litho of log cabin. "Respectfully Dedicated to the Friends of Harrison and Tyler." Page 78: Advertising. [M-012]. [Crew/WHH-68].

- **AmPM-912A MCCARTHY**, James W. (Judge, Court of Common Pleas, Hudson County, ca. 1918)

912A.1 The Blue Star Turned To Gold. w. Hon. James W. McCarthy. m. M.E. Schwarz. [ca. 1918]. R/w/b/bk/gd drawing of the Statue of Liberty, crosses, Gold Star Flag. "Dedicated to the memory of Albert Louis Quinn." 4pp. Page 3; At the bottom of page— "Cover page designed, and cut in linoleum, by Miss Ruth Johnson. Printing done in the William L. Dickinson High School, Jersey City." Page 4: Blank.

- **AmPM-913 MCCLELLAN**, George Brinton (Democratic Candidate for President, 1864; Governor, 1878–1881) [ALSO SEE: DOC/PSM-GBM]

913.1 Abraham's Daughter. w. No composer indicated. m. No tune indicated. Lyrics published by Mudcat Café online at <http://www.mudcat.org/kids/@displaysong.cfm?SongID=117>. [1997].

913.2 All Hail Our Nominee. w. Sidney Herbert. m. "Air—*God Save The Queen*." In: *McClellan Campaign Melodist*, page 25. c. Sidney Herbert. Published by [V-1 and 2: Benjamin Russel, Boston, MA] [V-3: American News Co., New York, NY] [V-4-7: B.W. Hitchcock, No. 14 Chambers Street, New York, NY]. 1864. [4⅜" × 6⅝"]. B/w litho of "McClellan" and "Pendleton." "A Collection of Patriotic Campaign Songs in Favor of the Constitution and the Union, the Election of General McClellan, the Restoration of the Federal Authority, and the Speedy Extermination of Treason." "The Union Must Be Preserved At All Hazards." 34pp. [M-137-143]. [Crew/GBM-24].

913.3 Are We Freedom's Friends? w. C.J.F., Jr. m. "Air—*Old Dog Tray*." In: *Lincoln Campaign Songster*, page 10. Published by Mason & Company, Philadelphia, PA. 1864. [4" × 6⅜"]. B/w litho of a beardless Abraham Lincoln, bold striped border. 20pp. "For the use of Clubs, Containing all of the most popular songs." [M-126]. [Crew/AL-81].

913.4 Banner Song. w. Sidney Herbert. m. "Arranged from a song by Mrs. S.E. Wallace, Air—*The Flag Of Our Union*." In: *McClellan Campaign Melodist*, page 14. e. Sidney Herbert. Published by Benjamin B. Russell, No. 515 Washington Street, Boston, MA. [4⅜" × 6¹¹⁄₁₆"]. 1864. Bl/bk litho of an eagle—"E Pluribus Unum," cotton bales, crops. "A Collection of Patriotic Campaign Songs in Favor of the Constitution and the Union, the Election of General McClellan, the Restoration of the Federal Authority and the Speedy Extermination of Treason." "The Union must be Preserved at all Hazards!" 36pp. [Crew/GBM-27].

913.5 Battle-Cry Of Union. w. Sidney Herbert. m. "Arranged from *Battle-Cry Of Freedom*, Air—*Battle-Cry Of Freedom*." In: *McClellan Campaign Melodist*, page 129. e. Sidney Herbert. Published by Benjamin B. Russell, No. 515 Washington Street, Boston, MA. [4⅜" × 6¹¹⁄₁₆"]. 1864. Bl/bk litho of an eagle—"E Pluribus Unum," cotton bales, crops. "A Collection of Patriotic Campaign Songs in Favor of the Constitution and the Union, the Election of General McClellan, the Restoration of the Federal Authority and the Speedy Extermination of Treason." "The Union must be Preserved at all Hazards!" 36pp. [Crew/GBM-27].

913.6 Battle Of Williamsburgh. w. No composer indicated. m. "Air—*The Land Of America*." Published by H. De Marsan, No. 54 Chatham Street, New York, NY. [ca. 1862]. B/w litho border of Naval scenes. "H. De Marsan, Dealer in Songs, Toy Books, &c., 54 Chatham St, N.Y." 2pp. Page 2: Blank. [AMC].

913.7 Behold, They Come! w. Sidney Herbert. m. "Air—*Old Folks At Home*." "Arranged form a Campaign song." In: *McClellan Campaign Melodist*, page 24. c. Sidney Herbert. Published by [V-1 and 2: Benjamin Russel, Boston, MA] [V-3: American News Co., New York, NY] [V-4-7: B.W. Hitchcock, No. 14 Chambers Street, New York, NY]. 1864. [4⅜" × 6⅝"]. B/w litho of "McClellan" and "Pendleton." "A Collection of Patriotic Campaign Songs in Favor of the Constitution and the Union, the Election of General McClellan, the Restoration of the Federal Authority, and the Speedy Extermination of Treason." "The Union Must Be Preserved At All Hazards." 34pp. [M-137-143]. [Crew/GBM-24].

913.8 Better Times Are Coming. w.m. Stephen Foster. Lyrics published online at <http://www.mudcat.org/kids/@displaysong.cfm?SongID=610>. [199-].

913.9 The Bold Engineer. w. No composer indicated. m. "Air—*Young Locinvar*." No publisher indicated. [ca. 1862]. [Approx. 3¼" × 9½"]. Pk/bk litho of an elephant with a blanket reading—"George B. McClellan," and holding a banner reading—"Oh dear! Oh Dear! What have we here," black line border. 2pp. Page 2: Blank. [WFU].

913.10 The Brave Sons Of Erin. w. Sidney Herbert. m. "Arranged from an Army song, Air—*The Red, White And Blue*." In: *McClellan Campaign Melodist*, page 17. e. Sidney Herbert. Published by Benjamin B. Russell, No. 515 Washington Street, Boston, MA. [4⅜" × 6¹¹⁄₁₆"]. 1864. Bl/bk litho of an eagle—"E Pluribus Unum," cotton bales, crops. "A Collection of Patriotic Campaign Songs in Favor of the Constitution and the Union, the Election of General McClellan, the Restoration of the Federal Authority and the Speedy Extermination of Treason." "The Union must be Preserved at all Hazards!" 36pp. [Crew/GBM-27].

913.11 The Broker's Stamp Act Lament. w.m. No composer or tune indicated. No publisher indicated. [July, 1862. [Approx. 3½" × 7½"]. Y/bk non-pictorial black line border, line under title. 2pp. Page 2: Blank. [WFU]. [AMC].

913.12 Campaign Song. w. No composer indicated. m. "Air—*Old Zip Coon*." In: *The Lincoln And Johnson Union Campaign Songster*, page 15. Published by A. Winch, No. 505 Chestnut Street, Philadelphia, PA. 1864. [3⅞" × 6"]. Be/bk lithos of Abraham Lincoln and Andrew Johnson, geometric design border. 58pp. [M-124] [Crew/AL-379].

913.13 Cast Your Votes For Abraham. w. "By a Republican." m. "Air—*The Watcher*." In: *Lincoln Cam-*

paign Songster, page 6. Published by Mason & Company, Philadelphia, PA. 1864. [4" × 6⅜"]. B/w litho of a beardless Abraham Lincoln, bold striped border. 20pp. "For the use of Clubs, Containing all of the most popular songs." [M-126]. [Crew/AL-81].

913.14 The Chicago Convention. w. No composer indicated. m. "Air—*The Little Tailor Boy.*" In: *The Lincoln And Johnson Union Campaign Songster*, page 12. Published by A. Winch, No. 505 Chestnut Street, Philadelphia, PA. 1864. [3⅞" × 6"]. Be/bk lithos of Abraham Lincoln and Andrew Johnson, geometric design border. 58pp. [M-124] [Crew/AL-379].

913.15 Colored Volunteer. w. Tom Craig. m. No tune indicated. Published by [V-1: Johnson, No. 7 Tenth Street] [V-2: A.W. Auner, N.E. Cor. Of Eleventh and Market], Philadelphia, PA. [186-]. [Approx. 6" × 9"]. B/e geometric design border. [V-1: "See Prof. Brooks' Ball Room Monitor, it will give you more Instruction in Dancing than say book ever Published. Sold by Johnson, No. 7 North Tenth Street, Phila. Price 15 cts."]. 2pp. Page 2: Blank. [V-1 & 2: AMC]. [V-2: VBL, p. 385].

913.16 The Colored Volunteers. w. No composer indicated. m. No tune indicated. Published by Charles Magnus, 12 Frankfort Street, New York, NY. [186-]. H/c litho of a Black man on stage playing a banjo. "500 Illustrated Ballads, lithographed and printed by Charles Magnus, No. 12 Frankfort Street, New York. Branch Office: No. 520 7th St., Washington, D.C." 2pp. Page 2: Blank. [AMC].

913.17 Come On, Boys, Come On! w. No composer indicated. m. "Air—*Adam And Eve.*" In: *Democratic Presidential Campaign Songster (No. 1)*, page 9. Published by J.F. Feeks, No. 26 Ann Street, New York, NY. 1864. [3¾" × 5½"]. Y/bk litho of George B. McClellan, chain link frame. "McClellan & Pendleton." "Original Campaign Songs, Choruses, &c." 74pp. [M-135, 136]. [Crew/GBM-23].

913.18 Conservative Union Mass Convention Song Sheet. Published under the direction of the National Committee, R.F. Stevens, Secretary. 1864. [12" × 18"]. Non-pictorial. Published for a rally in Chicago, Illinois, August 27, 1864. [Crew/GBM-91].

913.19 The Constitution, Our Platform!—McClellan Our Choice! [Crew/GBM-96].

913.20 The Constitution Wagon. w. No composer indicated. m. "Air—*Wait For The Wagon.*" In: *Democratic Presidential Campaign Songster (No. 1)*, page 32. Published by J.F. Feeks, No. 26 Ann Street, New York, NY. 1864. [3¾" × 5½"]. Y/bk litho of George B. McClellan, chain link frame. "McClellan & Pendleton." "Original Campaign Songs, Choruses, &c." 74pp. [M-135, 136]. [Crew/GBM-23].

913.21 Corcoran's Ball! w. John Mahon, Esq. m. "Air—*Lanigan's Ball.* Published by H. De Marsan, 54 Chatham Street, New York, NY. [186-]. [Approx. 5½" × 9¼"]. B/w litho border of naval scenes. "Written expressly for Thomas I. Donnelly, Esq., and sung by him, with tremendous applause, at the New-Bowery Theatre." 2pp. Page 2: Blank. [AMC].

913.22 The Cry Is Mac, My Darling. w. No composer indicated. m. "Air—*Oh My Nora Creina, Dear.*" In: *Democratic Presidential Campaign Songster (No. 1)*, page 37. Published by J.F. Feeks, No. 26 Ann Street, New York, NY. 1864. [3¾" × 5½"]. Y/bk litho of George B. McClellan, chain link frame. "McClellan & Pendleton." "Original Campaign Songs, Choruses, &c." 74pp. [M-135, 136]. [Crew/GBM-23].

913.23 The Democratic Rally. w. No composer indicated. m. "Air—*Wait For The Wagon.*" In: *Democratic Presidential Campaign Songster (No. 1)*, page 63. Published by J.F. Feeks, No. 26 Ann Street, New York, NY. 1864. [3¾" × 5½"]. Y/bk litho of George B. McClellan, chain link frame. "McClellan & Pendleton." "Original Campaign Songs, Choruses, &c." 74pp. [M-135, 136]. [Crew/GBM-23].

913.24 The Democratic Rally. w. No composer indicated. m. "Tune—*Wait For The Wagon.*" Published by J.F. Feeks, No. 26 Ann Street, and No. 636 Broadway, New York, NY. [1864]. Non-pictorial geometric and black line border. "From the *Democratic Presidential Campaign Songster.*" 2pp. Page 2: Blank. [Crew/GBM-88].

913.25 The Democratic Slogan. w. No composer indicated. m. "Air—*Fine Old English Gentleman.*" In: *Democratic Presidential Campaign Songster (No. 1)*, page 28. Published by J.F. Feeks, No. 26 Ann Street, New York, NY. 1864. [3¾" × 5½"]. Y/bk litho of George B. McClellan, chain link frame. "McClellan & Pendleton." "Original Campaign Songs, Choruses, &c." 74pp. [M-135, 136]. [Crew/GBM-23].

913.26 The Fame Of Our Leader. w. No composer indicated. m. "Air—*Soldiers Of The Union.*" "From the *Boston Post.*" In: *McClellan Campaign Melodist*, page 23. c. Sidney Herbert. Published by [V-1 and 2: Benjamin Russel, Boston, MA] [V-3: American News Co., New York, NY] [V-4-7: B.W. Hitchcock, No. 14 Chambers Street, New York, NY]. 1864. [4⅜" × 6⅝"]. B/w litho of "McClellan" and "Pendleton." "A Collection of Patriotic Campaign Songs in Favor of the Constitution and the Union, the Election of General McClellan, the Restoration of the Federal Authority, and the Speedy Extermination of Treason." "The Union Must Be Preserved At All Hazards." 34pp. [M-137-143]. [Crew/GBM-24].

913.27 Father Abraham We Are Coming. w. No composer indicated. m. "Air—*Jeannett And Jeanot.*" In: *Democratic Presidential Campaign Songster (No. 1)*, page 19. Published by J.F. Feeks, No. 26 Ann Street, New York, NY. 1864. [3¾" × 5½"]. Y/bk litho of George B. McClellan, chain link frame. "McClellan & Pendleton." "Original Campaign Songs, Choruses, &c." 74pp. [M-135, 136]. [Crew/GBM-23].

913.28 The Father Of All Songs. w. Wm. Dunne. m. "Air—*The Glorious Sixty-Ninth.*" Published by H. De Marsan, 54 Chatham Street, New York, NY. [186-]. [Approx. 5¾" × 9¼"]. B/w litho border of minstrels, Black children, jester. Composed by Wm. Dunne, ad sold at the Stationary-Store, 223 Ninth Avenue." 2pp. Page 2: Blank. [AMC].

913.29 The Final Victory (Ballad No. 3). w. A. Anderson. m. "Air—*Johnny Fill Up The Bowl.*" Published by A. Anderson, 420 South Tenth Street, Philadelphia, PA. 1864. [Approx. 6" × 9½"]. B/w non-pictorial geometric design border. "See numbers one and two." "A. Anderson, 420 South Tenth Street, Philadelphia, Where all Ballads bearing his name may be had; also all the most Popular Songs of the times, Wholesale and Retail." 2pp. Page 2: Blank. [AMC].

913.30 The Flag Of Our Union. w. George P. Morris. m. "Air—*The Flag Of Our Union*." In: *McClellan Campaign Melodist*, page 31. e. Sidney Herbert. Published by Benjamin B. Russell, No. 515 Washington Street, Boston, MA. [4⅜" × 6$^{11}/_{16}$"]. 1864. Bl/bk litho of an eagle—"E Pluribus Unum," cotton bales, crops. "A Collection of Patriotic Campaign Songs in Favor of the Constitution and the Union, the Election of General McClellan, the Restoration of the Federal Authority and the Speedy Extermination of Treason." "The Union must be Preserved at all Hazards!" 36pp. [Crew/GBM-27].

913.31 Flip Flap. w.m. No composer or tune indicated. Published by H. De Marsan, Publisher, 54 Chatham Street, New York, [186-]. B/w litho border of allegorical figures, geometric designs. "As sung by Frank Lum, the celebrated Ethiopian comedian." 2pp. Page 2: Blank. [AMC].

913.32 Forward One And All! w. Sidney Herbert. m. "Air—*Scots Wha Hae*." "Arranged from a song by Walter Anonym." In: *McClellan Campaign Melodist*, page 12. c. Sidney Herbert. Published by [V-1 and 2: Benjamin Russel, Boston, MA] [V-3: American News Co., New York, NY] [V-4–7: B.W. Hitchcock, No. 14 Chambers Street, New York, NY]. 1864. [4⅜" × 6⅝"]. B/w litho of "McClellan" and "Pendleton." "A Collection of Patriotic Campaign Songs in Favor of the Constitution and the Union, the Election of General McClellan, the Restoration of the Federal Authority, and the Speedy Extermination of Treason." "The Union Must Be Preserved At All Hazards." 34pp. [M-137–143]. [Crew/GBM-24].

913.33 Funeral March In Memory Of General Geo. B. McClellan. m. H.J. Bennertt. Published by White, Smith & Co., Chicago, IL. 1885. B/w litho of laurel branches, geometric designs. 6pp. Page 2: Blank. Page 6: Advertising, black border. [Crew/GBM-89].

913.34 Gallant Pennsylvania 69th, Irish Volunteers. w. M. Fay. m. "Air—*McKenney's Dream*." Published by J.H. Johnson, Song Publisher, &c., No. 7 N. Tenth Street, 3 doors above Market, Philadelphia, PA. 1863. Non-pictorial. "To the Sixty-ninth Regiment Pennsylvania Volunteers." 2pp. Page 2: Blank. [AMC].

913.35 Gen Lee, Is Pretty Good Looking (But He Can't Come To Maryland). w. No composer indicated. m. "Air—*Oh, Carry Me Back To Old Virginia*." No publisher indicated. [1862–1863]. [Approx. 6" × 9½"]. B/w litho of a military man, geometric design border. 2pp. Page 2: Blank. [AMC].

913.36 Genl. McClellan's Grand March. Published by John Church, Jr., No. 66 West 4th Street, Cincinnati, OH. 1864. B/w litho of General George McClellan, geometric designs. 6pp. Pages 2 and 6: Blank. [Crew/GBM-86].

913.37 Gen. McLellan's [sic] ***Farewell Address To His Army***. w. A. Anderson. m. "Air—*Highland Mary*." Published by Harris, Printer, 4th & Vine Street, Philadelphia, PA. November, 1862. Non-pictorial geometric design border. 2pp. Page 2: Blank. [AMC].

913.38 Give Us Noble Leaders. w. "By An Invincible." m. "Air—*Give Us Back Our Old Commander*." In: Lincoln Campaign Songster, page 3. Published by Mason & Company, Philadelphia, PA. 1864. [4" × 6⅜"]. B/w litho of a beardless Abraham Lincoln, bold striped border. 20pp. "For the use of Clubs, Containing all of the most popular songs." [M-126]. [Crew/AL-81].

913.39 God Is With The Right. w. Sidney Herbert. m. "Air—*Columbia, The Pride Of Nations*." "Arranged from a song by M. Bingham." In: *McClellan Campaign Melodist*, page 26. c. Sidney Herbert. Published by [V-1 and 2: Benjamin Russel, Boston, MA] [V-3: American News Co., New York, NY] [V-4–7: B.W. Hitchcock, No. 14 Chambers Street, New York, NY]. 1864. [4⅜" × 6⅝"]. B/w litho of "McClellan" and "Pendleton." "A Collection of Patriotic Campaign Songs in Favor of the Constitution and the Union, the Election of General McClellan, the Restoration of the Federal Authority, and the Speedy Extermination of Treason." "The Union Must Be Preserved At All Hazards." 34pp. [M-137–143]. [Crew/GBM-24].

913.40 God Save Our Noble Land! w.m. No composer or tune indicated. In: *Democratic Presidential Campaign Songster (No. 1)*, page 70. Published by J.F. Feeks, No. 26 Ann Street, New York, NY. 1864. [3¾" × 5½"]. Y/bk litho of George B. McClellan, chain link frame. "McClellan & Pendleton." "Original Campaign Songs, Choruses, &c." 74pp. [M-135, 136]. [Crew/GBM-23].

913.41 Good Advice! w. W.C. m. No tune indicated. No publisher indicated. [ca. 1861–1862]. B/w geometric design border. 2pp. Page 2: Blank. [AMC].

913.42 The Goose Hung High, No. 2. w.m. No composer or tune indicated. Published by H. De Marsan, No. 54 Chatham Street, New York, NY. [186-]. B/w litho border of four people, one in each corner, geometric designs. "As sung with great success by Wm. Jennings." 2pp. Page 2: Blank. [AMC].

913.43 Grant At The Head Of The Nation. w.m. W.O. Fiske. In: *The Grant And Colfax Republican Songster, Containing Campaign Songs, Ballads And Choruses. Adapted To The Most Popular And Stirring Tunes*, page 40. Published by R.M. Dewitt, Publisher, No. 13 Frankfort Street, New York, NY. 1868. [4" × 6$^{3}/_{16}$"]. R/w/b litho of flag. Advertising. 100pp. [M-150]. [Crew/USG-63].

913.44 Hail To McClellan! w. Sidney Herbert. m. "Air—*Hail To The Chief*." "Arranged from a song by John F. Poole." In: *McClellan Campaign Melodist*, page 7. c. Sidney Herbert. Published by [V-1 and 2: Benjamin Russel, Boston, MA] [V-3: American News Co., New York, NY] [V-4–7: B.W. Hitchcock, No. 14 Chambers Street, New York, NY]. 1864. [4⅜" × 6⅝"]. B/w litho of "McClellan" and "Pendleton." "A Collection of Patriotic Campaign Songs in Favor of the Constitution and the Union, the Election of General McClellan, the Restoration of the Federal Authority, and the Speedy Extermination of Treason." "The Union Must Be Preserved At All Hazards." 34pp. [M-137–143]. [Crew/GBM-24].

913.45 Hail To McClellan! w. No composer indicated. m. "Air—*Hail To The Chief*." In: *Democratic Presidential Campaign Songster (No. 1)*, page 62. Published by J.F. Feeks, No. 26 Ann Street, New York, NY. 1864. [3¾" × 5½"]. Y/bk litho of George B. McClellan, chain link frame. "McClellan & Pendleton."

"Original Campaign Songs, Choruses, &c." 74pp. [M-135, 136]. [Crew/GBM-23].

913.46 Hey! Uncle Abe, Are You Joking Yet? w. No composer indicated. m. "Tune—*Johnny Cope.*" Published by J.F. Feeks, 26 Ann Street, and 636 Broadway, New York, NY. 1864. B/w non-pictorial geometric design border. 2pp. Page 2: Blank. [AMC].

913.47 Hey! Uncle Abe, Are You Joking Yet? w. No composer indicated. m. "Air—*Johnny Cope.*" In: *Democratic Presidential Campaign Songster (No. 1)*, page 30. Published by J.F. Feeks, No. 26 Ann Street, New York, NY. 1864. [3¾" × 5½"]. Y/bk litho of George B. McClellan, chain link frame. "McClellan & Pendleton." "Original Campaign Songs, Choruses, &c." 74pp. [M-135, 136]. [Crew/GBM-23].

913.48 Hoist The Flag For Abraham. w. "By a Veteran." m. "Air—*Hoist Up The Flag.*" In: *Lincoln Campaign Songster*, page 7. Published by Mason & Company, Philadelphia, PA. 1864. [4" × 6⅜"]. B/w litho of a beardless Abraham Lincoln, bold striped border. 20pp. "For the use of Clubs, Containing all of the most popular songs." [M-126]. [Crew/AL-81].

913.49 Hoist Up The Flag, Long May It Wave. w. No composer indicated. m. No tune indicated. Published by Johnson Song Publisher, No. 7 No. 10th Street, Philadelphia, PA. [ca. 1863]. [Approx. 6" × 9"]. B/w non-pictorial geometric design border. 2pp. Page 2: Blank. [AMC].

913.50 Hold On, Abraham. w.m. No composer or tune indicated. "Copied by permission of Firth, Pond & Co., Music Publishers, 547 Broadway, N.Y., Owners of the copyright." In: *Beadle's Dime Knapsack Songster: Containing The Choicest Patriotic Songs, Together With Many New And Original Ones, Set To Old Melodies*, page 46. Published by Beadle and Company, No. 141 William Street, New York, NY. 1862. [3¾" × 5¾"]. Litho of coin—"One Dime, United States of America." 74pp. [Crew/GBM-78].

913.50A Honest Abe. w. Michael Pacholek. m. "*Honesty*, based on a performance by Billy Joel." "For the greatest of American Presidents, my favorite musical performer of all time (not to mention my most parodied performer)." Published online at <http://www.amiright.com/parody/70s/billyjoel152.shtml>. 2004.

913.51 The Hour And The Man. w. No composer indicated. m. "Air—*The Bonnets Of Bonnie Dundee.*" n: *Democratic Presidential Campaign Songster (No. 1)*, page 46. Published by J.F. Feeks, No. 26 Ann Street, New York, NY. 1864. [3¾" × 5½"]. Y/bk litho of George B. McClellan, chain link frame. "McClellan & Pendleton." "Original Campaign Songs, Choruses, &c." 74pp. [M-135, 136]. [Crew/GBM-23].

913.51A [How Are You, Mister Little Mac?]. w. No composer indicated. m. "Air—*Yankee Doodle.*" Lyrics published online at <http://libwww.syr.edu/digital/exhibits/l/Lincoln/campsong.htm>.

913.52 How McClellan Took Manassas. w. "By Old Napoleon." m. No tune indicated. In: *Songs For The Union*, page 1. "Printed for the Union Congressional Committee by John A. Gray & Geen, New York," NY. [ca. 1864]. Non-pictorial. 8pp. [AMC].

913.53 A Hundred Years Hence. w. Tony Pastor. m. No tune indicated. Published by Charles Magnus, 12 Franklin Street, New York, NY. [1863–1864]. N/c lithos of an Indian with a American flag inscribed "For The Union," and a litho of a bull and man chopping a tree titled "Indiana." 2pp. Page 2: Blank. [AMC].

913.54 A Hunkey Boy Is A Yankee Doodle. w.m. No composer or tune indicated. Published by Auner's Printing Office, 110 N. Tenth Street, ab. Arch, [Philadelphia, PA]. [186-]. [Approx. 6" × 9½"]. B/w non-pictorial geometric design border. "As sung by Frank Kerns, at the Kossuth Concert Saloon." 2pp. Page 2: Blank. [AMC]. MIDI and lyrics online at <http://mariah.stonemarche.org/livhis/whack.htm>.

913.55 Hurrah For Lincoln And Johnson! w. C.J.F., Jr. m. "Air—*John Brown's Body.*" In: *Lincoln Campaign Songster*, page 11. Published by Mason & Company, Philadelphia, PA. 1864. [4" × 6⅜"]. B/w litho of a beardless Abraham Lincoln, bold striped border. 20pp. "For the use of Clubs, Containing all of the most popular songs." [M-126]. [Crew/AL-81].

913.56 I'm Going To Fight Mit Sigel. w.m. No composer or tune indicated. In: T*he Good Old Songs We Used To Sing ('61 to '65)*, page 4. Published by O.H. Oldroyd, Lincoln Homestead, Springfield, IL. [ca. 1880]. [5¹¹⁄₁₆" × 8⅝"]. Ma/bl litho from "Photo from Life—1864—General Ulysses S. Grant." 36pp. [Crew/USG-301].

913.57 The Irish Volunteer. w. John L. Davenport. "As Sung by John L. Davenport." In: *John L. Davenport's Own Comic Vocalist*, page 10. Published by H.R. Hildreth, No. 5 Olive Street, St. Louis, MO. 1864. [2⅞" × 4¼"]. B/w non-pictorial double black line border. [18pp?]. [Crew/GBM-85]

913.58 Jeff Davis Is Getting Tired Of The War. m. "Air—*Maryland, My Maryland.*" [186-]. B/w litho of two women, geometric design border. [186-]. 2pp. Page 2: Blank. [Crew/JD-80]. [AMC].

913.59 Jeff Davis' Last Proclamation To His Council. m. "Air—*The Girl I Left Behind Me.*" [186-]. Non-pictorial geometric design border. 2pp. Page 2: Blank.

913.60 John Bull's Blockade Played Out. w. F. Collins. m. "Air—*Lovely Molly O!*" Published by J. Wrigley, 27 Chatham Street, New York, NY. [186-]. [Approx. 5¾" × 9⅞"]. B/w litho order of man and woman, two figures playing trumpet, geometric designs. "J. Wrigley, Publisher of songs, ballads, and toy books, conversation, age and playing cards, alphabet wood blocks, valentines, motto verses and cat motto paper, &c., No. 27 Chatham Street (Opp. City Hall fare), New York." 2pp. Page 2: Blank. [AMC].

913.61 John C. Fremont, My Jo. w. "As Sung by the soldiers of General McClellan's Army." m. "*John Anderson, My Jo.*" No publisher indicated. [ca. 1964]. [5⅛" × 9"]. B/w geometric and floral design border. Civil War penny song sheet. 2pp. Page 2: Blank. [Crew/GBM-90].

913.62 Lift High The Standard. w. Sidney Herbert. m. "Air—*Auld Lang Syne.*" In: *McClellan Campaign Melodist*, page 8. c. Sidney Herbert. Published by [V-1 and 2: Benjamin Russel, Boston, MA] [V-3: American News Co., New York, NY] [V-4-7: B.W. Hitchcock, No. 14 Chambers Street, New York, NY]. 1864. [4⅜" × 6⅝"]. B/w litho of "McClellan" and "Pendleton." "A Collection of Patriotic Campaign

Songs in Favor of the Constitution and the Union, the Election of General McClellan, the Restoration of the Federal Authority, and the Speedy Extermination of Treason." "The Union Must Be Preserved At All Hazards." 34pp. [M-137–143]. [Crew/GBM-24].

913.63 Lincoln Campaign Song. w. No composer indicated. m. "Air — *Yankee Doodle.*" In: *Lincoln Campaign Songster*, page 14. Published by Mason & Company, Philadelphia, PA. 1864. [4" × 6⅜"]. B/w litho of a beardless Abraham Lincoln, bold striped border. 20pp. "For the use of Clubs, Containing all of the most popular songs." [M-126]. [Crew/AL-81].

913.64 Little Mac. w.m. No composer or tune indicated. "First in peace, first in war and first in the hearts of his Countrymen!" In: *Democratic Presidential Campaign Songster (No. 1)*, page 43. Published by J.F. Feeks, No. 26 Ann Street, New York, NY. 1864. [3¾" × 5½"]. Y/bk litho of George B. McClellan, chain link frame. "McClellan & Pendleton." "Original Campaign Songs, Choruses, &c." 74pp. [M-135, 136]. [Crew/GBM-23].

913.65 Little Mac. w. No composer indicated. m. "Air — *Nelly Bly.*" *The Lincoln And Johnson Union Campaign Songster*, page 10. Published by A. Winch, No. 505 Chestnut Street, Philadelphia, PA. 1864. [3⅞" × 6"]. Be/bk lithos of Abraham Lincoln and Andrew Johnson, geometric design border. 58pp. [M-124] [Crew/AL-379].

913.65A Little Mac Campaign Songster. Published by E.P. Patten, The World Office, 35 Park Row, New York, NY. 1864. [4" × 5¾"]. B/w litho of George B. McClellan. "'The Union is the one condition of peace' — we ask no more — Letter of Acceptance." 15pp.

913.66 Little Mac Shall Be Restored. w. Sidney Herbert. m. "Air — *Auld Lang Syne.*" In: *McClellan Campaign Melodist*, page 13. c. Sidney Herbert. Published by [V-1 and 2: Benjamin Russel, Boston, MA] [V-3: American News Co., New York, NY] [V-4–7: B.W. Hitchcock, No. 14 Chambers Street, New York, NY]. 1864. [4⅜" × 6⅝"]. B/w litho of "McClellan" and "Pendleton." "A Collection of Patriotic Campaign Songs in Favor of the Constitution and the Union, the Election of General McClellan, the Restoration of the Federal Authority, and the Speedy Extermination of Treason." "The Union Must Be Preserved At All Hazards." 34pp. [M-137–143]. [Crew/GBM-24].

913.67 Long Live McClellan. w. No composer indicated. m. "Air — *Happy Land Of Canaan.*" No publisher indicated. [1862–1864]. B/w litho border. 2pp. Page 2: Blank. [AMC

913.68 Mac's The Boy. w. No composer indicated. m. "Air — *Old Dan Tucker.*" In: *Democratic Presidential Campaign Songster (No. 1)*, page 39. Published by J.F. Feeks, No. 26 Ann Street, New York, NY. 1864. [3¾" × 5½"]. Y/bk litho of George B. McClellan, chain link frame. "McClellan & Pendleton." "Original Campaign Songs, Choruses, &c." 74pp. [M-135, 136]. [Crew/GBM-23].

913.69 Major General G.B. McClellan's Triumphal March. m. J.C. Beckel. Published by Marsh, No. 1102 Chesnut Street, Philadelphia, PA. 1861. Non-pictorial. "Composed and Dedicated to that Gallant Officer." 6pp. Pages 2 and 6: Blank. [Crew/GBM-98].

913.70 Marching Along. w.m. No composer or tune indicated. Published by J.H. Johnson, No. 7 Tenth Street, Philadelphia, PA. [186-]. Non-pictorial. "The music for this beautiful marching song is published by Firth, Pond & Co., No. 547 Broadway, New York. Send them 25 cents and they will send you the Music by return of mail." List of other titles available from the publisher. "J.H. Johnson, No. 7 Tenth Street, Philada. publishes all the new and popular songs. See his large assortment of Union Songs." "N.B. — Soldiers in the Field sending 25 cts. Will receive 100 Union Songs, assorted, Which may be remitted in postage stamps." 2pp. Page 2: Blank. [AMC].

913.70A McClellan And Freedom. w. No composer indicated. m. "Air — *Battle Cry Of Freedom.*" In: *Little Mac Campaign Songster*. Published by E.P. Patten, The World Office, 35 Park Row, New York, NY. 1864. [4" × 5¾"]. B/w litho of George B. McClellan. "'The Union is the one condition of peace' — we ask no more — Letter of Acceptance." 15pp.

913.71 McClelland And Union. w. No composer indicated. m. "Music — *Bonnie Dundee.*" On 33⅓ rpm LP: *Sing Along With Millard Fillmore*. Life Records #RB 360 T2/#61 P3. "The Life Album of Presidential Campaign Songs." 1964.

913.72 McClellan Campaign Song. w. John A. McSorley, "of New York City." m. "Air — *Wait For The Wagon.*" Published by Theodore Dutton, No. 13 Spruce Street, New York, NY. 1864. B/w penny song sheet with a litho border of geometric designs. "Dedicated to Horatio Seymour." [Crew/GBM-92].

913.73 McClellan For 1865! w. J. Lovelock. m. "Air — *Billy O'Rourke.*" Published by H. De Marsan, No. 54 Chatham Street, New York, NY. [ca. 1864). [6½" × 10"]. B/w border lithos of naval scenes. "H. De Marsan, Publisher of Songs, Ballads, toy Books, &c., 54 Chatham St., N.Y." 2pp. Page 2: Blank. [AMC]. [Crew/GBM-95].

913.74 McClellan Is Our Man. w. Sidney Herbert. m. "Air — *America.*" In: *McClellan Campaign Melodist*, page 21. c. Sidney Herbert. Published by [V-1 and 2: Benjamin Russel, Boston, MA] [V-3: American News Co., New York, NY] [V-4–7: B.W. Hitchcock, No. 14 Chambers Street, New York, NY]. 1864. [4⅜" × 6⅝"]. B/w litho of "McClellan" and "Pendleton." "A Collection of Patriotic Campaign Songs in Favor of the Constitution and the Union, the Election of General McClellan, the Restoration of the Federal Authority, and the Speedy Extermination of Treason." "The Union Must Be Preserved At All Hazards." 34pp. [M-137–143]. [Crew/GBM-24].

913.75 The McClellan Legion. w.m. No composer or tune indicated. Published in the Boston *Daily C* [?], October 18, 1864.

913.76 McClellan The Brave. w. No composer indicated. m. "Air — *Columbia The Gem Of The Ocean.*" In: *Democratic Presidential Campaign Songster (No. 1)*, page 68. Published by J.F. Feeks, No. 26 Ann Street, New York, NY. 1864. [3¾" × 5½"]. Y/bk litho of George B. McClellan, chain link frame. "McClellan & Pendleton." "Original Campaign Songs, Choruses, &c." 74pp. [M-135, 136]. [Crew/GBM-23].

913.77 McClellan The Brave And True. w. No composer indicated. m. "Air — *The Red, White And*

Blue." In: *Democratic Presidential Campaign Songster (No. 1)*, page 6. Published by J.F. Feeks, No. 26 Ann Street, New York, NY. 1864. [3¾" × 5½"]. Y/bk litho of George B. McClellan, chain link frame. "McClellan & Pendleton." "Original Campaign Songs, Choruses, &c." 74pp. [M-135, 136]. [Crew/GBM-23].

913.77A McClellan The Hope Of The Nation. w. No composer indicated. m. "Air — *Red, White, And Blue*." In: *Little Mac Campaign Songster*, page 12. Published by E.P. Patten, The World Office, 35 Park Row, New York, NY. 1864. [4" × 5¾"]. B/w litho of George B. McClellan. "'The Union is the one condition of peace' — we ask no more — Letter of Acceptance." 15pp.

913.78 McClellan Will Be President. w. No composer indicated. m. "Air — *Whack, Row De Dow!*" In: *Democratic Presidential Campaign Songster (No. 1)*, page 3. Published by J.F. Feeks, No. 26 Ann Street, New York, NY. 1864. [3¾" × 5½"]. Y/bk litho of George B. McClellan, chain link frame. "McClellan & Pendleton." "Original Campaign Songs, Choruses, &c." 74pp. [M-135, 136]. [Crew/GBM-23].

913.79 McClellan Will Be President. w. M.J. Million. m. "Air — *Whack, Row De Dow!*" Published by H. De Marsan, No. 54 Chatham Street, New York, NY. [ca. 1864]. [6½" × 10"]. B/w border lithos of cherubs, minstrel, women, geometric designs. 2pp. Page 2: Blank. [Crew/GBM-97].

913.80 McClellan's Battle & Victory (At Antietam, MD, Sept. 17th, 1862). w. A. Anderson "(Philadelphia)." m. "Arranged from *Lutzow's Wild Hunt*." [1862]. B/w geometric design border. "Arranged from Lutzow's *Wild Hunt*, the music of which may be obtained at No. 722 Chestnut Street, Philadelphia." "Address of the Author. A. Anderson, a member of the discharges Band of the 82d (late 31st) Regiment, P.V., (Col. D.H. Williams) respectfully informs the public that he resides at No. 420 South Tenth Street, Philadelphia, where all pieces bearing his name may be had, wholesale and retail, viz: *The Soldier's Farewell; or The Battle Of The War; The Dying Hero's Request; The Heroes Of '62; Interrogatory-1776 And 1862; The Star Of The North*, &c., &c., &c. N.B. — He will sing his own pieces at Fairs, Festivals, &c., which may have for their object the benefit of Sick and Wounded Soldiers, Oct. 24, 1862." [Crew/GBM-87].

913.80A McClellan's Coming. w. No composer indicated. m. "Air — *Kingdom Coming*." In: *Little Mac Campaign Songster*. Published by E.P. Patten, The World Office, 35 Park Row, New York, NY. 1864. [4" × 5¾"]. B/w litho of George B. McClellan. "'The Union is the one condition of peace' — we ask no more — Letter of Acceptance." 15pp.

913.81 McClellan's In The Field. w. No composer indicated. m. "Air — *Watchman, Tell Us Of The Night*." In: *Democratic Presidential Campaign Songster (No. 1)*, page 14. Published by J.F. Feeks, No. 26 Ann Street, New York, NY. 1864. [3¾" × 5½"]. Y/bk litho of George B. McClellan, chain link frame. "McClellan & Pendleton." "Original Campaign Songs, Choruses, &c." 74pp. [M-135, 136]. [Crew/GBM-23].

913.82 Noble Lads Of Brooklyn. w.m. No composer or tune indicated. Published by H. De Marsan, 39 & 60 Chatham Street, New York, NY. [1863]. [Approx. 6" × 9"]. B/w litho border of ethnic minstrel characters. 2pp. Page 2: Blank. [AMC].

913.83 Old Abe's Last Run. w. No composer indicated. m. "Air — *Old Dan Tucker*." n: *Democratic Presidential Campaign Songster (No. 1)*, page 48. Published by J.F. Feeks, No. 26 Ann Street, New York, NY. 1864. [3¾" × 5½"]. Y/bk litho of George B. McClellan, chain link frame. "McClellan & Pendleton." "Original Campaign Songs, Choruses, &c." 74pp. [M-135, 136]. [Crew/GBM-23].

913.84 The Old Ship Of State. w. Sidney Herbert. m. "Air — *Red, White, And Blue*." "Arranged from a Campaign song." In: *McClellan Campaign Melodist*, page 30. c. Sidney Herbert. Published by [V-1 and 2: Benjamin Russel, Boston, MA] [V-3: American News Co., New York, NY] [V-4-7: B.W. Hitchcock, No. 14 Chambers Street, New York, NY]. 1864. [4⅜" × 6⅝"]. B/w litho of "McClellan" and "Pendleton." "A Collection of Patriotic Campaign Songs in Favor of the Constitution and the Union, the Election of General McClellan, the Restoration of the Federal Authority, and the Speedy Extermination of Treason." "The Union Must Be Preserved At All Hazards." 34pp. [M-137–143]. [Crew/GBM-24].

913.85 On To Victory (Gen. McClelan's [sic] War Song!). w.m. No composer or tune indicated. No publisher indicated. [186-]. [Approx 4⅞" × 11"?]. Litho of bugler on horseback, globe labeled "America," American flag, geometric design border. 2pp. Page 2: Blank.

913.86 Our Country. w. No composer indicated. m. "Air — *America*." In: *Democratic Presidential Campaign Songster (No. 1)*, page 23. Published by J.F. Feeks, No. 26 Ann Street, New York, NY. 1864. [3¾" × 5½"]. Y/bk litho of George B. McClellan, chain link frame. "McClellan & Pendleton." "Original Campaign Songs, Choruses, &c." 74pp. [M-135, 136]. [Crew/GBM-23].

913.87 Our Country Right Or Wrong. w. Thomas A. Becket. m. "Tune — *Few Days*." Published by Weaver & Royal, Printer, Harrisburg, PA. [1862-1863]. B/w non-pictorial geometric design border. "Tho's a'Becket, author of *Columbia The Gen Of The Ocean, Pennsylvania Battle Cry*, &c., &c. Sung nightly at Sanford's Opera House." 2pp. Page 2: Blank. [AMC].

913.88 Our Flag With Every Star. w. Sidney Herbert. m. "Air — *Bonnie Blue*." "Arranged from a Campaign song." In: *McClellan Campaign Melodist*, page 11. c. Sidney Herbert. Published by [V-1 and 2: Benjamin Russel, Boston, MA] [V-3: American News Co., New York, NY] [V-4-7: B.W. Hitchcock, No. 14 Chambers Street, New York, NY]. 1864. [4⅜" × 6⅝"]. B/w litho of "McClellan" and "Pendleton." "A Collection of Patriotic Campaign Songs in Favor of the Constitution and the Union, the Election of General McClellan, the Restoration of the Federal Authority, and the Speedy Extermination of Treason." "The Union Must Be Preserved At All Hazards." 34pp. [M-137–143]. [Crew/GBM-24].

913.89 Our German Volunteers. w. No composer indicated. m. "Air — *New-York Volunteers*." Published by H. De Marsan, Publisher, 54 Chatham Street, New York, NY. [ca. 1861]. [Approx. 6¼" × 9"]. H/c litho border of U.S. flags, eagle, soldier, Black man. 2pp. Page 2: Blank. [AMC].

913.90 Our Mac Shall March To Washington. w. No composer indicated. m. "Air—*Johnny Fill Up The Bowl.*" In: *Democratic Presidential Campaign Songster (No. 1),* page 65. Published by J.F. Feeks, No. 26 Ann Street, New York, NY. 1864. [3¾" × 5½"]. Y/bk litho of George B. McClellan, chain link frame. "McClellan & Pendleton." "Original Campaign Songs, Choruses, &c." 74pp. [M-135, 136]. [Crew/GBM-23].

913.91 Our Union Is In Peril. w. Sidney Herbert. m. "Air—*Health To All Good Lassies.*" "Arranged from an Army song." In: *McClellan Campaign Melodist,* page 28. c. Sidney Herbert. Published by [V-1 and 2: Benjamin Russel, Boston, MA] [V-3: American News Co., New York, NY] [V-4–7: B.W. Hitchcock, No. 14 Chambers Street, New York, NY]. 1864. [4⅜" × 6⅝"]. B/w litho of "McClellan" and "Pendleton." "A Collection of Patriotic Campaign Songs in Favor of the Constitution and the Union, the Election of General McClellan, the Restoration of the Federal Authority, and the Speedy Extermination of Treason." "The Union Must Be Preserved At All Hazards." 34pp. [M-137–143]. [Crew/GBM-24].

913.92 Our Yankee Generals. w.m. No publisher or tune indicated. Published by J.H. Johnson, Song Publisher, Stationer and Printer, No. 7 North Tenth Street, 3 Doors above Market, Philadelphia, PA. [186-]. [Approx. 6" × 9"]. Non-pictorial geometric design border. 2pp. Page 2: Blank. [AMC].

913.93 Preserve The Union. w. No composer indicated. m. "Air—*Gay And Happy.*" In: *Lincoln Campaign Songster,* page 13. Published by Mason & Company, Philadelphia, PA. 1864. [4" × 6⅜"]. B/w litho of a beardless Abraham Lincoln, bold striped border. 20pp. "For the use of Clubs, Containing all of the most popular songs." [M-126]. [Crew/AL-81].

913.94 The President's Ball. w. No composer indicated. m. "Air—*Lannegan's Ball.*" Published by H. De Marsan, 54 Chatham Street, New York, NY. [1860–1862]. [Approx. 6" × 9"]. B/w litho border of theatrical-type figures, leaves, lion's head, stars. "Sung by Joe English." 2pp. Page 2: Blank. [AMC].

913.95 Quamdiu Yendem Abutere Patientiae Nostra? Ad Quen Finem Sese Jactabit Audacia? (Come gentle muse, Give me Your Aid). w. "B." m. No tune indicated. No publisher indicated. Published in Baltimore, June 30, 1861. B/w geometric design border. 2pp. Page 2: Blank. [AMC].

913.96 Rag-Baby Money (Greenback Campaign Song). w. No composer indicated. m. "Air—*Rosin The Bow.*" In: *Greenback Song-Book,* page 7. Published by M.S. Cadwell, Grand Ledge, MI. [ca. 1880]. [3¹⁵⁄₁₆" × 7¹⁵⁄₁₆"]. Gn/w litho of a "Greenback" bank note. 20pp. [Crew/BFB-18].

913.97 Rally For The Union. w. No composer indicated. m. "Air—*Few Days.*" No publisher indicated. [186-]. Non-pictorial geometric design border. 2pp. Page 2: Blank. [AMC].

913.98 Rebellion's Weak Back. w.m. F. Wilmarth. Published by Russell & Patee, Boston, MA. [ca. 1862]. Non-pictorial geometric designs. "As sung by Billy Morris at Morris Bros., Pell and Trowbridge." 6pp. Pages 2 and 6: Blank. [AMC].

913.99 The Rebel's Retort (Song). w. No composer indicated. m. "Air—*Cocachelunk.*" No publisher indicated. [ca. 1861]. [Approx. 4⅝" × 9½"]. Litho of mill house, trees, geometric design border. 2pp. Page 2: Blank. [WFU].

913.100 The Retreat Of The Grand Army From Bull Run. w. Ernest Cliftan. m. "Air—*Sweet Evelina.*" No publisher indicated. Published at Baltimore. [1861–1862]. [Approx. 3⅝" × 5⅝"]. Y/bk non-pictorial line border. 2pp. Page 2: Blank. [WFU].

913.101 Richmond Is A Hard Road To Travel (Or The New Jordan). w. No composer indicated. m. *Jordan Is A Hard Road To Travel.* No publisher indicated. [ca. 1862]. "Respectfully Dedicated to Gen. Ambrose E. Burnside." "As sung with enthusiastic applause in all the Northern States." 2pp. Page 2: Blank. [AMC].

913.102 Root Yank Or Die! w. No composer indicated. m. "Air—*Root Hog Or Die.*" No publisher indicated. [186-]. [Approx. 6" × 9"]. B/w non-pictorial geometric design between title and text. 2pp. Page 2: Blank. [AMC].

913.103 Seven Days Fight (From June 26th, to July 4th, 1862). w. James Smith, "Co. H." m. "Air—*Louisiana Lowlands.*" Published by J.H. Johnson, Song Publisher, Stationer & Printer, No. 7 Tenth Street, 3 Doors above Market, Philadelphia, PA. 1862. Non-pictorial. 2pp. Page 2: Blank. [AMC].

913.104 Seven Days Fight Before Richmond. w.m. No composer or tune indicated. Published by H. De Marsan, 54 Chatham Street, New York, NY. [186-]. [Approx. 6" × 9"]. B/w litho border of an ethnic men's heads in each corner—Irish, Black, etc.—and geometric designs. 2pp. Page 2: Blank. [AMC].

913.105 Seymour's Now The People's Choice. w. No composer indicated. m. "Air—*When Johnny Comes Marching Home.*" In: *Seymour Campaign Songster,* page 21. Published by Pattee & Hubbard, Democratic State Committee Rooms, World Building, No. 37 Park Row, New York, NY. 1868. [4" × 5¼"]. Gn/bk litho of Horatio Seymour and Francis Blair. "In the spirit of George Washington and the Patriots of the Revolution, Let us take the steps to re-inaugurate our Government, to start it once again on its course to greatness and prosperity—Horatio Seymour." 38pp. [M-173]. [Crew/HS-8].

913.106 The Shekinah. w. B. Danforth. m. No tune indicated. Published by E.L. Mitchell, Printer, 24 Congress Street, Boston, MA. 1862. Non-pictorial geometric design border. "Composed on reading Geo. McClellan's Vision." 2pp. Page 2: Blank. [AMC].

913.107 Shout A Song Of Triumph. w. Sidney Herbert. m. "Air—*The Old Granite State.*" In: *McClellan Campaign Melodist,* page 16. c. Sidney Herbert. Published by [V-1 and 2: Benjamin Russel, Boston, MA] [V-3: American News Co., New York, NY] [V-4–7: B.W. Hitchcock, No. 14 Chambers Street, New York, NY]. 1864. [4⅜" × 6⅝"]. B/w litho of "McClellan" and "Pendleton." "A Collection of Patriotic Campaign Songs in Favor of the Constitution and the Union, the Election of General McClellan, the Restoration of the Federal Authority, and the Speedy Extermination of Treason." "The Union Must Be Preserved At All Hazards." 34pp. [M-137–143]. [Crew/GBM-24].

913.108 Shout Aloud For Lincoln. w. "Occasional." m. "Air—*Wait For The Wagon.*" In: *Lincoln Campaign Songster,* page 5. Published by Mason & Company,

Philadelphia, PA. 1864. [4" × 6⅜"]. B/w litho of a beardless Abraham Lincoln, bold striped border. 20pp. "For the use of Clubs, Containing all of the most popular songs." [M-126]. [Crew/AL-81].

913.109 Shouting Our Battle Cry — McClellan! w. No composer indicated. m. "Air — *Battle Cry Of Freedom.*" In: *Democratic Presidential Campaign Songster (No. 1)*, page 5. Published by J.F. Feeks, No. 26 Ann Street, New York, NY. 1864. [3¾" × 5½"]. Y/bk litho of George B. McClellan, chain link frame. "McClellan & Pendleton." "Original Campaign Songs, Choruses, &c." 74pp. [M-135, 136]. [Crew/GBM-23].

913.110 Soldier's Song. w. No composer indicated. m. "Air — *John Brown.*" In: *Democratic Presidential Campaign Songster (No. 1)*, page 26. Published by J.F. Feeks, No. 26 Ann Street, New York, NY. 1864. [3¾" × 5½"]. Y/bk litho of George B. McClellan, chain link frame. "McClellan & Pendleton." "Original Campaign Songs, Choruses, &c." 74pp. [M-135, 136]. [Crew/GBM-23].

913.111 Song. w. No composer indicated. m. "Tune — *Happy Land Of Canaan.*" No publisher indicated. [ca. 1863]. [Approx. 4½" × 13"]. Y/bl non-pictorial. 2pp. Page 2: Blank. [WFU].

913.112 A Song Dedicated To The Colored Volunteer. w. Tom Craig. m. No tune indicated. Published by J.Mc. C. Crummill, Printer, No, 449 N. 3d St. [186-]. B/e geometric design border. 2pp. Page 2: Blank. [AMC].

913.113 A Song For Our Banner. w. Sidney Herbert. m. "Air — *Star Spangled Banner.*" "Arranged from a Patriotic song." In: *McClellan Campaign Melodist*, page 22. c. Sidney Herbert. Published by [V-1 and 2: Benjamin Russel, Boston, MA] [V-3: American News Co., New York, NY] [V-4-7: B.W. Hitchcock, No. 14 Chambers Street, New York, NY]. 1864. [4⅜" × 6⅝"]. B/w litho of "McClellan" and "Pendleton." "A Collection of Patriotic Campaign Songs in Favor of the Constitution and the Union, the Election of General McClellan, the Restoration of the Federal Authority, and the Speedy Extermination of Treason." "The Union Must Be Preserved At All Hazards." 34pp. [M-137–143]. [Crew/GBM-24].

913.114 Stand To Your Guns. w. Sidney Herbert. m. "Air — *Vive La America.*" "Arranged from an Army song." In: *McClellan Campaign Melodist*, page 19. c. Sidney Herbert. Published by [V-1 and 2: Benjamin Russel, Boston, MA] [V-3: American News Co., New York, NY] [V-4-7: B.W. Hitchcock, No. 14 Chambers Street, New York, NY]. 1864. [4⅜" × 6⅝"]. B/w litho of "McClellan" and "Pendleton." "A Collection of Patriotic Campaign Songs in Favor of the Constitution and the Union, the Election of General McClellan, the Restoration of the Federal Authority, and the Speedy Extermination of Treason." "The Union Must Be Preserved At All Hazards." 34pp. [M-137–143]. [Crew/GBM-24].

913.115 Tardy George. w. No composer indicated. m. No tune indicated. In: *Songs For The Union*, page 51. "Printed for the Union Congressional Committee by John A. Gray & Geen, New York," NY. [ca. 1864]. Non-pictorial. 8pp. [AMC].

913.116 Then Up With This Banner. w. Sidney Herbert. m. "Air — *Hear Ye The Bugles.*" "Arranged from a Campaign song." In: *McClellan Campaign Melodist*, page 20. c. Sidney Herbert. Published by [V-1 and 2: Benjamin Russel, Boston, MA] [V-3: American News Co., New York, NY] [V-4-7: B.W. Hitchcock, No. 14 Chambers Street, New York, NY]. 1864. [4⅜" × 6⅝"]. B/w litho of "McClellan" and "Pendleton." "A Collection of Patriotic Campaign Songs in Favor of the Constitution and the Union, the Election of General McClellan, the Restoration of the Federal Authority, and the Speedy Extermination of Treason." "The Union Must Be Preserved At All Hazards." 34pp. [M-137–143]. [Crew/GBM-24].

913.117 Three Cheers For Abe And Andy (A Song For The Times). w.m. Chas. B. Brigham. Published by H.M. Higgins, No. 117 Randolph Street, Chicago, IL. 1964. Non-pictorial geometric designs. "Inscribed to Capt. H.G. Brigham, 107 N.Y. Vol." 6pp. Pages 2 and 6: Blank. [Crew/AL-540].

913.118 Three Cheers For Siegel. w. No composer indicated. m. "Air — *Sparkling And Bright.*" In: *Beadle's Dime Knapsack Songster: Containing The Choicest Patriotic Songs, Together With Many New And Original Ones, Set To Old Melodies*, page 50. Published by Beadle and Company, No. 141 William Street, New York, NY. 1862. [3¾" × 5¾"]. Litho of coin — "One Dime, United States of America." 74pp. [Crew/GBM-78].

913.119 To Whom It May Concern. w. No composer indicated. m. "Air — *Johnny Fill Up The Bowl.*" n: *Democratic Presidential Campaign Songster (No. 1)*, page 50. Published by J.F. Feeks, No. 26 Ann Street, New York, NY. 1864. [3¾" × 5½"]. Y/bk litho of George B. McClellan, chain link frame. "McClellan & Pendleton." "Original Campaign Songs, Choruses, &c." 74pp. [M-135, 136]. [Crew/GBM-23].

913.120 'Tis Our Country's Cause. w. Sidney Herbert. m. "Air — *O Heed The Invitation.*" "Arranged from a Campaign song." In: *McClellan Campaign Melodist*, page 9. c. Sidney Herbert. Published by [V-1 and 2: Benjamin Russel, Boston, MA] [V-3: American News Co., New York, NY] [V-4-7: B.W. Hitchcock, No. 14 Chambers Street, New York, NY]. 1864. [4⅜" × 6⅝"]. B/w litho of "McClellan" and "Pendleton." "A Collection of Patriotic Campaign Songs in Favor of the Constitution and the Union, the Election of General McClellan, the Restoration of the Federal Authority, and the Speedy Extermination of Treason." "The Union Must Be Preserved At All Hazards." 34pp. [M-137–143]. [Crew/GBM-24].

913.121 Traitors, Yield To Law. w. Sidney Herbert. m. "Air — *Scots Wha Hae.*" "Arranged from a song by Walter Anonym." In: *McClellan Campaign Melodist*, page 18. c. Sidney Herbert. Published by [V-1 and 2: Benjamin Russel, Boston, MA] [V-3: American News Co., New York, NY] [V-4-7: B.W. Hitchcock, No. 14 Chambers Street, New York, NY]. 1864. [4⅜" × 6⅝"]. B/w litho of "McClellan" and "Pendleton." "A Collection of Patriotic Campaign Songs in Favor of the Constitution and the Union, the Election of General McClellan, the Restoration of the Federal Authority, and the Speedy Extermination of Treason." "The Union Must Be Preserved At All Hazards." 34pp. [M-137–143]. [Crew/GBM-24].

913.121A Union. w. No composer indicated. m. "Air — *We'll Be Gay And Happy.*" In: *Little Mac Cam-*

paign Songster, page 9. Published by E.P. Patten, The World Office, 35 Park Row, New York, NY. 1864. [4" × 5¾"]. B/w litho of George B. McClellan. "'The Union is the one condition of peace'—we ask no more—Letter of Acceptance." 15pp.

913.122 Union And Freedom. w. No composer indicated. m. "Air—*Rally Round The Flag*." In: *Lincoln Campaign Songster*, page 14. Published by Mason & Company, Philadelphia, PA. 1864. [4" × 6⅜"]. B/w litho of a beardless Abraham Lincoln, bold striped border. 20pp. "For the use of Clubs, Containing all of the most popular songs." Lyrics published online at <http://libwww.syr.edu/digital/exhibits/1/Lincoln/campsong.htm>. [M-126]. [Crew/AL-81].

913.123 Union And Lincoln. w. C.J.F., Jr. m. "Air—*Marching Along*." In: *Lincoln Campaign Songster*, page 12. Published by Mason & Company, Philadelphia, PA. 1864. [4" × 6⅜"]. B/w litho of a beardless Abraham Lincoln, bold striped border. 20pp. "For the use of Clubs, Containing all of the most popular songs." [M-126]. [Crew/AL-81].

913.124 The Union Boys. w. No composer indicated. m. "Air—*Flip Flap*." Published by H. De Marsan, Chatham Street, New York, NY. [1861–1863]. [Approx. 5¾" × 9¼"]. B/w litho of minstrels, Black cherubs, geometric designs. 2pp. Page 2: Blank. [AMC].

913.125 Union Forever. w. Sidney Herbert. m. "Air—*We'll Be Gay And Happy*." "Arranged from a favorite song." In: *McClellan Campaign Melodist*, page 27. c. Sidney Herbert. Published by [V-1 and 2: Benjamin Russel, Boston, MA] [V-3: American News Co., New York, NY] [V-4-7: B.W. Hitchcock, No. 14 Chambers Street, New York, NY]. 1864. [4⅜" × 6⅝"]. B/w litho of "McClellan" and "Pendleton." "A Collection of Patriotic Campaign Songs in Favor of the Constitution and the Union, the Election of General McClellan, the Restoration of the Federal Authority, and the Speedy Extermination of Treason." "The Union Must Be Preserved At All Hazards." 34pp. [M-137–143]. [Crew/GBM-24].

913.126 The Union—Right Or Wrong. w. Sidney Herbert. m. No tune indicated. "Arranged from a song by G.P. Morris." In: *McClellan Campaign Melodist*, page 14. c. Sidney Herbert. Published by [V-1 and 2: Benjamin Russel, Boston, MA] [V-3: American News Co., New York, NY] [V-4-7: B.W. Hitchcock, No. 14 Chambers Street, New York, NY]. 1864. [4⅜" × 6⅝"]. B/w litho of "McClellan" and "Pendleton." "A Collection of Patriotic Campaign Songs in Favor of the Constitution and the Union, the Election of General McClellan, the Restoration of the Federal Authority, and the Speedy Extermination of Treason." "The Union Must Be Preserved At All Hazards." 34pp. [M-137–143]. [Crew/GBM-24].

913.127 The Union! The Hope Of The Free. w. Sidney Herbert. m. "Arranged from a song by Francis De Haes Janvier, Air—*The Union Forever*." In: *McClellan Campaign Melodist*, page 10. e. Sidney Herbert. Published by Benjamin B. Russell, No. 515 Washington Street, Boston, MA. [4⅜" × 6¹⁄₁₆"]. 1864. Bl/bk litho of an eagle—"E Pluribus Unum," cotton bales, crops. "A Collection of Patriotic Campaign Songs in Favor of the Constitution and the Union, the Election of General McClellan, the Restoration of the Federal Authority and the Speedy Extermination of Treason." "The Union must be Preserved at all Hazards!" 36pp. [Crew/GBM-27].

913.128 Vir-Gin-A. w. William Buckley, "of New York." m. "Air—*New Jers-A*." Published by Charles Magnus, 12 Franklin Street, New York, NY. [ca. 1863]. H/c lithos of Miss Liberty standing on a globe of the "U.S." while blowing a trumpet and holding an American flag inscribed "For The Union, vignette of an eagle holding a ribbon and shield over the sea and labeled "Illinois." 2pp. Page 2: Blank. [AMC].

913.129 Vote For McClellan. w. No composer indicated. m. "Air—*Wait For The Wagon*." In: *Democratic Presidential Campaign Songster (No. 1)*, page 20. Published by J.F. Feeks, No. 26 Ann Street, New York, NY. 1864. [3¾" × 5½"]. Y/bk litho of George B. McClellan, chain link frame. "McClellan & Pendleton." "Original Campaign Songs, Choruses, &c." 74pp. [M-135, 136]. [Crew/GBM-23].

913.130 Vote For McClellan. w. No composer indicated. m. "Air—*Uncle Sam Is Rich Enough To Give Us All A Farm*." In: *Little Mac Campaign Songster*, page 9. Published by E.P. Patten, The World Office, 35 Park Row, New York, NY. 1864. [4" × 5¾"]. B/w litho of George B. McClellan. "'The Union is the one condition of peace'—we ask no more—Letter of Acceptance." 15pp.

913.131 Wanamaker's Session Song. w. Samuel R. Wanamaker. m. "Air—*Wait For The Wagon*." Published by Samuel R. Wanamaker, Provision Dealer, 619 Federal Street, above Sixth, Philadelphia, PA. [186-]. Non-pictorial. "Samuel R. Wanamaker, Provision Dealer, 619 Federal Street, above Sixth, Philadelphia, Dealer in Butter, Eggs, Lard, Hams, Dried Beef, Fresh and Salt Beef, Mutton, Pork, Veal, Fruits and Vegetables, &c. All Orders sent to the Store promptly filled and delivered." 2pp. Page 2: Blank. [AMC].

913.132 Wandering Poet's Songs! [1864]. Non-pictorial song sheet with two McClellan songs: **The Song Of O Dear, Dear Little Mac** {913.132–1}. m. "Air—*Widow Machree*," and **Whitewashing The Chicago Platform** {193.132–2}. m. "A Parody on *Lord Ullen's Daughter*." 2pp. Page 2: Blank. [Anti-McClellan]. [Crew/GBM-93].

913.133 We Will Have The Union Still. w. Robert Smith. m. "Air—*Free And Easy*. Published by Auner's Printing Office, 110 N. Tenth Street, ab. Arch, [Philadelphia, PA]. [ca. 1861]. [Approx. 5½" × 9¼"]. B/w non-pictorial geometric design border. 2pp. Page 2: Blank. [AMC].

913.134 Whack, Row De Dow. w. John L. Davenport. "As Sung by John L. Davenport." In: *John L. Davenport's Own Comic Vocalist*, page 15. Published by H.R. Hildreth, No. 5 Olive Street, St. Louis, MO. 1864. [2⅞" × 4¼"]. B/w non-pictorial double black line border. [18pp?]. [Crew/GBM-85].

913.135 When Little Mac Takes The Helm. w. Sidney Herbert. m. "Air—*When Johnny Comes Marching Home*." "Arranged from a Song of Welcome." In: *McClellan Campaign Melodist*, page 32. c. Sidney Herbert. Published by [V-1 and 2: Benjamin Russel, Boston, MA] [V-3: American News Co., New York,

NY] [V-4-7: B.W. Hitchcock, No. 14 Chambers Street, New York, NY]. 1864. [4⅜" × 6⅝"]. B/w litho of "McClellan" and "Pendleton". "A Collection of Patriotic Campaign Songs in Favor of the Constitution and the Union, the Election of General McClellan, the Restoration of the Federal Authority, and the Speedy Extermination of Treason." "The Union Must Be Preserved At All Hazards." 34pp. [M-137–143]. [Crew/GBM-24].

913.136 When The Demmies Were In Power. w. Logan S. Porter. m. W.G. Thomas. In: *McKinley Campaign Songster For 1900 (For Male Voices)*, page 26. e. W.G. Thomas. Published by The Home Music Company, Logansport, IN. 1900. Gn/bk litho of "William McKinley for President" and "Theo. Roosevelt For Vice President," eagle, flags, shield. "Send cash with order." "All orders will be promptly filled if accompanied by cash." "Single copy 15 cts. $.50 per dozen." "Note: Our McKinley Campaign Songster No. 2, Entirely Different from this will be issued September 10th. Same Price." 36pp. [M-373]. [Crew/WM-275].

913.137 Who Will Care For Old Abe Now? (A parody). w.m. No composer or tune indicated. Published by H. De Marsan, No. 54 Chatham St., NY. [ca. 1864]. B/w litho border of minstrels, cherubs, geometric designs. 2pp. Page 2: Blank. [Crew/GBM-94]. [AMC].

913.138 Whom Shall We Send To Washington. w. No composer indicated. m. "Air—*A Man's A Man For A' That.*" In: *Democratic Presidential Campaign Songster (No. 1)*, page 34. Published by J.F. Feeks, No. 26 Ann Street, New York, NY. 1864. [3¾" × 5½"]. Y/bk litho of George B. McClellan, chain link frame. "McClellan & Pendleton." "Original Campaign Songs, Choruses, &c." 74pp. [M-135, 136]. [Crew/GBM-23].

• **AmPM-913A** MCGREEVEY, James E. (State General Assembly, 1990–1991; Mayor, Township of Woodbridge, 1991–1994; State Senate, 1994–1997; Governor, 2001–Present)

913A.1 Drag Queen With Fever. w. Guy DiRito. "*Day Dream Believer* based on the performance by The Monkies." "Just some more on our favorite New Jersey Governor." Published on line at <http://www.amiright.com/parody/60s/themonkees55.shtml>. 2004.

913A.1A The Girlie Governor. w. Alan Dover, "alvindover@hotmail.com." m. "Sung to the tune of *The Lonely Goat Herd* from *The Sound of Music* by Rogers and Hammerstein." "As sung by Cahleefornia Governor Arnold Schwarzenegger about New Jersey Governor James McGreevy [sic]." 2004.

913A.2 Jimmy McGreevey. w. Guy DiRito. "*Lady Madonna* based on the performance by The Beatles." "Taking center stage this week on all the news circuits is none other than New Jersey Governor James McGreevy. And we thought old Grey was bad…" Published on line at <http://www.aimright.com/parody/60s/thebeatles787.shtml>. 2004.

913A.3 Uncle McGreevey Song. w.m. No composer indicated. "Kids! Sing along with the Uncle McGreevey Song! Just follow the bouncing Uncle McGreevey Head." N/c photo of the head of James McGreevey, sheet music. Published online at <http://www.njleek.com/funhouse/UnMcGSong.htm>. [ca. 2004].

913A.4 You've Lost That Gov'nor Feelin'. w. Michael Pacholek. m. "*You've Lost That Lovin' Feelin'* based on the performance by The Righteous Brothers." "For my State's Governor, James I. McGreevey. He's just like any other Governor: He puts his pants on one leg at a time. The difference is in what he did with them before." Published on line at <http://www.aimright.com/parody/60s/therighteousbrothers3.shtml>. 2004.

• **AmPM-914** MEYNER, Robert B. (State Senate, 1947–1951; Governor, 1954–1962)

914.1 Make Mine Meyner. w.m. Bing Shopa and Jo Frances. No publisher indicated. Copyright 1957 by Gary Stephens Music Publications, 1466 Whipple Walk, Camden, NJ. Bl/w photo of Robert Meyner. 4pp. Page 4: Bl/w photo of "Gov. Robert B. Meyner." "Re-Elect."

• **AmPM-915** MILLER, Jacob Welsh (State Assembly, 1832; State Council, 1838–1840; U.S. Senate, 1841–1853)

915.1 Song Of The First Of Arkansas. w. Lindley Miller. m. No tune indicated. Published by the Supervisory Committee for Recruiting Colored Regiments. [Approx. 6" × 11"]. Non-pictorial. "The following song was written by Captain Lindley Miller, of the First Arkansas Colored Regiment. Captain Miller says the 'boys' sing the song on dress parade with the effect which can hardly be described, and he adds that 'while it is not very conservative, it will do to fight with.' Captain Miller is a song of the late ex–Senator Miller, of New Jersey." 2pp. Page 2: Blank. [AMC].

• **AmPM-916** MUNLEY, Francis E. (Candidate for Freeholder, Bergan County, 1949)

916.1 We'll Change The Scene With Elmer Wene. w. Walter E. Brill. m. Frank T. Grasso. Published by Valemont Music Co., Montvale, NJ. 1949. Bl/w photo of Elmer Wene. R/w/b printing, stars. "The Campaign Song of Elmer H. Wene, Democratic Candidate for Governor of New Jersey." 4pp. + 2pp. insert. Page 4: Bergan County ticket including "Karl D. Van Wagner for State Senator, Lloyd S. Carr, David B. Foley, Patrick Tedesco, Robert Eichler, George B. Chelius, Jr., and Otto J. Stellato for General Assembly, Jacob Schneider, for Surrogate, and James A. Bishop and Francis E. Munley for Freeholders." "On Election Day Nov. 8, 1949."

NEWELL, William Augustus (U.S. House, New Jersey, 1847–1851 & 1865–1867; Governor, New Jersey, 1857–1860) [See: Washington State]

• **AmPM-917** NICHOLS, Armand T. (Candidate for Sheriff, Atlantic County, 1941)

917.1 For Sheriff Armand T. w. Roy J. Walsh. m. Art Stanley. a. George Johnson. Published by the candidate. 1941. B/w photo of Armand T. Nichols. R/w/b drawing of a pretty girl sitting under a tree near the shore, sailboat. "Paid for by Roy L. Walsh." 6pp. Page 2: Blank. Page 6: Campaign poem by William J. Bates.

• **AmPM-918** NICHOLSON. (Candidate for Assembly, 1886)

918.1 Prohibition Song. [4¼" × 6¹⁵⁄₁₆"]. Non-pictorial. 2pp. Page 2: Blank. [Crew/CBF-3].

• **AmPM-919** NORTON, Mary Teresa (County Freeholder, Hudson County, 1922; U.S. House, 1925–1951)

919.1 Franklin Roosevelt We're With You w. Maud Michael. m. Charles Gilpin. Published by Maud Michael, 1819 Chestnut Street, Philadelphia, PA. 1935. [5⅜" × 8½"]. Non-pictorial. "Notice: Endorsed and Sponsored by the Roosevelt Citizens' Committee of Philadelphia, PA., and many Democratic leaders throughout the United States as the Official Democratic Campaign Song for 1936." "Notice: Endorsed by the Atlantic County Democratic Campaign Committee of New Jersey, with a request this song be used to open all Democratic Political Meetings and Public Assemblies, Charles J. Lafferty, Chair." "Notice: Mrs. Mary T. Norton, Democratic Congressman and Chairman of the District of Columbia Committee which supervises local government in Washington, D.C., and the Federal District endorses this song and recommends its use at all Political Meetings and claims it to be a Real Patriotic Promoter." "This song was introduced as the Official Democratic Campaign Song at the Testimonial Dinner of 1200 guests at the Pennsylvania Athletic Club, January 10, 1935, for the Hon. H. Edgar Barnes, Secretary of Revenue of Pennsylvania." "A Meeting without a Song is like a Meal without Salt — It's Flat." 2pp. Page 2: Blank.

• **AmPM-920 PIERSON**, George. (Candidate for State House, 1899)

920.1 How Can I Make A Dollar. "In German: ***Wie Kann Man Geld Verdienen?"*** (Campaign Song). w.m. Paul G. Zimmerman. Published by Paul G. Zimmerman, Morristown, NJ. 1899. B/w photos of "For President William Jennings Bryan," "For Vice-President Adlai E. Stevenson," and "For Congress Joshua S. Salmon." "For Assembly John Bergen, George Pierson [No photos]." "The 1900 Common Sense Campaign Song." "Respectfully Dedicated to Mrs. Mary B. Bryan." 4pp. [Crew/WJB-42].

• **AmPM-921 POTTER**, Francis D. (Candidate for U.S. House, 1912)

921.1 Progressive League Of Burlington County [Song Sheet]. [1912]. [6" × 8¼"]. B/w litho of U.S. flag. "For President Theodore Roosevelt, For Vice-President Hiram Johnson, For Congressman Francis D. Potter; For State Senator William B. Shedaker, For Assemblyman Joseph Beck Tyler." "This folder ordered and paid for by the Progressive League of Burlington Co." 4pp.

• **AmPM-922 ROBESON**, George Maxwell (State Attorney General, 1867–1869; Secretary of the Navy, 1867–1877; U.S. House, 1879–1883)

922.1 After The Election Is Over. w.m. No composer indicated. m. "Air — *After The Opera Is Over*." In: *The Sun's Greeley Campaign Songster*, page 10. c. Amos J. Cumming. Published from *The Sun* Office, New York, NY. 1872. [4⅛" × 6½"]. Be/bk litho of Horace Greeley, wreath. "He shines for all." 64pp. [Crew/HG-5].

922.2 Bryan Campaign Songster For 1900 (For Male Voices). e. Logan S. Porter. Published by Home Music Company, Logansport, IN. 1900. Pk/bk litho of William Jennings Bryan and Adlai E. Stevenson. 36pp. [M-386]. [Crew/WJB-71].

922.3 Carry The News To 'Lysses. w. No composer indicated. m. "Air — *Carry The News To Mary*." In: *Greeley Campaign Songster*, page 40. "Respectfully dedicated to the Greeley Clubs of the Country." Published by Halpin & McClure, Chicago, IL. 1872. [4" × 5$\frac{11}{16}$"]. Pl/bk litho of Horace Greeley, geometric design border. "Chicago: Western News Company, Wholesale Agents." 72pp. [M-187]. [Crew/HG-21].

922.4 Cocachilunk, &c. w.m. No composer or tune indicated. In: *Illustrated Campaign Song And Joke*, page 39. Published by The American News Company, New York, NY. [4¾" × 7½"]. 1876. Y/bk litho of Samuel J. Tilden, geometric design border. 50pp. [?]. Page 5: Title — *The Illustrated Campaign Tilden Song And Joke Book*. [Crew/SJT-8].

922.5 The Hat Of Chappaqua. w.m. No composer or tune indicated. In: *The Sun's Greeley Campaign Songster*, page 28. c. Amos J. Cumming. Published from *The Sun* Office, New York, NY. 1872. [4⅛" × 6½"]. Be/bk litho of Horace Greeley, wreath. "He shines for all." 64pp. [Crew/HG-5].

922.6 Hayes, Make Way For Tilden. w. No composer indicated. m. "Air — *Tommy, Make Room For Your Auntie*." In: *Illustrated Campaign Song And Joke*, page 36. Published by The American News Company, New York, NY. [4¾" × 7½"]. 1876. Y/bk litho of Samuel J. Tilden, geometric design border. 50pp. [?]. Page 5: Title — *The Illustrated Campaign Tilden Song 922.7 And Joke Book*. [Crew/SJT-8].

922.7 Hiram's Menagerie. In: *The Sun's Greeley Campaign Songster*. c. Amos J. Cummings. Published from *The Sun* Office, New York, NY. 1872. [4⅛" × 6½"]. Be/bk litho of Horace Greeley, wreath. "He shines for all." 64pp. [M-183]. [Crew/HG-5].

ROSS, Edmund Gibson (Territorial Governor, 1885–1889) [See: Kansas]

• **AmPM-923 RODINO**, Peter Wallace, Jr. (U.S. House, 1949–1989)

923.1 I'm So Lonesome Tonight. w. No composer indicated. m. "Tune — *Are You Lonesome Tonight*." In: *Thoroughly Mad-ern Malcolm or He Didn't Need A Course In Forensics To Become A Famous Public Speaker*, page 13. Published by the New York State Legislative Correspondents' Association, Albany, NY. 1974. N/w photo of Malcolm Wilson as Alfred E. Newman — "What — Me Governor?" "Featuring the New York Correspondents' Association, March 16. 1974." 32pp.

• **AmPM-924 RYALL**, Daniel Bailey (State House, 1831 & 1833–1835; U.S. House, 1839–1841)

924.1 A Parody On Up Salt River. w. No composer indicated. m. "Tune — *All On Hobbies*." In: *Songs For The People (Or Tippecanoe Melodies)* [Songster], page 37. "Dedicated to the Democratic Whig Young Men of the City and County of New York." Published for the Authors by James P. Giffing, No. 56 Gold Street, New York, NY. 1840. [3¾" × 6"]. Litho of William Henry Harrison, log cabin, flag. "Original and Selected." 76pp. [M-019]. [Crew/WHH-63].

924.2 Up Salt River (A New Whig Song). w. G.B.W. (Toledo, OH). m. "Tune — *All On Hobbies*." Published by Firth & Hall, No. 1 Franklin Square, New York, NY. 1840. Non-pictorial. "Respectfully Dedicated to the Toledo Tippecanoe Club." "Pr. 25 c nett [sic]." 4pp. [Crew/ WHH-38].

924.3 Up Salt River (A New Whig Song). w. G.B.W. "of Toledo, Ohio." m. "Tune — *All On Hobbies*." "Respectfully dedicated to the Toledo Tippecanoe Club."

In: *The Log Cabin & Hard Cider Melodies, A Collection Of Popular And Patriotic Songs*, page 65. Published by Charles Adams, No. 23 Tremont Street, Boston, MA. 1840. [3¾" × 6"]. [V-1: Pk/bk] [V-2: Gn/bk] litho of William Henry Harrison. "The Freeman's glittering Sword be Blest, For ever blest the Freeman's Lyre." 78pp. Pages 2 and 77: Blank. Page 3: Inside title page. B/w litho of log cabin. "Respectfully Dedicated to the Friends of Harrison and Tyler." Page 78: Advertising. [M-012]. [Crew/WHH-68].

• **AmPM-925 SALMON**, Joshua S. (State House, 1877–1878; Prosecuting Attorney, Morris County, 1893–1898; U.S. House, 1899–1902)

925.1 How Can I Make A Dollar. "In German: ***Wie Kann Man Geld Verdienen?*** (Campaign Song). w.m. Paul G. Zimmerman. Published by Paul G. Zimmerman, Morristown, NJ. 1899. B/w photos of "For President William Jennings Bryan," "For Vice-President Adlai E. Stevenson," and "For Congress Joshua S. Salmon." "For Assembly John Bergen, George Pierson [No photos]." "The 1900 Common Sense Campaign Song." "Respectfully Dedicated to Mrs. Mary B. Bryan." 4pp. [Crew/WJB-42].

• **AmPM-926 SCALIA**, Antonin (General counsel, Office of Telecommunications Policy, Executive Office of the President, 1971–1972; Chairman, Administrative Conference of the United States, 1972–1974; Assistant Attorney General, Office of Legal Counsel, U. S. Department of Justice, 1974–1977; U.S. Court of Appeals 1982–1986; Supreme Court, 1986–Present)

926.1 Bush Lacks Authority. w. Skisics Surus. m. "*Authority Song*, originally by John Cougar Mellencamp." Published online at <http://amiright.com/parody/80s/johncougarmellencamp1.shml>. [ca. 2000].

926.2 Diff'rent Votes. w. Attmay. m. "Sung to the tune of the theme from *Diff'rent Strokes*." Published online at <http://www.geocities.com/wmktong/bootnewt/diffvotes.htm>. [ca. 2000].

926.3 Don't Cry For Me Judge Scalia. w. Bill Strauss and Elaina Newport. On CD: *Unzippin' My Doo-Dah*. Published by Capitol Steps Productions, 1505 King Street, Alexandria, VA. 1998. CD Cover: Gn/bl/y drawing of George Bush and George W. Bush as Seuss characters.

926.4 Dubya, The Bogus POTUS. w. William Tong. m. "*Rudolph The Red-Nosed Reindeer*, originally by Gene Autry." Published online at <http://amiright.com/parody/misc/geneautry0.shml>. [ca. 2000].

926.5 Fiasco. w. William Tong. m. "*El Paso*, originally by Marty Robbins." Published online at <http://www.amiright.com/parody/70s/martyrobbins0.shml>. [ca. 2001].

926.6 How Do You Solve A Problem Like Scalia? w. Bill Strauss and Elaina Newport. On CD: *Sixteen Scandals*. Published by Capitol Steps Productions, 1505 King Street, Alexandria, VA. 1997. CD Cover: Gn/bl/y drawing of George Bush and George W. Bush as Seuss characters.

926.7 Scalia. w. William K. Tong. m. "Sung to the tune of *Maria* from the musical *West Side Story*." "From a suggestion by Leslie Allison." Published online at <http://www.bootnewt.envy.nu.scalia.html>.

926.8 Shady Scalia. w. William K. Tong. m. "Sung to the tune of *Lady Madonna* by The Beatles." N/c computer photo of Antonin Scalia—"The Coup Father, Antonin 'lightfingers' Scalia, the alleged brains behind the Judicial Coup which appointed His Fradulency, G.W. Bush to the U.S. presidency, is rumored to become the new 'made man' of the GOP controlled Extreme Court. When asked to confirm the rumor, he said 'Ged Oudda heah, I don' no nuttin' ablut it." Published online at <http://www.bootnewt.envy.nu.shadyscalia.html>.

926.9 Supreme Court's Installation. w. William Tong. m. Tune—"*You're My Soul And Inspiration*, originally by The Righteous Brothers." "Sung by Scalia to Dubya." Published online at <http://www.amiright.com/parody/misc/therighteousbrothers0.shtml>. [ca. 2000]

926.10 To Hell With Vote Machines. w. William Tong. m. Tune—"*Yellow Submarine*, originally by The Beatles." Published online at <http://amiright.com/parody/misc/thebeatles7.shml>. [ca. 2000].

926.11 Won't The Courts Be Loverly? w. Lydia Theys. m. "*Wouldn't It Be Loverly?* originally by *My Fair Lady*." "As Sung by Antonin Scalia." Published online at <http://amiright.com/parody/misc/myfairlady0.shml>. [ca. 2000].

• **AmPM-927 SCHNEIDER**, Jacob (Candidate for Surrogate, Bergan County, 1949)

927.1 We'll Change The Scene With Elmer Wene. w. Walter E. Brill. m. Frank T. Grasso. Published by Valemont Music Co., Montvale, NJ. 1949. Bl/w photo of Elmer Wene. R/w/b printing, stars. "The Campaign Song of Elmer H. Wene, Democratic Candidate for Governor of New Jersey." 4pp. + 2pp. insert. Page 4: Bergan County ticket including "Karl D. Van Wagner for State Senator, Lloyd S. Carr, David B. Foley, Patrick Tedesco, Robert Eichler, George B. Chelius, Jr., and Otto J. Stellato for General Assembly, Jacob Schneider, for Surrogate, and James A. Bishop and Francis E. Munley for Freeholders." "On Election Day Nov. 8, 1949."

• **AmPM-928 SEAGRAVE**, R.T. (Candidate for Assembly, 1886)

928.1 Prohibition Song. [4¼" × 6¹⁵⁄₁₆"]. Non-pictorial. 2pp. Page 2: Blank. [Crew/CBF-3].

• **AmPM-929 SHEDAKER**, William B. (Candidate for State Senate, 1912)

929.1 Progressive League Of Burlington County [Song Sheet]. [1912]. [6" × 8¼"]. B/w litho of U.S. flag. "For President Theodore Roosevelt, For Vice-President Hiram Johnson, For Congressman Francis D. Potter; For State Senator William B. Shedaker, For Assemblyman Joseph Beck Tyler." "This folder ordered and paid for by the Progressive League of Burlington Co." 4pp.

• **AmPM-930 SOUTHARD**, Samuel Lewis (State House, 1815; State Supreme Court, 1815–1820; U.S. Senate, 1821–1823 & 1833–1842; Secretary of the Navy, 1823–1829; Secretary of War, 1824; Secretary of the Treasury, 1825; State Attorney General, 1829–1833; Governor, 1832–1833)

930.1 Keep The Ball Rolling. w. No composer indicated. In: *The Log Cabin*, page 4, Vol. 1, No. 26, Oct. 24, 1840. Published by Horace Greeley & Company, New York, NY. 1840. Non-pictorial. [Crew/WHH-91(A)].

• **AmPM-931 STELLATO**, Otto J. (Candidate for State House, 1949)
931.1 We'll Change The Scene With Elmer Wene. w. Walter E. Brill. m. Frank T. Grasso. Published by Valemont Music Co., Montvale, NJ. 1949. Bl/w photo of Elmer Wene. R/w/b printing, stars. "The Campaign Song of Elmer H. Wene, Democratic Candidate for Governor of New Jersey." 4pp. + 2pp. insert. Page 4: Bergan County ticket including "Karl D. Van Wagner for State Senator, Lloyd S. Carr, David B. Foley, Patrick Tedesco, Robert Eichler, George B. Chelius, Jr., and Otto J. Stellato for General Assembly, Jacob Schneider, for Surrogate, and James A. Bishop and Francis E. Munley for Freeholders." "On Election Day Nov. 8, 1949."

• **AmPM-932 STOCKTON**, Richard (State Executive Council, 1768–1776; State Supreme Court, 1774–1776; Continental Congress, 1776; Signer of the Declaration of Independence, 1776)
932.1 The Declaration Of Independence Of The United States Of North America, July 4, 1776. w. From the Declaration of Independence. m. John E. Wilson. Published by John E. Wilson, Baltimore, MD. 1863. B/w litho of the interior of Independence Hall. "Arranged and adapted for Vocal and Instrumental Music as the Great National Chant." 4pp. [?]. Page 4: Facsimile signatures of all signers.
932.2 Old Independence Hall. w. A. Fletcher Stayman. m. Francis Weiland. Published by Stayman & Brothers, No. 210 Chesnut Street, Philadelphia, PA. 1855. Non-pictorial. "Respectfully dedicated to the Memory of the Signers of the Declaration of Independence." "Fac Simile of their signatures" including John Adams, Sam Adams, Elbridge Gerry, Thomas Jefferson. 8pp. Pages 2 and 8: Blank. [Crew/MISC-34].

• **AmPM-933 STRATTON**, Charles Creighton (General Assembly, 1821, 1823 & 1829; U.S. House, 1837–1839 & 1841–1843; State Constitutional Convention, 1844; Governor, 1845–1848)
933.1 A Parody On Up Salt River. w. No composer indicated. m. "Tune—*All On Hobbies.*" In: *Songs For The People (Or Tippecanoe Melodies)* [Songster], page 37. "Dedicated to the Democratic Whig Young Men of the City and County of New York." Published for the Authors by James P. Giffing, No. 56 Gold Street, New York, NY. 1840. [3¾" × 6"]. Litho of William Henry Harrison, log cabin, flag. "Original and Selected." 76pp. [M-019]. [Crew/WHH-63].
933.2 Up Salt River (A New Whig Song). w. G.B.W. "of Toledo, Ohio." m. "Tune—*All On Hobbies.*" "Respectfully dedicated to the Toledo Tippecanoe Club." In: *The Log Cabin & Hard Cider Melodies, A Collection Of Popular And Patriotic Songs*, page 65. Published by Charles Adams, No. 23 Tremont Street, Boston, MA. 1840. [3¾" × 6"]. [V-1: Pk/bk] [V-2: Gn/bk] litho of William Henry Harrison. "The Freeman's glittering Sword be Blest, For ever blest the Freeman's Lyre." 78pp. [M-012]. [Crew/WHH-68].

• **AmPM-934 TEDESCO**, Patrick (Candidate for State House, 1949)
934.1 We'll Change The Scene With Elmer Wene. w. Walter E. Brill. m. Frank T. Grasso. Published by Valemont Music Co., Montvale, NJ. 1949. Bl/w photo of Elmer Wene. R/w/b printing, stars. "The Campaign Song of Elmer H. Wene, Democratic Candidate for Governor of New Jersey." 4pp. + 2pp. insert. Page 4: Bergan County ticket including "Karl D. Van Wagner for State Senator, Lloyd S. Carr, David B. Foley, Patrick Tedesco, Robert Eichler, George B. Chelius, Jr., and Otto J. Stellato for General Assembly, Jacob Schneider, for Surrogate, and James A. Bishop and Francis E. Munley for Freeholders." "On Election Day Nov. 8, 1949."

• **AmPM-935 THOMAS**, John Parnell (Borough Council, Allendale, 1925; Mayor, Allendale 1926–1930; State House, 1935–1937; U.S. House, 1937–1950)
935.1 The Unfriendly 19. w. Earl Robinson. m. *Tam Pierce*. In: *Battle Hymn Of '48*. w. Bryant M. French. m. "Tune—*John Brown's Body.*" In: *People's Songs, Songs Of Labor And The American People (Vol. 3, Nos. 1 And 2)*, page 21. Published by People's Songs, Inc., No. 126 West 21st Street, New York, NY. 1948. [8⅞" × 10⅛"]. B/w drawing of farmer. [Crew/HAW-8(A)].

• **AmPM-936 TORRICELLI**, Robert Guy (Assistant to the Governor of New Jersey, 1975–1977; Counsel to Vice President Walter Mondale, 1978–1980; U.S. House, 1983–1997; U.S. Senate, 1997–2003)
936.1 Glenn, Torricelli And Associates. w. Paul Shanklin. On CD: *Bill Clinton Comeback Kid Tour*. Published by Narodniki Records. CD Cover: Caricature of Bill Clinton. See: www.paulshanklin.com. 2002.
936.2 Toricelli. w. Bill Strauss and Elaina Newport. On CD: *Between Iraq And A Hard Place*. Published by Capitol Steps Productions, 1505 King Street, Alexandria, VA. 2003. CD Cover: N/c drawing of a U.N. vehicle.

• **AmPM-937 TREAT**, Robert (Surveyor of Milford Lands, 1639–1640 & 1652; Tax Collector, Wethersfield, 1647; Deputy, New Haven Colony General Court, 1653,1655–1659; Chief Military Officer of Milford, 1654; Magistrate, New Haven Colony, 1660–1664; Founder and Town Clerk, Newark, New Jersey, 1666–1667; State Legislature, New Jersey, 1667–1672; Assistant, General Court of the Colony of Connecticut, 1673–1676; Deputy Governor, Colony of Connecticut, 1676–1683, 1699–1709; Governor, Colony of Connecticut, 1683–1698)
937.1 The 250th Anniversary Of Dear Old Newark, N.J. 1666-1916 (Novelty March Song). w.m. T. Geo. Callahan. Published by Callahan, 627–629 Market Street, Newark, NJ. 1916. B/w drawing of a key marked "Welcome to our City," geometric designs. "In loving memory of our dear old friend "Hon. Robert Treat and his followers."

• **AmPM-938 TRIPP**, Linda (Executive Assistant to the President's Counsel, 1993; Pentagon Public Affairs Office, 1994–2001)
938.1 Bill Clinton Got Run Over By A Taxi. w. Billy Florio. m. "*Grandma Got Run Over By A Reindeer,* originally by Elmo & Patsy." Published online at <http://amiright.com/parody/80s/elmoandpatsy0. shml>. [ca. 2001].
938.2 Bill So Horney. w.m. Mark Ross, Chris Wong Won, David Hobbs and Luther Campbell. On 33⅓ rpm EP: *Bill So Horney* by 2 Live Crew. Lil' Joe

Records, 6157 NW 167th St., Miami, FL. Record #LJR 900-1. 1998. Performed by 2 Live Crew and Amos Braxton. Cover art: Drawing of Bill Clinton and Monica Lewinsky; 2 Live Crew. [2 versions—Clean and Explicit]. 1998.

938.3 Bleaque Alley. w. "Melhi." m. "*Creeque Alley*, originally by The Mamas and Papas." Written as the Monica Lewinsky scandal was fading." Published online at <http://amiright.com/parody/60s/themamasandpapas0.shml>. [ca. 2000].

938.4 Hail To The Chief, O. w. Raymond Frost. m. No tune indicated. [Sir Arthur Sullivan]. Published online at <http://lightjunkie.org/parody/starr2.html>. 1998.

938.5 Help Republicans Fail. w. William K. Tong. m. "Sung to the tune of *The Ballad Of Gilligan's Isle*." In: *The Sting The Right Wing Song Book* at <http://www.geocities.com/wmktong/bootnewt/repfail.htm>.

938.6 Hey Now (Your [sic] an Ex Pres). w. Vermonter. m. Tune—"*Hey Now (Your* [sic] *An All Star)*, originally by Smash Mouth." Published online at <http://www.amiright.com/parody/90s/smashmouth2.shtml>. [ca. 2001].

938.7 Hide Willie Hide. w. Charles Baum. m. "My son about Bill and Monica el al, parodying *The Two Magicians*." "This was written in February 1998, before most of the events happened as a short shelf-life song that just lasted longer than I thought possible ..." Lyrics and sound file published online at <http://www.mudcat.org/kids/@displaysong.cfm?SongID=8883>. 1998.

938.8 Hotel Pennsylvania. w. Malcolm Higgins. m. Tune—"*Hotel California*, originally by The Eagles." Published online at <http://www.amiright.com/parody/70s/theeagles4.shtml>. [ca. 2001].

938.9 I Got You Bill. w. Malcolm Higgins. m. Tune—"*I Got You Babe*, originally by Sonny and Cher." Published online at <http://amiright.com/parody/misc/sonnyandcher1.shml>. [ca. 1999].

938.10 Linda Is A Tripp. w. Bill Strauss and Elaina Newport. On CD: *Unzippin' My Doo-Dah*. Published by Capitol Steps Productions, 1505 King Street, Alexandria, VA. 1998. CD Cover: Gn/bl/y drawing of George Bush and George W. Bush as Seuss characters.

938.11 Lirty Dies: Imbos In The Office. w.m. The Capitol Steps. Published by The Capitol Steps online at<http://capsteps.com/lirty/imbos.htm>. 1998.

938.12 Name Is Bill Clinton. w. S.T.G. m. "*Dreams In Digital (Fiction)*, originally by Orgy." Published online at <http://amiright.com/parody/2000s/orgy0.shml>. [ca. 2001].

938.13 Scandal Time. w. William K. Tong. m. "Sung to the tune of *Summer Time* from Porgy & Bess." In: *The Sting The Right Wing Song Book* at <http://www.geocities.com/wmktong/bootnewt/scandtim.htm>.

938.14 Trida Lipp. w. Bill Strauss and Elaina Newport. On CD: *Unzippin' My Doo-Dah*. Published by Capitol Steps Productions, 1505 King Street, Alexandria, VA. 1998. CD Cover: Gn/bl/y drawing of George Bush and George W. Bush as Seuss characters.

938.15 A Yucky Woman (Ode to Linda Tripp). w. William K. Tong. m. "Sung to the tune of *Kentucky Woman* by Neil Diamond." In: *The Sting The Right Wing Song Book* at <http://www.geocities.com/wmktong/bootnewt/yucky.htm> and <http://amiright.com/parody/70s/neildiamond1.shml>. [ca. 2000].

- **AmPM-939 TROAST**, Paul L. (Delegate to Republican National Convention from New Jersey, 1948 & 1952. Chairman, New Jersey Turnpike Authority, 1949; Republican Candidate for Governor, 1953)

939.1 A Toast To Troast. w. Lou Cunningham. m. Harry Link. Published by Edward B. Marks Music Corporation, R.C.A. Building, New York, NY. 1953. B/w photo of "Paul Troast." 6pp. Page 6: Advertising.

- **AmPM-940 TUMULTY**, Joseph Patrick (State House, 1907-1910; Private Secretary to Woodrow Wilson, 1911-1921)

940.1 My Pretty Little Indian Maid. w.m. M.J. Fitzpatrick. Published by Fitzpatrick Brothers. R/w/br/bk drawing of an Indian girl. Background of newspaper clippings including headlines and articles such as "Wilson Love Song Can't Be Stopped;" "A Brooklyn song writer, Michael J.F. Fitzgerald who wrote the song, Pretty Little Indian Maid, using the White House romance as a basis, has received a letter from Secretary Tumulty a request that the song not be published;" and "While the name of Mrs. Galt, the President's fiancée, is not mentioned, the reference in the song is unmistakable, because of the fact that Mrs. Galt is descended from Pocahontas, the Indian Princess." [Crew/WW-220].

- **AmPM-941 TURNER**, Benjamin Franklin (Commissioner of Parks, NJ., 1935)

941.1 Return Ben Turner. w.m. Frank 'Duke' Feher. Published by the Ben Turner campaign. 1935. Bl/w photo of Ben Turner. "True, Unbiased, Resolute, Needed, Efficient, Resourceful." "Return Ben Turner for Commissioner, Tuesday, May 14th, 1935, Official Campaign song by Duke Feher." 4pp. Page 4: Narrative—"Turner's Candidacy Greeted With Enthusiasm in Passaic!"

- **AmPM-942 TYLER**, Joseph Beck (Candidate for State Assemblyman, 1912)

942.1 Progressive League Of Burlington County [Song Sheet]. [1912]. [6" × 8¼"]. B/w litho of U.S. flag. "For President Theodore Roosevelt, For Vice-President Hiram Johnson, For Congressman Francis D. Potter; For State Senator William B. Shedaker, For Assemblyman Joseph Beck Tyler." "This folder ordered and paid for by the Progressive League of Burlington Co." 4pp.

- **AmPM-943 VAN WAGNER**, Karl D. (Candidate for State Senate, 1949)

943.1 We'll Change The Scene With Elmer Wene. w. Walter E. Brill. m. Frank T. Grasso. Published by Valemont Music Co., Montvale, NJ. 1949. Bl/w photo of Elmer Wene. R/w/b printing, stars. "The Campaign Song of Elmer H. Wene, Democratic Candidate for Governor of New Jersey." 4pp. + 2pp. insert. Page 4: Bergan County ticket including "Karl D. Van Wagner for State Senator, Lloyd S. Carr, David B. Foley, Patrick Tedesco, Robert Eichler, George B. Chelius, Jr., and Otto J. Stellato for General Assembly, Jacob Schneider, for Surrogate, and James A. Bishop and Francis E. Munley for Freeholders." "On Election Day Nov. 8, 1949."

• **AmPM-944 WALL**, Garret Dorset (Clerk of the State Supreme Court, 1812–1817; State Quartermaster General, 1815–1837; General Assembly, 1827; U.S. District Attorney for New Jersey, 1829; U.S. Senate, 1835–1841; Court of Errors and Appeals, 1848–1850)
944.1 The Aristocracy Of Democracy. w. "An Old Democrat, 1798." m. "Tune—*John Anderson, My Jo.*" "The Following song was written by an Old Democrat of 1798, an original Jackson man, but not an admirer of such modern or patent democracy as is professed by 'Nor-a-single-drop-of-democratic-blood' Buchanan, or 'As-long-as-the-federal-flag-waved-in-New-Jersey-I-was-proud-to-rally-under-it' Garret D. Wall." In: *The Clay Minstrel Or National Songster*, page 224. c. John Stockton Littell. Published by Greeley & M'Elrath, Tribune Building, New York, NY. 1844. [3⅛" × 4⅞"]. Non-pictorial. 396pp. [Crew/HC-18].
• **AmPM-945 WENE**, Elmer H. (U.S. House, 1937–1939 & 1941–1945; Board of Freeholders, Cumberland County, 1939–1941; State Senate, 1946; Candidate for Governor, NJ., 1949)
945.1 We'll Change The Scene With Elmer Wene. w. Walter E. Brill. m. Frank T. Grasso. Published by Valemont Music Co., Montvale, NJ. 1949. Bl/w photo of Elmer Wene. R/w/b printing, stars. "The Campaign Song of Elmer H. Wene, Democratic Candidate for Governor of New Jersey." 4pp. + 2pp. insert. Page 4: Bergan County ticket including "Karl D. Van Wagner for State Senator, Lloyd S. Carr, David B. Foley, Patrick Tedesco, Robert Eichler, George B. Chelius, Jr., and Otto J. Stellato for General Assembly, Jacob Schneider, for Surrogate, and James A. Bishop and Francis E. Munley for Freeholders." "On Election Day Nov. 8, 1949."
• **AmPM-946 WHITMAN**, Christie (Governor, 1994–2001; EPA Administrator, 2002)
946.1 Christie Todd Whitman. w. Ed Smiley. m. Tune—"*American Woman,* originally by Guess Who." Published online at <http://www.amiright.com/parody/70s/guesswho0.shtml>. [ca. 2001].
946.2 Christie Whitman Went To Town. w. Madeleine Begun Kane. Published online at <http://www.madkane.com/christie_whitman.html>. "In honor of Christie Whitman's resignation as Dubya's EPA Administrator, I present my *Christie Whitman Went To Town* to be sung to *Yankee Doodle*. Feel free sing-along, using this midi link." 2003.
946.3 Talking Cabinet Blues. w. Dave Lippman. m. No tune indicated. Published online at <http://www.davelippman.com/Cabinet.html>. N/c photo of Dave Lippman. [ca. 2001].

• **AmPM-946x WILSON**, Woodrow (Governor, 1911–1913; President, 1913–1921; Winner, Nobel Peace Prize, 1919) [SEE: DOC/PSM-WW]
• **AmPM-947 WITHERSPOON**, John (Committee on Correspondence, Somerset County, 1775; Provincial Congress of New Jersey, 1776; Continental Congress, 1776–1782; Signer of the Declaration of Independence, 1776; Secret Committee of the Congress on the Conduct of the War and the Board of War, 1778; State Council, 1780; General Assembly, 1783 & 1789)
947.1 The Declaration Of Independence Of The United States Of North America, July 4, 1776. w. From the Declaration of Independence. m. John E. Wilson. Published by John E. Wilson, Baltimore, MD. 1863. B/w litho of the interior of Independence Hall. "Arranged and adapted for Vocal and Instrumental Music as the Great National Chant." 4pp. [?]. Page 4: Facsimile signatures of all signers.
947.2 Old Independence Hall. w. A. Fletcher Stayman. m. Francis Weiland. Published by Stayman & Brothers, No. 210 Chesnut Street, Philadelphia, PA. 1855. Non-pictorial. "Respectfully dedicated to the Memory of the Signers of the Declaration of Independence." "Fac simile of their signatures" including John Adams, Sam Adams, Elbridge Gerry, Thomas Jefferson. 8pp. Pages 2 and 8: Blank. [Crew/MISC-34].
• **AmPM-948 YORKE**, Thomas Jones (County Collector, Salem County, 1830; Common Pleas Court Judge, Salem County, 1833–1834 & 1845–1854; State House, 1835; U.S. House, 1837–1839 & 1841–1843)
948.1 A Parody On Up Salt River. w. No composer indicated. m. "Tune—*All On Hobbies.*" In: *Songs For The People (Or Tippecanoe Melodies)* [Songster], page 37. "Dedicated to the Democratic Whig Young Men of the City and County of New York." Published for the Authors by James P. Giffing, No. 56 Gold Street, New York, NY. 1840. [3¾" × 6"]. Litho of William Henry Harrison, log cabin, flag. "Original and Selected." 76pp. [M-019]. [Crew/WHH-63].
948.2 Up Salt River (A New Whig Song). w. G.B.W. (Toledo, OH). m. "Tune—*All On Hobbies.*" Published by Firth & Hall, No. 1 Franklin Square, New York, NY. 1840. Non-pictorial. "Respectfully Dedicated to the Toledo Tippecanoe Club." "Pr. 25 c nett [sic]." 4pp. [Crew/ WHH-38].
• **AmPM-949 MISCELLANEOUS MUSIC**
949.1 Atlantic City Municipal Band March. m. J.C. Simpson. Published by J.C. Simpson, Pleasantville, NJ. 1917. Non-pictorial geometric designs. 4pp. Page 2: "Respectfully Dedicated to J. Frank Merrick and Members of the Band." Page 4: Blank.

NEW MEXICO

• **AmPM-950 BARKER**, Squire Omar (aka: Philip Squires) (State Legislature, 1924)
950.1 Tall Men Riding. w. S. Omar Baker. m. "Tune—*Tramps And Hawkers.*" "Squire Omar Baker (b. 1894), honorary president of the Western Writers of America, has been a rancher and a teacher, and was

once elected to the New Mexico legislature. Look for more of his poems in *Vientos de las Sierras* (1924) and *Buckaroo Ballads!* (1928)..." Lyrics and sound file published online at <http://www.mudcat.org/kids/@displaysong.cfm?SongID= 5677>. [199-].

ELKINS, Stephen Benton (Territorial House, New Mexico, 1864–1865; Territorial District Attorney, New Mexico, 1866–1867; Territorial Attorney General, New Mexico, 1867; U.S. District Attorney, Territory of New Mexico, 1867–1870; U.S. House Delegate, Territory of New Mexico, 1873–1877) [See: West Virginia]

• **AmPM-951** FALL, Albert Bacon (Territorial House, 1891–1892; Judge of the Third Judicial District, 1893; State Supreme Court, 1893; Territorial Attorney General, 1897 & 1907; Territorial Council, 1897; U.S. Senate, 1912–1921; Secretary of the Interior, 1921–1923)

951.1 The Farmer's Prayer. w. No composer indicated. m. "Sung to the tune *After The Ball*." In: *Democratic Song Book*, page 5. Published by Charles W. Stewart, No. 439 Arlington Place, Chicago, IL. July 21, 1928. [3¾" × 6⅛"]. Non-pictorial geometric design border. "Dedicated to sane government and honest administration with 'Life, Liberty and The Pursuit of Happiness' without blue laws or fool laws. The most damnable tyranny is the tyranny of small things. 'Give me the writing of a nation's songs and I care not who writes its laws.' The best way to cure a fool of his folly — to Laugh him out of it." "Sing Brother Sing!" 6pp. Various Christian and anti-prohibition sayings throughout — "Would Christ have joined the Ku Klux Klan or the Anti-Saloon League?, &c." [M-418]. [Crew/AES-70].

• **AmPM-952** MECHEM, Edwin L. (Governor, 1951–1955, 1957–1959 & 1961–1962)

952.1 In New Mexico. w.m. Bernie Williams. Published by Crowell Music Publishing Co., 1645 West Palmer Drive, Phoenix, AZ. 1951. B/w photo of "His Excellency Gov. Edward Mechem of the State of New Mexico" and a mountain scene. "Dedicated to the People of the State of New Mexico." 4pp. Page 4: Advertising.

• **AmPM-952A** MONTOYA, Joseph Manuel (State, 1936–1940; State Senate, 1940–1946 & 1953–1954; Lt. Governor, 1947–1951 & 1955–1957; U.S. House, 1957–1964, U.S. Senate, 1964–1977)

952A.1 Joe Montoya (For Senator). w. Gloria White. m. Ralph Williams. 33⅓ rpm microgroove 5⅞" vinyl record. Band arrangement, Dr. Ted Crager. Jimmy Brown vocal. #20051. [ca. 1964]. Side 2: Blank. Record sleeve: B/w photo of President John F. Kennedy and Joseph Montoya.

WALLACE, Lewis (Governor, New Mexico Territory, 1878–1881) [See: Indiana]

NEW YORK

• **AmPM-953** ADLER, Simon Louis (State Assembly, 1911–1926; U.S. District Court Judge, 1927–1934)

953.1 Over There. w. No composer indicated. m. "Air — *Over There*." In: *The Public Frutilities Of 1923*, page 8. Published by The Albany Legislative Correspondents' Association of New York State, Albany, NY. 1923. [8" × 10¾"]. N/c drawing by Fred O. Seibel of Al Smith and Jimmy Walker at the seashore trying to hold back waves of "Traction Lobby," "Electric Light Trust," Water Power Ring," and "GOP Bloc of 81." "A ribald revue, redolent of guff, gestures, gold-bricks, hydrohokum, horse-cars, trackless telephones, transit thugs, synthetic budgets, five-cent fare fiascos, blackjacks, blue noses, monkey wrenches and the 'M.M.M.' (Machold's Minute Men." "At Ten Eyck, Albany, NY., April, 5, 1923."

• **AmPM-954** ALDRIDGE, George W. (Delegate to Republican National Convention, 1900–1916)

954.1 How Many? w. No composer indicated. m. "Air — *Tammany*." "In which the Governor unloads his mind on pork, pastry and patronage." In: *The Bacchanal Of 1919*, page 7. Published by The Legislative Correspondents' Association of New York, Albany, NY. 1919. [7¾" × 10½"]. N/c drawing by Fred O. Seibel of the "Last Chance Cafe," sign — "Headquarters Hard Liquor Club," "Senator Sage" as bellboy, and "Al Smith Tonight" on sign marquee. "A Product of the Capitoline Vineyard, Staged for the Delertation of People Still on Earth by The Legislative Correspondents' Association at The Ten Eyck, Albany, the Night of April 3, 1919." [Crew/AES-65].

• **AmPM-955** AMBRO, Jerome G. (State Assembly, 1925–1933)

955.1 Love Lyric. w. No composer indicated. m. "Air — *I'm Through With Love*." In: *The Scrappy Warriors, A Merry, Martial Medley, Mingling-Wrenches And Muck-Rakers, Presidential Pipe-Dreams, Partisan Perfidies And Prohibition Planks — All Revolving 'Round Convulsive Conclave Of Delirious Delegates, Shellshocked Spellbinders And Rabid Rivals For White House Honors*, page 12. Published by Albany Legislative Correspondents' Association, Albany, NY. 1933. [8¼" × 12"]. N/c drawing of Franklin Roosevelt with spear and on horseback charging Al Smith and others holding axes and knives. "Staged at Ten Eyck Hotel Rathskeller, Albany, New York, the evening of Thursday, March 3, 1932, at Seven o'clock." 16pp.

• **AmPM-956** AMOS, William C. (State Assembly, 1919)

956.1 Oh, Amos. m. "Air — *Frenchy*." In: *Fourth Internationale*, page 14. Published by The Legislative Correspondents' Association of the State of New York, Albany, NY. 1920. [8" × 11¼"]. N/c drawing by Fred

O. Seibel of a statue of House Speaker Thaddeus "Sweet" on horseback, "Governor's Chair," "Assemblyman Roosevelt," other politicians. "A Session of Soviets, Seething with Socialism, Sweetism, Sedition, Seven-Cent Fares, School-Ma'ams, Soda-Water, Slams, Slander, Simps and Strangulation, and Bristling with Booms, Boobs and Bunk." "Called by The Legislative Correspondents' Association of the State of New York, at The Ten Eyck, Albany, April 22, 1920." [Crew/AES-66].

- **AmPM-957** ANDERSON, William Henry (Anti-Saloon League)

957.1 The Executioner. w. No composer indicated. m. "Air—*Got A Little List—The Mikado.*" "The sword of the Governor falls slowly, but it chops exceeding small." In: *The Bacchanal Of 1919*, page 9. Published by The Legislative Correspondents' Association of New York, Albany, NY. 1919. [7¾" × 10½"]. N/c drawing by Fred O. Seibel of the "Last Chance Cafe," sign—"Headquarters Hard Liquor Club," "Senator Sage" as bellboy, and "Al Smith Tonight" on sign marquee. "A Product of the Capitoline Vineyard, Staged for the Delertation of People Still on Earth by The Legislative Correspondents' Association at The Ten Eyck, Albany, the Night of April 3, 1919." [Crew/AES-65].

957.2 Hymn Of Hydra. w. No composer indicated. m. "Air—*The Old Oaken Bucket.*" "With a heavy heart the Legislature beseeches you to unite in this nonintoxicating dirge." In: *The Bacchanal Of 1919*, page 10. Published by The Legislative Correspondents' Association of New York, Albany, NY. 1919. [7¾" × 10½"]. N/c drawing by Fred O. Seibel of the "Last Chance Cafe," sign—"Headquarters Hard Liquor Club," "Senator Sage" as bellboy, and "Al Smith Tonight" on sign marquee. "A Product of the Capitoline Vineyard, Staged for the Delertation of People Still on Earth by The Legislative Correspondents' Association at The Ten Eyck, Albany, the Night of April 3, 1919." [Crew/AES-65].

957.3 On To Havana! w. No composer indicated. m. "Air—*Over There.*" "In which Senators James J. Walker, Henry M. Sage, Henry Walters, Charles C. Lockwood and Alvah W. Burlingame offer a solution for the 'dry capitol' bugaboo. Let's Go!" In: *Fourth Internationale*, page 7. Published by The Legislative Correspondents' Association of the State of New York, Albany, NY. 1920. [8" × 11¼"]. N/c drawing by Fred O. Seibel of a statue of House Speaker Thaddeus "Sweet" on horseback, "Governor's Chair," "Assemblyman Roosevelt," other politicians. "A Session of Soviets, Seething with Socialism, Sweetism, Sedition, Seven-Cent Fares, School-Ma'ams, Soda-Water, Slams, Slander, Simps and Strangulation, and Bristling with Booms, Boobs and Bunk." "Called by The Legislative Correspondents' Association of the State of New York, at The Ten Eyck, Albany, April 22, 1920." Page 5: "Toast List" including "Comrade Alfred E. Smith, Dictator of the Proletariat." [Crew/AES-66].

- **AmPM-958** ANDREWS, Walter Gresham "Ham" (Supervisor of the Fifteenth Federal Census, New York, 1929–1930; U.S. House, 1931–1949)

958.1 When I Left The Hill Behind. w. No composer indicated. m. "Air—*When I Left The World Behind.*" "In which 'Ham' Ward proclaims himself happily out of the game and admits his preference for the flagon and shotgun to the inkwell and opinion pen." In: *Jays In Jungleland, Or The Curry-Combers, Starring The Snarling, Scornful, Sinew-Set Political Puma And Rampant, Rural Republican Ravagers, Bent On Battering The Beast's Bailiwick And Leveling His Lair In A Scrambled Salmagundi Studded With Sachems, Satchels, Swag, Scuttlers, Sang Froid, Seaburyisms, Etc.—Plus A Peep At That Tammany Masterpiece—"The Tiger's Knightmare,"* page 8. Published by The Legislative Correspondents' Association of New York, Albany, NY. 1931. [7¾" × 10½"]. N/c drawing a "Tammany" tiger perched overlooking "GOP" elephants, New York City skyline. "Launched at Ten Eyck Hotel, Albany, New York, On the evening of Thursday, March 26, 1931, at seven o'clock." 16pp.

- **AmPM-958x** ARTHUR, Chester Alan (State Inspector General & State Quartermaster General 1861–1862; Collector, Port of New York, 1871–1878; Chairman, Republican State Committee, 1879–1881; Vice President, 1881; President, 1881–1885) [SEE: DOC/PSM-JAG & CAA]

- **AmPM-958A** ASBOTH, Alexander Sandor (U.S. Minister to Argentina and Uruguay, 1866–1868)

958A.1 Fremont Hussars March. m. Charles Fradel. Published Beer & Schirmer, No. 701 Broadway, New York, NY. 1862. B/w beige tinted litho by Sarony, Major & Knapp of mounted troops in battle, eagle, floral designs. "Respectfully dedicated to Brig. General Asboth." 8pp. Pages 2 and 8: Blank. [Crew/JCF-53].

- **AmPM-959** BARNES, William, Jr. (New York Republican State Committee, 1892–1915; Delegate to Republican National Convention, 1904, 1908 & 1912; New York State Republican Party Chairman, 1911–1914)

959.1 The Candidates' Lament. w. No composer indicated. m. "Air—*Everyone Knows, But Nobody Seems To Care.*" In: *Fourth Internationale*, page 6. Published by The Legislative Correspondents' Association of the State of New York, Albany, NY. 1920. [8" × 11¼"]. N/c drawing by Fred O. Seibel of a statue of House Speaker Thaddeus "Sweet" on horseback, "Governor's Chair," "Assemblyman Roosevelt," other politicians. "A Session of Soviets, Seething with Socialism, Sweetism, Sedition, Seven-Cent Fares, School-Ma'ams, Soda-Water, Slams, Slander, Simps and Strangulation, and Bristling with Booms, Boobs and Bunk." "Called by The Legislative Correspondents' Association of the State of New York, at The Ten Eyck, Albany, April 22, 1920." Page 5: "Toast List" including "Comrade Alfred E. Smith, Dictator of the Proletariat." [Crew/AES-66].

959.2 Carpenters' Chorus. w. No composer indicated. m. "Air—*Sidewalks Of New York, Daisy Bell, Sweet Annie Moore, Tramp, Tramp, Tramp, Hang Jeff Davis.*" "All Kinds of Hammers Save Gavels Appropriate." In: *The Modest Art Of Self Advance Sporting Annual, Containing Correct Records Of White House Hopes, State Champions, Has Beens, Handlers And Never-Wases,* page 27. Published by the Legislative Correspondents' Association, Albany, NY. 1915. [5" × 7"]. Gy/r/bk cover drawing of a crowd watching a boxing match. 34pp.

959.3 How Many? w. No composer indicated. m. "Air — *Tammany*." "In which the Governor unloads his mind on pork, pastry and patronage." In: *The Bacchanal Of 1919*, page 7. Published by The Legislative Correspondents' Association of New York, Albany, NY. 1919. [7¾" × 10½"]. N/c drawing by Fred O. Seibel of the "Last Chance Cafe," sign — "Headquarters Hard Liquor Club," "Senator Sage" as bellboy, and "Al Smith Tonight" on sign marquee. "A Product of the Capitoline Vineyard, Staged for the Delertation of People Still on Earth by The Legislative Correspondents' Association at The Ten Eyck, Albany, the Night of April 3, 1919." [Crew/AES-65].

959.4 I Want To Go Back To My Job In Second Place. w. No composer indicated. m. "Air — *I Want To Go Back To My Home In Michigan*." In: *The Modest Art Of Self Advance Sporting Annual, Containing Correct Records Of White House Hopes, State Champions, Has Beens, Handlers And Never-Wases*, page 25. Published by the Legislative Correspondents' Association, Albany, NY. 1915. [5" × 7"]. Gy/r/bk cover drawing of a crowd watching a boxing match. 34pp.

959.5 In The Good Old Summer Time. w.m. No composer or tune indicated. "An Unconventional Bit of Satire on the Convention." In: *The Modest Art Of Self Advance Sporting Annual, Containing Correct Records Of White House Hopes, State Champions, Has Beens, Handlers And Never-Wases*, page 28. Published by the Legislative Correspondents' Association, Albany, NY. 1915. [5" × 7"]. Gy/r/bk cover drawing of a crowd watching a boxing match. 34pp.

959.6 Oh, Jimmy! w. No composer indicated. m. "Air — *Please*." In: *Foam Sweet Foam*, page 11. Published by Albany Legislative Correspondents' Association, Albany, NY. 1933. [8" × 11¾"]. N/c drawing by Jerry Costello of Franklin D. Roosevelt, Al Smith and other politicians riding a bottle of beer — "The Lager Limited." "A Rollicking Review Rotating on Resurrection of Bouncing Beverages, Tipsily Tapped at Ten Eyck Hotel Rathskeller, Albany, New York, the evening of Thursday, February 23, 1933, at Seven-Thirty O'clock." 20pp. [Crew/FDR-277].

959.7 Tammany. w. No composer indicated. m. "*Tammany*." "A Sore Cry, Not A War Cry." In: *The Modest Art Of Self Advance Sporting Annual, Containing Correct Records Of White House Hopes, State Champions, Has Beens, Handlers And Never-Wases*, page 30. Published by the Legislative Correspondents' Association, Albany, NY. 1915. [5" × 7"]. Gy/r/bk cover drawing of a crowd watching a boxing match. 34pp.

959.8 There Ain't No G.O.P. w. No composer indicated. m. "Air — *Where The River Shannon Flows*." In: *The Red Book, Containing Portraits And Biographies Of Some Persons More Or Less Prominent Public Life Written Entirely Without Respect To The Libel Laws, In A Studious Effort To Conceal Everything But The Truth; Some Songs Built Upon The Same Principle, And Other Important (?) Material Entirely Unfit To Print*, page 22. Published by Legislative Correspondents' Association of the State of New York, Albany, NY. 1913. [5" × 7¼"]. R/w/bk hardback book with drawing of State House, seal of New York, geometric designs. 90pp.

• **AmPM-960** BAUMES, Caleb Howard (State Assembly, 1909–1913; State Senate, 1919–1930; Candidate for Lt. Governor, 1930)

960.1 Sing A Song O'Candidates. w. H.P.L. m. "Air — *Heidelberg*." In: *Breaks And Outbreaks*, page 10. Published by Albany Legislative Correspondents' Association of New York State, Albany, NY. 1930. [8" × 11¾"]. N/c drawing of Franklin Roosevelt as warden, other politicians in jail — "A Paroxysmic, Penological Panorama, Pillorying Prison Probes, Partisan Pap-Grabbers, Peanut Policies, Phony Philanthropies, Punctured Pledges and Public Service Piffle, and Redolent with Republican Rebels Riddling Rooseveltian Ruses and Mocking Mogenthau Ministrations and Lehman Loquacities — Topped by That Toothsome Tidbit, 'Cells and Sell-Outs.'" "Detonated at Ten Eyck Hotel Terminal, Albany, NY., On the Evening of March 20, 1930, at 7:00 p.m." [Crew/FDR-362].

960.2 What's The Answer? w. No composer indicated. m. "Air — *On A Dew, Dew, Dewey Day*." In: *Roundups And Showdowns*, page 12. Published by The Albany Legislative Correspondents' Association, Albany, NY. 1928. [8" × 11¾"]. N/c drawing labeled "Ride Her, Cowboy" of "Al" Smith on bucking horse — "Solid Dixie Vote," James "Cox," John "Davis," other politicians — "Heflin, Reed, Ritchie," pennant — "The Great Houston Rodeo." "A Rollicking Rodeo and Sizzling Stampede, Laid in the Light of Western Stars and Set to the Hammer of Heifrer Hoofs, Plus a Perspiration-proof Potpourri of Presidential Piffle and Proxy Prattle, Topped by the Miniature Mirthquake, 'Who's Who in Houston.'" "Ride Her, Cowboy!" "Staged at The Ten Eyck, Albany, The Evening of March 8, 1928." 20pp. [Crew/AES-69].

• **AmPM-961** BEACH, Allen C. (Lt. Governor, 1869–1872; New York Secretary of State, 1878–1879)

961.1 Governor Beach's Schottisch. m. No composer indicated. Published by Charles W. Harris, 481 Broadway, New York, NY. 1871. B/w litho of Allen C. Beach. "Composed and Dedicated to Lieut. Gov. Allen C. Beach by A Friend and Townsman." 8pp. Pages 2, 7 and 8: Advertising.

• **AmPM-962** BEAGLE, Fred (Delegate to Republican National Convention, 1940)

962.1 Let's Reapportion! w. No composer indicated. m. "Air — *Rainbow On The River*." In: *Wake Up And Scream*, page 12. Published by Albany Legislative Correspondents' Association, Albany, NY. 1937. [8" × 11¾"]. N/c drawing by Jerry Costello of Dr. Bill Murray, King Macy, New York GOP, and Ham Fish as patients undergoing transfusions. "A Trumpet Call to the G.O.P. Eagle to Snap out of Coma and Rally Ravaged Republicans with New Volley of Vocal Vim — the Same Being Enacted 'mid a Merry Medley of Mountain Madness, Dutch Delirium, Liberalization Legendry, Melancholy Maidens and Rapscallion Redskins, at Ten Eyck Hotel, Albany, N.Y., Thursday, March eleventh, 1937, at Seven-Thirty o'clock." 20pp.

• **AmPM-963** BEAME, Abraham D. (Mayor, New York City, 1974–1977)

963.1 Abie's On His Toes. w. No composer indicated. m. "Tune — *Sweet Gypsy Rose*." In: *Thoroughly Mad-ern Malcolm Or He Didn't Need A Course In Forensics To Become A Famous Public Speaker*, page 11. Published by the New York State Legislative Correspondents' Association, Albany, NY. 1974. N/w photo of Malcolm Wilson as Alfred E. Newman—"What—Me Governor?" "Featuring the New York Correspondents' Association, March 16. 1974." 32pp.

963.2 Abraham Beame For Mayor. No composers indicated. Published by the Independent Committee for the Election of Abraham Beame—Mayor, Hotel Summit, New York, NY. [1974]. Published as a post card. Obv: B/w photo of Abraham Beame. Song. "Sing." Rev: Postal mailing information. "Frank O'Connor, Pres. City Council." Mario Procaccino, Comptroller."

- **AmPM-964 BEDENKAPP**, Glenn R. (State Republican Party Chairman, 1945–1949; Delegate to Republican National Convention, 1948)

964.1 Song Of Bedenkapp And Jaeckle. w.m. No composer or tune indicated. "Before Republican State Committee." In: *Visions And Revisions*, page 20. Published by The Albany Legislative Correspondents' Association, Albany, NY. March 6, 1947. [8½" × 11"]. R/w/gn/y/bk drawing of Thomas "Dewey" as Santa Claus, sign—"Santa's Workshop," other New York politicians. "Revealing in Rhapsodic Revelry of Song and Stunt How a Political Scrooge Became a Political Saint; or, What Happened When Many Paws Raided the Wonderful Workshop of Santa Claus Dewey; Together with Other Strange and Silly Scenes." "Hotel Ten Eyck, Albany, March 6, 1947." 24pp. [Crew/TED-34].

- **AmPM-965 BEHAN**, Thomas F. (State Insurance Dept)

965.1 The Executioner. w. No composer indicated. m. "Air—*Got A Little List—The Mikado*." "The sword of the Governor falls slowly, but it chops exceeding small." In: *The Bacchanal Of 1919*, page 9. Published by The Legislative Correspondents' Association of New York, Albany, NY. 1919. [7¾" × 10½"]. N/c drawing by Fred O. Seibel of the "Last Chance Cafe," sign—"Headquarters Hard Liquor Club," "Senator Sage" as bellboy, and "Al Smith Tonight" on sign marquee. "A Product of the Capitoline Vineyard, Staged for the Delertation of People Still on Earth by The Legislative Correspondents' Association at The Ten Eyck, Albany, the Night of April 3, 1919." [Crew/AES-65].

- **AmPM-966 BELMONT**, August [a.k.a. Schönberg] (Consul-General of Austria in New York, 1844–1850; U.S. Chargé d'Affaires The Hague, 1853–1855; U.S. Minister to Netherlands, 1855–1858; Chairman of the National Democratic Committee, 1860–1872)

966.1 The Greeley Pill. w. No composer indicated. m. "Air—*The Mistletoe Bough*." "Mixed at Cincinnati and taken to Baltimore." "Sung by the Union Glee Club at a Grant Republican rally at Cooper Institute." Published in the *New York Times*, September 26, 1872. [VBL, p. 456].

966.2 Mary Blaine. w. Ben Warren. m. Air—*Mary Blane*. Published by Hitchcock's Music Store, No. 166 Nassau Street, New York, NY. 1884. Litho of James G. Blaine in woman's dress, slogans—"Side Contracts," "Sentenced to Go Up Salt River, Nov. 6, 1884," "Little Rock RR Bonds," "20 Years in Congress," "Mulligan Letters," "To J.G.B. form the King of the Lobby,"
"Belmont," "Crooked Paths," "Self." Oriental man with sign inscribed "Blain-E Must-E Go-E." "Utilizing the old air of Mary Blane for Patriot Purposes." 4pp. Page 4: Blank. [Crew/GC-70].

966.3 Nothing To Do (Greenback Song). w. No composer indicated. m. "Air—*Wearing Of The Green*." In: *Greenback Song-Book*, page 7. Published by M.S. Cadwell, Grand Ledge, MI. [ca. 1880]. [3⁵⁄₁₆" × 7⅝⁄₁₆"]. Gn/w litho of a "Greenback" bank note. 20pp. [Crew/BFB-18].

966.4 Pay The Bonds In Greenbacks (Greenback Campaign Song). w. No composer indicated. m. "Air—*Hold The Fort*." In: *Greenback Song-Book*, page 8. Published by M.S. Cadwell, Grand Ledge, MI. [ca. 1880]. [3⁵⁄₁₆" × 7⅝⁄₁₆"]. Gn/w litho of a "Greenback" bank note. 20pp. [Crew/BFB-18].

966.5 Tar And Turpentine. w. Carl Brent. m. No tune indicated. m. "Air—*The Groves Of Blarney*." From the "Missouri Democrat." In: *National Republican Grant And Wilson Campaign Song-Book*, page 50. Published by The Union Republican Congressional Committee, Washington, DC. 1872. [3¹³⁄₁₆" × 8⅝⁄₁₆"]. Be/bk litho of Ulysses S. Grant. "We'll Sing a Song for U.S. Grant." 100pp. [M-182]. [Crew/USG-110].

966.6 When The Demmies Were In Power. w. Logan S. Porter. m. W.T. Giffe. In: *Roosevelt Campaign Songster 1904 (For Male Voices)*, page 18. c. Logan S. Porter. Published by The Home Music Company, Logansport, IN. 1904. [6" × 9"]. Be/bk photos of Theodore Roosevelt and Charles Fairbanks. Be/bk drawing of a star, geometric designs. "Single Copy 15 cts—$1.60 per Dozen." 36pp. [M-391]. [Crew/TR-356].

966.7 The White House Gate (Solo and Chorus). w.m. Logan S. Porter. In: *Roosevelt Campaign Songster 1904 (For Male Voices)*, page 26. c. Logan S. Porter. Published by The Home Music Company, Logansport, IN. 1904. [6" × 9"]. Be/bk photos of Theodore Roosevelt and Charles Fairbanks. Be/bk drawing of a star, geometric designs. "Single Copy 15 cts—$1.60 per Dozen." 36pp. [M-391]. [Crew/TR-356].

966.8 Wilson And Grant. w. Sam Booth. m. "Tune—*Bonnie Dundee*." In: *Grant And Wilson Campaign Songster*, page 2. Published by Frank Eastman, Book and Job Printer, No. 509 Clay Street, San Francisco, CA. [4¼" × 5⅝"]. 1872. Bk/bl geometric design border. 40pp. [Crew/USG-69].

- **AmPM-967 BENNETT**, John James (State Attorney General, 1931–1942; Candidate for Governor, 1942)

967.1 Don't Run Again. w. No composer indicated. m. "Air—*Let's Sing Again*." In: *Wake Up And Scream*, page 10. Published by Albany Legislative Correspondents' Association, Albany, NY. 1937. [8" × 11¾"]. N/c drawing by Jerry Costello of Dr. Bill Murray, King Macy, New York GOP, and Ham Fish as patients undergoing transfusions. "A Trumpet Call to the G.O.P. Eagle to Snap out of Coma and Rally Ravaged Republicans with New Volley of Vocal Vim—the Same Being Enacted 'mid a Merry Medley of Mountain Madness, Dutch Delirium, Liberalization Legendry, Melancholy Maidens and Rapscallion Redskins, at Ten Eyck Hotel, Albany, N.Y., Thursday, March eleventh, 1937, at Seven-Thirty o'clock." 20pp.

967.2 I'll Get Away With Murder. w. No composer indicated. m. "Air — *Without A Word Of Warning.*" In: *Tory, Tory Hallelujah*, page 13. Published by Albany Legislative Correspondents' Association, Albany, NY. 1936. [8" × 11¾"]. N/c drawing of Franklin D. Roosevelt, other politicians dressed as Revolutionary soldiers in battle scene — "A Dashing Delirious Drama, Lampooning Loyalists and Liberty Leaguers, Daggering Despots, Dictators and Dummy Donkey-Drivers to music by Red-Coats and Lyrics by Turn-Coats, the Combat Being Played Against a Spangled Back-Drop." "Furiously Fought at Ten Eyck Hotel, Albany, New York, The Evening of Thursday, March 12, 1936, at Seven-Thirty o'clock." [Crew/FDR-325].

967.3 Mr. Sir Exit. w. No composer indicated. m. "Air — *Chattanooga Choo Choo.*" In: *Lehman Unlimited*, page 7. Published by The Legislative Correspondents' Association of New York, Albany, NY. 1942. [7¾" × 10½"]. N/c drawing of Herb Lehman as a train engineer, others dressed as bandits trying to block the way including Dewey, Mead, Poletti, Willkie, Marvin Bennett and Farley — "The Great Train Hold-Up!" "Featuring that Famous Political Personality and Star of 'There'll Always be a Herbie' on an Uncensored Double Bill with 'Fifty Million Candidates Won't be Wronged.'" "Exploded At Hotel Ten Eyck, Albany, New York, on the evening of Thursday, March 12th, 1942, at seven-thirty o'clock."

967.4 Paean Of Perpetuity. w. No composer indicated. m. "Airs — *Streets Of New York, Because You're You* and *Every Day Is Ladies Day With Me.*" In: *Lehman Unlimited*, page 6. Published by The Legislative Correspondents' Association of New York, Albany, NY. 1942. [7¾" × 10½"]. N/c drawing of Herb Lehman as a train engineer, others dressed as bandits trying to block the way including Dewey, Mead, Poletti, Willkie, Marvin Bennett and Farley — "The Great Train Hold-Up!" "Featuring that Famous Political Personality and Star of 'There'll Always be a Herbie' on an Uncensored Double Bill with 'Fifty Million Candidates Won't be Wronged.'" "Exploded At Hotel Ten Eyck, Albany, New York, on the evening of Thursday, March 12th, 1942, at seven-thirty o'clock."

967.5 Rah, Rah, Rah For Robert! w. No composer indicated. m. "Air — *You're A Sweetheart.*" In: *Sock-A-Bye Baby, A No Punches-Pulled Potpourri, Pillorying Political Palookas On Parade And Set To 'Swing' Time, Plus That Mad Maternal Masterpiece — Labor's Love Lost*, page 9. Published by The Legislative Correspondents' Association of New York, Albany, NY. 1938. [7¾" × 10½"]. N/c drawing of politicians as boxers: "Tom Dewey, Gotham Gamecock, Morry Tremaine Queen City's Idol, Bob-Jackson, Jamestown's Mighty Atom, Ripper Rolly Marvin, Syracuse Fistic Sensation, Jabber Bennett, Brooklyn Bomber and Promoter's Dream, Billy Bleakley, Westchester Wildcat, Killer Lehman, Knockerouter De Luxe." "Ace Cards for 1838 Golden Gloves Combat." "At Ten Eyck Hotel, Albany, New York, the evening of Thursday, March Tenth, 1938, at seven o'clock." 16pp. [Crew/TED-28].

967.6 Six Snappy Candidates. w. No composer indicated. m. "Air — *Ten Pretty Girls.*" In: *Sock-A-Bye Baby, A No Punches-Pulled Potpourri, Pillorying Political Palookas On Parade And Set To 'Swing' Time, Plus That Mad Maternal Masterpiece — Labor's Love Lost*, page 12. Published by The Legislative Correspondents' Association of New York, Albany, NY. 1938. [7¾" × 10½"]. N/c drawing of politicians as boxers: "Tom Dewey, Gotham Gamecock, Morry Tremaine Queen City's Idol, Bob-Jackson, Jamestown's Mighty Atom, Ripper Rolly Marvin, Syracuse Fistic Sensation, Jabber Bennett, Brooklyn Bomber and Promoter's Dream, Billy Bleakley, Westchester Wildcat, Killer Lehman, Knockerouter De Luxe." "Ace Cards for 1838 Golden Gloves Combat." "At Ten Eyck Hotel, Albany, New York, the evening of Thursday, March Tenth, 1938, at seven o'clock." 16pp. [Crew/TED-28].

967.7 Swing, Baby, Swing. w. No composer indicated. m. "Air — *Danny Deever.*" In: *Lehman Unlimited*, page 8. Published by The Legislative Correspondents' Association of New York, Albany, NY. 1942. [7¾" × 10½"]. N/c drawing of Herb Lehman as a train engineer, others dressed as bandits trying to block the way including Dewey, Mead, Poletti, Willkie, Marvin Bennett and Farley — "The Great Train Hold-Up!" "Featuring that Famous Political Personality and Star of 'There'll Always be a Herbie' on an Uncensored Double Bill with 'Fifty Million Candidates Won't be Wronged.'" "Exploded At Hotel Ten Eyck, Albany, New York, on the evening of Thursday, March 12th, 1942, at seven-thirty o'clock."

• **AmPM-968   BENNETT**, William (Chairman, National Endowment for the Humanities, 1981–1985; U.S. Secretary of Education, 1985–1988; Director of the National Drug Control Policy, 1989–1990)

968.1 Blinded By The Right. w. William K. Tong. m. "Sung to the tune of *Blinded By The Light* by Manfred Mann/Bruce Springsteen." In: *The Sting The Right Wing Song Book* at <http://www.geocities.com/wmktong/bootnewt/blindrit.htm>.

968.2 Guerrillas In The Mist. Consolidated. On CD: *Play More Music.* #X2–0777–7-13171–25. Amusement Control Records, Universal City, California. 1992.

• **AmPM-969   BENSEL**, John A. (State Engineer and Surveyor, 1911–1914)

969.1 The Grand March In January. w. No composer indicated. m. "Air — *It's A Long Way To Tipperary.*" "A modern political Tango." In: *The Modest Art Of Self Advance Sporting Annual, Containing Correct Records Of White House Hopes, State Champions, Has Beens, Handlers And Never-Wases*, page 29. Published by the Legislative Correspondents' Association, Albany, NY. 1915. [5" × 7"]. Gy/r/bk cover drawing of a crowd watching a boxing match. 34pp.

969.2 The Sharing Of The Green. w. No composer indicated. m. *Wearing Of The Green.* In: *The Red Book, Containing Portraits And Biographies Of Some Persons More Or Less Prominent Public Life Written Entirely Without Respect To The Libel Laws, In A Studious Effort To Conceal Everything But The Truth; Some Songs Built Upon The Same Principle, And Other Important (?) Material Entirely Unfit To Print*, page 14. Published by Legislative Correspondents' Association of the State of New York, Albany, NY. 1913. [5" × 7¼"]. R/w/bk hardback book with drawing of State House, seal of New York, geometric designs. 90pp.

- **AmPM-970 BIRD**, John (State Assembly, 1796–1798, U.S. House, 1799–1801)

970.1 Poor Jude, Or The Death Of The Judiciary. w. No composer indicated. m. "An AmPMified Parody of the celebrated Song *Cock-Robin.*" Published in the *Washington Federalist,* December 8, 1802. [VBL, p. 173].

- **AmPM-971 BLEAKLEY**, William F. (New York Supreme Court, 1933; Candidate For Governor, 1936)

971.1 Madison Square Garden Rally (Musical Program Booklet]. Published by New York Republican State Committee, [New York, NY]. 1936. [6¼" × 10⅞"]. Y/bk drawing of sunflower, eagle. "For President Alf. M. Landon; For Vice President Frank Knox; For Governor Wm. F. Bleakley; For Lieut. Governor Ralph K. Robertson; For Comptroller John E. May; For Atty. General Nathan D. Pearlman." "Richard W. Lawrence, General Chairman; Carleton Greenwald, Chairman General Arrangements Committee." "Madison Square Garden Rally, October 29th, 1936, under the auspices of New York Republican State Committee." 4pp. Page 2: "George McEverett, Director, Music by Melville Monis Orchestra, Capt. Francis W. Southerland and his 7th (107th) Regiment Band, Soloists, Queena Mario, Sporano [sic] Metropolitan Opera Co., Martio Chamlee, Tenor, Metropolitan Opera Co., Republican Men's Glee Club, University of New York, Arthur Hill, Conductor."

971.2 Six Snappy Candidates. w. No composer indicated. m. "Air—*Ten Pretty Girls.*" In: *Sock-A-Bye Baby, A No Punches-Pulled Potpourri, Pillorying Political Palookas On Parade And Set To 'Swing' Time, Plus That Mad Maternal Masterpiece—Labor's Love Lost,* page 12. Published by The Legislative Correspondents' Association of New York, Albany, NY. 1938. [7¾" × 10½"]. N/c drawing of politicians as boxers: "Tom Dewey, Gotham Gamecock, Morry Tremaine Queen City's Idol, Bob-Jackson, Jamestown's Mighty Atom, Ripper Rolly Marvin, Syracuse Fistic Sensation, Jabber Bennett, Brooklyn Bomber and Promoter's Dream, Billy Bleakley, Westchester Wildcat, Killer Lehman, Knockerouter De Luxe." "Ace Cards for 1838 Golden Gloves Combat." "At Ten Eyck Hotel, Albany, New York, the evening of Thursday, March Tenth, 1938, at seven o'clock." 16pp. [Crew/TED-28].

- **AmPM-973 BLISS**, Cornelius Newton (State Republican Party Chairman, 1887–1889; U.S. Secretary of the Interior, 1897–1899)

973.1 The Cabinet Grand March. m. Hans S. Line, Op. 64. Published by National Music Company, Nos. 215–221 Wabash Avenue, Chicago, IL. 1897. R/w cover. B/w photo of William McKinley and eight Cabinet members. "Dedicated to Hon. Lyman J. Gage." 6pp. Page 6: Advertising. [Crew/WM-15].

- **AmPM-974 BLOOM**, Sol (U.S. House, 1923–1949; Chairman, George Washington Bicentennial Commission, 1931–1932)

974.1 Father Of The Land We Love. w.m. George M. Cohan. Published by The United States George Washington Bicentennial Commission, Washington, DC. Copyright 1931 by Hon. Sol Bloom. B/w medallions of George Washington—"George Washington Bicentennial 1732–1932." "Written for the American People." "To Commemorate the Two Hundredth Anniversary of the Birth of George Washington." 2pp. [This piece was documented here because of the use of his Congressional title "Hon." Sol Bloom was one of the largest Tin Pan Alley publishers, and it is not practical to list all his publications].

- **AmPM-975 BLOOMBERG**, Michael (Mayor, 2002–Present)

975.1 Hot Tempers In The City. w. Michael Pacholek. m. Tune—"*Hot Child In The City* originally by Nick Gilder." "Dedicated to Mayor Michael Bloomberg, who has proven once and for all It takes a politician to run a city, and businessmen should stay out of it! I like the smoking ban—what are smokers, but drug addicts?—but homelessness, garbage and potholes are reaching their 1990 or so peak, and as Mick Jagger would say, the crime rate's going up up up up UUU-UUUUUUUP!" Published online at <http://www.amiright.com/parody/70s/nickgilder0.shtml>. 2003.

975.2 Oy Vey (The Blackout Song). w. Michael Pacholek. m. Tune—"*Day-O, The Banana Boat Song* originally by Harry Belafonte." Published online at <http://www.amiright.com/parody/misc/harrybelafonte8.shtml>. 2003.

- **AmPM-976 BOARDMAN**, William (Alternate Delegate to Republican National Convention, 1916)

976.1 The Candidates' Lament. m. "Air—*Everyone Knows, But Nobody Seems To Care.*" In: *Fourth Internationale,* page 6. Published by The Legislative Correspondents' Association of the State of New York, Albany, NY. 1920. [8" × 11¼"]. N/c drawing by Fred O. Seibel of a statue of House Speaker Thaddeus "Sweet" on horseback, "Governor's Chair," "Assemblyman Roosevelt," other politicians. "A Session of Soviets, Seething with Socialism, Sweetism, Sedition, Seven-Cent Fares, School-Ma'ams, Soda-Water, Slams, Slander, Simps and Strangulation, and Bristling with Booms, Boobs and Bunk." "Called by The Legislative Correspondents' Association of the State of New York, at The Ten Eyck, Albany, April 22, 1920." Page 5: "Toast List" including "Comrade Alfred E. Smith, Dictator of the Proletariat." [Crew/AES-66].

BOIES, Horace (State Assembly, New York, 1855) [See: Iowa]

- **AmPM-977 BONTECOU**, Frederic H. (State Senate, 1935–1938 & 1943–1947)

977.1 Each Monday Night Is The Screwiest Night Of The Week. w.m. No composer or tune indicated. In: *Cash & Carry–On Or It Ain't Hay, A Stirring Saga Suggesting Scrimping, Scrooging And Spending Twixt The Highlands And Lowlands Of State Street; Also, A Loony Lift To Luna For Leaders Looking For Less O'Lockwood; All Pieced Together With A Paralyzing Portrayal Of Pickets Putting Pay Ahead Of Party,* page 16. Published by The Legislative Correspondents' Association of New York, Albany, NY. 1946. [8½" × 11"]. N/c drawing of politicians fighting over the "Castle Surplus, Irish dressed "O'Dwyer, Hannegan, Farley, Mead" against Scottish dressed "Lockwood, Bedenknap, MacDewey, Burton." "Hotel Ten Eyck, Albany, March 14, 1946." 24pp. [Crew/TED-20].

- **AmPM-978 BORKOWSKI**, Ansley B. (State Assembly, 1921 & 1924–1930; Candidate for State Senate, 1932 & 1934; Delegate to Republican National Convention, 1956)

978.1 Let's Reapportion! w. No composer indicated. m. "Air — *Rainbow On The River.*" In: *Wake Up And Scream*, page 12. Published by Albany Legislative Correspondents' Association, Albany, NY. 1937. [8" × 11¾"]. N/c drawing by Jerry Costello of Dr. Bill Murray, King Macy, New York GOP, and Ham Fish as patients undergoing transfusions. "A Trumpet Call to the G.O.P. Eagle to Snap out of Coma and Rally Ravaged Republicans with New Volley of Vocal Vim — the Same Being Enacted 'mid a Merry Medley of Mountain Madness, Dutch Delirium, Liberalization Legendry, Melancholy Maidens and Rapscallion Redskins, at Ten Eyck Hotel, Albany, N.Y., Thursday, March eleventh, 1937, at Seven-Thirty o'clock." 20pp.

- **AmPM-979 BOUCK**, William C. (Sheriff; Schoharie County, 1814; State Assembly, 1814–1818; State Senate, 1820–1822; Governor, 1843–1845)

979.1 Governor Bouck's Grand Quick Step. m. Oliver J. Shaw. Published by Boardman & Grey, No. 4 & 6 North Pearl Street, Albany, NY. 1842. B/w litho by Thayer & co., Boston, of a "View of the State and City Halls taken from the Capitol." "As performed by the National Brass Band, Albany." "Composed and arranged for the Piano Forte and respectfully dedicated to His Excellency by Oliver J. Shaw." 4pp. Page 4: Blank.

- **AmPM-980 BOUTON**, Arthur F. (State Senate, 1923–1926)

980.1 Party Pals (Passionate Paean of Praise by Damon Fearon for his Playmate, Pythias Knight). w. No composer indicated. m. "Air — *Little Annie Rooney.*" In: *Statutes And Statuettes*, page 10. Published by Albany Legislative Correspondents' Association, Albany, NY. 1925. N/c drawing by Fred O. Seibel of "Venus DeMilo Smith," other politicians as historical figures. "A Private Presentation of Immortal Images and Matchless Masterpieces From the 1925 Legislative Louvre Frivolously Fashioned in Political Pigments and Capitoline Colors and Featuring Etchers and Fetchers, Chisels and Fizzles, Hues and Hewitts, G.O.P. Gargoyles, Democratic Dorics, Prohibition Pastels, Lowman Landscapes and McGinnies Models, Combined with a Superficial Squint into the Gallery of Gee-Gaws, Freaks and Flim Flam." "Viewed at Ten Eyck Hotel, Albany, N.Y., on the Evening of March 12, 1925, Seven o'clock." 20pp. [Crew/AES-17].

- **AmPM-981 BRAY**, M. William (Delegate, Democratic National Convention, 1928, 1932, 1940, & 1948; Democratic State Party Chairman, 1928–1930; Lt. Governor, 1932–1938)

981.1 Don't Run Again. w. No composer indicated. m. "Air — *Let's Sing Again.*" In: *Wake Up And Scream*, page 10. Published by Albany Legislative Correspondents' Association, Albany, NY. 1937. [8" × 11¾"]. N/c drawing by Jerry Costello of Dr. Bill Murray, King Macy, New York GOP, and Ham Fish as patients undergoing transfusions. "A Trumpet Call to the G.O.P. Eagle to Snap out of Coma and Rally Ravaged Republicans with New Volley of Vocal Vim — the Same Being Enacted 'mid a Merry Medley of Mountain Madness, Dutch Delirium, Liberalization Legendry, Melancholy Maidens and Rapscallion Redskins, at Ten Eyck Hotel, Albany, N.Y., Thursday, March eleventh, 1937, at Seven-Thirty o'clock." 20pp.

981.2 It's An Old Roosevelt Custom. w. No composer indicated. m. "Air — *It's An Old Southern Custom.* In: *Tory, Tory Hallelujah*, page 7. Published by Albany Legislative Correspondents' Association, Albany, NY. 1936. [8" × 11¾"]. N/c drawing of Franklin D. Roosevelt, other politicians dressed as Revolutionary soldiers in battle scene — "A Dashing Delirious Drama, Lampooning Loyalists and Liberty Leaguers, Daggering Despots, Dictators and Dummy Donkey-Drivers to music by Red-Coats and Lyrics by Turn-Coats, the Combat Being Played Against a Spangled Back-Drop." "Furiously Fought at Ten Eyck Hotel, Albany, New York, The Evening of Thursday, March 12, 1936, at Seven-Thirty o'clock." [Crew/FDR-325].

981.3 Now That The Wurzburger Flows. m. "Air — *Down Where The Wurzburger Flows*" In: *Foam Sweet Foam*, page 14. Published by Albany Legislative Correspondents' Association, Albany, NY. 1933. [8" × 11¾"]. N/c drawing by Jerry Costello of Franklin D. Roosevelt, Al Smith and other politicians riding a bottle of beer — "The Lager Limited." "A Rollicking Review Rotating on Resurrection of Bouncing Beverages, Tipsily Tapped at Ten Eyck Hotel Rathskeller, Albany, New York, the evening of Thursday, February 23, 1933, at Seven-Thirty o'clock." 20pp. [Crew/FDR-277].

- **AmPM-982 BREES**, Orlo M. (State Assembly, 1941–1952; State Senate, 1952)

982.1 Each Monday Night Is The Screwiest Night Of The Week. w.m. No composer or tune indicated. In: *Cash & Carry–On Or It Ain't Hay, A Stirring Saga Suggesting Scrimping, Scrooging And Spending Twixt The Highlands And Lowlands Of State Street; Also, A Loony Lift To Luna For Leaders Looking For Less O'Lockwood; All Pieced Together With A Paralyzing Portrayal Of Pickets Putting Pay Ahead Of Party*, page 16. Published by The Legislative Correspondents' Association of New York, Albany, NY. 1946. [8½" × 11"]. N/c drawing of politicians fighting over the "Castle Surplus, Irish dressed "O'Dwyer, Hannegan, Farley, Mead" against Scottish dressed "Lockwood, Bedenknap, MacDewey, Burton." "Hotel Ten Eyck, Albany, March 14, 1946." 24pp. [Crew/TED-20].

982.2 Singing Commercials (With their sponsors). w.m. No composer or tune indicated. "Sponsor — The State Assembly." In: *Alice In Blunderland Or Through The Rooking Class* [Program and Songbook], page 18. Published by The Legislative Correspondents' Association of New York State, Albany, NY. 1949. [8⅝" × 11"]. N/c drawings of Harry Truman, Thomas Dewey, Franklin Roosevelt, Henry Wallace, Harold Stassen, Alben Barkley, Robert Taft, Earl Warren, other politicians. "A Scintillating Satire of Sadistic Surprises and Surprising Successes Featuring a Dramatic Disclosure of How Tom Did Not Go Down to D.C. in Slips; Together with a Give-Away-Nothing Radio Broadcast and Epic Melodrama of the Indian Wars Entitled 'When the Cat's Away the Mice Will Play.'" "Done With Music and Mirrors — Particularly Mirrors in Three Acts at Hotel Ten Eyck, Albany, March 12, 1949." [Crew/HST-20].

- **AmPM-983 BREITEL**, Charles D. (State

Supreme Court, 1950–58; State Court of Appeals, 1966–1979)

983.1 All We Want For Taxes. w. No composer indicated. m. "Tune—*All I Want For Christmas Is My Two Front Teeth.*" Sung by "Henry Wallace." In: *Alice In Blunderland Or Through The Rooking Class* [Program and Songbook], page 17. Published by The Legislative Correspondents' Association of New York State, Albany, NY. 1949. [8⅝" × 11"]. N/c drawings of Harry Truman, Thomas Dewey, Franklin Roosevelt, Henry Wallace, Harold Stassen, Alben Barkley, Robert Taft, Earl Warren, other politicians. "A Scintillating Satire of Sadistic Surprises and Surprising Successes Featuring a Dramatic Disclosure of How Tom Did Not Go Down to D.C. in Slips; Together with a Give-Away-Nothing Radio Broadcast and Epic Melodrama of the Indian Wars Entitled 'When the Cat's Away the Mice Will Play.'" "Done With Music and Mirrors—Particularly Mirrors in Three Acts at Hotel Ten Eyck, Albany, March 12, 1949." [Crew/HST-20].

- **AmPM-983A BROOKS**, Erastus (State Senate, 1854–1857; Candidate For Governor, 1856)

983A.1 The Erastus Brooks Library Schottisch. m. W.D. Raphaelson. Published by Dressler & Clayton, 933 Broadway, New York, NY. 1855. B/w litho on copper by F. Melville of a large library building, street scene, people talking—"How about that three Million Library." "To Erastus Brooks, Esq." 6pp. Pages 2 and 6: Blank.

- **AmPM-984 BROWDER**, Earl Russel (Candidate for U.S. House, 1930; General Secretary, Communist Party of the U.S., 1934–1944; Candidate for President, 1936 & 1940)

984.1 Give Our Regards To Dewey. w. No composer indicated. m. "Tune—*Give My Regards To Broadway.*" In: *Cash & Carry–On Or It Ain't Hay, A Stirring Saga Suggesting Scrimping, Scrooging And Spending Twixt The Highlands And Lowlands Of State Street; Also, A Loony Lift To Luna For Leaders Looking For Less O'Lockwood; All Pieced Together With A Paralyzing Portrayal Of Pickets Putting Pay Ahead Of Party*, page 17. Published by The Legislative Correspondents' Association of New York, Albany, NY. 1946. [8½" × 11"]. N/c drawing of politicians fighting over the "Castle Surplus, Irish dressed "O'Dwyer, Hannegan, Farley, Mead" against Scottish dressed "Lockwood, Bedenknap, MacDewey, Burton." "Hotel Ten Eyck, Albany, March 14, 1946." 24pp. [Crew/TED-20].

984.2 Swarmin' To Reform. w. No composer indicated. m. "Tune—*Make Believe.*" As sung by "Conklin, Margiotta, Steingut and Zaretzki." In: *Thoroughly Mad-ern Malcolm Or He Didn't Need A Course In Forensics To Become A Famous Public Speaker*, page 21. Published by the New York State Legislative Correspondents' Association, Albany, NY. 1974. N/w photo of Malcolm Wilson as Alfred E. Newman—"What—Me Governor?" "Featuring the New York Correspondents' Association, March 16. 1974." 32pp.

984.3 We're All For F.D.R. w. No composer indicated. m. "Tune—*By The Beautiful Sea.*" In: *Again And Again And Again Or All At Sea*, page 9. Published by Albany Legislative Correspondents' Association of New York State, Albany, NY. 1945. [8¾" × 11"]. N/c drawing of Franklin Roosevelt as pirate, Thomas Dewey as "Black Tom," Henry Wallace, Sidney Hillman, others on ship—"Union Ship C.I.O.–P.A.C." "Black Tom" Dewey walking plank. "Featuring Political Craft and Cunning and Contortions; Also Summoned by Subpoena, or Hit-Toddy and the Shady Lady, the Indestructible Dame Known as Lu-Lu; Together with Mystical Midsummer Mummery of '46, in a Roaring and Raucous and Revealing Racing Scene Entitled 'Hoots and Straddles.'" "All Done with Music, Magic, and Mirrors—In Three Acts at Hotel Ten Eyck, Albany, March 15, 1945." [Crew/FDR-371].

984.4 We Wish We Had A Governor! w. No composer indicated. m. "Tune—*Paper Doll.*" In: *Dealers Choice or Back-To-Back Biting*, page 13. Published by the Albany Legislative Correspondent's Association of New York State, Albany, NY. 1944. [8" × 11¾"]. N/c drawing of Franklin Roosevelt, Thomas Dewey, "Chiang," "Winnie" and "Joe" playing cards—"Featuring the World's Most Exciting Egomaniacs in a Marvelous Musical of Messianic and Mystery: Showing Sinners, Sycophants, Suckers, and Sleuths Saving Civilization with Sound; or Find the Joker!" "Dealt Off the Bottom of a Hot Deck—In Three Acts at Ten Eyck, Albany, March 9, 1944." [Crew/FDR-364].

- **AmPM-985 BROWN**, Elon R. (State Senate, 1898–1904, 1913–1918; Delegate, Republican National Convention, 1900, 1904 & 1916)

985.1 Battle Hymn Of The Internationale. w. No composer indicated. m. "Air—*Battle Hymn Of The Republic.*" In: *Fourth Internationale*, page 7. Published by The Legislative Correspondents' Association of the State of New York, Albany, NY. 1920. [8" × 11¼"]. N/c drawing by Fred O. Seibel of a statue of House Speaker Thaddeus "Sweet" on horseback, "Governor's Chair," "Assemblyman Roosevelt," other politicians. "A Session of Soviets, Seething with Socialism, Sweetism, Sedition, Seven-Cent Fares, School-Ma'ams, Soda-Water, Slams, Slander, Simps and Strangulation, and Bristling with Booms, Boobs and Bunk." "Called by The Legislative Correspondents' Association of the State of New York, at The Ten Eyck, Albany, April 22, 1920." Page 5: "Toast List" including "Comrade Alfred E. Smith, Dictator of the Proletariat." [Crew/AES-66].

985.2 Carpenters' Chorus. w. No composer indicated. m. "Air—*Sidewalks Of New York, Daisy Bell, Sweet Annie Moore, Tramp, Tramp, Tramp, Hang Jeff Davis.*" "All Kinds of Hammers Save Gavels Appropriate." In: *The Modest Art Of Self Advance Sporting Annual, Containing Correct Records Of White House Hopes, State Champions, Has Beens, Handlers And Never-Wases*, page 27. Published by the Legislative Correspondents' Association, Albany, NY. 1915. [5" × 7"]. Gy/r/bk cover drawing of a crowd watching a boxing match. 34pp.

985.3 I Want To Go Back To My Job In Second Place. w. No composer indicated. m. "Air—*I Want To Go Back To My Home In Michigan.*" In: *The Modest Art Of Self Advance Sporting Annual, Containing Correct Records Of White House Hopes, State Champions, Has Beens, Handlers And Never-Wases*, page 25. Published by the Legislative Correspondents' Association, Albany, NY. 1915. [5" × 7"]. Gy/r/bk cover drawing of a crowd watching a boxing match. 34pp.

985.4 Tammany. w. No composer indicated. m. "*Tammany.*" "A Sore Cry, Not A War Cry." In: *The Modest Art Of Self Advance Sporting Annual, Containing Correct Records Of White House Hopes, State Champions, Has Beens, Handlers And Never-Wases,* page 30. Published by the Legislative Correspondents' Association, Albany, NY. 1915. [5" × 7"]. Gy/r/bk cover drawing of a crowd watching a boxing match. 34pp.

985.5 This Is The Life! w. No composer indicated. m. No tune indicated. "Rapid Roll Call—Ayes, 201; Noes, 0." In: *The Modest Art Of Self Advance Sporting Annual, Containing Correct Records Of White House Hopes, State Champions, Has Beens, Handlers And Never-Wases,* page 26. Published by the Legislative Correspondents' Association, Albany, NY. 1915. [5" × 7"]. Gy/r/bk cover drawing of a crowd watching a boxing match. 34pp.

- **AmPM-986** BROWNELL, Herbert, Jr. (State Assembly, 1933–1937; Chairman, Republican National Committee, 1944–1946; U.S. Attorney General, 1953–1957)

986.1 Keep 'Em Pure. w. No composer indicated. m. "Air—*If I Had Rhythm In My Nursery Rhymes.*" In: *Tory, Tory Hallelujah,* page 9. Published by Albany Legislative Correspondents' Association, Albany, NY. 1936. [8" × 11¾"]. N/c drawing of Franklin D. Roosevelt, other politicians dressed as Revolutionary soldiers in battle scene—"A Dashing Delirious Drama, Lampooning Loyalists and Liberty Leaguers, Daggering Despots, Dictators and Dummy Donkey-Drivers to music by Red-Coats and Lyrics by Turn-Coats, the Combat Being Played Against a Spangled Back-Drop." "Furiously Fought at Ten Eyck Hotel, Albany, New York, The Evening of Thursday, March 12, 1936, at Seven-Thirty o'clock." [Crew/FDR-325].

986.2 Let's Reapportion! w. No composer indicated. m. "Air—*Rainbow On The River.*" In: *Wake Up And Scream,* page 12. Published by Albany Legislative Correspondents' Association, Albany, NY. 1937. [8" × 11¾"]. N/c drawing by Jerry Costello of Dr. Bill Murray, King Macy, New York GOP, and Ham Fish as patients undergoing transfusions. "A Trumpet Call to the G.O.P. Eagle to Snap out of Coma and Rally Ravaged Republicans with New Volley of Vocal Vim—the Same Being Enacted 'mid a Merry Medley of Mountain Madness, Dutch Delirium, Liberalization Legendry, Melancholy Maidens and Rapscallion Redskins, at Ten Eyck Hotel, Albany, N.Y., Thursday, March eleventh, 1937, at Seven-Thirty o'clock." 20pp.

- **AmPM-987** BRUSH, Edw. F. (Mayor, Mt. Vernon, 1892–1894, 1903–1907 & 1918–1919)

987.1 The Brush March. m. A. Charles Stegman, Mount Vernon, NY. Published by Carl Fischer, 6 & 8 Fourth Avenue, New York, NY. Copyright 1901 by E.F. Brush. R/w/b flag with b/w inset photo of Edw. F. Brush. "Dedicated to Edw. F. Brush." "1901 Mayoralty Campaign." 6pp. Page 6: Blank.

- **AmPM-988** BRYCE, Lloyd Stephens (U.S. House, 1887–1889; U.S. Ambassador to The Netherlands, 1911–1913)

988.1 March Of The Boy Scouts. m. Howard Kocian. Published by Buck & Lowney, "Publishers of Music that Sells," St. Louis, MO. 1912. N/c drawing by Kissack of Boy Scouts marching. "Dedicated to the Boy Scouts of America. "Also published for band and orchestra." 6pp. Page 6: Bl/w photo—"This photo contains photos of President Taft, Ambassador Bryce, Gen. Baden Powell, Mr. Colin H. Livingston, President of Boy Scouts of America, Mr. A.C. Moses, President of Washington Local Council and Major Archibald Butt." Advertising.

988.2 University Club Banquet. [Song Book]. Published by The University Club, Washington, DC. 1911. Bk/br/w drawing of buildings, grapes, glasses, geometric designs. 30pp. Page 3: "The Seventh Annual Banquet, the New Willard Hotel, Monday, February 27, 1911, 7:00 p.m." Page 5: Menu. Pages 6 to 10: Drawings of Senator Thomas Carter, William H. Taft, Ambassador Bryce, Senator Depew and Hon. Martin Littleton.

- **AmPM-988A** BUCCI, Richard A. (Mayor, Binghamton, 199-)

988A.1 Binghamton, New York. w.m. Jim Ford. Published by James R. Ford Musical Enterprises (ASCAP), P.O. Box 406, Binghamton, NY. 1989. B/w photo of "Broome County Courthouse, Binghamton, New York—Photo by Jim Ford." "Proclaimed the Official Song of the City of Binghamton by Mayor Richard A. Bucci, May 21, 1998." "As Recorded by Jim Ford & Company Featuring vocalist Dan Hibbard, available on audio cassette)." "This song dedicated to everyone who has ever called greater Binghamton, New York home. The purchaser of this music has permission to make one copy of final page to eliminate the need to turn page during performance." 4pp.

- **AmPM-989** BUCK, Ellsworth Brewer (Board of Education, New York City, 1935–1944; U.S. House, 1944–1949)

989.1 Don't Pass The Buck. w.m. Clarence Gaskill. Published by Oscar Mayer, St. George Building, Staten Island, New York, NY. 1944. [9½" × 12½"]. Non-pictorial. 2pp. Page 2: Blank.

- **AmPM-990** BUCKLEY, James Lane (U.S. Senate, 1971–1977; U.S. Under Secretary of State, 1981–1982; President, Radio Free Europe/Radio Liberty, Inc., 1982–1985; U. S. Court of Appeals, District of Columbia Circuit, 1985–Present)

990.1 Embraceable Me. w. No composer indicated. m. "Tune—*Five Foot Two, Eyes Of Blue.*" In: *Thoroughly Mad-ern Malcolm Or He Didn't Need A Course In Forensics To Become A Famous Public Speaker,* page 10. Published by the New York State Legislative Correspondents' Association, Albany, NY. 1974. N/w photo of Malcolm Wilson as Alfred E. Newman—"What—Me Governor?" "Featuring the New York Correspondents' Association, March 16, 1974." 32pp.

- **AmPM-991** BUCKLEY, John L. (State Assembly, 1925–1926; State Senate 1927–1942)

991.1 I'll Get Away With Murder. w. No composer indicated. m. "Air—*Without A Word Of Warning.*" In: *Tory, Tory Hallelujah,* page 13. Published by Albany Legislative Correspondents' Association, Albany, NY. 1936. [8" × 11¾"]. N/c drawing of Franklin D. Roosevelt, other politicians dressed as Revolutionary soldiers in battle scene—"A Dashing Delirious Drama, Lampooning Loyalists and Liberty Leaguers, Daggering Despots, Dictators and Dummy Donkey-Drivers to music by Red-Coats and Lyrics by Turn-Coats, the

Combat Being Played Against a Spangled Back-Drop." "Furiously Fought at Ten Eyck Hotel, Albany, New York, The Evening of Thursday, March 12, 1936, at Seven-Thirty o'clock." [Crew/FDR-325].

• **AmPM-992 BURCHILL**, Thomas Francis (State Assembly, 1920–1924; State Senate, 1925–1938; U.S. House, 1943–1945)

992.1 Lehman Lullaby. w. No composer indicated. m. "Air — *Let's Put Out The Lights And Go To Sleep*." In: *Foam Sweet Foam*, page 10. Published by Albany Legislative Correspondents' Association, Albany, NY. 1933. [8" × 11¾"]. N/c drawing by Jerry Costello of Franklin D. Roosevelt, Al Smith and other politicians riding a bottle of beer — "The Lager Limited." "A Rollicking Review Rotating on Resurrection of Bouncing Beverages, Tipsily Tapped at Ten Eyck Hotel Rathskeller, Albany, New York, the evening of Thursday, February 23, 1933, at Seven-Thirty o'clock." 20pp. [Crew/FDR-277].

• **AmPM-993 BURLEIGH**, Henry Gordon (Town Supervisor, Ticonderoga, 1864–1865; State Assembly, 1876; U.S House, 1883–1887)

993.1 Burleigh Two Step. m. Alonzo F. Burt. Published by Standard Music Co., (Grasmuk & Schott), 180 East 88th Street, New York, NY. 1897. Br/w photo of "Hon. H.G. Burleigh, Whitehall, N.Y." B/w geometric designs. 6pp. Pages 2 and 6: Blank.

• **AmPM-994 BURLINGAME**, Alvah W., Jr. (State Senator, 1909–1910 & 1915–1922)

994.1 On To Havana! w. No composer indicated. m. "Air — *Over There*." "In which Senators James J. Walker, Henry M. Sage, Henry Walters, Charles C. Lockwood and Alvah W. Burlingame offer a solution for the 'dry capitol' bugaboo. Let's Go!" In: *Fourth Internationale*, page 7. Published by The Legislative Correspondents' Association of the State of New York, Albany, NY. 1920. [8" × 11¼"]. N/c drawing by Fred O. Seibel of a statue of House Speaker Thaddeus "Sweet" on horseback, "Governor's Chair," "Assemblyman Roosevelt," other politicians. "A Session of Soviets, Seething with Socialism, Sweetism, Sedition, Seven-Cent Fares, School-Ma'ams, Soda-Water, Slams, Slander, Simps and Strangulation, and Bristling with Booms, Boobs and Bunk." "Called by The Legislative Correspondents' Association of the State of New York, at The Ten Eyck, Albany, April 22, 1920." Page 5: "Toast List" including "Comrade Alfred E. Smith, Dictator of the Proletariat." [Crew/AES-66].

• **AmPM-994A BURR**, Aaron (State Assembly, 1784–1785 & 1798–1799; New York Attorney General, 1789–1790; Commissioner of Revolutionary Claims, 1791; U.S. Senate, 1791–1797; Vice President; 1801–1805) [ALSO SEE: DOC/PSM-TJ]

994A.1 The Dutchman. w. No composer indicated. m. "Air — *The Poachers*." In: *A Miniature Of Martin Van Buren (With A Selection Of The Best And Most Popular Tippecanoe Songs)*, page 49. 1840. [3½" × 6½"]. [V-1: Br/bk] [V-2: Gn/bk] [V-3: Y/bk] litho of man, chain around neck. Van Buren quote. "Amos Kendall's Veracity — Tom Benton's Honesty — Francis Blair's Beauty." "What is wanting cant be numbered [sic]." 58pp. [M-016]. [Crew/WHH-88].

994A.2 Jefferson And Liberty. w. No composer indicated. m. "Tune — *To Anacreon In Heav'n*." In: *The Republican Harmonist (Being A Select Collection Of Republican, Patriotic, And Sentimental Songs, Odes, Sonnets, &c, American And European: Some Of Which Are Original, And Most Of The Others Now Come For The First Time From An American Press)*, page 64. c. D.E. [Daniel Ebsworth] (A Citizen of the World). Printed "for the People," Boston, MA. 1801. Non-pictorial. 152pp. [Crew/TJ-10].

994A.3 On The Murder Of Hamilton (A Scotch Ballad). w. Composer not indicated. m. "Tune — *Good Night, And Joy Be Wi' Ye A'!*" In: *Collection Of The Facts And Documenta Relative To The Death Of A. Hamilton; With Comments: Together With The Various Orations, Sermons, And Eulogies That Have Been Published Or Written On His Life & Character*. e. William Coleman. 1804. [VBL, p. 179].

• **AmPM-995 BURTON**, John E. (State Budget Director, 1943–1950)

995.1 All We Want For Taxes. w. No composer indicated. m. "Tune — *All I Want For Christmas Is My Two Front Teeth*." Sung by "Henry Wallace." In: *Alice In Blunderland Or Through The Rooking Class* [Program and Songbook], page 17. Published by The Legislative Correspondents' Association of New York State, Albany, NY. 1949. [8⅝" × 11"]. N/c drawings of Harry Truman, Thomas Dewey, Franklin Roosevelt, Henry Wallace, Harold Stassen, Alben Barkley, Robert Taft, Earl Warren, other politicians. "A Scintillating Satire of Sadistic Surprises and Surprising Successes Featuring a Dramatic Disclosure of How Tom Did Not Go Down to D.C. in Slips; Together with a Give-Away-Nothing Radio Broadcast and Epic Melodrama of the Indian Wars Entitled 'When the Cat's Away the Mice Will Play.'" "Done With Music and Mirrors — Particularly Mirrors in Three Acts at Hotel Ten Eyck, Albany, March 12, 1949." [Crew/HST-20].

995.2 Five Birds In A Gilded Cage. w. No composer indicated. m. "Tune — *Bird In A Gilded Cage*." "As sung to and by Heck, Feinberg, Wicks, Mailler, Stephens." In: *Visions And Revisions*, page 11. Published by The Albany Legislative Correspondents' Association, Albany, NY. March 6, 1947. [8½" × 11"]. R/w/gn/y/bk drawing of Thomas "Dewey" as Santa Claus, sign — "Santa's Workshop," other New York politicians. "Revealing in Rhapsodic Revelry of Song and Stunt How a Political Scrooge Became a Political Saint; or, What Happened When Many Paws Raided the Wonderful Workshop of Santa Claus Dewey; Together with Other Strange and Silly Scenes." "Hotel Ten Eyck, Albany, March 6, 1947." 24pp. [Crew/TED-34].

995.3 Locked Up In The Reconstruction Fund. w.m. No composer or tune indicated. In: *Cash & Carry — On Or It Ain't Hay, A Stirring Saga Suggesting Scrimping, Scrooging And Spending Twixt The Highlands And Lowlands Of State Street; Also, A Loony Lift To Luna For Leaders Looking For Less O'Lockwood; All Pieced Together With A Paralyzing Portrayal Of Pickets Putting Pay Ahead Of Party*, page 8. Published by The Legislative Correspondents' Association of New York, Albany, NY. 1946. [8½" × 11"]. N/c drawing of politicians fighting over the "Castle Surplus, Irish dressed "O'Dwyer, Hannegan, Farley, Mead" against Scottish dressed "Lockwood, Bedenknap, MacDewey, Burton."

"Hotel Ten Eyck, Albany, March 14, 1946." 24pp. [Crew/TED-20].

995.4 Next Year. w. No composer indicated. m. "Tune—*Santa Claus Is Coming To Town.*" In: *Visions And Revisions*, page 13. Published by The Albany Legislative Correspondents' Association, Albany, NY. March 6, 1947. [8½" × 11"]. R/w/gn/y/bk drawing of Thomas "Dewey" as Santa Claus, sign—"Santa's Workshop," other New York politicians. "Revealing in Rhapsodic Revelry of Song and Stunt How a Political Scrooge Became a Political Saint; or, What Happened When Many Paws Raided the Wonderful Workshop of Santa Claus Dewey; Together with Other Strange and Silly Scenes." "Hotel Ten Eyck, Albany, March 6, 1947." 24pp. [Crew/TED-34].

- **AmPM-996 BUTLER, Benjamin Franklin** (State Assembly, 1827–1833; U.S. Attorney General, 1833–1837 & 1837–1838; Secretary of War, 1836–1837; U.S. District Judge, 1838–1841 & 1845–1848)

996.1 Behold The Man! w. No composer indicated. m. "Air—*A Little More Cider Too.*" In: *The Republican Campaign Songster, A Collection Of Lyrics, Original And Selected, Specifically Prepared For The Friends Of Freedom In The Campaign Of Fifty-Six*, page 105. Published by Miller, Orton & Mulligan, No. 25 Park Row, New York, NY. 1856. [3¹³⁄₁₆" × 6"]. Be/bk litho of "Colonel John C. Fremont" facing to viewer's left, black line border. 112pp. [M-097]. [Crew/JCF-24].

996.2 King Andrew (Glee). w. No composer indicated. m. "Tune—*Dame Durden.*" Published by S.H. Parker, No. 141 Washington Street, Boston, MA. August, 1834. Non-pictorial. "As Sung at the Salem Whig Festival." 4pp. Pages 1 and 4: Blank. [Crew/AJK-7].

996.3 King Andrew. w. No composer indicated. m. "Air—*Dame Durden.*" In: *A Miniature Of Martin Van Buren (With A Selection Of The Best And Most Popular Tippecanoe Songs)*, page 46. 1840. [3½" × 6½"]. [V-1: Br/bk] [V-2: Gn/bk] [V-3: Y/bk] litho of man, chain around neck. Van Buren quote. "Amos Kendall's Veracity—Tom Benton's Honesty—Francis Blair's Beauty." "What is wanting cant be numbered [sic]." 58pp. [M-016]. [Crew/WHH-88].

996.4 A Miniature Of Martin Van Buren. w.m. No composer or tune indicated. In: *A Miniature Of Martin Van Buren (With A Selection Of The Best And Most Popular Tippecanoe Songs)*, page 3. 1840. [3½" × 6½"]. [V-1: Br/bk] [V-2: Gn/bk] [V-3: Y/bk] litho of man, chain around neck. Van Buren quote. "Amos Kendall's Veracity—Tom Benton's Honesty—Francis Blair's Beauty." "What is wanting cant be numbered [sic]." 58pp. [M-016]. [Crew/WHH-88].

996.5 Polk Is A Used Up Joke. w.m. No composers or tune indicated. [1844]. Non-pictorial geometric design border. 2pp. Page 2: Blank.

996.6 The Rubber; Or Mat's Third And Last Game. w. No composer indicated. m. "Tune—*Miss Bailey.*" In: *The National Clay Minstrel (And True Whig's Pocket Companion For The Presidential Canvass Of 1844)*, page 46. Published by [V-1: George Hood, No. 15 North 6th Street, Philadelphia, PA] [V-2: James Fisher, No. 71 Court Street, Boston, MA]. 1843. [3¼" × 5⅛"]. Y/bk litho of raccoon—"That Coon" and flag—"Henry Clay," log cabin. "New and Improved Edition." 128pp. Page 10: Dedication—"To the National Clay Club this work is respectfully dedicated by the Publisher." [Crew/HC-11].

- **AmPM-997 BUTLER, Nicholas Murray** (Board of Education, New Jersey, 1887–1895; President of Columbia University, 1901–1945; Delegate, Republican National Convention, New York, 1888, 1904, 1912, 1916, 1924, 1928, & 1932; Republican Candidate for Vice-Presidency, 1912; Winner, Nobel Peace Prize, 1931].

997.1 Oh, Jimmy! w. No composer indicated. m. "Air—*Please.*" In: *Foam Sweet Foam*, page 11. Published by Albany Legislative Correspondents' Association, Albany, NY. 1933. [8" × 11¾"]. N/c drawing by Jerry Costello of Franklin D. Roosevelt, Al Smith and other politicians riding a bottle of beer—"The Lager Limited." "A Rollicking Review Rotating on Resurrection of Bouncing Beverages, Tipsily Tapped at Ten Eyck Hotel Rathskeller, Albany, New York, the evening of Thursday, February 23, 1933, at Seven-Thirty O'clock." 20pp. [Crew/FDR-277].

- **AmPM-998 CAMBRELENG, Churchill Caldom** (U.S. House, 1821–1839; Ambassador to Russia, 1840–1841)

998.1 Lost Hopes. w. No composer indicated. m. "Tune—*The Last Rose Of Summer.*" In: *Log Cabin Song Book* (A Collection of Popular and Patriotic Songs), page 8. Published at *The Log Cabin* office, No. 30 Ann-Street, New York, NY. 1840. [4⅞" × 7"]. [V-1: Br/bk] [V-2: Y/bk] litho of log cabin, cider barrel, farmer with plow, flag—"Harrison and Tyler," geometric design border. "The Freeman's glittering Sword be Blest, For ever blest the Freeman's Lyre" Page 3: B/w litho of "Major-General William Henry Harrison, of Ohio," facsimile signature. 74pp. [M-020]. [Crew/WHH-56].

998.2 A Parody On Up Salt River. w. No composer indicated. m. "Tune—*All On Hobbies.*" In: *Songs For The People (Or Tippecanoe Melodies)* [Songster], page 37. "Dedicated to the Democratic Whig Young Men of the City and County of New York." Published for the Authors by James P. Giffing, No. 56 Gold Street, New York, NY. 1840. [3¾" × 6"]. Litho of William Henry Harrison, log cabin, flag. "Original and Selected." 76pp. [M-019]. [Crew/WHH-63].

998.3 The Sub Treasury Waltz. m. "Composed by A. Jackson." [1837–1840]. Non-pictorial. "As Composed by A. Jackson and Dedicated to Martin Van Buren." Non-pictorial. 2pp. Page 2: Blank. [Crew/MVB-9].

- **AmPM-999 CAREY, Hugh Lee** (State Chairman, Young Democrats of New York, 1946; U.S. House, 1961–1974; Governor; 1975–1983)

999.1 What Beats Four Of A Kind? w. No composer indicated. m. "Tunes—*Playground In My Mind* and *Around The World.*" As sung by "Samuels, Stratton, Reid and Carey." In: *Thoroughly Mad-ern Malcolm Or He Didn't Need A Course In Forensics To Become A Famous Public Speaker*, page 27. Published by the New York State Legislative Correspondents' Association, Albany, NY. 1974. N/w photo of Malcolm Wilson as Alfred E. Newman—"What—Me Governor?" "Featuring the New York Correspondents' Association, March 16. 1974." 32pp.

- **AmPM-1000 CARLINO, Joseph F.** (State Assembly, 1945–1964; Delegate, Republican National Convention, 1956–1964)

1000.1 A Losing Entry. w. No composer indicated. m. "Tune—*Matchmaker.*" As sung by "Mosbacher and Carlino." In: *Thoroughly Mad-ern Malcolm or He Didn't Need A Course In Forensics To Become A Famous Public Speaker*, page 6. Published by the New York State Legislative Correspondents' Association, Albany, NY. 1974. N/w photo of Malcolm Wilson as Alfred E. Newman—"What—Me Governor?" "Featuring the New York Correspondents' Association, March 16. 1974." 32pp.

• **AmPM-1001 CARLISLE**, John G. (State Public Service Commission

1001.1 The Grand March In January. w. No composer indicated. m. "Air—*It's A Long Way To Tipperary.*" "A modern political Tango." In: *The Modest Art Of Self Advance Sporting Annual, Containing Correct Records Of White House Hopes, State Champions, Has Beens, Handlers And Never-Wases*, page 29. Published by the Legislative Correspondents' Association, Albany, NY. 1915. [5" × 7"]. Gy/r/bk cover drawing of a crowd watching a boxing match. 34pp.

1001.2 The Sharing Of The Green. w. No composer indicated. m. *Wearing Of The Green*. In: *The Red Book, Containing Portraits And Biographies Of Some Persons More Or Less Prominent Public Life Written Entirely Without Respect To The Libel Laws, In A Studious Effort To Conceal Everything But The Truth; Some Songs Built Upon The Same Principle, And Other Important (?) Material Entirely Unfit To Print*, page 14. Published by Legislative Correspondents' Association of the State of New York, Albany, NY. 1913. [5" × 7¼"]. R/w/bk hardback book with drawing of State House, seal of New York, geometric designs. 90pp.

• **AmPM-1002 CASEY**, William Joseph (Chairman, Securities and Exchange Commission, 1973–1974; Head of the Export-Import Bank, 1975; Chairman, President Reagan's Campaign Committee, 1980; Director, Central Intelligence Agency, 1981–1987)

1002.1 Mighty Casey. w. Bill Strauss and Elaina Newport. On Cassette: *Workin' 9 To 10*. Published by Capitol Steps Productions, 1505 King Street, Alexandria, VA. 1987. Cassette Cover: N/c Reagan at desk.

• **AmPM-1003 CHAPIN**, Alfred C. (State Assembly, 1882–1883; Mayor, Brooklyn, 1888–1891; U.S. House, 1891–1892)

1003.1 Quick Step Mayor Chapin. m. Alfred D. Fohs, "Bandmaster 23rd Reg't N.G.S.N.Y." 6pp. Page 6: Blank. Published by Chas. W. Held, Brooklyn, NY. 1890. B/w floral and geometric designs. "Respectfully Dedicated with permission to the Ho. Alfred C. Chapin, Mayor of Brooklyn, N.Y." "For Piano." 1890.

• **AmPM-1003A CHASE**, "Canon" William Sheafe (Sunday Law Enforcement Fanatic; Movie Reformer; Law Preservation Candidate for U.S. Senate, 1934)

1003A.1 Off To Wonderland Ballad. w. No composer indicated. m. "Air—*When The Midnight Choo Choo Leaves For Alabam.*" In: *Al S. In Wonderland*, page 13. Published by The Albany Legislative Correspondents' Association of New York State, Albany, NY. 1924. [8½" × 10½"]. N/c drawing by Fred O. Seibel of Statue of Liberty with Beer, "Al Smith," Calvin "Coolidge" as a dragon, other politicians. "A Jocose Junket in Phantom Pullmans to that Roisterous Realm, where Hectic Hopes, Hocus-Pocus Harmonies, Folly, Froth and Flim Flam Blend Blithely with Becalmed Booms, Budget Butchers, Bubbles, Blunders and Barters." "Departing from at Ten Eyck Hotel Terminal, Albany, NY., at 7 o'clock, Eastern Time, on the evening of Thursday, March, 27, 1924." [Crew/AES-67].

• **AmPM-1004 CLARK**, William W. (State Supreme Court, 1920–1925)

1004.1 Everybody's Getting' It Now—The Gate. w. No composer indicated. m. "Air—*Everybody's Doing It.*" In: *The Red Book, Containing Portraits And Biographies Of Some Persons More Or Less Prominent Public Life Written Entirely Without Respect To The Libel Laws, In A Studious Effort To Conceal Everything But The Truth; Some Songs Built Upon The Same Principle, And Other Important (?) Material Entirely Unfit To Print*, page 13. Published by Legislative Correspondents' Association of the State of New York, Albany, NY. 1913. [5" × 7¼"]. R/w/bk hardback book with drawing of State House, seal of New York, geometric designs. 90pp.

1004.2 The Sharing Of The Green. w. No composer indicated. m. *Wearing Of The Green*. In: *The Red Book, Containing Portraits And Biographies Of Some Persons More Or Less Prominent Public Life Written Entirely Without Respect To The Libel Laws, In A Studious Effort To Conceal Everything But The Truth; Some Songs Built Upon The Same Principle, And Other Important (?) Material Entirely Unfit To Print*, page 14. Published by Legislative Correspondents' Association of the State of New York, Albany, NY. 1913. [5" × 7¼"]. R/w/bk hardback book with drawing of State House, seal of New York, geometric designs. 90pp.

• **AmPM-1005 CLARK**, Myron Holley (State Senate, 1852–1854; Governor, 1855–1857)

1005.1 The State Staff Polka. m. Thomas Baker. Published by Firth, Pond & Co., 1 Franklin Square, New York, NY. 1856. N/c litho by Sarony & Co. of Major Samuel Thompson on horseback. "Composed and respectfully dedicated to Major Samuel C. Thompson of the staff of His Excellency Govr. Clark of N.Y." 8pp. [?]. Pages 2, 7 and 8: Blank. [LL/JH].

• **AmPM-1006 CHENEY**, Nelson W. (State Assembly, 1916–1917 & 1918–1929; State Senate, 1930–1938)

1006.1 Let's Reapportion! w. No composer indicated. m. "Air—*Rainbow On The River.*" In: *Wake Up And Scream*, page 12. Published by Albany Legislative Correspondents' Association, Albany, NY. 1937. [8" × 11¾"]. N/c drawing by Jerry Costello of Dr. Bill Murray, King Macy, New York GOP, and Ham Fish as patients undergoing transfusions. "A Trumpet Call to the G.O.P. Eagle to Snap out of Coma and Rally Ravaged Republicans with New Volley of Vocal Vim—the Same Being Enacted 'mid a Merry Medley of Mountain Madness, Dutch Delirium, Liberalization Legendry, Melancholy Maidens and Rapscallion Redskins, at Ten Eyck Hotel, Albany, N.Y., Thursday, March eleventh, 1937, at Seven-Thirty o'clock." 20pp.

• **AmPM-1006x CLEVELAND**, Stephen Grover (Sheriff, Erie County, 1870–1873; Mayor of

Buffalo, NY, 1882 Governor, 1883–1885; President, 1885–1889 & 1893–1897) [SEE: DOC/PSM-GC]

• **AmPM-1007 CLINTON, De Witt** (State Assembly, 1790–1795; State Senate, 1798–1802 & 1806–1811; U.S. Senate, 1802–1903; Mayor, New York City, 1803–1807, 1808–1810, 1811–1815; Lt. Governor, 1811–1813; Governor, 1817–1821 & 1825–1828) [ALSO SEE: DOC/PSM-DWC]

1007.1 Celebration Ode. w. No composer indicated. m. *Hail Columbia.* "Sheldon Smith, Esq. delivered a well written ... address, after which was sung by the choir to the tune of *Hail Columbia*, the following *Ode*, with fine effect." Published in *Buffalo Journal*, October 27, 1825. [VBL, p. 234].

1007.2 Gov. Clinton's Grand March. m. William C. Swan. Published for the Author by S. Wetherbee, Boston, MA. [1820?]. Non-pictorial. "Composed and arranged for the Piano Forte by William C. Swan. With an accompaniment for the Flute." 4pp. Pages 1 and 4: Blank. [W-9160].

1007.3 Governor Dewitt Clinton's Grand March. m. F. Meline. Published by the Author, New York, NY. [1817–1821]. Non-pictorial. "Composed for the piano forte." "Approved of by His Excellency." "Pr. 37 cts." 6pp. Page 6: Blank. [W-5824].

1007.4 A Miniature Of Martin Van Buren. w.m. No composer or tune indicated. In: *A Miniature Of Martin Van Buren (With A Selection Of The Best And Most Popular Tippecanoe Songs)*, page 3. 1840. [3½" × 6½"]. [V-1: Br/bk] [V-2: Gn/bk] [V-3: Y/bk] litho of man, chain around neck. Van Buren quote. "Amos Kendall's Veracity — Tom Benton's Honesty — Francis Blair's Beauty." "What is wanting cant be numbered [sic]." 58pp. [M-016]. [Crew/WHH-88].

• **AmPM-1007A CLINTON, George** (Clerk of the Court of Common Pleas, New York, 1759; District Attorney, New York, 1765; State Assembly. 1768; New York Committee of Correspondence, 1774; Continental Congress, 1775–1776, Governor, 1777–1795 & 1801–1804; Vice President 1805–1812)

1007A.1 A Miniature Of Martin Van Buren. w.m. No composer or tune indicated. In: *A Miniature Of Martin Van Buren (With A Selection Of The Best And Most Popular Tippecanoe Songs)*, page 3. 1840. [3½" × 6½"]. [V-1: Br/bk] [V-2: Gn/bk] [V-3: Y/bk] litho of man, chain around neck. Van Buren quote. "Amos Kendall's Veracity — Tom Benton's Honesty — Francis Blair's Beauty." "What is wanting cant be numbered [sic]." 58pp. [M-016]. [Crew/WHH-88].

• **AmPM-1008 CLINTON, Hillary Rodham** (House Judiciary Committee, Impeachment Inquiry Staff, 1974; First Lady of Arkansas, 1983–1993; First Lady of the United States, 1993–2001; U.S. Senate, 2001–Present) [ALSO SEE: DOC/PSM-WJC]

1008.1 All I'm Turning To (Is Rush Limbaugh). w. S.T.G. m. "*All I Wanna Do* (Is Have Some Fun), originally by Sheryl Crow Published online at <http://www.amiright.com/parody/90s/shetylcrow0.shtml>. [199-].

1008.2 Amazing Bush. w. Static. m. "*Amazing Grace*, based on the performance by Traditional." "Gotta flip it around this time for personal reasons." Published online at <http://www.amiright.com/parody/misc/traditional304.shtml>. 2003.

1008.3 The Ballad Of Jeb's Brother. w. William Tong. m. "*The Ballad Of Jed Clampett*, based on a performance by Lester Flatt and Earl Skruggs." Published online at <http://www.amiright.com/parody/60s/lesterflattandearlskruggs0.shtml>. [ca. 2003].

1008.4 Bill And Hillary. w. Scott Loeb. m. "This is a parody of *Jack & Diane* by John Cougar about our President & Co." Published online at <http://www.geocities.com/sldice/bill_hillary.htm>. [199-].

1008.5 Bill Clinton Got Run Over By A Taxi. w. Billy Florio. m. "*Grandma Got Run Over By A Reindeer*, originally by Elmo & Patsy." Published online at <http://amiright.com/parody/80s/elmoandpatsy0.shml>. [ca. 2001].

1008.6 Bill Clinton Rhapsody. w. Tom Stevens. m. "*Another Bohemian Rhapsody*, originally by Queen." Published online at <http://www.amiright.com/parody/70s/queen14.shtml>. [ca. 2000].

1008.7 Bill So Horney. w.m. Mark Ross, Chris Wong Won, David Hobbs and Luther Campbell. On 33⅓ rpm EP: *Bill So Horney* by 2 Live Crew. Lil' Joe Records, 6157 NW 167th St., Miami, FL. Record #LJR 900-1. 1998. Performed by 2 Live Crew and Amos Braxton. Cover art: Drawing of Bill Clinton and Monica Lewinsky; 2 Live Crew. [2 versions — Clean and Explicit]. 1998.

1008.8 Bleaque Alley. w. "Melhi." m. "*Creeque Alley*, originally by The Mamas and Papas." Written as the Monica Lewinsky scandal was fading." Published online at <http://amiright.com/parody/60s/themamasandpapas0.shml>. [ca. 2000].

1008.9 The Boogie-Woogie Tenor Sax Commander-In-Chief. w. Paul Silhan. m. "Sung to *The Boogie-Woogie Bugle Boy Of Company B* by The Andrews Sisters." On: Cassette: *Running On Empty*. Lyrics published at <http://www.paulsilhan.com/roe-10.htm>. [ca. 1996].

1008.10 Bored Of Elections. w. Keith H. Peterson. m. "Warren's *The Song Of The Marines*." "View and hear the original piano version of this song at The Harry Warren Web Site, courtesy of Davis Jenkins." Published online at <http://mysite.verizon.net/vze1q1d3/id48.html>. [ca. 1992].

1008.11 Brother Lib's Traveling Salvation Show. w. Paul Silhan. m. "Sung to *Brother Love's Traveling Salvation Show* by Neil Diamond." On: Cassette: *Brother Lib*. Lyrics published at <http://www.paulsilhan.com/bl-1.htm>. [ca. 1993].

1008.12 Bye Bye Bill. w. Vermonter. m. Tune — "*Bye Bye Bye*, originally by N'Sync." Published online at <http://www.amiright.com/parody/90s/nsync12.shml>. [ca. 2001].

1008.13 The Chipwonk Song. w. Paul Silhan. m. "Sung to *The Chipmunk Song (Hurry Christmas Don't Be Late)* by David Seville and the Chipmunks." On: Cassette: *Lie-A-lot*. Lyrics published at <http://www.paulsilhan.com/lal-2.htm>. 1993.

1008.14 Clinton Administration Highlights. w. Steve Krulin. m. "With apologies to Billy Joel's *We Didn't Start The Fire*." Published online by Steve Krulin at <http://www.hsc.sunysb.edu/apap/archives/1996/2316.html>. November 4, 1996. [Crew/WJC-15].

1008.15 The Clintonian So-Slick Blues. w. Paul

Silhan. m. "Sung to Bob (Zimmerman) Dylan's *Subterranean Homesick Blues*." "As heard on Rush's radio Show." Lyrics published online at <http://www.paulsilhan.com/dylan.htm>. 1996.

1008.16 *Clinton's Wife*. w. Mike Armstrong. m. "*Stacy's Mom*, based on a performance by Fountains of Wayne." "After seeing her on *The Daily Show* ... jees." Published online at <http://www.amiright.com/parody/2000s/fountainsofwayne9.shtml>. 2003.

1008.17 *Connie, Do You Want To Know A Secret?* w. No composer indicated. m. "Parody of *Do You Want To Know A Secret?* by The Beatles." Lyrics published by *The Bob Rivers Show* with Bob, Spike & Joe and Twisted Tunes online at <http://www.twistedradio.com/player/lyrics.asp?songID=838>. [199-].

1008.18 *Dean, Dean*. w. "Stray Pooch." m. "*Green, Green* by The New Christie Minstrels." "Well, Dean's power is growing — he's up to overestimating 3200 people..." Published online at <http://amiright.com/parody/60s/thenewchristieminstrels0.shtml.

1008.19 *Democracy Bites*. w. S.G.T. m. "*Misc Songs*, originally by Pearl Jam." Published online at <http://amiright.com/parody/90s/pearljam6.shml>. [ca. 2001].

1008.20 *Don't Stop* (Thinking About Hillary). w. Tim Hall. m. "*Don't Stop Thinking About Tomorrow*, based on the performance by Fleetwood Mac." Published online at <http://amiright.com/parody/70s/fleetwoodmac12.shml>. [ca. 2003].

1008.21 *Don't Worry, Hillary*. w. Paul Silhan. m. "Sung to *Don't Worry, Baby* by The Beach Boys." On: Cassette: *Spinball Wizard*. "As heard on Rush's Radio Show." Lyrics published at <http://www.paulsilhan.com/dontworr.htm>. 1997.

1008.22 *Eleanor*. w. Paul Silhan. m. "Sung to *Eleanor* by The Turtles." On: Cassette: *Running On Empty*. Lyrics published at <http://www.paulsilhan.com/roe-5.htm>. [ca. 1996].

1008.23 *Election Day*. w. Mike Florio. m. "*Minority*, originally by Green Day." Published online at <http://amiright.com/parody/70s/greenday5.shml>. [ca. 2001].

1008.24 *Electoral Rhapsody 2000*. w. Kevin Dunlap. m. "Sung to the tune of *Bohemian Rhapsody* by Queen." Published online at <http://www.analyticalq.com/music/parodies/rhapsody.htm>. 2000.

1008.25 *Everyone Knows It's Hillary*. w. Paul Silhan. m. "Sung to *(Everyone Knows It's) Windy* by The Association." On: Cassette: *Running On Empty*. Lyrics published at <http://www.paulsilhan.com/roe-1.htm>. [ca. 1996].

1008.26 *For What It's Worth 2003*. w. Steve Kalafut. m. "*For What It's Worth* originally by *Buffalo Springfield*." Published online at <http://www.amiright.com/parody/60s/buffalospringfield2.shtml>. 2003.

1008.27 *George And Al*. w. Tom Smith. m. "*You Can Call Me Al* by Paul Simon." "The beauty of this one is I wrote it at ConClave 2000, about two-and-a-half weeks before the Presidential election." "Published online at <http://www.tomsmithonline.com/lyrics/george_and_al.htm>. 2000.

1008.28 *Gov Finks*. w. Kev O'Keefe. m. "*Love Stinks*, based on the performance by J. Geils Band." "Socialist Hillary is teaming up with that ex-KKK Bryd & other Dems to filibuster time & time again." Published online at <http://amiright.com/parody/80s/jgeilsband0.shml>. [2003].

1008.29 *He Gets Around*. w. Paul Silhan. m. "Sung to *I Get Around* by The Beach Boys." On: Cassette: *Lie-A-lot*. Lyrics published at <http://ww.paulsilhan.com/lal-9.htm>. 1994.

1008.29A *The Heart Of Hillary*. w. Lionel Mertens. m. "*The Heart Of Rock-N-Roll*, based on the performance by Huey Lewis and the News." Published online at <http://amiright.com/parody/80s/hueylewisandthenews25.shtml>. 2004.

1008.30 *Hello Muddahs, Hello Faddahs*. w. Paul Silhan. m. "Sung to *Hello Muddah, Hello Faddah (A Letter From Camp)* by Allan Sherman." On CD: *Scandal In The Wind*. Lyrics published online at <http://www.paulsilhan.com/muddahs.htm>. 1998.

1008.31 *Hillary*. w. Michael Florio. m. "*Kryptonite* originally by Three Doors Down." Published online at <http://www.amiright.com/parody/2000s/threedoorsdown0.shtml>.

1008.32 *Hillary*. w. "S.G.T." m. "Parody of Pearl Jam's *Jeremy*." Published online at <http://www.angelfire.com.music/parodies/sentinpearljamparody.html>. [199-].

1008.33 *Hillary Clinton*. w. Mike Florio. m. "*Elanor [sic] Rigby*, originally by The Beatles." Published online at <http://amiright.com/parody/misc/thebeatles10.shml>. [ca. 2001].

1008.34 *Hillary Clinton's Socialist Health Care Plan*. w. Paul Silhan. m. "Sung to the reprise version of *Sergeant Pepper's Lonely Hearts Club Band* by The Beatles." On: Cassette: *Lie-A-lot*. Lyrics published at <http://www.paulsilhan.com/lal-7.htm>. 1994.

1008.35 *Hillary, Oy! Hillary*. w.m. Henry and Bobbie Shaffner. Published by Keynote Associates, One Montgomery Avenue, Bala Cynwyd, PA. 2000. Lyrics printed on a "New Release For Immediate Release, October, 2000." "*Hillary, Oy! Hillary* Song (In Yiddish) Helps Mrs. Clinton Attract the Jewish Vote." 2pp. Page 2: Blank.

1008.36 *Hillary Queen*. w. Tim Bowlby. m. "*Killer Queen* originally by Queen." Published online at <http://www.amiright.com/parody/70s/queen13.shtml>. 2003

1008.37 *Hillary The 1st*. w. Craig Pritchett. m. "*Henry The VIII* originally by Herman's Hermits." Published online at <http://www.amiright.com/parody/60s/hermanhermits17.shtml>.

1008.38 *Hillary* (You're A Fine Girl). w. Mediamike. m. "*Brandy (You're A Fine Girl*, based on a performance by Looking Glass." "This was the first song I did for the Album." Published online at <http://www.amiright.com/parody/70s/lookingglass7.shtml>. 2003.

1008.39 *Hillary's Song* (Open Fire). w. S.T.G. m. "*Ana's Song* (Open) originally by Silverchair." Published over the Internet online by Amiright.com at <http://www.amiright.com/parody/90s/silverchair0.shtml>. 2000. [Crew/WJC-16].

1008.40 *Hillary's Suits*. w. Bruce Decker. m. "*Joseph's Coat*, originally by Andrew Lloyd Webber." "The musical *Joseph And His Amazing Technicolor*

Dream Coat is now Hillary and Her Amazing Mono Colored Pant Suits." Published online at <http://amiright.com/parody/80s/andrewlloydwebber0.shml>. [ca. 2000].

1008.41 *Hill'rita*. w. Bill Strauss and Elaina Newport. On CD: *One Bush, Two Bush, Old Bush, New Bush*. Published by Capitol Steps Productions, 1505 King Street, Alexandria, VA. 2001. CD Cover: Gn/bl/y drawing of George Bush and George W. Bush as Seuss characters.

1008.42 *Hotel Pennsylvania*. w. Malcolm Higgins. m. "*Hotel California*, originally by The Eagles." Published online at <http://www.amiright.com/parody/70s/theeagles4.shtml>. [ca. 2001].

1008.43 *I Am A Prime Example Of Transactional Immunity*. w. Lady Gale [Gale Stevenson]. m. Sir Arthur Sullivan. Published online at <http://light junkie.org/parody/major-intern.html>. 1998.

1008.44 *I Got You Bill*. w. Malcolm Higgins. m. "*I Got You Babe*, originally by Sonny and Cher." Published online at <http://amiright.com/parody/misc/sonnyandcher1.shml>. [ca. 1999].

1008.45 *If You Could Just Not Lie*. w. Billy Florio. m. "*If You Could Read My Mind* originally by Gordon Lightfoot." Published online at <http://www.amiright.com/parody/70s/gordonlightfoot0.shtml>. [ca. 2000].

1008.46 *I'll Tax The Rich*. w. Edward Goldstein. m. "Parody *I Want To Be Rich*." Published online at <http://www.bagelfather.com/funstuff/parody/parody7.htm>. [199-].

1008.47 *Impeachment Time In Georgia*. w. Art Thieme. m. "Tune—*Peach Pickin' Time In Georgia* by Jimmie Rogers." Lyrics published online at <http://www.mudcat.org/kids/@displaysong.cfm?SongID=3000>. 1999.

1008.48 *Indecision 2000*. w. Gary S. O'Connor. m. "*Mack The Knife*, based on a performance by Bobby Darin." "I finally got to write my editorial on the Presidential Election of 2000. This is political fodder for your ears. The story of Al, Walker, Kathy, Hillary, Jessie and all the rest is set to the melody of Mack the Knife in this parody. By the way, this is not the Rush Limbaugh theme song, but it could be!" Published online at <http://www.amiright.com/parody/60s/bobbydarin2.shtml>. [ca. 2003].

1008.49 *The Inevitable Return Of A Texan Dope*. w. S.T.G. m. "*The Inevitable Return Of The Great White Dope*, originally by Bloodhound Gang." Published online at <http://amiright.com/parody/2000s/bolldhoundgang1.shml>. [ca. 2000].

1008.50 *Instant Clinton*. w. Tom Smith. m. "*Where The Hell Is Bill?* by Camper Van Beethoven." "This mid-80s demented classis ... is a perfect forum for riffing on the Clinton Administration." "Published online at <http://www.tomsmithonline.com/lyrics/instantclinton.htm>. 1999.

1008.51 *Itsy Bitsy Teenie Weenie Yellow Spot Of Something Seamy*. w. Paul Silhan. m. "Sung to *Itsy Bitsy Teenie Weenie Yellow Polk Dot Bikini* by Bryan Hyland." On CD: *Scandal In The Wind*. Lyrics published online at <http://www.paulsilhan.com/itsy.htm>. 1998.

1008.52 *Kenneth Starr Is Coming To Town*. w. H.R. Yeager. m. "Sung to the tune of *Santa Claus Is Coming To Town*." Published online at <http://www.geocities.com/CapitolHill/Congress/3950>. 1998.

1008.53 *Liberalcation*. w. Mike Florio. m. "*Californication*, originally by Red Hot Chili Peppers." Published online at <http://amiright.com/parody/2000s/redhotchilipeppers4.shml>. [ca. 2001].

1008.54 *The Little First Lady With Megalomania*. w. Paul Silhan. m. "Sung to *The Little Old Lady From Pasadena* by Jan & Dean." On: Cassette: *Lie-A-lot*. Lyrics published at <http://www.paulsilhan.com/lal-1.htm>. 1995.

1008.55 *Lirty Dies: The Kesidntial Prandidates*. w. Bill Strauss and Elaina Newport. Published by The Capitol Steps online at <http://capsteps.com/lirty/prandidates.html>. [ca. 1992].

1008.56 *Living Next Door To Al Gore*. w. Smokie. m. "*Living Next Door to Alice*, originally by Gail Smith." Published online at <http://amiright.com/parody/80s/gailsmith0.shml>. [ca. 2001].

1008.56A *Me And Hillary*. w. Paul Shanklin. On CD: *Bill Clinton Comeback Kid Tour*. Published by Narodniki Records. CD Cover: Caricature of Bill Clinton. See: www.paulshanklin.com. 2002.

1008.57 *Miss Lewinsky* (The Opera). w. No composer indicated. m. Tune of *Miss Gradenko* by The Police." "The Half-Baked Institute for Political Parody." "The following duet was inspired by *Miss Gradenko* by The Police. It is the writer's opinion that Bill, Hillary, Monica, Paula and Gennifer should all go into group therapy together to uncover their past-life karma." Published online at <http://www.houstonprogressive.org/parody2.html>. [ca. 1997–1998].

1008.58 *Musical Impeachment*. w. No composer indicated. m. Tune of *Beauty School Dropout* from *Grease*." "The Half-Baked Institute for Political Parody." "The following is a re-write of Beauty School Dropout (from the musical Grease) sung at a church picnic, proving that people will laugh at just about anything I sing about, as long as I'm dressed up like Marilyn Monroe!" Published online at <http://www.houstonprogressive.org/parody2.html>. [ca. 1992–1993].

1008.59 *My Wife* (Bill Clinton's Song). w. Big Boecky. m. "*My Life*, originally by Billy Joel." Published online at <http://amiright.com/parody/70s/billyjoel0.shml>. [ca. 2001].

1008.60 *Name Is Bill Clinton*. w. S.T.G. m. "*Dreams In Digital (Fiction)*, originally by Orgy." Published online at <http://amiright.com/parody/2000s/orgy0.shml>. [ca. 2001].

1008.61 *New Hampshire Primary Marching Cadence*. w. Guy DiRito. m. "*Military Cadence (Sound Off)*, based on a performance by Traditional." "This song is done to the traditional military cadence beat. Practice marching as you sound off to this." Published online at <http://www.amiright.com/parody/misc/traditional430.shtml>. 2004.

1008.61A *O Hillary*. w. Paul Shanklin. On CD: *Holiday Classics*. Published by Narodniki Records. CD Cover: Caricature of Bill Clinton as Santa. See: www.paulshanklin.com. 2002.

1008.62 *Oh, I'm A Good Ol' Republican*. w. Stuart Schimler. m. "*Oh, I'm A Good Ol' Rebel*, originally by Anonymous writer." "The original song is from right after the Civil War. It is the same tune as *Lily Of The West*." Published online at <http://amiright.com/parody/misc/anonymouswriter0.shml>. [ca. 2002].

1008.63 1. .2. .3 Volunteer Some More. w. Paul Silhan. m. "Sung to (As is commonly known) *1. .2. .3. . What Are We Fighting For?* (although — as Country Joe fans know- the song's real title is the *I-Feel-Like-I'm-Fixin'-To-Die-Rag*) by Country Joe & The Fish." On: Cassette: *Spinball Wizard.* "As heard on Rush's Radio Show." Lyrics published at <http://www.paulsilhan.com/1-2-3.htm>. 1997.

1008.64 Oops He Did Her Again. w. Alex. m. "*Oops I Did It Again*, originally by Britney Spears." Published online at <http://www.amiright.com/parody/90s/britneyspears25.shtml>. [ca. 1999].

1008.65 Oval Office Thumpin'. w. Mel. m. "This is to the tune of that old *Tubthumping* song." Published online at <http://foreardgarden.com/forward/6625.html>.

1008.66 Pardoned. w. Michael Florio. m. Tune — "*Jaded*, based on a performance by Aerosmith." Published online at <http://www.amiright.com/parody/2000s/aerosmith0.shtml>. [ca. 2002].

1008.67 Please Go Home. w. Michael Florio. m. "*If Your Gone*, originally by Matchbox Twenty." "A note to Hillary." Published online at <http://amiright.com/parody/70s/matchboxtwenty0.shml>. [ca. 2001].

1008.68 Poor Bill Can't Tell The Truth. w. Peter Hicks and Geoff Francis. m. No tune indicated. "Isn't it heart warming to know that the man responsible for the continuing genocide against the Iraqi people has finally come clean about his little dalliances — or has he? Published online at <http://www.trump.net.au/glazfolk/songs/clinton.htm>. [ca. 1999].

1008.69 President Clinton's Costly Health Care Plan. w. No composer indicated. m. "Parody of *Sgt. Pepper's Lonely Hearts Club Band* by The Beatles." Lyrics published by *The Bob Rivers Show* with Bob, Spike & Joe and Twisted Tunes online at <http://www.twistedradio.com/player/lyrics.asp?songID=958>. [199-].

1008.70 The Real Rick Lazio. w. "Weird Alan." m. "Parody of Eminem's *The Real Slim Shady*." "This was a song about the New York Senate race but it ended, it was about Rick Lazio, who most of you probably won't know in 4 years..." Published online at <http://www.angelfire.com.music/parodies/orgyparody.html>. [ca. 2000].

1008.71 Re-callin' (The Gray Davis Song). w. Malcolm Higgins. m. "*Free Fallin'* originally by Tom Petty." Published online at http://www.amiright.com/parody/90s/tompetty11/ html>. 2003.

1008.72 Re-Election. w. Michael Florio. m. "*Again*, based on a performance by Lenny Kravitz." Published online at <http://www.amiright.com/parody/2000s/lennykravits0.shtml>. [ca. 2000].

1008.73 Rudolph The New York Mayor. w. William K. Tong. m. "Sung to the tune of *Rudolph The Red-Nosed Reindeer*." In: *The Sting The Right Wing Song Book* at <http://www.geocities.com/wmktong/bootnewt/rudymayr.htm>.

1008.74 Runaround Sue. w. Paul Silhan. m. "Sung to *Runaround Sue* by Dion." On: Cassette: *Lippo Tiptoe*. "As heard on Rush's Radio Show." Lyrics published at <http://www.paulsilhan.com/runarnd.htm>. 1997.

1008.75 Senator. w. Michael Florio. m. "*Piano Man*, based on a performance by Billy Joel." Published online at <http://www.amiright.com/parody/70s/billyjoel8.shtml>. [ca. 2000].

1008.76 Story Of Hillary. w. Michael Florio. m. *Story Of A Girl* originally by Nine Days." Published online at <http://www.amiright.com/parody/2000s/ninedays1.shtml>.

1008.77 Taxman. w. Paul Silhan. m. "Sung to *Taxman* by The Beatles." On: Cassette: *Lie-A-lot*. Lyrics published at <http://www.paulsilhan.com/lal-2.htm>. 1993.

1008.78 The Payroll Comes (Hillary's Song). w. Michael Florio. m. "*The Morning Comes*, originally by Smashmouth." Published online at <http://amiright.com/parody/90s/smashmouth3.shml>. [ca. 2000].

1008.79 Tie A Yellow Ribbon 'Round The Ol' Pee-Pee. w. Paul Silhan. m. "Sung to *Tie A Yellow Ribbon 'Round The Ol' Oak Tree* by Tony Orlando & Dawn." On CD: *Scandal In The Wind*. Lyrics published online at <http://www.paulsilhan.com/yellow.htm>. 1998.

1008.80 Vote. w. Moscowman. m. "*Vogue*, based on a performance by Madonna." "The Election is coming in November, voters reading the magazines and think what's their decision on the upcoming election." Published online at <http://amiright.com/parody/90s/thekinks3.shtml. [2004].

10008.80A Warren Harding. w. Michael Pacholek. m. "*Garden Party*, based on a performance by Rick Nelson." "The way things have worked out, Elizabeth Cochrane, the daughter of Warren Harding and Nan Britton, is, at 85, the oldest living child of a President ... First Lady hating didn't begin with Hillary Clinton or even Eleanor Roosevelt ... some still believe that the Duchess poisoned him for his infidelities ..." Published online at <http://www.amiright.com/parody/60s/theshirelles2.shtml>. 2004.

1008.81 Was Bill Clinton Blown. w. S.G.T. m. "*Is Anybody Home*, originally by Our Lady Peace." Published online at <http://amiright.com/parody/2000s/ourladypeace0.shml>. [ca. 2001].

1008.82 We Are The Champions (Senator Shoplift). w. Doug from Upland. m. "*We Are The Champions* by Queen." Published by Freerepublic.com at <http://freerepublic.com/forum/a3a78c1372989.htm>. 1/31/2001.

1008.83 West Palm Beach. w. Weird O'l Yankee Vic. m. "*Green Acres*, originally by Theme." Published online at <http://www.amiright.com/parody/misc/theme0.shml>. [ca. 2000].

1008.84 Where' Slick Willie Lay. w. Joseph Hayes. m. "*Barbara Allen*, based on a performance by Dolly Parton. "The oldest known song that the Pilgrims brought over. Go to <http://theromanceclub.com/aurthirs/lauramillsalcott/lyrics.htm> and see the original lyrics and scroll down to a choice of three who sing it." Published online at <http://www.amiright.com/parody/misc/dollyparton0.shtml>. [ca. 2004].

1008.85 Whitewater Debacle. w. Paul Silhan. m. "Sung to *Winchester Cathedral* by The New Vaudeville Band." On: Cassette: *Lie-A-Lot*. Lyrics published at <http://www.paulsilhan.com/lal-4.htm>. 1993.

1008.86 The (Willie) White House. w. Leo Jay. m. "*Copacabana*, based on a performance by Barry Manilow." "I know this is ancient history, but a little nostalgia never hurt...;-) it came to me while I was working on something else, and figured I might as well publish it — I'm trying to rack up 10 parodies. Plus, this looks forward to what may be yet to come...;-) Besides, I've done some bush-wacking, so I owe a bit to the left. I mean. 'left of Center' ... Or is that 'Left-inching-toward-center-while-pandering-to-the-base? Whatever..." Published online at <http://www.amiright.com/parody/70s/barrymanilow27.shtml>. [2004].

1008.87 Wouldn't It Be Hillary? w. Bill Strauss and Elaina Newport. On CD: *The Joy Of Sax*. Published by Capitol Steps Productions, 1505 King Street, Alexandria, VA. 1993. CD Cover: Saxophone with Bill Clinton's likeness.

1008.88 Yankee Baseball Booster. w. No composer m. "Tune — *I'm A Yankee Doodle Dandy*." B/w photo of Hillary Clinton in Yankee's ball cap. Published online at <http://.www.presidentialelection2000.com/yankee-baseball-booster.html>. 2000.

1008.89 Yes, The SOB Is Insane. w. "Doug form Upland." m. "*You're So Vain* by Carly Simon." "Carly, baby. How about doing this more appropriate version for the rapist scumbag degenerate pervert evil SOB." Published online at <http://www.freerepublic.com/forum/a398e3c0b22a3.htm>. 2000.

1008.90 You Don't Mess With Jesse And Win. w. Paul Silhan. m. "Sung to *You Don't Mess Around With Jim* by Jim Croce." On: Cassette: *Spinball Wizard*. "As heard on Rush's Radio Show." Lyrics published at <http://www.paulsilhan.com/jesse.htm>. 1997.

1008.91 Zany Politics. w. Edward Goldstein. m. "Parody of *Animaniac's Opening Theme* song." Published online at <http://www.bagelfather.com/funstuff/parody/parody12.htm>. [199-].

• **AmPM-1009** COCHRANE, John (Surveyor, Port of New York, 1853–1857; U.S. House, 1857–1861; State Attorney General, 1863–1865; Collector of Internal Revenue, New York, 1869; Board of Aldermen, New York City, 1872?-1883?; Police Justice, New York City, 1889)

1009.1 Witches' Scene From MacGreeley (Which is Seen to be a Fact). w.m. No composer or tune indicated. From the "*New York Standard*." In: *National Republican Grant And Wilson Campaign Song-Book*, page 34. From the *New York Standard*. Published by The Union Republican Congressional Committee, Washington, DC. 1872. [3³⁄₁₆" × 8⅝"]. Be/bk litho of Ulysses S. Grant. "We'll Sing a Song for U.S. Grant." 100pp. [M-182]. [Crew/USG-110].

• **AmPM-1010** COCKRAN, William Bourke (U.S. House, 1887–1889, 1991–1995, 1904–1909 & 1921–1923)

1010.1 Sharing Of The Green. w. No composer indicated. m. "Air — *Wearing Of The Green*." In: J*ays In Jungleland, Or The Curry-Combers, Starring The Sanrling, Scornful, Sinew-Set Political Puma And Rampant, Rural Republican Ravagers, Bent On Battering The Beast's Bailiwick And Leveling His Lair In A Scrambled Salmagundi Studded With Sachems, Satchels, Swag, Scuttlers, Sang Froid, Seaburyisms, Etc.— Plus A Peep At That Tammany Masterpiece — 'The Tiger's Knightmare*," page 13. Published by The Legislative Correspondents' Association of New York, Albany, NY. 1931. [7¾" × 10½"]. N/c drawing a "Tammany" tiger perched overlooking "GOP" elephants, New York City skyline. "From 1920 Dinner." "Launched at Ten Eyck Hotel, Albany, New York, On the evening of Thursday, March 26, 1931, at seven o'clock." 16pp.

1010.2 Sharing Of The Green. w. No composer indicated. m. "Air — *Wearing Of The Green*." In: *Fourth Internationale*, page 8. Published by The Legislative Correspondents' Association of the State of New York, Albany, NY. 1920. [8" × 11¼"]. N/c drawing by Fred O. Seibel of a statue of House Speaker Thaddeus "Sweet" on horseback, "Governor's Chair," "Assemblyman Roosevelt," other politicians. "A Session of Soviets, Seething with Socialism, Sweetism, Sedition, Seven-Cent Fares, School-Ma'ams, Soda-Water, Slams, Slander, Simps and Strangulation, and Bristling with Booms, Boobs and Bunk." "Called by The Legislative Correspondents' Association of the State of New York, at The Ten Eyck, Albany, April 22, 1920." Page 5: "Toast List" including "Comrade Alfred E. Smith, Dictator of the Proletariat." [Crew/AES-66].

1010.3 Since Cockran Turned His Back On Tammany Hall. w. No composer indicated. m. "Tune — *The Picture With Its Face Turned Toward The Wall*." In: *Republican Campaign Parodies And Songs* [Songster], page 9. Published by Betts and Burnett, South Butler, Wayne County, NY. 1896. [7¾" × 5½"]. Be/bk non-pictorial. "McKinley and Hobart." "1896." 28pp. [M-340]. [Crew/WM-67].

• **AmPM-1011** COLLINS, William T. (New York Supreme Court, 1933–1945)

1011.1 Floating Fantasy. w. No composer indicated. m. "Air — *When My Dreamboat Comes Home*." In: *Wake Up And Scream*, page 11. Published by Albany Legislative Correspondents' Association, Albany, NY. 1937. [8" × 11¾"]. N/c drawing by Jerry Costello of Dr. Bill Murray, King Macy, New York GOP, and Ham Fish as patients undergoing transfusions. "A Trumpet Call to the G.O.P. Eagle to Snap out of Coma and Rally Ravaged Republicans with New Volley of Vocal Vim — the Same Being Enacted 'mid a Merry Medley of Mountain Madness, Dutch Delirium, Liberalization Legendry, Melancholy Maidens and Rapscallion Redskins, at Ten Eyck Hotel, Albany, N.Y., Thursday, March eleventh, 1937, at Seven-Thirty o'clock." 20pp.

• **AmPM-1012** COLUMBO, Joseph (Founder, Italian-American Civil Rights League, 1970–1971)

1012.1 (Official Song Of) The Italian-American Civil Rights League. w. Henri Gine. m. Bert Mann (ASCAP). Published by Hengine & Adrienne Music, 25 Central Park West, New York, NY. 10023. 1970. Gn/y litho of the logo of the Italian-American Civil Rights League. 4pp.

• **AmPM-1013** CONKLING, Roscoe (District Attorney, Oneida County, 1850; Mayor, Utica, 1858; U.S. House, 1859–1863 & 1865–1867; U.S. Senate, 1867–1881)

1013.1 Brave Hancock Is The Man (A Campaign Song And Chorus). w. Colonel T.G. Morrison "(Formerly of the 12th and 66th Regts., Ind. Inf.)." m.

William B. Richardson. Published by John Church & Company, No. 66 West 4th Street, Cincinnati, OH. 1880. B/w litho of Winfield S. Hancock, star border. "Democratic Campaign Music." List of other songs in series. 6pp. Page 6: Blank. [Crew/WSH-19].

1013.2 ***Carry The News To 'Lysses.*** w. No composer indicated. m. "Air—*Carry The News To Mary.*" In: *Greeley Campaign Songster*, page 40. "Respectfully dedicated to the Greeley Clubs of the Country." Published by Halpin & McClure, Chicago, IL. 1872. [4" × 5 11/16"]. Pl/bk litho of Horace Greeley, geometric design border. "Chicago: Western News Company, Wholesale Agents." 72pp. [M-187]. [Crew/HG-21].

1013.3 ***Hark! How Sweet Those Organs Play!*** w. No composer indicated. m. "Air—*Hieland Laddie, Bonnie Laddie!*" In: *Tilden And Hendricks' Reform Songs (For The Centennial Campaign Of 1876)*, page 8. Published by The National Democratic Committee, Box 3637, New York, NY. 1876. [3⅞" × 5 15/16"]. Gn/bk litho of Samuel J. Tilden and Thomas A. Hendricks, geometric design border. 40pp. [M-203]. [Crew/SJT-21].

1013.4 ***Hayes.*** w. No composer indicated. m. "Air—*Life On The Ocean Wave.*" In: *Hayes & Wheeler Campaign Song Book (For The Centennial Year)*, page 37. Published by the American News Company, Nos. 117, 119, 121, 123 Nassau Street, New York, NY. 1876. [3⅞" × 6 5/16"]. Y/bk litho of Rutherford B. Hayes and William A. Wheeler, liberty cap, geometric designs. 74pp. Pages 2, 4, 73 and 74: Blank. Page 3: "Containing Over Sixty Original Songs Adapted to Popular Melodies." [M-193]. [Crew/RBH-11].

1013.5 ***O, The Crow, The Beautiful Crow.*** w. No composer indicated. m. "Air—O, *The Snow, The Beautiful Snow.*" "As sung by the Blaine men, Conklingites, Morton men and other defeated Republican leaders." In: *Illustrated Campaign Song And Joke*, page 26. Published by The American News Company, New York, NY. [4¾" × 7½"]. 1876. Y/bk litho of Samuel J. Tilden, geometric design border. 50pp. [?]. Page 5: Title—*The Illustrated Campaign Tilden Song And Joke Book.* [Crew/SJT-8].

1013.6 ***The Soreheads On Our Block.*** w. No composer indicated. m. Dave Braham, "Air—*Babies On Our Block.*" In: *Hancock And English Campaign Songster*, page 4. Published by New York Popular Publishing Company, A.J. Dick, Manager, No. 32 Beekman Street, New York, NY. 1880. Be/bk litho of Winfield Scott Hancock. "Containing the Largest and Most Complete Collection of Songs, All Written to the Most Popular Airs of the Day." "The Most Popular Edition Of Hancock And English Campaign Songster." 68pp. Page 68: Be/bk litho of William H. English. [M-217]. [Crew/WSH-41].

1013.7 ***Treason's Fate.*** w. S.N. Holmes. m. "Tune—*A Thousand Years*, &c." In: *The Republican Campaign Song Book, With Music, 1892*, page 15. e. Samuel Newall Holmes. Published by Samuel Newall Holmes, Syracuse, NY. 1892. Be/bk non-pictorial. "Composed and especially prepared by Judge S.N. Holmes of Syracuse, N.Y." "Headquarters: Syracuse, N.Y." "Price twenty-five cents." 60pp. [M-308]. [Crew/BFH-107].

1013.8 ***Uncle Sam's A Coming.*** w. No composer indicated. m. "Air—*Babylon Is Fallen.*" In: *Tilden And Hendricks' Reform Songs (For The Centennial Campaign Of 1876)*, page 19. Published by The National Democratic Committee, Box 3637, New York, NY. 1876. [3⅞" × 5 15/16"]. Gn/bk litho of Samuel J. Tilden and Thomas A. Hendricks, geometric design border. 40pp. [M-203]. [Crew/SJT-21].

1013.9 ***Who Killed Jim Garfield?*** (Humorous Campaign Song). w. No composer indicated. m. H.S. Aubry. Published by Geo. D. Newhall & Co., Cincinnati, OH. 1880. B/w non-pictorial geometric designs, black border. 4pp. [?]. Page 4: Advertising.

1013.10 ***Who Killed Jim Garfield?*** w. No composer indicated. m. "Tune—*Cock Robin.*" In: *Music For The Campaign (A Collection Of Original And Selected Songs, Adapted To Familiar Tunes For Use At Campaign Meetings, For 1880)*, page 6. Published by The Indianapolis Sentinel as a newspaper supplement, Indianapolis, IN. 1880. [7¾" × 10⅝"]. B/w lithos of Winfield Scott Hancock and William H. English. "This Collection of fifty one first-class Campaign Songs will be sent to any address, postage paid as follows: 25 for 30 cts.; 50 for 60 cts.; 100 for $1.00. Address Sentinel Company, Indianapolis, Ind." 8pp. Foldover. [Crew/WSH-11].

• **AmPM-1014 CONNOLLY**, Richard (City Comptroller, New York City, 1871?)

1014.1 ***The Bummer's Evening Hymn.*** w. No composer indicated. m. "Air—*Benny Havens, Oh!*" In: *Hayes & Wheeler Campaign Song Book (For The Centennial Year)*, page 25. Published by the American News Company, Nos. 117, 119, 121, 123 Nassau Street, New York, NY. 1876. [3⅞" × 6 5/16"]. Y/bk litho of Rutherford B. Hayes and William A. Wheeler, liberty cap, geometric designs. 74pp. Pages 2, 4, 73 and 74: Blank. Page 3: "Containing Over Sixty Original Songs Adapted to Popular Melodies." [M-193]. [Crew/RBH-11].

1014.2 ***Rally, Boys, Rally Boys.*** w. T.K. Preuss. a. J. Starr Holloway. m. "Tune—*Wrecker's Daughter Quickstep.*" In: *Hayes & Wheeler Song Book*, page 26. Published by The Union Republican Congressional Committee, Washington, DC. 1876. [5¾" × 9¼"]. Br/bk litho of Rutherford B. Hayes and William A. Wheeler, shield, geometric design border. "I'll be on hand again shortly." [V-1: "Series I" under title on cover] [V-2: Series not indicated on cover]. 52pp. Page 2: Contents. Page 52: State-by-state electoral vote totals for 1876. [M-196, 197]. [Crew/RBH-20].

1014.3 ***The Rogues March.*** a. M. Woolfe. "Dedicated with Great Respect to the Ring." Published in Harper's Weekly, November 18, 1871, page 1076. [26" × 11½"]. B/w litho of William Tweed, holding a bag labeled "Spoils," Richard Connolly, the city comptroller, and Peter Sweeny, the county chamberlain, holding bags labeled "cash box" and "hauls." "Arranged for the Piano Forte." Music marked "Allegro Grabspoilioso." In the background are drawings of "Tammany" and "Penitentiary."

1014.4 ***Tilden's Battle Song.*** w. No composer indicated. m. "Air—*The Governor's Own.*" In: *Hayes & Wheeler Campaign Song Book (For The Centennial Year)*, page 33. Published by the American News Company, Nos. 117, 119, 121, 123 Nassau Street, New York, NY. 1876. [3⅞" × 6 5/16"]. Y/bk litho of Rutherford B. Hayes and William A. Wheeler, liberty cap, geometric designs. 74pp. [M-193]. [Crew/RBH-11].

1014.5 Voting For Hayes, My Boys, And Wheeler. w. No composer indicated. m. "Air—*Marching Thro' Georgia.*" In: *Hayes & Wheeler Campaign Song Book (For The Centennial Year)*, page 57. Published by the American News Company, Nos. 117, 119, 121, 123 Nassau Street, New York, NY. 1876. [3⅞" × 6⅟₁₆"]. Y/bk litho of Rutherford B. Hayes and William A. Wheeler, liberty cap, geometric designs. 74pp. Pages 2, 4, 73 and 74: Blank. Page 3: "Containing Over Sixty Original Songs Adapted to Popular Melodies." [M-193]. [Crew/RBH-11].

1014.6 We'll Put Him In His Little Bed. w. No composer indicated. m. "Air—*Put Me In My Little Bed.*" In: *Hayes & Wheeler Campaign Song Book (For The Centennial Year)*, page 55. Published by the American News Company, Nos. 117, 119, 121, 123 Nassau Street, New York, NY. 1876. [3⅞" × 6⅟₁₆"]. Y/bk litho of Rutherford B. Hayes and William A. Wheeler, liberty cap, geometric designs. 74pp. Pages 2, 4, 73 and 74: Blank. Page 3: "Containing Over Sixty Original Songs Adapted to Popular Melodies." [M-193]. [Crew/RBH-11].

• **AmPM-1015 COOPER**, Peter (Alderman, New York City; Candidate for President, 1876) [ALSO SEE: DOC/PSM-PC]

1015.1 The Greenback Yankee Medley. w. No composer indicated. m. "Air—*Cork Leg.*" In: *National Greenback Labor Songster*, page 43. c. B.M. Lawrence, M.D. Published by D.M. Bennett, Liberal and Scientific Publishing House, No. 141 8th Street, New York, NY. 1878. [3¾" × 6¼"]. Gn/bk litho of arm with hammer. 52pp. Page 3: "Containing Original, Practical, Patriotic, Progressive and Stirring Songs, Adapted to the Most Popular Airs in addition to which will be found choice and humorous readings, including 'The Bankers and I Are Out,' "Men and Monkeys,' 'What We Want,' &c."

1015.2 The Hero Of Our Day! w. Frank Myrtle. m. John M. Loretz, Jr. Published by Frank Myrtle Music Company, Brooklyn, NY. Copyright 1881 by C. Aug. Haviland. Non-pictorial geometric designs. "Respectfully Dedicated to Peter Cooper, America's Great Philanthropist." 6pp. Pages 2 and 6: Blank. [Crew/PC-5].

1015.3 March Cooper-Union. m. A.W. Lilienthal. Copyright 1880 by Fred Finder. Non-pictorial. Parts for orchestra. [Crew/PC-4].

1015.4 Rally Men Of Michigan. w. Julia A. Moore. m. "Air—*Yankee Doodle.*" In: *The Sentimental Song Book*, page 39. Published by Julia A. Moore, Grand Rapids, MI. 1876. [4⅛" × 5¹³⁄₁₆"]. Gn/bk non-pictorial back line border. "Centennial, 1876." 62pp. [Crew/PC-3].

1015.5 Who Shall Be The Man? (A Serio Comic Campaign Song & Chorus). w.m. Henry Schroeder. Published by S.T. Gordon, No. 13 East 14th Street, New York, NY. 1876. Non-pictorial geometric designs. "To The Presidential Victor." "Showing the trials of the Independent Citizen." 6pp. Page 2: Blank. Page 6: Advertising. [Crew/MISC-204].

• **AmPM-1016 COOPER**, William (Founded Cooperstown; Judge of the Court of Common Pleas, Otsego County, 1791; U.S. House, 1795–1797 & 1799–1801)

1016.1 Beauties Of Anglo-Federalism, Displayed (Or State Tricks Developed). w. No composer indicated. m. "Tune—*Moderation And Alteration.*" In: *The Republican Harmonist (Being A Select Collection Of Republican, Patriotic, And Sentimental Songs, Odes, Sonnets, &c, American And European: Some Of Which Are Original, And Most Of The Others Now Come For The First Time From An American Press)*, page 29. c. D.E. [Daniel Ebsworth] "(A Citizen of the World)." Printed "for the People," Boston, MA. 1801. Non-pictorial. 152pp. [Crew/TJ-10].

• **AmPM-1017 COPELAND**, Royal Samuel (Mayor, Ann Arbor, 1901–1903; Park Board, Ann Arbor, 1905–1906; Board of Education, Ann Arbor, 1907–1908; U.S. Senate, New York, 1923–1938) [ALSO SEE: DOC/PSM-MISC]

1017.1 Marble Madrigal (Inspired by Senator Copeland's Apt Characterization of our Guv.). w. No composer indicated. m. "Air—*The Kind Of A Girl That Men Forget.*" In: *Statutes And Statuettes*, page 12. Published by Albany Legislative Correspondents' Association, Albany, NY. 1925. N/c drawing by Fred O. Seibel of "Venus DeMilo Smith," other politicians as historical figures. "A Private Presentation of Immortal Images and Matchless Masterpieces From the 1925 Legislative Louvre Frivolously Fashioned in Political Pigments and Capitoline Colors and Featuring Etchers and Fetchers, Chisels and Fizzles, Hues and Hewitts, G.O.P. Gargoyles, Democratic Dorics, Prohibition Pastels, Lowman Landscapes and McGinnies Models, Combined with a Superficial Squint into the Gallery of Gee-Gaws, Freaks and Flim Flam." "Viewed at Ten Eyck Hotel, Albany, N.Y., on the Evening of March 12, 1925, Seven o'clock." 20pp. [Crew/AES-17].

1017.2 When I Leave The Chair Behind (In Which 'Al' Proclaims Himself Weary of the Game and Admits His Preference for the Golf-Stick to the Veto-Power Pen). w. No composer indicated. m. "Air—*When I Leave The World Behind.*" In: *Statutes And Statuettes*, page 11. Published by Albany Legislative Correspondents' Association, Albany, NY. 1925. N/c drawing by Fred O. Seibel of "Venus DeMilo Smith," other politicians as historical figures. "A Private Presentation of Immortal Images and Matchless Masterpieces From the 1925 Legislative Louvre Frivolously Fashioned in Political Pigments and Capitoline Colors and Featuring Etchers and Fetchers, Chisels and Fizzles, Hues and Hewitts, G.O.P. Gargoyles, Democratic Dorics, Prohibition Pastels, Lowman Landscapes and McGinnies Models, Combined with a Superficial Squint into the Gallery of Gee-Gaws, Freaks and Flim Flam." "Viewed at Ten Eyck Hotel, Albany, N.Y., on the Evening of March 12, 1925, Seven o'clock." 20pp. [Crew/AES-17].

• **AmPM-1018 CORNING**, Erastus (State Senate 1842–1845; Alderman, Albany; Mayor, Albany, 1834–1837; U.S. House, 1857–1859 & 1861–1863; Delegate, State Constitutional Convention, in 1867)

1018.1 Rally 'Round The Clan, Boys! w. No composer indicated. m. "Tune—*Oklahoma.*" In: *Dealers Choice Or Back-To-Back Biting*, page 12. Published by the Albany Legislative Correspondent's Association of New York State, Albany, NY. 1944. [8" × 11¾"]. N/c drawing of Franklin Roosevelt, Thomas Dewey, "Chiang," "Winnie" and "Joe" playing cards—"Featuring the World's Most Exciting Egomaniacs in a Marvelous Musical of Messianic and Mystery: Showing Sinners, Sycophants, Suckers, and Sleuths Saving Civilization with Sound; or Find the Joker!" "Dealt Off the Bottom of a Hot Deck—In Three Acts at Ten Eyck, Albany, March 9, 1944." [Crew/FDR-364].

• **AmPM-1019   CORTELYOU**, George Bruce (Stenographer to President Cleveland, 1895–1896; Secretary to the President, 1898–1903; U.S. Secretary of Commerce and Labor, 1903–1904; Chairman of Republican National Committee, 1904–1907; U.S. Postmaster General, 1905–1907; U.S. Secretary of the Treasury, 1907–1909)

1019.1 The White House Gate. w.m. Logan S. Porter. In: *Parker Campaign Songster, 1904*, page 26. e. Logan S. Porter. Published by The Home Music Company, Logansport, IN. 1904. [6" × 9"]. O/bk litho of Alton Parker and Henry Gassaway Davis. 36pp. [M-394]. [Crew/ABP-7].

• **AmPM-1020   COX**, Samuel "Sunset" Sullivan (Editor, *Columbus Statesman*, 1853–1854; Secretary U.S. Legation, Lima, Peru, 1855; Delegate to the Democratic National Convention, 1864 & 1868; U.S. House, Ohio, 1857–1865, from New York, 1869–1873–1885 & 1886–1889; Envoy Extraordinary and Minister Plenipotentiary, Turkey, 1885–1886)

1020.1 Hayes And Wheeler. w. No composer indicated. m. "Air—*The King Of The Cannibal Islands*." In: *Tilden And Hendricks' Reform Songs (For The Centennial Campaign Of 1876)*, page 22. Published by The National Democratic Committee, Box 3637, New York, NY. 1876. [3⅞" × 5⅚"]. Gn/bk litho of Samuel J. Tilden and Thomas A. Hendricks, geometric design border. 40pp. [M-203]. [Crew/SJT-21].

1020.2 Tweed's Lament. a. A. Watt. In: *Helmick's Republican Campaign Song Book*, page 12. Published by F.W. Helmick, Music dealer and Publisher, No. 50 West 4th Street, Cincinnati, OH. 1876. [5¼" × 7½"]. [V-1: Y/bk] [V-2: Pl/bk] lithos of Rutherford B. Hayes and William A. Wheeler, geometric design border. "Arranged for Four Voices." "As Sung by the Springfield, (O.) Glee Club." 24pp. [M-198]. [Crew/RBH-14].

• **AmPM-1021   CRANGLE**, Joseph, F. (Democratic Party Chairman, Erie County, 1965–1988; State Democratic Party Chairman, 1974)

1021.1 Outrageous Fortunes. w. No composer indicated. m. "Tune—*You're Getting To Be A Habit With Me*." As sung by "Crangle and Rosenbaum." In: *Thoroughly Mad-ern Malcolm Or He Didn't Need A Course In Forensics To Become A Famous Public Speaker*, page 7. Published by the New York State Legislative Correspondents' Association, Albany, NY. 1974. N/w photo of Malcolm Wilson as Alfred E. Newman—"What—Me Governor?" "Featuring the New York Correspondents' Association, March 16. 1974." 32pp.

• **AmPM-1022   CRANE**, Frederick E. (Chief Judge, State Court of Appeals, 1939)

1022.1 Ditty Of Smitty. w. No composer indicated. m. Air—*Franklin D. Roosevelt Jones*." "Sung by Crane." In: *Knighty—Knighty (Or A Michigan Yankee In King Herbie's Court)*, page 9. Published by The Legislative Correspondents' Association of New York State, Albany, NY. March 23, 1939. [8" × 11¾"]. N/c drawing of Thomas Dewey and Herbert Lehman jousting—"A Bouncing Blend, Mellowly Medieval, of Tangy Tunes, Balmy Buffoons, Flashing Blades and Ravishing Maids, Featuring the Glamour Gink of Gotham and the Caliph of Capitol Hill in 'Let's Tangle Tinware.'" "Thursday, March Twenty-Third, 1939, at Seven-Thirty o'clock. "Ribbingly Ripped Off at Hotel Ten Eyck, Albany, New York." [Crew/TED-30].

• **AmPM-1023   CRAWFORD**, Thomas J. (Candidate for Justice of New York Supreme Court, 1948)

1023.1 Dewey-Warren Victory Rally [Program/Songster]. Published by the New York Republican County Committee, New York, NY. 1948. [5¼" × 8¾"]. Bl/w photos of Thomas Dewey and Earl Warren. Bl/w drawing of two eagles. "Madison Square Garden, Saturday, October 30, 1948." "Gov. Thomas E. Dewey, Lt. Gov. Joe R. Hanley, Sen. Irving M. Ives, Mrs. Preston Davie, Hon. Thomas J. Curran, Hon. George Frankenthaler, Hon. Thos. J. Crawford, Mrs. Lillian Sharp Hunter, Hon. Daniel J. Riesner." 8pp. Foldout. Pages 2, 3 and 8: List of committee members. Pages 4 to 7: Songs including: **We All Want Dewey** {1023.1–1}. w. Douglas D. Ballin.

• **AmPM-1024   CREWS**, John R. (State Assembly, 1921–1922; Delegate, Republican National Convention, 1928–1960; Chairman, Kings County Republican Committee, 1939)

1024.1 Keep 'Em Pure. w. No composer indicated. m. "Air—*If I Had Rhythm In My Nursery Rhymes*." In: *Tory, Tory Hallelujah*, page 9. Published by Albany Legislative Correspondents' Association, Albany, NY. 1936. [8" × 11¾"]. N/c drawing of Franklin D. Roosevelt, other politicians dressed as Revolutionary soldiers in battle scene—"A Dashing Delirious Drama, Lampooning Loyalists and Liberty Leaguers, Daggering Despots, Dictators and Dummy Donkey-Drivers to music by Red-Coats and Lyrics by Turn-Coats, the Combat Being Played Against a Spangled Back-Drop." "Furiously Fought at Ten Eyck Hotel, Albany, New York, The Evening of Thursday, March 12, 1936, at Seven-Thirty o'clock." [Crew/FDR-325].

1024.2 Let's Reapportion! w. No composer indicated. m. "Air—*Rainbow On The River*." In: *Wake Up And Scream*, page 12. Published by Albany Legislative Correspondents' Association, Albany, NY. 1937. [8" × 11¾"]. N/c drawing by Jerry Costello of Dr. Bill Murray, King Macy, New York GOP, and Ham Fish as patients undergoing transfusions. "A Trumpet Call to the G.O.P. Eagle to Snap out of Coma and Rally Ravaged Republicans with New Volley of Vocal Vim—the Same Being Enacted 'mid a Merry Medley of Mountain Madness, Dutch Delirium, Liberalization Legendry, Melancholy Maidens and Rapscallion Redskins, at Ten Eyck Hotel, Albany, N.Y., Thursday, March eleventh, 1937, at Seven-Thirty o'clock." 20pp.

1024.3 Stowaway Ballad. w. No composer indicated. m. "Air—*Rendezvous With A Dream*." In: *Wake Up And Scream*, page 11. Published by Albany Legislative Correspondents' Association, Albany, NY. 1937. [8" × 11¾"]. N/c drawing by Jerry Costello of Dr. Bill Murray, King Macy, New York GOP, and Ham Fish as patients undergoing transfusions. "A Trumpet Call to the G.O.P. Eagle to Snap out of Coma and Rally Ravaged Republicans with New Volley of Vocal Vim — the Same Being Enacted 'mid a Merry Medley of Mountain Madness, Dutch Delirium, Liberalization Legendry, Melancholy Maidens and Rapscallion Redskins, at Ten Eyck Hotel, Albany, N.Y., Thursday, March eleventh, 1937, at Seven-Thirty o'clock." 20pp.

• **AmPM-1025** CROKER, Richard (Alderman, New York City, 1868; Leader, Tammany Society, 1886–1902; City Chamberlain, 1889–1890)

1025.1 [Bill McKinley In The Chair]. w. H.D. Tutewiler. m. "To the tune *Bull Frog On The Bank.*" In: *The March Of The Flag Songbook*, page 20. Published by H.D. Tutewiler, No. 133 West Market Street, Indianapolis, IN. 1900. [5" × 7⅝"]. Be/bk litho of flag. "The Only Republican Campaign Songs for 1900 Having the Authorized Endorsement [sic] of Both National Republican Committees." 28pp. [M-374]. [Crew/WM-155].

1025.2 Caw Caw. w. D.E. Bryer. m. No tune or composer indicated. In: *The Harrison Campaign Songster*, page 3. w. D.E. Bryer (The Old Campaigner). m. Popular tunes. Published by The Home Music Company, No. 200 Fourth Street, Logansport, IN. 1892. [5¾" × 8½"]. Non-pictorial. Table of Contents. 36pp. Page 36: Advertising. [M-301]. [Crew/BFH-87].

1025.3 The Cuckoos. w. No composer indicated. m. "Tune — *Billy Magee McGaw*." In: *The Rough Rider (Republican Campaign Song Book)*, page 8. c. J. Burgess Brown. Published by J. Burgess Brown, Indianapolis, IN. 1900. [6" × 9"]. Br/bk non-pictorial. "ROUGH ON DemocRATS." 28pp. Page 3: B/w litho of William McKinley. Page 28: "Republican National Ticket — 1900. [Crew/WM-330].

1025.4 Dick Croker's English Pup. w. Roland. m. Roland — "Air — *What's That A Lighthouse!*" In: *The People's Searchlight.* Published by The 20th Century Music & Souvenir Pub. Co., P.O. Lock Box 1274, New York, NY. 1901. Bl/w drawing of Father Knickerbocker looking over the "East River" where a boat sailing a flag that reads — "Dick's Yacht Deception" has hit a rock — "Public Vigilance" and is sinking. Tammany tiger overboard. A Lighthouse is beaming "The Searchlight of Honest Uncorrupted City Government." Page 1 song — *The People's Searchlight!* (Waltz Refrain) {1025.4–1}. "Chorus by the Tammany Five — "Over board with Jonah we've struck a snag, It's the only chance to save out sinking flag." 4pp. Page 4: Blank. Page 2: At title — "Dick Croker's English Pup, A Parody companion song on *What's That? A Lighthouse!* By the same author."

1025.5 Holding Hands. w.m. J.A. Parks. In: *Park's Republican Songs Campaign Of 1904 (For Male Voices)* [Song Book], page 15. Published by J.A. Parks Company, York, NE. 1904. [6⁵⁄₁₆" × 9¾"]. Br/br non-pictorial geometric design border. 40pp. [M-390]. [Crew/TR-157].

1025.6 Marching To The Bugle Call. w. No composer indicated. m. "Tune — *Swinging In The Grape Vine Swing.*" In: *The Rough Rider (Republican Campaign Song Book)*, page 19. c. J. Burgess Brown. Published by J. Burgess Brown, Indianapolis, IN. 1900. [6" × 9"]. Br/bk non-pictorial. "ROUGH ON DemocRATS." 28pp. Page 3: B/w litho of William McKinley. Page 28: "Republican National Ticket — 1900. [Crew/WM-330].

1025.7 Since Cockran Turned His Back On Tammany Hall. w. No composer indicated. m. "Tune — *The Picture With Its Face Turned Toward The Wall.*" In: *Republican Campaign Parodies And Songs* [Songster], page 9. Published by Betts and Burnett, South Butler, Wayne County, NY. 1896. [7¾" × 5½"]. Be/bk non-pictorial. "McKinley and Hobart." "1896." 28pp. [M-340]. [Crew/WM-67].

1025.8 Since I Joined Tammany Hall. (Song). w.m. Lou. Edmunds. Published by Wm. A. Pond & Co., 25 Union Square, New York, NY. 1893. Non-pictorial geometric designs.

1025.9 The Son Of A Gambolier. w. Gen. Stillman F. Kneeland. m. "*The Son Of A Gambolier.*" In: *Campaign College Songs* 1900 [Song Book], page 6. w. Gen. Stillman F. Kneeland. Published for the Wholesale Dry Goods Republican Club, No. 350 Broadway, New York, NY. 1900. [5⅞" × 9⅛"]. Y/bk photos of William "McKinley" and Theodore "Roosevelt." Y/bk drawings of eagle, shield, flags. "A bird that can sing and won't sing must be made to sing." 16pp. Page 16: "If any one pulls down the Flag, shoot him on the spot — John A. Dix." "Will you vote for a man who will pull down the American Flag in the Philippines?" [Crew/WM-214].

1025.10 The Tammany Society (Polka Caprice). m. J.N. Pattison, Op. 100. Published by J.N. Pattison, 1659 Madison Avenue, New York, NY. 1898. B/w photo of Richard Croker. Bl/w/bk/gd floral and geometric designs. "To the Hon. Richard Croker." 6pp. Page 6: Blank.

1025.11 Refrigeration. w. F.H.M. m. "Tune — *There's Music In The Air.*" "For the Wholesale Dry Goods Republican Club, September 20, 1900." In: *McKinley & Roosevelt Campaign 1900,* page 9. Published for the Wholesale Dry Goods Republican Club, No. 350 Broadway by C.G. Burgoyne, New York, NY. 1900. [4¾" × 7"]. Y/bk litho of William McKinley and Theodore Roosevelt, eagle, shield. "Meetings daily from 12 Noon until 2 p.m." "A bird that can sing and won't must be made to sing." 20pp. [M-376]. [Crew/WM-84].

1025.12 We'll All Be Happy Then. w.m. J.A. Parks. In: *Park's Republican Songs Campaign Of 1904 (For Male Voices)* [Song Book], page 4. Published by J.A. Parks Company, York, NE. 1904. [6⁵⁄₁₆" × 9¾"]. Br/br non-pictorial geometric design border. 40pp. [M-390]. [Crew/TR-157].

1025.13 We've Waited, Billy, Waited Long For You. w. Stephen Laskey. m. "Tune — *I've Waited, Honey, Waited Long For You.*" In: *McKinley & Roosevelt Campaign 1900* [Song Book], page 16. Published for the Wholesale Dry Goods Republican Club, No. 350 Broadway by C.G. Burgoyne, New York, NY. 1900. [4¾" × 7"]. Y/bk litho of William McKinley and Theodore Roosevelt, eagle, shield. "Meetings daily from 12 Noon until 2 p.m." "A bird that can sing and won't must be made to sing." 20pp. [M-376]. [Crew/WM-84].

1025.14 [When Bill Bryan Talks About The Presidential Chair]. w. H.D. Tutewiler. m. "To the tune *There'll Be A Hot Time In The Old Town Tonight.*" In:

The March Of The Flag Songbook, 11. Published by H.D. Tutewiler, No. 133 West Market Street, Indianapolis, IN. 1900. [5" × 7⅝"]. Be/bk litho of flag. "The Only Republican Campaign Songs for 1900 Having the Authorized Endorsement [sic] of Both National Republican Committees." 28pp. [M-374]. [Crew/WM-155].

1025.15 When Knighthood Was In Clover. w. No composer indicated. m. "Air—*Song Of The Vagabonds.*" In: *Knighty—-Knighty (Or A Michigan Yankee In King Herbie's Court)*, page 7. Published by The Legislative Correspondents' Association of New York State, Albany, NY. March 23, 1939. [8" × 11¾"]. N/c drawing of Thomas Dewey and Herbert Lehman jousting—"A Bouncing Blend, Mellowly Medieval, of Tangy Tunes, Balmy Buffoons, Flashing Blades and Ravishing Maids, Featuring the Glamour Gink of Gotham and the Caliph of Capitol Hill in 'Let's Tangle Tinware.'" "Thursday, March Twenty-Third, 1939, at Seven-Thirty o'clock. "Ribbingly Ripped Off at Hotel Ten Eyck, Albany, New York." [Crew/TED-30].

• **AmPM-1026 CROOKE**, Philip Schuyler (Board of Supervisors, Kings County, 1844–1852 & 1858–1870, General Assembly, 1863; U.S. House, 1873–1875)

1026.1 Captain Grant. w. No composer indicated. m. "Air—*Captain Jenks.*" In: *Tilden And Hendricks' Reform Songs (For The Centennial Campaign Of 1876)*, page 33. Published by The National Democratic Committee, Box 3637, New York, NY. 1876. [3⅞" × 5¹⁵⁄₁₆"]. Gn/bk litho of Samuel J. Tilden and Thomas A. Hendricks, geometric design border. 40pp. [M-203]. [Crew/SJT-21].

• **AmPM-1027 CUVILLIER**, Louis A. (State Assembly, 1907–1909, 1911–1913, 1920, 1922–1933 & 1935)

1027.1 Battle Hymn Of The Internationale. w. No composer indicated. m. "Air—*Battle Hymn Of The Republic.*" In: *Fourth Internationale*, page 7. Published by The Legislative Correspondents' Association of the State of New York, Albany, NY. 1920. [8" × 11¼"]. N/c drawing by Fred O. Seibel of a statue of House Speaker Thaddeus "Sweet" on horseback, "Governor's Chair," "Assemblyman Roosevelt," other politicians. "A Session of Soviets, Seething with Socialism, Sweetism, Sedition, Seven-Cent Fares, School-Ma'ams, Soda-Water, Slams, Slander, Simps and Strangulation, and Bristling with Booms, Boobs and Bunk." "Called by The Legislative Correspondents' Association of the State of New York, at The Ten Eyck, Albany, April 22, 1920." Page 5: "Toast List" including "Comrade Alfred E. Smith, Dictator of the Proletariat." [Crew/AES-66].

1027.2 Oh, Amos. w. No composer indicated. m. "Air—*Frenchy.*" In: *Fourth Internationale*, page 14. Published by The Legislative Correspondents' Association of the State of New York, Albany, NY. 1920. [8" × 11¼"]. N/c drawing by Fred O. Seibel of a statue of House Speaker Thaddeus "Sweet" on horseback, "Governor's Chair," "Assemblyman Roosevelt," other politicians. "A Session of Soviets, Seething with Socialism, Sweetism, Sedition, Seven-Cent Fares, School-Ma'ams, Soda-Water, Slams, Slander, Simps and Strangulation, and Bristling with Booms, Boobs and Bunk." "Called by The Legislative Correspondents' Association of the State of New York, at The Ten Eyck, Albany, April 22, 1920." Page 5: "Toast List" including "Comrade Alfred E. Smith, Dictator of the Proletariat." [Crew/AES-66].

1027.3 Political Pastels. w. No composer indicated. m. "Air—*O, Mr. Dooley.*" "Pertinent and Personal Portraits of Party Patriots, Publists and Pap-Peddlers." In: *Al S. In Wonderland*, page 4. Published by The Albany Legislative Correspondents' Association of New York State, Albany, NY. 1924. [8½" × 10½"]. N/c drawing by Fred O. Seibel of Statue of Liberty with Beer, "Al Smith," Calvin "Coolidge" as a dragon, other politicians. "A Jocose Junket in Phantom Pullmans to that Roisterous Realm, where Hectic Hopes, Hocus-Pocus Harmonies, Folly, Froth and Flim Flam Blend Blithely with Becalmed Booms, Budget Butchers, Bubbles, Blunders and Barters." "Departing from at Ten Eyck Hotel Terminal, Albany, NY., at 7 o'clock, Eastern Time, on the evening of Thursday, March, 27, 1924." [Crew/AES-67].

1027.4 Tammany. w. No composer indicated. m. *No tune indicated.* In: *The Red Book, Containing Portraits And Biographies Of Some Persons More Or Less Prominent Public Life Written Entirely Without Respect To The Libel Laws, In A Studious Effort To Conceal Everything But The Truth; Some Songs Built Upon The Same Principle, And Other Important (?) Material Entirely Unfit To Print*, page 17. Published by Legislative Correspondents' Association of the State of New York, Albany, NY. 1913. [5" × 7¼"]. R/w/bk hardback book with drawing of State House, seal of New York, geometric designs. 90pp.

1027.5 The Wail Of The Vets. w. No composer indicated. m. "Air—*O, How I Hate To Get Up In The Morning.*" "In which the ex-service boys in the legislature, with Dry Districts, get something off their chests." In: *Fourth Internationale*, page 11. Published by The Legislative Correspondents' Association of the State of New York, Albany, NY. 1920. [8" × 11¼"]. N/c drawing by Fred O. Seibel of a statue of House Speaker Thaddeus "Sweet" on horseback, "Governor's Chair," "Assemblyman Roosevelt," other politicians. "A Session of Soviets, Seething with Socialism, Sweetism, Sedition, Seven-Cent Fares, School-Ma'ams, Soda-Water, Slams, Slander, Simps and Strangulation, and Bristling with Booms, Boobs and Bunk." "Called by The Legislative Correspondents' Association of the State of New York, at The Ten Eyck, Albany, April 22, 1920." [Crew/AES-66].

• **AmPM-1028 CUOMO**, Mario Matthew (State Secretary of State, 1975–1978; Lt. Governor, 1979–1982; Governor, 1983–1995)

1028.1 All The Way With Mondale. w.m. Joseph Erdelyi, Jr., "No. 358 West 51st Street, New York, NY." 10019. 1984. [8½" × 11"]. Non-pictorial. "Campaign Song for Walter Mondale, 1984 Democratic Candidate for President of the United States, with Special adaptation of the song for New York State residents and the Primary Election of April 3, 1984." "Dedicated to the Honorable Governor of the State of New York Mario Cuomo, who encouraged the Author to write a song for the Democrats." 2pp. Page 2: Blank. [Crew/WFM-1].

1028.2 Cuomo. w. Bill Strauss and Elaina Newport. On CD: *A Whole Newt World.* Published by Capitol Steps Productions, 1505 King Street, Alexandria, VA. 1995. CD Cover: Gn/bl/y drawing of George Bush and George W. Bush as Seuss characters.

1028.3 We Need A Change In Washington. w.m. Joseph Erdelyi, Jr., No. 358 West 51st Street, New York, NY. 10019. July 18, 1984. [8½" × 11"]. B/w photos of Walter Mondale on a campaign button inscribed "America Needs A Change, Mondale in '84," Joseph Erdelyi, Jr. "Campaign Song for Walter Mondale, 1984 Democratic Candidate for President of the United States." "Dedicated to the Honorable Governor of the State of New York Mario Cuomo, who encouraged the Author to write a song for the Democrats." 2pp. Page 2: Blank. [Crew/WFM-2].

- **AmPM-1029 CURRAN**, Thomas J. (New York Secretary of State, 1943–1944; Delegate, Republican National Convention, 1944, 1948, 1952, 1956; Candidate for U.S. Senate, 1944)

1029.1 Dewey-Warren Victory Rally [Program/Songster]. Published by the New York Republican County Committee, New York, NY. 1948. [5¼" × 8¾"]. Bl/w photos of Thomas Dewey and Earl Warren. Bl/w drawing of two eagles. "Madison Square Garden, Saturday, October 30, 1948." "Gov. Thomas E. Dewey, Lt. Gov. Joe R. Hanley, Sen. Irving M. Ives, Mrs. Preston Davie, Hon. Thomas J. Curran, Hon. George Frankenthaler, Hon. Thos. J. Crawford, Mrs. Lillian Sharp Hunter, Hon. Daniel J. Riesner." 8pp. Foldout. Pages 2, 3 and 8: List of committee members. Pages 4 to 7: Songs including: **We All Want Dewey** {1029.1–1}. w. Douglas D. Ballin.

- **AmPM-1030 CURRY**, John F. (Leader of Tammany Hall, 1930s; Delegate to Democratic National Convention, 1928, 1932)

1030.1 Gambling Wheels. w. No composer indicated. m. "Air — *Wagon Wheels.*" In: *Scars And Strifes, A Jungle Jamboree And Carnivorous Carnival, Cracking With Clashes And Seething With Slams, Socks, Strangle-Holds And Skullduggery*, page 12. Published by The Albany Legislative Correspondents' Association, Albany, NY. 1934. [8" × 11¾"]. N/c drawing of jungle animals fighting in the legislative chamber. "Riotously Revealed at Ten Eyck Hotel Rathskeller, Albany, New York, the evening of Thursday, March 22, 1934, at Seven-thirty o'clock." 16pp.

1030.2 Good Night Herbie. w. No composer indicated. m. "Air — *Good Night, Sweetheart.*" In: *The Scrappy Warriors, A Merry, Martial Medley, Mingling-Wrenches And Muck-Rakers, Presidential Pipe-Dreams, Partisan Perfidies And Prohibition Planks — All Revolving 'Round Convulsive Conclave Of Delirious Delegates, Shellshocked Spellbinders And Rabid Rivals For White House Honors*, page 8. Published by Albany Legislative Correspondents' Association, Albany, NY. 1933. [8¼" × 12"]. N/c drawing of Franklin Roosevelt with spear and on horseback charging Al Smith and others holding axes and knives. "Staged at Ten Eyck Hotel Rathskeller, Albany, New York, the evening of Thursday, March 3, 1932, at Seven o'clock."16pp.

1030.3 Lehman Lullaby. w. No composer indicated. m. "Air — *Let's Put Out The Lights And Go To Sleep.*" In: *Foam Sweet Foam*, page 10. Published by Albany Legislative Correspondents' Association, Albany, NY. 1933. [8" × 11¾"]. N/c drawing by Jerry Costello of Franklin D. Roosevelt, Al Smith and other politicians riding a bottle of beer — "The Lager Limited." "A Rollicking Review Rotating on Resurrection of Bouncing Beverages, Tipsily Tapped at Ten Eyck Hotel Rathskeller, Albany, New York, the evening of Thursday, February 23, 1933, at Seven-Thirty O'clock." 20pp. [Crew/FDR-277].

1030.4 Stalling Stanzas. w. No composer indicated. m. "Air — *Bidin' My Time.*" In: *Jays In Jungleland, Or The Curry-Combers, Starring The Snarling, Scornful, Sinew-Set Political Puma And Rampant, Rural Republican Ravagers, Bent On Battering The Beast's Bailiwick And Leveling His Lair In A Scrambled Salmagundi Studded With Sachems, Satchels, Swag, Scuttlers, Sang Froid, Seaburyisms, Etc. — Plus A Peep At That Tammany Masterpiece —'The Tiger's Knightmare,* page 12. Published by The Legislative Correspondents' Association of New York, Albany, NY. 1931. [7¾" × 10½"]. N/c drawing a "Tammany" tiger perched overlooking "GOP" elephants, New York City skyline. "Launched at Ten Eyck Hotel, Albany, New York, On the evening of Thursday, March 26, 1931, at seven o'clock." 16pp.

- **AmPM-1031 DAILEY**, Vincent (Chairman, State Democratic Party; Delegate, Democratic National Convention, 1940–1952)

1031.1 Our Albany Zoo. w. No composer indicated. m. "Air — *Easter Parade.*" In: *Scars And Strifes, A Jungle Jamboree And Carnivorous Carnival, Cracking With Clashes And Seething With Slams, Socks, Strangle-Holds And Skullduggery*, page 7. Published by The Albany Legislative Correspondents' Association, Albany, NY. 1934. [8" × 11¾"]. N/c drawing of jungle animals fighting in the legislative chamber. "Riotously Revealed at Ten Eyck Hotel, Albany, New York, the evening of Thursday, March 22, 1934, at Seven-thirty o'clock." 16pp.

1031.2 Those Fighting Irish. w. No composer indicated. m. "Air — *The Bold McIntyre.*" In: *Knighty — Knighty (Or A Michigan Yankee In King Herbie's Court)*, page 10. Published by The Legislative Correspondents' Association of New York State, Albany, NY. March 23, 1939. [8" × 11¾"]. N/c drawing of Thomas Dewey and Herbert Lehman jousting — "A Bouncing Blend, Mellowly Medieval, of Tangy Tunes, Balmy Buffoons, Flashing Blades and Ravishing Maids, Featuring the Glamour Gink of Gotham and the Caliph of Capitol Hill in 'Let's Tangle Tinware.'" "Thursday, March Twenty-Third, 1939, at Seven-Thirty o'clock. "Ribbingly Ripped Off at Hotel Ten Eyck, Albany, New York." [Crew/TED-30].

1031.3 When Knighthood Was In Clover. w. No composer indicated. m. "Air — *Song Of The Vagabonds.*" In: *Knighty — Knighty (Or A Michigan Yankee In King Herbie's Court)*, page 7. Published by The Legislative Correspondents' Association of New York State, Albany, NY. March 23, 1939. [8" × 11¾"]. N/c drawing of Thomas Dewey and Herbert Lehman jousting — "A Bouncing Blend, Mellowly Medieval, of Tangy Tunes, Balmy Buffoons, Flashing Blades and Ravishing Maids, Featuring the Glamour Gink of Gotham and the Caliph of Capitol Hill in 'Let's Tangle Tinware.'" "Thursday, March Twenty-Third, 1939, at Seven-Thirty o'clock. "Ribbingly Ripped Off at Hotel Ten Eyck, Albany, New York." [Crew/TED-30].

• **AmPM-1032 D'AMATO**, Alfonse Marcello (Public Administrator, Nassau County, 1965–1968; Tax Assessor, Hempstead, 1969; Town Supervisor, Hempstead, 1971–1977?; Board of Supervisors, Nassau County, 1977–1980; U. S. Senate, 1981–1999)

1032.1 D'Amato. w. William K. Tong. m. "Sung to the tune of *Tomorrow* from the Broadway musical *Annie*." In: *The Sting The Right Wing Song Book* at <http://www.geocities.com/wmktong/bootnewt/damato.htm>. [ca. 199-].

1032.2 Funds, Funds, Funds. w. Paul Silhan. m. "Sung to *Fun, Fun, Fun* by The Beach Boys." On: Cassette: *Running On Empty*. "Well, they thanked their lucky stars they slipped through Al D'Amato's hands..." Lyrics published at <http://www.paulsilhan.com/roe-11.htm>. [ca. 1996].

• **AmPM-1033 DAVENPORT**, Frederick M. (Candidate for Lt. Governor, 1912)

1033.1 National Progressive Party Song Sheet Of Roosevelt-Straus Ratification. In: *[Program For Madison Square Garden Rally]*. [7⅞" × 11¼"]. Nonpictorial. "For Madison Square Garden, Friday Night, November 1st, 1912. Let The Whole Assembly Sing!" "Speakers Oscar S. Straus, Candidate for Governor, Frederick M. Davenport, Candidate for Lieutenant Governor." Program contains 10 songs. 14pp. [Crew/TR-397].

• **AmPM-1034 DAVIDSON**, Irwin Delmore (State Assembly, 1936–1948; Court of Special Sessions, New York City, 1948–1954; U.S. House, 1955–1956; Court of General Sessions, New York County, 1956–1963; State Supreme Court, 1963–1974)

1034.1 Each Monday Night Is The Screwiest Night Of The Week. w.m. No composer or tune indicated. In: *Cash & Carry–On Or It Ain't Hay, A Stirring Saga Suggesting Scrimping, Scrooging And Spending Twixt The Highlands And Lowlands Of State Street; Also, A Loony Lift To Luna For Leaders Looking For Less O'Lockwood; All Pieced Together With A Paralyzing Portrayal Of Pickets Putting Pay Ahead Of Party*, page 16. Published by The Legislative Correspondents' Association of New York, Albany, NY. 1946. [8½" × 11"]. N/c drawing of politicians fighting over the "Castle Surplus, Irish dressed "O'Dwyer, Hannegan, Farley, Mead" against Scottish dressed "Lockwood, Bedenknap, MacDewey, Burton." "Hotel Ten Eyck, Albany, March 14, 1946." 24pp. [Crew/TED-20].

• **AmPM-1035 DAVIS**, Richard David (U.S. House, 1841–1845)

1035.1 The Rubber (Or Mat's Third And Last Game). w. No composer indicated. m. "Tune — *Miss Bailey*." In: *The National Clay Minstrel (And True Whig's Pocket Companion For The Presidential Canvass Of 1844)*, page 46. Published by [V-1: George Hood, No. 15 North 6th Street, Philadelphia, PA] [V-2: James Fisher, No. 71 Court Street, Boston, MA]. 1843. [3¼" × 5⅛"]. Y/bk litho of raccoon — "That Coon" and flag — "Henry Clay," log cabin. "New and Improved Edition." 128pp. Page 10: Dedication — "To the National Clay Club this work is respectfully dedicated by the Publisher." [Crew/HC-11].

• **AmPM-1036 DEPEW**, Chauncey Mitchell (State Assembly, 1861–1862; New York Secretary of State, 1863; U.S. Senate, 1899–1911)

1036.1 Ben And Levi. w. No composer indicated. m. "Air — *Solomon And Levi*." In: *Democratic Song Book For The Campaign Of 1888*, page 8. c. John R. East. Published by John R. East, Bloomington, IN. 1888. [4¼" × 5¹³⁄₁₆"]. Bl/bl litho of Grover Cleveland and Allen Thurman. "Price 10 cents, postage prepaid, Liberal Discounts to Dealers." 20pp. [Crew/GC-140].

1036.2 Empire State March. m. Alfred H. Aarons. Published by Cluett & Sons, Troy and Albany, New York. 1896. B/w photo of Chauncey Depew. Bl/w litho of a train, geometric designs. "Dedicated to Hon. Chauncey M. Depew." 6pp. Pages 2 and 6: Blank.

1036.3 [Here's To Chauncey M. Depew]. w. No composer indicated. m. "Air — *Hold Your Hand Out, You Naughty Boy*." B/w drawing of Taft walking to Chicago. In: *Gridiron Nights*, page 314. Published by Frederick A. Stokes Company, Publishers, New York, NY. Copyright 1915 by Arthur Wallace Dunn. [7½" × 10½"]. B/gd imprinting of comedy mask, lamps, floral designs. 406pp.

1036.4 Our Own Waltz. m. A. B. de Frece. Published by Wm. A. Pond & Co., 124 Fifth Avenue, New York, NY. 1896. B/w photo of Chauncey Depew. R/w floral designs. "Dedicated to Hon. Chauncey M. Depew, IL.D." 8pp. Page 8: Blank. [LL/JH].

1036.5 Tammany (A Pale Face Pow-Wow). w. Vincent Bryan. m. Gus Edwards. Published by M. Witmark & Sons, New York, New York. 1905. [11" × 13⅞"]. Br/bl/o litho of a stereotypic Indian in headdress. O/w photo of Jefferson DeAngelis. "Sung with Great Success by Jefferson DeAngelis in Sam S. Shubert's Production of *Fantana*." [Different editions have different performers pictured on the cover]. "50¢." 6pp. Pages 2–5 music. Page 6 advertising. Page 2: Dedication — "Respectfully Dedicated to the Hon. Timothy D. Sullivan." [Crew/S-1905-1].

1036.6 University Club Banquet. [Song Book]. Published by The University Club, Washington, DC. 1911. Bk/br/w drawing of buildings, grapes, glasses, geometric designs. 30pp. Page 3: "The Seventh Annual Banquet, the New Willard Hotel, Monday, February 27, 1911, 7:00 p.m." Page 5: Menu. Pages 6 to 10: Drawings of Senator Thomas Carter, William H. Taft, Ambassador Bryce, Senator Depew and Hon. Morton Littleton.

1036.7 We've Got Him On The List. w. No composer indicated. m. "Arr. by Tariff Reform." In: *Red Hot Democratic Campaign Songs For 1888*. page 16. e. John Bunyon Herbert. Published by The S. Brainard's Sons Company, Chicago, IL. 1888. [5⅜" × 7⁷⁄₁₆"]. R/bk geometric designs. 36pp. Pages 2, 31 and 32: Advertising. Page 3: Contents. [M-294]. [Crew/GC-141].

1036.8 Will You Ever Give The Colored Race A Show? (An Appeal To Congress). w.m. Robert P. Jackson. Copyright 1898? by Robert P. Jackson, 3143 Dearborn Street, Chicago, IL. B/w photos of Abraham "Lincoln — The Shackles Fell 1863," Charles "Sumner — The Original Champion of the Slaves 1856," William "McKinley — Prosperity 1896." Photo of Robert P. Jackson. Drawing of soldiers marching labeled "The U.S. 25th Inft. Colored Soldiers, the first called on to fight to free Cuba," "white laborers going to work" at a factory labeled "Prosperity & at peace with all nations," "Negroes waiting" behind a "Color Line." 6pp. Page 2: Narrative on "The Negro In The Field Of Labor." Page 6: Blank. [Crew/WM-341]

• **AmPM-1037 DESMOND**, Thomas Charles (State Senate, 1934-1958)

1037.1 Bedtime Ballad. w. No composer indicated. m. "Air—*Lights Out.*" In: *Tory, Tory Hallelujah*, page 10. Published by Albany Legislative Correspondents' Association, Albany, NY. 1936. [8" × 11¾"]. N/c drawing of Franklin D. Roosevelt, other politicians dressed as Revolutionary soldiers in battle scene—"A Dashing Delirious Drama, Lampooning Loyalists and Liberty Leaguers, Daggering Despots, Dictators and Dummy Donkey-Drivers to music by Red-Coats and Lyrics by Turn-Coats, the Combat Being Played Against a Spangled Back-Drop." "Furiously Fought at Ten Eyck Hotel, Albany, New York, The Evening of Thursday, March 12, 1936, at Seven-Thirty o'clock." [Crew/FDR-325].

1037.2 Got To Pick A Nag. w. No composer indicated. m. "Tune—*Camptown Races.*" In: *Again And Again And Again Or All At Sea*, page 19. Published by Albany Legislative Correspondents' Association of New York State, Albany, NY. 1945. [8¾" × 11"]. N/c drawing of Franklin Roosevelt as pirate, Thomas Dewey as "Black Tom," Henry Wallace, Sidney Hillman, others on ship—"Union Ship C.I.O.-P.A.C." "Black Tom" Dewey walking plank. "Featuring Political Craft and Cunning and Contortions; Also Summoned by Subpoena, or Hit-Toddy and the Shady Lady, the Indestructible Dame Known as Lu-Lu; Together with Mystical Midsummer Mummery of '46, in a Roaring and Raucous and Revealing Racing Scene Entitled 'Hoots and Straddles.'" "All Done with Music, Magic, and Mirrors—In Three Acts at Hotel Ten Eyck, Albany, March 15, 1945." [Crew/FDR-371].

1037.3 Let's Reapportion! w. No composer indicated. m. "Air—*Rainbow On The River.*" In: *Wake Up And Scream*, page 12. Published by Albany Legislative Correspondents' Association, Albany, NY. 1937. [8" × 11¾"]. N/c drawing by Jerry Costello of Dr. Bill Murray, King Macy, New York GOP, and Ham Fish as patients undergoing transfusions. "A Trumpet Call to the G.O.P. Eagle to Snap out of Coma and Rally Ravaged Republicans with New Volley of Vocal Vim—the Same Being Enacted 'mid a Merry Medley of Mountain Madness, Dutch Delirium, Liberalization Legendry, Melancholy Maidens and Rapscallion Redskins, at Ten Eyck Hotel, Albany, N.Y., Thursday, March eleventh, 1937, at Seven-Thirty o'clock." 20pp.

1037.4 Our Albany Zoo. w. No composer indicated. m. "Air—*Easter Parade.*" In: *Scars And Strifes, A Jungle Jamboree And Carnivorous Carnival, Cracking With Clashes And Seething With Slams, Socks, Strangle-Holds And Skullduggery*, page 7. Published by The Albany Legislative Correspondents' Association, Albany, NY. 1934. [8" × 11¾"]. N/c drawing of jungle animals fighting in the legislative chamber. "Riotously Revealed at Ten Eyck Hotel, Albany, New York, the evening of Thursday, March 22, 1934, at Seven-thirty o'clock." 16pp.

• **AmPM-1038 DEWEY**, Thomas Edmund (U.S. District Attorney, 1933; Candidate for Republican Nomination for President, 1940; Governor, 1943-1955; Republican Candidate for President, 1944 & 1948; Delegate, Republican National Convention, 1952 & 1956) [ALSO SEE: DOC/PSM-TED]

1038.1 Accentuate The Politics! w. No composer indicated. m. "Tune—*Accentuate The Positive.*" In: *Again And Again And Again Or All At Sea*, page 17. Published by Albany Legislative Correspondents' Association of New York State, Albany, NY. 1945. [8¾" × 11"]. N/c drawing of Franklin Roosevelt as pirate, Thomas Dewey as "Black Tom," Henry Wallace, Sidney Hillman, others on ship—"Union Ship C.I.O.-P.A.C." "Black Tom" Dewey walking plank. "Featuring Political Craft and Cunning and Contortions; Also Summoned by Subpoena, or Hit-Toddy and the Shady Lady, the Indestructible Dame Known as Lu-Lu; Together with Mystical Midsummer Mummery of '46, in a Roaring and Raucous and Revealing Racing Scene Entitled 'Hoots and Straddles.'" "All Done with Music, Magic, and Mirrors—In Three Acts at Hotel Ten Eyck, Albany, March 15, 1945." [Crew/FDR-371].

1038.2 All Alone—Washington D.C. (President Truman). w. No composer indicated. m. "Tune—*All Alone* and *Civilization.*" In: *Alice In Blunderland Or Through The Rooking Class* [Program and Songbook], page 9. Published by The Legislative Correspondents' Association of New York State, Albany, NY. 1949. [8⅝" × 11"]. N/c drawings of Harry Truman, Thomas Dewey, Franklin Roosevelt, Henry Wallace, Harold Stassen, Alben Barkley, Robert Taft, Earl Warren, other politicians. "A Scintillating Satire of Sadistic Surprises and Surprising Successes Featuring a Dramatic Disclosure of How Tom Did Not Go Down to D.C. in Slips; Together with a Give-Away-Nothing Radio Broadcast and Epic Melodrama of the Indian Wars Entitled 'When the Cat's Away the Mice Will Play.'" "Done With Music and Mirrors—Particularly Mirrors in Three Acts at Hotel Ten Eyck, Albany, March 12, 1949." [Crew/HST-20].

1038.3 Always True To Fashion. w. No composer indicated. m. "Tune—*Always True To You In My Fashion.*" "Quartette—Stassen, Taft, Warren and Martin." In: *Alice In Blunderland Or Through The Rooking Class* [Program and Songbook], page 6. Published by The Legislative Correspondents' Association of New York State, Albany, NY. 1949. [8⅝" × 11"]. N/c drawings of Harry Truman, Thomas Dewey, Franklin Roosevelt, Henry Wallace, Harold Stassen, Alben Barkley, Robert Taft, Earl Warren, other politicians. "A Scintillating Satire of Sadistic Surprises and Surprising Successes Featuring a Dramatic Disclosure of How Tom Did Not Go Down to D.C. in Slips; Together with a Give-Away-Nothing Radio Broadcast and Epic Melodrama of the Indian Wars Entitled 'When the Cat's Away the Mice Will Play.'" "Done With Music and Mirrors—Particularly Mirrors in Three Acts at Hotel Ten Eyck, Albany, March 12, 1949." [Crew/HST-20].

1038.4 Ballots And Votes. w. No composer indicated. m. "Tune—*Buttons And Bows, On A Slow Boat To China* and *What Did I Do.*" In: *Alice In Blunderland Or Through The Rooking Class* [Program and Songbook], page 11. Published by The Legislative Correspondents' Association of New York State, Albany,

NY. 1949. [8⅝" × 11"]. N/c drawings of Harry Truman, Thomas Dewey, Franklin Roosevelt, Henry Wallace, Harold Stassen, Alben Barkley, Robert Taft, Earl Warren, other politicians. "A Scintillating Satire of Sadistic Surprises and Surprising Successes Featuring a Dramatic Disclosure of How Tom Did Not Go Down to D.C. in Slips; Together with a Give-Away-Nothing Radio Broadcast and Epic Melodrama of the Indian Wars Entitled 'When the Cat's Away the Mice Will Play.'" "Done With Music and Mirrors—Particularly Mirrors in Three Acts at Hotel Ten Eyck, Albany, March 12, 1949." [Crew/HST-20].

1038.5 A Bee In My Bonnet. w. No composer indicated. m. "Tune—*A Tree In The Meadow*." "Duet—Hack and Moore." In: *Alice In Blunderland Or Through The Rooking Class* [Program and Songbook], page 23. Published by The Legislative Correspondents' Association of New York State, Albany, NY. 1949. [8⅝" × 11"]. N/c drawings of Harry Truman, Thomas Dewey, Franklin Roosevelt, Henry Wallace, Harold Stassen, Alben Barkley, Robert Taft, Earl Warren, other politicians. "A Scintillating Satire of Sadistic Surprises and Surprising Successes Featuring a Dramatic Disclosure of How Tom Did Not Go Down to D.C. in Slips; Together with a Give-Away-Nothing Radio Broadcast and Epic Melodrama of the Indian Wars Entitled 'When the Cat's Away the Mice Will Play.'" "Done With Music and Mirrors—Particularly Mirrors in Three Acts at Hotel Ten Eyck, Albany, March 12, 1949" [Crew/HST-20].

1038.6 The Biggest Dog-Gone Surplus In The World. w. No composer indicated. m. "Tune—*The Biggest Aspidastra In The World*." "Miss November's Victory Song." In: *Cash & Carry—On Or It Ain't Hay, A Stirring Saga Suggesting Scrimping, Scrooging And Spending Twixt The Highlands And Lowlands Of State Street; Also, A Loony Lift To Luna For Leaders Looking For Less O'Lockwood; All Pieced Together With A Paralyzing Portrayal Of Pickets Putting Pay Ahead Of Party*, page 10. Published by The Legislative Correspondents' Association of New York, Albany, NY. 1946. [8½" × 11"]. N/c drawing of politicians fighting over the "Castle Surplus, Irish dressed "O'Dwyer, Hannegan, Farley, Mead" against Scottish dressed "Lockwood, Bedenknap, MacDewey, Burton." "Hotel Ten Eyck, Albany, March 14, 1946." 24pp. [Crew/TED-20].

1038.7 Brush Those Tears From Your Eyes. w. No composer indicated. m. "Tune—*I Wonder Who's Kissing Her Now*." In: *Alice In Blunderland Or Through The Rooking Class* [Program and Songbook], page 26. Published by The Legislative Correspondents' Association of New York State, Albany, NY. 1949. [8⅝" × 11"]. N/c drawings of Harry Truman, Thomas Dewey, Franklin Roosevelt, Henry Wallace, Harold Stassen, Alben Barkley, Robert Taft, Earl Warren, other politicians. "A Scintillating Satire of Sadistic Surprises and Surprising Successes Featuring a Dramatic Disclosure of How Tom Did Not Go Down to D.C. in Slips; Together with a Give-Away-Nothing Radio Broadcast and Epic Melodrama of the Indian Wars Entitled 'When the Cat's Away the Mice Will Play.'" "Done With Music and Mirrors—Particularly Mirrors in Three Acts at Hotel Ten Eyck, Albany, March 12, 1949" [Crew/HST-20].

1038.8 But He Wouldn't Say Yes! w. No composer indicated. m. "Air—*I Can't Say No*." In: *Dealers Choice Or Back-To-Back Biting*, page 15. Published by the Albany Legislative Correspondent's Association of New York State, Albany, NY. 1944. [8" × 11¾"]. N/c drawing of Franklin Roosevelt, Thomas Dewey, "Chiang," "Winnie" and "Joe" playing cards—"Featuring the World's Most Exciting Egomaniacs in a Marvelous Musical of Messianic and Mystery: Showing Sinners, Sycophants, Suckers, and Sleuths Saving Civilization with Sound; or Find the Joker!" "Dealt Off the Bottom of a Hot Deck—In Three Acts at Ten Eyck, Albany, March 9, 1944." [Crew/FDR-364].

1038.8A Campaign Songs. w. O.M. Brees, "Editor of the *Endicott Times*." m. Popular tunes. 1938. Non-pictorial songsheet. Three songs: **Battle Hymn Of '38** {1038.8A-1}. m. Air—"*Battle Hymn of the Republic*;" **Yankee Doodle And Dewey** {1038.8A-2}. m. Air—"*Yankee Doodle*;" and **Fighting Bonnet** {1038.8A-3}. m. Air—"*Put On Your Old Gray Bonnet*." 2pp. Page 2: Blank.

1038.9 Congratulations, Tom Dewey. w.m. Richard M. Sherman and Milton Larsen. On 33⅓ rpm LP: *Smash Flops*. Lemon Records #PLP1905. Performed by Richard M. Sherman and Milton Larsen. [ca. 1960s].

1038.10 Congratulations, Tom Dewey. w. No composer indicated. "Based on a host of polls and media predictions of a Dewey landslide in the 1948 Presidential campaign ... songs like this one were poised on the nation's bandstands..." Lyrics and sound file published online at <http://www.mudcat.org/kids/@displaysong.cfm?SongID=1326>. [199-].

1038.11 Cutting Down The Budget. w. No composer indicated. m. "Tune—*Cruising Down The River*." As sung by "Senator MaHoney." In: *Alice In Blunderland Or Through The Rooking Class* [Program and Songbook], page 25. Published by The Legislative Correspondents' Association of New York State, Albany, NY. 1949. [8⅝" × 11"]. N/c drawings of Harry Truman, Thomas Dewey, Franklin Roosevelt, Henry Wallace, Harold Stassen, Alben Barkley, Robert Taft, Earl Warren, other politicians. "A Scintillating Satire of Sadistic Surprises and Surprising Successes Featuring a Dramatic Disclosure of How Tom Did Not Go Down to D.C. in Slips; Together with a Give-Away-Nothing Radio Broadcast and Epic Melodrama of the Indian Wars Entitled 'When the Cat's Away the Mice Will Play.'" "Done With Music and Mirrors—Particularly Mirrors in Three Acts at Hotel Ten Eyck, Albany, March 12, 1949." [Crew/HST-20].

1038.12 Dance Of The Liberal Republicans. w.m. Gerald Gardner. In: *These Are The Songs That Were* [Song Book], page 10. e. Gerald Gardner (Writer of *Who's In Charge Here?*, *News-Reals*, and *That Was The Week That Was*). Published by Edwin H. Morris and Company, No. 31 West 54th Street, New York, NY. 10019. 1965. B/w photo of Lyndon B. Johnson, Hubert Humphrey, Everett Dirksen, others. R/w/bk cover. List of contents. 36pp. Pages 8, 23 and 25: Photos of politicians. [Crew/LBJ-6].

1038.13 Dewey Lowers The Boom. w. No composer indicated. m. "Tune—*Clancy Lowered The Boom*." Sung by "Henry Wallace." In: *Alice In Blunderland Or Through The Rooking Class* [Program and Songbook], page 16. Published by The Legislative Correspondents' Association of New York State, Albany, NY. 1949. [8⅜" × 11"]. N/c drawings of Harry Truman, Thomas Dewey, Franklin Roosevelt, Henry Wallace, Harold Stassen, Alben Barkley, Robert Taft, Earl Warren, other politicians. "A Scintillating Satire of Sadistic Surprises and Surprising Successes Featuring a Dramatic Disclosure of How Tom Did Not Go Down to D.C. in Slips; Together with a Give-Away-Nothing Radio Broadcast and Epic Melodrama of the Indian Wars Entitled 'When the Cat's Away the Mice Will Play.'" "Done With Music and Mirrors—Particularly Mirrors in Three Acts at Hotel Ten Eyck, Albany, March 12, 1949." [Crew/HST-20].

1038.14 Don't Bring Back Dewey To Me. w. No composer indicated. m. "Tune—*Bring Back My Bonnie To Me*." In: *Alice In Blunderland Or Through The Rooking Class* [Program and Songbook], page 21. Published by The Legislative Correspondents' Association of New York State, Albany, NY. 1949. [8⅜" × 11"]. N/c drawings of Harry Truman, Thomas Dewey, Franklin Roosevelt, Henry Wallace, Harold Stassen, Alben Barkley, Robert Taft, Earl Warren, other politicians. "A Scintillating Satire of Sadistic Surprises and Surprising Successes Featuring a Dramatic Disclosure of How Tom Did Not Go Down to D.C. in Slips; Together with a Give-Away-Nothing Radio Broadcast and Epic Melodrama of the Indian Wars Entitled 'When the Cat's Away the Mice Will Play.'" "Done With Music and Mirrors—Particularly Mirrors in Three Acts at Hotel Ten Eyck, Albany, March 12, 1949." [Crew/HST-20].

1038.15 [Don't Vote For Dewey]. w. Bill Leader. m. "Sing to the tune of *Four Leaf Clover*." [1948]. [4½" × 6"]. R/w/b litho of clover leafs, geometric design border. 2pp. Page2: Blank. [Crew/TED-39].

1038.16 Down The Up Staircase. w. No composer indicated. m. "Tune—*If My Friends Could See Me Now!*" As sung by "Wilson and Chorus." In: *Thoroughly Mad-ern Malcolm Or He Didn't Need A Course In Forensics To Become A Famous Public Speaker*, page 28. Published by the New York State Legislative Correspondents' Association, Albany, NY. 1974. N/w photo of Malcolm Wilson as Alfred E. Newman—"What—Me Governor?" "Featuring the New York Correspondents' Association, March 16. 1974." 32pp.

1038.17 The Elephant Boys. w. No composer indicated. m. "Air—*Battle Hymn Of The Republic*." In: *Knighty—Knighty (Or A Michigan Yankee In King Herbie's Court)*, page 10. Published by The Legislative Correspondents' Association of New York State, Albany, NY. March 23, 1939. [8" × 11¾"]. N/c drawing of Thomas Dewey and Herbert Lehman jousting—"A Bouncing Blend, Mellowly Medieval, of Tangy Tunes, Balmy Buffoons, Flashing Blades and Ravishing Maids, Featuring the Glamour Gink of Gotham and the Caliph of Capitol Hill in 'Let's Tangle Tinware.'" "Thursday, March Twenty-Third, 1939, at Seven-Thirty o'clock. "Ribbingly Ripped Off at Hotel Ten Eyck, Albany, New York." [Crew/TED-30].

1038.18 Five Birds In A Gilded Cage. w. No composer indicated. m. "Tune—*A Bird In A Gilded Cage*." "As sung by Heck, Feinberg, Wicks, Mailler, Stephens." In: *Visions And Revisions*, page 10. Published by The Albany Legislative Correspondents' Association, Albany, NY. March 6, 1947. [8½" × 11"]. R/w/gn/y/bk drawing of Thomas "Dewey" as Santa Claus, sign—"Santa's Workshop," other New York politicians. "Revealing in Rhapsodic Revelry of Song and Stunt How a Political Scrooge Became a Political Saint; or, What Happened When Many Paws Raided the Wonderful Workshop of Santa Claus Dewey; Together with Other Strange and Silly Scenes." "Hotel Ten Eyck, Albany, March 6, 1947." 24pp. [Crew/TED-34].

1038.19 Forward Goes The New Advance. w.m. No composer or tune indicated. In: *Cash & Carry—On or It Ain't Hay, A Stirring Saga Suggesting Scrimping, Scrooging And Spending Twixt The Highlands And Lowlands Of State Street; Also, A Loony Lift To Luna For Leaders Looking For Less O'Lockwood; All Pieced Together With A Paralyzing Portrayal Of Pickets Putting Pay Ahead Of Party*, page 9. Published by The Legislative Correspondents' Association of New York, Albany, NY. 1946. [8½" × 11"]. N/c drawing of politicians fighting over the "Castle Surplus, Irish dressed "O'Dwyer, Hannegan, Farley, Mead" against Scottish dressed "Lockwood, Bedenknap, MacDewey, Burton." "Hotel Ten Eyck, Albany, March 14, 1946." 24pp. [Crew/TED-20].

1038.20 Give Our Regards To Dewey. w. No composer indicated. m. "Tune—*Give My Regards To Broadway*." In: *Cash & Carry-On or It Ain't Hay, A Stirring Saga Suggesting Scrimping, Scrooging And Spending Twixt The Highlands And Lowlands Of State Street; Also, A Loony Lift To Luna For Leaders Looking For Less O'Lockwood; All Pieced Together With A Paralyzing Portrayal Of Pickets Putting Pay Ahead Of Party*, page 17. Published by The Legislative Correspondents' Association of New York, Albany, NY. 1946. [8½" × 11"]. N/c drawing of politicians fighting over the "Castle Surplus, Irish dressed "O'Dwyer, Hannegan, Farley, Mead" against Scottish dressed "Lockwood, Bedenknap, MacDewey, Burton." "Hotel Ten Eyck, Albany, March 14, 1946." 24pp. [Crew/TED-20].

1038.21 Got To Pick A Nag. w. No composer indicated. m. "Tune—*Camptown Races*." In: *Again And Again And Again Or All At Sea*, page 19. Published by Albany Legislative Correspondents' Association of New York State, Albany, NY. 1945. [8¾" × 11"]. N/c drawing of Franklin Roosevelt as pirate, Thomas Dewey as "Black Tom," Henry Wallace, Sidney Hillman, others on ship—"Union Ship C.I.O.-P.A.C." "Black Tom" Dewey walking plank. "Featuring Political Craft and Cunning and Contortions; Also Summoned by Subpoena, or Hit-Toddy and the Shady Lady, the Indestructible Dame Known as Lu-Lu; Together with Mystical Midsummer Mummery of '46, in a Roaring and Raucous and Revealing Racing Scene Entitled 'Hoots and Straddles.'" "All Done with Music, Magic, and Mirrors—In Three Acts at Hotel Ten Eyck, Albany, March 15, 1945." [Crew/FDR-371].

1038.22 Hang Down Your Head, Tom Dewey. w. Noel E. Parmentel, Jr. and Marshall J. Dodge. In: *Folk Songs For Conservatives*, page 11. Published by Unicorn Press, Inc., No. 790 Madison Avenue, New York, NY. 10021. 1964. [5" × 8⅜"]. Bl/w drawings of Barry Goldwater, Bill Buckley, Ray Cohn, eagle. List of contents.

"Sung by Noel E. Parmentel, Jr. and His Unbleached Muslims, Greatest Political Satirists Since Cohn and Schine." "Right Wing Hootenanny." 36pp. [Crew/BMG-13].

1038.23 Hold That Hanley! w. No composer indicated. m. "Air—*MacNamara's Band*." In: *Gone With The Winner*, page 13. Published by Albany Legislative Correspondents' Association of New York State, Albany, NY. March 20, 1941. [9" × 11¹⁶⁄₁₆"]. R/w/bl/y drawing of Franklin Roosevelt and Wendell Willkie riding "A Bicycle Built For Two" labeled—"Roosevelt-Willkie Axis." Wheels—"New Deal" and "Lend Lease Bill." "Or 'Back in the Lap of God.' A Hoosier-Hyde Park Honeymoon Hit, Staring the G. Oomph P.'s Lost Leader and the King of Krum Elbow in 'Lucky Partners.' Says F.D.R.—'He's My Man.' Says the Republican Party—'Once a New Dealer, Sometimes a Double- Dealer.' Says the Public—'Willkie's the Life of the Party, But What Party?" "Served Piping Hot at Hotel Ten Eyck, Albany, New York, Thursday Night, March 20, 1941, at 7:30 o'clock. [Crew/FDR-394].

1038.24 How Are Things With You? w. No composer indicated. m. "Tune—*How Are Things In Glocca Morra?*" In: *Visions And Revisions*, page 18. Published by The Albany Legislative Correspondents' Association, Albany, NY. March 6, 1947. [8½" × 11"]. R/w/gn/y/bk drawing of Thomas "Dewey" as Santa Claus, sign—"Santa's Workshop," other New York politicians. "Revealing in Rhapsodic Revelry of Song and Stunt How a Political Scrooge Became a Political Saint; or, What Happened When Many Paws Raided the Wonderful Workshop of Santa Claus Dewey; Together with Other Strange and Silly Scenes." "Hotel Ten Eyck, Albany, March 6, 1947." 24pp. [Crew/TED-34].

1038.25 I Can Pass On My Troubles. w. No composer indicated. m. "Tune—*I've Got The Sun In The Morning.*" In: *Visions And Revisions*, page 8. Published by The Albany Legislative Correspondents' Association, Albany, NY. March 6, 1947. [8½" × 11"]. R/w/gn/y/bk drawing of Thomas "Dewey" as Santa Claus, sign—"Santa's Workshop," other New York politicians. "Revealing in Rhapsodic Revelry of Song and Stunt How a Political Scrooge Became a Political Saint; or, What Happened When Many Paws Raided the Wonderful Workshop of Santa Claus Dewey; Together with Other Strange and Silly Scenes." "Hotel Ten Eyck, Albany, March 6, 1947." 24pp. [Crew/TED-34].

1038.26 Let's All Be Happy. w.m. Joe Lock, Herman Parris and Morty Berk. Published by Lock-O'Malley Music Publishing Co., No. 45 South 17th Street, Philadelphia, PA. 1948. Bl/w drawing of mask, music notes. "Featured by the Trilby String Band & Rice Club Octette." 4pp. Page 4: Special Version for the G.O.P. with special words for the 1948 presidential election. [Crew/TED-38].

1038.27 Locked Up In The Reconstruction Fund. w.m. No composer or tune indicated. In: *Cash & Carry—On Or It Ain't Hay, A Stirring Saga Suggesting Scrimping, Scrooging And Spending Twixt The Highlands And Lowlands Of State Street; Also, A Loony Lift To Luna For Leaders Looking For Less O'Lockwood; All Pieced Together With A Paralyzing Portrayal Of Pickets Putting Pay Ahead Of Party*, page 8. Published by The Legislative Correspondents' Association of New York, Albany, NY. 1946. [8½" × 11"]. N/c drawing of politicians fighting over the "Castle Surplus, Irish dressed "O'Dwyer, Hannegan, Farley, Mead" against Scottish dressed "Lockwood, Bedenknap, MacDewey, Burton." "Hotel Ten Eyck, Albany, March 14, 1946." 24pp. [Crew/TED-20].

1038.28 Much Obliged, Pal. w. No composer indicated. m. "Air—*Thanks For The Memories.*" In: *Sock-A-Bye Baby, A No Punches-Pulled Potpourri, Pillorying Political Palookas On Parade And Set To 'Swing' Time, Plus That Mad Maternal Masterpiece—Labor's Love Lost*, page 13. Published by The Legislative Correspondents' Association of New York, Albany, NY. 1938. [7¾" × 10½"]. N/c drawing of politicians as boxers: "Tom Dewey, Gotham Gamecock, Morry Tremaine Queen City's Idol, Bob-Jackson, Jamestown's Mighty Atom, Ripper Rolly Marvin, Syracuse Fistic Sensation, Jabber Bennett, Brooklyn Bomber and Promoter's Dream, Billy Bleakley, Westchester Wildcat, Killer Lehman, Knockerouter De Luxe." "Ace Cards for 1838 Golden Gloves Combat." "At Ten Eyck Hotel, Albany, New York, the evening of Thursday, March Tenth, 1938, at seven o'clock." 16pp. [Crew/TED-28].

1038.29 Mutual 'Shun Society. w. No composer indicated. m. "Air—*The Last Time I Saw Paris.*" In: *Gone With The Winner*, page 8. Published by Albany Legislative Correspondents' Association of New York State, Albany, NY. March 20, 1941. [9" × 11¹⁶⁄₁₆"]. R/w/bl/y drawing of Franklin Roosevelt and Wendell Willkie riding "A Bicycle Built For Two" labeled—"Roosevelt-Willkie Axis." Wheels—"New Deal" and "Lend Lease Bill." "Or 'Back in the Lap of God.' A Hoosier-Hyde Park Honeymoon Hit, Staring the G. Oomph P.'s Lost Leader and the King of Krum Elbow in 'Lucky Partners.' Says F.D.R.—'He's My Man.' Says the Republican Party—'Once a New Dealer, Sometimes a Double- Dealer.' Says the Public—'Willkie's the Life of the Party, But What Party?" "Served Piping Hot at Hotel Ten Eyck, Albany, New York, Thursday Night, March 20, 1941, at 7:30 o'clock. [Crew/FDR-394].

1038.30 Next Year! w. No composer indicated. m. "Tune—*Santa Claus Is Coming To Town.*" In: *Visions And Revisions*, page 13. Published by The Albany Legislative Correspondents' Association, Albany, NY. March 6, 1947. [8½" × 11"]. R/w/gn/y/bk drawing of Thomas "Dewey" as Santa Claus, sign—"Santa's Workshop," other New York politicians. "Revealing in Rhapsodic Revelry of Song and Stunt How a Political Scrooge Became a Political Saint; or, What Happened When Many Paws Raided the Wonderful Workshop of Santa Claus Dewey; Together with Other Strange and Silly Scenes." "Hotel Ten Eyck, Albany, March 6, 1947." 24pp. [Crew/TED-34].

1038.31 No Second Floor! m. "Tunes—*My Sweetheart's The Man In The Moon, Singin' In The Rain, In The Evening By The Moonlight* And *When The Moon Comes Over The Mountain.*" In: *Cash & Carry–On Or It Ain't Hay, A Stirring Saga Suggesting Scrimping, Scrooging And Spending Twixt The Highlands And Lowlands Of State Street; Also, A Loony Lift To Luna For*

Leaders Looking For Less O'Lockwood; All Pieced Together With A Paralyzing Portrayal Of Pickets Putting Pay Ahead Of Party, page 12. Published by The Legislative Correspondents' Association of New York, Albany, NY. 1946. [8½" × 11"]. N/c drawing of politicians fighting over the "Castle Surplus, Irish dressed "O'Dwyer, Hannegan, Farley, Mead" against Scottish dressed "Lockwood, Bedenknap, MacDewey, Burton." "Hotel Ten Eyck, Albany, March 14, 1946." 24pp. [Crew/TED-20].

1038.32 Oh, The Budget's Growing. w. No composer indicated. m. "Tune—*Red Silk Stockings And Green Perfume*." Sung by "Henry Wallace." In: *Alice In Blunderland Or Through The Rooking Class* [Program and Songbook], page 13. Published by The Legislative Correspondents' Association of New York State, Albany, NY. 1949. [8⅝" × 11"]. N/c drawings of Harry Truman, Thomas Dewey, Franklin Roosevelt, Henry Wallace, Harold Stassen, Alben Barkley, Robert Taft, Earl Warren, other politicians. "A Scintillating Satire of Sadistic Surprises and Surprising Successes Featuring a Dramatic Disclosure of How Tom Did Not Go Down to D.C. in Slips; Together with a Give-Away-Nothing Radio Broadcast and Epic Melodrama of the Indian Wars Entitled 'When the Cat's Away the Mice Will Play.'" "Done With Music and Mirrors—Particularly Mirrors in Three Acts at Hotel Ten Eyck, Albany, March 12, 1949." [Crew/HST-20].

1038.33 Paean Of Perpetuity. w. No composer indicated. m. "Airs—*Streets Of New York*, *Because You're You* and *Every Day Is Ladies Day With Me*." In: *Lehman Unlimited*, page 6. Published by The Legislative Correspondents' Association of New York, Albany, NY. 1942. [7¾" × 10½"]. N/c drawing of Herb Lehman as a train engineer, others dressed as bandits trying to block the way including Dewey, Mead, Poletti, Willkie, Marvin Bennett and Farley—"The Great Train Hold-Up!" "Featuring that Famous Political Personality and Star of 'There'll Always be a Herbie' on an Uncensored Double Bill with 'Fifty Million Candidates Won't be Wronged.'" "Exploded At Hotel Ten Eyck, Albany, New York, on the evening of Thursday, March 12th, 1942, at seven-thirty o'clock."

1038.34 Parade Of The Rent Marchers. w. No composer indicated. m. "Tunes—*Battle Hymn Of The Republic* and *The Battle-Cry Of Freedom*." In: *Visions And Revisions*, page 14. Published by The Albany Legislative Correspondents' Association, Albany, NY. March 6, 1947. [8½" × 11"]. R/w/gn/y/bk drawing of Thomas "Dewey" as Santa Claus, sign—"Santa's Workshop," other New York politicians. "Revealing in Rhapsodic Revelry of Song and Stunt How a Political Scrooge Became a Political Saint; or, What Happened When Many Paws Raided the Wonderful Workshop of Santa Claus Dewey; Together with Other Strange and Silly Scenes." "Hotel Ten Eyck, Albany, March 6, 1947." 24pp. [Crew/TED-34].

1038.35 Pipe The Pachyderms. w. No composer indicated. m. "Air—*When I Saw An Elephant Fly*." In: *Lehman Unlimited*, page 14. Published by The Legislative Correspondents' Association of New York, Albany, NY. 1942. [7¾" × 10½"]. N/c drawing of Herb Lehman as a train engineer, others dressed as bandits trying to block the way including Dewey, Mead, Poletti, Willkie, Marvin Bennett and Farley—"The Great Train Hold-Up!" "Featuring that Famous Political Personality and Star of 'There'll Always be a Herbie' on an Uncensored Double Bill with 'Fifty Million Candidates Won't be Wronged.'" "Exploded At Hotel Ten Eyck, Albany, New York, on the evening of Thursday, March 12th, 1942, at seven-thirty o'clock." 16pp.

1038.36 The Pollster's Song. w. No composer indicated. m. "Tune—*Yale Whiffenpoof Song*." Original publication not located. 1948. Published, with lyric sheet, in *Winners & Losers, Campaign Songs From The Critical Elections In American History, Volume 2—1896-1976*. Sung with notes by Peter Janovsky. 33⅓ rpm LP. Folkways Records FSS 37261. 1980.

1038.37 Presidential Fox Trot (A Song). w. Mary Salinda Foster. m. J. Wm. Sontag. Published by Schuldt Publishing Company, Mankato, MN. Copyright 1948 by J. Wm. Sontag, Minneapolis, Minnesota. 6pp. including a 2pp insert with words. [Crew/TED-36].

1038.39 Rock's Big Candy Mountain. w. Noel E. Parmentel, Jr. and Marshall J. Dodge. In: *Folk Songs For Conservatives*, page 25. Published by Unicorn Press, Inc., No. 790 Madison Avenue, New York, NY. 10021. 1964. [5" × 8⅜"]. Bl/w drawings of Barry Goldwater, Bill Buckley, Ray Cohn, eagle. List of contents. "Sung by Noel E. Parmentel, Jr. and His Unbleached Muslims, Greatest Political Satirists Since Cohn and Schine." "Right Wing Hootenanny." 36pp. [Crew/BMG-13].

1038.40 School Daze. w. No composer indicated. m. "Tune—*School Days*." "Dedicated to the Little Red School House." In: *Visions And Revisions*, page 15. Published by The Albany Legislative Correspondents' Association, Albany, NY. March 6, 1947. [8½" × 11"]. R/w/gn/y/bk drawing of Thomas "Dewey" as Santa Claus, sign—"Santa's Workshop," other New York politicians. "Revealing in Rhapsodic Revelry of Song and Stunt How a Political Scrooge Became a Political Saint; or, What Happened When Many Paws Raided the Wonderful Workshop of Santa Claus Dewey; Together with Other Strange and Silly Scenes." "Hotel Ten Eyck, Albany, March 6, 1947." 24pp. [Crew/TED-34].

1038.40A Sing Something Simpson. w. No composer indicated. m. "Air—*I Stole The Prince—The Gondoliers*." In: *So You Won't Talk, A Rollicking Rhapsody Ribbing Strong Silent Statesmen With Twelve Year Itch, Twitting Third Termites And Starring The G.O.P. White House Hopeful In 'Mr. Myth Goes To Washington.' Plus That Pari-Muted Phantasy, 'Three Million Men On A Horse,'* page 6. Published by The Legislative Correspondents' Association of New York, Albany, NY. 1942. [7¾" × 10½"]. N/c drawing of two Veiled brides labeled "Democratic Presidential Nominee" and "Republican Presidential Nominee" and a donkey and elephant dressed as grooms standing on the street at "1940" Convention Corner." Drawing titled "Blind Dates." "Daringly Unreeled at Hotel Ten Eyck, Albany, New York, on the evening of Thursday, February 29th, 1940, at seven-thirty o'clock."16pp.

1038.41 Singing Commercials (With their sponsors). w. No composer indicated. m. No tune indicated. Sponsor—"Governor Dewey." In: *Alice In*

Blunderland Or Through The Rooking Class [Program and Songbook], page 18. Published by The Legislative Correspondents' Association of New York State, Albany, NY. 1949. [8⅝" × 11"]. N/c drawings of Harry Truman, Thomas Dewey, Franklin Roosevelt, Henry Wallace, Harold Stassen, Alben Barkley, Robert Taft, Earl Warren, other politicians. "A Scintillating Satire of Sadistic Surprises and Surprising Successes Featuring a Dramatic Disclosure of How Tom Did Not Go Down to D.C. in Slips; Together with a Give-Away-Nothing Radio Broadcast and Epic Melodrama of the Indian Wars Entitled 'When the Cat's Away the Mice Will Play.'" "Done With Music and Mirrors — Particularly Mirrors in Three Acts at Hotel Ten Eyck, Albany, March 12, 1949." [Crew/HST-20].

1038.42 Six Snappy Candidates. w. No composer indicated. m. "Air — *Ten Pretty Girls.*" In: *Sock-A-Bye Baby, A No Punches-Pulled Potpourri, Pillorying Political Palookas On Parade And Set To 'Swing' Time, Plus that Mad Maternal Masterpiece — Labor's Love Lost*, page 12. Published by The Legislative Correspondents' Association of New York, Albany, NY. 1938. [7¾" × 10½"]. N/c drawing of politicians as boxers: "Tom Dewey, Gotham Gamecock, Morry Tremaine Queen City's Idol, Bob-Jackson, Jamestown's Mighty Atom, Ripper Rolly Marvin, Syracuse Fistic Sensation, Jabber Bennett, Brooklyn Bomber and Promoter's Dream, Billy Bleakley, Westchester Wildcat, Killer Lehman, Knockerouter De Luxe." "Ace Cards for 1838 Golden Gloves Combat." "At Ten Eyck Hotel, Albany, New York, the evening of Thursday, March Tenth, 1938, at seven o'clock." 16pp. [Crew/TED-28].

1038.43 Song Of The Legislative Leaders. w. No composer indicated. m. "Tune — *Trolley Song.*" In: *Again And Again And Again Or All At Sea*, page 15. Published by Albany Legislative Correspondents' Association of New York State, Albany, NY. 1945. [8¾" × 11"]. N/c drawing of Franklin Roosevelt as pirate, Thomas Dewey as "Black Tom," Henry Wallace, Sidney Hillman, others on ship — "Union Ship C.I.O.-P.A.C." "Black Tom" Dewey walking plank. "Featuring Political Craft and Cunning and Contortions; Also Summoned by Subpoena, or Hit-Toddy and the Shady Lady, the Indestructible Dame Known as Lu-Lu; Together with Mystical Midsummer Mummery of '46, in a Roaring and Raucous and Revealing Racing Scene Entitled 'Hoots and Straddles.'" "All Done with Music, Magic, and Mirrors — In Three Acts at Hotel Ten Eyck, Albany, March 15, 1945." [Crew/FDR-371].

1038.44 Spring Fantasy! w. No composer indicated. m. "Air — *Flowers That Bloom In The Spring.*" In: *Sock-A-Bye Baby, A No Punches-Pulled Potpourri, Pillorying Political Palookas On Parade And Set To 'Swing' Time, Plus That Mad Maternal Masterpiece — Labor's Love Lost*, page 11. Published by The Legislative Correspondents' Association of New York, Albany, NY. 1938. [7¾" × 10½"]. N/c drawing of politicians as boxers: "Tom Dewey, Gotham Gamecock, Morry Tremaine Queen City's Idol, Bob-Jackson, Jamestown's Mighty Atom, Ripper Rolly Marvin, Syracuse Fistic Sensation, Jabber Bennett, Brooklyn Bomber and Promoter's Dream, Billy Bleakley, Westchester Wildcat, Killer Lehman, Knockerouter De Luxe." "Ace Cards for 1838 Golden Gloves Combat." "At Ten Eyck Hotel, Albany, New York, the evening of Thursday, March Tenth, 1938, at seven o'clock." 16pp. [Crew/TED-28].

1038.44A Stalling Stanzas. w. No composer indicated. m. "Air — *The Little Man Who Wasn't There* and *I'm Bidin' My Time.*" "Sung by Hanley and Lehman." In: *So You Won't Talk, A Rollicking Rhapsody Ribbing Strong Silent Statesmen With Twelve Year Itch, Twitting Third Termites And Starring The G.O.P. White House Hopeful In 'Mr. Myth Goes To Washington.' Plus That Pari-Muted Phantasy, 'Three Million Men On A Horse,'* page 12. Published by The Legislative Correspondents' Association of New York, Albany, NY. 1942. [7¾" × 10½"]. N/c drawing of two Veiled brides labeled "Democratic Presidential Nominee" and "Republican Presidential Nominee" and a donkey and elephant dressed as grooms standing on the street at "1940" Convention Corner." Drawing titled "Blind Dates." "Daringly Unreeled at Hotel Ten Eyck, Albany, New York, on the evening of Thursday, February 29th, 1940, at seven-thirty o'clock."16pp.

1038.45 Swing, Baby, Swing. w. No composer indicated. m. "Air — *Danny Deever.*" In: *Lehman Unlimited*, page 8. Published by The Legislative Correspondents' Association of New York, Albany, NY. 1942. [7¾" × 10½"]. N/c drawing of Herb Lehman as a train engineer, others dressed as bandits trying to block the way including Dewey, Mead, Poletti, Willkie, Marvin Bennett and Farley — "The Great Train Hold-Up!" "Featuring that Famous Political Personality and Star of 'There'll Always be a Herbie' on an Uncensored Double Bill with 'Fifty Million Candidates Won't be Wronged.'" "Exploded At Hotel Ten Eyck, Albany, New York, on the evening of Thursday, March 12th, 1942, at seven-thirty o'clock."

1038.46 There Goes That Man Again! w. No composer indicated. m. "Tune — *There Goes That Tune Again.*" In: *Again And Again And Again Or All At Sea*, page 11. Published by Albany Legislative Correspondents' Association of New York State, Albany, NY. 1945. [8¾" × 11"]. N/c drawing of Franklin Roosevelt as pirate, Thomas Dewey as "Black Tom," Henry Wallace, Sidney Hillman, others on ship — "Union Ship C.I.O.-P.A.C." "Black Tom" Dewey walking plank. "Featuring Political Craft and Cunning and Contortions; Also Summoned by Subpoena, or Hit-Toddy and the Shady Lady, the Indestructible Dame Known as Lu-Lu; Together with Mystical Midsummer Mummery of '46, in a Roaring and Raucous and Revealing Racing Scene Entitled 'Hoots and Straddles.'" "All Done with Music, Magic, and Mirrors — In Three Acts at Hotel Ten Eyck, Albany, March 15, 1945." [Crew/FDR-371].

1038.47 There's A Mansion White (Governor Dewey). w. No composer indicated. m. "Tune — *There's A Small Hotel.*" In: *Alice In Blunderland Or Through The Rooking Class* [Program and Songbook], page 5. Published by The Legislative Correspondents' Association of New York State, Albany, NY. 1949. [8⅝" × 11"]. N/c drawings of Harry Truman, Thomas Dewey, Franklin Roosevelt, Henry Wallace, Harold Stassen, Alben Barkley, Robert Taft, Earl Warren, other politicians. "A Scintillating Satire of Sadistic Surprises and Surprising Successes Featuring a Dramatic

Disclosure of How Tom Did Not Go Down to D.C. in Slips; Together with a Give-Away-Nothing Radio Broadcast and Epic Melodrama of the Indian Wars Entitled 'When the Cat's Away the Mice Will Play.'" "Done With Music and Mirrors — Particularly Mirrors in Three Acts at Hotel Ten Eyck, Albany, March 12, 1949." [Crew/HST-20].

1038.48 They Knew What They Wanted. w. No composer indicated. m. "Air — *One, Two, Three Kick*." In: *Gone With The Winner*, page 14. Published by Albany Legislative Correspondents' Association of New York State, Albany, NY. March 20, 1941. [9" × 11 1/16"]. R/w/bl/y drawing of Franklin Roosevelt and Wendell Willkie riding "A Bicycle Built For Two" labeled — "Roosevelt-Willkie Axis." Wheels — "New Deal" and "Lend Lease Bill." "Or 'Back in the Lap of God.' A Hoosier-Hyde Park Honeymoon Hit, Staring the G. Oomph P.'s Lost Leader and the King of Krum Elbow in 'Lucky Partners.' Says F.D.R. — 'He's My Man.' Says the Republican Party — 'Once a New Dealer, Sometimes a Double- Dealer.' Says the Public — 'Willkie's the Life of the Party, But What Party?" "Served Piping Hot at Hotel Ten Eyck, Albany, New York, Thursday Night, March 20, 1941, at 7:30 o'clock. [Crew/FDR-394].

1038.49 Tom Dewey For President. w.m. Roslyn Wells. Published by The Eighth South Republican Club, Inc., 157 East 48th Street, New York, NY. Copyright 1948 by Roslyn Wells. B/w photo of Thomas Dewey. B/w litho of an eagle, geometric designs. "1949 National Republican Campaign Song." 4pp. Page 4: B/w drawing of two elephants. "Photo-offset by Passantino Printing Co., 250 W. 49th St., N.Y.C." [Crew/TED-40].

1038.50 Try Uniting (Governor Dewey). w. No composer indicated. m. "Tune — *The Girl That I Marry*." In: *Alice In Blunderland Or Through The Rooking Class* [Program and Songbook], page 8. Published by The Legislative Correspondents' Association of New York State, Albany, NY. 1949. [8 5/8" × 11"]. N/c drawings of Harry Truman, Thomas Dewey, Franklin Roosevelt, Henry Wallace, Harold Stassen, Alben Barkley, Robert Taft, Earl Warren, other politicians. "A Scintillating Satire of Sadistic Surprises and Surprising Successes Featuring a Dramatic Disclosure of How Tom Did Not Go Down to D.C. in Slips; Together with a Give-Away-Nothing Radio Broadcast and Epic Melodrama of the Indian Wars Entitled 'When the Cat's Away the Mice Will Play.'" "Done With Music and Mirrors — Particularly Mirrors in Three Acts at Hotel Ten Eyck, Albany, March 12, 1949." [Crew/HST-20].

1038.51 Wanted: A Winner. w. No composer indicated. m. "Air — *Stout-Hearted Men*." In: *Gone With The Winner*, page 6. Published by Albany Legislative Correspondents' Association of New York State, Albany, NY. March 20, 1941. [9" × 11 1/16"]. R/w/bl/y drawing of Franklin Roosevelt and Wendell Willkie riding "A Bicycle Built For Two" labeled — "Roosevelt-Willkie Axis." Wheels — "New Deal" and "Lend Lease Bill." "Or 'Back in the Lap of God.' A Hoosier-Hyde Park Honeymoon Hit, Staring the G. Oomph P.'s Lost Leader and the King of Krum Elbow in 'Lucky Partners.' Says F.D.R. — 'He's My Man.' Says the Republican Party — 'Once a New Dealer, Sometimes a Double- Dealer.' Says the Public — 'Willkie's the Life of the Party, But What Party?" "Served Piping Hot at Hotel Ten Eyck, Albany, New York, Thursday Night, March 20, 1941, at 7:30 o'clock. [Crew/FDR-394].

1038.52 We Wish We Had A Governor! w. No composer indicated. m. "Tune — *Paper Doll*." In: *Dealers Choice or Back-To-Back Biting*, page 13. Published by the Albany Legislative Correspondent's Association of New York State, Albany, NY. 1944. [8" × 11 3/4"]. N/c drawing of Franklin Roosevelt, Thomas Dewey, "Chiang," "Winnie" and "Joe" playing cards — "Featuring the World's Most Exciting Egomaniacs in a Marvelous Musical of Messianic and Mystery: Showing Sinners, Sycophants, Suckers, and Sleuths Saving Civilization with Sound; or Find the Joker!" "Dealt Off the Bottom of a Hot Deck — In Three Acts at Ten Eyck, Albany, March 9, 1944." [Crew/FDR-364].

1038.53 Who All Is Goin' My Way? w. No composer indicated. m. No tune indicated. In: *Dealers Choice or Back-To-Back Biting*, page 14. Published by the Albany Legislative Correspondent's Association of New York State, Albany, NY. 1944. [8" × 11 3/4"]. N/c drawing of Franklin Roosevelt, Thomas Dewey, "Chiang," "Winnie" and "Joe" playing cards — "Featuring the World's Most Exciting Egomaniacs in a Marvelous Musical of Messianic and Mystery: Showing Sinners, Sycophants, Suckers, and Sleuths Saving Civilization with Sound; or Find the Joker!" "Dealt Off the Bottom of a Hot Deck — In Three Acts at Ten Eyck, Albany, March 9, 1944." [Crew/FDR-364].

1038.54 Who Will It Be? — I Hope! w. No composer indicated. m. "Tune — *Who Do You Love, I Hope*." In: *Visions And Revisions*, page 7. Published by The Albany Legislative Correspondents' Association, Albany, NY. March 6, 1947. [8 1/2" × 11"]. R/w/gn/y/bk drawing of Thomas "Dewey" as Santa Claus, sign — "Santa's Workshop," other New York politicians. "Revealing in Rhapsodic Revelry of Song and Stunt How a Political Scrooge Became a Political Saint; or, What Happened When Many Paws Raided the Wonderful Workshop of Santa Claus Dewey; Together with Other Strange and Silly Scenes." "Hotel Ten Eyck, Albany, March 6, 1947." 24pp. [Crew/TED-34].

• **AmPM-1039 DINKINS**, David Norman (State Assembly, 1966; Mayor, New York City, 1990–1993)

1039.1 Abie's On His Toes. w. No composer indicated. m. "Tune — *Sweet Gypsy Rose*." In: *Thoroughly Mad-ern Malcolm or He Didn't Need A Course In Forensics To Become A Famous Public Speaker*, page 11. Published by the New York State Legislative Correspondents' Association, Albany, NY. 1974. N/w photo of Malcolm Wilson as Alfred E. Newman — "What — Me Governor?" "Featuring the New York Correspondents' Association, March 16. 1974." 32pp.

• **AmPM-1040 DIX**, John Adams (State House, 1842; U.S. Senate, 1845–1849; U.S. Secretary of the Treasury, 1861; U.S. Ambassador to France, 1866–1869; Governor, 1873–1875)

1040.1 Audax Omnia Perpeti Gens Lincolna Ruit Per Vetitum Nefas. w.m. No composers or tune indicated. No publisher indicated. [1861–1862]. B/w non-pictorial geometric design border. 2pp. Page 2: Blank. [AMC].

1040.2 Campaign College Songs 1900 [Song Book]. w. Gen. Stillman F. Kneeland. Published for the Wholesale Dry Goods Republican Club, No. 350 Broadway, New York, NY. 1900. [5⅞" × 9⅛"]. Y/bk photos of William "McKinley" and Theodore "Roosevelt." Y/bk drawings of eagle, shield, flags. "A bird that can sing and won't sing must be made to sing." 16pp. Page 16: "If any one pulls down the Flag, shoot him on the spot—John A. Dix." "Will you vote for a man who will pull down the American Flag in the Philippines?" [Crew/WM-214].

1040.3 Dix's Manifesto. w. "B." m. "Air—*Dearest Mae*." No publisher indicated. Published in Baltimore, September 11th, 1861. [Approx. 3⅛" × 9⅜"]. Litho of a man in a barrel. 2pp. Page 2: Blank. [WFU].

1040.3A Funeral March In Memory Of Genl. John A. Dix. m. H. Maylath. Published by C.H. Ditson & Co., 843 Broadway, New York, NY. 1879. Black litho border, v/w geometric designs. 8pp. Pages 2 and 8: Blank.

1040.4 John A. Dix's Revenge. w. No composer indicated. m. "A Ballad by the Former Governor, Entitled *Somebody Else Is Getting; It Where I Got Mine*." In: *The Red Book, Containing Portraits And Biographies Of Some Persons More Or Less Prominent Public Life Written Entirely Without Respect To The Libel Laws, In A Studious Effort To Conceal Everything But The Truth; Some Songs Built Upon The Same Principle, And Other Important (?) Material Entirely Unfit To Print*, page 16. Published by Legislative Correspondents' Association of the State of New York, Albany, NY. 1913. [5" × 7¼"]. R/w/bk hardback book with drawing of State House, seal of New York, geometric designs. 90pp.

1040.5 Our General's Grand March. m. C.S. Grafulla. Published by E.A. Daggett, New York, NY. 1861. N/c litho [horizontal format] of Union generals, including "Scott, Butler, McClellan, Sprague, Prentiss, Tyler, Burnside, Hunter, Blenker, M'Dowell, Anderson, M'Call, Woll, Rosecrans, Lander, Dix, Curtis, Stone, Heintzelman, Banks, and Fremont. 8pp. Pages 2 and 8: Blank. Page 3: Title—***Our General's Quickstep*** {1040.5-1}. "As Performed by the 7th Reg. National Guard Band." [Crew/WS-14]

1040.6 The Psalm Of Sammy Tilden. w. No composer indicated. m. "Air—*Auld Lang Syne*." In: *Hayes & Wheeler Campaign Song Book (For The Centennial Year)*, page 9. Published by the American News Company, Nos. 117, 119, 121, 123 Nassau Street, New York, NY. 1876. [3⅞" × 6$\frac{5}{16}$"]. Y/bk litho of Rutherford B. Hayes and William A. Wheeler, liberty cap, geometric designs. 74pp. [M-193]. [Crew/RBH-11].

1040.7 Unlimited Gall. w. C.M. Maxon. m. "Tune—*Dennis M'Carthy*." In: *The Alliance And Labor Songster (Third Edition), A Collection Of Labor And Comic Songs For Use Of Alliances, Debating Clubs, Political Gatherings*, page 58. Published by R. & L. Vincent, Printers, Winfield, KS. 1890. [4¾" × 7½"]. 66pp.

• **AmPM-1041 DONNELLEY**, Charles S. (Mayor, Utica)

1041.1 Re-Elect Mayor Donnelley. No composer indicated. No publisher indicated. [ca. 1933] B/w photo of Charles S. Donnelley [facsimile signature]. 4pp. Page 4: Campaign advertising for "Re-Elect Mayor Donnelley."

• **AmPM-1042 DONOVAN**, William J. (Candidate for Governor, 1932)

1042.1 Lehman Lullaby. w. No composer indicated. m. "Air—*Let's Put Out The Lights And Go To Sleep*." In: *Foam Sweet Foam*, page 10. Published by Albany Legislative Correspondents' Association, Albany, NY. 1933. [8" × 11¾"]. N/c drawing by Jerry Costello of Franklin D. Roosevelt, Al Smith and other politicians riding a bottle of beer—"The Lager Limited." "A Rollicking Review Rotating on Resurrection of Bouncing Beverages, Tipsily Tapped at Ten Eyck Hotel Rathskeller, Albany, New York, the evening of Thursday, February 23, 1933, at Seven-Thirty o'clock." 20pp. [Crew/FDR-277].

1042.2 Wild Bill Donovan Song Of Victory. w.m. Tom Donahue. Published by the Independent Donovan-For-Governor Independent Veterans Committee. [1932]. Non-pictorial handwritten manuscript. 4pp. Page 4: Blank.

1042.3 Wild Bill Donovan Victory Song. w.m. Tom Donahue. Published by the Independent Veterans Committee State Headquarters, Hotel Lexington, New York, NY. 1932. Br/w photo of William Donovan in WWI uniform. "Donovan for Governor." 4pp. Page 4: Blank.

• **AmPM-1043 DOOLING**, James J. (State Assembly, 1930–1942)

1043.1 Floating Fantasy. w. No composer indicated. m. "Air—*When My Dreamboat Comes Home*." In: *Wake Up And Scream*, page 11. Published by Albany Legislative Correspondents' Association, Albany, NY. 1937. [8" × 11¾"]. N/c drawing by Jerry Costello of Dr. Bill Murray, King Macy, New York GOP, and Ham Fish as patients undergoing transfusions. "A Trumpet Call to the G.O.P. Eagle to Snap out of Coma and Rally Ravaged Republicans with New Volley of Vocal Vim—the Same Being Enacted 'mid a Merry Medley of Mountain Madness, Dutch Delirium, Liberalization Legendry, Melancholy Maidens and Rapscallion Redskins, at Ten Eyck Hotel, Albany, N.Y., Thursday, March eleventh, 1937, at Seven-Thirty o'-clock." 20pp.

1043.2 It's An Old Roosevelt Custom. w. No composer indicated. m. "Air—*It's An Old Southern Custom*. In: *Tory, Tory Hallelujah*, page 7. Published by Albany Legislative Correspondents' Association, Albany, NY. 1936. [8" × 11¾"]. N/c drawing of Franklin D. Roosevelt, other politicians dressed as Revolutionary soldiers in battle scene—"A Dashing Delirious Drama, Lampooning Loyalists and Liberty Leaguers, Daggering Despots, Dictators and Dummy Donkey-Drivers to music by Red-Coats and Lyrics by Turn-Coats, the Combat Being Played Against a Spangled Back-Drop." "Furiously Fought at Ten Eyck Hotel, Albany, New York, The Evening of Thursday, March 12, 1936, at Seven-Thirty o'clock." [Crew/FDR-325].

• **AmPM-1044 DUBINSKY**, David (President of International Ladies' Garment Workers Union, 1932; Founder of the American Labor Party, 1936; Presidential Elector, 1936; Co-founder & Vice-Chairman of New York Liberal Party, 1944 & 1958)

1044.1 Clear It With Sidney. w. No composer indicated. m. "Tune—*Bellbottom Trousers*." In: *Again And Again And Again Or All At Sea*, page 10. Published by Albany Legislative Correspondents' Association of New York State, Albany, NY. 1945. [8¾" × 11"]. N/c drawing of Franklin Roosevelt as pirate, Thomas Dewey as "Black Tom," Henry Wallace, Sidney Hillman, others on ship—"Union Ship C.I.O.–P.A.C." "Black Tom" Dewey walking plank. "Featuring Political Craft and Cunning and Contortions; Also Summoned by Subpoena, or Hit-Toddy and the Shady Lady, the Indestructible Dame Known as Lu-Lu; Together with Mystical Midsummer Mummery of '46, in a Roaring and Raucous and Revealing Racing Scene Entitled 'Hoots and Straddles.'" "All Done with Music, Magic, and Mirrors—In Three Acts at Hotel Ten Eyck, Albany, March 15, 1945." [Crew/FDR-371].

1044.2 Spring Fantasy! w. No composer indicated. m. "Air—*Flowers That Bloom In The Spring.*" In: *Sock-A-Bye Baby, A No Punches-Pulled Potpourri, Pillorying Political Palookas On Parade And Set To 'Swing' Time, Plus That Mad Maternal Masterpiece—Labor's Love Lost*, page 11. Published by The Legislative Correspondents' Association of New York, Albany, NY. 1938. [7¾" × 10½"]. N/c drawing of politicians as boxers: "Tom Dewey, Gotham Gamecock, Morry Tremaine Queen City's Idol, Bob-Jackson, Jamestown's Mighty Atom, Ripper Rolly Marvin, Syracuse Fistic Sensation, Jabber Bennett, Brooklyn Bomber and Promoter's Dream, Billy Bleakley, Westchester Wildcat, Killer Lehman, Knockerouter De Luxe." "Ace Cards for 1838 Golden Gloves Combat." "At Ten Eyck Hotel, Albany, New York, the evening of Thursday, March Tenth, 1938, at seven o'clock." 16pp. [Crew/TED-28].

1044.3 Swing, Baby, Swing. w. No composer indicated. m. "Air—*Danny Deever.*" In: *Lehman Unlimited*, page 8. Published by The Legislative Correspondents' Association of New York, Albany, NY. 1942. [7¾" × 10½"]. N/c drawing of Herb Lehman as a train engineer, others dressed as bandits trying to block the way including Dewey, Mead, Poletti, Willkie, Marvin Bennett and Farley—"The Great Train Hold-Up!" "Featuring that Famous Political Personality and Star of 'There'll Always be a Herbie' on an Uncensored Double Bill with 'Fifty Million Candidates Won't be Wronged.'" "Exploded At Hotel Ten Eyck, Albany, New York, on the evening of Thursday, March 12th, 1942, at seven-thirty o'clock."

• AmPM-1045   DUFFIE, Ed (State Highway Commissioner)

1045.1 The Executioner. w. No composer indicated. m. "Air—*Got A Little List—The Mikado.*" "The sword of the Governor falls slowly, but it chops exceeding small." In: *The Bacchanal Of 1919*, page 9. Published by The Legislative Correspondents' Association of New York, Albany, NY. 1919. [7¾" × 10½"]. N/c drawing by Fred O. Seibel of the "Last Chance Cafe," sign—"Headquarters Hard Liquor Club," "Senator Sage" as bellboy, and "Al Smith Tonight" on sign marquee. "A Product of the Capitoline Vineyard, Staged for the Delertation of People Still on Earth by The Legislative Correspondents' Association at The Ten Eyck, Albany, the Night of April 3, 1919." [Crew/AES-65].

• AmPM-1046   DULLES, John Foster (State Banking Board, 1946–1949; U.S. Senate, 1949, 1949; U.S. Secretary of State, 1953–1959)

1046.1 Who's In Charge Of Killing In Vietnam? w.m. Jim Bowden, 1968. "How I feel about the war? The song says it..." In: *The Vietnam Songbook*, page 112. c. Barbara Dane and Irwin Silber. Published by The Guardian, No. 32 West 22nd Street, New York, NY. Copyright 1969 by Barbara Dane and Irwin Silber. [7" × 10"]. B/w photo of a protest march. O/y/r/bk cover. 228pp.

• AmPM-1047   DUNMORE, Russell G. (State Assembly, 1922–1935)

1047.1 Now That The Wurzburger Flows. w. No composer indicated. m. "Air—*Down Where The Wurzburger Flows.*" In: *Foam Sweet Foam*, page 14. Published by Albany Legislative Correspondents' Association, Albany, NY. 1933. [8" × 11¾"]. N/c drawing by Jerry Costello of Franklin D. Roosevelt, Al Smith and other politicians riding a bottle of beer—"The Lager Limited." "A Rollicking Review Rotating on Resurrection of Bouncing Beverages, Tipsily Tapped at Ten Eyck Hotel Rathskeller, Albany, New York, the evening of Thursday, February 23, 1933, at Seven-Thirty o'clock." 20pp. [Crew/FDR-277].

• AmPM-1048   DUNNIGAN, John J. (State Senate, 1915–1944)

1048.1 Johnny's On The Junk. w. No composer indicated. m. "Air—*If I Had My Way.*" "Sung by Dunnigan." In: *So You Won't Talk, A Rollicking Rhapsody Ribbing Strong Silent Statesmen With Twelve Year Itch, Twitting Third Termites And Starring The G.O.P. White House Hopeful In 'Mr. Myth Goes To Washington.' Plus That Pari-Muted Phantasy, 'Three Million Men On A Horse,'"* page 11. Published by The Legislative Correspondents' Association of New York, Albany, NY. 1942. [7¾" × 10½"]. N/c drawing of two Veiled brides labeled "Democratic Presidential Nominee" and "Republican Presidential Nominee" and a donkey and elephant dressed as grooms standing on the street at "1940" Convention Corner." Drawing titled "Blind Dates." "Daringly Unreeled at Hotel Ten Eyck, Albany, New York, on the evening of Thursday, February 29th, 1940, at seven-thirty o'clock." 16pp.

1048.2 Lady's Lament. w. No composer indicated. m. "Air—*Melancholy Baby Heaven.*" In: *Wake Up And Scream*, page 14. Published by Albany Legislative Correspondents' Association, Albany, NY. 1937. [8" × 11¾"]. N/c drawing by Jerry Costello of Dr. Bill Murray, King Macy, New York GOP, and Ham Fish as patients undergoing transfusions. "A Trumpet Call to the G.O.P. Eagle to Snap out of Coma and Rally Ravaged Republicans with New Volley of Vocal Vim—the Same Being Enacted 'mid a Merry Medley of Mountain Madness, Dutch Delirium, Liberalization Legendry, Melancholy Maidens and Rapscallion Redskins, at Ten Eyck Hotel, Albany, N.Y., Thursday, March eleventh, 1937, at Seven-Thirty o'clock." 20pp.

1048.3 Leonine Lament. w. No composer indicated. m. "Air—*If I Only Had A Brain.*" "Sung by Twomey." In: *So You Won't Talk, A Rollicking Rhapsody Ribbing Strong Silent Statesmen With Twelve Year Itch, Twitting Third Termites And Starring The G.O.P. White House Hopeful In 'Mr. Myth Goes To Washington.' Plus That Pari-Muted Phantasy, 'Three Million Men On A Horse,'"* page 10. Published by The Legislative Correspondents' Association of New York, Albany, NY. 1942.

[7¾" × 10½"]. N/c drawing of two Veiled brides labeled "Democratic Presidential Nominee" and "Republican Presidential Nominee" and a donkey and elephant dressed as grooms standing on the street at "1940" Convention Corner." Drawing titled "Blind Dates." "Daringly Unreeled at Hotel Ten Eyck, Albany, New York, on the evening of Thursday, February 29th, 1940, at seven-thirty o'clock."16pp.

1048.4 Love Lyric. w. No composer indicated. m. "Air—*I'm Through With Love*." In: *The Scrappy Warriors, A Merry, Martial Medley, Mingling-Wrenches And Muck-Rakers, Presidential Pipe-Dreams, Partisan Perfidies And Prohibition Planks—All Revolving 'Round Convulsive Conclave Of Delirious Delegates, Shellshocked Spellbinders And Rabid Rivals For White House Honors*, page 12. Published by Albany Legislative Correspondents' Association, Albany, NY. 1933. [8¼" × 12"]. N/c drawing of Franklin Roosevelt with spear and on horseback charging Al Smith and others holding axes and knives. "Staged at Ten Eyck Hotel Rathskeller, Albany, New York, the evening of Thursday, March 3, 1932, at Seven o'clock."16pp.

1048.5 Our Albany Zoo. w. No composer indicated. m. "Air—*Easter Parade*." In: *Scars And Strifes, A Jungle Jamboree And Carnivorous Carnival, Cracking With Clashes And Seething With Slams, Socks, Strangle-Holds And Skullduggery*, page 7. Published by The Albany Legislative Correspondents' Association, Albany, NY. 1934. [8" × 11¾"]. N/c drawing of jungle animals fighting in the legislative chamber. "Riotously Revealed at Ten Eyck Hotel, Albany, New York, the evening of Thursday, March 22, 1934, at Seven-thirty o'clock." 16pp.

1048.6 You Lose! We Win. w. No composer indicated. m. "Air—*Nya, Nya, Nya Said The Little Fox.*" In: *So You Won't Talk, A Rollicking Rhapsody Ribbing Strong Silent Statesmen With Twelve Year Itch, Twitting Third Termites And Starring The G.O.P. White House Hopeful In 'Mr. Myth Goes To Washington.' Plus That Pari-Muted Phantasy, 'Three Million Men On A Horse,'* " page 9. Published by The Legislative Correspondents' Association of New York, Albany, NY. 1942. [7¾" × 10½"]. N/c drawing of two Veiled brides labeled "Democratic Presidential Nominee" and "Republican Presidential Nominee" and a donkey and elephant dressed as grooms standing on the street at "1940" Convention Corner." Drawing titled "Blind Dates." "Daringly Unreeled at Hotel Ten Eyck, Albany, New York, on the evening of Thursday, February 29th, 1940, at seven-thirty o'clock."16pp.

• **AmPM-1049** DURYEA, Perry B., Jr. (State Assembly, 1960–1978)

1049.1 Lou's Blues. w. No composer indicated. m. "Tune—*Why Do I Love You?*" As sung by "Lefkowitz and Duryea." In: *Thoroughly Mad-ern Malcolm Or He Didn't Need A Course In Forensics To Become A Famous Public Speaker*, page 20. Published by the New York State Legislative Correspondents' Association, Albany, NY. 1974. N/w photo of Malcolm Wilson as Alfred E. Newman—"What—Me Governor?" "Featuring the New York Correspondents' Association, March 16. 1974." 32pp.

1049.2 Troubles To Boot. w. No composer indicated. m. "Tune—*I Get A Kick Out Of You*." As sung by "Wilson, Anderson and Duryea." In: *Thoroughly Mad-ern Malcolm Or He Didn't Need A Course In Forensics To Become A Famous Public Speaker*, page 20. Published by the New York State Legislative Correspondents' Association, Albany, NY. 1974. N/w photo of Malcolm Wilson as Alfred E. Newman—"What—Me Governor?" "Featuring the New York Correspondents' Association, March 16. 1974." 32pp.

• **AmPM-1050** EATON, Melvin C. (Chairman, New York State Republican Party, 1934–1936; Delegate, Republican National Convention, 1936 & 1940; Presidential Elector, 1952)

1050.1 Keep 'Em Pure. w. No composer indicated. m. "Air—*If I Had Rhythm In My Nursery Rhymes*." In: *Tory, Tory Hallelujah*, page 9. Published by Albany Legislative Correspondents' Association, Albany, NY. 1936. [8" × 11¾"]. N/c drawing of Franklin D. Roosevelt, other politicians dressed as Revolutionary soldiers in battle scene—"A Dashing Delirious Drama, Lampooning Loyalists and Liberty Leaguers, Daggering Despots, Dictators and Dummy Donkey-Drivers to music by Red-Coats and Lyrics by Turn-Coats, the Combat Being Played Against a Spangled Back-Drop." "Furiously Fought at Ten Eyck Hotel, Albany, New York, The Evening of Thursday, March 12, 1936, at Seven-Thirty o'clock." [Crew/FDR-325].

1050.2 Paean Of Liberalization. w. No composer indicated. m. "Air—*Sing, Baby, Sing*." In: *Wake Up And Scream*, page 6. Published by Albany Legislative Correspondents' Association, Albany, NY. 1937. [8" × 11¾"]. N/c drawing by Jerry Costello of Dr. Bill Murray, King Macy, New York GOP, and Ham Fish as patients undergoing transfusions. "A Trumpet Call to the G.O.P. Eagle to Snap out of Coma and Rally Ravaged Republicans with New Volley of Vocal Vim—the Same Being Enacted 'mid a Merry Medley of Mountain Madness, Dutch Delirium, Liberalization Legendry, Melancholy Maidens and Rapscallion Redskins, at Ten Eyck Hotel, Albany, N.Y., Thursday, March eleventh, 1937, at Seven-Thirty o'clock." 20pp.

• **AmPM-1051** HUTCHINSON, Eberly (State Assembly, 1919–1931)

1051.1 G.O.P. Hunting Ballad. w. M.G.T. m. "Air—*Singin' In The Rain*. In: *Breaks And Outbreaks*, page 12. Published by Albany Legislative Correspondents' Association of New York State, Albany, NY. 1930. [8" × 11¾"]. N/c drawing of Franklin Roosevelt as warden, other politicians in jail—"A Paroxysmic, Penological Panorama, Pillorying Prison Probes, Partisan Pap-Grabbers, Peanut Policies, Phony Philanthropies, Punctured Pledges and Public Service Piffle, and Redolent with Republican Rebels Riddling Rooseveltian Ruses and Mocking Mogenthau Ministrations and Lehman Loquacities—Topped by That Toothsome Tidbit, 'Cells and Sell-Outs.'" "Detonated at Ten Eyck Hotel Terminal, Albany, NY., On the Evening of March 20, 1930, at 7:00 p.m." [Crew/FDR-362].

1051.2 Steingut Stanzas. w. No composer indicated. m. "Air—*Down Where The Wurzburger Flows*." "Dashing Ditty of Dutiful Democrat Loyally Lauding Leader With Lager Libations." In: *Breaks And Outbreaks*, page 8. Published by Albany Legislative Correspondents' Association of New York State, Albany,

NY. 1930. [8" × 11¾"]. N/c drawing of Franklin Roosevelt as warden, other politicians in jail—"A Paroxysmic, Penological Panorama, Pillorying Prison Probes, Partisan Pap-Grabbers, Peanut Policies, Phony Philanthropies, Punctured Pledges and Public Service Piffle, and Redolent with Republican Rebels Riddling Rooseveltian Ruses and Mocking Mogenthau Ministrations and Lehman Loquacities — Topped by That Toothsome Tidbit, 'Cells and Sell-Outs.'" "Detonated at Ten Eyck Hotel Terminal, Albany, NY., On the Evening of March 20, 1930, at 7:00 p.m." [Crew/FDR-362].

• **AmPM-1052** EDSON, Franklin (Mayor, New York City, 1883–1884)

1052.1 19th Century Wonder Collection. m. F. Miller. Published by Anderson & Co., Fulton Street, New York, NY. 1893. O/bk litho of the Brooklyn Bridge [horizontal format]. "Respectfully dedicated to Mayors Edson and Low." 24pp. Pages 2 and 24: Advertising. Page 23: Blank.

1052.2 19th Century Wonder March. m. F. Miller. Published y Frank P. Anderson, No. 298 Fulton Street, New York, NY. 1893. B/w litho of the Brooklyn Bridge [horizontal format]. "Written for the Opening Festivities of the Brooklyn and New York Suspension Bridge, Thursday, May 24th, 1883." "Respectfully dedicated to Mayors Edson and Low." 8pp. Pages 2, 7 and 8: Advertising.

1052.3 New York Produce Exchange Galop. m. Theodore Wenzlik. a. F.W.M. Published by Spear & Dehnoff, 717 Broadway, New York, NY. 1884. B/w litho of "Hon. F. Edson," Miss Liberty and Columbia, cherubs with trumpets, exchange building. "Advertising at top—"Don't fail to get the favorite *Silver King Waltz*— Same Composer." 6pp. Page 6: Advertising.

• **AmPM-1053** ELY, Alfred (U.S. House, 1859–1863)

1053.1 Congressman Ely (Song). w. No composer indicated. m. "Air—*Hi Ho Dobbin*." No publisher indicated. Probably published in Baltimore. [1861]. [Approx. 5" × 10¼"]. [V-1: B/w geometric design border] [V-2: Non-pictorial design in title, geometric design border]. 2pp. Page 2: Blank. [V-2: WFU].

• **AmPM-1054** EMERSON, James A. (State Senate, 1907–1918)

1054.1 I Want To Go Back To My Job In Second Place. m. "Air—*I Want To Go Back To My Home In Michigan*." In: *The Modest Art Of Self Advance Sporting Annual, Containing Correct Records Of White House Hopes, State Champions, Has Beens, Handlers And Never-Wases*, page 25. Published by the Legislative Correspondents' Association, Albany, NY. 1915. [5" × 7"]. Gy/r/bk cover drawing of a crowd watching a boxing match. 34pp.

• **AmPM-1055** EURICH, Alvin Christian (President, Northwestern University; President, State University of New York; VP, Fund for Advancement of Ed., Ford Foundation)

1055.1 The Board Of Regents — The Board Of Trustees. w. No composer indicated. m. "Tune — *That Certain Party.*" Sung by "Henry Wallace." In: *Alice In Blunderland Or Through The Rooking Class* [Program and Songbook], page 14. Published by The Legislative Correspondents' Association of New York State, Albany, NY. 1949. [8⅝" × 11"]. N/c drawings of Harry Truman, Thomas Dewey, Franklin Roosevelt, Henry Wallace, Harold Stassen, Alben Barkley, Robert Taft, Earl Warren, other politicians. "A Scintillating Satire of Sadistic Surprises and Surprising Successes Featuring a Dramatic Disclosure of How Tom Did Not Go Down to D.C. in Slips; Together with a Give-Away-Nothing Radio Broadcast and Epic Melodrama of the Indian Wars Entitled 'When the Cat's Away the Mice Will Play.'" "Done With Music and Mirrors — Particularly Mirrors in Three Acts at Hotel Ten Eyck, Albany, March 12, 1949." [Crew/HST-20].

• **AmPM-1056** EVERITT, William Theodore (Candidate for Town Councilman, Webster, ca. 1955–1963)

1056.1 The Ballad Of Row B (Keep A Voice In Your Government with Garnham Everitt Littell). Published by Webster Democratic Record, KRC-336. Record label has a bl/w drawing of a donkey and a megaphone. Side 2: No recording. 33⅓ rpm, 6" diameter record. Six page foldout sleeve with information on the candidates. [ca. 1955].

• **AmPM-1057** EWING, Oscar Ross (Vice-Chairman of Democratic National Committee, 1943–1945; Delegate to Democratic National Convention, 1944 & 1948)

1057.1 Got To Pick A Nag. w. No composer indicated. m. "Tune—*Camptown Races.*" In: *Again And Again And Again Or All At Sea*, page 19. Published by Albany Legislative Correspondents' Association of New York State, Albany, NY. 1945. [8¾" × 11"]. N/c drawing of Franklin Roosevelt as pirate, Thomas Dewey as "Black Tom," Henry Wallace, Sidney Hillman, others on ship—"Union Ship C.I.O.–P.A.C." "Black Tom" Dewey walking plank. "Featuring Political Craft and Cunning and Contortions; Also Summoned by Subpoena, or Hit-Toddy and the Shady Lady, the Indestructible Dame Known as Lu-Lu; Together with Mystical Midsummer Mummery of '46, in a Roaring and Raucous and Revealing Racing Scene Entitled 'Hoots and Straddles.'" "All Done with Music, Magic, and Mirrors — In Three Acts at Hotel Ten Eyck, Albany, March 15, 1945." [Crew/FDR-371].

• **AmPM-1058** FARLEY, James Aloysius (State Assembly, 1923; Secretary of New York Democratic Party, 1928–1930; Chairman of Democratic National Committee, 1932–1940; U.S. Postmaster General, 1933–1940) [ALSO SEE: DOC/PSM-FDR]

1058.1 Accentuate The Politics! w. No composer indicated. m. "Tune—*Accentuate The Positive.*" In: *Again And Again And Again Or All At Sea*, page 17. Published by Albany Legislative Correspondents' Association of New York State, Albany, NY. 1945. [8¾" × 11"]. N/c drawing of Franklin Roosevelt as pirate, Thomas Dewey as "Black Tom," Henry Wallace, Sidney Hillman, others on ship—"Union Ship C.I.O.–P.A.C." "Black Tom" Dewey walking plank. "Featuring Political Craft and Cunning and Contortions; Also Summoned by Subpoena, or Hit-Toddy and the Shady Lady, the Indestructible Dame Known as Lu-Lu; Together with Mystical Midsummer Mummery of '46, in a Roaring and Raucous and Revealing Racing Scene Entitled 'Hoots and Straddles.'" "All Done with

Music, Magic, and Mirrors — In Three Acts at Hotel Ten Eyck, Albany, March 15, 1945." [Crew/FDR-371].

1058.2 Barry's Boys. w.m. June Reizner. On 33⅓ rpm LP: *Reflecting* by The Chad Mitchell Trio. Performed by The Chad Mitchell Trio. Mercury Records #SR 60891/MG 20891. [ca. 1964]. Lyrics Published online by Mudcat Café at <http://mudcat.org/@displaysong.cfm?SongID=519>. 1997.

1058.3 Big Jim Farley. w. No composer indicated. m. "Air — *San Francisco.*" In: *Wake Up And Scream*, page 9. Published by Albany Legislative Correspondents' Association, Albany, NY. 1937. [8" × 11¾"]. N/c drawing by Jerry Costello of Dr. Bill Murray, King Macy, New York GOP, and Ham Fish as patients undergoing transfusions. "A Trumpet Call to the G.O.P. Eagle to Snap out of Coma and Rally Ravaged Republicans with New Volley of Vocal Vim — the Same Being Enacted 'mid a Merry Medley of Mountain Madness, Dutch Delirium, Liberalization Legendry, Melancholy Maidens and Rapscallion Redskins, at Ten Eyck Hotel, Albany, N.Y., Thursday, March eleventh, 1937, at Seven-Thirty o'clock." 20pp.

1058.4 Charlie Boy. w. No composer indicated. m. "Air — *Sonny Boy.*" In: *Gone With The Winner*, page 10. Published by Albany Legislative Correspondents' Association of New York State, Albany, NY. March 20, 1941. [9" × 11⅞"]. R/w/bl/y drawing of Franklin Roosevelt and Wendell Willkie riding "A Bicycle Built For Two" labeled — "Roosevelt-Willkie Axis." Wheels — "New Deal" and "Lend Lease Bill." "Or 'Back in the Lap of God.' A Hoosier-Hyde Park Honeymoon Hit, Staring the G. Oomph P.'s Lost Leader and the King of Krum Elbow in 'Lucky Partners.' Says F.D.R. — 'He's My Man.' Says the Republican Party — 'Once a New Dealer, Sometimes a Double- Dealer.' Says the Public — 'Willkie's the Life of the Party, But What Party?" "Served Piping Hot at Hotel Ten Eyck, Albany, New York, Thursday Night, March 20, 1941, at 7:30 o'clock. [Crew/FDR-394].

1058.5 The End Of The New Deal Dream (WPA, AAA, IEC or What Have We?) (A Burlesque). w.m. Charles Hammond Frye. Published by Sunset Song Bureau, Monrovia, CA. 1936. Bl/w photo of child playing with alphabet blocks — "Big AAA house fa' down." Bl/w drawing of Capitol building — "AAA, IEC, WPA, NRA." "There's a dreamer in The White House, building castles in the air, Like a child with lettered blocks, That he piles with greatest care." "Today's Most Popular Song." 4pp. Page 4: "Suggested spoken interludes." [Anti-FDR]. [Crew/FDR-330].

1058.6 Floating Fantasy. w. No composer indicated. m. "Air — *When My Dreamboat Comes Home.*" In: *Wake Up And Scream*, page 11. Published by Albany Legislative Correspondents' Association, Albany, NY. 1937. [8" × 11¾"]. N/c drawing by Jerry Costello of Dr. Bill Murray, King Macy, New York GOP, and Ham Fish as patients undergoing transfusions. "A Trumpet Call to the G.O.P. Eagle to Snap out of Coma and Rally Ravaged Republicans with New Volley of Vocal Vim — the Same Being Enacted 'mid a Merry Medley of Mountain Madness, Dutch Delirium, Liberalization Legendry, Melancholy Maidens and Rapscallion Redskins, at Ten Eyck Hotel, Albany, N.Y., Thursday, March eleventh, 1937, at Seven-Thirty o'clock." 20pp.

1058.7 [Four Years We Have Drifted And Wandered]. w. No composer indicated. m. "Air — *My Bonnie Lies Over The Ocean.*" In: *Campaign Songs For The Liberty Quartette*, page 6. Published for The Liberty Quartette, Utica, NY. [1936]. [4¼" × 8¹¹⁄₁₆"]. Bk/br litho of four men singing, eagle. 18pp. [Crew/AML-36].

1058.8 Got To Pick A Nag. w. No composer indicated. m. "Tune — *Camptown Races.*" In: *Again And Again And Again Or All At Sea*, page 19. Published by Albany Legislative Correspondents' Association of New York State, Albany, NY. 1945. [8¾" × 11"]. N/c drawing of Franklin Roosevelt as pirate, Thomas Dewey as "Black Tom," Henry Wallace, Sidney Hillman, others on ship — "Union Ship C.I.O.–P.A.C." "Black Tom" Dewey walking plank. "Featuring Political Craft and Cunning and Contortions; Also Summoned by Subpoena, or Hit-Toddy and the Shady Lady, the Indestructible Dame Known as Lu-Lu; Together with Mystical Midsummer Mummery of '46, in a Roaring and Raucous and Revealing Racing Scene Entitled 'Hoots and Straddles."' "All Done with Music, Magic, and Mirrors — In Three Acts at Hotel Ten Eyck, Albany, March 15, 1945." [Crew/FDR-371].

1058.9 Hi, Ho, Hail The New Deal. w.m. Major A.L. James, Jr. 1935. R/w/bk drawing of James "Farley" conducting choir of people from various walks of life representing New Deal scandals. One man holding a "Slaughtering knife," another holding "B & L Stock." 4pp. Page 4: Blank. [Crew/FDR-261].

1058.10 [Hiram Said To Aunt Miranda]. w. No composer indicated. m. "Air — *Put On Your Old Gray Bonnet.*" In: *Campaign Songs For The Liberty Quartette*, page 12. Published for The Liberty Quartette, Utica, NY. [1936]. [4¼" × 8¹¹⁄₁₆"]. Bk/br litho of four men singing, eagle. 18pp. [Crew/AML-36].

1058.11 Hymn Of Hate. w. No composer indicated. m. "Air — *The Spaniard That Blighted My Life.*" In: *Tory, Tory Hallelujah*, page 12. Published by Albany Legislative Correspondents' Association, Albany, NY. 1936. [8" × 11¾"]. N/c drawing of Franklin D. Roosevelt, other politicians dressed as Revolutionary soldiers in battle scene — "A Dashing Delirious Drama, Lampooning Loyalists and Liberty Leaguers, Daggering Despots, Dictators and Dummy Donkey-Drivers to music by Red-Coats and Lyrics by Turn-Coats, the Combat Being Played Against a Spangled Back-Drop." "Furiously Fought at Ten Eyck Hotel, Albany, New York, The Evening of Thursday, March 12, 1936, at Seven-Thirty o'clock." [Crew/FDR-325].

1058.12 It's An Old Roosevelt Custom. w. No composer indicated. m. "Air — *It's An Old Southern Custom.* In: *Tory, Tory Hallelujah*, page 7. Published by Albany Legislative Correspondents' Association, Albany, NY. 1936. [8" × 11¾"]. N/c drawing of Franklin D. Roosevelt, other politicians dressed as Revolutionary soldiers in battle scene — "A Dashing Delirious Drama, Lampooning Loyalists and Liberty Leaguers, Daggering Despots, Dictators and Dummy Donkey-Drivers to music by Red-Coats and Lyrics by Turn-Coats, the Combat Being Played Against a Spangled Back-Drop." "Furiously Fought at Ten Eyck Hotel, Albany, New

York, The Evening of Thursday, March 12, 1936, at Seven-Thirty o'clock." [Crew/FDR-325].

1058.13 Lehman Lullaby. w. No composer indicated. m. "Air—*Let's Put Out The Lights And Go To Sleep.*" In: *Foam Sweet Foam*, page 10. Published by Albany Legislative Correspondents' Association, Albany, NY. 1933. [8" × 11¾"]. N/c drawing by Jerry Costello of Franklin D. Roosevelt, Al Smith and other politicians riding a bottle of beer—"The Lager Limited." "A Rollicking Review Rotating on Resurrection of Bouncing Beverages, Tipsily Tapped at Ten Eyck Hotel Rathskeller, Albany, New York, the evening of Thursday, February 23, 1933, at Seven-Thirty o'clock." 20pp. [Crew/FDR-277].

1058.14 Mr. Sir Exit. w. No composer indicated. m. "Air—*Chattanooga Choo Choo.*" In: *Lehman Unlimited*, page 7. Published by The Legislative Correspondents' Association of New York, Albany, NY. 1942. [7¾" × 10½"]. N/c drawing of Herb Lehman as a train engineer, others dressed as bandits trying to block the way including Dewey, Mead, Poletti, Willkie, Marvin Bennett and Farley—"The Great Train Hold-Up!" "Featuring that Famous Political Personality and Star of 'There'll Always be a Herbie' on an Uncensored Double Bill with 'Fifty Million Candidates Won't be Wronged.'" "Exploded At Hotel Ten Eyck, Albany, New York, on the evening of Thursday, March 12th, 1942, at seven-thirty o'clock."

1058.15 [The Nation Of Our Fathers Is Assailed By Foes Within]. w. No composer indicated. m. "Air—*Battle Hymn Of The Republic.*" In: *Campaign Songs For The Liberty Quartette*, page 8. Published for The Liberty Quartette, Utica, NY. [1936]. [4¼" × 8¹⁄₁₆"]. Bk/br litho of four men singing, eagle. 18pp. [Crew/AML-36].

1058.16 [O Listen While We Sing About The Billions Spent]. w. No composer indicated. m. "Air—*Jingle Bells.*" In: *Campaign Songs For The Liberty Quartette*, page 10. Published for The Liberty Quartette, Utica, NY. [1936]. [4¼" × 8¹⁄₁₆"]. Bk/br litho of four men singing, eagle. 18pp. [Crew/AML-36].

1058.17 Our Albany Zoo. w. No composer indicated. m. "Air—*Easter Parade.*" In: *Scars And Strifes, A Jungle Jamboree And Carnivorous Carnival, Cracking With Clashes And Seething With Slams, Socks, Strangle-Holds And Skullduggery*, page 7. Published by The Albany Legislative Correspondents' Association, Albany, NY. 1934. [8" × 11¾"]. N/c drawing of jungle animals fighting in the legislative chamber. "Riotously Revealed at Ten Eyck Hotel, Albany, New York, the evening of Thursday, March 22, 1934, at Seven-thirty o'clock." 16pp.

1058.18 Paean Of Perpetuity. w. No composer indicated. m. "Airs—*Streets Of New York, Because You're You* and *Every Day Is Ladies Day With Me.*" In: *Lehman Unlimited*, page 6. Published by The Legislative Correspondents' Association of New York, Albany, NY. 1942. [7¾" × 10½"]. N/c drawing of Herb Lehman as a train engineer, others dressed as bandits trying to block the way including Dewey, Mead, Poletti, Willkie, Marvin Bennett and Farley—"The Great Train Hold-Up!" "Featuring that Famous Political Personality and Star of 'There'll Always be a Herbie' on an Uncensored Double Bill with 'Fifty Million Candidates Won't be Wronged.'" "Exploded At Hotel Ten Eyck, Albany, New York, on the evening of Thursday, March 12th, 1942, at seven-thirty o'clock."

1058.19 Paging One Pitcher. w. No composer indicated. m. "Air—*I Wonder What's Become Of Sally.*" In: *Gone With The Winner*, page 9. Published by Albany Legislative Correspondents' Association of New York State, Albany, NY. March 20, 1941. [9" × 11¹⁄₁₆"]. R/w/bl/y drawing of Franklin Roosevelt and Wendell Willkie riding "A Bicycle Built For Two" labeled—"Roosevelt-Willkie Axis." Wheels—"New Deal" and "Lend Lease Bill." "Or 'Back in the Lap of God.' A Hoosier-Hyde Park Honeymoon Hit, Staring the G. Oomph P.'s Lost Leader and the King of Krum Elbow in 'Lucky Partners.' Says F.D.R.—'He's My Man.' Says the Republican Party—'Once a New Dealer, Sometimes a Double- Dealer.' Says the Public—'Willkie's the Life of the Party, But What Party?" "Served Piping Hot at Hotel Ten Eyck, Albany, New York, Thursday Night, March 20, 1941, at 7:30 o'clock. [Crew/FDR-394].

1058.20 Party Pals. w. No composer indicated. m. "Air—*I Just Couldn't Say Good-Bye.*" In: *Foam Sweet Foam*, page 7. Published by Albany Legislative Correspondents' Association, Albany, NY. 1933. [8" × 11¾"]. N/c drawing by Jerry Costello of Franklin D. Roosevelt, Al Smith and other politicians riding a bottle of beer—"The Lager Limited." "A Rollicking Review Rotating on Resurrection of Bouncing Beverages, Tipsily Tapped at Ten Eyck Hotel Rathskeller, Albany, New York, the evening of Thursday, February 23, 1933, at Seven-Thirty o'clock." 20pp. [Crew/FDR-277].

1058.21 Poor Jim. w. No composer indicated. m. "Tune—*Poor Jud Is Dead.*" In: *Dealers Choice Or Back-To-Back Biting*, page 9. Published by the Albany Legislative Correspondent's Association of New York State, Albany, NY. 1944. [8" × 11¾"]. N/c drawing of Franklin Roosevelt, Thomas Dewey, "Chiang," "Winnie" and "Joe" playing cards—"Featuring the World's Most Exciting Egomaniacs in a Marvelous Musical of Messianic and Mystery: Showing Sinners, Sycophants, Suckers, and Sleuths Saving Civilization with Sound; or Find the Joker!" "Dealt Off the Bottom of a Hot Deck—In Three Acts at Ten Eyck, Albany, March 9, 1944." [Crew/FDR-364].

1058.22 Rah, Rah, Rah For Robert! w. No composer indicated. m. "Air—*You're A Sweetheart.*" In: *Sock-A-Bye Baby, A No Punches-Pulled Potpourri, Pillorying Political Palookas On Parade And Set To 'Swing' Time, Plus That Mad Maternal Masterpiece—Labor's Love Lost*, page 9. Published by The Legislative Correspondents' Association of New York, Albany, NY. 1938. [7¾" × 10½"]. N/c drawing of politicians as boxers: "Tom Dewey, Gotham Gamecock, Morry Tremaine Queen City's Idol, Bob-Jackson, Jamestown's Mighty Atom, Ripper Rolly Marvin, Syracuse Fistic Sensation, Jabber Bennett, Brooklyn Bomber and Promoter's Dream, Billy Bleakley, Westchester Wildcat, Killer Lehman, Knockerouter De Luxe." "Ace Cards for 1838 Golden Gloves Combat." "At Ten Eyck Hotel, Albany, New York, the evening of Thursday, March Tenth, 1938, at seven o'clock." 16pp. [Crew/TED-28].

1058.23 Song Of Big Jim Farley. w. No composer indicated. m. No tune indicated. "Before Democratic State Committee." In: *Visions And Revisions*, page 17. Published by The Albany Legislative Correspondents' Association, Albany, NY. March 6, 1947. [8½" × 11"]. R/w/gn/y/bk drawing of Thomas "Dewey" as Santa Claus, sign—"Santa's Workshop," other New York politicians. "Revealing in Rhapsodic Revelry of Song and Stunt How a Political Scrooge Became a Political Saint; or, What Happened When Many Paws Raided the Wonderful Workshop of Santa Claus Dewey; Together with Other Strange and Silly Scenes." "Hotel Ten Eyck, Albany, March 6, 1947." 24pp. [Crew/TED-34].

1058.24 Spring Fantasy! w. No composer indicated. m. "Air—*Flowers That Bloom In The Spring.*" In: *Sock-A-Bye Baby, A No Punches-Pulled Potpourri, Pillorying Political Palookas On Parade And Set To 'Swing' Time, Plus That Mad Maternal Masterpiece—Labor's Love Lost*, page 11. Published by The Legislative Correspondents' Association of New York, Albany, NY. 1938. [7¾" × 10½"]. N/c drawing of politicians as boxers: "Tom Dewey, Gotham Gamecock, Morry Tremaine Queen City's Idol, Bob-Jackson, Jamestown's Mighty Atom, Ripper Rolly Marvin, Syracuse Fistic Sensation, Jabber Bennett, Brooklyn Bomber and Promoter's Dream, Billy Bleakley, Westchester Wildcat, Killer Lehman, Knockerouter De Luxe." "Ace Cards for 1838 Golden Gloves Combat." "At Ten Eyck Hotel, Albany, New York, the evening of Thursday, March Tenth, 1938, at seven o'clock." 16pp. [Crew/TED-28].

1058.24A Stalling Stanzas. w. No composer indicated. m. "Air—*The Little Man Who Wasn't There* and *I'm Bidin' My Time.*" "Sung by Hanley and Lehman." In: *So You Won't Talk, A Rollicking Rhapsody Ribbing Strong Silent Statesmen With Twelve Year Itch, Twitting Third Termites And Starring The G.O.P. White House Hopeful In 'Mr. Myth Goes To Washington.' Plus That Pari-Muted Phantasy, 'Three Million Men On A Horse,'* page 12. Published by The Legislative Correspondents' Association of New York, Albany, NY. 1942. [7¾" × 10½"]. N/c drawing of two Veiled brides labeled "Democratic Presidential Nominee" and "Republican Presidential Nominee" and a donkey and elephant dressed as grooms standing on the street at "1940" Convention Corner." Drawing titled "Blind Dates." "Daringly Unreeled at Hotel Ten Eyck, Albany, New York, on the evening of Thursday, February 29th, 1940, at seven-thirty o'clock." 16pp.

1058.25 That Little Guy In Washington (Song of the Republicans). w. No composer indicated. m. "Tune—*A Gal In Calico.*" In: *Visions And Revisions*, page 9. Published by The Albany Legislative Correspondents' Association, Albany, NY. March 6, 1947. [8½" × 11"]. R/w/gn/y/bk drawing of Thomas "Dewey" as Santa Claus, sign—"Santa's Workshop," other New York politicians. "Revealing in Rhapsodic Revelry of Song and Stunt How a Political Scrooge Became a Political Saint; or, What Happened When Many Paws Raided the Wonderful Workshop of Santa Claus Dewey; Together with Other Strange and Silly Scenes." "Hotel Ten Eyck, Albany, March 6, 1947." 24pp. [Crew/TED-34].

1058.26 Those Fighting Irish. w. No composer indicated. m. "Air—*The Bold McIntyre.*" In: *Knighty—Knighty (Or A Michigan Yankee In King Herbie's Court)*, page 10. Published by The Legislative Correspondents' Association of New York State, Albany, NY. March 23, 1939. [8" × 11¾"]. N/c drawing of Thomas Dewey and Herbert Lehman jousting—"A Bouncing Blend, Mellowly Medieval, of Tangy Tunes, Balmy Buffoons, Flashing Blades and Ravishing Maids, Featuring the Glamour Gink of Gotham and the Caliph of Capitol Hill in 'Let's Tangle Tinware.'" "Thursday, March Twenty-Third, 1939, at Seven-Thirty o'clock." "Ribbingly Ripped Off at Hotel Ten Eyck, Albany, New York." [Crew/TED-30].

• **AmPM-1059 FASSETT**, Jacob Sloat (State Senate, 1884–1891; Candidate for Governor, 1891; U.S. House, 1905–1911)

1059.1 Campaign 1891. w. C.P. Woodworth, Lodi, NY. Published in the *Democrat And Chronicle*, 1891. [Music taped to a CDV of Jacob Fassett].

• **AmPM-1060 FAY**, Ernest A. (Clerk of the State Senate)

1060.1 The Executioner. w. No composer indicated. m. "Air—*Got A Little List—The Mikado.*" "The sword of the Governor falls slowly, but it chops exceeding small." In: *The Bacchanal Of 1919*, page 9. Published by The Legislative Correspondents' Association of New York, Albany, NY. 1919. [7¾" × 10½"]. N/c drawing by Fred O. Seibel of the "Last Chance Cafe," sign—"Headquarters Hard Liquor Club," "Senator Sage" as bellboy, and "Al Smith Tonight" on sign marquee. "A Product of the Capitoline Vineyard, Staged for the Delertation of People Still on Earth by The Legislative Correspondents' Association at The Ten Eyck, Albany, the Night of April 3, 1919." [Crew/AES-65].

• **AmPM-1061 FEARON**, George R. (State Assembly, 1916–1920; State Senate, 1921–1936)

1061.1 G.O.P. Hunting Ballad. w. M.G.T. m. "Air—*Singin' In The Rain.*" In: *Breaks And Outbreaks*, page 12. Published by Albany Legislative Correspondents' Association of New York State, Albany, NY. 1930. [8" × 11¾"]. N/c drawing of Franklin Roosevelt as warden, other politicians in jail—"A Paroxysmic, Penological Panorama, Pillorying Prison Probes, Partisan Pap-Grabbers, Peanut Policies, Phony Philanthropies, Punctured Pledges and Public Service Piffle, and Redolent with Republican Rebels Riddling Rooseveltian Ruses and Mocking Mogenthau Ministrations and Lehman Loquacities—Topped by That Toothsome Tidbit, 'Cells and Sell-Outs.'" "Detonated at Ten Eyck Hotel Terminal, Albany, NY., On the Evening of March 20, 1930, at 7:00 p.m." [Crew/FDR-362].

1061.2 I'll Get Away With Murder. w. No composer indicated. m. "Air—*Without A Word Of Warning.*" In: *Tory, Tory Hallelujah*, page 13. Published by Albany Legislative Correspondents' Association, Albany, NY. 1936. [8" × 11¾"]. N/c drawing of Franklin D. Roosevelt, other politicians dressed as Revolutionary soldiers in battle scene—"A Dashing Delirious Drama, Lampooning Loyalists and Liberty Leaguers, Daggering Despots, Dictators and Dummy Donkey-Drivers to music by Red-Coats and Lyrics by Turn-

Coats, the Combat Being Played Against a Spangled Back-Drop." "Furiously Fought at Ten Eyck Hotel, Albany, New York, The Evening of Thursday, March 12, 1936, at Seven-Thirty o'clock." [Crew/FDR-325].

1061.3 It's All 'Jake' With Us. w. No composer indicated. m. "Air—*I Must See Annie Tonight.*" In: *Knighty—-Knighty (Or A Michigan Yankee In King Herbie's Court)*, page 8. Published by The Legislative Correspondents' Association of New York State, Albany, NY. March 23, 1939. [8" × 11¾"]. N/c drawing of Thomas Dewey and Herbert Lehman jousting—"A Bouncing Blend, Mellowly Medieval, of Tangy Tunes, Balmy Buffoons, Flashing Blades and Ravishing Maids, Featuring the Glamour Gink of Gotham and the Caliph of Capitol Hill in 'Let's Tangle Tinware.'" "Thursday, March Twenty-Third, 1939, at Seven-Thirty o'clock. "Ribbingly Ripped Off at Hotel Ten Eyck, Albany, New York." [Crew/TED-30].

1061.4 Lehman Lullaby. w. No composer indicated. m. "Air—*Let's Put Out The Lights And Go To Sleep.*" In: *Foam Sweet Foam*, page 10. Published by Albany Legislative Correspondents' Association, Albany, NY. 1933. [8" × 11¾"]. N/c drawing by Jerry Costello of Franklin D. Roosevelt, Al Smith and other politicians riding a bottle of beer—"The Lager Limited." "A Rollicking Review Rotating on Resurrection of Bouncing Beverages, Tipsily Tapped at Ten Eyck Hotel Rathskeller, Albany, New York, the evening of Thursday, February 23, 1933, at Seven-Thirty o'clock." 20pp. [Crew/FDR-277].

1061.5 Party Pals (Passionate Paean of Praise by Damon Fearon for his Playmate, Pythias Knight). w. No composer indicated. m. "Air—*Little Annie Rooney.*" In: *Statutes And Statuettes*, page 10. Published by Albany Legislative Correspondents' Association, Albany, NY. 1925. N/c drawing by Fred O. Seibel of "Venus DeMilo Smith," other politicians as historical figures. "A Private Presentation of Immortal Images and Matchless Masterpieces From the 1925 Legislative Louvre Frivolously Fashioned in Political Pigments and Capitoline Colors and Featuring Etchers and Fetchers, Chisels and Fizzles, Hues and Hewitts, G.O.P. Gargoyles, Democratic Dorics, Prohibition Pastels, Lowman Landscapes and McGinnies Models, Combined with a Superficial Squint into the Gallery of Gee-Gaws, Freaks and Flim Flam." "Viewed at Ten Eyck Hotel, Albany, N.Y., on the Evening of March 12, 1925, Seven o'clock." 20pp. [Crew/AES-17].

1061.6 Political Pastels. w. No composer indicated. m. "Air—*O, Mr. Dooley.*" "Pertinent and Personal Portraits of Party Patriots, Publists and Pap-Peddlers." In: *Al S. In Wonderland*, page 4. Published by The Albany Legislative Correspondents' Association of New York State, Albany, NY. 1924. [8½" × 10½"]. N/c drawing by Fred O. Seibel of Statue of Liberty with Beer, "Al Smith," Calvin "Coolidge" as a dragon, other politicians. "A Jocose Junket in Phantom Pullmans to that Roisterous Realm, where Hectic Hopes, Hocus-Pocus Harmonies, Folly, Froth and Flim Flam Blend Blithely with Becalmed Booms, Budget Butchers, Bubbles, Blunders and Barters." "Departing from at Ten Eyck Hotel Terminal, Albany, NY., at 7 o'clock, Eastern Time, on the evening of Thursday, March, 27, 1924." [Crew/AES-67].

1061.7 Six Snappy Candidates. w. No composer indicated. m. "Air—*Ten Pretty Girls.*" In: *Sock-A-Bye Baby, A No Punches-Pulled Potpourri, Pillorying Political Palookas On Parade And Set To 'Swing' Time, Plus That Mad Maternal Masterpiece—Labor's Love Lost*, page 12. Published by The Legislative Correspondents' Association of New York, Albany, NY. 1938. [7¾" × 10½"]. N/c drawing of politicians as boxers: "Tom Dewey, Gotham Gamecock, Morry Tremaine Queen City's Idol, Bob-Jackson, Jamestown's Mighty Atom, Ripper Rolly Marvin, Syracuse Fistic Sensation, Jabber Bennett, Brooklyn Bomber and Promoter's Dream, Billy Bleakley, Westchester Wildcat, Killer Lehman, Knockerouter De Luxe." "Ace Cards for 1838 Golden Gloves Combat." "At Ten Eyck Hotel, Albany, New York, the evening of Thursday, March Tenth, 1938, at seven o'clock." 16pp. [Crew/TED-28].

- **AmPM-1062** FENTON, Ruben Eaton (Town Supervisor, Carroll, 1846–1852; U.S. House, 1853–1855 & 1857–1864; Governor, 1865–1868; U.S. Senate, 1869–1875)

1062.1 The Greeley Pill. w. No composer indicated. m. "Air—*The Mistletoe Bough.*" "Mixed at Cincinnati and taken to Baltimore." "Sung by the Union Glee Club at a Grant Republican rally at Cooper Institute." Published in the *New York Times*, September 26, 1872. [VBL, p. 456].

1062.2 The Voice Of The Army. w.m. James G. Clark "(Author of *Moonlight And Starlight, Let Me Die With My Face To The Foe, Beautiful Annie, Children Of The Battlefield, &c. &c.*)." Published by Horace Waters, 481 Broadway, New York, NY. 1864. Nonpictorial geometric frame. "And sung by him [Clark] at his popular entertainments." "Dedicated to Governor Fenton." 6pp. Page 8: Advertising.

- **AmPM-1062x** FILLMORE, Millard (State Assembly, 1829–1831; U.S. House, 1833–1835, 1837–1843, 1833–1835, 1837–1841, & 1841–1843; State Comptroller, 1848–1849; Vice President, 1849–1850; President, 1850–1853; Candidate for President, 1852 & 1856) [SEE: DOC/PSM-MF]

- **AmPM-1063** FEINBERG, Benjamin F. (State Senate, 1933–1949; Delegate to Republican National Convention, 1940–1948)

1063.1 Dewey Lowers The Boom. w. No composer indicated. m. "Tune—*Clancy Lowered The Boom.*" Sung by "Henry Wallace." In: *Alice In Blunderland Or Through The Rooking Class* [Program and Songbook], page 16. Published by The Legislative Correspondents' Association of New York State, Albany, NY. 1949. [8⅝" × 11"]. N/c drawings of Harry Truman, Thomas Dewey, Franklin Roosevelt, Henry Wallace, Harold Stassen, Alben Barkley, Robert Taft, Earl Warren, other politicians. "A Scintillating Satire of Sadistic Surprises and Surprising Successes Featuring a Dramatic Disclosure of How Tom Did Not Go Down to D.C. in Slips; Together with a Give-Away-Nothing Radio Broadcast and Epic Melodrama of the Indian Wars Entitled 'When the Cat's Away the Mice Will Play.'" "Done With Music and Mirrors—Particularly Mirrors in Three Acts at Hotel Ten Eyck, Albany, March 12, 1949." [Crew/HST-20].

1063.2 Each Monday Night Is The Screwiest Night Of The Week. w.m. No composer or tune indicated.

In: *Cash & Carry—On Or It Ain't Hay, A Stirring Saga Suggesting Scrimping, Scrooging And Spending Twixt The Highlands And Lowlands Of State Street; Also, A Loony Lift To Luna For Leaders Looking For Less O'Lockwood; All Pieced Together With A Paralyzing Portrayal Of Pickets Putting Pay Ahead Of Party*, page 16. Published by The Legislative Correspondents' Association of New York, Albany, NY. 1946. [8½" × 11"]. N/c drawing of politicians fighting over the "Castle Surplus, Irish dressed "O'Dwyer, Hannegan, Farley, Mead" against Scottish dressed "Lockwood, Bedenknap, MacDewey, Burton." "Hotel Ten Eyck, Albany, March 14, 1946." 24pp. [Crew/TED-20].

1063.3 Five Birds In A Gilded Cage. w. No composer indicated. m. "Tune—*A Bird In A Gilded Cage*." "As sung by Heck, Feinberg, Wicks, Mailler, Stephens." In: *Visions And Revisions*, page 10. Published by The Albany Legislative Correspondents' Association, Albany, NY. March 6, 1947. [8½" × 11"]. R/w/gn/y/bk drawing of Thomas "Dewey" as Santa Claus, sign—"Santa's Workshop," other New York politicians. "Revealing in Rhapsodic Revelry of Song and Stunt How a Political Scrooge Became a Political Saint; or, What Happened When Many Paws Raided the Wonderful Workshop of Santa Claus Dewey; Together with Other Strange and Silly Scenes." "Hotel Ten Eyck, Albany, March 6, 1947." 24pp. [Crew/TED-34].

1063.4 Let's Call The Whole Thing Off. w. No composer indicated. m. "Tunes—*Let's Call The Whole Thing Off, There'll Be A Hot Time In The Old Town Tonight* and Medley." In: *Dealers Choice or Back-To-Back Biting*, page 5. Published by the Albany Legislative Correspondent's Association of New York State, Albany, NY. 1944. [8" × 11¾"]. N/c drawing of Franklin Roosevelt, Thomas Dewey, "Chiang," "Winnie" and "Joe" playing cards—"Featuring the World's Most Exciting Egomaniacs in a Marvelous Musical of Messianic and Mystery: Showing Sinners, Sycophants, Suckers, and Sleuths Saving Civilization with Sound; or Find the Joker!" "Dealt Off the Bottom of a Hot Deck—In Three Acts at Ten Eyck, Albany, March 9, 1944." [Crew/FDR-364].

1063.5 No Second Floor! m. "Tunes—*My Sweetheart's The Man In The Moon, Singin' In The Rain, In The Evening By The Moonlight* And *When The Moon Comes Over The Mountain*." In: *Cash & Carry-On Or It Ain't Hay, A Stirring Saga Suggesting Scrimping, Scrooging And Spending Twixt The Highlands And Lowlands Of State Street; Also, A Loony Lift To Luna For Leaders Looking For Less O'Lockwood; All Pieced Together With A Paralyzing Portrayal Of Pickets Putting Pay Ahead Of Party*, page 12. Published by The Legislative Correspondents' Association of New York, Albany, NY. 1946. [8½" × 11"]. N/c drawing of politicians fighting over the "Castle Surplus, Irish dressed "O'Dwyer, Hannegan, Farley, Mead" against Scottish dressed "Lockwood, Bedenknap, MacDewey, Burton." "Hotel Ten Eyck, Albany, March 14, 1946." 24pp. [Crew/TED-20].

1063.6 Phony Farewell. w.m. No composer or tune indicated. "With a bow to Mr. Jerry Colonna." As "sung by Lehman." In: *Lehman Unlimited*, page 9. Published by The Legislative Correspondents' Association of New York, Albany, NY. 1942. [7¾" × 10½"]. N/c drawing of Herb Lehman as a train engineer, others dressed as bandits trying to block the way including Dewey, Mead, Poletti, Willkie, Marvin Bennett and Farley—"The Great Train Hold-Up!" "Featuring that Famous Political Personality and Star of 'There'll Always be a Herbie' on an Uncensored Double Bill with 'Fifty Million Candidates Won't be Wronged.'" "Exploded At Hotel Ten Eyck, Albany, New York, on the evening of Thursday, March 12th, 1942, at seven-thirty o'clock."

1063.7 Singing Commercials (With their sponsors). w.m. No composer or tune indicated. "Sponsor—The State Senate." In: *Alice In Blunderland Or Through The Rooking Class* [Program and Songbook], page 18. Published by The Legislative Correspondents' Association of New York State, Albany, NY. 1949. [8⅝" × 11"]. N/c drawings of Harry Truman, Thomas Dewey, Franklin Roosevelt, Henry Wallace, Harold Stassen, Alben Barkley, Robert Taft, Earl Warren, other politicians. "A Scintillating Satire of Sadistic Surprises and Surprising Successes Featuring a Dramatic Disclosure of How Tom Did Not Go Down to D.C. in Slips; Together with a Give-Away-Nothing Radio Broadcast and Epic Melodrama of the Indian Wars Entitled 'When the Cat's Away the Mice Will Play.'" "Done With Music and Mirrors—Particularly Mirrors in Three Acts at Hotel Ten Eyck, Albany, March 12, 1949." [Crew/HST-20].

1063.8 You Can't Pass A Bill Without Votes. w. No composer indicated. m. "Tune—*You Can't Get A Man Without A Gun*." In: *Visions And Revisions*, page 12. Published by The Albany Legislative Correspondents' Association, Albany, NY. March 6, 1947. [8½" × 11"]. R/w/gn/y/bk drawing of Thomas "Dewey" as Santa Claus, sign—"Santa's Workshop," other New York politicians. "Revealing in Rhapsodic Revelry of Song and Stunt How a Political Scrooge Became a Political Saint; or, What Happened When Many Paws Raided the Wonderful Workshop of Santa Claus Dewey; Together with Other Strange and Silly Scenes." "Hotel Ten Eyck, Albany, March 6, 1947." 24pp. [Crew/TED-34].

- **AmPM-1064** FINLEY, Dr. John F. (Commissioner of Education, 1913–1921)

1064.1 Our Yankeeland. w.m. Rose H. Walton. Published by The Progress Publishing Company, Caldwell, NJ. 1919. [7¼" × 11 1/16"]. B/w photo of John Finley. B/w drawing of an eagle, shield. "A Patriotic Song dedicated to Dr. John H. Finley, Commissioner of Education of the State of New York." "Designed for use in Public Schools and for Community Singing." 4pp. Pages 2 and 4: Long narrative on the history of the song.

- **AmPM-1065** FINN, Daniel E. (County Clerk, New York; Supreme Court Clerk, New York County)

1065.1 The Neighbors' Ballad (To 'Our Al'). w. No composer indicated. m. "Air—*Because You're Irish*." In: *The Bacchanal Of 1919*, page 12. Published by The Legislative Correspondents' Association of New York, Albany, NY. 1919. [7¾" × 10½"]. N/c drawing by Fred O. Seibel of the "Last Chance Cafe," sign—"Headquarters Hard Liquor Club," "Senator Sage" as bellboy, and "Al Smith Tonight" on sign marquee. "A Product of the Capitoline Vineyard, Staged for the Delertation of People Still on Earth by The Legislative Correspondents' Association at The Ten Eyck, Albany, the Night of April 3, 1919." [Crew/AES-65].

• **AmPM-1066 FINO**, Paul Albert (Assistant State Attorney General, 1943–1944; State Senate, 1945–1950; Civil Service Commission, New York City, 1950–1952; U.S. House, 1953–1968; State Supreme Court, 1969–?)

1066.1 Lefkowitz, Gilhooley & Fino (Campaign Song). w.m. Ted Eddy, Frank Davis and Mario Del Guercio. 45 rpm record. Studio Records #9912/M90W 4980. Performed by The Campaigners. Produced for the New York City Mayoralty Race, Nov., 1961. Delaware Music. 1961. Side 2: Latin version.

• **AmPM-1067 FISH**, Hamilton (U.S. House, 1843–1845; Lt. Governor, 1848–1849; Governor, 1849–1850; U.S. Senate, 1851–1857; U.S. Secretary of State, 1869–1877)

1067.1 Governor Fish's Grand March. m. Oliver J. Shaw. Published by Boardman & Gray, No. 4 & 6 N. Pearl Street, Albany, NY. [ca.1849]. B/w litho by Thayer & Co. from a Daguerreotype by Johnson & Mead of "View of the State and City Halls taken from the Capitol." "Composed and arranged for Piano Forte & respectfully dedicated to His Excellency." 6pp. Pages 2 & 6: Blank.

1067.2 The Hat Of Chappaqua. w.m. No composer or tune indicated. In: *The Sun's Greeley Campaign Songster*, page 28. c. Amos J. Cumming. Published from *The Sun* Office, New York, NY. 1872. [4⅛" × 6½"]. Be/bk litho of Horace Greeley, wreath. "He shines for all." 64pp. [Crew/HG-5].

1067.3 A White House Epilogue. w.m. No composer or tune indicated. In: *The Sun's Greeley Campaign Songster*, page 45. c. Amos J. Cumming. Published from *The Sun* Office, New York, NY. 1872. [4⅛" × 6½"]. Be/bk litho of Horace Greeley, wreath. "He shines for all." 64pp. [Crew/HG-5].

1067.4 Who Killed Jim Garfield? w. No composer indicated. m. "Tune — *Cock Robin*." In: *Music For The Campaign (A Collection Of Original And Selected Songs, Adapted To Familiar Tunes For Use At Campaign Meetings, For 1880)*, page 6. Published by The *Indianapolis Sentinel* as a newspaper supplement, Indianapolis, IN. 1880. [7¾" × 10⅝"]. B/w lithos of Winfield Scott Hancock and William H. English. "This Collection of fifty one first-class Campaign Songs will be sent to any address, postage paid as follows: 25 for 30 cts.; 50 for 60 cts.; 100 for $1.00. Address Sentinel Company, Indianapolis, Ind." 8pp. Foldover. [Crew/WSH-11].

1067.5 Ye Doleful Lament Of A Dismal Office-Holder. w. No composer indicated. m. "Air — *Dear Father, Come Home*." In: *The Sun's Greeley Campaign Songster*, page 43. c. Amos J. Cummings. Published from *The Sun* Office, New York, NY. 1872. [4⅛" × 6½"]. Be/bk litho of Horace Greeley, wreath. "He shines for all." 64pp. [M-183]. [Crew/HG-5].

1067.6 Ye Doleful Lament Of A Dismal Office-Holder. w. No composer indicated. m. "Air — *Dear Father, Come Home*." In: *Greeley Campaign Songster*, page 38. Published by Halpin & McClure, Chicago, IL. 1872. [4" × 5¹⁵⁄₁₆"]. Pl/bk litho of Horace Greeley, geometric design border. "Chicago: Western News Company, Wholesale Agents." 72pp. [M-187]. [Crew/HG-21].

• **AmPM-1068 FISH**, Hamilton (State Assembly, 1914–1916; U.S. House, 1920–1945)

1068.1 Bedtime Ballad. w. No composer indicated. m. "Air — *Lights Out*." In: *Tory, Tory Hallelujah*, page 10. Published by Albany Legislative Correspondents' Association, Albany, NY. 1936. [8" × 11¾"]. N/c drawing of Franklin D. Roosevelt, other politicians dressed as Revolutionary soldiers in battle scene — "A Dashing Delirious Drama, Lampooning Loyalists and Liberty Leaguers, Daggering Despots, Dictators and Dummy Donkey-Drivers to music by Red-Coats and Lyrics by Turn-Coats, the Combat Being Played Against a Spangled Back-Drop." "Furiously Fought at Ten Eyck Hotel, Albany, New York, The Evening of Thursday, March 12, 1936, at Seven-Thirty o'clock." [Crew/FDR-325].

1068.2 Every Day You Meet Quite A Few! w. No composer indicated. m. "Tune — *Swinging On A Star*." In: *Again And Again And Again Or All At Sea*, page 12. Published by Albany Legislative Correspondents' Association of New York State, Albany, NY. 1945. [8¾" × 11"]. N/c drawing of Franklin Roosevelt as pirate, Thomas Dewey as "Black Tom," Henry Wallace, Sidney Hillman, others on ship — "Union Ship C.I.O.-P.A.C." "Black Tom" Dewey walking plank. "Featuring Political Craft and Cunning and Contortions; Also Summoned by Subpoena, or Hit-Toddy and the Shady Lady, the Indestructible Dame Known as Lu-Lu; Together with Mystical Midsummer Mummery of '46, in a Roaring and Raucous and Revealing Racing Scene Entitled 'Hoots and Straddles.'" "All Done with Music, Magic, and Mirrors — In Three Acts at Hotel Ten Eyck, Albany, March 15, 1945." [Crew/FDR-371].

1068.3 He's Got Them On The List. w. No composer indicated. m. "Tune — *I've Got A Little List*." In: *Again And Again And Again Or All At Sea*, page 13. Published by Albany Legislative Correspondents' Association of New York State, Albany, NY. 1945. [8¾" × 11"]. N/c drawing of Franklin Roosevelt as pirate, Thomas Dewey as "Black Tom," Henry Wallace, Sidney Hillman, others on ship — "Union Ship C.I.O.-P.A.C." "Black Tom" Dewey walking plank. "Featuring Political Craft and Cunning and Contortions; Also Summoned by Subpoena, or Hit-Toddy and the Shady Lady, the Indestructible Dame Known as Lu-Lu; Together with Mystical Midsummer Mummery of '46, in a Roaring and Raucous and Revealing Racing Scene Entitled 'Hoots and Straddles.'" "All Done with Music, Magic, and Mirrors — In Three Acts at Hotel Ten Eyck, Albany, March 15, 1945." [Crew/FDR-371].

1068.4 Paean Of Liberalization. w. No composer indicated. m. "Air — *Sing, Baby, Sing*." In: *Wake Up And Scream*, page 6. Published by Albany Legislative Correspondents' Association, Albany, NY. 1937. [8" × 11¾"]. N/c drawing by Jerry Costello of Dr. Bill Murray, King Macy, New York GOP, and Ham Fish as patients undergoing transfusions. "A Trumpet Call to the G.O.P. Eagle to Snap out of Coma and Rally Ravaged Republicans with New Volley of Vocal Vim — the Same Being Enacted 'mid a Merry Medley of Mountain Madness, Dutch Delirium, Liberalization Legendry, Melancholy Maidens and Rapscallion Redskins, at Ten Eyck Hotel, Albany, N.Y., Thursday, March eleventh, 1937, at Seven-Thirty o'clock." 20pp.

1068.5 The Sharing Of The Green. w. No composer indicated. m. *Wearing Of The Green.* "Reminiscent." In: *The Modest Art Of Self Advance Sporting Annual, Containing Correct Records Of White House Hopes, State Champions, Has Beens, Handlers And Never-Wases*, page 31. Published by the Legislative Correspondents' Association, Albany, NY. 1915. [5" × 7"]. Gy/r/bk cover drawing of a crowd watching a boxing match. 34pp.

• **AmPM-1069 FITZMAURICE**, Robert M. (Executive Assistant to the Governor, ca. 1920s)

1069.1 Jungle Jingle (A Discordant Ditty Denouncing Depletion of Tropics and Timberlands to Stock Smith's Mansion Menagerie). w. No composer indicated. m. "Air—*Where The River Shannon Flows.*" In: *Statutes And Statuettes*, page 8. Published by Albany Legislative Correspondents' Association, Albany, NY. 1925. N/c drawing by Fred O. Seibel of "Venus De-Milo Smith," other politicians as historical figures. "A Private Presentation of Immortal Images and Matchless Masterpieces From the 1925 Legislative Louvre Frivolously Fashioned in Political Pigments and Capitoline Colors and Featuring Etchers and Fetchers, Chisels and Fizzles, Hues and Hewitts, G.O.P. Gargoyles, Democratic Dorics, Prohibition Pastels, Lowman Landscapes and McGinnies Models, Combined with a Superficial Squint into the Gallery of Gee-Gaws, Freaks and Flim Flam." "Viewed at Ten Eyck Hotel, Albany, N.Y., on the Evening of March 12, 1925, Seven o'clock." 20pp. [Crew/AES-17].

1069.2 War Whoops (In which 'Al' Rises to Resent Rough Reception Meted out to His Manifold Messages and Parchment Pleas by Paleface Phalanxes). w. No composer indicated. m. "Air—*Tammany.*" In: *Statutes And Statuettes*, page 6. Published by Albany Legislative Correspondents' Association, Albany, NY. 1925. N/c drawing by Fred O. Seibel of "Venus De-Milo Smith," other politicians as historical figures. "A Private Presentation of Immortal Images and Matchless Masterpieces From the 1925 Legislative Louvre Frivolously Fashioned in Political Pigments and Capitoline Colors and Featuring Etchers and Fetchers, Chisels and Fizzles, Hues and Hewitts, G.O.P. Gargoyles, Democratic Dorics, Prohibition Pastels, Lowman Landscapes and McGinnies Models, Combined with a Superficial Squint into the Gallery of Gee-Gaws, Freaks and Flim Flam." "Viewed at Ten Eyck Hotel, Albany, N.Y., on the Evening of March 12, 1925, Seven o'clock." 20pp. [Crew/AES-17].

• **AmPM-1070 FITZPATRICK**, James Martin (Commissioner of Street Openings, New York City, 1919; Broad of Aldermen, New York City, 1919–1927; U.S. House, 1927–1945)

1070.1 The Biggest Dog-Gone Surplus In The World. w. No composer indicated. m. "Tune—*The Biggest Aspidastra In The World.*" "Miss November's Victory Song." In: *Cash & Carry—On Or It Ain't Hay, A Stirring Saga Suggesting Scrimping, Scrooging And Spending Twixt The Highlands And Lowlands Of State Street; Also, A Loony Lift To Luna For Leaders Looking For Less O'Lockwood; All Pieced Together With A Par-alyzing Portrayal Of Pickets Putting Pay Ahead Of Party*, page 10. Published by The Legislative Correspondents' Association of New York, Albany, NY. 1946. [8½" × 11"]. N/c drawing of politicians fighting over the "Castle Surplus, Irish dressed "O'Dwyer, Hannegan, Farley, Mead" against Scottish dressed "Lockwood, Bedenknap, MacDewey, Burton." "Hotel Ten Eyck, Albany, March 14, 1946." 24pp. [Crew/TED-20].

• **AmPM-1071 FLOYD**, William (Continental Congress, 1774–1776 & 1779–1783; Signer, Declaration of Independence, 1776; State Senate, 1777–1778, 1784–1788 & 1808; U.S. House, 1789–1791)

1071.1 The Declaration Of Independence Of The United States Of North America, July 4, 1776. w. From the Declaration of Independence. m. John E. Wilson. Published by John E. Wilson, Baltimore, MD. 1863. B/w litho of the interior of Independence Hall. "Arranged and adapted for Vocal and Instrumental Music as the Great National Chant." 4pp. [?]. Page 4: Facsimile signatures of all signers.

1071.2 Old Independence Hall. w. A. Fletcher Stayman. m. Francis Weiland. Published by Stayman & Brothers, No. 210 Chesnut Street, Philadelphia, PA. 1855. Non-pictorial. "Respectfully dedicated to the Memory of the Signers of the Declaration of Independence." "Fac Simile of their signatures" including John Adams, Sam Adams, Elbridge Gerry, Thomas Jefferson. 8pp. Pages 2 and 8: Blank. [Crew/MISC-34].

• **AmPM-1072 FLYNN**, Edward J. (State Assembly, 1918–1921; Delegate to Democratic National Convention, 1924–1952; New York Secretary of State, 1929–1939; Democratic National Committee, 1944–1945)

1072.1 Bedtime Ballad. w. No composer indicated. m. "Air—*Lights Out.*" In: *Tory, Tory Hallelujah*, page 10. Published by Albany Legislative Correspondents' Association, Albany, NY. 1936. [8" × 11¾"]. N/c drawing of Franklin D. Roosevelt, other politicians dressed as Revolutionary soldiers in battle scene—"A Dashing Delirious Drama, Lampooning Loyalists and Liberty Leaguers, Daggering Despots, Dictators and Dummy Donkey-Drivers to music by Red-Coats and Lyrics by Turn-Coats, the Combat Being Played Against a Spangled Back-Drop." "Furiously Fought at Ten Eyck Hotel, Albany, New York, The Evening of Thursday, March 12, 1936, at Seven-Thirty o'clock." [Crew/FDR-325].

1072.2 Big Jim Farley. w. No composer indicated. m. "Air—*San Francisco.*" In: *Wake Up And Scream*, page 9. Published by Albany Legislative Correspondents' Association, Albany, NY. 1937. [8" × 11¾"]. N/c drawing by Jerry Costello of Dr. Bill Murray, King Macy, New York GOP, and Ham Fish as patients undergoing transfusions. "A Trumpet Call to the G.O.P. Eagle to Snap out of Coma and Rally Ravaged Republicans with New Volley of Vocal Vim—the Same Being Enacted 'mid a Merry Medley of Mountain Madness, Dutch Delirium, Liberalization Legendry, Melancholy Maidens and Rapscallion Redskins, at Ten Eyck Hotel, Albany, N.Y., Thursday, March eleventh, 1937, at Seven-Thirty o'clock." 20pp.

1072.3 Floating Fantasy. w. No composer indicated. m. "Air—*When My Dreamboat Comes Home.*" In: *Wake Up And Scream*, page 11. Published by Albany

Legislative Correspondents' Association, Albany, NY. 1937. [8" × 11¾"]. N/c drawing by Jerry Costello of Dr. Bill Murray, King Macy, New York GOP, and Ham Fish as patients undergoing transfusions. "A Trumpet Call to the G.O.P. Eagle to Snap out of Coma and Rally Ravaged Republicans with New Volley of Vocal Vim—the Same Being Enacted 'mid a Merry Medley of Mountain Madness, Dutch Delirium, Liberalization Legendry, Melancholy Maidens and Rapscallion Redskins, at Ten Eyck Hotel, Albany, N.Y., Thursday, March eleventh, 1937, at Seven-Thirty o'clock." 20pp.

1072.4 Hymn Of Hate. w. No composer indicated. m. "Air—*The Spaniard That Blighted My Life.*" In: *Tory, Tory Hallelujah*, page 12. Published by Albany Legislative Correspondents' Association, Albany, NY. 1936. [8" × 11¾"]. N/c drawing of Franklin D. Roosevelt, other politicians dressed as Revolutionary soldiers in battle scene—"A Dashing Delirious Drama, Lampooning Loyalists and Liberty Leaguers, Daggering Despots, Dictators and Dummy Donkey-Drivers to music by Red-Coats and Lyrics by Turn-Coats, the Combat Being Played Against a Spangled Back-Drop." "Furiously Fought at Ten Eyck Hotel, Albany, New York, The Evening of Thursday, March 12, 1936, at Seven-Thirty o'clock." [Crew/FDR-325].

1072.5 It's A Grand Time For Striking! w.m. No composer or tune indicated. In: *Cash & Carry–On Or It Ain't Hay, A Stirring Saga Suggesting Scrimping, Scrooging And Spending Twixt The Highlands And Lowlands Of State Street; Also, A Loony Lift To Luna For Leaders Looking For Less O'Lockwood; All Pieced Together With A Paralyzing Portrayal Of Pickets Putting Pay Ahead Of Party*, page 19. Published by The Legislative Correspondents' Association of New York, Albany, NY. 1946. [8½" × 11"]. N/c drawing of politicians fighting over the "Castle Surplus, Irish dressed "O'Dwyer, Hannegan, Farley, Mead" against Scottish dressed "Lockwood, Bedenknap, MacDewey, Burton." "Hotel Ten Eyck, Albany, March 14, 1946." 24pp. [Crew/TED-20].

1072.6 It's Been A Long, Long Time. w. No composer indicated. m. "Tune — The Same, but with real feeling!" In: *Cash & Carry–On Or It Ain't Hay, A Stirring Saga Suggesting Scrimping, Scrooging And Spending Twixt The Highlands And Lowlands Of State Street; Also, A Loony Lift To Luna For Leaders Looking For Less O'Lockwood; All Pieced Together With A Paralyzing Portrayal Of Pickets Putting Pay Ahead Of Party*, page 7. Published by The Legislative Correspondents' Association of New York, Albany, NY. 1946. [8½" × 11"]. N/c drawing of politicians fighting over the "Castle Surplus, Irish dressed "O'Dwyer, Hannegan, Farley, Mead" against Scottish dressed "Lockwood, Bedenknap, MacDewey, Burton." "Hotel Ten Eyck, Albany, March 14, 1946." 24pp.

1072.7 Song Of Big Jim Farley. w.m. No composer or tune indicated. "Before the State Committee." In: *Visions And Revisions*, page 17. Published by The Albany Legislative Correspondents' Association, Albany, NY. March 6, 1947. [8½" × 11"]. R/w/gn/y/bk drawing of Thomas "Dewey" as Santa Claus, sign — "Santa's Workshop," other New York politicians. "Revealing in Rhapsodic Revelry of Song and Stunt How a Political Scrooge Became a Political Saint; or, What Happened When Many Paws Raided the Wonderful Workshop of Santa Claus Dewey; Together with Other Strange and Silly Scenes." "Hotel Ten Eyck, Albany, March 6, 1947." 24pp. [Crew/TED-34].

1072.8 Those Fighting Irish. w. No composer indicated. m. "Air—*The Bold McIntyre.*" In: *Knighty—Knighty (Or A Michigan Yankee In King Herbie's Court)*, page 10. Published by The Legislative Correspondents' Association of New York State, Albany, NY. March 23, 1939. [8" × 11¾"]. N/c drawing of Thomas Dewey and Herbert Lehman jousting—"A Bouncing Blend, Mellowly Medieval, of Tangy Tunes, Balmy Buffoons, Flashing Blades and Ravishing Maids, Featuring the Glamour Gink of Gotham and the Caliph of Capitol Hill in 'Let's Tangle Tinware.'" "Thursday, March Twenty-Third, 1939, at Seven-Thirty o'clock. "Ribbingly Ripped Off at Hotel Ten Eyck, Albany, New York." [Crew/TED-30].

1072.9 We Are More To Be Pitied Than Censured. w. No composer indicated. m. "Tune —*She Is More To Be Pitied Than Censured.*" In: *Cash & Carry–On Or It Ain't Hay, A Stirring Saga Suggesting Scrimping, Scrooging And Spending Twixt The Highlands And Lowlands Of State Street; Also, A Loony Lift To Luna For Leaders Looking For Less O'Lockwood; All Pieced Together With A Paralyzing Portrayal Of Pickets Putting Pay Ahead Of Party*, page 18. Published by The Legislative Correspondents' Association of New York, Albany, NY. 1946. [8½" × 11"]. N/c drawing of politicians fighting over the "Castle Surplus, Irish dressed "O'Dwyer, Hannegan, Farley, Mead" against Scottish dressed "Lockwood, Bedenknap, MacDewey, Burton." "Hotel Ten Eyck, Albany, March 14, 1946." 24pp. [Crew/TED-20].

1072.10 When Knighthood Was In Clover. w. No composer indicated. m. "Air—*Song Of The Vagabonds.*" In: *Knighty—Knighty (Or A Michigan Yankee In King Herbie's Court)*, page 7. Published by The Legislative Correspondents' Association of New York State, Albany, NY. March 23, 1939. [8" × 11¾"]. N/c drawing of Thomas Dewey and Herbert Lehman jousting—"A Bouncing Blend, Mellowly Medieval, of Tangy Tunes, Balmy Buffoons, Flashing Blades and Ravishing Maids, Featuring the Glamour Gink of Gotham and the Caliph of Capitol Hill in 'Let's Tangle Tinware.'" "Thursday, March Twenty-Third, 1939, at Seven-Thirty o'clock. "Ribbingly Ripped Off at Hotel Ten Eyck, Albany, New York." [Crew/TED-30].

• **AmPM-1073 FOLEY, Samuel J.** (District Attorney, New York City, 1933–?)

1073.1 Floating Fantasy. w. No composer indicated. m. "Air—*When My Dreamboat Comes Home.*" In: *Wake Up And Scream*, page 11. Published by Albany Legislative Correspondents' Association, Albany, NY. 1937. [8" × 11¾"]. N/c drawing by Jerry Costello of Dr. Bill Murray, King Macy, New York GOP, and Ham Fish as patients undergoing transfusions. "A Trumpet Call to the G.O.P. Eagle to Snap out of Coma and Rally Ravaged Republicans with New Volley of Vocal Vim—the Same Being Enacted 'mid a Merry Medley of Mountain Madness, Dutch Delirium, Liberalization Legendry, Melancholy Maidens and Rapscallion Redskins, at Ten Eyck Hotel, Albany, N.Y., Thursday, March eleventh, 1937, at Seven-Thirty o'clock." 20pp.

• **AmPM-1074** FOLEY, Thomas F. (Delegate to Democratic National Convention, 1924)

1074.1 Hang Down Your Head, Tom Foley. w. Bill Strauss and Elaina Newport. On CD: *A Whole Newt World.* Published by Capitol Steps Productions, 1505 King Street, Alexandria, VA. 1995. CD Cover: Gn/bl/y drawing of George Bush and George W. Bush as Seuss characters.

1074.2 The Neighbors' Ballad (To 'Our Al'). w. No composer indicated. m. "Air — *Because You're Irish.*" In: *The Bacchanal Of 1919,* page 12. Published by The Legislative Correspondents' Association of New York, Albany, NY. 1919. [7¾" × 10½"]. N/c drawing by Fred O. Seibel of the "Last Chance Cafe," sign — "Headquarters Hard Liquor Club," "Senator Sage" as bellboy, and "Al Smith Tonight" on sign marquee. "A Product of the Capitoline Vineyard, Staged for the Delertation of People Still on Earth by The Legislative Correspondents' Association at The Ten Eyck, Albany, the Night of April 3, 1919." [Crew/AES-65].

1074.3 Off To Wonderland Ballad. w. No composer indicated. m. "Air — *When The Midnight Choo Choo Leaves For Alabam.*" In: *Al S. In Wonderland,* page 13. Published by The Albany Legislative Correspondents' Association of New York State, Albany, NY. 1924. [8½" × 10½"]. N/c drawing by Fred O. Seibel of Statue of Liberty with Beer, "Al Smith," Calvin "Coolidge" as a dragon, other politicians. "A Jocose Junket in Phantom Pullmans to that Roisterous Realm, where Hectic Hopes, Hocus-Pocus Harmonies, Folly, Froth and Flim Flam Blend Blithely with Becalmed Booms, Budget Butchers, Bubbles, Blunders and Barters." "Departing from at Ten Eyck Hotel Terminal, Albany, NY., at 7 o'clock, Eastern Time, on the evening of Thursday, March, 27, 1924." [Crew/AES-67].

1074.4 Volstead Vaporings. w. No composer indicated. m. "Air — *Sidewalks Of New York.*" In: *The Public Frutilities Of 1923,* page 10. Published by The Albany Legislative Correspondents' Association of New York State, Albany, NY. 1923. [8" × 10¾"]. N/c drawing by Fred O. Seibel of Al Smith and Jimmy Walker at the seashore trying to hold back waves of "Traction Lobby," "Electric Light Trust," Water Power Ring," and "GOP Bloc of 81." "A ribald revue, redolent of guff, gestures, gold-bricks, hydrohokum, horse-cars, trackless telephones, transit thugs, synthetic budgets, five-cent fare fiascos, black-jacks, blue noses, monkey wrenches and the 'M.M.M.' (Machold's Minute Men." "At Ten Eyck, Albany, NY., April, 5, 1923."

• **AmPM-1075** FOSTER, William Z. (Candidate for President, 1924, 1928 & 1932; Candidate for Governor, 1930)

1075.1 Worker's Songs And Cheers. [1932]. [8½" × 11"]. Non-pictorial. 2pp. Page 1: Worker songs. Page 2: Worker cheers for Foster and Ford for President/Vice President [Communist Party]. WZF-1].

• **AmPM-1076** FRANKENTHALER, George (Delegate, Republican National Convention, 1932, 1936, 1940; New York Supreme Court, 1944; Surrogate, New York County, 1948)

1076.1 Dewey-Warren Victory Rally [Program/Songster]. Published by the New York Republican County Committee, New York, NY. 1948. [5¼" × 8¾"]. Bl/w photos of Thomas Dewey and Earl Warren. Bl/w drawing of two eagles. "Madison Square Garden, Saturday, October 30, 1948." "Gov. Thomas E. Dewey, Lt. Gov. Joe R. Hanley, Sen. Irving M. Ives, Mrs. Preston Davie, Hon. Thomas J. Curran, Hon. George Frankenthaler, Hon. Thos. J. Crawford, Mrs. Lillian Sharp Hunter, Hon. Daniel J. Riesner." 8pp. Foldout. Pages 2, 3 and 8: List of committee members. Pages 4 to 7: Songs including: *We All Want Dewey* {1076.1–1}. w. Douglas D. Ballin.